I0819977

IN THE SHADOW OF TYRANNY

Volume One

IN THE SHADOW OF TYRANNY

Between Hitler & Stalin

Volume One

Peter E. Vlčko

Edited by
Peter B. Vlčko

Tatra International Publishers Corp.

Tatra International Publishers Corp.
524 Riverside Drive
Wyandotte, Michigan 48192

REVISED DEFINITIVE
SECOND EDITION

Library of Congress Control Number: 2019920307

Printed in the United States of America

Cover by dePinho Design

Hardbound Volume One ISBN: 978-1-7343777-6-7
Hardbound Volume Two ISBN: 978-1-7343777-7-4
Paperback Volume One ISBN: 978-0-578-34293-1
Paperback Volume Two ISBN: 978-1-7343777-9-8
Paperback Volume Three ISBN: 978-0-578-34294-8
eBook ISBN: 978-1-7343777-4-3

Kto za pravdu horí

Kto za pravdu horí v svätej obeti,
kto za ľudstva právo život posvätí,
kto nad krivdou biednych slzu vyroní:
tomu moja pieseň slávou zazvoní.

Who burns for truth in holy sacrifice,
Who dedicates his life to human rights,
Who sheds a tear for those whom wrongs have bound:
For him my song with glory shall resound.

— ThDr. Karol Kuzmány, *Sláva šľachetným*, 1848,
translated by Reverend Dr. Jaroslav J. Vajda

ACKNOWLEDGEMENTS

IT TOOK FIVE YEARS TO WRITE AND PREPARE THIS MANUSCRIPT FOR PUBLISHING. Although I compiled it first in my native Slovak, an English version was more appealing. With some assistance of my two older sons, Miroslav and Vladimír, I finished the translation. However, this work, done in haste, had to be revised and edited.

Fortunately enough, I became acquainted with two wonderful persons who gained great merit in this work. They gladly took time from their normal duties and gave me the assistance I was looking for.

Mrs. Sandra Ratliff, an instructor of English at the Oakland University, at Rochester, Michigan, was a most cooperative and kind lady, when she revised my work. To her belongs my sincere gratitude for showing me how inadequate my English was. Nevertheless, this was not the end of my endeavor. New inspiration with the following changes in the manuscript confronted me with the necessity of re-editing it. Then Mrs. Ratliff's time ran out. Lee William Slazinski, a teacher of English composition at the high school in Lincoln Park, Michigan, soon found himself engaged with this new task. His admiration of my life experiences and the drama which has been presented was a compelling force that made him completely involved, despite many hardships of his own. His advice and the assistance he offered me, as well as his knowledge of English grammar, were great advantages to my manuscript. To this fine gentleman I am wholeheartedly indebted for the opportunity to have my book written in a more universal language.

My gratitude also goes to Mrs. Mary-Ellen Zell of Dearborn, Michigan, a very pleasant lady and careful in this work. She had the whole manuscript typed and retyped in a required time.

Needless to say, in depth of my heart I am indebted to the utmost to my beloved wife Georgina, as well as to my two younger children, Zora Tamara and Peter Boris; for it was their patience that gave me the strength I really needed for my endurance. Of course, they missed me often, mainly in that I was absent as their husband and father when they needed me most. Although it was hard for them to comprehend my involvement, they were not in doubt that they would be reimbursed, after I had finished this work, with yet a greater love and affection which I owe them all.

Peter E. Vlčko

CONTENTS

PART THREE

SLOVAKIA NO LONGER ABOVE THE FRAY

Part Four
Peril and Fear Hit Home

Volume Two

Part Five
Courage & Survival

PART SIX
TURNING THE TIDE

Part Seven
Rejecting a Second Tyranny

LIST OF TABLES, FIGURES, MAPS, AND DIAGRAMS

PREFACE TO THE SECOND EDITION

IN RESPONSE TO THE PASSING OF JOZEF STALIN ON 5 MARCH 1953, cultural, political, and economic events in Czechoslovakia began to slowly evolve in the late 1950s and early 1960s. The process of de-Stalinization in Czechoslovakia began in 1956 under the once hardline Stalinist President and General Secretary Antonín Novotný but progressed more slowly than in most other states of the Eastern Bloc. Rehabilitation of the condemned in Czechoslovakia during the Stalinist-era, such as those convicted in the Slánský trials in November 1952, was considered as early as 1963, but did not come to pass until 1968. In the early 1960s, Czechoslovakia underwent an economic recession. The obligatory Soviet model of industrialization applied poorly to Czechoslovakia. From the time of its origin on 28 October 1918, Czechoslovakia managed under the leadership of its founder and first president Tomáš Garrigue Masaryk to rapidly consolidate and expand the strong industrial base it inherited after the collapse of the Austro-Hungarian Empire. The new nation had a population of over thirteen-and-one-half million. It acquired seventy to eighty percent of the industry formerly under the Austro-Hungarian Empire that was located on Czech territory, including the porcelain and glass industries and the sugar refineries, more than forty percent of all its distilleries and breweries, the Škoda Works of Pilsen (Plzeň), which produced armaments, locomotives, automobiles, and machinery, and the chemical industry of northern Bohemia. Seventeen percent of all Hungarian industry that had developed in Slovakia during the late nineteenth century, including mining, forestry, and agriculture, also fell to the new republic. During the interwar period, Czechoslovakia was one of the world's ten most industrialized nations. The Soviet economic model mainly took into account less developed economies and was therefore ineffective, even counterproductive, in postwar Czechoslovakia. Novotný's attempt at restructuring the economy under the 1965 New Economic Model had unintended, although predictable consequences spurring increased demand for political reform. A series of cultural and political events between 1965 and 1968 led to the fall of Antonín Novotný and rise to power of

Alexander Dubček who launched a series of liberalizations under the name "Action Program," which included increasing freedom of the press, freedom of speech, and freedom of movement, with economic emphasis on consumer goods and the possibility of a multiparty government with limited powers and federalization into "two equal fraternal nations" (Czech Socialist Republic and Slovak Socialist Republic). The "Action Program" was to be a ten-year transition through which Democratic elections would be made possible and a new form of Masaryk-style Democratic Socialism would replace the *status quo*. These changes came to be known as "Socialism with a human face" and led to the failed "Prague Spring" of 1968.

At the height of the Cold War, the Soviets under Leonid Brežnev became increasingly alarmed at the prospect of another of their satellite states departing from traditional Marxism-Leninism and proletarian internationalism that could lead to a counter-revolution similar to what occurred in Hungary in 1956. After the failure of a series of bilateral negotiations between the leaders of the Soviet Union and Czechoslovakia in July 1968, Moscow executed the Brežnev Doctrine and ordered the military forces of the Warsaw Pact—the Soviet Union, the German Democratic Republic, Bulgaria, Poland, and Hungary (Romania and Albania abstained)—to invade Czechoslovakia. On the night of 20 August 1968, 200,000 troops and 2,000 tanks entered and occupied the country. During the invasion, seventy-two Czechs and Slovaks were killed (nineteen of those in Slovakia) and 700 wounded. Although Alexander Dubček called upon his people not to resist, there was scattered resistance in the streets. An estimated 70,000 Czechoslovak citizens fled the country immediately with an eventual total of some 300,000 that managed to follow before the borders were sealed.

In the aftermath, the United Nations and governments across the globe mounted only symbolic condemnation. The invasion and occupation of an established sovereign state seeking by its own volition Democratic reforms was once again reluctantly accepted by the international community. This seemed to be Czechoslovakia's fate since its inception. However, the late provocateur, author, critic, and journalist Christopher Hitchens recapitulated the repercussions of the Prague Spring to western Communism in *Slate* on 28 August 2008: "What became clear, however, was that there was no longer something that could be called the world communist movement. It was utterly, irretrievably, hopelessly split. The main spring had broken. And the Prague Spring had broken it."

In light of these historic, cyclical eruptions of a people longing for freedom, General Peter Vlčko felt the moment had come to finally document his memoirs recalling the events he lived through in Czechoslovakia during the turbulent decade of 1938–1948. The original 1,500-page manuscript was drafted and translated into English but judged too massive to economically publish by any available traditional means at the time. Moreover, in the late 1960s and early 1970s publishing houses were averse to publishing biographies, histories, or personal memoirs with traditional military and political themes. The culture at the time demanded more counter-cultural themes. In order to bring this project into reality, General Vlčko was forced to significantly revise and condense his memoirs into the form of a novel emphasizing the romantic, sensual dynamic between his two principal characters under the alias *Hronský*. In the end, much of the vital political and historical context in the book was excised and whittled down to 860 pages with library cataloging organizations miscategorizing the book as fiction. Correcting this improper genre categorization over three decades later required much work that finally placed this book into its correct genre among world cataloging organizations and academic libraries.

Since the publication of *In the Shadow of Tyranny* in January 1973 and particularly since the collapse of the Soviet Union in September 1991, vast resources of previously classified government archives from the Soviet Union and its satellite states have become progressively available to academic researchers and the public. Over the course of the ensuing decades since the fall of the Soviet Union and continuing to date, libraries of works analyzing the formerly secret archives have been steadily published, critiqued, and rewritten as twentieth century history is redebated, reinterpreted, and rebooted. Furthermore, extensive official German archives that have slowly become increasingly available for government research (1952) and public access (1988)—the reunited Federal *Reich* Archives, or *Bundesarchiv*, comprised of the Central State Archives of the GDR, formerly held by the Soviet government in Potsdam since 1946, and the Federal Archives in Koblenz since 1952, finally became an integrated archive physically accessible to the general public in 1990 and by Internet access in 1997—have found new interest among academic and independent researchers combing Eastern Bloc secret archives. The plethora of academic works produced since the declassification of state secret archives in Europe, Russia, the United States, and the Vatican have helped reframe the contextual understanding of landmark historical events of the twentieth century and beyond.

Moreover, in his attempt to quickly crystallize his memories and thoughts in order to publish and meet the pressing events of the 1968 Prague

Spring, General Vlčko was forced to bypass consulting her and write about events and conversations involving his beloved Jirka, details of which he had no first-hand knowledge. Consequently, he created facts and dialogue in the book involving Jirka that were not entirely accurate and projected a misleading message that would later require revision.

The availability of this new information and life circumstances that in 2014 led Georgina Vlčko to come under the care of her youngest child Dr. Peter B. Vlčko, provided an extraordinary opportunity to move forward with this second edition of *In the Shadow of Tyranny* with the added subtitle, *Between Hitler and Stalin*. My mother and I worked closely together to revise the history of the events and interactions that she was involved in while separated from her husband during periods of the Second World War, and thereafter. Through years of personal discussion with my father and extensive research of secondary sources analyzing primary source archival materials declassified since 1990, I was also able to expand my father's memoirs in the greater historical, political, and philosophical context of the tragic events in Europe and Russia during the nineteenth and twentieth centuries that laid the foundation to the Second World War and the Holocaust. Added to the first edition of the book is a relatively in-depth exploration of the origins of the Nazi movement, as well as brief biographies of the lives of Peter Vlčko and Georgina Reichsfeld before they met, that lay the foundation for the remainder of the book. Preserved from the original, however, is the moving story of a love affair between a young, beautiful, hunted and condemned Jew trapped in the lion's den and a handsome, well-positioned Aryan Slovak Army officer in the Ministry of National Defense whose unlikely fates and disparate backgrounds amalgamate in symbiotic harmony. Their story is the perfect antithesis to, yet microcosm in the thunderous backdrop of aggression, war, military occupation, insurrection, political oppression, and the racist policies of extermination that exploded in Europe during the 1940s. The stark contrast of these two settings epitomize the two extremes of the human experience: the insanity and chaos of war and the blissful serenity of love.

Underpinning the motivation for this project was the maturing interest of my youngest child, Sonja Georgina, whose teachers at Grosse Ile High School expressed deep interest in my parents' story. I felt that the passage of time inevitably dilutes the younger generation's interest in and true understanding of the series of events and *Zeitgeist* that led up to one of history's most notable human tragedies. Pressing upon me was the latent resignation among secondary school educators that the lessons of the nineteenth and twentieth centuries with their reflection on human nature had not been fully explored, understood, and taught, and are losing their significance to approaching generations of students. For this reason, *Epimythium* (or "moral of the story") was added at the end of the book to touch on some of the lessons intended by this edited work. It is my sincere hope this new and expanded edition will help future generations move beyond the mere study of historical facts, to become metahistorians with a deeper understanding of history, the world, and human nature when developing their *Weltanschauung*.

Peter B. Vlčko

PROLEGOMENON

Live as if you were to die tomorrow; learn as if you were to live forever.

— MOHANDAS (MAHATMA) KARAMCHAND GANDHI

Man becomes what he thinks about all day long.

— RALPH WALDO EMERSON

What we learn from history is that no one learns from history.

— OTTO VON BISMARCK

BY THE UNIVERSAL LAW OF CAUSE AND EFFECT, ALL MAJOR MOVEMENTS and causes are the offspring of preceding events or their antithesis—the quagmire or impasse. By this same causality, the Nazi movement was the archetypical reactionary response to erupting revolutionary trends that had been building momentum over two centuries and permanently changing the *status quo* that had existed in Europe for millennia. A great deal of serious study and scholarship has been invested over the decades since the fall of the Third *Reich* into understanding the Nazi movement and the events leading up to it in an effort to satisfy humanity's intense thirst for answers to the perplexity created by the Second World War and its catastrophe known as the Holocaust. In response to the growing loss of interest in and true understanding of the series of events and *Zeitgeist* that led up to one of history's most notable human tragedies and the latent resignation among educators that the lessons of the nineteenth and twentieth centuries with their reflection on human nature are losing their significance to approaching generations of students, Part One to the second edition of this book was added as a foundational prologue to the moving story of Peter Vlčko and Georgina Reichsfeld, and two of history's greatest tragedies. At the risk of presenting a novel interpretation of this complex history and raising uncomfortable, potentially offensive cultural, philosophical, psychological, theological, and political issues, Part One delves deeply into the who, what, where, when, why, and how of the Nazi movement. Without a thorough grasp of these issues, a true understanding of and empathy for what those who experienced and lived through the decade-long tragedy of 1938–1948 will remain beyond reach. Growing misunderstanding of that period will inevitably result in a repeat of history, in one form or another.

The reader is cordially invited—no, forcefully urged—to wade through this complex discussion. The rewards will be self-evident by the end of this book and the dialogue among and the events in the lives of the various participants in this story of Peter Vlčko and Georgina Reichsfeld will have much richer meaning. If the reader choses to undertake this scholarly journey, they are strongly encouraged to look up and read the discursive endnotes for each chapter represented by superscript numerals throughout this manuscript and found in the back of the last volume of this title. These important endnotes provide greater insight to the issue being referenced that was at the time of this writing deemed too lengthy of a parenthetical digression to include in the main body of the manuscript. With this foundation, the reader will be teleported into the dramatic scenes unfolding throughout this book. However, if the reader is convinced that they are simply not interested in the complexities of how the Nazi movement became a reality and would rather jump directly into the story of Peter Vlčko and Georgina Reichsfeld beginning in Part Two, then the reader can be assured to enjoy their story without this foundation.

Part One

THE ORIGINS OF THE NAZI MOVEMENT

National Socialism could not have come to power in Germany if it had not found, in broad strata of the population, soil prepared for its sowing of poison.

— KONRAD ADENAUER, first Chancellor of the Federal Republic of Germany, 1949

Das war ein Vorspiel nur, dort wo man Bücher verbrennt, verbrennt man auch am Ende Menschen. ("That was but a prelude; where they burn books, they will ultimately burn people as well.")

— The Muslim Hassan, when he heard that the Christian conquerors had burned the Qur'an at the marketplace of Granada. In HEINRICH HEINE'S 1821 play *Almansor*.

Christianity—and this is its greatest merit—has somewhat mitigated that brutal Germanic love of war, but it could not destroy it. Should that subduing talisman, the cross, be shattered, the frenzied madness of the ancient warriors, that insane Berserk rage of which Nordic bards have spoken and sung so often, will once more burst into flame. This talisman is fragile, and the day will come when it will collapse miserably. Then the ancient stony gods will rise from the forgotten debris and rub the dust of a thousand years from their eyes, and finally Thor with his giant hammer will jump up and smash the Gothic cathedrals.

* * *

Do not smile at my advice—the advice of a dreamer who warns you against Kantians, Fichteans, and philosophers of nature. Do not smile at the visionary who anticipates the same revolution in the realm of the visible as has taken place in the spiritual. Thought precedes action as lightning precedes thunder. German thunder is of true Germanic character; it is not very nimble, but rumbles along ponderously. Yet, it will come and when you hear a crashing such as never before has been heard in the world's history, then you know that the German thunderbolt has fallen at last. At that uproar the eagles of the air will drop dead, and lions in the remotest deserts of Africa will hide in their royal dens. A play will be performed in Germany which will make the French Revolution look like an innocent idyll.

— HEINRICH HEINE, 1834 *The History of Religion and Philosophy in Germany*

PROLOGUE

SIMPLISTICALLY—POSSIBLY, OVER-SIMPLISTICALLY—THE NAZI movement has been generally characterized as one of militant Nationalism, xenophobia, racism, and genocide. Xenophobia and racism are intimately related to three of the four basic human emotions—anger, fear, and sadness—and have deep roots in human psychopathology. Exploring these complex origins is far beyond the scope and intent of this work. Inquiry into the origins of Nazi ideology leading to the Holocaust invariably draws historians into Adolf Hitler's mind. To date, examination of the origins of the Nazi movement falls into one of two schools of thought: the Intentionalist interpretation that Nazi genocide stemmed directly from Adolf Hitler's personal racist prejudices that were imposed upon the German people as part of a master plan; and the Functionalist interpretation, which contends that historic, economic, and "bureaucratic" forces determined events leading up to the Holocaust to a greater extent than Hitler's own will.

A branch of the Functionalist school of thought that arose early during World War II as a consequence of the rise of Nazi Germany, came to be known as the *Sonderweg* or "special path." Its proponents argued that the way Germany developed over the centuries virtually ensured the evolution of a social and political order along the lines of Nazi Germany. In their view, German mentalities, the structure of society, and institutional developments followed a different course in comparison with the other nations of the West, which had a "normal" development of their histories. Proponents of the *Sonderweg* theory were in conflict with the more liberal proponents of the Intentionalist theory.

Starting in the 1960s, *Sonderweg* historians such as Fritz Fischer and Hans-Ulrich Wehler argued that, unlike France and Britain, Germany had experienced only "partial modernization," in which industrialization was not followed by changes in the political and social spheres, which in the opinion of Fischer and Wehler continued to be dominated by a "pre-modern" aristocratic elite. In the opinion of the proponents of the *Sonderweg* thesis, the crucial turning point was the Revolution of 1848, when German liberals failed to seize power and consequently either emigrated or chose to resign themselves to being ruled by a reactionary elite, living in a society that taught its children obedience, glorification of militarism, and pride in a very complex notion of German culture. During the latter half of the Second *Reich*, from about 1890 to 1918, this pride, they argued, developed into hubris. Since 1950, historians such as Fischer, Wehler, and Hans Mommsen have drawn a harsh indictment of the German elite of the period 1870–1945, who were accused of promoting authoritarian values during the Second *Reich*, being solely responsible for launching World War I, sabotaging the Democratic Weimar Republic, and aiding and abetting the Nazi dictatorship in internal repression, war, and genocide. In the view of Wehler, Fischer, and their supporters, only the German defeat in 1945 put an end to the "premodern" social structure which had led to and then sustained traditional German authoritarianism and its more radical variant, National Socialism. Wehler has asserted that the effects of the traditional power elite in maintaining power up to 1945 "and in many respects even beyond that" took the form of:

> a penchant for authoritarian politics; a hostility toward democracy in the educational and party system; the influence of preindustrial leadership groups, values and ideas; the tenacity of German state ideology; the myth of the bureaucracy; the superimposition of caste tendencies and class distinctions; and the manipulation of political antisemitism (Hamerow 1983, 53–72).

Another version of the *Sonderweg* thesis emerged in the United States in the 1950s–1960s, when historians such as Fritz Stern and George Mosse examined ideas and culture in nineteenth-century Germany, especially those of the virulently anti-Semitic *völkisch* movement. Mosse and Stern both concluded that the intellectual and cultural elites in Germany by and large chose to consciously reject modernity and along with it those groups they identified with modernity, such as Jews, and embraced anti-Semitism as the basis for their *Weltanschauung* (worldview). However, in recent years, Stern has abandoned his conclusion and now argues against the *Sonderweg* thesis, holding the views of the *völkisch* movement to be a mere "dark undercurrent" in the Second *Reich.*

Another variant of the *Sonderweg* theory has been provided by Nationalist German historian Michael Stürmer who, echoing claims of conservative historians during the Imperial and Weimar periods, argues that it was geography that was the key to German history. Stürmer contends that what he regards as Germany's precarious geographical situation in the heart of Central Europe left successive German governments no other choice but to engage in authoritarianism. Stürmer's views have been very controversial; they would become one of the central issues in the notorious *Historikerstreit* ("Historians' Quarrel," see *infra*) of the mid-1980s. One of Stürmer's leading critics, German historian Jürgen Kocka, himself a proponent of the *Sonderweg* view of history, argued that "Geography is not destiny" (Kocka 1993, 85–92), suggesting that the reasons for the *Sonderweg* were political and cultural instead.

Immediately after World War II, intense debates arose in intellectual circles about how to interpret Nazi Germany, a contested discussion that continues today. Two of the more hotly debated questions were whether Nazism was in some way part of the "German national character" and how much responsibility, if any, the German people bore for the crimes of Nazism. Various non-German intellectuals in the immediate postwar era, such as British historians Alan John Percivale Taylor and Sir Lewis Namier, argued that Nazism was the culmination of German history, and that the vast majority of Germans were responsible for Nazi crimes. Different assessments of Nazism were common among Marxists, who insisted on the economic aspects of Nazism and conceived of it as the culmination of a Capitalist crisis, and liberals, who emphasized Hitler's personal role and responsibility and bypassed the larger problem of the relation of ordinary German people to the regime. Within West Germany, then, most liberal historians were strongly defensive and advocated for the Intentionalist construct focusing solely on Hitler and his gang of cohorts. In the assessment of Gerhard Ritter and other Intentionalists, Nazism was a totalitarian movement that represented only the work of a small criminal clique; Germans were victims of Nazism, and the Nazi era represented a total break in German history.

Starting in the 1960s, that assessment was challenged by younger German historians. Fritz Fischer argued in favor of a *Sonderweg* conception of German history that saw Nazism as the result of the way German society had developed. In the late 1960s and early 1970s, the Functionalist school of historiography emerged; its proponents argued that medium- and lower-ranking German officials were not just obeying orders and policies but actively engaged in the making of the policies that led to the Holocaust. The Functionalists thereby cast blame for the Holocaust across a wider circle. Many liberal German historians disliked the implications of the *Sonderweg* conception and the Functionalist school; they were generally identified with Socialism and were seen by the Nationalists as being derogatory toward Germany. From this growing controversy between the two schools, particularly the *Sonderweg* branch, arose the contentious *Historikerstreit* that played out in 1986–1989. The debate attracted much media attention in West Germany, with its participants frequently giving television interviews and writing op-ed pieces in newspapers.

The debate centered on four questions:

1. Were the crimes of Nazi Germany uniquely evil in history, or were other crimes, such as those of Josef Stalin in the Soviet Union, comparably evil?
2. Did German history follow a "special path" (*Sonderweg*) leading inevitably to Nazism?
   a. If that teleological interpretation was accepted, then most or all of pre-1945 German history bore the taint of the impending Nazism, while Nazism was considered inevitable. If the *Sonderweg* analysis were valid, it would undermine German historian Ernst Nolte's[*] argument that the Holocaust was a

[*] Ernst Nolte (1923–2016) - German historian and philosopher. Nolte's major interest was the comparative studies of Fascism and Communism. Originally trained in philosophy, he was professor emeritus of modern history at the Free University of Berlin, where he taught from 1973 until his 1991 retirement. He was previously a professor at the University of Marburg from 1965 to 1973. He was best known for his seminal work *Fascism in Its Epoch*, which received widespread acclaim when it

defensive reaction to Soviet crimes, and would suggest that the origins of Nazism predated World War I. The *Sonderweg* analysis, however, did not necessarily consider Nazism from a teleological perspective, but tried to identify historical factors explaining its rise (the popularity of anti-Semitism in pre-Nazi Germany, Prussian militarism, etc.)

b. The West German historians Klaus Hildebrand, Gerhard Ritter, and Andreas Hillgruber rejected the *Sonderweg* view, while the British historian A. J. P. Taylor and the West German historians Hans-Ulrich Wehler, Wolfgang Mommsen, Hans Mommsen, and Fritz Fischer supported it.

c. A sub-issue of the *Sonderweg* thesis concerned the reasons for the alleged *Sonderweg*. Stürmer argued for geographical factors as the reason for the *Sonderweg*, while Wehler insisted on cultural and social factors. One of Stürmer's leading critics, Jürgen Kocka, himself a proponent of the *Sonderweg* view of history, argued that "Geography is not destiny."

3. Were other genocides comparable to the Holocaust? Many people believed that such comparisons tended to trivialize the Holocaust, but others maintained that the Holocaust could best be understood in the context of the twentieth century by means of these comparisons.
4. Were the crimes of the Nazis a reaction to Soviet crimes under Stalin, as German historian Ernst Nolte contended? Should the German people bear a special burden of guilt for Nazi crimes, or could new generations of Germans find sources of pride in their history?

---

was published in 1963. Nolte was a prominent Nationalist academic from the early 1960s and was involved in many controversies related to the interpretation of the history of Fascism and Communism, including the *Historikerstreit* in the late 1980s. In recent years, Nolte focused on Islamism and "Islamic fascism." During the *Historikerstreit*, Nolte argued that because there was no moral difference between the crimes of the Soviet Union and those of Nazi Germany—and even more controversially that because the Holocaust was something that the Germans were allegedly forced to do out of a fear of what the Soviet Union might do to them—that Germans should not feel any guilt over the Holocaust and should essentially forget about it.

The answers to the above four questions will become evident throughout Part One of this book and revisited in *Epimythium* at the end of the book. According to the now prevailing opinion of historians, Germany's history did not differ from the history of the great European nations to an extent that would justify speaking of a "unique German path." However, no matter how extreme or eccentric any single movement may be, major historical events are never the product of a single individual's ideations and will and are not born out of a vacuum unimpacted by the world and events around them. Drawing definitive conclusions solely under the Intentionalist paradigm is like making a diagnosis of disease and drafting a therapeutic plan in a patient based solely on physical examination without intimately considering the full medical and social history of the patient. In order to better understand the origins of the Nazi movement and its ageless implications (see *Epimythium* at the end of this book), an examination of specific historical events and developments over a relatively narrow period of time is most helpful. Understanding these past events and developments is critical to understanding the *Zeitgeist* of cyclical contemporary and future developments. At the risk of being loquacious, dense, and pedantic, let us now digress for a moment to more closely examine the historical developments in historiography, political theory, philosophy, the arts, theology, the occult, and the German Revolution leading to the Nazi movement and the Holocaust of the 1940s.

The following discussion is not based on this author's own novel research of the primary source historical documents but on this author's analysis and summation of the vast extant research done by scholars and experts in the various disciplines addressed below. By no means should this author's writing here be considered comprehensive. It is merely intended to be a coherent summation. The extant research on the origins of the Nazi movement and its analysis and conclusions remain somewhat specialized, disjointed, narrowly focused, episodic, esoteric, and inchoate. Without committing the reader to years of study, this discussion will attempt to unify the extant research to crystalize a panoptic, holistic, global picture hopefully enabling the reader to better understand the natural pathogenesis by which a series of events over a period of human history may predictably lead to tragedy. With this understanding, it is the hope and goal of this writer to enlighten and prepare the reader for his or her independent critical analysis of human events, past and present. Finally, it is this writer's firm belief that the penultimate objective of all scholarship has historically been to better understand ourselves, human nature, and the world we live in—self-awareness—in order to ultimately enlighten us and answer humanity's ageless and most vexing dilemmas as to our origins, purpose, and destiny.

CHAPTER 1

HISTORIOGRAPHY

History . . . is indeed little more than the register of the crimes, follies, and misfortunes of mankind.

— EDWARD GIBBON, *The Decline and Fall of the Roman Empire*

The very ink with which all history is written is merely fluid prejudice.

— MARK TWAIN, *Following the Equator*

That's one of the central problems of history, isn't it, sir? The question of subjective versus objective interpretation, the fact that we need to know the history of the historian in order to understand the version that is being put in front of us.

— JULIAN BARNES, *The Sense of an Ending*

LIKE MUCH OF DOCUMENTED HISTORY, THE HISTORIOGRAPHY OF THE Holocaust in twentieth-century Europe has been tainted with deep emotion, political ideology, and hubris. Before we delve into the deep, it would be appropriate to say a few words on historiography, in general.

Hayden White (1928–2018) was a historical theorist in the tradition of literary criticism and perhaps most famous for his work *Metahistory: The Historical Imagination in Nineteenth-Century Europe* (1973 and 2014). His central argument in this seminal work was that every modern historian since the nineteenth century to present has written history in an ideological narrative—either anarchist, conservative, radical, or liberal—hidden or overt, subconscious or unconscious. Being an historian is like being a witness in the courtroom; the witness, whether eyewitness or hearsay, conveys their version of the facts from their viewpoint, memory, and interpretation with their unique set of inherent biases (conscious and unconscious) and motivations.

"All stories are fictions," wrote Hayden White, viewed by many as one of the most influential and revolutionary thinkers in the humanities in the last fifty years, and known for going beyond the surface level of historical text to a deeper structural level of linguistic form. White believes that history is not a science, or a story told only in facts, but rather a form of discourse that relies on conventional narrative forms and the imagination. He claims that the manifest historical text is marked by strategies of explanation, which include explanation by argument, explanation by emplotment, and explanation by ideological implication (White 1973a, 7). He has argued that historical writing mirrors literary writing in many ways, sharing the strong reliance on narrative for meaning, therefore ruling out the possibility for objective or truly scientific history (White 1973b, 281–314). White has also argued, however, that history is most successful when it embraces this "narrativity," since it is what allows history to be meaningful. Below is an excerpt from White's *Metahistory: The Historical Imagination in Nineteenth-Century Europe* (1973), pages 45–9.

> Nineteenth-century European culture displayed everywhere a rage for a realistic apprehension of the world. The term "realistic," of course, meant something other than a "scientific" comprehension of the world, although certain self-designated "realists," such as the Positivists and Social Darwinists, identified their "realism" with the kind of comprehension of natural processes which the physical sciences provided. Even here, however, the term "realism" had connotations which suggested that more was involved than a simple application of "scientific method" to the data of history, society, and human nature. For, in spite of their generally "scientistic" orientation, the "realistic" aspirations of nineteenth-century thinkers and artists were informed by an awareness that any effort to understand the historical world offered special problems, difficulties not presented in the human effort to comprehend the world of merely physical process.
>
> The most important of these problems was created by the fact that the student of the historical process was enclosed within it or involved in it in a way that the student

of the natural process was not. There was a sense in which one could legitimately maintain that man was both in nature and outside it, that he *participated* in the natural process, but that he could also *transcend* that process in consciousness, assume a position outside it, and *view* the process as manifested in those levels of natural integration which were demonstrably non- or prehuman. But, when it came to reflection on history, only man of all the beings of nature appeared to *have* a history; for all practical purposes, the "historical process" existed only in the form of a generally human process. And, since "humanity" constituted the sole conceivable manifestation of that process which was called "historical," it seemed impossible to make about the process, as a whole, generalizations of the sort that one could legitimately make about "nature" in its purely physical, chemical, and biological dimensions. "Realism" in the natural sciences could be identified with the "scientific method" developed since Newton at the latest for the analysis of natural processes. But what a "realistic" conception of history might consist of was as much a problem as the definition of such similarly illusive terms as "man," "culture," and "society." Each of the most important cultural movements and ideologies of the nineteenth century—Positivism, Idealism, Naturalism, (literary) Realism, Symbolism, Vitalism, Anarchism, Liberalism, and so on—claimed to provide a more "realistic" comprehension of social reality than its competitors. Even the Symbolist contention that "the world is a forest of symbols" and the Nihilist denial of confidence in *any* possible system of thought were attended by arguments on behalf of the "realistic" nature of their world views.

To be a "realist" meant both to see things clearly, as they *really* were, and to draw appropriate conclusions from this clear apprehension of reality for the living of a possible life on its basis. As thus envisaged, claims to an essential "realism" were at once epistemological and ethical. One might stress the purely analytical or perceptual nature of one's "realism," as the Impressionist painters did, or the moral and prescriptive implications of one's clarity of vision, as did the so-called Neo-Machiavellians in political theory, such as Treitschke. But the claim to represent a "realistic" position on any matter entailed defense of that position on at least two grounds, epistemological and ethical.

From our vantage point in the eighth decade of the twentieth century, we can now see that most of the important theoretical and ideological disputes that developed in Europe between the French Revolution and the World War I were in reality disputes over which group might claim the right to determine of what a "realistic" representation of social reality might consist. One man's "reality" was another man's "utopia," and what appeared to be the quintessence of a "realistic" position on one issue might represent the quintessence of "naiveté" from a different perspective of that same issue. What is most interesting about this whole period, considering it as a finished drama of inquiry and expression, is the general authority which the notion "realism" itself commanded. For every age, even the most fideistic, such as the Medieval period, gains its integral consistency from the conviction of its own capacities to know "reality" and to react to its challenges with appropriately "realistic" responses. The express desire to *be* "realistic," then, must reflect a specific conception not so much of what the essence of "realism" is as of what it means to be "unrealistic." The problematics of a "realistic" approach to reality are much the same as those contained in the notions of "sanity" and "health." Such notions are more easily defined by what men of a given time and place recognize as their opposites, "madness" and "sickness." So, too, the specific content of a given age's conception of "realism" is more easily defined by what that age as a whole took to be "unrealism" or "utopianism." And, when it is a matter of trying to characterize the historical thinking of an age in which many different conceptions of "historical realism" were contending for hegemony, it is necessary to ask what it was that these different conceptions of "realism" agreed upon as "unrealism" or "utopianism" in historical thinking in general.

Nineteenth-century historical theorists generally agreed that the principal forms of historical thought of the period which immediately preceded them—that is, those of the Enlightenment [1685–1815]—provided models of the dangers confronting any historical theory that claims the authority of a "realistic" world view. This is not to say that they rejected out of hand the entire historiographical productivity of Enlightenment thinkers. In fact, certain of the *philosophes,* and most notably Voltaire, continued to exercise a profound influence during the period of Romanticism, and Voltaire himself was regarded as an ideal worthy of emulation by even as Romantic a historian as Michelet. Nonetheless, in general, what nineteenth-century historical thought aspired to in the way of a "realistic" historiography can best be characterized in terms of what it objected to in its eighteenth-century predecessors. And what it objected to most in Enlightenment historiography was its *essential irony,* just as what it objected to most in its cultural reflection was its *skepticism.*

It did not, be it noted, object to what is usually regarded as the principal characteristic of Enlightenment philosophy of history—that is to say, its presumed "optimism" and the doctrine of progress which usually accompanied it. For historical thinkers during the greater part of the nineteenth century were as interested as their eighteenth-century counterparts had been in providing the bases for belief in the possibility of "progress" on the one hand and some kind of justification for historical "optimism" on the other. For most of them, the concept of "progress" and the feeling of "optimism" were compatible with the "realistic" world view to which they hoped to contribute through their historical writings. For them, the important point was that the concept of progress and its accompanying optimism had *not yet* been provided with adequate cognitive justification. Some of them—most notably, Tocqueville and Burckhardt—feared that such justification could never be provided, and consequently a somewhat soberer tone pervades their work than that which we find in more sanguine spirits such as Michelet (in his early works) and Marx (in all of his).

In general, then, the "realism" of nineteenth-century historical thought consists in its search for adequate grounds for belief in progress and optimism *in the full awareness* of the failure of eighteenth-century historical thinkers to provide those grounds. If one is to understand the specific nature of nineteenth-century historical realism, considered as the matrix of shared beliefs that make of the different schools of historical thought of that time inhabitants of a single universe of discourse, one must specify the nature of the eighteenth century's failure in historical thinking. This failure, I will argue, did not consist in a lack of scholarly achievement—that is to say, a failure of learning—or in an inadequate theory of historical reflection. Rather, it consisted in the Ironic mode in which both scholarly inquiry and theoretical syntheses were cast by the Enlightenment's outstanding historical thinkers.

The Dialectics of Enlightenment Historiography

Eighteenth-century historical reflection originated in an attempt to apply Metonymical strategies of reduction to the data of history in such a way as to justify belief in the possibility of a human community conceived in the Synecdochic mode. To put it another way, the Enlightenment attempted to justify an Organicist conception of the ideal human community on the basis of an analysis of social process which was essentially Mechanistic in nature. It thus criticized society in the light of an ideal that was moral and valuative, but it pretended to base that criticism on a purely causal analysis of historical processes. As a consequence, the end to which historical representation was meant to contribute was inconsistent with the means actually used in the construction of historical narratives. The result of this conflict between the *means* of historical representation and the *end* to which it was meant to contribute was to drive thought about history into a position that was overtly and militantly Ironic. What started out as a creative tension in early Enlightenment historical thinking, between Comic and Tragic conceptions of the plot of history, between Mechanistic and Organicist conceptions of its processes, and between the Conservative and Radical implications that might be drawn from these, gradually degenerated into an ambiguity, and ultimately an ambivalence, concerning all the principal problems of both historiographical representation and general social goals. By the last quarter of the eighteenth century, this ambivalence had been transformed into irony, which expressed itself in a historical epistemology that was Skeptical in the extreme and in an ethical attitude, generated by Skepticism, that was manifestly relativistic. By the end of the Enlightenment, such thinkers as Gibbon, Hume, and Kant had effectively dissolved the distinction between history and fiction on which earlier thinkers such as Bayle and Voltaire had based their historiographical enterprises. It was against this "fictionalization" of history, this Ironic stance before the "scientific" tasks which early eighteenth-century historians had set for themselves, that Herder, Burke, and the *Stürmer und Dränger* rebelled.

CHAPTER 2

POLITICAL THEORY

> [Politics:] *The struggle in any group for power that will give one or more persons the ability to make decisions for the larger group.* (O'Neil 2004, 5)
>
> — PATRICK H. O'NEIL

> *Those who believe religion and politics aren't connected don't understand either.*
>
> — MAHATMA GANDHI

AMONG PRIMITIVE PEOPLES, THE IDEAS THAT LATER COME TO BE designated as political are inextricably blended with conceptions known to us as legal, ethical, theological, ecclesiastical, and even mathematical. The disentanglement of this confused mass and the isolation and definition of what is purely political is practically never fully accomplished. From the fact that political philosophy in all ages has stood in such intimate relationship with other philosophy, it is inevitable that a historical treatment of the special should involve a good deal of attention to the general field. Particularly obstinate is the entanglement of politics with ethics and jurisprudence. A by no means insignificant proportion of the thought of political philosophers has been devoted to defining the interrelationship of the three, or to demonstrating that no distinction can be drawn between them. Ethical and juristic concepts, therefore, must figure largely in a history of political concepts (Dunning 1919, xix–xxi).

Let us digress for a moment to clarify some important definitions that are used and consistently adhered to throughout this discussion. Liberalism and Conservativism are terms that have over centuries of Western history taken on many meanings and implications. Liberal theories form a broad continuum, from those that constitute full-blown philosophical systems, to those that rely on a full theory of value and the good, to those that rely on a theory of the right (but not the good), all the way to those that seek to be purely political doctrines. Nevertheless, it is important to appreciate that, though Liberalism in the modern era has been primarily a political theory, it has been associated with broader theories of ethics, value, and society. Indeed, many believe that Liberalism cannot rid itself of all controversial metaphysical (Hampton 1989, 791–814) or epistemological (Raz 1990, 3–46) commitments (Gaus, Courtland, and Schmidtz 2014). In our examination here on the origins of the Nazi movement, the terms Liberalism and Conservativism are used in three arenas: political; theological; and sociological.

The term "Liberalism" has its origin in the Latin root *liber* whose original meaning and intent was rebellion against traditional authority, truth, and culture. In pre-republican Rome, *liber* referred to a man who has "freed" or unbridled himself by rejecting and thwarting traditional authority. Such men were seen as rebellious and "free, unrestricted, unimpeded, unbridled, unchecked, licentious." Later, during republican Roman times, the term *liber* took on the meaning of a "noble born" or "free man."

> The contrary of the *liber*, or free, person in Roman, republican usage was the *servus*, or slave, and up to at least the beginning of the . . . [nineteenth] century, the dominant connotation of freedom, emphasized in the long republican tradition, was not having to live in servitude to another: not being subject to the arbitrary power of another (Pettit 1996, 576–604).

The term "liberal" was used in the sixteenth and seventeenth centuries as a pejorative term of reproach with the meaning "free from restraint in speech or action." The Enlightenment adopted some of the neo-Roman republican characteristics of *liber* men revolting against injustice and oppression and redefined "liberal" in a positive sense "free from prejudice, tolerant, not bigoted or narrow," whose use emerged in 1776–1788. In the nineteenth century, "liberal" was more often used in the theological rather than political sense as meaning "opposed to orthodoxy."

"Liberal" in the modern political sense meaning "tending in favor of freedom and Democracy," dates only from *circa* 1801, from the French *libéral*. In English, the political label was at first applied by opponents (often in the French form and with pejorative suggestions of foreign lawlessness) to the party more favorable to individual political freedoms. But also (especially in U.S. politics) tending to mean "favorable to government action to effect social change," which seems at times to draw more from liberal theological use of the term as meaning "free from prejudice of traditional opinions and established institutions" (and thus open to new ideas and plans of reform—"progressive"), which dates from 1823.

The Left-Right "wing" label originates from the 1789 French Revolution when members of the National Assembly divided into supporters of the king seated to the Assembly president's right and supporters of the revolution seated to his left. By 1914, the Left half of the legislature in France was composed of Unified Socialists, Republican Socialists, and Socialist Radicals, while the parties that were called "Left," now sat on the right side. The post-Enlightenment use of the words Left and Right spread from France to other countries and came to be applied to a large number of political parties worldwide, which often differed in their political beliefs.

However, as we will come to learn, the single-axis Left-Right political spectrum defining and categorizing various political theories that has become conventional wisdom in academia, journalism, literature, and all forms of common communication is a contrived system that is based on emotion rather than fact. The single-axis Left-Right system of political labeling has completely misled generations to believe vast and polar differences exist between various political ideologies, which in fact and reality do not exist. This misinformation has resulted in vitriolic debate and even violence and death. Few theologians over history have managed to recognize the simple factor that differentiates all religions that have ever existed. Likewise, few philosophers and political theorists have managed to recognize the simple factor that differentiates all political theories that have existed over history. The Left-Right or Liberal-Conservative visions of our world have given us a bum steer in guiding our understanding of ourselves and how best to govern (Vlčko *Bum Steer*).

The earliest scholastic use of the term Liberalism was in theology and specifically refers to any deviation from orthodox dogma and doctrine. This concept arose from the legal doctrines of statutory interpretation, which was the basis of magisterial code in Roman law and of English common law, which interpreted and established the intended meaning of statutory law. Historical jurisprudence has taught that no legislation perfectly, unambiguously, and specifically addresses all matters that may arise over time. In ancient monarchical systems, the lawmaker (king) was most often also the interpreter of the law. As societies grew in complexity and size, the sheer volume of legal challenges made it impossible for the monarch alone to judge all cases. Therefore, societies established hierarchical systems of magistrates or judges charged with interpreting and applying legislation to specific challenges leaving the final word on appeal to the supreme authority (the monarch). Universal to the various systematic philosophies of statutory interpretation that developed over time was the concept of "narrow" (conservative) versus "broad" (liberal) interpretation of the intended meaning of specific words in the statute. Words are imperfect symbols to communicate intent. They are at times ambiguous and change in meaning over time; hence, their "broad" and "narrow" interpretation. Unforeseen situations are inevitable, and new technologies and cultures may change the meaning of words and/or change the basis, on which the legislation was originally written—*e.g.*, what was once thought to be scientifically or causally true may one day be proven to be false, yet the intent of the legislation remains apropos. One of the most fundamental factors that differentiates political, theological, and sociological ideologies is the meaning of key terms. Hence, the meaning of Liberalism remains controversial. To mitigate this controversy in our discussion here, let us stipulate that the meaning of Liberalism in the three arenas that we use the term is as follows:

- THEOLOGICAL LIBERALISM – any deviation from or alteration of literal orthodox (meaning "original") teachings. Theological Liberalism is a form of religious thought that establishes religious inquiry on the basis of a norm other than the authority of Scripture and tends to emphasize ethics over doctrine and experience over Scriptural authority. This applies to all religious faiths. According to orthodox Christian doctrine, Scripture is *norma normans* ("the rule that rules") while Christian Confessions, Creeds, and traditions are *norma normata* ("the rule that is ruled"). Above all, theological Liberalism asserts the freedom of the will of man (humanism) in matters of justification (salvation); this issue alone is what separates all heterodox from orthodox Christian faiths.

- POLITICAL LIBERALISM – 1) Classical Liberalism: was founded on ideas of liberty and equality and above all else values the freedom of individuals and property rights, including the freedom of religion, speech, press, assembly, and markets, as well as limited government; 2) Neoclassical Liberalism or Libertarianism: is Classical Liberalism with the added extreme *laissez-faire* political philosophy advocating only minimal state intervention in the lives and wider property rights of citizens. Classical and neoclassical Liberalism view government as a counter-productive force to liberty; and 3) Progressive Liberalism: defines liberty as social justice; social justice is the ultimate objective. Here, the chief task of government is to actively remove obstacles that prevent society from living freely or from fully realizing their potential in the struggle to achieve the ultimate objective of social justice. Greater value is placed on collective social justice than individual liberty; the government's *modus operandi* is to promote a legalistic milieu of policies, rules, regulations, and laws that "engineer" a more perfect and just society, even if they impinge on individual freedoms. When balancing the tradeoffs between collective social justice (the greater good) and individual liberty, collective social justice always supersedes in value. Outcome is valued over method as ethics are relative to outcome.

- SOCIOLOGICAL LIBERALISM – a philosophy that human nature is fundamentally good, and that mankind's latent "goodness" needs to be guided, nurtured ("educated"), and teased out by the policies of an elite ("wise") overseer through societal apparatus of government and academia. As the fundamental "goodness" of more and more individuals is manifested, society approaches true social justice. Whereas classical Liberalism emphasizes the role of individual liberty and believes that any attempt to ensure that market transactions and property rights conform to any predefined specific pattern of holdings to create "equality," "egalitarianism," and "social justice" will involve constant interferences with individual freedom, social Liberalism stresses the importance of equality and social justice that challenges the intimate connection between personal liberty and a private-property-based free market order.

Politics is the art of self-government. Historically, when people have collectively submitted to a governing authority, they did not do so out of preference; they did so out of necessity. What form of government they oblige and how that government exercises its authority has been and continues to be most often a reflection of their baser instincts and the ethics and values of their culture. These elements are what constitute politics. To fully examine a political theory, on which governance is based, one cannot ignore the culture and times in which it originates and operates. In essence, politics is merely a manifestation of human nature with all its contradictions, and political theory reflects mankind's efforts to bridle human nature for the collective good.

Having stipulated the aforementioned definitions, we start this discussion on the role of political theory in the origins of the Nazi movement with the writings and thesis of British cultural metahistorian Christopher Dawson (1889–1970)—a man who has been called "[t]he greatest English-speaking Catholic historian of the twentieth century" (Daniel Callahan, *Harvard Theological Review*), and "[o]ne of the foremost prophets of our age" (Herbert Musurillo, S.J., American classical philologist and church historian). However, before demonstrating how Dawson applied his Christian interpretation of history to particular periods, it is necessary to situate it theologically. As his conversion reading indicates, Dawson drew on Augustinianism and Thomism in forming his outlook. He acknowledged Augustine's influence, and the affinities in their thought have led Dawson critics to posit correctly that his worldview was "essentially Augustinian" (Schwartz 2005, 245; see also footnote at 245). Dawson deemed Augustine's work seminal in shaping the approach to history he had inherited: "it is impossible to exaggerate the influence of St. Augustine's thought on the development of the Christian view of history and on the whole tradition of Western historiography" (Dawson 1951, 312–27).

Dawson had much to say on political movements and their intimate relationship with religion and culture.

> The work of Christopher Dawson is very relevant to those who want to understand the role of religion in Western history and the Christian roots of European history in particular. . . . Dawson's vast erudition, his historical intuition, his profound understanding of human nature, and his vision of Western culture as a living and dynamic entity, make him an essential starting point in the study—and understanding of—the spiritual tradition at the root of Western culture. Without this, all else that follows in Western history is incomprehensible (Duque 2016).

In Dawson's mind, culture is the essence of civilization. Therefore, in order to understand the evolution of civilization, one must understand the history of culture.

Dawson possessed a "cultural mind." What was this "cultural mind"? Some writers suggested that Dawson was an "historian of ideas."[44] While it is true that ideas and beliefs played a significant role in his historiography, and that he shared the typical interdisciplinarity of the intellectual historian, it is important to note that his main concern was not with ideas-in-themselves. Even in *Progress and Religion* (1929), the topic was not so much the idea of Progress as it was *culture* and cultural change, the factors present in cultural morphology and authentic human development. Dawson's object of knowledge in that book, and in much of his work, was "culture," which he described fundamentally as a common way of life of a particular people in a particular place. For him, "culture" was not simply the higher intellectual achievements of a people. It was also not simply the ways that people of the past represented themselves to themselves, or the meanings attached to objects or social mores, as it is for cultural historians of today. Dawson drew from the anthropology of the 1920s to view culture as broader than these descriptions: "The unity of a culture rests not only on a community of place—the common environment, a community of work—the common function, and the community of blood—the common race, it springs also, and above all, from a community of thought."[45]

Because culture embraced the whole of life, the intellectual and the material elements, Dawson had to study culture with the aid of many different disciplines. Thus the understanding of culture (and cultural change) was the goal that united the many disciplines of knowledge in Dawson's mind. They cooperated in this common intellectual goal (of understanding), as in *Progress and Religion*, where each chapter of the first part of the book studied the history of a separate discipline (sociology, history, anthropology, and comparative religion) (Stuart 2009, 31–2).

[44] [Footnote in original] Dawson 2001, xv; see also Oliver 1992, 212, 213, 214.

[45] [Footnote in original] Dawson 2001, 66.

Dawson saw Nationalism (and Liberalism) at the heart of the movements leading to totalitarianism. In his famous essay *On Nationalism*, published in London on the eve of the attempted German invasion of Britain, Dawson wrote about Nationalism as . . .

> a development which had its centre and origin in Western Europe, and it is only by the study of the European development that any understanding of the nature of Nationalism can be reached. It is true that the roots of Nationalism lie deep in history and in human nature. If the peoples of antiquity were not nations in our sense of the word, it is impossible to deny them a certain national character. When Herodotus asserts the duty of loyalty "to the bond of the Hellenic race by which we are of one blood and speech, the common temples of the gods and the common sacrifices, the manners of life which are the same for all," he comes very near to affirming the existence of Hellenic nationality. The one essential element that was missing was political unity which found its classical expression in the city state which was only transcended by the supernational imperialism of the Hellenistic and Roman empires. Hence the possibility of a true national development did not emerge till the Middle Ages with the rise of the European monarchies, which almost from the beginning had a quasi national character and which under favourable circumstances, as in France and England, developed into true nation-states. The nation-state had, in fact, become the political ideal to which every European monarchy aspired long before the appearance of Nationalism in its modern form, and the latter was due above all to the attraction which this achieved ideal exercised on peoples which possessed national culture and self consciousness but which had failed to attain political unity. It was not however until the French Revolution had challenged the vested interests of the territorial and dynastic monarchy and had asserted the rights of man and the freedom of peoples that the nationalist ideology became one of the dominant forces in European society. It is therefore intimately connected with the parallel movements of

democracy and liberalism, though the circumstances of its origin in Germany caused it to ally itself with the forces of the old regime which were carrying on the struggle against the French hegemony in Europe. It may even seem that there are two rival nationalist ideologies which have been in conflict throughout modern times: a conservative Nationalism which was the creation of German romanticism, and a democratic Nationalism based on the rights of man and popular plebiscites which was the creation of the French Revolution. In fact, however, the two types of Nationalism are inextricably mixed. The founders of the cult of Nationalism in Germany, such as Fichte, F. von Schlegel and Görres, had themselves been ardent disciples of the French Revolution, while the liberal and democratic Nationalism of the nineteenth century was deeply influenced by the ideas of the German philosophers and historians of the Napoleonic age.

Thus the Nationalism which has spread from Europe all over the world during the last century and a quarter was from the beginning a rather unstable compound of different elements. It has not been sufficiently recognized that Nationalism and democracy are so closely connected that they are two sides of the same social movement. How far Nationalism can survive democracy or democracy Nationalism is a problem that is still undecided. The attempt to create a world order of democratic nation-states—the League of Nations—has made shipwreck on the rocks of intransigent Nationalism. But we have no reason to suppose that an anti-democratic and totalitarian Nationalism will prove any more successful. On the contrary, the fate of Czecho-Slovakia and Poland and the Baltic States suggests that totalitarianism is as great a danger to the principle of nationality, as it is to democracy. The ultimate goal towards which totalitarianism aspires is not the nation-state but world empire, and if democracy disappears, it is probable that the nation-state will disappear also, as in the ancient world political freedom and the city-state went down together before the world empire of a deified autocrat. (Dawson 1940, 348–9.) [Emphasis added.]

Nationalism, secularism,* humanism,† and Liberalism are at the heart of the philosophical, theological, artistic, and political developments leading up to the Bolshevik and Nazi movements. Although essentially present since the formation of the first societies in human history, European Nationalism in its earliest form surfaced during the decline and fall of the Roman Empire in *AD* fifth century. Nationalism in meaning and practice has always been and continues to be the subject of fierce controversy. Like Liberalism, Nationalism is a term that over time has been associated with various meanings, uses, and interpretations—either pejorative or approbatory. Since Lord Acton condemned it in 1862, and Ernest Renan broadly approved its more liberal manifestations in 1882, observers and scholars have been divided, not only over its alleged beneficial or harmful effects, but as to the real meaning and nature of this elusive phenomenon. Nationalism's various meanings, uses, and interpretations generally fall into one of two categories: 1) sectarian Nationalism that is based on personal identity elitism (supremacy), which embraces militant xenophobia, racism, and ethnic and religious discrimination; or 2) patriotic Nationalism that derives from collective allegiance to a nation or nationality (national supremacy) and categorically rejects discrimination against its own nationals based on race, ethnicity, or religion. Nationalism of the first definition has

---

* Secularism is a hedonic, nihilistic, utilitarian doctrine that morality should be based on the well-being of man in the present life, without regard to religious belief or a hereafter, an indifference to or rejection or exclusion of religion and religious considerations in moral, political, and philosophical matters. Secularism draws its intellectual and ethical roots from Greek and Roman philosophers such as Epicurus and Marcus Aurelius; from Enlightenment thinkers such as John Locke, Jean-Jacques Rousseau, Denis Diderot, Voltaire, Benedict (Baruch) de Spinoza, James Madison, Thomas Jefferson, and Thomas Paine; and from more recent freethinkers and atheists such as Robert Ingersoll and Bertrand Russell.

† Humanism was a Renaissance artistic, literary, and political movement that sought to reorder society along the artistic and moral examples of the pre-Christian Classical World. The movement was especially invigorated by the ancients' previous accomplishments in aesthetics, ethics, and applied reason. The modern study of "the humanities" derives from this term and period. The humanists, including pioneers like Dante and Petrarch, emphasized the ancient Greek values of individualism and human excellence (virtue) over the divine and helped to reintegrate Classical thought, especially neo-Platonic thought, into the Western tradition. Humanists were avid collectors and translators of ancient Greek and Roman texts, many of which had been largely unknown prior to the revival but which became widely disseminated through the aid of the printing press.

predominated human history and produced many of the worst man-made tragedies; Nationalism of the second definition when based in Democratic representative governance (Aristotelian polity) has been integral to advancing dignity and ethics that have resulted in some of the most valued advances in the human condition. Clearly, the second type of Nationalism has been relatively rare but has produced many of the most significant and enduring positive changes for humanity.* When Christopher Dawson refers to Nationalism, he is employing the first, pejorative use of the term and not the second. Despite his own definitions differentiating the two types of Nationalism ("conservative" versus "democratic"), Dawson ends up confounding the two uses of the term, claiming "the two types of Nationalism are inextricably mixed."

Has patriotic Nationalism at times also espoused sectarian Nationalism? Certainly, in societies without a national constitution that enshrines individual human rights and universal suffrage for all its citizens, militant discrimination and sectarianism find fertile ground to flourish—colonialism, paternalism, National Socialism, Fascism, Socialism, Communism, autocracy, aristocracy, and military juntas have all at one time or another ostracized, oppressed, or excluded a segment of their population. Immutable characteristics of human nature make it impossible to completely eliminate from human behavior discrimination and xenophobia in all their forms. To believe otherwise would be naïve Utopianism and any legalistic effort to achieve such a sterile society would effectively result in totalitarianism. Yet, patriotic Nationalism that respects its diverse constituency is an historic reality from ancient and Classical times (Western, Middle Eastern, and Eastern cultures) that has positively contributed to humanity. A proper distinction between different forms of Nationalism is essential to an intellectually honest appraisal of political history.

In defining the word *Nationalism*, at least five senses can be identified: (1) a sentiment of loyalty to a nation (a form of patriotism); (2) a propensity, as applied to policies, to consider exclusively the interests of one's own nation, especially in cases where these compete with the interests of other nations; (3) an attitude that attaches high importance to and identification with the distinctive characteristics of a nation (race, ethnicity, language, heritage, religion) and, therefore, (4) a doctrine that maintains that

---

* For more on this distinction between forms of Nationalism, see Rich Lowry, *The Case for Nationalism: How It Made Us Powerful, United, and Free* (New York, NY: Broadside Books, 2019).

national culture should be preserved; and (5) a political and an anthropological theory that asserts that humankind is naturally divided into nations, that there are determinate criteria for identifying a nation and for recognizing its members, that each nation is entitled to an independent government of its own, that states are legitimate only if constituted in accordance with this principle, and that the world would be rightly organized, politically speaking, only if every nation formed a single state and every state consisted exclusively of the whole of one nation (Benn 2006, 481–5).

> Nationalism is "primarily a political principle, which holds that the political and the national unit should be congruent." See: Ernest Gellner, *Nations and Nationalism* (Ithaca: Cornell University Press, 1983), 1. The concept "nation" has been notoriously difficult to define. Benedict Anderson argues that nationality or nation-ness, as well as nationalism, are cultural artifacts of a particular kind. They emerged toward the end of the eighteenth century as the older sacral culture of Christendom declined, with its sacred language (Latin). Before that time, fundamental conceptions about "social groups" depicted them as "centripetal and hierarchical, rather than boundary-oriented and horizontal." Religiously imagined communities gave way to politically imagined communities. For Anderson, then, the nation was "an imagined political community—and imagined as both inherently limited and sovereign." *Boundaries* (limitation) were always central to the concept of the nation (no one imagines a nation as coterminous with mankind). *National sovereignty* was important because, during the age of Enlightenment and Revolution the divinely-ordained, hierarchical and dynastic idea of the realm, was challenged. *Community* was important because the nation was imagined as a deep horizontal comradeship; a sense of fraternity then made it possible for some members to die for the nation. Anderson used the word "imagination" because no one ever met all the members of the national community and thus it primarily had to live in their minds. See Benedict Anderson, *Imagined Communities:*

Reflections on the Origin and Spread of Nationalism (London: Verso, 1991), 6–7, 15, 16. [Stuart 2009, 180.]

Next to religion, the consensus among historians, has been to regard Nationalism as one of the most powerful and influential political, philosophical, social, and economic forces in the modern world (from Middle Ages to present)—despite the fact that Nationalism is merely a manifestation as opposed to an essence of human nature—and to regard it as a necessary and fundamental element of modernity. Nationalism (in the third, fourth, and fifth senses, above) is at the heart of our discussion on militant xenophobia, racism, and totalitarianism undergirding Nazism.

Let us revisit for a moment the Liberalism referred to in this work believed by many historians and philosophers to be responsible for playing a role in the development of the totalitarian regimes of the twentieth century. The liberalization of traditional paradigms of morality, scriptural authority, Christian or Jewish doctrine, and of the strict division of divine law and Christian Gospel is at the heart of the destructive liberal movement that Christopher Dawson saw as commencing in the late Reformation period. (The Reformation period began with Martin Luther's 95 Theses in 1517 and ended in 1648 with the Peace of Westphalia concluding the Thirty-Years' and Eighty-Years' Wars.) Dawson lays the culpability for this liberalization directly at the feet of the French Huguenots and their Atlantic Diaspora. The Huguenot Diaspora is one of the most important and most spectacular dispersions of a religious minority in early modern Europe. Traditionally known as *le Refuge*, this migration led to the exodus of nearly 200,000 Protestants out of France in 1685 at the time of the revocation of the Edict of Nantes with the signing of the Edict of Fontainebleau by Louis XIV of France.

Sometime between 1550 and 1580, members of the Protestant Reformed church in France came to be commonly known as *Huguenots*. Historically, Huguenots were inspired by the writings of French theologian and humanist lawyer Jehan Cauvin (John Calvin). A series of religious conflicts known as the French Wars of Religion, fought intermittently from 1562 to 1598, finally concluded with the Edict of Nantes by King Henry IV of France, which granted the Huguenots substantial religious, political, and military autonomy. When conditions of the Edict of Nantes deteriorated culminating in its revocation by the Edict of Fontainebleau under Louis XIV, the Huguenots faced an ultimatum—either convert to Roman Catholicism or face brutal consequences. Mass migration of French Protestants ensued. The bulk of Huguenot émigrés relocated to Protestant nations such as England, Wales, Scotland, Denmark, Sweden, Switzerland, the Dutch Republic (Netherlands), the Electorate of Brandenburg and Electorate of the Palatinate in the Holy Roman Empire, the Duchy of Prussia, the Channel Islands, and Ireland. They also spread to the Dutch Cape Colony in South Africa, the Dutch East Indies, the Caribbean, New Netherland, several of the English colonies in North America (particularly South Carolina and New York), and Quebec, where they were generally accepted and allowed to prosper and worship freely.

In preparing the manuscript for his biography of Christopher Dawson, *Sanctifying the World: The Augustinian Life and Mind of Christopher Dawson* (Christendom Press, 2007), Professor of American History Bradley J. Birzer planned to include a section on Dawson's critique of Liberalism. The following are excerpts from that section, which ended up never being included in the biography. Despite its length, understanding this crystallized summary of Dawson's critique of Liberalism is important to laying the foundation to this discussion on the origins of the Nazi movement.

> [It should be noted that Dawson saw liberalism (19th and 20th century varieties) as a whole. And, while he was extremely anti-statist to the point of quasi-anarchism, Dawson thought liberalism of any sort could exist only as a transition state from true culture, liberty, and order to chaos and totalitarianism.] — Bradley J. Birzer, 2012
>
> The Rise of Liberalism
>
> As a revolt against authority, the Protestant Reformation opened the door to western secularization and economic individualism, otherwise known as liberalism, a word that Dawson sometimes mistrusted as too vague. "Liberalism is an unsatisfactory word since it has been used to describe three quite distinct movements," Dawson wrote to the editor of Notre Dame's Review of Politics, in 1954. "But the very fact that it has been used so widely and loosely increases the need for a fuller historical examination."
>
> The three movements, to which Dawson referred, were the English, the American, and the French, each represented by a revolution—the revolutions of 1688, 1776,

and 1789, respectively. Each, though, had a common origin in the Protestant Reformation. The ideals of liberalism spread with the Huguenot Diaspora of the early seventeenth century. "Wherever they settled in Holland and England and North Germany, they formed centres of militant anti-Catholic opinion and carried on an organized campaign of public propaganda and secret agitation" against the Sun King and the Roman Catholic Church.

Most of the intellectual strains of thought and economic forces that would promote liberalism first came together in Holland. "Here, I think," Dawson argued, "17th century Holland and Dutch culture are the decisive points, for it was in Holland that we find the first developments of secularism and toleration, of bourgeois control of the state, of bourgeois capitalism and finance."

The greatest successes of liberalism, Dawson wrote, came with the so-called "Glorious Revolution" of 1688 and 1689, in which the Dutch and the English, as well as the Puritans and the Episcopalians, united.

Led by the rising middle-classes, Dawson argued, Protestantism had stressed the need for economic individualism. The rising middle-classes, as best expressed and represented by the Classical Economists of the eighteenth century, argued that the well-being of the community could only result from the individual pursuit of profit. The riches of the few would indirectly benefit the masses. But with *laissez faire* in Northern Europe, the old world of tradition and communal protection of the aged and indigent withered, Dawson contended.

* * *

The justification of the avarice of the individual, Dawson seems to have suggested, was the greatest accomplishment of liberalism. "The capitalist organization of industry has led, no less than military conquest, to the exploitation of subject classes and nationalities."

Such an argument can be found in John Locke's *Second Treatise on Government*. The so-called philosopher of the Glorious Revolution of 1688 and 1689, completely redefined political society. This nominal Anglican moved even farther away from the traditional Platonic-Aristotelian-Augustinian-Thomist attempt to make virtue the basis of all good society than had Machiavelli. Indeed, whereas Machiavelli at least acknowledged the existence and importance of a God and then dismissed Him, Locke seems just to have dismissed God and His sacred law. Locke argued that society is no longer about a sublime covenant between the cult and God, but between insecure property-rights bearers who desire little more than worldly security and prosperity.

To protect one's self and one's material acquisitions, property rights define us and our neighbors. Rather than being created in the Image of God, the liberal philosophers of the seventeenth-century argued, men became *homo economicus* and formed society not for the common good or the will of God, but for individual benefit and profit. The world began not with the Creator making His creation, but with an amorphous "state of nature." And, man, rather than possessing a soul with the natural law written on his heart, as St. Paul had assured the Romans, is merely the *tabula rasa*, ready to be molded by society itself.

Despite all of Dawson's rhetoric against liberalism, he did not outright reject the importance of benefits of the market. In the early and middle 1930s, for example, Dawson issued several caveats regarding his views on capitalism. "When I say Capitalism, I do not, of course, mean the institution of private property or even the co-operative use of private capital for economic production," Dawson argued in 1934. "I mean that whole system and philosophy of economic liberalism which allowed the economic process to develop without moral guidance and with no end but its own interest."

A year earlier, in a letter to *The Cambridge Review*, Dawson noted that while capitalism could be as materialist as communism in its most liberal aspects, a Christian fared much better in the capitalist world than he would in a totalitarian society. "In our Capitalist society the Christian may be a misfit," Dawson claimed, "but in a Communist society he is a traitor and a pariah."

Additionally, capitalism has provided an immense increase in the production of wealth and enjoyment of life. The most significant problem with capitalism, Dawson argued, is that it fails to see the human person as an end in and of himself. It attempts to mechanize the human person for some goal or profit.

Dawson also noted, rather strongly, that the Catholic must live according to the rules of charity, never to the desires of the market order or the laws of supply and demand. As with the economy as a whole, wealth is morally neutral. It must never become an end, but only serve as a means to something greater. In the 1920s, Dawson wrote a three-part series on *Catholicism and Economics*. He wrote approvingly of the Church Fathers and their understanding of the market and charity. Ultimately, the market is only good if one uses it "as a vehicle of spiritual love."

One of the Church Fathers, St. Ambrose, had taken this argument to its logical conclusion. "What you give to the poor man is not yours but his. For what was given for the common use, you alone usurp. The earth is all men's and not the property of the rich."

Another Church Father, St. Basil, stated: "He who strips a man of his garments will be called a thief. Is not he who fails to clothe the naked when he could do so worthy of the same title? It is the bread of the hungry that you hold, the clothing of the naked that you lock up in your cupboard."

Each of these men was following the beliefs of the first Archbishop of Jerusalem, St. James. In his Catholic epistle, he wrote of the wealthy: "You have feasted upon earth: and in riotousness you have nourished your hearts, in the day of slaughter."

When liberal political and economic notions combined with the ideas introduced by the Scientific Revolution of 1543 to 1687, Dawson feared, liberalism almost shattered all of Christianity's significance in the eighteenth century. The universe, according to Newton, for example, was no longer moved by Love. It was, instead, a vast mechanism that could be discovered through science and observation. Even the understanding of God changed. In his dedication to the pope, Copernicus tellingly labeled Him "the Best and Most Orderly Workman of all" who had built "the machinery of the world."

This was indeed a far cry from the Divine Love of the Divine Comedy that "moves the sun and the other stars," pulling all things back to Him.

The Fulfillment of Liberalism

In the end, Dawson believed, liberalism destroyed far more than it created. By the end of the eighteenth century, he feared, little of traditional western culture—beyond the Protestant Americans and the Lutheran and Catholic peasants of Europe—remained religious. The dominant political philosophy of that century, liberalism, "retained the inherited moral standards and values of a Christian civilization," Dawson wrote. However, "as Liberalism did not create these moral ideals, so, too, it cannot preserve them."

Further, economic liberalism "laid the foundations of the technological order in the new industrial society of the nineteenth century."

By 1935, Dawson claimed that all of England and western civilization was "bourgeois from top to bottom," and its philosophy was spreading quickly beyond western civilization to all parts of the world.

While the Middle Ages had kept the profit-motive in its proper perspective, liberalism had allowed it to dominate all aspects of society and remake even nature itself. "The devastated areas of industrial England and the cancerous growth of the suburbs" has destroyed the "aesthetic sense" of the English as well destroying "almost everything that made life worth living." Most important, Dawson thought, was liberalism's destruction of the agrarian way of life, a foundation of English culture. "It involves the divorce of man from nature and the from the life of the earth," and "the very face of nature is changed," as the beauty of the Created Order is marred by man's order.

With free competition, England witnessed the destruction of community norms, church moral standards, and the family. Liberalism led directly to the rise of what Dawson and many of his fellow twentieth-century Augustinians called "the machine." The end result: "the individual has become a cog in the vast machinery of modern industrial life," Dawson wrote in 1930. "He is the servant of the machine and his whole life tends to become mechanized."

The human person becomes nothing more than a tool. As England became the "workshop of the world," he argued, "society was brought into a state of dependence on material and non-moral factors such as had not existed since the days of the slave dealers and publicans of the later Roman Empire."

While the capitalists chanted slogans about freedom, they promoted "conquest and exploitation" of the laborers and of the world.

Equally important, while the liberals and Classical Economists claimed to have found an order within nature, they have actually just subordinated western civilization to a quantitative way of thinking, enslaving them to the importance and movement of money.

But, Christianity, "is essentially hostile to the spirit of calculation, the spirit of worldly prudence and above all to the spirit of religious self-seeking and self-satisfaction." The modern liberal capitalist descends from the Pharisee, who becomes a mere "hoarder of merits." Importantly, Dawson claimed, St. Augustine had understood the divide that the liberals would create in the City of God. The liberals—possessors of "the bourgeois soul"—focused on the material, rather than the spirit. The Metaxy—man, as the possessor of a spirit within the physical—grew lop-sided under liberalism, with the soul neglected. Ultimately, while the Catholic should not reject capitalism as a vital part of a free society, he should reject the liberal capitalist order as society's prime mover. "For the soul that is closed to love is closed to grace," Dawson concluded.

Dawson put the Catholic understanding of the Protestant "work ethic" in historical comparison. "The bourgeois culture had the mechanical rhythm of a clock," he wrote in 1935, "the Baroque the musical rhythm of a fugue or a sonata."

Unlike northern European Protestant culture, "the baroque spirit lives in and for the triumphant moment of creative ecstasy."

Within Catholic cultures, peasants often vehemently defended the Baroque spirit, challenging liberalism at the political, religious, and cultural levels. The peasant uprisings, "fought with desperate resolution and heroism in defense of the old Catholic order," of the French in 1793, the Tyrolers under Andreas Hofer in 1809, and the Basques throughout the nineteenth century especially impressed Dawson.

They had been preceded by the famous 1536 defense against Protestantism in northern England, "under the banners of St. Cuthbert and the Five Wounds." Dawson found great inspiration from this earlier defense, noting proudly that it had come from his father's ancestral home.

Ultimately, Dawson claimed, liberalism created nothing. It merely tore down the old, the venerable, and the traditional. But just as every culture and people long for and need a religion, so did the liberals of the Enlightenment. They found their new religion in democracy and unrestrained nature. Dawson claimed the exemplar of the new religion of democracy and its natural man to be the French/Swiss educational theorist and philosopher Jean-Jacques Rousseau, who found "that all the ills of man and the evils of society were due not to man's own sin or ignorance but to social injustice and the corruptions of an artificial civilization."

In the thought of Rousseau, Dawson claimed, the liberals, the democrats, the revolutionaries, and the anarchists each found solace.

The liberals also embraced the utilitarianism of Jeremy Bentham. At base, utilitarianism argued for "the greatest good for the greatest number," words that even Edmund Burke had used. The difference between Burke and Bentham, though, came in their differing uses of "great." For Burke, "great" meant society ordered according to God and tradition, embracing the virtues and piety.

For Bentham, great meant that each man pursues his own "pleasure principle," what the modern or neo-classical economists call "utility." His pleasure principle, though, far from the morally and religiously-infused "pursuit of happiness" of the Declaration of Independence—meaning to do what is right in the sight of God—embraced only materialism. Bentham despised the old virtues as mere platitudes and the idea of sin as the result of mere ignorance. Instead, he believed in blanket uniformity in politics and education, especially. Uniformity for Bentham meant liberty, equality, abstract rights, and efficiency. But, Dawson cautioned in his Harvard lectures, the "elimination of all supernatural motives and all metaphysical truths," inherent in Bentham's utilitarianism, leads "not to liberty, but to slavery, since there was no appeal from the tribunal of social utility and majority opinion."

Bentham's philosophy, in Dawson's words, is nothing more than a "bleak rationalism."

Speaking through Newman, Dawson argued that "the colorless neutral phraseology of social utility and efficiency" of Bentham and others served merely as a "screen behind which mighty inhuman powers were marshalling their forces for the conquest of humanity." These are the powers St. Paul warned were the true rulers of the world. "These spiritual powers are the real actors behind the veil of events," Dawson continued. "They are invisible and apparently non-existent to the politician and the economist." They "decide the fate of nations."

The Americans also experienced the influence of the Enlightenment. Dawson labeled Benjamin Franklin, "the greatest representative of this American

Enlightenment," but he claimed Thomas Jefferson as the greatest Liberal.[*]

Dawson argued that radical forms of Protestantism—especially the rhetoric of the Anabaptists—had inspired many of the more radical elements of both the American and French Revolutions.

In America, such traditions of thought continued through men such as Ralph Waldo Emerson and movements such as Unitarianism, which attempted to fuse "the two traditions of the rationalist-Enlightenment and of Protestant Christianity."

If nothing else, the American Revolution provided for European liberals a model of the possibilities of success. America, as embodied by the Franklin, Jefferson, and the ideals of the Declaration of Independence, represented the future, according to Dawson. Buoyed by these successes in North America, liberalism in Europe took on a political cast.

And yet, the liberals of Europe focused only on the traditions of Revolutionary America. Almost immediately,

---

* Thomas Jefferson was an admirer of Bavarian philosopher and professor of law Johann Adam Weishaupt. Weishaupt founded the Order of the Illuminati—a secret society to combat religion and foster rationalism in its place by "illumination, enlightening the understanding by the sun of reason, which will dispel the clouds of superstition and of prejudice" with the goal of "perfecting human nature" through re-education to achieve a communal state with nature, freed of government and organized religion. Augustin Barruel (1741–1820) was a French publicist and Jesuit priest known for setting forth the conspiracy theory involving the Bavarian Illuminati and the Jacobins in his 1797 book *Memoirs Illustrating the History of Jacobinism* (original title *Mémoires pour servir à l'Histoire du Jacobinisme* [Barruel 1797–1803]). In short, Barruel wrote that the French Revolution was planned and executed by the secret societies. Augustin Barruel regarded Weishaupt as a "human devil" and saw his mission as one of malevolent destructiveness. Others such as Thomas Jefferson, who wrote in a letter to James Madison that "Barruel's own parts of the book are perfectly the ravings of a Bedlamite" and considered Weishaupt as an "enthusiastic Philanthropist" who believed in the indefinite perfectibility of man and his intention was simply to "reinstate natural religion, and by diffusing the light of his morality, to teach us to govern ourselves." In this light, Jefferson and Weishaupt were true pupils of the Enlightenment who saw traditional religious beliefs as superstitious prejudice that needed to be replaced with rational science ("natural religion") in the struggle over "perfecting human nature."

more conservative elements took over in America during the Patriot movement of the 1770s and 1780s. Indeed, with Jefferson absent [in France], the American Founders rooted the American constitution in the principles of Plato, Aristotle, Cicero, Livy, and Montesquieu. Much of the intense religiosity and inherent conservatism of the American founders such as George Washington, John Adams, John Dickinson, and Alexander Hamilton also tempered the more radical elements of the American revolutionary generation, and America became as strongly traditional as it was liberal. By 1959, Dawson came to recognize that "the American Revolution does not coincide with the French and cannot be taken as equivalent."

Only a temporal accident links the two revolutions.

Additionally, no matter how secular or liberal America proved itself to be, it also plowed the soil in which a thriving Catholicism [and confessional Lutheranism] would grow from 1848 to the present. In America, Catholics of every ethnic variety came together, united not only by their faith but also by the larger culture's hostility to them. "The creation of this great American Church out of nothing in the midst of a society that seemed as remote from Catholicism as any society in Christendom was not the result of human planning or design," Dawson wrote. "It is God's work, not man's."

America served as the refuge of Catholics [and Lutherans] from the secular, liberal, and atheist places of the world, Dawson believed. If its men and women embrace the graces given specifically to America, Dawson argued, it will "play an increasing part in the life of Christendom."

It was the French Revolution in which liberalism revealed its darkest side, Dawson wrote. "The French Revolution marked the triumph of the movement towards secularization of Western culture which had been advancing" for the entirety of the eighteenth century. [Emphasis added.]

Once accomplished, the French Revolution unleashed inhumane and uncontrollable forces. Indeed, the forces [Communism] that would imprison much of the world's population from 1917 to 1991 (and continues, to be sure, through this present writing), have their origins with the French disciples of Jean Jacques Rousseau and their assault on a Parisian prison in the summer of 1789. Dawson explained its significance in the context of the very short nineteenth century. [Emphasis added.]

The history of the nineteenth century developed under the shadow of the French Revolution and the national liberal revolutions that followed it. A century of political, economic and social revolution, a century of world discovery, world conquest and world exploitation, it was also the great age of capitalism; and yet saw too the rise of socialism and communism and their attack upon the foundation of capitalist society. . . . When the century began, Jefferson was president of the United States, and George III was still King of England. When it ended Lenin already was planning the Russian Revolution. [Emphasis added.]

More than any other event in world history to that point, the leaders of the French Revolution murdered the past.

Burke called the introduction of the French revolutionary spirit the "most astonishing [thing] that has hitherto happened in the world."

The French Revolutionaries introduced the concept of ideology into the world, a concept that has yet to be contained. "Out of the tomb of the murdered Monarchy in France, has arisen a vast, tremendous, unformed spectre, in a far more terrific guise than any which ever yet overpowered the imagination and subdued the fortitude of man," one of Dawson's heroes, Edmund Burke, concluded in the last year of his life.

Rejecting the laws of nature, the French Revolution instigated much havoc: "Laws overturned; tribunals subverted; industry without vigour; commerce expiring; the revenue unpaid, yet the people impoverished; a church pillaged, and a state not relieved; civil and military anarchy made the constitution of the kingdom; every thing human and divine sacrificed to the idol of the public credit, and national bankruptcy the consequence."

The French revolutionaries attempted to overturn and remake all of society in their image (or images, more accurately). Inspired by the vision of Rousseau, the revolutionaries attempted to abolish all institutions of subsidiarity, institutions such as family, school, and church that make life worth living. As early as the fall of 1789, the revolutionaries emphasized this in the Declaration of the Rights of Man. Article Three states: "The principle of all sovereignty resides essentially in the nation. No body nor individual may exercise any authority which does not proceed directly from the nation."

Brutality and terror, Dawson wrote, were the logical conclusions to Rousseau's argument regarding the General Will. As the Revolution progressed, or regressed as the case was, "it gradually revealed the naked reality that had been veiled by the antiquated trappings of royalty and tradition." And, the revolution revealed the General Will for what it really was, the raw, naked will to power, destructive of any opposition.

Their most vehement attacks on institutions of subsidiarity were against the Roman Catholic Church, then seen as an ally to the hated French monarchy and aristocracy. Priests and other religious were beaten, tortured, raped, and exiled or executed. Church property was confiscated, and a prostitute was put on the altar of Notre Dame Cathedral and declared a goddess. One apostate abbot desired to distribute the bodily remains of "reactionaries" as a "Republican Eucharist."

Those who opposed the new revolutionary regimes (for they came and went based on who momentarily had the most might to rule) paid with their lives. True to Burke's prediction, at least twenty-five thousand forfeited their lives to the insatiable hunger of the guillotine between 1791 and 1794. Indeed, the revolutionaries were so blood thirsty, they tended to turn on each other. The worst modern case of this would be in Cambodia under the Khmer Rouge, 1975–1978, which almost collapsed due to so much internal bloodletting. Tellingly, many of the Khmer Rouge leadership, known as Ankor (The Organization), had studied under the French Communist existentialist philosopher, Jean Paul Sartre.

Contending Against Liberalism

As Dawson attempted to discover the sources of the ideological disruptions of the twentieth century as well as solutions to the death and terror they caused, he often produced some of his most impassioned work. The forerunner to such brutal terrors as Communism and Fascism was liberalism, Dawson claimed. In his own research and writing, Dawson then took a special interest in those things which countered the growth of liberalism. From their successes and failures, this twentieth-century Augustinian figure thought the world might learn from its follies and unify around some healing solution. As Dawson saw it, four forces worked against the growing power of liberalism, to varying degrees of success: the rise of Protestant Evangelicalism; the anti-Revolutionary traditionalist thought of Edmund Burke and Joseph De Maistre; the Romantic movement; and John Henry Cardinal Newman. [Emphasis added.]

John Wesley, a high-church Anglican, heavily influenced by the pietism of German Moravians, led the first counter-liberal movement.

In daily sermons, given throughout England, he preached the need for a rigorous personal, moral discipline as well as for an intense pietism and a personal relationship with Christ. Methodism decreased the chances of a liberal or radical revolution by serving as a conservative force attracting the disenfranchised and economically downtrodden in England and, through the revivalists George Whitfield and Francis Asbury, numerous and various peoples of all backgrounds in the American colonies.[*]

In almost every way, Dawson argued, the Wesleyan movement ran counter to the liberalism and Deism of its day.

"Wesley was undoubtedly one of the greatest Englishmen of the eighteenth century and a great religious genius," Dawson wrote in his unpublished, *Return to Christian Unity*. "But no man of his religious stature was more unphilosophical and more anti-metaphysical, and more out of touch with the new intellectual currents of his time than Wesley."

Wesley's movement, despite its many successes, shared the flaw that all Protestantism shared, according to Dawson. It was individualistic, decentralized, and, hence, unable to deal effectively with social and cultural problems.[†]

The anti-Revolutionary movement of the late eighteenth and early nineteenth centuries founds its greatest intellectual representatives in Joseph de Maistre and Edmund Burke, each of whom Dawson considered a brilliant prophet. [Joseph-Marie, Comte] De Maistre, a Frenchman by birth, "hid the spirit of a Hebrew prophet," attempting to discern "the problem of suffering and evil and the justification of the obscure purposes of God in history."

However, Dawson cautioned, de Maistre focused so much on the dark side of creation, however, that he eventually could only see darkness as the cause of anything. An extreme Augustinian, de Maistre believed that man was so dark that "impersonal forces which move to their appointed ends" moved men, denying them any free will.

---

* Essentially, Dawson viewed the effectiveness of Methodism in countering the destructive forces of Liberalism as stemming from its adoption of Liberalism's social justice methods under the guise of pietism and its power of persuasion with the masses (works righteousness).

† Like most Catholics, Dawson believed God intended religion to not only provide the path to divine salvation for the afterlife, but also to help relieve the suffering and promote social justice in the temporal life.

This resulted in war and revolutions as natural parts of humanity. De Maistre held a special hatred for any aspect of liberalism. "The contempt of Locke is the beginning of wisdom," de Maistre firmly believed.

He viewed the French Revolution as the birth of "a new age" of "hollow abstractions." Still, de Maistre conceded, perhaps God intended the Revolution as a necessary punishment and purifier for men and their sinful ways. Ultimately, though those present may not see the how or why, God would use the violence and terror of the revolution to remake Christendom.

"We have been grievously and justly broken," de Maistre wrote, "but if such eyes as mine are worthy to foresee the divine purpose, we have been broken only to be made one."

Dawson cautioned that de Maistre took this belief too far, veering into a heterodox view closely resembling the Hindu belief of Karma, in which an evil will be repaid with an evil.

Despite de Maistre's minor heterodoxies, Dawson strongly identified with him.

As he did with de Maistre, Dawson considered the Anglo-Irish statesman Edmund Burke a kindred spirit. Dawson never read Burke during his formative intellectual period, but he valued his thoughts on ideologies greatly, especially in the 1930s. "Burke has said certain things better than any one else can hope to again," Dawson told John J. Mulloy.

Dawson especially appreciated Burke's organic approach to culture and history.

Society, Burke argued, was never merely political or legal. At its most fundamental, society was spiritual as well as material, transcending any one generation, but embracing all living beings, past, present, and future.

It was from this standpoint, that Burke attacked the French Revolutionaries as the harbingers of terror not just for the French, but for all of Christendom. Their movement was the unloosing of chaos upon the world.

Much of Burke's and de Maistre's thought resurfaced with the early nineteenth-century Romantics. The Romantics were diverse in their thought, and though they often shared de Maistre's and Burke's fears of pure rationalism, they just as usually rejected the traditionalist love of order, often preferring chaos and anarchy as seemingly free and liberating of the individual.

Still, the Romantics typically agreed that the rationalism of the Enlightenment came from the dividing of Christendom and the Protestant attempt to de-mythologize the sacraments and Creation. Hence, those Romantics who eventually embraced theism, more often than not embraced a medieval form of Roman Catholicism.

Even the extreme William Blake, one of the greatest of the Romantics, traversed a tortuous path from spiritual darkness and Gnosticism "among beasts and devils" to Christian heterodoxy to something closely resembling Catholic orthodoxy.

Through it all, he conceded, he had traveled "on the strength of the Lord God," finding his greatest enemy in the rationalist, liberal Deism of his day.

But, according to Dawson, Blake embraced the Logos and the moral imagination as a "Divine Vision."

It, and it alone, could heal the divisions of Christendom. And, though "religion failed to reconquer and reunite European Civilization," as the traditionalists and Romantics had desired, Dawson argued, "it recovered its vitality and once more asserted itself as an autonomous force in European culture."

John Henry Cardinal Newman offered the last great opposition to the rising tide of liberalism before it both turned into—and succumbed to—the deadly ideologies of the twentieth century. As with many of the other figures mentioned above, Dawson felt a true kinship to Newman.

Both had been converts to Roman Catholicism, both were Augustinians, and both did everything in their intellectual power to combat liberalism. Indeed, Dawson considered his book on the Oxford Movement, *The Spirit of the Oxford Movement*, one of his two greatest intellectual accomplishments.

Newman's *Development of Christian Doctrine* and his *Apologia* especially influenced Dawson. The former impressed Dawson because it had been "inspired by an intense faith in the boundless powers of assimilation which the Christian faith possessed and which made it a unitive principle in life and thought."

Dawson admired Newman's *Apologia* because it recognized that "it was only in history that the divine process of progressive revelation and spiritual renovation could be fulfilled."

Because all of history had a purpose, Newman argued, history seemed to have changed its direction with the coming of Christ. It no longer runs straight forward, but is, as it were, continually verging on eternity."

Newman's near mysticism and inspired foresight—his understanding of being on the edge of eternity—also impressed Dawson. Newman, more clearly than any of his contemporaries, understood the coming war of the Church against the ideologues. Evil and iniquity were attempting to enter the world in any way that they could, and they found their first and perhaps most important vehicles in the French Revolution, utilitarianism, and secularization, Newman feared. Newman's vision can best be seen in the poetry of William Butler Yeats, in the fiction of Father R. H. Benson, or in the gulags and killing fields of the twentieth century. Newman's words were a call to arms in defense of the Church before the Enemy gained control of its own institutions, Dawson believed.

Ultimately, Dawson argued, future scholars would remember Newman as the paragon of the nineteenth century. "The personality and genius of Newman will be seen as a key point of the whole development" of nineteenth-century religious development and thought, "as at once the embodiment and contradiction of the spirit of his age."

He was the greatest and best defender of the West and Christendom in his day.

Despite the opposition of those discussed above, the liberalism of the eighteenth and nineteenth century that Dawson abhorred became the academic liberalism of the twentieth century. This academic liberalism, as conformist one as one could imagine, seemed utterly devoid of any real history or purpose to Dawson. Significantly influenced by the various materialist philosophies of the previous century, these typical liberal academics in the first half of the twentieth century often referred to man as *homo economicus*, economic man. Greed, self-interest, and material pursuit occupied and shaped one's every decision, or so many of these academics confidently argued and firmly believed. Often the materialist economic man arguments melded seamlessly with other materialist philosophies such as scientific evolutionary theories or Freudian psychological theories.

Coincident with Dawson's declining health in the early 1960s, academic interest in theories of modernity and economic development lost some of their verve, and, within much of the academy and government agencies, economic man became political man. Though the transition occurred (and is still occurring) slowly, one sees the trend in its infancy in the 1930s in the speeches and writings of such diverse figures as-soon-to-be president Franklin D. Roosevelt and public intellectual Dorothy Thompson. The former explained in the early 1930s that America must accept the private as public and all things as political.

His various New Deal policies soon reflected his beliefs, and the nation, economy, and culture were suddenly politicizing at an unprecedented rate.

Many of Dawson's fears regarding the purposelessness of liberalism can be seen in the life and career of American Dorothy Thompson. One of the most important and profound liberal intellectuals of her day, Thompson flirted with the New Deal, communism, and fascism. She rejected each, as well as rejecting her father's evangelical Christian faith. The loss of so many beliefs left her adrift. "I am in search of a living faith in which to believe, and a body of faith in which to belong," lamented Thompson. "I cannot bear this world!"

After all, once the progressive and more materialist visions of Marx, Freud, and Darwin had obscured the tradition and faith that ordered the human person, little solid or tangible seemed to remain. Aristotelian purpose seemed quaint and tired. Rather than a balance of the spirit and the material, the material dominated, and the spirit was forgotten. Further, Thompson admitted, "individualism and skepticism had set [her] adrift in a world where everything was challenged, and nothing believed."

The author of Deuteronomy had predicted such an outcome, thousands of years before Thompson recognized the plight of many within modernity. Those who ignored the law of God would find themselves with "no resting place for the sole of" one's foot.

All shall be in doubt, and the individual person adrift and soon to drown in the depths of his subjective reality.

With the death of liberal faith in religion, tradition, and all things spiritual, the community could then start anew and define itself and its members. In short, culture could be born again, liberal thinking ran. And, in hindsight, it should surprise no one that the progressivism of the early-twentieth century became the New Deal of the 1930s, the Great Society of the 1960s, and, at century's end, the existential "politics of meaning," "it takes a village," and the "desire to redefine the human person" of the last decade of the twentieth century. Liberalism, as Dawson argued, merely inherited the Christian world view without God or natural authority. It, therefore, can never transcend its limited inheritance. It must always remain merely derivative. As a creature rather than a creative force, liberalism can produce nothing truly new, for it has no roots. Even more important for Dawson, by neglecting the spiritual side of man—or, at best, relegating it to the private judgment of autonomous individuals—liberalism ignored or mocked the source of true creativity, the Holy Spirit. Since all life—in its creation and its animation—comes from the love of the Holy Trinity,

> liberalism has no substantial life of its own. As noted several times earlier, liberalism serves merely as a transition within western society, Dawson argued. Christendom came before it, and the killing fields and gulag followed it, Dawson contended (Brizer 2012).

While Great Britain worked out in comparative calm the adaptation of her political system to the needs of the nineteenth century, progress in the same direction in the rest of Europe was attended with a long series of convulsions. For a full two-thirds of a century from the fall of Napoléon's empire agitation on the European continent was continuous and wars were not infrequent for the realization of political ideas that had been made prominent by the French Revolution. Until the middle of the nineteenth century, the history of the period is punctuated with insurrections; after 1850, the type of disturbance changed to international war (Dunning 1920, 248).

Insurrection made its first imposing appearance in the early twenties, when the Carbonari and the Free Masons rose in Italy and Spain, respectively, and temporarily converted Bourbon despotism into a semblance of constitutional governments. At the same time, Portugal went through a similar experience, and the Greeks won the interest and sympathy of Christendom by throwing off the yoke of the Sultan (Dunning 1920, 248).

Before the widespread ferment attending these movements had subsided, a more terrifying shock was given to Conservatism by the reappearance of revolution in France. In July 1830, the Bourbon Charles X was driven from the throne and the Orléanist Louis Philippe was put in his place. All Europe was filled with unrest and alarm in fear these events should be the prelude to such developments as had followed the uprising against the brother of Charles in 1789. Only at two widely separated centers, however, were there serious consequences. Poland rose against the Tsar and was ruthlessly crushed back into subjugation; the Belgians broke away from the Dutch, whose union had been arranged by the great powers at Vienna and were assisted by these same powers to set up an independent neutralized monarchy (Dunning 1920, 248–9).

After the turmoil of these affairs, there was a fretful interval of peace. Then came the most violent of all the insurrectionary convulsions, that of 1848. France was again the first to set up the standard of revolt, and she was easily first in the unexpectedness of the outcome. None would have predicted when the insurrection began that the French government was about to pass from constitutional monarchy to republic and from that, within four years, to a second Napoleonic empire. Central Europe on this occasion furnished tumults that in fervor and complexity fairly rivalled those in France. All the German and Italian peoples were aflame with political passion. Berlin, Vienna, and Rome were the scenes of bloody conflicts. At Frankfort, a famous assembly of Germans labored long but futilely on the project of uniting Germany under a constitutional government. At Budapest, a short-lived independence of the Hapsburger cheered the hopes and stimulated the florid eloquence of the Magyars. On every side it seemed as if the old order was finally destroyed. But when after two tempestuous years the tumult ceased, the Hapsburger and the Hohenzollern ruled their dominions and their neighbors as before, and on the face of things central and southern Europe showed little change (Dunning 1920, 249–50).

Beneath the surface, however, a transformation had been effected that was readily perceived when trouble again appeared among the nations. Not internal but international conflicts assumed the chief place in European politics, and the projects of the warring powers were in an ever-increasing measure determined by considerations of national growth and consciousness. The operation of this influence is not hard to discern in the Crimean War (1853–1856) and the Italian War of 1859; in the great Bismarckian conflicts of 1866 and 1870, the consolidation of German national unity was the avowed end and the most efficient instrument of the triumphant Prussian policy. Nor was the notion of nationality lacking to the Russo-Turkish War of 1877–1878 (relitigation of Crimean War); for Serb and Bulgar received through this war the birthright of substantial independence (Dunning 1920, 250).

Looked at from the viewpoint of political philosophy, the sixty-five years (1815–1880) of strenuous statecraft just surveyed shows three bodies of doctrine occupying successively the chief place in the current speculation. The first was constitutionalism, which dominated thought until the middle of the century. The second was Nationalism, which reached the climax of its sway over men's minds in the sixties. The third was Socialism, which was on the high road to universal absorption of philosophy when the period closed (Dunning 1920, 250–1).

Despite the strong reactionary and obscurantist influence manifested in the Holy Alliance, the governments actually organized in the states whose monarchs were restored by the Congress of Vienna, furnished abundant evidence that the ideas of the 1848 Revolutions had not lost all their force. Especially conspicuous was the idea that some kind of constitution—of fundamental law, written or unwritten—was of the essence of a rational and workable system. Various practical conditions* confirmed the old tendency to regard a formal written document as in the only full and precise sense a constitution. Hence the demand for some such well-defined legal basis for the government, whether monarchic, aristocratic, or Democratic, became the central feature in the program of the Liberal Party in every state. Concession to this demand went steadily on among the princes of the continent, strongly resisted only by Austria, Russia, and Prussia. After the crisis of 1848, the Hohenzollern and later the Hapsburger gave way, and by 1880 practically every Christian state of the continent save Russia was governed under a written constitution (Dunning 1920, 251).

During the agitations and conflicts that attended the progress to this end, theoretical debate developed new and striking doctrines only as to the content, not as to the desirability of the written code. There was the greatest diversity among the actual constitutions as to the organization and action of the governments. In every state there was continuous strife between parties devoted to the application of liberal and conservative interpretations respectively to the fundamental law, or to the expansion of it in the sense of their interests. As to the essential requirements of constitutional government, theory was practically unanimous in holding that there must be some guarantee of rights to the individual and some reciprocal check and balance among the legislative, executive, and judicial powers. It was further held by all but the ultra-conservatives that rational government required the participation of some form of deliberative assembly, representing in some way the body politic. All these requirements had been understood and met in France in 1789 and the following years, but the swift evolution of those years into anarchy remained a potent warning to the Liberals of the next generation and interposed a barrier for decades against every suggestion of republicanism. Hence, the chief problem of those who speculated on the theory of constitutional government was to find a safe and useful niche in the system for the monarch (Dunning 1920, 252).

Thus, until after 1848, the theories of the constitutional state, *Rechtsstaat*, as the Germans called it, were largely concerned with the effort to reconcile the functions of a representative assembly with those of a

---

* Among them the fact that where French dominion, after long sway, was destroyed and a sweeping reorganization was necessary, the restored princes were almost compelled to formulate the principles that were to characterize their government, in order to save their subjects from hopeless confusion and anarchy (Dunning 1920, 251 fn).

hereditary monarch, to insure the liberty of the subject individual against the historical and traditional omnipotence of the reigning individual, and to partition sovereignty neatly between the prince and the people or banish the troublesome concept from the ken of philosophy (Dunning 1920, 252–3). Side by side with the development of constitutionalism in political philosophy the conception and influence of nationality received elaborate investigation and assumed much prominence (Dunning 1920, 291).

These rival political ideologies from the old and new Europe battled for the hearts and minds of the peoples of Europe. Centers of power and control over the masses were rapidly shifting from traditional, *status quo* regimes held for centuries by the nobility (kleptocratic aristocracies, autocracies, and plutocracies) to polities elected by the masses. This rapid tectonic upheaval in nineteenth-century Europe produced the 1848 Revolutions, end to feudalism and serfdom, *The Communist Manifesto*, and other radical political ideologies. French diplomat, political scientist, and historian Alexis de Tocqueville remarked in his *Recollections* of the period, "society was cut in two: those who had nothing united in common envy, and those who had anything united in common terror." Although philosophically intended to be a Democratic liberation of the masses from the oppression of the ruling classes, these upheavals created anarchy and a vast vacuum in governance opening the door widely for totalitarian ideologies to seize the day. Quickly filling this vacuum were ideologies like Socialism and Marxism; again, initially intended to be a liberation of the working class endeavoring for a Utopian egalitarian society free of outdated oppressive traditions such as socioeconomic classes, religion, and concentration of wealth. However, like all Utopian endeavors, these liberation movements were inherently naïve, philosophically romantic, and vulnerable to abuse and corruption like all other humanistic political systems.

Marxist Communism infected the masses of Europe like a novel bacterium or virus against which the host possesses no immunity. Throughout the latter half of the nineteenth century, it spread like wildfire across the European continent and beyond, culminating in the Revolutions of 1917–1924, which was a period of political unrest and revolts around the world inspired by the success of the Russian Bolshevik Revolution and the disorder created by the aftermath of the First World War. The Bolsheviks sought to coordinate this new wave of revolution in the Soviet-led Communist International (Comintern). Communist revolutionaries during this period inspired by the Comintern revolted in Ukraine (1918), Hungary (1918–1920), Netherlands (1918), Germany (1918–1923), Slovakia (1919;

part of Czechoslovakia), Italy (1921), Canada (1919), Georgia (1920), Mongolia (1921), South Africa (1921–1922), Bulgaria (1923), Romania (1924), and Estonia (1924). The uprisings were mainly Socialist or anti-colonial in nature and were mostly short-lived, failing to have a long-term impact. The primary exceptions were the Bolshevik revolution in Russia in 1917 and the German Revolution of 1918–1919. Despite ambitions for world revolution, the sweeping Comintern movement had more setbacks than successes. To counter these revolutionary forces, another totalitarian ideology was born of the Liberalism of the time to compete for the working class—National Socialism.

The First World War was the final blow to monarchism that had ruled for a millennium in Continental Europe. By the end of 1918, all twenty-two royals ruling in Germany (emperor, lesser kings, princes, grand dukes, and ruling dukes) had been deposed, and over the ensuing five years, most of the ruling aristocracy in Europe had been removed from power. The fate of these deposed aristocrats ranged from poverty and obscurity at home to a life in exile, while some were met with execution. The radicalism that jumped into the void after the fall of monarchism prevented republican (parliamentary) Democracy from gaining any ground in mainland Europe—the primary exception being Czechoslovakia. In a practical sense, Communism and National Socialism became political and philosophical stereoisomers competing for power and were at the time seen as the most effective solutions to the chaos engulfing Europe. Although they identify each other as their primary enemy, their fundamental ideology and *modus operandi* in their approach to governance, the economy, and prioritizing state over individual is in fact innately and systematically homologous. (National Socialist or Fascist economic ideology supports the profit motive and limited private property, but like Communism, emphasizes that production must serve the state and uphold the national interest over private profit and wealth. Both political models effectively claim *prima ius* over all property, labor, and production. Neither model permits a free-market economy; both models exercise central planning of the economy. Neither model equalizes wages and social class standing. Both models are based on the "dictate of the 'elite'" in law and economics.) Until these evil totalitarian ideologies destined for mutual destruction completed their natural evolutions (see *inter alia*: Plato's *The Republic*), representative Democracy, individual human rights over the rights of the state, and a free-market economy remained only a Utopian concept for most Continental Europeans.

One of academia's biggest deceptions over the past century has been the polar political differentiation of Fascism and Communism. The established standard in the field of political "science" has been to classify on the single-axis political spectrum Fascism on the far right just beyond Conservativism and Communism on the far left just beyond Socialism. The origin and history of this false dogma separating the two totalitarian ideologies is relatively new and well identified. Every citizen of a Democratic society approaching majority age preparing to exercise their civic right to vote would provide themselves great benefit to fully understand the brief history of this tragic lie still propagated throughout the world by mainstream academia.

The polar differentiation of Fascism (best represented by Nazism at the time) and Communism (best represented by Marxism or Bolshevism at the time) originated in Frankfurt, Germany in 1924. After the First World War, the son of wealthy Jewish German Argentine parents, Lucio Félix José Weil (1898–1975), was a doctoral student in economics (*Nationalökonomie* or *Wirtschaftswissenschaften*) at *Eberhard Karls Universität Tübingen*. In 1919, Weil was banned from doing his doctorate in Tübingen because of his revolutionary political sentiments. Like Theodor W. Adorno, Weil belonged "to the generation of turn-of-the-century intellectuals born of *bourgeois*, mostly Jewish families, attracted by philosophical Marxism beyond the workers' parties in the 1920s." Weil managed to transfer his studies to *Königliche Universität zu Frankfurt am Main* (Royal University of Frankfurt on Main), known since 1932 as *Goethe Universität Frankfurt am Main*. His doctoral thesis, titled "Socialization: An Attempt at a Conceptual Foundation, with a Critique of the Plans for Socialization," dealt with the practical problems of implementing Socialism. In 1922, Weil organized the First Marxist Workweek (*Erste Marxistische Arbeitswoche*), a conference in the Thuringian town of Ilmenauin as an effort to synthesize different trends of Marxism into a coherent, practical philosophy; the first symposium included famous Marxists such as György Lukács, Karl Korsch, Karl August Wittfogel, Richard Sorge, and Friedrich Pollock. The success of this event led Weil and his friend Friedrich Pollock, with the help of an endowment from Weil's father Hermann, to found in Frankfurt, Germany on 3 February 1923 a permanent institute for social research—the *Institut für Sozialforschung* (*IfS*; Institute for Social Research) commonly known as the Frankfurt School. Weil negotiated with the Prussian Ministry of Education for a university professor to be director of the *IfS*, thereby formally ensuring that the Frankfurt School would be an adjunct organization at *Königliche*

Universität zu Frankfurt am Main. The first director of *IfS*, Kurt Albert Gerlach, died shortly after accepting his post and was swiftly followed in 1924 by Jewish-Bessarabian German Marxist philosopher of law and history, and chair of history of economy at the University of Vienna, Carl Grünberg ("Father of Austro-Marxism"; 1861–1940). Grünberg gathered together fellow "orthodox" Marxists at the Institute, including Max Horkheimer, Theodor W. Adorno, Herbert Marcuse, Friedrich Pollock, Erich Fromm, Otto Kirchheimer, Leo Löwenthal, Franz Leopold Neumann, and Grünberg's former pupil Henryk Grossman. After having suffered from a stroke, Grünberg retired in 1929 and left leadership of the Institute to Max Horkheimer.

Founded in the Weimar Republic during the European interwar period and early years of National Socialism, the Frankfurt School was a Marxist response to the rise of National Socialism in the wake of the failed German Revolution. The Institute comprised intellectuals, academics, and political dissidents who sought rational answers for contemporary political developments in Germany. In their reactionary analysis, the Institute's theoreticians developed the single-axis political spectrum and placed Fascism on the far right just beyond Conservativism and Communism on the far left just beyond Socialism to represent their view of the conflict between these two competing political ideologies of the time. The Institute's theoreticians developed their new Critical Theory* that proposed Marxist social theory was inadequate for explaining the turbulent political factionalism and reactionary politics occurring in ostensibly liberal Capitalist societies in the twentieth century. The Frankfurt School perspective of critical investigation is based upon Freudian, Marxist, and Hegelian premises of idealist philosophy. To fill the omissions of nineteenth-century classical Marxism, which could not address twentieth-century social problems, they applied the methods of anti-Positivist sociology, of psychoanalysis, and of existentialism. The School's sociologic works derived from syntheses of the thematically pertinent works of Immanuel Kant, Georg Wilhelm Friedrich Hegel, Karl Marx, Sigmund Freud, Max Weber, Georg Simmel, and Georg Lukács. Essentially, the Institute's

---

* "[The Institute's] Critical Theory was initially developed in Horkheimer's circle to think through political disappointments at the absence of revolution in the West, the development of Stalinism in Soviet Russia, and the victory of fascism in Germany. It was supposed to explain mistaken Marxist prognoses, but without breaking Marxist intentions" (Habermas 1987, 116).

principles and methodology heavily drew from Hegelian dialectic, Freudian psychology, and Marxist scientific materialism.

As the threat of Nazism increased to political violence, the founders of *IfS* decided to move the Institute out of Nazi Germany. Soon after Adolf Hitler's rise to power in 1933, the Institute first moved from Frankfurt to Geneva, and then to New York City in 1935, where the Frankfurt School joined Columbia University. The Institute's journal, *Zeitschrift für Sozialforschung* ("Magazine of Social Research"), was renamed "Studies in Philosophy and Social Science." Thenceforth, began the period of the Institute's important work in Marxist critical theory; the scholarship and the investigational method gained acceptance throughout academia in the U.S. and in the U.K. and the false dogma that Fascism and Communism are polar political opposites persists, to date. By the 1950s, the direction of scholarship led Horkheimer, Adorno, and Pollock to return to West Germany, while Marcuse, Löwenthal, and Kirchheimer remained in the U.S. In 1953, the Institute was formally re-established in Frankfurt, West Germany.

Austrian Nobel Laureate economist and political philosopher Friedrich August von Hayek whose 1944 book *The Road to Serfdom* made the startling claim that Western welfare-state Democracies, having defeated Fascism, were themselves moving inexorably in the Fascist direction. Von Hayek identified Fascism as a phenomenon of the Left, a cousin of Socialism and progressivism. And he warned, "The rise of fascism and Nazism was not a reaction against the socialist trends of the preceding period but a necessary outcome of those tendencies" (von Hayek 2007, 59). Von Hayek recalled that Hitler once declared in one of his public speeches as late as February 1941, that "basically National Socialism and Marxism are the same" (von Hayek 1994, 35 fn 9).

"The founder of modern management" Austrian American Peter Ferdinand Drucker opined in his 1939 book *The End of Economic Man: The Origins of Totalitarianism*:

> The complete collapse of the belief in the attainability of freedom and equality through Marxism has forced Russia to travel the same road toward a totalitarian, purely negative, non-economic society of un-freedom and inequality which Germany has been following. Not that communism and fascism are essentially the same. Fascism is the stage reached after communism has proved an illusion, and it has

> proved as much an illusion in Stalinist Russia as in pre-Hitler Germany. (Drucker 1939, 230.)

In his *The Road to Serfdom*, von Hayek continues in the same vein as Drucker:

> No less significant is the intellectual history of many of the Nazi and Fascist leaders. Everyone who has watched the growth of these movements in Italy or in Germany has been struck by the number of leading men, from Mussolini downward (and not excluding Laval and Quisling), who began as socialists and ended as Fascists or Nazis. And what is true of the leaders is even more true of the rank and file of the movement. The relative ease with which a young communist could be converted into a Nazi or vice versa was generally known in Germany, best of all to the propagandists of the two parties. Many a university teacher during the 1930's has seen English and American students return from the Continent uncertain whether they were communists or Nazis and certain only that they hated Western liberal civilization.
>
> It is true, of course, that in Germany before 1933, and in Italy before 1922, communists and Nazis or Fascists clashed more frequently with each other than with other parties. They competed for support of the same type of mind and reserved for each other the hatred of the heretic. But their practice showed how closely they are related. To both, the real enemy, the man with whom they had nothing in common and whom they could not hope to convince, is the liberal of the old type. While to the Nazi the communist, and to the communist the Nazi, and to both the socialist, are potential recruits who are made of the right timber, although they have listened to false prophets, they both know there can be no compromise between them and those who really believe in individual freedom. (von Hayek 1994, 33–4.)

The National Socialist German Workers' Party (*NSDAP*) was founded on a doctrine of inequality between races, but it also promised Germans greater equality among themselves than they had enjoyed during either the Wilhelmine empire or the Weimar Republic. In practice, this goal was achieved at the expense of other groups, by means of a racist war of conquest. Nazi ideology conceived of racial conflict as an antidote to Marxist class conflict. By framing its program in this way, the party was propagating two age-old dreams of the German people: national and class unity. That was the key to the Nazis' popularity, from which they derived the power they needed to pursue their criminal aims. The ideal of the *Volksstaat*—a state of and for the people—was what we would now call a welfare state for Germans with the proper racial pedigree. In one of his central pronouncements, Hitler promised "the creation of a socially just state," a model society that would "continue to eradicate all [social] barriers" (Aly 2006, 16–17).

> Another source of the Nazi Party's popularity was its liberal borrowing from the intellectual tradition of the socialist left. Many of the men who would become the movement's leaders had been involved in communist and socialist circles in the waning years of the Weimar Republic. In his memoirs, Adolf Eichmann repeatedly asserted: "My political sentiments inclined toward the left and emphasized socialist aspect every bit as much as nationalist ones" [Eichmann 2015]. In the days when the movement was still doing battle in the streets, Eichmann added, he and his comrades had viewed Nazism and Communism as "quasi-siblings" [Eichmann 2015, 75; see also Aly 2003, 141–51].

Hence, the current conventional wisdom that Fascism and Communism are polar opposites on the political spectrum is based on a false narrative created by the very Communists that competed with the Fascists for power. The Communists sought to monopolize the liberal workers' liberation movement sweeping the industrialized world, so, they cleverly reserved for themselves the Left on their contrived political spectrum and placed Fascism (National Socialism) as far opposite as they could to create the impression of a polar difference between the two ideologies. This false narrative persists as conventional wisdom throughout the world and continues as a foundational principle in academia. Although it may be expedient to their objectives, those who continue to subscribe to and propagate this falsity are deceiving themselves and the communities in which they live and serve. The danger of this lie rests in the false inference that Socialism and Communism are liberation movements for social justice against the evils and despotism of Fascism. The lie implies that the so-called political Left is morally superior to the political Right. This same false implication has been extended by much of academia and mainstream journalism to the Liberal-Conservative debate.

CHAPTER 3

PHILOSOPHY & THE ARTS

There are many questions in philosophy to which no satisfactory answer has yet been given. But the question of the nature of the gods is the darkest and most difficult of all. . . . So various and so contradictory are the opinions of the most learned men on this matter as to persuade one of the truth of the saying that philosophy is the child of ignorance. . . .

— CICERO, *The Nature of the Gods*

WHEN SPEAKING OF CULTURE, WE REFER HERE TO THE SET OF CUSTOMS (way of life), traditions, morals (mores), laws, arts, knowledge, worldviews, self-concepts, goals, values, and idiosyncrasies of a society or community. When speaking of philosophy (Greek: "the love of wisdom"), we here refer to the study of ideas about knowledge, truth, morality, causality, the nature and meaning of life, and fundamental problems concerning matters such as existence, values, purpose, reasoning, logic, and rhetoric.

From the fall of the Holy Roman Empire on 6 August 1806, when the last Holy Roman Emperor Francis II (also known as Emperor Francis I of Austria) abdicated, following a military defeat by the French under Napoléon at Austerlitz (2 December 1805) and concluding with the Treaty of Pressburg (26 December 1805), Europe faced a rising tide of chaos and anarchy as tectonic shifts in political and philosophical theories accelerated at this crossroads of history. The English philosopher and political theorist John Locke (1632–1704), the "Father of Liberalism," set the stage while the French-Swiss philosopher and educational theorist Jean-Jacques Rousseau (1712–1778) was Liberalism's greatest evangelist leading up to the 1789 French Revolution. From the outbreak of the French Revolutionary Wars in 1792 to the exile of Napoléon to Saint Helena in 1815, Europe had been almost constantly at war. During this time, the military conquests of France had resulted in the spread of Liberalism throughout much of the continent, driving many states to adopt the anti-feudal Napoleonic code (*Code civil des Français*). Largely as a reaction to the radicalism of the French Revolution, most victorious powers of the Napoleonic Wars resolved to suppress Liberalism and Nationalism and revert largely to the *status quo ante* of Europe prior to 1789. The Concert of Europe (from the end of the Napoleonic Wars in 1815 to the formation of the German Empire in 1871) was Europe's last collective convulsive attempt to preserve the political *status quo ante* in maintaining traditional monarchism, opposing revolutionary movements, suppressing the forces of Liberalism and Nationalism, and upholding aristocratic power. The Concert of Europe failed to halt the tidal forces of Liberalism and Nationalism that were moving to redefine Europe and the world. It was the middle of the Romantic period.

Romanticism (late eighteenth to mid-nineteenth centuries) had a significant and complex effect on politics, philosophy, and the arts, and while for much of the Romantic period it was associated with Liberalism and radicalism, its long-term effect on the growth of Nationalism was perhaps most significant. In 1920, Herbert Leslie Stewart, the George Munro Professor of Philosophy and Head of the Department of Philosophy and Psychology at Dalhousie University in Halifax, Nova Scotia, published his treatise *Theology and Romanticism* for the Harvard Divinity School. In *Theology and Romanticism*, Stewart makes the following observations on the Romantic period: "If we describe it [Romanticism] as 'the revolt of the nineteenth century against the eighteenth,' we shall have spoken with a larger degree of justice than is usually compressed into an epigram" (Stewart 1920, 365). Stewart goes on to explain that during the Romantic period:

> Three new ideas were especially in the air, and each of them was represented in some form by writers of the Romantic school. There was a startling and widely prevalent distrust in the strength of human reason. There was an immensely deepened interest in the past, and at least the beginning of a far more adequate appreciation of history. And there was the assertion as a definite principle of the trustworthiness of feeling, of instinct, of the "impulses of the heart," against dialectic, ratiocination, intellectual "proof" or "disproof." (Stewart 1920, 365.)

* * *

The two great Romantic poets who collaborated in the production of *Lyrical Ballads* [Bentham and Coleridge] were at once the representatives and the stimulators of a profound disbelief both in the perfecting of the world through science and in the salvation of souls through philosophy.

The general literature of the period has an unmistakable tone of despair both about the possibilities of higher knowledge and about the value of knowledge for life. (Stewart 1920, 366.)

* * *

Again and again in his [Byron's] poetry we meet with such laments as that all science is but the replacing of one sort of ignorance by another [*Manfred* Vol. II, p. iv, 1816–17], that the tree of knowledge has not fulfilled its promise [*Cain* Vol. I, p. i, 1821], that happiness can be the lot only of those like the sleeping babe in Cain, who have not plucked the fruit and know not they are naked (Stewart 1920, 366).

* * *

A second main idea to which the men of the Romantic impulse gave expression was a deepened feeling for history . . . at a time of profound historical ignorance and no historical sympathy. The life and ideals of one period were freely projected into another, and bygone ages were reconstructed with the utmost arbitrariness to buttress some favorite dogma or programme. As Lord Morley says in speaking of Rousseau, history was less a teacher than the meagerly nourished handmaid of the imagination.

The revulsion from a period in which men spoke of believing only what they could see produced a new sympathy with that long-derided time when it was the pride of faith to leave evidence far behind. (Stewart 1920, 368–9.)

* * *

> This discord between the tone of the two centuries, appearing almost at the moment of transition from the one to the other, is among the great significant things in the history of thought (Stewart 1920, 369).
>
> * * *
>
> The word "romantic" is perhaps ill chosen to describe the new spirit that spread over Europe just one hundred years ago, but it has the sanction of long usage, and for want of a better it may still serve. Alike in art, in literature, in philosophy, in religion, a single impulse had revealed itself. It was the impulse to look backward rather than forward, reverence for the primitive, distrust of "march of intellect," a dim yet insistent faith that there had been no age of darkness towards which a philosophic age of light could rightly be contemptuous, a suspicion that science was about to overleap its limits to the eternal undoing of the human spirit, a passionate return to the natural instincts against the artificial contrivances of an arrogant Reason. (Stewart 1920, 370.)
>
> II
>
> How did these tendencies act upon theology? When one's despair of human knowledge is intensified, his appreciation of history deepened, and his new respect for feeling supersedes his old respect for reasoning, will he become more amenable or less amenable to the direction of the church? The result is sure to vary in part at least with individual temperament. (Stewart 1920, 370.)

Stewart goes on to describe the movement of thought that was in progress during this Romantic period by citing what he advocates are the two most important figures in this movement.

> There was a widespread belief that authority is mankind's sole refuge, and it was inevitable that in France return to authority should mean return to Rome. Some of the leaders of this movement were priests, and—at least until the July

Revolution of 1830—the sacerdotal hand is conspicuous in French politics. Monasteries were restored, sacrilege was punished with a rigor almost unknown since the Middle Ages, even the applicant for poor-law relief was required to produce his certificate of attendance at confession. The divine right of the monarchy was reasserted by Polignac, the last minister who served the ill-fated Charles X, and whose constantly recurring visions confirmed his faith that he was himself appointed by God to restore the kingship and the Church. It is an obvious suggestion that all this was the work of Jesuits, and we know well that the Jesuits as usual were busy. But the two most important figures for our present purpose were both laymen, one a cultivated diplomat of the old *noblesse*, who for fourteen years represented the Sardinian kingdom at the Russian capital, the other a man of letters, formerly an emigrant of the Revolution, but afterwards high in favor at the restored court of Louis XVIII, and for many years French Minister of Public Instruction. Both were reactionary in politics, eager to reestablish autocratic rule in things spiritual no less than in things temporal, and ready to take advantage of that failure of public nerve which gave its chance to the propaganda of absolutism.

De Maistre is very generally known to all students of the period, and it is needless to recall his famous argument in *Du Pape* or in the *Soirèes de Saint Petersbourg*. We have the usual picture of that moral anarchy which calls for a supreme spiritual head, even as political anarchy can be dealt with only by a supreme head of the state. We have the usual arraignment of that whole theory of life which, according to the Roman [Catholic] view, had begun at the Renaissance, developed in Lutheranism, found its expositors in the *Encyclopédie*, and reached its practical culmination in the September massacres.* But, although

* [Footnote in original] How persuasive this line of thought appeared, even to some thinkers who never joined the Roman Church, may be seen from A. W. Schlegel's letter to M. de Montmorency: "The Protestant system does not satisfy me any longer. . . . I am convinced that the time is not far off when all Christians will reunite in the

much less familiar than these books by de Maistre, the *Recherches Philosophiques* by the Vicomte de Bonald can cast more significant light on the movement of thought that was in progress. The author concentrates attention on two facts, of which each taken by itself is quite intelligible but whose combination is a curious enigma. The first is the prolonged failure of philosophy to reach any secure solution of its cosmic problems, a failure which in the hopeless discord of philosophers from Thales to Kant seemed long since as well attested as historical evidence could make it. The second is the unquenchable ardor with which, despite the disappointments of two thousand years and the demonstrated impotence of our intellectual machinery for the task, mankind refuses to draw the inference that seems so obvious, and the fruitless effort continues to be tried again. The rolling of the stone of Sisyphus was no mere poet's dream; it was rather a quite inadequate parable of the metaphysician's sublime folly.

How is this persisting impulse to be explained? De Bonald suggests that the human mind had imprinted upon it at the beginning certain truths of capital importance for moral and social development. Providence, duty, future rewards and punishments, were ideas not reached by reasoning, but implanted—as Descartes said about the notion of an Infinite Being—by God Himself upon our race at the first. The mythopoetic imagination corrupted them, and the grotesque legends by which they became overlaid called for that repudiation with which philosophy has been so copious. But philosophy destroyed good and evil alike. It discredited not only the myths but the principle round which the myths had grown up. It presumed, for example, to demand proof for that purposive structure of the universe which must be assumed as often as we prove anything, and

old faith. The work of the Reformation is accomplished, the pride of human reason, which was evident in the first Reformers, and still more in their successors, has guided us so ill, especially during the last century, that it has come into antagonism with itself and has destroyed itself. It is perhaps ordained that those who have influence on the opinions of their contemporaries shall publicly renounce it, and then assist in preparing a union with the one Church of former days."

which consequently cannot itself be proved at all. Small wonder then that *petitio principii* should abound in theistic argument. "We take within ourselves the resting-place on which we want to climb up; in a word, we gauge our own thought by itself, which puts us in the position of a man who wished to weigh himself without scales or weights. Playthings of our own illusions, we interrogate ourselves, and we take the echo of our own voice for the response of truth." Thus for De Bonald the spiritual anarchies of private judgment are like the social anarchies of individualism. In speculations purely theoretical, like some parts of astronomy for instance, each inquirer has to depend on his own gift of reasoning. But in ascertaining the truths by which we have to live, no such desperate task is laid upon us. We are not forced to make an independent chemical analysis before we eat our food, and neither have we to conduct for ourselves a logical investigation into the ultimate things we are to believe. The Most High has implanted convictions in mankind for the life of the spirit, just as He has made the earth yield her fruit for the life of the body. In each case tradition, common consent, verification by long trial, are our sufficient guides. (Stewart 1920, 370–3.)

* * *

III

But there was another and a very different side to Romanticism, a side so prominent that the historians of literature dwell upon it almost to the exclusion of the tendencies we have mentioned. It was the glorifying of impulse as against reason, of the individual as against controlling authority, of self-fulfillment and self-expression as against self-denial and self-restraint. . . . Goethe, who in some of his work may be looked upon as its prophet. . . . Germany was once the special home of this law-defying individualism. . . . (Stewart 1920, 379–80.)

* * *

> Yet enthusiasm for what was called "return to nature" is perhaps the most characteristic common element in the Romanticists, and "nature" was curiously identified with the emotional rather than the ratiocinative impulse in mankind. It was an odd reaction against a still odder myth, the myth endorsed by [Anglican Bishop of Gloucester William] Warburton when he said that "the image of God in which man was at first created lay in the faculty of reason only." (Stewart 1920, 381.)

Christopher Dawson begins his analysis of the tragedies of the twentieth century with the claim that the Reformation was disastrous in terms of precipitating the latent Nationalism of Europe that he argues led to the Enlightenment, 1789 French Revolution, Romanticism, Liberalism, Communism, and National Socialism (Nazi movement). The following is an excerpt from Professor of American History Dr. Bradley J. Birzer's Introduction to the 2013 edition of Dawson's 1959 work: *The Movement of World Revolution* (Dawson 1959).

> Having witnessed the loss of an idyllic Edwardian world to the deadening trenches of the first world war, the rise of communism and the gulag state in Slavic Europe and China, and the advent of national socialism and the holocaust camps in Germanic Europe, Christopher Dawson found the ideologies that spawned such twentieth-century atrocities profoundly disturbing.[*]
>
> * * *
>
> One of his last books published during his life time, Dawson's 1959 *Movement of World Revolution*, not surprisingly, explored almost all of the themes he had considered most important in his own time: nationalism, ideology, and Christian Humanism. Dawson preferred to write on non-political subjects, but he believed the necessities of the moment required solid political analysis.

---

[*] [Footnote in original] On Dawson's formative views of the pre-1914 world, see Dawson 1970 and Dawson 1949.

He wrote extensively on political issues in the 1930s and early 1940s, and he returned to the topic in this 1959 book. . . .

Christendom

* * *

The [fifth-century Germanic] barbarians . . . contributed much that was dangerous to the classical/Christian synthesis and antithetical to the very heart of Christendom, the church universal. Their most important contribution, which the Church had to combat repeatedly in the middle ages, was the tendency toward nationalism. Roman Catholic historian Lord Acton stressed that the end of Christendom and the western ideals would mean the rise of nationalism. "Christianity rejoices at the mixture of races," he wrote in his famed essay, "Nationalism." Paganism, however, "identifies itself with their differences, because truth is universal, errors various and particular" [Dalberg-Acton 1985, 409–33]. For Dawson, ideologies served as the glue that kept modern nations together, for each nation needed something to overcome and, more often than not, overwhelm, those who would be different. And, when Christendom could no longer contain the inherent nationalisms of the Germanic elements of medieval society, Christendom disintegrated.

Before that, though, the Middle Ages were *sui generis* for six centuries. Culturally, the church unified Christendom through a common language, Latin, and a common liturgy, tying men together with other men of their own time, but also to the whole communion of saints. Politically, nearly every type of entity imaginable existed: free cities, abbeys, fiefs, bishoprics, counties, duchies, and those lands controlled by the various Orders, military or religious [Dawson 1965, 20]. In other words, Christendom embraced a cultural unity and beheld a polycentric political system. It was the *Christiana Res Publica.* "I saw monarchy without tyranny, aristocracy without factions, democracy without tumult, wealth without luxury," Dawson quoted Erasmus approvingly. "Would that it had been your lot, divine Plato, to come upon such a republic" [Dawson 1991, 173–4]. Perhaps most important, medieval man believed that he knew his place in the Economy of Grace, in God's universe. He had, Dawson wrote, "an intuition of the eternal verities which is itself an emanation from the Divine Intellect" [Dawson 1931, 161].

The Rise of Nationalism

Dawson found nationalism emerging in a number of different ways in the western tradition. As noted, it was already inherent within German barbarianism [Dawson 1940, 349]. It was latent, ready to emerge at any time it found opportune, especially if Christendom was divided against itself. Christendom disintegrated because of the barbarian propensity for nationalism, but not all at once. And, it was certainly not unique to the Germans in the western tradition, as Hellas may have been a proto-type of nationalism. The process began in earnest in the early fourteenth century and continues through the present day. The French first experienced a budding nationalism in 1302 and then again in the French Revolution [Pettit 1996, 576–604; Dawson 1965, 21].

The rise of a nation-state in any western area by necessity must witness the corresponding decline of religious influence and thought.* Christianity, through Grace and mercy, especially embraces the universal rather than the particular, as Lord Acton correctly stated. The nation, though, demands a unity of thought, culture, and politics. "And in each case what we find is a substitute religion or counter religion which transcends the juridical limits of the political State and creates a kind of secular

* [Foot note in original] Perhaps the most insightful examination and microhistory of this process is a book often regarded as superficial by many scholars, though published in the same year as Dawson's *Movement of World Revolution*. This author [Birzer], however, found it to be one of the most insightful and artfully written books he's ever read: William L. Shirer, *The Rise and Fall of the Third Reich: A History of Nazi Germany* (Shirer 1959).

Church" [Dawson 1957, 425]. It unifies its disparate peoples and cultures through ideology, which takes "the place of theology as the creator of social ideals and the guide of public opinion" [Dawson 1956, 139].

Though the process of nationalism began long before the sixteenth century, Dawson viewed the Reformation as disastrous in terms of precipitating the latent nationalism of Europe. One should not be surprised, Dawson argued, that Martin Luther [1483–1546] came from northern Germany where the "spirit of the old gods was imperfectly exorcised by the sword and . . . has continued to haunt the background of the German mind" [Dawson 1942a, 30]. Following other nationalists of the previous centuries such as Wycliffe and Hus, Luther "embodies the revolt of the awakening German national spirit" [Dawson 2001, 142]. Like all nationalisms, Luther's rejected the complexity of Christendom–its culture and polycentric political system–and de-intellectualized "the Catholic tradition," Dawson wrote. "He took St. Paul without his Hellenism, and St. Augustine without his Platonism."[11] The Reformation also habituated the populations of Europe to think in ideological terms, thus preparing them for the Enlightenment world [Dawson 1956, 140].

Indeed, for Dawson, the Enlightenment and the French Revolution completed the work of the Reformation. The Enlightenment, after all, witnessed more neglect of Christian ideals and more selling of church property than any other time. The Enlightenment, in essence, extended the desires of the Reformers even into cultural and geopolitical areas that had resisted the Reformation of the sixteenth and seventeenth centuries.[12] It should not surprise the modern mind, Dawson claimed, that the philosophy of the Enlightenment spawned both liberalism and communism. Each rejected the intellectual contributions of Christendom and instead embraced materialist understandings of the world. Each also developed propaganda as a means of undermining the "social order and traditional morality" [Dawson 1932, 320]. Both the liberals and the communists understood the spiritual underpinnings of Europe even better than do present-day European Christians. Hence, each ideological group attempted to undermine the Christian understanding of spirituality, and, instead, have Christians embrace Christ as a political revolutionary. Finally, each destroyed without rebuilding [Dawson 1957b, 50].

> But it is Christianity which is at once the original bond of European unity, and the source of the spiritual ideals and the attitude to life which inspired our civilization. The enemies of Europe recognize this fact more clearly than we do ourselves, and that is why Christianity is everywhere the first object of Communist attacks, and why the creation of a materialist ideology and a new moral attitude is regarded by the Russian government as essential to the success of the Communist experiment. [Dawson 1932, 332.]

The undermining of the spiritual bond of Europe and its substitution with ideologies has had numerous profound effects on European culture, in addition to the loss of religious fervor and the destruction of Europe itself. First, it has led to substitute religions. God created us to find religion, to find Him. Man without true religion is empty. He finds himself devoid of something, but that something remains elusive. He will seek until he finds either true religion or a substitute that temporarily fills the void.* "The

---

* [Footnote in original] "'Every living culture must possess some spiritual dynamic, which provides the energy necessary for that sustained social effort which is civilization,' Dawson wrote in the preface to *Progress and Religion*. 'Normally this dynamic is supplied by a religion, but in exceptional circumstances the religious impulse may disguise itself under philosophical or political forms.' Even in a secular, modern age, Dawson thought, the 'religious impulse' does not go away. Unable to express itself fully through traditional channels, it can emerge in philosophical forms (such as the idea of progress or the 'religion of democracy' in the eighteenth century) or political forms (political religion in the twentieth century) as a powerful propellant force behind human action. *The Gods of Revolution* examines the sources of these philosophical forms of religious forces in the eighteenth century and how they spread through modern, secular prophets such as

ordinary man will never stand for nihilism; it is against all his healthier instincts," Dawson wrote in 1955 [Devon Dawson 1955]. To find his substitute, man turns in many directions: utopianism, drugs, and cults, "leaving the enemy in possession of the field" (Dawson *Essays in Order* 1931, 158).

Second, the substitute of ideology for true religion has yielded to the unwieldiness and ultimate tyranny of science and technology. If Christianity cannot delimit the growth of technology, providing the scientists with an ethical understanding of the world, technology soon masters man. "He becomes a subordinate part of the great mechanical system that his scientific genius has created," Dawson lamented. "In the same way, the economic process, which led to the exploitation of the world by man and the vast increase of his material resources, ends in the subjection of man to the rule of the machine and the mechanisation of human life" [ibid., 162]. Romano Guardini stated the problem equally well. Man could work with nature, or he could seek to dominate it. Of the first type of technology, "the aim is to penetrate, to move within, to live with," Guardini argued. "The other, however, unpacks, tears apart, arranges in compartments, takes over and rules" [Guardini 1994, 43]. The dominating kind of technology, though, soon takes on a life of its own, and man loses his control over it and becomes subsumed by it. "It is destructive because it is not under human control," Guardini concluded. "It is surging ahead of unleashed forces that have not yet been mastered, raw material that has not yet been put together, given a living and spiritual form, and related to humanity" [Guardini 1994, 79].

Unrestrained science and technology has resulted in mechanized man and the mechanized government. Bureaucratic states–whether democratic or tyrannical–are the "coldest of cold monsters" [Dawson *Essays in Order* 1931, 162]. In 1942, Dawson argued that Soviet

---

Jean-Jacques Rousseau or Thomas Paine to emerge as real forces in the French Revolution." (Stuart 1972, xv.)

> Communism, German National Socialism, and America's New Deal were all variants of a theme (Dawson 1942a, 114). The Soviets "may have deified mechanism in theory," Dawson argued, "but it is the Americans who raised it in practice" [Dawson 1931, 167; Dawson 1972, 163–4]. Ultimately, Dawson claimed, the alliance of science and political power was forcing humanity "helplessly towards the abyss" [Dawson 1942a, 6].

Clearly, Dawson held strong, controversial views on what many other scholars judge in a different light. Over the centuries from Charlemagne to Francis II, the Roman Catholic Church, particularly in the office of the Papacy, had become deeply involved in the political life of Europe. The resulting intrigues and political manipulations, combined with the Church's increasing power and wealth, contributed to the bankrupting of the Church as a spiritual force. Abuses such as the sale of indulgences (or spiritual privileges) and relics and the corruption of the clergy exploited the pious and further undermined the Church's spiritual authority. Corruption among the clergy showed the need for reform and Lutheran ideas made impressions of such hope (Cairns 1996, 309). Criticisms from the populace played a part in spreading anticlerical sentiments, such as the publication *Heptaméron* by Marguerite of Navarre, sister of French King Francis I (1494–1547), a collection of stories that depicted immorality among the clergy (Lindberg 1972, 279). Furthermore, the reduction of salvation to a business scheme based on a good-works-for-sale system added to the injury. Under these circumstances, salvation by grace through faith in Jesus was a pleasant alternative. Works such as Guillaume (William) Farel's 1524 French translation of the Lord's Prayer, *Le Livre de vraye et parfaicte oraison* (*The Book of True and Perfect Prayer*) and the Apostles' Creed with a Lutheran leaning, became the most popular book of evangelical piety in France and was reprinted fourteen times between 1528 and 1545 (Greengrass 1987, 13; see also Higman 1992, 26–31]. It echoed Luther's emphasis on justification by grace alone, faith as the free gift of God, complete human dependence on God for salvation, and the scriptural basis for these evangelical positions. It also contained criticisms of the clergy for their immorality, idolatry, and superstition in religious practices that hampered growth of true faith.

Most scholars, secular and religious, agree that Roman Catholic authority and excesses had reached unprecedented heights in the late Middle

Ages, which saw the Church going through a period of real doctrinal confusion. There arose generations of Christians who did not understand what the Gospel was all about. To many scholars, the Reformation brought with it a rediscovery of the truths of the Christian faith. A rebirth of Christian understanding and Christian knowledge. To these scholars, Martin Luther was a true reformer and not a rebel, liberal revolutionary, or anarchist, as Dawson may suggest. Martin Luther's movement intended to theologically and politically reform Roman Catholicism and not destroy it. Luther claimed that what distinguished him from previous reformers was that while they attacked corruption in the life of the Church, he went to the theological root of the problem—the perversion of the Church's doctrine of redemption and grace. Luther deplored the entanglement of God's free gift of grace in a complex system of indulgences and good works. In his Ninety-Five Theses, he attacked the indulgence system, insisting that the pope had no authority over purgatory and that the doctrine of the merits of the saints had no foundation in the Gospel. Here lay the key to Luther's concerns for the ethical and theological reform of the Church: Scripture alone is authoritative (*sola scriptura*); justification is by faith alone (*sola fide*), not by works; and faith is solely an unmerited gift of divine grace (*sola gracia*)—in other words: scripture over tradition, faith over works, and grace over merit.

While he did not intend to break with the Catholic Church, a confrontation with the Papacy over the *power and primacy of the pope** was not long in coming. In 1521, Luther was tried before the Imperial Diet of Worms and was eventually excommunicated. However, what began as an internal reform movement had, in part due to the corruption and obstinacy of the pope and the Church's doctrinal theologians, become a fracture in western Christendom. Also responsible for this fracture was the fact that Luther's movement for reform was to a certain extent ultimately hijacked by Nationalists, anarchists, theological legalists, power and warmongers among the nobles and royals, and militant anti-Catholics resulting in the Great

---

* *Tractatus de Potestate et Primatu Papae* (*Treatise on the Power and Primacy of the Pope*) was a 1537 monograph or tractate in Latin by Philip Melanchthon that defined the Lutheran stance on the papacy declaring: 1) The Pope is not head of the Christian Church and superior to all other bishops by divine right (*de iure divino*); 2) The Pope and bishops do not hold civil authority by divine right; and 3) The claim of the Bull *Unam sanctam* (1302) that obedience to the Pope is necessary for salvation is invalid since it contradicts the doctrine of justification by faith alone. This monograph became the seventh of ten Lutheran credal documents in the *Book of Concord* (German 1580; Latin 1584).

Peasants' Revolt, Huguenot Wars, and the Thirty-Years' War. To Roman Catholics such as Dawson, Martin Luther was an ideologue who along with his Reformation was to blame for stirring Nationalism, dumbing down or trivializing "the Catholic tradition," and laying the foundation for the Enlightenment that turned out to be so devastating to Roman Catholicism and social harmony. But Dawson fails to differentiate the Lutheran Reformation from the *Reformed Protestant* Reformation that ensued and managed to sectarianize Christendom with heterodox ideology emphasizing reason, humanism, and works-righteousness (legalism), the very heterodoxies that motivated Luther's pen and voice in the beginning. Although Dawson acknowledges in so many words the corruption of the Catholic Church's divine mission as the primary impetus for the Reformation, he nonetheless has never articulated any good that came from the Reformation. To the contrary, Dawson has clearly concluded the Reformation was just another cog in the great wheel of secularization and liberalization that ushered in the destruction of Christendom and the rise of Nazi and Marxist totalitarianism (Dawson 1942b, 93–109). Dawson ostensibly placed the social benefits of the temporal Church over theological orthodoxy as if the Church's primary mission is more social (communal) rather than evangelical; a social gospel for the sake of temporal harmony, peace, and justice as opposed to the Gospel of individual salvation in an ever more secular, scientific, materialistic, and spiritually decaying world.

However, in at least two areas Dawson can be trusted, namely, in his historical scholarship and his ability to atomize, dissect, clarify, and link complex historical movements in lucid metahistorical terms; he was effective at capturing the very *Zeitgeist* behind the historical movements.

> The fourteenth century was . . . the age of the Great [Western] Schism and the Black Death and the Hundred Years' War, but it was also the age of Dante and Petrarch, of St. Catherine and St. Bridget, of Tauler and Suso and Ruysbroeck, an age of poets and mystics and saints. It was the breakdown of the universal theocratic order of mediaeval Christendom and the rise of political nationalism and religious division, and at the same time it witnessed the passing of the old agrarian and feudal society and the rise of capitalism and urban industrialism. [Dawson 1933, 160–1.]

Dawson is correct in his interpretation of how the Reformation successfully pierced the unquestionable authority and veil of infallibility and irreproachability of the Papacy with its bureaucracy, and how it aided in the push towards Nationalism, helping to lay the foundations to the Enlightenment and 1789 French Revolution. The Reformation was one of the greatest of all revolutions in terms of impact on culture and history. This stormy, often brutal conflict hijacked from Luther fractured Christendom and divided the Christians of Western Europe into Protestants and Catholics. So far-reaching were the consequences of this division that the Reformation has been declared a major turning point in history. It ushered in the Modern Age because once the people's religious unity was destroyed, they began to think in terms of their own regional interests and national identities. From the diversity of those interests arose new political, social, and economic philosophies. To this extent, Dawson strongly lamented the separation of church and state initiated during the Reformation. The loss of the unifying political and moral influence of the one Christian Church that existed up until the Reformation with the growing factionalism and divided loyalties that infected all of Europe in the form of Nationalism eventually led to totalitarian ideologies redefining morality and manipulating the masses.

In 1939, Christopher Dawson interrupted his work on the French Revolution (posthumously published in 1972 as *The Gods of Revolution*) to focus on his *opus* of social criticism, *Beyond Politics* (Dawson 1939). In *Beyond Politics*, Dawson addressed the problems vexing him in the mid-1930s that he saw were intimately connected to the loss of spiritual community. The loss of such community, Dawson believed, pushed people toward revolutionary Nationalism and Socialism, culminating in dangerous totalitarian states. Dawson argued that the Jacobin Democracy of 1793–1794 was the prototype of the totalitarian state and the matrix in which modern totalitarian ideology was born. The republic of Robespierre and Saint-Just, as conceived of by French-Swiss philosopher and educational theorist Jean-Jacques Rousseau, was a spiritual community "based on definite moral doctrines and finding direct religious expression in an official civic cult." It operated by means of dictatorship and the enforcement of a uniform ideology. It gave full license to Nationalism and Socialism, which later realized their latent possibilities in the new spiritual communities of Hitler and Stalin with their political religions similarly aimed at social regeneration (Stuart and Dawson 1972, x). Yes, Fascism, Communism, and Nazism; Dawson viewed these movements as symptoms of mental crises, partly because they developed in the psychological and spiritual vacuum left by the separation of Europe's traditional religion (Christianity) from its culture (Stuart 2009, 9).

Dawson blamed the separation between religion and culture (secularization) as a leading factor in the contemporary situation of the 1930s. Christian disunity since the Reformation had created a "neutral territory which gradually expanded till it came to include almost the whole of social life." The wars of religion led to the eventual exclusion of religion to a private world (Dawson 1942, 104). For a Christian "who believes in the existence of a divine and universal society all such ideas are blasphemy against Christ the King," he wrote (Dawson 1935). In this way, in *The Judgment of the Nations* he blamed Christian disunity for the division between religion and culture that led to secularization (Stuart 2009, 295).

Dawson saw the Reformation as a subplot of the Renaissance (1307–1789), which he believed ushered in the Modern Age and its associated religious, political, Nationalist, social, and moral sectarianism. In *The Gods of Revolution*, Dawson argues the following:

> In order to understand European history we must first understand what Europe is—not a mere geographical expression, nor a heterogeneous collection of independent nationalities, but a true society of peoples possessing a common tradition of culture and of religion. In the past this social organism was known as Christendom, and it is in fact in medieval Christendom that its unity is most plainly visible.
>
> It is true that in its origins western Christendom was conterminous neither with Christendom as a whole nor with Europe. To an oriental observer it must have appeared little more than an outlying barbaric province of the Christian world, isolated between the pagan north and the Moslem south and unworthy to be compared with the wealthy and civilized society of Byzantine Christendom. Yet this semi-barbarous society of western Christendom possessed a vitality and power of growth that its more civilized neighbours lacked.
>
> From its original centre in the Frankish dominions it gradually extended its range, until by the end of the Middle Ages it had embraced the whole of western and northern Europe and had begun its career of colonial

expansion beyond the seas, while the fortunes of eastern Christendom had steadily declined until Byzantium had become the capital of Islam and the Christian peoples of the Balkans were the slaves of the Turk.

This triumphant expansion was, however, accompanied by a loss of internal unity; western Christendom was a synthesis of Nordic and Latin elements, ordered and directed by the Church and the Papacy. The state, as it was under the tutelage of the Church and the clergy, who possessed a monopoly of the higher education, took a leading part in its administration and policy. But with the decline of feudalism and the growth of a centralized monarchical power, the state asserted its independence and attempted to deprive the territorial Church of its international character and to weaken the bonds that attached it to the Holy See.

At the same time the development of national feeling and vernacular culture brought to the surface the underlying elements of racial and cultural diversity which had been held in abeyance but not removed by the unifying forces of medieval Catholicism. Both the Latin south and the Germanic north rejected the medieval synthesis as an impure mixture of discordant elements and attempted to go behind the Middle Ages and to recover the unalloyed traditions of classical culture and evangelical religion.

Thus the sixteenth century saw the first great European revolution, a revolt carried out by the Italian Renaissance in the name of the purity of culture, and by the German Reformation in the name of the purity of the Gospel. The Middle Ages were rejected by the humanists as barbarous and by the reformers as superstitious and corrupt. To both alike they were the Dark Ages, and to both it seemed as though mankind, after a thousand years of barbarism and error, was being born again and that religion and culture were destined to be renewed after the model of primitive Christianity and classical antiquity. (Dawson 2015, 4–5.)

Out of the late Middle Ages emerged the Renaissance, regarded as the cultural bridge between the Middle Ages and the Enlightenment and modern history. The Renaissance—beginning with Marco Polo's literary recollections in 1307 of his voyages or with the crowning of Petrarch as Rome's poet laureate in 1341 and ending with the French Revolution in 1789—was a period of nostalgia for classical antiquity with its humanism focusing education on ancient texts in the original Classical Greek and Latin to recover, reinterpret, and assimilate the language, literature, art, learning, and values of ancient Greece and Rome, thereby asserting "the genius of man . . . the unique and extraordinary ability of the human mind" (Manetti 1452 or 1453). Humanism, until the late 1520s, served as a breeding ground for the French Protestant Reformation. The humanist perspective on understanding Scriptures had irreversible theological and ecclesiastical implications.

Despite its fascination with antiquity and the glorification of man, the Renaissance was actually an intellectual revolution in that it revisited ancient concepts of man, reinterpreted those concepts, and produced new ideas, particularly about science and experimentation, that went on to inform the events of the Age of Reason, commonly referred to as the Enlightenment (1685–1815). In response, Romanticism (roughly 1770–1848) arose out of the notion that not everything could be coldly rationalized, and that beauty and aesthetics were important parts of existence. Whereas Renaissance art looked back constantly to the ancient Greeks and Romans, the Romantics celebrated the wilder aspects of the creativity of medieval man with his strong, irrational emotions—particularly horror, mysticism, and the occult—along with the more tender sentiments of affection, sorrow, and romantic longing.

Romanticism was characterized by its emphasis on emotion and individualism as well as glorification of nature and the past, preferring the medieval rather than the classical. Romanticism is a philosophical movement during the latter stages of the Enlightenment, which emphasizes emotional self-awareness as a necessary pre-condition to improving society and bettering the human condition. Like German Idealism and Kantianism, with which it is usually linked in a philosophical context, Romanticism was largely centered in Germany during the late eighteenth and early nineteenth century. It was a reaction against the Enlightenment's emphasis on the primacy of reason and stands in opposition to the Rationalism and Empiricism of the Age of Reason, representing a shift from the objective to the subjective. Enlightened rationality gave way to the wildness of

Romanticism, but nineteenth-century Liberalism and Classicism—not to mention twentieth-century Modernism—all owe a heavy debt to the thinkers of the Enlightenment. John Locke of the Enlightenment was the "father of Liberalism"; Jean-Jacques Rousseau of the Romantic period was Liberalism's greatest evangelist.

In general, Romanticism was a reaction against the Industrial Revolution, the aristocratic social and political norms of the Enlightenment, and the scientific rationalization of nature during the Age of Reason, which left little room for the freedom and creativity of the human spirit. Romanticism stressed strong emotion as a source of aesthetic experience. It was embodied most strongly in the visual arts, music, and literature, but it also had a counterpart in philosophical thought and religion. Although Romanticism was rooted in the German *Sturm und Drang* counter-Enlightenment movement,* which preferred intuition and emotion to the rationalism of the Enlightenment, the events and ideologies of the 1789 French Revolution were also influential factors.

Philosophical Romanticism holds that the universe is a single unified and interconnected whole, and full of values, tendencies and life, not merely objective lifeless matter. The Romantic view is that reason, objectivity, and analysis radically falsify reality by breaking it up into disconnected lifeless entities, and the best way of perceiving reality is through some subjective feeling or intuition, through which we participate in the subject of our knowledge, instead of viewing it from the outside. To the Romanticist, nature is an experience, not an object for manipulation and

---

* *Sturm und Drang* is a proto-Romantic movement in German literature and music that took place from the late 1760s to the early 1780s, in which individual subjectivity and, in particular, extremes of emotion were given free expression in reaction to the perceived constraints of rationalism imposed by the Enlightenment and associated aesthetic movements. The period is named for Friedrich Maximilian Klinger's play *Sturm und Drang*, which was first performed by Abel Seyler's famed theatrical company in 1777. The philosopher Johann Georg Hamann is considered to be the ideologue of *Sturm und Drang*, with Jakob Michael Reinhold Lenz, H. L. Wagner, and Friedrich Maximilian Klinger also significant figures. Johann Wolfgang von Goethe was also a notable proponent of the movement, though he and Friedrich Schiller ended their period of association with it by initiating what would become Weimar Classicism. ("Sturm und Drang," *Wikipedia, The Free Encyclopedia,* https://en.wikipedia.org/w/index.php?title=Sturm_und_Drang&oldid=739674932. Accessed 21 October 2016.)

study, and, once experienced, the individual becomes in tune with his feelings enabling him to create moral values.

The roots of Philosophical Romanticism can be found in the work of Jean-Jacques Rousseau (1712–1778) and Immanuel Kant (1724–1804). Rousseau—credited with the idea of the "noble savage," uncorrupted by artifice and society—thought that civilization fills man with unnatural wants and seduces him away from his true nature and original freedom. Kant's theory of Transcendental Idealism posited that we do not directly see "things-in-themselves"; we only understand the world through our human point of view, an idea developed by American Transcendentalism of the mid-nineteenth century.

The German Idealists who followed on from Kant and adapted and expanded his work with their own interpretations of Idealism, can all be considered Romanticists in their outlook. The German Idealists injected Rousseau's "noble savage" into the Aryan *Völkisch Bewegung* of "*blut und boden*" (blood and soil) and the notion of "the organic community" (*Volksgemeinschaft*) that became essential pillars of the early National Socialist movement in Germany. Among these German Idealists, the most important were Johann Gottlieb Fichte (1762–1814), Friedrich Wilhelm Joseph von Schelling (1775–1854), Georg Wilhelm Friedrich Hegel (1770–1831), and Arthur Schopenhauer (1788–1860). Hegel was perhaps the most influential of the German Idealist philosophers, and his idea that each person's individual consciousness or mind is really part of the Absolute Mind (Absolute Idealism) had far-reaching effects.

The key step in secularizing dialectic theology, and thus in paving the way for Marxism, was taken by the lion of German philosophy, Georg Wilhelm Friedrich Hegel. Born into a family of pietist Lutherans in Stuttgart, Hegel studied theology at the University of Tübingen, and then taught theology and philosophy at the Universities of Jena and Heidelberg before becoming the leading philosopher at the new jewel in the Prussian academic crown, the University of Berlin.* Coming to Berlin in 1817, Hegel remained there until his death, ending his days as rector of the university.

Hegel was an important figure of German idealism. He achieved wide recognition in his day and—while primarily influential within the continental tradition of philosophy—has become increasingly influential in

---

* University of Berlin – founded in 1809 as University of Berlin; renamed Friedrich Wilhelm University in 1828; renamed *Humboldt-Universität zu Berlin* in 1949.

the analytic tradition as well. Although Hegel remains a divisive figure, his canonical stature within Western philosophy is universally recognized.

Hegel's principal achievement was his development of a distinctive articulation of idealism, sometimes termed *absolute idealism*, in which the dualisms of, for instance, mind and nature and subject and object are overcome. His philosophy of spirit conceptually integrates psychology, the state, history, art, religion, and philosophy. His account of the master–slave dialectic has been highly influential, especially in twentieth-century France. Of special importance is his concept of spirit (*Geist*, sometimes also translated as "mind") as the historical manifestation of the logical concept and the "sublation" (*Aufhebung*, integration without elimination or reduction) of seemingly contradictory or opposing factors: examples include the apparent opposition between necessity and freedom and between immanence and transcendence. Hegel has been seen in the twentieth century as the originator of the thesis, antithesis, synthesis triad, but as an explicit phrase it originated with Johann Gottlieb Fichte.

Along with Johann Gottlieb Fichte and, at least in his early work, Friedrich Wilhelm Joseph von Schelling, Hegel belongs to the period of German idealism in the decades following Kant. The most systematic of the post-Kantian idealists, Hegel attempted, throughout his published writings as well as in his lectures, to elaborate a comprehensive and systematic philosophy from a purportedly logical starting point. He is perhaps most well-known for his teleological account of history, an account that was later taken over by Marx and "inverted" into a materialist theory of an historical development culminating in Communism.

In the spirit of the Romantic movement in Germany, Hegel pursued the goal of unifying man and God by virtually identifying God as man, and thereby submerging the former into the latter. Johann Wolfgang von Goethe had recently popularized the Faust theme, centering on Faust's intense desire for divine, or absolute knowledge, as well as divine power. In orthodox Christianity, of course, the overweening pride of man in trying to achieve God-like knowledge and power is precisely the root cause of sin and man's fall (Genesis, chapter 3). But, on the contrary, Hegel, a most heretical Lutheran indeed, had the temerity to generalize the Faustian urge into a world-philosophy, and into an alleged insight into the inevitable workings of the historical process (Rothbard 1995).

In Professor Tucker's words, Hegelianism was a "philosophic religion of self in the form of a theory of history. The religion is founded on an identification of the self with God" (Tucker 1961, 39). It should not be necessary to add at this point that "the self here is not the individual, but the collective organic species 'self.'" In a youthful essay on "The Positivity of the Christian Religion," written at the age of twenty-five, Hegel revealingly objects to Christianity for "separating" man and God except "in one isolated individual" (Jesus), and placing God in another and higher world, to which man's activity could contribute nothing (Rothbard 1995). Four years later, in 1799, Hegel resolved this problem by offering his own religion, in his "The Spirit of Christianity" (Rothbard 1995). In diametrical contrast to orthodox Christianity, in which God became man in Jesus, for Hegel Jesus's achievement was, as a man, to become God! Tucker sums this up neatly. To Hegel, Jesus

> is not God become man, but man become God. This is the key idea on which the entire edifice of Hegelianism was to be constructed: there is no absolute difference between the human nature and the divine. They are not two separate things with an impassable gulf between them. The absolute self in man, the *homo noumenon*, is not mere godlike . . . it is God. Consequently, in so far as man strives to become "like God," [Genesis 3:5] he is simply striving to be his own real self. And in deifying himself, he is simply recognizing his own true nature. (Tucker 1961, 41.)

If man is really God, what then is history? Why does man, or rather, do men, change and develop? Because the man-God is not perfect, or at least he does not begin in a perfect state. Man-God begins his life in history totally unconscious of his divine status. History, then, for Hegel, is a process by which the man-God increases his knowledge, until he finally reaches the state of absolute knowledge, that is, the full knowledge and realization that he is God. In that case, man-God finally realizes his potential of an infinite being without bounds, possessed of absolute knowledge. (Rothbard 1995.)

Why then did man-God, also termed by Hegel the "world-self" (*Weltgeist*) or "world-spirit," create the universe? Not, as in the Christian account, from overflowing love and benevolence, but out of a felt need to become conscious of itself as a world-self. This process of growing consciousness is achieved through creative activity by which the world-self externalized itself. This externalization occurs first by creating nature or the original world, but second—and here of course is a significant addition to other theologies—there is a continuing self-externalization through human history. The most important is this second process, for by this means man, the collective organism, expands his building of civilization, his creative externalizing, and *hence* his increasing knowledge of his own divinity, and therefore of the world as his own self-actualization. This latter process: of knowing ever more fully that the world is really man's self, is the process which Hegel terms the gradual putting to an end of man's "self-alienation," which of course for him was also the alienation of man from God. To Hegel, in short, man perceives the world as hostile *because* it is not himself, because it is alien. All these conflicts are resolved when he realizes at long last that the world really *is* himself. This process of realization is Hegel's *Aufhebung,* by which the world becomes de-alienated and assimilated to man's self. (Rothbard 1995.)

But why, one might ask, is Hegel's man so odd, so neurotic, that he regards everything that is not himself as alien and hostile? The answer is crucial to the Hegelian mystique. It is because Hegel, or Hegel's man, cannot stand the idea of himself not being God, and therefore not being of infinite space and without limits. Seeing any other being, or any other object, exist, would mean that he himself is not infinite or divine. In short, Hegel's philosophy is severe and cosmic solipsistic megalomania on a grand and massive scale (Rothbard 1995). Professor Tucker develops the case with characteristic acuity:

> For Hegel alienation is finitude, and finitude in turn is bondage. The experience of self-estrangement in the presence of an apparent objective world is an experience of enslavement. . . . Spirit [or the world-self], when confronted with an object or "other," is *ipso facto* aware of itself as merely finite being, as embracing only so much and no more of reality, as extending only so far and no farther. The object is, therefore, a "limit" (*Grenze*). And a limit, since it contradicts spirit's notion of itself as absolute being, i.e., being-without-limit, is necessarily apprehended as a "barrier" or "fetter" (*Schranke*). It is a barrier to spirit's awareness of itself as that which it conceives itself truly to be—the whole of reality. In its confrontation with an apparent object, spirit feels imprisoned in limitation. It experiences what Hegel calls the "sorrow of finitude."
>
> The transcendence of the object through knowing is spirit's way of rebelling against finitude and making the

> break for freedom. In Hegel's quite unique conception of it, freedom means the consciousness of self as unbounded: it is the absence of a limiting object or non-self. . . . This consciousness of "being alone with self" . . . is precisely what Hegel means by the consciousness of freedom. . . . Accordingly, the growth of spirit's self-knowledge in history is alternatively describable as a progress of the consciousness of freedom. (Tucker 1961, 53ff.)

After Hegel's death, his followers were split between the "Old Hegelians" who uncritically accepted Hegel's Romantic views, and the "Young Hegelians" who wanted to continue the revolution of ideas using his concept of dialectics—initially, Marx and Engels were enjoined in this movement.

In the labor movement of early to mid-nineteenth-century Europe, the problem of the emerging proletariat also had its sympathetic analysts among German intellectuals. As early as 1800, Johann Gottlieb Fichte (1762–1814) in his *Geschlossene Handelsstaat* had described the anarchy of *laissez faire*, which deprived the worker of the full product of his labor and gave an undue share of the profits to the merchant class. In 1835, social theorist Ludwig Gall (1791–1863), sometimes called the first German Socialist, issued a pamphlet in Trier (Rhineland Prussia) titled *Mein Wollen und mein Wirken* (*My Will and My Work*) which foreshadowed the class struggle and maintained that labor was the sole source of wealth. Georg Büchner (1813–1837), a dramatist of merit and medical student who died in exile, founded the "Society for Human Rights" in 1834 in Giessen (Grand Duchy of Hesse and by Rhine), and typesetter, revolutionary Stephan Born (1824–1898) published his first plea for the working classes when he was only twenty. The ideas of the German Idealists and the rapidly evolving social developments in the wake of the 1789 French Revolution influenced a generation of:

Romantic writers, such as:

- Johann Wolfgang von Goethe (1749–1832) – German
- William Blake (1757–1827) – English
- Samuel Coleridge (1772–1834) – English
- William Wordsworth (1770–1850) – English
- Lord Byron (1788–1824) – Anglo-Scottish

- John Keats (1795–1821) – English
- Percy Bysshe Shelley (1792–1822) – English
- Victor Marie Hugo (1802–1885) – French

Artists, such as:

- John Constable (1776–1837) – English
- Joseph Mallord William Turner (1775–1851) – English
- Jean-Louis André Théodore Géricault (1791–1824) – French
- Ferdinand Victor Eugène Delacroix (1798–1863) – French

And composers, such as:

- Ludwig van Beethoven (1770–1827) – Belgian-German
- Franz Schubert (1797–1828) – Austrian
- Hector Berlioz (1803–1869) – French
- Frédéric François Chopin (1810–1849) – Polish
- Robert Alexander Schumann (1810–1856) – German
- Franz Liszt (1811–1886) – Hungarian
- Pyotr Ilyich Tchaikovsky (1840–1893) – Russian

The literary features of Romanticism involved certain philosophical writings and lifestyles along with occultism and occult practice. Their main themes included:

- An embrace of paganism that more closely reflected pantheism, especially in artistic and imaginative ways. This is sometimes called a *mythopoeic* approach (related to the making of myths).
- A marriage to certain philosophical movements, especially the thinking of Hegel, an extremely influential nineteenth-century German philosopher-theologian. Like many philosophers at the time, Hegel was trying to build a philosophy and religion that was mystical and spiritual but that denied the biblical God and Christianity. At times Hegel's ideas took on an outward Christian appearance. For example, Hegel often used the word "spirit," but he was actually referring to the soul of the universe not the Holy Spirit of the Judeo-Christian God. In essence, Hegel believed that the universe *was* God (monism). His thinking became foundational to Marxism, Nazism, and Liberalism. Hegel's followers were even more complex because some held select Christian doctrines while

also subscribing to Hegelian ideas and embracing pagan mythology. In the Romantic movement, mythology became equal or superior to or even absolutely replacing the traditional written Word of God. Out of this strange blend of classic Christian theology and Romantic philosophy sprang Prussian Friedrich Schleiermacher (1768–1834), who elevated experience to the highest realm of revelation and became known as the "father of modern liberal theology." In his first major work, *On Religion: Speeches to Its Cultured Despisers* (1799), he defended religion against its Enlightenment critics. Religion, he argued, was not a philosophy, nor abstract metaphysical thought, nor natural science, nor adherence to dogmatic formulae, but the "sense and taste for the infinite" consisting primarily in feeling; belief and action are secondary.

- A powerful unifying theme in Romantic literature is the elevation of imagination to equality with the written Word of God, and even to the worship of imagination. Such a view holds that humans create like God, or that God creates anew through human imagination.

In addition to further developments in Enlightenment movements such as German Idealism (1750–1820), Kantianism, and Romanticism, the Modern period (1500–1815) saw the rise of: Continental Philosophy; Hegelianism; Transcendentalism; Existentialism; Marxism; Modernism; Positivism; Utilitarianism; Pragmatism; Analytic Philosophy; Logical Positivism; Ordinary Language Philosophy; Logicism; Phenomenology; Theosophy; Anthroposophy; Ariosophy; Fascism; and the more contemporary Structuralism; Post-Structuralism; Post-Modernism; and Deconstructionism, among others. All of these movements created a cauldron of boiling stew in Europe that moved individuals and peoples to question all established theological, political, and social presuppositions and dogmas and reject and rise against the *status quo* power structures, traditions, and mores that had existed throughout Europe for nearly a millennium.

Neo-Kantianism was the dominant philosophical movement in Germany from roughly 1870 until the First World War. This movement drew inspiration from a diverse cast of philosophers—principally, Kuno Fischer (1824–1907), Hermann von Helmholtz (1821–1894), Friedrich Albert Lange (1828–1875), Otto Liebmann (1840–1912), and Eduard Gottlob Zeller (1814–1908)—who in the middle of the nineteenth century were calling for a return to Kant's philosophy as an alternative to both speculative metaphysics and materialism (Heis 2018). During the 1870s, the movement formed into two schools, one based around Hermann Cohen at Marburg University, and another based in southwest Germany (in the province of Baden) around Wilhelm Windelband.

"Classical" neo-Kantians were not only intellectually influential, but they were also great successes academically in Germany. They held prominent academic chairs, and were successful in placing their students, shaping curricula, and editing important journals and books. Most of the German philosophers who came to prominence in Germany after the First World War were educated by neo-Kantians—an impressive and comprehensive list of students that includes Rudolf Carnap, Hans-Georg Gadamer, Martin Heidegger, and Hans Reichenbach (Heis 2018). Neo-Kantianism is the common root out of which both the so-called "analytic" and "continental" traditions grew (Heis 2018). But the reputation of Neo-Kantianism shifted dramatically in the decades after 1918 (Heis 2018). Neo-Kantians were associated with the old order, and so became the primary targets of the many philosophers (including their own students) wanting to make a completely fresh start (Heis 2018). The subsequent geopolitical upheavals, not the least of which was Hitler's rise to power in 1933, nearly erased the institutional memory of Neo-Kantianism within the emerging analytic and continental traditions (Heis 2018).

CHAPTER 4

THEOLOGY, ROMANTICISM, AND THE *KULTURKAMPF*

Since religion is the heart of culture then religion is the key to history . . . we cannot understand the inner form of a society unless we understand its religion.

— CHRISTOPHER DAWSON

It is the religious impulse which supplies the cohesive force which unifies a society and a culture. . . . A society which has lost its religion becomes sooner or later a society which has lost its culture.

— CHRISTOPHER DAWSON

In Dawson's picture, religion is not an obstacle that has to be pushed out of the way before the rise of culture can begin; it is the inspiration and the driving force to which the rise of culture has been due. (Toynbee 1950, 4)

— ARNOLD TOYNBEE, on Christopher Dawson's thesis

The history of Greece and Rome is a witness and an example of the intimate relation which always exists between men's ideas and their social state. Examine the institutions of the ancients without thinking of their religious notions, and you find them obscure, whimsical, and inexplicable. (Coulanges 1877, 11)

— COULANGES

All modern systems of order based on a totalitarian ideology contain a pseudo-religious claim.

— JOACHIM C. FEST, *The Face of the Third Reich*

> *Democracy bases its appeal on the sacredness of the People—the consecration of Folk; Socialism on the sacredness of Labor—the consecration of Work; and Nationalism on the sacredness of the Fatherland—the consecration of Place. These concepts still arouse transcendent religious values or sanctions. It is religious emotion divorced from religious belief.*
>
> — CHRISTOPHER DAWSON, *Dynamics of World History*

> *Now the serpent was more crafty than any of the wild animals the Lord God had made. He said to the woman, "Did God really say . . . ?"*
>
> — Genesis 3:1, *New International Version*

HISTORIANS OF CHRISTIANITY LIKE OWEN CHADWICK AND CHRISTOPHER Dawson have viewed the "secularization of the European mind in the nineteenth century" as the primary prism, through which the interpretation and understanding of religion under the conditions of modernity are to be viewed. They firmly believed that the animating force of traditional Christianity on the cultural imagination of the West increasingly dwindled during this period, making modern religious history marginal, if not entirely irrelevant, to other domains of public life and thought. Since apostolic times, Christianity has faced continuous challenges of revisionism and heterodox interpretations. The Dark Ages set the stage for the Liberalism and skepticism of long-established dogmas that blossomed during the Renaissance and Enlightenment. Although the Reformation was a sister to the Renaissance, Martin Luther was actually an opponent of the Liberalism and humanistic rationalism of the time. Most historians fail to distinguish Luther's Reformation from the *Reformed* Protestant Reformation that began during Luther's lifetime and spiraled out of control after Luther's death, ushering in the prevailing militant Liberalism and humanism of the Renaissance. Dawson viewed this liberal evolution in Christian thought and official doctrine as the motivating factor behind Martin Luther's

Reformation to return the Church to its orthodox roots.* However, during no other period of time has the Christian Church experienced a more radical transformation and diversification than under the influence of the forces of modernity during the eighteenth and nineteenth centuries—particularly, the nineteenth century. There is no doubt that the rise of historical criticism, with its applications to Scripture and Christian dogmatics, shattered many assumptions that seemed fundamental for Christianity. Various causes contributed to the intellectual developments that influenced the transformation and diversification of Christianity in the eighteenth and nineteenth centuries. Kantian dialectic and its Romantic and Idealist offshoots undoubtedly exerted a strong influence on the changing views of the transcendence and immanence, selfhood and relationality, and the

---

* Christopher Dawson overstates or incorrectly asserts the influence that Liberalism had on Martin Luther. Martin Luther was one of the few ardent enemies of Liberalism in his time. He, himself, affirmed over and over at great risk to his life how Rome's heterodox teachings on indulgences, the power and primacy of the pope, purgatory, tradition over Scripture, the necessity of works in salvation, and many other false teachings had strayed from orthodox doctrine and stemmed from liberal (humanistic) influences that infected church dogma over the centuries. In his many debates and writings, Luther denigrated scholastic theology whose critically rationalistic approach to Scripture and exaltation of human reason almost to divine status as the final arbiter of truth. This places Luther in direct conflict with the prophets of the Renaissance and Enlightenment, for which Dawson indicts Luther. Dawson fails to properly decipher the Reformation, its true impetus, objective, and place in history. The Liberalism that bore the Enlightenment and the 25-years of revolution, wars, and anti-Catholicism in 19th-century Europe blossomed in the Renaissance. Moreover, Dawson fails to recognize how the Reformation after Martin Luther was hijacked by theological liberals who insisted on taking the movement further than Luther ever envisioned necessary and ended up reinfecting Christian doctrine with the same kind of rationalistic, works-based heterodox teachings that prompted Luther's Reformation in the beginning. Out of blind loyalty to Rome, Dawson inappropriately places the blame for these latter destructive liberal developments of the Reformation on Luther's shoulders. Did Luther awaken and empower the revolutionary and Nationalistic animal in European culture? Certainly, that was not his objective. Luther never intended to divide Christendom or the Catholic Church or to encourage general rebellion against established authority. It was Rome's intransigence to Luther's Scripturally based reforms, which threatened the power of the Roman Church, that caused its own division and set the stage for a reactionary liberal movement (the Enlightenment) that was never intended by Luther.

relationship between faith and reason. Broader social and cultural trends also played an influential role in these paradigm shifts.

By definition, theological Liberalism is a form of religious thought that establishes religious inquiry on the basis of a norm other than the authority of Scripture and tends to emphasize ethics over doctrine and experience over Scriptural authority ("Theological liberalism," 2018). Theological Liberalism disavows the long-standing dogma that Scripture is *norma normans* and demotes Scripture to *norma normata*. Liberal Christian scholars embrace and advocate the higher biblical criticism of modern biblical scholarship that employs the historical-critical rather than the traditional historical-grammatical method of biblical interpretation. Theological Liberalism takes a page from Satan's personal playbook; *sow doubt in what God says* (Genesis 3:1).

To understand the root of how Liberalism caused a paradigm shift in theology one must be absolutely clear on how biblical exegesis and hermeneutics changed in the seventeenth century. To understand this change one must know how the historical-critical method differed from the historical-grammatical method of Scriptural interpretation. The historical-critical method is a specific hermeneutical interpretive method used to examine an ancient text's historical origins, such as the time, the place in which the text was written, its sources, and the events, dates, persons, places, things, and customs that are mentioned or implied in the text, and thereby make conclusions on the "probability" of the text's veracity. Historical critics compare texts to other texts written around the same time. Pioneers of historical criticism include the Dutch scholars Desiderius Erasmus and Benedict (Baruch) de Spinoza. Historical criticism took hold in the seventeenth century and gained popular recognition in the nineteenth and twentieth centuries. The perspective of the early historical critic was rooted in post-Luther Protestant Reformation ideology since its approach to biblical studies was free from the influence of traditional interpretation (theological Liberalism). Where historical investigation was unavailable, historical criticism rested on humanistic philosophical and theological interpretation. The phrase "higher criticism" became popular in Europe from the mid-eighteenth century to the early twentieth century to describe the work of German biblical scholars of the Tübingen School. After the revolutionary work on the New Testament by Friedrich Schleiermacher, the next generation, which included scholars such as David Friedrich Strauss and Ludwig von Feuerbach, analyzed in the mid-nineteenth century the historical records of the Middle East from biblical times, in search of independent confirmation of events in the Bible. The latter scholars built on the tradition of Enlightenment and Rationalist thinkers such as John Locke, David Hume, Immanuel Kant, Gotthold Lessing, Gottlieb Fichte, G. W. F. Hegel, and the French rationalists. With each passing century, historical criticism became refined into various methodologies used today: source criticism, form criticism, redaction criticism, tradition criticism, canonical criticism, and related methodologies (Soulen 2001, 79).

A study of Biblical interpretation down through the centuries reveals that various methods have been employed. One of the oldest is some form of *allegorizing*. This dates back to the Jewish interpretation of the Old Testament in the Targums and the Talmud and was employed in the early Christian church by such men as Clement of Alexandria and Origen. Even Jerome and Augustine used this method extensively. The latter distinguished a four-fold sense of Scripture, the *literal/historical*, the *tropological/moral*, the *anagogical*, and the *allegorical*. This four-fold sense was the common approach to interpretation in the Middle Ages. The literal sense was the evident meaning of the words themselves. The tropological moral sense was regarded as the advice these words give us concerning our conduct—what to do. The allegorical sense told men what to believe, and the anagogical sense told them what to hope for (Vogel 1974).

The early Reformation rejected this four-fold sense and concentrated on the *unus simplex sensus* again. Martin Luther, himself, was still taught the four-fold sense, but soon rejected it in favor of the one simple sense of Scripture. When Scripture seemed to conflict with human reason, Luther was willing to submit reason to God's truth. French theologian Jehan Cauvin (John Calvin), on the other hand, felt that all Scripture had to be "reasonable" because of its absolute clarity. This was just one more of a long line of movements to inject human reasoning and logic into the meaning of the Scriptures. The doctrinal controversies that followed the solidification of Roman Catholic dogma in the Decrees of the Council of Trent led to intensive study of Scripture in the Lutheran church and resulted in the Formula of Concord (1577), in which the doctrines in controversy at the time are thoroughly stated thetically and antithetically. (Vogel 1974.)

Soon, there were reactions to this tendency to make thorough exegesis the basis for the formulation of doctrine. The Lutheran church experienced a period of pietism which tended to disregard dogmatics and to substitute subjective psychological interpretation which aimed primarily at edification. (Vogel 1974.)

This was followed by the age of rationalism and higher criticism which attempt to verify everything in Scripture by modern methods of historical research. Since divine revelation and divine intervention (miracles) are not verifiable in this way, the only religious truth in the Bible is that which agrees with man's understanding. Reason and logic are used to distinguish between fact in the Bible and what is regarded as the interpretation of the first century believers. This process denies verbal inspiration and the infallibility of the Scriptures; more importantly, it denies the dual nature of Christ and his divine works on earth. The human side of the Bible and humanistic Progressive revelation are stressed. Literary criticism is said to supply the method of identifying sources behind the Bible. The main purpose of religious truth is said to be to maintain Christian morality. Supernatural elements such as miracles are denied or disparaged and are usually explained as historical influences on the writers of ancient beliefs in gods who control or influence events among men. (Vogel 1974.)

The historical-grammatical method, on the other hand, is a Christian hermeneutical method that strives to discover the biblical writers' original intended meaning in the text. This method *primus et præcipuus* holds Scripture as *norma normans* and *sola fide* divinely inspired and *emendatæ necesse est*. The process for determining the original meaning of the text is through examination of the grammatical and syntactical aspects, the historical background, the literary genre as well as theological (canonical) considerations. The historical-grammatical method distinguishes between the one original meaning of the text and its significance. The significance of the text is essentially the application or contextualization of the principles from text (Johnson 1990). The historical-grammatical method is the primary method of interpretation for many conservative Protestant exegetes who reject the historical-critical method to various degrees (from complete rejection by some orthodox Lutherans and fundamentalist Protestants to moderated acceptance of it in the Roman Catholic tradition since Pope Pius XII), in contrast to liberal Christianity's overwhelming reliance on historical-critical interpretation, often to the exclusion of all other hermeneutics.

Those who adopted the historical-critical method are convinced that they have found the key to the mysteries of God and thereby made spiritual progress. They are convinced that by this adoption they have done God and the Church a service and made it easier for the Church to defend its position against its enemies.

> It is difficult to overestimate the significance the nineteenth century has for biblical interpretation. The result was a revolution of viewpoint in evaluating the Bible. The Scriptures were, so to speak, secularized. The biblical books became historical documents to be studied and questioned like any other ancient sources. The Bible was no longer the criterion for the writing of history; rather history had become the criterion for understanding the Bible. . . . The history it reported was no longer assumed to be everywhere correct. The Bible stood before criticism as defendant before judge. (Krentz 1975, 30.)

The proponents of the historical-critical method admit that theirs is a method of doubt. Historical criticism is to decide what is more or less probable. Swedish Biblical scholar and professor of theology Birger Gerhardsson (1926–2013) says that "the task of critical scholarship is only to estimate probability on the basis of the evidence of the source materials" (Gerhardsson 1969, 34). Dutch-born Reformed theologian and biblical scholar Martin Woudstra (1922–1991) says that "the historical method by its own admission cannot accept at face value the Biblical contentions concerning past events as being true and subject to no contradiction or doubt" (Woudstra 1970, 70).

The result of this historical-critical method has been hopeless confusion among the scholars. What one scholar holds to be very probable another considers to be very unlikely. The great diversity of their conclusions drawn from the same evidence demonstrates how unreliable the method is. It is a common view among liberal theologians today that the only thing we can be certain about is that nothing is certain—again, *Did God really say . . . ?* (Genesis chapter 3, verse 1 [*NIV*]).

Theological Liberalism has been an important influence in Protestantism from about the mid-seventeenth century and continues to be so. One of the central tenets of theological Liberalism is that man has a free will in matters of his justification (salvation). This was the central controversy that led to the infamous debates between the Roman Catholic humanist theologian Desiderius Erasmus of Rotterdam and the German Augustinian monk Martin Luther early in the Reformation. These debates on the doctrine of the will of man produced Martin Luther's *magnum opus* in December 1525, *De Servo Arbitrio* (*On the Bondage of the Will*) as a rebuttal to Erasmus's 1524 first public attack on Luther in his diatribe *De libero* *arbitrio diatribe sive collatio* (*On the Freedom of the Will Discourse or Confrontation*). This single issue on the doctrine of the will of man goes to the very heart of what separates all heterodox and orthodox Christian faiths—in truth, it separates all religions (Christian and non-Christian) over the course of human history.*

The defining trait of this Liberalism is a will to be liberated from the coercion of external controls and a consequent concern with inner motivation. Although some earlier indications of the liberal temper of mind existed, it became overtly evident during the Renaissance (1300–1600), when curiosity about natural man and appreciation for the human spirit developed, and during the Reformation. The Renaissance had a profound effect on contemporary theology, particularly in the way people perceived the relationship between man and God. Many of the period's foremost theologians were followers of the humanist method, including John Wycliffe (1330–1384), Jan Hus (1369–1415), Desiderius Erasmus (1466–1536), Huldrych Zwingli (1484–1531), Thomas More (1478–1535), and Jehan Cauvin or John Calvin (1509–1564).

The modern historical period of theological Liberalism began, however, with the seventeenth-century French philosopher and mathematician René Descartes (1596–1650). This first phase, called Rationalism or the Enlightenment (Age of Reason), lasted until about the mid-eighteenth century. In designating the thinking self as the primary substance from which the existence of other realities was to be deduced (except that of God), Descartes initiated a mode of thinking that remained in force through the nineteenth century and laid the ground for the presuppositions of this modern consciousness: (1) confidence in human reason, (2) primacy of the person, (3) immanence of God, and (4) meliorism (the belief that human nature is improvable and is improving). The many persons influencing religious thought in this period included the philosophers (Baruch) Benedict de Spinoza (Jewish-Dutch, 1632–1677), Gottfried Wilhelm Leibniz (1646–1716) and Gotthold Ephraim Lessing

---

* All religions that have existed over human history can be systematically divided into two categories: 1) the religion of the "do" that professes humans have the power and are required to do something (a deed, work, or act) towards their reconciliation (salvation) with God; and 2) religion of the "done" that professes humans are entirely incapable of doing anything towards their reconciliation (salvation) with God and that God does it all for the believer through a vicarious atonement. This system of categorization is predicated on the doctrine of the will of man (see Luther's *On the Bondage of the Will*).

(1729–1781) (both German), John Locke (1632–1704) and Samuel Clarke (1675–1729) (both English), and the English writers and philosophers known as the Cambridge Platonists and the Deists, who hoped to reconcile Christian ethics with Renaissance humanism, religion with the new science, and faith with rationality.

The writings of the liberal Lutheran chaplain at the Charité hospital and *Invalidenkorps* in Berlin, Johann Heinrich Friedrich Ulrich (1751–1798), best exemplify the theological thinking of this time. Ulrich noted in the chapter on the Lutheran Church in the eighteenth century of his lengthy 1782 work, *Geschichte der Christlichen Kirche für christliche Leser aus allen Ständen. Zweiter Band. Von der Reformation bis auf unsre Zeiten* (*A History of the Christian Church for Christian Readers from all Social Standings. Volume 2: From the Reformation to Our Times*) how, "biblical criticism has advanced tremendously in this century" and that as a result there had transpired "very great changes in the study of sacred philology and exegesis," "a significant change in the dogmatic theology of the Lutheran church," "manifold changes in the articles of our doctrine," "an indisputable change of a very excellent kind in Christian moral theology," and "distinct, excellent changes in the public preaching at worship services" (Ulrich 1782, 671–5, 681–6). Ulrich claimed that out of these developments there had emerged a new principle that was used by proponents of religious Enlightenment for evaluating whether various doctrines were essential articles of faith: did they or did they not promote moral behavior? Those doctrines that clearly did were retained in the churches, whereas those that did not were dismissed as "mere speculations, the vestigial remains of scholastic sophistry, and the words of men" (Ulrich 1782, 677). In order to illustrate more fully how Protestant theology was changing, Ulrich identified fourteen major late Reformation-era doctrines that enlightened theologians regarded as having failed this test, and which they now labelled as "incomprehensible and useless, not to be taught to children, nor mentioned in public worship services" (Ulrich 1782, 677–9).

Ulrich maintained that enlightened reformers of Protestantism believed that God had inspired "the authors of the Holy Scriptures," but not every word of the Bible (Ulrich 1782, 677). As a result, the Bible consisted of an admixture of inspired and uninspired materials, whose parsing required the expertise of highly educated exegetes. The work of disentangling the authoritative elements of biblical texts from the unauthoritative ones formed the basis for reconsidering theological dogmas.

Concerning the doctrine of God, Ulrich reported how "those who wish to promote an improvement in religion" taught that it was "improper and unbiblical to speak of there being one God in three persons" (Ulrich 1782, 676–8). Rather, God the Father alone was almighty God. While "Jesus was the greatest of God's messengers," neither the Son, nor the Holy Spirit, were equal to the Father in the degree of their divinity, especially as "the personhood of the Holy Spirit is not taught anywhere in Bible" (Ulrich 1782, 678). Ulrich noted additional departures from historical orthodoxy in how enlightened theologians discussed soteriology. "They claim that the former doctrines of original sin and of mankind's innate inability to do good are both unbiblical and harmful and instead teach that man must first act to improve himself and become good before he can receive the grace and pleasure of God" (Ulrich 1782, 679). Regarding the atonement, "They claim that it is false and unbiblical to believe that Christ died on our behalf to make satisfaction for our sins before God. . . . God is not so cruel as to want to be reconciled to us through the blood of Christ, but rather he forgives our sins when we sincerely commit to living more faithfully. . . . [another page taken from Satan's playbook—enticing people into a performance trap of works-righteousness, by which they can never know for certain if they have satisfied God enough]. The doctrine of the eternal punishment of sinners in hell contradicts both the love of God and reason" (Ulrich 1782, 679). Ulrich observed how enlightened theologians believed that "the sacraments are not actually means of conveying grace to us but are merely external ceremonies that have neither divine power nor effect" (Ulrich 1782, 679). Ulrich's and University of Göttingen professor of ecclesiastical history Ludwig Timotheus Freiherr von Spittler's contentions regarding the changes in Protestant theology comports with those of a number of contemporary eighteenth-century ecclesiastical historians (Kloes 2015, 76–8). Von Spittler noted: "All in all, we have realized extraordinary gains through the revolution of the last thirty years [c. 1760–1790] and in the future this period will surely be distinguished as one of the brightest eras in the history of the Lutheran church" (Spittler 1788, 486–7).

The second phase of theological Liberalism, Romanticism, lasted from the late eighteenth to the middle of the nineteenth century. Marked by the discovery of the uniqueness of the individual and the consequent significance of individual experience as a distinctive source of infinite meaning, this premium upon personality and upon individual creativity exceeded every other value. The American and French revolutions provided the symbol of this spirit of independence and dramatically exemplified it in political action.

Jean-Jacques Rousseau (1712–1778) and Immanuel Kant (1724–1804) were the architects of Romantic Liberalism. In theology, the German Friedrich Schleiermacher (1768–1834), called the "father of modern liberal theology," was enormously influential. Unlike Kant, who saw in moral will the clue to man's higher nature, Schleiermacher seized upon the feeling of absolute dependence as being simultaneously that which "signifies God for us" and that which is distinctive in the religious response. Thus, self-consciousness in this deep religious sense becomes God-consciousness. According to Schleiermacher, the Christian is brought to this deeper vein of self-consciousness through the man Jesus, in whom the God-consciousness had been perfected. The nurture of God-consciousness in relation to Jesus Christ, Schleiermacher believed, led to the creation of the church as a fellowship of believers.

The German Albrecht Ritschl (1822–1889) dominated liberal Protestant theology after Schleiermacher, and two other German theologians, Wilhelm Herrmann (1846–1922) and Adolf von Harnack (1851–1930), were Ritschl's most prominent followers. In the United States, Horace Bushnell (1802–1876) was the most significant liberal theologian. Another important liberal was Walter Rauschenbusch (1861–1918), leader of the Social Gospel movement.

Religion was a topic of considerable dispute in the Romantic period, with several perspectives vying for ascendancy and credibility. The Church of England held the status of establishment church, and as such Protestantism enjoyed the privileges of this position; for instance, members of parliament were required to be Anglican. The nature of this religious influence was fundamentally connected with the political context. The 1789 French Revolution advocated rebellion against all forms of social authority, with British propaganda labelling this attitude paradoxically as Catholic as well as atheist, attempting to discredit the ideological perspective and maintain the institutions of the monarchy and church (Morris 1998, 101–16). In some ways, however, there was a growing tolerance of other religions—for instance, the Doctrine of the Trinity Act 1813, which legalized non-trinitarianism (Medley 1925, 653). The limitations of this relative tolerance, however, were tested by the increasing prominence of divergent religious beliefs. Pantheism, for instance, flourished particularly in the Romantic period and arguably became one of its defining characteristics (Reardon 1985, 5). Atheism was also increasingly defended, adhering to the empirical principles of the Age of Enlightenment (Israel 2010, vii–viii). This religious diversity is reflected in the literature produced by the period; Wordsworth's *Ode: Intimations of Immortality* and Shelley's *The Necessity of Atheism*, for example, both portray a representation of their authors' religious identities, exemplifying the complexity of reactions to the religious *status quo* of the Romantic period in a variety of ways.

In *Necessity*, Shelley argues that there is no empirical evidence for the existence of God, finding "no proofs" in "the three sources of conviction" (Shelley 1813). His subsequent line of argument indicates the influence of the Enlightenment philosophers on his perspective. As Ellen Wilson explains, they, like Shelley, "promoted science and intellectual interchange and opposed superstition" (Wilson 2004, 577); this approach was particularly hostile to organized religion, with Hume, for instance, advancing "a systematic, skeptical critique of the philosophical foundations of various theological systems" (Russell 2005). Shelley develops and refines these anti-theist principles in *Necessity*; however, that is not to say that the text actively promotes atheism, instead merely pursuing the hypothetical limits of theological rationality, as indicated by his conclusion that there is "no proof of the existence of a Deity" rather than denying the existence of God outright. Despite its title, *Necessity* does not even indicate that Shelley himself is an atheist. He begins with the caveat that "the hypothesis of a pervading Spirit co-eternal with the universe remains unshaken," which he only later recognizes as pantheism. This recognition implies that Shelley's complaints in *Necessity* are reactionary and directed at organized religion and its political ties rather than the concept of theism itself. This is supported by a consideration of his other works; S. F. Gingerich describes *Queen Mab* as "an outspoken and unblushing attack upon Christianity" (Gingerich 1918, 446), while *England in 1819* refers to "Religion Christless, Godless" (Shelley 2006, 1180–1). Shelley's argument in *Necessity*, then, is that theoretically speaking the existence of God (in the sense that Christianity conceives it) cannot be proven, thereby directly opposing the dominant religious system.

The third phase of theological Liberalism, Modernism, from the mid-nineteenth century through the 1920s, was marked by the discovery of the significance of historical time and an emphasis upon the notion of progress. The decisive events stimulating these interests were the Industrial Revolution and the publication of Charles Darwin's *Origin of Species* (1859). A determined course emerged among Modernists to bring religious thought into accord with modern knowledge and to solve issues raised by modern culture. The study of Christian doctrine was transformed into the psychological study of religious experience and into the sociological study of religious institutions and customs and the philosophical inquiry into religious knowledge and values. Among important figures during this period were Thomas Huxley (1825–1895) and Herbert Spencer (1820–1903) in England, William James (1842–1910), John Dewey (1859–1952), Shailer Mathews (1863–1941), and Harry Emerson Fosdick (1878–1969) in the United States, and Ernst Troeltsch (1865–1923) in Germany.

After the 1920s, many theologically liberal ideas were challenged by Neo-orthodoxy, a theological movement in Europe and the United States that used the traditional language of Protestant orthodoxy and advocated a return to biblical faith centered in Christ, although it accepted modern historical-critical methods of biblical interpretation.

Nationalism has sometimes been singled out as the one most influential novel form of political religion gaining ground in the nineteenth century, specifically in response to the decline of the early modern model of an absolutist monarchy with an established Church. Even more obviously, the Socialist movement appeared as an anti-religious force to its conservative and *bourgeois* opponents at the time and to many critics to this day. And while the proponents of Capitalism did not usually challenge openly the ideological authority of the Church, the social discipline and the economization of all areas of human life (*homo economicus*) that came with its establishment interrupted traditional patterns of life, shattered long-held values, and in this way, it appears, undercut much of the basis on which traditional religion had rested. Socialism, however, has not always been propagated on the basis of an atheistic platform; in fact, even its Marxist version has its own theological dimension. It was the early Socialist movement that drew much of its inspiration from a radical reading of Christian sources.

Nationalism, finally, was frequently presented and perceived as merely a novel interpretation of Christianity and its story cannot be divested of its complex marriage of convenience with organized religion. Closely connected with Western colonial missionary activity was the increasing fascination with the world of non-Christian religions. Empirical knowledge of non-Western religious traditions grew exponentially throughout the nineteenth century—especially at the height of colonialism ("New Imperialism")—and fundamentally transformed the Western understanding of the world of religions. The impact of this development on Christian thought can hardly be exaggerated; embedding theology within the history of religions seemed inevitable to many. Consequently, understanding of Christianity—and arguing for its validity—was increasingly dependent on tackling the obvious challenge that it was one of many religions. At the same time, growing interest in non-Christian religions was inevitably inspired also by "higher criticism" resulting in an increasing sense of detachment from the Christian heritage, and some of the most dramatic advances in the field came from scholars detached from or at least dissatisfied with traditional Christianity. Throughout the nineteenth century, competing reflections on non-Christian religions were produced by theological and non-theological scholars, until the turn of the twentieth century saw the eventual establishment of the study of comparative religions as a secular discipline.

One particular aspect linking Western intellectual developments of the nineteenth century with a country's global activities was the emergent concept of race. Its fascinating and troubling story combines various obsessions of the century: the rising allure of scientific and pseudo-scientific patterns of explanation; the search for new categories of social and cultural differentiation in the fact of the collapse of traditional hierarchies; and the reality of early globalization driven by colonial expansion. The case of slavery and abolitionism in the United States is instructive. The fateful legacy of the "peculiar institution" and its social economic ramifications came to a head in the American Civil War, but the history of the transatlantic slave trade continued to reverberate in the segregationist "Jim Crow" laws that sought to preserve the racial hierarchies of a colonialist past. Abolitionists and their successors in northeast United States—Congregationalists and Unitarians, especially—worked to help ameliorate some of the worst consequences of this heritage but, yet again, the role of Christian thought is ambivalent. On the one hand, racial patterns of thought gain plausibility as a result of the decline of traditional theological notions of humanity. On the other hand, their attractiveness also benefited from attempts to synthesize racial and Christian ideas. In the most notorious case of anti-Semitism (the Dreyfuss affair, 1894–1906), these two aspects are particularly distinct: while it is apparent that racial anti-Semitism rose to prominence at a time of declining religious sensitivities, seeking to supplant and replace the older anti-Judaism, it is equally clear that it could never have taken hold of the Western imagination the way it did without the enduring power of anti-Scriptural Christian anti-Jewish sentiments. It is therefore hardly coincidence that some of anti-Semitism's most vocal proponents came from heretical, liberal Christian and even clerical backgrounds, though others combined their adherence to racist ideology with a strenuously anti-religious, secular creed.

The tendency of nineteenth-century artists to understand their product as autonomous on the basis of aesthetic principles alone may have rattled traditional ideas about the subordination of art to religion. But it also opened new opportunities for a genuine encounter between Christian thought and the world of art. The history of art in the nineteenth century may be to some extent a story of conflicts with established religious authorities and with traditional religious thoughts and sentiments, but this period equally represents one of the most creative, powerful, and mutually enriching encounters between the arts and Christianity.

Slovak-American Lutheran theologian and historian Jaroslav Pelikan once noted that what is distinctive about the modern period in the history of Christianity is that, for the first time, "doctrines that had been assumed more than debated for most of Christian history were themselves called into question: the idea of [divine] revelation, the uniqueness [divinity] of Christ, the authority of Scripture, the expectation of life after death, even the very transcendence of God." Our brief study here on the intimate interrelationships between Christian thought, philosophy, psychology, political theory, the arts, literature, science—the humanities in general—and the tragedies of the twentieth century reveals how Christians grappled with these issues and set the agenda that incorporated and influenced the paradigm shifts and emerging ideologies of the times.

Ludwig Andreas von Feuerbach (1804–1872) was a German philosopher and anthropologist best known for his book *The Essence of Christianity* (1841), which provided a critique of Christianity that strongly influenced generations of thinkers, including Karl Marx, Friedrich Engels, Richard Wagner, and Friedrich Nietzsche. As an associate of the Young Hegelians,* von Feuerbach advocated Liberalism, atheism, and materialism.

* The Young Hegelians (*Junghegelianer*), or Left Hegelians (*Linkshegelianer*), or the Hegelian Left (*die Hegelsche Linke*), were a group of German intellectuals who, in the decade or so after the death of Georg Wilhelm Friedrich Hegel in 1831, reacted to and wrote about his ambiguous legacy. The Young Hegelians drew on his idea that the purpose and promise of history was the total negation of everything conducive to restricting freedom and reason; and they proceeded to mount radical critiques, first of religion and then of the Prussian political system. They rejected anti-Utopian aspects of his thought that "Old Hegelians" have interpreted to mean that the world has already essentially reached perfection. It was the outcry caused by David Friedrich Strauss's *The Life of Jesus* in 1835, which first made the Young

Many of his philosophical writings offered a critical analysis of religion. His thought was influential in the development of historical materialism,* where

---

Hegelians aware of their existence as a distinct group, and it was their attitude to religion that distinguished the Left and Right from then onwards. Despite the lack of political freedom of speech in Prussia at the time, King Wilhelm III, under the influence of his minister of religion, health and education Karl vom Stein zum Altenstein, allowed pretty much anything to be said about religion so long as there was practical obedience to his enforced merging of Calvinism and Lutheranism and spreading of Protestantism in Catholic ghetto strongholds. Thus, the Young Hegelians at first found it easier to direct their critical energies towards religion than politics. The Young Hegelians interpreted the entire state apparatus as ultimately claiming legitimacy based upon religious tenets. While this thought was clearly inspired by the function of Lutheranism in contemporary Prussia, the Young Hegelians held the theory to be applicable to any state backed by any religion. All laws were ultimately based on religious tenets. As such, their plan to undermine what they felt was the corrupt and despotic state apparatus was to attack the philosophical basis of religion. The Young Hegelians secularized Hegel's idea of *Geist* (spirit), removing the religious link. The resulting philosophy ultimately replaces spirit as the subject of history with that of man.

* Historical materialism – the scientific methodological approach of Marx's *materialist conception of history* that focuses on human societies and their development over time, arguing that they follow a number of observable tendencies. It is centered around the idea that forms of society rise and fall as they further and then impede the development of human productive power. Marx saw the historical process as proceeding through a necessary series of modes of production, characterized by class struggle, culminating in Communism. It is principally a theory of history according to which the material conditions of a society's way of producing and reproducing the means of human existence or, in Marxist terms, the union of its technological and productive capacity and social relations of production, fundamentally determine society's organization and development. Historical materialism looks for the causes of developments and changes in human society in the means by which humans collectively produce the necessities of life. It posits that social classes and the relationship between them, along with the political structures and ways of thinking in society, are founded on and reflect contemporary economic activity. Marx and Engels first state and detail their materialist conception of history within the pages of *The German Ideology*, written in 1845. The book is a lengthy polemic against Marx's and Engels's fellow Young Hegelians and contemporaries Ludwig von Feuerbach, Bruno Bauer, and Max Stirner. Stirner's 1844 work *The Unique and its Property* had a particularly strong impact on the worldview of Marx and Engels: Stirner's blistering critique of morality and whole-hearted embrace of egoism prompted the pair to formulate a conception of Socialism along lines of self-

he is often recognized as a bridge between Hegel and Marx. In rejecting Hegel's philosophy and advocating materialism, criticizing religion and idealism, von Feuerbach emphasized the individual, purely "biological" nature of man. He saw thought as a purely reflective, contemplative process, and in his understanding of history remained an idealist. Nevertheless, his critique of Hegel's idealism laid the basis for Marx's and Engels's work. Two years before his death, von Feuerbach joined the German Social Democratic Party, but he was not politically active.

In his Preface to *The Essence of Christianity*, von Feuerbach states:

> If therefore my work is negative, irreligious, atheistic, let it be remembered that atheism—at least in the sense of this work—is the secret of religion itself; that religion itself, not indeed on the surface, but fundamentally, not in intention or according to its own supposition, but in its heart, in its essence, believes in nothing else than the truth and divinity of human nature.

And in his *Lectures on the Essence of Religion* (1851), von Feuerbach declares:

> Though I myself am an atheist, I openly profess religion in the sense just mentioned, that is, a nature religion. I hate the idealism that wrenches man out of nature; I am not ashamed of my dependency on nature; I openly confess that the workings of nature affect not only my surface, my skin, my body, but also my core, my innermost being, that the air I breathe in bright weather has a salutary effect not only on my lungs but also on my mind, that the light of the sun illumines not only my eyes but also my spirit and my heart. And I do not, like a Christian, believe that such dependency is contrary to my true being or hope to be delivered from it. I know further that I am a finite moral being, that I shall one day cease to be. But I find this very natural and am therefore perfectly reconciled to the thought. (Von Feuerbach 1967, 35–6).

---

interest rather than simple humanism alone, grounding that conception in the scientific study of history.

* * *

God did not, as the Bible says, make man in His image; on the contrary man, as I have shown in *The Essence of Christianity*, made God in his image [Lecture XX, von Feuerbach 1967, 187].

* * *

Christianity set itself the goal of fulfilling man's unattainable desires, but for that very reason ignored his attainable desires. By promising man eternal life, it deprived him of temporal life, by teaching him to trust in God's help it took away his trust in his own powers; by giving him faith in a better life in heaven, it destroyed his faith in a better life on earth and his striving to attain such a life. Christianity gave man what his imagination desires, but for that very reason failed to give him what he really and truly desires. [Lecture XXX – *Atheism alone a Positive View*, von Feuerbach 1967, n.p.]

THE MARRIAGE OF THEOLOGY & ROMANTICISM

A romantic theologian does not mean one who is romantic about theology but one who is theological about romance, one who considers the theological implications of those experiences which are called romantic.

— C. S. LEWIS

Now as myth transcends thought, Incarnation transcends myth. The heart of Christianity is a myth which is also a fact . . . To be truly Christian we must both assent to the historical fact and also receive the myth (fact though it has become) with the same imaginative embrace which we accord to all myths . . . For this is the marriage of heaven and earth: Perfect Myth and Perfect Fact: claiming not only our love and our obedience, but also our wonder and delight, addressed to the savage, the child, and the poet in each one of us no less than to the moralist, the scholar, and the philosopher.

— C. S. LEWIS

The religious element in Romanticism, whether Catholic or non-Catholic, goes much deeper than the superficial aesthetic appeal. It has its roots in the fundamental principles of the movement.

— CHRISTOPHER DAWSON

It is not difficult to imagine the peculiar excitement and joy that one would feel, if any specially beautiful fairy-story were found to be "primarily" true, its narrative to be history, without thereby necessarily losing the mythical or allegorical significance that it had possessed . . . God is the Lord of angels, and of men—and of elves. Legend and History have met and fused . . . The Evangelium has not abrogated legends; it has hallowed them, especially the "happy ending."

— J. R. R. TOLKIEN

MANY SCHOLARS AGREE IT IS HARD TO OVERSTATE THE IMPACT OF THE 1789 French Revolution on history, including the rise of Romanticism and the European Nationalist movements, as well as the religious revival that followed in wake of the Romantic Movement. Moreover, one cannot fully understand history without recognizing the integral dynamic force that religion has played in shaping history. For this reason, many scholars also recognize the role scholastic theology of the *Reformed* Protestant Reformation played in setting to motion the changes leading to the Enlightenment and the French Revolution. The disillusions and tragedies of the 1789 French Revolution became the key to a new philosophy of society dramatically opposed to the philosophies of the Enlightenment. This reaction became known as the Romantic movement.

As he did with other such movements, like the Renaissance, Reformation, and Enlightenment, Dawson assessed the 1789 French Revolution by religious, Catholic standards. He claimed that the revolutionaries adopted the *philosophes'*—the intellectuals of the Enlightenment who systematically questioned every aspect of French government and society—conscious anti-Catholicism by undertaking a radical reconstruction of the Church according to Enlightenment principles, plus measures of "positive de-Christianization" (Schwartz 2005, 257). These policies signaled to Dawson how fundamentally hostile to Catholicism the French Revolution was: "it was a religion of human salvation, the salvation of the world by the power of man set free by Reason. The Cross has been replaced by the Tree of Liberty, the Grace of God by the Reason of Man, and Redemption by Revolution" (Schwartz 2005, 257). If the Enlightenment was a qualitative break with the Renaissance, Dawson thought, the French Revolution was an equally substantial split from the Reformation: "In sheer material destruction of monasteries and churches, in confiscation of property and abrogation of privileges, the Age of the Revolution far surpassed that of the Reformation; it was in fact a second Reformation, but a frankly anti-religious one" (Schwartz 2005, 257). During the Reign of Terror in revolutionary France (5 September 1793–27 July 1794), of the nearly 115,000 Catholic clergy in France at the time, nearly fifty percent abdicated the priesthood, handed over their letters of ordination, and swore loyalty to the revolutionary government—this group was called "constitutional" or "juring" clergy. Of the remaining "non-juring" clergy, 30,000 were forced abroad into exile (French Guiana), thousands went underground and continued to minister in clandestine settings, thousands were imprisoned, and hundreds were executed by guillotine, including bishops and abbots (Lewis 1993, 96). Most French parishes were left without the services of a priest and deprived of the sacraments. By Easter 1794, few of France's forty thousand churches remained open; many had been shuttered, sold, destroyed, or converted to other uses.

In chapter nine, *Religion and the Romantic Movement*, of his book *The Gods of Revolution* (posthumously published in 1972), Dawson expounds on the nexus between evolving liberal theology in Europe during twenty-five years of war (French Revolution [5 May 1789–9 November 1799], French revolutionary wars [20 April 1792–25 March 1802], and Napoleonic wars [18 May 1803–20 November 1815]) and emerging Romanticism that was a reaction to the empiricism and rationalism of the Enlightenment. The following is an extended excerpt of that chapter (Dawson 2015a, 115–24).

> The revival of religion that followed the French Revolution was not confined to any one country or to any single Church. It was common to the Latin and Germanic peoples and to

Catholic and Protestant countries. Indeed it made itself felt far beyond the limits of organized Christianity and imparted a religious tendency to social and intellectual movements of the most diverse kinds, even though they were apparently in revolt against everything orthodox and traditional, whether in the sphere of religion or morals. Christianity, which had been relegated by Voltaire to the stables and the scullery, was brought back to the court and the salon, and even those who still rejected it no longer did so in the contemptuous and cocksure manner of the man of the Enlightenment. Perhaps the most remarkable instance of this is the attitude of Auguste Comte, whose denial of all metaphysical validity to religious belief does not prevent his wholesale acceptance of the moral and ritual tradition of Catholic Christianity as one of the essential elements in the spiritual life of humanity. Thus on the one hand we have a series of religious thinkers that represents the movement of revival within the limits of organized Christianity—men such as Count Joseph [-Marie] de Maistre, Maine de Biran, Ballanche, and Lamennais and Lacordaire in France, Coleridge, Newman in England, Möhler and Görres in Germany, and Kierkegaard in Denmark, while on the other, there is a series of no less eminent names of men who stood outside the frontiers of Christian orthodoxy and who attempted to build up a new religious edifice on humanitarian or idealist foundations—as, for example, did St. Simon, Leroux, Comte, Bazard and Guinet in France, and Fichte and Hegel in Germany.

This revival of belief in religion, or at least a respect for religion, is the more remarkable when we contrast it with the external losses that religion had suffered during the preceding period. In sheer material destruction of monasteries and churches, in confiscation of property and abrogation of privileges, the Age of the Revolution far surpassed that of the Reformation; it was in fact a second Reformation, but a frankly anti-religious one. Throughout Europe the old regime had based itself on a union between Church and State so close that any revolt against the political system involved a corresponding revolt against the established Church. Moreover, the Church was singularly ill-prepared to stand a shock of this kind. For more than half a century—first in the Bourbon kingdoms and Portugal and then in Germany and the Austrian dominions—the policy of enlightened despotism had been at work, reducing the Church to complete dependence on the secular power. The princes and statesmen who carried out this policy, Choiseul in France, Pombal in Portugal, Florida Blanca in Spain, and Joseph II and Leopold II in Austria, were themselves the disciples of the philosophers, and in some cases were animated by the same spirit that inspired Voltaire's campaign against Christianity. It was, however, not their intention to destroy the Church, but rather to make it a part of the machinery of the new bureaucratic state—and to limit its functions to that of an educational institution whose business it was to make men useful and obedient citizens. This ideal was most completely realized by the Emperor Joseph II, who set himself to rationalize and socialize the Church in his dominions with Teutonic thoroughness. No detail of ecclesiastical usage was too small to escape his meticulous regulation, and the parish priest was expected to supervise the rural economy as well as the morals of his parish. And while in Austria the Church was thus reformed by an enlightened despotism inspired by the rational and progressive ideas of eighteenth-century Freemasonry, in the rest of Germany every kind of abuse continued to reign. Nothing could be darker than the picture which the papal nuncio, Cardinal Pacca, paints of the Catholic Rhineland at the close of the century. The prince bishops lived a thoroughly secular life and squandered the resources of their sees on their courts and their mistresses. Of the electors of Mainz, the primates of Germany, Ostein was the friend of Voltaire and Erthal was the patron of the neo-pagan Heinse, and things were no better in the archdiocese of Cologne for the greater part of the eighteenth century, though the best elector, the Archduke Maximilian, was a well intentioned "enlightened despot" of the type of his brother Joseph II. But underneath this corruption in high places the faith of the masses remained as strong as ever.

* * *

[T]he net result of the [French] revolutionary wars and the wholesale secularization that followed the Treaty of Lunéville [1801] was to leave the Catholic Church in Germany weaker and more at the mercy of the secular power than ever before.

* * *

Yet the very violence of the [French revolutionary] storm revealed the strength of those religious forces which the eighteenth century had ignored. The persecution [of the French Catholic Church] itself did much to restore the prestige of religion and of the clergy by investing them with the halo of martyrdom. . . . The effect of such things was, in fact, just the opposite of what the Jacobins intended. Fifty years earlier, when religious conformity was enforced by law, and people were obliged to produce certificates of confession, the rising generation grew up as infidels: but now that the churches were closed and the "refractory" clergy said Mass in secret at the peril of their lives, religion took on a new lease of life and the *new* generation—the generation of Lamennais and the Cure d'Ars—turned to Christianity with an enthusiasm and conviction which in the preceding century had been found only among the Methodists and the Moravians.

Thus the [French] Revolution, which was the child of the Enlightenment, also proved to be its destroyer. The philosophic rationalism of the eighteenth century was the product of a highly civilized and privileged society which was swept away by the catastrophe of the *ancien régime*. In the salons of Madame de Pompadour, Madame du Deffand, or Madame Geoffrin, it was easy to believe that Christianity was an exploded superstition which no reasonable man could take seriously. But the same men and women felt very differently when the brilliant society that had worshipped at the shrine of Voltaire was decimated by the guillotine and scattered to the four winds. Many of them, like

Chateaubriand, recovered their faith in Christianity by the stress of personal suffering and bereavement, but even those who did not recover their faith in God, lost that faith in man and in the law of progress that had been characteristic of the previous age. Rationalism flourishes best in a prosperous age and a sheltered society; it finds few adherents among the unfortunate and the defeated.

The course of the Revolution was equally fatal to the hopes of every party. It seemed as though fate had determined to explode the hollowness of any kind of idealism by the destruction of all that was best in France and by permitting only the basest elements—the Barras and the Fouchés—to survive and prosper. There were some to whom this sense of the malignity of fate came with a force of a personal revelation. One of the writers of the French emigration has described in a striking passage how this happened to him while he was making the terrible march over the frozen Zuyder Zee with the defeated English army in 1796. As he marched over the ice he felt all the illusions of the Enlightenment falling away from him under the cold light of the winter stars until he realized with a flash of blinding conviction that his life had hitherto been based on a lie. And a similar experience was had by many of the most distinguished minds of the age in many different countries.

No more terrible answer could have been given to the facile optimism of the age of Louis XVI than the twenty-five years of revolution and war from 1790 to 1815, and it is not surprising that the more sensitive minds who contemplated this long drawn out spectacle of human misery were led not only to surrender their illusions but to question the principles which had been the foundations of their whole thought. In many cases, as for instance with Senancourt, the author of *Obermann* (who is so well known to us through the poems of Matthew Arnold), or Mallet du Pan, or the young Chateaubriand, these doubts found expression in a pessimistic fatalism which left no room for human effort. There were some, however, who found in the disillusions and tragedies of the Revolution the key to a new philosophy of society dramatically opposed to those of the Enlightenment.

The chief representative of this tendency was Joseph [-Marie, Comte] de Maistre, one of the most original thinkers and brilliant writers of his age, and one of the most important formative influences on French thought in the early nineteenth century. . . .

Although he [de Maistre] belonged to the pre-Romantic generation, it was not until after the Restoration [1815–1830] that his influence was fully felt, owing to the circumstances of his life. He had spent the whole of the period from the Revolution to the Restoration in exile, and the greater part of it in Russia, as the penniless ambassador of an exiled dynasty—that of Savoy—for de Maistre, though a man of French culture and speech, was never a French citizen. But the intellectual isolation and material failure which marked his whole career only served to strengthen the almost fanatical singleness of purpose and force of conviction that characterized his thought. Beneath the exterior of a diplomat and a man of the world he hid the spirit of a Hebrew prophet, and in fact the problems that preoccupied him were fundamentally the same as those that confronted Job and Jeremiah—the problem of suffering and evil and the justification of the obscure purposes of God in history. The men of the Enlightenment had lived on the surface of life. They had rejected the very idea of mystery [particularly divine mystery] and had done their best to eliminate and ignore everything that was irrational and obscure; they explained the problem of existence by denying that there was a problem to explain. De Maistre, on the other hand, concentrated his attention on the other side of life and made the suffering and evil of the world the key to the understanding of it.

* * *

The Revolution was not an event, he [de Maistre] wrote as early as 1794, it was an epoch in the history of humanity [Goyau 1921, 88], the birth pangs of a new age. And its real significance was not to be found in its conscious ideals, as for instance in the Declaration of the Rights of Man, which were nothing but hollow abstractions concealing the real trend of events by a sort of rationalizing mirage; it was to be found on a much deeper plane in profound spiritual changes of which the contemporary mind was still unconscious. "What we are witnessing," he writes, "is a religious revolution; the rest, immense as it seems, is but an appendix."

* * *

Of course de Maistre's philosophy of history is not quite so Christian as this. It has a certain Hindu or Buddhist element in it—history is governed by an impersonal law of retribution or Karma. Every evil will or act produces an inevitable fruit of suffering—the innocent may pay for the guilty, but history shows that the full payment must be made. The only way out of this circle of guilt and suffering is to be found in detachment and in the voluntary acceptance of suffering.

And this view of history as a superhuman process which transcended the aims and ideas of the men who were apparently the makers of history was to influence all the thinkers of the next generation in both camps—on the one hand the founders of socialism and Positivism like the St Simonians, especially Bazard and Comte, on the other the founders of liberal Catholicism, like Lamennais and his school, and of the Catholic conservatives like Donoso Cortes.

But in his own time de Maistre was an isolated figure standing between "two worlds, one dead, the other powerless to be born." He belongs neither to the eighteenth nor the nineteenth century, neither to the Enlightenment nor to the Romantic movement. But though this simple and austere gentleman of the old regime has little in common with the undisciplined, emotional, unstable spirit of Romanticism, there is a curious parallelism between his thought and that of the leaders of the Romantic movement.

This parallelism is seen most clearly in the essay on *Europe or Christendom* composed by the young Navalis in 1798, only two years after de Maistre's *Considerations on France*. In spite of his Protestant origins, Navalis exalts the religious ideal of the Middle Ages and condemns the Reformation for its sacrilegious attempt to divide the indivisible Church and to imprison religion within political frontiers. Like de Maistre, he regards the Reformation as the source of rationalism and free thought, which found its culmination in the work of the Revolution. But at the same time he sees in the Revolution the dawn of a new era and shares de Maistre's belief that the signs of the times pointed to a great spiritual renewal which would bring Europe back to religious unity. All the early Romantics were inspired by the same consciousness of an imminent spiritual revolution, all of them were enemies of the Enlightenment and admirers of medieval Catholicism, and many of them, such as Friedrich and Dorothea Schlegel, Adam Müller, Zacharias Werner, Franz von Baader, Görres and Clemens Brentano found their spiritual home in the Catholic Church.

It would of course be a mistake to ignore the existence of a Protestant element in the movement. Schleiermacher, perhaps the chief formative influence on Protestant religious thought in the nineteenth century, was a friend of the Schlegels and was closely associated with the origins of the movement, while at a later date the most original Protestant thinker of the nineteenth century, the Dane, Søren Kierkegaard, was a true Romantic in spite of his isolation and his hostility to everything for which Schleiermacher stood.

Nevertheless contemporary opinion was not unjustified in regarding Romanticism as a Catholicizing movement. The tendency is to be seen most clearly years before the conversion of the Schlegels in the writings of early Romantics like Wackenroder and Novalis, who never themselves became Catholics and whose admiration was in no way inspired by propagandist motives.

I have already referred to Novalis' remarkable panegyric of medieval Catholicism and his criticism of the

> Reformation, and in the same way Wackenroder in 1797 initiated that return to the religion of the Middle Ages through the art of the Middle Ages which became so typical of the Catholic revival in the nineteenth century. This Catholicizing tendency, which was denounced by Heine and the young German school as mere reactionary sentimentalism, did much to render Romanticism unpopular in the later nineteenth century, as we see for example in the well-known volumes of George Brandes, *The Romantic Movement in Germany* (1873), which for all their ability are biased by an almost sectarian bitterness. In reality, however, the religious element in Romanticism, whether Catholic or non-Catholic, goes much deeper than the superficial aesthetic appeal. It has its roots in the fundamental principles of the movement, which differed not merely aesthetically but also metaphysically and psychologically from those of both seventeenth-century Classicism and eighteenth-century Rationalism.

Christopher Dawson brings the total revolutionary movement up to date in the final chapter, *Revolution and the Modern World*, of his *The Gods of Revolution*. How well that world can ponder one of the closing lines in his book, "And a free society requires a higher degree of spiritual unity than a totalitarian one, hence the spiritual integration of western culture is essential to its temporal survival" (Dawson 2015, 147).

Theology in Germany during the nineteenth century was dominated by pietist Lutheran Friedrich August Gottreu Tholuck, rationalist Friedrich Daniel Ernst Schleiermacher, and Schleiermacher's pupils: Albrecht Ritschl, Wilhelm Hermann, and Adolf von Harnack. Common to all of these leaders were liberal theology, higher criticism, and Lutheran Neo-Kantianism. Throughout the nineteenth century and leading up to the mid-twentieth century, theology in Germany continued in its long-standing liberal tradition as defined earlier in this writing based on higher criticism and the historical-critical method of Scriptural interpretation.*

---

* For a more in-depth exposition of the changes in German theology during the first half of the nineteenth century, see Kloes 2019. Andrew A. Kloes, Ph.D. (History of Christianity, University of Edinburgh) has since 2016 been research historian at the

THE MARRIAGE OF POLITICS & RELIGION

KING OF PRUSSIA FRIEDRICH WILHELM III (1770–1840), WAS OF THE Hohenzollern Dynasty ruling Brandenburg since 1415 and Prussia since 1525. The Dynasty ended at the conclusion of the First World War with the abdication of German Emperor Kaiser Wilhelm II and establishment of the Weimar Republic under Social Democratic Party of Germany (*SPD*) party chairman Friedrich Ebert on 9 November 1918. The Hohenzollern family converted from Roman Catholicism to Lutheranism during the time of Martin Luther, but later converted to Calvinism under Hohenzollern Prince-Elector of Brandenburg Johann Sigismund (1572–1619). Sigismund was probably won over to Calvinism during a visit to Heidelberg in 1606, but it was not until 1613 that he publicly took communion according to the Calvinist rite. The vast majority of his subjects in Brandenburg, including his wife Anna of Prussia, remained deeply Lutheran, however. After the Elector and his Calvinist court officials drew up plans for mass conversion of the population to the new faith in February 1614, as provided for by the rule of *Cuius regio, eius religio* within the Holy Roman Empire, there were serious protests, with his wife backing the Lutherans. Resistance was so strong that in 1615, Sigismund backed down and relinquished all attempts at forcible conversion. Instead, he allowed his subjects to be either Lutheran or Calvinist according to the dictates of their own consciences. Henceforward, Brandenburg-Prussia would be a bi-confessional state.

One year after he ascended to the throne in 1798, Friedrich William III, being *summus episcopus* (Supreme Governor of the Protestant Churches), decreed a new common liturgical agenda (service book) to be published, for use in both the Lutheran and Reformed congregations. The king, a Reformed Calvinist, lived in a denominationally mixed marriage with the Lutheran Queen Louise (1776–1810), which is why they never partook of Holy Communion together. A commission was formed in order to prepare this common agenda. This liturgical agenda was the culmination of the efforts of his predecessors to unify these two Protestant churches in Prussia and in its predecessor, the Electorate of Brandenburg, becoming later its core province. In 1808, Reformed theologian and philosopher Friedrich

Mandel Center for Advanced Holocaust Studies, United States Holocaust Memorial Museum in Washington, D.C.

Schleiermacher (1768–1834),* pastor of Trinity Church (Berlin-Friedrichstadt), issued his ideas for a constitutional reform of the Protestant Churches, also proposing a union. Under the influence of his Minister of Church and Educational Affairs Karl vom Stein zum Altenstein, Wilhelm III allowed pretty much anything to be said about religion so long as there was practical obedience to his enforced merging of Calvinism and Lutheranism and spreading of liberal Protestantism in Catholic strongholds. Altenstein was named minister in 1817 and charged with re-founding the Evangelical Church in Prussia by forming a union of Lutheran and Calvinist (Reformed) churches, which on the 300th anniversary of the Reformation (31 October 1817), united into one Evangelical Christian congregation and celebrated the first conjoined Lutheran-Reformed Eucharist in Potsdam (Brandenburg Prussia). The new unified church was called the Prussian Union of Churches (1817–1821) followed by the Evangelical Church in the Royal Prussian Lands (1821–1845), the Evangelical State Church of Prussia (1845–1875), the Evangelical State Church of Prussia's older Provinces (1875–1922), the Evangelical Church of the old-Prussian Union (1922–1953), the Evangelical Church of the Union (1953–2004), and the current Union of Evangelical Churches.

David Friedrich Strauss' two-volume *Life of Jesus Critically Examined* (1835–1836) was one of the few books which Socialist revolutionary Wilhelm Weitling owned, and it may be assumed that he was thoroughly familiar with its contents. David Friedrich Strauss (1808–1874) was a German liberal Lutheran theologian and writer, who with his portrayal of the "historical Jesus," denied Jesus's divine nature. Strauss' attempt to combine Hegelian philosophy with Christianity and to reconcile science and religion started a veritable spiritual renaissance in Germany and Switzerland. Karl Gutzkow (German writer notable in the Young Germany movement)

* Friedrich Daniel Ernst Schleiermacher was known for his attempt to reconcile the criticisms of the Enlightenment with traditional Protestant Christianity. He also became influential in the evolution of higher criticism, and his work forms part of the foundation of the modern field of hermeneutics. Because of his profound effect on subsequent Christian thought, he is often called the "Father of Modern Liberal Theology" and is considered an early leader in liberal Christianity. However, his lack of faith in foundational Christian dogma such as the divinity of Jesus can be surmised from his letter (dated 21 January 1787) to his Calvinist chaplain father, in which he states: "I cannot believe that he who called himself the Son of Man was the true, eternal God; I cannot believe that his death was a vicarious atonement." (Gerrish 1984, 25.)

referred to the book as "the yeast of Germany's intellectual ferment" (Gutzkow 1875, 140, 290–1).

The event that precipitated the gradual dissolution of the Hegelian synthesis of faith and knowledge that Marx and Engels later referred to sardonically as the "putrefaction of absolute spirit" was Strauss' *The Life of Jesus Critically Examined.* Here, Strauss used the Schleiermacher's tools of "higher criticism" (historical-critical method) he had acquired from his University of Tübingen professor of ecclesiastical and doctrinal history, Ferdinand Christian von Baur (1792–1860),* to reveal the historical unreliability of the accounts of the life of Jesus preserved in the canonical gospels, and interpreted the doctrine of the incarnation of Christ as a mythological expression of the philosophical truth of the identity of the divine spirit and the human species (conceived as the community of finite spirits existing throughout history, and not as the historical individual, Jesus of Nazareth). The appearance of Strauss' book confirmed the suspicions of theological Conservatives like Lutheran clergyman and theologian Ernst Wilhelm Hengstenberg (1802–1869) and Prussian historian Heinrich Leo (1799–1878) that Hegel's philosophy, despite its use of Christian terminology, is incompatible with the historical faith, and the editors of the Berlin Annals felt compelled to publicly discredit Strauss' Hegelian credentials. It was in the wake of these events that Arnold Ruge established in 1837 the *Hallesche Jahrbücher für deutsche Kunst und Wissenschaft* (*Halle Annals for German Science and Art*), which served for several years as the principal literary organ of the Young Hegelians, and to which German philosopher and religious theorist Ludwig von Feuerbach (1804–1872) began to contribute essays and reviews in 1838, including in 1839 an essay entitled "Toward a Critique of the Hegelian Philosophy," in which he first began to distance himself publicly from the Hegelian cause, calling for a "return to nature"—and to a naturalistic explanation of the mysteries of Christianity, and of religion more generally (Gooch 2016).

---

* Ferdinand Christian von Baur – German Protestant theologian and founder and leader of the (now debunked) Tübingen School of theology that followed Hegel's theory of dialectic. By the late 1840s, the Tübingen School came under severe attack and the various members gradually drifted away. Baur himself became isolated within the Tübingen faculty, as well as the German academic community, and spent his last years defending his views and producing a multivolume history of the church from a naturalistic standpoint, which explained all events by a combination of political, social, cultural, and intellectual causes but without any consideration of divine influence.

Ludwig von Feuerbach's *The Essence of Christianity* (1841) represented a further challenge to orthodoxy that by Karl Marx's admission marked the end of the period of classical German philosophy (Hegelianism). "Man had created God," von Feuerbach argued, but now the time had come for him to recognize his own true nature, to fuse within himself the moral and the natural, the divine and the animal. For man to find his true nature, it was not enough to abolish the concept of a transcendental Deity and seek God within himself; he also had to abolish all forms of social inequality. The era of theology was over; the era of "anthropology" and "humanism" had arrived in its stead. At a time when the altar supported not only the throne but practically every other institution of the established order, von Feuerbach sought to emancipate human beings from being "the valets of His Heavenly Majesty." Von Feuerbach's friend, firebrand revolutionary poet Georg Herwegh (1817–1875), who believed that only revolution would bring about freedom, announced that he was ready for revolution and issued his mighty call to arms in his poem *Aufruf* (*The Call*) (Herwegh 1841):

Reißt die Kreuze aus der Erden!
Alle sollen Schwerter werden,
Gott im Himmel wird's verzeih'n.
Laßt, o laßt das Verseschweißen!
Auf den Amboß legt das Eisen!
Heiland soll das Eisen sein.

Break the crosses out of the earth!
All should become swords,
God in heaven will forgive them.
Let go, o let go of the welding!
The iron is laid on the anvil!
The Savior should be the iron.

Eure Tannen, eure Eichen
Habt die grünen Fragezeichen
Deutscher Freiheit ihr gewahrt?
Nein, sie soll nicht untergehen!
Doch ihr fröhlich Auferstehen
Kostet eine Höllenfahrt.

Your firs, your oaks
Have you noticed the green question
marks of German freedom?
No, she should not go down!
But you reborn joyfully
Cost a hellish journey.

Deutsche, glaubet euren Sehern,
Unsre Tage werden ehern,
Unsre Zukunft klirrt in Erz;
Schwarzer Tod ist unser Sold nur,
Unser Gold ein Abendgold nur,
Unser Rot ein blutend Herz!

Germans, believe your seers,
Our days will be brave,
Our future clinks in brass;
Black death is our only pay,
Our gold only evening gold,
Our red a bleeding heart!

Reißt die Kreuze aus der Erden! *Alle sollen Schwerter werden,* *Gott im Himmel wird's verzeihn.* *Hört er unsre Feuer brausen* *Und sein heilig Eisen sausen,* *Spricht er wohl den Segen drein.*	*Break the crosses out of the earth!* *All should become swords,* *God in heaven will forgive them.* *Does he hear our fires roar* *And whirl his holy iron,* *Does he speak the blessing?*
Vor der Freiheit sei kein Frieden, *Sei dem Mann kein Weib beschieden* *Und kein golden Korn dem Feld;* *Vor der Freiheit, vor dem Siege* *Seh kein Säugling aus der Wiege* *Frohen Blickes in die Welt!*	*There is no peace before freedom,* *let no man be given a wife* *And no golden grain in the field;* *Before freedom, before victory* *See no baby from the cradle* *Glance into the world!*
In den Städten sei nur Trauern, *Bis die Freiheit von den Mauern* *Schwingt die Fahnen in das Land;* *Bis du, Rhein, durch freie Bogen* *Donnerst, laß die letzten Wogen* *Fluchend knirschen in den Sand.*	*In the cities, only mourning,* *Until freedom from the walls* *Swing the flags in the land;* *Until you, Rhine, through free arch* *Thunder, leave the last waves* *Cursing crunching in the sand.*
Reißt die Kreuze aus der Erden! *Alle sollen Schwerter werden,* *Gott im Himmel wird's verzeihn.* *Gen Tyrannen und Philister!* *Auch das Schwert hat seine Priester,* *Und wir wollen Priester sein!*	*Break the crosses out of the earth!* *Everyone should become swords,* *God in heaven will forgive them.* *Enough tyrants and philistines!* *The sword also has its priests,* *and we want to be priests!*

Austrian poets Alfred Meissner (1822–1885) and Karl Isidor Beck (1817–1879) were active along similar revolutionary and Socialistic lines in Austria, the former publishing the epic poem *Žižka* (1846) and the latter publishing the poem *Songs of the Poor Man* (1846). Also, radical ideas, which somehow managed to escape the vigilance of the censors, appeared in some of the papers of Rhenish Prussia, Hesse, Westphalia, and Frankfurt. These were the ingredients from which a social revolution could be fashioned.

Von Feuerbach achieved the height of his brief literary fame with the publication in 1841 of *The Essence of Christianity*. Engels recalled the appearance of von Feuerbach's book as having a profoundly "liberating effect" on him and Marx by "breaking the spell" of the Hegelian system and establishing the truths that human consciousness is the only consciousness or spirit that exists, and that it is dependent upon the physical existence of human beings as part of nature (Engels 1888: 12–13). In 1844, Marx wrote to von Feuerbach, with reference to the latter's *Principles of the Philosophy of the Future* (1843) and *The Essence of Faith According to Luther* (1844), that in them he had, intentionally or not, "given socialism a philosophical foundation" (Schuffenhauer 1981, 376). In fact, von Feuerbach was only then beginning to acquaint himself with Socialist ideas through his reading of authors like Lorenz von Stein and Wilhelm Weitling. In the end, he declined Marx's request for a contribution to the radical Socialist Parisian newspaper *Deutsch-Französische Jahrbücher* (*German French Annals*), as well as Ruge's urging that he become more politically engaged. He did come out of rural seclusion to observe fairly passively the ultimately disappointing events in Frankfurt in 1848, and to deliver a series of public lectures at Heidelberg beginning the same year. He unfortunately failed to develop with much specificity or argumentative rigor the "philosophy of the future" for which he himself called in the early 1840s, continuing instead to focus his attention mainly on religion in works like *The Essence of Religion* (1845), *Lectures on the Essence of Religion* (1851), and *Theogony According to the Sources of Classical, Hebrew and Christian Antiquity* (1857). The five years of philological labor that von Feuerbach invested in the latter work, which he considered his crowning achievement, went largely unnoticed both by his contemporaries and by posterity.

During the 1840s, von Feuerbach corresponded and occasionally visited and maintained close personal relationships with several leading German radicals, including, in addition to Ruge and Marx, the publishers Otto Lüning, Otto Wigand, and Julius Fröbel; the revolutionary poet Georg Herwegh and his wife Emma; Hermann Kriege, a freelance activist and early German Socialist who emigrated to America; and scientific materialists like Jacob Moleschott and Carl Vogt. The impression made by him on several leading lights of the younger generation is reflected in Gottfried Keller's *Bildungsroman, Green Henry*, first published in 1855, and in the dedication (to von Feuerbach) of Richard Wagner's early book, *The Art-Work of the Future* (1850).

Partly as the result of a global financial crisis, the porcelain factory that had supported von Feuerbach's literary existence went bankrupt in 1859. The following year he, his wife, and their daughter were forced to relocate to the village of Rechenberg, located then on the outskirts of Nuremberg, where von Feuerbach lived out the remainder of his life under severely strained financial circumstances and in increasingly ill health. Although his productivity as a writer declined sharply during this period, he was able to bring out in 1866 the tenth and final volume of his collected works (which had begun to appear in 1846), bearing the title *God, Freedom and Immortality from the Standpoint of Anthropology*, and including a fairly substantial, though fragmentary, essay "On Spiritualism and Materialism, Especially in Relation to the Freedom of the Will." In this essay, and in an essay on ethics that von Feuerbach left incomplete at his death, we find him beginning to sketch out a moral psychology and a eudemonistic ethical theory in which the concept of the "drive-to-happiness" (*Glückseligkeitstrieb*) plays a central role (Gooch 2016).

THE *KULTURKAMPF*

AFTER TWENTY-FIVE YEARS OF ENDLESS WARS IN EUROPE, 1815 brought the beginnings of a spiritual revolution in Germany against the liberal Church and clerical class, and a plea for the return to the ethics of medieval Christianity. This was the Protestant Awakening movement (*die Erweckungsbewegung*) that unfolded during the *Vormärz* period (1815–1848) in German history. The Protestant Awakening in Prussia involved a nexus between political conservatism and Prussia's neo-pietist religious revival, especially in Brandenburg and Pomerania. Awakened Conservatives waged a cultural struggle against the political and religious Liberalism of the 1789 French Revolution, impacting the state church, the outcome of the revolution, and Prussia's later controversial neutrality in the Crimean War (1853–1856). "The Awakening" was the last major nationwide Protestant reform and revival movement to occur in Germany. The Awakening was a product of the larger social changes that were re-shaping German society during the early decades of the nineteenth century. Theologically, Awakened Protestants were traditionalists. They affirmed religious doctrines that orthodox Protestants had professed since the confessional statements of the Reformation era. Awakened Protestants rejected the changes that Enlightenment thought had introduced into Protestant theology and preaching since the mid-eighteenth century. However, Awakened Protestants were also themselves distinctly modern. Their efforts to spread their religious beliefs were successful because of the new political freedoms and economic opportunities that the Enlightenment had introduced. These social conditions gave German Protestants new means and abilities to pursue their religious goals. Awakened Protestants were leaders in the German churches and in the universities. They used their influence to establish many voluntary organizations for evangelism, in Germany and abroad. They also established many institutions to ameliorate the living conditions of those in poverty. Adapting Protestantism to modern society in these ways was the most original and innovative aspect of the German Awakening movement (Kloes 2019; see also Kloes, doctoral thesis 2015).

Awakened leaders, in their effort to recover and adapt a pre-Napoleonic order, ironically modernized Conservatism with individualistic rhetoric, widely circulated newspapers, and political organization. The Protestant Awakening in Prussia began in 1815 as a response to the secularization and fallout of the 1789 French Revolution being witnessed in Prussia and manifested as the transition of these revivalist Prussian Protestants from cultural pariahs to powerbrokers in an effort to win a cultural struggle against both religious and political "liberals." The Awakening represented a reappraisal of the role of religion in modern Europe. An older narrative of secularization portrayed the period after the Scientific Revolution and the Enlightenment as a time in which rationalistic ways of viewing the world fairly steadily but at times dramatically eroded the profoundly religious worldview of Europeans, ultimately producing societies that were wealthier, more socially mobile, more egalitarian, more merit oriented, more materialistic, and more individualistic—essentially, more modern. The first half of the nineteenth century witnessed tremendous evangelistic revivals in religion across the Western world, challenging secularization in many Protestant and Catholic states. It coincided with German Romanticism and the longing for the old medieval religion. However, through its theological egalitarianism and its neo-pietist emphasis on the individual's direct experience of God, the Prussian Awakening was unintentionally a powerful transformative force, which in practice enhanced the Liberalism of individual agency. These "culture wars" sought to resolve the political stalemate between revolutionaries and reactionaries in the post-Napoleonic era through a complex battle carried out in the spheres of religion and culture that culminated in the *Kulturkampf* of Otto von Bismarck in the 1870s.

Kulturkampf (culture war) was a power struggle between emerging constitutional Democratic nation states and the Roman Catholic Church over the place and role of religion in modern polity, usually in connection with secularization campaigns. From 1871 to 1876, the Prussian state parliament (*Landtag*) and the federal legislature (*Reichstag*), both with liberal majorities, enacted twenty-two laws in the context of the *Kulturkampf*. They were mainly directed against clerics—bishops, priests, and religious orders—and enforced the supremacy of the state over the church. While several laws were specific to the Catholic Church (Jesuits, parishes, etc.), the general laws affected both Catholic and Protestant churches. In an attempt to overcome growing resistance by the Catholic Church and its defiance of the laws, new regulations increasingly went beyond state matters referring to purely internal affairs of the Church. Even many Liberals saw them as encroachment on civil liberties, compromising their own credo. This clash in the German Empire laid the groundwork for the repression of Catholics in Germany and Europe under Adolf Hitler and the Nazis.

Catholic Professor of Church History Matthew Bunson (born 1966) has written extensively on the developments in Germany during the nineteenth century and their impact on the Roman Catholic Church. The following is an excerpt from his publicly posted writings on this subject of the *Kulturkampf*.

The history of the Church in Europe is replete with conflict over secular and ecclesiastical rights and privileges. The Middle Ages witnessed the Investiture Controversy between the Holy Roman Emperors and the Holy See and the sometimes-violent disputes between the popes and the monarchs of England and France. The Protestant Reformation and the Enlightenment ushered in a new age of monarchial despotism marked by the promotion of Enlightenment rationalism, the central authority of the crown, and the ruthless suppression of all opposition or Democratic tendencies in the population. The period was characterized by a willingness to remove the Catholic Church from all areas of public life, as Church teachings were seen as a hindrance to the formation of national unity and scientific progress. The chief exemplar of such absolutism was Holy Roman Emperor Austrian Joseph II (reign 1764–1790), whose program against the Church was dubbed Josephinism—a policy that influenced German Chancellor Otto von Bismarck a century later.

The nineteenth century brought more despotism under Napoléon Bonaparte, who persecuted the Church across the French Empire and even imprisoned Pope Pius VII from 1808 to 1813. Napoléon's fall in 1815 was greeted with joy by Catholics in Europe, but his time as emperor had wrought lasting changes to European politics. One of the most significant was the dissolution of the Holy Roman Empire in 1806 and the subsequent ascendancy in German-speaking regions of a Protestant state, Prussia, at the expense of Catholic Austria. In 1866, Austria and several Austrian-aligned German states were defeated by Prussia at the Battle of Königgrätz in Bohemia (3 July 1866). Henceforth, Prussia was the driving force for German cultural, religious, and national unity.

As Prussia amassed greater authority over the other German states, Catholic populations found themselves suddenly under Protestant rule. The risks of this became apparent in the 1830s in the Rhineland and Westphalia. There, a disagreement between civil and ecclesiastical authorities over mixed marriages climaxed with the two-year imprisonment of the Catholic archbishop of Cologne, Clemens August von Droste zu Vischering. In 1852, decrees were issued against the Jesuits in Prussia.

A new era began in Prussia in 1858 with the appointment of Prince Wilhelm Friedrich as prince regent for his mentally incapacitated monarch brother Prussian King Friedrich Wilhelm IV. On 2 January 1861, Friedrich Wilhelm IV died, and Wilhelm Friedrich was crowned King of Prussia. As head of the Prussian state, he inherited a long-simmering dispute with the Prussian Parliament, the *Landtag*, over military reforms. His solution was the appointment in 1862 of Otto von Bismarck as Prime Minister (*Ministerpräsident*) and Foreign Minister of Prussia. Upon unification of German and creation of the *Deutsches Reich* (German Empire) in 1871, von Bismarck was also named the first Chancellor of Germany.

Von Bismarck gave the crown a firm hand in its dealings with the *Landtag* and soon earned both his reputation as the most feared diplomat and statesman in Europe and his title of "Iron Chancellor." He took as one of the central objectives for Prussian ambitions the unification of Germany. In this he was joined by the two other chief figures of the Prussian government, Helmuth von Moltke, the Chief of Staff for the Prussian Army, and Albrecht von Roon, Prussian Minister of War. This triad of ministers-built Prussia into a military juggernaut and shocked Europe with their triumph over Austria in 1866 (Battle of Königgrätz). The final achievement of German unification followed swiftly from Prussia's shattering defeat of France and Napoléon III in 1870–1871 in the Franco-Prussian War. On 18 January 1871, Prussian King Wilhelm Friedrich was proclaimed German Emperor, or Kaiser Wilhelm I in the Chateau de Versailles's Hall of Mirrors in conquered France. The patchwork of German kingdoms, grand duchies, duchies, principalities, and free cities was now brought together into one collective polity called the *Deutsches Reich*, the German Empire, under the Kaiser and his ministers (chiefly von Bismarck), but with some legislative authority vested in the bicameral parliament, including a lower house elected by universal male suffrage, the *Reichstag*.

For von Bismarck, the solidification of German national and cultural unity faced obstacles, and one was the sizable Catholic population in the new Germany, whose loyalties he deeply suspected. Von Bismarck's long mistrust of the Roman Church was only exacerbated by the definition of papal infallibility by the First Vatican Council (1869–1870), which to a pragmatic politician seemed to suggest supremacy for the pope that outweighed loyalty to the state among the Catholic faithful. As a point of statecraft, then, Catholic influence had to be subjugated to the new imperial order.

Von Bismarck found allies against the Catholic Church in two seemingly disparate political parties. On the one hand, there were his natural supporters, the Conservatives, and especially their leader Moritz von Blankenburg. Von Blankenburg was openly opposed to the Catholic Church in Germany and determined to maintain the Protestant character of the government.

Surprisingly, however, von Bismarck's strongest supporters in the Prussian *Landtag* and then in the *Reichstag* were the Liberals. The liberal wing in the Prussian *Landtag* had long opposed absolutism and called for constitutional government, but they were also united in their antipathy for the Catholic Church; many liberal leaders were anti-clerical and ardent students of the German Enlightenment. This hatred for the Catholic Church naturally extended into their calls for a pure German culture freed from the supposed superstitions, dogmatism, and obscurantism of the Church. Their influence in German politics increased in the middle of the nineteenth century, when they used public sentiment for German Nationalism to their advantage. Their presence increased steadily in the *Landtag* after 1860, and in that year, they were permitted to introduce harsh anti-Catholic educational measures in traditionally Catholic Bavaria.

Having found common ground with the Liberals, von Bismarck allowed them to hold many offices in the imperial government, climaxing in 1870 with the role of the Liberals in waging the Franco-Prussian War. When, therefore, von Bismarck set out upon the *Kulturkampf*, the Liberals were his most enthusiastic foot-soldiers. In fact, it was a liberal member of the Prussian *Landtag* in 1873, eminent pathologist Dr. Rudolf Virchow (German Progressive Party [*Deutsche Fortschrittspartei, DFP*]), who first used the term *Kulturkampf*.

The program was inaugurated through a legal measure appended to the *Strafgesetzbuch*, the German Criminal Code, that threatened two years in prison should a clergyman address any political topics from the pulpit. Passed in 1871, the new law was termed the *Kanzelparagraf* (or pulpit paragraph). That same year, the Roman Catholic department for religious affairs in the Prussian government was closed for being pro-Polish. The following year, the Jesuits were expelled from the German Empire (only returning in 1917) and all religious schools were required to accept official government inspections. In June, all religious teachers were removed from government schools. In December, the German government broke off diplomatic relations with the Holy See.

In March 1873, the Prussian *Landtag* passed a series of laws drafted by Adalbert Falk, the German minister of education, that regulated Catholic life in Prussia. The new laws were then approved for the entire German Empire on 15 May 1873, by the *Reichstag* and came to be called the *Maigesetze* (May Laws). Ecclesiastical punishments were prohibited save in purely spiritual matters. In areas of religious law, appeal was permitted to the state, and from the state's decision there would be no further ecclesiastical appeal.

All seminarians, both Catholic and Protestant, had to study at state-controlled high schools and universities, where they had to pass an examination in German culture, including history, philosophy, and literature. Once ordained, all priests and clergy faced state approval before they could be appointed to any positions. If the Church installed an unapproved priest or bishop, the offending cleric was removed and charged with a civil infraction.

Once the basic framework was in place through the May Laws of 1873, a new round of even tighter restrictions was launched. In 1874, the government decreed bishops who were deposed by the state could be replaced only by a prelate acceptable to the state. Appointments of pastors over parishes were no longer the right of local bishops but were given to the parishioners or local government officials. In 1875, all priests were stripped of any stipends or endowments granted by the government. That same year, all religious orders and communities in the Empire were outlawed except for those engaged directly in nursing or hospital care. Marriage was decreed a mandatory civil ceremony and taken completely out of ecclesiastical hands. These acts climaxed on 20 June 1875, when all Catholic Church property was confiscated. By 1875, over 200 Catholic priests had been arrested, along with over 130 newspaper editors. Five bishops in Prussia had been forcibly deposed, and nearly 1,000 parishes had been stripped of their priests.

The May Laws were felt most harshly in German-occupied Poland (the so-called *Provinz Posen*) where the *Kulturkampf* went hand in hand with anti-Polish and anti-Slavic prejudices. As the Catholic Church was the primary defender of Polish rights and culture, Catholic leaders were singled out. The seminaries in Poznari and Gniezno were shut down, and the monasteries were ordered to close. When Polish priests and bishops resisted the measures, German police arrested and imprisoned 185 priests and bishops, including the primate of Poland, Archbishop Mieczyslaw Leddchowski. Even when, at last, the German government released the priests and bishops, most were sent immediately into exile. And, when the *Kulturkampf* was eventually eased in most of the German Empire, it continued largely unabated in Poland for many more years, a grim harbinger of the anti-Catholic and anti-Polish terror that descended on the Poles under the Nazis.

On 21 November 1873, Pope Pius IX issued the encyclical *Etsi Multa* on the persecution of the Church in Italy, Germany, and Switzerland. He wrote of Germany: "No wonder, then, that the former religious tranquility has been gravely disturbed in that Empire by this kind of law and other plans and actions of the Prussian government most hostile to the Church. But who would wish to falsely cast the blame of this disturbance on the Catholics of the German Empire!" (*EM 15*).

On 5 February 1875, Pio Nono (Pius IX) wrote again, this time addressing Germany exclusively in a new encyclical, *Quod Nunquam*. He declared that the May Laws were invalid, "insofar as they totally oppose the divine order of the Church" (*QN 5*). In harsh reply, the German state proceeded to arrest more priests, nuns, laypeople, bishops, and archbishops.

The Catholic bishops of Prussia, meanwhile, issued a pastoral letter in May 1873 in which they called on the faithful to resist the new laws and informed the Prussian government that they would not cooperate. Minister Falk grew irate at the obdurate stubbornness of Prussian bishops and their priests. He imposed steep fines and then punitively collected them from parishes to the outrage of the parishioners. When this did not budge the priests and laypeople, arrests began anew.

German Catholics had already recognized the need to resist anti-Catholic political moves by forming popular associations, called *Vereinswesen*. By 1870, a greater sense of cohesion was needed, and German Catholic associations formed a new national political party, the *Zentrum* (or

Center) Party. Its goals were to preserve Catholic rights as promised and to defend the practice of the Catholic faith and Catholic education. The party also spoke for the rights of minorities in the German Empire, including the Poles and the Jews. The party took its name from the fact that its members sat in the *Reichstag* between the Liberals and the Conservatives.

The leader of the *Zentrum* from 1874, and one of the great forgotten heroes of German Catholic history, was a Hanoverian by the name of Ludwig Windthorst. Windthorst had already proven himself an able opponent to von Bismarck in the Prussian *Landtag*, but as leader of the *Zentrum*, he emerged as the Iron Chancellor's primary legislative nemesis.

Like Napoléon before him, von Bismarck found that crushing the Catholic Church was far more difficult than he had initially anticipated. With each new piece of legislation and every new outrage and arrest, the levels of Catholic anger grew. But Catholics did not riot in the streets or plot violent revolution. Windthorst called repeatedly for a patient and moderate reply to the government's actions lest the Catholic cause be damaged by violence. The German bishops adopted a similar approach. Catholics instead celebrated more fervently the Catholic faith, supported their priests and bishops, and organized politically. Parish councils declined to elect new pastors or accept parish administrators. Parishioners used their own money to buy back Church property or the priests' possessions sold off by the government. Exiled or imprisoned bishops used underground networks to stay in touch with their faithful and continued to run their dioceses. In the elections of 1873, the Center Party nearly doubled its membership in the Prussian *Landtag* and jumped to 91 members in the *Reichstag*. In the 1874 elections, the *Zentrum* doubled its membership in the *Reichstag*.

By 1878, von Bismarck accepted that the *Kulturkampf* had failed. The Iron Chancellor realized as well that the circumstances for the German Empire had also changed. No longer worried about Austrian influence in Germany, von Bismarck determined closer relations with the Catholic Austrian Empire were essential as a counterweight to Imperial Russia. To pave the way for diplomacy with Austria, an improved understanding with the Church was needed. Catholic support in the *Reichstag* was also becoming more crucial as the inevitable rupture with the liberals took place over their Socialist agenda. The Conservatives likewise had grown disenchanted with the anti-Christian tenor of the legislation of the liberal Minister Falk.

With the passing of Pope Pius IX in February 1878, von Bismarck was presented with an off-ramp from his hardline position. The Chancellor sought reconciliation with the new pontiff, Pope Leo XIII, but he did so slowly and at times grudgingly. In 1879, he sacked the hated Minister Falk, and in 1882, von Bismarck allowed Prussia to establish an embassy to the Holy See. The Chancellor reached out even to his great enemy Windthorst, whom he invited to receptions at the von Bismarck estate.

In 1882, the Conservatives reclaimed power in the *Reichstag* and declared no interest in perpetuating a liberal policy against the Church. Years of negotiations followed, but in 1886 and 1887 the May Laws were modified so significantly that the *Kulturkampf* could be considered dead. In the succeeding years, all remaining laws were lifted. Still, the infamous *Kanzelparagraf* remained in effect until 1953.

Von Bismarck's own titanic career ended pathetically with the accession of Kaiser Wilhelm II in 1888 upon the deaths of his grandfather, Wilhelm I, and then his father, Frederick III (Frederick William), who had reigned only 99 days because of incurable throat cancer. Raised by von Bismarck, Wilhelm II was determined from the first to be a true ruler, unlike his grandfather, who had left the government in the hands of the Chancellor. Wilhelm II opposed von Bismarck's conservative foreign policy, and the Chancellor refused to embrace Wilhelm's desired social reform. The two suffered a final rupture in 1890, and the seventy-five-year-old von Bismarck resigned at the insistence of his onetime pupil.

The actors in these culture wars in Prussia under Chancellor Otto von Bismarck saw religion and politics as inextricably and usefully entwined. The Awakened Protestants helped to crush the liberal revolution of 1848 in Prussia. In mobilizing to do so, the Awakened helped to transform the justification for political Conservatism from relying on estate-based identities to emphasizing the benefits to each individual in a Burkean world of gradual renovations in tradition. Moreover, in their efforts, the Awakened introduced means of semi-formal political parties and widely circulated newspapers that established an additional dimension of modernization. Ironically, by contributing to a different understanding of conservative values and to a new means to mobilize support, the Awakened more effectively undermined the older model of Conservatism and the prerevolutionary order than the liberal revolutionaries of 1848. They used the ideological, rhetorical, and organizational weapons of their perceived liberal enemies, not fully understanding the weapons were double-edged. These were the times when the "theoretical foundations of Prussian conservativism were laid" before von Bismarck (Beck 2001, 87). Prussian Conservatives in this period did not so much restore old ways of life as create a convincing *memory* of tradition (Levinger 2000; see also Ellis 2017, 4).

The Protestant Awakening in Prussia was not so much about theology as political power. Hence, any debate over theological orthodoxy versus heterodoxy that may have existed early in the movement, was quickly drowned out by debates over the primacy of traditional natural law over the chaos and anarchy of the "dictatorship of the proletariat." This religious revival in nineteenth-century Germany laid the foundation to the dichotomous character (Liberalism versus traditionalism) of twentieth-century German culture that set the stage for the tragic conflict between Communism and National Socialism.

CHAPTER 5

THE OCCULT

BRITISH HISTORIAN AND PROFESSOR OF WESTERN ESOTERICISM Nicholas Goodrick-Clarke was considered one of the world's foremost experts on esoteric traditions. His University of Oxford doctoral dissertation was the basis for his most celebrated work, *The Occult Roots of Nazism: The Ariosophists of Austria and Germany, 1890–1935*. This book has been continually in print since its first publication in 1985 (Wellingborough, UK: The Aquarian Press), and has been translated into twelve languages. Much of the following information on the occult in the Nazi movement is taken from Dr. Goodrick-Clarke's 1985 masterpiece.

"Occult" is generally associated with secret knowledge and practices dealing with the supernatural or "psychic" phenomena, the study of a deeper spiritual reality that extends beyond pure reason and the physical sciences, often for the purpose of obtaining personal power. Occultism has its basis in a religious way of thinking, the roots of which stretch back into antiquity, and which may be described as the Western esoteric tradition. From its beginning, occultism spontaneously filled the void as traditional understanding of the natural, the supernatural, and their relationship was adulterated, forsaken, or totally lost in society. Its more recent principal ingredients have been identified as Gnosticism (see endnote 5 under *Epimythium*, *infra*), the Hermetic treatises on alchemy and magic, Neoplatonism,* and the Cabbala, all originating in the eastern Mediterranean

---

* Neoplatonism is a strand of Platonic philosophy that emerged in *AD* third century against the background of Hellenistic philosophy and religion. For much of the history of Platonism, it was commonly accepted that the doctrines of the Neoplatonists were essentially the same as those of Plato. Although it is unclear precisely when scholars began to disassociate the philosophy of the historical Plato from the philosophy of his Neoplatonic interpreters, they had clearly begun to do so at least as early as the first decade of the nineteenth century. Neoplatonism is a philosophical movement based on the teachings of Plotinus (c. *AD* 204/5–271), an Egyptian. Crucial to Neoplatonism was the doctrine of emanation. At the center of

area during the first few centuries CE. Gnosticism properly refers to the beliefs of certain heretical sects among the early Christians that claimed to possess *gnosis*, or special esoteric knowledge of spiritual matters. Although their various doctrines differed in many respects, two common Gnostic themes exist: first, an oriental (Persian) dualism, according to which the two realms of Good and Evil, Light and Darkness, order and chaos are viewed as independent battling principles; and second, the conviction that this material world is utterly evil, so that man can be saved only by attaining the gnosis of the higher realm. The Gnostic sects disappeared in the fourth century, but their ideas inspired the dualistic Manichaean religion of the second century and also the *Hermetica*. These Greek texts were composed in Egypt between *AD* third and fifth centuries and developed a synthesis of Gnostic ideas, Neo-Platonism, and cabbalistic theosophy. Since these mystical doctrines arose against a background of cultural and social change, a correlation has been noted between the proliferation of the sects and the breakdown of the stable agricultural order of the late Roman Empire. When the basic assumptions of the medieval world were shaken by new modes of enquiry and geographical discoveries in the fifteenth century, Gnostic and Hermetic ideas enjoyed a brief revival. Prominent humanists and scholar magicians edited the old classical texts during the Renaissance and thus created a modern corpus of occult speculation. But after the triumph of empiricism in the seventeenth-century scientific revolution, such ideas became the preserve of only a few antiquarians and mystics. By the eighteenth century, these unorthodox religious and philosophical concerns were well defined as "occult," inasmuch as they lay on the outermost fringe of accepted forms of knowledge and discourse. However, a reaction to the rationalist Enlightenment, taking the form of a quickening romantic temper, an interest in the Middle Ages and a desire for mystery, encouraged a revival of occultism in Europe from about 1770.

---

all reality was the One. Outside the One were various levels that had emanated from the One but were inferior to it to the extent that they were removed from the One and lacked its attributes. The purpose of philosophy was to lead individuals back through the various levels until they had reunited themselves with the One that was the source of all being. For Neoplatonists, evil as such did not exist; there was merely an absence of good as an individual fell away from the One. Christian thinkers tried to square Neoplatonism with Christianity, although the Neoplatonic universe lacked Satan and the concept of emanation was rather different from the Jewish and Christian account of God's conscious creation of the world.

Germany boasted several renowned scholar magicians in the Renaissance, and a number of secret societies devoted to Rosicrucianism, theosophy, and alchemy also flourished there from the seventeenth to the nineteenth centuries. However, the impetus for the neo-Romantic occult revival of the nineteenth century did not arise in Germany. It is attributable rather to the reaction against the reign of materialist, rationalist, and positivist ideas in the utilitarian and industrial cultures of America and England. The modern German occult revival owes its inception to the popularity of theosophy in the Anglo-Saxon world during the 1880s. Here, theosophy refers to the international sectarian movement deriving from the activities and writings of the Russian adventuress and occultist, Helena Petrovna Blavatsky (1831–1891). Her colorful life and travels in the 1850s and 1860s, her clairvoyant powers and penchant for supernatural phenomena, her interest in American spiritualism during the 1870s, followed by her foundation of the Theosophical Society at New York in 1875 and the subsequent removal of its operations to India between 1879 and 1885, have all been fully documented in several biographies.

How can one explain the enthusiastic reception of Blavatsky's ideas by significant numbers of Europeans and Americans from the 1880s onwards? Theosophy offered an appealing mixture of ancient religious ideas and new concepts borrowed from the Darwinian theory of evolution and modern science. This syncretic faith thus possessed the power to comfort certain individuals whose traditional outlook had been upset by the discrediting of orthodox religion, by the very rationalizing and de-mystifying progress of science, and by the culturally dislocative impact of rapid social and economic change in the late nineteenth century. George L. Mosse has noted that theosophy typified the wave of anti-positivism sweeping Europe at the end of the century and observed that its *outré* notions made a deeper impression in Germany than in other European countries. (Goodrick-Clarke 2004, 22.)

Although a foreign hybrid combining Romantic Egyptian revivalism, American spiritualism and Hindu beliefs, theosophy enjoyed a considerable vogue in Germany and Austria. Its advent is best understood within a wider neo-Romantic protest movement in Wilhelmine Germany known as *Lebensreform* (life reform). This movement represented a middle-class attempt to palliate the ills of modern life, deriving from the growth of the cities and industry. A variety of alternative lifestyles—including herbal and natural medicine, vegetarianism, nudism, and self-sufficient rural communes—were embraced by small groups of individuals who hoped to restore themselves to a natural existence. The political atmosphere of the movement was apparently liberal with its interest in land reform, but there were many overlaps with the *völkisch* movement. Marxian critics have even interpreted it as mere *bourgeois* escapism from the consequences of Capitalism. Theosophy was appropriate to the mood of *Lebensreform* and provided a philosophical rationale for some of its groups. (Goodrick-Clarke 2004, 22.)

Occult science tended to stress humanity's intimate and meaningful relationship with the cosmos in terms of "revealed" correspondences between the microcosm and macrocosm and strove to counter materialist science, with its emphasis upon tangible and measurable phenomena and its neglect of invisible qualities respecting the spirit and the emotions. These new "metaphysical" sciences gave individuals a holistic view of themselves and the world in which they lived. This view conferred both a sense of participation in a total meaningful order and, through divination, a means of planning one's affairs in accordance with this order. Occultism had flourished coincident with the decline of the Roman Empire and once again at the waning of the Middle Ages. It exercised a renewed appeal to those who found the world out of joint due to rapid social and ideological changes at the end of the nineteenth century. Certain individuals, whose sentiments and education inclined them towards an idealistic and romantic perspective, were drawn to the modern occult revival in order to find that sense of order, which had been shaken by the dissolution of former conventions and beliefs.

Ariosophy originated in Vienna in response to the problems of German nationality and metropolitanism and is a particular kind of theosophy which the Ariosophists adapted to their *völkisch* ideas. Whereas the earlier Austrian theosophical movement had been defined by the mystical Christianity and personal Gnosticism of cultivated individuals, its later manifestation in Vienna corresponded to a disenchantment with Catholicism coupled with the popularization of mythology, folklore, and comparative religion. Theosophy in Vienna after 1900 appears to be a quasi-intellectual sectarian religious doctrine of German importation, current among persons wavering in their religious orthodoxy but who were inclined to a religious perspective. The attraction of theosophy for Guido von List, Jörg Lanz von Liebenfels, and their supporters consisted in its eclecticism with respect to exotic religion, mythology, and esoteric lore, which provided a universal and non-Christian perspective upon the cosmos and the origins of mankind, against which the sources of Teutonic belief, customs, and identity, which were germane to *völkisch* speculation, could be located. Given the antipathy towards Catholicism among *völkisch* Nationalists and pan-Germans in Austria at the turn of the century, theosophy commended itself as a scheme of religious beliefs which ignored Christianity in favor of a *mélange* of mythical traditions and pseudo-scientific hypotheses consonant with contemporary anthropology, etymology, and the history of ancient cultures. Furthermore, the very structure of theosophical thought lent itself to *völkisch* adoption. The implicit elitism of the hidden mahatmas with superhuman wisdom was in tune with the longing for a hierarchical social order based on the racial mystique of the *Volk*. The notion of an occult gnosis in theosophy, notably its obscuration due to the superimposition of alien (Christian) beliefs, and its revival by the chosen few, also accorded with the attempt to ascribe a long pedigree to *völkisch* Nationalism, especially in view of its really recent origins. In the context of the growth of German Nationalism in Austria since 1866, we can see how theosophy, otherwise only tenuously related to *völkisch* thought by notions of race and racial development, could lend both a religious mystique and a universal rationale to the political attitudes of a small minority. Given this occult subculture in Vienna, one can better appreciate the local background of the movements around Guido von List and Jörg Lanz von Liebenfels, whose racist writings after 1906 owed so much to the modern occult revival in Central Europe.

The Ariosophists, initially active in Vienna before the First World War, combined German *völkisch* Nationalism and racism with occult notions borrowed from the theosophy of Helena Petrovna Blavatsky, in order to prophesy and vindicate a coming era of German world rule. Their writings described a prehistoric golden age when wise gnostic priesthoods had expounded occult-racist doctrines and ruled over a superior and racially pure society. They claimed that an evil conspiracy of anti-German interests (variously identified as the non-Aryan races, the Jews, or even the early Church) had sought to ruin this ideal Germanic world by emancipating the non-German inferiors in the name of a spurious egalitarianism. The resulting racial confusion was said to have heralded the historical world with its wars. Economic hardship, political uncertainty, and the frustration of German world power. In order to counter this modern world, the Ariosophists founded secret religious orders dedicated to the revival of the lost esoteric knowledge and racial virtue of the ancient Germans, and the corresponding creation of a new pan-German empire. The Ariosophists were cultural pessimists. An obvious link exists between their fantasies and the grievances of German Nationalists in the Habsburg Empire of Austro-Hungary towards the end of the nineteenth century. Such factors as Catholicism, the rapid urban and industrial changes in society, the conflict of Slav and German interests in a multinational state, the rise of the Austrian Pan-German movement under Georg von Schönerer, and the vogue of Social Darwinism and its racist precepts were also crucial influences upon their thinking. The role and importance of occultism in their doctrines is principally explicable as a sacred form of legitimation for their profound reaction to the present and their extreme political attitudes. The fantasies of the Ariosophists concerned elitism and purity, a sense of mission in the face of conspiracies, and millenarian visions of a felicitous national future. An ideological preoccupation with the *Volk* arose for two reasons: firstly, this cultural orientation was the result of the delayed political unification of Germany; secondly, it was closely related to a widespread romantic reaction to modernity. The Nazi leaders themselves were mostly men of limited education who seized hold of these ideas and prejudices which came most naturally to them, as to others. As romantic reactionaries and millenarians, the Ariosophists stood on the margin of practical politics, but their ideas and symbols filtered through to several anti-Semitic and Nationalist groups in late Wilhelmine Germany, from which the early Nazi Party emerged in Munich after the First World War.

Unlike generic anti-Semitism that existed throughout Europe since the first century of the Common Era Jewish Diaspora, Nazi anti-Semitism was founded on the occult concept of German "*blut und boden*" (blood and soil) drawn from a mystical relationship between man and nature (the peasant and the "Eternal Forest") and the notion of "the organic community" (*Volksgemeinschaft*). In the post-Versailles era, Nazi ideology opportunistically managed to resurrect, manipulate, and exploit this latent Romantic "allegory of [German] history and life," which evoked 2,000 years of Germanic (Nordic) civilization, in order to create national solidarity and the need for space in which to live and grow (*Lebensraum*). But in order to do so, National Socialism needed a scapegoat to blame for the humiliation of Versailles and its paralyzing war debts.

The Nazis opportunistically adapted ancient German and Nordic mythology to the *Zeitgeist* in postwar Germany by integrating the mythology with General Erich Ludendorff's "stab-in-the-back legend" (see further discussion on this topic later) and the growing public awareness of *The Protocols of the Elders of Zion*, an Imperial Russian fabricated text imported by Baltic German and White Russian émigrés and distributed throughout Germany in the 1920s (see further discussion on this topic later). Nazi ideology propagated the belief that the crooked Jew adulterated Aryan blood and community—a theory for which philosopher Eugen Dühring, and composer Richard Wagner and his son-in-law political philosopher Houston Stewart Chamberlain were particularly responsible. Hitler justified the persecution of the Jews under the generalization and pretense that Jews are the "great Master in Lying" (economic and political parasites, scoundrels, and crooks) and the progenitors of and driving force behind Marxism (Bolshevism)—a creed advocating "dictatorship of the proletariat" that Hitler viewed as antithetical to natural law. Historians have assumed that the combination of pervasive anti-Semitism in Bavaria and the prominent involvement of Jews in the Russian Revolution of 1917 and the Munich revolutions of November 1918 and April 1919 fully explain the widespread acceptance of the Jewish-Communist conspiracy theory in Munich and its centrality to Nazi ideology. According to English historian and author Ian Kershaw, Hitler, in his "ferocious attacks on the Jews" beginning in the second half of 1919, was "doing no more than reflect sentiments which were widespread at the time among the people of Munich" (Kershaw 1998, 124–5). Canadian historian and author Robert Ventresca likewise opined that because of Munich's experience with Jewish radical political figures after the First World War, "it was a logical step to view Bolsheviks and Jews as indistinguishable" (Ventresca 2013, 54–5). Hitler's (and a significant portion of European's) hypocrisy and projection of his own irrationality on the Jews was not clearly understood until decades after the war and continues to be a topic of debate.

The Thule Society, from which the Nazi Party originated, was one of the Ariosophic groups of the 1920s. *Thule-Gesellschaft* had initially been the name of the Munich lodge of the *Germanenorden*. It took its name from an alleged lost continent Thule, which was assumed to be the mythical homeland from which the Aryan race had originated. Atlantis at least, and most likely also Hyperborea, were taken to be identical with Thule (Strohm 1997, 57). The superiority of Aryans over all other races was a key concept and the members of various *Germanenorden* lodges saw themselves (as Teutons or Germanic peoples) as the "purest" branch of the Aryan race.

Some of von Liebenfels's proposals for racial purification anticipate the Nazis. The sterilization of those deemed to be genetically "unfit" was in fact implemented under the Nazi eugenics policies, but its basis lay in the theories of scientific racial hygienists.

Following Goodrick-Clarke's caution in assessing the relation between von Liebenfels and Nazi sterilization programs (Goodrick-Clarke 1985, preface), Adolf Hitler cannot be considered a pupil of von Liebenfels, as von Liebenfels himself had claimed (Goodrick-Clarke 1985, 192). However, it has been suggested with some evidential basis that the young Hitler did read and collect von Liebenfels's *Ostara* magazine while living in Vienna:

> In view of the similarity of their ideas relating to the glorification and preservation of the endangered Aryan race, the suppression and ultimate extermination of the non-Aryans, and the establishment of a fabulous Aryan-German millennial empire, the link between the two men looks highly probable (Goodrick-Clarke 1985, 194).

Nevertheless: "It also remains a fact that Hitler never mentioned the name of von Liebenfels in any recorded conversation, speech, or document. If Hitler had been importantly influenced by [von Liebenfels], he cannot be said to have ever acknowledged this debt" (Goodrick-Clarke 1985, 198).

As a National Socialist, Hitler's primary domestic priority was to unite the despondent and directionless German people in a "community of struggle" (*Kampfgemeinschaft*), to arm Germany mentally and materially for reconstruction and preparation for a war to revenge Versailles and to rightfully secure Germany's destiny and "living space" (*Lebensraum*)—a concept Hitler adopted from his friend Karl Haushofer, professor of geopolitics at the *Institut für Geopolitik* of the University of Munich, who was introduced to Hitler by his cellmate at Landsberg Prison and Haushofer's former student, Rudolf Heß. *Lebensraum* was a modified colonial imperialism whose justification, even at the cost of other nations' existence, was based on the belief that conquest was a biological necessity for a state's growth. Germany had a high population density, but the old colonial powers had a much lower density, a virtual mandate for German expansion into resource-rich areas such as Alsace-Lorraine (France), North European Lowlands, Poland, the Baltics, Russia, northern Italy, and all German-speaking lands such as Austria, Switzerland, and Lichtenstein. Hitler planned to accomplish these goals by eliminating all those elements who, he believed, threatened to undermine Greater Germany's unity, morale, and strength—liberals, Marxists, "reactionaries," "asocials," the eugenically "unfit," foreigners, and, above all, the Jews; once accomplished, domestic conflict in the Third *Reich* would no longer exist under the National Socialist vision.

CHAPTER 6

The (R)Evolution of Communism, Liberation Theology, the Unification of Germany, and the German Revolution of 1918–1919

It is not religion but revolution that is the opiate of the people.

— SIMONE WEIL, 1942

Revolutions are the locomotives of history.

— KARL MARX, 1895
The Class Struggles in France, 1848–1850

Let the ruling classes tremble at a Communist revolution. The proletarians have nothing to lose but their chains. They have a world to win. Workingmen of all countries, unite!

— KARL MARX, 1848
Manifest der Kommunistischen Partei

I don't care what becomes of Russia. To hell with it. All this is only the road to a World Revolution.

— VLADIMÍR ILYICH ULYANOV (LENIN), 1917

Fascism was the shadow or ugly child of Communism. . . . As Fascism sprang from Communism, so Nazism developed from Fascism. Thus were set on foot all these kindred movements which were soon destined to plunge the world into even more hideous strife, which none can say has ended with their destruction.

— SIR WINSTON CHURCHILL, 1948
The Second World War, Volume 1: The Gathering Storm

> *On the other hand, we do want, and want very much, to make men treat Christianity as a means; preferably, of course, as a means to their own advancement, but, failing that, as a means to anything—even to social justice. The thing to do is to get a man at first to value social justice as a thing which the Enemy* [God] *demands, and then work him on to the stage at which he values Christianity because it may produce social justice. For the Enemy will not be used as a convenience.*
>
> — Screwtape to his nephew Wormwood, *The Screwtape Letters*, C. S. LEWIS, 1942

INTRODUCTION

THE GERMAN REVOLUTION (29 OCTOBER 1918–11 AUGUST 1919) WAS the penultimate result of the movement of consequential world political and cultural revolutions, which accelerated and became more intimately related to one another in 1215 with the signing of the *Magna Carta Libertatum*—an unsuccessful attempt to bring peace between royalist and rebel factions in England that promised the protection of church rights, the rights of free men and serfs, protection from illegal imprisonment, access to swift justice, and, most importantly, limitations on taxation and other feudal payments to the Crown requiring baronial consent. As of this writing, the last consequential revolution in modern times has been the collapse of Marxism and state Communism in 1989. In 1980, 1.5 billion people, out of a global population of about 4.4 billion, lived in one of the world's seventeen Communist countries. Today, there are still about 1.5 billion living under Communism in the remaining five holdouts—China, North Korea, Vietnam, Laos, and Cuba—but the world's population is now 7.4 billion. Of the five remaining Communist countries, only North Korea's version of Communism continues to be Marxist, and theirs too is quickly changing. The rest have incorporated Socialist principles into their model of Communism and can no longer be considered pure Marxist. Thus, it is accurate to conclude that Marxism and official state Communism, which began as a liberation movement and strove to engulf the globe in the twentieth century, has, for all intents and purposes, collapsed and become a victim of its own liberation movement. However, human societies undergo continual revolutions as they exist in a perpetual state of ideological struggle (see *inter alia*, Sowell: *A Conflict of Visions: The Ideological Origins of Political Struggles*). Although the Nazi movement was the product of a 150-year-long series of liberal philosophic, theological, political, industrial, and sociological cultural developments, defeat in the First World War, the Versailles Treaty,[1] economic collapse, an explosion of Marxism, and the German Revolution exerted the most proximate and precipitating influence on the Nazi movement.

Liberalism and Marxism can be safely attributed as *the* primary catalysts of German National Socialism. Counterintuitively, in his memoirs, German-Austrian Adolf Eichmann repeatedly asserted: "My political sentiments inclined toward the Left and emphasized the Socialist aspect every bit as much as Nationalist ones." In the days when the Nazi movement was still doing battle in the streets, Eichmann added, he and his comrades had viewed Nazism and Communism as "quasi-siblings" (Aly 2006, 16–17; see also Aly 2003, 141–51). In his memoirs written while in Israeli custody in 1961–1962, Eichmann recollected his and the sympathies of his fellow Austrian *SS* comrades . . .

> I still remember the feeling that filled me when I heard of the preparations for the war against the Soviets. Even in the SS there were two *personal* orientations that were never outwardly manifested. One that was politically left-wing and another attitude tending to the extreme right. My personal political feelings lay towards the left, at least emphasising the socialistic aspect as much as the nationalistic.
>
> Our opinion at the time was that National Socialism and the Communism of the Soviet Republic were sort of "siblings." And it may also be that this attitude was peculiar especially to an Austrian SS member. For his enemies at that time were not Social Democracy and Communism; these were combated by the Austrian aristocracy as much as he himself was; the former at that time occupied the leading positions in the "Home Guards" [*Heimwehr*] and their challenge was to the National Socialists, Social Democrats and Communists equally.
>
> Indeed, there were times when the followers of these two orientations were united through party truce and mutual help and support in the battle against their chief

> opponent [Austrian aristocracy]. In no way however did they betray each other and in the worst case be "prepared for battle," as one used to say. It may be that this attitude of a left-wing tendency began at this time. However it may have been, it was in any case present, and 22 June 1941 saw us sullen and discontented, but we obeyed as the oath ordered us to. (Eichmann 2015, 74–5.)

Some scholars date the concept of a liberal, classless, egalitarian society back to ancient Greece. At times in some Roman provinces, various small Communist communities existed, generally under the heterodox interpretation of Jewish and Christian Scripture that viewed the Torah as communal law or Jesus's and the Apostles' teachings as a social gospel (a legalistic form of social justice).[2] One example of such a Jewish community was the Essenes in Roman Judaea from second century BC to *AD* first century. In condemning the growing wealth of those in the Church, the Bishop of Milan Aurelius Ambrosius (ca. 340–397), better known as Ambrose, stated: "What you give to the poor man is not yours but his. For what was given for the common use, you alone usurp. The earth is all men's and not the property of the rich." Other examples include some monastic communities and religious orders of the medieval Christian church who shared their land and other property. The fifth-century Zoroastrian priest and religious activist Mazdak instituted communal possessions and social welfare programs in Persia. His has been seen as a proto-Socialist movement, which can be described as "Communistic" for challenging the enormous privileges of the noble class and the clergy, for criticizing the institution of private property, and for striving to create an egalitarian society. Communist thought has also been traced back to the works of the sixteenth-century English writer Sir Thomas More. In his treatise *Utopia* (1516), More portrayed a society based on common ownership of property, whose benevolent rulers administered it through the application of reason. In the seventeenth century, Communist thought surfaced again in England, where a Puritan religious group known as the "Diggers" advocated the abolition of private ownership of land. In his 1895 *Cromwell and Communism*, Eduard Bernstein (see *infra*) argued that several groups during the English Civil War (1642–1651)—not to be confused with the English Revolution of 1688—especially the Diggers, espoused clear Communistic, agrarian ideals.

Criticism of the idea of private property continued into the Age of Reason (the Enlightenment) through the eighteenth century by such thinkers as Jean-Jacques Rousseau (1712–1778) in France— "you are undone if you once forget that the fruits of the earth belong to us all, and the earth itself to nobody" (*Discours sur l'origine et les fondements de l'inégalité parmi les hommes*, 1755 [*Discourse on the Origin and Foundations of Inequality Among Men*]). John Locke (1632–1704) was the "father of modern Liberalism" and Jean-Jacques Rousseau was its greatest evangelist. Although Locke and Rousseau disagreed over Locke's labor theory on property entitlement, the two shared many common liberal viewpoints such as man's natural morality and the need for a government that "nurtures" man's natural morality. In the tradeoff between individual rights and the greater collective good, both Locke and Rousseau favored the greater good.

Not long after the upheaval of the 1789 French Revolution, Communism finally emerged as a political doctrine. The *Declaration of the Rights of Man and of the Citizen*, first codified in 1789 in France by the Marque de Lafayette, Thomas Jefferson, and Honoré Mirabeau, is a foundational document of both Liberalism and human rights. The intellectual "progress" of the Enlightenment, which questioned old traditions about societies and governments, eventually coalesced into powerful revolutionary movements that toppled what the French called the *ancien régime*, the belief in divinely instituted absolute monarchy and established religion, especially in Europe, Latin America, and North America. A new world order was struggling to be born, not only in France but throughout western Europe and to a lesser degree in the Americas as well. The greatest challenge to the old order in Europe came primarily from the rise of the proletarian class and from the introduction of the factory system during the Industrial Revolution, which was destined to break down large segments of the middle class and start the movement of workers from the poor countryside into the cities.* There is abundant statistical evidence that the

---

* The Industrial Revolution was the transition to new manufacturing processes in the period from about 1760 to sometime between 1820 and 1840. This transition included going from hand production methods to machines, new chemical manufacturing and iron production processes, the increasing use of steam power, the development of machine tools and the rise of the factory system. The Industrial Revolution began in Great Britain, and many of the technological innovations were of British origin. The precipitating developments to the Industrial Revolution occurred between 1712 and 1774 and included: Newcomen's steam engine (1712); Lombe's Mill (1719); Kay's Flying Shuttle (1733); Hargreaves' Spinning Jenny

economic revolution was on the march and that the ancient bonds which had held medieval society together were beginning to break. Moreover, labor was becoming more highly specialized and therefore more monotonous, and skilled workers (artisans) already were being forced to yield their highly respected standing in the guilds to become mere cogs of a factory system.

In the late eighteenth century, these developments still were in their earliest stages, and the transformation in Germany lagged far behind England and France in this respect; but a century later after the unification of Germany in 1871, the march of "big industry" exploded along the Rhine, in Saxony, and in Silesia, and theories of *laissez-faire* economics and modern Capitalism were beginning to replace the medieval concepts which had held the feudal and guild systems together in the German states (Wittke 1950, 12).

Early in the German industrial transformation, Aachen (Rhineland Prussia) was the scene of workers' riots against the introduction of laborsaving machines in the early 1830's. Solingen and Cologne (Rhineland Prussia) experienced serious labor troubles. The number of journeymen increased, but the number of masters remained stationary. Tailors complained about "ready-made" suits and consequent unemployment; workers in Bonn (Rhineland Prussia) protested the use of steam engines; and labor demonstrations in Breslau (Silesia Prussia) indicated the decline of the crafts and the rise of the class struggle. The year 1844 brought the tragic insurrection of Silesian weavers. Goaded by the decline in demand for their products, and by low wages and exploitation under a "truck system" which forced them to accept inadequate food in lieu of wages, the starving and desperate workers attacked the factories and mills of their employers, only to have their demonstrations ruthlessly suppressed by the military. Long before Gerhart Hauptmann thought of making their tragedy the subject of one of his most stirring dramas (*Die Weber* [*The Weavers*] 1892), the

---

(1764); Arkwright's water frame (1768); Watt's "atmospheric" steam engine (1769); and Crompton's spinning mule (1774). Textiles were the dominant industry of the Industrial Revolution in terms of employment, value of output, and capital invested. The textile industry was the first to use these modern production methods. The Industrial Revolution marks a major turning point in history; almost every aspect of daily life was influenced in some way. In particular, average income and population began to exhibit unprecedented, sustained growth. Some economists say that the major impact of the Industrial Revolution was that the standard of living for the general population began to increase consistently for the first time in history. These events led to the creation of the proletarian working middle class.

sufferings of the Silesian weavers figured in the novels of the 1840's and in the poems of Heinrich Heine (1797–1856) and Ferdinand Freiligrath (1810–1876). The year 1844 also produced an epidemic of strikes in the calico factories of Berlin (Brandenburg Prussia), among the railway workers of Westphalia (Prussia), and in Hamburg (free state) and Saxony (kingdom). In 1843, a "society for the education of the children of the helpless proletariat" was organized in Breslau, and workers' organizations of several kinds were formed in leading cities of the states of the German Confederation (1815–1866; a loose association of 39 independent German states, Principalities, and Duchies), in vain efforts to solve the labor problem. Hence, by the mid-nineteenth century the labor movement was born in Germany (Bernstein 1913, 60–71; see also Quarck 1924, 2 and Wendel 1921, *passim*).

In the early nineteenth century, various social reformers founded communities based on common ownership. However, unlike many previous Communist communities, they replaced the religious emphasis with a rationalistic and philanthropic basis. Notable among them were Englishmen Robert Owen (1771–1858), who founded New Harmony in Indiana (1825), as well as Charles Fourier (1772–1837), whose followers organized other settlements in the United States such as Brook Farm (1841–1847).

In its modern form, Communism grew out of the Socialist movement in nineteenth-century Europe born after the decade-long 1789 French Revolution. As the Industrial Revolution (1760–1840) advanced, a generation of Socialist critics emerged in Europe, who blamed Capitalism for the misery of the proletariat—a new class of urban factory workers who labored under often-hazardous conditions. As the elders among these critics vanished in history, two up and coming Socialist revolutionaries who would eventually become the icons of Communism were German political philosopher Karl Marx (1818–1883) and his German associate Friedrich Engels (1820–1895). In February 1848, Marx and Engels offered a refined political definition of Communism and popularized the term in their infamous pamphlet *Manifest der Kommunistischen Partei* (*Manifesto of the Communist Party*).

THE FOUNDING FATHERS OF MODERN COMMUNISM

> *Society must be made to operate in such a way that it eradicates once and for all the desire of a man to become richer, or wiser, or more powerful than others.*[*]
> — FRANÇOIS-NOËL ("GRACCHUS") BABEUF

> *The French Revolution was nothing but a precursor of another revolution, one that will be bigger, more solemn, and which will be the last.*
> — SYLVAIN MARECHAL,
> in his *Manifesto of the Equals*, 1796

> *Out of the tomb of the murdered Monarchy in France, has arisen a vast, tremendous, unformed spectre, in a far more terrific guise than any which ever yet overpowered the imagination and subdued the fortitude of man.*
> — SIR EDMUND BURKE, 1797

THE FIRST UNIFICATION OF GERMANY AS A NATION-STATE OCCURRED under King of Prussia Kaiser Wilhelm I in the form of the *German Empire* (1871–1918) that arose from the short-lived *North German Confederation* (1866–1870; an alliance of 22 German states north of the river Main) under Wilhelm I and his Minister-President Otto von Bismarck (1815–1898)—south German states outside the confederation, namely, Baden, Wuerttemberg, and Bavaria, were tied to Prussia only by military alliances—which arose from the ashes of the much larger *German Confederation* (1815–1866; a loose association of 39 independent German states, Principalities, and Duchies in Central Europe), which itself eventually arose from the ashes of the *Confederation of the Rhine* (formed by Napoléon after his victory at the Battle of Austerlitz in 1806 and lasted until Napoléon's defeat at the Battle of Leipzig in 1813), which in turn was born upon the disintegration of the *Holy Roman Empire* (from Charlemagne in 800 or Otto I in 962 to 1806 when Napoléon dissolved it).

Out of the crucible of Romanticism (late eighteenth to mid-nineteenth centuries) and the French Revolution (1789–1799), modern Communism originated in the mid-nineteenth century in Germany, England,

---

[*] Stated during his defense before the High Court of Vendôme in February 1797.

and France with the radical idea that anarchic Socialism was the only path to social justice for the working class. The following were influential figures and prophets the early modern Communist movement. Among all of these individuals exists a common denominator the reader should recognize.

Joseph Alexandre Victor d'Hupay de Fuveau (1746–1818) – Catholic French writer and philosopher who is best known as the first theoretician of modern Communism. His first book, *Projet de Communauté Philosophe* (*Project for a Philosophical Community*), published in 1777, advocated the idea of living in a sort of commune. This book can be seen as the cornerstone of proto-Communist philosophy as d'Hupay defines this lifestyle as a "commune" and advises to "share all economic and material products between inhabitants of the commune, so that all may benefit from everybody's work." In 1785, just before the French Revolution, he was referred to as a *Communiste* in a book review by novelist and shoe fetishist Rétif de la Bretonne (1734–1806); according to some sources, this was the first time that the word "Communist" was used in print in its modern sense (Grandjonc 1983, 143–8).

François-Noël ("Gracchus") Babeuf (1760–1797) – "The first revolutionary Communist." He was a French political agitator, former Catholic priest, and journalist of the French Revolutionary period. His newspaper *Le Tribun du peuple* (*The Tribune of the People*) was best known for his advocacy for the poor. In Issue Number 40 (24 February 1796) of his paper, Babeuf created an immense sensation, openly praising the authors of the September Massacres (1792)—a wave of killings in Paris and other cities during the French Revolution resulting in the murder of 1,200–1,400 people, including 233 Catholic priests, incarcerated in various prisons—as "deserving well of their country," and declaring that a more complete "Second September" was needed to annihilate the actual government, which consisted of "starvers, bloodsuckers, tyrants, hangmen, rogues and mountebanks." On 11 April 1796, *Le Tribun du peuple* published posters and posted them all over Paris. The opening line on the posters read: "Nature has given to every man the right to the enjoyment of an equal share in all property." Babeuf openly called for a popular revolt against the *Directoire* (1795–1799) under Paul Barras. Babeuf was a leading advocate for Socialism, redistribution of wealth, equal pay for all workers, the "equality of outcome," all under a benevolent dictatorship of himself. He angered the *Directoire* authorities who were clamping down hard on their radical enemies. Despite the efforts of his Jacobin friends to save him, Babeuf was imprisoned in May 1796 and executed by guillotine on 27 May 1797 for his role in the Conspiracy of the Equals—a failed *coup de main* planned for 11 May 1796 joining the Jacobin and Socialist forces to overthrow the *Directoire* and replace it with an egalitarian and proto-Socialist republic, inspired by Jacobin ideals. The plot was a milestone, because Communism, with Babeuf, became a political program rather than an abstract *vue de l'esprit* of use primarily to titillate the habitués of Parisian salons. Although the words "anarchist" and "Communist" were not in wide use in Babeuf's lifetime, they have both been used by later scholars to describe his ideas. Communism during the French Revolution was a flare that illumined the future and had at the time little to do with the actual business of revolutionary politics. But it was a sign of things to come, and conceptually does have a great deal to do with the French Revolution. The roots of Babouvism were emphatically in the Revolution, though its fruits may have been indigestible and its conclusions too bold at the time. Communism was reintroduced into France in 1830 by Italian Utopian Socialist, writer, agitator, freemason, and revolutionary conspirator Philippe Buonarroti (1761–1837), a protégé of Babeuf (Marx 1845). The word "Communism" was first used in English by John Goodwyn Barmby (1820–1881; a British Victorian Utopian Socialist) during his visit to Paris in 1840 when he engaged in a conversation with those he described as the "disciples of Babeuf."

Claude Henri de Rouvroy, comte de Saint-Simon (1760–1825) – a Catholic French political and economic theorist, businessman, and the founder of French Socialism, whose thought played a substantial role in influencing politics, economics, sociology, and the philosophy of science. In the wake of the 1789 French Revolution, Saint-Simon proposed a new and positive reorganization of society, controlled by the chiefs of industry, with scientists in the role of priests. The objective of this society would be to produce things useful to life, and peace would be assured by universal association. Saint-Simon's call for a "science of society" influenced the development of sociology and economics as fields of "scientific" study. Saint-Simon's vision influenced French and European society throughout the nineteenth century. Henri was born in Paris to an impoverished aristocratic family. His grandfather's cousin, the duc de Saint-Simon, had written a famous memoir of the court of Louis XIV. Henri often claimed he was a descendant of Charlemagne. At an early age, Saint-Simon showed a certain disdain for tradition; at thirteen he refused to make his first Communion and was punished by imprisonment at Saint Lazare, from which he escaped. After being educated by private tutors, he entered military service at the age of seventeen. His regiment was among those sent by France to aid the American colonies. He served as captain of artillery at Yorktown in 1781, was later taken prisoner and freed only after the 1783 Treaty of Versailles (Peace of Paris). He remained in France during the French Revolution (1789) and bought up newly nationalized land with funds borrowed from a friend. During the Reign of Terror (1793–1794), he was imprisoned in the Palais de Luxembourg, and emerged extremely wealthy because the value of Revolutionary currency had depreciated. Saint-Simon lived a life of luxury, entertaining prominent people from all walks of life at his lavish and glittering salons. Within several years he was on the point of bankruptcy, and began to study science, taking courses at the École Polytechnique and acquainting himself with distinguished scientists. His first published work, *Lettres d'un habitant de Genève à ses contemporains* (1803; *Letters of an Inhabitant of Geneva to His Contemporaries*), proposed that scientists should replace priests in the social order, and that the property owners who held political power could only hope to maintain themselves against those without property if landowners subsidized the advance of knowledge. In reaction to the destructive Liberalism of the Revolution, he insisted on the necessity of a new and positive reorganization of society. In opposition to the military and feudal system, which remained prevalent in France, Saint-Simon advocated an arrangement by which the industrial chiefs should control society. In place of the medieval church, the spiritual direction of society should fall to the men of science. Saint-Simon envisioned an industrialist state directed by modern science, in which universal association should suppress war. He believed that the men who are successfully able to organize society for productive labor are entitled to govern it. The social aim was to produce things useful to life. The conflict between labor and capital so much emphasized by later Socialism was not present to Saint-Simon, who assumed that the industrial chiefs, to whom the control of production was to be committed, would rule in the interest of society.

In his greatest work, *Le Nouveau Christianisme* (1825; *The New Christianity*), his cause for the poor took the form of a religion—a social gospel. In *Le Nouveau Christianisme*, He announced that the world had arrived at the crisis, predicted by the Old Testament, which was to end in the establishment of a truly universal religion, the adoption by all nations of a peaceful social organization, and the speedy betterment of the condition of the poor. Saint-Simon attempted to clear away the dogma which had developed in Catholicism and Protestantism, and to reduce Christianity to its simple and temporal elements. Though he had few followers in his lifetime, shortly after his death, Olinde Rodrigues, Barthélemy Prosper Enfantin, and Amand Bazard founded the school of Saint-Simonism, which attracted many able young scientists and thinkers. Saint-Simonism declared that history was progressing toward an era of peace and industrial development, and advocated state ownership of property. Saint-Simon proposed, as the precept of *The New Christianity*, that "The whole of society ought to strive towards the amelioration of the moral and physical existence of the poorest class; society ought to organize itself in the way best adapted for attaining this end." Saint-Simon's *The New Christianity* was a vision of a society that practiced the legalistic teachings of Jesus by devoting itself to the betterment of its least fortunate members. Saint-Simon rejected many of the doctrines and rituals which had been developed by the Christian churches and returned to the words of Jesus in the New Testament. He developed a concept in which the state owned and administered the means of production for the benefit of all. Later thinkers took these concepts in two directions, Christian Socialism (Weitlingism, Liberation Theology) and atheistic Communism. His influence on modern thought remains undeniable, both as the historic founder of French Socialism and as the origin of many ideas that were later elaborated into Comtism. His "scientism" also influenced the development of Marxist theories on historical materialism and scientific Socialism. Saint-Simon died on 19 May 1825 and was interred in Le Père Lachaise Cemetery in Paris.

Robert Owen (1771–1858) – the "father of British Socialism." Robert Owen was born in Newtown, mid Wales on 14 May 1771. His father, also named Robert Owen, was an ironmonger, saddler, and local postmaster. The Owens family was most likely part of the nonconformist Calvinist Welsh Methodist Revival that was popular in the eighteenth century and revitalized Christianity in Wales. "The Calvinistic Methodists are intensely national in sentiment and aspirations, beyond all suspicion loyalists. They take a great interest in social, political and educational matters, and are on public bodies. . . . They thus form a living, Democratic body, flexible and progressive in its movements. . . ." (David Erwyd Jenkins, *Encyclopædia Britannica*, 1911.) Robert Jr. received little formal education, but he was an avid reader. At the age of 10, he was taken away from school and sent to work as an apprentice at a local draper in Stamford, Lincolnshire. After three years of apprenticeship, he moved briefly to London, before finding work at a large drapery business in Manchester. In Manchester, Owen became interested in the new business of textile manufacturing which was prospering in Lancashire. Despite being only nineteen-years of age, he borrowed £100 from his brother William and set up a business manufacturing clothes with engineer John Jones. This experience of running his own textile business gave Owen the opportunity to gain work as a manager of a large spinning factory in Manchester. Owen cultivated many contacts with other businessmen in the Manchester area. He also became involved in local philosophy groups who discussed the utilitarianism of Jeremy Bentham and other writers of the Enlightenment. In 1799, he married Caroline Dale, the daughter of David Dale, a successful businessman who owned the Chorton Twist textile company in New Lanark, Scotland. With the help of other Manchester businessmen, Owen arranged to buy the mill complex from his father-in-law for £60,000.

By the early 1790s, Owen's entrepreneurial spirit, management skills, and progressive moral views were emerging. In 1793, he was elected as a member of the Manchester Literary and Philosophical Society, where the ideas of reformers and philosophers of the Enlightenment were discussed. He also became a committee member of the Manchester Board of Health, which was instigated to promote improvements in the health and working conditions of factory workers. In July 1799, Owen and his partners bought the New Lanark mill and Owen became the mill's manager in January 1800. Encouraged by his success in the management of cotton mills in Manchester, Owen hoped to conduct the New Lanark mill on higher principles than purely commercial ones. He was not just interested in running a successful business. He was also keen to improve the working conditions and life of the workers. At the time, factory conditions were often dire, with people working long hours for little pay. Workers received little, if any, education and had few prospects. Owen was a great believer that man was shaped by his environment and surroundings. Therefore, he felt it his duty as a manager to offer education and respectable surroundings for his extended family. On taking over the New Lanark business, Owen ordered the building of a school. He also banned corporal punishment. Owen also restricted the employment of children under the age of 10 (children as young as 5 had been working in the factories). These young children were instead sent to school. Owen's philanthropy towards his own workers was rare and his other business partners feared that the profitability of their investment would be reduced. This conflict between profit maximization and social concerns was a continual source of tension. To resolve it, Owen borrowed money from a Quaker, Archibald Campbell, to buy out the other businessmen. He later sold shares to investors more sympathetic to his aims. Owen raised the demand for an eight-hour day in 1810 and instituted the policy at New Lanark. In 1813, Owen authored and published *A New View of Society, or Essays on the Principle of the Formation of the Human Character*, the first of four essays that he wrote to explain the principles behind his reform-minded and Socialist philosophy. Owen had originally been a follower of the classical Liberal and utilitarian Jeremy Bentham, who believed that free markets, in particular, the right of workers to move and choose their employers, would release the workers from the excessive power of Capitalists. However, Owen developed his own, pro-Socialist outlook. Owen was also a religious free thinker. He was critical of organized religion, such as the Church of England. He argued that religion tended to create prejudice in men, which was a barrier to peace and harmony.

> I was forced, through seeing the error of their foundation, to abandon all belief in every religion which had been taught to man. But my religious feelings were immediately replaced by the spirit of universal charity—not for a sect, or a party, or for a country or a colour—but for the human race, and with a real and ardent desire to do good.
>
> – *Life of Robert Owen* (1857), his autobiography.

This religious criticism divided him from other social reformers, such as William Wilberforce (1759–1833) and made his works less popular. In addition, Owen, a deist, developed a belief system of his own. An example of his philosophy:

> What ideas individuals may attach to the term "Millennium" I know not; but I know that society may be formed so as to exist without crime, without poverty, with health greatly improved, with little, if any misery, and with intelligence and happiness increased a hundredfold; and no obstacle whatsoever intervenes at this moment except ignorance to prevent such a state of society from becoming universal.
>
> – Extract from Robert Owen's
> "Address to the Inhabitants of New Lanark"
> New Year's Day, 1816.

Despite expressing agnostic views, towards the end of his life he became interested in spiritualism. He had several "sittings" where he became convinced he had mediumistic contact with great spirits like Benjamin Franklin and Thomas Jefferson who sought "to prepare the world for universal peace, and to infuse into all the spirit of charity, forbearance and love." Owen felt that human character is formed by circumstances over which individuals have no control. As a result, individuals cannot be praised or blamed for their behavior or situation in life. This principle led Owen to the conclude that the secret behind the correct formation of people's characters is to place them under proper environmental influences—physical, moral, and social—from their earliest years. These principles of the irresponsibility of humans and of the effect of early influences on an individual's character formed the basis of Owen's system of education and social reform. Relying on his own observations, experiences, and thoughts, Owen considered his view of human nature to be original and "the most basic and necessary constituent in an evolving science of society." Owen's philosophy was influenced by Sir Isaac Newton's views of natural law and shared similar views with those of Plato, Denis Diderot, Claude Adrien Helvétius, William Godwin, John Locke, James Mill, and Jeremy Bentham, among others. Owen embraced Socialism in 1817, a turning point in his life, and began making specific efforts to implement what he described as his "New View of Society." By 1817, he had formulated the goal of the eight-hour workday and coined the slogan: "Eight hours labour, Eight hours recreation, Eight hours rest." Owen's work at New Lanark continued to have significance throughout Britain and in Continental Europe. He was a "pioneer in factory reform, the father of distributive cooperation, and the founder of nursery schools." His schemes for the education of his workers included the opening of the Institute for the Formation of Character at New Lanark in 1818. The institute and other educational programs at New Lanark provided free education from infancy to adulthood. In addition, he zealously supported factory legislation that culminated in the Cotton Mills and Factories Act of 1819. Owen also had interviews and communications with the leading members of the British government, including its premier, Robert Banks Jenkinson, and Lord Liverpool, as well as providing testimony. Owen met with many of the rulers and leading statesmen of Europe. Owen was disappointed with the response from Parliament, feeling that the Cotton Mills and Factories Act of 1819 was woefully inadequate. He increasingly began to feel that the solution was the creation of independent "Utopian communities" of between 500 to 3,000 people who would work cooperatively for the common good. In these Utopian communities, there would be no private property, just a community based on sharing the common good with equal wages.

> There is but one mode by which man can possess in perpetuity all the happiness which his nature is capable of enjoying—that is by the union and co-operation of all for the benefit of each.
>
> — Robert Owen, 1826 *The Social System: Constitution, Laws, and Regulations of a Community*

In 1825, he sought to implement his vision of a Utopian community in America, called "New Harmony." He sank much of his capital into this experiment, but unfortunately it was not a lasting success. His son, who helped manage the community, wryly noted that the Utopian community attracted a diverse mixture of charlatans, vagrants, and lazy theorists. A more successful Communistic experiment was tried in Ralahine, County Clare, Ireland. For three years, this cooperative society was a great success, until the owner had to sell out after ruining himself from gambling. Other Utopian experiments in the United States included communal settlements at Blue Spring, near Bloomington, Indiana; Yellow Springs, Ohio; and the Owenite community of Forestville Commonwealth at Earlton, New York, as well as other projects in New York, Pennsylvania, and Tennessee. Nearly all these experiments ended before New Harmony was dissolved in April 1827. Having invested most of his personal fortune in the failed New Harmony communal experiment, Owen was no longer a wealthy Capitalist; however, he remained the head of a vigorous propaganda effort to promote industrial equality, free education for children, and adequate living conditions in factory towns. In addition, he delivered lectures in Europe and published a weekly newspaper to gain support for his ideas. Owen attempted to gain support for his Socialist vision among American thinkers, reformers, intellectuals, and public statesmen. On 25 February and 7 March 1825, Owen delivered addresses in the United States House of Representatives and others in the United States government that outlined his vision and plans for the Utopian community at New Harmony, Indiana, as well as his Socialist beliefs. Among the audience to hear his ideas were three former United States presidents (John Adams, Thomas Jefferson, and James Madison), in addition to outgoing United States president James Monroe, and president-elect John Quincy Adams. His meetings were possibly the first discussions about Socialism in the Americas; they were certainly a major step towards the beginnings of discussions about Socialist thought in the United States. Owenism, among the first Socialist ideologies active in the United States, is considered the origin point of the modern Socialist movement in the United States.

Owen was one of the first to use the term "Socialist" in publications such as the *New Westminster Review* (1839). Owen also founded early Socialist/cooperative groups such as the Grand National Consolidated Trades Union of 1834 and Association of All Classes of All Nations (1835). His approach, however, was to rely more on the philanthropy of the Capitalist class to set up Utopian communities. His Socialism was a different brand to the later Socialist movements which emphasized relying on the working classes to agitate for better conditions. However, he still raised in the public consciousness the ideal of communities working together and ending inequality based on ownership of property. Friedrich Engels described him as "a man of almost sublime, childlike character," and also "one of the few born leaders of men." Engels also said: "Every social movement and real advance in England on behalf of the workers links with the name of Robert Owen." Owen's agitation for social change and the Owenites whose work he inspired, including the efforts of his own five children, helped to establish and promote long-lasting social reforms in the area of women's and workers' rights; the establishment of free public libraries and museums; childcare and public, co-educational schools; pre-Marxian Communism; and the development of the cooperative and the trade union movement. Although he had spent most of his life in England and Scotland, Owen returned to his native village of Newtown at the end of his life. He died at Newtown on 17 November 1858 and was buried there on 21 November. Apart from an annual income drawn from a trust established by his sons in 1844, Owen died penniless.

François Marie Charles Fourier (1772–1837) – a Catholic Jesuit French philosopher, influential early Socialist thinker, and one of the founders of Utopian Socialism. Some of Fourier's social and moral views, held to be radical in his lifetime, have become mainstream thinking in modern society. For instance, Fourier is credited with having originated the word "feminism" (*féminisme*) in 1837. Born in Besançon, France, Charles was the son of a wealthy textile merchant. He was more interested in architecture than in his father's trade. He wanted to become an engineer, but the local military engineering school accepted only sons of noblemen. He received a classical education at the Jesuit College de Besançon (1781–1787) but was mostly self-taught. In 1791, he moved from his native Besançon to Lyon, the second largest city in France. As the sole surviving son in his family, he was expected to succeed his father as head of the family business, and he began his apprenticeship in the cloth trade at the age of six. He found himself unsuited for commerce and deplored its chicanery as immoral. Nevertheless, upon the death of his father in 1781, according to the terms of his will, Charles was compelled to enter a commercial career by age twenty or forfeit a substantial patrimony. Fourier lived through the events of the 1789 French Revolution, the Napoleonic Empire, the Bourbon Restoration, and the revolution of 1830, but though they affected his personal fortunes, they did not seem to influence his ideas or his writing. During the early years of the 1789 Revolution, Fourier lived in Lyons, where he fought on the counter-revolutionary side and lost his inheritance in a series of business failures. He barely escaped being executed by Jacobin forces when they purged that royalist stronghold in 1793. In 1794, he was drafted for service in the Army of the Rhine but was discharged two years later because of illness. He spent the remainder of his life in Lyons and Paris, earning his living by doing odd jobs, living in cheap rooming houses, preaching "universal harmony," and searching for a wealthy patron to finance a prototype of his Utopian community.

As a twenty-year-old man, Fourier worked for a short period as the head of the Office of Statistics in Paris in the midst of the Revolution. He later worked as a traveling salesman and correspondence clerk, but often complained of "serving the knavery of merchants" and the stupefaction of "deceitful and degrading duties." It was during this period that Fourier developed his disdain for Capitalism, and it was after his experiences as a traveling salesman and correspondence clerk that he produced most of his writings (1816–1821). Fourier based his Socialist Utopia on the transformation of labor into pleasure. In Fourier's system of harmony, all creative activity, including industry, craft, agriculture, etc. will arise from liberated passion—this is the theory of "attractive labor." Fourier sexualizes work itself—life in Fourier's community is a continual orgy of intense passion, intellection, and creativity, a society of lovers and wild enthusiasts. "Attractive labor" (*travail attrayant*) derives from the release of libidinal forces. Fourier assumed the existence of an attraction *industrielle* which makes for pleasurable cooperation. It is based on the attraction *passionnée* in the nature of man, which persists despite the opposition of reason, duty, prejudice. This attraction *passionnée* tends toward three principal objectives: the creation of "luxury, or the pleasure of the five senses"; the formation of libidinal groups (of friendship and love); and the establishment of a harmonious order, organizing these groups for work in accordance with the development of the individual "passions" (internal and external "play" of faculties). In the 1830s, a schism among the followers of Utopian Socialist Henri de Saint-Simon increased Fourier's following and led to the establishment of the Fourierist movement in France. A journal, the *Phalanstere* (1832–1834), was begun, and a model Fourierist community (a phalanx), the Societary Colony, was established in Conde-sur-Vesgre (1833–1836). Fourier also developed a following in Romania. Through the popularization of his ideas by the social reformer Albert Brisbane (1809–1890), approximately 40 phalanxes were established in the United States between 1843 and 1858, including one of the most famous, Utopia, Ohio. The influence of Fourier's ideas in French politics was carried forward into the 1848 Revolutions and the Paris Commune of 1871 by followers such as French Utopian Socialist Victor-Prosper Considerant (1808–1893). Fourier died in Paris in 1837.

Étienne Cabet (1788–1856) – Catholic French lawyer, philosopher, Utopian Socialist, and founder of the Icarian movement, who coined the term *Communisme* (Cabet n.d.). Cabet was born in Dijon, Côte-d'Or, the youngest son of a cooper from Burgundy, Claude Cabet, and his wife Francoise Berthier. He went on to study medicine before abandoning it for law. Entering practice in Dijon, Cabet acquired an effective reputation as a lawyer, and by 1825 had moved to Paris. He soon fell in with the republican circles around Dupont de l'Eure. Étienne Cabet was briefly appointed procurator-general in Corsica, before being forced to resign. He represented the Orléanist government of Louis Philippe, despite having headed an insurrectionary committee during the July Revolution of 1830 which led to the ouster of the "Republican Monarch" King Charles X (and the ascent of Louis Philippe). However, Cabet lost this position for his attack upon the Conservatism of the government in his *Histoire de la révolution de 1830.* Nonetheless, in July 1831, Cabet was elected to the Chamber of Deputies in France as the representative of Côte d'Or and sat with the extreme radicals. Accused of treason in 1834 because of his bitter attacks on the government both in the history book and subsequently, Cabet was convicted. To eliminate the dangerous Democratic agitator, the French Orléanist regime (1830–1848) gave Cabet the choice of two-years' imprisonment or five years in foreign exile. He decided upon the latter punishment and immediately went into exile in England. During his five years of English exile, Cabet dedicated himself to philosophical and economic study, carefully considering the relationship between political structures and economic welfare throughout history. Cabet turned to the idea of reorganization of society on a communal basis—known as "Communism" in the terminology of the day in France. His ideas for the modification of society closely paralleled those of a man he met in England, Robert Owen (1871–1858; a Welsh textile manufacturer, philanthropic social reformer, and one of the founders of Utopian Socialism and the cooperative movement establishing experimental Socialistic communities in the United States, Canada, and the United Kingdom between 1821 and 1827). In 1839, his exile in England completed, Cabet returned to his native France. After his return to France, Cabet promptly published a laudatory history of the Jacobins of 1789–1792. He went on in 1840 to write *Voyage en Icarie* (*Voyage to Icaria*) to expound his economic and social ideas, following the example of Sir Thomas More and using the form of an allegorical novel, which allowed not only the exposition of the ideal form of public administration but an opportunity for cloaked criticism of the Orléanist regime in France. Cabet introduced the idea of "Communism" (a term of his invention) as the greatest realization of Democracy and the direct descendent of Christian principles. The novel was popular, but his embrace of Utopian Communism broke his remaining links to radical republicans. Cabet's Icarianism led to French political exiles traveling to New Orleans, Louisiana in 1848–1849, who then traveled north with 280 French settlers to establish "Icaria," a communal settlement at Nauvoo, Illinois. His Utopian Socialist-Communist movement established similar egalitarian communes in Texas, Iowa, Missouri, and California. Cabet died in St. Louis in 1856. By 1895, most Icarian communes dissolved.

Moses (Moshe, Moritz) Heß (1812–1875) – French-German Jewish philosopher, anarchic Socialist, founder of Labor Zionism, and one of several primary influential people to Karl Marx and Friedrich Engels. Moses Heß was born in Bonn on 21 June 1812, which was under Napoleonic rule at the time. His father was an ordained rabbi, but never practiced the profession. Moses Heß received a Jewish religious education from his grandfather, and later studied philosophy at the University of Bonn, but never graduated. From his student days, Moses Heß was strongly attracted to Liberalism and Socialism. He was a disciple of the transcendental philosophy of Dutch Jewish philosopher Benedict (Baruch) de Spinoza (1632–1677) and German Continental philosopher Georg Wilhelm Friedrich Hegel (1770–1831). As a rebel, Moses Heß gravitated toward the liberal Young Hegelian circle in Berlin, a group which boasted among its members David Friedrich Strauss (1808–1874), Ludwig von Feuerbach (1808–1872), Bruno Bauer (1809–1882), Karl Marx, and Friedrich Engels. It was not by chance that already in the 1840's his Socialist comrades had dubbed him "the Communist Rabbi." Moses Heß was Wilhelm Weitling's colleague in the League of the Just.

From 1841 to 1845, Moses Heß was accepted as an equal and even as a guide by Marx and Engels. It was Heß who encouraged Marx to join the editorial staff of the *Rheinische Zeitung*, the Young Hegelian journal he had helped found in his home city of Cologne; there Marx gained his first intimate experience of day-to-day politics. It was Heß, too, who persuaded Engels that the logical culmination of German philosophy must be an uncompromising demand for the total abolition of private property. ("My conversion to Communism was definitely due to Heß." – Engels.) And it was Heß, again, who saw in the British proletariat a national prototype of what was to come into being everywhere, thereby giving Engels the incentive to undertake his crucial study of Manchester factory life, which was published in 1844 as *The Condition of the Working Class in England.* In 1845, Moses Heß and Engels launched a campaign to rally the workers of the Rhineland to their program. Though the enterprise did not get much further than a popular journal and a series of public rallies, it marked the first attempt of those Young Hegelians who now referred to themselves as "Communists" to organize the emergent industrial proletariat in Germany along political lines. While Engels and Heß were thus seeking action, Marx was laying the philosophical groundwork for his new-found Communist faith—until his journey to Paris in 1843, Marx had been more of a radical Democrat than Socialist. In his new synthesis, Marx now included both Heß's conception of private property as the "self-alienation" of man, and his view of the future Communist society as an expression of man's true nature. Heß collaborated with Marx in writing *Die deutsche Ideologie* (1845); part of the manuscript is in his own handwriting. Heß's contribution to the *Manifesto of the Communist Party* (1848) was the phrase "religion is the opiate for the masses." But the year 1848 saw the end of the partnership, at least so far as Heß was concerned. Marx was now at the point of beginning to assert his claim to the leadership both of European Socialist thought and of the early German Communist movement. Marx gradually fell out with his former allies one by one: Karl Grün, Arnold Ruge, Wilhelm Weitling, were the first to go; in 1847, he launched his attack on the anarchist Socialist Pierre-Joseph Proudhon, and a year later, in the *Manifesto of the Communist Party*, he and Engels jointly denounced Heß as the proponent of a viewpoint that "objectively strengthened" *bourgeois* society. There was a good deal of irony in this denunciation, not only because Marx and Engels had until a short time before held those very same views, but also because Moses Heß, now under the intellectual sway of Marx, was in the process of eagerly adopting the latter's conception of the primacy of economics and the class struggle.

From 1861 to 1863, Heß lived in Germany, where he became acquainted with the rising tide of German anti-Semitism. It was then that he reverted to his Jewish roots and original name Moses (after apparently going by Moritz) to protest Jewish assimilation. Moses Heß's most prominent work published in 1862, the early Zionist *Rom und Jerusalem, die letzte Nationalitätsfrage* (*Rome and Jerusalem: A Study of the Question of Jewish Nationalism*), was ignored at the time of publication, but it significantly influenced such later renowned Zionist leaders as Aḥad Haʿam and Theodor Herzl. Heß viewed the struggle of races, or nationalities, as the prime factor of history as opposed to the view of Marx and Engels who based all history on economic causes and class struggle. Moses Heß interpreted history as a circle of race and national struggles. He contemplated the rise of Italian Nationalism and the German reaction to it, and from this he arrived at the idea of Jewish national revival, and at his prescient understanding that the Germans would not be tolerant of the national aspirations of others and would be particularly intolerant of the Jews. His book called for the establishment of a Jewish Socialist commonwealth in Palestine, in line with the emerging Nationalist movements in Europe and as the only way to respond to anti-Semitism and assert Jewish identity in the modern world. The fallout between Heß, Marx, and Engels was primarily over the degree of radical militancy integral to promotion of the proletarian movement and how race rather than materialism was the primary influence on history. This man who, in the mid-1840's, together with Marx, was condemning the Jews as a race of shopkeepers doomed to speedy disappearance, could proclaim in 1862 that "every Jew, even the converted, should cling to the cause and labor for the regeneration of Israel." In essence, Moses Heß had given up on Christian Europe and saw the future freedom and equality of the Jews only in a new Israel in Palestine. Marx had far less of a bond with his Jewish roots than Heß, and this at the core is what divided them.

Karl Schapper (1812–1870) – Catholic German Socialist labor leader, son of Roman Catholic priest, and friend of Karl Marx. Karl Friedrich Schapper was born on 30 December 1812, in Weinbach, Grand Duchy of Hesse. His father, Christian Schapper, was a priest serving in the local Roman Catholic parish. Karl studied forestry in Giessen. As a student, he joined a radical fraternity (*Burschenschaft*), and on 3 April 1833, he participated in an insurrection known as *Frankfurter Wachensturm*—an attempt to gain control over the treasury of the German Confederation to start a revolution in all German states. However, because the plot had been betrayed to the police, it was easily crushed. The would-be revolutionaries, about fifty in total—organized by students, most of them members of the *Burschenschaft*, Gustav Körner,* Gustav Bunsen,† and others—seized an arsenal and wanted to overthrow the Frankfurt diet and proclaim a republic. Schapper was imprisoned, but after three months, he managed to escape, making his way to Switzerland. There he worked as a forestry worker and typesetter. He joined the radical organization "Young Germany" and became a follower of Utopian Communist Wilhelm Weitling. "Young Germany" was a group of German writers that existed from about 1830 to 1850. It was essentially a youth ideology (like those that had swept France, Ireland, America, and Italy). Its main proponents were Karl Gutzkow, Heinrich Laube, Theodor Mundt, and Ludolf Wienbarg; **Heinrich Heine**, Ludwig Börne, Georg Büchner, and **Georg Herwegh** were also considered part of the movement. It was modelled on, and affiliated with, Giuseppe Mazzini's "Young Italy," and in 1834, Schapper participated in Mazzini's attempt at an armed invasion of Savoy from Switzerland. This was Mazzini's second attempt; like the first, in 1833, it was unsuccessful. Schapper was once again imprisoned. On his release, Schapper resumed his activities in "Young

---

* Gustav Körner – a revolutionary, journalist, lawyer, politician, judge, and statesman in Illinois and Germany and a Colonel of the U.S. Army who was a confessed enemy of slavery. He was one of the co-founders and first members of the Grand Old Party (Republican; founded in 1854); and he was a close confidant of Abraham Lincoln and his wife Mary Todd and had an essential role in his nomination and election for president in 1860. During the *Frankfurter Wachensturm* in 1833, Körner was injured and, to avoid being prosecuted by the authorities and held captive for high treason which would threaten capital punishment, he escaped in female dress to France. A warrant was issued but he managed to evade capture. He is counted as one of the *Dreißiger* (Thirtiers)—liberal intellectuals who left Germany and came to the United States in the 1830s to escape political repression, much like the Forty-Eighters after the 1848 Revolutions.

† Gustav Bunsen – a medical student who aborted his studies to participate in the failed Warsaw (1830) and Frankfurt (1833) uprisings. After the *Frankfurter Wachensturm*, he and his compatriot Adolph Berchelmann managed to escape to America (Illinois, later moving to Cincinnati, Ohio). In 1835, he became involved in Sam Houston's Texas independence movement with the promise of fame and fortune. In 1836, he joined 63 fellow rebel riders in a rather hopeless and foolishly planned campaign at San Patricio, Texas against the Mexican government, during which he and 58 of his comrades were killed.

Germany" and was associated with the exiled German Democrat Georg Fein (1803–1869) in setting up workers' educational circles. In 1836, Schapper was deported from Switzerland for his political activities and went to Paris where he joined the French section of "Young Germany" and the Communist "League of Outlaws" (an international revolutionary fellowship organization of German exiled expatriate artisans and political activists in Paris from 1834–1838).

In 1836, Schapper broke away from Theodore Schuster's League of Outlaws and founded the League of the Just (*Bund der Gerechten*)—an organization comprised of German journeymen artisans whose stated goal was "the establishment of the Kingdom of God on Earth, based on the ideals of love of one's neighbor, equality and justice," whose motto was "All men are brothers," and who anticipated a social revolution, which Karl Schapper, described as "the great resurrection day of the people" that will sweep away not just the "aristocracy of money," but also the "aristocracy of the mind." Revolutionaries should beware, however, of intellectuals, who "think little of the people and believe that heads filled with book learning make them better than other people [and entitled] to make laws and govern." Shapper's anti-intellectual religiosity was intensified and popularized by the tailor Wilhelm Weitling, who wrote the principal manifesto for the League: *Humanity as it is and as it ought to be*. Schapper and Wilhelm Weitling were colleagues in the League of the Just but over the years became bitter revolutionary rivals in London.

In 1839, the League was implicated in the unsuccessful Blanquist revolt by the "Society of the Seasons," led by Auguste Blanqui and Armand Barbès. Schapper, who had been involved, was arrested and imprisoned. In 1840, Schapper and Weitling were expelled from France and went to London, where they re-organized the League of the Just. The League had originally followed Weitling's lead, but in the 1840s it came under the growing influence of Karl Marx and Friedrich Engels, despite the fact they were not official members of the League of the Just. The League of the Just eventually merged with Marx's Brussels Communist Correspondence Committee on 1 June 1847, to form the Communist League. After the merger, Schapper became head of the Communist Correspondence Committee, which now functioned under the merger, and organized the publication of Marx's and Engels's *Manifesto of the Communist Party* in 1848.

Schapper played a role in the 1848 Revolution in Germany and, subsequently, in founding the First International.* The Communist League maintained relations with French Utopian Communist Étienne Cabet who now resided in the United States and the neo-Babouvists in France. In 1850, a bitter disagreement led to a split, with Marx and Engels on one side and Karl Schapper and August Willich (born Johann August Ernst von Willich; a military officer in the Prussian Army and a leading early proponent of Communism in Germany who in 1847 discarded his title of nobility) on the other. Schapper's conflict with Marx had been building for some time. The final break came over the question of how to react to the defeat of the 1848 Revolutions. Marx argued for building a mass workers' movement for the future; Schapper and Willich wanted to prepare for further insurrections. Schapper and Willich formed their own group, the Communist Central Committee, modelled on the conspiratorial Blanquist organizations they knew from the 1830s. However, their efforts came to naught, and Willich emigrated to the United States in 1853, where he became a general in the Union Army during the American Civil War. Schapper and Marx were reconciled in 1856. Schapper's long-standing contacts with French, British, Swiss, Italian, Belgian, and American radicals, Socialists, and trade unionists were a valuable asset to Marx. In 1865, Schapper was elected to the General Council of the First International, the organization's governing body. In the factional conflicts within the International, Schapper loyally supported Marx. However, Schapper's health had been poor for some time. He suffered from tuberculosis. Karl Schapper died in London on 28 April 1870.

Schapper was important for several reasons: As a Communist of working-class background, he was one of the pioneers of the labor movement in Germany. As a member of Young Germany, he was one of the most important links between the German *Vormärz* (see *infra*) and the Italian Risorgimento—the political and social movement that consolidated different states of the Italian peninsula into the unified Kingdom of Italy in the nineteenth century. As a member of the League of the Just, Schapper helped forge links between German Socialists and the radical French Communist

* The International Workingmen's Association (IWA), often called the First International (1864–1876), was an international organization which aimed at uniting a variety of different Socialist, Communist, and anarchist groups and trade unions that were based on the working class and class struggle. It was founded in 1864 in a workers' meeting held in St. Martin's Hall, London.

and Blanquist groups of the 1830s and 1840s. In the Communist League, Schapper helped pave the way from the Utopian Socialism of Weitling to the "scientific" Communism of Marx and Engels. In the 1840s, Schapper helped build bridges between German Socialists and the radical wing of the British Chartist movement.

Wilhelm Weitling (1808–1871) – Despite his relative obscurity, Weitling remains a towering figure and, next to Karl Marx, one of the most influential in the early Communist movement. Weitling was a Catholic French-Prussian journeyman tailor and self-educated writer, populist, and radical political activist, who was a friend of Karl Schapper and Theodore Schuster, and eventually was a Forty-Eighter in America (European revolutionaries of the 1848 Revolutions that fled to America). Much of the following information is adopted from *The Utopian Communist: A Biography of Wilhelm Weitling* by Carl Frederick Wittke (Baton Rouge: Louisiana State University Press, 1950, pages 18–122).

Born out of wedlock on 5 October 1808 to a French artillery officer (Guillaume Terijon) and a young Prussian maidservant Christine Erdmuth Friedericke Weidlingen in the town of Magdeburg during the Napoleonic occupation and the *Grande Armée*'s eventual march to Moscow. In March 1812, only six months after Wilhelm's third birthday, his biological French father left Magdeburg with the Grand Army and was never seen or heard from again by the Weitling's. Wilhelm's education ended with elementary school. He then apprenticed and by the age of eighteen-years began his wandering from city to city as a journeyman tailor (*Handwerksbursche*). Living in relative poverty most of his youth, his restless spirit became absorbed in other things, and tailoring was merely the means of keeping body and soul together while his inquiring mind was engrossed in ambitious plans for the reconstruction of the social order. After reaching Leipzig in Saxony, he befriended and lived with August Schilling from 1830–1832, who also became interested in Socialism and Communism, and the correspondence between these old friends continued until shortly before Weitling's death in New York. While in Leipzig, Weitling may have participated in the revolutionary revolt of 1830 in Saxony. He also spent two years (1832–1834) in Dresden, Saxony.

After a hurried departure from his second stay in Vienna (first visit was in 1834–1835, second visit was in 1836), he fled a second time to post-revolutionary Paris in the autumn of 1837 (first visit was in 1835–1836). In the French capital, the most important formative period of his life was about to begin. Paris was the intellectual center from which the new revolutionary movements derived much of their sustenance, and Weitling was there during one of its most exciting periods. Moreover, the traditions of the French Revolution lingered on and provided the germs from which many of the economic and philosophical principles of modern Socialism and Communism developed. Weitling so deeply admired Babeuf that many years later he named one of his sons after the French revolutionary conspirator. Weitling was also familiar with Cabet's program and knew the French Utopian personally, visited his colony in Illinois, and carried on a considerable correspondence with him while both were residents of the United States. Thus, during the years which Weitling spent in Paris, revolutionary propaganda filled the air; and the ideas of Charles Fourier (1772–1837), Henri de Saint-Simon (1760–1825), Victor-Prosper Considerant (1808–1893), Cabet the Communist priest, and many others already had affected the thinking of many people and had seeped down from the intellectual groups to the workers, to whom Weitling belonged. He owed nothing to the universities, and he had the honest craftsman's contempt for mere theory. His contacts were largely with fellow workers, whose problems and reactions he understood because they were his own. He entered upon the path of social revolution through the door of the worker's movement by way of the secret societies to which he and many of his class belonged, for, after the suppression of the workers' uprisings in Paris and Lyons in 1834, there was no other place for radicals to go except underground.

At the time, Paris also was the home of thousands of German craftsmen like Weitling—estimates place the number of Germans in Paris in 1842 at 80,000 to 100,000. German was heard on every Paris street. Upon his second arrival in Paris, Weitling joined Schapper's fledgling League of the Just and quickly rose to leadership authority. As one of its members, Weitling achieved fame in the early history of Communist activities in France, Germany, Belgium, Switzerland, and England. In Paris, the young tailor developed rapidly into a militant Communist and became one of the most eloquent orators and literary champions of the proletariat well before Marx and Engels arrived on the scene. He learned typesetting and was commissioned to prepare the League's first major publication *Die Menschheit, wie sie ist und wie sie sein sollte* (*Humanity as it is and as it ought to be*) for distribution throughout France, Switzerland, and the German states. The publication eventually was codified into a booklet that poet, journalist, and essayist Heinrich Heine later described as "the catechism of the German Communists." Its two thousand copies were widely distributed and discussed as the booklet became the model for subsequent manifestoes of social revolution. Weitling proclaimed himself to be a "social Luther." Inequality, Weitling argued, was increasing rather than vanishing in the face of industrialization. All exploitation and corruption could be traced to one disease carrier: money. All the goods made by honest workers, as well as their wives, their families, and their very souls have been put up for sale and subjected to the rule of money.

Against the artificial world of this false narrative Weitling juxtaposed a Utopian alternative to be based on a fusion of the "law of nature" with the "law of charity"—a mélange of Buonarroti and Lamennais, and of radical secular enlightenment with visionary Christian sentiment. All individual property ownership and right of inheritance were to be abolished. The value of all products was henceforth to be calculated in terms not of money, but of hours of work. Conflict was to be resolved and rights guaranteed not by republican political institutions, but by two totally new social authorities: the "order of families" and the "order of production."

On 12 May 1839, Weitling, Schapper, and many members of the League of the Just were involved the Blanquist revolt in Paris to overthrow the French government. The members fought bravely side by side with their French comrades on the barricades around the Hôtel de Ville. This led to the group being expelled from France. The League moved to London. In 1840 London, they established a front organization called the Educational Society of German Workingmen. They continued to grow, until reaching a peak membership of over one thousand. Later in 1840, Weitling accepted a commission to carry the Communist gospel of the League of the Just to the workers of Switzerland. Consistent with its virtue-based legalistic Calvinism, Switzerland at the close of the 1830's was a center of revolutionary social justice propaganda. Though the impact for the revolutionary eruptions of 1848 in Germany came from Paris, Switzerland was the spiritual home, in which many of the German revolutionaries nurtured their ideas to maturity. During his time in Switzerland, Weitling was imprisoned for two years for his revolutionary activities. In the summer of 1844, he returned to London. In 1845, a rift occurred within the League between Weitling, who advocated for an immediate uprising of workers, and Karl Schapper, who considered this premature, especially after his experience in the 1839 uprising. Schapper advocated for a longer campaign of popular education to prepare the masses for revolution. Weitling refused to give ground. He emphasized the emotions and the primitive-Christian virtues as important factors in social reform and insisted upon his plan to crush the old order by a temporary dictatorship of a well-organized revolutionary minority. Schapper took sharp issue with his former Paris colleague about religion, and Weitling resented all attacks on Christianity, especially by those who rejected faith and relied wholly on cold science. Not much historical imagination is needed to sense the fire and heat, with which these radicals and former members of the same persecuted league in Paris now debated their differences in the smoke-filled rooms of their London clubhouse. As was the custom in workers' clubs, a vote was taken at the end of each discussion and Weitling consistently lost by a heavy majority.

In 1846, Weitling departed for Brussels, where his decisive conflict with the much younger Karl Marx was about to take place. Weitling was then far better known in Communist circles than the young man who was destined to become a world figure as the oracle of modern scientific Communism. In the years before their encounter in Brussels, Marx and Engels held high regard for all that Weitling had done for the Communist movement. Marx and Engels regarded his program as "the only existing German Communist system." At the root of the fracture between Weitling and Marx was religion. Marx originally met Weitling in London and received reports of the London controversy from his friends there. It is also known that long before the Brussels conference, Marx had begun to work on a plan to divorce Communism from religious sentimentality and reduce it to a scientific, materialistic doctrine. Weitling was not an avowed atheist like Ludwig von Feuerbach, nor a materialist like Marx or Karl Heinzen. He was not a churchman either. But he wanted to use Christian faith to stir the emotions necessary for revolution. "Cold reason has never produced a revolution," he repeatedly said, and "there is as little reason in atheism as in deism." Knowledge alone would not solve all human problems nor completely satisfy the craving of the human spirit. Much of life remained a mystery, and like most men Weitling groped in vain for a solution for the riddle of the universe. He believed that "the mysterious emotions of love" often prove more powerful than reason, and lead men to comprehend that "image of highest love" which they seek in their search for God. "Only when the last riddle of human existence has been solved," he wrote, "can we know what God is." In the meantime, he preferred man take God on faith, rather than to "sink his thoughts into empty space." Weitling was an agnostic, but his bruised spirit yearned for the balsam of religion, and he was not prepared to dismiss the whole world of religious experience as a mere opiate for the people. As a product of poverty and life on the road, Weitling was conscious of an impenetrable mystery surrounding the origin of life, and to him that mystery suggested an "eternal, omnipotent, unifying cause."

Though his extravagant references to religious terminology irritated Marx and his followers, Weitling refused to abandon his efforts to unite "intelligence and morality," "head and heart," the joint products of "the harmony of creation," in the quest for the communal society. Still another essential difference between Marx and Weitling must be emphasized. The former was a university man who had enjoyed all the advantages of higher education, which culminated in a doctorate from the University of Jena. Marx was a pedantic neo-Hegelian, who even on minor questions could mobilize "his whole artillery of logic, dialectic, stylistic and learning." Weitling could not find his way around in the "fog" of Hegelianism, and he referred to von Schelling and Schleiermacher with equal disdain.

In October 1843, Marx and his young wife moved to Paris to help edit Arnold Ruge's *Deutsch-Französische Jahrbücher* (*German French Annals* established in February 1844 as the successor to the German *Hallesche Jahrbücher für deutsche Kunst und Wissenschaft* [*Halle Annals for German Science and Art*]). In Paris, Marx engaged in an intensive study of "political economy" (Adam Smith, David Ricardo, James Mill, etc.), the French Utopian Socialists (especially Henri de Saint-Simon, Charles Fourier, Pierre-Joseph Proudhon, Étienne Cabet, etc.), the history of France, and the writings of Weitling. Through this study, Marx completed the transition from being a *bourgeois* Democrat to a committed Communist. Marxism is based in large part on three influences: Hegel's dialectics, French Utopian Socialism, and English economics. Together with his earlier study of Hegel's dialectics, the studying that Marx did during this time in Paris meant that all major components of "Marxism" (or "political economy" as Marx called it) were in place by the autumn of 1844. Marx rejected Weitling's state of nature, natural law, primitive Christianity, and even social ethics as appropriate bases for Communism. With the able collaboration of Friedrich Engels, Marx slowly evolved a scientific basis for his philosophy of economic determinism, materialism, the class struggle, and the ultimate and inevitable proletarian revolution.

Between 1843 and 1847, Marx mixed his Hegelianism with large doses of von Feuerbach's materialism. Thus, Marxism was derived from the French Revolution, great German philosophers such as Hegel and von Feuerbach, French theorists such as Fourier and Saint-Simon, and English industrialism. According to "scientific Communism" *à la* Marx and Engels, the economic structure of society was decisive for all social institutions, moral, legal, political and religious; and even "moral theories" were the product of "the economic stage which society has reached" at a particular time. In short, even morality and religion were determined by the processes of production and the exchange of goods. In view of the ideological conflicts, the break between Weitling and Marx was inevitable. It represented the clash between a master of economics, scientific abstractions, and Hegelian dialectics, and a simple-minded prophet of the brotherhood of man who had no other formula for world betterment. It marked the collision between a champion of the class struggle determined by scientific economic laws, and a new Messiah who had faith in a kingdom of love and science. Marx was winning the race to organize an international Communist party with himself at the helm.

Marx finally succeeded in London on 1 June 1847 when the Communist Correspondence Committee of Brussels merged with Schapper's League of the Just to form the Communist League (*Bund der Kommunisten*)—the world's first Marxist international political party. Weitling could hardly be ignored in the launching of the new party, and so he was invited to participate in the preliminary discussions. The group consisted originally of seventeen of the faithful, the majority of whom definitely belonged to the *bourgeoisie*. Among them were Freiligrath, Heß, Marx's brother-in-law, Edgar von Westphalen, Weydemeyer, a former artillery officer, Seiler, Heilberg, Gigot, an employee of the Brussels library, Ernst and Ferdinand Wolff, two German typesetters, Ernst Dronke, later editor of Marx's *Neue Rheinische Zeitung: Organ der Demokratie*, Weitling, and several others. The group met twice a week under the name of a workers' educational society for discussion and debate, amateur theatricals, singing, and lectures. It was this small group who eventually hammered out the Communist doctrine which became a powerful force in world history.

The final dispute resulting in the break between the two fiercest competitors to lead the world Communist movement (Marx and Weitling) occurred during the conference in 1846 in Brussels organized to discuss preliminary steps to establish the first Communist party. The two lions turned on each other resulting in a series of drawn out campaigns by Marx and Engels lasting several years to libel Weitling in the international Communist community and excommunicate and extricate him, his followers, and his ideology from the party. It is interesting to speculate on what might have happened in the history of Communism and in the history of modern Europe if Weitling's suggestion of bridging the gap between scientific materialism and humanitarianism had been accepted at the Brussels conference. Marx and Engels demonstrated that they had the intelligence, the education, and the determination necessary to develop a system that was destined to become a powerful force in world affairs. Weitling lacked the qualifications for such a task; his head was not equal to his heart. But he saw clearly that a system which eschewed all considerations of morality, social ethics, and religious emotionalism, and frankly proceeded on the amoral principle that the end justifies the means, might be turned into the devil's own philosophy leading to a new form of tyranny. Weitling decided to leave Europe and test the waters for social change in America.

According to Weitling's own account, he landed in New York on the last day of 1846. Other evidence, however, fixes the date at 25 January 1847. In the United States, Weitling traveled widely organizing local lodges of workers under his new League of Deliverance, or Emancipation, the *Befreiungsbund* (in 1899, it amalgamated with the Philadelphia *Harmonie*). At the outbreak of the 1848 Revolutions (Spring of Nations) in Europe, Weitling returned to Germany. There, he lasted just over a year when the Hamburg authorities expelled him. He gave up on Europe for good and returned to the Unites States. Weitling was never to set foot on German soil again. He spent the remaining twenty-one years of his life in America attempting to convert workers, especially the large number of German immigrants, to the Communist cause. Shortly after settling in New York, he started another newspaper (*Die Republik der Arbeiter*) and revived the League of Emancipation as the Workingmen's League (*Arbeiterbund*). During this period, Weitling visited the many Communist communes throughout America established by Owen, Fourier, and Cabet. By 1855, both the Workingmen's League and the Communia colony had virtually collapsed because of factionalism, financial disorders, and widespread disillusionment with Weitling's authoritarian style of leadership. Weitling recognized his failed efforts to organize a Communist movement under his ideals and decided that the time had come to give up the life of a political activist. He devoted his attention to private life and in 1854 married a German immigrant. They settled in New York and Weitling resumed his work as a tailor. The couple had a large family (five sons and one daughter). During the 1860s, the family's financial situation steadily deteriorated and ended in bankruptcy. His health also deteriorated with diabetes mellitus. On 25 January 1871, following a stroke, he died just a few hours after making a rare appearance at a meeting organized by the Workers' International of New York.

Karl Marx (1818–1883) – German Jewish philosopher, economist, historian, political theorist, sociologist, journalist, and revolutionary Communist, who was a third cousin once removed and friend of German

Jewish Romantic poet Heinrich Heine. Karl was born on 5 May 1818 as one of nine children born to Heinrich (Herschel) Marx (1777–1838) and Henriette Pressburg (1788–1863). Karl was born in Trier, then part of the Kingdom of Prussia's Lower Rhine province. The Marxs were ethnically Jewish. Karl's maternal grandfather was a Dutch rabbi, while his paternal line had supplied Trier's rabbis since 1723, a role taken by his grandfather Meier Halevi Marx. His father, as a child known as Herschel, was the first in the line to receive a secular education. He became a successful lawyer and lived a relatively wealthy middle-class existence, with his family owning several Moselle vineyards. Largely non-religious, Herschel was a man of the Enlightenment, interested in the ideas of the philosophers Immanuel Kant and Voltaire. A classical Liberal, he took part in agitation for a constitution and reforms in Prussia, then governed by an absolute monarchy. His wife, Henriette, was a Dutch Jewish woman from a prosperous business family that later founded the company Philips Electronics. Her sister Sophie Pressburg married Lion Philips (1794–1866) and was the grandmother of both Gerard and Anton Philips and great-grandmother to Frits Philips. Lion Philips was a wealthy Dutch tobacco manufacturer and industrialist, upon whom Karl and Jenny Marx would later often come to rely for loans while they were exiled in London. Prior to Karl's birth, and after the 1815 abrogation of Jewish emancipation in the Rhineland, Herschel converted from Judaism in 1816 at the age of thirty-five-years to join the state Evangelical Lutheran Church of Prussia, taking on the German forename of Heinrich over the Yiddish Herschel. Hershel's conversion to Christianity was likely a professional concession in response to an 1815 law banning Jews from high society. Herschel was baptized a Lutheran, rather than a Catholic, which was the predominant faith in Trier, because he "equated Protestantism with intellectual freedom." At the age of six-years, Karl and his surviving six siblings (two died in childhood) were baptized into the Lutheran Church in August 1824 and their mother in November 1825. Despite their attempt at assimilation, their Jewish roots remained firmly ensconced.

Karl was privately educated by his father until 1830, when he entered Trier Gymnasium, whose headmaster, Hugo Wyttenbach, was a friend of his father. By employing many liberal humanists as teachers, Wyttenbach incurred the contempt of the local conservative government. Subsequently, police raided the school in 1832 and discovered that literature espousing political Liberalism was being distributed among the students. Considering the distribution of such material a seditious act, the authorities instituted reforms and replaced several staff during Karl's attendance. In October 1835, at the age of seventeen-years, Karl enrolled at the University of Bonn wishing to study philosophy and literature, but his father insisted on law as a more practical field. Due to a condition referred to as a "weak chest," Karl was excused from military duty when he turned 18. While at the University at Bonn, Karl joined the Poets' Club, a group of political radicals that were monitored by the police. Karl also joined the Trier Tavern Club drinking society (*Landsmannschaft der Treveraner*), at one point serving as club co-president. Additionally, Karl was involved in certain disputes, some of which became serious: in August 1836 he successfully took part in a duel with a member of the university's *Borussian Korps*. His academic performance was unsatisfactory, leading his father to force a transfer to the more serious and academic University of Berlin, then known as Friedrich Wilhelm University since 1828.

Spending summer and autumn 1836 in Trier, Karl became more serious about his studies and his life. He became engaged to Jenny von Westphalen, an educated baroness of the Prussian ruling class who had known Karl since childhood. As she had broken off her engagement with a young aristocrat to be with Karl, their relationship was socially controversial owing to the differences between their religious and class origins, but Karl befriended her father Ludwig von Westphalen (a liberal aristocrat) and later dedicated his doctoral thesis to him. Seven years after their engagement, on 19 June 1843, they got married in a Lutheran church in Kreuznach.

In October 1836, Karl arrived in Berlin, matriculating in the university's faculty of law. Although studying law, he was fascinated by philosophy and looked for a way to combine the two, believing that "without philosophy nothing could be accomplished." Karl became interested in the recently deceased German philosopher Hegel, whose ideas were then widely debated among European philosophical circles. He joined the Doctor's Club (*Doktorklub*), a student group which discussed Hegelian ideas and through them became involved with a group of radical thinkers known as the Young Hegelians* in 1837. They gathered around Ludwig von Feuerbach and Bruno Bauer, with Karl developing a particularly close friendship with Adolf

* Founding members of the Young Hegelians included: David Friedrich Strauss; Bruno Bauer; Ludwig von Feuerbach; Carl Nauwerck; Arnold Ruge; and Max Stirner. Younger members included: Karl Marx; August von Cieszkowski; Karl Schmidt; and Edgar Bauer (anarchist, political terrorist, and younger brother of Bruno).

Rutenberg. Like Karl, the Young Hegelians were critical of Hegel's metaphysical assumptions, but adopted his dialectical method to criticize established society, politics, and religion from a liberal perspective. Karl's father died in May 1838, resulting in a diminished income for the family. Karl had been emotionally close to his father and treasured his memory after his death.

By 1837, Karl was writing both fiction and non-fiction and engrossed himself in the study of English and Italian, art history, and the translation of Latin classics. He began co-operating with Bruno Bauer on editing Hegel's Philosophy of Religion in 1840. Marx was also engaged in writing his doctoral thesis, *The Difference Between the Democritean and Epicurean Philosophy of Nature*, which he completed in 1841. British journalist, writer, and BBC broadcaster Francis James Baird Wheen described Marx's doctoral thesis as "**a daring and original piece of work in which Marx set out to show that theology must yield to the superior wisdom of philosophy**" (Wheen 2001, 32). The essay was controversial, particularly among the conservative professors at the University of Berlin, then known as Friedrich Wilhelm University since 1828. Marx decided instead to submit his thesis to the more liberal University of Jena, whose faculty awarded him his doctorate in April 1841. As Marx and Bauer were both atheists, they began plans in March 1841 for a journal entitled *Archiv des Atheismus* (*Archives of Atheism*), but it never came to fruition. In July 1841, Marx and Bauer took a trip to Bonn where they scandalized their class by getting drunk, laughing in church, and galloping through the streets on donkeys.

Marx was considering an academic career, but this path was barred by the Prussian government's growing opposition to Liberalism and the Young Hegelians. Marx moved to Cologne in 1842 where he became a journalist writing for the radical newspaper *Rheinische Zeitung* (*Rhineland News*), expressing his early views on Socialism and his developing interest in economics. Marx criticized both conservative European governments, as well as figures in the Liberal and Socialist movements whom he thought ineffective or counterproductive. The newspaper attracted the attention of the Prussian government censors, who checked every issue for seditious material before printing, as Marx lamented: "Our newspaper has to be presented to the police to be sniffed at, and if the police nose smells anything un-Christian or un-Prussian, the newspaper is not allowed to appear." After the *Rheinische Zeitung* published an article strongly criticizing the Russian monarchy, Tsar Nicholas I requested it be banned and Prussia's government complied in March 1843. The intelligentsia of the Rhineland saw the suppression of the newspaper as a personal affront and a delegation was sent to Berlin to forestall the paper's final closure. Subscriptions had risen to more than 3,000—very few German papers of the day were larger, and none more widely quoted. Moreover, thousands of citizens signed petitions calling for the publication's continuation. Prussian King Friedrich Wilhelm IV ignored all petitions and pleas. The Prussian authorities then promptly ran Marx out of town.

In October 1843, Marx and his wife moved to Paris. During the time they lived at 38 *Rue Vanneau* in Paris (from October 1843 until January 1845), Marx engaged in an intensive study of "political economy" (Adam Smith, David Ricardo, James Mill, etc.), the French Utopian Socialists (especially Henri de Saint-Simon, Charles Fourier, Pierre-Joseph Proudhon, Étienne Cabet, etc.), the history of France, and the writings of Weitling. His stay in Paris lasted barely fifteen months. But they were fifteen months that meant a revolution in his life.

The 1830s and 1840s were exceptionally creative decades. Paris was at the focal point for everything new. Social projects blossomed, at least in ideas and dreams. Most of Henri de Saint-Simon's many followers were in Paris, Charles Fourier's visions of the future drew people to the city, and it was here that Étienne Cabet's plans for a new kingdom of happiness enjoyed success. Pierre Leroux, who helped redefine Socialism, was in Paris. And another term, "Communism," was also turning up more and more frequently.

During these tumultuous decades, Paris was a melting pot of ideologies in literature, music, art, and politics. It was this remarkable environment which greeted Marx and his pregnant wife Jenny. Domestic happiness did not prevent the young husband and father from making himself at home in the simmering new environment. He was not the only German who had taken refuge in Paris. There was an entire German colony that included everyone from poets to craftsmen. In Paris, they could live a freer, richer life than they could in their German homelands.

One of them was the great author Heinrich Heine. Marx came to know his distant cousin in December 1843, and he, Jenny, and Heine began a deep friendship. Through Heine, Marx began to frequent one of the real focal points of Parisian life: the salon of Marie d'Agoult (pen name Daniel Stern), where many musicians, artists, authors, and many of the great personages of the era met. At that time, Paris was the cultural capital of Europe, but it also constituted a center for new, revolutionary political ideas. Culture and politics met at Madame d'Agoult's. Many of the more or less regular visitors to her salon were living in exile. Heinrich Heine and Karl Marx were just two of them. It was at her salon that Marx met several of the great personages of the time: Franz Liszt, Frédéric Chopin, George Sand, Charles-Augustin Saint-Beuve, Jean-Auguste-Dominique Ingres, and likely the prose author whom he would rank highest of all throughout his life—Honoré de Balzac.

Heinrich Heine's importance to Marx during this momentous time in Paris is often underestimated. Marx deeply admired Heine's poetry, as Heine just as highly appreciated the intelligence and acumen of his twenty-one-year-old friend and distant cousin. But Heine's influence was certainly greater than mutual admiration. Heine introduced the young Marx to much that could not be found in Trier, Bonn, or Berlin.

Like many other Germans, Heine initially had a positive view of the 1830 revolution in France; in fact, it was the direct reason Heine settled in Paris in 1831. In the art of painter Léopold Robert, Heine found signs that people were abandoning their dreams of finding happiness in the life to come and were now instead looking for it in this world. But the more that cold economic calculations prevailed in 1830s France, the darker Heine's image of the times became. He sought escapes from the society of egoism in various Socialist and Communist ideas. The world of ideas that Marx first encountered in Paris was thus well known to his new friend, who was significantly older.

Like his new fellow traveler, Heine gladly talked about the need for revolution. At the same time, his political radicalism was mostly aesthetic. It was in art, literature, and music that Heine could most clearly read the need for a new and better society. He was not alone in this. The Socialist tendency he sympathized with above all—Saint-Simonism—contained a crucial aesthetic component. In it, the artist was the central figure in the new society of the future taking over the role of the priests.

Marx did not make his most important contacts in the salons of Paris but in significantly darker locales where the worker and craftsman dwelt. However, both the salons and the back alleys of the commoners shared the idea that society had to be changed completely, but while this topic was the subject of smart conversation at Madame d'Agoult's, it was a matter of life and livelihood in the poorer quarters (Liedman 2018, 107–112).

During his time in Paris, Marx became co-editor of a new, radical Socialist Parisian newspaper, the *Deutsch-Französische Jahrbücher* (*German French Annals*), established by the German Socialist Arnold Ruge to bring together German and French radicals. In 1844, Marx contributed two essays to the paper, "Introduction to a Contribution to the Critique of Hegel's Philosophy of Right" and "On the Jewish Question," the latter was in response to Bruno Bauer's 1843 provocative anti-Semitic treatise *Die Judenfrage*[3] and introduced Marx's belief that the proletariat were a revolutionary force and marking his embrace of Communism. Only one issue was published in 1844, but it was relatively successful, largely owing to the inclusion of Heinrich Heine's satirical odes on King Ludwig of Bavaria, leading the German states to ban it and seize imported copies. After the paper's collapse, Marx began writing for the only uncensored German-language radical newspaper left, *Vorwärts!* (*Forward!*). Based in Paris, the paper was connected to the League of the Just. Marx attended some of their meetings but did not join.

In *Vorwärts!* Marx refined his views on Socialism based upon Hegelian and Feuerbachian ideas of historical materialism, at the same time criticizing Liberals and other Socialists in Europe. On 28 August 1844, Marx met the German Communist Friedrich Engels at the Café de la Régence, beginning a lifelong friendship. By late 1844, Marx had pretty much solidified the outline of his vision of Communism ("Marxism"). In 1845, after receiving a request from the Prussian king, the French government shut down *Vorwärts!* with the interior minister, François Guizot, expelling Marx from France in February 1845. At this point, Marx moved from Paris to Brussels, where Marx hoped to continue his study of Capitalism and political economy once again.

To stay in Belgium, he had to pledge not to publish anything on the subject of contemporary politics. In Brussels, Marx associated with other exiled Socialists from across Europe, including Moses Heß, Karl Heinzen, and Joseph Weydemeyer. In April 1845, Engels moved from Barmen in Germany to Brussels to join Marx and the growing cadre of members of the League of the Just now seeking home in Brussels.

Marx and his wife Jenny had seven children in total, but partly owing to the poor conditions in which they lived in London (their final residence), only three survived to adulthood. Following the death of his wife on 2 December 1881 (liver cancer), Marx's health quickly deteriorated over the last fifteen months of his life. Developing bronchitis and pleurisy, he died in London on 14 March 1883 (age 64) a stateless person. (The remainder of Marx's biography can be read under Friedrich Engels, below.)

Friedrich Engels (1820–1895) – German political philosopher, social scientist, journalist, businessman, and son of wealthy industrialist and pietist Lutherans. Friedrich was born in Barmen, Rhineland Prussia. The

Engels had British connections. Friedrich Engels, Sr. was a partner in Ermen & Engels cotton mill in Manchester, England. Attending the excellent gymnasium (university preparatory high school) in Barmen, Friedrich Jr. was a gifted student. However, as his interests in literature and poetry deepened, his father withdrew his son from gymnasium one year before his graduation (1838). He was sent to the larger, northern port city of Bremen where at the age of seventeen-years he began working as an unsalaried apprentice in the export business. During his time in Bremen, Friedrich began to lead a double life, pleasing his father developing a business career while secretly pursuing his own pleasures in literature, the arts, languages, philosophy, revolutionary political theory, and athletics. He became particularly fond of the writings of Hegel. The Young Hegelians wanted to accelerate historical change and direct it toward rational progress. As a result, they criticized all that they found irrational, outmoded, and repressive. And as an outgrowth of the Enlightenment, one of their primary targets was Christianity. It is at this time that because of his readings and conversations an already agnostic Engels was converted unto a militant atheist. This perhaps more than his political and economic views greatly disturbed his pious parents. While still in Bremen, Engels began his journalism career and found that despite the lack of a normal education he was good at it. In 1841, he returned to his family in Barmen and enlisted as a one-year volunteer in a Berlin artillery regiment. In cosmopolitan Berlin, he continued his double life, even attending university lectures and joining the Young Hegelians. His officers had no idea their young recruit was becoming a revolutionary. He anonymously published articles in Cologne's *Rheinische Zeitung* addressing the poor working and living conditions of factory workers. Ten months after the newspaper's first publication (January 1842), Marx was appointed to the editorial board of the *Rheinische Zeitung*, whose chief editor at the time was Moses Heß, although Marx and Engels did not meet until later. In his debates among his circle of Young Hegelians, Friedrich became known as a formidable debater on philosophical matters, particularly religion.

While in Berlin, Friedrich met Moses Heß, with whom he had intense discussions. Their connection was the Hegelian dialectic. It was Heß who converted Engels to Communism, although he was yet to become a "Marxist." Moses Heß and Engels agreed that the future of the proletarian revolution lied in Britain, the capital of the Industrial Revolution. In 1842, Friedrich moved to Manchester, England where his father owned a textile mill. While continuing his business training, Friedrich wrote articles on Communism for both European and English journals and read books and

British parliamentary reports on economic and political issues. He decided to write a history of England focusing on the Industrial Revolution and the poverty of the workers. By this time, Friedrich had begun to formulate many of his key political concepts of "scientific" Socialism. He concluded the industrial system developing in Britain and Germany based on ownership of private property would ultimately lead to a world consisting of "millionaires and paupers." He advocated a Communist revolution that would eliminate private property and reconcile humanity with nature.

In 1844, Friedrich traveled to Paris where he first met Karl Marx. Marx fled Prussia after encountering problems with the German authorities and traveled to Paris in 1843 to work on a journal to promote his ideas on social reform. After much exchange of views, the two concluded that social reform was not possible without revolution. Marx followed Engels back to England and the two collaborated on *Die deutsche Ideologie* (*German Ideology*) but did not publish it until decades later. Together, they denounced and ridiculed many of their earlier Young Hegelian comrades and sharply attacked German Socialists who rejected the idea of revolution. This shift began a division that would fundamentally split the world Socialist movement into Marxist revolutionaries and Socialist reformers.

In 1845, Engels joined Marx at the Brussels conference where Marx and Weitling would battle over the role of religion in the Communist movement and result in a major split between the two schools. After the failure of the 1848 Revolutions, Marx and Engels returned to England in November 1849 disappointed. Marx and his family would remain based in London for the rest of his life. In London, Marx and Engels reorganized the Communist League (originally formed on 1 June 1847 with the merging of the Communist Correspondence Committee of Brussels and Karl Schapper's League of the Just) and began sending directives to operatives on the European mainland, convinced a second stronger wave of revolutions would soon follow. In the early period in London, Marx committed himself almost exclusively to revolutionary activities such that his family endured extreme poverty. Engels financed their entire organization and program, as well as their two immediate families. In February 1848, Engels collaborated with and financed Marx to publish *Manifesto of the Communist Party* (*Manifest der Kommunistischen Partei*) for the Communist League. To continue collecting his family's wealth and help finance his and Marx's collaborative work, Friedrich accepted a clerk's position in his father's Manchester textile factory. He was a successful businessman and eventually became full partner in the factory in 1864, five years before his retirement. Despite his work at the mill, Engels found time to write his monumental work on Martin Luther, the Protestant Reformation, and the 1525 revolutionary war of the peasants. This work, entitled *The Peasant War in Germany* (*Der deutsche Bauernkrieg*), was published in 1850. While Engels lived and worked in Manchester, Marx operated out of London. The two maintained constant correspondence (after Marx's death in 1883, Engels destroyed over 1,500 letters to conceal the details of their secretive lifestyle and revolutionary activities). After Engels's retirement from the textile factory, one of the ideas that he and Marx contemplated was the possibility and character of a potential revolution in Russia. As early as April 1853, Engels and Marx anticipated an aristocratic-*bourgeois* revolution in Russia, which would begin in St. Petersburg with a resulting civil war in the interior.

In 1867, Marx finally completed his eighteen-year-long project and published the first of three planned volumes of the landmark *Das Kapital, Kritik der politischen Ökonomie* (*Capital, Critique of Political Economy*). *Das Kapital* is a foundational theoretical text in materialist philosophy, economics, and politics revealing the economic patterns underpinning the Capitalist mode of production and Marx's view that the motivating force of Capitalism is in the exploitation of labor, whose unpaid work is the ultimate source of surplus value protected by the ruling regime through property rights and distribution of shares, which are by law only to be distributed to company owners and their board members. In his historical review of these property rights, Marx explains how these rights were originally acquired chiefly through plunder, conquest, and the activity of the merchant and "middle-man." University of London professor of history and director of the Centre for History and Economics at the University of Cambridge, UK, Gareth Stedman Jones wrote in the journal *Nature*:

> What is extraordinary about *Das Kapital* is that it offers a still-unrivalled picture of the dynamism of Capitalism and its transformation of societies on a global scale. It firmly embedded concepts such as commodity and capital in the lexicon. And it highlights some of the vulnerabilities of Capitalism, including its unsettling disruption of states and political systems. [. . .] If *Das Kapital* has now emerged as one of the great landmarks of nineteenth-century thought, it is [because it connects] critical analysis of the economy of his time with its historical roots. In doing so, he inaugurated a debate about how best to reform or transform politics and

social relations, which has gone on ever since. (Jones 2017, 401–2.)

In 1870, Engels moved to London where he and Marx lived until Marx's death in 1883. After Marx's death, Engels devoted much of his remaining years to editing and publishing Marx's unfinished two volumes (1885 and 1894) of *Das Kapital.* Despite his disappointing political and religious views, his family in Barmen remained loyal to Friedrich. His doting mother, to whom Engels was closely attached throughout her life, and her love prevented a breech in the frayed ties between father and son. As a result, Engels never suffered the adult poverty and dependency that his friend and colleague Karl Marx experienced. Fredrich Engels died of throat cancer in London on 5 August 1895, at age 74 without any children. He left Marx's two surviving daughters a "significant portion" of his considerable estate (valued in 2011 at 4.8 million U.S. Dollars).

Ferdinand Lassalle (1825–1864) – German Jewish jurist, philosopher, Socialist, political activist, and friend of Moses Heß. Ferdinand Lassalle, the son of a successful silk merchant, was born in Wrocław, Silesia, on 11 April 1825. He studied philosophy and law in Berlin, and he became a strong supporter of German philosopher Georg Hegel (1770–1831). He developed a working professional relationship with then Minister-President of Prussia Otto von Bismarck and managed to influence state policy. In the 1850s and 1860s, Karl Marx was in frequent contact with Lassalle, with them regularly exchanging letters with each other from 1858 to 1862. Lassalle was a member of Marx's Communist League. On 23 May 1863, together with Eduard Bernstein, Lassalle founded the first Marxist organization in Germany, the *Allgemeiner Deutscher Arbeiterverein, ADAV* (General German Workers' Association), the precursor to the *Sozialdemokratische Partei Deutschlands, SPD* (Social Democratic Party of Germany)—the first and longest-lasting Marxist-influenced political party in world history that actually wielded political power. He was a proponent of the revisionist theory of Marxism (see Eduard Bernstein, *infra*). In Berlin, Lassalle met a young woman, Helene von Dönniges, and during the summer of 1864, they decided to marry. She was the daughter of an historian then living in Geneva, who would have nothing to do with Lassalle. The elder von Dönniges prevented Helene from seeing Ferdinand. Lassalle protested vehemently, but soon, apparently under duress, she renounced Lassalle in favor of another suitor, a Wallachian prince named Iancu Racoviță, to whom she had previously been engaged. Lassalle sent dueling challenges both to Helene's father von Dönniges, and to Racoviță, who accepted. At the Carouge, a suburb of Geneva, a duel was held on the morning of 28 August. Lassalle was shot in the abdomen by Racoviță, and Lassalle died three days later on 31 August 1864. Lassalle is best remembered as the initiator of national-style Socialism in Germany known as Lassallism—the strategy of the pursuit of Socialism through the use of the state political apparatus.

Eduard Bernstein (1850–1932) – German Jewish Socialist propagandist, political theorist, and historian. Together with Ferdinand Lassalle, he helped found the *ADAV* in 1863. In 1898, he was one of the first Socialists to attempt a revision of Karl Marx's tenets, such as abandoning the ideas of the imminent collapse of the Capitalist economy and the seizure of power by the proletariat. Bernstein, called "the father of revisionism," envisaged a type of Social Democracy that combined private initiative with social reform. Bernstein distinguished between early Marxism as being its immature form, as exemplified in *Manifesto of the Communist Party*, which he opposed for what he regarded as its violent Blanquist tendencies. He instead favored Marxism in its mature form, which holds that Socialism could be achieved by peaceful means through incremental legislative reform in Democratic societies.

Die Voraussetzungen des Sozialismus (*The Prerequisites of Socialism*, 1899) was Bernstein's most significant work. Bernstein was principally concerned with refuting Marx's predictions about the imminent and inevitable demise of Capitalism, and Marx's consequent *laissez faire* policy which opposed ameliorative social interventions before the demise. Bernstein indicated simple facts that he considered to be evidence that Marx's predictions were not being borne out: he noted that the centralization of Capitalist industry, while significant, was not becoming wholescale and that the ownership of capital was becoming more, and not less, diffuse. Bernstein's analysis of agriculture (according to which Bernstein believed that land ownership was becoming less concentrated) was largely based on the work of Eduard David and was in its marshalling of facts impressive enough that even his orthodox opponent Karl Kautsky acknowledged its value.

As to Marx's belief in the disappearance of the middleman, Bernstein declared that the entrepreneur class was being steadily recruited from the proletariat class, and therefore all compromise measures, such as the state regulation of the hours of labor, provisions for old-age pensions, and so on, should be encouraged. For this reason, Bernstein urged the labor classes to take an active interest in politics. Bernstein also indicated what he considered to be some of the flaws in Marx's labor theory of value.

Looking especially at the rapid growth in Germany, Bernstein argued that middle-sized firms would flourish, the size and power of the middle class would grow, and Capitalism would successfully adjust, and not collapse. He warned that violent proletarian revolution, as in France in 1848, produced only reactionary successes that undermined workers' interests. Therefore, he rejected revolution and instead insisted the best strategy was patiently building up a durable social movement working for continuous nonviolent incremental change through Democratic legislative means.

In her publication *Sozialreform oder Revolution?* (1889; *Social Reform or Revolution?*), Rosa Luxemburg categorically opposed Bernstein's revisionist theory and defended Marxist orthodoxy and the necessity of violent revolution, arguing that parliament was nothing more than a *bourgeois* sham. Karl Kautsky, the leading theoretician of the Second International, agreed with her, and revisionism consequently became viewed as a Socialist heresy both in Germany and abroad, though it continued to make headway, especially in the labor movement.

Wilhelm Liebknecht (1826–1900) – German Socialist, close associate of Karl Marx, and later cofounder of the *Sozialdemokratische Arbeiterpartei Deutschlands*, *SDAP* (Social Democratic Workers' Party of Germany). Wilhelm Liebknecht was born in 1826 in Gießen (Grand Duchy of Hesse), the son of pietist Lutheran parents Katharina Elisabeth Henrietta (née Hirsch) and Hessian public official Ludwig Christian Liebknecht. Wilhelm grew up with relatives after the death of his parents in 1832. From 1832 to 1842, he went to school at the gymnasium of Gießen. Between 1842 and 1847, he studied philology, philosophy, and pietistic Lutheran theology in Gießen, Berlin, and Marburg where he was strongly influenced by republican and Utopian Socialist ideas. After some trouble with German authorities, consequent to his participating in student radicalism, Wilhelm decided to emigrate to America. However, while on a train to a port city, he met the headmaster of the famous Friedrich Wilhelm Fröbel model school in Zürich, Switzerland and impulsively decided to accept an offer to be an unpaid teacher at that school. He found himself in Switzerland in 1847 in the midst of civil war. In September 1848, he participated in the uprising in Lörrach (Kingdom of Württemberg) and in May 1849 in the Baden (Grand Duchy) Revolution as Gustav Struve's adjutant. In Baden, he was arrested and managed to escape back to Switzerland. In Geneva, he joined the German Workers' Association. Wilhelm soon departed Geneva and took flight to London in 1850 where he met and befriended Karl Marx and Friedrich Engels. In 1862, amnesty was granted to 1848–49 revolutionaries arrested in Germany. Wilhelm left London and returned to Germany where he soon joined the General German Workers' Association (*ADAV*) of Ferdinand Lassalle in 1863. Consistent criticism of Otto von Bismarck's Conservative-Nationalist policies led in 1865 to Liebknecht's expulsion from Prussia, as well as the *ADAV*. He traveled to Leipzig where he met and befriended Socialist August Bebel (1840–1913). In Chemnitz, Saxony, Liebknecht and Bebel founded the *Sächsische Volkspartei* (Saxon People's Party—an alliance between liberal, anti-Prussian *bourgeois* and Socialist workers' organizations in Saxony) in 1866. In 1869, he helped found the Social Democratic Workers' Party (*SDAP*). He was a member of the *Reichstag* under the new German Empire in 1871. In 1872–1874, he served two years in prison for high treason for his opposition to the annexation of Alsace and Lorraine. In 1875, he was responsible for the merging of the *SDAP* and *ADAV* to form the Socialist Workers' Party of Germany (*SAPD*). In 1876, he became editor of the Socialist biweekly newspaper *Vorwärts!* During the period of Anti-Socialist Laws outlawing all Socialist political parties (1878–1890), he was imprisoned several times, yet managed to publish several important programmatic statements of the German labor movement. From 1890 until his death, he was the chief editor of *Vorwärts!* and remained an active member of the *Reichstag* representing the *SPD* (formerly known as *SAPD*). He played a leading role in the international Socialist movement spreading Socialism in the United States (1886), Britain (1896), and the Netherlands (1897). He died in the Charlottenburg district of Berlin on 7 August 1900. He was the father of Karl Liebknecht, the Communist revolutionary who collaborated with the Polish-German Jewish Communist revolutionary Rosa Luxemburg in the January 1919 Spartacist Uprising in Germany. Luxemburg and Karl Liebknecht formed the *Kommunistische Partei Deutschlands, KPD* (Communist Party of Germany) on 1 January 1919. Both were executed during the Spartacist Uprising.

Leopold Sonnemann (1831–1909) – Wealthy German Jewish textile merchant, journalist, newspaper publisher, political party activist, and public patron who in 1863 helped found the *Verband Deutscher Arbeitervereine, VDAV* (League of German Worker Associations), the rival to the *ADAV*. He was born in Höchberg near Würzburg, Bavaria to a successful cloth merchant. Well-educated in his youth, he became an astute businessman and organizer. He built upon his family business by converting it into a banking company and amassed enough wealth by 1856 to establish a Bavarian market publication, the *Frankfurter Geschäftsbericht*, changing the name the same year to *Frankfurt Handelszeitung*. In 1859, he added the title *Neue Frankfurter Zeitung* when he added a political section. Rechristening it in 1866 to simply *Frankfurter Zeitung* (also known as *Handelsblatt*), Sonnemann devoted himself wholeheartedly to the paper as owner, editor, and contributing writer. Their editors were committed to creating a liberal, Social-Democratic society. The paper developed an influential position in the business community of southern Germany. Using this position, Sonnemann successfully attracted and organized a workers' movement in Germany. In 1868, he and fellow leaders of the *VDAV* broke from the German Progress Party and founded the German People's Party on a working-class political platform that opposed Chancellor Otto von Bismarck's *kleindeutsche* Prussian solution to German unification. After the founding of the *Reich* in 1871, the *Frankfurter Zeitung* became an important forum for extra-parliamentary liberal-*bourgeois* opposition to the conservative government. Of the established political parties, the *Frankfurter Zeitung* was the closest to the strongly liberal German People's Party. Sonnemann represented his German People's Party in the *Reichstag* from 1871 to 1884. Leopold Sonnemann died on 30 October 1909 in Frankfurt am Main. During the period of the Weimar Republic, the *Frankfurter Zeitung* drew hostility from Nationalist circles when in 1918 it supported acceptance of the Versailles Treaty. The *Frankfurter Zeitung* was kept running by Sonnemann's coterie, providing an alternative national media outlet for German Liberals. It survived precariously after the Nazi assumption of power but was finally acquired by a subsidiary of the Nazi publishing organ *Eher Verlag* in 1938, and ultimately closed by Adolf Hitler's order in August 1943.

Rosa Luxemburg (1871–1919) – Polish-German Jewish Marxist theorist, philosopher, political economist, prolific author, lecturer, orthodox Marxist revolutionary, and antiwar activist who became a naturalized German citizen at the age of twenty-eight-years. Luxemburg was born on 5 March 1871 in Zamość, then Russian-controlled Poland. She was the fifth and youngest child of timber trader Eliasz Luxemburg and Line (Helena) Löwenstein. Rosa later stated that her father imparted an interest in liberal ideas in her, while her mother was religious and well-read with books kept at home. The family spoke German and Polish, and Rosa also learned Russian. The family moved to Warsaw in 1873. After being bedridden with a hip ailment at the age of five-years, she was left with a permanent limp. In 1880, Luxemburg began her *gymnázium* ("gymnasium" in German) education.

From 1886, she belonged to the Polish Marxist Proletariat Party (founded in 1882, anticipating Russian political parties by twenty years). She began political activities by organizing a general strike; as a result, four of the Proletariat Party leaders were put to death and the party was disbanded, though the remaining members, including Luxemburg, kept meeting in secret. In 1887, she passed her *Maturita* (*gymnázium* graduation) examinations two years earlier than her peers.

After fleeing to Switzerland to escape detention in 1889, she matriculated at the University of Zurich where she met Marxist revolutionaries the Russian Anatoly Lunacharsky (1875–1933, future first Bolshevik Soviet People's Commissar of Ministry of Education) and Polish Jew Leon Jogiches (1867–1919). She studied philosophy, history, politics, economics, and mathematics and specialized in *Staatswissenschaft* (political science), the Middle Ages, and the history of crises in economics and stock exchanges. Rosa and Leo Jogiches fell in love while in Zurich and became both close political allies and personal companions for many years. Rosa's doctoral dissertation, *Die Industrielle Entwicklung Polens* (*The Industrial Development of Poland*), was officially presented in the spring of 1897 at the University of Zurich, which awarded her a Doctor of Philosophy degree. She was an oddity in Zurich as she was one of the very few women with a doctorate.

After completing the bulk of her university studies in 1893, she plunged immediately into the politics of international Marxism, following in the footsteps of Marxist revolutionaries Russian Georgi Plekhanov (1856–1918) and Lithuanian Jew Pavel Axelrod (1850–1928). In 1893, she moved to Paris where with Leon Jogiches, Julian Marchlewski (alias Julius Karski), and Adolf Warski founded the magazine *Sprawa Robotnicza* (*The Workers' Affairs*)—published in Paris in the Polish language and distributed internationally from 1893–1896—which opposed the Nationalist policies of the Polish Socialist Party. Also in 1893, she and Leo Jogiches co-founded the *Socjaldemokracja Królestwa Polskiego, SDKP* (Social Democracy of the Kingdom of Poland) later known as the *Socjaldemokracja Królestwa Polskiego i Litwy, SDKPiL* (Social Democracy of the Kingdom of Poland and Lithuania), the precursor to the *Komunistyczna Partia Robotnicza Polski, KPRP* or *KPP* (Communist Workers' Party of Poland), founded on 16 December 1918. In August 1893, she traveled to Zurich to attend the Second International Congress. Despite living in Germany for most of her adult life, Luxemburg was the principal theoretician of the *SDKPiL* and led the party in a partnership with Jogiches, its principal organizer. In 1896,

Luxemburg traveled to London to attend the next International Socialist Congress, during which the right of nations to self-determination and opposition to colonialism was affirmed. However, Luxemburg believed that an independent Poland could arise and exist only through Socialist revolutions in Germany, Austria, and Russia. She maintained that the struggle should be against Capitalism and not just for Polish independence. Her position of denying a national right of self-determination under Socialism provoked a philosophic disagreement with Vladimír Lenin. After considerable success in Paris, Rosa Luxemburg wanted to immigrate permanently to Germany to be at the epicenter of Communist activism, which in the late nineteenth century was in Germany. However, she had no way of obtaining permanent residence status in Germany. In April 1897 after successfully defending her doctoral dissertation at the University of Zurich, she traveled to Germany and married the son of an old friend, Gustav Lubeck, to gain German citizenship. They never lived together, and they formally divorced five years later. She returned briefly to Paris, then in May 1898, settled permanently in Berlin to begin her fight for Eduard Bernstein's constitutional reform movement. Luxemburg hated the stifling conservatism of Berlin. She despised Prussian men and resented what she saw as the grip of urban Capitalism on Social Democracy.

The Russian Revolution of 1905 erupted abruptly on "Bloody Sunday," 22 January with the shooting deaths of hundreds of peaceful protesters who were attempting to present a petition to Tsar Nicholas II at his Winter Palace in St. Petersburg. Within days, protests and strikes calling for establishment of a Constitutional Monarchy swept the empire, which rocked the state censorship and threatened the stability of the government for months.

"Bloody Sunday" was an historical milestone deserving closer examination in this review of revolutionary movements. "Bloody Sunday" (*Крова́вое воскресе́нье* or *Krovávoye voskresén'e*) was just one of many in a long line of revolts that occurred in Imperial Russia that began with the Enlightenment and concluded with the founding of the Soviet Union on 30 December 1922. Although palace revolts occurred throughout Russia's history, grassroots revolts began in earnest during the reign of Russian Emperor Alexander I (reign 1801–1825) shortly after the American and French Revolutions. Alexander's father, Emperor Paul I (Pavel Petrovich), son of Empress Catherine the Great (Prussian-born) and Peter III (of Schleswig-Holstein-Gottorp), began instituting social reforms shortly after ascending to the Russian throne in 1796. Paul I's reforms attempted to clean up corruption in the Russian treasury, grant greater rights for the peasantry, and better treatment for serfs; most of his policies were viewed as a great threat to the noble class whose wealth and power depended on free serf labor. In 1801, Paul I was assassinated by a band of dismissed aristocratic military officers. Shortly after his son Alexander I ascended to the Russian throne, he continued his father's liberal reforms in education and social matters. He also had plans to establish a Constitutional Monarchy sharing power with a parliament. After defeating Napoléon in 1815, Alexander I continued his liberal reforms abolishing serfdom in Baltic provinces in 1816 and initiating drafting of a constitution in 1818. However, internal and external unrest, which the Tsar believed stemmed from political liberalization, led to a series of repressions and a return to absolutist monarchism. A revolutionary conspiracy among the officers of the Imperial Guard, and a foolish plot to kidnap him on his way to the Congress of Aix-la-Chapelle, are said to have shaken the foundations of his Liberalism.

Alexander I died of typhus on 1 December 1825 without an heir and confusion ensued when Alexander's first younger brother, Constantine, refused the throne. Alexander's second younger brother, the political conservative Nicholas I, then assumed the throne. This succession eventually led to the Decembrist Revolt on 26 December 1825 when a group of Royal Guards officers (themselves members of the aristocratic class) commanding about 3,000 men in Peter's Square in St. Petersburg refused to swear allegiance to Nicholas I, proclaiming instead their loyalty to Constantine and their Decembrist Constitution. The Constitution was essentially a Russian translation of the U.S. Constitution. But Decembrists were against U.S. slavery. Any slaves and serfs from all countries were to become free in Russia immediately. The Decembrists were members of the secret and illegal Northern Society—an offspring of the first underground Russian political societies the Union of Salvation (1816) and the Union of Prosperity (1818). Unlike the more radical Union of Salvation, the objectives of the Union of Prosperity were abolishment of autocracy and serfdom and introduction of constitutional form of government through peaceful means. Northern Society's sister organization, the Southern Society, was more radical and, in the spirit of Western European revolutionaries of the time, wanted to abolish the monarchy, establish a republic, and redistribute land: taking half into state ownership and dividing the rest among the peasants. When it became clear the Russian nobility rejected the notions of the Northern and Southern Societies, members of the Northern Society decided to revolt in St. Petersburg on 26 December 1825.

The revolt was a bloody disaster for the Decembrists. A subsequent revolt in Tulchin, Ukraine by the Southern Society on 15 January 1826 met with a similar disastrous outcome. Those who survived the battles were either tried and executed or sent to gulags in Siberia, Kazakhstan, and the Far East. The exile of the Decembrists led to the permanent implantation of an intelligentsia in Siberia. For the first time, a cultural, intellectual, and political elite came to Siberian society as permanent residents; they integrated with the country and participated alongside natives in its development.

Although the revolt was a proscribed topic during Nicholas I's reign, Alexander Herzen placed the profiles of executed Decembrists on the cover of his radical periodical *Polar Star*. Alexander Pushkin addressed poems to his Decembrist friends, Nikolai Nekrasov wrote a long poem about the Decembrist wives, and Leo Tolstoy started writing a novel on that liberal movement, which would later evolve into *War and Peace*. In the Soviet era, Yuri Shaporin produced an opera entitled *Dekabristi* (*The Decembrists*), about the revolt, with the libretto written by Aleksey Nikolayevich Tolstoy (a remote relative of Leo Tolstoy). It premiered at the Bolshoi Theatre on 23 June 1953. The Decembrist revolt has been considered the beginning of the revolutionary movement in Russia. The uprising was the first open breach between the government and reformist elements of the Russian nobility, which would subsequently widen.

The revolutionaries were handed another opportunity in the mid-nineteenth century. Russia, as a member of the Holy Alliance (Russia-Austria-Prussia) under Alexander I, had operated as the "police of Europe," maintaining the balance of power that had been established in the Treaty of Vienna in 1815. Russia helped save several European monarchies including Austria's during the 1848 Revolutions and expected gratitude; it wanted a free hand in settling its problems with the declining Ottoman Empire, the "sick man of Europe." Britain could not tolerate Russian dominance of Ottoman affairs, as that would challenge its domination of the eastern Mediterranean.

Starting with Peter the Great (reign 1689–1725), after centuries of Ottoman northward expansion and Crimean-Nogai raids (1441–1774), Russia had been expanding southwards across the sparsely populated "Wild Fields" toward the warm water ports of the Black Sea, which did not freeze over like the handful of ports it controlled in the north. The goal was to promote year-round trade and a year-round navy. Pursuit of this goal brought the emerging Russian state into conflict with the Ukrainian Cossacks and then with the Tatars of the Crimean Khanate and Circassians. When Russia under Nicholas I conquered these groups and gained possession of their territories, the Ottoman Empire lost its buffer zone against Russian expansion, and Russia and the Ottoman Empire came into direct conflict in what was to be known as the Crimean War (1853–1856).

> In some sense the Crimean war was predestined and had deep-seated causes. Neither Nicholas I nor Napoleon III nor the British government could retreat in the conflict for prestige once it was launched. Nicholas needed a subservient Turkey for the sake of Russian security; Napoleon needed success for the sake of his domestic position; the British government needed an independent Turkey for the security of the Eastern Mediterranean. . . . Mutual fear, not mutual aggression, caused the Crimean war. (Taylor 1954, 60–1.)

Due to the Industrial Revolution in Western Europe, British and French militaries were far more advanced than the Russian military, which suffered from decades of deterioration and neglect after defeating Napoléon in 1815. Russia faced defeat after defeat from the superior and more modern British and French forces. The Crimean War was one of the first conflicts to use modern technologies such as explosive naval shells, railways, and telegraphs. The war was one of the first to be documented extensively in written reports and photographs. The war quickly became an iconic symbol of logistical, medical, and tactical failures and mismanagement.

Before the conclusion of the war, Nicholas I died of pneumonia in March 1855. His son Alexander II inherited the throne and the disastrous war, and immediately conceded defeat and began calling home his troops from the front. The Crimean War was a sobering military and psychological defeat for Russia. Like his grandfather Alexander I before him, Alexander II instituted reforms to modernize the military, pardon the Decembrists, abolish corporal punishment, institute trial by jury, relax censorship, license new industries, commission a railway line to the Black Sea, and emancipate Russia's serfs. The nobility vehemently opposed the emancipation of the serfs since doing so would evaporate their fortunes and threaten the Russian economy built on serfdom. But Alexander II believed this was the only way to save the autocracy—either the autocracy emancipated the serfs, or the serfs would emancipate themselves and bring down the autocracy. Two years before Abraham Lincoln freed American slaves, Alexander II freed Russian serfs in March 1861. The emancipation of the serfs did not suddenly end the state of grim rural poverty in Russia, and the autocracy headed by the Tsar of Russia and the nobles around him, as well as the privileged state bureaucracy, remained in firm control of the nation's economy from which it extracted pecuniary benefits. The landed aristocracy raised land prices, which the freed serfs needed to survive and produce crops. Agricultural production plummeted and the Russian economy came to the brink of collapse. By the beginning of the 1870s, dissent regarding the established political and economic order had begun to take concrete form among many members of the intelligentsia, which sought to foster a modern and Democratic society in Russia in place of the economic backwardness and political repression which marked the old regime. In 1877, in an effort to divert attention from his domestic problems, Alexander II exploited an opportunity of political instability in the Balkans to relitigate the disastrous Crimean War—this time better prepared leading a new Eastern Orthodox coalition with independence-aspirational Bulgaria, Romania, Serbia, and Montenegro. This time, the Russian-led coalition won the war. As a result, Russia succeeded in claiming several provinces in the Caucasus, namely Kars and Batum, and also annexed the Budjak region. And Bulgaria, Romania, Serbia, and Montenegro effectively won their independence from the Ottoman Empire.

Despite military conquest in the Balkans, conditions back home remained dire for the working class. Consequently, the revolutionary underground became increasingly vocal in its demand for action. Socialist radicals (*Narodnaya Volya* or *People's Will*) called for free distribution of land, elections, and the Tsar's execution. Ironically, at least seven attempts on the Tsar's life occurred before they succeeded on 13 March 1881, just two days before he planned to present his proposal to share power with a parliament under a constitution. Alexander II's son, Alexander III, ascended the throne with a vengeance towards the revolutionaries and reform. Many of the revolutionaries were captured, tried, and executed or imprisoned. Six years later in 1887, the *Narodnaya Volya* attempted to assassinate Alexander III but failed. One of the ringleaders of this attempt, Alexander Ulyanov, the older brother of Vladimír Ilyich Ulyanov (later known as Lenin), was captured, tried, and executed. Young Ulyanov never forgot the loss of his brother and vowed to carry on his legacy of revolution.

The Russian Industrial Revolution of the 1890s brought many peasant workers into the cities where an industrial worker's class quickly evolved as it had in Western Europe six decades earlier. Russian revolutionary ideology was built upon the philosophical foundation of Russia's *Narodnik*—a populist movement of the 1860s–1870s whose worldview was developed primarily by Alexander Herzen and Pyotr Lavrov. After a period of decline and marginalization in the 1880s, the *Narodnik* school of thought about social change in Russia was revived and substantially modified by a group of writers and activists known as *neonarodniki* (neo-populists), particularly Viktor Chernov. Their main innovation was a renewed dialogue with Marxism and integration of some of the key Marxist concepts into their thinking and practice. In this way, with the economic spurt and industrialization in Russia in the 1890s, they attempted to broaden their appeal in order to attract the rapidly growing urban workforce to their traditionally peasant-oriented program. The intention was to widen the concept of the people so that it encompassed all elements in society that opposed the Tsarist regime. This Marxist ideology began to make its way into the large industrial centers in Russia. In 1893, as a young lawyer Lenin, already well-indoctrinated in Marxist ideology, traveled to one of the largest industrial centers, St. Petersburg, to help organize a Socialist workers' party. This period soon proved to be a critical juncture in Russian political history. On 1 November 1894, Alexander III died, and his son Nikolai Aleksandrovich Romanov ascended to the throne as Nicholas II. Nicholas II was psychologically and intellectually completely unprepared to lead at this challenging and rapidly evolving time in Russian history. Both he and his German princess wife were disinterested in the plight of ordinary Russians, and this proved to be the Romanov dynasty's downfall.

Revolutionary Marxist cells sprang up in the larger industrial centers of Russia with Lenin leading the way. In 1895, Lenin was arrested for his revolutionary activities and exiled to Siberia. After his release three years later, Lenin fled to the West, from where he continued his revolutionary agitation. Disinterested and ignorant of the growing plight and unrest of the working classes, Nicholas II foolishly ventured into an expansionist military campaign against Japan on 8 February 1904 (Russo-Japanese War) over rival imperial ambitions in Manchuria and Korea and a warm-water port on the Pacific Ocean for the Russian navy and for maritime trade. Russia repeated the same hubristic mistakes it made in the Crimean War and suffered multiple defeats. The complete victory of the Japanese military in September 1905 surprised world observers. The consequences transformed the balance of power in East Asia, resulting in a reassessment of Japan's recent entry onto the world stage. It was the first major military victory in the modern era of an Asian power over a European one. Scholars continue to debate the historical significance of the Russo-Japanese war.

Meanwhile, the autumn of 1904 brought soaring inflation and winter brought hunger and hardship to the streets of Russia. News of the string of defeats in the Russo-Japanese War demolished any remaining confidence in the Tsar's leadership. A wave of mass political and social unrest spread through vast areas of the Russian Empire with worker strikes, peasant unrest, and military mutinies. In December 1904, a strike occurred at the Putilov plant (a railway and artillery supplier) in St. Petersburg. Sympathy strikes in other parts of the city raised the number of strikers to 150,000 workers in 382 factories. By 21 January 1905, the city had no electricity and newspaper distribution was halted. All public areas were declared closed.

Controversial Orthodox priest Georgy Gapon, who headed a police-sponsored workers' association, led a huge workers' procession of about 150,000 peaceful demonstrators to the Winter Palace to deliver a petition to the Tsar on Sunday, 22 January 1905. Instead of carrying revolutionary placards, they carried religious icons and a petition with over 100,000 signatures pleading the Tsar to grant representative government, freedom of speech, workers' rights, and to make peace with Japan. The Palace Guards were ordered to tell the demonstrators not to pass a certain point but Gapon and the workers demanded to hand the petition to the Tsar—who, unbeknownst to the demonstrators, left the day before for his residence at Tsarskoye Selo 24 kilometers (15 mi) south of St. Petersburg. At some point, the Guards opened fire on the peaceful demonstrators, causing up to 1,000 deaths and many thousands wounded. The event became known as "Bloody Sunday," and is considered by many scholars as the start of the active phase of the 1905 revolution. The tragedy finally shattered the long-standing myth that the Tsar simply was unaware of the suffering of the Russian people.

The events in St. Petersburg provoked public indignation and a series of massive strikes that spread quickly throughout the industrial centers of the Russian Empire, including the Russian partition of the Polish-Lithuanian Commonwealth and the Russian Caucasus. By March 1905, all higher academic institutions were forcibly closed for the remainder of the year, adding radical students to the striking workers. A strike by railway workers on 21 October 1905 quickly developed into a general strike in St. Petersburg and Moscow. This prompted the setting up of the short-lived St. Petersburg Soviet of Workers' Delegates, an admixture of Bolsheviks and Mensheviks. By 26 October 1905, over two million workers were on strike and there were almost no active railways in all of Russia. Growing interethnic confrontation throughout the Caucasus resulted in Armenian-Tatar massacres (1905–1907),* heavily damaging the cities and the Baku oilfields. The overall estimates of lives lost vary widely, ranging from 3,000 to 10,000. Anti-Jewish pogroms, ongoing since 1903, increased in fervor and severity throughout the Russian Empire. These pogroms occurred during a time when Jews comprised a growing membership in terrorist revolutionary organizations like the Combat Organization (Боевая Организация) wing of the Social Revolutionary Party of Russia (*Партия социалистов-революционеров, ПСР*), of which Jews made up one-third of the membership willing to undertake bombings and assassinations of aristocratic leaders of Imperial Russia (Gorodnitsky 1998, 235–6). It was also during this revolutionary time that the Tsar's secret police *Okhrana* distributed the forged *The Protocols of the Elders of Zion* for mass publication to incite anti-Semitic reaction and divert attention from the Tsar's domestic problems (see: "Commentary on *The Protocols of the Elders of Zion*" by Professor Daniel Keren, Ph.D., *infra*).

With the unsuccessful and bloody Russo-Japanese War there was unrest in army reserve units. On 2 January 1905, Port Arthur was lost; in February 1905, the Russian army was defeated at Mukden, losing almost 80,000 men. On 18 February 1905, under great pressure, Tsar Nicholas II agreed to the creation of a State Duma of the Russian Empire but with consultative powers only. When its slight powers and limits on the electorate were revealed, unrest redoubled. On 27–28 May 1905, the Russian Baltic Fleet was defeated at Tsushima. In June and July 1905, there were many peasant uprisings in which peasants seized land and tools. Disturbances in Russian-controlled Polish-Lithuania culminated in June 1905 in the Łódź insurrection.

Throughout 1905, there were naval mutinies at Sevastopol, Vladivostok, and Kronstadt, peaking in June with the mutiny aboard the battleship Potemkin. The mutinies were disorganized and quickly crushed. Some sources claim over 2,000 sailors died in the suppression. Instead of fighting the Japanese, the Russians were killing each other. The Tsar's emissary Sergei Witte was dispatched to make peace with Japan, negotiating the Treaty of Portsmouth (signed 5 September 1905). The complete victory of the Japanese military surprised world observers. The consequences

* Armenian-Tatar Massacres – not to be confused with the Armenian Genocide of 1915–1923 by the Ottoman Turks, in which 1.5 million Armenians died.

transformed the balance of power in East Asia, resulting in a reassessment of Japan's recent entry onto the world stage. It was the first major military victory in the modern era of an Asian power over a European one. Scholars continue to debate the historical significance of the Russo-Japanese war.

In October 1905, the St. Petersburg Soviet was formed and called for a general strike, refusal to pay taxes, and the withdrawal of bank deposits. The October Manifesto, written by Count Sergei Witte (soon-to-be Prime Minister of the Constitutional Monarchy) and Prince Alexey Alexandrovitch Obolensky, was presented to the Tsar on 14 October. It granted basic civil rights, allowing the formation of political parties, extending the franchise towards universal suffrage, and establishing the Duma as the central legislative body. The Tsar waited and argued for three days, but finally signed the manifesto on 17 October 1905, citing his desire to avoid a massacre and his realization that there was insufficient military force available to pursue alternative options. He regretted signing the document, saying that he felt "sick with shame at this betrayal of the dynasty . . . the betrayal was complete." The Manifesto served as the precursor to the first Russian Constitution of 1906. While Russian liberals were satisfied by the October Manifesto and prepared for upcoming Duma elections, radical Marxists and revolutionaries denounced the elections and called for an armed uprising to destroy the Empire. Scattered revolts continued throughout the Empire. After a final spasm in Moscow, the uprisings ended in December 1905. According to figures presented in the Duma by Professor Maksim Kovalevsky, by April 1906, more than 14,000 people had been executed and 75,000 imprisoned. The Russian Constitution of 1906, also known as the Fundamental Laws or formally Code of Laws of the Russian Empire (*Сводъ законовъ Россійской имперіи*), set up a multiparty system and a limited Constitutional Monarchy. The revolutionaries were quelled and satisfied with the reforms, but it was not enough to prevent the 1917 revolution that would later topple the Tsar's regime and Russian Empire.

During the 1905 Revolution in Russia, Leo Jogiches and his common-law wife, Rosa Luxemburg, remained in German exile, their eyes set firmly on the German Communist movement. Jogiches returned to Poland first, traveling to Warsaw in the spring of 1905 to establish the Central Committee of the *SDKPiL*. Luxemburg remained in Berlin as the representative of the *SDKPiL* abroad, representing it before the Socialist International and attempting to win support for the organization and its activities among the German Communist movement. Within the *SPD*, Luxemburg, drawing upon the ongoing Russian experience, pushed the idea of the "mass strike" as a strategic tool for the achievement of power, over the objections of trade unionists and more conservative and electorally driven party leaders. Jogiches would return to delegate to the annual congress of the *SPD*, held at Jena in the middle of September 1905.

At the end of November 1905, Jogiches returned to Warsaw for a meeting with his fellow *SDKPiL* leaders. He regularly sent Luxemburg updates as to the revolution in Warsaw. As part of an ongoing battle to radicalize the *SPD*'s daily newspaper, *Vorwärts!* (*Forward!*), Luxemburg was named to the paper's editorial board in the fall of 1905. Using Jogiches communiqués, she would spend the months of November and December 1905 churning out aggressive commentary about Russian events for her German readers, attempting to draw analogies between the Russian and German situations whenever possible, her contributions appearing almost daily. It was not until the morning of 28 December 1905, that she would board a train for Warsaw to directly participate in the ongoing revolutionary effort to overthrow the Tsarist government of the Russian Empire. It was a two-day undercover journey on a train carrying soldiers; Luxemburg traveled under the alias "Anna Matschke."

On 4 March 1906, Luxemburg and Jogiches were arrested by Russian authorities for their revolutionary activity. Jogiches was sentenced by the court to eight years of hard labor followed by lifetime exile to Siberia. He served only months in prison before managing to escape across the border back to Berlin. Rosa served four months at the infamous Pavilion X of the Warsaw Citadel, reserved for the most "dangerous" political prisoners. After appeals from her German Social-Democratic comrades (including August Bebel), threats of further anti-government attacks from Polish Socialist organizations and the payment of a substantial bribe (2,500 Russian Rubles) and bail (3,000 Rubles), Rosa was eventually released from the Citadel. Later, when she discovered that her friends and family had paid this money, Rosa was furious. Finally, on 30 July 1906, she was able to leave Russian-occupied Warsaw and made to her way to Finland via St. Petersburg where she met with the Russian Communists, including Vladimír Lenin. She wrote about her encounter with Lenin that: "It is a pleasure to talk to him, he is sophisticated and knowledgeable, with the kind of ugly mug I like so much." Her experience in Warsaw influenced Rosa deeply, as was expressed particularly in her 1906 prison work *The Mass Strike, The Political Party, and the Trade-Unions*. Rosa eventually returned to Berlin on 13 September 1906, after a sea voyage via Sweden. On 12 December, she was sentenced to two-months imprisonment by the German authorities, ever keen to work in conjunction with the Tsarist police across the border. In January 1907, Rosa was sentenced by the Warsaw court in absentia. Between 1904 and 1906, she was imprisoned for her political activities on three occasions.

In 1907, Luxemburg and Jogiches are finally together back in Berlin, but the early magic of their relationship proves impossible to recapture. Instead, their life is an inferno of fights and reconciliations, against the background of which (and perhaps not unrelated to their domestic difficulties), Rosa Luxemburg begins to overshadow her lover decisively in the worlds of politics and journalism. Although an intelligent person and dedicated revolutionary Socialist thinker, Jogiches was virtually incapable of translating his ideas into written words: "the mere thought of putting his ideas on paper paralyzes him," Luxemburg later recalled (Falcoff 1980). Consequently, the chief contribution of Jogiches was that of literary stimulant to the skilled publicist Luxemburg as well as behind-the-scenes organizer of the fledgling underground political party that he had helped to establish. As Luxemburg grew in fame as a Marxist theoretician, Jogiches became gradually more embittered about his life, until by his mid-thirties, he had come, as Luxemburg biographer Elzbietta Ettinger phrased it, to have "fully realized the gap between his youthful aspirations and the disillusionments of reality" (Falcoff 1980, 135). Interpersonal conflict followed, exacerbated by the different trajectories of personal achievement, with the pair permanently ending their personal, but not political, relationship in 1907. In the *SPD*'s women's section, she met Marxist theorist and feminist Klara Zetkin, of whom she made a lifelong friend. Having broken off with Jogiches in 1907, Luxemburg takes up with a man twenty years her junior, Kostja Zetkin, the son of the German Marxist (and later Communist Party luminary) Klara Zetkin. Approximately 600 surviving letters (now mostly published) bear testimony to this eight-year romance. By this time the tone of her letters to Jogiches ranges from coldly hostile to crisply businesslike. Even so, there are brief periods of friendly reconciliation, particularly in several remarkable letters from prison in spring 1915 which Rosa Luxemburg, for reasons of censorship, was required to phrase as if they were intended for another woman. Throughout the entire life of her relationship with Jogiches, the one thing which does not change is Luxemburg's dependence on Jogiches for financial support; her appeals for money are quite open and undisguised in the early periods of their relationship; in the final phase (1907–1914), they are made in the name of "the party."

From her experiences in Poland emerged her theory of revolutionary mass action, which she propounded in *Massenstreik, Partei und Gewerkschaften* (1906; *The Mass Strike, the Political Party, and the Trade Unions*). Her continual advocacy for mass strike became a major point of contention in the German Social Democratic Party and was primarily opposed by August Bebel and Karl Kautsky. For such passionate and relentless agitation, Luxemburg earned the nickname "Bloody Rosa." Luxemburg was a combative intellectual and brilliant Marxist who opposed World War I and favored revolution over parliamentary Democracy.

Together with Karl Liebknecht, she founded the *Kommunistische Partei Deutschlands, KPD* (Communist Party of Germany) on 1 January 1919, and was involved in the Spartacist Uprising from 5–15 January 1919 resulting in her and Liebknecht's brutal beating and execution by the *Freikorps* in Berlin. Luxemburg remains a heroine to many in Germany—from both the East and West—as well as to fans across the world. Old Communists and young Socialists march through the streets of former East Berlin every year to place red carnations on her grave. While many other former Communist leaders have had their memory erased from Berlin's street names since the fall of the Wall, Rosa Luxemburg, whose early death left her untainted by the terror and totalitarianism of Communist rule, has retained a place of honor. In the former East Germany, the annual mass march by tens of thousands of admirers to the graves of Karl Liebknecht and Rosa Luxemburg in the Friedrichsfelde Cemetery on the Sunday before the anniversary became a state ritual and today it is still an occasion to commemorate the two early Communist leaders. In Germany, where there is a resurgence of interest in Marxism, with readings of *Das Kapital* all the rage, Rosa Luxemburg is looking ripe for a renaissance.

LIBERATION THEOLOGY

Facilis descensus Averno [*the descent to hell is easy*].
— VIRGIL, 29–19 BC *Aeneid*

L'enfer est plein de bonnes volontés ou désirs [*hell is full of good wishes or desires*].
— SAINT BERNARD OF CLAIRVAUX, c. *AD* 1150

Der weg zur Hölle ist jedoch mit guten Absichten [*The road to hell, however, is with good intentions*]

— KARL MARX, 1867

Das Kapital: Kritik der politischen Ökonomie

Those who promise us paradise on earth never produced anything but a hell. (Winokur 2005, 144)

— KARL POPPER

AS AN IMPORTANT TAKEAWAY FROM THE ABOVE BIOGRAPHICAL vignettes, one cannot help but recognize a pattern, namely, the nexus of liberal theology or Jewish apocalyptic chiliasm common to their backgrounds. Whether they had a Jewish or Christian (Roman Catholic or Protestant) background and irrespective of their belief in and observance of religious tenets, the common denominator can clearly be identified as early familial immersion in a liberal, heterodox interpretation of these two historic, symbiotic religions and their admixture to a growing humanistic Hegelian philosophy. During the lifetimes of these central figures of the early Socialist-Communist movement and of its contemporary movements in philosophy, theology, politics, economics, and the arts, it was as if the radical liberal wings of the two ancient traditional religions (Judaism and Christianity) decided to secede from their more traditional roots and unite under one new religion focused entirely on the temporal world. Clearly, as the movement evolved particularly under Marx and Engels, religion and God were extirpated and condemned. The more moderate, Socialist wing of the movement that was eventually excommunicated by Marx and Engels retains to this day much of the liberal theology (albeit secularized) the movement was wed to from the beginning.

Christians and Jews experiencing the social ills of Industrial Age Capitalism, and the promise of Socialism in the nineteenth-century Western world evidently drew on the thought patterns of their ancestors' faith in diverse ways but from common roots. For many, the traditional paternalist theologies of the past were not to be disregarded, but rediscovered and reinterpreted in "progressive" terms and understanding through "higher criticism." For pietistic evangelical Protestants, the agency and freedoms of markets were seen in a different light—from their more traditional counterparts—as spheres of God's providence and domain for Christians to employ their own agency and freedom for the common good. Christian responses to Socialism repeatedly agonized over anti-Christian, secular propensities. Many nonetheless viewed the cooperative and communal principles of Socialism to be more consistent with the social messages of Christianity than values of selfish materialistic competition. Under the tremendous and growing social pressure of the times, Roman Catholic attempts to devise a social theology mediating between free market Capitalism and secular Socialism acknowledged a vision of the Church as a unique temporal arbiter and upholder of social justice and universal human dignity, representing in some sense the institutional rule of the Christian God in the present. In reality, this was nothing more than a desperate attempt by Rome to hold on to the last vestiges of the rapidly decaying spiritual and moral authority it solely possessed in Western culture for over a millennium. But by the time Friedrich Nietzsche (1844–1900) so audaciously declared "God is dead. God remains dead. And we have killed him" (Nietzsche 1882, section 125), traditional Christianity and Judaism in Europe had all but died also.

The idea of God's rule was also latent within the repeated evocation of the idea of the Kingdom of God in reflections on Capitalism and Socialism. The history of Socialism and Communism traces its primordial roots to the misinterpretation of the Beatitudes and the "Kingdom of God" in Jesus's Sermon on the Mount (*sermo in monte*). Precise theological understandings of when and where this Kingdom would be realized clearly differed. Trends in liberal Protestantism encouraged a view of a Kingdom already proclaimed and present in the world, yet to be brought to fruition; alternative theologies more influenced by Pietism[4] looked to an eschatological horizon from which such a Kingdom could dramatically commence. Jewish apocalyptic eschatology also foretells such a Kingdom on earth.

The resonance of this theme of the Kingdom is hardly surprising. Nineteenth-century Christians were growing increasingly conscious of Capitalism becoming the system which dominated, determined, and *ruled* their societies. And as the social effects of the unchecked market became clearer, it was evident that baser human instincts were holding the reins of society. Socialism represented the romantic attempt to introduce more rational, harmonious orders of human relating, seeking to empower human "goodness" to "regulate" social relationships. Any Christian acknowledging the fallen condition of humanity was liable to doubt the potential of humans themselves to overcome this state. A coming divine Kingdom where all is subject to God's rule offered the ready theological answer—an end to

Capitalism's disorderly reign and the realizing of a Christian society superseding any Socialist hope.

As previously discussed, anti-traditionalism and Liberalism in all its forms gradually infected the traditional values and belief systems that were the glue holding European society together for nearly two millennia by the time the Age of Reason (Enlightenment) entered Western culture. A new and growing skepticism of all established principles and this deepening liberal inflection on traditional religious beliefs cast their influence on all aspects of society—theology, philosophy, ethics, logic (critical reasoning), politics, economics, education, academia, the arts, the professions, and the interrelationships of the evolving socioeconomic classes. Long-established definitions and principles were being redefined in entirely novel terms. Expectations were taking on new meaning. Mankind was moving from his long-standing position of subordination to the principles and will of a loving, benevolent, supernatural deity to a new position of being the liberated master of his own destiny, disgusted with his past impotence and inaction to effectuate change for the better, eager to turn the *status quo* on its head at all costs and without careful introspection of the possible consequences. These reactionary upheavals and convulsions of the masses led by their hubristic sages in their perceived newfound liberation are what led to the tragedies of the twentieth century. The heterodox liberal misinterpretations of long-standing traditional (orthodox) religious dogma that emanated from the Enlightenment and Romantic eras eviscerated the central doctrines of the Judeo-Christian tradition and paved the road to a new humanistic theology of social justice—*A Theology of Liberation* deeply rooted in Pietism, legalism, and man-defined virtue (relativistic situational ethics) focused primarily on temporal (natural) rather than eternal (supernatural) matters. Even though the victorious figures of the struggle to lead the Communist movement eventually divested themselves and their program from all traditional religious beliefs, their newfound religion was unwittingly rooted in the liberal theology of their conquered rivals—they just redefined the deities in anthropomorphic, materialistic terms and promulgated a new, secular set of "pietistic" doctrines. A new political correctness had been born.

Catholic Liberation Theology, which developed within the Roman Catholic Church in Latin America in the 1950s and 1960s, was a direct descendant of the Utopian social justice Babouvist, Weitlingist, chiliastic, millenarian, populist, Communist movement of the nineteenth century. It arose principally as a moral reaction to the poverty and social injustice in the region. The term Liberation Theology was coined in 1971 by the Peruvian Catholic priest Gustavo Gutiérrez, who wrote one of the movement's defining books, *A Theology of Liberation*, in which he combined populist ideas with the social teachings of the Catholic Church (Gutiérrez 1971). Gutiérrez emphasized practice (or, more technically, "praxis") over Christian doctrine but later under Vatican pressure recanted and clarified the "symbiotic" circular relationship that he saw existed between orthopraxis and orthodoxy. This still did not satisfy the Vatican who saw Gutiérrez's interpretation of the Scriptures as heterodoxy by his elevating orthopraxis to the level of orthodoxy—in other words, Gutiérrez's Liberation Theology promoted the works-righteousness achieved through the struggle for social justice in this life to the same level as Christianity's central dogma of Christ's vicarious atonement for the afterlife. Many theologians recognize Marxist principals inherent to Liberation Theology. According to theologians such as Leonardo Boff, the Latin American branch of Christian Communist Liberation Theology is rooted in the concept that "prudence is the understanding of situations of radical crisis." A narrative of the nature of contemporary social struggles ("radical crisis") is developed via "materialist analysis" utilizing historiographic concepts developed by Karl Marx. One concrete example is the Paraguayan *Sin Tierra* (landless) movement, who engage in direct land seizures and the establishment of socialized agricultural cooperative production in *asentamientos* (settlements, communes). The *Sin Tierra* operate in a very similar manner as that of the English Reformation era Diggers. For Camilo Torres (the founder of the Colombian guerrilla group *ELN*), developing this orthopraxis meant celebrating the Catholic Eucharist only among those engaged in armed struggle against the national army of the Colombian state. Many other Latin American armed revolutionary movements exploited Liberation Theology as a means of attracting followers. From its very beginning, the de-deification of Jesus, the abolition of God, and the socialization and politicization of Christian teachings in the struggle for social justice in this life have been a potent means of propagating Socialist-Communist ideology for well over 170 years.

Jews of the liberal chiliastic persuasion have also been strongly drawn to the Socialist-Communist movement in their hope to realize the prophecies made in the apocryphal and apocalyptic books of Enoch, Ezra, Daniel, Baruch, and Jubilees that predict the establishment of a Golden Age or Paradise on Earth. This interpretation no doubt helped some Jews to cope with the socio-political conflicts that they faced since the first-century diaspora (after the Roman destruction of the Second Temple). This interpretation served as a means of justice for the previous period of evil and suffering, rewarding the virtuous for their courage while punishing evildoers, with a clear separation of those who are good from those who are evil. The vision of an age of bliss for the faithful, to be enjoyed here in the physical world as "heaven on earth," exerted an irresistible power over the imagination of some Jews in the inter-testament period, as well as early Christians.

Millennialism, which had already existed in liberal Jewish thought, received a new liberal interpretation and fresh impetus with the arrival of Christianity and the book of Revelation. Liberal Christians and Jews of the Modern Era retain much of the Utopian vision held by their liberal ancestors, if not consciously, then certainly subconsciously, despite formal rejection of millennialism or chiliasm by their respective orthodox religious schools.* With respect to good works achieving righteousness before God, Judaism has always held that Mosaic Law functions in three spheres: moral, civil (juridical), and ceremonial. And only by strict adherence to Mosaic Law in these three spheres can one be declared "righteous" (justified) before God. Roman Catholicism, likewise, holds to a central doctrine that faith and righteousness are completed through fulfilling one's ethical duty and divine command to do good works ("charity") including the struggle for social justice in this life—a form of social gospel (Liberation Theology behind a different façade known as semi-Pelagianism,† synergism, Molinism, or

* American economist Murray Newton Rothbard (1926–1995) was S. J. Hall Distinguished Professor of Economics at the University of Nevada, Las Vegas, cofounder of the Ludwig von Mises Institute in Alabama, and a central figure in the 20th-century American Libertarian movement. He wrote over twenty books on political theory, economics, and other subjects. In his "Origins of the Welfare State in America" (1996; originally delivered by the author at the von Mises Institute's "Evils of the Welfare State" conference in Lake Bluff, Illinois, April 30–May 2, 1993), Rothbard had pointed out that progressives had evolved from elitist Gilded Age pietist Protestants that wanted to bring a secularized version of millennialism under a welfare state, which was spearheaded by a coalition of Yankee Protestant and Jewish women and "lesbian spinsters" (Rothbard 1996, 193–232).

† Pelagianism: heterodox religious doctrine associated with a British monk named Pelagius (c. *AD* 354–418). Pelagianism maintained that human beings did not need grace to fulfill God's moral commands and, thus, could achieve salvation through their own efforts. It minimized or denied entirely the debilitating effects of original sin on the human will. Pelagianism was decisively condemned at the 418 Council of Carthage and is still regarded as heretical by Christianity.

Massilianism). Many other Christian denominations, indeed, most of all known religions over the course of human history, have held to a dogma *dictating* some form of human action to achieve reconciliation with (justification by) God (or gods) that includes a compassionate struggle for social justice to alleviate suffering in this life. For non-Christian faiths, the error of this teaching lies in a fundamental, humanistic misunderstanding of the will of man and his ability to achieve or satisfy the supernatural. For Christians, the heterodoxy of this teaching lies in the misunderstanding of the doctrine on the will of man and its role in justification, and the common misinterpretation of the teachings of Jesus (the eight Beatitudes given in the Sermon on the Mount*), as documented in the Gospel of Matthew chapters 5 through 7, and the parallel writings of James, the "biological" brother of Jesus, in his paraenetic epistle, particularly chapter 2 verses 17, 24, and 26.[5] What is lost on the masses of people and their teachers who misinterpret both of these passages (Matthew chapters 5–7 and James chapter 2) is the fact that these passages were exhortation and rebuking messages intended for believers and not to bring unbelievers to faith (justification) via the law. This kind of error in interpretation is commonly known among theologians as "improper distinction between Law and Gospel" (Walther 1929, 6). According to the teachings of Jesus and the Apostles, the false teaching dictating human action to achieve social justice (moral imperatives) as necessary to completing salvation (justification) is grounded exclusively in religious law and is antithetical to the message of the Gospel and the orthodox doctrines on the will of man, justification, and Christ's sole vicarious atonement. Many of the leaders of the early Socialist movement confounded religious Law and Gospel in their political program to achieve social justice for the masses. This error continues perpetually among those political leaders advocating for Socialist policies under the guise of social

* The Beatitudes – according to many Christian denominations, the Beatitudes have an eschatological meaning, that is, they promise salvation—not in this world, but in the next. They believe the Beatitudes initiate one of the main themes of Matthew's Gospel, that the Kingdom so long awaited in the Old Testament is not of this world, but of the next, the Kingdom of Heaven. According to this viewpoint, while the Beatitudes of Jesus provide a way of life (protrepsis) that promises salvation, they also bring peace in the midst of our trials and tribulations on this earth. This viewpoint, however, totally misses the nature of the audience, to whom the Sermon on the Mount was given. Matthew 5:1–2 clearly indicates the intended audience for the Sermon on the Mount was his "disciples" who were already believers and did not need to perform any acts to attain salvation.

justice. It is also a fundamental reason why Socialist ideology continues to attract so many who place such high value on virtue-based social justice. Eugen Richter (see *infra*) would persuasively instruct them that Utopian Socialism travels on an inevitable one-way road to totalitarian Communism and dictatorial despotism.

For those with the aforementioned liberal Christian or Jewish background who forsook the faith of their ancestors and turned agnostic or atheistic (such as Marx and Engels), unwittingly retained the objectives of the liberal theology of their ancestors—they just replaced the supernatural with the natural and the eternal with the temporal (materialistic and "scientific"), and declared their end moral objective justifies the violent revolutionary means that they advocate is necessary to achieve their objective. It was these rabbis and ministers of atheism and humanism that gave birth to the Luxemburgs, Liebknechts, Lenins, Trotskys, Stalins, Eckarts, Rosenbergs, von Sebottendorffs, von Scheubner-Richters, Vinbergs, Heßes, Feders, and Hitlers of the twentieth century (see *DRAMATIS PERSONÆ*, *infra*).

KALEIDOSCOPIC MOVEMENT OF WORLD REVOLUTION THE 33-YEAR *VORMÄRZ*

SCHOOLED IN THE LESSONS OF THE 1789 FRENCH REVOLUTION AND Communist movements that ensued, Marx and Engels established the Communist Correspondence Committee in Brussels in early 1846 with the aim of ideologically and organizationally consolidating the Socialists of different countries and preparing the formation of an international proletarian party. They organized local working classes with the objective of overthrowing the *bourgeoisie*, establishing the "rule of the proletariat," and the construction of a new (Utopian) society free of both private property and social classes. In London, on 1 June 1847, the Communist Correspondence Committee of Brussels merged with Karl Schapper's League of the Just to form the *Bund der Kommunisten* (Communist League)—the first Marxist international political party, for which Marx and Engels wrote *Manifest der Kommunistischen Partei* (*Manifesto of the Communist Party*) in London in February 1848. These developments laid the foundation for the long-awaited Revolutions of 1848 (Spring of Nations) that swept Europe like a firestorm in an attempt to overthrow the feudal system and the barons of the Industrial

Revolution oppressing the working classes, as well as the old monarchical structures that had dominated Europe since the Middle Ages, and to create independent nation states governed by liberal secular political systems. Although the 1848 Revolutions were crushed by the elite monarchial powers, there was no going back; the seeds had been planted for a political revolution that, as Sylvain Marechal predicted in his *Manifesto of the Equals* (1796), would sweep the world only a few decades later.

The failures of the 1848 Revolutions taught the revolutionary leaders what they needed to change in their messaging and *modus operandi*, particularly relative to the proletariat class, which they failed to fully enlist; they were convinced their political theory of "dictatorship of the proletariat" was correct and sacrosanct. The promise of social justice, egalitarianism (classless societies), and liberation of the oppressed working classes became the central mantra to appeal to the growing masses that yearned for change. For the more militant wing in the rising Communist organizations throughout Europe, change was not occurring fast enough. They ardently pushed for anarchy and violent revolution to achieve their goals. Vladimír Lenin (1870–1924) with his Bolshevik revolution and Mao Zedong (1893–1976) with his People's Liberation Army were just two of the many in the next generation of disciples of the more radical, militant wing in the Communist movement of the nineteenth and twentieth centuries.

The primary reason a significant segment of the weary and beleaguered working class, avant-garde, literary, and liberal academic populations in parts of late nineteenth- and early twentieth-century Europe, Asia, and the Americas were captivated and mesmerized by the Communist movement was the movement's romantic, altruistic message of a better world that was just, and one where all people were equal with no one enriching themselves with property or wealth above others—power was now to be equally distributed among those that actually built and maintained society, and denied to those who had enriched themselves off the broken back of the laborer. Like the Reformation, the 1776 American Revolution was hijacked and imported by Utopian radicals in Europe with far less understanding of human nature than what America's Founding Fathers possessed. The pop culture of a communal society is best exemplified in history by the 1789 French Revolution and the mass following of romantic, Utopian revolutionaries like French-Prussian Wilhelm Weitling (an important source of inspiration to Marx and Engels) whose "highly emotional mix of Babouvist Communism, chiliastic Christianity, and millenarian populism" captivated the masses of Europe (chiliasm or millennialism is rooted in Judaic Messianic eschatology). Theirs was a bastardized, humanistic, legalistic plagiarism of the Christian Gospels devoid of the divinity of Jesus that twisted the orthodox evangelical message into a social gospel for temporal social justice. For the struggling common masses, this was, and remains, a powerful message—if only it were true. Interestingly, once the generation of America's Founding Fathers had passed, several of the early movers and shakers in the late nineteenth-century European Communist movement exiled to the United States, which at that time was also a vulnerable and welcoming crucible for social and political experimentation.

The late eighteenth century was a tumultuous period of rapid political, economic, intellectual, and cultural reforms stemming from the Enlightenment—represented by figures such as Locke, Rousseau, Voltaire, and Adam Smith—and early Romanticism, climaxing with the French Revolution, where freedom of the individual and nation was asserted against privilege and custom. Representing a vast mosaic of types and theories, these developments were largely a catalyst and response to the disintegration of previous long-standing cultural traditions, coupled with new patterns of industrial production, specifically the rise of industrial Capitalism. However, the defeat of Napoléon at Leipzig in October 1813 enabled conservative and reactionary regimes such as those of the Kingdom of Prussia, the Austrian Empire, and Tsarist Russia to survive, laying the groundwork for the Congress of Vienna* and the alliance that strove to oppose radical demands for change ushered in by the French Revolution. The Great Powers (Austria, United Kingdom, Russia, Prussia, and Bourbon France) at the Congress of Vienna in 1815 aimed to restore Europe (as far as possible) to its prewar conditions by combating both Liberalism and Nationalism and by creating barriers around France. With Austria's position on the continent now intact and ostensibly secure under its reactionary premier Klemens von Metternich, the Habsburg empire would serve as a barrier to contain the emergence of

---

* A meeting of ambassadors of European states chaired by Austrian statesman Klemens von Metternich, and held in Vienna from November 1814 to June 1815, though the delegates had arrived and were already negotiating by late September 1814. The objective of the Congress was to provide a long-term peace plan for Europe by settling critical issues arising from the French Revolutionary Wars and the Napoleonic Wars. The goal was not simply to restore old boundaries but to reframe the main powers, so they could balance each other and remain at peace. The leaders were Conservatives with little use for Republicanism or revolution, both of which threatened to upset the *status quo* in Europe.

Italian and German nation-states as well, in addition to containing France. But this reactionary balance of power, aimed at blocking German and Italian Nationalism on the continent, was precarious.

After Napoléon's final defeat at Waterloo in July 1815, the surviving member states of the defunct Holy Roman Empire joined to form the *Deutscher Bund* (German Confederation)—a rather loose organization, especially because the two great rivals, the Austrian Empire and the Kingdom of Prussia, each feared domination by the other. In Prussia, the Hohenzollern rulers forged a centralized state. By the time of the Napoleonic Wars (1803–1815), Prussia was a socially and institutionally backward state, grounded in the virtues of its established military aristocracy (the *Junkers*), stratified by rigid hierarchical lines. After 1815, Prussia's defeats by Napoleonic France highlighted the need for administrative, economic, and social reforms to improve the efficiency of the bureaucracy and encourage practical merit-based education. Inspired by the Napoleonic organization of German and Italian principalities, the Prussian reforms of Karl August von Hardenberg and Karl Freiherr vom Stein (1806–1815) were conservative, enacted to preserve aristocratic privilege while modernizing institutions.

Outside Prussia, industrialization in German states progressed slowly, and was held back because of political disunity, conflicts of interest between the nobility and merchants, and the continued existence of the guild system, which discouraged competition and innovation. While this kept the middle class at bay, affording the old order a measure of stability not seen in France, Prussia's vulnerability to Napoléon's military proved to many among the old order that a fragile, divided, and traditionalist Germany would be easy prey for its cohesive and industrializing neighbor.

The Stein-Hardenberg Reforms laid the foundation for Prussia's future military dominance by professionalizing the military and decreeing universal military conscription. In order to industrialize Prussia, working within the framework provided by the old aristocratic institutions, land reforms were enacted to break the monopoly of the *Junkers* on land ownership, thereby also abolishing, among other things, the feudal practice of serfdom.

Although the forces unleashed by the 1789 French Revolution were seemingly under control after the Vienna Congress, the conflict between conservative forces and liberal Nationalists was only deferred at best. The thirty-three-year era from the defeat of Napoléon in 1815 to the outbreak of the 1848 Revolutions, in which these tensions amassed, is commonly referred to among historians as *Vormärz* ("before March")—meaning before the outbreak of riots in March 1848.

This conflict pitted the forces of the old order against those inspired by the French Revolution and the Rights of Man. The sociological breakdown of the conflict was, roughly, one side engaged mostly in commerce, trade, and industry, and the other side associated with landowning aristocracy or military aristocracy (the *Junkers*) in Prussia, the Habsburg monarchy in Austria, and the conservative notables of the small princely states and city-states in Germany.

Meanwhile, demands for change from the commoners had been fomenting since the 1789 French Revolution. Throughout the German Confederation (1815–1866), Austrian influence was paramount, drawing the ire of the German Nationalist movements. Austria's von Metternich considered Nationalism, especially the Nationalist youth movement, the most pressing danger: German Nationalism might not only repudiate Austrian dominance of the Confederation, but also stimulate Nationalist sentiment within the Austrian Empire itself. In a multi-national polyglot state in which Slavs and Magyars outnumbered the Germans, the prospects of Czech, Slovak, Hungarian, Polish, Serb, or Croatian sentiment along with middle class Liberalism was certainly horrifying to the ruling class.

Figures with influential voices like Johann Wolfgang von Goethe, Johann Gottlieb Fichte, Friedrich von Schelling, August Heinrich Hoffmann von Fallersleben, Ludwig Uhland, Georg Herwegh, Heinrich Heine, Georg Büchner, Ludwig Börne, and Bettina von Arnim ushered in the *Vormärz* era. Deeply influenced by the French Revolution, these prominent German writers, philosophers, artists, and intellectuals turned to Romanticism and neo-Nationalism. Father Friedrich Jahn's gymnastic associations exposed middle class German youth to Nationalist and Democratic ideas, which took the form of the Nationalist and liberal Democratic college fraternities known as the *Burschenschaften*. In another example of hijacking the Reformation, the Wartburg Festival in 1817 celebrated Martin Luther as a proto-German Nationalist, linking Lutheranism to German Nationalism, and helping arouse religious sentiments for the cause of German nationhood. The festival culminated in the burning of several books and other items that symbolized reactionary attitudes. One item was a book by August von Kotzebue. In 1819, von Kotzebue was accused of spying for Russia, and then murdered by a theological student, Karl Ludwig Sand, who was executed for the crime. Sand belonged to a militant Nationalist faction of the *Burschenschaften*. Von Metternich used the murder as a pretext to issue the Carlsbad Decrees of

1819, which dissolved the *Burschenschaften*, cracked down on the liberal press, and seriously restricted academic freedom.

In academia, high-powered professors developed international reputations, especially in the humanities led by history and philology, which brought a new historical perspective to the study of political history, theology, philosophy, language, and literature. With Georg Wilhelm Friedrich Hegel (1770–1831) in philosophy, Friedrich Schleiermacher (1768–1834) in theology, and Leopold von Ranke (1795–1886) in history, the University of Berlin, founded in 1809, became the world's leading university. Von Ranke, for example, professionalized history and set the world standard for historiography. By the 1830s, mathematics, physics, chemistry, and biology had emerged as world-class sciences, led by Alexander von Humboldt (1769–1859) in natural science and Carl Friedrich Gauss (1777–1855) in mathematics. Young intellectuals of the Romantic era often turned to politics, but their support for the failed Revolutions of 1848 forced many into exile. Out of this boiling cauldron of revolutionary stew nourishing the proletariat masses and their higher society sympathizers of Europe and the Americas, which accelerated with the 1789 French Revolution and 1848 Spring of Nations, activists in Europe began emulating what Marx and Engels achieved in establishing the Communist League (1847) and taking their achievement to the next predicted natural step in the *(r)evolution* of the movement.

CHAPTER 7

THE UNIFICATION OF GERMANY AND THE POLITICIZATION OF ANTI-SEMITISM

A BASIC UNDERSTANDING OF HOW GERMANY BECAME A NATION AND OF the political upheavals and machinations that preceded and accelerated after unification are vital to understanding the tragedy of mid-twentieth-century Europe. The long-anticipated unification of Germany into a politically and administratively integrated nation state officially occurred on 18 January 1871 in the Hall of Mirrors at the Chateau de Versailles in France. Princes of the German states, excluding Austria, gathered there to proclaim Wilhelm I of Prussia as German Emperor after the French capitulation in the Franco-Prussian War. Unofficially, the *de facto* transition of most of the German-speaking populations into a federated organization of states had been developing for some time through formal and informal alliances between princely rulers but punctuated in spasms and false starts. The self-interests of the various principals hampered the process over nearly a century of autocratic experimentation, beginning in the era of the Napoleonic Wars, which prompted the dissolution of the Holy Roman Empire of the German Nation in 1806, and the subsequent rise of German Romanticism and Nationalism. Attempts at unification exposed tensions due to established religious, dialectal, social, and cultural differences among the inhabitants of the various regions, suggesting that 1871 only represented one moment in a continuum of the larger unification processes.

The Holy Roman Empire of the German Nation,[1] which had included 360 independent states, was effectively dissolved when Holy Roman Emperor Francis II abdicated on 6 August 1806 during the War of the Third Coalition (1803–1806, Britain, Austria, Russia, Sweden, and some German states against the allied armies under Napoléon I) ending with France's victory at Austerlitz and the Treaty of Pressburg. Despite the legal, administrative, and political disruption associated with the end of the Holy Roman Empire, the people of the German-speaking areas of the old Empire had many common linguistic, cultural, and legal traditions further enhanced by their shared experience in the French Revolutionary Wars (1792–1802) and Napoleonic Wars (1803–1815). European Liberalism offered an intellectual basis for unification by challenging historic dynastic and absolutist models of social and political organization; its German manifestation emphasized the importance of cultural tradition, education, and linguistic unity of peoples in a geographic region. Economically, the creation of the Prussian customs union beginning in 1818, and its subsequent expansion to the *Zollverein* to include other states of the German Confederation, reduced competition between and within states.

The Napoleonic Wars continued to rage throughout Europe until Napoléon's defeat by the Seventh Coalition at Waterloo on 18 June 1815. From a German perspective, the model of diplomatic spheres of influence resulting from the Congress of Vienna—ongoing since September 1814 and finally concluded just nine days before the battle of Waterloo—ratified Austrian dominance in Central Europe. The negotiators at Vienna took no account of Prussia's growing strength within and among the German states and so failed to foresee that Prussia would rise to challenge Austria for leadership of the German peoples. This German dualism presented two solutions to the problem of unification: *Kleindeutsche Lösung*, the small Germany solution (Germany without Austria), or *Großdeutsche Lösung*, the greater Germany solution (Germany with Austria). By establishing a Germany without Austria, the political and administrative unification in 1871 at least temporarily solved the problem of dualism.

To better understand the rapidly evolving political developments in Germany culminating in its geopolitical unification as the *Deutsches Reich* (German Empire) in 1871 and the rise of the modern German political party system, the table below provides a brief timeline of the major events in this momentous and long-anticipated development in the affairs of Europe.

1797 The French First Republic annexes the Left Bank of the Rhine as a result of the War of the First Coalition.

1802 Previous annexations by France are confirmed following its victory in the War of the Second Coalition.

1804 Francis I of Austria declares the new Austrian Empire as a reaction to Napoléon Bonaparte's proclamation of the First French Empire in 1804.

1806 As a result of the War of the Third Coalition, Napoléon I annexes some territories East of the Rhine and replaces the Holy Roman Empire by the Confederation of the Rhine as a French client-state.

1807 Prussia loses one half of its territory following the War of the Fourth Coalition.

1815 After the defeat of Napoléon, the Congress of Vienna reinstates the Germanic states into the German Confederation under the leadership of the Austrian Empire.

1819 The Carlsbad Decrees suppress any form of pan-Germanic activities to avoid the creation of a "German state"; the Kingdom of Prussia, however, initiates a customs union with other Confederation states.

1834 The Prussian-led customs union evolves into the *Zollverein* that includes almost all Confederation states except the Austrian Empire.

1848 Revolts across the German Confederation, such as in Berlin, Dresden and Frankfurt, force King Frederick Wilhelm IV of Prussia to grant a constitution to the Confederation. In the meantime, the Frankfurt Parliament (*Landtag*) is set up in 1848 and attempts to proclaim a united Germany, but this is refused by Wilhelm IV. The question of a united Germany under the *Kleindeutsch* solution (to exclude Austria) or the so-called *Großdeutsch* (to include Austria) begins to surface.

1850 The Erfurt Union is a short-lived attempt at a union of German states under a federation, proposed by the Kingdom of Prussia. The Erfurt Union Parliament (*Erfurter Unionsparlament*), lasting from March 20 to April 29, 1850, is opened at the former Augustinian monastery at Erfurt. The union never comes into effect, and is completely undermined by the Punctation of Olmütz, a treaty between Prussia and Austria, signed 29 November 1850, by which Prussia abandons the Erfurt Union and accepts the revival of the German Confederation under Austrian leadership.

1861 – 1862 Prince Regent Wilhelm Friedrich Ludwig becomes Wilhelm I King of Prussia and appoints Otto von Bismarck on 23 September 1862 Minister-President and Foreign Minister, who favors an "iron-and-blood" policy to create a united Germany under the leadership of Prussia.

1864 The Danish-Prussian War starts as Prussia protests Danish incorporation of Schleswig into the Kingdom of Denmark. The Austrian Empire is deliberately drawn into this war by Otto von Bismarck, Chancellor of Prussia. The Austro-Prussian victory leads to Schleswig, the northern part, being governed by Prussia and Holstein, the southern part, being governed by Austria, as per the Treaty of Vienna (1864).

1866 Von Bismarck accuses the Austrian Empire of stirring up troubles in Prussian-held Schleswig. Prussian troops drive into Austrian-held Holstein and take control of the entire state of Schleswig-Holstein. Austria declares war on Prussia and, after fighting the Austro-Prussian War (Seven-Weeks' War), is swiftly defeated. The Treaty of Prague (1866) formally dissolves the German Confederation and Prussia creates the North German Confederation to include all Germanic states except the pro-French, southern kingdoms of Bavaria, Baden, and Württemberg.

1870 When French Emperor Napoléon III demands territories of the Rhineland in return for his neutrality amid the Austro-Prussian War, von Bismarck uses the Spanish Succession Question (1868) and Ems Telegram (1870) as an opportunity to incorporate the southern kingdoms. Napoléon III declares war against Prussia.

1871 The Franco-Prussian War ends with Prussian troops capturing Paris, the capital of the Second French Empire. Bavaria, Baden, and Württemberg are incorporated into the North German Confederation in the Treaty of Frankfurt (1871). Von Bismarck proclaims King Wilhelm I, now Kaiser (Emperor) Wilhelm I, as leader of the new, united Germany (*Deutsches Reich*), excluding Austria. With German troops remaining in Paris, Napoléon III dissolves the French Empire and a new republic, the Third French Republic, is created under Adolphe Thiers.

The new Imperial Constitution of the German Empire (16 April 1871) made no reference to political parties, whose activities were governed by the law on associations. Indeed, prior to 1908 political parties were subject to the legislation of the individual federal states regulating the activities of associations, but in that year the statutory provisions governing associations were standardized throughout the German Empire, and this codification was accompanied by a liberalization of the right of association and the right of assembly, which lifted existing restrictions prohibiting women from becoming members of associations, and public political gatherings in enclosed spaces required authorization by the police.

The dominant type of political party in the German Empire was an elite-based party, in which all the crucial political functions were performed by small groups of personalities whose role as leading representatives of their respective sectors of society gave them an exalted position. Party organizations were still in their infancy and only existed at the constituency level. After 1871, the way in which parties were led and organized began to change, and during the German Empire the (Catholic) Center Party and the Social Democratic Party became the first mass-membership parties of the modern type. Although many political parties sprouted during this period, a six-party landscape may be said to have prevailed throughout the duration of the Empire, as the various splinter parties never came to exert any real influence. Each of the six major political camps was largely linked with a particular milieu. The model of the people's party, drawing support from various milieu, was still in its infancy.

As in present times, no political party was ideologically homogenous in nineteenth-century Germany. Every party was comprised of some degree of ideological heterogeneity, on a spectrum from strongly liberal to strongly conservative interpretations and praxes of their respective party platforms. The strongest political force in the early days of the German Empire was Liberalism, which relied chiefly on the *bourgeoisie* for its votes, although it was weakened by division into the Social Liberals and Nationalist Liberals. Despite common basic liberal convictions—belief in the market economy, the rule of law and respect for individual freedoms—there were major differences of opinion between the two tendencies on specific political issues. The Social Liberals wanted parliament to have greater powers within the political system, although it had no wish to undermine the Constitutional Monarchy. It also advocated an active government social policy. Many splits and mergers occurred within the Social Liberals camp, giving birth to a plethora of political parties in Germany. Among the leading representatives of the Social Liberals were **Eugen Richter** (1838–1906) and **Friedrich Naumann** (1860–1919). Liberal Nationalists were also torn by factional fighting. Rudolf von Bennigsen (1824–1902) and Ernst Bassermann (1854–1917) set their seal on the liberal Nationalism of their time. Liberal

Nationalists were largely supportive of the policies pursued by Chancellor Otto von Bismarck and his successors and, unlike the Social Liberals, backed a foreign policy based on the quest for power through the build-up of military and naval armaments.

True ideological Conservatives were scarce in nineteenth-century German politics as Liberalism dominated the political scene, counterintuitively, even on the conservative side. Several conservative-leaning parties and leaders, however, are noteworthy: Free Conservative Party (1867, Karl Ludwig Aegidi, Duke Victor of Ratibor, Prince Karl Max von Lichnowsky, General Hans Hartwig von Beseler, Otto Hoetzsch); German Conservative Party (1876, Prussian Field Marshal Helmuth von Moltke, Elard von Oldenburg-Januschau); Christian Social Party (1878, Adolf Stöcker); the General German League (1886, Karl Peters) and Pan-German League (1891, Emil Kirdorf, Max Weber, Ernst Hasse); German Fatherland Party (1917, Wolfgang Kapp, Admiral Alfred von Tirpitz, Alfred Hugenberg, Anton Drexler); and German National People's Party (1918, Hugo Stinnes, Alfred Hugenberg, Ernst Oberfohren).

Eugen Richter was a German politician and journalist in Imperial Germany. He was one of the leading advocates of Liberalism in the Prussian *Landtag* and German *Reichstag*. However, over the course of his political career, Richter became an outspoken opponent of Socialism and effectively removed himself from the Social Liberal movement. In hindsight, he can more accurately be viewed as Libertarian.

Eugen Richter was born in Düsseldorf (Rhineland Prussia) on 30 July 1838 to an army regimental doctor. Upon completion of his studies in the local gymnasium in 1856, he studied political science and law with Friedrich Christoph Dahlmann at University of Bonn and with Robert von Mohl at University of Heidelberg, where he also studied public finance with Karl Heinrich Rau, then the most celebrated expert in the field. While still a student he went to Berlin, where the proceedings of the Prussian *Landtag* interested him much more than his university lectures at the local Friedrich Wilhelm University. He began attending the meetings of the *Kongress deutscher Volkswirte* (Congress of German Economists), a liberal reformist organization and, through newspapers and journal articles, avidly took part in the growing movement for classical economic Liberalism;* he was also

* Economic Liberalism: an economic system organized on individual lines, which means the greatest possible number of economic decisions are made by individuals or households rather than by collective institutions or organizations (Adams 2001,

active in the consumer-cooperative movement. In 1859, Richter completed his studies in Bonn and successfully passed the civil service examination. He took a position as a trainee civil servant in the judiciary. Richter became a strong advocate of free trade, a market economy, and a *Rechtsstaat*;* views he held for all his life. He achieved some renown for his 1862 essay *Über die Freiheit des Schankgewerbes* (*On the Freedom of the Tavern Trade*) in which he criticized the Prussian trade police for their arbitrary and illegal basis of enforcement. His liberal views caused some trouble with the conservative Prussian bureaucracy resulting in a disciplinary reprimand. Already as a young journalist, Richter emphasized not only the economic disadvantages of the antiquated mercantilist system but at the same time the infringement of civil and political freedom bound up with that system. Thus, in his essay *On the Freedom of the Tavern Trade* he attacked the concessions system, which invested the political authorities with wide-ranging licensing and regulatory authority for all trades and professions: "As long as the police administration in our state unites in itself such legislative, judicial, and executive powers, Prussia does not yet deserve the name of a *Rechtsstaat*" (Rachfahl 1912, 226). Thus, from the start the cornerstone of Richter's social philosophy was the connection between political and economic freedom, a conception that distinguished him, and Social Liberalism in general, from the mass of liberal Nationalists. Two decades later, Richter closed his great speech against von Bismarck's protective tariffs with the words, "Economic freedom has no security without political freedom, and political freedom can

---

20). It is the economic component of classical Liberalism. The highest aim of economic Liberalism is efficiency. It includes a spectrum of different economic policies, such as freedom of movement, but its basis is on strong support for a *laissez-faire* market economy and private property in the means of production. Although economic Liberals can also be supportive of government regulation to a certain degree, they tend to oppose government intervention in the free market when it inhibits free trade and open competition. Historically, economic Liberalism arose during the Enlightenment, opposing mercantilism and feudalism. Today, economic Liberalism is also considered opposed to non-Capitalist economic orders, such as Socialism and planned economies (Brown 2005, 39). It also contrasts with protectionism because of its support for free trade and open markets. An economy that is managed according to these precepts may be described as a liberal economy.

* *Rechtsstaat* is a doctrine in Continental European legal thinking, originating in German jurisprudence. It can be translated into English as "rule of law," alternatively "legal state," "state of law," "state of justice," "state of rights," or "state based on justice and integrity."

find its security only in economic freedom" (Richter 1894–1896, 114). This tenet determined Richter's continuing political strategy. All his life, he conducted a "two-front war" against Bismarckian "pseudo-constitutionalism" and a recrudescent mercantilism on the one hand, and the rising Socialist movement on the other. Richter rejected any alliance with the Socialists. He saw himself faced with a Socialist party that did not care to conceal its ultimate aim—**abolition of the system of private property and the market economy—and its view on "the class-struggle between bourgeoisie and proletariat as the 'pivot of all revolutionary socialism'"** (Engelberg 1983, 26). After 1875, the Social Democratic Party of Germany (*SPD*) was officially a Marxist party, and despite later revisionist tendencies by Bernstein *et al.*, its acknowledged leaders like Bebel, Liebknecht, and Kautsky were confirmed orthodox Marxists. Of course, the *SPD* initially presented various Democratic demands; its ultimate goal remained, however, the **social elimination of all non-proletarians**.

Richter left the civil service and became the parliamentary correspondent of the *Elberfelder Zeitung* in Berlin. In 1867, during the North German Confederation he entered the *Reichstag* representing the German Progress Party (*DFP*), and from 1869 to 1905 was a member of the Prussian *Landtag* Lower House (*Abgeordnetenhaus*). He became the leader of the *DFP*, then after dissolution of the *DFP* and the Liberal Union in 1884, he became leader of the German Free-minded Party that boasted more than 100 seats in the *Reichstag*. In 1893, when the German Free-minded Party split, he became leader of the German Free-minded People's Party and was one of the leading critics of the policies of Chancellor Otto von Bismarck throughout his political career. In response to the Anti-Socialist Law passed in 1878 banning the Social Democrat Party, Richter said: "I fear Social-Democracy more under this law than without it." When von Bismarck proposed in 1889 a system of social insurance for retired and disabled workers paid by the state, Richter denounced it as "not Socialistic, but Communistic." From 1885 to 1904, Richter was the chief editor of the liberal newspaper *Freisinnige Zeitung*.

Richter viewed Socialism as the great modern counterrevolution and believed that the achievement of the Socialist goal would lead both to appalling poverty and to state absolutism. Richter attempted to make this evident to the public in his 1891 publication *Sozialdemokratische Zukunftsbilder, Frei nach Bebel* (*Pictures of the Socialistic Future, Freely Adapted from Bebel*). In its time, this little book, with its ironic subtitle referring to August Bebel, was a sensation. It was translated into a dozen languages, with more than a quarter-million copies printed in Germany alone. This dystopian novel predicts what would happen to Germany if the Socialism espoused by the trade unionists, Social Democrats, and Marxists was put into practice. It is a nineteenth-century version of George Orwell's *1984* (published in 1949). Richter aims to show that government ownership of the means of production and central planning of the economy would lead to shortages, not abundance as the Socialists claim. He seeks to draw attention to the problem of incentives in the absence of profits, and the public choice vested interests of bureaucrats and politicians. He also focuses on the connection between economic and political liberty. Written in the form of a diary by a supporter of the Socialist revolution who comes to see the horrors he has wrought, the narrator begins by applauding expropriation, the use of force to prevent emigration, and the reassignment of people to new tasks, all the while assuring doubters that paradise is just around the corner. To date, the book remains a potent antidote to cyclical Socialist flirtation.

During the latter half of the nineteenth century, anti-Semitism reared its ugly head among formal organs of the German Empire. In the 1870s, Kaiser Wilhelm I made anti-Semitism even more prevalent in Germany, but when historian Heinrich von Treitschke (1834–1896)[2] and Imperial Court Chaplain pietist Lutheran Adolf Stöcker (1835–1909)[3] endorsed it in 1879 (based on his misinterpretation of Martin Luther's 1543 treatise *Von den Juden und ihren Lügen* [*On the Jews and Their Lies*]), what had been a fringe phenomenon gained national attention. Various newspapers (such as the *Berliner Antisemitismusstreit*) published articles attacking Jews. A petition (*Antisemitenpetition*) to the *Reich* Chancellor Otto von Bismarck in April 1881 called for administrative measures banning Jewish immigration and restricting their access to positions in education and the judiciary.

Although anti-Semitism was opposed by Eugen Richter's Progress Party and some members of the National Liberal Party led by Theodor Mommsen and Heinrich Rickert, other National Liberals and the other parties, including the Conservatives, Center Party, and Socialists, mostly either stayed aloof or flirted with anti-Semitism. In November 1880, a declaration by seventy-five leading scientists, businessmen, and politicians was published in major newspapers condemning anti-Semitism (*Notabeln-Erklärung*). It was signed by among others the Mayor of Berlin Max von Forckenbeck, eminent pathologist Dr. Rudolf Virchow, historian Theodor Mommsen, and entrepreneur and inventor Werner Siemens (founder of Siemens *AG*). On 20 November 1880, the Progress Party brought the issue before the Prussian *Landtag*, asking the government to take a stand on whether legal restrictions were to be introduced (*Interpellation Hänel*). The government confirmed that the legal status of Jews was not to be altered but fell short of condemning anti-Semitism. Dr. Rudolf Virchow complained in the ensuing debate: "Well, *meine Herren*, even if I have called the reply given by the Royal state government correct, I cannot deny that on the whole it could have been somewhat warmer. It was correct, but cold down to the heart" (*Die Judenfrage* 1880). While on the first day of the debate a consensus seemed to emerge against the anti-Semitic movement, on the second day 22 November 1880, some politicians began to brazenly declare their anti-Semitism. In his speech, Eugen Richter predicted the eventual consequences of the anti-Semitic movement (*Die Judenfrage* 1880, 63):

> *Meine Herren*, the whole movement has by all means a similar character regarding its final goal, regarding its methods, as the Socialist movement. (Call from the floor.) That is what matters. The small gradual differences completely cede into the background, that is what is particularly insidious about the whole movement, that while the Socialists only turn against the economically better-off, here racial hatred is nourished, that is, something the individual cannot alter and that can only be ended by either killing him or forcing him out of the country.

He concluded his speech with the words:

> Exactly to give the government the opportunity to speak its mind, how it stands on the matter, including the *Reich* Chancellor, that is why we have introduced this interpellation, and we are pleased about the success and wish that from now on throughout the country a sturdy reaction will crush this anti-Semitic movement, which truly does not confer honor and adornment on our country.

Responding to an anti-Semitic meeting on 17 December 1880, the Progress Party invited all electors for the Prussian *Landtag* to a meeting in the upper hall of the *Reichshallen* on 12 January 1881 to demonstrate that the citizens of Berlin did not support anti-Semitism. Eugen Richter delivered a speech before an audience of 2,500 electors, attacking anti-Semitic university students (Richter 1881):

> And what do we see now as an outrageous phenomenon? Young people* who have not lived a great time with a political consciousness like we have—because they were still in 6th and 5th grade (Amusement)—Young people who have not yet proved what they are worth, force their way to the fore and dare to hurl at the Jewish cavaliers of the Iron Cross, and at the fathers who have given their sons to Germany, that they do not belong to the German nation?!! (Long-lasting, tempestuous applause. Calls of Boo!)

He turned the anti-Semitic accusations around:

> Nowadays it is seen as the act of a hero if you drink more than the Jews, and as an educated nation you reproach the Jews for sending so many children to higher education.† And after you have worked all those valiant deeds, then you sing: *Deutschland, Deutschland über Alles!*‡ (Tempestuous amusement.) Truly! Our friend Hoffmann von Fallersleben has been saved by a kind fate from experiencing this abuse of his magnificent song. Since, that's something I admit openly, if this is supposed to be German, if this is supposed

---

* "Young people" refers to the popularity of the anti-Semitic movement among university students. By law, full adulthood started only at age twenty-five-years.

† Jews were eager to send their children to high schools and universities where they were over-represented. Over-representation was also due to the fact Jews would focus on subjects like medicine and the law that could lead to careers outside of the government service or the military from which they were effectively barred. The anti-Semites were clamoring for affirmative action for non-Jews.

‡ "Deutschland, Deutschland über alles" ("Germany, Germany above All") was the refrain of the Song of the Germans (*Deutschlandlied* or *Lied der Deutschen*) written by Hoffmann von Fallersleben in 1841. The original meaning of the refrain was that a unified Germany should be above the lesser states. But at the time of Richter's speech, the song (to music from Haydn) had taken on a more chauvinistic overtone and was a signature song of the anti-Semites. It was not yet the German national anthem, but "Heil Dir im Siegerkranz" ("Hail to you in the Victor's Wreath," with the same tune as "God Save the Queen"). It would become the national anthem only in the Weimar Republic in 1922 and stay so until today, albeit now with a focus on the third stanza with the refrain "Einigkeit und Recht und Freiheit" ("Unity and Justice and Liberty").

> to be Christian, then I want to be anywhere else in the world but in Christian Germany! (Vigorous applause.)

Already in February 1880, the German Crown Prince and latter Emperor Frederick III (Frederick William) had called the anti-Semitic movement in a private conversation with the president of the Jewish corporation of Berlin, Meyer Magnus, "a disgrace for Germany" (in some reports also "a disgrace of our time" or "a disgrace for our nation"). Eugen Richter referred to these words, which the Crown Prince confirmed two days later:

> One day, it will not be the smallest leaf of laurel in the wreath of our Crown Prince* that already at the first stirrings of this movement, something that our deceased colleague Wulffsheim† overheard with his own ears and which has also been confirmed otherwise as trustworthy—he declared to the president of the Jewish corporation of Berlin [Meyer Magnus] that this movement is a disgrace for the German nation! (Tempestuous, long lasting applause.)

He rejected the claim that the anti-Semitic movement had grown from the ranks of craftsmen, workers, and businessmen:

> It confers honor on the German craftsmen, workers, and businessmen that this movement, which is supposed to be in their interest, did not arise from their circles, (Vigorous applause), just like the corn tariff propaganda did not arise from peasant circles. It arose from young people who do not earn anything at all but live out of their parents' pockets.

---

* Frederick William (1831–1888), at the time Crown Prince of Prussia and Germany and, for only 99 days, King of Prussia, and Emperor Frederick III of Germany. Eugen Richter is referring to a statement the Crown Prince made in early 1880 calling the anti-Semitic movement "a disgrace for Germany" (there are different versions: "a disgrace for our nation," "a disgrace of our time"). The anti-Semites attacked the authenticity of the quote. Days after Richter's speech, the Crown Prince reaffirmed his statement and made this known through the newspapers. Nonetheless, the anti-Semites would continue to cast doubt on its authenticity well into the 1890s.

† Emanuel Gustav Wulffshein (1807–1880), a member of the National Liberals and later of Eugen Richter's Progressive Party acting as representative in the *Reichstag*.

> Furthermore, from people who in positions of trust as officials obtain their salaries from the public coffers and often cannot have any idea of how a businessman sometimes feels who struggles to earn his daily bread and to pay the obligatory taxes! (Tempestuous, general applause). Such people who call themselves "educated" have put Jew baiting into action. Indeed, here it shows again that superior mental culture if it is not aligned with a culture of the heart and true religiosity—not a religiosity that has God on its lips, but the devil in its heart—often only leads to nothing more than barbarity in a more refined form!

In his concluding words, Richter called upon his audience of electors at the Prussian *Landtag*:

> In this vein, let us also fight against the depravity of this movement in a league without party distinction and let us feel united in this resolution—drawing on the New Year's Address of the city councilors to the Kaiser and his reply—that only if all powers of national life, before which no distinction of denominations is justified, work peacefully and peaceably together, the welfare of the German *Reich* and her individual citizens can prosper. (Vigorous, continuous applause.)

On 27 October 1881, the German Progress Party defeated the anti-Semitic *Berliner Bewegung* (Berlin Movement),* winning all six seats for

---

* The Berlin Movement (*Berliner Bewegung*) was an anti-Semitic intellectual and political movement in the German Empire in the 1880s. The movement developed in the aftermath of the six-year financial Panic of 1873 that led to a recession in the United States and parts of the Western European economy. It assailed Jews and Capitalism; along with this critique it opposed Liberalism and it represented a fear of Social Democracy. The movement came out of a racial conception of national identity on the part of the German middle class. The journalist and author Otto Glagau led a journal, *Der Kulturkämpfer* (*The Culture Warrior*), that propagated these ideas. The pietist Lutheran theologian and politician, Adolf Stöcker, led the Christian Social Party in support of the movement. The movement lost strength after the *CSP*'s losses in the 1887 elections. The significance of the movement laid in its being the first political anti-Semitic movement in modern Germany.

the capital, with Eugen Richter gaining 66 percent of the vote in the first round.

Eugen Richter died of natural causes in Berlin on 10 March 1906.

Friedrich Naumann was a German liberal politician and pietist Protestant pastor. He was born 25 March 1860 in the vicarage of Großpösna near Leipzig in Saxony. He attended school in Leipzig and the *Fürstenschule* in Meissen, thereafter he studied theology at the universities of Leipzig and Erlangen. From 1883, he worked at the *Rauhes Haus* charity institution established by Johann Hinrich Wichern in Hamburg, before in 1886 he took over the rectorate of Lengenberg near Glauchau in Saxony. From 1890, he also served in the Inner mission in Frankfurt.

Originally a follower of the conservative-clerical and anti-Semitic *Berliner Bewegung* led by Adolf Stöcker and his Christian Social Party, Naumann later became interested in the social theories advocated by his friend jurist, sociologist, and political philosopher and economist Max Weber (1864–1920), one of the most pronounced critics of Emperor Wilhelm II. His ideal was that of helping the workers, whose miserable life circumstances he had witnessed in Hamburg. His goal was to raise interest in this issue among the middle class; however, initially he was hindered by the middle-class's fear of the proletariat, who were regarded as potential revolutionaries.

Together with Rudolph Sohm and Caspar René Gregory, Naumann founded the National-Social Association in 1896 in an attempt to provide a social liberal alternative to the Social Democrats that could address the growing social rift between rich industrialists and the poor working class. It sought to synthesize Liberalism, Nationalism, and revisionist-Marxist Socialism with Protestant Christian values in order to cross the ideological front lines and draw workers away from a Marxist class struggle.

Later in his life, Naumann worked for rapprochement of German Social Democrat and liberal movements but faced major opposition from Conservatives. Industrialists called Naumann and his associates "Allies of the Socialists." Naumann wanted to preserve Christian values, which he hoped would improve the fraught relations between workers and corporate businessmen. The National-Social Association failed in the German elections of 1898 and 1903 and was then dissolved into the German Free-minded Union. Naumann became a member of the *Reichstag* upon the 1907 federal election.

In 1907, Naumann co-founded the *Deutscher Werkbund* association. On the eve of World War I, Naumann proved to be a monarchist and devotee of Wilhelm II. He espoused a kind of liberal imperialism, signing the 1914 Manifesto of the Ninety-Three, and still in 1918 backed the Anti-Bolshevist League of Eduard Stadtler.

In 1918, Friedrich Naumann was among the founders of the *Deutsche Demokratische Partei*, *DDP* (Social Liberal German Democratic Party) with Theodor Wolff and Hugo Preuß. As a member of the Weimar National Assembly, he became one of the "Fathers of the Constitution" of the Weimar Republic, and shortly before his death in 1919 was elected as the first president of the *DDP*.

CHAPTER 8

THE BIRTH OF GERMAN POLITICAL PARTIES

My political sentiments inclined toward the Left and emphasized the Socialist aspects every bit as much as Nationalist ones. (Eichmann 2015, 75; also quoted in Aly 2006, 16)

— ADOLF EICHMANN,
False Gods: The Jerusalem Memoirs

Basically, National Socialism and Marxism are the same. (von Hayek 1994, 35)

— ADOLF HITLER, 1941

THE FRUIT OF THE ENLIGHTENMENT, EUROPEAN LIBERALISM, AND German Romanticism included Socialism, Communism, and early National Socialism representing movements seeking to counter the long-established *status quo* in governance and privilege, and to liberate the working class from its overlord, viewed as despotic and exploitive: the aristocrat, industrial baron, usurper, landed gentry. In the mid-nineteenth century, a new political movement arose—Socialism. Germany was its epicenter. Usurping its early Utopian founders, Karl Marx became its leading thinker before divorcing himself from Socialism and its leading organization the Social Democratic Party of Germany (*SPD*). The Socialists denounced Capitalist inequality and argued that the obvious solution was government ownership of property and the means of production.

From the outset, many questioned the practicality of the Socialist solution. "After you equalize incomes, who will take out the garbage?" Eugen Richter posited to the leading Socialists in the *Reichstag*. Yet almost no one questioned the Socialists' idealism. By 1961, however, the descendants of the *radical* wing of the *SPD* had built the Berlin Wall—and were shooting anyone who tried to flee their "Workers' Paradise." A movement founded to liberate the worker turned its guns on the very people it vowed to save.

Who could have foreseen such a mythic transformation? Out of all the critics of Socialism, one stands out as uniquely prescient: Eugen Richter. During the last decades of the nineteenth century, Eugen Richter was the leading Libertarian in the *Reichstag*, as well as the chief editor of the *Freisinnige Zeitung.* Seventy years before the Berlin Wall, Richter's dystopian novel, *Sozialdemokratische Zukunftsbilder, Frei nach Bebel* (*Pictures of the Socialistic Future, Freely Adapted from Bebel* [Berlin: Verlag Fortschritt Aktiengesellschaft, November 1891]), boldly predicted that victorious German Socialism would inspire a mass exodus—and that the Socialists would respond by banning emigration and punishing violators with deadly force. (Excerpts and quotes taken from Bryan Caplan's 21 June 2010 Forward, titled "The Writing on the Wall," to Henry Wright's 1893 translation of Richter's novel [Auburn, Alabama: Ludwig von Mises Institute, 2010].)

> [U]seful people, and people who had really learnt something, went away in ever-increasing numbers to Switzerland, to England, to America, in which countries Socialism has not succeeded in getting itself established. Architects, engineers, chemists, doctors, teachers, managers of works and mills, and all kinds of skilled workmen, emigrated in shoals. The main cause of this would appear to be a certain exaltation of mind which is greatly to be regretted. These people imagine themselves to be something better, and they cannot bear the thought of getting only the same guerdon as the simple honest day labourer. (Page 53)
>
> [A] decree has been issued against all emigration without the permission of the authorities. . . . Old persons who are beyond work, and infants, are at liberty to go away, but the right to emigrate cannot be conceded to robust people who are under obligations to the State for their education and culture, so long as they are of working age. (Page 51)
>
> Under these circumstances the Government is to be commended for stringently carrying out its measures to prevent emigration. In order to do so all the more effectually, it has been deemed expedient to send strong

> bodies of troops to the frontiers, and to the seaport towns. The frontiers towards Switzerland have received especial attention from the authorities. It is announced that the standing army will be increased by many battalions of infantry and squadrons of cavalry. The frontier patrols have strict instructions to unceremoniously shoot down all fugitives. (Page 54)

English Catholic historian, moderate conservative politician, and writer Lord Acton (1834–1902)* and Austrian-British Libertarian economist and philosopher Friedrich August von Hayek (1899–1992) have inspired the two most popular explanations for the crimes of Socialism. While Acton never lived to see Socialists gain power in England, their behavior seems to perfectly illustrate his aphorism that "Power tends to corrupt, and absolute power corrupts absolutely." For all their idealism, *even Socialists* will do bad things if left unchecked. Von Hayek, with the benefit of hindsight, suggested a slightly different explanation: under Socialism, "the worst get on top" (von Hayek 1994, 148–67). On this theory, the Utopian founders of Socialism were gradually pushed out by brutal cynics as their movement's power increased.

Richter's novel advances a very different explanation for Socialism's "moral decay": the movement was born bad. While the early Socialists were indeed "idealists," their ideal was in reality totalitarianism. Their overriding goals were to engineer a new society and a New Socialist Man. If this meant treating workers like slaves—depriving them of the freedom to choose their occupation or location, forbidding them to quit, splitting up families without their consent, and imposing draconian punishments on malcontents—so be it.

Richter admittedly presents some of the Socialists' uglier policies—increased work hours, stringent rationing, massive military spending, corporal punishment—as slippery-slope responses to deteriorating conditions. But many of their worst offenses happen early in the novel, and Mr. Schmidt, the novel's Socialist narrator, happily supports them. In chapter 6, workers lose the freedom to choose their trade. Schmidt's reaction:

---

* John Emerich Edward Dalberg-Acton, first Baron Acton, otherwise known simply as Lord Acton.

> [W]hat has the Government to do in order to bring their scheme for organising production and consumption into some sort of harmony with the entries made by the people? Should Government attempt a settlement by fixing a lower rate of wages for those branches which showed any over-crowding, and a higher rate for those labours which were not so coveted? This would be a subversion of the fundamental principles of Socialism. (Page 20)

The period of Austrian and Prussian police-states and vast censorship before the Revolutions of 1848 in Germany later became widely known as the *Vormärz*, the "before March," referring to March 1848 when the revolutions spread to Vienna and Germany. During this period, European Liberalism gained momentum; the agenda included economic, social, and political issues. Most European Liberals in the *Vormärz* sought unification under Nationalist principles, promoted the transition to Capitalism, sought the expansion of male suffrage, among other issues. Their "radicalness" depended upon where they stood on the spectrum of male suffrage: the wider the definition of suffrage, the more radical. The first political opportunities for German workers grew out of the originally non-political workers' educational associations that were sponsored by middle-class reformers. These associations expressed the liberal conviction that education and self-help would be the main means of working-class improvement. At this time, there was still no clear organizational distinction between Liberal and working-class movements in Germany. In the 1860s, as the constitutional struggles in Prussia intensified, Liberals sought to enlist the support of these workers' associations on behalf of national unification and constitutional reform. Marx's and Engel's Communist League (the world's first Marxist political party), formed in London on 1 June 1847 by the merging of Communist Correspondence Committee of Brussels and Karl Schapper's League of the Just, had by the 1860s not yet managed to elect representation in any European parliament. However, the early Socialist movement had managed to not only find its way into but to take control of many parliaments throughout late nineteenth- and early twentieth-century Europe.

Six major political parties were active in Imperial Germany: Free Conservative Party (1867); National Liberal Party (1867); Center Party (1870); German Conservative Party (1876); Social Democratic Party of Germany (1890, *SPD*); and Progressive People's Party (1910). Only *SPD* survived both the Empire and the Weimar Republic and came to play a vital role in the Federal Republic after the Second World War. Even though the German Empire lacked a genuinely Democratic system, the six main parties accurately reflected the interests and hopes of most of its people.

Although many blocs and coalitions were formed between parties in the years 1871 to 1918, these never lasted long enough to become stable "governing coalitions." The parties were too much at odds to conclusively develop the rights of Parliament or establish a more parliamentary system of government. Moreover, apart from the *SPD*, which formed the largest parliamentary group in the *Reichstag* from 1912, no party saw any lasting benefit in constitutional change, and even within the ranks of the Social Democrats there was an ambivalent attitude to parliamentary Democracy.

Not until September 1918 during the closing chapter of the First World War when Germany was on the brink of economic and military collapse, did the majority parties thrust their way into government. The military high command (*Oberste Heeresleitung*, *OHL*) under Generals Paul von Hindenburg and Erich Ludendorff did not wish to take responsibility for the defeat, although over the course of the war they had increasingly determined imperial policy and had done so almost dictatorially. For this reason, they were finally willing to compromise with the political parties—of course, in a conscious effort to shift the blame for defeat to the political parties. The advances made by the majority parties and the military high command and, not least, the pressure exerted by President Woodrow Wilson, who did not wish to make peace with anything other than a Democratic government, paved the way for the introduction of parliamentary Democracy. By a large majority, Parliament amended the Imperial Constitution, and on 28 October 1918 the Empire became a parliamentary monarchy, albeit only for a moment. On 9 November 1918, Kaiser Wilhelm II abdicated the throne and Philipp Scheidemann of the Social Democratic Party proclaimed the Weimar Republic from a window in the *Reichstag* building, thereby completing the constitutional transformation.

The most conservative of the six majority parties was the German Conservative Party, which represented Prussian Nationalism, aristocracy, and landed gentry. Many of its members remained opposed to German unification because they feared Prussia's gradual subjugation to the Empire. The Conservatives also detested the *Reichstag* because it was elected by universal male suffrage. The Free Conservative Party represented industrialists and large commercial interests. The views of this party most closely matched those of von Bismarck. Its members supported unification because they saw it as unavoidable. The National Liberal Party was composed of liberal Nationalists who had accepted Germany's lack of full Democracy because they valued national unity more. They continued to favor a *laissez-faire* economic policy and secularization. In time, National Liberals became some of the strongest supporters of the acquisition of colonies and a substantial naval buildup, both key issues in the 1880s and 1890s.

Unlike the members of the National Liberal Party, members of the German Progress Party and its two primary offspring remained faithful to all the principles of European Liberalism and championed the extension of parliament's powers. This party was in the forefront of those opposed to the authoritarian rule of von Bismarck and his successors. The Center Party was Germany's Roman Catholic party and had strong support in southern Germany, the Rhineland, and in parts of Prussia with significant Polish populations. It was conservative regarding monarchical authority but progressive in matters of social reform.

Formally organized political Liberalism in Germany developed in the 1860s, combining the previous Liberal and Democratic currents. Between 1867 and 1933, Liberalism was divided into liberal progressive (Socialist and Communist) and liberal Nationalist factions. The Socialists and Communists sought a complete break with the monarchal system of rule of the past and the rise of the proletariat class—the Communists sought to replace aristocratic rule with the "dictate of the proletariat"—while the liberal Nationalists sought to liberalize the monarchal aristocratic rule but not eliminate it.

Let us examine how the political party system began and evolved in Germany with some of the more prominent political parties pertinent to our topic. Weaving through the intricacies, strategies, and intrigues of German politics during the late nineteenth and early twentieth centuries is not the intent of this writing. The only interest here is in briefly introducing the various significant political movements and their key players from one ideologically liberal extreme to the other liberal extreme, that facilitated the dramatic developments taking Germany from Empire (First *Reich*) to the Third *Reich*. Throughout this discussion it is important to remember that it was Liberalism that was the primary driving force in the political evolution of the period. Many minor, insignificant political movements and parties have been left out of this discussion. Although the following examination may seem tedious, pedantic, and esoteric to some, it is useful to gain insight into the German political movements born of the Enlightenment, 1789 French Revolution, Industrial Revolution, and 1848 Spring of Nations

Revolutions that led to the German Revolution and rise of National Socialism.

I. ON THE SOCIALIST/MARXIST SIDE OF THE GERMAN POLITICAL SPECTRUM (See Figure 1)

THE **GERMAN NATIONAL ASSOCIATION (UNION)** (*Deutscher Nationalverein*) was a liberal political organization that existed from 1859 to 1867 and precursor of the German Progress Party (*Deutsche Fortschrittspartei, DFP*)—one of the six major political parties during the German Empire. The Union was founded in Frankfurt, Prussia (German Confederation) by Liberals and moderate Democrats and aimed at forming a liberal, parliamentary Lesser German (*kleindeutsch*), Prussia-led nation-state. When repeated efforts between 1848 and 1862 to unify the many states of Germany into a single nation-state failed, the moderate liberal "New Era" in Prussia ended. The German National Association had to change its strategy of influence to unify Germany under Prussian leadership. Leading up to these changes were the naming of *Generalleutnant* Albrecht von Roon Minister of War in 1859 and Otto von Bismarck Minister-President in 1862. Prussian King Friedrich Wilhelm IV suffered a stroke in 1857 and could no longer rule. This led to his younger brother Wilhelm Friedrich Ludwig becoming Prince Regent of the Kingdom of Prussia in 1858. Von Roon and Wilhelm Friedrich began reorganizing the Prussian army. Beginning in 1860, Prussian army reforms (especially the power to levy taxes to pay for them) caused a constitutional crisis of the 1849 German Confederation Constitution because both parliament and Wilhelm Friedrich—via his minister of war—claimed control over the military budget. Wilhelm Friedrich Ludwig, crowned King Wilhelm I upon the death of his brother Wilhelm IV in 1861, appointed Otto von Bismarck to the position of Minister-President of Prussia in 1862. Von Bismarck aggravated the Prussian constitutional crisis when he further pushed the army reform plan designed by his Minister of War von Roon and levied taxes to support it, effectively ignoring and bypassing the power of the Prussian parliament (*Landtag*).[1] The controversy over levying taxes to reform the army and budgetary control over the army persisted until von Bismarck resolved the constitutional crisis in favor of the war minister in 1866. The liberal German

National Association could no longer support the Prussian government and its power grab. Earlier in 1862, the National Association adopted the Democratic constitution of 1849 (*Paulskirchenverfassung*) into its political program, illustrating the organization's swing further to the left. Parallel to these events, the German National Association established the German Progress Party (*Deutsche Fortschritsspartei*, or *DFP*) in Prussia in 1861—the first modern political party in Germany. The *DFP* was immediately successful in the Prussian parliamentary election of the same year. The strategy was to exert pressure on the governments of the German states to promote German unification via parliamentary means. During the Austro-Prussian War (1866) and subsequent establishment of the North German Confederation (1866–1867), the conflict between the Social Liberals and National Liberals inside the German National Association grew deeper over the question whether to support von Bismarck. Ultimately, the liberal Nationalists decided to accept the Indemnity bill (*Indemnitätsvorlage*)* in 1866, leading to the final split of the Social Liberal, staunchly oppositional German Progress Party and the pro-government National Liberal Party, that was established in 1867. Thus, the German National Association ceased to exist.

German Progress Party (*Deutsche Fortschrittspartei*, *DFP*) was the **first modern political party in Germany**, founded on 6 June 1861 by liberal members of the Prussian *Landtag*'s lower House of Representatives (*Abgeordnetenhaus*), in opposition to Minister-President Otto von Bismarck. When under the regency of Wilhelm I of Prussia the Prussian policies of the

---

* Indemnity Bill of 1866 – As soon as peace was concluded in the Austro-Prussian War, von Bismarck introduced in the Prussian *Landtag* a bill of indemnity granting the government retroactive approval for its operation without a legal budget. The consequence, as von Bismarck had foreseen, was a split in the ranks of his adversaries. Those who argued that there could be no compromise on the principle of constitutional government rejected the indemnity bill, but many more moderate Liberals, who eventually formed the National Liberal Party in 1867, decided to accept the settlement offered by von Bismarck. Their reasoning was that an obstinate resistance against the cabinet would only condemn them to sterile dogmatism, whereas a willingness to accept what could not be prevented would enable them to influence official policy in the direction of greater freedom. With the support of these moderate Liberals, on 3 September 1866, parliament approved the Bill of Indemnity, 230 to 75. By dividing the forces of reform and weakening their sense of purpose, von Bismarck won as important a success in domestic political affairs as the victory on the field of battle.

"New Era" turned towards a more centrist stance, a Socialist group under Max von Forckenbeck (1821–1892) seceded and allied with remaining members of the German National Association to form the German Progress Party. Among the more infamous founding members were: eminent pathologist Dr. Rudolf Virchow (1821–1902); classical historian, jurist, Lutheran, and Nobel laureate Theodor Mommsen (1817–1903), inventor and industrialist Werner von Siemens (1816–1892), strongly-liberal deputy of Prussian National Assembly of 1848 Benedict Waldeck (1802–1870), economist Hermann Schulze-Delitzsch (1808–1883), President of the Prussian National Assembly of 1848 Hans Victor von Unruh (1806–1886), Frankfurt physician Dr. Wilhelm Loewe (1814–1886), and Jewish activist and physician Dr. Johann Jacoby (1805–1877). The party supported the unification of the German states with the central power in Prussia under the Small Germany solution (*Kleindeutsche Lösung*). It demanded representative Democracy, implementation of the rule of law, and greater responsibility for local governments. Before the rise of the Social Democrats, the Progress Party was the main liberal party in Germany, as well as the first German party with its candidates and deputies acting on a common party platform. In the mid-1860s, von Bismarck continued to rule against the parliamentary majority, while the members of the German Progress Party found themselves unable to overthrow his government. In 1866, upon the Prussian victory of the Austro-Prussian War, von Bismarck capitulated and introduced a law (Indemnity Bill) confirming parliament's power of the purse, but also granting an amnesty for the arbitrary conduct of his government relative to budgetary matters and the army. Meant as an attempt for reconciliation, a large majority of the *Landtag* approved it, however the Liberals disagreed among themselves, and the German Progress Party finally split apart. In 1867, the right wing (National Liberals) that supported von Bismarck seceded to form the National Liberal Party. And in 1868, the left wing (Social Liberals) in southern Germany that opposed von Bismarck seceded from the German Progress Party to form the German People's Party. After the 1867 split, the remaining German Progress Party members under Benedict Waldeck and Eugen Richter principally supported von Bismarck's formation of the North German Confederation with the objective of establishment of a Prussian-led German nation state. In the first federal election of 1871, the German Progress Party gained 8.8 percent of the votes cast and 46 seats in the *Reichstag*, largely outnumbered by its National Liberal rivals.

To characterize von Bismarck's politics toward the Catholic Church, the pathologist Dr. Rudolf Virchow used the term *Kulturkampf* the first time on 17 January 1873, in the Prussian *Landtag* House of Representatives. In the later years of von Bismarck's incumbency, the German Progress Party again kept its distance from his government. Under the new leadership of Eugen Richter, the Progress Party eventually evolved into a pan-German liberal Democratic party, rejecting von Bismarck's *Kulturkampf*, Anti-Socialist Laws, and free trade restrictions. In the 1881 federal election, the German Progress Party reached its best results ever with 12.7 percent of the votes cast and 56 seats in the *Reichstag*, becoming the second strongest faction after the Catholic Center Party. However, the German Progress Party progressively declined in popularity and support thereafter and eventually folded in 1884 when Eugen Richter and his fellow Social Liberals joined the Liberal Union to form the German Free-minded Party.

The **Social Democratic Party of Germany** (*Sozialdemokratische Partei Deutschlands, SPD*) remains, to date, the oldest extant political party represented in the *Reichstag* (now known as *Bundestag*) and, as an amalgamation of two precursor organizations, was one of the first Marxist-influenced political parties in the world. Although the *SPD* did not officially call itself the Social Democratic Party of Germany until January 1890, some historians date the founding of the *SPD* to as far back as 23 May 1863 when one of its predecessor constituents, the **General German Workers' Association** (*Allgemeiner Deutscher Arbeiterverein, ADAV*), was established in Leipzig, Kingdom of Saxony by the German-Jewish jurist, philosopher, Socialist, and political activist Ferdinand Lassalle (1825–1864). Within the early Communist movement in Germany, Lassalle was of the revisionist Marxist camp. The revisionists, led at various times by Lassalle and Eduard Bernstein, argued that social and economic justice could be achieved for the working class through Democratic elections and institutions and without the violent class struggle and revolution advocated by Marx and Engels. The orthodox Marxists insisted that free elections and civil rights would not create a truly Socialist society and that the ruling class would never cede power without a fight. Lassalle's idea of defeating Capitalism through the establishment of producers' co-operatives was strongly opposed by several Communists who supported the orthodox teachings of Karl Marx.

In Leipzig, Kingdom of Saxony, the first distinctively working-class movement appeared with the formation in 1863 of Ferdinand Lassalle's

ADAV. The *ADAV* ultimately became the leading North German force in the making of the *SPD*, so its origins are worth our attention.

The *ADAV* was initially a non-Marxist workers' party whose main aim was universal suffrage. It came into being because of the break between the **Leipzig Workers' Educational Association** (founded in 1861) and the Liberals' **German National Association (Union)** (*Deutscher Nationalverein*). This break was provoked when the Leipzig Workers' Educational Association sought full membership within the liberal *Deutscher Nationalverein* for manual workers. This appeal for equal status was rebuffed by the Liberals. In doing so, the Liberals revealed their reluctance to accede to the Leipzig Educational Association's principal aim, universal suffrage. This was a turning point because, in substance, the Liberals were acknowledging their unwillingness to collaborate on equal terms with workers even within a liberal association. It was only in consequence of this that the Leipzig Association was willing to participate in the founding of the autonomous, but still non-Marxist, *ADAV*.

The Leipzig Educational Association's importance here is more than merely illustrative: it provided the leadership of the newly created *ADAV*. After its establishment, *ADAV* found itself in constant conflicts with the Liberals over universal suffrage and the place of state-supported workers' cooperatives in the new Germany. It is important to stress, however, that *ADAV* remained open to cooperation with anyone willing to accommodate these ambitions. It was even willing to work with the conservative Prussian government; so, at this point it was certainly not a radical working-class movement rejecting cooperation with its social "betters." Rather, the rejection came mainly from the more liberal members of the *ADAV* and the conservative Prussian government. The turning point was the Prussian military victory over Austria in 1866. In the aftermath of that victory, the Liberals began to disintegrate and as a large faction abandoned the demands for constitutional reform and moved to support the government. Here, it is important to recall that von Bismarck was able to manipulate Prussian Liberals in this fashion because he could play on their obsession with unification via the *kleindeutsch* strategy. In the absence of the regional and religious cleavages in the larger German liberal community that gave meaning to it, von Bismarck's ability to make good the *kleindeutschland* dream would have had little pull among the northern Liberals.

The Liberal's retreat was accelerated in 1867 when von Bismarck introduced a general suffrage in the elections to the North German Confederation, for a general suffrage in such a heterogeneous society made the Liberals even more vulnerable and correspondingly more dependent on the state for the enactment of their own program. With the Liberals' enthusiasm for Democratic reform thus waning, the workers' *ADAV* could expect neither governmental concessions in return for support against the Liberals nor a reformist alliance with the Liberals. Instead, *ADAV* now found itself faced with a united front of the conservative Prussian government and most Liberals. Thus, the settlement of the Prussian constitutional conflicts over a military reform budget and the resulting collaboration between von Bismarck and the Liberals forced *ADAV* to pursue an independent political course to advance its working-class movement. It was only at this juncture that *ADAV* adopted an explicitly Socialist program.

Even as the *ADAV* was forming an autonomous workers' organization, most workers remained politically wedded to the Liberals. In this, their main vehicle was the **League of German Worker Associations** or *VDAV* (*Verband Deutscher Arbeitervereine*), founded on 8 June 1863 as the stronger rival to Lassalle's *ADAV* by the Jewish journalist, newspaper publisher, and political activist Leopold Sonnemann (1831–1909). In 1865, *VDAV* included about 100 local associations with more than 20,000 members, mostly from Saxony and south of the river Main. In time, *VDAV* became the principal organization of workers in the non-Prussian territories brought into the North German Confederation in 1866. Like its original sister organization *ADAV*, the *VDAV* was not a Socialist movement at its inception, but rather a radical liberal movement of workers in close cooperation with the newly formed (1868) liberal German People's Party (*Deutsche Volkspartei*, *DVP*) also under Leopold Sonnemann. Leaders of the *VDAV* sought to make the *DVP* a part of the larger Liberal movement and bind it to their ambition of reform through parliamentary government rather than revolution. At the same time, these leaders sought to discourage the revolutionary tendencies within *VDAV*, then in a minority, which wanted an independent, not to mention Socialist, workers' organization. Like its northern counterpart (*ADAV*), the *VDAV* moved toward a break with moderate Social Liberalism and further to the radical Liberalism of Socialism only after the Prussian victory in 1866 in the Franco-Prussian War. Before the war, a sound basis for cooperation had been provided by the preoccupation of southern German workers with national rather than social issues. The 1866 war resolved the national question of Austria, however. Moreover, von Bismarck's provision of a general suffrage satisfied one of the *VDAV*'s main constitutional aspirations. In consequence, the attention of the rank-and-file workers in *VDAV* turned to social issues. Whereas in the north (mainly Prussia), moderate Social Liberalism came to an end because Liberals rejected it, in the southern German territories brought into the North German Confederation in 1866, Liberalism eventually came to an end because the only Liberals willing to align with *VDAV*, namely, the German People's Party (*DVP*), were incapable of offering the *VDAV* an effective ally on the social issues. This conclusion was driven home to the *VDAV* by the *DVP*'s inability to protect the interests of workers in the *Reichstag* of the North German Confederation, which in 1867 legislated a series of economic reforms largely at the expense of workers. *VDAV*'s adoption of a Socialist program at its Nuremberg Congress in 1868 was a consequence of the weakness of the Democratic Liberals. The Liberals' desperate efforts to stem the tide and even Karl Liebknecht's reluctance to sever the relationship with them could not prevent the evolution of the *VDAV* into an independent Socialist party, the **Social Democratic Workers' Party of Germany** (*Sozialdemokratische Arbeiterpartei Deutschlands*, *SDAP*) at Eisenach in 1869.

The other precursor organization to the *SPD* was the *SDAP* founded in the city of Eisenach, Kingdom of Saxony on 9 August 1869, by Wilhelm Liebknecht (1826–1900, father of Karl) and August Bebel (1892–1913)—both close friends of Marx and Engels. Karl Marx and Friedrich Engels steered the party toward more Marxian Communism and welcomed them (as far as German law would allow) into their International Workingmen's Association (IWA or *Internationale Arbeiterassoziation*, *IAA*), also known as the First International—in which Moses Heß in collaboration with Karl Marx was very active. The *SDAP* was at times referred to as the *Eisenachers*, named after the town in the province of Thuringia, Germany where the *SDAP* was founded. The *SDAP* endorsed Marx's teachings and commitment to class struggle and revolution. The *ADAV* and the *SDAP* differed markedly in their views on Socialist theory, the First International, the role of the state, trade unions, universal suffrage, and on supporting Chancellor Otto von Bismarck. Despite these differences, members of both parties knew that unity meant strength. The *SDAP* was itself the child of Sonnemann's *VDAV* (see *supra*). At the Socialist Unity Conference in the central German city of Gotha from 22–27 May 1875 the Lassallean (*ADAV*) and Marxist Liebknecht/Bebel (*SDAP*) wings debated a new program and decided to merge their two organizations to form the **Socialist Workers' Party of Germany** (*Sozialistische Arbeiterpartei Deutschlands*, *SAPD*). The program contained some of Lassalle's controversial ideas, whereas Socialist commitment to violent revolution did not appear in the text. The manifesto of the new organization was the Gotha program (*Gothaer Parteiprogramm*), which urged "universal, equal, direct suffrage." On 25 January 1890, when the German *Reichstag* refused to renew the Anti-Socialist Laws,* Socialist parties could resume presenting their electoral lists. Shortly thereafter, the *SAPD* adopted its current name, the **Social Democratic Party of Germany** (*Sozialdemokratische Partei Deutschlands, SPD*). The *SPD* remains the longest, continuous Socialist party in the world with roots to some of the original major movers and shakers of the Communist movement.

The unification of the nation, the alliance of the National Liberals and von Bismarck, and the growing estrangement of *VDAV* and *ADAV* from the moderate Social Liberals made most of the differences between the two working-class movements (National Liberals and Social Liberals) inconsequential and laid the foundations for a unified, and now Socialist, working-class movement in Germany under the newly-formed *SAPD* (*SPD* since 25 January 1890). Working-class consciousness certainly remained inchoate in the mid-1870s. The new Socialist party had no more than 30,000 or 40,000 members and it polled just seven percent of the vote. The great majority of wage earners remained loyal to the other parties or did not bother to vote. This was true even if we limit our attention solely to urban Protestant workers. The period of Social Democratic growth was framed by the Anti-Socialist Laws. In the year when the Anti-Socialist Laws were enacted, 1878, the *SAPD* was still receiving just 7.6 percent of the vote. It had perhaps 35,000 members. By 1890, when the *Reichstag* refused to renew the Anti-Socialist Laws, the formerly-outlawed *SAPD* (as of January 1890 known as *SPD* – see *supra*) had 19.7 percent of the vote and 100,000 members. It was

* The Anti-Socialist Laws (officially, *Gesetz gegen die gemeingefährlichen Bestrebungen der Sozialdemokratie*, approximately "Law against the public danger of Social Democratic endeavors") were a series of acts, the first of which was passed on 19 October 1878 by the *Reichstag* lasting until 31 March 1881 and extended four times (May 1880, May 1884, April 1886, and February 1888). The legislation was passed after two failed attempts by Marxist radicals Max Hödel and Dr. Karl Nobiling to assassinate Kaiser Wilhelm I; it was meant to curb the growing strength of the *SAPD*, which was blamed for influencing the assassins. The laws' main proponent was Chancellor Otto von Bismarck, who feared the outbreak of a Socialist revolution like the one that created the Paris Commune in 1871. Despite the government's attempts to weaken the *SAPD*, the party continued to grow in popularity. A bill introduced by von Bismarck in 1888, which would have allowed for the denaturalization of Social Democrats was rejected. After von Bismarck's resignation in 1890, the *Reichstag* did not renew the legislation, allowing it to lapse.

by then, in terms of electoral strength, the largest party in the *Reich*. Eugen Richter's prediction of the consequences of the Anti-Socialist Laws had come true. By the autumn of 1890, the *SPD* had developed a refined sense of parliamentary tactics, a more coherent Marxian ideology, a close relationship with the trade unions, and a greatly broadened electoral base.

The *Reich*'s break with the Social Liberals was made definitive by the enactment of the Anti-Socialist Laws of 1878, which the National Liberals endorsed. The law allowed the police to arrest hundreds of Socialist leaders, suppress the party press, close down Socialist trade unions, and prevent public meetings. It did not prevent party candidates from running for office. That the National Liberals embraced the Anti-Socialist Laws was itself a direct consequence of their own desperate position after national unification. Unalterably subordinated by the conservative state and apparently under siege by the mobilization of workers, Catholics, particularists, and minorities, the Anti-Socialist Laws (like the failed *Kulturkampf* [2] before it) seemed to provide a mechanism by which Social Liberals could secure themselves and their middle-class interests. It was because German Social Liberalism became the first working-class movement in a society of failed National Liberalism that it exerted such an influence on working-class movements in other comparatively situated societies. Socialist movements did not "arrive," that is, achieve enduring electoral breakthroughs, elsewhere in Europe until about 1900. In retrospect, the timing of these breakthroughs can be pinpointed with some precision: 1894 in Belgium, 1895 in Denmark, 1900 in Italy, 1903 in Norway, 1905 in Sweden, 1906 in the Netherlands, 1917 in Spain.

By the middle of the 1890s, at a time when other Socialist parties were still in their infancy, the Social Democrats were the largest party in Germany, so it is no surprise that they exerted such an influence on the thinking of Socialists elsewhere in Europe. Just as the *SPD* became a model for other Socialists, the response of the German Liberals and the Bismarckian state to Social Democracy also became a model of sorts for governments and Liberals elsewhere. The Bismarckian strategy, supported by the National Liberal Party (National Liberals or liberal Nationalists), of attempting to wean the working class from Socialism through welfare-state measures and anti-Socialist legislation, became a negative model because the Anti-Socialist Laws so patently backfired. The growth of Social Democracy in Germany between 1878 and 1890 made it clear that such a blunt instrument as the Anti-Socialist Laws was counterproductive. That it was inadequate to stem the growth of a Socialist working-class movement was apparent, after all, even to the Kaiser and the *Reichstag*'s National Liberals, who refused to renew the legislation without modifications in 1890 and consequently caused its expiration. However, the fact that such laws were not adopted elsewhere does not tell us, *ipso facto*, that Liberals in other societies were more tolerant of Socialism. It merely tells us that liberal parties and government offices elsewhere in Europe were comprised of men capable of learning from two decades of German experience. In fact, Liberals in other European societies were often even more hostile to Social Democracy than German moderate Social Liberals. But because they had the benefit of the German experience, they could articulate that hostility in subtler, and often more effective, ways. Moreover, whether that hostility was articulated bluntly or subtly, would ultimately be of no enduring consequence. The labor movements that took shape in either case were remarkably similar.

The **National Liberal Party** (*Nationalliberale Partei*, *NLP*) was a liberal political party of the North German Confederation and the German Empire, which flourished between 1867 and 1918. After the Prussian-led unification of Germany in 1871, it became the dominant party in the *Reichstag*. A liberal Nationalist parliamentary faction or caucus first arose among liberal Nationalist members of the German Progress Party (*DFP*) during debate and vote in the Prussian *Landtag* House of Representatives on the Indemnity Bill in September 1866 redressing the constitutional crisis sparked by Minister-President Otto von Bismarck, who in 1862, levied taxes for military reforms of the Prussian Army and delivered his martial "iron and blood" speech.* The liberal Nationalist faction supported von Bismarck and

* In September 1862, when the Prussian *Landtag* (lower) House of Representatives was refusing to approve an increase in military spending desired by Kaiser Wilhelm I, the monarch appointed Otto von Bismarck Minister-President and Foreign Minister. A few days later, von Bismarck appeared before the House's Budget Committee and stressed the need for military preparedness to solve the German Question (*Kleindeutschland* or *Großdeutschland*). He concluded his speech with the following statement: "The position of Prussia in Germany will not be determined by its liberalism but by its power [. . .] Prussia must concentrate its strength and hold it for the favorable moment, which has already come and gone several times. Since the treaties of Vienna, our frontiers have been ill-designed for a healthy body politic. Not through speeches and majority decisions will the great questions of the day be decided—that was the great mistake of 1848 and 1849—but by iron and blood [*Eisen und Blut*]." This phrase, relying on a patriotic poem written by Max von Schenkendorf during the Napoleonic Wars, was popularized as the more euphonious

his Indemnity Bill. This first National Liberal faction in the Prussian *Landtag* was formally formed on 17 November 1866, around Max von Forckenbeck, Eduard Lasker, Rudolf von Bennigsen, and Hans Victor von Unruh. The National Liberal Party was founded shortly after the North German federal election of 12 February 1867. They gathered support from the Prussian annexed territories of Hanover and Hesse-Nassau, as well as from the other states of the North German Confederation, emerging as the largest faction in the newly established *Reichstag*. An inaugural declaration was adopted on 12 June 1867. One year later in 1868, more liberal members of the *Reichstag*, particularly German Progress Party (*DFP*) members, also broke away from *DFP* to join Socialist Leopold Sonnemann to form the German People's Party (*DVP*), which supported the *Großdeutsch* solution to unification under Austria.

The *NLP* came to be closely associated with the interests of big business, maintaining strong relations with mighty industrialist advocacy groups, as well as with imperialist and Nationalist associations like the Pan-German League. Increasingly threatened by the growing strength of the Socialists, the party gradually became more conservative, although it was generally split between a more liberal wing that sought to strengthen ties with the dissident Liberals to their left, and a right wing that came to support more economic and military protectionist policies and close relations with the Conservatives and the imperial government. The party strongly advocated the interests of the Grand Burgher (*Großbürger*) dynasties and business magnates, as well as Nationalist-minded Protestant circles of the educated *bourgeoisie* (*Bildungsbürgertum*). The key points of the party manifesto focused on national unification and von Bismarck's policies, which resulted in the emergence of a German nation-state as a Constitutional Monarchy and highly industrialized country.

The *NLP*'s period of dominance was between 1871 and 1879, when it was von Bismarck's chief ally in the *Reichstag* where its members were avid supporters of the anti-Catholic *Kulturkampf* measures and the Anti-Socialist Laws. In the first all-German federal election held on 3 March 1871, the party reached 30.1 percent of the votes, becoming the strongest group in the *Reichstag* with 125 seats.

Blut und Eisen (Blood and Iron), and became symbolic of Bismarckian *Machtpolitik* (power politics).

PARTY	**VOTES**	**%**	**SEATS**
National Liberal Party	1,171,000	30.1	125
Center Party	724,000	18.6	63
German Conservative Party	549,000	14.1	57
German Progress Party	342,000	8.8	46
Imperial Liberal Party	281,000	7.2	30
Social Democratic Party	124,000	3.2	2
German People's Party	19,000	0.5	1

Lindner and Schultze, 2010, 762.

The stabilization of the new empire was in a large degree only feasible because of *NLP*'s support as the *de facto* ruling party and their guidance of von Bismarck's domestic policies, especially regarding the economy and legal foundations of the German Empire. Weights and measurements were standardized, a common German market and a national bank, the *Reichsbank*, was created and the numerous regional currencies replaced with the *Reichsmark*. The liberal economic policies, although temporarily unpopular in the recession of the 1870s, laid the groundwork for the economic boom the German nation experienced at the turn of the nineteenth century. In 1871, a growing chasm between the liberal and conservative wings of the party resulted in the conservative faction (half were Nationalist Protestants while the other half were liberal Catholics) forming the short-lived Imperial Liberal Party (*Liberale Reichspartei*), which disbanded in 1874 with members returning to the *NLP* or joining more conservative political parties that supported von Bismarck.

In 1879, von Bismarck's alliance with the *NLP* broke over his abandonment of free trade policies through his implementation of tariffs. In the economic crisis following the Panic of 1873, several lobbying associations exerted pressure on von Bismarck who increasingly favored a more protectionist approach. Von Bismarck's protectionist trade policy benefited the infant industries of middle-class Liberals and the agricultural production of *Junker* Conservatives. Von Bismarck established an autonomous tariff wall and concluded a host of most-favored-nation agreements. The result was that, with the European community still clinging to relatively free trade, protectionist Germany acquired low tariff rates abroad without reciprocating. Its economy naturally initially flourished. Impressed by this example, other European nations began turning toward protectionism. Most of Germany's trade treaties expired in early 1892. Unless it established more equitable trade relationships before then, its exports could face prohibitive tariffs everywhere. Foreign markets would dry up just when industry expected to expand. However, these policies violated the classical Liberal principles of both the *NLP* and the more left-leaning liberal *DFP*. The shift was so important, that it has been characterized as von Bismarck's "conservative turn." This meant an enduring shift of the chancellor to the more conservative viewpoint, which changed the political climate of the fledgling nation and soured relations between von Bismarck and several leading German Liberals. The *NLP* lost its status as the dominant party beginning with the 1880 splinter of the left wing of the party that formed the short-lived Liberal Union. On 5 March 1884, the Liberal Union merged with the remains of the German Progress Party (*DFP*) forming the German Free-minded Party.

During the First World War, most of the members of the *NLP*, including such leaders of their left wing as Gustav Stresemann (1878–1929), avidly supported the expansionist goals of the imperial government, although they also called for reform at home. However, following the devastating defeat in the war in November 1918, the *NLP* collapsed and the political scene in Germany became significantly more complicated as the German Revolution unfolded. Political parties rapidly evolved with mixed factions of former parties forming new parties in nearly every major city. For the first time in German history, political parties had real power. They could determine policy and had patronage available for supporters. However, the large number of political parties made coalitions necessary and made it difficult to obtain and maintain legislative majorities. At times, there were more than thirty political parties on the ballot although only about six commanded substantial voting blocs. Making life even more difficult for the Weimar Republic were extremist parties on both sides of the political spectrum who were opposed to the existence of the Republic itself. The most important of these radical anti-Republican parties were the Communists on and the National Socialists (Nazis). Most of the twenty-two Weimar government coalitions were made up of members of the Catholic Center, Social Democratic, Democratic, and People's Workers' parties.

The **German People's Party** (*Deutsche Volkspartei*, *DVP*) was a liberal party created in 1868 by the wing of the German Progress Party (*DFP*) and members of Leopold Sonnemann's *VDAV*, who supported

Austria (*Großdeutsch* solution) during the conflict over whether the unification of Germany should be led by the Kingdom of Prussia or Austria. The party was most popular in Southern Germany, particularly Bavaria. Initially, the South German Democrats supported the Greater German solution of the German unification question. After the establishment of the German Empire in 1871 under Prussia at the exclusion of Austria, the *DVP* advocated federalist structures, and defended the South German states' rights against the growing strength of the central government in Berlin. Tenaciously, the party demanded Democratic reforms, particularly strengthening of the position of the *Reichstag*, which had no say in the formation of the government and little influence on government policies as the government was appointed and dismissed by the Kaiser alone.

Majority-Catholic Bavaria in southern Germany and majority-Protestant Prussia in northern Germany have a long history of rivalry and conflict that reflects the North-South conflict in the United States during the first century after its founding. The Bavarian-Prussian rivalry traces back to the Napoleonic Wars of the early nineteenth century, when Bavaria fought on the side of France against Prussia; as a reward for its help in Napoléon's initial victories, the emperor made Bavaria a kingdom in 1806, a designation that survived until 1918. Sixty years after becoming a kingdom, Bavaria again went to war against Prussia, this time as an ally of Austria in a contest among German-speaking rivals over which power would determine the political future of the region. Von Bismarck's Prussia prevailed in this confrontation, allowing Berlin, not Munich, to take the lead in the 1870–71 war against France that produced a unified German empire under Prussian domination. Bavaria had joined Prussia and the other German states in this epic conflict, but only after its unstable king, Ludwig II, received handsome bribes from Prussian Minister-President Otto von Bismarck (Large 2017).

Germany's unification in 1871 papered over, but did not diminish, the socio-political and cultural divide between the largely Protestant north and the heavily Catholic south. That divide was heightened (literally) by a mountainous wooded terrain (Franconian and Thuringian Forests) that in earlier times impeded access and fostered distinct Alpine folkloric costumes and traditions: *tracht*, *lederhosen,* alpen-horns, the knee-and-shoe-slapping *Schuhplattler* dance, and so on. The kingdom's ruling Wittelsbach dynasty explicitly encouraged the perpetuation of these traditions as a way of "increasing a feeling of national cohesion among Bavarians, enabling them to hold their heads high in the face of Prussian self-confidence." Bavarians also spoke a distinct language (Bayerisch) that was totally incomprehensible to other Germans; even their rendition of standardized High German (*Hochdeutsch*) baffled northerners, who, like their counterparts in the United States, viewed Southerners as backwards hillbillies. Finally, the Catholic Church in Bavaria played, and continues to play, an outsize role in public life, fielding a church-based political party (the Bavarian People's Party from 1870 to 1933; the Christian Social Union [*CSU*] in the post-World War II era), and exerting considerable influence in education, culture, and social policy. (Large 2017.)

The world war into which Wilhelmine Germany so avidly plunged in 1914 exacerbated these internal divisions. At the outset, Bavaria fielded its own royal army (this was the outfit young Adolf Hitler joined). When Bavarian units later fell under a centralized command dominated by Prussians, Bavarian officials complained that their boys were being used as cannon fodder by "Saupreuss" (pig-Prussian) officers and, even worse, that the quality of their beer was being undermined by confiscations of raw materials mandated by Berlin. (Large 2017.)

With the German empire's defeat and destruction in 1918, some Bavarians agitated for the creation of a separate southern state. Instead, Bavaria became a state within the new "Weimar Republic," whose highly progressive constitution and avant-garde culture occasioned considerable hostility among more conservative Bavarians, steeped as they were in regional royalism, political Catholicism, and rustic rural values. (Large 2017.)

It was in malcontented Munich that the Nazi Party was born in 1919, and from there, in 1923, that Hitler launched his ill-starred "Beer Hall *Putsch*" to topple the republic. Although the *putsch* failed, Bavaria remained a haven for strongly conservative opponents of Berlin's experiment in Social Democracy. When, ten years after the abortive *putsch*, Hitler assumed power in Germany legally, many of his Bavarian followers registered dismay over his decision to keep the national capital in Berlin rather than moving it to Munich. They could, however, take consolation in Munich's ongoing status as "Capital of the [Nazi] Movement" and "Capital of German Art" (that is, the kind of conventional, homey, literalist art that the Nazis considered "German" as opposed to the experimental modernism they denounced as "degenerate"). (Large 2017.)

In contrast to the National Liberal Party, the *DVP* stood in staunch opposition to the unification policy of Otto von Bismarck in the establishment of the German Empire. The party put the Classical Liberal notion of liberty above the prospect of a German unification led "from above." The German People's Party was highly critical of the Prusso-German monarchy and advocated the separation of church and state but rejected von Bismarck's *Kulturkampf* against the Catholic Church, as well as the Anti-Socialist Laws.

The *DVP* was the most radical liberal among non-Marxist parties in Germany whose platform was closer to that of a Social Democracy. It was the sole Liberal party to cooperate with the Socialists in the *Reichstag*. Most of the party's members were craftsmen, small traders, farmers, and clerks. However, the leadership consisted of upper-class intellectuals. Leopold Sonnemann (proprietor of the Bavarian newspaper *Frankfurter Zeitung*), who represented the party in the *Reichstag* from 1871 until 1884, and the lawyer Friedrich von Payer served as Chairmen.

On 6 March 1910, the *DVP* ceased to exist when in order to unify various fragmented Liberal groups represented in the *Reichstag*, the Social Liberal *DVP* merged with two National Liberal parties (the German Free-minded People's Party and the German Free-minded Union) to form the Progressive People's Party (*Fortschrittliche Volkspartei, FVP*).

The **Liberal Union** (*Liberale Vereinigung*) was a short-lived liberal party in the German Empire. It originated as a break-away from the National Liberal Party in 1880 and eventually merged with the remnant of the strongly liberal German Progress Party (*DFP*) under Eugen Richter to form the German Free-minded Party (*Deutsche Freisinnige Partei*) in March 1884. The Socialist faction of the National Liberal Party (*NLP*), which had supported von Bismarck's policies in the past, now expressed discontent with the party leadership's support for Otto von Bismarck's conservative government. Most importantly, they supported free trade, whereas *NLP* leaders Rudolf von Bennigsen and Johann von Miquel (1828–1901) sustained, against classically Liberal principles, von Bismarck's prohibitive tariffs strategy (*Schutzzollpolitik*). Other contentious points included the Anti-Socialist Laws (*Sozialistengesetze*), the *Kulturkampf* against the Catholic Church and the septennial military budget (*Septennat*). Franz August Schenk von Stauffenberg (1834–1901), Jewish economist, banker, revolutionary, and writer Ludwig Bamberger (1823–1899), Berlin's mayor Max von Forckenbeck, Heinrich Edwin Rickert (1833–1902), and Eduard Lasker led the secession from the *NLP* in 1880. Other notable members of the new German Free-minded Party included historian and future Nobel laureate Theodor Mommsen, Friedrich Kapp (1824–1884), publicist Theodor Barth (1849–1909), and Georg von Siemens (1839–1901; Werner's nephew). The Liberal Union was a notables' party (*Honoratiorenpartei*), having its electorate mainly among the North and East German upper classes: wholesale merchants, industrialists, bankers, and intellectuals. The organizational structure was rather loose. Nevertheless, the new grouping was initially successful, gaining 46 seats of the *Reichstag* in the 1881 federal election—as many as the preceding *NLP*. Ultimately the secessionists planned to merge all German Liberals into a single, "whole" liberal party with classically Liberal and parliamentary monarchist positions, modelled after the British Liberal Party and ideally to govern under a future Emperor Frederick III (Frederick William). However, the remaining members of the *NLP* made clear they preferred to not leave the majority loyal to von Bismarck. Therefore, secessionist representative Franz von Stauffenberg negotiated with Eugen Richter, the leader of the remaining portion of the strongly liberal *DFP* in early 1884. On 5 March 1884, both parties' legislators (Liberal Union and *DFP*) formed a joint parliamentary group totaling 100 seats establishing the German Free-minded Party.

The **German Free-minded Party** (*Deutsche Freisinnige Partei*) was a short-lived liberal party (1884–1893) in the German Empire, founded as a result of the merger of the remnants of the German Progress Party (*DFP*) under Eugen Richter and Liberal Union under von Stauffenberg on 5 March 1884. The German Free-minded Party supported the extension of parliamentarism in the German Constitutional Monarchy, separation of church and state, as well as Jewish emancipation. However, under party chairman Franz von Stauffenberg with his deputy eminent pathologist Dr. Rudolf Virchow, the German Free-minded Party received a disappointing 17.6 percent of the votes in the 1884 election. The main beneficiaries of this Liberal defection were the conservative forces supporting the protectionist, colonialist, and anti-Socialist policies of Chancellor Otto von Bismarck. In the 1887 election, the German Free-minded Party again lost half of their seats in the *Reichstag*, dropping down to thirty-two. During the decline of the German Free-minded Party, the differences between Richter's "Progressives" and the moderately-conservative Liberals became irreconcilable. Upon von Bismarck's dismissal from government in March 1890, German Free-minded Party members lost their common adversary. In 1893, the party split in conflict over the new *Reich* chancellor's (Georg von Caprivi) policies into the German Free-minded People's Party (*Freisinnige Volkspartei*)—under Eugen Richter, party leader from 1893 until his death in 1906—and the German Free-minded Union—under industrialist Georg von Siemens, Jewish economist, banker, revolutionary, and writer Ludwig Bamberger, and publicist Theodor Barth. In 1903, the German Free-minded

Union absorbed the National-Social Association with Friedrich Naumann and Theodor Barth. In 1908, the more liberal elements of this combined party broke away from the German Free-minded Union to form the Democratic Union with Theodor Barth and Hellmut von Gerlach. A reunion between the remnants of the German Free-minded Union and German Free-minded People's Party took place on 6 March 1910, when both further weakened liberal parties merged with the Socialist German People's Party of 1868 (*DVP*) to form the Progressive People's Party—disbanded eight years later after the fall of the German Empire, with most of its members joining the new German Democratic Party (1918–1930) of the Weimar Republic, merging the Progressive People's Party with the left wing of the old National Liberal Party (*NLP*).

The **German Free-minded Union** (*Freisinnige Vereinigung*) existed from 1893 to 1910. Inside its predecessor, the German Free-minded Party, there have always been policy tensions between the strongly liberal and the moderate wing. Adding to these tensions was the personal style of leader Eugen Richter. When chancellor Georg von Caprivi presented the Army Bill in parliament on 6 May 1893,* seven German Free-minded Party representatives, among them Georg von Siemens, decided to accept Caprivi's motion. Consequently, Eugen Richter successfully pushed the expulsion of the Caprivi supporters causing a split in the German Free-minded Party. Other moderate party members, including Jewish economist, banker, revolutionary, and writer Ludwig Bamberger (1823–1899) and publicist Theodor Barth (1849–1909), left voluntarily and formed the German Free-minded Union. The remaining Social Liberal wing of the German Free-minded Party loyal to Richter assembled in the German Free-minded People's Party. The new German Free-minded Union focused on

---

* Army Bill of 1892–93: Introduced into the *Reichstag* at a time of acute economic crisis, this bill proposed an unprecedented increase in the peacetime strength of the Imperial German Army. The resulting deliberations led to widespread unrest and agricultural agitation, turbulent intra-party disputes, the dissolution of the *Reichstag*, and national elections. The Bill grew out of military plans formulated in the late 1880s. After the Franco-Prussian War in 1871, Chancellor Otto von Bismarck and most German military leaders believed that France would never accept the loss of Alsace-Lorraine. France, they were convinced, was bent on a "war of revenge." But the French would never attack Germany unilaterally; first, they would form an alliance with another great power like Russia, thereby forcing Germany to fight on two fronts. The Army Bill was intended to prepare Germany for the likelihood of such a scenario.

classically and economically liberal policies. In the 1893 federal election, it won thirteen seats. The Union was initially more a loose electoral alliance than a real party. Its organizational structure was very weak. Its strongholds were in the northern and eastern regions of the German Empire. Together with the governing National Liberal Party and unlike the former German Free-minded Party, the German Free-minded Union supported National Liberal policies like the Imperial Navy arms race and German colonial policy. In 1903, the German Free-minded Union absorbed members of the liberal National-Social Association (1896) led by Friedrich Naumann. This brought new members, including publicist and political pacifist Hellmut von Gerlach (1866–1935), to the party. Both the organizational structure and the program outlook changed from this moment on. The German Free-minded Union tended now to seek compassion towards the masses of the working class, but also tried to strengthen the German national position by closing the ranks of the middle and working classes. It sought to synthesize Liberalism, Nationalism and revisionist-Marxist Socialism with Protestant Christian values in order to cross the ideological front lines and draw workers away from a Marxist class struggle. This was compatible with the Union's National Liberal line. The gain of local Social Liberal organizational structures led to a loose association towards a workers' party. However, the party could not really win the support of the working class and did not become a major party.

From 1905 on, the German Free-minded Union cooperated increasingly with the other Social Liberals including the German Free-minded People's Party and the German People's Party (of 1868). In 1907, the three parties drafted a common electoral program for the elections to the *Reichstag*. Afterwards, they formed a common parliamentary group, which was part of the pro-government imperialist Bülow-Bloc (Imperial Chancellor Bernhard von Bülow) together with the Conservatives and National Liberals. The party's own left wing and pacifist faction, including publicist Theodor Barth, Hellmut von Gerlach, Rudolf Breitscheid, and feminist Helene Lange, were discontent with this step and left to form the Democratic Union in 1908. On 6 March 1910, the remaining members of the German Free-minded Union, German Free-minded People's Party, and German People's Party of 1868 joined to form the Progressive People's Party.

The **German Free-minded People's Party** (*Freisinnige Volkspartei*) was a moderate liberal party in the German Empire, founded as a result of the split of the German Free-minded Party in 1893. One of its most notable members was Eugen Richter, who was party leader from 1893 to 1906. The party advocated classical Liberalism, social progressivism, and parliamentarism. On 6 March 1910, it merged with the German Free-minded Union and German People's Party to form the Progressive People's Party.

The **National-Social Association** (*Nationalsozialer Verein, NSV*) was a moderate liberal party in the German Empire, founded in 1896 by Friedrich Naumann (1860–1919). It sought to amalgamate Liberalism, Nationalism, and non-Marxist Socialism with Protestant Christian values, in order to cross the ideological lines and draw workers away from Marxist class struggle and the dominant Marxist Social Democratic Party of Germany (*SPD*). The party's founding is seen as a reaction to the rise of Socialism and an attempt to offer a moderate, Social Liberal alternative guided by Protestant Christian principles, as opposed to the atheism of the *SPD*, to the working-class masses. The party was influenced by the political theories of eminent sociologist, jurist, and political philosopher and economist Max Weber, who helped found the party. Weber is best known for his thesis combining economic sociology and the sociology of religion, elaborated in his 1904 book *The Protestant Ethic and the Spirit of Capitalism*, in which he proposed that ascetic Protestantism was one of the major "elective affinities" associated with the rise in the Western world of market-driven Capitalism and the rational-legal nation-state. He argued that it was in the basic tenets of Protestantism to promote Capitalism. Thus, it can be concluded from Weber's thesis that the spirit of Capitalism is inherent to Protestant religious values. Against Marx's historical materialism, Weber emphasized the importance of cultural influences embedded in religion as a means for understanding the genesis of Capitalism. Per Weber's teachings, the party believed that the working class and *bourgeoisie* should join hands for a strong German empire, economic growth, and social progress. The party strove to dismantle the ideological divisions between Socialist, National Liberal, and Christian political parties. Naumann first labeled the party's ideology as "National Socialism on a Christian basis" (*nationaler Sozialismus auf christlicher Grundlage*) and "Social Imperialism" (*soziales Kaisertum*), later as "proletarian-bourgeois integral liberalism" (*proletarisch-bürgerlicher Gesamtliberalismus*), meaning a mix of Nationalism, Christian Socialism, and Social Liberalism. Naumann's party advocated a stronger role for the parliament but did not question the leading position of the monarch. The party never grew beyond a minor party of intellectuals which failed to gain mass support in elections. In the 1903 federal elections, the candidates of the Association failed win a single seat in the *Reichstag* and Naumann dissolved the party, merging into the moderate liberal German Free-minded Union.

The **Democratic Union** (*Demokratische Vereinigung, DV*) was formed in 1908 and lasted only ten years. From 1905 on, the German Free-minded Union cooperated increasingly with the other Social Liberal parties to the point of drafting a common electoral program for the 1907 federal elections to the *Reichstag* and forming a common parliamentary group, which was part of the pro-government imperialist Bülow-Bloc (Imperial Chancellor Bernhard von Bülow) together with the conservatives and National Liberals. The party's own left wing and pacifist faction, including publicists Theodor Barth (1849–1909) and Hellmut von Gerlach, economist, journalist, and politician Rudolf Breitscheid (1874–1944), and pedagogue and feminist Helene Lange (1848–1930), were discontent with these developments and left the party to form the Democratic Union in 1908. The party demanded universal suffrage and a strict separation of Church and State. It was not, however, considered "revolutionary" against Wilhelmine Germany. The close of the First World War brought an end to the party when Hellmut von Gerlach and some of his followers joined members of the Progressive People's Party (*FVP*) and the more liberal remnants of the National Liberal Party (*NLP*) founded the German Democratic Party (*DDP*) in November 1918.

The **Progressive People's Party** (*Fortschrittliche Volkspartei, FVP*) was formed on 6 March 1910 as a merger of German Free-minded People's Party, German Free-minded Union, and German People's Party of 1868 in order to unify various fragmented Social Liberal groups represented in the newly created *Reichstag*. The *FVP* demanded universal suffrage, the abolition of the Prussian three-class franchise system,[3] a new local elections law, and amendments to the Imperial Constitution transforming the Empire into a parliamentary Democratic monarchy. They also advocated the separation of Church and State, free trade, a progressive taxation, as well as safety, health, and welfare of workers. The *FVP*, thereby, distanced itself from Conservatives and the National Liberal Party. Leading members of the *FVP* like pietist Lutheran Pastor Friedrich Naumann (1860–1919) were still favoring economic Liberalism, but gradually turned to the Socialist concept of a welfare state. The *FVP* was disbanded in November 1918 after the fall of the Empire, with most of its members joining the new German Democratic Party (*DDP*) of the Weimar Republic, merging the *FVP* with the more liberal remnants of the old National Liberal Party (*NLP*) and the Democratic Union (*DV*). Remnants of the *DDP* are still found in the current classical-Liberal, moderately conservative Free Democratic Party (*Freie Demokratische Partei, FDP*) founded in Germany in 1948.

The **Independent Social Democratic Party of Germany** (*Unabhängige Sozialdemokratische Partei Deutschlands, USPD*) split from the *SPD* on 6 April 1917 after the *SPD* leadership under Friedrich Ebert excluded the opponents of the war from his party. On 21 December 1915, several *SPD* members in the *Reichstag* voted against the authorization of further credits to finance World War I, an incident that emphasized existing tensions between the party's leadership under Ebert and the Socialist pacifists surrounding Hugo Haase and ultimately led to the expulsion of the group from the *SPD* on 24 March 1916. To be able to continue their parliamentary work, the group formed the Social Democratic Working Group (*Sozialdemokratische Arbeitsgemeinschaft, SAG*). The *SPD* members of parliament who opposed the war included the Spartacists under Rosa Luxemburg and Karl Liebknecht, the so-called "Revisionists" under Eduard Bernstein, and Centrists such as Karl Kautsky. These three disparate factions joined to found the fully antiwar *USPD* under the leadership of Hugo Haase. Other members of the *USPD* included Kurt Eisner, Julius Leber, Ernst Thälmann, Rudolf Breitscheild, Ernst Toller (eventual leader of the first Bavarian Soviet Republic), Rudolf Hilferding, Gustav Landauer, Silvio Gesell, Erich Mühsam, and Franz Lipp. To clarify the difference from *USPD*, the remaining *SPD* was now known as the Majority Social Democratic Party of Germany (*MSPD*) and continued to be led by Friedrich Ebert. The *USPD* demanded an immediate end to the war and a further democratization of Germany but did not have a unified agenda for social policies. The Spartacus League (*Spartakusbund*), which until then had opposed a split of the party, now made up the left wing of the *USPD*. Both the *USPD* and the Spartacists continued their antiwar propaganda in factories, especially in the armament plants. On 29 December 1918, the *Spartakusbund*, led by Rosa Luxemburg and Karl Liebknecht, separated from the *USPD* to merge with other Marxist groups and form the Communist Party of Germany (*Kommunistische Partei Deutschlands, KPD*) on 1 January 1919 just before calling for mass workers' strikes commencing the Spartacist Uprising. Eugen Leviné (eventual co-leader of the second Bavarian Soviet Republic) was one of the first people to join the Spartacus League.

In Petrograd and Moscow from 19 July to 7 August 1920, four delegates from the *USPD* attended the Second World Congress of the Comintern (Communist International), Ernst Däumig, Arthur Crispien,

Walter Stoecker, and Wilhelm Dittmann to discuss participating in the Comintern. While Däumig and Stoecker agreed with the International's 21 conditions of membership, Crispien and Dittmann opposed them, leading to a controversial debate in the *USPD* over joining the Comintern. Many members felt that the necessary requirements for joining would lead to a loss of the party's independence and a perceived "dictate from Moscow," while others, especially younger members such as Ernst Thälmann, argued that only the joining of the Comintern would allow the party to implement its Socialist ideals. Ultimately, the proposition to join the Comintern was approved at a party convention in Halle in October 1920 by 237 votes to 156. The *USPD* split up in the process, with both groups seeing themselves as the rightful *USPD* and the other one as being outcast. On 4 December 1920, the left wing of the *USPD*, with about 400,000 members, merged into the *KPD*, forming the United Communist Party of Germany (*Vereinigte Kommunistische Partei Deutschlands*, *VKPD*), while the other half of the party, with about 340,000 members and including three quarters of the 81 *Reichstag* members, continued under the name *USPD*; led by Georg Ledebour and Arthur Crispien, they advocated a parliamentary Democracy.

Over time, the political differences between *SPD* and *USPD* dwindled, and following the assassination of Foreign Minister Walther Rathenau by Nationalist extremists in June 1922, the two parties' factions in the *Reichstag* formed a common working group on 14 July 1922; two months later, on 24 September, the parties officially merged again after a joint party convention in Nürnberg, adopting the name United Social Democratic Party of Germany (*Vereinigte Sozialdemokratische Partei Deutschlands*, *VSPD*), which was shortened back to *SPD* in 1924.

The **German Democratic Party** (*Deutsche Demokratische Partei*, *DDP*) was founded in November 1918 at the close of the First World War and fall of the German Empire by leaders of the former Progressive People's Party (*FVP*), the more liberal members of the National Liberal Party (*NLP*), and a new group calling themselves the Democrats (remnants of Democratic Union, *DV*). The *DDP* was Center Liberal. Many of the leading figures in the party had been supporters of Imperial Germany's aim of *Weltpolitik* and *Mitteleuropa*. Along with the Socialists and the Center Party, the *DDP* was most committed to maintaining a Democratic, republican form of government. Its social bases were middle-class entrepreneurs, civil servants, teachers, scientists, and craftsmen. It considered itself also a devotedly National party and opposed the Treaty of Versailles, while emphasizing the need for international collaboration and the protection of ethnic minorities.

The *DDP* enjoyed the support of most German Jews and was attacked by some for being a party of Jews and professors.

The party's first leader was Protestant parish priest Friedrich Naumann (1860–1919), who was popular and influential, but failed with his National-Social Association ten years earlier to link progressive intellectuals with the working class. He died early in 1919. Other well-known politicians of the *DDP* were Hugo Preuß, the main author of the Weimar Constitution, and the eminent sociologist, jurist, and political philosopher and economist Max Weber (1864–1920). Hjalmar Schacht, president of the *Reichsbank* and one of the founders of the party, left the party in 1926 and became a supporter of Adolf Hitler.

Nearly all German governments from 1918 to 1931 included ministers from the *DDP*, such as Walther Rathenau, Eugen Schiffer, Hugo Preuß, Kurt Riezler, Otto Gessler, Max Weber, and Erich Koch-Weser. From their eighteen percent share of the first German federal election under proportional representation in 1919, they dropped to 4.9 percent in the 1928 German federal election, and to one percent in the November 1932 German federal election as the German State Party.

The party merged with the more conservative-leaning Young German Order (*Jungdo*) to form the German State Party in 1930. With Ludwig Quidde (Nobel Peace Prize winner of 1927) and others, the party had a pacifist wing which left the Party in 1930 and founded the Radical Democratic Party (*RDP*), which represented radical Democratic and more Socialist policies.

The **Communist Party of Germany** (*Kommunistische Partei Deutschlands*, *KPD*) was established at a founding congress held in Berlin during 30 December 1918–1 January 1919, the Spartacist League joined with another Jewish Marxist leader Arthur Goldstein and his International Communists of Germany (*Internationalen Kommunisten Deutschlands*; *IKD*) to form the *KPD* under the leadership of Karl Liebknecht and Rosa Luxemburg. While most war weary Germans just wanted peace, these few radicals still favored the establishment of a revolutionary alternative to the burgeoning parliamentary Democracy. They immediately called for labor strikes throughout Germany precipitating a simultaneous second revolution—the Spartacist Uprising. Under the leadership of Liebknecht and Luxemburg, the *KPD* was committed to a revolution in Germany, and during 1919 and 1920 attempts to seize control of the government continued. Germany's Social Democratic government, which had come to power after the fall of the Monarchy, was vehemently opposed to the *KPD*'s version of socialism that was more in line with Marxism and Bolshevism. With the new regime terrified of a Bolshevik Revolution in Germany, Defense Minister Gustav Noske formed a series of anti-Communist paramilitary groups, dubbed *Freikorps*, out of demobilized World War I veterans.[4] During the failed Spartacist Uprising in Berlin of January 1919, Liebknecht and Luxemburg were captured by the *Freikorps* and murdered.

After the death of Luxemburg and Liebknecht, the party became ever more committed to Leninism and later Stalinism. During the Weimar Republic, the *KPD* usually polled between 10 and 15 percent of the vote and was represented in the *Reichstag* and in state parliaments. The party directed most of its attacks on the Social Democratic Party of Germany, which it considered its main opponent. On 3 April 1920, the *KPD* split into two factions, the *KPD* and the Communist Workers' Party of Germany (*Kommunistische Arbeiterspartei Deutschlands*, *KAPD*). On 4 December 1920, the left wing of the *USPD*, with about 400,000 members, merged into the *KPD*, forming the United Communist Party of Germany (*Vereinigte Kommunistische Partei Deutschlands*, *VKPD*). Then at the Jena Congress of the German Social-Democratic Workers' Party in August 1921, the *VKPD* rejoined the *KDP*. After 1921, when the *KAPD* still had over 43,000 members, the party's influence declined, and it separated in 1922 into the Berlin Faction and the Essen Faction around Alexander Schwab, Arthur Goldstein, Bernhard Reichenbach, and Karl Schröder. The main reason was the Essen Faction's rejection of participation in workers' struggles in factories, a situation seen as revolutionary. The Essen Faction founded the Communist Workers' International (Fourth Communist International) but dissolved in 1927. The Berlin Faction was the larger and more enduring group, surviving until 1933, when it merged into the underground Communist Workers' Union. In 1923, new *KPD* leadership more favorable to the newly established Union of Soviet Socialist Republics was elected. This leadership, headed by Ernst Thälmann, abandoned the goal of immediate revolution, and from 1924 onwards contested *Reichstag* elections, with some success.

During the years of the Weimar Republic the *KPD* was the largest Communist party in Europe and was seen as the "leading party" of the Communist movement outside the Soviet Union. It maintained a solid electoral performance, usually polling more than 10 percent of the vote, and gaining 100 deputies in the November 1932 federal elections. In the presidential election of the same year, Thälmann took 13.2 percent of the vote, compared to Hitler's 30.1 percent.

In July 1932, the *KPD* formed the *Antifaschistische Aktion* (Antifa) network.[5] Critics of the *KPD* accused it of having pursued a sectarian policy—the Social Democratic Party criticized the *KPD*'s thesis of "Social Fascism." This scuttled any possibility of a united front with the *SPD* against the rising power of the National Socialists. These allegations were repudiated by supporters of the *KPD*: the conservative faction of the leadership of the *SPD*, it was said, rejected the proposals of the *KPD* to unite for the defeat of Fascism. The *SPD* leaders were accused of having countered *KPD* efforts to form a united front of the working class. Banned in Nazi Germany one day after Adolf Hitler emerged triumphant in the federal elections in March 1933, the *KPD* maintained an underground organization in Germany throughout the Nazi period, but the loss of many core members severely weakened the party's infrastructure. The most senior *KPD* leaders fled to the Soviet Union. Several senior *KPD* leaders in exile were caught up in Joseph Stalin's Great Purge of 1937–38 and executed or sent to the gulags. Others denounced their fellow exiles to the *NKVD*. Willi Münzenberg, the *KPD*'s propaganda chief, was murdered in mysterious circumstances in France in 1940. The *NKVD* is believed to have been responsible for this operation in German-occupied France.

The party was revived in divided postwar West and East Germany and won seats in the first *Bundestag* (West German Parliament) elections in Bonn in 1949, but its support collapsed following the establishment of a Communist state in the Soviet occupation zone of Germany. In East Germany, the party was merged, by Soviet decree, with the Social Democratic Party to form the Socialist Unity Party (*SED*) which ruled East Germany until 1989–1990. After the fall of the Berlin Wall, the *SED* was renamed the Party of Democratic Socialism and subsequently merged into *Die Linke*. The *KPD* was banned in West Germany in 1956 by the Constitutional Court. Some of its former members founded an even smaller fringe party in 1969, the German Communist Party, which remains legal, and multiple tiny splinter groups claiming to be the successor to the *KPD* have also subsequently been formed.

FIG. 1 – ON THE SOCIALIST/MARXIST SIDE OF THE GERMAN POLITICAL SPECTRUM

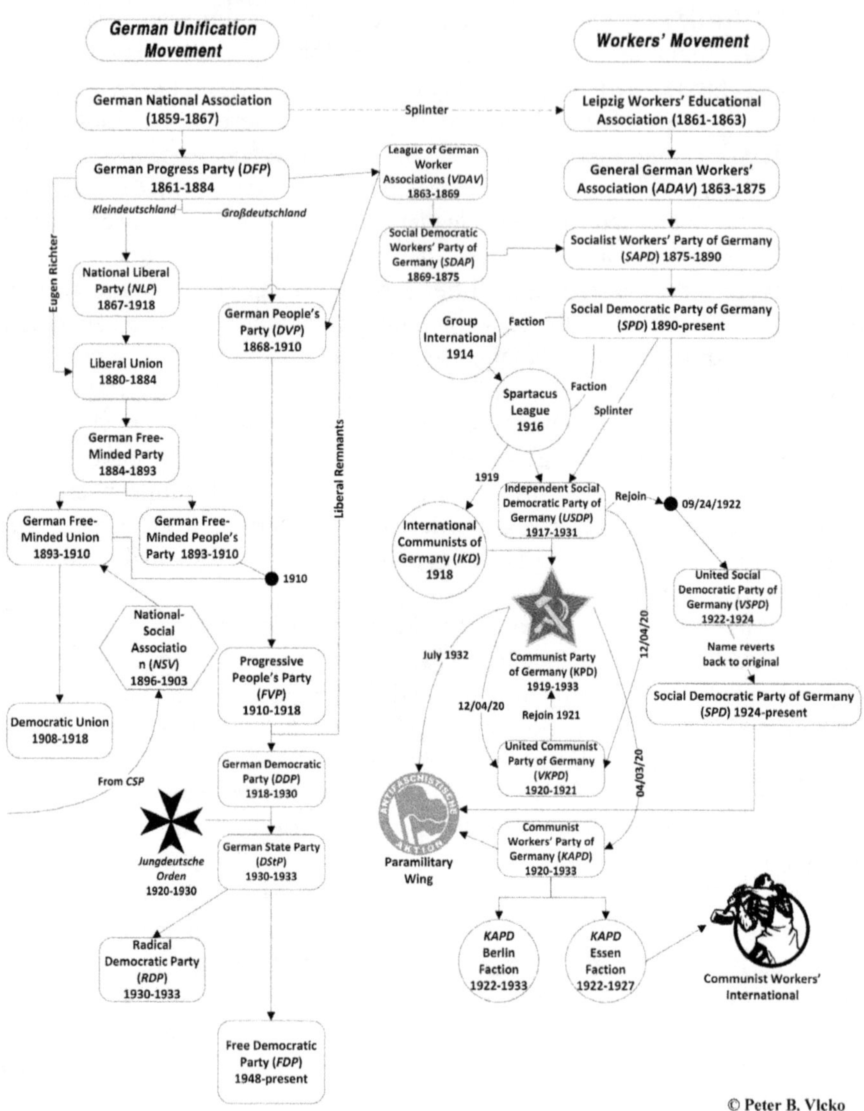

II. IN THE CENTER OF THE GERMAN POLITICAL SPECTRUM

THE **GERMAN CENTER PARTY** (*Deutsche Zentrumspartei* or just *Zentrum*) founded in 1870 is a moderately-conservative lay Catholic political party in Germany, primarily influential during the German Empire and the Weimar Republic. It is often called the Catholic Center Party. The Center Party belongs to the movement of "Political Catholicism" that, emerging in the early nineteenth century after the turmoil of the Napoleonic wars, had changed the political face of Germany. Many Catholics found themselves in Protestant dominated states. At that time, one of the founding fathers of Political Catholicism was journalist Joseph Görres, who called upon Catholics to "stand united" for their common goals of "religious liberty and political and civil equality of the denominations." Following the 1848 Revolutions, German Catholics organized themselves into "Catholic Federations" and "Catholic Clubs" to consolidate their political power. Growing anti-Catholic sentiment and policies, including plans for dissolving all monasteries in Prussia, made it clear that a reorganization of the groups was urgently needed in order to protect Catholic minority rights enshrined in the 1849 Frankfurt Constitution, and to bring them over to the emerging nation-state. In the midst of the First Vatican Council (8 December 1869 to 20 October 1870), on 18 July 1870, Pope Pius IX formally defined and reconfirmed the long-held dogma of papal infallibility in the Roman Catholic Church's apostolic constitution *Pastor aeternus*, which also openly condemned Liberalism in all forms, and had given strong impetus to the formation of Catholic political parties. In June 1870, German Catholic jurist and parliamentarian Peter Reichensberger called on Catholics to unite and, in October, priests and representatives of Catholic federations and the Catholic gentry met at Soest (Westphalia, Prussia) and drew up an election program. The main points were:

- Preservation of the Church's autonomy and rights, as accepted by the constitution. Defense against any attack on the independence of Church bodies, on the development of religious life and on the practice of Christian charity.
- Effectual implementation of parity for recognized denominations.
- Rejection of any attempt to de-Christianize marriage.
- Preservation or founding of denominational schools.

There were also more general demands such as for a more federal, decentralized state, a limitation of state expenditure, a just distribution of taxes, the financial strengthening of the middle class, and the legal "removal of such evil states that threaten the worker with moral or bodily ruin." With such a manifesto, the number of Catholic representatives in the Prussian *Landtag* rose considerably. It was shortly after the close of Vatican I in October 1870 that von Bismarck and the National Liberal Party embarked on their *Kulturkampf* against the Catholic Church. On 13 December 1870, Catholic politicians formed a new "Center" faction in the *Landtag*, also called the "Constitution Party" to emphasize its adherence to constitutional liberties. Three months later, early in 1871, the Catholic representatives to the new Imperial *Reichstag*, also formed a "Center" faction. The party not only defended the Church's liberties but also supported representative government and minority rights in general, in particular those of German Poles, Alsatians, and Hannoverians. The Center's leader was the Hannoverian lawyer Ludwig Windthorst. In the age of Nationalism, Protestant Germans, whether conservative (like Otto von Bismarck) or liberal, accused the Center Party of Ultramontanism or having a greater loyalty towards the Pope (his power and primacy) than to their own nation.

Catholic parties also formed in other German states that cooperated with the Prussian Center Party in the *Reichstag*, namely: the **Bavarian People's (Patriotic) Party**, formed in the winter of 1868–69 with a particularistic-conservative bent. In 1887, it changed its name to **Bavarian Center Party**. In Heidelberg, the **Catholic People's Party** formed in 1869 demanding the separation of Church and State, freedom for the Church to manage her own affairs, unification of Germany under Catholic Austria, and universal male suffrage (to drown liberal urbanites with more traditional rural Catholics). Likewise, in Baden, the Catholic People's Party formed in 1869, and since 1881 was formally linked to the national Center Party, in 1888 adopting the name Center Party.

The Center Party successfully battled the *Kulturkampf*. It soon won a quarter of the seats in the *Reichstag*, and its centrist position on most political issues allowed it to play a decisive role in the formation of ruling majorities. The Center Party remained a party of opposition to von Bismarck, but after his resignation in 1890, it frequently supported the new administration's policies in the *Reichstag*, particularly in the social welfare issues as social security. In the early days of the Weimar Republic, the Center Party was the second-largest party in the *Reichstag*. After the *Reichstag* fire in late February 1933, the Center Party found itself coerced into supporting the National Socialists on several key issues, including anti-Semitism. In an act of total submission like Mephistopheles selling his soul to the Devil, the Center Party voted for the Enabling Act in March 1933, which granted dictatorial powers to Adolf Hitler. By this vote, the Center Party effectively destroyed itself, as the Nazi Party became the only legally permitted party in the country shortly thereafter (14 August 1933). Had the Center Party held out and resisted Nazi coercion, the Enabling Act never would have passed, and Hitler could not have outlawed all other political parties. The continuing political competition would have forced the National Socialists to produce economic victories in order to remain in power under a coalition.

After the Second World War, the Center Party was reestablished, but could not rise to its former importance, as most of its members joined the new Christian Democratic Union (*CDU*). The Center Party was represented in the German *Bundestag* until 1957. It remains a marginal party, mainly based in the state of North Rhine-Westphalia.

III. ON THE NATIONALIST AND ANTI-SEMITIC SIDE OF THE GERMAN POLITICAL SPECTRUM (See Figure 2)

THE **FREE CONSERVATIVE PARTY** (*Freikonservative Partei, FKP*) was a moderate conservative political party in Prussia and the German Empire, which in 1867 emerged from the Conservatives in the Prussian *Landtag* and the Free Conservative Association. Notable members included Karl Ludwig Aegidi, Duke Victor of Ratibor, Karl Rudolf Friedenthal, Johann Viktor Bredt, Hermann von Hatzfeldt, Hermann von Dechend, Prince Karl Max von Lichnowsky, Prussian General Hans Hartwig von Beseler, Hans Delbrück, and Otto Hoetzsch. For federal elections to the *Reichstag* beginning in 1871, it ran under the name German *Reich* Party (*Deutsche Reichspartei, DRP*) but otherwise retained its original name *FKP*. The *FKP* comprised German nobles and East Elbian *Junkers* (landowners east of the Elbe River), industrialists, government officials, and scholars. It was distinguished from the German Conservative Party established in 1876 by its unqualified support of German unification and was seen as the political party which beside the National Liberals was closest in views to those of Chancellor Otto von Bismarck, including his Anti-Socialist Laws and *Kulturkampf* policies.

The party was generally dominated by conservative industrialists, and while it opposed political Liberalism, it also tended to support free trade and the development of industry. Upon the accession of Emperor Wilhelm II in 1888, the party backed his naval policies and the formation of the German colonial empire, approaching the Nationalist Pan-German League pressure group. The *FKP* disbanded in November 1918. Several members had supported the formation of the Fatherland Party in 1917, but most of its constituency turned to the newly established conservative Nationalist German National People's Party, while some joined the new liberal Nationalist German People's Party of 1918.

The **German Conservative Party** (*Deutschkonservative Partei, DKP*) was a conservative political party founded on 7 June 1876 by members of the Prussian Conservative Party. It largely represented the wealthy landowning elite Prussian *Junkers* and the Evangelical Church of the Prussian Union. Notable party members included Prussian Field Marshal Helmuth von Moltke and Elard von Oldenburg-Januschau. The party was a response in opposition to German unification, universal suffrage, and rapid industrialization. It changed from a diffuse party of broad ideology into a special interest party in Bismarckian Germany. In the early 1870s, von Bismarck formed his majority with the base in the National Liberal Party, which emphasized the *kleindeutsche lösung* to German unification, free trade, and anti-Catholicism. He broke with the *NLP* in the late 1870s, by which time the Free Conservative Party and the German Conservative Party had brought together the landed *Junkers* in the East, and the rapidly growing industrial leadership in the major cities. They now became the main base of von Bismarck's support, and successive chancellors up to 1918. As Germans moved from rural areas to new industrial centers in the west (*Ostflucht*), the party suffered heavy losses and was forced to forge an alliance with rabidly anti-Semitic Adolf Stöcker's Christian Social Party, opportunistically embracing anti-Semitism. The 1892 *DKP* platform denounced a "demoralizing Jewish influence"; however, when this attitude failed to halt the party's continued fall in the polls, this element was de-emphasized. Stöcker finally revoked the alliance in 1896. Though predominantly Protestant, the *DKP* opposed the *Kulturkampf*, but supported von Bismarck during the Long Depression (1873–1896) when the Chancellor implemented protectionist policies by imposing tariffs and restricting grain imports from Russia and the United States. The party supported Kaiser Wilhelm II's naval policies and Germany's arms race with the United Kingdom, but initially kept its distance from colonialism and the activists of the Pan-German

League. The party was dissolved following the fall of the monarchy in November 1918. Most of its supporters turned to the newly established German National People's Party.

The **Christian Social Party** (*Christlichsoziale Partei, CSP*) was an extremist political party founded on 1 February 1878 as the Christian Social Workers' Party (*Christlichsoziale Arbeiterpartei*) by Imperial Court Chaplain and rabid anti-Semite Adolf Stöcker. The party combined a strong pietistic Christian and conservative program with progressive ideas on labor and tried to provide an alternative for disillusioned Social Democrat Party voters. As part of the Berlin movement, it increasingly focused on the "Jewish question" with a vociferous anti-Semitic stand and supported the Anti-Semites' Petition of 1881. The party linked anti-Capitalism with hatred toward Jews, denoting both big business and social liberal or Socialist movements as "Judaized" and fulfilling the plans of the "world Jewry" to exterminate the German people (which according to the *CSP* did not include Jews). In 1896, a liberal group around Friedrich Naumann (1860–1919) split off to launch the National-Social Association, which merged with the German Free-minded Union in 1903 and together with the liberal pacifist faction of the German Free-minded Union formed the Democratic Union in 1908, which in turn helped form the German Democratic Party (*DDP*) in 1918. The demise of the Christian Social Party came in the early 1900s. Adolf Stöcker died in 1909 and in November 1918, most members of the *CSP* stepped over to the conservative Nationalist German National People's Party (*DNVP*).

The **General German League** and **Pan-German League**. (Much of the information below regarding these two leagues is taken from a publication by doctoral candidate Martin Urban, Department of Historical Studies, Faculty of Philosophy and Arts, University of West Bohemia in Pilsen, Czech Republic [Urban 2016, 60–71].) The German League was unofficially founded by Karl Peters (1856–1918). Karl Peters was a German colonial ruler, explorer, Nationalist politician, and author. After spending some time in London where he became acquainted with the British way of life and principles of colonization and imperialism, Karl Peters returned to Berlin and on 28 March 1884 founded the *Gesellschaft für Deutsche Kolonisation* (Society for German Colonization) whose goal was to accumulate capital for the acquisition of German colonial territories outside of Germany. During the autumn of 1884, Peters proceeded to East Africa and signed treaties with the chiefs of four African nations that later became known as German East Africa (modern Uganda, Tanzania, Burundi, and

Rwanda). Upon his return to Germany in 1885, he changed the name of the Society for German Colonization to the German East Africa Company. Peters was a proponent of Social Darwinism and *völkisch* philosophy. At the First General German Congress in Berlin in 1886, Peters founded the *Allgemeiner Deutscher Verband zur Förderung überseeischer deutsch-nationaler Interessen* (General German League to Support Overseas German National Interests) converging many national organizations espousing Pan-Germanism (*Alldeutsche Bewegung*).[6] His German East Africa Company began disintegrating with the Heligoland-Zanzibar Treaty (1 July 1890)* between Germany and the United Kingdom and with the Abushiri Revolt in Zanzibar (1888–1889), which the German government crushed and assumed ownership of the German East Africa Company's possessions as a colony.

Karl Peters was one of many similar pan-German Nationalist colonialists that sprouted in late nineteenth-century Germany, particularly after the ascension of Kaiser Wilhelm II. Notably among these colonialists were their patriotic financiers. Jews dominated many of the prominent positions in German banking and finance at the time. In the early 1900s, major Jewish banking families like the Warburgs of Hamburg and the Rothschilds of Frankfurt were still subject to great prejudice and excluded from much of German society. This led them to become hyperpatriotic, reasoning that to gain greater acceptance, they needed to go beyond their Christian banking contemporaries in supporting the state. And so it was that they participated vigorously in helping finance German colonial expansion in the early 1900s. But it was their high profile in helping the state that made

---

* Heligoland-Zanzibar Treaty – Under the terms of this treaty, Germany gained the Heligoland archipelago in the North Sea—which its new navy needed to control the new Kiel Canal and the approaches to Germany's North Sea ports—originally part of Danish Holstein-Gottorp but since 1814 a British possession, the so-called Caprivi Strip in what is now Namibia, and a free hand to control and acquire the coast of Dar es Salaam that would form the core of German East Africa (later Tanganyika, now the mainland component of Tanzania). In exchange, Germany handed over to Britain the protectorate over the small sultanate of Wituland on the Kenyan coast and parts of East Africa vital for the British to build a railway to Lake Victoria and pledged not to interfere with British actions *vis-à-vis* the independent Sultanate of Zanzibar (*i.e.*, the islands of Unguja and Pemba). In addition, the treaty established the German sphere of interest in German Southwest Africa (most of present-day Namibia) and settled the borders between German Togoland and the British Gold Coast (now Ghana), as well as between German Cameroon and British Nigeria.

them easy target for blame by rising Nationalist parties for Germany's defeat in World War I, the hyperinflation of 1923, and Germany's Great Depression in the 1930s.

> [Warburg family head] Max Warburg attained eminence in the heyday of imperial intrigue, when statesmen picked countries ripe for exploitation on unfurled maps and bankers served their will. Private bankers were ideal channels for such covert action because they didn't answer to shareholders or publish balance sheets. They also prized intelligence and operated with sphinxlike discretion that mimicked diplomatic activity. The involvement of Jewish bankers in often sub-rosa colonial activity fed popular fantasies that they ran a secret empire, when, in fact, they operated under the strict guidance of the German Foreign Office. Like other private bankers, Jewish bankers mixed business and politics in a way that made them liable to a later political backlash.
>
> On the eve of World War I, Jewish bankers enjoyed such official favor as to make their later persecution the more perplexing to them. Some analysts have suggested that these Jews, still insecure at bottom, financed colonial expansion to certify their patriotism and to curry favor with the Kaiser. If so, their talents were abundantly exploited. Service to the imperial state lashed them to Germany's presumed mission in the world.
>
> Max believed unhesitatingly that bankers should advance the overseas interests of their governments. Noting how his British counterparts stimulated an economic rebound from the Boer War, he observed in his bank's 1904 report, "This shrewd merger of finance and politics didn't occur equally well in Germany." A liberal imperialist who thought Germany needed colonies to sustain a booming economy and population, he wished to extend German power by peaceful settlement, not by military domination. A close friend of Colonial Secretary Bernhard Dernburg [1865–1937], Max boasted that no German bank more steadfastly supported colonial enterprises than his own. At Dernburg's prompting, he cofounded the Colonial Institute

in Hamburg to train Germans to run the country's colonies. As an institute adviser, he stressed that these pioneers must preserve their German identity in exotic settings. He also helped to cofound—then twice rescued from bankruptcy—a Tropical Hygiene Institute.

Max's colonial work strengthened his ebullient, enterprising presence in official Berlin. If his judgment was later badly clouded by patriotism, we must note that his early success was premised on government patronage. It was during its period of colonial involvement that M. M. Warburg & Co. leaped into the first rank of world banking, its balance sheet expanding from assets of 46 million Marks in 1900, to 127 million Marks in 1914.

Germany was infused with a sense of manifest destiny about overseas development. Von Bismarck had displayed only grudging interest in colonies, regarding them as economic burdens that might spark friction with England and France. In contrast, Wilhelm II wanted to compete for colonies and bumptiously asserted German interests. With truculent pride and notable self-pity, German leaders deplored the discrepancy between their robust domestic economy and the relative paucity of their overseas holdings. As late comers to imperial adventure, they tried to compensate by boldly exploiting opportunities to make inroads against the French and British.

In 1904, Max joined a Deutsche Bank loan to the Imperial Ottoman Empire to bankroll the Baghdad railway. The next year, the Foreign Office lured him into tangled Liberian intrigue. After spurning loans from French and British banks to avoid submission to their governments, Monrovia appealed to Germany. Working with [his brother] Paul at [U.S. investment bank] Kuhn, Loeb, Max organized an international loan for Liberia to thwart England and guarantee a market for German goods, a loan so successful that most Liberian commerce ended up in German hands. By 1907, M. M. Warburg & Co. tied for first place in securities issues among German banks, sharing top honors with the globe-straddling Deutsche Bank.

> As the great powers jockeyed for influence in Asia and Africa, they formed syndicates with other creditor countries to regulate the competition. The elaborate cartel for China included Germany. By the late 1890s. HAPAG ran freight service there, and major Chinese ports swarmed with German merchants. In 1909, U.S. president William Howard Taft insisted that American banks join in financing Chinese railways. With [Kuhn, Loeb leaders] Jacob Schiff and Paul Warburg participating in the American group, Max was recruited by the German Foreign Office to ensure German-American harmony. He later said, "We succeeded through our good offices, in constant contact with Washington and the Wilhelmstraße, in achieving an understanding between America and Germany." Max relished such a middleman role, which proved that international bankers could transcend national differences—a fond Warburg belief. (Chernow 1993, 141–4.)

The **Pan-German League** (1891–1939) was founded on 9 April 1891. In response to the widely unpopular Heligoland-Zanzibar Treaty, the idea arose to establish a new, more firmly organized Nationalist organization which would better defend the interests of proponents of colonialism if needed, and which would be able to put greater efforts into promoting a decisive colonial policy. A then young Alfred Ernst Christian Alexander Hugenberg (1865–1951) promoted this idea, exploiting the situation after publication of the Heligoland-Zanzibar Treaty, and set about organizing this new association. His successful initiative resulted in him later being named the "true father of the Pan-German League." On Hugenberg's invitation, a meeting of supporters of his ideas took place on 28 September 1890. The group around Hugenberg managed to achieve cooperation with the General German League to Support Overseas German National Interests, and convinced Karl Peters to support their idea. The constitutive assembly of the new organization took place on 9 April 1891 in Berlin. The name of the new organization was shortened to the General German League (*Allgemeiner Deutscher Verband*). The League embraced a brand of Nationalism that called for the uncompromising unification of all Germans into an ethnically and politically homogeneous German Empire. Several founding members of the new league came from the German colonial movement of the 1880s, including Emil Kirdorf, Max Weber, Ernst Hasse, and Karl von der Heydt, a banker from Elberfeld who became its head. From its beginning, the organization promoted itself as a pressure group of German "patriots" and defenders of broadly conceived "national interests." A significant portion of their activities were focused on criticizing the imperial government's foreign and domestic policies. The league's core ideology was a conviction of the German nation's exclusive mission, right, and duty to build a strong Central European and colonial power. To this end, it pursued an aggressive and confident expansionist policy, demanded the broadening of its colonial domination in the world, and promoted the building of a strong navy and other measures which were meant to secure the German Empire a place among the great powers of the world. During the first years of its existence, the league's program managed to attract a large number of important figures. The league's top management, for example, included people such as lawyer, Prussian politician, and entrepreneur Wilhelm von Kardoff, Conservative Party leader and eminent Professor of Chemistry and Rector at University of Leipzig Johannes Wislicenus, and Director of the German East Africa Company Alexander Lucas. Some of the members of the *Reichstag* and *Bundesrat* featured in the league's other bodies. Representatives of heavy industry also held influential positions within the league, including, for example, Emil Kirdorf, President of the Rhenish-Westphalian Coal Syndicate, Theodor Reismann-Grone, later Secretary General of the Mining Association in Dortmund and publisher of *Rheinisch-Westfälischen Zeitung*, and finally Alfred Hugenberg himself, who in 1909 became Chairman of the Board of Krupp Steel—the world's largest armaments manufacture and the largest supplier of weapons to the German Empire and Weimar Republic. This is no surprise, because as the league was pursuing an expansionist policy and the arming of the navy, its activities were clearly in the interests of representatives of big industry. Hugenberg undertook a comprehensive reorganization of the league in July 1893. On 5 July 1893, University of Leipzig's Professor of Statistics Ernst Hasse (1846–1908) became its new president. Its previously irregularly issued magazine was transformed into the regular weekly periodical *Alldeutsche Blätter*. The complete reorganization culminated in a change in the league's name to the Pan-German League (*Alldeutscher Verband*) on 1 July 1894.

The Pan-German League's interests and priorities underwent significant re-evaluation under Ernst Hasse's presidency. The pan-Germans' attention turned from overseas and colonial policies to an expansionist strategy within Europe. The Pan-German League's change in priorities, however, was expressed in the building of mutual relations with German Nationalist associations in Central Europe. An example of this is the contacts it developed with German associations within the Habsburg Monarchy, in particular in Bohemia. Some of the Pan-German League's first confidants within Austro-Hungary included Josef Taschek (1857–1939), president of the *Deutscher Böhmerwaldbund* association in Česke Budějovice (Budweis), and Josef Wenzel Titta (1863–1923), later president of the so-called *Deutscher Volksrat in Böhmen*. Ernst Hasse, himself, was welcomed to Bohemia and Austria with his close associates at the end of 1896. Together, they visited German Nationalist associations in Prague, Liberec (Reichenberg), Litoměřice (Leitmeritz), and Most (Brux), and several other organizations in the Austrian lands. During their journey across the monarchy, they endeavored to establish links between local Nationalist associations and the Pan-German League. The leaders of these organizations, of which the Union of Germans in Bohemia (*Bund der Deutschen in Böhmen*) would later come to prominence, provided the Pan-German League with information on nationality statistics within the Habsburg Monarchy. The League then used this information for its scaremongering in the *Alldeutsche Blätter* paper, thus sowing the seeds of German hatred towards other nationalities in Austro-Hungary and Germany. This practice was also meant to demonstrate the solidarity of all Germans against the "danger" from the "enemy of the German nation." This tendency for hatred towards other nations, however, is notable prior to this. In 1894, Ernst Hasse wrote an article published in *Alldeutsche Blätter*, in which he refused to countenance the very possibility of autonomy for, or even the separate national existence of Czechs and Slovenians. He wrote:

> Looking at the map of nations shoes that this relationship is geographically unavoidable. The German nation can never give up Bohemia or Moravia, nor its access to the Adriatic Sea. When existential issues are at stake, in the light of cultural history there can be no doubt that Czechs and Slovenians must be subservient to the German nation. (Urban 2016, 69.)

In subsequent years, pan-German campaigns escalated further. In 1895, an anonymous brochure was published in Berlin entitled *Germany Triumphant* (*Germania triumphans*), which predicted the events of 1900–1915. The author anticipated a war between Germany and Great Britain and

Russia in which Germany would be victorious along with Austro-Hungary. Germany would then acquire huge amounts of territory in Poland, the Baltic, and southern Russia as far as the Volga and Don Rivers, while Austria would govern the Balkan states, together creating a federal state with Austria in the leading role. Not only did the author assume the gradual Germanization of the Slavic population of the expanded Habsburg Monarchy, but, above all, the forced Germanization of the newly acquired territories of the German Empire. Furthermore, Germany wanted to secure the right to deport the Slavic population of annexed areas. The abandoned land would then be repopulated by emigrants returning from America and overseas. A review of this document appeared in *Alldeutsche Blätter* written by the president of the Pan-German League, himself. Hasse gave quite a positive assessment of the brochure's content, agreeing with the expulsion (*Vertreibung*) of much of the non-German nations in the territories confiscated.

Over subsequent years, a large number of similar *Pangermanismus* and *Alldeutschtum* tracts were published. They all had a similar content. Their difference was only in how far the writer dared to go. It is hard to estimate to what extent the spreading of these publications influenced public opinion in wider German society, or the policies of the central government. What is certain is that these theoretical reflections on the future of the German nation became ever more radical. In addition, criticism of the central government also grew. The organization's behavior began to resemble the behavior of *enfants terribles*. At the beginning of the new century, however, the organization's nature changed. In 1908 the hitherto president of the organization, Ernst Hasse, died and was replaced as head of the Pan-German League by pietist Lutheran lawyer Heinrich Claß (1868–1954).

Close connections with the language movement (*Sprachbewegung*) in Germany and Austria signaled the league's aspirations to use language as a cultural marker for ethnic belonging. The pan-German concerns over the limitations of the German nation-state of 1871, the challenges of transnational migration, and the ethnic complexity of German society were to be solved by a comprehensive social rearrangement. Twenty million ethnic Germans lived outside of Germany in other nation-states. Foreign expansion of the German Empire, ethnic homogenization, and political reform were all elements of the comprehensive program of the Pan-German League, which Heinrich Claß had laid out in a series of publications since he became chairman in 1908. Claß demanded the suppression of religious and ethnic minorities in Imperial Germany (Jews and Slavs), and the political suppression of Social Democracy, radical Liberalism, and the Catholic Center Party as domestic "enemies of the empire."

The **German Fatherland Party** (*Deutsche Vaterlandspartei*) was a short-lived radically conservative party, active during the closing phase of World War I. It played a vital role in the emergence of General Erich Ludendorff's "stab-in-the-back legend" and the defamation of the politicians who agreed to the Armistice as the "November Criminals." Backed by the Pan-German League, the party was founded on 2 September 1917 and represented conservative, Nationalist, anti-Semitic, and *völkisch* political circles, united in their opposition against the *Reichstag* Peace Resolution of July 1917. The party's leaders were Wolfgang Kapp (of the Kapp *Putsch* fame) and Admiral Alfred von Tirpitz (a naval minister and post-war party leader). Media baron Alfred Hugenberg was also a prominent member who would later support and coordinate with Hitler and his National Socialist party in the 1933 elections. One other member, Anton Drexler, went on to form a similar organization in Munich on 5 January 1919, the German Workers' Party (*Deutsche Arbeiterpartei, DAP*), which on 24 February 1920 became the National Socialist German Workers' Party (*Nationalsozialistische Deutsche Arbeiterpartei*, *NSDAP*, Nazi Party), which in coalition with Hugenberg's German National People's Party (*DNVP*) consolidated majority power status in the *Reichstag* in 1933 under Adolf Hitler (see: NATIONAL SOCIALISM'S RISE TO POWER, *infra*, for further details). Several defecting members of the disintegrating Free Conservative Party also joined the ranks of the Fatherland Party in 1917. Its political influence peaked in summer 1918 when it had around 1,250,000 members. Its main source of funding was the Third Supreme Command (*OHL*) under the duumvirate of Generals von Hindenburg and Ludendorff.* The party was officially dissolved during the German Revolution on 10 December 1918. Most of its members later joined the conservative Nationalist German National People's Party (*DNVP*), the major Nationalist party of the Weimar Republic under Alfred Hugenberg.

German National People's Party (*Deutschnationale Volkspartei, DNVP*) was an alliance of Nationalists, reactionary monarchists, *völkisch*, and anti-Semitic elements, and supported by the Pan-German League. The

---

* The *Oberste Heeresleitung* (*OHL*) was the highest echelon of command of the army (*Heer*) of the German Empire. In the latter part of World War I, the Third *OHL* assumed dictatorial powers and became the *de facto* political authority in the Empire.

party was formed in December 1918 by a merger of the German Conservative Party (1876) and the Free Conservative Party (1867) of the old monarchic German Empire. It was soon joined thereafter by the remaining radically conservative members of the former National Liberal Party (1867), most supporters of the dissolved extreme Nationalist German Fatherland Party (1917), and the anti-Semitic Christian Social Party (1878). Thus, the party united most of the former fragmented radically conservative political spectrum of the Empire. The founding of the *DNVP* was a response to the November Revolution of 1918 and the sense of extreme crisis it had engendered among German Conservatives, where there were widespread fears that society was on the verge of destruction. As a result of the crisis atmosphere of late 1918, a very wide assortment of different Nationalist parties came together to form the *DNVP* (Hertzman 1958, 24–36). British historian Ian Kershaw wrote that ever since the late nineteenth century there had been tension among German Conservatives between traditional Conservatives and the more radical, populist *völkisch* elements, and that "Even the German National People's Party, itself with many fascistic characteristics, could only uneasily accommodate the new strength of the populist forces on the radical Right" (Kershaw 1983, 165). The more prominent members of the party included Hugo Stinnes, Alfred Hugenberg, Ernst Oberfohren, Count Kuno von Westarp, Ulrich von Hassell, and Oskar Hergt.

Reflecting a strong anti-Semitic orientation, Jews were banned from joining the *DNVP*. In the elections of 19 January 1919, the *DNVP* produced a pamphlet entitled "The Jews—Germany's Vampires!" intended to influence the Weimar National Assembly, which was tasked with drafting the new constitution. Generally hostile towards the republican Weimar Constitution, the *DNVP* spent most of the inter-war period in opposition. The party was largely supported by landowners, especially from the agricultural, conservative and Protestant Prussian east (East Elbia), wealthy industrialists, monarchist academics, pastors, high-ranking government officials, farmers, craftsmen, small traders, and Nationalist white-collar and blue-collar workers (Winkler 2000, 352). Because most of the Protestant aristocracy, high civil servants, Lutheran clergy, the *Bildungsbürgertum* (the upper middle-class), university professors, and gymnasium (university preparatory high school) teachers supported the *DNVP* until 1930, the party had a cultural influence on German life far beyond what its share of the vote would suggest (Beck 2009, 19–20). Because so many university professors and gymnasium teachers supported the *DNVP*, everyone who went to university in Germany under the Weimar Republic was exposed in some way to *Deutsch-National* influence. More women than men voted for the *DNVP*, and despite the party's traditionalist values, women were very active in the *DNVP* (Scheck 2001, 547–60). The women in the *DNVP* came mostly from evangelical Protestant church leagues and associations representing housewives who had become politically active during World War I, and groups like the Pan-German League, the Colonial League, and the Navy League, in which voting women had been active (Scheck 2001, 558). The women in the *DNVP* tended to be most concerned with wiping out "trash and dirt" which was their term for pornography and prostitution that had increasingly become part of German society (Scheck 2001, 547–8). Israeli historian Yehuda Bauer called the *DNVP* "the party of the traditional, often radical anti-Semitic elites . . ." (Bauer 2000, 101). From 1920, Hugenberg represented the party in the *Reichstag* and was made sole chairman of the party on 21 October 1928. As a result of the party's increasing radicalization under the leadership of Alfred Hugenberg, the more moderate elements broke away from the *DNVP* to form the Conservative People's Party (*Konservative Volkspartei, KVP*) on 23 July 1930 under the leadership of Kuno von Westarp (former *DNVP* chairman) and Gottfried Treviranus.

Extremely Nationalistic, reactionary, and originally favoring restoration of the Hohenzollern monarchy, the *DNVP* later recognized the monarchy was not returning and as a substitute supported, unwittingly to its own demise, the creation of an authoritarian state under the National Socialism on 28 June 1933.

The **German People's Party** of 1918 (not to be confused with the German People's Party of 1868) was a National Liberal or Conservative-Liberal party in Weimar Germany and successor to the National Liberal Party of the German Empire. Its most famous member was Chancellor and Foreign Minister Gustav Stresemann (1878–1929), a 1926 Nobel Peace Prize laureate. It was essentially the main body of the old National Liberal Party (mostly its moderate and conservative factions) combined with some of the more moderate elements of the Free Conservative Party (*FKP*) and the Economic Union and was formed in the early days of the Weimar Republic by Stresemann. During the Weimar Republic, it was one of two large liberal parties in Germany, the other being the Social Liberal German Democratic Party (*DDP*). The party was generally thought to represent the interests of the great German industrialists. Its platform stressed Christian family values, secular education, lower tariffs, opposition to welfare spending and agrarian subsidies, and hostility to Marxism (that is, the Communists and the Social

Democrats). The party was initially seen, along with the German National People's Party (*DNVP*), as part of the "national opposition" to the Weimar Republic, particularly for its grudging acceptance of Democracy and its ambivalent attitude towards the *Freikorps* and the Kapp *Putsch* in 1920. By late 1920, Stresemann gradually moved to cooperation with the strongly- and moderately-liberal parties—possibly in reaction to political murders like that of Walther Rathenau. However, he remained a monarchist at heart.

The party wielded an influence on German politics beyond its numbers, as Stresemann was the Weimar Republic's only statesman of international standing. He served as foreign minister continuously from 1923 until his death in 1929 in nine governments (one of which he briefly headed in 1923) ranging from the moderately conservative to the moderately liberal. Despite Stresemann's international standing, he was never really trusted by his own party, large elements of which never really accepted the republic. After Stresemann's death, the German People's Party of 1918 veered sharply towards radical Conservativism.

The party's rightward turn accelerated soon after the September 1930 federal election, in which it lost fifteen of its forty-five parliamentary seats, and many of its more liberal members resigned. It began angling for a coalition of all Nationalist parties, including the Nazis, but this was not enough to stave off collapse in the March 1933 federal election, in which it was reduced to only two seats. After the passage of the Enabling Act of 1933, the party was subjected to increased harassment. Civil servants resigned in droves out of fear for their jobs. Party Chairman Eduard Dingeldey fended off calls to merge with the Nazis only with difficulty. However, the harassment against the party grew to the point that Dingeldey was forced to dissolve the party on 4 July 1933 out of fear for the safety of its remaining members.

Fig. 2 – On the Nationalist and Anti-Semitic Side of the German Political Spectrum

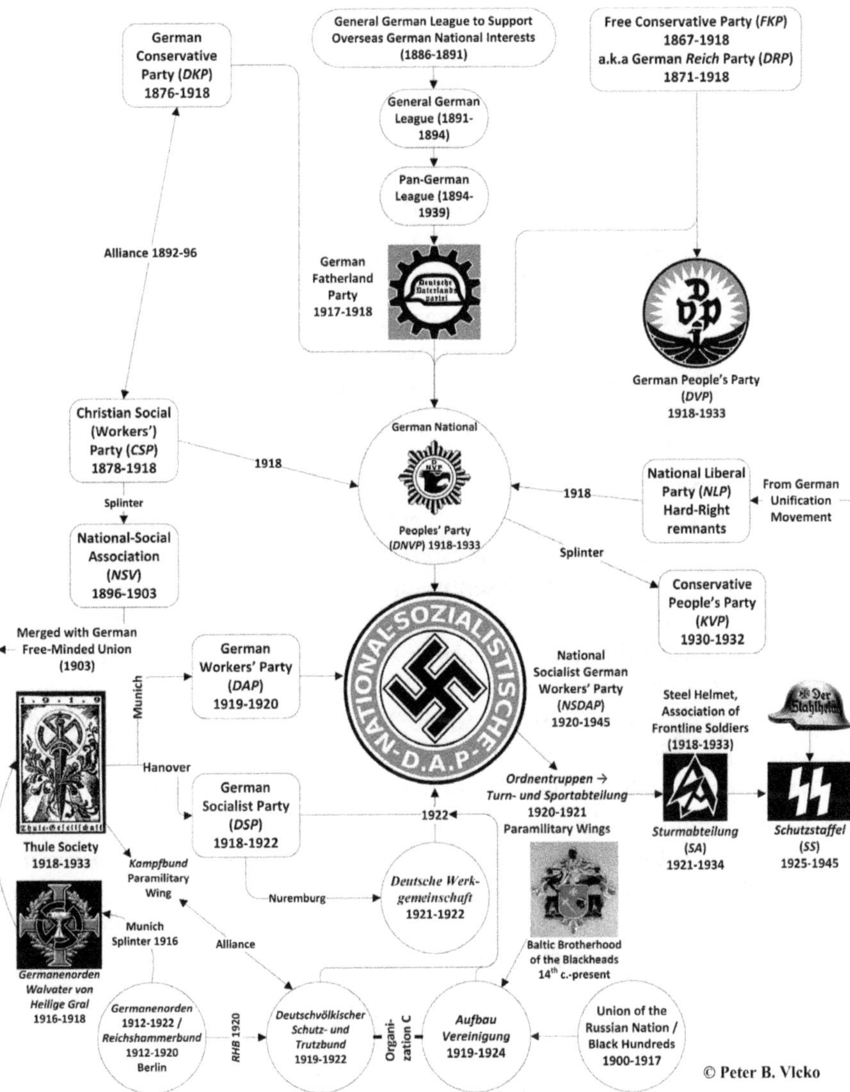

© Peter B. Vlcko

CHAPTER 9

THE STAGE IS SET FOR REVOLUTION

AFTER THE "FEBRUARY" (MARCH 1917) REVOLUTION IN RUSSIA AND THE abdication of Tsar Nicholas II on 15 March 1917, the Russian Provisional Government, led by Alexander Kerensky as of 21 July 1917, continued the war on the side of the Entente powers. Nevertheless, Russian society was severely strained by the opposing motivations of patriotism and antiwar sentiment. There was significant support for continuing the war to defend Russia's honor and territory, but also a strong desire to remove Russia from the conflict and let the other countries of Europe destroy one another without Russian involvement.

The German Imperial Government under the Third Supreme Command (*Oberste Heeresleitung, OHL*) now saw one more chance for victory. To support the antiwar sentiment in Russia and perhaps turn the tide in Russia toward a separate peace, it permitted the leader of the Russian Bolsheviks, Vladimír Lenin, to pass in a sealed train wagon from his place of exile in Zurich, Switzerland through Germany, Sweden, and Finland to Petrograd (Volkogonov 1994). Since he had heard about the February Revolution, Lenin had been scheming on how to get back into Russia, but no option previously available to him proved successful. Within months of his return, Lenin led the "Great October Socialist Revolution" (November 1917) in which the Bolsheviks seized power from Kerensky's Democrats and withdrew Russia from the world war. Leon Trotsky (born Lev Davidovich Bronstein) observed that the October Revolution could not have succeeded if Lenin had remained trapped in Switzerland.

Thus, the Imperial German government had an important influence in the creation of what would become the Soviet Union by turning over Russia's Socialist transformation decisively into the hands of the Bolsheviks, whereas in March 1917, it had been oriented towards parliamentary Democracy.

In early and mid-1918, many people in both Russia and Germany expected that Russia would now "return the favor" by helping to foster a Communist revolution on German soil. European Communists had long looked forward to a time when Germany, the homeland of Karl Marx and Friedrich Engels, would undergo such a revolution. The success of the Russian proletariat and peasantry in overthrowing their ruling classes raised fears among the German *bourgeoisie* that such a revolution could take place in Germany as well. Furthermore, the proletarian internationalism of Marx and Engels was still very influential in both Western Europe and Russia at the time, and Marx and Engels had predicted that for a Communist revolution to succeed in Russia, there would probably need to be a Western European Communist revolution earlier or at least simultaneously. Lenin had high hopes for world revolution in 1917 and 1918 (Volkogonov 1994). The Communism of Marx and Engels had had a significant following among German workers for decades, and there were many German revolutionaries eager to see revolutionary success in Russia and have help from Russian colleagues in a German revolution.

The moderate *SPD* leadership under Friedrich Ebert noted that a determined and well-managed group of the Bolsheviks might well try to seize power in Germany, quite possibly with Russian help. Otto Braun, board member of the *SPD* and later Prime Minister of Prussia, clarified the position of his party in a leading article in the *SPD* newspaper *Vorwärts!* (October 1918) under the title "The Bolsheviks and Us":

> Socialism cannot be erected on bayonets and machine guns. If it is to last, it must be realized with Democratic means. Therefore of course it is a necessary prerequisite that the economic and social conditions for socializing society are ripe. If this was the case in Russia, the Bolsheviks no doubt could rely on the majority of the people. As this is not the case, they established a reign of the sword that could not have been more brutal and reckless under the disgraceful regime of the Tzar. . . . Therefore we must draw a thick, visible dividing line between us and the Bolsheviks. (Schulze 1982, 158.)

In the same month in which Otto Braun's article appeared, another series of strikes swept through Germany with the participation of over one million workers. For the first time during these strikes, the so-called "Revolutionary Stewards" (*Revolutionäre Obleute*) took action. They were to play an important part in further developments. They called themselves "Councils" (*Räte*) after the Russian "Soviets." To weaken their influence,

Ebert joined the Berlin strike leadership and achieved an early termination of the strike.

On 3 March 1918, the newly established Soviet government agreed to the Treaty of Brest-Litovsk negotiated with the Germans by Leon Trotsky. The settlement arguably contained harsher terms for the Russians than the later Treaty of Versailles would demand of the Germans. The Bolsheviks' principal motivation for acceding to so many of Germany's demands was to stay in power at any cost amid the backdrop of the Russian civil war. Lenin and Trotsky also believed at the time that all of Europe would soon see world revolution and proletarian internationalism, and *bourgeois* Nationalistic interests as a framework to judge the treaty would become irrelevant.

With Russia knocked out of the war, the German Supreme Command (Third *OHL*) could now move part of the eastern armies to the Western Front. Most Germans believed that victory in the west was now at hand.

Despite the optimism created by the surrender of Russia early in 1918, there is no question that the military situation on the Western Front had become more precarious for the Germans after the United States entered the war in April 1917. In the wake of the United States declaration of war, the *SPD* in the *Reichstag* joined the "Interfactional Committee" with the Center Party and the German Progressive People's Party. In summer 1917, these three parties passed a peace resolution providing for a peace through rapprochement without annexations and payments, as opposed to a peace through victory and annexations, as the political Conservatives were demanding. The Committee still believed in victory, as did most people in the country. The *OHL* did not like this resolution, and in the negotiations with Russia from December 1917 to March 1918, it imposed a harsh peace by victory.

The Third *OHL* also rejected outright the "Fourteen Points" set out by United States President Woodrow Wilson on 8 January 1918. Wilson wanted peace based on "self-determination of peoples" without victors or conquered. Generals von Hindenburg and Ludendorff rejected the offer because they believed themselves to be in a stronger position than they were before their victory over Russia. They continued to bet on a "peace through victory," with far-reaching annexations at the expense of Germany's enemies.

After the victory in the east, the Third *OHL* on 21 March 1918 launched its so-called "Spring Offensive" in the west to turn the war decisively in Germany's favor, but by July 1918, their last reserves were used up, and Germany's military defeat became certain. The Allied forces scored numerous successive victories in the Hundred Days Offensive between August and November 1918 that yielded huge territorial gains at the expense of Germany. The arrival of large numbers of fresh troops from the United States was a decisive factor.

In mid-September 1918, the Balkan Front collapsed. The Kingdom of Bulgaria, an ally of the German Empire and Austro-Hungary, capitulated on 27 September. The political collapse of Austro-Hungary itself was now only a matter of days away.

On 29 September 1918, the Third *OHL*, at army headquarters in Spa, Belgium, informed Emperor Wilhelm II and the Imperial Chancellor Count Georg von Hertling that the military situation was hopeless. General Ludendorff said that he could not guarantee to hold the front for another 24 hours and demanded a request be sent to the Entente powers for an immediate ceasefire. In addition, he recommended the acceptance of the main demand of President Wilson to put the Imperial Government on a Democratic footing in hopes of more favorable peace terms. This enabled Ludendorff to protect the reputation of the Imperial Army and put the responsibility for the capitulation and its consequences squarely at the feet of the Socialist parties in the *Reichstag*. Thus, the so-called "stab-in-the-back legend" (*Dolchstoßlegende*; see *infra*) was born, according to which the Socialist revolutionaries had attacked the undefeated army from the rear and turned an almost-certain victory into a defeat.

Upon the defeat of Germany and collapse of the German Empire at the close of the First World War, Germany fell into a state of anarchy, chaos, and social upheaval resulting in revolution and civil war. Two of the perceived paths forward were either Social Democracy or a council-based Soviet republic like the one recently established through violent revolution by the Bolshevik Party in Russia. The German Revolution resulted in the replacement of the German federal constitutional monarchy with a Social Democratic parliamentary republic that later became known as the Weimar Republic. The revolutionary period lasted from 29 October 1918 until the adoption on 11 August 1919 of the Weimar Constitution.

The causes of the revolution were the extreme burdens suffered by the population during the four years of war, the strong impact of the defeat on the German Empire, and the social tensions between the general population and the elite of aristocrats and *bourgeoisie* who held power and had just lost the war. Before establishment of the Weimar Republic in November 1918, the majority parties of the *Reichstag*, including Ebert's *SPD*, were quite satisfied with the state of affairs; what they now needed was a period of calm to deal with the issue of negotiating an armistice and a peace treaty. However, events quickly spiraled out of control as rumblings of revolution permeated the air. The plans of the new German government were thrown into disarray when a confrontation between officers and crews on board the German fleet at Wilhelmshaven on 29 October 1918 (Wilhelmshaven Mutiny) set in motion a chain of events that would result in a revolution that spread over a substantial part of the country over the ensuing nine months. In October 1918, the Imperial Naval Command in Kiel under Admiral Franz von Hipper planned to dispatch the fleet for a final battle against the British Royal Navy in the English Channel. These first acts of revolution were triggered by the policies of the German Supreme Command (Third *OHL*) and its lack of coordination with the Naval Command. In the face of defeat, the Naval Command insisted on trying to precipitate a climactic battle with the British Royal Navy by means of its naval order of 24 October 1918. The battle never took place. Instead of obeying their orders to begin preparations to fight the British, German sailors led a revolt in the naval ports of Wilhelmshaven on 29 October 1918, followed by the Kiel mutiny on 3 November. By the evening of 4 November, Kiel was firmly in the hands of about 40,000 rebellious sailors, soldiers, and workers, as was Wilhelmshaven two days later. On the same evening, the *SPD* deputy Gustav Noske arrived in Kiel and was welcomed enthusiastically, but he had orders from the new government and the *SPD* leadership to bring the uprising under control. He had himself elected chairman of the soldiers' councils (Soviets) and reinstated peace and order. During the following weeks, Noske succeeded in reducing the influence of the councils in Kiel, but he could not prevent the spread of the revolution throughout Germany. These disturbances spread the spirit of civil unrest across Germany and ultimately led to the simultaneous proclamation of a parliamentary Democratic Republic (Ebert/Scheidemann – *SPD*) and Free Socialist Republic (Liebknecht – *USPD*) on 9 November 1918. Shortly thereafter, Emperor Wilhelm II abdicated his throne and fled the country.

The revolutionaries, inspired by Socialist ideas, did not hand over power to Soviet-style councils as the Bolsheviks had done in Russia, because with only a few exceptions for soldiers the leadership of the Social Democratic Party of Germany (*SPD*) opposed their creation. The *SPD* opted instead for a national assembly that would form the basis for a parliamentary system of government. This strategy placed the *SPD* at direct odds with the more radical liberal *USPD* (see *infra*) that aligned itself with the revolutionaries. Fearing an all-out civil war in Germany between militant workers and reactionary Conservatives, the *SPD* did not plan to strip the old German upper classes completely of their power and privileges. Instead, it sought to integrate them into the new Social Democratic system. In this endeavor, *SPD* radical Liberals sought an alliance with the German Supreme Command (Third *OHL*). This allowed the army and the *Freikorps* (Nationalist militias) to quell the Communist Spartacist Uprising of 4–15 January 1919 by force. The same alliance of political forces succeeded in suppressing uprisings of the radical Liberals in other parts of Germany, with the result that the country was completely pacified by late summer 1919. Elections for the new Weimar National Assembly, tasked with drafting a new constitution, were held on 19 January 1919. The German Revolution ended on 11 August 1919, when the Weimar Constitution was adopted.

During the nine-month (October 1918 to August 1919) upheaval and revolution in Germany near the time of the Armistice that ended the First World War (11 November 1918), German Jewish Social-Democrat Kurt Eisner organized the Socialist revolution in Bavaria that on 8 November 1918 overthrew the Wittelsbach monarchy under King Ludwig III (ruling Bavaria since 1180) and declared the independent Socialist People's State of Bavaria (*Volksstaat Bayern*). Eisner informed King Ludwig III that the situation in Bavaria was desperate, that the revolutions breaking out all over Germany were now happening in Bavaria and that the new republican government could not guarantee the safety of the monarch and his family. Packing what possessions from the *Residenz Palace* in Munich they could into an automobile, Ludwig III along with his wife Maria Theresa von Austria-Este went into exile on 7 November 1918, and took up residence in *Schloss Anif*, near Salzburg, Austro-Hungary. After a short stay in Salzburg, he and his family fled to Switzerland, Liechtenstein, and finally to a personal estate in Hungary, where he would pass away in 1921. He was the first of the twenty-two of Germany's lesser kings, princes, grand dukes, and ruling dukes that had been deposed, the last was Günther Victor, Prince of Schwarzburg, on 23 November (Watt 1968). On 8 November, the People's State of Bavaria was proclaimed by Eisner.

Between July 1917 and October 1918, four individuals held the office of Chancellor of the German Empire under Kaiser Wilhelm II—Theobald von Bethmann-Hollweg, Georg Michaelis, Count Georg von Hertling, and Prince Max von Baden. On 3 October 1918, Prince Maximillian von Baden (1867–1929) was named the final chancellor of the German Empire by Wilhelm II under the hope he could negotiate an armistice and save the monarchy. The fanatical anti-Jewish German Emperor and King of Prussia Kaiser Wilhelm II (grandson of Wilhelm I) was at the Imperial Army headquarters in Spa, Belgium when the uprisings in Berlin and other centers took him by surprise in late October and early November 1918. Mutiny among the ranks of his beloved *Kaiserliche Marine*, the imperial navy, profoundly shocked him. Two days after the Bavarian royal family fled, Wilhelm II finally relented to demands for his abdication on 9 November 1918. On 10 November, he and his family boarded a train, crossed the German border, and sought refuge in the neutral Netherlands. By the intervention of his royal English cousin King George V and American President Woodrow Wilson, Wilhelm II managed to avoid extradition and execution in Germany and died in exile in 1941. On 9 November 1918, the abdication of Wilhelm II was announced by his Chancellor Prince Maximilian von Baden at the Imperial Chancellery in Berlin. Later the same day, under pressure from *SPD* party chairman Roman Catholic Friedrich Ebert, whose party held majority in the *Reichstag* (parliament of Germany), Prince Max von Baden resigned and unconstitutionally designated Ebert his successor as "Imperial Chancellor" and "Minister-President" of Prussia. Meanwhile, Karl Liebknecht, just released from prison, had returned to Berlin, and re-founded the Spartacus League the previous day. At lunch in the *Reichstag*, the *SPD* deputy chairman and recently named *Staatssekretär* (Secretary of State without portfolio) Philipp Scheidemann learned that Liebknecht planned the proclamation of a Socialist republic. Scheidemann did not want to leave the initiative to the Spartacists and without further ado, he stepped out onto a balcony of the *Reichstag*. From there, he proclaimed a republic before a mass of demonstrating people on his own authority (against Ebert's expressed will). A few hours later the Berlin newspapers reported that from a balcony of the Berlin *Stadtschloß* (City Palace) facing *Unter den Linden Straße* opposite the Berlin *Lustgarten* and *Altes Museum*—at probably around the same time as Scheidemann's declaration—Liebknecht had proclaimed a Socialist republic, which he affirmed to an assembled crowd at around 4:00 p.m.

By this time, all twenty-two of Germany's lesser kings, princes, grand dukes, and ruling dukes had been deposed (Watt 1968). Ebert did not favor exchanging the monarchy for a republic, but like many others, he was worried about the danger of a growing Bolshevik revolution, which seemed more likely with every day that passed. Earlier on 28 October 1918, the constitution was changed to transfer power to the *Reichstag*—a reluctant last-minute attempt by Kaiser Wilhelm II to appease revolutionary voices—paving the way for the founding of the Weimar Republic on 9 November 1918.

It was only on 5 October 1918 that the German public was informed of the dismal situation that it faced. In the general state of shock about the defeat, which now had become obvious, the constitutional changes, formally decided by the *Reichstag* on 28 October, went almost unnoticed. From then on, Imperial Chancellor von Baden and his ministers depended on the confidence of the parliamentary majority. After the Supreme Command (Third *OHL*) had passed from the emperor to the Imperial Government, the German Empire changed from a Constitutional to a Parliamentary Monarchy. As far as the Social Democrats were concerned, the so-called October Constitution met all the important constitutional objectives of the party. Ebert already regarded 5 October 1918 as the birthday of German democracy since the emperor voluntarily ceded power and so he considered a revolution unnecessary.

When Karl Liebknecht's declared a Socialist republic from the balcony of the Berlin *Stadtschloß* on 9 November 1918, his intentions were little known to the public. The Spartacus League's demands of 7 October for a far-reaching restructuring of the economy, the army, the judiciary, and among other things, abolishing the death penalty, had not yet been publicized. The biggest bone of contention with the *SPD* was to be the Spartacists' demand for the establishment of "unalterable political facts" on the ground by social and other measures before the election of a constituent National Assembly, while the *SPD* wanted to leave the decision on the future economic system to the Assembly.

Ebert was faced with a dilemma. The first proclamation he had issued on 9 November was addressed "to the citizens of Germany." Ebert wanted to take the sting out of the revolutionary mood and to meet the demands of the demonstrators for the unity of the labor parties. He offered the *USPD* participation in the government and was ready to accept Liebknecht as a minister. Liebknecht in turn demanded the control of the workers' councils over the army; *USPD* Chairman Hugo Haase was still in Kiel and the deliberations were ongoing. The *USPD* deputies were unable to reach a decision that day.

Neither the early announcement of the emperor's abdication, Ebert's assumption of the chancellorship, nor Scheidemann's proclamation of the new republic was covered by the constitution. These were all revolutionary actions by protagonists who did not want a revolution, but nevertheless took action. However, a real revolutionary action took place the same evening that would later prove to have been in vain.

Around 8:00 p.m. on 9 November 1918, a group of 100 Revolutionary Stewards (*Revolutionäre Obleute*) from the larger Berlin factories occupied the *Reichstag*. Led by their spokesmen Richard Müller and Emil Barth, they formed a revolutionary parliament. Most of the participating stewards had already been leaders during the strikes earlier in the year. They did not trust the *SPD* leadership and had planned a *coup* for 11 November independently of the sailors' revolt but were surprised by the rapidly unfolding revolutionary events since the Kiel Mutiny (3 November 1918). In order to snatch the initiative from Ebert, they now decided to announce elections for the following day on Sunday, 10 November. On that Sunday, every Berlin factory and every regiment was to elect workers' and soldiers' councils that were then in turn to elect a revolutionary government from members of the two workers' parties (*SPD* and *USPD*). This Council of the People's Deputies (*Rat der Volksbeauftragten*) was to execute the resolutions of the revolutionary parliament as the revolutionaries intended to replace Ebert's function as chancellor and president.

The same Saturday evening, the *SPD* leadership heard of these plans. As the elections and the council's meeting could not be prevented, Ebert sent speakers to all Berlin military garrisons and into the factories on the same night and early Sunday morning. They were to influence the elections in his favor and announce the intended participation of the *USPD* in the government.

In turn, these activities did not escape the attention of Richard Müller and the Revolutionary Stewards. Seeing that Ebert would also be running the new government, they planned to propose to the assembly not only the election of a government, but also the appointment of an Action Committee. This committee was to co-ordinate the activities of the Workers' and Soldiers' Councils. For this election, the stewards had already prepared a list of names on which the *SPD* was not represented. In this manner, they hoped to install a monitoring body acceptable to them watching the government.

In the assembly that convened on 10 November in the Berlin Circus Busch, the majority stood on the side of the *SPD*: almost all soldiers' councils and a large part of the workers' representatives. They repeated the demand for the "Unity of the Working Class" that had been put forward by the revolutionaries the previous day and now used this motto in order to push through Ebert's line. As planned, three members of each Socialist party were elected into the "Council of People's Representatives": from the *USPD*, their Chairman Hugo Haase, the deputy Wilhelm Dittmann, and Emil Barth for the Revolutionary Stewards; from the *SPD* Ebert, Scheidemann, and the Magdeburg deputy Otto Landsberg.

The proposal by the Revolutionary Stewards to elect an Action Committee additionally took the *SPD* leadership by surprise and started heated debates. Ebert finally succeeded in having this twenty-four-member "Executive Council of Workers' and Soldiers' Councils" equally filled with *SPD* and *USPD* members. The Executive Council was chaired by Richard Müller and Brutus Molkenbuhr.

On the evening of 10 November, there was a private phone call between Ebert and General Wilhelm Groener, the new First General Quartermaster in Spa, Belgium. Assuring Ebert of the support of the army, the general in return was given Ebert's promise to reinstate the military hierarchy and, with the help of the army, to take action against the Councils.

In the turmoil of this day, the Ebert government's acceptance of the harsh terms of the Entente for an armistice, after a renewed demand by the Supreme Command (*OHL*), went almost unnoticed. At the eleventh hour on the eleventh day of the eleventh month of 1918, the Center Party deputy Matthias Erzberger, on behalf of Berlin, signed the Armistice agreement in Compiègne, France, and the First World War came to an end.

Although Ebert had saved the decisive role of the *SPD*, he was not happy with the results. He did not regard the Council Parliament and the Executive Council as helpful, but only as obstacles impeding a smooth transition from empire to a new system of government. The whole *SPD* leadership mistrusted the councils rather than the old elites in army and administration, and they considerably overestimated the old elite's loyalty to the new republic. What troubled Ebert most was that he could not now act as chancellor in front of the councils, but only as chairman of a revolutionary government. Though he had taken the lead of the revolution only to halt it, Conservatives saw him as a traitor.

In theory, the Executive Council was the highest-ranking council of the revolutionary regime and therefore Müller the head of state of the new declared "Socialist Republic of Germany" (*SPD-USPD* diarchy). But in practice, the council's initiative was blocked by internal power struggles. The Executive Council decided to summon to Berlin an "Imperial Council Convention" in December to resolve political infighting and hammer out the mechanism of how government was to operate. In the eight weeks of double rule of councils (*SPD-USPD* shared power) and imperial government (*SPD*), the latter always was dominant. Although Haase was formally a chairman in the Council with equal rights, the whole higher-level administration reported only to Ebert.

The *SPD* worried that the revolution would end in a Council (Soviet) Republic, following the Russian example. However, the secret Ebert-Groener pact (made in a private telephone conversation on the evening of 10 November) did not win over the Imperial Officer Corps for the republic. As Ebert's behavior became increasingly puzzling to the revolutionary workers, the soldiers, and their stewards, the *SPD* leadership lost more and more of their supporters' confidence, without gaining any sympathies from the conservative opponents of the revolution.

Over the ensuing month, political machinations and jockeying over how the new power structures of government would be set up and who would command them escalated between those on the one hand (mostly *USPD* supporters) who supported a government under workers' and soldiers' revolutionary councils represented by a Council of People's Representatives and a supreme Executive Council of Workers' and Soldiers' Councils, and those on the other hand who preferred a parliamentary Social Democracy elected by universal suffrage of all citizens over the age of twenty-years (mostly *SPD* supporters).

This conflict was finally decided at the First General Convention of Workers' and Soldiers' Councils (*Erster Allgemeiner Kongress der Arbeiter- und Soldatenräte*) at the Prussian House of Representatives in Circus Busch in Berlin between 16 and 19 December 1918. The Convention consisted mainly of *SPD* followers. Not even Karl Liebknecht had managed to get a seat. The Spartacus League was not granted any influence. On 19 December 1918, the councils voted 344 to 98 against the creation of a council system as a basis for a new constitution. Instead, they supported the government's decision to call for elections for a constituent National Assembly as soon as possible. This Assembly was to draft a new constitution and decide upon the form of government.

On 19 January 1919, a Constituent National Assembly (*Verfassungsgebende Nationalversammlung*) was elected. Aside from *SPD* and *USPD*, the Catholic Center Party took part, and so did several middle-class parties that had established themselves since November 1918: Social Liberal German Democratic Party (*DDP*), National Liberal German People's Party (*DVP*), and the conservative Nationalist German National People's Party (*DNVP*). In spite of Rosa Luxemburg's earlier recommendation, the *KPD* did not participate in these elections.

With 37.4 percent of the vote, the *SPD* became the strongest party in the *Reichstag* and secured 165 out of 423 deputies. The *USPD* received only 7.6 percent of the vote and sent twenty-two deputies into the parliament. The popularity of the *USPD* temporarily rose one more time after the Kapp-Lüttwitz *Putsch* in 1920, but the party dissolved in 1922. The Center Party was runner-up to the *SPD* with ninety-one deputies, the *DDP* had seventy-five, the *DVP* nineteen, and the *DNVP* forty-four. As a result of these first elections of the new republic, the *SPD* formed the so-called Weimar Coalition with the Center Party and the *DDP*. To get away from the post-revolutionary confusion in Berlin, the National Assembly met on 6 February 1919 in the town of Weimar, Thuringia, some 250 kilometers southwest of Berlin, where Friedrich Ebert was elected temporary *Reich* President on 11 February. Philipp Scheidemann was elected as Prime Minister (*Ministerpräsident*) of the newly formed coalition on 13 February. Ebert was then constitutionally sworn in as *Reichspräsident* on 21 August 1919.

The German Revolution of 1918–1919 is one of the most important events in the modern history, yet it is poorly understood and embedded in the historical memory of most people. The failure of the Weimar Republic that this revolution brought into being and the Nazi era that followed it obstructed the view of these revolutionary events for a long time. To this very day, the interpretation of these events has been determined more by legends than by facts.

Both the radical Conservatives and the radical Liberals—out of different aspirations—nurtured the idea that a Communist uprising was aiming to establish a Soviet Republic following the Russian example. The Democratic parties closer to the Center, especially the *SPD*, were uninterested in assessing the events which turned Germany into a Republic. At closer look, these events turned out to be a revolution supported by the Social Democrats only to be brutally stopped by their party leadership. These processes helped to weaken the legitimacy of the Weimar Republic from its very beginning.

After the imperial government and the Supreme Command (Third *OHL*) shirked their responsibilities for the war and the defeat at an early stage, the majority parties of the *Reichstag* were left to cope with the resulting burdens. In his autobiography, Ludendorff's successor General Wilhelm Groener states, "It suited me just fine, when the army and the Supreme Command remained as guiltless as possible in these wretched truce negotiations, from which nothing good could be expected" (Schulze 1982, 149).

Thus, the "stab-in-the-back legend" was born, according to which the revolutionaries stabbed the army, "undefeated on the field," in the back and only then turned the almost sure victory into defeat. It was mainly General Ludendorff who contributed to the spread of this falsification of history to conceal his own role in the defeat. In Nationalistic and anti-Semitic circles, the myth fell on fertile ground given the fact that the leadership of the regime that took control of government after the monarchy abdicated and fled was strongly represented by Socialist-leaning Jews. Nationalists and anti-Semites soon defamed the Socialist revolutionaries and even politicians like Ebert, who never wanted the revolution and had done everything to channel and contain it, as "November Criminals" (*Novemberverbrecher*). In 1923, Hitler and Ludendorff deliberately chose symbolic 9 November as the date of their attempted Beer Hall *Putsch.*

From its very beginning, the Weimar Republic was afflicted with the stigma of the military defeat of the First World War and the disastrous peace negotiations that followed. A large part of the *bourgeoisie* and the old elites from big industry, landowners, military, judiciary, and government administration never accepted the Democratic Weimar Republic and hoped to get rid of it at the first opportunity. For the radical Liberals, the violent actions of the *SPD* leadership during the revolution drove many of its former adherents to the Communists. The contained revolution gave birth to a "democracy without democrats" (Sontheimer 1962).

Revolutions continued to erupt throughout Germany as all the monarchies of the German Empire melted away, their families heading into exile, and the Imperial Army still demobilizing on the front lines remained completely in the dark about the situation inside Germany. In Munich, a drama critic-turned revolutionary now headed the government of Bavaria. A question now arises: just who was this man, who saw off the world's longest reigning monarchy, the Bavarian royal family, into exile?

Kurt Eisner was 51 years old when he assumed control of one of the oldest continuous nations in Europe. Ironically, he took over Bavaria despite not having been a Bavarian; Eisner was born in 1867 to a Jewish family in Berlin, and graduated from the university there having studied economics, living his entire life in the Kingdom of Prussia. In 1897, Eisner wrote an article satirizing the virulent anti-Semite German Emperor and King of Prussia Wilhelm II and was sentenced to nine months in a Prussian jail. In 1898, after his release he joined the *SPD* where he met Wilhelm Liebknecht, a legend among the German Socialist movements. In 1869, Wilhelm Liebknecht cofounded the Social Democratic Workers' Party of Germany

(*Sozialdemokratische Arbeiterpartei Deutschlands, SDAP*)—known as the *SPD* since 1890. Liebknecht duly converted Eisner to his cause and made him an editor of the Communist revolutionary magazine *Vorwärts!* (*Forward!*). Eisner would likely have spent the rest of his life as a theorist and editor for the *SPD* were it not for him getting caught up in a vicious interparty war between revolutionaries and revisionists. But Eisner was not a rigid Marxist; his resolve to link Socialism and Kantian ethics provoked his dismissal from the party. Savagely denounced by Rosa Luxemburg (another legendary Jewish figure of the German Marxist movement) as being too insincere in his studies of economics and social theory, and being too inclined towards literary critiques, Eisner was given the boot from the *SPD* and, leaving his wife and five children behind in Prussia, fled south to Nuremberg, Bavaria in 1907, then on to Munich in 1910. Eisner took up residence at a small cottage of an old Socialist's daughter and until the later phases of the war, lived a simple life as a drama critic, essayist, theoretician, and writer, all of which ensured he would blend in as Munich during this time was replete with artists and writers.

After considerable success in Paris, Rosa Luxemburg (1871–1919) wanted to immigrate permanently to Germany to be at the epicenter of Communist activism, which in the late nineteenth century was in Germany. However, she had no way of obtaining legal permanent residency in Germany. She returned to Berlin and in April 1897, she married the son of an old friend, Gustav Lubeck, to gain German citizenship. They never lived together, and they formally divorced five years later. Her real lover had been the Polish Jew and Marxist revolutionary Leon Jogiches (1867–1919) since her days at the University of Zurich. She returned briefly to Paris, then in May 1898, settled permanently in Berlin to begin her fight for Eduard Bernstein's imperial constitutional reform movement. Along with Karl Liebknecht, Luxemburg was a member of the uncompromising Marxist wing of the *SPD*. While serving time in a Polish-Russian prison in Warsaw in 1906, she published her paper *Massenstreik, Partei und Gewerkschaften* (*The Mass Strike, the Political Party, and the Trade Unions*), in which Luxemburg delineated her theory of revolutionary mass action, which sharply defined the bright line separating the views of her radical-liberal faction and the revisionist-Marxist theory of Eduard Bernstein. Luxemburg advocated the mass strike as the single most important tool of the proletariat, Western as well as Russian, in attaining a Socialist victory. The mass strike, the spontaneous result of "objective conditions," would radicalize the workers and drive the revolution forward. In contrast to Lenin, she deemphasized the need for a tight party structure, believing that organization would emerge naturally from the struggle. For this she was repeatedly chastised by mainstream Communist parties. Luxemburg's rhetorical skill made her a leading spokesperson in denouncing the *SPD*'s reformist parliamentary course. She argued that the critical difference between capital and labor could only be countered if the proletariat assumed power and effected revolutionary changes in methods of production. She wanted the revisionists ousted from the *SPD*. Between 1904 and 1906, she was imprisoned for her political activities on three occasions. From 30 April to 19 May 1907, she attended the Russian Social Democrats' Fifth Party Day in London, where she met Vladimír Lenin a second time—the first being in Finland in 1906 on her way back to Berlin from her imprisonment in Warsaw (see: Rosa Luxemburg, *supra*). At the Seventh Socialist Congress of the Second International in Stuttgart (18–24 August 1907), her resolution demanding that its member parties in belligerent countries use the social and economic crises brought about by war to promote social revolution was adopted.

Before the First World War, Luxemburg taught Marxism and economics at the *SPD*'s Berlin training center. Her former student, Friedrich Ebert, became the *SPD* leader, and later Weimar Republic's first president. When World War I broke out and the *SPD* voted in the *Reichstag* to support Germany's participation in the war on the side of the Central Powers (4 August 1914), Luxemburg and her close companion feminist and Marxist theorist Klara Zetkin contemplated suicide; the "revisionism" she had fought against since 1899 had triumphed in German politics.

Immediately after the *Reichstag* vote on war credits, Luxemburg invited the friendly *SPD* opponents of war to her Berlin apartment. At this evening meeting on 4 August 1914, six guests—Hermann Duncker, Hugo Eberlein, Julian Marchlewski, Franz Mehring, Ernst Meyer, and Wilhelm Pieck—together with Luxemburg established the independent Group International (*Gruppe Internationale*), the nucleus of the future Spartacus League (*Spartakusbund*). In the following week, ten additional supporters joined the Group International, including Leo Jogiches, Karl Liebknecht, August and Bertha Thalheimer, and Eugen Leviné (eventual co-leader of the second Bavarian Soviet Republic).

The vote to approve war credits was a stunning reversal of the Second International's position on Capitalist war that came as a shock to radical internationalist elements in the *SPD*, including Jogiches. Luxemburg's immediate inclination was to publish and clandestinely circulate a manifesto signed by antiwar leaders of the *SPD* calling for spontaneous resistance—an effort which Jogiches criticized as no substitute for actual political organization. Luxemburg's idea was soon abandoned due to lack of support from the 300 party leaders canvassed via telegram for the effort, of whom no more than a small handful responded. The Group International saw the *SPD* approval of the war credits as a betrayal of the goals of pan-European Socialism, and especially of the principles affirmed by the Second International in solidarity with the working-class movement against the war. It adhered to these prewar aims and rejected the war as an imperialist genocide of the ruling *bourgeoisie* against the interests of the peoples and the proletariat.

Karl Liebknecht and Luxemburg became prominent members of the radical-liberal faction of the *SPD*. Their clear position was that the objectives of liberation for the industrial working class and all minorities could be achieved by revolution only. Besides their opposition to what they saw as an imperialist war, Luxemburg and Liebknecht maintained the need for revolutionary methods, in contrast to the leadership of the *SPD*, who were revisionist Marxists and participated in the parliamentary process.

The next vote in the *Reichstag* to extend budgetary credits for the war was held on 2 December 1914. This time, Karl Liebknecht was the only member of parliament to vote against extending war credits. Liebknecht was not permitted to speak in the *Reichstag* to explain his vote, but what he had planned to say was made public through the circulation of a leaflet that was declared unlawful:

> The present war was not willed by any of the nations participating in it and it is not waged in the interest of the Germans or any other people. It is an imperialist war, a war for capitalist control of the world market, for the political domination of huge territories and to give scope to industrial and banking capital.

Because of high demand, this leaflet was soon printed and evolved into the so-called *Politische Briefe* (*Political Letters*), collections of which were later published by Group International in defiance of the censorship laws under the name *Die Internationale* (*The International*) and edited by Luxemburg and Mehring. Rosa Luxemburg and a small network of her friends and like-minded thinkers began to organize themselves politically from the summer of 1914 and into 1915. These included Leo Jogiches, Julian

Marchlewski, Franz Mehring, and Klara Zetkin, her lawyer Paul Levi, and second secretary of the *SPD* in Berlin Wilhelm Pieck. It would be several months after getting together before the first leaflet *Die Internationale* (*The International*) of the Group International would be published. The short-lived paper did provide a handle for the burgeoning underground organization.

Imperial authorities were not deaf to the threat of antiwar radicalism gaining a foothold and despite his immunity as a member of parliament, they conscripted Marxist antiwar *SPD* parliamentary official Karl Liebknecht on 7 February 1915, only to begin transferring him from one military unit to another on the Eastern Front to isolate him and neutralize his influence. Refusing to fight, Liebknecht was enlisted as an *Armierungssoldat*—a military unit that provided labor to the fighting divisions, and which consisted of men unwilling or not permitted to directly bear arms (for example, because of criminal records or poor health). In this role, he experienced life on the Eastern Front and was directly involved in the clearing of bodies. As an enlisted man he was forbidden from engaging in any political activity. Due to his rapidly deteriorating health on the Front, he was permitted to return to Germany in October 1915. On 18 February 1915, Rosa Luxemburg began a twelve-month prison sentence in Berlin's *Barnimstraße* Women's Prison for an antiwar speech delivered in September 1913 to workers at Fechenheim, near Frankfurt. In her Fechenheim speech Luxemburg had called on German workers to refuse to shoot their French brothers in the event of war. As a result, she was charged with "inciting public disobedience" and put on trial in Frankfurt in February 1914. Declared a flight risk by the public prosecutor, Luxemburg famously replied: "Sir, I do believe that you would run away. A Social Democrat never does. A Social Democrat stands by his deeds and laughs at your judgements. Now sentence me." The judge did indeed sentence her to one year in prison, but the trial was a propaganda success and made Luxemburg a hero of the antiwar Liberals and villain of the Nationalist press.

The implementation of her sentence was delayed while Luxemburg underwent hospital treatment, but on 18 February 1915, she was suddenly arrested and informed that her sentence would begin immediately. Luxemburg served her entire twelve months in *Barnimstraße* Prison for Women in Berlin and was released on 18 February 1916. Antiwar sentiment was short-circuited by arrests of leaders and suppression of antiwar publications, but not silenced entirely, with more than 1,000 women demonstrating for peace in front of the *Reichstag* on 28 May 1915, further adding to the government's unease.

From Group International emerged the Spartacus League (*Spartakusbund*) on 1 January 1916 under Liebknecht and Luxemburg, with Luxemburg still serving her prison sentence in Berlin. When Luxemburg was released from prison on 18 February 1916, she rejoined Liebknecht and Jogiches to resume her antiwar activities with the League. The Spartacus League vehemently rejected the *SPD*'s support for fighting World War I by the German Empire, trying to lead Germany's proletariat to an antiwar general strike. Group International's leaflet *Die Internationale* eventually evolved into the leaflet *Spartakusbriefe* (*Spartacus Letters*), from which the organization drew its new name on 1 January 1916. Included in the early publications of the leaflet were *Klassenkampf gegen den Krieg* (*Class Struggle against the War*) and *Der Hauptfeind steht im eigenen Land* (*The Main Enemy is in Your Own Country*), two of Liebknecht's most important antiwar polemics. Beginning in September 1916, the illegal, antiwar *Spartakusbriefe* was changed to a journal and pseudonymously renamed *Spartacus* (after the slave-liberating Thracian gladiator who opposed the Romans); Luxemburg's pseudonym was "Junius" (after Lucius Junius Brutus, founder of the Roman Republic). *Spartacus* appeared irregularly for 25 issues until November 1918. The League published and distributed the outlawed journal *Spartacus* against German involvement in the war and organized antiwar demonstrations in Frankfurt, calling for conscientious objection to military conscription and the refusal to obey orders. The League sought to contact Socialists from other European countries through letters to the Swiss Socialist press condemning the war effort and linking the struggle for peace with the class struggle to overthrow autocracy.

The antiwar faction in the *SPD* was becoming a growing annoyance to the party and the government. When, on 24 March 1916, the opposition rejected the *Notetat* (emergency budget) in the *Reichstag* after a speech from Hugo Haase, the opposition split off into an independent faction. Under the leadership of Haase, Bernstein, and Kautsky, the minority formed the *Sozialdemokratische Arbeitsgemeinschaft* (*Social Democratic Working Group*, *SAG*).

Because of their continued antiwar activism, Liebknecht and Luxemburg were arrested again. In early 1916 Liebknecht was one of very few German politicians to publicly question the German government's response to the genocidal massacre of Armenians by their Ottoman-Turkish allies. A day after raising this issue in the *Reichstag*, he was expelled from the parliamentary party (*Reichstagsfraktion*) of the Social Democratic Party because of his opposition to the war and criticism of the party leadership. On 1 May 1916, the Spartacus League organized a massive antiwar demonstration with nearly 10,000 participants on the *Potsdamer Platz* in central Berlin where Liebknecht was arrested as he delivered his antiwar speech. He was stripped of his parliamentary immunity (an unprecedented move by parliament), tried, and sentenced to two and one-half years in jail for high treason; the sentence was later increased to four years and one month.

Rosa Luxemburg managed to avoid arrest at the mass gathering on *Potsdamer Platz* on 1 May 1916 but was finally arrested on 10 July 1916 and placed under "protective custody" for the rest of the war. Leo Jogiches took over leadership of the Spartacus League overseeing the publication of the official newsletter *Spartacus*, launched in September 1916, while Liebknecht and Luxemburg were imprisoned. Luxemburg was held first in Wronke Fortress in Posen (now Poznań, Poland) and then Breslau Prison (now Wrocław, Poland). During her two incarcerations between 1915 and 1918, Luxemburg produced some of her most important works, including the antiwar *Junius* Pamphlet (February–April 1915), the economic work *The Accumulation of Capital: An Anti-Critique* (1915), and her analysis of events in Russia, *The Russian Revolution* (1918). Friends smuggled out and illegally distributed many of her articles. Among them was *The Russian Revolution*, criticizing the Bolsheviks and prophetically warning of their dictatorship. Nonetheless, she continued to call for a "dictatorship of the proletariat," albeit not of the Bolshevik model. In that context, she wrote the words "Freiheit ist immer die Freiheit des Andersdenkenden" ("Freedom is always the freedom of the one who thinks differently") and continues in the same chapter: "The public life of countries with limited freedom is so poverty-stricken, so miserable, so rigid, so unfruitful, precisely because, through the exclusion of Democracy, it cuts off the living sources of all spiritual riches and progress" (Luxemberg 1940). Another article, written in February-April 1915 and published in June 1916, was *Die Krise der Sozialdemokratie* (*The Crisis of Social Democracy*), written in prison under the pseudonym *Junius*. In this work she agreed with Lenin in advocating the overthrow of the existing regime and the formation of a new International strong enough to prevent a renewed outbreak of mass slaughter.

After two years of war, opposition to the official party line grew inside the *SPD*. More and more members of parliament refused to vote for war bonds and were expelled. While in prison, Luxemburg wrote *Die russische Revolution* (*The Russian Revolution*), first published in 1922 by Paul Levi, in which she criticized Lenin's party on its agrarian and national self-determination stands and its dictatorial and terrorist methods. At the end of the war, a general amnesty was declared in Germany for all revolutionaries and Luxemburg and Liebknecht were released from prison. They immediately resumed their political activism in Berlin.

After the outbreak of the Russian February Revolution in 1917, the first organized strikes erupted in German armament factories in March and April 1917, with about 300,000 workers going on strike. The strike was organized by a group called the Revolutionary Stewards (*Revolutionäre Obleute*), led by their spokesman Richard Müller. The group emerged from a network of Marxist unionists who disagreed with the support of the war that came from the union leadership (Hoffrogge 2014, 35–61). The American entry into World War I on 6 April 1917 threatened further deterioration in Germany's military position. Generals von Hindenburg and Ludendorff had called for an end to the moratorium on attacks on neutral shipping in the Atlantic, which had been imposed when the *Lusitania*, a British ship carrying United States citizens, was sunk off Ireland in 1915. Their decision signaled a new strategy to stop the flow of United States war matériel to France to make a German victory (or at least a peace settlement on German terms) possible before the United States entered the war as a combatant. Emperor Kaiser Wilhelm II tried to appease the population in his Easter address of 7 April 1917 by promising Democratic elections in Prussia after the war, but lack of progress in bringing the war to a satisfactory end blunted its effect. Opposition to the war among munitions workers continued to rise, and what had been a united front in favor of the war split into two sharply divided groups (Winkler 2000, 362).

After the *SPD* leadership under Friedrich Ebert excluded the opponents of the war from his party, the Spartacists joined with so-called "Revisionists" such as Eduard Bernstein and Centrists such as Karl Kautsky to found the fully antiwar Independent Social Democratic Party of Germany (*Unabhängige Sozialdemokratische Partei Deutschlands, USPD*) under the leadership of Hugo Haase on 6 April 1917. The *SPD* was now known as the Majority Social Democratic Party of Germany (*MSPD*) and continued to be led by Friedrich Ebert. The *USPD* demanded an immediate end to the war and a further democratization of Germany but did not have a unified agenda for social policies. The Spartacus League, which until then had opposed a split of the party, now made up the left wing of the *USPD*. Both the *USPD* and the Spartacists continued their antiwar propaganda in factories, especially in the armament plants.

In Bavaria, it was the unfolding catastrophe of the war that thrust Eisner onto the political stage. Splitting from the *SPD* and establishing the fully antiwar *USPD* on 6 April 1917, Eisner led countless strikes among the armaments workers all over Munich and the surrounding areas in January 1918. Authorities tossed him into prison in February 1918 until 14 October 1918. He resided in the infamous Cell 70 of *Stadelheim*, the Bavarian state prison—the very same cell later occupied by Eisner's assassin, Count von Arco auf Valley in 1919–1922, Adolf Hitler from 24 June to 27 July 1922, and Ernst Röhm when he was executed in 1934 during the Nazis purge of rival elements in their party (Night of the Long Knives). Eisner, along with other antiwar demonstrators including Karl Liebknecht, was granted amnesty by Prince Max of Baden and was released from prison in October 1918. He then formed a cabinet and effectively rode the wave of discontent and uncertainty to power in Bavaria. The Marxist revolutionary Spartacus League under Luxemburg and Liebknecht was part of the *USPD* in its formation period. After the Russian Revolution of 1917, the Spartacus League began agitating for a similar course in Germany—a government based on local workers' councils (Soviets). After the abdication of Bavarian King Ludwig III, Kurt Eisner, a member of the *USPD*, declared the independent Socialist People's State of Bavaria (*Volksstaat Bayern*) on 8 November 1918. Upon abdication of Kaiser Wilhelm II on 9 November 1918, Friedrich Ebert was unconstitutionally appointed "Imperial Chancellor" and "Minister-President" of Prussia. However, earlier on the same night, Philipp Scheidemann of the *SPD* had declared from a balcony of the *Reichstag* a new parliamentary republic. It was Ebert and Scheidemann who ultimately won control of the government in Berlin and consolidated power under the new Weimar Republic. And to further complicate matters in Germany, on 9 November 1918, from a balcony of the Kaiser's *Berliner Stadtschloss*, Karl Liebknecht declared all of Germany a "Free Socialist Republic." These events were the result of the chaos spreading across Germany and created further instability resulting in violent armed conflicts throughout the country.

Rosa Luxemburg's timely re-entry to the center of revolutionary activity—the original motive behind her desire to permanently immigrate to Germany in 1898—was now realized with her release from Breslau Prison on 9 November 1918. She immediately immersed herself in the rapidly developing events surrounding her, believing this was the moment she had been writing about and preparing and waiting for all her adult life. Little did she foresee the tragedy awaiting her and her fellow comrades.

After their experiences with the *SPD* and the *USPD*, the Spartacists concluded that their goals could be met only in a party of their own. At a founding congress held in Berlin during 30 December 1918–1 January 1919, the Spartacus League under Luxemburg separated from the *USPD* and joined with another Jewish Marxist leader Arthur Goldstein and his International Communists of Germany (*Internationalen Kommunisten Deutschlands*; *IKD*) to form the Communist Party of Germany (*Kommunistische Partei Deutschlands*, *KPD*) under the leadership of Karl Liebknecht and Rosa Luxemburg. While most war weary Germans just wanted peace, these few radicals still favored the establishment of a revolutionary alternative to the burgeoning parliamentary Democracy. They immediately called for labor strikes throughout Germany precipitating a simultaneous second revolution.

From 4 to 15 January 1919, general workers' strikes devolved into armed battles on the streets throughout major cities in Germany. The conflict became known as the Spartacist Uprising (*Spartakusaufstand*) or January Uprising (*Januaraufstand*). The uprising was primarily a power struggle between the moderate *SPD* under Friedrich Ebert and the radical Communists of the *KPD* under Liebknecht and Luxemburg. Luxemburg saw that things were rapidly spiraling out of control. She attempted to distance herself from the armed hostilities, but it was too late. The *USPD* joined with the *KPD*. In Berlin, some of the participants organized a plan to oust the *SPD* and launch a Communist revolution emulating the Bolshevik revolution in Russia. Insurgents seized key buildings, which led to a standoff with the *SPD* government. However, the strike leadership (known as the *ad hoc* "Interim Revolutionary Committee"), from which Luxemburg was conspicuously absent, failed to resolve the division between militarized revolutionaries committed to a genuinely new society and reformists advocating deliberations with the government. Meanwhile, the strikers obtained weapons. On 8 January, the *KPD* resigned from the Interim Revolutionary Committee after *USPD* representatives invited Ebert (*SPD*) for talks.

In a move that remains highly controversial among political historians, the *SPD* leadership then gave Nationalist paramilitaries, the *Freikorps*, the go-ahead to crush the Marxist revolution. While talks were taking place, the workers discovered the *Freikorps* (heavily armed Nationalist paramilitary militias opposing Soviet-backed German Communists attempting to overthrow the Weimar Republic) were being hired to suppress the revolting workers. Ebert had ordered his defense minister, Gustav Noske, to do so on 6 January. When the talks broke off, Liebknecht and the *KPD* then called on its members to engage in armed combat to precipitate a Bolshevik-style *coup*. During the fighting, 156 insurgents and 17 *Freikorps* volunteer soldiers died. On the evening of 15 January, Luxemburg and Liebknecht were found in a Berlin-Wilmersdorf apartment. They were arrested and handed over to the largest *Freikorps* unit, the heavily armed *Gardekavallerie Schützendivision*, also ominously known as *Freikorps Mördenzentrale* (Murder Central). Their commander, Captain Waldemar Pabst, had them brutally interrogated at the luxury Hotel Eden. That same night, both prisoners were beaten unconscious with rifle butts and shot in the head in nearby Tiergarten park. Because of her Jewish ancestry, Rosa Luxemburg's body was thrown into the Landwehr Canal, where it was found on 1 June. Karl Liebknecht's body was delivered anonymously to a morgue. By taking part in the second revolution (against parliamentary Democracy) in January 1919 Luxemburg sealed her fate and disastrously, the Socialist Social Democrats turned to anti-Democratic forces to murder their Marxist rivals. Eminent historian Heinrich August Winkler of Humboldt University in Berlin says that the tragedy of their murders was a heavy burden for the German workers' movement and ultimately the Weimar Republic to bear (Dowling 2009). In the words of historian Isaac Deutscher: "In her assassination Hohenzollern Germany celebrated its last triumph, and Nazi Germany its first" (Dowling 2009). Winkler has argued that it would be incorrect to restyle her and Liebknecht as Social Democrats. "They were opponents of the form of Democracy that then and now was the only way to create a pluralistic Democracy with different social groups," he argues, adding that their support for Soviets would have eventually led to a dictatorship akin to that imposed in Russia (Dowling 2009).

Similar uprisings occurred in January 1919 and were suppressed by the *Freikorps* in Bremen, the Ruhr, Rhineland, Saxony, Hamburg, Thuringia, and Bavaria, and another round of even bloodier street battles occurred in Berlin in March 1919 with between 1,200 and 1,500 dead and roughly 12,000 wounded, which led to popular disillusionment with the Weimar Government.

Leo Jogiches remained in his role with the underground Spartacus League as well as the *KPD* until his own arrest in Berlin on 24 March 1919. He was investigating the murder of Rosa Luxemburg when arrested. A few weeks later, Jogiches was assassinated in Berlin by members of the *Freikorps* supporting the *SPD*'s brutal campaign against Communists and anyone threatening the *SPD*'s leadership of the republic. The leadership of the Spartacus League then passed into the hands of Klara Zetkin's lawyer Paul Levi.

Though he advocated a Socialist republic, Kurt Eisner (*USPD*) distanced himself from the Russian Bolsheviks, declaring that his government would protect individual property rights. The new People's State of Bavaria under Eisner started out with many strikes against it. None of the leaders were native Bavarians, and they were bohemians and intellectuals—many of them Jewish—who were conspicuous in their anti-*bourgeois* bias. Conservatives called Eisner a "foreign, racially alien vagabond" and a Bolshevik, and his associates as "unscrupulous alien scoundrels," "Jewish rascals," and "misleaders of labor." Eisner did not help matters by declaring his regime would have "government by kindness," and would create a "realm of light, beauty and reason." There were frequent spectacles such as parades, demonstrations, concerts, and speeches, but the regime's philosophical Utopianism won over few converts.

On 23 November 1918, he leaked documents dated July and August 1914, kept with the Bavarian plenipotentiary in Berlin, which he thought proved that the war was caused by "a small horde of mad Prussian military" men, as well as "allied" industrialists, Capitalists, politicians, and princes. These documents were published to prove that Bavaria was an innocent party in the war, having been dragged along by Imperial Germany. Essentially, Eisner was playing upon Bavarian feelings that the war was strictly the fault of Prussian intransigence and thus Bavaria should be treated as a separate political entity by the Allies. Naturally, that did not go well with Chancellor Ebert when Eisner traveled to Berlin the day after those documents were published. Ebert ripped into Eisner over the release of the documents, stating emphatically (and quite correctly) that Eisner was being incredibly naïve regarding the feelings of the Allies, informing Eisner that the only government the Allies were going to be dealing with was the one in Berlin, and that the elections for the new German National Assembly were to continue regardless of how Eisner felt about them or about the fact that the new German government, along with its new constitution, was going to be exerting a more centralizing influence over the various constituent states. Eisner, of course, thought all of this was sheer nonsense and booked it back to Munich, where on 26 November 1918, his government severed diplomatic relations with Ebert's government and proceeded to set up their own foreign policies.

At the International Labor and Socialist Conference held in Bern, Switzerland on 26 January–10 February 1919, Eisner attacked moderate

German Socialists over their refusal to acknowledge Germany's role in bringing about World War I. For that speech, and for his uncompromising hostility to Prussia, Eisner became bitterly hated by large segments of the German populace. Moreover, the economy of Eisner's Bavaria was in total freefall, with resources being sent away to the victors as part of reparations payments (surrender of assets and material looted from Belgium, Romania, and Russia) under the terms of the Armistice, which was extended three times beyond the original 36 days of the agreement before the Treaty of Versailles was finally ratified on 10 January 1920. By the end of 1918, demonstrations were surging against the drama critic and his status as a Jewish man from Berlin did not help his image among those in the countryside. Rumors abounded that he was really a Russian agent named Salomon Kuchinsky, and demonstrators screamed slogans such as "Out with the Israelite Devil!" and other remarks. (Most of the demonstrators were students in the universities of Bavaria at this time, which, quite contrary to modern times, were regarded by radical-Liberals as hotbeds of monarchists, radical Conservatives, and those favoring restoration of the monarchy.)

As the new government was unable to provide basic services, Eisner's Independent Social Democrats (*USPD*) were soundly defeated in the January 1919 Bavarian *Landtag* election, winning only two and one-half percent of the vote. Eisner, apparently because he was loath to give up power, delayed calling the *Landtag* into session until public pressure from all quarters—including a death threat from the Thule Society if he did not give up his office—forced him to. Finally, he set the legislature to meet on 21 February 1919, more than a month after the election. As he was on his way to the *Landtag* to announce his resignation, Eisner was shot dead from behind by the Nationalist Anton Graf von Arco auf Valley, a decorated aristocratic former cavalryman now a student at the University of Munich, who was a believer in General Ludendorff's growing "stab-in-the-back legend" (*Dolchstoßlegende*) that the German loss in World War I was caused by betrayal of the German Army by Marxists, Bolsheviks, and Jews who were later responsible for the disastrous settlement negotiated for Germany in the Treaty of Versailles.* Returning from the frontlines to the wreckages

---

* The "stab-in-the-back legend" (*Dolchstoßlegende*), for which General Erich Ludendorff is believed to be primarily responsible, was the notion, widely believed and promulgated in Nationalist circles in Germany after 1918, that the German Army did not lose World War I on the battlefield but was instead betrayed by the civilians on the home front, especially the republicans who overthrew the monarchy in the German Revolution of 1918–19. Advocates denounced the German

of postwar Bavaria, von Arco auf Valley was disillusioned and furious like many other veterans returning from the front over the state of affairs in Germany. After the war, he was humiliated when his emblematic military insignia of rank—the cockade—was torn off his hat by a radical liberal mob. He tried to mollify these feelings of disillusionment and humiliation by joining a local *völkisch*[1] organization called the Thule Society. He was rejected membership based on his mother's Jewish heritage. Desperate to prove himself, von Arco auf Valley—knowing that the Thule Society had failed to kidnap Kurt Eisner in December, decided to one-up them—he set out to assassinate the now-deposed revolutionary.

As a Jew, Socialist, bohemian, and Berliner, Eisner was the perfect target. Eisner's assassination resulted in the elected members of Eisner's government of the People's State of Bavaria fleeing Munich and paving the way for the establishment of the short-lived Bavarian Soviet Republic (*Bayerische Räterepublik*).

Over the ensuing six weeks after Eisner's murder, a heated struggle for power emerged in Bavaria between Bavarian members of the *SPD*, *USPD*, and *KPD*. Attempts to capture power and restore stability were made by Munich's *SPD* leader Johannes Hoffmann (1867–1930)* and the more

---

government leaders who signed the Armistice on 11 November 1918 as the "November Criminals" (*Novemberverbrecher*). When the Nazis came to power in 1933, they made the legend an integral part of their official history of the 1920s, portraying the Weimar Republic as the work of the "November Criminals" who used the "stab-in-the-back legend" to seize power while betraying the nation. Nazi propaganda depicted Weimar as "a morass of corruption, degeneracy, national humiliation, ruthless persecution of the honest 'national opposition'—fourteen years of rule by Jews, Marxists, and 'cultural Bolsheviks,' who had at last been swept away by the National Socialist movement under Adolf Hitler and the victory of the 'national revolution' of 1933."

* Johannes Hoffmann was a German politician and member of the Social Democratic Party since 1907. He represented the *SPD* in the *Reichstag* when Kurt Eisner declared the People's State of Bavaria on 8 November 1918. As a former teacher, Hoffmann was named Bavarian Minister of Education in Eisner's government. As minister of education, Hoffmann removed the Bavarian schooling system from the supervision of the Catholic ghetto Church. After Eisner's assassination on 21 February 1919, he succeeded him as minister-president of the People's State of Bavaria on 17 March 1919 as the first freely elected Bavarian Minister-President. Ousted from Munich by the forces of the Bavarian Soviet Republic and the local worker's council on 6 April 1919 led by Hoffmann's former *SPD* fellow Ernst Niekisch, the Bavarian *Landtag* and government fled north to Bamberg in April

radical leaders of Munich's *USPD* Ernst Toller and the *KPD*'s Bolshevik revolutionary Max Levien. On 6 April 1919, the first Bavarian Soviet Republic was declared by Ernst Toller and the more radical elements of his fellow *USPD* colleagues in Munich, including Gustav Landauer, Silvio Gesell, Erich Mühsam, and Franz Lipp. Toller called on the non-existent "Bavarian Red Army" to support the new dictatorship of the proletariat and ruthlessly deal with any counter-revolutionary behavior. Hoffmann's government was forced to flee north to Bamberg, which it declared as the new seat of government—although most of Hoffmann's cabinet ministers resigned.

The administration of the first Bavarian Soviet Republic failed to consolidate power, and the following week on 12 April 1919, hardline Marxist Russian-Jewish émigrés, *KPD* members, and Bolshevik revolutionaries Max Levien (1885–1937; descendant of Huguenot and German immigrants to Russia under the name of Lavigne; participant in 1905 Russian Revolution), Eugen Leviné (1883–1919; Spartacus League; participant in 1905 Russian Revolution; executed in Munich 3 June 1919), and Towia Axelrod (Tobias Akselrod; 1887–1938) took over the leadership and declared the second Bavarian Soviet Republic. Hitler would later call them the "Jewish kings of Munich." These three individuals were protégés of Lenin and Trotsky. Max Levien assisted Vladimír Lenin with his exile in Zurich from 21 February 1916, until his infamous journey back to Petrograd, Russia on 9 April 1917.* Towia Axelrod accompanied Lenin from Zurich to Petrograd until Axelrod was assigned to Berlin as part of Adolph Joffe's revolutionary embassy. Adolph Abramovich Joffe (1883–1927) was a highly-ranked Trotskyist Communist revolutionary, Bolshevik politician, member of the Central Committee, and Soviet diplomat of Karaite descent (Crimean Tatar Turkic-speaking adherents of Karaite Judaism). After the collapse of the Bavarian Soviet Republic, Axelrod managed to ultimately evade execution and returned to Russia in 1920 only to be eventually executed in Stalin's Great Purge in 1938.

1919, where Hoffmann took part in the drafting of the Bavarian Constitution ("Bamberg Constitution"). Many of Hoffmann's cabinet ministers defected to the Bavarian Soviet Republic. The remaining members escaped with Hoffmann to Bamberg.

* Max Levien managed to escape the *Freikorps* summary executions of Communists in Munich in 1919 and returned to Russia only to face execution by order of Stalin during the Great Purge.

PALM SUNDAY *PUTSCH*
13 APRIL 1919

AN ATTEMPT BY TROOPS LOYAL TO THE HOFFMANN GOVERNMENT TO mount a counter-*coup* and overthrow the Bavarian Soviet Republic was put down on Palm Sunday 13 April 1919 by the new "Bavarian Red Army" created from factory workers and members of the soldiers' and workers' councils. On 13 April, the *Republikanischen Schutztruppe* (Republican Protection Force) an ostensibly pro-Republic *Freikorps Schutzwehr* founded in December 1918 and commanded by Alfred Seyffertitz, a supporter of the Thule Society, staged the Palm Sunday *Putsch* in a bid to overthrow the Bavarian Soviet regime from within Munich. Seyffertitz's *Schutztruppe* broke into the former royal *Residenz* (*Wittelsbacher Palais*)—headquarters of the new second Bavarian Soviet Republic in Munich—before dawn and arrested thirteen people, including eight members of the Central Soviet. Among those rounded up were the eccentric People's Representative for Foreign Affairs (*Volksbeauftragter für Äußeres*) Franz Lipp and Erich Mühsam, a cabaret writer and anarchist essayist who had been part of the first Bavarian Soviet Republic's leadership and would later undergo four months of brutal torture at three different concentration camps ending in death at Oranienburg Concentration Camp on 9 July 1934. However, key decision-makers escaped arrest, including Ernst Toller, Gustav Landauer, and leading *KPD* politicians. The *coup* was supported by Hoffmann and his comrade-in-arms, Bavarian Minister of Military Affairs Ernst Schneppenhorst.

As boss of the Nuremberg lumbermen's union, Schneppenhorst had become the Social Democrats' political commissar to the 3rd Bavarian Army Corps, headquartered at Nuremberg, following the collapse of Imperial Germany in November 1918. During the week after Eisner's assassination, Schneppenhorst arranged for thousands of leaflets to be scattered over Munich from airplanes, promising that the Third Corps would "reject the domination of Dr. Levien and his armed supporters." He was rewarded for his enterprise by being named military affairs minister in Hoffmann's cabinet on 18 March 1919. Exemplifying the murkiness of postwar Bavaria, Schneppenhorst supported the proclamation of the Bavarian Soviet Republic on 6 April. Like many other fence-sitters at the time, Schneppenhorst himself did not have a clear idea of what he was doing.

The Palm Sunday plan called for Schneppenhorst and his men to liberate Munich once Seyffertitz's *Schutztruppe* occupied key positions.

Schneppenhorst gathered six hundred infantry, cavalry, and artillery for the operation at Ingolstadt, a city on the Danube thirty miles north of Munich. The propaganda aspect of the *putsch* was well planned. In the days before Palm Sunday, airplanes from Bamberg showered Munich with a leaflet urging the "confused and discouraged" masses to "[c]ome to your senses and take courage!" and "[r]ise up!" to "protect their Socialist government . . . Free State of Bavaria! . . . of Hoffmann-Segitz!," which von Sebottendorff claimed the Thule Society reprinted and distributed throughout the city.

Seyffertitz's claim to represent the Munich garrison was spurious. He could count only on support of Thule Combat League (*Kampfbund*) units within the city. An alleged eyewitness account, an anonymous letter supposedly written by Seyffertitz himself, was critical of Thule's contributions to the *coup*. It claimed that only a dozen Thulists arrived at the barricades. One of them was a captain "in gala uniform! Patent leather riding boots, riding whip, monocle!" Von Sebottendorff claimed that his forces returned to headquarters after seeing the hopelessness of the situation, realizing that the loyalty of the Munich garrison to the Reds (or at least their indifference to the Whites) and the failure of Schneppenhorst's force to advance doomed the adventure. Schneppenhorst claimed his trucks were stuck in the April mud. Others murmured that his plans had been sabotaged (Luhrssen 2012, 127).

Many soviet officials escaped arrest, warned by frantic phone calls from the wife of Erich Mühsam. After a five-hour gun battle, which began in the *Marienplatz* where the *Schutztruppe* was opposed by the Red Guards—a crowd of armed workers and revolutionary sailors under *Münchner Stadtkommandanten* (Munich City Commander) Rudolf Egelhofer—and the pro-Red 1st Infantry Regiment from the Munich Garrison, the *Schutztruppe* retreated to the Munich Central Station. Enduring shelling by Red mortars, the counterrevolutionaries fled by train before the end of the night to Bamberg, taking with them thirteen officials arrested that morning. The Palm Sunday *Putsch* claimed more than twenty deaths and a hundred injuries.

Von Sebottendorff managed to travel to Bamberg on 16 April 1919 to meet with Schneppenhorst, from whom he begged permission to establish a new *Freikorps* from elements of the Thule Society's *Kampfbund* and fresh volunteers. Von Sebottendorff asserted that the Hoffmann regime, acting "through a well-known attorney in Augsburg," requested him to expand the *Kampfbund* into a force capable of helping retake Munich. Von

Sebottendorff claimed that he went to Augsburg to negotiate with the legitimate government through the attorney, and narrowly escaped arrest by Red sailors at his lodgings at the Golden Lamb Inn. Von Sebottendorff received authorization on 19 April to form a new paramilitary group:

> By order of the Cabinet and the State Soldiers Soviet, Rudolf von Sebottendorff receives permission to establish, at Treuchtlingen, Freikorps Oberland.
>
> State Soldiers Soviet Minister for Military Affairs
>
> Signed—Simon
> Signed—Schneppenhorst

The Bavarian Soviet Republic forces—led by, of all people, Ernst Toller—were victorious in the first battle at Dachau (on the northern outskirts of Munich) on 16 April, when Hoffmann's 8,000 soldiers met the Bavarian Soviet Republic's 20,000. Toller took Dachau and Freising, ten miles northeast of Dachau, with casualties numbering only a few wounded. On principle, Toller ignored orders from the bloodthirsty Egelhofer to shell Dachau and shoot all captured White officers. After a victory parade through the streets of Munich, complete with a short procession of prisoners from the recent engagements, Max Levine promptly rearrested the "liberator of Dachau" Ernst Toller for disobedience. In any event, Dachau and Freising would soon slip from Red hands into the grasp of the advancing *Freikorps*.

After the humiliating defeat at Dachau, Hoffmann came to grips with the fact that he could not retake Munich on his own and had to indeed turn to Berlin for help. His deal with Ebert's government in Berlin gave him the services of 22,000 men of the *Freikorps* plus various units of the *Vorläufige Reichswehr* (Provisional National Defense) placed under the command of Major General Burghard Franz Viktor von Oven (1861–1935). The rival governments then clashed again militarily at Dachau. Von Oven and the *Freikorps* then took Dachau and surrounded Munich, panicking Rudolf Egelhofer, who on 30 April had eight hostages (mostly Thule Society members) he was holding executed at Luitpold Gymnasium, despite the efforts of Toller to prevent it.

On 6 November 1918, the Soviet delegation in Berlin headed by Ambassador Joffe was expelled from the country on charges of preparing a Communist uprising in Germany. Axelrod, however, managed to stay on in

Berlin. With the news of Eisner's takeover of Bavaria in November 1918, Axelrod fled south to Munich to avoid Berlin police interrogation during the inevitable hostilities in the wake of the expulsion of Wilhelm II and Bavaria's Ludwig III. On 13 April 1919, the Bavarian Soviet triumvirate named Kiel Mutiny veteran twenty-three-year-old marine and charismatic militaristic Communist Rudolf Egelhofer as *Münchner Stadtkommandanten* (Munich City Commander) and four days later on 17 April, as commander of the newly established Bavarian Red Army (known as *Rote Garde* "Red Guard"). Only four months earlier, Egelhofer was amnestied from a sentence of death for his part in the Kiel Mutiny, and with 600 other navy mutineers fled south to Munich.

In January 1919, *SPD* leader and prime minister of the new Weimar Republic in Berlin Friedrich Ebert through his defense minister Gustav Noske enjoined *Reichswehr* Colonel Franz Ritter von Epp to form a *Freikorps* unit in Bavaria as a border guard unit. However, fearing the *Freikorps* would be used against his government in Bavaria, Bavarian *SPD* leader Hoffmann forbade any such military border guard formation. On 10 February 1919, Colonel von Epp secretly traveled to Berlin to meet with Weimar Defense Minister Gustav Noske to discuss how to force the rebellious Bavarian state back under the Weimar Republic. Many student unions of Bavarian universities defied Hoffmann's ban and joined *Freikorps Epp* organizing in Ohrdruf and Ulm, Bavaria as the "Bavarian Rifle Corps." By 23 April 1919, *Freikorps Epp* boasted 700 men. Notable members included von Epp's Adjutant Captain Ernst Röhm. Most members of the Thule Society Combat League (*Kampfbund*) wishing to join military units to fight the Bolsheviks managed—with the help of Thule Society's President Rudolf von Sebottendorff's contacts in Munich's transportation ministry—to circumvent travel restrictions in Munich at the time and flee north via train to join the men in Treuchtlingen (140 km north of Munich) and Eichstätt (110 km north of Munich) where von Sebottendorff's *Freikorps Oberland* depots were located. Munich University student and Thule Society *Kampfbund* member Lieutenant Rudolf Heß (future Deputy *Führer* under Hitler) was instrumental in recruiting many of his fellow university students to join *Freikorps Oberland* associated with the *Kampfbund*. Hans Frank (future legal counsel to the Nazi Party and Governor-General of the occupied Polish territories) was another notable member of *Freikorps Oberland*.

Time was of the essence, given the rapid development of revolutionary events in Bavaria and elsewhere throughout Germany threatening the Weimar government in Berlin. The Republic's Defense

Minister Noske moved rapidly to form a large, heavily armed force by combining *Freikorps Epp*, *Görlitz*, *Lützow*, *Regensburg*, *Chiemgau*, *Marinebrigade Ehrhardt*, 3,750 Württemberg troops including a security company under the command of Captain Erwin Rommel that occupied Lindau and Schwäbisch-Gmünd, and 1,650 men of Thule Society Combat League's *Freikorps Oberland*. These pro-government troops under supreme command of Major General Burghard von Oven totaled about 22,000 and were commonly referred to by the Reds as "Whites," as if the ongoing Russian civil war was now being played out in Bavaria. The march south towards Munich began on 27 April from the gathering point at Freising (forty kilometers north of Munich). First engagements with Red Guards occurred on 28 April in four cities about thirty miles north of Munich, including Dachau. The pro-Republic troops encircled Munich by 30 April 1919 striking fear and causing panic among the remaining 2,000- to 3,000-strong Red Guards holding Munich (many Red Guards were untrained civilians who went AWOL when news of the Weimar forces reached the gates of Munich). The following day on 1 May, an uncoordinated attack proceeded against the Red Guards within the city and by the end of the day, Munich was completely occupied by pro-Republic troops with only some scattered skirmishes remaining. Estimated casualties between 27 April and 3 May were 1,000 Reds dead and seventy Whites dead. After armed engagement ended, aggressive roundup and purges ensued, including the infamous *Feme* murders executed by members of *Freikorps Oberland* and *Epp*. After the Second World War, and particularly after partition of Germany and Berlin, the leaders and victims of the six months of civil war in Germany were honored and memorialized in archetypical propaganda form by political Liberals and Conservatives in statuary, memorials, literature, the arts, street-building-place names, and calendar days, depending on which side of the political divide the powers resided.

The followers of the Thule Society were, by von Sebottendorff's own admission, little interested in his occultist theories. They were more interested in racism and combating Jews and Communists—the pressing social issue of the times. Through their Combat League (*Kampfbund*; established 10 November 1918), they are also said to have planned to kidnap the Socialist Prime Minister Kurt Eisner of the People's State of Bavaria. After Eisner's assassination and the establishment of the more radical Bavarian Soviet Republic, members of the Thule Society and their lightly armed Combat League were also accused of trying to infiltrate the Bavarian Soviet government and of having attempted a *coup* on 13 April 1919. In response to this attempt, Bavarian Soviet Republic's Max Levien received a tip from a clerk in the Four Seasons Hotel that the offices of the Thule Society were located in the hotel. Levien interrogated the two Walterspiel brothers (Alfred and Otto)* and discovered Rudolf von Sebottendorff was leader of the Thule Society. Levien then sent three plainclothesmen of the Munich Military Police to search the Thule offices on 26 April. They discovered large quantities of incriminating material, including membership rosters, notes on Red Guards positions throughout Munich, Red Army commander Rudolf Egelhofer's official rubber stamp and seal, anti-Semitic literature, and a stock of weapons and ammunition. A detail of Red sailors was sent to guard the offices. Learning of the raid, Thule's spy network immediately warned members of the Society to lie low. However, the Reds managed to find five Thulists. Further interrogations of hotel employees, neighbors, and friends of the suspects revealed the whereabouts of other Thule members. Countess Heila von Westarp, a young woman who functioned as Thule's secretary, was seized at the hotel, briefly questioned, and released the same day on 26 April 1919. She was arrested again at six o'clock that evening in her apartment and release again only to be rearrested two hours later. Thule Society's other aristocrat Prince Gustav Franz Maria von Thurn und Taxis, a member of Bavaria's wealthiest family and relative of several royal houses, arrived in Munich via rail on 26 April on a mission to secure von Sebottendorff's secret papers in the offices of the Thule Society. He was arrested at Park Hotel before he could execute his mission. Franz Cronauer, Chief of the Revolutionary Tribunal, a Thule mole, managed to free von Thurn und Taxis granting him a safe conduct pass to

---

* Walterspiel brothers – businessman Alfred (1881–1960) and international chef Otto (1884–1974) began a partnership in 1910 when they purchased the Hiller Restaurant in Berlin from Lorenz Adlon (founder of Hotel Adlon), which they turned into a success. However, the approaching end to the First World War and collapse of the monarchy left the restaurant without its regular patrons, and it had to close in 1917. The Walterspiel brothers decided to go to Munich and obtained a license to run a restaurant there—under the condition that they also take over a hotel. Although they did not want to become hoteliers, they bought the Hotel Drei Löwen on Schillerstraße. Their real interest, however, was their Restaurant Walterspiel, originally on Fürstenstraße. It was opened on 1 February 1922 and quickly became the most popular address in Munich. Later, when they purchased the Four Seasons Hotel in 1926, they moved the restaurant to the Four Seasons on Maximilianstraße. The restaurant and hotel were soon considered among the best in all of Europe with a guest list of some of the most famous people of the time.

get out of town. But von Thurn und Taxis was rearrested the same day before he could leave and Cronauer's efforts to save his life were no longer effective as the situation in Munich was quickly deteriorating. Over the ensuing 48 hours, the Reds searched high and low for other Thule Society members but could find no more; most of the rank and file had left Munich to join the *Freikorps*, and most of the Society's leadership had managed to evade capture. As chief of the Red Army, twenty-three-year-old navy marine mutineer Rudolf Egelhofer interrogated all the detainees at the War Ministry except von Thurn und Taxis. They were all kept in the cellar of the Luitpold Gymnasium (where Albert Einstein had been a student)—converted to a temporary prison since the Palm Sunday *Putsch* of 13 April 1919—under guard by a contingent of the Bavarian Soviet Red Army.

As reports circulated of summary executions of Red Guards by approaching *Freikorps*, the mood at Luitpold Gymnasium darkened. The Bavarian First Infantry Regiment, the only *Vorläufige Reichswehr* unit at the Munich garrison to enthusiastically support the second Bavarian Soviet Republic, passed a Soldiers' Council resolution demanding the execution of five *bourgeois* hostages for every Red prisoner murdered. Other units of the Munich garrison, commanded by soldiers' councils since Eisner's revolution in November 1918, sat out the fight. The Red Army in Munich was urged to prepare for "a battle to the death." In the face of defeat, it began to melt away. Panic sized the Levine regime, and they began looking for support. Red workers' and soldiers' committees were dispatched throughout the city in hopes of getting anyone to join them. In desperation, and counter to all their ideals, they even implored the detested troops of the *Vorläufige Reichswehr* to turn out for a last-ditch battle. Their appeals fell on deaf ears. Other than the Bavarian First Infantry Regiment, there was virtually no response from the *Vorläufige Reichswehr*.

At Hitler's barracks (as in a few others) the soldiers were called together to vote on the appeal. There was a loud debate between those who favored joining the Reds and those who wished to remain neutral. Hitler, who had turned thirty a week before, had recently been elected as one of the barrack's representatives. Surprisingly, he had little to say. The debate went on for some time. Finally, Hitler, wearing his Iron Cross First Class (in defiance of the Red cause), climbed on a chair and shouted: "Those who say we should remain neutral are right! After all, we're no pack of Revolutionary Guards for a bunch of Jews from who knows where!" (Fest 1974, 85). Hitler's Bavarian Second Infantry Regiment in Munich remained silent and withdrawn to their barracks, despite having supported the Bavarian Soviet government in earlier Soldiers' Council referendums.

Rifles were loaded at Luitpold Gymnasium on the morning of 30 April, after the arrival of a courier with orders from Egelhofer to execute some prisoners. The seven Thule prisoners, plus an elderly Jewish professor named Berger who had been caught tearing down a Red poster on a Munich street, were taken from their cells in pairs to be executed in the school's courtyard and shot against the courtyard wall in front of a rowdy, cheering crowd of some 200 drunk Red Guards and their girlfriends. As news of the executions at Luitpold Gymnasium and elsewhere in the city reached the approaching Weimar government forces, the more radical elements such as *Freikorps Epp* and *Regensburg* broke ranks and stormed the city against supreme commander Major General Burghard von Oven's orders; thus, commenced a White terror of their own.

The *Freikorps*, along with vengeful Munich citizens, hunted down and murdered hundreds of "suspected" Red leaders or resisters. Lucky ones were shot. In retaliation for the murders of the hostages (especially the *Freikorps* men) at Luitpold Gymnasium, Landauer and most of the other members of the "Soviet" government were beaten to death. Max Levine was captured, tried, and shot even though the government in Berlin attempted to save him. Ernst Toller was captured but because of his actions in stopping the "Soviet executions" at Luitpold Gymnasium, he was sentenced to five years in prison. (Toller would later depart for the United States. He committed suicide in 1939 while living in New York city.) Within a week it was all over.

During the Red terror, a small contingent of untrained Red Army grunts reportedly showed up on the morning of 27 April at the Munich garrison barracks where Adolf Hitler resided and attempted to arrest him. Hitler briefly recalls this incident:

> As the new Soviet Revolution began to run its course in Munich my first activities drew upon me the ill-will of the Central Council [*Münchner Räterepublik*]. In the early morning of April 27th, 1919, I was to have been arrested; but the three fellows [Red Guards] who came to arrest me did not have the courage to face my rifle and withdrew just as they had arrived. (Hitler 1942, 167.)

Most historians dispute this account of Hitler's and see it as his and the Nazi Party's attempt to cover up Hitler's support of the revolutionary "Councils" under the *Münchner Räterepublik*. In *Hitler 1889–1936: Hubris*, Ian Kershaw dismisses Hitler's account of his attempted arrest by pointing out that the "Central Council" had already been dissolved on 13 April, but this may be a matter of imprecision rather than deception (Kershaw 1998, 639). By using the term "Central Council," Hitler could have referred generically to the Red authorities clinging to power in Munich through the end of April.

If true, Hitler was to have been taken in the wave of arrests following the 26 April 1919 raid by Red Guards on Thule Society headquarters at the Four Seasons Hotel, which netted the Thule Society's membership list and the arrest of the seven members executed at Luitpold Gymnasium on 30 April.

On 7 April 1919, the day after the first Bavarian Soviet Republic (*Münchner Räterepublik*) was declared, Hitler's regiment elected to support the revolutionary Councils against the legitimate Weimar government. Video and still-photographic evidence have surfaced showing Hitler attending the funeral of Kurt Eisner on 26 February 1919, and in solidarity with the Socialist People's State of Bavaria and with Eisner, a Jewish Socialist reformer, he wore a black armband of mourning on one arm and a red Communist brassard on the other. In the footage, Hitler and a few men from his unit are seen walking in Eisner's funeral procession. Furthermore, surviving photographs of the procession taken just before Eisner was eulogized show Hitler in attendance.

Hitler's activities from his return to Munich in March 1919 through the city's liberation from the Reds in May 1919 remain obscure and subject to speculation. In *Hitler, 1889–1936: Hubris*, Kershaw wonders about the odd "political indolence" of Hitler, who returned to a barracks flying the red flag rather than joining his officers who fled Munich to join a *Freikorps* (Kershaw 1998, 84). Hitler was arrested by *Freikorps Epp* after the battle for Munich in early May, but according to German historian Joachim Clemens Fest, "some officers who knew him intervened, and he was released again." Hitler claims, "A few days after the liberation of Munich I was ordered to appear before the Inquiry Commission which had been set up in the Second Infantry Regiment for the purpose of watching revolutionary activities" (Hitler 1942, 208). Were those officers known to him from wartime service, or was he familiar with them from a connection through the Thule Society?

Could Hitler have been masking his early *völkisch* ties by obscuring his activities under the Soviet Republics?

In *Hitler: Legend, Myth & Reality* (NY: Harper & Row, 1973, pages 101–3), Werner Maser takes the conventional, entirely plausible position that Hitler "remained in barracks, awaiting developments" and even adapted himself to circumstances by wearing a red armband. Maser derives this from a 1952 letter to him by Otto Straßer, a leader of the radical Socialist wing of the Nazi Party. As his brother, Gregor Straßer, was murdered on Hitler's orders during the Night of the Long Knives, his recollections may not be entirely disinterested. Rumors had long placed Hitler in the Social Democratic camp during the early months of 1919 (Heiden 1936, 54).

More recent research uncovers a more interesting, if still tantalizingly incomplete picture. A routine military order of 3 April 1919 referred to Hitler as the representative (*Vertrauensmann*) of his company, a task apparently involving the distribution of Social Democratic materials to the troops. On 15 April, Hitler was elected deputy (*Ersatz*) battalion representative.* "How to interpret this evidence is, nevertheless, not clear" (Kershaw 1998, 118). Given the Thule Society's admitted cooperation with the Social Democrats beginning in the early weeks after the November 1918 revolution, it is possible that Hitler was acting in concert with a Thule front group, which would explain his hasty release from captivity by investigators from *Freikorps Epp*.

Hitler's account does capture the irresolution of many Red Guards in the final days before the fall of Munich. The machinist Anton Drexler, who under the auspices of the Thule Society organized the Political Workers' Circle, the nucleus of the Nazi Party, was also on a list of suspects to be arrested by Red Guards. Drexler was spared when a Communist coworker at his railroad workshop told Red Guards that the frail, nearsighted man "can't shoot and he is a bit touched in the head as well." Both the co-founder of the Nazi Party and its future leader may have narrowly escaped arrest and execution in the waning hours of Red rule in Munich. (Luhrssen 2012, 128.)

---

* Kershaw 1998, 117–18 citing Bavarian *Hauptstaatsarchiv Abt. IV, 2 I.R. Batl. Anordnungen Bl. 1504/1505/1516.*

CHAPTER 10

GERMANENORDEN, *DEUTSCHVÖLKISCHER SCHUTZ- UND TRUTZBUND*, THE THULE SOCIETY, AND THE KAPP *PUTSCH*

At bottom, every German has one foot in Atlantis, where he seeks a better Fatherland and a better patrimony. This double nature of Germans, this faculty they have of splitting their personality which enables them to live in the real world and at the same time to project themselves into an imaginary world, is especially noticeable in Hitler and provides the key to his magic socialism.

— HERMAN RAUSCHNING, 1940

The association of revolution and Jewry in the minds of the German masses...(will) threaten the very existence of German Jews.

— SIGMUND AVIEZRI HALEVI FRAENKEL (1860–1925)*

THE *GERMANENORDEN* (TEUTONIC ORDER) WAS FOUNDED AS A *VÖLKISCH* secret society in Leipzig on 24–25 May 1912, by the virulent anti-Jew Theodor Fritsch (1852–1933) and some twenty prominent pan-German occultists and anti-Semites including Philipp Stauff and Hermann Pohl, who became the *Germanenorden*'s first leader. In addition to occult and magical philosophies, the *Germanenorden* taught to its initiates Nationalist

* In his prophetic "Open Letter to the Gentlemen Erich Mühsam, Dr. Arnold Wadler, Dr. Otto Neurath, Ernst Toller, and Gustav Landauer" (6 April 1919) intended to be published in the *Münchener Neueste Nachrichten.*

ideologies of Nordic racial superiority and anti-Semitism. The group was aimed at the upper echelons of society and was a sister movement to the more open and mainstream *Reichshammerbund.*

Philipp Stauff (1876–1923) was a prominent German-Austrian journalist and publisher in Berlin and founding member of the List Society who held the rank of High Armanen Order (Guido von List's intimate inner circle).[1] Theodore Fritsch trained as a milling engineer but soon became politically active as a community organizer in protecting his rapidly changing profession. Fritsch was concerned that small tradesmen and craftsmen were threatened by the growth of larger firms, factories, and mass production. He sought to mitigate these threats through his new German Millers' League. Undeterred by the failure of the Anti-Semites' Petition (*Antisemitenpetition*) of 1881, his championship of small-business interests was complemented by anti-Semitic, anti-modernistic *völkisch* attitudes. Fritsch attributed the new economic order in Germany to the growing influence of Jewish business and finance. By 1887, he had published a collection of pan-German and anti-Semitic writings. His first anti-Semitic organization was the *Leipziger Reformverein*, established in 1884, for which he issued a periodical, *Antisemitische Korrespondenz*. Although at the time anti-Semitism existed in the deep fabric of German (and greater European) society, given the fact that Jews had made tremendous inroads throughout nineteenth-century German society in the professions, arts, politics, finance, and academia, it remained latently submerged in practice. When Kaiser Wilhelm II was enthroned on 15 June 1888, latent anti-Semitism progressively surfaced to overt racist policies of the government that affected much of German society and culture. By 1889, two anti-Semitic parliamentary political parties were established in the *Reichstag*: the *Deutsch-Soziale Partei* and the *Antisemitische Volkspartei*. The two parties merged in 1894 under the *Deutsch-Soziale Reformpartei*, but it proved ineffective in promoting its anti-Semitic platform. By 1912, with only three seats, the *Reformpartei* was essentially unrepresented in the *Reichstag* (Goodrick-Clarke 1993, 123–34).

Theodore Fritsch wanted to establish a broad and powerful anti-Semitic movement outside parliament, where it would be most effective. By 1910, the *völkisch* societies had identified two main enemies of their pure Aryan Germany: Freemasons and Jews, who embodied French Enlightenment ideas and cosmopolitan Capitalism, respectively. Fritsch, whose explicitly political *Hammerbund* anti-Semitic movement was going nowhere, decided he needed a counter-Masonry to promote anti-Semitism.

In 1911, Fritsch recruited Magdeburg bureaucrat Hermann Pohl to help organize a *Germanenorden* along the lines of Guido von List's and Jörg Lanz von Liebenfels's writings. The year 1912 was crucial for those *völkisch* activists most worried about the direction Germany was heading and the state of the nation. The January 1912 parliamentary elections shocked the anti-Semitic movement. The *SPD* won 110 seats, an increase from 43, and the Conservatives and anti-Semites were the greatest losers retaining only 68 of the 109 seats they had held in the *Reichstag* since 1907. Given the strong Jewish membership in the Socialist *SPD*, these alarming losses stirred the anti-Semitic forces to call for suspension of parliament, establishment of a dictatorship, and denunciation of the Jews.

At a meeting at his Leipzig home on 24–25 May 1912, Fritsch and some twenty prominent *völkisch* pan-German anti-Semites—including Philipp Stauff, Hermann Pohl, Karl Hellwig, Georg Hauerstein, Bernhard Koerner, and retired Captain Eberhard von Brockhusen—formally founded the *Germanenorden* and *Reichshammerbund* to promote their cause and indoctrinate German society. The *Reichshammerbund* was a confederation of all existing Hammer (the emblem of Nordic god Thor) groups throughout Germany. Magdeburg's bureaucrat seal-maker of weights and measures Hermann Pohl became the first chancellor of the *Germanenorden* while retired Colonel Karl August Hellwig (List Society member since 1908) became the first president of the *Reichshammerbund* (Levy 2005, 269). When Hellwig died in 1914, Alfred Roth (1879–1948) replaced him as president of the *Reichshammerbund.* A set of guidelines prepared in advance in April 1912, urged collaboration with Catholics and broad distribution of propaganda among workers, farmers, teachers, civil servants, and officers of the armed forces, with particular efforts among university students. As a secret society, *Germanenorden* lodges were positioned to quietly keep watch on the Jews. In an internal manifesto of 12 January 1912, Hermann Pohl wrote of a rebirth of Aryan Germany, which necessitated the deportation of Jews and Gypsies. By the end of 1912, the *Germanenorden* numbered over 300 "brothers and sisters" with lodges in Breslau, Dresden, Königsberg, Hamburg, Berlin, Nuremberg, Munich, and Duisburg. Their numbers increased by many hundreds by the start of the First World War. (Goodrick-Clarke 1993, 123–34.)

In spring of 1914, a *Reichshammerbund* chapter was established in the Thule Society's future home of Munich. It was founded by Wilhelm Rohmeder, who later joined Thule. With the outbreak of the First World War, membership in *Germanenorden* had reached several thousand with over 100 lodges. However, 95 percent of *Germanenorden* brothers volunteered for military service and lost their lives at the front. Lodge activity became relatively dormant. During the first two years of the war, Pohl was increasingly criticized for his leadership. After the Leipzig lodge had politely asked him to resign in mid-1914, the Berlin lodge in 1915 made a split-off attempt. At the end of 1915, the Master of the Order of the Nuremberg lodge wrote "that the brothers were tired of the rituals, ceremonies and banquets which Pohl evidently regarded as the main purpose of the Order" (Goodrick-Clarke 1993, 118). In October 1916, during a major religious assembly, argument arose over a power struggle between Hermann Pohl and Philipp Stauff, a close associate of Theodore Fritsch and fellow founding member of the *Germanenorden*. By the end of the evening, Pohl was dismissed from office. He and his faithful followers then split off and founded a new secret society, the *Germanenorden Walvater von Heilige Gral* (Teutonic Order of the All-Father of the Holy Grail).

Initially, Pohl remained with his new organization in Berlin and placed advertisements in newspapers throughout Germany written in cryptic runes recruiting new members for his *völkisch* order. Stauff remained president of the "loyalist" *Germanenorden*. The original organization with its "loyalist" members under Stauff fell into chaos and lethargy losing many of its members. Driven by the horrendous political changes in the German *Reich* from a *völkisch* point of view, the order under Stauff was reorganized in the years after 1918 following fellow List Society member retired Captain Eberhart von Brockhusen's ideas and increasingly developed into a terrorist organization that saw itself as a combat organization (*Kampfverband*). Captain von Brockhusen (1869–1939) took over the "loyalist" *Germanenorden* and closely associated it with *Aufbau*'s and the *Deutschvölkischer Schutz- und Trutzbund*'s Organization C (see *infra*), with which von Brockhusen's *Germanenorden* was involved in several infamous assassinations of prominent Weimar notables, including on 26 August 1921 the former head of the Armistice Commission and Minister of Finance Matthias Erzberger.

The *Deutschvölkischer Schutz- und Trutzbund* (German Nationalist Protection and Defensive Federation) was one of three front organizations that were the primary ideological principals and shepherds of the Nazi movement—the other two being, *Thule-Gesellschaft* and *Aufbau Vereinigung*. Only one person was the common denominator to all three organizations—Max von Scheubner-Richter.[2] Founded during a meeting of the *Alldeutscher Verband* (Pan-German Union) on 18 February 1919 in

Bamberg, Bavaria by Alfred Roth (1879–1948; president of *Reichshammerbund*) as a subsidiary of the Pan-German Union with the objective of "fighting" Judaism, the *Schutz- und Trutzbund* was the largest anti-Semitic organization in the early Weimar Republic. The first secret chairman was Konstantin von Gebastelt (1854–1932) under the director Alfred Roth with national headquarters in Hamburg. *Schutz- und Trutzbund* was one of the largest and most important organizations of the German *völkisch* movement during the Weimar Republic, whose Democratic parliamentary system it unilaterally rejected. Its publishing arm put out many of the books that greatly influenced the opinions of those who later organized the Nazi Party, and after the *Bund* folded (1922, except in Bavaria, Württemberg, Anhalt, and Mecklenburg-Strelitz) its members eventually joined and comprised about one third of the Nazi Party. The *Schutz- und Trutzbund* used as its symbols a blue cornflower and the *Hakenkreuz*, and its motto was *Wir sind die Herren der Welt!* ("We are the masters of the world!"), which in fact is a verse from the song *Der mächtigste König im Luftrevier* ("The mightiest king in the skies"), as well as *Deutschland den Deutschen* ("Germany for the Germans"). Theodore Fritsch, Max von Scheubner-Richter, Dietrich Eckart, Julius Lehmann, Gottfried Feder, Heinrich Himmler, Julius Streicher, Reinhard Heydrich, and Max Sesselmann were among the prominent members of the *Schutz- und Trutzbund.* On 1 April 1920, it merged with the *Reichshammerbund.* Membership grew from 25,000 in 1919 to 110,000 in 1920, and by the summer of 1922 just before the organization was banned following the murder of Walther Rathenau, membership rolls reached 180,000. Like the Thule Society, the Munich branch of the *Schutz- und Trutzbund* had offices at the Four Seasons Hotel (Lohalm 1970). Lohalm described the social composition of the *Schutz- und Trutzbund* as "a middle-class *petite-bourgeois* movement" (Lohalm 1970, 114). The organization struggled to penetrate the general labor force, with the main exception being in Nuremberg. The *Schutz- und Trutzbund* actively engaged and collaborated with the Thule Society, *Aufbau Vereinigung*, Ehrhardt's Organization C (Consul), and the *Germanenorden* not only in supporting the National Socialist movement but also in some of the more secretive underground terrorist activities. The leaders of these militant anti-Semitic *völkisch* German organizations were the very same influential figures who chose and molded the outspoken Hitler to lead the *NSDAP* (Nazi Party) to power in 1933.

The Thule Society and *NSDAP* both emanated from the *Germanenorden* founded by Theodore Fritsch, Philipp Stauff, Hermann Pohl and others in 1912. The *Germanenorden* attempted to unite various anti-Semitic splinter groups so that they could more effectively battle "the worldwide Jewish conspiracy." Hitler read Fritsch's *Hammer* Magazine and Handbook on the Jewish Question during his years as a struggling artist in Vienna, and Philipp Stuaff's racist articles while serving on the Western Front.

Hermann Pohl of the *Germanenorden Walvater von Heilige Gral* violently opposed Freemasonry as being international and Jew-ridden, but used Masonic terminology and organizational structure, believing this would insure secrecy of his new organization. He was joined in the same year (1916) by Rudolf von Sebottendorff (formerly Rudolf Glauer), the wealthy adventurer with wide-ranging occult and mystical interests. Von Sebottendorff claimed to have discovered the *Germanenorden Walvater von Heilige Gral* through a cryptic Munich newspaper advertisement, placed by Pohl, seeking "fair-haired and blue-eyed German men and women." In September 1916, von Sebottendorff traveled to Berlin to meet Pohl. A Freemason and a practitioner of Sufism and astrology, von Sebottendorff was also an admirer of Austrian Nationalist, occultist, journalist, playwright, and novelist Guido von List and *völkisch* Austrian political and racial theorist, occultist, anti-Semite, former Cistercian monk, and pioneer of Ariosophy Jörg Lanz von Liebenfels. Convinced that the Islamic and Germanic mystical systems shared a common Aryan root, von Sebottendorff was attracted by Pohl's runic lore.

Von Sebottendorff had a twofold mission in mind when he entered Munich in 1916. He wanted to interest the German general staff in an armored vehicle invented by his friend Friedrich Gobel, and also revive Theodor Fritsch's failing *Germanenorden*. Gobel's "tank car" never panned out, but interest in the *Germanenorden* flourished. The Russian Revolution erupted that November in Moscow, nullifying Germany's victory over the Tsarist Empire. American, British, and French forces pounded German forces on the Western Front. Liberals urged the Kaiser to surrender. Recognizing the gravity of the situation, von Sebottendorff became a leading spokesman for the *völkisch* reaction against "Jewish Bolshevism" spreading to Hungary and Germany.

Now fully entrusted by Pohl, von Sebottendorff was charged with reviving the original *Germanenorden*'s dormant Bavarian province decimated by losses in the war. Membership in Bavaria under von

Sebottendorff increased from about a hundred in 1917 to 1,500 by the autumn of the following year with 250 members in Munich. During ceremonies in Berlin at the winter solstice on 21 December 1917, the order's Bavarian province branch was officially rededicated and von Sebottendorff was officially elected Master of the Bavarian Order Province, the nucleus of what soon became the Thule Society. The Munich lodge of the *Germanenorden Walvater* when it was formally dedicated on 18 August 1918 was given the cover name, the Thule Society, which is notable chiefly as the organization that sponsored the *Deutsche Arbeiterpartei* (*DAP*), which was later transformed by Adolf Hitler into the National Socialist German Workers' Party (*NSDAP*, Nazi Party). A mere four months later, the German Empire would disintegrate, and the postwar chaos would give the *völkisch* Thule Society opportunity to rise from the margins and into the heart of the fray. The shock of defeat, and the political and economic collapse that followed, ensured an audience for even the most fantastic explanations of what was, for most Germans, an inexplicable chain of events. (Luhrssen 2012, 69.)

The secretive *Germanenorden*, whose symbol was the *Hakenkreuz*,[3] had a hierarchical fraternal structure based on Freemasonry. The *völkisch Germanenorden*'s anti-Semitic, pan-German Nationalism was colored by Theosophical accounts of human prehistory, which assigned prominent roles to proto-Aryans, and by a neo-pagan fascination with the old Nordic gods (Luhrssen 2012, xix). Local groups of the sect met to celebrate the summer solstice, an important neopagan festivity in *völkisch* circles (and later in Nazi Germany), and more regularly to read the *Prose and Poetic Edda*'s[*] as well as some of the German mystics. In addition to occult and Romantic philosophies, the *Germanenorden* taught its initiates Nationalist ideologies of Nordic racial superiority and anti-Semitism. As was becoming increasingly typical of German *völkisch* organizations, it required its candidates and spouses to prove that they had no non-Aryan bloodlines and required from each a promise to maintain purity of his stock in marriage. (Goodrick-Clarke 1993, 123–34.)

---

* Edda – an Old Norse term that has been attributed by modern scholars to the collective of two Medieval Icelandic literary works: what is now known as the *Prose Edda* and an older collection of poems without an original title now known as the *Poetic Edda*. Both works were written down in Iceland during the thirteenth century in Icelandic, although they contain material from earlier traditional sources, reaching into the Viking Age. The books are the main sources of medieval skaldic tradition in Iceland and Norse mythology.

ADAM ALFRED RUDOLF GLAUER (1875–1945) ALIAS RUDOLF FREIHERR VON SEBOTTENDORFF

THE FUTURE BARON WAS BORN ADAM ALFRED RUDOLF GLAUER ON 9 November 1875, in the Saxon market town of Hoyerswerda west of Görlitz, near the cosmopolitan city of Dresden. His father, no aristocrat but a skilled worker, a railroad engineer, left his son enough money at the time of his death (1893) to study engineering. He studied at the Ilmenau Technical School and later continued at Berlin-Charlottenburg Polytechnic. Glauer apprenticed with the engineering firm of J. E. Christoph in Niesky, a town in Prussian Silesia. Rejected by the imperial navy in 1897 due to a hernia, and his small inheritance exhausted, Glauer found employment as a private tutor for two small boys in Hanover through 1898. He forfeited his position following what he described as a romantic flight that took him and the boys' mother, an attractive young widow, to a string of cities on the French and Italian Riviera. Scandalized, penniless, and lacking the engineering diploma he coveted, Glauer went to sea as a stoker aboard the steamship *H. H. Meier*, sailing from Bremerhaven to New York in April 1898. By September 1899, he was a crewman aboard the steamer *Ems*, and from there became an electrician on the *Prinzregent Luitpold*, which sailed from Naples for Australia on 15 February 1900. Glauer and a crew mate jumped ship at Fremantle (13 March) in scantly populated West Australia and trekked inland for Coolgardie, where they prospected for gold at the rim of the Great Victoria Desert (Luhrssen 2012, 45).

In July 1900, after the death of his prospecting companion one month earlier, Glauer journeyed to Egypt, armed with a letter of introduction to a wealthy, influential pasha given him in Coolgardie by a Parsee, a follower of Zoroaster. There he met the secretary of Hussein Pasha, a Turkish landowner who was summering near Constantinople. By von Sebottendorff's account, a telegram from Hussein Pasha summoned him to Turkey. Glauer met the pasha at his mansion on the Bosporus, two-hours' journey from the old imperial capital in a narrow-hulled caique. What set Glauer apart from the better-known explorers and expatriates of the period were his obscure and modest origins. He came without academic credentials, cultural cachet, or aristocratic pedigree, but not without ambition. He would return to Europe with a noble title, a changed outlook, and a novel's worth of experience.

Glauer enjoyed the friendly concern of the pasha after his arrival in Turkey and was offered a position as surveyor of his estate in the vilayet of

Hudawengiar (Khudarinddighair). Glauer apparently learned Turkish at this time, studying Arabic calligraphy under the imam of the mosque at Beikos. By 1901, he was employed on the pasha's Anatolian estates near Bandirma and Bursa, on the slopes of Uluda, known to the ancients as Mount Olympus. Glauer's interest in the occult increased during long conversations on the inner life with the pasha, who was devoted to Sufism. He was also befriended by a Kabbalist and alchemist called Termudi, a descendant of Sephardic Jews who had emigrated in the sixteenth century to Salonika (Thessaloniki), a crossroads city where Eastern Orthodox Christians and Sunni Muslims mingled with Jews and Sufis. Before the Second World War, Salonika had the largest Jewish community in Greece. At the time of the German occupation, the Jewish population in Salonika was about 50,000.

While living in Turkey, von Sebottendorff was introduced to occultism, esoterism, Freemasonry, Sufi Islam, Jewish mysticism (Kabbalism), and Rosicrucianism. He became friends with the Termudi family, who were involved in banking and the silk trade in Turkey. The Termudis were Freemasons. They initiated von Sebottendorff into the lodge where the Termudis were members. Before Termudi died, he bequeathed his library of occult, Kabbalistic, Rosicrucian, and Sufi texts to von Sebottendorff. By 1912, von Sebottendorff became convinced from his studies of the texts that he had discovered what he called "the key to spiritual realization," described by a later historian as "a set of numerological meditation exercises that bear little resemblance to either Sufism or Masonry" (Sedgwick 2004, 66). The Parsee from Coolgardie and the Turk and the Jew from Bursa were links in an occult network stretching across the globe, crossing lines of ethnicity and the outer forms of religion. The image von Sebottendorff presented in his autobiographical writings as an adventurer traveling in those circles is at odds with the militant racism and anti-Semitism, he later expounded in the Thule Society. By the end of his first Turkish sojourn, Glauer had become acquainted with the seminal teachings of European occultism in Rosicrucianism and alchemy, along with the Eastern practices of the Sufis and dervishes. He was also initiated into his first secretive lodge. All these influences would be apparent in his occult writings.

From September 1902 to April 1903, he journeyed to Munich, where he registered with the police as an engineering fitter by trade and a freethinker by religion. From there, he moved to the small Thuringian town of Probstzella. In March 1905, he moved to Dresden, the same year he married a farmer's daughter from the Saxon town of Bischofswerda, some sixty kilometers from his hometown, and divorced her in Berlin in 1907. In 1908, he returned to Turkey. Unable, however, to find work with the German-financed Anatolian Railroad Company or the many other construction projects under way in Turkey, von Sebottendorff accepted a teaching post in a Jewish community on the slopes of Alemdag near Scutari (Uskuedar), the town on the Asiatic shore of the Bosporus where Florence Nightingale had treated British wounded during the Crimean War (1853–1856). He soon met and befriended an expatriate Prussian nobleman Baron Heinrich von Sebottendorff (1825–?), who in 1908 adopted Glauer as his stepson (under Turkish law), and on this basis, he asserted his claim to the Sebottendorff surname and to the title of *Freiherr* (equivalent to baron in British society; the third-lowest titled rank within the nobility, above *Ritter* [knight] and *Edler* [nobility without a specific title] and below *Graf* [count, earl] and *Herzog* [duke]). Baron Heinrich von Sebottendorff was also reportedly an American national, although the status of his American citizenship remains unclear; his brother Hugo died in the United States. There exists very little information on what Baron Heinrich von Sebottendorff was doing in Turkey at the time as a German expat and American national.

In 1911, Rudolf von Sebottendorff became an Ottoman citizen. He claimed a period of military service under the Ottoman-Turkish sultan. By his account, from October to December 1912, he volunteered as a medical orderly at the onset of the First Balkan War (October 1912–May 1913), in which Greece, Montenegro, Bulgaria, and Serbia defeated the Turks and expelled them from all but a small corner of Europe. Agreeing to command a company of men recruited from Jenikioj, the refugee village he had helped construct years before, von Sebottendorff was injured in combat, struck on the head by a Bulgarian rifle butt.

After fighting in the First Balkan War, Rudolf von Sebottendorff returned to Berlin with a Turkish passport in early 1913. Under German law, an adoption involving nobility required the Kaiser's assent, but the Sebottendorff family appears to have accepted the railroad engineer's son as one of its own. He exchanged his legally dubious baronage for a more tenable baronetcy by being readopted on German soil, at Wiesbaden in 1914, by a nobleman from the Austrian branch of the Sebottendorffs (residing near Glauer's birthplace), a retired major, Sigmund Freiherr von Sebottendorff von der Rose. He was exempted from military service during the First World War because of his Ottoman citizenship and because of a wound received during the First Balkan War. By the time he emerged from the occult underground of the Near East and Central Europe to play a hand in the turmoil that nearly tore Germany apart after World War I, von Sebottendorff possessed an Ariosophical agenda and the will and resources, based in part on his second wife's inherited fortune, to shape events on a local level in Bavaria, where he had settled during the war years.

Von Sebottendorff exhibited no trace of hostility toward Jews earlier in life. Indeed, his relationship with the Jewish occultist Termudi was by his own telling a formative experience. His writings preserve no turning point on the road to anti-Semitism. It is likely that his anti-Semitism dates from his immersion, after returning to Germany, in the deepening racism of many Central European Theosophists of the *Völkische Bewegung*. Von Sebottendorff's rising anti-Semitism could only have been sharpened after a clash with a Jewish lawyer, Max Alsberg, over the substantial trust fund of his second wife. Alsberg possessed power of attorney over the trust belonging to the divorcée, Berta Anna Iffland, who after her marriage to von Sebottendorff in Vienna in 1915 was known as Anna Freifrau von Sebottendorff. When he dismissed Alsberg, his wife's Berlin solicitor and executor of her estate, the outraged lawyer incited a Dresden police official called Heindl to defame him as a fortune hunter. At one point his accounts were placed under court supervision and he was forbidden to withdraw funds without its permission. He later added that Alsberg, a Jewish convert to Christianity and a "relative by marriage," tried to sabotage his home life. Evidence exists that von Sebottendorff may have entertained regrets about his anti-Semitism and *völkisch* political activism. In *Der Talisman des Rosenkreuzers*, he complained on behalf of his alter ego that "he who did not wish to become involved in politics was now editing a political newspaper. He who had always stood up for the equality of human rights was getting more and more involved in anti-Semitism. He was now becoming more and more entangled in the mess." Von Sebottendorff's protagonist, Torre, also stated, "I am not anti-Semitic in the present sense of the expression. And even less am I pro-Jew. But I am not indifferent to the question." That von Sebottendorff later returned to Germany and tried to take a measure of credit for the birth of Nazism speaks to a current of opportunism than ran alongside his genuine devotion to the occult and opposition to Bolshevism and scientific materialism. (Luhrssen 2012, 59.)

(For developments in the life of von Sebottendorff between the years 1918 and 1919, see the Thule Society, *infra*.)

Von Sebottendorff survived the terror of the Bavarian Soviet Republic and its Red Guards in April 1919. However, by July 1919, von

Sebottendorff had left the Thule Society and Bavaria, having been accused of negligence in allegedly allowing the names of Thule Society members to fall into the hands of the Bavarian Soviet Republic, resulting in the execution of seven members of the Thule Society in April 1919. Von Sebottendorff fled Germany for Switzerland and then Turkey in 1923. In 1926, the Turkish government appointed von Sebottendorff consul to Mexico. Between 1929 and 1931, he traveled to the United States and Central America as Turkey's official representative. He visited Germany in January 1933 and published his controversial *Bevor Hitler kam: Urkundlich aus der Frühzeit der Nationalsozialistischen Bewegung* (*Before Hitler Came: Documents from the Early Days of the National Socialist Movement*), dealing with the Thule Society and the *DAP* (von Sebottendorff 1933). Hitler himself understandably disliked this book, which was banned by the Nazis. Himmler had von Sebottendorff imprisoned for a few days in 1934, but von Sebottendorff managed to escape, presumably, due to some friendly contacts in Munich. While escorting him to the border an *SS* agent supposedly offered him a position as a spy, which he turned down. Eight years later economic necessity impelled him to reconsider, and during the years 1942 to 1945, he reportedly served as an agent of the German military intelligence (*Abwehr* under Admiral Wilhelm Canaris) in neutral Istanbul with the code name "Hakawaki" (teller of tales) while apparently also working as a double agent for British military intelligence (Secret Intelligence Service, SIS later known as MI6—Military Intelligence, Section 6). Istanbul *Abwehr* bureau chief Rittlinger liked the "penurious old gentleman," but thought him ill-suited to espionage because of his brash and open manner. Depressed over Germany's defeat and his deteriorating financial situation, von Sebottendorff committed suicide by jumping into the Bosporus Strait on 8 May 1945, the day after Germany's unconditional surrender.

THE THULE SOCIETY

THE THULE SOCIETY (*THULE-GESELLSCHAFT*, ORIGINALLY THE *Studiengruppe für germanisches Altertum*, "Study Group for Germanic Antiquity") was a German occultist and *völkisch* group in Munich consisting of intellectuals dedicated to the study of Germanic culture. The Society was formally founded in Munich on 18 August 1918, by Adam Alfred Rudolf Glauer—better known under his adopted pseudo-aristocratic alias Rudolf

Freiherr von Sebottendorff—as the Bavarian branch of the *Germanenorden Walvater von Heilige Gral* (Teutonic Order of the All-Father of the Holy Grail),* a schismatic offshoot of the secret society *Germanenorden*, also known as the "Order of the Teutons." The Munich lodge of the *Germanenorden Walvater* when it was formally dedicated on 18 August 1918 was given the cover name "Thule Society." The young sculptor and wounded First World War veteran Walter Nauhaus was already one of the members of the dormant Munich's parent *Germanenorden*. By the time von Sebottendorff contacted him from Pohl's former membership list, Nauhaus had already organized his own group called the Thule Society, whose members met to discuss the Edda and Nordic mythology (Phelps 1963a, 245, citing a letter by Nauhaus, *NSDAP Hauptarchiv HA* no. 886). Von Sebottendorff later wrote: "A cover name for the Society was proposed by Mr. Nauhaus, which was Thule." Pleased by its Listian connotations, von Sebottendorff accepted the suggestion, "for not only was the name somewhat esoteric sounding, but an informed person knew immediately what it referred to" (von Sebottendorff 1933, 52; see also Howe 1968, 28). Membership in the Thule Society was synonymous with membership in *Germanenorden Walvater*; both organizations employed the same emblematic symbol—the *Hakenkreuz*.

Earlier in July 1918, von Sebottendorff purchased for 5,000 *Reichsmarks* the weekly *Münchener Beobachter* (*Munich Observer*)—originally founded in November 1867 by publisher Johann Naderer (1852–

---

* *Walvater* – ("All Father") Guido von List (1848–1919), born Guido Karl Anton List, founding father of the German *völkisch* movement. He also founded Ariosophy by cementing *völkisch* Aryan ideology together with Hindu Theosophy by way of Wodan and the old Nordic gods of northern Europe. In the tradition of *völkisch* German Romanticism, von List was a prolific writer of historical fiction, folklore, mythology, and culture. The drift of von List's writing grew increasingly and overtly occult. He was prominent in the revival of Wodanism, the conscious reconstruction of beliefs surrounding Wodan (or Odin), the paramount deity of the Nordic pantheon. Von List's Wodanism centered around a Trinitarian godhead, *Walvater* (or Allvater, "All Father"), whose persons he called Wodan, Wili, and We. Although Christian parallels are visible, he made his god from the clay of Helen Blavatsky's notion of the three Logoi or manifestations of the deity. Linking the worship of Wodan with the evolutionary doctrine of Hindu Theosophy, von List held that Wodanism "grew out of the intuitive recognition of evolutionary laws in natural life, out of the 'primal laws of nature.' . . . It set for itself the final goal of bringing into being a noble race, whose destiny it was to be to educate itself and the rest of humanity to the actual task of human beings." (Luhrssen 2012, 20, 21, 29.)

1912) under the title *Merkur*—from Friederike Eher, the widow of the weekly's publisher anti-Semite Franz Xaver Josef Eher (1851–22 June 1918), for Pohl's Bavarian branch of the *Germanenorden Walvater von Heilige Gral*. In his weekly, Eher had since 1899 been highly critical of the social corruption of Jewish businessmen and politicians in German society. On 31 May 1908 (edition number 22), Eher under the acronym "Ek" first commented on the "Jewish Question" under the heading "Antisemitisch und Nationalsozial" ("Anti-Semitic and National Social") writing "I do not deny that even a Jew can have the ability to think and act as a German-National and National Socialist, but they can and do it as white ravens [racist pejorative], and at any rate, they should not push themselves in any way, because they only frighten off. . . . Moreover, the Jew is ruining every union he joins."

After purchasing the paper in 1918, von Sebottendorff immediately altered the weekly's name to *Münchener Beobachter und Sportblatt* (*Munich Observer and Sports Sheet*) to increase readership and thereby more effectively spread its racist, anti-Semitic, and Social Darwinist propaganda. However, its new subtitle *Unabhängige Zeitung für nationale und völkische Politik* (*Independent Newspaper for National and Ethnic Politics*) left no doubt about its true character. After inauguration of the *Thule-Gesellschaft* in August 1918, the weekly was absorbed from the Bavarian *Germanenorden* keeping the same editorial board and publisher—Franz Eher Verlag, owned by von Sebottendorff's wealthy girlfriend Käthe Bierbaumer; his sister Dora Kunze was also a shareholder. Upon the founding in Munich of the German Socialist Party (*Deutschsozialistische Partei, DSP*) in May 1919, von Sebottendorff and his Thule Society's *Münchener Beobachter und Sportblatt* openly supported the *DSP*'s *völkisch* anti-Semitic program. On 9 August 1919, von Sebottendorff changed the weekly's name to *Völkischer Beobachter* (*People's Observer*) and in October 1919, the Munich book trade house M. Müller & Sohn took over publication and increased the paper's frequency to twice weekly. However, poor management of the twice weekly and its new publisher led to financial ruin for von Sebottendorff's paper. In mid-1920, von Sebottendorff had seriously—but in vain—tried to sell the publisher to the *Centralverein deutscher Staatsbürger jüdischen Glaubens* (*Central Association of German citizens of Jewish faith*) (Hoser 2006). Determined that Thule Society's *Völkischer Beobachter*, threatened by bankruptcy and takeover by a rival Nationalist group such as the *DSP*, Hitler with the help of Dietrich Eckart, Captain Ernst Röhm, and *Freikorps* Colonel Franz Xaver Ritter von Epp urgently purchased the paper for 120,000 *Papiermarks* ($1,333.33) from the Thule Society on 17 December 1920 for the new *NSDAP*. Under the *NSDAP*, the name changed to *Völkischer Beobachter und Freiwirtschaftzeitung* (. . . *and Free Newspaper*) and became a daily newspaper. Dietrich Eckart became the paper's editor in chief from 12 August 1921 to March 1923, followed by Alfred Rosenberg from 1923 to 1938, and ending with Wilhelm Weiß as editor in chief from 1938 to 1945.

On 17 August 1918, von Sebottendorff rented five club rooms at Munich's posh Four Seasons Hotel (*Vierjahreszeiten*) to stage *Thule-Gesellschaft*'s founding ceremony the following evening. In a fervent speech before a crowd of 300, he proclaimed Germany's mission to elevate humanity and promised to fight the forces of international Jewry with his last ounce of strength. Wielding a ceremonial gavel, he shrieked: "I intend to commit the Thule Society to this struggle, as long as I hold the Iron Hammer . . . I swear it on this swastika, on this sign which for us is sacred" (Angebert 1974, 169). Von Sebottendorff emphasized that the present emergency called for united action from all the scattered pan-German societies. He invited Heinrich Claß's *Alldeutscher Verband*, Wilhelm Rohmeder's *Deutscher Schulverein*, Theodore Fritsch's *Hammerbund*, Hans Dahn's National Liberal Party, The Iron Fist, Old *Reich* Flag Association, *Der Stahlhelm, Bund der Frontsoldaten* (The Steel Helmet, Association of Frontline Soldiers), and other *völkisch* groups to make common cause against the forces of darkness now engulfing Germany. He concluded his talk by reciting an Ariosophical poem by Armanist Philipp Stauff.

When Jewish pundit Kurt Eisner took over the Bavarian government in a bloodless *coup* on 7 November 1918, von Sebottendorff's worst fears were confirmed. Two days later, he issued a "plangent call to arms against Judah."

> [Recently] we experienced the collapse of everything which was familiar, dear, and valuable to us. In place of our prince of Germanic blood rules our deadly enemy: Judah. . . . Now we shall declare the Jew to be our mortal enemy . . . and from today we will begin to act" (Maser 1973b, 110).

New members continued to flock to the Thule Society. Included among them were Gottfried Feder, Alfred Rosenberg, Rudolf Heß, and Dietrich Eckart, who gave a speech before the group on 30 May 1919. Due to this influx, von Sebottendorff relaxed entrance requirements. Candidates no longer had to undergo one year's probation, provide footprints to a committee of elders, or permit inspectors to view the color of their pubic hair (Tyson 2008, 119). Thule's membership list reveals that the Thule supporters were drawn principally from lawyers, judges, university professors, aristocratic members of the Wittelsbach royal entourage, industrialists, doctors, scientists, and wealthy businessmen like the future proprietor Alfred Walterspiel of the elegant Hotel *Vierjahreszeiten* (Goodrick-Clarke 1993, 149; von Sebottendorff 1933).

The primary focus of the Thule Society was a claim concerning the origins of the Aryan race. "Thule" was a land located by Greco-Roman geographers at the furthest point north. The society was named after *Ultima Thule* ("most distant north") mentioned by the Roman poet Virgil in his epic poem *Aeneid*, which was the far northern segment of Thule and is generally understood to mean Scandinavia. Said by Nazi mystics to be the capital of ancient Hyperborea, they placed *Ultima Thule* in the extreme north near Greenland or Iceland. The Thule Society counted among its goals the desire to prove that the Aryan race came from a lost continent, perhaps Atlantis. The Society maintained close contacts with followers of Theosophy and of Helena Petrovna Blavatsky (1831–1891), a famous aristocratic Ukrainian-German occultist who cofounded the Theosophical Society in New York in 1875. Her Theosophical doctrines, a pantheistic philosophical-religious system stemming from Hinduism, influenced the spread of Hindu and Buddhist ideas in the West, as well as the development of Western esoteric movements that eventually merged into what is now known as the New Age movement.

In the spring of 1918, the Thule Society numbered only 200 members; by fall the number had swelled to 1,500. The official banner of the Thule Society bore their insignia consisting of the date of its founding (1919 official registration with government authorities) at the top and the name of the organization (*Thule-Gesellschaft*) at the bottom, both in *Leipzig Fraktur* font. Centered underneath the date of founding is the clockwise *Hakenkreuz* in a circle representing the sun with four sunrays representing the four corners of the globe emanating down from the encircled *Hakenkreuz*; running vertical throughout the emblem is a Knightly dagger with its crowned handle over the encircled *Hakenkreuz* and its four-edged cruciform blade pointing down between the four sunrays; finally, branches of oakleaf and acorn cross over the dagger blade and rise upwards under the encircled *Hakenkreuz*. Thule Society members greeted each other by crying out "*Sieg Heil!*"

Many members of the Thule Society became prominent figures in Nazi Germany. Joachim Clemens Fest (1926–2006) was a German historian, journalist, critic, editor, and a leading figure in the *Historikerstreit* (historians' dispute) of 1986–1989 among German historians relative to the Nazi period (more on the *Historikerstreit* is found under *Epimythium* at the end of this book). Fest made a significant and valuable contribution to the literature on Nazism when in 1963 he published *Das Gesicht des Dritten Reiches. Profile einer totalitären Herrschaft* [*The Face of the Third Reich: Portraits of the Nazi Leadership*] (Fest 1963; Fest 1970). His was an in-depth character study of the leading figures of the Nazi movement that collectively presented a clearer picture of the *Zeitgeist* in Germany during the interwar period that no biography of any individual Nazi figure has produced, to date. The following short biographies of some of the more prominent members of the Thule Society who became influential figures in the Nazi movement are excerpts from Fest's *The Face of the Third Reich,* as well as other publicly available sources. The membership list comes from von Sebottendorff's *Bevor Hitler kam* (Munich: Deukula Verlag Grassinger & Co., 1933).

DRAMATIS PERSONÆ

ANTON DREXLER (1884–1942) – WAS BORN IN MUNICH ON 13 June 1884. Drexler was a machine-fitter before becoming a railway toolmaker and locksmith in Berlin. Deemed physically unfit to join the ranks of soldiers fighting in the First World War, he joined the German Fatherland Party. Drexler is usually depicted as a naïve and unworldly character who gladly became the tool of more ambitious figures. Anton Drexler was a man of proletarian background. His father had been a Social Democrat; his anti-Marxism resulted from negative encounters with trade unions, and his anti-Semitism came from a period of employment under a brutal Jewish cattle dealer. Barred for a time from his trade, he earned a living by playing a zither in cafes. After causing a minor stir for writing a pro-war article in the *Münchener Zeitung* in January 1918, the Munich railroad repairman set up in Berlin on 7 March 1918 the *Freier Arbeiterausschuss für einen guten Frieden* (Free Workers' Committee for a Good Peace), a branch of the North German Association for the Promotion of Peace along Working Class Lines. "We were all poor, powerless, unknown," Drexler later recalled. (Luhrssen 2012, 153.) The organization he founded was small as well as unknown. At its inception in March 1918, the committee numbered only twenty-seven men, most of them Drexler's coworkers. After Drexler penned a few more articles for the *Münchener Zeitung*, membership climbed to around forty by October. However, the chaos that existed in post-war Weimar Germany meant that the country was littered with many small groups that classed themselves as political parties. Drexler's Free Workers' Committee was one of many in Berlin. Drexler eventually left Berlin to return home to Munich where he joined the Thule Society. He befriended fellow Thulist Karl Harrer who convinced him to join their efforts in forming a political party. In Munich in *Fürstenfelderhof* hotel on 5 January 1919, together with fellow Thule Society members Gottfried Feder and Dietrich Eckart, Drexler decided to merge his Free Workers' Committee with the larger Political Workers' Circle, led by sports journalist and Thule Society member Karl Harrer. Once joined together, they adopted a new name for their organization: *Deutsche Arbeiterpartei* (*DAP*, German Workers Party)—whose idea was to form an organization that would "combat the Marxism of the free trade unions" and to agitate for a "just" peace for Germany. His long-term objective was to create a party which would be both working class and *völkisch* Nationalist. He promoted the concept that there existed a diabolical Jewish-Capitalistic-Masonic conspiracy which had to be counteracted. He saw on the one side the innocent German worker, farmer, and soldier; on the other the common enemy . . . Capitalist Jews (as opposed to Marxist Bolshevik Jews). Initially, its small group of faithful followers—workmen, craftsmen, members of the lower-middle-class—assembled each week in the Leiber Room of the *Sternecker-Bräu* "for the discussion and study of political matters." The trauma of the lost war, anti-Semitic feelings, and complaints about the snapping of all the "bonds of order, law and morality" set the tone of its meetings. It stood for the dissemination of the idea of a National Socialism "led only by German leaders" and aiming at the "ennoblement of the German worker"; instead of socialization it called for profit-sharing, demanded the formation of an association for national unity, and proclaimed that its "duty and task" was "to educate its members in an ideal sense and raise them up to a higher conception of the world." It was not so much a political party in the usual sense, as a mixture of secret society and drinking club typical of the Munich of those years; it did not address itself to the public. Obscure visionaries would hold forth to the thirty or forty who had gathered together, discuss Germany's disgrace and rebirth, or write postcards to like-minded societies in northern Germany.

The party's ideas captivated Hitler when under assignment he began attending *DAP* meetings on 12 September 1919, as a liaison officer (*Verbindungsmann*) of a reconnaissance detail (*Aufklärungskommando*) in the Intelligence Division's Education and Propaganda Department (Ib/P) of the *Vorläufige Reichswehr* (Provisional National Defense) Group Headquarters 4 (Bavaria) during the early Weimar Republic. The mission of Department Ib/P was to influence other soldiers against joining Marxist groups and to infiltrate movements such as the *DAP*. At the time, Hitler was still enlisted and serving in the army until his formal discharge on 13 March 1920 (2,050 days of military service).

On 12 September, Gottfried Feder spoke on "How and by what means is Capitalism to be eliminated?" When in the ensuing discussion a visitor demanded that Bavaria should break away from the *Reich*, Hitler attacked him so violently that Drexler whispered to a neighbor, "My, he's got the gift of the gab. We could use him." When Hitler soon afterwards left the "dreary society," Drexler hurried after him and asked him to come back soon. He pressed into Hitler's hand a small pamphlet written by himself, *Mein politisches Erwachen* (*My Political Awakening*), and evidently arranged for him to receive un-requested, a few days later, a membership card numbered 555. Having nothing else to do, Hitler attended a few more meetings. At his instigation, on 16 October 1919, the little party risked a meeting in the *Hofbräukeller*. One hundred and eleven people turned up, and Hitler rose to address his first public meeting as the second speaker of the evening. In a bitter stream of words, the dammed-up emotions and the lonely man's suffocated feelings of hatred and impotence burst out. Like an explosion after the restriction and apathy of the past years, hallucinatory images and accusations came pouring out. Abandoning restraint, Hitler talked until he was sweating and exhausted. "I talked for thirty minutes," he recalled in *Mein Kampf*, "and what I had always felt deep down in my heart, without being able to put it to the test, was here proved to be true" (Hitler 1942, 278). Jubilantly he made the overwhelming, liberating discovery. "I could make a good speech!"

The small number of party members were quickly won over to Hitler's political beliefs. He organized their biggest meeting yet of 2,000 people, for 24 February 1920 in Munich's *Staatliches Hofbräuhaus*. To make the party more broadly appealing to larger segments of the population, the *DAP* was renamed the *Nationalsozialistische Deutsche Arbeiterpartei* (*NSDAP*, National Socialist German Workers [Nazi] Party) on 24 February. Such was the significance of Hitler's publicity stunt that Karl Harrer resigned from the party in disagreement. As Hitler gained more influence and power in the party, Anton Drexler became more and more marginalized, eventually resigning from *NSDAP* after the failed Beer Hall *Putsch* in November 1923. In April 1924, Drexler was elected to the Bavarian *Landtag* representing the People's Bloc. From 1924 to 1930, Drexler steered clear of the Nazi Party and he played no part in the party's political comeback in 1925. After the reorganization of the *NSDAP* in February 1925, Drexler became one of Hitler's opponents. Reportedly, their dispute was over long-term political objectives.

> Hitler was as much interested in the working class and the lower middle class as Drexler, but he had no more sympathy for them than he had had in Vienna: he was interested in them as material for political manipulation. Their grievances and discontents were the raw stuff of politics, a means, but never an end. Hitler had agreed to the socialist clauses of the programme, because in 1920 the German working class and the lower middle classes were saturated in a radical anti-capitalism; such phrases were essential for any politician who wanted to attract their support. But they remained phrases. (Bullock 1962.)

There was an attempt in 1930 to reabsorb Drexler into the much larger Nazi Party but it came to naught. However, Drexler did rejoin the party in 1933 and was awarded the "Blood Order" badge in 1934. The badge was considered the highest honor a Nazi Party member could be given but in Drexler's case the whole process was done merely for propaganda purposes as opposed to Hitler wanting to rekindle any true relationship with Drexler. After this, Drexler became an obscure figure within Nazi Germany. Anton Drexler died in Munich on 24 February 1942.

Karl Harrer (1890–1926) – a German journalist, politician, and in partnership with Anton Drexler, Gottfried Feder, and Dietrich Eckart, he established the *Deutsche Arbeiterpartei* (*DAP*, German Workers Party). Harrer was "commissioned" by the Thule Society to try and politically influence German workers in Munich after war to sway them from swelling the ranks of Communist parties and organizations. At the time, Harrer was a reporter for the Nationalist publication *Münchner-Augsburger Abendzeitung* (*Munich-Augsburg Evening Times*). Harrer convinced Anton Drexler and several others to form the *Politischer Arbeiterzirkel* (Political Workers'

Circle) in 1918. The members met periodically for discussions with themes of Nationalism and racism directed against the Jews. Although Harrer preferred that the small group remain a semi-secret Nationalistic club, Drexler wanted to make it a political party. Thereafter, Drexler proposed the founding of the *DAP* in December 1918. On 5 January 1919, the *DAP* was formed in Munich. With the *DAP* founding, Drexler was elected chairman and Harrer was given the honorary title of "*Reich* Chairman." Harrer became increasingly unhappy with the direction in which the party was going after Adolf Hitler became an influential force within it. Early in 1920, Hitler moved to sever the party's link with the Thule Society, and to redefine the policies of the *DAP*. On 24 February 1920, in the *Staatliches Hofbräuhaus* in Munich, Hitler, for the first time, enunciated the Twenty-Five Points of the *DAP* manifesto that had been drawn up by Drexler, Feder, and Hitler. The program contained twenty-five articles, and was anti-Semitic, anti-Capitalist, anti-Democratic, anti-Marxist, and anti-Liberal. The same day, the party changed its name by adding two words: "National" and "Socialist" either at Hitler's suggestion or over his objection—the history remains unclear on this matter. Hitler had always been hostile to Socialist ideas, especially those that involved racial or sexual equality. However, Socialism was a popular political movement in Germany after the First World War. This was reflected in the growth in the German Social Democrat Party (*SPD*), the largest political party in Germany. Hitler, therefore redefined Socialism by placing the word "National" before it. He claimed he was only in favor of equality for those who had "German blood." Jews and other "aliens" would lose their rights of citizenship, and immigration of non-Germans should cease. At the *Hofbräuhaus* meeting on 24 February 1920, Hitler changed the name of the party to *Nationalsozialistische Deutsche Arbeiterpartei* (*NSDAP*, National Socialist German Workers' [Nazi] Party). The new name was borrowed from an Austrian party active at the time (*Deutsche Nationalsozialistische Arbeiterpartei*, German National Socialist Workers' Party), although Hitler earlier suggested the party to be renamed the "Social Revolutionary Party"; it was Sudeten German Rudolf Jung who persuaded Hitler to adopt the *NSDAP* naming. Expanding the party's public profile in this way finally moved Harrer to resign from the party in disagreement, as he had always believed that it should be a semi-secret elite group rather than a mass popular movement. The Thule Society subsequently fell into decline, and went silent about six years later, well before Hitler came to power in the German government in 1933. Karl Harrer died of natural causes in Munich on 5 September 1926 at the age of thirty-five-years.

Dietrich Eckart (1868–1923) – the "spiritual father of National Socialism." Accurate analysis of the background and character of Dietrich Eckart is as complex as that of Adolf Hitler. Much has been written in an attempt to understand Hitler; little western scholarship exists on Eckart. Both men deserve a dedicated in-depth appraisal (a psychological autopsy) to truly understand the ideological origins of the Nazi movement. Much of the following biographical information is taken from Joseph Howard Tyson's *Hitler's Mentor: Dietrich Eckart, His Life, Times, & Milieu* (Bloomington, IN: iUniverse, 2008), unless otherwise referenced.

Johann Dietrich Eckart was born on 23 March 1868 in Neumarkt in der Oberpfalz, an Upper Palatinate town of 4,500 residents near Nuremberg. His mother, Anna Bosner Eckart, was the daughter of a Bavarian Army quartermaster. She tried to raise Dietrich and his three siblings as Catholics, though her husband was Evangelical Lutheran. Her youngest child, a daughter, died as a young child. Dietrich suffered from a variety of illnesses. Family members recollected that his mother always seemed to be nursing him back to health. Anna has been described as a dreamy and sensitive soul. Unfortunately, this delicate *hausfrau* died of influenza in her thirties during the winter of 1878. Ten-year-old Dietrich never recovered psychologically from that blow. Episodes of depression plagued him for the rest of his life.

Dietrich's father, Georg Christian Eckart, practiced law and served as Neumarkt's royal notary. In 1888, Prince Regent Luitpold appointed him a district justice. Christian Eckart had a reputation for being tough but fair. Judge Eckart assumed a dictatorial mien and treated local farmers as country bumpkins. Dietrich later emulated his father's decisiveness, air of authority, and readiness to pass judgment on others.

Eckart senior's professional duties completely preoccupied him. In 1879, one year after his wife's death, he accepted a civil service post in Nuremberg, twenty miles northwest from Neumarkt in der Oberpfalz. Like most workaholics, Georg Christian left something to be desired as a father, alternately ignoring and browbeating Dietrich and Dietrich's brother Wilhelm. A Franconian Lutheran himself, the brusque official neglected his sons' Catholic education when his wife died. They could empathize with criminals brought before their father, who viewed him as arbitrary and reluctant to temper justice with mercy. Possibly due to his mother's coddling, restraints of any kind were always onerous to Dietrich. Despite his intelligence, he became a disciplinary problem at several different schools.

Adversaries could quickly provoke his volatile temper and sharp tongue. He found it difficult to follow rules. Members of a rival political party later dubbed this tough guy as "the man with elephant skin," but his rough exterior concealed a hypersensitive psyche. Dietrich's chronic misbehavior resulted in expulsion from a school in Nuremberg circa 1884. Georg Christian then sent him to Schwabach's *Lateinschule*. When he found himself in trouble there, Judge Eckart enrolled his obstreperous son at Regensburg *Realgymnasium*, from where he finally graduated.

Twenty-year-old Dietrich went off to the University of Erlangen in 1888. At his father's insistence, he studied law, but hated the subject. Eckart's lifelong abhorrence of lawyers stemmed in part from resentment toward his father. He changed his major to medicine and transferred to Ludwig Maximilian University of Munich where he joined his father's old dueling fraternity, The Onoldia Corps Erlangen (originally founded by Carl Freiherr von Pollnitz in 1798). Onoldia Corps fostered Eckart's life-long penchants for drinking, male camaraderie, song, and factionalism. German dueling fraternities served as hothouses for German Nationalism and anti-Semitism. Although it had more of a reputation for partying than political activism, Onoldia Corps adopted the Teutonia Fraternity's "Aryan Clause" of 1877 which barred Jews and foreigners from membership.

While at Erlangen, Eckart proposed to the daughter of a local schoolteacher. When the girl's father learned of the engagement, he broke it off immediately. This involuntary separation from a beloved female rekindled the trauma of his mother's untimely death, triggering a nervous breakdown that required hospitalization in a private sanitarium. During his confinement, Eckart wrote an article entitled "Hypnosis and the Novel" for Rudolf Heinrich Greinz's *Cultural & Literary Illustrated*. He theorized that the fictional characters dreamed up in creative "trance states" often represented authors' own alter egos. This topic suggests that Eckart underwent hypnosis therapy in the course of his treatment—fashionable among physicians and psychiatrists in several European countries, including Germany, during the late 1880s and early 1890s, having been imported from France by visitors to neurologist Hippolyte Bernheim's clinic in Nancy, France.

Dietrich Eckart became addicted to morphine in his early 20s. His friend Albert Reich claimed that a doctor administered the drug to treat a serious illness. Another story alleged that Eckart had access to morphine as a medical student. To deaden the pain of depression he sampled the drug and soon became hooked. Whatever the circumstances, his father had to send him back to the sanitarium for nearly two years. Eckart battled morphine dependency for the rest of his life. He would kick the habit a while, then go back to it. About his narcotic use Alfred Rosenberg wrote:

> Without his sweet poison he could not live, and applied the whole cunning of a possessor of this craving to get himself dose after dose. Eventually he was taking measures from which a normal man, not (endowed with) such bear-like strength, would have died (Webb 1976, 283; see also Rosenberg 1928).

Eckart was a cultured man, well-versed in works by Plutarch, Plato, Luther, Angelus Silesius, Pascal, de Spinoza, Shakespeare, Ibsen, von Goethe, Kant, Nietzsche, Schopenhauer, Heine, and von Bismarck. However, he could not resist the temptation to dip into sub-literature such as the anti-Semitic writings of German biblical scholar, orientalist, and pan-German Paul Anton de Lagarde (born Böttischer, 1827–1891), the bogus psychology of Jewish Austro-Hungarian philosopher Otto Weininger (1880–1903), the pseudo-scientific theories of German biologist, naturalist, philosopher, and physician Ernst Haeckl (1834–1919), and the Ariosophy fantasies of Guido von List. Of the mainstream thinkers, German Jewish-Lutheran Romantic poet, journalist, essayist, and literary critic Heinrich Heine (1797–1856), Dutch-German philosopher Arthur Schopenhauer (1788–1860), and German Catholic priest (converted from Lutheranism), physician, mystic, and religious poet Angelus Silesius (1624–1677) exerted the most influence on him as a young man.

In the course of his unsystematic reading at the University of Erlangen, Eckart discovered Heinrich Heine and Arthur Schopenhauer, two authors of opposite temperament. The German-Jewish poet Heinrich Heine was his first literary model. He admired the "realistic Romanticism" espoused by Heine's Young Germany movement, and his original style, which creatively utilized irony, slang, and poetic license. Like Heine, Eckart was attracted to poetry, theater, journalism, and philosophy. In later years, Eckart would repudiate the hero of his youth, as well as his own juvenile Liberalism. Though he outgrew his enthusiasm for Heine, the pessimism of Arthur Schopenhauer's philosophy stayed with Eckart for life. Eckart also became an avid admirer of Wagner's operas, particularly *Tannhäuser*, as a young man.

In adolescence, Eckart found Jews exotic and intriguing. As the years went on and under the growing influence of anti-Jewish sentiment in the writings of de Lagarde and French ultramontane Catholic Henri-Roger Gougenot des Mousseaux (1805–1876), and the operas of German composer Wilhelm Richard Wagner (1813–1883), the Jewish image morphed into his nemesis, an alien "alter ego" which he reviled. Eckart lapped up the scathing misrepresentations of Gougenot des Mousseaux, paying special heed to his prophecy that Jews would create much mischief in Germany, then suffer a devastating payback in return. During the early 1920s Eckart persuaded Alfred Rosenberg to translate Gougenot's 1869 book *Le Juif, le judaïsme et la judaïsation des peuples chrétiens* (*The Jew, Judaism and the Judaization of Christian Peoples*) into German under the new title, *The Eternal Jew*.

Eckart moved to Berlin in the autumn of 1899. Germany's new capital, with its forty theaters, plethora of newspapers, and world-class orchestra, had become the empire's cultural center. Thirty-four-year-old Eckart turned into an intellectual thug by 1902. His excessive drinking produced characteristic behavioral changes: egocentricity, mood swings, excitability, strong biases, and a propensity to turn against former friends. He had the alcoholic's tender and swollen ego, which made him unable to accept criticism, and quick to blame others for his problems. Fault-finding became his *modus operandi*. To preserve his own unassailable dignity he tore down others, including close associates. During his Berlin period, Eckart decided that his career setbacks were not due to personal shortcomings, but the pernicious influence of Jewish-controlled media. Ugly words such as "stooges" and "Judenkitsch" crept into his vocabulary. Though he did not yet have the temerity to attack individual Jews by name in signed articles, Eckart employed such derogatory terms as "yids" and "slick Cohns" (Engelman 1971, 42).

Between 1906 and 1910 Eckart led a threadbare existence, surviving by freelance writing, pawnshop barter, hand-outs from friends, and credit extended by the owner of the *Alt Bayern* pub on *Potsdammerstraße*, where he was a regular. Painter, graphic artist, draftsman, and illustrator Albert Reich grew up with Eckart in Neumarkt in der Oberpfalz and reconnected with him in the Steglitz section of southwestern Berlin. According to Reich, Eckart occupied various tenements during his "Hunger Years." The many different return addresses on Eckart's correspondence with Georg Graf von Hülsen-Haeseler (superintendent of The Royal State Theater in Berlin) indicated frequent changes of residence between 1905 and 1910. For a while he shared a "rear bachelor flat" in The Black Piglet Rooming House at 11

Felderstraße with an impecunious actor named Otto Fitzsche, and Paul Haase, an underemployed painter. Eckart's niece, *Frau* Claire Lormer-Schneider, heatedly denied rumors that her uncle had lived like a bum in Berlin. On 31 January 1936, she sent a letter to the National Socialist Archive insisting that Eckart never had to bunk on park benches, since loving family members resided in a comfortable suburb of Berlin. However, his friend Albert Reich claimed that during the lowest period, circa 1908, Eckart occasionally slept on a "favorite park bench" (Reich 1933, 60) in Berlin's Tiergarten (zoological gardens.)

In the course of his 1906–1910 downward spiral, friends mailed Eckart "care packages" containing toiletries, food, and Schnapps. He freeloaded on his brother Wilhelm and family in Döberlitz for weeks at a time. While there, he developed closer relationships with nephew Hans and nieces Claire and Mitzi. Though Eckart never suffered from physical starvation during the "Hunger Years," his longing for professional fulfillment went unsatisfied. These failure pangs, combined with feelings of being wronged, scarred him for life, and intensified his revulsion toward Jews.

To his young friend Xaver Steinbach in Neumarkt in der Oberpfalz he wrote that he might adopt a "Jewish pseudonym" (Plewnia 1970, 20) in order to win over the critics. Believing himself to be an unappreciated genius, Eckart let his anti-Semitic prejudices burgeon between 1902 and 1918. He joined the Nationalistic *Fichte-Bund*, Theodor Fritsch's anti-Semitic *Hammerbund*, and studied the racial theories of Guido von List and Jörg Lanz von Liebenfels. His paranoia about Jews repeatedly surfaced in letters to von Hülsen-Haeseler: "the enemies of my convictions, that is, the Jews, are everywhere I go—busy with their crafty work" (Plewnia 1970, 57). He thought they would cause him to have another nervous collapse. In an apparent cry from the heart, Eckart subsequently wrote that Jews drove "men to despair, to madness, to ruin" (Eckart 1966, section VIII). Traumatized by early twentieth-century Germany's accelerating pace of change, he blamed the disconnectedness of contemporary life on Jewish influence.

Roommate Otto Fritzsche noticed Eckart's extreme moodiness. He would be affable one day, and anti-social the next. By 1909 "his sense of shame and rage led him to withdraw progressively into a small group of intimates. . . . He developed a habit of locking himself in his room and refusing to see anyone in order to avoid creditors, publishers, agents, and all others to whom he had obligations" (Engelman 1971, 60). Eckart's manic depression produced mood swings that made him a truculent blowhard one day and shrinking violet the next. After his relationship with a seventeen-year-old named Eleonore unraveled, he again slid into the "Slough of Despond," moping in his room for days. One of his neighbors, architect Ernst Rossius-Rhyn, observed that he seemed "a most lonely man . . . always sunk in his thoughts . . ." (Engelman 1971, 15). Physically ravaged by substance abuse, dejected about his stalled career and failed romance, Eckart again checked into an asylum (Tyson 2008, 20).

In the fall of 1911, Dietrich Eckart finished his "translation" of Henrik lbsen's *Peer Gynt*. Since he knew only a smattering of Norwegian, Eckart did not translate the play but transliterated the earlier German versions of Louis Lassarge and Christian Morgenstern. He rendered the dialogue into rhymed couplets and transformed the work from an adult fairy tale to a racist allegory. It would take him another three years to market this work. Based on a Scandinavian folk tale, *Peer Gynt* presented a humorous but pessimistic view of the human condition. On his sojourn through our mad world protagonist Peer, a compound of animal and angel, veered between criminal and virtuous behavior. The work appealed to Eckart on multiple levels. Eckart took liberties with the play. He consciously transformed the trolls into Jewish caricatures and insisted that Yiddish actor Max Pohl be cast as the troll king. Ibsen characterized Peer as a Norwegian peasant engaged in picaresque misadventures while vainly striving to become "World Emperor." Eckart changed him into a rustic sage—the antithesis of modern phonies. This re-invented Peer came across as a humorously unpretentious Nordic always in touch with his *völkisch* roots. In one passage, Ibsen's Peer stated that he learned "patience" from the Jews. Eckart's version substituted the word "cunning."

The Jewish firm of S. Fischer Verlag owned rights to Christian Morgenstern's 1880 German translation of *Peer Gynt*. Fischer Verlag refused Eckart the rights to stage his version of the play. Eckart raised money to incorporate Herold Verlag and published the play at his own expense. His friend Georg von Hülsen-Haeseler staged the first production in February 1914. *Peer Gynt* turned out to be a big hit. However, many critics, including Jewish editors Julius Bab and Fritz Engel condemned Eckart's translation as a bungled job, untrue to the original. They realized that he had smuggled in pan-German sentiments and transformed Peer from Ibsen's impish peasant into a Faustian figure. Jewish reviewer Siegfried Jacobsohn "ridiculed The Royal Theater's pretense of modernity by presenting Eckart's adulterated rendition of Peer Gynt" (Engelman 1971, 75).

Former Onoldia Corps swordsman Eckart could not allow such insults to go unanswered. Baron Wolfgang Graf von Gersdorff, a Royal Theater official, counseled him to remain above the fray. "Let these Jewish dogs howl," he wrote. Incapable of restraint, Eckart furiously scribbled a 104-page pamphlet, "Ibsen, Peer Gynt, the Boyg, & I," which maligned his Hebrew detractors. Eckart's vanity press, Herold Verlag, published this diatribe. Because the "Jewish literary Mafia" denied him a voice, he once again had to resort to a "tribune outside existing institutions." His subsidy publishing followed a pattern of increasing virulence, beginning with Eckart's innocuous book on Heine in 1893, continuing through his drama career, *Auf gut Deutsch* period, and ending with final testament, "Bolshevism from Moses to Lenin." (Tyson 2008, 51.)

Despite the carping of critics, Eckart's version of *Peer Gynt* delighted audiences and lifted him from rags to riches. Kaiser Wilhelm saw it twice. Between 1914 and 1918, Berlin's *Königliches Schauspielhaus* theater put on 183 performances to packed houses. The play toured all over Germany and was translated into Czech, Hungarian, and Dutch. In 1919, *Peer Gynt* ran continuously in twelve cities. Ten of those theaters utilized Eckart's version, two used Morgenstern's translation. Nationalist critic Paul Schulze-Berghof weighed in with qualified praise but cautioned that Eckart and Ibsen were Jeremiahs (prophets of doom), not messiahs who could show a better way. Hitler's personal library contained a leather-bound edition of *Peer Gynt* illustrated by Otto Sager and signed by Eckart who wrote: "intended for my dear friend Adolf Hitler, Dietrich Eckart, Munich, 22 October 1921." The resounding commercial success of *Peer Gynt* bailed Eckart out. He paid off an estimated 11,000 Marks in debts and received a steady income from royalties for the rest of his life. (Tyson 2008, 51–2.)

Eckart ended up a law school and medical school dropout, playwright, poet, journalist, politician, and recovering alcohol and morphine addict. Since late 1913, Eckart had been living in Munich with his new wife Rose and her three daughters from a previous marriage. Generally regarded as a likeable rogue, Eckart had no trouble making friends in the Bavarian capital. He felt right in at the famous Schwabing Quarter—a "Greenwich Village" where artists, writers, philosophers, and political radicals gathered every night to drink and talk into the early hours. Beginning in 1916, Eckart made the transition from drama to politics and built a reputation as a defender of traditional German culture. While the war continued, Eckart became involved in November 1916 in launching an abortive Nationalist periodical, *Unser Vaterland*, published by Julius Lehmann. The publication was short lived and apparently suppressed by government censors (Engelman 1971, 42). He would enjoy greater success in newspaper publishing in the revolutionary upheaval of postwar Bavaria, where he launched a periodical called *Auf gut Deutsch.* Its early editions (December 1918), produced at Thule's office,* were written almost entirely by Eckart in his characteristically earthy, mocking style. Soon enough he attracted other writers from his circle, including Feder. For Eckart, Germany's cultural, political, and international problems stemmed from a common source, the Jews. Like the Ariosophists, Eckart proclaimed a German-Jewish polarity representing opposing values of idealism and materialism. Along with letters from readers and opinion pieces on current events, *Auf gut Deutsch* published Eckart's poems and scenes from his plays. Of these publications, Professor and Chair of Journalism and Communication Studies at Long Island University Ralph Engelman writes, "In its pages Eckart outlined a comprehensive anti-Semitic *Weltanschauung* which had previously been expressed in an incomplete and symbolic form in his plays" (Engelman 1971, 125). For the first time in his writings he denounced individual Jews such as Trotsky, Eisner, and Rathenau. Companions observed that the patriotic bard constantly smoked cigars and sipped beverages. While examining Eckart's papers in 1969, Ralph Engelman noticed that most of them were "pocked with wine or coffee stains" (Engelman 1971, 125), because he usually wrote at tavern tables. Rumor had it that in 1919 he had dashed off his famous poem *Feuerjo!* (*Fire!*) that in 1922 became the Nazi *SA* battle cry (*Sturmlied* [Assault Song]) and Nazi Party anthem (1923–1930) in one sitting at the *Bratwurstglockl Café* (Tyson 2008, 53).

---

* This despite a dispute between von Sebottendorff and Eckart over who would finance the paper. Eventually, Eckart received 10,000 Marks from Hans Duchner, publisher of the *Münchener Zeitung*. The industrialist Wolfgang Kapp, who would lead a failed *putsch* against the Weimar Republic, donated 1,000 Marks. Other funds were provided by the tireless Captain Mayr through the good offices of the *Vorläufige Reichswehr*'s District IV Command. An additional 25,000 Marks came from the printer of *Auf gut Deutsch*, who in exchange was made a partner in Eckart's publisher *Hoheneichen Verlag*. The premiere issue of *Auf gut Deutsch* was mailed to 25,000 addresses. (Plewnia 1970, 33; von Sebottendorff 1933, 77–8; Engelman 1971, 103–4.) *Auf gut Deutsch* attracted such writers as the *Germanenorden*'s founder, Theodore Fritsch, dramatist Ernst Wachler, a List Society member, and List's ardent admirer, the *völkisch* author Ellegaard Ellerbek, who claimed that Germans were descendants of the old Nordic gods. (Luhrssen 2012, 254.)

As defeat in the First World War became more and more evident, anger, chaos, and armchair politics sprouted in every beerhall, social club, and household across Germany. Germany's defeat, announced on 11 November 1918, radicalized Eckart. Like many of his fellow Germans, Eckart joined the fledgling postwar Nationalist anti-Jewish political club *Deutschvölkischer Schutz- und Trutzbund*, as well as the Thule Society. It was after joining the Thule Society that Eckart founded and edited the anti-Semitic periodical *Auf gut Deutsch, Wochenschrift für Ordnung und Recht* (*In Plain German, A Weekly for Order and Law*) in December 1918, which would elucidate Germany's plight with utter frankness in the tone of Viennese pan-German anti-Semite Georg von Schönerer's (1842–1921) virulently Nationalist newspaper *Unvefälschte Deutsche Worte* (*Unadulterated German Words*), and Heinrich Claß's 1912 blunt imperialist pan-German anti-Semitic potboiler *Wenn ich der Kaiser wär* (*If I were Kaiser*) (Tyson 2008, 130).

Eckart worked on the paper with fellow Thulists Alfred Rosenberg and Gottfried Feder. A fierce critic of the German Revolution and the Weimar Republic, Eckart vehemently opposed the Treaty of Versailles, which he viewed as treason, and was an advocate of General Erich Ludendorff's so-called "stab-in-the-back legend" (*Dolchstoßlegende*), according to which the Social Democrats and Capitalist Jews were to blame for Germany's defeat in the war. In his scandalous tabloid *Auf gut Deutsch*, Eckart put a face on modern day angst by making the enemy palpable. *Auf gut Deutsch* notified patriotic Germans of an unfolding "pan-Jewish World Conspiracy." Eckart censured Jews for undermining national morale and accused them of masterminding the Bolshevik Revolution, which now spread like a cancer toward Germany (Tyson 2008, 132). In his mind, "the Jew" had mobilized the destructive forces of finance Capitalism, Bolshevism, Democracy, and technological mass culture to destroy "the good old days." Eckart believed that removing the Jewish spirit from Europe would solve this crisis, and thereby transfigure Germany into an Aryan Utopia. With a Nationalist mailing list in hand, Eckart sent out 25,000 copies of *Auf gut Deutsch* on 7 December 1918. Over the next two and one-half years, he published fifty-six issues, totaling 1,500 pages, for fifty *pfennigs* per copy. By 1920, *Auf gut Deutsch* had a circulation of approximately 30,000 (Tyson 2008, 132).

Auf gut Deutsch's lead article "Men!" declared that Germany needed a statesman of von Bismarck's caliber to lead it out of perdition. Unlike the current crop of petty politicians, the former Iron Chancellor refused to affiliate himself with any one party. Eckart, too, vowed to remain independent. "Whoever wants to help my effort is welcome. But I cannot bind myself to him: neither to any individual nor . . . party." Germany's multitudinous political parties merely raised weaklings to the heights. Despite Eckart's pledge of political neutrality, he soon plugged Anton Drexler's German Workers' Party, which sought "the ennoblement of the German worker . . . profit-sharing, not socialization . . . a full pot, prospering children" while combatting "usury . . . inflation, and drones . . . who create no value. . . ." Eckart promised that *Deutsche Arbeiterspartei* workers would form a protective rampart against Reds who took orders from Jewish Bolsheviks (Tyson 2008, 133).

Using his family's social connections, Eckart became a go-between for Bavaria's *völkisch* far right and its more pragmatic conservatives. After the Bavarian *Landtag* elections of January 1919, Eckart negotiated on behalf of Hans Georg Müller with Gustav Ritter von Kahr (1862–1934).[4] Müller proposed the union of his German Socialist Party (*DSP*) with von Kahr's Bavarian People's Party. Müller, a Thulist and an editor of the *Münchener Beobachter* (March 1919), formed the German Socialist Party (*Deutschsozialistische Partei*) in collaboration with his two coeditors, the Thulists Max Sesselman and Dr. Fritz Wieser. The German Socialists were yet another organization by which von Sebottendorff hoped to reach the working class, although its Gottfried Feder–based economic theory was indistinguishable from the ideology of the German Workers' Party (*DAP*). The German Socialists numbered in its rank the future *Mittelfranken Gauleiter* (Middle Franconia District Superintendent) Nazi Julius Streicher (see *infra*), the regional party boss whose pornographic anti-Semitic periodical *Der Stürmer* contributed so much to the obscenity of the Third *Reich* that the Nuremberg Tribunal sent him to the gallows. The German Socialist Party (*DSP*) voluntarily dissolved in December 1922 and advised its members to join the Nazis (Orlow 1969, 27, 42). Sesselman later marched with Hitler in the Beer Hall *Putsch*. (Luhrssen 2012, 157.)

On 5 January 1919, Eckart, Gottfried Feder, Anton Drexler, and Karl Harrer founded the German Workers' Party (*Deutsche Arbeiterspartei, DAP*). The recognized spiritual leader of this small group was Eckart, the journalist and poet, twenty-one years older than Hitler. After their meeting in September 1919, Eckart was by far the most influential figure in Hitler's early political life. The two were inseparable. Both men were self-educated bohemians who grew up in rural towns, then moved to big cities as young adults in attempts to fulfill artistic ambitions. They experienced setbacks that scarred them for life. Each man attributed his personal failures to the expanding power of Jews. The tragedy of the First World War and its harrowing aftermath further exacerbated their anti-Semitism. The journalist, Konrad Heiden, pointed out: "Eckart was the same sort of uprooted, agitated, and far from immaculate soul. . . . He could tell Hitler that he [like Hitler himself] had lodged in flop-houses and slept on park benches because of Jewish machinations which [in his case] had prevented him from becoming a successful playwright" (Heiden 1944). Alan Bullock, the author of *Hitler: A Study in Tyranny* (1962) agrees: "He [Eckart] talked well even when he was fuddled with beer and had a big influence on the younger and still very raw Hitler. He lent him books, corrected his style of expression in speaking and writing, and took him around with him." Eckart was described by Edgar Ansel Mowrer as "a strange drunken genius." His anti-Semitism likely arose from various esoteric schools of mysticism; he spent hours with Hitler discussing art and the place of the Jews in world history and has been called the "spiritual father of National Socialism." Hitler never forgot his early mentor, calling him his "North Star." Hitler spoke emotionally of his fatherly friend, and there were often tears in his eyes when he mentioned Eckart's name after his death.

In issues of *Auf gut Deutsch* published after the end of the Bavarian Soviet regime, when a common front against radical Liberals was no longer necessary, Eckart attacked the Roman Catholic Church and conservative, monarchist Bavarian separatists as well as Jews with increasing bitterness. All of these were to become favorite targets of the coming Nazi movement. In *Mein Kampf*, Hitler claimed to have shouted down a monarchist separatist, a spectator like himself, during his first visit to the German Workers' Party.

In May 1919, Eckart founded the Citizens' Union (*Bürgervereinigung*), an anti-Semitic league that aspired to bridge class differences between the proletariat and the *bourgeoisie*. In the group's manifesto, Eckart stressed that a German renewal could not occur unless Jews were stripped of economic and political power. The short-lived Citizens' Union met at Thule's office until it faded from existence in August 1919. Some of its members, including Fritz von Treutzschler, were veterans of the Thule Combat League and had helped Eckart circulate anti-Liberalism propaganda under the Bavarian Soviet Republic. The group never achieved its goal of reaching a broad constituency and was viewed by its founder as a failure. But the Citizens' Union had barely expired before Eckart pinned his hopes on another association, one that would prove more enduring. On 15 August 1919, the *völkisch* polemicist spoke for the first time before a meeting of the German Workers' Party (*DAP*). His topic was "Bolshevism and the Jewish Question." (Luhrssen 2012, 157.)

While it is true that the *DAP* was growing, the appearance of Eckart and Feder as speakers becomes less remarkable if one is cognizant of the role of the Thule Society as the network connecting Eckart and Feder with Drexler and Harrer. Eckart was not present at Hitler's first Workers' Party meeting on 12 September 1919 and missed all of the party's October sessions because of illness. Although the two men swam the same waters, it is not possible to positively link Hitler and Eckart until late November 1919, during the drafting of the party's program. (Luhrssen 2012, 160.)

Before meeting Hitler, Eckart was a successful playwright, especially with his 1912 adaptation of Henrik Ibsen's *Peer Gynt*, one of the best attended productions of the age with more than 600 performances in Berlin alone. In Eckart's version, the play became a powerful dramatization of *völkisch* Nationalist and anti-Semitic ideas, in which Gynt represents the superior Germanic hero, struggling against implicitly Jewish "trolls" and the Great Boyg—a clammy blob described as "not dead, not alive, . . . slimy, misty, shapeless . . . [which] wins without fighting." (To some, the Boyg represents society's resistance to excellence. In subsequent polemical writings, Eckart compared the Boyg to materialistic culture, which slowly suffocates individual creativity by its sheer bulk, thus preventing earth's "valley dwellers" from reaching the peaks of idealism.) As Ralph M. Engelman says, "Eckart meant his adaptation of *Peer Gynt* to represent a racial allegory in which the trolls and Great Boyg represented what [Otto] Weininger conceived to be the Jewish spirit." This success not only made Eckart wealthy, but it also gave him the social contacts that he later used to introduce Hitler to dozens of important German citizens. These introductions proved to be pivotal in Hitler's ultimate rise to power. It was Eckart who introduced his fellow Thulist Alfred Rosenberg to Adolf Hitler. Between 1920 and 1923, Eckart and Rosenberg labored tirelessly in the service of Hitler and the party. Through Rosenberg, Hitler was introduced to the anti-Jewish writings of the Germanophile racist British-born philosopher Houston Stewart Chamberlain (son-in-law of composer Wilhelm Richard Wagner), who was Rosenberg's inspiration. In his 1899 book, *Die Grundlagen des 19 Jahrhunderts* (*The Foundations of the Nineteenth Century*), Chamberlain demands the "elimination" of the "Jewish infection." In *Mein Kampf*, Hitler laments "the indifference with which governments passed by [Chamberlain's] observations" (Hitler 1942, 211–12).

DIETRICH ECKART'S ROLE IN RESHAPING HITLER'S ANTI-SEMITISM*

ACCORDING TO HERMANN ESSER, WHO WORKED UNDER ECKART AT THE *Völkischer Beobachter*, Eckart usually wrote in solitude, whether in hotels, his apartment, or corner bar table. He often revised articles in the evening, with a glass of wine within easy reach. Eckart rarely consulted others about subject matter and would not tolerate editorial corrections. Although historians refer to him as a journalist, melodramatic fiction remained his specialty. He was a propagandist who loved to pontificate. The discipline of journalism, with its painstaking corroboration and double-checking of facts and sources, bored him. he liked to gossip and pass off droll bar chat as truth. Opponents successfully sued Eckart for libel on several occasions. In his work as a newspaper columnist and book reviewer, he lapsed into the habit of voicing controversial opinions, without bothering to research alternative views. Like Hitler, he was essentially an indolent know-it-all, who wanted a forum for his Judeophobic prejudices.

Certain interrelated themes pervade Eckart's tabloid *Auf gut Deutsch*: the "stab-in-the-back legend," which held that Jews in government undercut Germany's war effort; Russian Bolshevik atrocity stories; calls for patriotic working men to establish an anti-Communist party; dire warnings about an International "Jewish Conspiracy"; and prophecies that a "God-sent *Führer* with lion heart" would one day lead Germany out of its current predicament.

Eckart read Houston Stewart Chamberlain's bestselling *Kriegsaufsätze* (*Wartime Essays*) in 1915. Another believer in the "Coming Great One," Chamberlain also advanced General Erich Ludendorff's "stab-in-the-back legend," postulating a conspiracy of "International Jews." According to Chamberlain, Jewish financiers incited the present crisis in order to garner spoils after racially related English, French, Germans, Austrians, and Russians exhausted themselves in a deadly, internecine conflict. Patriotism means loyalty to one's homeland. Eckart's Nationalism exaggerated and perverted that hallowed ideal. Going beyond defense of the fatherland, he preached xenophobia, anti-Semitism, and imperialism. Liberals who disagreed with his jingoism were branded as traitors.

Both Eckart and Gottfried Feder agreed with Chamberlain, claiming that Jews had long planned an unwinnable two front war in order to

---

* Excerpted from Tyson 2008, 135–44 with some minor corrections and additions.

overthrow the Hohenzollern Dynasty and grab power for themselves. Feder wrote: "with the cowardly bravery of assassins (they) felled a swaying giant from behind." Germany's conservatives—including the nobility, officer corps, and all Nationalistically-minded men—refused to participate in the surrender process, leaving that task to Socialist politicians such as Haase, Landauer, and Erzberger. When things turned out badly due to French Revanchism, these agents became scapegoats. In Ernst Nolte's words, Nationalists blamed "the bankruptcy receivers for the bankruptcy." According to Eckart, the same "backstabbing malefactors" who arranged Germany's capitulation then created the Weimar Republic in order to arrogate power to themselves. The November 1918 disaster enabled "Jewish plutocrats" to install this sham government. Its American-style electioneering process staged media extravaganzas to gull proles. Anyone seeking office had to spend large sums for campaigning. Politics had become a part of show business. "Jewish wire pullers" bought candidates the way studios signed film stars. As a theater veteran, Eckart resolved to beat them at their own game.

Eckart's anti-Semitic prejudices were delusional, but he passionately believed in them. The struggling playwright, who thought Jews had stymied his literary career, was convinced that these wily adversaries now plotted Germany's ruin. The Entente victory deposed Kaiser Wilhelm and launched Jews such as Kurt Eisner and Walter Rathenau into thankless positions of power. Jewish Minister of the Interior Hugo Preuß wrote the Weimar Republic's Constitution, which Eckart viewed as a liberal-sounding hoax whose real intention was to establish Jewish authoritarianism down the road. According to him the Weimar Republic had been foisted upon Germany by "materialists, opportunists, and half-natures . . . devoid of Aryan attributes. . . ."

Alfred Rosenberg and other Russian émigrés provided Eckart with sensational stories about "the kosher Christian-butchering dictatorship of the Jewish world savior, Lenin, and his Elijah, Trotsky-Bronstein." When Eckart discovered that Lenin was an atheist of mixed Russian, Calmuck, German, Jewish, and Swedish extraction, he revised his slur to "that Tartar Lenin." Like Karl Marx, many Bolshevik leaders fit into the Jewish Messianic tradition, even though they repudiated Judaism. *Auf gut Deutsch* never tired of repeating Rosenberg's charges that five out of the seven members comprising the first Politburo of the Central Committee of the Russian Social Democratic Labor Party, founded on 10 October 1917 to direct the Bolshevik Revolution, including Leon Trotsky (born Lev Davidovich Bronstein), Lev

Kamenev (born Lev Borisovich Rozenfeld, brother-in-law of Trotsky), Vladimír Lenin (born Vladimír Ilyich Ulyanov), Grigori Zinoviev (born Hirsch Apfelbaum), and Grigori Sokolnikov (born Girsh Jankelevich Brilliant) were all ethnic Jews. Moreover, several other ethnic Jews comprised the Central Committee and Secretariat of the Sixth Party Congress (July–August 1917), including Karl Radek (born Karol Sobelsohn), Jakov Sverdlov (who ordered the Romanov murders), and Moisei Solomonovich Uritsky. Former Georgian Orthodox seminarian Josef Stalin (born Ioseb Besarionis Djughashvili) employed the code term "Left oppositionists" and "rootless cosmopolitans" for Jews and persecuted them with gusto. During purges in the 1920s, 1930s, and 1948–1952, Stalin ordered the murder of most of the above-mentioned men, plus another 500,000 Jews (five percent of the Jewish population in the Soviet Union).

After World War I, Bolsheviks spread terror far and wide. Hungarian Béla Kun (born Kohn, 1886–1938) toppled Hungary's rickety government. He and twenty of his twenty-six ministers were Jewish. Jewish revolutionaries Rosa Luxemburg and her former lover Leon Jogiches agitated during Berlin's ill-fated Spartacist uprising of January 1919. Russian-Jewish expats Eugen Leviné, Towia Axelrod, Max Levien (non-Jew), and German-Jew Ernst Toller fomented Munich's April 1919 Communist Revolution and declared the Bavarian Soviet Republic. German-Jew Kurt Eisner declared on 8 November 1919 the Socialist People's State of Bavaria (*Volksstaat Bayern*). In the Autumn of 1920, Jewish Soviet leader Grigori Zinoviev persuaded Berlin's Independent Socialists to affiliate with Moscow. Eckart recycled the false rumor that British-Jewish financier Samuel Landman conspired with American-Jewish stock market wizard Bernard Baruch to bring America into the First World War. He alleged that their colleagues subsequently took advantage of the unjust Versailles Treaty to buy up grain, steel, coal, and other commodities from Germany at bargain basement prices. Army staff officers hailed Eckart as a seer for unveiling these insidious Jewish plots. The battered playwright savored his new-found aura of self-importance.

Eckart stressed that a Bolshevik Revolution in Germany could only be prevented by a united effort on the part of *völkisch* workers, tradesmen, army veterans, and landowners. He wanted to take a page out of the Bolshevik playbook. To recruit dissatisfied laborers, Eckart proclaimed the radical populist view that "skilled resident workers have the right to be considered members of the middle class." The proletariat must have a voice in the New Germany, whether the aristocracy liked it or not. Intending to lure the masses away from Communist agitators, Eckart wrote:

> Is the factory hand not a citizen? Is every propertied person a good-for-nothing Capitalist? Down with envy! Down with pomp and false appearances! Our aim is to regain simplicity and to be once more German. Our demand is true Socialism. Power should only be given to him who has German blood alone in his veins! (Heiden 1971, 9).

These socio-economic notions reflected Gottfried Feder's influence. He believed that Marxist diches such as *bourgeoisie* and "proletariat" had no factual basis; they were just Jewish propaganda terms designed to divide and conquer Germany's native *Volk*. Eckart echoed the pan-German anti-Semitic sentiments of Georg Ritter von Schönerer when he wrote: "We have been goaded long enough. Let only those of pure German blood have influence" (Nolte 1966, 328).

In this age of mob-rule, it was imperative to recruit Fritz and Otto from the local beer hall. Thirty years of pub-crawling had given Eckart a sure touch with the common man. Without condescension he could trade jibes and drink rounds with mechanics, bricklayers, and railroad workers. He possessed "extensive knowledge consonant with his prejudices" (Fest 1974, 133), and passed for a savant among laborers. Over mugs of *Pilsner* and goblets of *Riesling* he would regale boon companions of all classes with barstool humor, anecdotes, Jewish jokes, and anti-French epithets. He was a "big bear of a man, a roughhewn comical figure," (Fest 1974, 132) who guffawed loudly at his own witticisms. His creative use of obscenities impressed army sergeants. In spite of respectable middle-class origins, Eckart loved ribald stories and prided himself on his mastery of the vernacular.

To woo working men, Eckart and Feder founded the German Union for the Abolition of Interest Slavery in September 1919. According to them, "Mammonism" caused most ills on earth. They defined it as "international money power," combined with "the insatiable acquisitive urge based on a purely temporal view of life, which has led to an appalling degeneration of all moral standards" (Webb 1976, 291).

Under this system "a minority of drones" collected steadily increasing amounts of interest from working stiffs. Feder, an engineer who specialized in concrete construction, drew a distinction between "rapacious capital" that swindled Germany's masses and "productive capital," which created goods and jobs. He identified the former with Jewish financiers and the latter with native German industrialists. Every year workers slaved to raise twelve million dollars just to pay off interest charged by bankers. As a consequence of compounding, the amount multiplied geometrically each year. To end this massive rip-off, Feder proposed the abolition of loan capital—even though modern finance had funded Wilhelmine Germany's "economic miracle." Eckart dramatized Feder's economic theories for the readers of *Auf gut Deutsch*:

> The greatest curse is omitted from all interpretations of Germany's crisis, namely loan capital, (which) earns money without work, by virtue of interest. I repeat: without budging a finger the capitalist increases his fortune at the expense of society. (Engelman 1971, 128.)

Eckart did not really want to outlaw interest. Such imbecility would arrest growth, and benefit France, England, and other competing nations. His compromise solution called for a state-controlled bank. Somehow, he thought that government bureaucrats would do a better job than professional bankers, a delusion which betrayed his naivete in business matters.

In *Auf gut Deutsch*, Eckart repeatedly lashed out against usurers.

> The tormentor of the German people is international finance, a financial militarism. On God's earth there is no more cold-blooded criminality than (that) which hide(s) behind the invisible empire of global economics. With a complete lack of scruples which defies description…the furtive Princes of Gold mix their pernicious brew, which makes mankind not only serve them, but crazy and blind enough to mistake evil for good and good for evil.… The Great Hunchback, a Hydra sucking up millions of our people's savings through his many banks and fattening himself with ever-increasing influence. Go ahead and put your last dime down, what kind of interest do you get for it? A trifle! The Great Hunchback, however, bears fruit a hundredfold. Shut him out, bring the state to your side, and you will have a double benefit: you'll yield a better interest

> on your money, and the state, being better served, can therefore pay debts and relieve you of your burdens. (Eckart 1918.)

According to Eckart, speculators fomented World War I behind the scenes. Native German manufacturers should not be blamed, only members of the "Gold International."

> They play one people off against another, cheating both. For these drones German . . . people are just objects of speculation! Not by the presumption of the military were we betrayed, but above all by usury, again by usury, and a third time through usury did we lose our power. . . . What? Did we die for the benefit of loan sharks? (The) uncrowned kings of the stock exchange are the international enemies of peace and law . . . who sowed a storm to salvage the jetsam beached between corpses. (Eckart 1918.)

Eckart's florid rhetoric presented a distorted picture. Nearly five times more Gentiles were defense contractors than Jews. Among the principal ones were Krupp, Siemens, Mercedes-Benz, and Thyssen Steel Workers: all gentile firms. Jewish concerns accounted for a relatively small percentage of military supplies—mostly uniforms and foodstuffs. Few manufactured arms or munitions, though some furnished chemicals or high-tech components to Krupp, Skoda, and Siemens. Many Jewish bankers provided loans to corporations with army contracts, but this was done with the government's blessing.

The war hurt more Jews than it helped. Shipping magnate Albert Ballin's experience was more typical than the nameless "Jewish war profiteers" mentioned by Eckart. Ballin started out as a travel agent. By dint of intelligence and hard work he built Hamburg-America into a major ocean liner company. He pioneered the concept of pleasure cruises to the Mediterranean and Caribbean for wealthy customers. A staunch German patriot, Ballin advised both Kaiser Wilhelm and Admiral von Tirpitz on naval matters. However, the foolishness of letting Austria pull the *Reich* into a pointless war distressed him. His depression deepened when wartime operations ruined his business. On 9 November 1918, he ended his life by taking an overdose of sleeping pills.

Eckart failed to grasp the obvious fact that recession and inflation adversely affected Jews. The hyperinflation of 1923 reduced Franz Kafka and many others to destitution. Why "engineer" an economic catastrophe that wiped out the savings of one's own people? But common-sense verities did not interest Eckart. He stubbornly insisted that "Jewish bankers" and "armament company directors" were responsible for World War I and its aftermath. Because of them "twenty-two dynasties have fallen or are clinging desperately to crumbling rocks" (Eckart 1918).

In December 1918, Eckart wrote "The Boyg," an article in *Auf gut Deutsch* comparing Jewish Capitalism to the noxious mass of gook which entangled wayfarers in *Peer Gynt*'s Valley of the Trolls. People could not ascend to the heights when stifled by materialism. To combat this nuisance, he advocated Gottfried Feder's idea of nationalizing credit. Of course, such a "remedy" would have devastated Germany's economy. During the first week of April 1919, Feder, Rosenberg, and Eckart tossed copies of "To All Workers" out of taxicab windows. This incendiary pamphlet characterized the banking system as "a Hydra" (Eckart *Auf gut Deutsch* 5 April 1919) with voracious appetite for money. If working men and women realized this problem's severity, they would "join arms and throttle the monster before tomorrow." (Eckart *Auf gut Deutsch* 5 April 1919.) According to Eckart, the Rothschild family began its banking operations in 1806 with approximately 15,000 Marks provided by "the abdicating Elector of Hesse." By 1919, their assets exceeded forty billion, whereas Germany's entire industrial capital only amounted to about twelve billion.

> It sounds like the ravings of a madman, but it's true. . . . Your money (is) drawn into the coffers of these insatiable people . . . not only the Rothschilds, but the Mendelssohns, Bleichroders, Friedlanders, and Warburgs— to name only a few of the most important. (Eckart *Auf gut Deutsch* 5 April 1919.)

Eckart feared that these foreign oligarchs had enough money to "buy" Germany. "Interest slavery . . . enabled Jewry to capture the entire cultural apparatus: painting, music, poetry, theater, and cinema." (Engelman 1971, 182.)

Eckart's mythic analysis of foreign policy displayed an anti-Semitic bias. Giving a new wrinkle to the age-old German encirclement phobia from the Napoleonic era, he interpreted current conditions as a conspiracy against the *Reich* by western Jewish Capitalists—the Gold International, and eastern Jewish Bolsheviks the Red International, both of whom allegedly worked in concert. In November 1917, Russia fell to Bolsheviks of Jewish extraction. According to Alfred Rosenberg 432 of the 537 Soviet commissars were Jewish. Eckart averred in 1922, that "the toll of Russians sacrificed since the beginning of Bolshevik domination is estimated by . . . authorities at about 30 million," (Eckart 1924, 31) a phony statistic later quoted by Hitler in *Mein Kampf* (Hitler 1942, 256). He never mentioned that approximately ninety percent of Germany's 400 political murders between 1919 and 1922 were perpetrated by Nationalist reactionaries, not radical Liberals.

Eckart's exotic conspiracy theories reveal him more as a liar than "mythmaker." The majority of American Jews were pro-German between 1914 and 1916. They perceived Germany and Austria as relatively liberal toward Jewry, especially when compared to anti-Semitic powers such as Russia and France. In 1914, German intelligence officers on the Eastern Front actually distributed propaganda leaflets in Jewish communities claiming to be their liberators. In postwar plebiscites, the majority of Jews living in the Polish Corridor voted for re-unification with Germany.

In addition to churning out newspaper articles and delivering speeches, former Onoldia Corps Master of Ceremonies Eckart composed songs and poems to trumpet the cause of Nazism. In August 1921, he wrote *Feuerjo!* which later became the storm trooper's fight song *Sturmlied.* Hans Gansser, brother of Dr. Emil Gansser, put his lyrics to music in January 1923. Hitler designated it the Nazi Party's official anthem. When befuddled by booze, Eckart would recite poems or belt out songs before tavern crowds. Professor Karl Alexander von Müller recalled his karaoke performance at the *Hofbrauhaus* one night.

> I still can see the large room before me, and how . . . the red, glowing head of . . . stocky, short-necked Dietrich Eckart sprang from the podium onto a table; and with gestures of furious violence shouted his song "Germany Awake!" into the crowd, who upon receiving his words accompanied by a brass band, appeared in a state of paroxysm. (Plewnia 1970, 88.)

Like Wotan the Awakener, Eckart sought to rouse the German masses out of their slumber by loudly declaiming apocalyptic doggerel:

> *Sound the alarm and let the earth rise up*
> *At the sound of avenging thunder.*
> *Woe to the nation that still slumbers!*
> *Germany, awake!*
>
> *The serpent, the dragon from hell has broken loose!*
> *Stupidities and lies have burst his chains asunder. . . . Red as with blood are the heavens in flames, The rooftops collapse, a sight to appall. . . . Ring out for the assault, now or never. Germany, awake!* (Köhler 2001, 22).

Because of his cultured veneer, Eckart appealed not only to conservative businessmen, but well-educated young men like Kurt Georg Wilhelm Lüdecke and Ernst Hanfstaengl. In Lüdecke's words:

> Eckart outshone all the others with his wit and common sense. He spoke in a lumbering, blustering bass, looking positively benign with good humor. But his great round head, powerful forehead, strong nose and chin and piercing little eyes, indeed his whole person and carriage revealed a dominating personality. When he slipped his shell-rimmed glasses up to his forehead and peered at you, there was a depth of joviality behind his fierce front . . . (but) . . . later I saw him in a rage when he seemed like an irate Teuton god grim and formidable. (Lüdecke 1937, 83).

Ernst "Putzi" Hanfstaengl recalled him as "humorous, sensual, hard-hitting, and omniscient. . . . Dietrich Eckart, to whom I took a distinct liking looked like an old walrus." The grizzled denizen of Stinging Nettle Win; Cellar had fashioned himself into the image of Peer Gynt: a local sage with back-slapping jollity and salty manner of speaking.

Friends remembered him as a showman, wit, and promoter. Hitler himself appreciated Eckart's gifts as a salesman and fundraiser for the movement while recognizing his limitations as an administrator.

> Would I have entrusted the editorship of a . . . newspaper to Dietrich Eckart? From the financial point of view there'd have been a terrifying mess. One day the paper would . . . come out, the next day not. If there'd been a pig

> to share out . . . Eckart would have promised . . . 24 hams. (Such) men are made like that, but without them it's impossible to get anything started. (Hitler 1953, 156.)

Because of his journalistic notoriety, Eckart built up credibility as a free-floating consultant among *völkisch* groups in Munich. Bavarian *Freikorps* leaders solicited his input on how to effectuate a coalition among anti-Communist Germans of all classes. His political savvy and outgoing nature earned him a key role in forging the German Workers' Party alliance of workers, soldiers, and *petite bourgeoisie*.

Shortly thereafter Eckart became an advisor to Julius Streicher's *Deutschvölkischer Shutz- und Trutzbund* (German Nationalist Protection and Defensive Federation) comprised mainly of recently discharged soldiers. This paramilitary group helped beleaguered civil authorities put down Communist disorders in Bavaria. On 22 August 1919, Eckart addressed a 1,000-man rally, citing allusions to *Peer Gynt*, and advising all to "thrust through the realm of illusion toward enlightenment" (Engelman 1971, 147).

The militant bard, like his father Georg Christian Eckart, now counseled *Herren* in worldly matters. He ebulliently dispensed ripe wisdom to "political dunderheads" in the officer corps, such as General Franz Ritter von Epp, Captain Karl Mayr, and Captain Ernst Röhm. Eckart persuaded *Freikorps* General von Epp and *Vorläufige Reichswehr* information officer Mayr to ally their legions with a party representing the laboring classes. The proletariat should be militarized and the military proletarianized. That would steal Communist thunder. A grassroots German type of Socialism must prevail over "Jewish Bolshevism."

Several months after forming the German Workers' Party (*DAP*), Dietrich Eckart urged the army to support this tiny group. On 14 August 1919, he addressed thirty-eight members of the *DAP* in a beer hall demanding united action against the "Jewish-Bolshevik peril."

Anton Drexler, a railroad tool and die maker interested in politics, embodied Eckart's ideal of the workingman. He had written an anti-Semitic pamphlet entitled "My Political Awakening." This booklet—which inspired Hitler to join *DAP* and later write *Mein Kampf*—recommended the disenfranchisement of Jews, dissolution of department stores, and repudiation of the Versailles Treaty. But the diffident and middle-aged Drexler felt more comfortable preaching to converted coworkers at a tavern table than dashing with Red gangs in the streets. The German Workers' Party needed a tougher leader to get its message out.

At 2:00 a.m. on 17 December 1920, Hitler and two other companions arrived at Drexler's flat determined that Thule Society's *Völkischer Beobachter*, threatened by bankruptcy and takeover by a rival Nationalist group, must be purchased by the *NSDAP* at once. Later the same day, Dietrich Eckart agreed to mortgage his house (at a time of worsening hyperinflation and property devaluation) to provide some of the funds necessary to complete the purchase. Captain Ernst Röhm joined the effort and together with Eckart they persuaded Röhm's commanding officer of the *Freikorps*, Colonel Franz Xaver Ritter von Epp, to provide the remaining funds necessary to purchase the *Völkischer Beobachter* from the Thule Society for 120,000 *Papiermarks* ($1,333.33). The money came from wealthy friends and secret *Vorläufige Reichswehr* funds embezzled by von Epp. To raise funds for the *NSDAP*, Eckart introduced Hitler into influential circles, including to his future social etiquette tutor, socialite Helene Bechstein.

Eckart became the editor of the *Völkischer Beobachter* and used it to publicize the policies of the *Nationalsozialistische Deutsche Arbeiterpartei* (*NSDAP*, National Socialist German Workers [Nazi] Party). Later in 1923, Ernst Hanfstaengel provided $1,000 to ensure the daily publication of the newspaper, which became the flagship periodical of the Nazi Party. As William L. Shirer, author of *The Rise and Fall of the Third Reich*, has pointed out: "It became a daily, thus giving Hitler the prerequisite of all German political parties, a daily newspaper in which to preach the party's gospels." When Alfred Rosenberg became editor of the *Völkischer Beobachter* in 1923, he published *The Protocols of the Elders of Zion* that he carried with him when he immigrated from Estonia to Germany in December 1918 along with other future members of the *Aufbau Vereinigung* (Reconstruction Organization)—See: Alfred Rosenberg, below.

> By 1923 Eckart's connections in Munich, added to Hitler's oratorical gifts, gave strength and prestige to the fledgling Nazi political movement. Eckart accompanied Hitler at rallies and was at his side in party parades. While Hitler stirred the masses, Eckart wrote panegyrics to his friend. The two were inseparable. Hitler never forgot his early sponsor. . . . Eckart, he said, was his North Star. . . . He spoke emotionally of his fatherly friend, and there were often tears in his eyes when he mentioned Eckart's name. (Snyder 1981, 51–2.)

Dietrich Eckart died of a heart attack on 26 December 1923 at the age of fifty-five-years while Hitler was in custody of the Bavarian police and awaiting trial for the failed Beer Hall *Putsch.* On his deathbed, Eckart reportedly said:

> *Follow Hitler!*
> *He will dance, but it is I who have called the tune!*
> *I have initiated him into the "Secret Doctrine,"*
> *opened his centers in vision and given him the means to communicate with the Powers.*
> *Do not mourn for me: I shall have influenced history more than any other German.*

In March 1924, Eckart's unfinished essay "Der Bolschewismus von Moses bis Lenin: Zwiegespräch zwischen Hitler und mir" ("Bolshevism from Moses to Lenin: Dialogue Between Hitler and Me") was published posthumously by Eckart's Munich publisher *Hoheneichen Verlag.* This writing remains a reliable indicator of Eckart's views on the nexus between Bolshevism and the Jews that became one of the primary pillars of the anti-Jewish program of the Nazi movement that formally began with the promulgation of the Twenty-Five Points, the first manifesto of the *NSDAP*, on 24 February 1920.

Gottfried Feder (1883–1941) – Gottfried Feder, the son of a government official, was born in Würzburg, Bavaria, on 27 January 1883. After attending schools in Ansbach and Munich, he studied engineering in Berlin and Zürich. In 1908, he started his own company constructing airplane hangars. During the First World War, Feder's travails in dealing with banking and finance for his business led to him developing a hostility to Germany's wealthy bankers and in 1919 he published his *Manifest zur Brechung der Zinsknechtschaft* (Manifesto on Breaking the Shackles of Interest) describing "Jewish finance Capitalism." Feder became convinced that his country's economic ruin could be attributed to manipulators of high finance. He initially favored retaining the Capitalist system, especially such productive assets as factories, mines, and machines, but he would abolish the idea of interest because it created no value. Over time, Feder preferred nationalization of major industries and therefore leaned more to Socialist economic policies.

On 30 May 1919, Captain Karl Mayr was appointed chief of Intelligence Division's Education and Propaganda Department (Ib/P) in the

Vorläufige Reichswehr (Provisional National Defense) Group Headquarters 4 (Bavaria). He was given considerable funding to build a team of agents and informants and to organize a series of educational courses to train selected officers and men in "correct" political and ideological thinking. Mayr recruited Feder to give lectures to soldiers at the University of Munich. Corporal Adolf Hitler would soon be one of those who attended his lectures in the summer of 1919 while working for Mayr.

Feder's views appealed to Hitler for political reasons. Feder's separation between stock exchange capital and the national economy supported opposing the internationalization of the German economy without threatening an independent national economy. Best of all, from Hitler's point of view, was the fact that he could identify international Capitalism as wholly Jewish-controlled. Hitler became a member of the *DAP* and Feder became his friend and guide on economic issues.

According to von Sebottendorff, Hitler was introduced to the Thule Society—most likely by Feder—and became a guest member in the summer of 1919 (Von Sebottendorff 1933). Gottfried Feder is the most likely nexus linking Hitler to the Thule Society at that time.

On 24 February 1920, the *NSDAP* published its first party platform which became known as the Twenty-Five Points. Its authors were Eckart, Hitler, Feder, and Drexler. In the manifesto, the party refused to accept the terms of the Versailles Treaty and called for the reunification of all German people. To reinforce their ideas on Nationalism, equal rights were only to be given to German citizens. "Foreigners" and "aliens" would be denied these rights. To appeal to the working class and Socialists, the program included several measures that would redistribute income and war profits, profit-sharing in large industries, nationalization of trusts, increases in old-age pensions and free education. Feder greatly influenced the anti-Capitalist aspect of the Nazi party platform and insisted on phrases such as the need to "break the interest thralldom of international Capitalism" and the claim that Germany had become the "slave of the international stock market."

Throughout the 1920s, Feder was a leader of the anti-Capitalist wing of the Nazi Party. In 1924, he was elected to the *Reichstag*, where he stayed until 1936 and demanded the freezing of interest rates and disenfranchisement of Jewish citizens. He put forward his views in *Das Programm der NSDAP und seine weltanschaulichen Grundlagen* (*The program of the NSDAP and its ideological bases*, 1927), *Kampf gegen die Hochfinanz* (*The struggle against high finance*, 1933), and *Die Juden* (*The Jews*, 1933) where he expressed his anti-Semitic views.

As Feder held the important post of chairman of the party's economic council, his anti-Capitalist views led to a decline in financial support from Germany's major industrialists. Hjalmar Schacht (President of *Reichsbank*) warned Hitler that Feder's economic planning apparatus would ruin the German economy. After pressure from German industrialists such as Albert Vögler (armaments), Gustav Krupp (heavy industries and armaments), Friedrich Flick (steel), Fritz Thyssen (mining, steel), and Emil Kirdorf (coal), Hitler decided to move the party away from Feder's anti-Capitalist economic theories.

When Adolf Hitler became chancellor in 1933, he appointed Feder as Vice Minister at the Ministry of Economics. Feder was disappointed that he had not been given a more senior position and had to serve under someone who completely opposed Feder's economic policies. The post of Vice Minister of Economics was a humiliating position to him. His superior in the Ministry, Doctor Karl Schmitt, general director of the largest German insurance company, was practically a stranger to the party, but familiar to the stock exchange. A bigger representative of avaricious capital would have been hard to find. Schmitt had spent his life lending money and collecting interest; he had literally bought his way into the National Socialist movement by generously financing the party in hard times. However, Schmitt soon lost the confidence of the Nazi leadership and on 3 August 1934, was replaced by Hjalmar Schacht with Feder remaining as Vice Minister.

Feder continued to campaign for nationalization, profit-sharing, the abolition of unearned incomes and the "thralldom of interest." Hitler refused to do this. As Alan Bullock, author of *Hitler: A Study in Tyranny* (1962) has pointed out: "Hitler had never been a Socialist; he was indifferent to economic questions. What he saw, however, was that radical economic experiments at such a time would throw the German economy into a state of confusion, and would prejudice, if not destroy, the chances of cooperation with industry and business to end the Depression and bring down the unemployment figures."

Hitler confirmed this in a speech he made on 6 July 1933:

> The revolution is not a permanent state of affairs, and it must not be allowed to develop into such a state. The stream of revolution released must be guided into the safe channel of evolution. . . . We must therefore not dismiss a business man if he is a good business man, even if he is not yet a National Socialist; and especially not if the National

> Socialist who is to take his place knows nothing about business. In business, ability must be the only authoritative standard. . . . History will not judge us according to whether we have removed and imprisoned the largest number of economists, but according to whether we have succeeded in providing work. . . . The ideas of the program do not oblige us to act like fools and upset everything, but to realize our trains of thought wisely and carefully. In the long run our political power will be all the more secure, the more we succeed in underpinning it economically.

As one of the leaders of the more Socialist wing of the Nazi Party, Hitler saw Feder as a threat to his leadership. After the Night of the Long Knives (*die Nacht der langen Messer*) on 30 June 1934 where other radical Socialists such as Gregor Straßer and Ernst Röhm were murdered, Feder resigned from the government telling his friends that Hitler had betrayed the Third *Reich.*[*] Gottfried Feder worked as a university lecturer until his death on 24 September 1941.

Hans Frank (1900–1946) – Hans Frank was one of the most equivocal figures among the National Socialist top leadership; weak, unstable, and full of strange contradictions. Behind the bloody image of the "slayer of Poles" and the party's leading jurist, we see on closer inspection an insecure and vacillating character; Frank's unrestrained veneration for the person of Hitler and for the party program of the *NSDAP*—which throughout his life he completely misinterpreted in keeping with illusions rooted in romantic idealism—carried him to the most abysmal depths of criminality. Governed by emotions and cranky ideas, ready to surrender himself and at the same time subject to sudden spells of self-destructive obstinacy springing from an awareness of normal standards from which in the last resort he could not escape, he seemed among all those cold manipulators of power as though made for the role of a sectarian, whose usual fate he actually avoided only with some difficulty (Fest 1970, 209). What prevented him from offering the ultimate challenge was solely a deeply rooted subservience and a remnant of

---

[*] First-Second-Third *Reich*s of Germany – The history of the German nation-state included the First *Reich* as the German Empire (1871–1918), the Second *Reich* was the Weimar Republic (1918–1933), and the Third *Reich* was Germany under Nazi rule (1933–1945). However, according to Hitler, the First *Reich* was the Holy Roman Empire, from the 10th to the 19th century and the Second *Reich* was the German Empire from 1871 to 1918.

devotion to the "glorious shaper" Hitler, which he preserved even "In the Face of the Gallows": "While I sit here in the solitude of Nuremberg [Adolf Hitler] goes striding through my earnest, profound thoughts as a concentrated, rich personality whose influence has attained gigantic proportions" (Frank 1955).

Hans, the middle child of three, was born in Karlsruhe (Grand Duchy of Baden) on 23 May 1900 to Karl Frank, a lawyer, and his wife, Magdalena (née Buchmaier), a daughter of a prosperous baker. He graduated from the renowned *Maximilian Gymnasium* in Munich, and right after, at seventeen, joined the German army fighting in World War I. After the war, in 1919, he was introduced to and became a member of the *völkisch* Thule Society. He also served in the *Freikorps* under Franz Ritter von Epp, taking part in the crackdown of the *Münchner Räterepublik* (Munich Soviet Republic). In 1919, as did other members of the Thule society, he joined the *DAP* at its founding. In September 1923, Frank joined the paramilitary wing of the *NSDAP Sturmabteilung* (*SA*), and in October 1923 he officially joined the *NSDAP*. In November of the same year, Frank took part in the Beer Hall *Putsch*. When the *putsch* failed, Frank fled to Austria returning to Munich in 1924 after the pending legal proceedings were stayed.

Frank studied law (passing the state examination in 1926) and rose to become Hitler's personal legal counselor. As the Nazis rose to power, Frank also served as the party's legal counsel representing it in over 2,400 cases. Frank was elected to the *Reichstag* in 1930, and in 1933 he was made Minister of Justice for Bavaria. From 1933, he was also the head of the National Socialist Jurists Association and President of the Academy of German Law. Frank objected to extrajudicial killings both at the Dachau Concentration Camp and during the Night of the Long Knives as it weakened the power of the legal system. Frank raised objections to the proposed executions without trial of 110 members of the *SA*. As a result of his intervention, only twenty men were shot. After this, Frank's influence in the *NSDAP* hierarchy waned.

In September 1939, Frank was assigned as Chief of Administration to Colonel-General (*Generaloberst*) Karl Rudolf Gerd von Rundstedt (1875–1953), commander of Army Group South in the German military administration in occupied Poland. Beginning 26 October 1939, Frank was assigned Governor-General of the occupied Polish territories (*Generalgouverneur für die besetzten polnischen Gebiete*). Frank oversaw the segregation of the Jews into *ghettos* and the use of Polish civilians as forced labor.

On 16 December 1941, Frank spelled out to his senior subordinates in the *Generalgouvernement* the approaching annihilation of the Jews:

> A great Jewish migration will begin in any case. But what should we do with the Jews? Do you think they will be settled in *Ostland*, in villages? We were told in Berlin, "Why all this bother? We can do nothing with them either in *Ostland* or in the *Reichskommissariat*. So, liquidate them yourselves." Gentlemen, I must ask you to rid yourself of all feelings of pity. We must annihilate the Jews wherever we find them and whenever it is possible.*

Frank was captured by American troops on 3 May 1945 at Tegernsee in southern Bavaria. While in custody, he attempted suicide twice but failed. He was indicted for war crimes and tried before the International Military Tribunal in Nuremberg. On 1 October 1946, he was found guilty of war crimes and crimes against humanity and was sentenced to death by hanging. The death sentence was carried out at Nuremberg Prison on 16 October 1946. He answered to his name quietly and when asked for any last statement, he replied "I am thankful for the kind treatment during my captivity and I ask God to accept me with mercy" (Lewis 2002, 565). His body and those of the other nine executed prisoners and the corpse of Hermann Göring were cremated at *Ostfriedhof* (Munich) and the ashes were scattered in the river Isar.

Rudolf Heß (1894–1987) – Like Dietrich Eckart, Rudolf Heß was a unique figure in the Nazi movement, and therefore deserves more extensive coverage here.

Rudolf Heß, the son of a wealthy German merchant based in Egypt, was born in Alexandria, Egypt on 26 April 1894 (five years Hitler's junior). One of his indelible memories was of his father Johann Fritz Heß—of his severity, which was so intimidating that Rudolf and his younger brother Alfred never dared to romp around in the morning until their father left for work. Their education was the finest that money could buy. The boy's inclinations were to study math and science, but Fritz Heß needed an heir to take over the import business, and that was the purpose of the expensive

---

* Speech by Frank to his senior officials, 16 December 1941, reprinted in *Office of Chief Counsel for Prosecution of Axis Criminality, OCCPAC*, quoted in Polonsky 2012, 434.

grooming. He sent Rudolf to the German Evangelical Lutheran School in Alexandria in 1900. From 1906, he was given two years of private tutoring, and then at the age of fourteen-years, his father enrolled him at the Evangelical Lutheran boarding school *Evangelisches Pädagogium* (*Oberrealschule*) in Godesberg (Bad Godesberg since 1925) near Bonn, Germany (known since 1937 as *Pädagogium Godesberg Otto-Kühne-Schule*). Heß graduated from the *Oberrealschule* in Godesberg in 1911. From Godesberg, he advanced in 1911 to the French-speaking *Ecole Supérieure de Commerce* at Neuchâtel, Switzerland, where he was initiated into the world of accounting. After just one year in Switzerland, he found this field uninspiring—a depressing conclusion that a two-year (1912–1914) apprenticeship at his father's import business in Hamburg served only to confirm.

At the outbreak of the First World War, Heß joined the German Army in August 1914 and served in the First Bavarian Infantry Regiment. He heroically fought in some major engagements and was thrice wounded. On 8 August 1917, he suffered a gunshot wound to the left chest while storming the Ungüreana, a hill in the Carpathian Mountains near Foscani, Romania with his Eighteenth Bavarian Reserve Infantry Regiment during the second battle of Oituz Pass. He nearly bled to death when the field dressing came off as he was manhandled down the mountain on an ammunition cart. He was awarded the Iron Cross Second Class on 27 April 1915, and after his battle wounds (left arm on 23 July and left chest on 8 August 1917) in Romania was recommended for the Iron Cross First Class but for unclear logistical reasons never received it. After a long convalescence in Hungarian and Saxon hospitals, he was allowed home on leave in the *Fichtelgebirge* (Fichtel Mountains in northeastern Bavaria). In March 1918, he volunteered as a fighter pilot, but the war had only one month left to run when he reached his operational unit, the 35th Fighter *Staffel*, on 1 November 1918. He saw limited action on the Western Front but scored no aerial victories. He was demobilized with the rank of lieutenant in reserve a month later but had acquired a taste for flying that was to obsess him for the next 25 years.

Heß was discharged from the armed forces in early 1919. After the war, the family fortunes had taken a serious downturn, as their business interests in Egypt had been expropriated by the British. He arrived in Munich in February 1919, depressed and embittered at the "treason" of the government in Berlin which had signed the Armistice. A Socialist government under Kurt Eisner had seized power in Bavaria in November

1918 with a Red "Soviet" regime threatening to seize power in April 1919. On 18 February 1919, he joined the secretive anti-Marxist, anti-Semitic, occultist *völkisch* Thule Society in Munich. In April 1919, Heß ran errands for Rudolf von Sebottendorff's Thule Society distributing inflammatory leaflets throughout Munich railing against the "Jewish" Soviet Republic of Bavaria. These were strange and turbulent months for him. He narrowly escaped a Red massacre of hostages by turning up late for a Thule meeting—in time to see his less fortunate Thulists loaded onto a truck, which took them to their execution. He joined Thule Society's *Freikorps Oberland* and partook in the battle of Munich. He was wounded for a fourth time, this time in the leg, while manning a howitzer during the street battles fought by the *Freikorps Oberland* to liberate Munich on 1 May 1919. After major hostilities against the Munich Bolsheviks ended, clean-up operations commenced with mass round ups of Red Guards and sympathetic supporters. On 7 May 1919, Heß resigned from *Freikorps Oberland* and formally joined *Freikorps Epp* renamed *Bayerischen Schützenkorps* (*4te Alarmkompanie*) under command of Franz Ritter von Epp.

> In his unbalanced approach to authority Hess strikingly resembles many National Socialists who, like him, had "strict" parents. There is a good deal of evidence that Hitler profited considerably from the damage wrought by an education system that took its models from the barracks and brought up its sons to be as tough as army cadets. The fixation on the military world, the determining feature of their early background, shows not only in the peculiar mixture of aggressiveness and doglike cringing so typical of the "Old Fighter," but also in the lack of inner independence and the need to receive orders. Whatever hidden rebellious feelings the young Rudolf Hess may have had against his father, who emphatically demonstrated his power for the last time when he refused to let his son go to a university but forced him, against his wishes and the pleas of his teacher, to train as a businessman with a view to taking over his own firm in Alexandria—the son, whose will was broken over and over again, henceforth sought fathers and father substitutes wherever he could find them. One must want the Führer! It fits into the picture of this complicated relationship that, of all the Hohenzollern kings, Rudolf Hess

> felt a particular admiration for Friedrich [*sic*] Wilhelm I, a blustering *roi sergent* with a fatherly roughness and strictness who has been interpreted in literature as a father figure. When Rudolf Hess volunteered for the Army at the outbreak of the First World War he was seeking to escape not only from the hated commercial career, but above all from the demands of his own father figure. He could not, of course, escape from himself. (Fest 1970, 189–90.)

In February 1920, against his father's wishes (Johann Fritz Heß, owner of the international wholesale importer-exporter Heß & Company), Rudolf chose to enroll in the University of Munich to study history and economics. There, he found a new "father." Two years earlier, a comrade on the training airfield at Lechfeld, Max Hofweber (member of Thule Society), told him about his gifted commanding major general in retirement Dr. Karl Haushofer (1869–1946) who now served as *Privatdozent* (*venia legend*) for political geography at the University of Munich. Intrigued, Heß had persuaded Hofweber to arrange an introduction, and they met on 4 April 1919—beginning an intimate friendship that was to prove fateful to both, despite Haushofer's wife Martha Mayer (née Doss) being half Jewish. Earlier, Hofweber introduced Heß to the Thule Society and its *Kampfbund.* Heß joined both secret organizations in Munich. During the period of his university studies, he was greatly influenced by the teachings of Dr. Haushofer, who argued that the state is a biological organism which grows or contracts, and that in the struggle for living space the strong countries take land from the weak. Professor Haushofer and Heß quickly became close friends and worked closely together over the ensuing twenty-two years.

In the summer of 1920, Heß first saw Adolf Hitler at an *NSDAP* meeting in the *Sternecker-Bräu* beerhall. Heß remarked: "Was this man a fool or was he the man who would save all Germany." Enthusiastic about this new figure in his life, who obviously provided Heß with yet another authoritative father figure, he persuaded Dr. Haushofer to go with him to the new party's meetings that June, and on 1 July 1920, enrolled himself as member number 16. But Heß failed to persuade the professor to also fall in behind the "tribune" (as he referred to Hitler).

In 1921, Haushofer's lectures and Hitler's speeches inspired Heß to enter a literary competition, which he won with his essay, answering the question: "What kind of leader does Germany need to regain her greatness?" It included the following passage:

> Profound knowledge of all matters of state and of history, the ability to learn from it, faith in the purity of his own cause and in ultimate victory, and an indomitable will to give him the power to carry away audiences with his speeches and cause the masses to cry out to him in jubilation. In the interests of the liberation of his nation, the leader does not shrink from using the weapons of his enemy: demagogy, slogans, street meetings, etc. Where all authority has vanished, only popularity creates authority. . . . The deeper the dictator's original roots are anchored in the broad masses, and the better he understands their psychology, the less the workers will mistrust him and the more followers he will win among these, the most energetic ranks of the people.
>
> He himself has nothing in common with the masses: he is a personality in his own right, like every great man.
>
> On every occasion the leader demonstrates his courage. This produces blind truth in the organized power; through this he achieves dictatorship. When necessity dictates he does not recoil from bloodshed. Great issues are always decided through blood and iron. And our issue is: to go under, or to arise anew. Whether or not the *Reichstag* continues to babble, this man will act. To reach his goal, he will crush even his closest friends. For the sake of the great ultimate goal he is able to endure seeming, temporarily, in the eyes of the majority, like a traitor to his nation.
>
> Thus we have the picture of the dictator: sharp of mind, clear and true, passionate and yet controlled, cold and bold, thoughtful and conscious of his aims when making decisions, uninhibited in swiftly putting them into execution, ruthless towards himself and others, mercilessly hard and then again soft in his love of his people, tireless in work, with a steel fist in a velvet glove, capable last of all of conquering himself.
>
> We do not yet know when "the man" will intervene to save us. But millions feel that he is coming.

In November 1923, Heß ended his studies at the University of Munich and took part in the failed Beer Hall *Putsch*. Heß escaped and sought the help of Professor Karl Haushofer. For several days he hid at the Haushofer's Munich apartment followed by a period in Haushofer's home, *Hartschimmelhof*, in the Bavarian Alps. Later, he was helped to escape to Austria. Hitler and his accomplices were put on trial early in 1924. Heß remained in exile but surrendered to the authorities in the trial's closing days. It was common sense rather than any kind of exhibitionism that motivated him: Haushofer had smuggled a letter to him warning that the favorably disposed court in Munich would transfer the trial of Heß to Leipzig, where a far stiffer sentence might result. In the end, Heß got off relatively mildly. The Bavarian court sentenced Heß to eighteen months in Landsberg Prison.

Heß had a small, quiet, whitewashed cell with a tranquil view across the countryside to the distant Alps. A former aviator friend was one of the warders. His cell was comfortably furnished, he had bookshelves, a modern reading lamp and writing desk. Hitler had attracted a five-year sentence in the same fortress-like jail. Surrounded by friendly and admiring warders, he and his twenty followers used these months to the full. They met each day at 10 a.m. around a long table in the common room, where Hitler held court beneath a swastika flag. The warders turned a blind eye, and Hitler and his accomplices conducted business as before.

They turned the same blind eye when Heß's young secretary Ilse Pröhl came to see him, bringing books and gifts—the old policeman yawned, turned away and pretended to fall asleep so that the young couple could be effectively alone. The prison's records show that between 24 June and 12 November 1924, Professor Haushofer came eight times to see Heß—always on a Wednesday—and stayed the whole morning and afternoon. He saw Hitler too, but stressed years later: "My visits to Landsberg were meant for Heß as he was my pupil" (Irving 1987, 12). Haushofer brought books to Heß to improve his mind—Karl von Clausewitz on war, and the improved second edition of Friedrich Ratzel's *Politische Geographie*—but he could see that neither Heß nor Hitler had grasped the essentials of geopolitics despite these private "tutorials." "I remember well," reminisced the professor in 1945, "that whenever Heß understood something and tried to explain it to Hitler, Hitler would come out with one of his new ideas about an autobahn or something completely irrelevant, while Heß just stood there and said nothing more about it." (Irving 1987, 12.)

The intimacy between Hitler and Heß dated from these months of shared imprisonment. He began to act as the *Führer*'s secretary, and Hitler dictated to him parts of his ideological testament *Mein Kampf*. It was no doubt here that the dominating idea of *Lebensraum* found its way into

National Socialist ideology; for through Karl Haushofer, who kept up a lively contact with the prisoners, the original idea of a political geography under the catchword "geopolitics" had undergone an imperialistic transformation into a "pseudo-scientific expansionist philosophy." It offered the humiliated national spirit the idea that the destiny of Germany would be decided in the East and thus added a fundamental ideological category of National Socialism, that of "space," to that of "race." These two ideas, linked by that of struggle, constituted the only more or less fixed structural elements in the intricate tactical and propagandist conglomerate of the National Socialist *Weltanschauung*. (Fest 1970, 191.)

On 1 November 1925, Heß formally joined the *SS* as *SS-Staffelführer* (squadron leader) eventually by 26 September 1933 reaching the rank of *SS-Obergruppenführer* (General) directly under *SS-Reichsführer* Heinrich Himmler. Acting as intermediary between Haushofer and Hitler was the most important and virtually the only personal contribution Rudolf Heß made towards the birth and shaping of National Socialism. Up to 1932, Heß held no rank in the party but belonged rather to Hitler's personal retinue as head of his private chancellery. As was his wish, he stood in the *Führer*'s shadow, high enough for his secretly burning ambition and yet as concealed as his insurmountable shyness demanded. To most people's surprise, in December 1932, after the fall of Gregor Straßer, Hitler thrust Heß out of this shadow to head the newly formed Political Central Commission, and very soon afterwards on 21 April 1933 appointed him *Stellvertreter des Führers* (Deputy to the *Führer*) and chief of the Party Chancellery with the words: "I appoint the director of the Political Central Commission, Rudolf Heß, as my deputy and authorize him to decide all matters concerning the direction of the Party in my name."

Shortly after being named *Stellvertreter des Führers* in April 1933, Heß began building a growing web of connections to the British, including learning to speak English. In *Mein Kampf*, Hitler repeatedly underlined his aspirations for a common cause, even a great alliance, with Britain. Based on Hitler's personal wishes shared with Heß over the years regarding cooperation and alliance with the British (Hitler envisioned world domination by the Germans, British, and the Anglo-Americans—all Nordic ancestors), Heß began developing a strategy to win over the British. Born under British rule in Egypt, he had a deep and natural predisposition towards their empire. Through the medium of Karl Haushofer's eldest son Dr. Albrecht Haushofer (1903–1945), Heß remained active in secret diplomacy, although the focus of interest shifted over time from the *Auslands-*

Organization's *Volksdeutsche* problem, the ethnic Germans abroad, to the English-speaking powers. For years, Heß and Albrecht—an expert on Great Britain and Heß's secret emissary abroad working under Heß's appointment to Hitler's alternate foreign office *Dienststelle Ribbentrop* in Berlin, which emphasized Anglo-German relations—arranged private meetings with British visitors, dozens of whom flocked to Hitler's Berlin in the mid-thirties eager to witness the revolution at first hand. Heß's basic political concept was that the Nordic countries (including the modern British descendants of historic Nordic ancestry, the Normans, Anglos, and Saxons) had a duty to avoid fighting any more wars with each other, if their dominant influence throughout the world was not to be totally destroyed. Ambassador to Great Britain Joachim von Ribbentrop, Heß, and Albrecht Haushofer were successful in finding common ground and support among a significant segment of British ruling aristocracy serving in British government. From his appointment as Deputy to the *Führer* in April 1933 until his shocking flight to England on 10 May 1941, Heß, in collaboration with von Ribbentrop and Albrecht Haushofer, engineered many communiqués and meetings with British officials in their effort to find common ground and cooperation, for which Hitler many times expressed hope and envisioned since early in his political career. Transcripts and documents of these communiqués and meetings were later destroyed by the British after the war.

Incompetence in the power struggles that naturally developed early on among the highest circles of power surrounding Hitler—particularly among the extreme militant *Sturmabteilung* (*SA*) wing, hardline party ideologists, and pure opportunists—effectively left Heß outside the inner circle of influence and real powerbrokers. Despite his official title and hungry loyalty to his *Führer*, Heß's responsibilities turned perfunctory and ceremonial as he soon found himself downgraded to a channel for petty grievances; he had become the movement's "wailing wall," as he put it at Nuremberg in September 1935. Eventually, nothing was left to him but subordinate representative functions; he became the party's status symbol, displaced increasingly by boorish and pushy subordinates, but still wheeled around the countryside to bedazzle the masses, reassure bankers and industrialists, and placate nervous foreign diplomats. "Decent, but sick and indecisive," was Rosenberg's ironic (see Alfred Rosenberg bio, below) verdict on Heß. Many others of the inner circle viewed Heß in the same light.

In strings of decrees during the party crises in 1933, Heß tried to halt the growing trend of violent attacks on town halls, banks and insurance firms, and non-Aryan executives of German businesses. He was then architect of a little-known law passed in May 1933 guaranteeing the freedom of religious thought. He forbade *SS*, *SA*, or other Party men to "intervene in the internal affairs of economic institutions." The *SA* paid no heed. Pointing out that every workplace was vitally needed, on 7 July 1933, Heß prohibited any Party operations calculated to harass the big chain-stores or force them out of business (they had previously been a target of Nazi propaganda). But the *SA*'s operations went on; nothing, it seemed, could damp down the fires of revolutionary fervor. Chief of the *SA* Ernst Röhm, in fact, was already acting as though he were the number two in Germany. It was plain that he had even greater ambitions, and Heß was determined to protect his *Führer* from them. On 9 September, he forbade Party functionaries to hold diplomatic receptions; Röhm ignored him and threw gala dinners for the Berlin diplomatic corps that were more lavish than those of the Foreign Ministry. On 22 January 1934, Heß published in the Party newspaper a warning that there was "not the slightest need" for the *SA* or other component organizations to "lead an independent existence." In a speech, he warned: "You want to be more revolutionary than the *Führer*—but the *Führer* alone determines the tempo of the revolution!" Still Röhm ignored him.

However, when the crisis approached the breaking point on 30 June 1934 ("Night of the Long Knives"; Operation Hummingbird–*Unternehmen Kolibri*), Heß pleaded with Hitler not to shed the blood of their closest friends. "The Röhm *putsch*," Heß's chief adjutant Alfred Leitgen stated afterwards, "was probably one of the worst strains on Heß. He was in Munich at the time. . . . He fought tooth and nail with Hitler to save some of those men and refused to be intimidated by even the most violent outbursts from Hitler. He saved a lot of men's lives—we'll never know how many" (Irving 1987, 22–3). Their argument lasted several hours, as Leitgen, in an adjacent room, could hear. "Heß was deeply affected by this eruption of personal brutality in Hitler. His pronounced—I would say almost feminine—instinct was hurt in every respect. In those few days he aged years" (Irving 1987, 23). Ironically, Karl Haushofer, of all people, sent Heß a fulsome letter of congratulations on the "great" deed, dated 1 July 1934; but this merely echoed the general public's sense of relief over the demise of the *SA* (Irving 1987, 23).

On 2 August 1935, Heß had issued a secret circular decree Number 160/35 prohibiting any kind of excesses by party members against "Jews or Jewish provocateurs" and insisting on the most rigorous prosecution of anybody causing criminal damage or bodily harm to Jews, or guilty of riotous assembly against them. When a Jewish terrorist murdered Heß's subordinate chief of *Auslands-Organization* Ernest Bohle's representative in Switzerland, Wilhelm Gustloff, in February 1936, Heß again issued secret orders to all party and state officials "to prevent outrages against Jews" (Irving 1987, 33). "It is for the *Führer* alone to decide what policy to adopt from case to case," ordered Heß. "No party member is to act off his own bat." A confidential speech by Heß to senior party officials at Nuremberg in September 1937 touched upon their campaign against Jews, freemasons, and the feuding clergy. "We are a soldierly movement," he said, "and we must keep discipline in this too!" He titillated them with the example of German firms who still employed Jews as their representatives abroad—"really magnificent specimens from East Galicia," he said (Irving 1987, 33). Yet, Heß continued to fully endorse the party's racial laws marginalizing Jews from every aspect of public life. Their enemies, boasted the Deputy *Führer*, were being forced to abandon one position after another. "Even if things seem to go slowly sometimes," Heß concluded his confidential speech at Nuremberg in September 1937, "what are a few years compared with a development which will determine the course of German history for centuries and which, in the field of race legislation, will still be showing results in thousands of years?" (Irving 1987, 34).

In 1936, Heß severed all ties with the *SS* as he did not wish to appear to be under Himmler. On 1 September 1939, Hitler replaced Heß with Hermann Göring as first in line to succeed Hitler, moving Heß to second in line. Field Marshal Göring was less enchanted to hear "that nincompoop" named as his successor, and afterwards told Hitler so. Hitler smiled. "But Hermann," he pointed out, giving his own interpretation of the *Führer* principle. "When you become Führer of the *Reich—pfui*! You can throw Heß out and choose your own successor." (Irving 1987, 47.)

Throughout the latter half of 1940, when Operation Sealion (*Unternehmen Seelöwe*) seemed inevitable, Heß began planning in earnest a secret diplomatic trip to England that would halt the devastating invasion of the British Isles and possibly reprise Hitler's long-held hopes for an Anglo-German alliance. The plan would include a generous German peace offer: Germany would withdraw all forces from France and the Low Countries and retain only those regions in Poland and Czechoslovakia which had earlier been Germany's; and Germany would assist the British empire against any enemies. This peace offer was turned down by Churchill in August 1940, but Heß thought it could be reintroduced in a modified form through the influence of Lord Clydesdale Douglas, fourteenth Duke of Hamilton (a friend of Dr. Albrecht Haushofer).

When Nazi Germany collapsed in 1945, more than 400 tons of Foreign Ministry (*Auswärtiges Amt*) archives, captured in the Harz Mountains, were assembled in Marburg Castle. The documents dated to the establishment of the new constitution and *Reichstag* (parliament) of the North German Confederation in 1867. This discovery was made 14–20 April 1945 by elements of the U.S. Ninth Infantry Division under the command of Major General Louis A. Craig. The Ninth Infantry Division was attached to the VII Corps (Lieutenant General J. Lawton Collins), First Army (General Courtney Hicks Hodges), and all under the Twelfth Army Group (General Omar N. Bradley). The 47th Infantry Regiment under Colonel Peter O. Ward was attached to the Ninth Infantry Division.

As the Ninth Infantry Division advanced eastward from Normandy (Operation Overlord D-Day invasion followed by Operation Eclipse), it crossed the Marne River into northeastern France and southwestern Germany (Saarland) on 28 August 1944—day before the outbreak of the Slovak National Uprising. The Ninth Infantry Division then fought its way across the Saar River and trekked north through western Germany along the Belgian-Dutch-German border, turning east at Aachen (North Rhine-Westphalia) towards Cologne to cross the Rur River at Düren on 30 January 1945 and then headed southeast to assist in Operation Lumberjack and over the infamous Ludendorff Bridge at Remagen[5] crossing the Rhine River on 7 March 1945—just after the Ninth Armored Division (Patton's Third Army) captured the Ludendorff bridge intact—and assisting in the sealing and clearing of the Ruhr Pocket,[6] then moving 150 miles (240 km) east to Nordhausen to attack remaining pockets of German resistance in the Harz Mountains on 14–20 April 1945. In and around Nordhausen at the southern edge of the Harz Mountains, a large complex of concentration slave labor camps and subcamps existed—Dora-Mittelbau with its 30 subcamps. These camps were liberated by advancing American forces. Beginning on 14 April and over the ensuing several days, fighting in the Harz Mountains was intense, with the 104th Infantry Division (Major General Terry de la Mesa Allen, Sr.) under VII Corps securing the southern region of the hills. The First (Major General Clift Andrus under Patton's Third Army) and Ninth Infantry Divisions with attached Target Force[7] Fourth Mechanized Cavalry Group (reconnaissance regiment comprising Fourth and Twenty-Fourth Cavalry Squadrons) eventually encircled the enemy and captured the Harz Mountains region along with nearly 84,000 German combatants under the command of Field Marshal Otto Moritz Walter Model.

U.S. Army First Lieutenant David Darwin Silberberg, Combat and Counter-Intelligence (CCI) Section of the 47th Infantry Regiment (under Colonel Peter O. Ward)—Ninth Infantry Division (under Major General Louis A. Craig) and General Hodges's First Army—was born on 20 March 1921 to Lee and Rosa Silberberg in Niedenstein, Germany in the Harz Mountains region from where he and his Jewish family fled in 1936 (113 Cong. Rec.). They eventually reached the United States where in 1942 David Silberberg joined the U.S. Army and became a naturalized citizen the same year. David longed to return to the region of Germany where he was born. While serving in mopping up operations in northern Germany in April 1945, he found himself near the Degenershausen region in the southeast part of the Harz Mountains. While moving in the area he noticed something that would have great consequences. David Silberberg recalled later: "While wrecked vehicles along the roads were commonplace, one truck caught my attention right outside the town of Degenershausen. It was lying in a ditch, with papers scattered all around it. I picked up one of the papers and saw that it was signed by Joachim von Ribbentrop, the foreign minister of Nazi Germany." Aware that he had found something worth investigating, Silberberg returned to Degenershausen to find some townspeople to talk to. "The mayor had already left town by then, but a villager told me that trucks had been bringing stuff to this area for two years. It turned out that every able-bodied person had been ordered to help unload and store the material." He then found the deputy mayor of Pansefelde who told him that in 1943, under the cover of darkness, a large contingent of trucks had unloaded tons of documents at a remote stately home called *Schloss Degenershausen* (Berghahn 2018, 32 and fn 23 to ch. 2, 306).

Together with Sergeants Herbert Schader, George Novak, and Charles Magnum, all members of the CCI, Silberberg went to *Schloss Degenershausen*. This turned out to be a 500-foot-long landmark chateau owned by Baroness von Bodenhausen. The baroness immediately handed Silberberg a note from British author and humorist P. G. Wodehouse (1881–1975). The men found out that the chateau was crammed with files. Silberberg exclaimed: "I couldn't believe what I saw. There were documents signed by the Kaiser, by Bismarck, by famous generals of World War I. A number of papers were even signed by Adolf Hitler!"

When Silberberg further interrogated the baroness, she told him not only about the Foreign Ministry files but also about another archive deposited with Countess von Der Asseburg at *Schloss Meisdorf*, which was located a few miles away. The countess also owned the nearby *Burg*

Falkenstein where Silberberg discovered hundreds of wooden boxes with books, paintings, and other art objects that had also come from Berlin. Upon reading Silberberg's report about his findings, Colonel Dickson of G2 (Intelligence) of the First U.S. Army sent intelligence officer Shepherd Stone to *Schloss Degenershausen* to investigate further. Stone discovered that the baroness was related to the Earl of Douglas and the note she showed Silberberg from P. G. Wodehouse confirmed that she was an anti-Nazi. Recognizing the importance of the find, Stone, fearing "that German paratroopers might try to destroy the castle," urged Colonel Dickson to take the archive to a safe place. Colonel Dickson gave the orders to transport the archive to *Schloss Marburg*. According to Stone, it took "a hundred or more 2 ½-ton trucks to evacuate the documents to Marburg" (Berghahn 2018, 306 fn 23). The collection of archives became known as the "Marburg Files."

In June 1946, the British Foreign Office and the United States Department of State agreed to publish jointly documents from the captured Marburg Files. France joined the effort in 1947. Although the captured archives go back to the year 1867, it was decided to limit the publication to papers relating to the years after 1918, since the objective of the publication was "to establish the record of German foreign policy preceding and during World War II." The large-scale publication of these documents in series from A to E is entitled *Akten zur deutschen auswärtigen Politik, 1918–1945* (*ADAP*; *Files on German Foreign Policy, 1918–1945*) and contains sixty-three volumes. Distinguished American, French, and British historians were selected to launch the series, and then formally and publicly were guaranteed untrammeled access to the records and complete freedom to use their professional judgment in determining what merited publication. Work to sift through the enormous volume of documents began immediately in 1946 and concluded in 1959. The series was published between 1950 and 1995. The Americans published their own English translation of Series C (six volumes covering 30 January 1933–14 November 1937) and D (thirteen volumes covering September 1937–11 December 1941) in nineteen volumes between 1949 and 1983, titled: *Documents on German Foreign Policy, 1918–1945* (*DGFP*; Washington, D.C.: U.S. Government Printing Office; London: H. M. Stationery Office).

As throughout mainland Europe, anti-Semitism resurfaced and gained momentum in England after the First World War. The historical affinity between British Anglo-Saxons and their German cousins manifested in growing overt support for conspiracy theories about a Jewish plot to dominate the world. In turn-of-the-century Russia, growing Jewish involvement in revolutionary fervor moved the Tsar's secret police to draft the scandalous forgery *The Protocols of the Elders of Zion* that was exported to Germany, England, France, and the United States after the First World War. Many prominent citizens, leaders, and industrial barons in the West bought into the *Protocol*'s conspiracy. Anti-Semitic writers such as Briton Nesta Helen Webster (née Bevan; 1876–1960)—who in 1920 was one of the contributing authors to *The Jewish Peril*, a series of articles in the London *Morning Post* centered on *The Protocols of the Elders of Zion*—began openly publishing anti-Semitic writings in England. *The Protocols* led Webster to believe that Jews were the driving force behind an international conspiracy, which in her 1921 book *World Revolution: The Plot Against Civilisation* she developed into a "Judeo-Masonic" conspiracy behind international finance and responsible for the Bolshevik revolution. Following this, she became the leading writer of *The Patriot*, an anti-Semitic paper financed by Alan Percy, eighth Duke of Northumberland.

In 1919, Webster published *The French Revolution: A Study in Democracy*. In the book she claimed that the Jews had prepared and carried out the French Revolution. Having bought into this theory, Winston Churchill praised her in a 1920 article entitled "Zionism versus Bolshevism: A Struggle for the Soul of the Jewish People" (Churchill 1920, 5. Quoted in Julius 2010, 719, fn. 387), in which he wrote:

> This movement among the Jews is not new. From the days of Spartacus-Weishaupt* to those of Karl Marx, and down to Trotsky (Russia), Bela Kun (Hungary), Rosa Luxembourg [*sic*] (Germany), and Emma Goldman (United States), this world-wide conspiracy for the overthrow of civilisation and for the reconstitution of society on the basis of arrested development, of envious malevolence, and impossible equality, has been steadily growing. It played, as a modern writer, Mrs. Webster, has so ably shown, a

---

* On 1 May 1776, German philosopher and professor of law Johann Adam Weishaupt (1748–1830) founded the "Illuminati" in the Electorate of Bavaria. He adopted the name of "Brother Spartacus" within the order. The Order of the Illuminati was a secret society to combat religion and foster rationalism in its place by "illumination, enlightening the understanding by the sun of reason, which will dispel the clouds of superstition and of prejudice" with the goal of "perfecting human nature" through re-education to achieve a communal state with nature, freed of government and organized religion.

> definitely recognisable part in the tragedy of the French Revolution. (Pyle 1920, 130–42.)

Webster also published *Secret Societies and Subversive Movements* (1924), *The Need for Fascism in Great Britain* (1926), and *The Origin and Progress of the World Revolution* (1932). In her books she argued that Bolshevism was a Jewish plot to take over the world. Webster became involved in several extreme groups including the British Fascists (Linehan 2000, 46), the Anti-Socialist Union, The Link, and the British Union of Fascists (Barberis, McHugh, and Tyldesley 2005, 176). In her books, Webster argued that Bolshevism was part of a much older and more secret, self-perpetuating conspiracy. She described three possible sources for this conspiracy: Zionism, Pan-Germanism, or "the occult power." She claimed that even if *The Protocols of the Elders of Zion* were fake, they still described how Jews think and behave. Webster dismissed much of the persecution of the Jews by Nazi Germany as exaggeration and propaganda, having abandoned her anti-German views due to her admiration for Hitler. In April 1933, she wrote: "those of us in England who have been subjected for years to a real boycott, organized by Jews can hardly be expected to shed tears over the turning of the tables." In 1938 Webster published *Germany and England*. In this book she developed the argument that Adolf Hitler had successfully halted the Jewish attempt to control the world. However, after the Molotov-Ribbentrop Pact she came to oppose Hitler. Webster's books and articles played an important role in the development of racist views in Britain and the United States. Such were the growing influences on British royal society.

From the time Hitler came to power in 1933 through the growing threat of war in 1938, the British "governing class" pursued a policy of appeasement with Hitler. According to American journalist and army intelligence (G2) officer Shepard Stone (born Shepard Arthur Cohen; 1908–1990), the appeasers were a small "gang" of upper-class men who controlled Britain politically and economically and who saw Nazi Germany merely as a bulwark against Bolshevism. They lived in a world that was "not the world of the vast majority of Englishmen or Americans." Rather it was "a world of privilege; a world which believes in its own prerogatives; a world convinced of its own wisdom and of its right to rule" (Berghahn 2018, 22–3).

Prime Minister Winston Churchill (1874–1965; prime minister May 1940–July 1945) was well aware of the fact that several British royals had kindred relations among German royalty and that these British royals held admiration for the Germans and the Nazis after they gained absolute power in 1933. After capture of the German Foreign Ministry and *Reich* Chancellery archives in 1945, Churchill in consultation with King George VI (younger brother of abdicated King Edward VIII, Duke of Windsor) commenced a top-secret scrubbing operation—Morshead-Blunt Mission—with a team called "the weeders" who were sent to Germany to find and conceal anything that documented the royals' interactions with Hitler and Nazi officials—particularly, ties binding the British royal House of Windsor to the German dynastic House of Hesse—to protect the Royal Family's reputation. Many Hessens were prominent members of the Nazi Party and blood relations to British royals (Petropoulos 2006).

Among the most secretive of the European royal houses is the House of Windsor. Of Germanic origin and cousins of the Hohenzollern and the Hessens* (among others), the British royals were viewed during the first half of the twentieth century as a source of hope by many who sought a rapprochement between Germany and Britain. The archives of the British royal family could indeed shed considerable light on the history of German princes during the Third *Reich.* Most of these records are housed in Windsor Castle in the so-called "Round Tower." While certain documents in the Royal Archives are accessible to researchers, it appears that many others have been held back. The royal family's connection to German princes is a subject that continues to raise uncomfortable questions, and the queen's staff has internalized this protective outlook: one experienced researcher who has received considerable support from the Windsors acknowledged that the subject of the royal family and the Nazis made the archivists "really nervous" (Petropoulos 2006, "Introduction").

After the Americans seized *Schloss Friedrichshof* in Kronberg in the spring of 1945, King George VI charged Royal Archivist Sir Owen Morshead with removing the letters from German Empress Victoria (wife of former German Emperor Fredrich III) to her mother, Queen Victoria, to the safekeeping of Windsor Castle. Major Anthony Blunt, who had just succeeded Kenneth Clark as surveyor of the king's (and later the queen's) pictures, also appeared on the scene. Until war's end, Blunt was a member of British Intelligence—the counterintelligence branch, MI5. In 1964, Blunt

* Hessian soldiers (30,000 in total) played an important role in the American Revolution. They fought on the side of the British because their royal leader Friedrich II, Landgraf of Hesse-Kassel, was married to Princess Mary, the fourth daughter of King George II of Great Britain and Caroline of Brandenburg-Ansbach.

was revealed as a traitor (member of the Cambridge Five) who had spied for the Soviet Union, and in turn was protected by the royal family (knighted by Queen Elizabeth II in 1956, despite suspicions since 1948 that he was a Soviet spy) lest he reveal the details of the secret mission he had undertaken at the end of the Second World War. But after public revelations of his espionage in 1979, the queen stripped Blunt of his knighthood and in short order he was removed as an Honorary Fellow of Trinity College and Fellow of the British Academy.

Eventually, "the weeders" also uncovered a cache of documents—ultimately known as the "Windsor File"—in the archives of the German Foreign Ministry and *Reich* Chancellery damaging to the royal family demonstrating close contacts between Nazi officials and certain British royals and government officials. Pressure on the editorial board overseeing the serial publication of the *ADAP* to omit these embarrassing and potentially damaging documents quickly grew. The most egregious documents involved the Duke of Windsor—formerly King Edward VIII of Great Britain who abdicated the throne on 10 December 1936—regarding his contacts with and support of the Nazi regime. Word of these embarrassing secret documents quickly reached Prime Minister Churchill who informed King George VI. Churchill wanted the most damaging documents destroyed regarding a conspiracy involving the Nazis and the Duke of Windsor to reinstate the duke to the British throne. However, the decision was made to classify and exclude these documents from publication. The classified file became known as the "Windsor File"—some 60 documents (letters, telegrams, and other papers) written by people working around the Duke of Windsor, including German agents, during the war.

Paul Robinson Sweet, formerly a historian in the Office of Strategic Services during the war (Winks 1987, 495–7), worked as chief historian for the United States Department of State after the war and was assigned as chief U.S. editor of the German documents publication series between 1952 and 1958, while also working from 1953 to 1963 at the U.S. Embassy in Bonn, West Germany. In Winter 1997, Sweet published an article in *The Historian* (December 1997; 59(2): 263–80) titled "The Windsor File" wherein he states the following:

> Controversy about Edward, Duke of Windsor and Nazi Germany had a long history before the fall of France in June 1940. From his youth, Edward had manifested a fondness for the German language and culture. As a war veteran, he

abhorred the thought of renewed conflict with Germany, and his political inclinations lay with Hitler's Germany rather than with Stalin's Russia. Like a large segment of contemporary Tory opinion, he hoped for an Anglo-German political settlement that would satisfy Germany's aspirations in Central and Eastern Europe. His pro-German feelings frequently found expression in indiscreet remarks that were not only insensitive to the brutalities of the Nazi regime but critical of "slip-shod democracy." In July 1933, he told former Kaiser Wilhelm II's grandson, Prince Louis Ferdinand, that it was "no business of ours to interfere in Germany's internal affairs either re Jews or re anything else." "Dictators are very popular these days," Edward had added, "We might want one in England before long."

In 1936 the Duke of Coburg,* another of Edward's [Duke of Windsor] German relatives and a committed Nazi, reported three conversations in which Edward, then king, resolved "to concentrate the business of government in himself" and asked for an appointment with Hitler "here or in Germany." A year after Edward's abdication in 1936 to marry American divorcee Wallis Simpson, he and his bride made a much-publicized visit to Germany. There they were entertained by Hermann Goering and received by Hitler at Berchtesgaden. On at least one occasion during this visit the duke apparently gave the Nazi salute.

The outbreak of war in 1939 only heightened tension between the British government and its former monarch. Still unwelcome in Britain, the duke and duchess had settled in France, where Edward was appointed a major-

---

* A welcome visitor to Buckingham Palace, former British prince Carl Eduard (Charles Edward), the Duke of Saxe-Coburg and Gotha with British titles of Duke of Albany, Earl of Clarence, and Baron Arklow, also known as "Charlie Coburg," was Queen Victoria's grandson, first cousin to King George V, and confidant to the Duke of Windsor. Coburg was employed by the *Führer* as a go-between for the German government to exploit the Royal Family's pro-German leanings. Coburg wrote in his diary of often visiting the royals at Buckingham and Sandringham Palace. His value as a key asset to Hitler was laid out in a telegram sent from the Nazi leader's bunker in April 1945: "The Führer attaches importance to the Duke of Coburg on no account falling into enemy hands."

general with rather nondescript liaison duties at French army headquarters. As a former field marshal, he considered this position demeaning, and before long Count Julius von Zech, the German minister at The Hague, reported "something like the beginning of a *fronde* [opposition]" around the disgruntled duke. "Under favorable circumstances," he suggested, this estrangement from the current British government might "acquire a certain significance." These reports were reviewed by Foreign Minister Joachim von Ribbentrop, and in one instance by Hitler himself.

When circumstances did become "favorable" upon the fall of France, eyes at the highest levels in Berlin turned appraisingly toward the duke. The Windsors had fled to neutral Spain, but upon reaching Madrid, they received the disappointing news that Prime Minister Winston Churchill, their strongest supporter in the abdication crisis, would not offer Edward a responsible position at home. Anxious to keep the Windsors "out of Hitler's grasp," however, he asked the duke to assume the governorship of the Bahamas. As Churchill delicately explained to President Franklin Roosevelt, "there are personal and family difficulties about his return to this country." On 2 July, the Windsors reached Lisbon, but instead of sailing for the new post as ordered they stayed for a month at the home of a rich Portuguese banker, Ricardo Ribeiro do Espírito Santo e Silva, while the duke pestered the prime minister about personal matters. Eventually Churchill became so frustrated that he reminded Edward in a telegram that even major generals could be court-martialed.

While the duke and the prime minister bickered over draft exemptions for personal servants, the German government considered the role Windsor might play in its plans. Ribbentrop told the German ambassador in Madrid on 11 July that "Germany is determined to force England to peace by every means of power and upon this happening would be prepared to accommodate any desire expressed by the duke, especially with a view to the assumption of the English throne by the duke and duchess." Germany had

> failed to prevent the Windsors' move to Lisbon, but now dispatched a top agent, Walter Schellenberg, to keep him there. As German intelligence reviewed various options, including kidnapping, it passed onto Berlin a stream of antiwar, anti-Churchill, anti-royal family remarks the duke allegedly had made to acquaintances. Reports stated that the duke believed "continued severe bombing would make England ready for peace," that he was considering a public declaration disassociating himself from Churchill's policy of carrying on the war, and that he was tempted by a Spanish offer of asylum in Granada or Malaga.
>
> Throughout July, as the Windsors lingered in Portugal, German agents tried to convince the duke that he had been targeted for assassination by his brother's secret service, while London sent increasingly peremptory demands that he leave for the Bahamas. Finally, Churchill dispatched Sir Walter Monckton, Edward's old friend and legal adviser during the abdication crisis, to get the duke on the boat, and on 1 August 1940 the Windsors finally sailed. Their departure did not end German hopes, however, as intelligence reported that the duke had left his Portuguese host a code word and promised to return to Europe if he received it. On 15 August the duke wired Silva to notify him "as soon as action might be desirable." A year later the German minister in Lisbon reported that "the intermediary familiar to us . . . has received a letter from the Duke of Windsor confirming his opinion as recently stated in a published interview that Britain has virtually lost the war already and the USA would be better advised to promote peace, not war." The British government certainly knew of many of these continued indiscretions, but made no real effort to restrain the former monarch beyond exiling him to the West Indies until victory was secure.

German historian Dr. Karina Urbach (doctorate from University of Cambridge), Senior Research Fellow at the Institute of Historical Research at the University of London (and author of *Go-Betweens for Hitler*, Oxford University Press, 2015), uncovered evidence of just how deep the duke's collusion with the Nazis went. She details a report from 25 June 1940 by

Spanish diplomat and friend of the duke Don Javier Bermejillo of a conversation where Edward went so far as to argue that bombing of England could bring World War II to an end. Dr. Urbach claims the report was passed on to Spain's military dictator, General Francisco Franco, and then to Germany. German aerial bombing of Britain began shortly after the 25 June Spanish report on 10 July 1940 and the Blitz—Operation *Loge* (*Unternehmen Loge*)—over London began on 7 September.

Among the Windsor File documents are details of the Nazi-devised plan *Unternehmen Willi* (Operation Willi), where the Germans would gain control of Britain and overthrow the monarchy, returning the Duke of Windsor to the throne. The Germans viewed the duke, who was perceived to be ambivalent about the war, as a better ally than his successor and younger brother King George VI. In order to get the duke on their side, German agents tried to manipulate the ostracized royal, even attempting to convince the duke that his brother, King George, had plans to assassinate him. Nazi Foreign Minister Joachim von Ribbentrop lavishly bestowed attention on the duke's American wife Duchess of Windsor Wallis Simpson. German Duke Carl Alexander of Württemberg (then a monk in an American monastery) had told the Federal Bureau of Investigation that the Duchess had slept with the German ambassador in London, Joachim von Ribbentrop, in 1936, had remained in constant contact with him, and had continued to leak secrets (Evans and Hencke 2002). The *Führer* and his key advisers were no doubt rubbing their hands together at the prospect of pulling the strings of a "puppet king" if their wish for Edward to be reinstalled was realized. In his autobiography *Inside the Third Reich*, Nazi *Reich* Minister of Armaments and War Production Albert Speer quoted Hitler directly: "I am certain through him [Duke of Windsor] permanent friendly relations could have been achieved. If he had stayed [on the throne], everything would have been different. His abdication was a severe loss for us (Speer 1970, 118)."

A pair of historians believe Edward VIII was not the only son of King George V to conspire with the Nazis to create a World War II Anglo-German alliance. John Harris and Richard Wilbourn, authors of *Rudolf Hess: Treachery and Deception* (Northampton, UK: Jema Publications, 2016), assert that Prince George, the Duke of Kent and uncle to Queen Elizabeth II, played a key part in planning a *coup d'état* with Hitler's deputy, Rudolf Heß, to remove Prime Minister Winston Churchill and forge a treaty with the *Führer*.

One of the most enduring mysteries of World War II is why Heß parachuted into Scotland in 1941. Harris and Wilbourn, after sifting through over 10,000 documents, believe the evidence "very strongly points" to an Anglo-German conspiracy. (Intriguingly, Prince George, who served in the RAF, is said to have been in Scotland when Heß arrived.)

"Having weighed up all the evidence, and in light of recent discoveries we have made, we now believe that it was, in fact, a *coup* attempt centred around Prince George," says Harris. "The aristocracy had the most to lose from Churchill staying in power. All they knew was that Germany was bombing Britain nightly, softening the country up prior to an invasion, which would surely cost them their wealth, their status and their lives."

After much negotiation and bickering between the British and American governments, an agreement to go forward with the project of publishing the captured German documents (Marburg Files) including the so-called "Windsor File" was concluded on 19 June 1946. The memorandum of agreement specified that editing was to be "performed on the basis of the highest scholarly objectivity" by "outside scholars of highest reputation." France and the Soviet Union were invited to participate in the project, but while France joined, the Soviets declined. However, over the ensuing eight years of the project's duration, controversy between the British and American editors over the Windsor File festered and threatened objectivity and integrity of the project. This ongoing controversy reached the highest levels of the British and American governments (Churchill and President Eisenhower) and caused the long delay in publishing Volume X containing the now infamous Windsor File. Volume X, with all the Windsor documents, finally was published in 1957.

British Royal Archives housed in Windsor Castle's Round Tower that deal with any relationship between the Windsors and the Nazis, however, remain sealed. They include correspondence between the British Royal Family and their German relatives, including the Victorian letters between mother and daughter seized by the Americans from *Schloss Friedrichshof* in Kronberg in the spring of 1945, that would reveal the full extent of the family's connections to the Third *Reich* in the lead-up to World War II. To date, there are no plans to ever declassify these British Royal Archives.

Most of the history of the Heß debacle in 1941 has been written by British historians. Given the inherent conflict of interest many British historians possess—loyalty to the ruling House of Windsor over academic integrity—much of the conclusions made on the Heß matter by these historians can be taken with a grain of salt. While many other captured and tried Nazis, who escaped a sentence of execution were eventually released from prison, after transferring him back to Germany for trial in 1947 and his conviction by the Nuremberg Tribunal, the British insisted Heß be sentenced to and remain imprisoned for life. For the British, Heß knew too much information that would be damaging to the British royals if it ever were to become public.

ON 8 SEPTEMBER 1940, ONE DAY AFTER COMMENCEMENT OF THE LONDON Blitz,* Albrecht Haushofer, wrote a letter to his British friend the Duke of Hamilton: "You . . . may find some significance in the fact that I am able to ask you whether you could find time to have a talk to me somewhere on the outskirts of Europe, perhaps in Portugal." Haushofer also referred to people who the German government believed wanted an "German-English agreement." This included senior British Conservative politicians Samuel John Gurney Hoare, First Viscount Templewood (1880–1959) and Richard Austen Butler (1902–1982), both of whom supported appeasement of Germany in 1938–1939. Two days later, Albrecht Haushofer sent a letter to his father, Karl. The letter discussed secret peace talks going on with Britain. Albrecht talked about "middlemen" such as the elderly General Sir Ian Standish Monteith Hamilton (1853–1947; head of the British Legion and founding member and vice-president of the Anglo-German Association), the Duke of Hamilton, and Violet Roberts, whose nephew Walter Roberts was

* The Blitz – Operation *Loge* (*Unternehmen Loge*) (the codename for London) was the air offensive against London and other industrial cities. Hitler's "Directive No. 17 – For the conduct of air and sea warfare against England" issued on 1 August 1940, reserved to himself the right to decide on terror attacks as measures of reprisal. The bombing operation over London occurred from 7 September 1940 to 11 May 1941. *Loge* continued for 57 nights. A total of 348 German bombers and 617 German fighters took part in the attack. Operation *Loge* was Hitler's last attempt to win the Battle of Britain (July 1940 to June 1941). The primary objective was to compel Britain to agree to a negotiated peace settlement. The Battle of Britain marked the first major defeat of Germany's military forces, with air superiority seen as the key to victory. For the RAF, Fighter Command had achieved a great victory in successfully carrying out Sir Thomas Inskip's 1937 air policy of preventing the Germans from knocking Britain out of the war. British historian Stephen Bungay cited Germany's failure to destroy Britain's air defenses to force an armistice (or even outright surrender) as the first major German defeat in World War II and a crucial turning point in the war that emboldened the Allies.

a close relative of the Duke of Hamilton and was working in the political intelligence and propaganda branch of the British Secret Intelligence Service (MI6). The Roberts were very close to Chief of MI6 Major General Sir Stewart Graham Menzies (1890–1968; Walter and Stewart had gone to school together). Violet Roberts was living in Lisbon in 1940. Portugal, Spain, Sweden, and Switzerland were the four main places where these secret negotiations were taking place.

On 19 September 1940, Albrecht Haushofer wrote to Rudolf Heß about his letter to the Duke of Hamilton. He explained that Hamilton would find it difficult to fly to Portugal without the permission of Lord Halifax, the British Foreign Secretary, and Archibald Sinclair, the Secretary of State for Air. Haushofer suggested that it would probably be better to work through Samuel Hoare but planned to send the letter via an old friend. The letter was intercepted by MI5, and Hamilton was persuaded to work as a double agent. Hamilton agreed to go to Lisbon to meet Haushofer. Colonel Tar Robertson, head of MI5's double-agent section, wrote in his report, dated 29 April 1941:

> Hamilton [was] at the beginning of the war, and still is, a member of the community which sincerely believes that Great Britain will be willing to make peace with Germany provided the present regime in Germany were superseded by some reasonable form of government. . . . He is a slow witted man but at the same time he gets there in the end; and I feel that if he is properly schooled before leaving for Lisbon he could do a very useful job of work (Douglas-Hamilton 1993, 132).

Despite the tide of the war in the Battle of Britain slowly shifting towards England at the close of 1940 and spring of 1941, Heß continued to believe he could effectuate peace between Great Britain and Germany. Heß knew of Hitler's plans for Operation Barbarossa and how its chances for ultimate success greatly depended on ending the war in Western Europe. Hitler knew this and repeatedly lamented to Heß how attractive of an offer he would be willing to make to the British were they only interested in peace. As late as May 1941 (one month before Hitler executed Operation Barbarossa), Heß fervently continued to plan how to improve Germany's chances in the East by ending war with Great Britain. In early May 1941, Heß began taking final steps to execute his plan by writing letters to his son, several of his closest friends and colleagues, and Hitler. Logistic planning and training on how to travel to England by air without detection had been in the works for months. Finally and unbeknownst to anyone else at the time, on the evening of 10 May 1941, Heß boarded his personal, modified Messerschmidt Bf 110 (modified by his friend Professor Willi Messerschmitt) at the airfield at Augsburg-Haunstetten and flew at low altitude across the North Sea to Scotland with the intended destination of Dungavel House (nineteenth-century hunting lodge and summer retreat of the Dukes of Hamilton linked to their then main house at Hamilton Palace) six miles from the town of Strathaven, Scotland. There, Heß hoped to meet with Douglas the fourteenth Duke of Hamilton, Lord Clydesdale to discuss a peace treaty between their two countries.

Heß parachuted out of his plane and landed at Floors Farm near the village of Eaglesham thirteen miles south of Glasgow and eighteen miles north of Dungavel House, where he was discovered still struggling with his parachute by local ploughman David McLean. Identifying himself as "Hauptmann Alfred Horn," Heß said he had an important message for the Duke of Hamilton. McLean helped Heß to his nearby cottage and contacted the local Home Guard unit, who escorted the captive to their headquarters in Busby, East Renfrewshire. He was next taken to the police station at Giffnock, arriving after midnight; he was searched, and his possessions confiscated. Heß repeatedly requested to meet with the Duke of Hamilton during questioning undertaken with the aid of an interpreter by Major Graham Donald, the area commandant of Royal Observer Corps. After the interview, Heß was taken under guard to Maryhill Barracks in Glasgow, where his ankle injury was treated. By this time, some of his captors suspected Heß's true identity, though he continued to insist his name was Horn.

Royal Air Force Air Commodore Hamilton had been on duty as wing commander at RAF Turnhouse near Edinburgh when Heß arrived, and his station had been one of those that had tracked the progress of the flight. He arrived at Maryhill Barracks the next morning, and after examining Heß's effects, he met alone with the prisoner. Heß immediately admitted his true identity and outlined the reason for his flight. Hamilton told Heß that he hoped to continue the conversation with the aid of an interpreter; Heß could speak English well but was having trouble understanding Hamilton. After the meeting, Hamilton examined the remains of the Messerschmitt in the company of an intelligence officer, then returned to Turnhouse, where he arranged through the Foreign Office to meet Churchill, who was at Ditchley for the weekend. They had some preliminary talks that night, and Hamilton accompanied Churchill back to London the next day, where they both met with members of the War Cabinet. Churchill sent Hamilton with foreign affairs expert Ivone Kirkpatrick, who had met Heß previously, to positively identify the prisoner, who had been moved to Buchanan Castle overnight. Heß, who had prepared extensive notes to use during this meeting, spoke to them at length about Hitler's expansionary plans and the need for Britain to let the Nazis have free rein in Europe, in exchange for being allowed to keep its overseas possessions. Kirkpatrick held two more meetings with Heß over the course of the next few days, while Hamilton returned to his duties. Heß, in addition to being disappointed at the apparent failure of his mission, began claiming that his medical treatment was inadequate and that there was a plot afoot to poison him.

Heß was not taken seriously by the British government who ignored his peace overtures. He spent the next thirteen months of his captivity undergoing interrogation and mental health examination. He was then interned at Maindiff Court Hospital until the end of the war. On 10 October 1945 (exactly four and one-half years, to the day, after his arrival in England), he was transferred to Nuremberg, Germany to appear before the International Military Tribunal as a war criminal. He was charged with four counts—conspiracy to commit crimes, crimes against peace, war crimes, and crimes against humanity, in violation of international laws governing warfare. His trial lasted from 7 February to 31 August 1946. Heß was found guilty on two counts: crimes against peace (planning and preparing a war of aggression) and conspiracy with other German leaders to commit crimes. On 1 October 1946, he was sentenced to life imprisonment. He was then transported by aircraft to the Allied military prison *Spandau* in Berlin on 18 July 1947.

Other than his stays in a hospital, Heß spent the rest of his life in *Spandau*. His fellow inmates Konstantin von Neurath, Walther Funk, and Erich Raeder were released because of poor health in the 1950s; Admiral Karl Dönitz, Baldur von Schirach, and Albert Speer served their time and were released; Dönitz in 1956, Schirach and Speer in 1966. The 600-cell prison continued to be maintained for its lone prisoner from 1966 until Heß's alleged suicide by hanging on 17 August 1987. Nearly immediately after his death, *Spandau* was demolished to prevent it from becoming a neo-Nazi shrine. His lawyer Dr. Alfred Seidl felt Heß was too old and frail to have managed to kill himself. Wolf Rüdiger Heß repeatedly claimed that his father had been murdered by the British Secret Intelligence Service to prevent him from revealing information about British royals and aristocrats connected to the British government who supported the Nazi Party during the 1930s and early 1940s.

Albrecht Haushofer became very distressed when he discovered that the Heß peace initiative had ended in failure. As Haushofer knew the true details of the operation, he feared for his life. He was right, and on 11 May 1941, Adolf Hitler ordered the arrest of Haushofer. The following day, he was taken to Berchtesgaden and ordered to write a full report on what he knew about the reasons for Rudolf Heß flying to Scotland. Haushofer also outlined his contacts with people like the Duke of Hamilton, Samuel Hoare (Viscount Templewood), British Foreign Secretary Edward Frederick Lindley Wood, First Earl of Halifax (Lord Halifax; 1881–1959), and parliamentary aide to Neville Chamberlain, Alexander Frederick Douglas-Home (Lord Dunglass; 1903–1995).

After reading Haushofer's report, Hitler ordered that he should be sent to the *Reich* Main Security Office (*Reichssicherheitshauptamt* or *RSHA*) on *Prinz Albrecht Straße* in Berlin to be interrogated by Heinrich Müller (1900–1945), the head of the *Gestapo*. Hitler believed that Haushofer could still play a key role in any future peace negotiations with Britain, so Haushofer was released from custody in July 1941. He was kept under surveillance and Chief of the Nazi Party Chancellery (*Reichsleiter Parteikanzlei*) Martin Bormann (1900–1945) sent a letter to important figures in the media that: "Professor Albrecht Haushofer should no longer be given any publicity."

After the 20 July 1944 attempt on Hitler's life at his Wolf's Lair field headquarters near Rastenburg, East Prussia, Albrecht feared for his life and went into hiding. On 7 December 1944, he was found and arrested by the *Gestapo* for his alleged involvement in the attempted 20 July 1944 assassination plot on Hitler. He was held at the remand holding Moabit Prison (*Untersuchungsgefängnis Moabit*) on *Lehrterstraße* in the Tiergarten-Moabit district of Berlin. Over the ensuing weeks, Haushofer was interrogated repeatedly. However, unlike the other conspirators, Haushofer was not executed. It is believed Hitler had the "intention to make use of Haushofer at a later date." Hitler and Himmler were both still hoping that they could exploit Haushofer's British connections to negotiate a peace deal with Britain and the United States. Haushofer was given special privileges and during this period he wrote what became known as the *Moabite Sonnets*, including the 38th Sonnet:

I lightly carry what the judge calls my guilt
Guilt in planning and caring
I would feel guilty had I not from inner duty
Planned for the people's future
But I am guilty other than you think:
I should have sooner seen my duty
I should have sharper condemned evil
I have too long delayed my judgement.
I now accuse myself
I have long betrayed my conscience
I have lied to myself and to others.
I soon foresaw the evil's frightful path;
I have warned,
But my warnings were too feeble.
I know today wherein lies my guilt

In February 1945, Heinrich Himmler explored the possibility of doing a deal that involved capitulating to the Western Allies but not to the Soviet Union. Winston Churchill and Harry Truman considered this offer but with the Red Army advancing on Berlin, it was not a realistic option. On 21 April 1945, Himmler instructed Heinrich Müller to execute Albrecht Haushofer. During the night of 22–23 April 1945, he and other alleged prisoners were walked out of the prison by an *SS* execution squad and were shot.

Karl Haushofer was imprisoned at Dachau Concentration Camp for eight months until the end of the war. Upon liberation of Dachau, Karl's identity was confirmed, and he was arrested by the Allies and interrogated. The British and American governments have never released the documents that include details of these interrogations. However, these documents remain in the archives of the Office of Strategic Services (now known as the CIA). Karl told his interrogators that Germany was involved in peace negotiations with Britain in 1940–1941. In 1941, his son Albrecht was sent to Switzerland to meet Samuel Hoare (Lord Templewood) the British ambassador to Spain. This peace proposal included a willingness to "relinquish Norway, Denmark and France." Karl goes onto say: "A larger meeting was to be held in Madrid. When my son returned, he was immediately called to Augsburg by Heß. A few days later Heß flew to England."

Karl was docketed to be tried in Nuremberg, but investigators found no basis for criminal charges, and he was released from custody. On the evening of 11 March 1946, Karl and his wife Martha set out for their last walk through the woods. They stopped about half a mile from their *Hartschimmelhof* estate at Pähl am Ammersee in a secluded hollow by the stream under a willow tree. There they drank arsenic. Martha was also hanged from the tree; the General was not strong enough to follow suit as the poison took effect.

ALFRED ROSENBERG (1893–1946) – ALFRED ROSENBERG, THE SON OF Baltic German* parents—Estonian mother (language teacher) and Lithuanian father (wealthy merchant)—was born in Tallinn, Russian Empire (now Estonia), on 12 January 1893. The family's German roots came into question in 1936 but were never definitively disproven. The young Rosenberg graduated from the *Petri-Realschule* (currently *Tallinna Reaalkool*) in 1911 and went on to study architecture at the Riga Polytechnical Institute (before it was evacuated to Moscow at the outset of World War I) where he joined a pro-German student group. After completing his architectural studies in Riga, he studied engineering at the Imperial Moscow Technical School (now Bauman Moscow State Technical University) earning his doctorate in 1917. During the German occupation of

---

* Baltic Germans: Ethnic German Catholic ghetto tradesmen and crusaders settled in the Baltics during the twelfth and thirteenth centuries as part of *Ostsiedlung* (east settlement; medieval eastward migration), *Ostkolonisation* (east colonization) or *Hochmittelalterlicher Landesausbau* (high medieval land consolidation). As Christianity was slowly rooted in the Baltics from the days of Charlemagne to the Prussian Crusade in 1224, Duchy of Estonia (1346), and Christianization of Lithuania (1387) by the Teutonic Order and Livonian Brothers of the Sword, control over the native pagan Baltic tribes was established resulting in the duchies of Mecklenburg and Saxony, as well as the Margraviate of Brandenburg. The landed nobility, bishops, and monasteries started to recruit farmers, tradesmen, artisans, and clerics from their Saxon and Frankish homelands. A second wave of Germanic colonization occurred in the sixteenth century and continued for several centuries, thereafter, as industrial craftsmen from Germany were needed for the exploitation of mines, processing of textile, forestry and carpentry, cultivation of depopulated lands and towns, and draining of marshes for agriculture. As Imperial Russian influence grew in the Baltics, German elites intermarried with Russian nobility and the German Baltic lineage was forever transformed (Emmert 2016.)

Estonia in 1918, Rosenberg served as a teacher at the *Gustav Adolf Gymnasium* (changed from *Gymnázium of Emperor Nikolai I* upon German occupation). Two days after the outbreak of the Estonian War of Independence against invading Russian Bolsheviks (28 November 1918–2 February 1920), Rosenberg held his first speech on Jewish Marxism on 30 November 1918 in Tallinn at the Brotherhood of the Blackheads (professional military and social association of ship owners, merchants, and foreigners dating to the fourteenth century whose mission was to protect Christianity and thwart enemy invasion).

The outbreak of World War I brought the end of the alliance of the Baltic Germans and Russian tsarist government as Germany and Russia were enemy belligerents in the war. German heritage was now viewed as a threat to Russians. Likewise, Baltic Germans were considered traitors by the German Empire if they remained loyal to Russia. Moreover, their loyalty to Imperial Russia was questioned by the tsar and rumors of a German Fifth Column increased as the Imperial Russian Army suffered a series of defeats under Russian General Paul von Rennenkampf who was of German Baltic descent. All German schools and societies were closed in the Estonian Governorate during the Estonian War of Independence. Hence, Rosenberg decided to emigrate to Germany with the retreating Imperial German Army in November 1918. Unable to find employment in Berlin, Rosenberg moved in December 1918 to Munich where he joined a Russian expatriate discussion circle, which convinced Rosenberg that Germany had to defend European civilization against the spread of Jewish-Marxist nihilism.

Like many Baltic Germans, Rosenberg supported the Whites during the Russian Revolution. Rosenberg later claimed that it was in Moscow in 1917 that he first saw a copy of *The Protocols of the Elders of Zion. The Protocols* was a Russian fabricated document believed to be written in the months after the second all-Russian Zionist Conference in Minsk in September 1902 (first all-Russian Zionist Conference was secretly held in Warsaw on 17 August 1898) when some of the most destructive anti-Jewish pogroms (1903–1906) began in the Russian Empire, in which thousands of Jews died or fled the empire. *The Protocols* was originally a French parody of Jewish idealism meant for internal circulation among anti-Semites until it was decided by the Tsar's secret police directly responsible for inciting the pogroms to alter and publish it as if it were real. In its fabricated form, *The Protocols* document the minutes of a sinister late nineteenth-century meeting attended by world Jewish leaders, the "Elders of Zion," who are conspiring to take over the world. In the forgery, the Jewish leaders enunciate a set of plans, most of which stem from conventional anti-Semitic canards such as subverting the traditional morals of the non-Jewish world, Jewish bankers controlling the world's economies and the press, and, ultimately, the replacement of established order, religion, and culture under sovereign governments with a new racist Jewish order, religion, and culture under a single government based on autocracy and control of wealth. The document consists of twenty-four "protocols," which confirm longstanding defamatory themes that appear repeatedly throughout *The Protocols*. The scandalous document made its way to Germany and throughout the West during the Russian Revolution and civil war when returning German expatriates, Baltic Germans, and monarchist White Russian émigrés living in the Russian Empire (future constituents of the *Aufbau Vereinigung* organization), most of which participated in the White Russian counter-revolution against the Reds, brought the forgery with them and distributed it for republication. One such individual carrying the forgery was Alfred Rosenberg who fully believed the document was authentic and enlightening. The threat of rapid spread of Bolshevism throughout Europe in the early nineteenth century generated tremendous fear among the establishment and anti-Marxist revolutionaries challenging burgeoning Socialist and Communist movements. With the widespread republication of *The Protocols*, first in Germany and then throughout the West, Bolshevism was soon seen as the vehicle, by which the Jews planned to destroy traditional Western culture and dominate the world. Through this forgery, the Thule Society and eventually the *NSDAP* were deeply infected with anti-Jewish sentiment that paved the way for the Holocaust of the 1930s and 1940s.

Aufbau: Wirtschaftspolitische Vereinigung für den Osten (Reconstruction: Economic-Political Organization for the East) was a secret counterrevolutionary monarchist conspiratorial organization formed in Munich in the aftermath of the German occupation of the Ukraine in 1918, the failed Latvian Intervention of 1919 (caused by British betrayal), and the mass murders and deportations by Bolshevik invaders in the Baltics in 1919. Defeated German soldiers, Baltic Germans, White Russians, and ethnic Balts fled to Germany. Some members of these groups radicalized in this period to unabashed haters of everything that was politically liberal, and of all nations within the Entente. Many members of the different ethnic groups fleeing the Baltics to Germany amalgamated into a group of extreme Nationalist militants under the colloquial names *Baltikumkämpfer* (Baltic fighter) or *Baltikumer*. It was the Baltic German émigré Lieutenant Max von Scheubner-Richter who unified these *Baltikumkämpferen* under the secret umbrella organization *Aufbau: Wirtschaftspolitische Vereinigung für den Osten* in early 1919. The White Russian émigrés and *völkisch*-minded Baltic German National Socialists sought to overthrow the Socialist governments of the Weimar Republic and the Soviet Union and restore their respective monarchies or, in the alternative, replace them with authoritarian regimes of radical Nationalists. The group was originally known as *Die Brücke* (The Bridge). *Aufbau* was also the name of a periodical the underground organization published (not to be confused with the New York-based Jewish international publication founded in 1934 for German-speaking Jews). In March 1920, *Aufbau* member Alfred Rosenberg introduced Hitler to von Scheubner-Richter. The *Aufbau Vereinigung* was a vital influence on the development of Nazi ideology in the years before the 1923 Beer Hall *Putsch*, as well as a source of financing *NSDAP* with considerable sums of money from wealthy industrialists such as Henry Ford. Its members introduced Hitler to the idea of a vast Jewish conspiracy propagated by the Russian forgery *The Protocols of the Elders of Zion* involving a close alliance between international finance and Bolshevism that threatened disaster for mankind.

Evidence has proven that Hitler's anti-Semitism during his early years in Vienna (1905–1913) was far less developed than it became under the influence of his closest members of the *Aufbau Vereinigung*, namely Baltic Germans Alfred Rosenberg, Max von Scheubner-Richter, and Fyodor Viktorovich Vinberg. Early anti-Bolshevik and anti-Semitic National Socialist thought in Germany developed largely as a post-World War I mixture of *völkisch* notions of Germanic racial and spiritual superiority with apocalyptic White émigré ideas of threatened world ruin at the hands of insidious international Jewish conspirators. Hitler only began to crystalize his anti-Bolshevik, anti-Semitic *Weltanschauung* in late 1919, when he started learning from his early mentors Eckart, Rosenberg, von Scheubner-Richter, and Vinberg. The *Aufbau* White émigrés von Scheubner-Richter, Vinberg, and Rosenberg, along with their *völkisch* German colleague Eckart, influenced National Socialist ideology as the "four writers of the apocalypse," who warned of ever-expanding "Jewish Bolshevik" destruction. Hitler assumed the apocalyptic stance of his four ideological colleagues by pledging to fight the alleged Jewish conspiracy to destroy the world through the spread of Bolshevism (Kellogg 2005, 278).

Flush with cash from like-minded wealthy international industrialists and strengthened by the successful organization and implementation of the Monarchical Congress at Bad Reichenhall (organized by *Aufbau*) in the May–June 1921, the White Russian and Baltic German *Aufbau Vereinigung* followed a two-pronged strategy of intensified anti-Bolshevik and anti-Weimar operations through means of political terror and secret military organization, all the while expanding its influence over Hitler's fledgling National Socialist movement. In its covert military undertakings, *Aufbau* forged a "league of the defeated" to overthrow both the prevailing Versailles system in Europe and Bolshevik rule to the East. Building upon the legacy of earlier German and White anti-Bolshevik campaigns, *Aufbau* exploited its vast resources to raise powerful armed forces intended for operation in the Baltic region. Among the aims of the *Aufbau*, as expressed by the Monarchical Congress at Bad Reichenhall, was a National Socialist campaign against the Bolsheviks, which would establish Nationalist Russian, Ukrainian, and Baltic successor states, and restoration of the Russian Monarchy under their tsarist candidate Grand Prince Kirill Romanov. Several *Aufbau* members also became involved in terrorist activities in collaboration with Organization C—a conspiratorial radical-Nationalist terrorist organization under leading Kapp *Putsch* figure Captain Hermann Ehrhardt that possessed considerable connections with the National Socialist Party—including the assassination of Weimar Republic's Minister of Finance Matthias Erzberger on 26 August 1921, and the Republic's Foreign Minister Walther Rathenau and the prominent constitutional Democrat Vladimir Dmitrievich Nabokov (both in 1922). Organization C arose around the same time as the White Russian Monarchical Congress of Bad Reichenhall in May–June 1921. Shortly after the conclusion of the Congress, officers of the disbanded II Marine Brigade (Ehrhardt Brigade) who had participated in the failed Kapp *Putsch*[*] and run

[*] The Kapp *Putsch*, also known as the Kapp-Lüttwitz *Putsch* after its leaders Wolfgang Kapp and General Walther von Lüttwitz, was an attempted *coup* on 13 March 1920, which aimed to undo the German Revolution of 1918–1919, overthrow the Weimar Republic, and establish a Nationalist autocratic government in its place. It was supported by parts of the *Vorläufige Reichswehr* (Provisional National Defense), including *Marine Brigade Ehrhardt*, and other conservative, Nationalist, and monarchist factions. The *coup* took place in Berlin, and the legitimate German government was forced to flee the city. The *coup* failed after a few days, when many Germans followed a call by the government to join a general strike. Most civil servants refused to cooperate with Kapp and his allies. Despite its failure, the *putsch* had significant consequences for the future of the Weimar Republic. It was the cause of the Socialist Ruhr uprising of March 1920, which the government suppressed by military force, while dealing leniently with those behind the Kapp *putsch*. These

out of Berlin in March 1920 formed Organization Consul, commonly known as Organization C, with "Consul" standing for Ehrhardt himself. Organization C became infamous for its attempted and successful assassinations of Socialist, often Jewish, leaders in the early years of the Weimar Republic. Chief of Bavarian police Ernst Pöhner was a mole for and great help to Organization C by embezzling state money to support Organization C and falsifying passports for indicted members to abscond before trial. Throughout the years 1921 to 1923, *Aufbau* increasingly coordinated its secretive activities with those of Organization C. In a manner similar to *Aufbau*, the ultra-Nationalist and conspiratorial Organization C rejected the Treaty of Versailles and the Weimar Constitution, and dedicated itself to fighting Socialism, Bolshevism, and "Jewry" under the motto of "struggle for Germany's rebirth."

After the death of von Scheubner-Richter in the Beer Hall *Putsch*, the *Aufbau* rapidly declined, and notions of *Lebensraum* and Slavic inferiority gained deeper roots in the Nazi movement during and after Hitler's imprisonment for the failed *putsch*—this is evident in Hitler's unpublished 1928 sequel to *Mein Kampf*. The long-term influence of *Aufbau* on Hitler has been traced in the implementation of the Final Solution and in Hitler's disastrous decision to divert troops away from Moscow towards Ukraine in 1941. Prominent members of *Aufbau Vereinigung* included:

- Lieutenant Max Erwin von Scheubner-Richter – Baltic German and Russian Imperial Army officer
- Alfred Rosenberg – Baltic German from the Russian Empire
- Colonel Fyodor Viktorovich Vinberg – Baltic German Russian Imperial Army officer, writer, publisher, influential anti-Jewish ideologue promoting *The Protocols* and total extermination of the Jews, central figure to Hitler's conversion to the idea of worldwide Jewish-Bolshevik conspiracy
- Lieutenant Piotr Shabelskii-Bork – Russian Imperial Army officer and assassin
- General Vasily Viktorovich Biskupskii – Ukrainian Russian Imperial Army officer and wealthy oil baron
- General Erich Ludendorff – World War I German army commander in the Baltics (*Ober Ost*), commander on the Western Front, and

---

events polarized the electorate, resulting in a shift in the majority after the June 1920 *Reichstag* elections.

partner to General von Hindenburg in the duumvirate leading the Third *OHL* during World War I

- Max Amann – Hitler's company sergeant during World War I, Nazi Party business manager, publisher of *Mein Kampf* and other Nazi literature
- Boris Brasol – Ukrainian Russian émigré and state prosecutor in Imperial Russia, immigrated in 1916 to U.S. where he published an English translation of *The Protocols*, which he sent to Henry Ford, and from whom he garnered financial support for *Aufbau* and Hitler

The following are excerpts from a timeline, titled "Antisemitism – 'The Longest Hatred'" (Anti-Semitism 2014) and from "Commentary on *The Protocols of the Elders of Zion*" by Professor Daniel Keren, Ph.D. (Keren 1993) that summarize the history behind *The Protocols*.

> *The Protocols of the Learned Elders of Zion*, perhaps the most notorious work of modern antisemitism, draws on popular antisemitic notions which have their roots in mediaeval Europe from the time of the Crusades. Accusations that the Jews used blood of Christian children for the Feast of Passover, spread the plague and poisoned wells were the pretexts for the wholesale destruction of Jewish communities throughout Europe. Other stories were circulated of secret rabbinical conferences whose aim was to subjugate and exterminate the Christians.
>
> The conceptual inspiration for *The Protocols* can be traced back to the time of the French Revolution when the Abbé Augustin Barruel [1741–1820] representing reactionary elements opposed to the Revolution, published four books in 1797, the last two blaming the Revolution on a secret conspiracy operating through the Order of Freemasons and Illuminati. Barruel's ideas were unsupportable. Before the Revolution, membership of the lodges was mostly comprised of the French nobility and landed gentry. By the time Napoléon declared the Revolution over, most of the lodges had closed and many of their members were either dead or in exile. Barruel had not blamed the Jews, who were emancipated as a result of the Revolution. However, in 1806, Barruel circulated a forged

letter—probably sent to him by members of the state police opposed to Napoléon Bonaparte's liberal policy toward the Jews—calling attention to the alleged part of the Jews in the conspiracy he had earlier attributed to the Freemasons. This myth of an international Jewish conspiracy reappeared later in nineteenth-century Europe.[1]

The literary predecessor of *The Protocols* can be found in the pamphlet *Dialogue in Hell Between Machiavelli and Montesquieu, or the Politics Machiavelli in the Nineteenth Century, by a Contemporary*, published by the non-Jewish French satirist Maurice Joly (1829–1878) in 1864, although it appears that Joly plagiarized Eugène Sue's 1843 serialized novel, *Les Mystères de Paris*. In Sue's work, the plotters were Jesuits.

In his *Dialogue*, which make no mention of the Jews, Joly attacked the political ambitions of the emperor Napoléon III using the imagery of a diabolical plot in hell. The *Dialogue* was discovered by the French authorities soon after their publication, and Joly was tried and sentenced to prison for his pamphlet.[2]

Joly's *Dialogue*, while intended as a political satire and defense of Liberalism, was adopted by a German postal clerk and *agent provocateur* for the Prussian secret police, Hermann Ottomar Friedrich Goedsche (1815–1878), writing under the pseudonym Sir John Retcliffe, despite being a Prussian chauvinist who held a profound aversion against Britain and everything British. He had been forced to leave the postal service due to his part in forging evidence in the prosecution against the Democratic leader Benedict Waldeck in 1849. Goedsche adapted Joly's *Dialogue* into a mythical tale of a Jewish conspiracy as part of a series of novels entitled *Biarritz*, which appeared in 1868. In a chapter called *The Jewish Cemetery in Prague and the Council of Representatives of the Twelve Tribes of Israel*, he concocts a secret centennial rabbinical conference held by the *Council of Representatives* which meets at midnight and whose purpose is to review the past hundred years and to make plans for the next century.

Goedsche's plagiary of Joly's *Dialogue* soon found its way to Russia. It was translated into Russian in 1872, and a summary of the *Council of Representatives* meeting under the name *The Rabbi's Speech* appeared in Russian in 1891. These works no doubt furnished the *Okhrana*, the Tsar's secret police, with a means by which to strengthen the position of the weak Tsar Nicholas II and discredit the reforms of the Liberals who sympathized with the Jews. During the Dreyfus affair of 1893–1895, Matvei Vasilyevich Golovinski (Mathieu Golovinski) (1865–1920), working for the *Okhrana* in Paris redacted the earlier works of Joly and Goedsche into a new edition in 1890 or 1891, which he called *The Protocols of the Learned Elders of Zion*. The manuscript of *The Protocols* was brought to Russia in 1895 and was printed privately for limited distribution in pamphlet form in 1897.[3]

The Protocols did not gain a wide audience until 1905, when Russia's defeat in the Russo-Japanese war was followed by the revolution the same year, leading to the promulgation of a constitution and institution of the Duma. In the wake of these events, the reactionary anti-Jewish "Union of the Russian Nation," or Black Hundreds organization, sought to incite popular sentiment against the Jews, who they blamed for the revolution and the constitution. To this end, they used *The Protocols*, which was first widely published by the self-styled [Russian] mystic, Sergius Nilus [1862–1929], in 1905. *The Protocols*, republished in the Black Hundreds' anti-Semitic newspaper *Russkoye Znamya* in 1905 and 1906, were part of a propaganda campaign which accompanied the ongoing pogroms incited by the *Okhrana* at the time. A variant text of *The Protocols* was published by George V. Butmi in 1906 and again in 1907. The 1906 edition was found among the tsar's collection, despite him already acknowledging the work was a forgery. In his later editions, Nilus claimed that *The Protocols* had been read secretly at the First Zionist Congress at Basel, Switzerland in 1897, while Butmi, in his editions, wrote that they had no connection with the new

Zionist movement, but rather were part of a Masonic conspiracy.

In the civil war following the Bolshevik Revolution of 1917, the reactionary White Armies made extensive use of *The Protocols* to incite widespread slaughter of Jews they were convinced were behind the Bolshevik movement. At the same time, emigrants escaping the Russian civil war brought *The Protocols* to Western Europe, where the Nilus editions served as the basis for many translations, starting in 1920. Just after its appearance in London in 1920, the British-Jewish journalist, historian of Anglo-Jewry, and champion of Jewish civil rights Lucien Wolf exposed *The Protocols* as a literary plagiary of the earlier works of Joly and Goedsche in a pamphlet of the Jewish Board of Deputies.[4] The following year, on 16–18 August 1921, the story of the forgery was published in a series of articles in *The Times* of London by Philip Graves, the paper's correspondent in Constantinople.[5] A book documenting the forgery was published the same year in the United States by Lithuanian Russian émigré Herman Bernstein. Nevertheless, *The Protocols* continued to circulate widely in the West. They were even sponsored and reprinted by Henry Ford in the United States, until a libel suit in 1927 forced him to retract his support and formed an important part of Nazi justification for genocide of the Jews in the Holocaust.

---

[1] *Encyclopædia Judaica* (Jerusalem, Israel: Keter Publishing House, 1971), entries on "Antisemitism" and "Elders of Zion, Protocols of the Learned."

[2] Herman Bernstein, *The Truth About "The Protocols of Zion,"* reprinted with introduction by Norman Cohn (New York, NY: Ktav Publishing House, 1971).

[3] Norman Cohn, *Warrant for Genocide: The Myth of the Jewish World Conspiracy and the Protocols of the Elders of Zion*, Brown Judaic Studies, No. 23 (Chico, CA: Scholars Press, 1981). See also: Eric Conan, "Les secrets d'une manipulation antisémite," *L'Express*, 24 November 1999; Patrick Bishop, "The Protocols of the Elders of Zion," *The Washington Times*, 21 November 1999, page C10; and *The London Telegraph*, 19 November 1999.

[4] Lucien Wolf, *The Jewish Bogey and the Forged Protocols of the Learned Elders of Zion* (London, UK: Press Committee of the Jewish Board of Deputies, 1920).
[5] "The Truth About 'The Protocols': A Literary Forgery," *The Times*, 16, 17, and 18 August 1921. London, UK: Printing House Square.

The nexus of Freemasonry and *The Protocols* was created by the self-styled Swiss-Russian Jewish mystic and lawyer, Sergei Aleksandrovich Nilus who converted to Orthodox Christianity and rose from poverty to become religious counselor in Tsar Nicholas II's court. Nilus was Rasputin's predecessor. While serving in the tsar's court, he married a lady-in-waiting, Grand Duchess Alexandra Feodorovna. After leaving the tsar's court, Nilus managed to convince the tsar to grant his wife a pension, with which in 1905 he published a second edition (417 pages) of his 1901 book, *The Great in the Small: Antichrist Considered as an Imminent Political Possibility. Notes of an Orthodox Believer* (Sergiev Posad, 1905) and included a full text of *The Protocols* in the final chapter. Throughout his book, Nilus weaves a fictitious web of conspiratorial interdependence between Freemasonry and *The Protocols*, whereby the Jewish leaders exploit Masonic lodges to attract public officials who can be manipulated to change the *status quo* and effectuate the Jewish plot.

Julius Streicher (1885–1946) – Streicher was born in Fleinhausen, in the Kingdom of Bavaria, one of nine children of the teacher Friedrich Streicher and his wife Anna (née Weiss). Like his father, Julius worked as an elementary school teacher. In 1913, Streicher married Kunigunde Roth, a baker's daughter, in Nuremberg. They had two sons, Lothar (born 1915) and Elmar (born 1918).

In 1914, Streicher joined the German Army. For his outstanding combat performance during the First World War, he was awarded the Iron Cross First and Second Class, as well as earning a battlefield commission as an officer (lieutenant), despite having several reported instances of poor behavior in his military record, and at a time when officers were primarily from aristocratic families. Following the end of World War I, Streicher was demobilized and returned to Nuremberg. Upon his return, Streicher took up another teaching position but something unknown happened in 1919, which turned him into a radical anti-Semite. Streicher was heavily influenced by the endemic anti-Semitism of prewar Germany, especially that of Theodor Fritsch. In February 1919, Streicher became active in the anti-Semitic *Deutschvölkischer Schutz- und Trutzbund*, one of the various radical-

Nationalist organizations that sprang up in the wake of the failed German Communist revolution of 1918. Such groups fostered the view that Jews and Bolsheviks were synonymous, and that they were traitors trying to subject Germany to Communist rule. In 1920, Streicher turned to the *Deutschsozialistische Partei* (German Socialist Party, *DSP*), a group whose platform was close to that of the Nazi Party. The German Socialist Party was created in May 1919 on an initiative of Rudolf von Sebottendorff as a child of the Thule Society, and its program was based on the ideas of the mechanical engineer Alfred Brunner (1881–1936). Leading members of the *DSP* were Hans Georg Müller, Max Sesselmann, and Friedrich Wiesel, the first two being editors of the *Münchener Beobachter*. Julius Streicher founded his local branch of the *DSP* in 1919 in Nuremberg. The *DSP* was officially inaugurated in 1919 in Hanover.

By the end of 1919, the *DSP* had branches in Düsseldorf, Kiel, Frankfurt am Main, Dresden, Nuremberg, and Munich. Streicher soon lost all interest in the *DSP*, for which he never held an official position. He sought to move the German Socialists in a more virulently anti-Semitic direction—an effort which aroused enough opposition that he abandoned the group and brought his now-substantial following to yet another organization in 1921, the *Deutsche Werkgemeinschaft* (German Working Community), which hoped to unite the various anti-Semitic *völkisch* movements. He established a magazine for this organization under the new name *Deutscher Volkswille* (*German People's Will*) and in November 1921 organized a Nuremberg *Ortsgruppe*. Meanwhile, Streicher's rhetoric against the Jews continued to intensify to such a degree that the leadership of the *Deutsche Werkgemeinschaft* thought he was dangerous and criticized him for his obsessive "hatred of the Jews and foreign races" (Rees 2017, 22). With his radical anti-Semitism and his dictatorial demeanor, he quickly fell out with the leadership of *Deutsche Werkgemeinschaft*.

The *DSP* continued to lose members and popularity. As it became apparent that the tightly organized *NSDAP* held its own better, Streicher formally resigned from the *DSP* in the fall of 1922 and subordinated himself to Hitler on 8 October.

In 1922, Streicher joined the Nazi Party, bringing with him enough members of the *DSP* and *Deutsche Werkgemeinschaft* to almost double the size of the Nazi Party overnight. Shortly thereafter, the *DSP* officially dissolved. Only three days after joining, he founded his first *NSDAP* local group in Hersbruck, which followed another in Nuremberg on 20 October. The Nuremberg branch quickly developed into the largest outside of Old

Bavaria. It became a vehicle for the spreading of the party to northern Germany. He would later claim that because his political work brought him into contact with German Jews, he "must therefore have been fated to become later on, a writer and speaker on racial politics" (Friedman 1998, 300). According to Streicher, his dislike of Jews stemmed from an incident when he was but five-years-old, during which he witnessed his mother weeping after claiming to have been cheated by the Jewish owner of a fabric shop (Rees 2017, 21). He visited Munich in order to hear Adolf Hitler speak, an experience that he later said left him transformed. When asked about that moment, Streicher stated:

> It was on a winter's day in 1922. I sat unknown in the large hall of the Bürgerbräuhaus . . . suspense was in the air. Everyone seemed tense with excitement, with anticipation. Then suddenly a shout. "Hitler is coming!" Thousands of men and women jumped to their feet as if propelled by a mysterious power . . . they shouted, "Heil Hitler! Heil Hitler!" . . . And then he stood on the podium . . . Then I knew that in this Adolf Hitler was someone extraordinary . . . Here was one who could wrest out of the German spirit and the German heart the power to break the chains of slavery. Yes! Yes! This man spoke as a messenger from heaven at a time when the gates of hell were opening to pull down everything. And when he finally finished, and while the crowd raised the roof with the singing of the "Deutschland" song, I rushed to the stage. (Dolibois 2000, 114.)

Nearly religiously converted by this speech, Streicher believed from this point forward that, "it was his destiny to serve Hitler" (Rees 2017, 22–3).

In May 1923, Streicher founded the sensationalist popular newspaper *Der Stürmer* (*The Stormer*, or, loosely, *The Attacker*) (Bytwerk 2001, 51–2). From the outset, the chief aim of the paper was to promulgate anti-Semitic propaganda; the first issue had an excerpt that stated, "As long as the Jew is in the German household, we will be Jewish slaves. Therefore he must go" (Bytwerk 2001, 52). Historian Richard J. Evans describes the newspaper:

> [*Der Stürmer*] rapidly established itself as the place where screaming headlines introduced the most rabid attacks on Jews, full of sexual innuendo, racist caricatures, made-up accusations of ritual murder and titillating, semi-pornographic stories of Jewish men seducing innocent German girls (Evans 2003, 188).

In November 1923, Streicher participated in Hitler's failed Beer Hall *Putsch* in Munich. Streicher marched with Hitler in the front row of the would-be revolutionaries and managed to escape injury. The Bavarian school authorities, which had always covered over his anti-Semitic failures, suspended him from the school service—formal dismissal of Streicher was only in 1928 (Zentner and Bedürftig 1991, 921). In January 1924, he was placed in protective custody in Landsberg Prison, but by April 1924 he functioned as a member of the *Völkischsozialer Block* (*VSB*) in the Bavarian *Landtag* (Zentner and Bedürftig 1991, 922), a position which gave him a margin of parliamentary immunity—a safety net that would help him resist efforts to silence his racist message (Showalter 1997).

With Alfred Rosenberg, he was involved in the founding on 30 January 1924 of *Großdeutscher Volksgemeinschaft* (Greater German National Community, *GVG*), a replacement organization for the banned Nazi Party. Their main objective was the release of Hitler and the assurance of the correct interpretation of National Socialism or of the "spirit and will of Adolf Hitler." Streicher, together with Hermann Esser, ousted Rosenberg from the leadership in July 1924 and became the first chairman of the *GVG*. His performances, in which he did not shy away from filthy insults of other "ethnic" men, repelled many supporters of the movement.

Beginning in 1924, Streicher used *Der Stürmer* as a mouthpiece not only for general anti-Semitic attacks, but for calculated smear campaigns against specific Jews, such as the Nuremberg city official Julius Fleischmann, who worked for Streicher's nemesis, mayor Hermann Luppe. *Der Stürmer* accused Fleischmann of stealing socks from his quartermaster during combat in World War I. Fleischmann sued Streicher and disproved the allegations in court, where Streicher was fined 900 marks but the detailed testimony exposed less-than-glorious details of Fleischmann's record, and his reputation was badly damaged. It was proof that Streicher's unofficial motto for his tactics was correct: "Something always sticks" (Showalter 1997). The slanderous attacks continued, and lawsuits followed. Like Fleischmann, other outraged German Jews defeated Streicher in court, but his goal was not necessarily legal victory; he wanted the widest possible dissemination of his message, which press coverage often provided. The rules of the court provided Streicher with an arena to humiliate his opponents, and he characterized the inevitable courtroom loss as a badge of honor. *Der Stürmer*'s infamous official slogan, *Die Juden sind unser Unglück* (the Jews are our misfortune) was deemed non-actionable under German statutes, since it was not a direct incitement to violence (Showalter 1997).

Streicher's opponents complained to authorities that *Der Stürmer* violated a statute against religious offense with his constant promulgation of the "blood libel"—the medieval accusation that Jews killed Christian children to use their blood to make *matzoh.* Streicher argued that his accusations were based on race, not religion, and that his communications were political speech, and therefore protected by the German constitution (Showalter 1997).

Streicher orchestrated his early campaigns against Jews to make the most extreme possible claims, short of violating a law that might get the paper shut down. He insisted in the pages of his newspaper that the Jews had caused the worldwide Depression and were responsible for the crippling unemployment and inflation which afflicted Germany during the 1920s. He claimed that Jews were white-slavers responsible for Germany's prostitution rings. Real unsolved killings in Germany, especially of children or women, were often confidently explained in the pages of *Der Stürmer* as cases of "Jewish ritual murder" (Snyder 1989, 47–51).

One of Streicher's constant themes was the sexual violation of ethnic German women by Jews, a subject which he used to publish semi-pornographic tracts and images detailing degrading sexual acts (Wistrich 2002, 128; see also Bytwerk 2001, 143–50). The fascination with the pornographic aspects of the propaganda in *Der Stürmer* was an important feature for many anti-Semites (Welch 2002, 75). With the help of his notorious cartoonist Phillip "Fips" Rupprecht, Streicher published image after image of Jewish stereotypes and sexually-charged encounters (Koonz 2005, 232–3). His portrayal of Jews as subhuman and evil is widely considered to have played a critical role in the dehumanization and marginalization of the Jewish minority in the eyes of common Germans—creating the necessary conditions for the later perpetration of the Holocaust and Final Solution (Fischer 1995, 135–6; see also Welch 2002, 76–7). Streicher also combed the pages of the Talmud and the Old Testament in search of passages potentially depicting Judaism as harsh or cruel. In 1929, this close study of Jewish scripture helped convict Streicher in a case known as "The Great Nuremberg Ritual Murder Trial." His familiarity with Jewish text was proof to the court that his attacks were religious in nature; Streicher was found guilty and imprisoned for two months. In Germany, press reaction to the trial was highly critical of Streicher; but the *Gauleiter* was greeted after his conviction by hundreds of cheering supporters, and within months Nazi Party membership surged to its highest levels yet (Showalter 1997). To protect himself from accountability, Streicher relied on Hitler's protection. Hitler declared that *Der Stürmer* was his favorite newspaper and saw to it that each weekly issue was posted for public reading in special glassed-in display cases known as *Stürmerkasten.* The newspaper reached a peak circulation of 600,000 in 1935 (Snyder 1989, 50). One of the possible solutions to the Jewish problem Streicher mentioned within the pages of *Der Stürmer* was shipping all of them to Madagascar (Kershaw 2000, 320).

He retained his position in the *Landtag* until 1932. His loyalty to the cause earned him Hitler's lifelong trust and protection; in the years that followed, Streicher would be one of the dictator's few true intimates (Showalter 1997). Streicher and Rudolf Heß were the only Nazis mentioned in *Mein Kampf* (Gunther 1940, 76); in the book Hitler praised him for subordinating the German Socialist Party to the Nazi Party, a move Hitler believed was essential to the success of the National Socialists (Bullock 1962, 124). When Hitler was released from his sentence at Landsberg Prison on 20 December 1924 for his role in the *putsch,* Streicher was one of the few remaining followers waiting for him at his Munich apartment (Fest 1974, 219).

Hitler—who would value loyalty and faithfulness very highly throughout his life—remained loyal to Streicher even when he landed in trouble with the Nazi hierarchy. Although Hitler would allow suppression of *Der Stürmer* at times when it was politically important for the Nazis to be seen as respectable, and although he would admit that Streicher was not a very good administrator, he never withdrew his personal loyalty (Evans 2003, 189).

As a reward for Streicher's dedication, when the Nazi Party was again legalized and re-organized in 1925, Streicher was appointed *Gauleiter* (district Superintendent) of the Bavarian region of Franconia, which included his hometown of Nuremberg (Zentner and Bedürftig 1991, 922). In the early years of the party's rise, *Gauleiters* were essentially party functionaries without real power, but in the final years of the Weimar Republic, as the Nazi Party grew, so did their power. During the 12 years of the Nazi regime, *Gauleiters* such as Streicher would wield immense power and authority, both over party matters and civil ones.

With the reestablishment of the *NSDAP* under Hitler on 27 January 1925, *völkisch* splinter groups reappeared together in the party. Hitler appointed Julius Streicher *Gauleiter* of Franconia. He responded by making it one of the largest member regions in the organization and giving himself the name *Frankenführer*.

Already on 16 April 1923, the first issue of his new and decidedly anti-Semitic weekly *Der Stürmer* was published. The occasion for his new project was his search for a journalistic platform for his desire for power within the *NSDAP*. In addition, he initially designed the newspaper as a general political local weekly with a circulation of about 3,000 copies. Increasingly, however, anti-Semitic incitement came to the fore and after a few years became almost the sole subject of the newspaper. At the same time, Streicher expanded the publication's geographic coverage and was able to increase circulation.

He spread his anti-Semitism and enmity with fanatic rage and at the same time brutal primitiveness. Fictitious stories about alleged rape, ritual murders, international conspiracies of "financial Jewry" or "Bolshevik world Jewry," racial defilement and denunciations dominated the pages of his *hetzblatt* (*smear-sheet*) *Der Stürmer*. He combined hatred, prejudice, and envy with pornographic portrayals and sexual obsessions. He regularly invited his readers to make concurring statements.

The circulation increased from about 10,000 copies in 1933 to nearly 500,000 just three years later and by the end of war 700,000 newspapers weekly. Streicher used modern sales and advertising methods, such as the "Striker Boxes"—public exhibition of the newspaper in small places in glass cases. The press organ was always privately owned by Julius Streicher and made him a multi-millionaire.

In April 1933, after Nazi control of the German state apparatus gave the *Gauleiters* enormous power, Streicher organized a one-day boycott of Jewish businesses which was used as a dress-rehearsal for other anti-Semitic commercial measures. As he consolidated his hold on power, he came to rule the city of Nuremberg and his *Gau Franken* more or less and boasted that every Jew had been removed from Hersbruck. Among the nicknames provided by his enemies were "King of Nuremberg" and the "Beast of Franconia." Because of his role as *Gauleiter* of Franconia, he also gained the nickname of *Frankenführer* (Nadler 1969, 5; see also Gunther 1940, 76).

After the National Socialist seizure of power in 1933, the *Frankenführer* became head of the "Central Committee for the Defense of Jewish Greed and Boycotts," an organization that was supposed to control anti-Semitic actions and boycotts centrally in the *Reich*. He used this function especially in Nuremberg to act against Jews and political opponents. In *Der Stürmer*, he launched a campaign that prepared the ground for the Nuremberg race laws of 1935. In 1934, he received the honorary rank of *SA* group leader.

Streicher later claimed that he was only "indirectly responsible" for passage of the anti-Jewish Nuremberg Laws of 1935, and that he felt slighted because he was not directly consulted. Perhaps epitomizing the "profound anti-intellectualism" of the Nazi Party, Streicher once opined that, "If the brains of all university professors were put at one end of the scale, and the brains of the Führer at the other, which end do you think would tip?" (Wall 1997, 98).

Streicher was ordered to take part in the establishment of the Institute for the Study and Elimination of Jewish Influence on German Church Life, that was to be organized together with the German Christians, the Ministry of Public Enlightenment and Propaganda, the *Reich* Ministry of Education, and the *Reich* Ministry of the Churches. Surgery prevented Streicher from being able to fully participate and engage in this endeavor (Kater, Mommsen, and von Papen 1999, 151). This anti-Semitic standpoint concerning the Bible can be traced back to the earliest time of the Nazi movement, *e.g.*, Dietrich Eckart's book *Bolshevism from Moses to Lenin: A Dialogue Between Adolf Hitler and Me*, where it was claimed that "Jewish forgeries" had been added to the New Testament (Steigmann-Gall 2003, 17–24).

The Great Synagogue of Nuremberg was built in 1874 and was ordered destroyed in 1938 by Julius Streicher—supposedly because he disapproved of its architecture, which in his opinion "disfigured the beautiful German townscape"—as part of what came to be known as *Kristallnacht* (Kershaw 2000, 132).

Beginning in 1935, Streicher's star began to decline. His newspaper was briefly banned because of the exposure of a Nazi official. To many National Socialists, the primitiveness of his appearance and his way of life seemed dangerous to the reputation of the party. American author and journalist John Gunther described Streicher as "the worst of the anti-Semites" (Gunther 1940, 61), and his excesses brought condemnation even from other Nazis. Streicher's behavior was viewed as so irresponsible that he was embarrassing the party leadership (Snyder 1989, 52–3); chief among his enemies in Hitler's hierarchy was *Reichsmarschall* Hermann Göring, who loathed him and later claimed that he forbade his own staff to read *Der Stürmer* (Maser 2000, 282).

After 1938 Streicher's position began to unravel, despite his special relationship with Hitler. He was accused of keeping Jewish property seized after *Kristallnacht* in November 1938; he was charged with spreading untrue stories about Göring—such as alleging that Göring's daughter Edda was conceived by artificial insemination; and he was confronted with his excessive personal behavior, including adultery, several furious verbal attacks on other *Gauleiters*, and striding through the streets of Nuremberg cracking a bullwhip (Snyder 1989, 47, 50–3). (Streicher's characteristic behavior is portrayed on screen in the 1944 Hollywood film *The Hitler Gang*.) But it was not until 1940 when Hermann Göring joined Streicher's opponents within the party, that a commission of inquiry was appointed by the highest party court. In February 1940, he was stripped of his party offices and withdrew from the public eye, although he was permitted to continue publishing *Der Stürmer*. Because of enrichment from Streicher's publication, however, Hitler, himself an avid reader of *Der Stürmer*, continued to protect him (Wistrich 1995, 251–2). He was still allowed to hold the title of *Gauleiter*, and Hitler also left the publisher and newspaper to him. From his estate *Pleikershof* near Cadolzburg, Streicher also ran his propaganda campaigns in the last years of the Nazi dictatorship.

Streicher's wife, Kunigunde Streicher (née Roth), died in 1943 after 30 years of marriage bearing two sons (Davidson 1997, 43).

When Germany surrendered to the Allied armies in May 1945, Streicher said later, he decided to commit suicide. Instead, he married his former secretary, Adele Tappe (Davidson 1997, 44). Streicher initially fled to the Austrian Alps. On 23 May 1945, he was captured in the town of Waidring, Austria by a group of American officers led by Major Henry Plitt (Tofahrn 2008, 163). At first Streicher claimed to be a painter named "Joseph Sailer," but misunderstanding Plitt's poor German, he came to believe the latter already knew who he was, and quickly admitted his identity ("U.S. Jewish Major" 1945).*

---

* "Oral history interview with Henry Plitt," Oral History | RG Number: RG-50.030.0181 (United States Holocaust Memorial Museum), https://collections.ushmm.org/search/catalog/irn506763 (retrieved 30 January 2019).

Streicher was held in custody until his trial before the International Military Tribunal in Nuremberg, Germany (20 November 1945 and 1 October 1946). Streicher was not a member of the military and did not take part in planning the Holocaust, or the invasion of other nations, yet his pivotal role in inciting the extermination of Jews was significant enough, in the prosecutors' judgment, to include him in the indictment of Major War Criminals before the International Military Tribunal. He complained throughout the process that all his judges were Jews (Snyder 1989, 54–6). Most of the evidence against Streicher came from his numerous speeches and articles over the years (Snyder 1989, 56–7). In essence, prosecutors contended that Streicher's articles and speeches were so incendiary that he was an accessory to murder and therefore as culpable as those who actually ordered the mass extermination of Jews. They further argued that he kept up his anti-Semitic propaganda even after he was aware that Jews were being slaughtered (Snyder 1989, 57).

During his trial, Streicher displayed for the last time the flair for courtroom theatrics that had made him famous in the 1920s. He answered questions from his own defense attorney with diatribes against Jews, the Allies, and the court itself, and was frequently silenced by the court officers. Streicher was largely shunned by all of the other Nuremberg defendants. He also peppered his testimony with references to passages of Jewish texts he had so often carefully selected and inserted into the pages of *Der Stürmer* (Conot 2000, 381–9).

Streicher was acquitted of crimes against peace (Count One) but found guilty of crimes against humanity (Count Four) and sentenced to death on 1 October 1946. The judgment against him read, in part:

> For his 25 years of speaking, writing and preaching hatred of the Jews, Streicher was widely known as "Jew-Baiter Number One." In his speeches and articles, week after week, month after month, he infected the German mind with the virus of anti-Semitism, and incited the German people to active persecution. . . . Streicher's incitement to murder and extermination at the time when Jews in the East were being killed under the most horrible conditions clearly constitutes persecution on political and racial grounds in connection with war crimes, as defined by the Charter, and constitutes a crime against humanity. ("Judgment : Streicher" 2008.)

On 16 October 1946, the sentence was executed by hanging. Streicher's was the most melodramatic of the hangings carried out that night. At the bottom of the scaffold, he cried out "Heil Hitler!" When he mounted the platform, he delivered his last sneering reference to Jewish scripture, snapping "*Purim Fest 1946!*" (Wistrich 1995, 252).* Streicher's final declaration before the hood went over his head was, "The Bolsheviks will hang you one day!" (Conot 2000, 506). Joseph Kingsbury-Smith, a journalist for the International News Service who covered the executions, said in his filed report that after the hood descended over Streicher's head, he also apparently said "*Adele, meine liebe Frau!*" ("Adele, my dear wife!") (Radlmeier 2001, 345–6).

The consensus among eyewitnesses was that Streicher's hanging did not proceed as planned, and that he did not receive the quick death from spinal severing typical of the other executions at Nuremberg. Kingsbury-Smith reported that Streicher "went down kicking," which may have dislodged the hangman's knot from its ideal position.† Smith stated that Streicher could be heard groaning under the scaffold after he dropped through the trap-door, and that the executioner intervened under the gallows, which was screened by wood panels and a black curtain, to finish the job (Kingsbury-Smith 1946). Streicher's body, along with those of the other nine executed men and the corpse of Hermann Göring, was cremated at *Ostfriedhof* (Munich) and the ashes were scattered (Manvell and Fraenkel 2011, 393).

---

* The Jewish holiday *Purim* celebrates the escape by the Jews from extermination at the hands of Haman, an ancient Persian government official. At the end of the *Purim* story, Haman is hanged, as are his ten sons. (Rubin 1946.)

† The hangman's knot or hangman's noose is a knot most often associated with its use in hanging a person. For a hanging, the knot of the rope is typically placed under or just behind the left ear, although the most effective position is just ahead of the ear, beneath the angle of the left lower jaw. The pull on the knot at the end of the drop levers the jaw and head violently up and to the right, which combines with the jerk of the rope becoming taut to wrench the upper neck vertebrae apart. This produces very rapid death, whereas the traditional position beneath the ear was intended to result in the mass of the knot crushing closed (occluding) the neck arteries, causing cessation of brain circulation. The knot is non-jamming but tends to resist attempts to loosen it. (Wikipedia contributors, "Hangman's knot," *Wikipedia, The Free Encyclopedia*, https://en.wikipedia.org/w/index.php?title=Hangman%27s_knot&oldid=819365081 [accessed 30 January 2019].)

Karl Fiehler (1895–1969) – Fiehler was born in Braunschweig, German Empire. He was the son of Baptist preacher Henry Fiehler and his wife Emma (née Wulff). He had four brothers and two sisters. Among his brothers was the writer Werner Fiehler, also a member of the *NSDAP*, who had been imprisoned for a short time in 1936 because of various frauds.

In 1902 Fiehler moved with his parents to Munich. There he attended secondary school, went through a commercial apprenticeship, and worked from 1914 in Schleswig-Holstein as an assistant. From May 1915, Fiehler served in the First World War, suffered a leg injury in 1918 and was awarded the Iron Cross second class (*EK II*). On 19 March 1919, he entered the administrative service of the city of Munich, first as temporary help in a food card distribution center. In February 1922, he was made official after successfully passing the administrative exam for state and local government service.

In 1920, he joined the Nazi Party. On 6 November 1923, he became a member of the *Stoßtrupp-Hitler* (Shock Troop-Hitler), that had been established to provide personal protection for Hitler, which in November 1925 became the *Schutzstaffel* (*SS*). On 8 and 9 November 1923, he participated in the failed Beer Hall *Putsch*. Fiehler was sentenced on 28 April 1924 by the People's Court to fifteen months imprisonment in Landsberg Prison and given a fine of 30 gold marks for aiding and abetting high treason.

From 1924 until 1933, he was an honorary Munich alderman and in 1929 he outlined the principles of Nazi local politics in his eighty-page booklet "National Socialist Municipal Policy," printed by the Munich publishing house Franz Eher Verlag, which was the publisher for the *NSDAP*. During the 1930s, he published on several occasions concerning local politics in Germany from a National Socialist point of view.

After the reestablishment of the *NSDAP* in February 1925, Fiehler joined the party again (membership number 37). As an "*Alter Kämpfer*" ("Old Fighter") or member of the "*Alte Garde*" ("Old Guard"), his career in the party rose rapidly: from 1927 to 1930, he was *Ortsgruppenleiter* of the *NSDAP* in Munich and from 1935 until the end of Nazi rule in the spring of 1945, he held the rank of *Reichsleiter*, of the *NSDAP*, first as secretary, then as head of the main office for local politics. He thus belonged to the highest leadership circle of the *NSDAP* and to the twenty closest associates of Adolf Hitler in the party. He was a member of the Academy of German Law and joined the *SS* (No. 91724) on 31 July 1933 with the rank of *SS-Standartenführer* (colonel). On 24 December 1933, he was promoted to *SS-Oberführer* (senior colonel), and finally on 27 January 1934, to *SS-*

Gruppenführer (lieutenant general, *Ehrenführer Oberabschnitt Süd*—Honorary Leader of the Upper Section of the South). On 30 January 1942, he was promoted to *SS-Obergruppenführer* (general) and was assigned to the staff of *Reichsführer-SS* Heinrich Himmler until 9 November 1944. From 1933 to 1945, Karl Fiehler was a member of the *Reichstag*. From 1934 to 1946, he was also a member of the Senate of the Kaiser Wilhelm Society.

On 9 March 1933, the *SA* occupied Munich city hall and unrolled a swastika flag. Mayor Karl Scharnagl defied the new rulers for eleven days, but on 20 March 1933 he had to "give way to violence." On this day, Adolf Wagner was appointed Bavarian Interior Minister and *Gauleiter* (district superintendent) of Upper Bavaria and Karl Fiehler was appointed Lord Mayor of Munich. During his time as mayor, Fiehler was zealously anti-Semitic and saw to it that the Jewish population of the city was persecuted. As a result of the National Socialist seizure of power, all parties and organizations that opposed the political program of the *NSDAP* were banned. The burning of books (*Bücherverbrennung*) on Munich's *Königsplatz* in front of the *Staatlichen Antikensammlungen* (National Antiquities Collections) on 10 May 1933, and the persecution of non-*völkisch* writers, artists, and scientists led to an exodus of the intellectual elite of Munich. On 22 March 1933, the provisional Munich police chief Heinrich Himmler opened the Dachau Concentration Camp sixteen kilometers (ten miles) northwest of Munich.

The first planned boycott of Jewish businesses (*Judenboykott*) in the spring of 1933 was zealously pursued by Fiehler. He ordered the shop-boycott in anticipatory obedience as early as 30 March, while the official date was actually 1 April. The *SA* and *SS* groups had already terrorized Jewish businessmen in Munich at the beginning of March 1933 with 280 of them being placed in "*Schutzhaft*" (protective custody). In the same year, Fiehler prohibited—without legal basis—urban contracts to "non-German companies." The *SA* smeared windows of Jewish shops with "*Juden*" or "On vacation in Dachau." Shop windows were smashed, and customers intimidated by being mobbed, registered, and sometimes even photographed by the *SA*. Munich hastened the demolition of Jewish synagogues. Propaganda Minister Joseph Goebbels had the main synagogue destroyed in June 1938 to find out if the "Aryan" public would be shocked or indifferent. The apathetic behavior of the population encouraged the Nazis to new excesses. On 9 November 1938, Fiehler invited Joseph Goebbels to deliver his wild anti-Semitic hate speech at Munich's *Alte Rathaus* (Old Townhall), which signaled the *SA* and party leaders for a general hunt for Jews. On that *pogrom* night, later euphemistically called the "*Kristallnacht,*" many people were killed, tortured, and injured. Many Jewish institutions, synagogues, and businesses fell victim to the devastation and plunder of that night.

The deprivation of Munich Jews was followed by the genocide of the Holocaust. On 20 November 1941, the first deportation transport with 1,000 Jews left Munich for Riga. The frightened people were told they were being "evacuated." The transport was diverted to the Kovno *ghetto* in the Lithuanian city of Kaunas because the Riga *ghetto* was overcrowded at that time. Shortly after their arrival at Fort IX of Kaunas on 25 November 1941, the deportees were arrested by members of *Einsatzgruppe A*, under the command of the *SS-Brigadeführer* Franz Walter Stahlecker, and were slaughtered in a mass shooting. By February 1945, a total of forty-two transports left Munich at irregular intervals to Kaunas, Piaski (near Lublin), and Auschwitz, as well as the "*Alters- und Prominentenghetto*" ("age and celebrity *ghetto*") Theresienstadt in northwestern Bohemia. From the end of February 1942 to November 1942, Piaski played a leading role in "*Aktion Reinhardt*"—the annihilation of the Jews in the *General Gouvernement.* The Jews in Piaski were deported to the Bełżec and Sobibór extermination camps. Fritz Reuter of the Lublin Population and Welfare Department quoted *SS-Hauptsturm* Hofle, the Deputy of "*Aktion Reinhardt*" as saying: "Piaski will be made free of Polish Jews and become the assembly point for Jews coming from the *Reich.*" The Piaski ghetto was finally liquidated in February or March 1943. In total, around 10,000 Jews from Germany, Bohemia, Moravia, Slovakia, Szczecin, Lublin, and many other locations went through the Piaski *ghetto* on to extermination camps in Bełżec and Sobibór. From 12,000 Munich Jews, 7,500 were able to escape deportation. Almost 3,000 were deported to concentration camps, of which more than half went to Theresienstadt. Only 430 surviving Munich Jews returned to their hometown in 1945.

On 30 April 1945, soldiers of the Seventh U.S. Army commanded by Lt. General Alexander Patch reached *Marienplatz* in central Munich. In the summer of 1945, Karl Fiehler was arrested and placed in internment by American military police. On 14 January 1949, Fiehler was classified by the Munich Main Court of Appeals as an "activist" under denazification laws and sentenced to two years in a labor camp, confiscation of one-fifth of his assets, the loss of active and passive right to vote in political elections, as well as a twelve-year ban on practicing his political profession. Fiehler's efforts to prevent the demolition of Isar bridges by the *Wehrmacht* served as a mitigating factor in his sentencing. In the end, Fiehler did not have to go to prison since they considered his three-and-a-half-year internment already served. He lived in Dießen am Ammersee (53 km/33 mi southwest of Munich on the western shores of Lake Ammersee) until his death on 8 December 1969 and worked as an accountant.

In 1962, an administrative court order obliged the city of Munich to pay Karl Fiehler the pension of a municipal senior secretary. He had held this position from the mid-1920s to 1933 before his appointment as Lord Mayor. Fiehler appealed this decision in order to obtain the pension of a mayor. In 1963, the appeal was rejected by the Bavarian Administrative Court. In 1965, the Federal Administrative Court upheld this ruling.

Wilhelm Frick (1877–1946) – Frick was born in the Palatinate municipality of Alsenz, then part of the Kingdom of Bavaria, the last of four children of Protestant teacher Wilhelm Frick and his wife Henriette (née Schmidt). He attended the *gymnasium* in Kaiserslautern, passing his *Abitur* exams in 1896. He went on studying philology at the University of Munich, but soon after turned to study law in Heidelberg and Berlin, taking the *Staatsexamen* in 1900, followed by his doctorate the next year. Serving as a referendary (administrative position in a government chancellery) since 1900, he joined the Bavarian civil service in 1903, working as an attorney at the Munich Police Department. He was appointed a *Bezirksamtassessor* (administrative district office assessor) in Pirmasens in 1907 and became acting district executive in 1914. Rejected as unfit, Frick did not serve in World War I. He was promoted to the official rank of a *Regierungsassessor* (government assessor) and, at his own request, resumed his post at the Munich Police Department by 1917.

On 25 April 1910, Frick had married Elisabetha Emilie Nagel (1890–1978) in Pirmasens. They had two sons and a daughter. The marriage ended in an ugly divorce in 1934. A few weeks later, on 12 March, Frick remarried in Münchberg to Margarete Schultze-Naumburg (1896–1960), the former wife of the Nazi *Reichstag* member Paul Schultze-Naumburg. Margarete gave birth to a son and a daughter.

In Munich, Frick witnessed the end of the war and the German Revolution of 1918–1919. He sympathized with *Freikorps* paramilitary units fighting against the Bavarian government of Prime Minister Kurt Eisner. Chief of Police Ernst Pöhner introduced him to Adolf Hitler, whom he helped willingly with obtaining permissions to hold political rallies and demonstrations.

Elevated to the rank of an *Oberamtmann* and head of the *Kriminalpolizei* (criminal police) from 1923, he and Pöhner participated in

Hitler's failed Beer Hall *Putsch.* Frick tried to suppress the State Police's operation, wherefore he was arrested and imprisoned, and tried for aiding and abetting high treason by the People's Court in April 1924. After several months in custody, he was given a suspended sentence of fifteen-months' imprisonment and was dismissed from his police post. Later, during the disciplinary proceedings, the dismissal was declared unfair and revoked on the basis that his treasonous intention had not been proven. Frick went on to work at the Munich social insurance office from 1926 onwards with the rank of a *Regierungsrat* first class (senior civil servant) by 1933.

On 1 September 1925, Frick joined the re-established Nazi Party. He associated himself with the radical Gregor Straßer; making his name through aggressive anti-Democratic and anti-Semitic *Reichstag* speeches, he climbed to the post of the Nazi parliamentary group leader (*Fraktionsführer*) in 1928.

On 23 January 1930, Frick was appointed Thuringia's provincial Minister of Interior and Education, becoming the first Nazi to hold a ministerial-level post at any level in Germany (though he remained a member of the *Reichstag*). Frick used his position to dismiss Communist and Social Democratic officials and replace them with Nazi Party members, so Thuringia's federal subsidies were temporarily suspended by *Reich* Minister of Interior Carl Severing. Frick also appointed the eugenicist Hans F. K. Günther as a professor of social anthropology at the University of Jena, banned several newspapers, and banned pacifist drama and anti-war films such as *All Quiet on the Western Front.* He was removed from office by a Social Democrat motion of no confidence in the Thuringian *Landtag* on 1 April 1931.

When *Reichspräsident* Paul von Hindenburg appointed Hitler chancellor on 30 January 1933, Frick joined his government as *Reich* Minister of the Interior. Together with *Reichstag* Speaker Hermann Göring, he was one of only two Nazi *Reich* Ministers in the original Hitler Cabinet, and the only one who actually had a portfolio; Göring served as minister without portfolio until 5 May 1933. Though Frick held a key position, especially in organizing the federal elections of March 1933, he initially had far less power than his counterparts in the rest of Europe. Notably, he had no authority over the police; in Germany law enforcement has traditionally been a state and local matter. Indeed, the main reason that von Hindenburg and Franz von Papen agreed to give the interior ministry to the Nazis was that it was almost powerless at the time. A mighty rival arose in the establishment of the Propaganda Ministry under Joseph Goebbels on 13 March 1933.

Frick's power dramatically increased as a result of the *Reichstag* Fire Decree and the Enabling Act of 1933. The provision of the *Reichstag* Fire Decree giving the cabinet the power to take over state governments on its own authority was actually his idea; he saw the fire as a chance to increase his power and begin the process of Nazifying the country. He was responsible for drafting many of the *Gleichschaltung* laws that consolidated the Nazi regime. Within a few days of the Enabling Act's passage, Frick helped draft a law appointing *Reichskommissare* to disempower the state governments. Under the Law for the Reconstruction of the *Reich*, which converted Germany into a highly centralized state, the newly implemented *Reichsstatthalter* (state governors) were directly responsible to him. In May 1934, he was appointed Prussian State Minister of the Interior under Prussian Minister-President Göring, which gave him control over the police in Prussia. By 1935, he also had near-total control over local government. He had the sole power to appoint the mayors of all municipalities with populations greater than 100,000 (except for the city states of Berlin and Hamburg, where Hitler reserved the right to appoint the mayors for himself). He also had considerable influence over smaller towns as well; while their mayors were appointed by the state governors, as mentioned earlier the governors were responsible to him.

Frick was instrumental in the racial policy of Nazi Germany drafting laws against Jewish citizens, like the Law for the Restoration of the Professional Civil Service and the notorious Nuremberg Laws in September 1935. Already in July 1933, he had implemented the Law for the Prevention of Hereditarily Diseased Offspring including forced sterilizations, which later culminated in the killings of the Action T4 "euthanasia" program supported by his ministry. Frick also took a leading part in Germany's re-armament in violation of the 1919 Versailles Treaty. He drafted laws introducing universal military conscription and extending the *Wehrmacht* service law to Austria after the 1938 *Anschluß*, as well as to the Sudetenland territories of the First Czechoslovak Republic annexed according to the Munich Agreement.

In the summer of 1938, Frick was named the patron (*Schirmherr*) of the *Deutsches Turn- und Sportfest* in Breslau, a patriotic sports festival attended by Hitler and much of the Nazi leadership. In this event he presided over the ceremony of handing over the new Nazi *Reich* Sports League (*NSRL*) standard to *Reichssportführer* Hans von Tschammer und Osten, marking the further Nazification of sports in Germany. On 11 November

1938, Frick promulgated the Regulations Against Jewish Possession of Weapons.

From the mid-to-late 1930s, Frick irreversibly lost favor within the Nazi Party after a power struggle involving attempts to resolve the lack of coordination within the *Reich* government. For example, in 1933 he tried to restrict the widespread use of "protective custody" orders that were used to send people to concentration camps, only to be begged off by *Reichsführer-SS* Heinrich Himmler. His power was greatly reduced in June 1936 when Hitler named Himmler the Chief of German Police, which for all intents and purposes effectively united the police with the *SS*. On paper, Frick was Himmler's immediate superior. In fact, the police were now independent of Frick's control since the *SS* was responsible only to Hitler. A long-running power struggle between Frick and Himmler culminated in Frick being replaced by Himmler as Minister of the Interior in 1943. However, Frick remained in the cabinet as a minister without portfolio. Besides Hitler, he and Lutz Graf Schwerin von Krosigk were the only members of the Third *Reich*'s cabinet to serve continuously from Hitler's appointment as Chancellor until his death.

Frick's replacement as *Reich* Minister of the Interior did not reduce the growing administrative chaos and infighting between party and state agencies. Frick was then appointed as Protector of Bohemia and Moravia, making him Hitler's personal representative in the Czech Lands. Its capital, Prague, where Frick used ruthless methods to counter dissent, was one of the last Axis-held cities to fall at the end of World War II in Europe.

Frick was arrested and tried before the International Military Tribunal in Nuremberg, where he was the only defendant besides Rudolf Heß who refused to testify on his own behalf. Frick was convicted of planning, initiating, and waging wars of aggression, war crimes and crimes against humanity, and for his role in formulating the Enabling Act as Minister of the Interior and the Nuremberg Laws. Frick was also accused of being one of the highest persons responsible for the existence of the concentration camps.

Frick was sentenced to death on 1 October 1946 and was hanged at Nuremberg Prison on 16 October. Of his execution, American journalist Joseph Kingsbury-Smith wrote:

> The sixth man to leave his prison cell and walk with handcuffed wrists to the death house was 69-year-old Wilhelm Frick. He entered the execution chamber at 2:05

a.m., six minutes after Rosenberg had been pronounced dead. He seemed the least steady of any so far and stumbled on the thirteenth step of the gallows. His only words were, "Long live eternal Germany," before he was hooded and dropped through the trap.

CHAPTER 11

THE FINAL ELEMENTS TO THE GATHERING STORM

THE **GERMAN WORKERS' PARTY** (*DEUTSCHE ARBEITERPARTEI, DAP*) WAS a short-lived political party established in Weimar Germany after World War I. The *DAP* only lasted from 5 January 1919 until 24 February 1920. It was the precursor of the Nazi Party, which was officially known as the National Socialist German Workers' Party (*Nationalsozialistische Deutsche Arbeiterpartei, NSDAP*).

On 7 March 1918, machinist and locksmith Anton Drexler set up in Berlin *Freier Arbeiterausschuss für einen guten Frieden* (Free Workers' Committee for a Good Peace), a branch of the North German Association for the Promotion of Peace along Working Class Lines. However, the chaos that existed in postwar Weimar Germany meant that the country was littered with many small groups that classed themselves as political parties. Drexler's Free Workers' Committee was one of many in Berlin. Karl Harrer (1890–1926), a sportswriter for the *Münchener-Augsburger Abendzeitung* (*Munich-Augsburg Evening Times*) and Thule Society member, witnessed a machinist, Anton Drexler, address a rally of Conservatives in Munich's Wagner Hall on 2 October 1918. Harrer was favorably impressed by the railroad worker's call for a national *Bürgerbund* representing politically unattached officials, *bourgeois*, and proletarians. "Citizens, workers, unite!" Drexler cried (Luhrssen 2012, 153). Within the month, Harrer, at the behest of the Thule Society, cofounded with Drexler the *Politischer Arbeiterzirkel* (Political Workers' Circle) in Munich, the organizational nucleus of the Nazi Party (Luhrssen 2012, 98). The Political Workers' Circle was one of several "rings of Thule" founded after the November Revolution in answer to Thule Society founder Rudolf von Sebottendorff's call for "inner struggle" against the new regime. Von Sebottendorff cited Gottfried Feder's ringing denunciations of Capitalism at Thule Society meetings as inspiration for founding the Workers' Circle under Thule Society member Karl Harrer. Feder immediately offered to edify the group with his lectures. Harrer is usually described as a shabbily dressed, club-footed man. Neither Harrer nor Drexler possessed the charisma of leadership, but their efforts created the vehicle for a magnetic leader's ascent to power. The members met periodically for discussions with themes of Nationalism and anti-Semitism. In December 1918, Drexler was encouraged to form the *DAP* by his mentor, Dr. Paul Tafel (1872–1953). Tafel was an engineer by education, leader of the *Alldeutscher Verband* (Pan-German League), member of the *Deutschvölkischer Schutz- und Trutzbund* (German Nationalist Protection and Defensive Federation, *DVSTB*), director of the *Maschinenfabrik Augsburg-Nürnberg*, member of the board of the Bavarian Industrialists' Association, and member of the Thule Society. Tafel's and Drexler's wish was for a political party which was both in touch with the working masses and Nationalist.

In the *Fürstenfelderhof* hotel in Munich on 5 January 1919, together with fellow Thule Society members Gottfried Feder and Dietrich Eckart, Drexler decided to merge the Free Workers' Committee with the larger Political Workers' Circle, led by sports journalist and Thule Society member Karl Harrer. Drexler was elected Chairman and Harrer was made "*Reich* Chairman," an honorary title. Once joined together, they adopted a new name for their organization: *Deutsche Arbeiterpartei* (German Workers' Party, *DAP*). Drexler's poor, powerless, unknown group was taken under wing by relatively sophisticated benefactors who systematized its inchoate Nationalism and anti-Semitism.

> He [Harrer] got together all sorts of books and facts about the war, the Russian Revolution—and our own Revolution—which we all set out to study hard, by way of trying to find some way out of the debacle. We discussed a new name for our combination and decided on a new departure. United, we numbered perhaps thirty-five members. We agreed to meet on 5 January in a little eating-house in Munich called *Fuerstenfelder Hof* to found the *Deutsche Arbeiter-Partei*. (Luhrssen 2012, 153–4.)

Drexler suggested "German National Socialist Party" as the group's name, but Harrer objected to the term "Socialist"; so, the term was removed, and a compromise found in "German Workers' Party." To ease concerns among potential middle-class supporters, Drexler made clear that unlike Marxists the party supported the middle-class and that its Socialist policy was meant to give social welfare to German citizens deemed part of the Aryan race. They became one of many *völkisch* movements that existed in

Germany. Like other *völkisch* groups, the *DAP* advocated the belief that through profit-sharing instead of Socialization Germany should become a unified "people's community" (*Volksgemeinschaft*) rather than a society divided along class and party lines. This ideology was explicitly anti-Semitic. As early as 1920, the party was raising money by selling a tobacco called *Anti-Semit*. The party's anti-Semitism, however, was couched in cautious terms: "Religious teachings contrary to the moral and ethical laws of Germany should not be supported by the state" (Luhrssen 2012, 154). Their idea was to form an organization that would "combat the Marxism of the free trade unions" and to agitate for a "just" peace for Germany—meaning renegotiate the Versailles Treaty. Their long-term objective was to create a party which would be both working-class and *völkisch* Nationalist. They promoted the concept that there existed a diabolical Jewish-Capitalistic-Masonic conspiracy which had to be counteracted. They saw on the one side the innocent German worker, farmer, and soldier; on the other the common enemy . . . Capitalistic Jews (as opposed to Marxist Bolshevik Jews). From the outset, the *DAP* was opposed to non-Nationalist political movements, including the Social Democratic Party of Germany (*SPD*) and the Communist Party of Germany (*KPD*). Members of the *DAP* saw themselves as fighting against Bolshevism and anyone considered a part of or aiding so-called "international Jewry." The *DAP* was also deeply opposed to the Versailles Treaty. The *DAP* did not attempt to make itself public and meetings were kept in relative secrecy, with public speakers discussing what they thought of Germany's present state of affairs or writing to like-minded societies in Northern Germany.

Initially, its small group of faithful followers—workmen, craftsmen, members of the lower-middle-class—assembled each week in the *Leiber* room of the *Sternecker-Bräu* "for the discussion and study of political matters." The trauma of the lost war, anti-Semitic feelings, and complaints about the snapping of all the "bonds of order, law and morality" set the tone of its meetings. The new party stood for the dissemination of the idea of a National Socialism "led only by German leaders" and aiming at the "ennoblement of the German worker"; instead of socialization it called for profit-sharing, demanded the formation of an association for national unity, and proclaimed that its "duty and task" was "to educate its members in an ideal sense and raise them up to a higher conception of the world." It was not so much a political party in the usual sense, as a mixture of secret society and drinking club typical of the Munich of those years; it did not address itself to the public. Obscure visionaries would hold forth to the thirty or forty who had gathered together, discuss Germany's disgrace and rebirth, or write postcards to like-minded societies in northern Germany. By 17 May 1919, only ten members were present at the meeting; a later meeting in August 1919 only noted 38 members attending.

Thule's Political Workers' Circle was not subsumed by the party but continued to function as the organization's ideological motor and leadership cadre. The Circle met once or twice a week, and was limited, at Harrer's insistence, to seven members. Although Drexler freely expressed his thoughts at meetings of the larger, more proletarian German Workers' Party, Harrer dominated Circle discussions held at Thule's office, Café Gasteig, or private apartments. Among Harrer's topics were anti-Semitism, the use of newspapers for political propaganda, and the implications of the lost war. "Harrer and not Drexler was the spiritual leader of this small group" (Luhrssen 2012, 155).

During the turbulent winter and spring of 1919, *DAP* also met regularly at Thule's offices or the *Sternecker-Bräu* brewery in Munich. Apparently, there were no other local chapters during that period. Records of a party meeting on 3 May 1919, held as White Guards mopped up Red stragglers in Munich, show the increasing stridence of Drexler's anti-Semitism in his address on "Jewish World-Bolshevism." At other meetings during that period, Drexler derided the rich and demanded laws limiting annual profits to ten thousand Marks. This was not your typical Fascist National Socialism; this was more Socialist Social Liberalism, so much so, that the party attracted the attention of Nationalist German authorities (Army Intelligence), who were suspicious of any Socialist organization that appeared to have subversive tendencies. Army Intelligence feared that this new party, led by Anton Drexler, might be advocating a Socialist revolution.

The **German Socialist Party** (*Deutschsozialistische Partei*, *DSP*), a sister organization of but in competition with the *DAP*, was founded in Munich in May 1919 by *Münchener Beobachter* editorial staff members Hans Georg Müller and Max Sesselmann under the impetus of Thule Society's founder Rudolf von Sebottendorff and several members of the *Deutschvölkische Schutz- und Trutzbund*. The *DSP* was predicated on the work of Düsseldorf mechanical engineer, anti-Capitalist, and *völkisch* anti-Semite Alfred Brunner (1871–1936), who on 1 December 1918 published "Denkschrift zu Gründung der deutschsozialistischen Partei auf judenreiner und kapitalloser Grundlage" ("Memorandum on the Founding of the German Socialist Party on a Jew-pure and Capital-less Basis"). Brunner wanted to replace long-standing Roman jurisprudence with relatively new German law and called for the union of the working class "on a German national basis" under emphatically anti-Semitic portent.

On 24 November 1919, a *DSP Ortsgruppe* (local branch) was founded in Nuremberg under the chairmanship of Hans Vey and Ludwig Käfer, both members of the *Deutschvölkische Schutz- und Trutzbund* (*DVSTB*). Numerous other *DVSTB* members joined the *DSP*, including elementary school teacher and decorated First World War veteran Julius Streicher (1885–1946). Although he never had an official function in the Nuremberg *DSP*, Streicher quickly expanded his position of power as a leading *DSP* man. He was helped by his newspaper *Deutscher Sozialist*, which he founded in 1920 for the *DSP*. In the *DSP*, Streicher achieved a similarly dominant position as Adolf Hitler did in the *NSDAP*. The two were aware of each other and fierce competitors. The Nuremberg *Ortsgruppe* had 350 members in the summer of 1920 and was thus next to Munich a regional focus of the party. In the fall of 1920, thirty-five local groups with around 2,000 members are said to have existed (Schuster 2004).

At a party congress from 23 to 25 April 1920 in Hanover, the *DSP* became a national party. However, in the *Reichstag* elections of 6 June 1920, the party ran in only five out of thirty-five electoral districts and remained politically uninfluential with just over 7,000 votes.

At the *DSP* party conference in the summer of 1920 in Leipzig, Streicher was unsuccessful in convincing party members to adopt his position regarding the clear demarcation between the *DSP*, *NSDAP*, and *DVSTB*. Consequently, an agreement between *DSP* and *NSDAP* provided for the demarcation of geographic regions of influence: The *DSP* would be limited to the area north of the river Main and the Nuremberg area while all of southern Germany would be in the *NSDAP*'s sphere of control. In October 1920, the *DSP* board moved its headquarters from Hanover to Berlin. Despite the small number of members, the *DSP* developed in Berlin into an important organization of Nationalist radicalism (Schuster 2004, 17). Overall, however, the *DSP* remained without organizational cohesion. It lacked an organizational center. An agreement between Streicher, other *DSP* members, and the *NSDAP* chairman Anton Drexler at the end of March 1921 provided an opportunity for the merger of *NSDAP*, *DSP*, and Austrian National Socialists into the German National Socialist Party, however, the plan failed two weeks later during negotiations in Munich because of Hitler's violent opposition the proposal. Streicher did not give up the fight with Hitler for supremacy. In the summer of 1921, Streicher undertook a new initiative to unite similar parties and oust Hitler. The *DSP* waned in importance.

Streicher's loose confederation of *völkisch* anti-Semitic groups limited to Nuremberg and Augsburg, however, recorded large growth and found new supporters in the rural communities of Schwaben and Central and Lower Franconia. At the end of 1921, Streicher's organization boasted about 1,000 members—nearly one-fifth of the *NSDAP*. Streicher's vitriolic leadership, however, failed to maintain unity. In March 1922, the Berlin branch of the *DSP* defected and joined the *NSDAP* in Munich. On 19 September 1922, Streicher resigned from the *DSP* and subordinated himself to Hitler on 8 October 1922 writing to Hitler "I hereby submit to the Munich main line, we still have to agree on the command conditions in Franconia." Shortly thereafter, the *DSP* dissolved all together. Numerous other *DSP* members, including Karl Holz and Wilhelm Grimm, moved to the *NSDAP*. "For the development of the *NSDAP* in Franconia and the northern administrative districts of Bavaria, it was an essential step that Streicher personally subordinated himself to Hitler in 1922" (Kershaw 1998, 229). The *NSDAP* practically doubled its membership: after about 2,000 members in early 1921 and 6,000 twelve months later, by the end of 1922, it counted about 20,000 members.

FRANZ EPP – KARL MAYR – ERNST RÖHM

FRANZ XAVER RITTER VON EPP (1868–1947) – WAS A GERMAN GENERAL and politician who started his military career in the Bavarian Army. Successful wartime military service earned him a knighthood in 1916. After the end of World War I and the dissolution of the German Empire, von Epp was a commanding officer in the *Freikorps* and the *Vorläufige Reichswehr*. Before joining the Nazi Party in 1928, he was a member of the particularistic-conservative Bavarian Center Party. Upon joining the Nazi Party, he was elected to the *Reichstag*, a position he held until the fall of Nazi Germany. Hitler appointed him *Reichskommissar*, later on 7 April 1933 *Reichsstatthalter* (*Reich* Governor), for Bavaria.

During the First World War, he served as the commanding officer of the Royal Bavarian Infantry Lifeguards Regiment in France, Serbia, Romania, and at the Isonzo Front. For his war service, von Epp received numerous medals, of which the *Pour le Mérite* (29 May 1918) was the most significant. He was also knighted, being made Ritter von Epp on 25 February

1918 and received the Bavarian Military Order of Max Joseph (23 June 1916).

After the end of the war, von Epp formed the *Freikorps Epp*, a Nationalist paramilitary unit mostly made up of war veterans, of which the future leader of the *SA* Ernst Röhm was a member and eventual chief of staff to von Epp. This unit took part in the crushing of the Bavarian Soviet Republic in Munich in May 1919, being responsible for various massacres. Von Epp joined the *Vorläufige Reichswehr* and was promoted to Major General in 1922. He took leave from the German Army after getting involved with Nationalist associations in 1923.

When it became necessary for the Nazi Party to purchase a newspaper to publicize its political creed, von Epp made available some 60,000 *Reichsmarks* from secret army funds to acquire the *Völkischer Beobachter*, which became the daily mouthpiece of the party.

As the *Sturmabteilung* (*SA*) expanded, it became an armed band of several hundred thousand men, whose function was to guard Nazi rallies and disrupt those of other political parties. When the *SA* was reorganized in 1926, von Epp became its area commander in Munich. Von Epp hoped to have the *SA* supplant the regular Army when Hitler came to power. He was in charge of a special defense political office called the *Wehrpolitisches Amt* [Army Political Office], the five divisions of which were concerned with external and defense policy, defense forces, and the like. But neither he nor Röhm was ever able to make the *SA* anything better than a motley band of street brawlers." Nothing came of this, as a distrustful Hitler had the *SA* crushed and many of its leaders killed during the Night of the Long Knives in the summer of 1934.

Suffering from a heart condition, von Epp was hospitalized at Bad Nauheim at the end of the Second World War. On 9 May 1945, a clerk at the hospital alerted agents from the U.S. Counterintelligence Corps that von Epp was a patient there, and he was arrested and sent to a prison camp in Munich to await trial at Nuremberg. He died in detention on 31 January 1947.

Karl Mayr (1883–1945) – was the son of a magistrate. After graduating from gymnasium, he was enrolled on 14 July 1901 in the First Bavarian Infantry Regiment in Munich as a cadet. Well-regarded by his superiors, he made rapid progress, becoming *Leutnant* in 1903 and *Oberleutnant* in 1911. From August 1914, Mayr was with the First *Bayerischen Jägerbattailon*. During the First World War he was in combat in Lorraine and Flanders and involved in early 1915 with the German Alpine Corps. On 1 June 1915, Mayr was promoted to *Hauptmann* (captain). In

1917, he was named to the General Staff of the Alpine Corps. On 13 March 1918, he was appointed commander of the First Bavarian *Jägerbattalion*, with whom he served in the Eastern Army Group in Turkey from 20 July to 15 October 1918.

Shortly after the war, from 1 December 1918, Mayr acted as company commander in the First Bavarian Infantry Regiment garrisoned in Munich (Hitler was in the Second Bavarian Infantry Regiment in Munich after the war). On 15 February 1919, he was on leave from the military, but returned in May as commander of the Sixth Battalion of the Guards Regiment in Munich and from 30 May as head of the "Education and Propaganda Department" (Department Ib/P) of the Intelligence Division in the Group Command No. 4 under Major General Arnold Ritter von Möhl (1867–1944) of the Bavarian Army Command under *Generalleutnant* Ernst von Oven (1859–1945).*

In 1921, Mayr was a Nazi Party supporter, but later became a critic. In 1925, he joined the *SPD*. Subsequently he was the leader of the *Reichsbanner Schwarz-Rot-Gold*, an *SPD* paramilitary force. In the early 1930s, Mayr collected among other things, information on *SA* member Georg Bell, an associate of *SA* chief Ernst Röhm, and other material against the Nazi Party, which he leaked in the Social Democratic press. After Hitler came to power in 1933, Karl Mayr fled to France. After the German invasion of France in 1940, he was arrested in Paris by the *Gestapo* under direct orders of Hitler. Mayr was taken back to Germany and was incarcerated in Sachsenhausen Concentration Camp until 1943, when he was transferred to Buchenwald Concentration Camp and forced to work at the Gustloff ammunition plant, where on 9 February 1945 he was murdered.

Ernst Röhm (1887–1934) – was a German military officer and an early member of the Nazi Party. As one of the members of its predecessor, the German Workers' Party, he was a close friend and early ally of Adolf Hitler and a co-founder of the *Sturmabteilung* (*SA*, "Storm Division"), the Nazi Party's militia, and later was its commander. By 1934, the German Army feared the *SA*'s influence and Hitler had come to see Röhm as a potential rival, so he was executed during the Night of the Long Knives, also known as the "Röhm Purge."

Although the family had no military tradition, Röhm entered the Royal Bavarian Tenth Infantry Regiment Prinz Ludwig at Ingolstadt as a cadet on 23 July 1906 and was commissioned on 12 March 1908. At the

---

* Ernst von Oven was unrelated to Burghard Franz Victor von Oven (1861–1935).

outbreak of World War I in August 1914, he was adjutant of the First Battalion, Tenth Infantry Regiment König. The following month, he was seriously wounded in the face at Chanot Wood in Lorraine and carried the scars for the rest of his life. He was promoted to first lieutenant (*Oberleutnant*) in April 1915. During an attack on the fortification at Thiaumont, Verdun on 23 June 1916, he sustained a serious chest wound and spent the remainder of the war in France and Romania as a staff officer. He was awarded the Iron Cross First Class on 20 June 1916, three days before being wounded at Verdun, and was promoted to captain (*Hauptmann*) in April 1917. In October 1918, while serving on the Staff of the *Gardekorps*, he contracted the deadly Spanish influenza and was not expected to live but recovered after a lengthy convalescence.

Following the armistice on 11 November 1918 that ended the war, Röhm continued his military career as an adjutant in the *Vorläufige Reichswehr* (Provisional National Defense). He was one of the senior members in Colonel von Epp's *Bayerisches Freikorps für den Grenzschutz Ost* (Bavarian Free Corps for Border Patrol East), formed in Ohrdruf in April 1919, which finally overturned the Bavarian Soviet Republic by force of arms on 3 May 1919. In 1919, he joined the German Workers' Party (*DAP*), which the following year became the National Socialist German Workers' Party (*NSDAP*). Not long afterward he met Adolf Hitler and they became political allies and close friends.

On 1 January 1923 *Generalmajor* Otto Herman von Lossow (1868–1938) became the commander (*Befehlshaber*) in *Wehrkreis VII* (Defense District 7), the *Reichswehr* military district which covered Bavaria. He held this assignment through the attempted Beer Hall *Putsch* until his replacement in March 1924. In 1923, Röhm's extremely cordial relationship with his commanding officer General von Epp turned sour because Röhm was made subordinate to Major General von Lossow, the new commander of the *Reichswehr* in Bavaria. "General von Epp found my collaboration with the new authorities awkward," Röhm wrote later. "Probably under the impression that I meant to detach myself from his influence by degrees, he turned cooler toward me." Thus their "loyal cooperation in the most difficult situations" culminated in "an estrangement from which I cannot, admittedly, exonerate myself." There are many indications that the relationship between Röhm and von Epp was homoerotic, and Hitler once let slip in later years that Röhm's homosexuality first became known around 1920. At the end of 1920, their relationship was still so close that the then *Freikorps* commander under urging from Röhm arranged the donation of 60,000 *Reichsmarks* to the Nazi Party to purchase a newspaper for party use from his secret fund "a purely personal matter," as von Epp termed it later. Thus, the Röhm-von Epp axis was of immense benefit to Hitler, not only personally but politically. The two soldiers had resources at their disposal that greatly augmented the influence of Hitler the "politician," whose assets had hitherto been limited to his charisma as an orator and actor.

ADOLF HITLER'S INDOCTRINATION IN PAN-GERMANISM AND ANTI-SEMITISM USHERING HIS PLUNGE INTO POLITICS

THE ULTIMATE LEGACY OF THE THULE SOCIETY IS THE IRREFUTABLE influence it had on awakening and perfecting Hitler's latent generic racial ideology that eventually became one of the pillars of National Socialism's political program beginning with the Twenty-Five Points. Thule's *dramatis personæ*, particularly Feder, Eckart, and Rosenberg, in intimate collaboration with the von Müllers, Heßes, Haushofers, and many others of the *Germanenorden*, *Deutschvölkischer Schutz- und Trutzbund*, and *Aufbau Vereinigund*, played a central role in molding the relatively uneducated Hitler into a pan-German racist charismatic leader of National Socialism and the Nazi Party. The tectonic and unprecedented developments in education, public speaking, self-confidence, leadership skills, and *Weltanschauung* that Hitler underwent in the years immediately following the war and German Revolution of 1919 were directly the consequence of the intimate influences of central figures in the *völkisch* anti-Semitic Ariosophical Thule Society.

Hitler had no familial legacy of anti-Semitism or personal reasons to hate Jews. Historians are generally in agreement that Ariosophy was at the root of Hitler's early anti-Semitism. Turn-of-the-century Vienna was the birthplace of Ariosophy and home to its founders, the Nationalist, occultist, journalist, playwright, and novelist Guido von List and *völkisch* political and racial theorist, occultist, anti-Semite, and former Cistercian monk Jörg Lanz von Liebenfels. Hitler's Vienna years provided his first exposure to Ariosophy through von Liebenfels's neo-pagan magazine *Ostara, Briefbücherei der Blonden und Mannesrechtler*, of which Hitler was an avid reader and collector during his years in Vienna. His time in Vienna laid the foundation for a generic anti-Semitism found among many Europeans at the time, albeit with a peculiar occult *völkisch* Viennese twist. However, Hitler's generic anti-Semitism remained dormant and nascent throughout the war years only to reawaken and make significant advancement shifting from romantic neo-pagan occultism to intellectual rationalism and materialism in the years immediately following the war and German Revolution of 1919. This occurred in no small part because of his introduction to and deepening connections with key figures of the Thule Society, some of whom became prominent figures in the Nazi Party. Dietrich Eckart was arguably the most influential figure among the Thulists in transforming Hitler's anti-Semitism from romantic neo-pagan occultism to intellectual rationalism and materialism.

Reorganization of German national military units stationed in Bavaria began after the fall of Munich and during the closing chapters of the German Revolution. On 30 May 1919, Captain Karl Mayr was appointed Chief of Intelligence Division's Education and Propaganda Department (Ib/P) in the new *Vorläufige Reichswehr* (Provisional National Defense) Group Headquarters 4 (Bavaria). He was given considerable funding to build a team of agents or informants and to organize a series of educational courses to retrain selected officers and men in "correct" political and ideological thinking.

On 19 November 1918, Hitler was diagnosed as unfit for military service and was discharged from Pasewalk Hospital in Pomerania and transferred to the Second Bavarian Infantry Regiment garrisoned in Munich. *Gefreiter* Adolf Hitler returned to Munich "[t]owards the end of November" (Hitler 1942, 167). Without formal education or career prospects, he remained in the army, now known as the *Vorläufige Reichswehr* in compliance with the Armistice and collected a meager salary at a time of widespread unemployment. By order of the Soldiers' Revolutionary Council, a detachment of soldiers including Hitler, was transferred on 6 December 1918 for guard duty in Traunstein (108 km southeast of Munich) where a prisoner-of-war camp holding Russian and Polish soldiers from the Eastern Front was located. The bulk of POWs left Traunstein before the end of January 1919. Between 23 January and 12 February 1919, Hitler returns to the Munich garrison and by mid-February, he successfully candidates for "spokesman" (*Vertrauensmann*) to represent his regiment at the self-governing regimental "Soldiers' Council" recognized by the *SPD* branch headquarters in Munich. Hitler's main responsibility was to "enlighten" his unit through pro-Republican propaganda. Between 20 February and 8 March 1919, Hitler began guard duty at the Munich central railway station, the site of the upcoming Palm Sunday *Putsch*.

On 21 February 1919, Kurt Eisner was assassinated, and the Socialist People's State of Bavaria quickly collapses. On 26 February 1919, Hitler and his *Ersatz* Battalion of the Second Infantry Regiment participate in the state funeral of Kurt Eisner walking directly behind the coffin-bearing carriage wearing the black band of mourning on the left arm and the red revolutionary brassard on the other showing support for the martyred Socialist.

On 7 March 1919, Hitler made the acquaintance of Captain Ernst Röhm. There, in that atmosphere of displaced fanaticism, he met a veteran of the Franco-German front, a pale and puny man with a look of exaltation in his eyes, fired by Nationalist passion and visionary ambition, a magnetic orator who spoke in short, sharp bursts. Hitler later recalled that they spent the evening "in a cellar where we racked our brains for ways of combating the revolutionary movement" (Gallo 1972, 14). It is believed that night Hitler was recruited by Röhm as a spy and informer on Socialist-Marxist organizations. Röhm was then chief of staff to Captain von Epp, the *Freikorps Epp* commander. The reference to the meeting in the "cellar" was likely due to the undercover nature of Röhm's clandestine work for *Freikorps Epp* at the time. Under orders of his commanding officer von Epp, Röhm had recently begun to recruit Bavarian mercenaries with the aid of a leaflet campaign.

When the *Freikorps* were fighting their way into Munich in May 1919, they had been greeted by gunshots from the barracks where Hitler was quartered. Only a few shots had been fired by a few Red sympathizers who hoped to draw the barracks into the fray, but the anger of the *Freikorps* troops had been aroused. The "neutrality" of the *Vorläufige Reichswehr* detachments in Munich during the political crises did not fare well with the *Freikorps* and they distrusted the Munich garrison. The short-tempered troops stormed the barracks. Everyone in it, including Hitler, was arrested and marched through the streets, hands above their heads, and imprisoned in the cellar of *Maximiliansgymnasium* where *Freikorps Lützow* quartered.

The officers of Hitler's regiment, who were forced to flee Munich during the Soviet Republic period, returned with the *Freikorps* and were soon in control of the city. An investigation was started to determine who had sided with the Reds. When they began to investigate the incident that occurred at Hitler's barracks, some officers recognized Hitler, testified to his character and war record, and ordered his release. It seems almost certain that Ernst Röhm, chief of staff to *Freikorps Epp*, protected him during this period. Hitler, nevertheless, was worried. Investigators were beginning to ask why the soldiers in the *Vorläufige Reichswehr* garrisoned in Munich, who claimed to be loyal to the conservative cause, did not join the guerrilla skirmishes within the city, or earlier flee Munich and join the *Freikorps*. To date, there is no record of how Hitler personally answered this challenge. But years later, several fellow members of the nascent Nazi Party revisited this issue and held his lack of action during the battle for Munich as contemptible. "A few days after the liberation of Munich," Hitler would later write, "I was ordered to appear before the Inquiry Commission." Hitler's hostility to Marxism and his cooperation with the Commission soon placed him above reproach (Bullock 1962, 64).

Many of the leaders of the revolution had been imprisoned at one time or another for their political activities. Hitler, consequently, felt the revolution had little to do with equality or freedom and was nothing but "a vast riot" led by "thugs, tramps, and typified by lootings and extortions." His account to the Commission about officers and troops sympathetic or supporting the Red cause was "mercilessly exact." Hitler's cooperation during the investigations caught the attention of his superiors. He subsequently joined the investigating Commission and appeared repeatedly as a witness against the accused.

"On one occasion," Hitler would later say:

> I was called as a witness in a case against an army deserter—a first class swine named Sauper. The [lawyer] rose and asked me a few questions, to which, like a silly fool, I answered quite frankly. . . . I told him in unmistakable terms what I thought of the swine. The [lawyer] smiled. "I object to this witness on the score of personal prejudice," he declared solemnly. The objection was upheld and the filthy Sauper got off scot-free. When the case ended, an officer who was in the public gallery came up to me with outstretched hand. "For God's sake, let's get out of here!" he cried.

The officer had reason to worry about Hitler. The Reds had been driven from the streets but there was still a teeming underground opposition. Those like Hitler, who had the courage to testify against the Reds, were often badly beaten or died mysteriously. Schmidt, who met Hitler shortly after he began giving testimony, stated that Hitler looked haggard and nervous. Hitler, nevertheless, continued to give testimony until it came to the point where he lost nearly all faith in the legal system and would later state: "I had no idea that a [lawyer] is a private individual who makes his living by defending scoundrels." He felt that lawyers were "irresponsible and useless" in obtaining justice, and that they shared a "kinship" with criminals because of their mutual need for one another.

Hitler, nevertheless, continued to supply information and give additional testimony. He also supplied information on the whereabouts of soldiers and officers who had taken part in the Bavarian Soviet regime. As many as ten Reds were executed because of the information Hitler supplied. As one admiring officer, A.V. von Körber, would state: "After joining the investigating commission, [Hitler] produced indictments which threw a merciless light on the unspeakably depraved military betrayals perpetrated by the Jewish dictatorship at the time of the Munich Soviets." As Hitler would later write: "This was my first more or less purely political activity."

It was through von Epp's connections and mutually-shared military and political sympathies with General Ludendorff that Captain Ernst Röhm was recommended as an undercover agent (*Verbindungsmann*) to Captain Karl Mayr's newly-established Education and Propaganda Department Ib/P in the Intelligence Division of the Bavarian Army Command under *General der Infanterie* Ernst von Oven—General Ludendorff's close friend.

> He [Röhm] was a stocky, bull-necked, piggish-eyed, scar-faced professional soldier – the upper part of his nose had been shot away in 1914 – with a flair for politics and a natural ability as an organizer. Like Hitler he was possessed of a burning hatred for the democratic Republic and the "November criminals" he held responsible for it. His aim was to re-create a strong nationalist Germany and he believed with Hitler that this could be done only by a party based on the lower classes, from which he himself, unlike most Regular Army officers, had come. A tough, ruthless, driving man – albeit, like so many of the early Nazis, a homosexual – he helped to organize the first Nazi strong-arm squads which grew into the S.A., the army of storm troopers which he commanded until his execution by Hitler in 1934. Roehm not only brought into the budding party large numbers of ex-servicemen and free-corps volunteers, who formed the backbone of the organization in its early years, but, as an officer of the Army, which controlled

> Bavaria, he obtained for Hitler and his movement the protection and sometimes the support of the authorities. Without this help, Hitler probably could never have got a real start in his campaign to incite the people to overthrow the Republic. Certainly he could not have got away with his methods of terror and intimidation without the tolerance of the Bavarian government and police. (Shirer 1960, 38.)

FROM SOLDIERS' SPOKESMAN TO UNDERCOVER LIAISON OFFICER, PROPAGANDA AGENT, AND EDUCATION OFFICER

THROUGHOUT JUNE 1919, CAPTAIN MAYR WORKED CLOSELY WITH Ernst Röhm in Department Ib/P. Röhm suggested that his new contact in the Second Bavarian Infantry Regiment, Corporal Adolf Hitler, was an outspoken speaker and leader (*Vertrauensmann*) in the "soldiers' council" of his *Ersatz* Battalion who held anti-Bolshevik views and should be recruited as an informant (*Verbindungsmann*). Hitler was particularly close to Munich's revolutionary "soldiers' councils" in the spring of 1919 but only two months later, he joined the Second Bavarian Infantry Regiment's "discharge and fact-finding board," a body set up immediately after the counterrevolutionaries had triumphed in the fall of Munich in May 1919. This job, which he would scarcely have obtained without Röhm's recommendation, entailed checking on the political convictions of comrade war veterans due for discharge and their political position during the revolution. Those discovered to have sympathies for the Bavarian Soviet regime were severely dealt with.

In June 1919, Hitler was introduced to Captain Mayr. There is some information to suggest that in the months after the Armistice, General Erich Ludendorff began looking for groups and outspoken individuals who were Nationalistic, anti-Entente, anti-Republican, and anti-Bolshevik—the opposite characteristics of those viewed among many Imperial Army officers as the culprits ("November Criminals") for the disastrous capitulation of the war effort leading to the Armistice and the greatest threat to Germany at the time. Ludendorff's contacts in the military (von Epp) made him aware of an outspoken corporal from the former *List Regiment* who served in leadership positions among his fellow demobilized army veteran groups. Some evidence exists suggesting that it was General Ludendorff who urged Captain Mayr to press Corporal Hitler to infiltrate the *DAP* and help direct it to win over the workers unions and the masses. This evidence implies that General Ludendorff believed the decorated veteran who was earning a reputation among his comrade veterans as an outspoken orator and leader would possibly be a good asset for the new chief of the *Vorläufige Reichswehr*'s Intelligence Division's Education and Propaganda Department in Bavaria, not only as a tool for reeducation and propaganda among army veterans who may be leaning Socialist, but also as a political leader to oust the Weimar government and restore the monarchy, or in the alternative, to establish a Nationalist government that would lead Germany (and its generals) with an iron fist back to its place of glory. Other historical information suggests that it was Ernst Röhm who introduced Hitler to Captain Mayr with Ludendorff only providing his and von Epp's recommendation supporting the propaganda aspirant.

In his capacity as head of the *Vorläufige Reichswehr*'s Education and Propaganda Department, Mayr recruited Adolf Hitler as an undercover agent or *Verbindungsmann* (liaison officer) in early June 1919. Hitler's role involved informing on soldiers suspected of Communist sympathies. On 22–26 July 1919, Hitler took part in the five-day "national thinking" course to train *Propagandaleute* (propaganda agents) at the *Reichswehrlager* at Lechfeld near Augsburg, which were organized by the Bavarian *Vorläufige Reichswehr* under Captain Mayr. Mayr believed demoralized and Bolshevized forces should be taught national sentiments. After this instructor training, Mayr issued Hitler the order to become "anti-Bolshevik educational speaker" to the soldiers at the Lechfeld and Munich barracks. Furthermore, Hitler was sent as an observer to the numerous meetings of the various newly formed political parties in Munich. Hitler spent much time at the meetings and wrote reports on the political ideas, goals, and methods of the groups. This included studying the activities of the *DAP* (German Workers' Party). At his first meeting with the *DAP* on 12 September 1919, Hitler became impressed with founder Anton Drexler's anti-Semitic, Nationalist, anti-Capitalist, and anti-Marxist ideas. Drexler was impressed with Hitler's oratory skills and invited him to join the *DAP*. After attending a further meeting on 3 October, Hitler stated to Mayr in his report "must join this club or party, as these were the thoughts of the soldiers from the front-line."

After learning of the outbreak of the Kapp–Lüttwitz *Putsch* in Berlin, Hitler, Captain Mayr, and Dietrich Eckart considered forming a parallel *putschist* government in Munich. The army in Munich wanted a liaison man in Berlin in order to coordinate the two revolts. Hitler and Eckart volunteered and their help was immediately accepted. Eckart's connections among the well-bred and well-fed, along with Hitler's power of arousing the working classes, was more than they could ask for. They were provided with two sets of credentials. One was to be used if they fell into the hands of Socialist sympathizers. The other was to introduce them to any conservative supporters. A plane and a military pilot were put at their disposal. On the morning of 17 March, Eckart and Hitler took off for Berlin to observe the events of the Kapp *Putsch*. Hitler and Eckart departed from the airfield at Augsburg landing in the outskirts of Berlin.

It was Hitler's first flight, and the weather was rough. He became air sick and started vomiting. Short of fuel, the pilot was forced to land at Juterbog, about 40 miles short of Berlin. The airport was in the hands of Socialists and Hitler, taking no chances that he might be recognized, put on his fake goatee. Eckart posed as a paper manufacturer on business. Hitler posed as his accountant. After some touch and go negotiating they were supplied with fuel and allowed to proceed. Hitler resumed vomiting.

After landing at Tempelhof in Berlin they proceeded to the *Reich* Chancellery where they met with Kapp's press secretary. They learned that the Kapp *Putsch* had turned into a fiasco. The Socialist government had called for a general strike to protest the *putsch*. The Communists, who knew their movement would suffer under a conservative regime, now wholeheartedly supported the ousted Socialist Republic. Red workers and their trade unions united with the Socialists. Electricity and water were turned off, transportation stopped, industry shut down, garbage piled up in the streets, and even small shops kept their doors closed. The civil servants in the ministries refused to cooperate with Kapp. No one of importance would accept a position in his cabinet. Kapp's position became hopeless, and his movement collapsed. The Weimar Republic, was in affect this time, saved by the Communists. Hitler and Eckart were informed that Kapp was already on his way out of the country. There was nothing for them to do.

In the meantime, Hitler and Eckart had adopted the role of tourists and remained in Berlin for over a week. The city was home to many Nationalist and *völkisch* organizations, as well as wealthy anti-Socialists whom Eckart knew well. Hitler, who at this stage, could never hope to enter such circles on his own, must have been greatly impressed. Though Hitler never mentioned his first introduction into Berlin's high society, it is highly likely that this was when he personally first met General Ludendorff. What

Hitler was very outspoken about, however, was, as he put it: "the great Babylonian whore . . . Red Berlin."

Hitler and Eckart had been sent to Berlin by Nationalist circles in Munich who were themselves preparing for a political takeover. One of them, Gustav von Kahr, became prime minister of Bavaria on the day after Hitler and Eckart reached Berlin. However, Hitler reached Berlin too late, after the *putsch* had failed. Feeling that the *putsch* must be in the wrong hands, they are disgusted to discover that Kapp's press chief was the adventurous Hungarian Jew, Ignaz Trebitsch-Lincoln, at one time also a member of the British Parliament. In Berlin, Eckart introduced Hitler to General Ludendorff and to the salon of Helene Bechstein, wife of the piano manufacturer (Hanser 1971, 221). Hitler also met Heinrich Claß, president of the *Alldeutscher Verband*, a major pan-German organization. Hitler and Eckart returned to Munich on 29 March 1920.

One year after his capture in France and imprisonment in Sachsenhausen Concentration Camp in Germany, Captain Mayr authored an essay providing an interesting recollection of his early days with Corporal Hitler and his view of who Hitler really is to the Nazi Party. The essay was published in *Current History: Incorporating Events, Forum and Century* (New York, NY: Events Publishing Company, November 1941, Volume I, Number 3, pages 193–9).

I WAS HITLER'S BOSS
By A Former Officer of the *Reichswehr*

For fifteen months I was in daily contact with Hitler, and I believe I know this strange man as well as, if not better than, anyone else. I knew him before he had to pretend and put on a leader's mask, sometimes even to the so-called men around him. after the First World War he was just one of the many thousands of ex-soldiers who walked the streets looking for work. For him it was especially hard, since he had not quite recovered from his war injuries and was without a family to which he could go back.

At this time Hitler was ready to throw in his lot with anyone who would show him kindness. He never had that "Death or Germany" martyr spirit which later was so much used as a propaganda slogan to boost him. he would have worked for a Jewish or a French employer just as readily as for an Aryan. When I first met him he was like a tired stray dog looking for a master. However fancifully writers describe him now, at that time he was totally unconcerned about the German people and their destinies.

Not long after the war, as soon as he was released from the hospital, Hitler tried to enter the postal service as a mail-carrier. His services were refused, because he was unable to pass the intelligence test. His school education in his Austrian village would have been quite sufficient, but his mental capacity suffered after he was gassed in the war.

I first met Hitler in 1919 when the Soldiers' Councils (Red Army) in Munich were smashed. Members of these councils disappeared from their barracks and offices, but it was known that they met secretly, and that they were far more numerous than their enemy, the newly organized Reichswehr. The Reichswehr was not exactly an army in the usual sense of the word, but rather a police force to protect citizens from terror groups. To forestall a surprise attack from its adversaries, the Reichswehr created an intelligence service. I was at the time an infantry captain and detailed to organized and supervise what was called the instruction department. I picked a handful of non-commissioned officers with exemplary war records; among them was Hitler.

The duties of these men were to organize patriotic lectures in the barracks and to attend labor meetings in civilian clothes, mingling with the workers and listening to their talk. I had an office in the officers' mess. My only assistant was a young sergeant who acted as my secretary. Twice a day my men reported to me and we discussed their findings.

Hitler was at first quartered in the same room with two other instruction officers, but not for long. His roommates complained about his physical habits, and that he talked and walked in his sleep and made himself generally a nuisance. We put Hitler in a small room on the second floor, with barred windows, which had been used until then as a lumber room. He seemed to be happy in this cubicle, and stayed there until he had to resign from the Reichswehr on June 10, 1920.

Inside the barracks Hitler had no friends. He was shy and self-conscious. The reason for this was probably the deformity (described in his medical report) that made him unlike other men. In my opinion it was this affliction that made Hitler a lone wolf and outsider. He felt keenly that he was different. That was also the reason why he was rated a permanently unfit for military service on his reporting, in 1911, as an Austrian conscript. This pariah was wild with joy when, after the outbreak of the war in 1914, the Germans disregarded his deformity and found him eligible to serve in the German Imperial Army. But I doubt if his army life was a happy one. A soldier has not the privacy that his deformity made him seek, and so he was continually chaffed by his comrades.

After the World War former officers were considered small potatoes in Germany. Their epaulettes were torn from their shoulders by the workers, and it was not safe to wear war decorations in the street. Ludendorff and his friends, former high officers and capitalists, met once a week in the "little conference room" at the Hotel Vier Jahrezeiten [Four Seasons] in Munich. There they were their former selves, wore their medals, clicked heels and saluted one another. They mourned over the past splendor, deplored their present condition and dreamed of a glorious future. Here in the Vier Jahrezeiten they talked about a Germany greater than ever and about the terrible revenge they would exact. To get all that another war—and the good-will of the workers to fight that war—was necessary. According to their belief Germany was never defeated.

While in the former enemy countries people thought that Germany was forever crushed, and became careless, here in Munich a group of almost desperate men, their wits sharpened by their misery, prepared. All causes that were responsible for their defeat had to be erased forever in Germany. The principal cause, starvation, would be made impossible if Germany could become self-supporting. But without the support of the workers they were helpless; a few thousand fanatics could not begin another war. The workers had to become war-minded again, but how? In their passion for revenge, this Ludendorff group thought of the most extraordinary ways to regain the good-will of the workers.

One general recalled the theory of Joan of Arc as the illiterate French shepherdess whose outbursts of exaltation were used to convince the common people and the soldiery that a goddess was leading them forward to battle. So inspired were the ignorant French warriors that they drove the English away from Orléans. The ruse worked once; why might it not work again? The Ludendorff group knew that nobody among them could ever influence the masses, let alone inspire them. No, a starry-eyed, more or less crazy girl must be found to bring the German people the glorious message that would inflame them. Ludendorff himself hunted diligently through the Bavarian mountains for a red-headed peasant girl to play the part of a German Joan of Arc who could be sold as a goddess, a divine messenger sent straight from Valhalla to wake up the Germans and save them from their bondage by leading them to victory and everlasting glory. But no girl was found with the right kind of vitality and glamor to incite the masses.

That is where Hitler came in. In discharging his duties he had visited a meeting of the newly founded German Workers Party. This handful of workers, though most of them were miserably poor, still felt a good deal of respect for eh former officers and capitalists. A day or two after I had received a report on this patriotic organization, Ludendorff came into my office to get details. At that time he and his friends were like Hollywood scouts looking for talent, in this case "loyal" workers, and they, too, almost at the same time as Hitler came across these extraordinary patriots of the German Workers Party.

Members of the Reichswehr were not allowed to join political parties, but to please Ludendorff, whose wishes were still respected in the Reichswehr, I ordered Hitler to join the Workers Party, and help to foster its growth. He was allowed at first the equivalent of twenty gold marks in the current inflation money weekly for this purpose.

Of course, other patriotic parties and lecturers cropped up like mushrooms after the war, but none of them attracted the masses. The lecturers were too gentlemanly; their meetings were held in bare, dreary lecture halls with notices, such as "Silence Please" and "Smoking Prohibited" on the walls.

With Hitler a new way of approaching the workers was tried. His meetings were announced in working-class saloons; there was free beer, and cigars if the funds allowed, also sausages and pretzels free. Instead of "Silence Please" on the wall, there was concertina music, and folk songs, and more free beer. Then everyone felt happy and grateful, Hitler jumped on a chair or a table and started with "Fellow-workers, Germany, awake!" In such a genial atmosphere it was of course a pleasure for the workers to "awake" and madly applaud everything. The experiment with Hitler was considered highly successful by his sponsors. Ludendorff and many others, who kept carefully behind the scenes at first, now began to associate openly with the workers Party, or Nazis, as they came to be called.

As the Nazi party grew and became popular in Munich, Ludendorff and his friends decided to put everything on a strict business basis. In fact, they copied American methods of salesmanship. The party in Munich was so organized that its ideas were gradually pushed by political salesmen into every home in Germany. The program was carefully concocted to fit in with the wishful thinking of the majority.

The leaders knew that to please the majority, a minority must suffer, and so the German Jews were made the chief scapegoats because their destruction would gain millions of votes for the Nazis. Small shopkeepers hated Jews, because they owned the chain stores; farmers wished their destruction because they were indebted to Jewish banks; even intellectuals were jealous because Jews held lucrative positions in the arts and sciences and professions.

The Communists also had to be destroyed, but that was because they took their orders from Russia and would never vote for an imperial Germany.

The Nazi salesmen offered anything and everything to make people war-minded. The Christian religion condemned war; so the old German gods, who took their heroes, killed in battle, straight to Valhalla, were peddled. The Nazis knew that few would trouble to fight and kill a beggar even if legally allowed, but most of them would kill a rich man to take his wealth, especially if such a killing were considered honorable and patriotic. Therefore, their sales-talk was: Germany is a have-not country; other nations have all the wealth; Germany must fight them successfully, and so be entitled to that wealth. Thus, in their program the Nazis catered always to the desires of the majority.

At that time the Nazi aim was to restore monarchy, a Wittelsbach or a Hohenzollern, then launch a successful war and regain their former splendor and riches. That patriotic slogan, "Everything for Germany," was nothing more than salesmanship; nobody cared in the least what would happen to the rest of Germany, so long as the result would be a restoration of the good old days. Hitler was looked upon as a good salesman for the Nazi ideology, who would be paid off when he was no longer needed.

After World War Germany swarmed with political adventurers. Roehm, a captain in the Reichswehr, was one of them. He was shunned by his fellow officers because of his abnormal vices. Nevertheless, he was a clever strategist. Seeing what possibilities the Workers Party had, he set to work to buy Hitler for himself. Hitler was astonished and flattered that a gentleman should offer him friendship and advice. This friendship began under cover as far back as 1920. Hitler, because of his physical defect, was indifferent about Roehm's vices; he saw in Roehm only the distinguished officer. When his friendship with Roehm became known, Hitler had to resign his position in the Reichswehr.

Beginning in 1922, the Reichswehr gradually became alarmed lest the Nazis should grow too powerful and turn against it. Generals von Lossow and von Seeckt therefore decided to advise Goering, who was considered a staunch imperialist, to join the Nazi party and report on its progress to the Reichswehr. But for an ambitious man like Goering it was too great a temptation to remain a spy for the Reichswehr; he soon decided to play his own game. He knew that should monarchy be restored, he would become, with so many princes waiting for glamorous jobs and medals, a mere nobody. On the other hand, if he should throw in his lot with the Nazis, there might be undreamed possibilities for him.

Though it is not generally known, there was a deadly enmity between Roehm and Goering right from the beginning. Each reckoned upon being one day the ruler of Germany and meanwhile waited for any chance to cut the other's throat. After the [Beer Hall] *putsch* in November 1923, Goering fled from Germany badly wounded, and was not allowed to return until after the amnesty in 1927. During this time Roehm was undisputed ruler of the Nazi party. He put his friends, all riff-raff and addicts to the same vices as himself, into the key positions and started organizing his own army, the Storm Troopers. But Goering paid Roehm back when the latter went to South America to "organize" the Bolivian army.

Roehm went to South America because he thought that there he could raise enough money to finance a *putsch* in Germany with his Storm Troopers and, though it is not well known, he obtained large amounts from Bolivian, Chilean and Argentine Nazi sympathizers. A German brewery in Argentina alone contributed 2,000,000 pesos as a loan. While Roehm was away, Goering discredited him and undermined his power wherever he could.

Why, it will be asked, did Hitler allow all this working over his head? Was he not the leader of the Nazis? The answer is that Hitler never was nor is he now anything of the kind. As a leader Hitler is probably the greatest hoax ever played on the world. The reports that Hitler brought me daily in the Reichswehr were scrupulously honest, but his style and grammar were lamentable. His reports always had to be rewritten before I could file them. His intellect was not higher than that of an eight-year-old child. After he left the Reichswehr, he was completely at the mercy of political freebooters. Those two would-be dictators, Roehm and Goering with their satellites, fought one another behind the scenes tooth and nail. They even ousted Ludendorff. Finally Goering won the battle in the "Blood Purge" of June 30, 1934.

The way was now clear for Goering and he lost no time. Conscription; occupation of the Rhineland; total rearmament; intervention in Spain; invasion of Austria, Czechoslovakia, Poland and other countries followed. "A bloodthirsty mad ogre," "a superman in leadership and strategy,"—in such terms was Hitler referred to. How little the world knows about the real Hitler!

The Nazi boast, "Tell people the most senseless lie again and again and they believe it to be sure and certain truth," has a right to stand after the world acknowledged Hitler as Germany's leader. As a rabble-rouser of the highest order Hitler was and still is of extreme value to the Nazis. So many people believe that without him Germany would have become a peace-loving country. Little do they know the true character of the Germans. Let the war bugle sound and show them a uniform, and they will follow their officers as the children followed the Pied Piper of Hamelin.

If all Germans had not more brains than Hitler, they would be a harmless lot. It is people with brains who use Hitler for their own ends that are dangerous-those who try to build their own prosperity and well-being upon the misery of others. Hitler has never been capable of making a decision of his own. He certainly never wrote a line of *Mein Kampf*; he merely signed his name to it. Many writers had their fingers in the *Mein Kampf* pie. Ludendorff, Rosenberg, Haushofer, Streicher, Epp, Eckart and probably several others contributed material for the book. Heß collected all their stuff, chose suitable parts fit for printing, and so *Mein Kampf* came into existence.

The chapter of *Mein Kampf* in which British-German collaboration is advocated was written by Heß himself. To attract the curiosity of the man in the street, the opinions of the political adventurers who collaborated were written in the form of Hitler's autobiography. Hitler, the man with the mind of a fourth-grade scholar, was of course proud to sign his name as author of a book.

Heß was Hitler's first and most successful mentor. Born in a British protectorate, and with his best friends amongst members of the British upper classes, he developed Anglomania. In his opinion a German allied with Great Britain could easily smash the rest of the world. Goering's belief was that Germany alone was qualified to rule the world. Heß's plane trip to Scotland last May was, in my opinion, for the purpose of trying to find a solution that would end the war between Germany and Britain.

A dabbler in mesmerism and faith healing, Heß certainly was most successful with Hitler. Before every important speech Hitler was, sometimes for days, closeted with Heß who in some unknown way got Hitler into that frenetic state in which he came forth to address the public. Just before Hitler had appointments to receive statesmen or foreign correspondents, he was minutely coached as what to say. Sometimes, when unexpected questions were put to him, he just walked away, or started his senseless political rantings.

At times Hitler sulks like a bad-tempered child; he locks himself up for days and holds conversations with himself, and his public speeches and receptions have to be postponed. When in such moods, music often has a soothing effect on him. he does not care what type of music it is so long as it is noisy; he is not in the least musical; he likes Wagner's music because it is loud. As a rule his coach has to play the piano wildly, while he makes weird noises in his mouth, imitating a trumpet, and bangs his fists on tables and chairs. Such concerts can last for hours before Hitler falls into a tranquil sleep.

Germany has many Fausts, but their Mephistopheles is Goering who was able, through crafty propagandists like Goebbels, to sell Hitler to the entire world as a patriotic superman. Goering alone engineered the

> burning of the Reichstag and had a feeble-minded boy executed for it. He arranged the "Blood Purge" of June 30, 1934; it was he who saw that Hitler got the false material to convince him that Roehm intended to kill him unless he killed Roehm first. Goering's references to Hitler as "My Fuehrer, the greatest living German of the ages" and his placing of Hitler's bust all over his house are sheer hypocrisy, designed to mislead public opinion.
>
> Those who call the present war "Hitler's war" or who say "We must defeat Hitlerism" do not know what role Hitler plays in Germany. Posed photographs in which Hitler is seen signing an agreement or, surrounded by generals, placing a finger on a war map are reproduced by the most serious newspapers as important documents and are regarded by the readers with awe.
>
> Yet the real power is Goering. If that is so, then why, it may be asked, does not Goering get rid of Hitler and take his place? Because the time has not yet come. Hitler is still a useful pawn in Goering's hands. If Germany loses the war, Goering can hypocritically declare: "Let us have an honorable peace. We Germans never wanted this war. It is this Austrian madman who is to blame. We will send him to a sanatorium for life." But if on the other hand, Germany should win, Hitler will have outlived his usefulness. He will die and Goering will come into his inheritance.
>
> Goering will even make use of Hitler when dead. Hitler would be declared the greatest of all German saints and heroes. Thousands of faithful Aryans would every year make a pilgrimage to his tomb. German theatres would boom by producing saintly Hitler plays, Joan of Arc style. The throne would be restored in Germany, with Goering as monarch. To rule over Europe would not satisfy his vanity; he would strive to bring the whole world under his imperial sway.

On 5 June 1919, under the direction of his new employer Captain Karl Mayr, Hitler began a course on political education at the University of Munich that had been organized by Mayr. Given the fact that Hitler's formal education was fragmented and ended at the age of sixteen-years, he had no formal training in higher critical thinking, polemics, rhetoric, world history, physical or biological sciences, economics, political theory, or literature. He was entirely unprepared to handle university-level subjects. Yet, Hitler attended courses entitled: German History After the Reformation; Germany from 1870–1900; Bavaria and the Unity of the *Reich*; The Political History of the War; The Significance of the Army; German Economic Conditions and the Peace Terms; State Control of Production; Price Policies in the Economic System; Russian and Communist Rule; Socialism in Theory and Practice; Foreign Policy; and Correlations Between Domestic and Foreign Policy. (Kershaw 1998, 123.)

The main objective of these courses was to promote his political philosophy favored by the army and help to combat the influence of the Russian Bolshevik Revolution on the German soldier. Speakers included Rhodes Scholar and Doctor of History Karl Alexander von Müller (future chief of the *Institut zum Studium der Judenfrage* [Institute for the Study of the Jewish Question] in the Nazi regime) and von Müller's brother-in-law the anti-Semite *Schutz- und Trutzbund* and Thule Society member and *DAP* co-founder Gottfried Feder. Both of these men proved to be foundational to transforming and perfecting Hitler's anti-Semitism, pan-Germanism, and political ideology. It is believed to be Feder who contemporaneously in the summer of 1919 introduced Hitler to the members of the Thule Society.

During the last days of June 1919, Hitler sat in class listening to von Müller's version of history in which the German's were exalted as a "master race." Because Hitler had been exposed to such teaching in Austrian schools, and since Europe was alive with Nationalist fervor, he took offense when after von Müller's speech, a student delivered a retort protesting the professor's negative view of the Jews. Hitler, therefore, entered his name "as wishing to take part in the discussion," and when his turn to speak came, he defended the professor's opinion with such passion that he held his audience and swayed it. This was Hitler's first and self-confessed anti-Semitic speech, and as he would later write: "The overwhelming majority of the students present took my standpoint." Von Müller was impressed with Hitler's contribution and told Mayr that he had "rhetorical talent," later describing his first impression of Hitler (Flood 1989, 63; see also Hanser 1971, 189 and Maser 1973, 104–7):

> My lecture and the lively discussion that followed it were over and the students had already begun to leave when my attention was caught by a small group of people in the hall.

> They were standing spellbound round a man who was vehemently haranguing them in a curiously guttural voice and with ever mounting passion. I had the peculiar feeling that he was feeding on the excitement he himself had whipped up. His face was pale and thin, his forehead partially concealed by an unmilitary lock of hair. He wore a close-cropped mustache and his striking large, clear-blue eyes had a cold passion in them.

At the next class, Captain Karl Mayr, the General Staff officer in charge of the soldier-speaker program, was present. Professor von Müller asked Captain Mayr if he was aware that he had among his students "a natural-born speaker." The Captain asked who the person was, and the professor pointed to Hitler.

"That's Hitler from the *List Regiment*," the Captain said and called out, "You Hitler, come up here." The Professor remembered that Hitler, still ill at ease among superiors, approached the Captain "awkwardly, with a kind of defiant embarrassment." Nothing came of the talk between Mayr and Hitler immediately, but Hitler was beginning to attract attention.

As a result of von Müller's recommendation, Hitler was selected as a prospective *Propagandaleute* (propaganda agent) in a team of twenty-three trainees that were to be sent to the *Reichswehrlager* at Lechfeld near Augsburg for a five-day indoctrination course. Hitler completed his indoctrination training as a standout among the first group. After this instructor training, Mayr issued Hitler the order to become "anti-Bolshevik educational speaker" to the soldiers at the Lechfeld and Munich barracks. This was arranged by Mayr in response to complaints about the political unreliability of men stationed there. The task of the squad was to inculcate Nationalist and anti-Bolshevik sentiments in the troops, described as being "infected" by Bolshevism and Spartacism.

Lechfeld was now being used as "transit center" and was receiving a regular flow of freed prisoners of war who were to be discharged or transferred. The huge camp was freely accessible to the many civilians employed there. Consequently, Independent Socialists (*USPD*) and other Marxist agitators were getting into the camp and were spreading their propaganda. The camp commander requested the Educational and Propaganda Department Ib/P to counter the Red propaganda with troop debriefings, or as Hitler put it: "The soldiers had to be taught to think and feel in a national and patriotic way."

When Hitler and his group arrived, they split into groups and set up shop in the various squad rooms scattered about the base. Because Allied and Communist propaganda was depicting Germany, the old Monarchy, and the army as those solely responsible for the war, the leader of Hitler's group would begin the proceedings with a speech titled: "Who Bears the Guilt for the World War?" In an informal way, the other soldier-speakers were expected to contribute to the proceedings.

Hitler went on to give lectures on "Peace Conditions and Reconstruction," "Emigration," and "Social and Political-Economic Catchwords." On 25 August 1919, the camp was in the act of processing the last of the returning prisoners of war and Hitler gave his last speech titled "Capitalism." Captain Lauterbach, who was in charge of troop indoctrination at Camp Lechfeld, wrote to Mayr that Hitler's speech, while "attractive, clear, and passionate," was also problematic:

> Within this speech he [Hitler] came to the question of the Jews—while Hitler was giving his presentation, there arose problems of differences of opinion about how clearly one should utter one's opinion about the Jews. If the question of the Jews were presented in a very clear way, with respect to our Germanic standpoint, if it were done like that, it could give Jews reason to regard these speeches as Jew-baiting. This is why I find it necessary to treat this question as carefully as possible, and too clear hints about a strange race should be avoided. (Flood 1989, 63.)

The soldiers were impressed with Hitler's lectures at Lechfeld. One soldier, Hans Knoden, pointed out that Hitler "revealed himself to be an excellent and passionate speaker and captured the attention of all the listeners with his comments." Another soldier, Lorenz Frank, argued that "Hitler is a born popular speaker who, through his fanaticism and his populist style in a meeting, absolutely compels his audience to take note and share his views." (Kershaw 1998, 107, 124, 125.)

In *Hitler, 1889–1936: Hubris*, Kershaw has argued:

> He (Hitler) threw himself with passion into the work. His engagement was total. And he immediately found he could strike a chord with his audience, that the way he spoke roused the soldiers listening to him from their passivity and

> cynicism. Hitler was in his element. For the first time in his life, he had found something at which he was an unqualified success. Almost by chance, he had stumbled across his greatest talent. (Kershaw 1998, 124)

Hitler wrote in *Mein Kampf* (Hitler 1942, 173):

> I took up my work with the greatest delight and devotion. Here I was presented with an opportunity of speaking before quite a large audience. I was now able to confirm what I had hitherto merely felt, namely, that I had a talent for public speaking. . . . I am able to state that my talks were successful. During the course of my lectures I have led back hundreds and even thousands of my fellow countrymen to their people and their fatherland.

Hitler was no longer isolated. The German soldiers who attended his lectures shared his sense of national failure. They found his message that they were not to blame attractive. He told them that Germany had not been beaten on the battlefield but had been betrayed by Jews and Marxists who had preached revolution and undermined the war effort.

> We were all more or less firmly convinced that Germany could not be saved from imminent disaster by those who had participated in the November treachery—that is to say, the Centre and the Social-Democrats; and also that the so-called Bourgeois-National group could not make good the damage that had been done, even if they had the best intentions. They lacked a number of requisites without which such a task could never be successfully undertaken. The years that followed have justified the opinions which we held at that time. (Hitler 1942, 167.)

At the beginning of September 1919, Hitler, now a *Bildungsoffizier* (Instruction Officer), returned to Munich and his work with Department Ib/P, where he was gaining a reputation as an expert in the "Jewish problem." Because anti-Semitism had not played a notable part in Bavarian politics prior to the revolutionary disturbances, *Herr* Adolf Gemlich, a *Vorläufige Reichswehr* soldier and fellow liaison officer (*Verbindungsmann*) (Jäckel and Kuhn 1980, 88–90), was prompted to send an inquiry about the growing importance of the "Jewish question" to Captain Karl Mayr, the officer in charge of the *Vorläufige Reichswehr* Education and Propaganda Department Ib/P in Munich. Mayr referred him to Hitler, who had distinguished himself in von Müller's courses at the University of Munich by the vehemence of his radical Nationalist and anti-Semitic views, and by his oratorical talents. Hitler was already feeling his way toward a political career; four days before responding to Gemlich in the letter translated below, he had paid his first visit to the German Workers' Party (eventually renamed, the National Socialist German Workers' Party) as a confidential agent of the *Vorläufige Reichswehr*.

In the letter to Gemlich, he appears anxious to establish his credentials as a knowledgeable and sober anti-Semite though his rhetoric is quite tame, stressing the need for a "rational" and "scientific" anti-Semitism. Hitler calls for the "irrevocable removal" of Jews from German life, but it is clear from the context that, at this point, Hitler meant only segregation or expulsion rather than systematic liquidation. The letter impressed Hitler's superiors and he soon gained a reputation as a man who could inoculate the masses against revolution and whose anti-Semitic rhetoric could help discredit the Weimar Republic. Because the letter, dated 16 September 1919 and paleographically authenticated in 1990, is the first record of Hitler's anti-Semitic views, and because it accompanied Hitler into politics, it is considered an important document in Holocaust studies.

Dear *Herr* Gemlich,

The danger posed by Jewry for our people today finds expression in the undeniable aversion of wide sections of our people. The cause of this aversion is not to be found in a clear recognition of the consciously or unconsciously systematic and pernicious effect of the Jews as a totality upon our nation. Rather, it arises mostly from personal contact and from the personal impression which the individual Jew leaves—almost always an unfavorable one. For this reason, antisemitism is too easily characterized as a mere emotional phenomenon. And yet this is incorrect. Antisemitism as a political movement may not and cannot be defined by emotional impulses, but by recognition of the facts. The facts are these: First, Jewry is absolutely a race and not a religious association. Even the Jews never designate themselves as Jewish Germans, Jewish Poles, or Jewish Americans but always as German, Polish, or American Jews. Jews have never yet adopted much more than the language of the foreign nations among whom they live. A German who is forced to make use of the French language in France, Italian in Italy, Chinese in China does not thereby become a Frenchman, Italian, or Chinaman. It's the same with the Jew who lives among us and is forced to make use of the German language. He does not thereby become a German. Neither does the Mosaic faith, so important for the survival of this race, settle the question of whether someone is a Jew or non-Jew. There is scarcely a race whose members belong exclusively to just one definite religion.

Through thousands of years of the closest kind of inbreeding, Jews in general have maintained their race and their peculiarities far more distinctly than many of the peoples among whom they have lived. And thus, comes the fact that there lives amongst us a non- German, alien race which neither wishes nor is able to sacrifice its racial character or to deny its feeling, thinking, and striving. Nevertheless, it possesses all the political rights we do. If the ethos of the Jews is revealed in the purely material realm, it is even clearer in their thinking and striving. Their dance around the golden calf is becoming a merciless struggle for all those possessions we prize most highly on earth.

The value of the individual is no longer decided by his character or by the significance of his achievements for the totality but exclusively by the size of his fortune, by his money.

The loftiness of a nation is no longer to be measured by the sum of its moral and spiritual powers, but rather by the wealth of its material possessions.

This thinking and striving after money and power, and the feelings that go along with it, serve the purposes of the Jew who is unscrupulous in the choice of methods and pitiless in their employment. In autocratically ruled states he whines for the favor of "His Majesty" and misuses it like a leech fastened upon the nations. In democracies he vies for the favor of the masses, cringes before the "majesty of the people," and recognizes only the majesty of money.

He destroys the character of princes with byzantine flattery, national pride (the strength of a people), with ridicule and shameless breeding to depravity. His method of battle is that public opinion which is never expressed in the press, but which is nonetheless managed and falsified by it. His power is the power of money, which multiplies in his hands effortlessly and endlessly through interest, and which forces peoples under the most dangerous of yokes. Its golden glitter, so attractive in the beginning, conceals the ultimately tragic consequences. Everything men strive after as a higher goal, be it religion, Socialism, Democracy, is to the Jew only means to an end, the way to satisfy his lust for gold and domination.

In his effects and consequences, he is like a racial tuberculosis of the nations.

The deduction from all this is the following: an antisemitism based on purely emotional grounds will find its ultimate expression in the form of the pogrom.[1] An anti-Semitism based on reason, however, must lead to systematic legal combating and elimination of the privileges of the Jews, that which distinguishes the Jews from the other aliens who live among us (an Aliens Law). The ultimate objective [of such legislation] must, however, be the irrevocable removal of the Jews in general.

For both these ends a government of national strength, not of national weakness, is necessary.

The Republic in Germany owes its birth not to the uniform national will of our people but the sly exploitation of a series of circumstances which found general expression in a deep, universal dissatisfaction. These circumstances however were independent of the form of the state and are still operative today. Indeed, more so now than before. Thus, a great portion of our people recognizes that a changed state-form cannot in itself change our situation. For that it will take a rebirth of the moral and spiritual powers of the nation.

And this rebirth cannot be initiated by a state leadership of irresponsible majorities, influenced by certain party dogmas, an irresponsible press, or internationalist phrases and slogans. [It requires] instead the ruthless installation of nationally minded leadership personalities with an inner sense of responsibility.

But these facts deny to the Republic the essential inner support of the nation's spiritual forces. And thus, today's state leaders are compelled to seek support among those who draw the exclusive benefits of the new formation of German conditions, and who for this reason were the driving force behind the revolution—the Jews. Even though (as various statements of the leading personalities reveal) today's leaders fully realized the danger of Jewry, they (seeking their own advantage) accepted the readily proffered support of the Jews and also returned the favor. And this pay-off consisted not only in every possible favoring of Jewry, but above all in the hindrance of the struggle of the betrayed people against its defrauders, that is in the repression of the anti-Semitic movement.

Respectfully,
Signed—Adolf Hitler

Sources: Jäckel and Kuhn 1980, 88–90.

[1] Pogrom in Russian means devastation. Until recently, the term described exclusively the organized or spontaneous massacres of Jews. In Russia, the worst pogroms occurred in 1881, 1903, 1905, and during the civil war following the Revolution of 1917 in areas controlled by the anti-Bolshevik White armies, especially the Ukraine.

Hitler's small step up the social ladder fed his self-respect, and he began looking for that something special that would distinguish him from other men. During the war he had experimented with several types of mustaches and by the end of the war was wearing one that was fairly bushy and ran along the length of the upper lip almost concealing it. During his training in propaganda and speaking, he thinned out his mustache and wore it close-cropped. Around this time, he chose to clip the ends which made it narrower than the width of his lips. This type of mustache was more prominent among the British, but some German officers (like Ernst Röhm) and Nationalist "intellectuals" (Dietrich Eckart, Gottfried Feder, etc.) to whom Hitler had been exposed in his speaker training period, sprouted such cropped clumps of hair over their upper lip. Hitler was undoubtedly attempting to emulate them; and like them, when he was off the military base, he dressed in a blue suit, white shirt, and tie with overcoat and broad brimmed hat.

The army in Munich, as well as the police, were still tense over the fact that a handful of Communist radicals had taken over Bavaria a few months before. The turbulent political situation had fostered over fifty political parties, associations, and societies which had formed as a direct challenge to the government. They covered the political spectrum from rabid Communists to rabid Nationalists. All of them, whether liberal or conservative, were subject to surveillance by the police or army intelligence. When Hitler was not lecturing troops, one of his other duties was to report on such organizations.

On 12 September 1919, as *Verbindungsmann*, Hitler was ordered to check out an organization calling itself the German Workers' Party. That evening, dressed in a dark blue suit, he attended the group's meeting which was held in one of the meeting rooms of the *Sternecker* Brewery. (*Biertischpolitik* [Beer-table politics] was an important factor in the political life of Germany.) Hitler had nothing to hide and signed the party's register as: *Gefreiter Munchen 2. I. Rgt* (Lance Corporal, Munich, Second Infantry Regiment).

Hitler's first impression of the party was "neither good nor bad . . . just another one of these many new societies which were being formed at that time" (Hitler 1942, 175). The main speaker that night was to have been the Nationalist poet and playwright Dietrich Eckart. When he fell ill, Gottfried Feder (engineer, amateur economist, and brother-in-law of Professor von Müller) substituted for him. Hitler, who had been exposed to Feder's speeches about the evils of Capitalism and the "yoke of high finance" during his training seminars at the University of Munich earlier the same year, was free to concentrate on the gathering. Over forty people had signed the register that night and Hitler noted that most of the participants were workers or soldiers "chiefly from among the lower walks of life" (Hitler 1942, 175). Present also were five students, a doctor, a writer, a pharmacist, two bank employees, four businessmen, two engineers, a daughter of a judge, and a professor.

Feder spoke for nearly two hours and by the time he finished, Hitler was dying of boredom. Although Hitler would have preferred to leave, he was obligated to make a report of the gathering to the army. An open discussion followed, and as Hitler expected, nothing of importance was mentioned. After a while, a visitor, Professor Baumann, rose and questioned the soundness of Gottfried Feder's arguments against Capitalism; Baumann proposed that Bavaria should break away from Prussia and found a new South German nation with Austria.

Hitler considered such talk "nonsense" and asked to be recognized. After introducing himself, he delivered a short opposing opinion of a strong united Germany with such passion that nearly everyone present was impressed with his sincerity and speaking abilities. According to Hitler, the professor left the hall acknowledging unequivocal defeat. Anton Drexler, co-founder of the party holding the meeting, and the so-called head of the "Munich District," was so impressed that he whispered to the party secretary: "This one has a great mouth, we could use him!"

When the meeting ended, Drexler, who made his living as a skilled worker for the railroad, approached Hitler and invited him to come again. He gave Hitler a copy of his forty-page pamphlet, "My Political Awakening—From the Diary of a German Socialist Worker," which he described was the basic outline of the party's position. As Hitler would later write: "I was quite pleased; because in this way, I could come to know about this association without having to attend its tiresome meetings" (Hitler 1942, 175).

One may wonder why Captain Mayr would order Hitler to spy on a group being addressed by one of Mayr's own minions—Gottfried Feder. The disingenuousness of the *Mein Kampf* account is demonstrated by a letter on 1 September 1919, from Captain Mayr to Eckart, ordering subscriptions for his men to Eckart's newspaper, *Auf gut Deutsch*. By enrolling his men as Eckart's subscribers, Mayr demonstrated the collusion prevailing between the Thule Society and Bavaria's military commanders. Evidence exists of an ongoing line of contact between Mayr and the *DAP* well before Hitler arrived on the scene. In December 1919, after Hitler had joined the party, Mayr arranged for the disbursement of army funds to provide the growing organization with its own office in the *Sternecker* Beer Hall, and for the June 1920 publication of a party brochure, which attacked the Versailles Treaty, by Thule member Julius Lehmann. Mayr would later claim that his office underwrote the party's earliest mass meetings. Even if von Sebottendorff lied by naming Hitler as a Thule guest-member, Hitler already traveled in circles defined by the Thule Society before he attended his first meeting of the German Workers' Party. (Luhrssen 2012, 151.)

Returning to his barracks on the evening of 12 September 1919, Hitler retired for the night. He had trouble sleeping and awoke early in the morning. "As I was not able to go to sleep again," he later wrote in *Mein Kampf* (Hitler 1942, 176), "I suddenly remembered the pamphlet that one of the workers had given me at the meeting . . . and I read it with interest to the end."

For nearly a week Hitler was unable to get Drexler's pamphlet out of his mind, when unexpectedly, he received a "postcard" from Drexler. Hitler was informed that he would be welcomed as a member of the German Workers' Party and was invited to attend a meeting of the officers the coming Wednesday. Although Hitler did not know exactly what to make of the invitation, the fact that he had been invited to the party committee meeting indicated that the party officials intended to offer him something—possibly a leading position.

The following Wednesday, Hitler attended the executive committee meeting at the rundown *Alte Rosenbad* restaurant. Hitler found the meeting to be utterly disappointing and noted that the party was disorganized and although the leaders claimed to have around fifty members, the six committee members were the only ones active. As Hitler would later write: "Apart from a few general principles, there was nothing—no program, no pamphlet, nothing at all in print, no membership cards, not even a party stamp, only obvious good faith and good intentions."

Hitler was completely let down and concluded that the organization would never amount to anything. He felt that the committee members had no "organizational abilities," no "adequate grasp" of the situation, and had no idea how to "develop a club into a party or a movement." He felt the party would "simply disappear silently after a time." Although Hitler was offered a position in the party, he left the meeting without making any commitment.

Over the next few days, Hitler had time to think and began to feel that he understood what the members of the party wanted to accomplish.

> The feeling which had induced those few young people to join in what seemed such a ridiculous enterprise was nothing but the call of the inner voice which told them—though more intuitively than consciously—that the whole

> party system as it had hitherto existed was not the kind of force that could restore the German nation or repair the damages that had been done to the German people by those who hitherto controlled the internal affairs of the nation." (Hitler 1942, 177–8)

"This ludicrous little formation," Hitler also observed, . . .

> with its handful of members, seemed to have the unique advantage of not yet being fossilized into an 'organization' and still offered a chance for real personal activity on the part of the individual. Here it might still be possible to do some effective work; and, as the movement was still small, one could all the easier give it the required shape. Here it was still possible to determine the character of the movement, the aims to be achieved and the road to be taken, which would have been impossible in the case of the big parties already existing. (Hitler 1942, 178.)

Over the ensuing two weeks, Hitler attended additional meetings and assisted with recruitment. By the time *Reich* Chairman Harrer began to speak at a meeting, around thirty new faces were present. Hitler, nevertheless, could not make up his mind whether to join the party, until "Fate," as he later wrote, "pointed out the way."

The army at this time, regarded it as a patriotic duty to support German Nationalism as a counterweight to Communist internationalism. Only paramilitary groups like the *Freikorps* were capable of putting down Red uprisings, so members of the officers' corps in Munich decided that the only other alternative to keep Bavaria from moving too far towards radical Liberalism was to support Nationalist political organizations. The army was rapidly down-sizing to the 200,000 men in its first reduction step required by the Armistice and was beginning to resemble an elite corps of officers. The need for soldier-speakers trained in lecturing troops was fast coming to an end. The men from the Education and Propaganda Department Ib/P were too valuable to lose and would be good assets working outside the army as propagandists of Nationalist views. In the meantime, their army salary of twenty *Geltmarks* (200 *Papiermarks*) would give them the time and ability to help expand acceptable organizations or parties until the next scheduled reduction in troop numbers.

Even though there was great competition for the few places available in the new army, Hitler was considered too valuable to let go. In keeping within the spirit of the Versailles Treaty, Hitler was actually discharged around this time but within one month he was accepted for re-enlistment into the *Vorläufige Reichswehr* (Provisional National Defense). Hitler, then received orders from Mayr to report on political parties with the hope of joining a "worker's party" and helping in its expansion.

At the beginning of October 1919, Hitler attended another meeting of the German Worker's Party. For the next two days he pondered on what "step" to take. There can be little doubt that Hitler would have preferred to have joined a larger and more established party, but he soon concluded that within a larger institution, he could never hope to rise to any important position because of his lack of "schooling." Coarse language, candidness, and appeals to the emotions are assets that have always troubled persons of "education or quality." Hitler held disdain for the so-called "educated class" of leaders who he viewed as typically lacking the qualities of leadership the times demanded.

On 4 October 1919, Hitler concluded his brief summary of the party to Mayr and added: "I request the Captain's permission to join this association or party." Ludendorff had already urged Mayr to push Hitler to join the *DAP*. Permission was quickly granted, and Hitler became member 555 (the party began counting membership at 500 to give the impression they were a much larger party) and number 7 in the party's executive committee in charge of "recruitment and propaganda." Among the party's earlier members were Ernst Röhm of the Army's District Command VII, Dietrich Eckart, who has been called the spiritual father of National Socialism, University of Munich student Rudolf Heß, *Freikorps* soldier Hans , and Alfred Rosenberg, often credited as the philosopher of the movement. All except Röhm were Thule Society members and all later became prominent figures in the Nazi regime. The party's *Reich* Chairman Karl Harrer, a journalist and the most "educated" within the executive committee, failed to see any value in the acquisition of Hitler, but Drexler was enamored with Hitler and insisted on his joining the executive committee. To a fellow committee member, Drexler commented: "Now we have an Austrian with a great mouth."

Hitler's first speech as a *DAP* member was held in the *Hofbräukeller* on 16 October 1919. He was the second speaker of the evening and spoke to 111 people. Hitler later declared that this was when he realized he could really "make a good speech" (Hitler 1942, 278).

At first, Hitler spoke only to relatively small groups, but his considerable oratory and propaganda skills were appreciated by the party leadership. With the support of Anton Drexler, Hitler became chief of propaganda for the party in early 1920. Over this time, Dietrich Eckart intimately worked with Hitler developing him into the charismatic leader and speaker that Eckart had searched for. Eckart provided the young man with his reading material, corrected his grammar, introduced him to Munich society, and spoke to him for hours about art, literature, music, and politics. Eckart saw in Hitler the leader he had spoken of in the summer of 1919. Germany needed, he said, "A guy who can stand the rattle of a machine gun, who won't fill his pants in fear. I can't use an officer; the people don't respect them any longer. Best of all would be a worker who's got his mouth in the right place." The phrase "I can't use an officer" indicates that Eckart actively sought such a leader; the verb "use" implies a master-apprentice relationship, with Eckart in the top position. "Best of all would be a worker" correlates with von Sebottendorff's motive of building a bridge between esoteric *völkisch* ideology and the working class, the objective behind Drexler's and Harrer's Political Workers' Circle. Eckart's search for the coming leader gave contemporary expression to the messianic strain of German social and political thought, nurtured by German Nationalists during the long prelude to Germany's unification in the nineteenth century, maintained by the *völkisch* discontents of von Bismarck's *Reich*. This element was amplified before World War I in the ruminations of Ariosophists, especially Guido von List in his call for a "Strong One from Above" to redeem the Germanic peoples and establish an Aryan-dominated world order. The trauma of German defeat and the upheavals that followed provided a larger contingent of the disaffected eager to follow a messiah to the German promised land. In appearance, Hitler was hardly the knight in white armor, the Teutonic thunder god, that *völkisch* activists had sought. Yet, his worldview and the conviction with which he expressed it transformed him into a personality of quite extraordinary dynamism, and his frothing rage found an echo in a society where fear and anger had been fed by Germany's unexpected defeat and the economic and political uncertainty that followed the Versailles peace. (Luhrssen 2012, 172.)

When Hitler was not involved in party matters, he was still called upon by his army superiors to deliver Nationalist pro-German, anti-Communist speeches to groups of officers and soldiers. In January and February 1920, "*Herr* Hitler" was listed besides such persons as University of Munich historian von Müller, and other notables as one of the main lecturers in the army's continuing patriotic course. On the afternoon following his presentation of the party's Twenty-Five-Points program, he delivered one of his lectures at the local barracks where he still lived. Though many of his lectures took place at the Munich barracks, he also lectured at the University and, still on occasion, traveled outside the city. In mid-March 1920, Hitler was to take his last trip outside of Munich as a member of the army.

On 16 March 1920, Captain Mayr sent Hitler and Dietrich Eckart to Berlin to observe the events of the Kapp *Putsch.*

THE KAPP-LÜTTWITZ *PUTSCH* BERLIN, 13–18 MARCH 1920

AFTER GERMANY LOST THE FIRST WORLD WAR, THE GERMAN Revolution of 1918–1919 ended the monarchy and the German Empire was replaced by a parliamentary Social Democracy, the Weimar Republic, by the Weimar National Assembly. Radical Nationalist and militarist circles opposed the new republic and promoted the "stab-in-the-back legend," claiming that the war had only been lost because the brave efforts of the undefeated German military had been undermined by politicians at home in power under the constitutional monarchy. In 1919–1920, the new government of Germany was formed by the Weimar Coalition, consisting of the Social Democratic Party (*SPD*), German Democratic Party (*DDP*), and the Center Party (conservative Catholics). President Friedrich Ebert, Chancellor Gustav Bauer, and Defense Minister Gustav Noske were all members of the *SPD.* According to the Weimar Constitution, the president was the commander-in-chief of the armed forces, represented in peace time by the minister of defense. The Third *Oberste Heeresleitung* (Supreme Army Command, *OHL*) under the duumvirate of *Generalfeldmarschall* Paul von Hindenburg (1847–1934) and *General der Infanterie* (General of Infantry) and *Erster Generalquartiermeister* (First Quartermaster General) Erich Ludendorff (1865–1937) was formed during the latter half of the First World War on the 29 August 1916. Von Hindenburg was mostly a figurehead and a representative of the military command to the public. Control was mainly exercised by his deputy General Ludendorff. Ludendorff's hand was everywhere. Every day he was on the telephone with the staffs of their armies and the Army was deluged with "Ludendorff's paper barrage" of orders, instructions, and demands for information. His finger extended into every aspect of the German war effort. He issued the two daily communiqués and often met with newspaper and newsreel reporters. Soon, the German public idolized him as their Army's brain. The duumvirate increasingly dominated decision making on the German war effort, to an extent that they are sometimes described as *de facto* military dictators, supplanting the Emperor and Chancellor. As the tide of the war turned against Germany with the Allied Hundred-Days Offensive in late September 1918, Ludendorff called for the "parliamentization" of the German government and immediate armistice negotiations. When he reversed course and demanded the fight to be resumed, Ludendorff was sacked on 26 October 1918. Von Hindenburg remained in his post until the *OHL* was disbanded on 3 July 1919. Von Hindenburg's son and two sons-in-law came though the war unscathed; Ludendorff had lost two beloved stepsons, and *SPD* Chairman Friedrich Ebert lost two sons.

Gustav Bauer, named Chancellor of Germany on 21 June 1919, was obliged to sign the Treaty of Versailles on 28 June 1919, even though he disagreed with it. The treaty had been dictated by the victorious Allies of World War I; it forced Germany to assume sole responsibility for the war, reduced the geographic area of Germany, and imposed harsh reparation payments and military restrictions on the nation. The treaty required the German Army to have no more than 100,000 men and abolished the General Staff. Therefore, on 6 March 1919, the army was reorganized and the *Vorläufige Reichswehr*, consisting of the *Vorläufiges Reichsheer* (Provisional National Army) and *Vorläufige Reichsmarine* (Provisional National Navy) were formally established. The *Vorläufige Reichswehr* was made up of 43 brigades. The 430,000 soldiers in Germany after the war competed for the limited assignments. In early 1919, more than 250,000 men were enlisted in the various *Freikorps*, volunteer paramilitary units, largely consisting of veterans returning from the war. The German government had repeatedly used *Freikorps* troops to put down Communist uprisings after the war and collapse of the German Empire. Under the terms of the Treaty of Versailles, which came into effect on 10 January 1920, Germany was required to reduce its land forces to a maximum of 100,000 men. The initial deadline was set for 31 March 1920 (later extended to the end of the year). On 30 September 1919, the army was again reorganized as the *Übergangsheer* (Transitional Army), and the force size was reduced to 20 brigades. Under the terms of the Treaty of Versailles, the *OHL* and General Staff were disbanded on 3 July 1919 and the most senior officer of the land forces was thereafter called *Chef der Heeresleitung*, a post held by *General der Infanterie* Walther Reinhardt (1872–1930) from 1 October 1919 until 26 March 1920; since May 1919, Reinhardt's provisional predecessor and primary competitor was *General der Infanterie* Walther von Lüttwitz (1859–1942). In May 1920, the army further was downsized to 200,000 men and restructured again, forming three cavalry divisions and seven infantry divisions. On 1 October 1920, the brigades were replaced by regiments and the manpower was now only 100,000 men as stipulated by the Treaty of Versailles (Articles 159 to 213). This lasted until 1 January 1921, when the *Reichswehr* was officially established according to the limitations imposed by the treaty. *Freikorps* units were expected to be disbanded. Since the reason for their creation—internal repression—had become obsolete with the crushing of the Socialist uprisings, they were becoming a threat to the government. Some senior military commanders connected to the *Freikorps* who vehemently resented the Weimar government had started discussing the possibility of a military *coup d'état* as early as July 1919.

Although the *putsch* has been named after Wolfgang Kapp,[1] a sixty-two-year-old Nationalist East Prussian civil servant, who had been planning a *coup* against the republic for a while, it was instigated by the military under the command of General Walther von Lüttwitz; Kapp played only a supporting role. On 29 February 1920, Defense Minister Noske ordered the disbandment of two of the most powerful *Freikorps*, the *Marinebrigade Loewenfeld* and *Marinebrigade Ehrhardt*. The latter, under command of *Korvettenkapitän* Hermann Ehrhardt, numbered from 5,000–6,000 men and had been stationed at the *Truppenübungsplatz* Döberitz, near Berlin, since January 1920. An elite force, it had been created from former Imperial Navy officers and NCOs, boosted later by *Baltikumer* (those who had fought the Bolsheviks in Latvia in 1919). During the German Revolution in 1919, the brigade had seen action in Berlin and in Munich where it played a central role in brutally crushing the Bavarian Socialist Republic in May 1919. The Brigade was extremely opposed to the Social Democrat government of Friedrich Ebert.

Korvettenkapitän Ehrhardt, declared that his *Freikorps* unit would refuse its dissolution. On 1 March, it staged a parade without inviting Noske. General Walther von Lüttwitz, commander-in-chief of all the regular troops in and around Berlin (*Oberbefehlshaber des Reichswehr-Gruppenkommandos I*) (Meyer 1987, 486–7), the highest ranking general in the army at the time and in command of many *Freikorps*, said at the parade that he would "not accept" the loss of such an important unit.

After failed negotiations with Ebert, General von Lüttwitz went on 11 March 1920 to Döberitz where the brigade was stationed and asked Ehrhardt whether he would be able to occupy Berlin that evening. Ehrhardt said he needed another day but in the morning of 13 March he could be in the center of Berlin with his men. Von Lüttwitz gave the order and Ehrhardt began the preparations. It was only at this point that von Lüttwitz brought the group known as *Nationale Vereinigung* into the plot. The *Vereinigung* included German National People's Party (*DNVP*) member Wolfgang Kapp, retired General Erich Ludendorff, Waldemar Pabst—of the infamous *Freikorps Mördenzentrale* (Murder Central), which had been behind the murder of Karl Liebknecht and Rosa Luxemburg in January 1919—and Traugott von Jagow, the last Berlin chief of police in the old *Reich*. Their goal was to establish an authoritarian regime (though not a monarchy) with a return to the federal structure of the Empire. General von Lüttwitz asked them to be ready to take over the government on 13 March. The group was unprepared but agreed to the schedule set by von Lüttwitz. One factor making them support quick action was that sympathetic members of the *Sicherheitspolizei* (*SiPo*) in Berlin informed them that warrants for their arrest had been issued that day.

On the evening of 12 March 1920, the *Marinebrigade Ehrhardt* went into action. Ehrhardt marched 5,000 of his men twelve miles from their military barracks to Berlin with Thule Society swastikas painted on their steel helmets. In his chronicle of the *Freikorps* movement, British historian Nigel H. Jones wrote, "Indeed, it was the Ehrhardt Brigade that first brought the evil symbol of the crooked cross, [later] adopted by Hitler as his emblem, to the notice of the world" (Jones 1987, 139). One wonders if Ehrhardt's men embraced the swastika while marching in Bavaria alongside Thulist contingents of *Freikorps Oberland*. Many members of the Erhardt Brigade later affiliated themselves with the Nazis by joining the *SA*.

Ebert's Minister of Defense Gustav Noske had only 2,000 men to oppose the rebel brigade. However, the leaders of the *Vorläufige Reichswehr* refused to put down the rebellion. General Hans von Seeckt informed Noske "*Reichswehr* does not fire on *Reichswehr*." Noske contacted the police and security officers but they had joined the *coup* themselves. He commented: "Everyone has deserted me. Nothing remains but suicide." At a confused meeting at the *Reichskanzlei* at 4:00 a.m. on 13 March, the undefended cabinet took two decisions: to flee the city and to issue a call for a general workers' strike. Ebert and the *SPD* ministers signed the call for a general strike. At 6:15 a.m. they had to interrupt the meeting and flee. Within ten minutes of their departure, the *Marinebrigade* reached the *Brandenburger Tor* (Brandenburg Gate), where it was met by General von Lüttwitz, General Ludendorff, Kapp, and their followers. Shortly thereafter, Kapp's men moved into the *Reichskanzlei*. Supported by a battalion of regular *Vorläufige Reichswehr*, they occupied the government quarter.

Kapp declared himself Chancellor (*Reichskanzler*) and formed a provisional government. Von Lüttwitz served as commander of the armed forces and minister of defense. Several well-known Conservatives and former secretaries of state were invited to assume government positions but declined. International con-man Ignaz Trebitsch-Lincoln became Kapp's press censor. Noske did not kill himself and instead fled to Dresden with President Friedrich Ebert. However, the local military commander, Major General Georg Maercker, refused to protect them and they were forced to flee to Stuttgart.

To defend the government, Noske ordered two regiments of *Sicherheitspolizei* and one regular regiment to take position in the government quarter but doubted that a *putsch* was imminent. The regimental commanders decided not to follow orders to shoot, a decision that received the approval of *Chef des Truppenamts* (cover name of the disbanded General Staff of the German Army [*Heer*]) General Hans von Seeckt. Noske asked the commanders to at least defend the government buildings but was turned down. The reluctance to shed blood was one-sided. Captain Ehrhardt met no resistance as they took over the ministries and proclaimed a new government headed by Wolfgang Kapp.

The regular troops in Berlin, *Sicherheitspolizei*, navy, the army commands of East-Prussia, Pomerania, Brandenburg, and Silesia, formally accepted the new minister of defense and *Reichskanzler*. Admiral Adolf von Trotha, the navy commander, came out in support of the *coup* as soon as he learned of it. In Bavaria, the *Vorläufige Reichswehr* toppled the Social Democratic state government under Minister-President of Bavaria Socialist Johannes Hoffmann and replaced it with the Nationalist regime of Gustav Ritter von Kahr. In the rest of the *Reich*, the commanders of the *Wehrkreise* (military districts) did not declare for or against Kapp but were not neutral and most sympathized more or less openly with the *putschists*. The upper echelons of the bureaucracy were still dominated by those who had risen to their positions under the Empire, and most were sympathetic to the *coup*, while remaining outwardly neutral and biding their time. In the eastern provinces, the bureaucracy fell in line behind Kapp and General von Lüttwitz.

The cabinet proclamation on 13 March, calling on German workers to defeat the *putsch* by means of a general strike met with enormous success and received massive support from the working class, which sympathized more with the Socialist government than the Nationalist military. The majority of trade unions, also sympathetic to the government dominated by Social Democrats, joined the call for a strike on the same day, as did the Independent Social Democratic Party (*USPD*) and the German Democratic Party (*DDP*); the Communist Party of Germany (*KPD*) followed one day later.

Berlin had been seized from the Social Democrat government. However, the trade union leaders refused to flee, and President of the International Federation of Trade Unions Carl Legien seconded the call for a general strike to take place. Chris Harman, the Socialist author of *The Lost Revolution: Germany, 1918 to 1923* (London, UK: Bookmarks, 1982), has pointed out:

> The appeal had an immediate impact. It went out at 11 a.m. on the day of the coup, Saturday, 13 March. By midday, the strike had already started. Its effects could be felt everywhere in the capital within 24 hours, despite it being a Sunday. There were no trains running, no electricity, and no gas. Kapp issued a decree threatening to shoot strikers. It had no effect. By Monday the strike was spreading throughout the country into the Ruhr, Saxony, Hamburg, Bremen, Bavaria, the industrial villages of Thuringia, even to the landed estates of rural Prussia.

It was the most powerful strike ever in Germany, involving up to twelve million workers leaving the country paralyzed. In Berlin, the gas, water, and power supply stopped. Adolf Hitler, who had been in contact with the members of the *Nationale Vereinigung* and was eager to help the *coup* along, was flown into Berlin from Munich by the Bavarian military district *Vorläufige Reichswehr*. He was met by striking workers at an airfield outside of Berlin, where he landed by mistake, and had to disguise himself.

With the country paralyzed, Kapp and von Lüttwitz were unable to govern; in Berlin, communication between military units was by courier only. The rank and file of the bureaucracy were on strike, and there were no newspapers. Proclamations asking the workers to return to their jobs, promises of new elections and even the threat of capital punishment for strikers remained without results and the *putsch* collapsed on 17 March, four days after it had begun. Kapp had put Prussian state Vice-Chancellor Schiffer and the members of the Prussian state government into protective custody on 13 March, but they were released the next day and on 15 March, negotiations began. Representatives of the Democratic Conservatives, Oskar Hergt and Gustav Stresemann also participated. The four big moderately-conservative parties (*DDP*, Center Party, German People's Party of 1918, and *DNVP*) agreed that the main threat was now Bolshevism and that they had to "win back" the officer corps. It was considered undesirable that Kapp and General von Lüttwitz should be toppled, they must be seen to resign voluntarily.

The four parties, supported by some Social Democrats who had remained in Berlin, offered fresh elections, a cabinet reshuffle, and an amnesty for all participants in the *putsch* if Kapp and von Lüttwitz were to resign. The *putschists* offered only the resignation of Kapp with von Lüttwitz pressing to hold on for another day as head of a military dictatorship but his commanders deserted him. They suggested to Schiffer, in charge of the government's affairs in Ebert's absence, that he appoint General von Seeckt as *Chef der Heeresleitung* (Chief of the Army), which Schiffer did in the name of Ebert. When General von Lüttwitz offered his resignation on 18 March, Schiffer accepted—again in Ebert's name—while granting him full military pension rights. Schiffer also suggested Pabst and von Lüttwitz should leave the country until the National Assembly had decided on the question of an amnesty and even offered them false passports and money.

On 18 March, *Chef der Heeresleitung* General von Seeckt praised the discipline of *Marinebrigade Ehrhardt* and the next day provided Ehrhardt with a written promise that he would not be arrested as long as he was in command of the brigade and the brigade left Berlin. When they were heckled by an unfriendly crowd of Socialist bystanders, the brigade opened fire with machine guns leaving twelve civilians dead and thirty severely wounded. Kapp remained in the country and only fled to Sweden in April. Kapp was arrested in Sweden on 16 April but not deported to Germany. He voluntarily returned to Germany in April 1922 to stand trial for treason but on 12 June 1922, died of cancer in prison awaiting trial. General von Lüttwitz first went to Saxony and only later left for Hungary. Both men used passports provided by supporters in the police. Ehrhardt went into hiding in Bavaria where he eventually formed Organization Consul. Pabst took refuge in Miklós Horthy's Hungary during the infamous White Terror where he was soon joined by co-conspirator General Walther von Lüttwitz. Von Lüttwitz returned to Germany as part of an amnesty in 1924. Despite the failure of the *putsch*, Pabst would often speak proudly of his involvement in the episode. For the remainder of his life, Pabst managed to escape justice. He left Hungary for Austria in 1922 shortly after a moderately-conservative government under Hungarian Prime Minister István Bethlen ousted Prime Minister Count Pál Teleki's radical Nationalist criminal enterprise. In Austria, Pabst immersed himself in the ultra-Nationalist *Heimwehr* movement in Tyrol (like the German *Freikorps*) and managed to secure funding for the *Heimwehr* from Benito Mussolini. However, Pabst had a falling out with Centrist Austrian Chancellor Johann Schober, who ordered Pabst be deported to Germany in 1930. Returning to Germany voluntarily, Pabst became a member of the Society for the Study of Fascism along with others such as Friedrich Minoux. In 1931, he wrote a pamphlet in which he set out a manifesto for a "White International";* in this he called for the replacement of the values of *liberté, égalité, fraternité* with a new pan-European order based on "a new Trinity: authority, order, justice." Despite meeting once with Hitler to discuss Pabst's activities in Austria, he was vaguely linked to the Nazi Party and never joined or became particularly active on the party's behalf. Rumors were floated that Pabst was in contact with Nazi *Abwehr* chief Admiral Wilhelm Canaris and his clandestine resistance to Hitler, but such rumors were never proven true. Pabst did manage to leave Germany just before the 20 July 1944 plot to assassinate Hitler (Operation Valkyrie, *Unternehmen Walküre*); he settled in Switzerland where he took a post with the Swiss arms manufacturer Werkzeugmaschinenfabrik Oerlikon, Bührle & Co. that sold over 7,000 of their 20 mm high-performance anti-aircraft auto-canons to the Axis powers during the Second World War (Heller 2002, 233). He returned to Germany in 1955, settling in Düsseldorf where he died in 1970 at the age of 89. In the 1986 West German drama *Rosa Luxemburg*, the role of Pabst was played by Hans-Michael Rehberg.

The legitimate government returned to Berlin on 20 March 1920 and asked for the general workers' strike to end. To achieve this, it offered some concessions to the unions, some of them made in bad faith. The unions demanded the creation of a new government made up of *SPD* and *USPD*, led by Carl Legien but only a new government based on the Weimar Coalition found a majority in the National Assembly and Hermann Müller (*SPD*)

---

* Named after the Nationalist White Russians who fought the Red Bolsheviks during the Russian Civil War.

replaced Gustav Bauer as Chancellor. The government then tried to negotiate with workers who refused to lay down their arms, after the unions called off the strike on 22 March. When the negotiations failed, the revolt in the Ruhr was suppressed by *Vorläufige Reichswehr* and *Freikorps* in early April 1920. Hundreds of people were killed, many in summary executions, some committed by units that had been involved in the Kapp *Putsch* less than one month earlier, including *Marinebrigade Ehrhardt*. As in 1918–1919, those radical Socialists had cause to accuse the *SPD* and the Ebert government of siding with the enemies of the workers and of the republic. Defense Minister Gustav Noske was forced to resign by the unions on 22 March 1920, as a condition for ending the general strike and because some in the *SPD* thought that he had not been tough enough facing up to the *putschists*; Otto Gessler succeeded Noske as Defense Minister. General Reinhardt also resigned out of protest at Noske's dismissal. General von Seeckt formally became his successor as *Chef der Heeresleitung* (Chief of the Army).

In the disturbed and unstable condition of Germany between 1918 and 1923, the power of the central government in Berlin was weakened, and the Bavarian State Government was able to exploit a situation in which the orders of the *Reich* Government were only respected if they were backed by the support of the authorities in Munich.

This anomalous position became more marked after March 1920, when the Kapp *Putsch* failed, but a simultaneous *coup d'état* succeeded in Bavaria. On the night of 13–14 March 1920, the District Commander of the *Vorläufige Reichswehr*, General Arnold von Möhl, presented the Social Democrat Premier of Bavaria Johannes Hoffmann with an ultimatum which led to the establishment of a Nationalist government under Gustav von Kahr, from which Socialist parties were excluded.

Bavaria was thenceforth ruled by a state government which had strong particularist leanings and a Nationalist bias quite out of step with the policies pursued by the Social Democrat government in Berlin. Bavaria thus became a natural center for all those who were eager to get rid of the republican regime in Germany, and the Bavarian government turned a blind eye to the treason and conspiracy against the legal government of the *Reich* which were being planned on its doorstep in Munich. It was in Bavaria that the irreconcilable elements of the *Freikorps Marinebrigade Ehrhardt* gathered under a new name "Organization Consul." Driven from Berlin by the failure of the Kapp *Putsch*, the notorious Captain Ehrhardt and his Ehrhardt Brigade found shelter in Bavaria, and here were arranged the murders of *Reich* Minister of Finance Matthias Erzberger (1875–1921), the man who had signed the Armistice of 1918, and the *Reich*'s Foreign Minister and Socialist Jew Walther Rathenau (1867–1922), who had initiated the policy of fulfilling the provisions of the Peace Treaty. The *Freikorps* were the training schools for the political murder and terrorism which disfigured German life up to 1924, and again after 1929. It was in this very same milieu that Adolf Hitler found his voice.

Reich Minister of Finance Matthias Erzberger was murdered on 26 August 1921 in Bad Griesbach, a spa in the Black Forest (Baden) while he was out for a walk. Due to his signing the Armistice of 1918, Erzberger was regarded as one of the "November Criminals" and a traitor by many political Conservatives. Manfred von Killinger, a leading member of the *Germanenorden*, masterminded his killing by recruiting two members (Heinrich Tillessen and Heinrich Schulz) of Ehrhardt's ultra-Nationalist death squad in Munich known as "Organization Consul." Both were former Imperial Navy officers and members of the disbanded *Marinebrigade Ehrhardt*. Erzberger's assassins were later smuggled into Horthy's Hungary and were prosecuted only after World War II.

Walther Rathenau was assassinated on Saturday, 24 June 1922, two months after the signing of the Treaty of Rapallo (which renounced German territorial claims from World War I). On this Saturday morning, Rathenau had himself chauffeured from his house in Berlin-Grunewald to the Foreign Office on *Wilhelmstraße*. During the trip, his NAG-Convertible was passed by a Mercedes-Touring car with Ernst Werner Techow behind the wheel, and Erwin Kern and Hermann Fischer on the backseats. Kern opened fire with a MP 18 submachine gun at close range, killing Rathenau almost instantly, while Fischer threw a hand grenade into the car before Techow quickly drove them away. Also involved in the plot were Techow's younger brother Hans Gerd Techow, future writer Ernst von Salomon, and Willi Günther (aided and abetted by seven others, some of them schoolboys). All conspirators were members of Ehrhardt's ultra-Nationalist secret Organization Consul. While Fischer and Kern prepared their plot, former Chancellor Philipp Scheidemann barely survived an attempt on his life by Organization Consul assassins on 4 June 1922.

Ehrhardt and his men believed that Rathenau's death would bring down the government and prompt the radical Liberals to act against the Weimar Republic, thereby provoking civil war, in which Organization Consul would be called on for help by the *Reichswehr*. After an anticipated victory, Ehrhardt hoped to establish an authoritarian regime or a military dictatorship. In order not to be completely delegitimized by the murder of

Rathenau, Ehrhardt carefully saw to it that no connections between him and the assassins could be detected. Although Fischer and Kern connected with the Berlin chapter of Organization Consul to use its resources, they mainly acted on their own in planning and carrying out the assassination.

The crime itself was soon cleared up. Willi Günther had bragged about his participation in public. After his arrest on 26 June, he confessed to the crime without holding anything back. Hans Gerd Techow was arrested the following day, and Ernst Werner Techow, who was visiting his uncle, three days later. Fischer and Kern, however, remained on the loose. After a daring flight, which kept Germany in suspense for more than two weeks, they were finally spotted at Saaleck Castle in Thuringia, whose owner was himself a secret member of the Organization Consul. On 17 July, they were confronted by two police detectives. While waiting for reinforcements during the stand-off, one of the detectives fired at a window, unknowingly killing Kern by a bullet in the head. Fischer then took his own life.

When the crime was brought to court in October 1922, Ernst Werner Techow was the only defendant charged with murder. Twelve more defendants were arraigned on various charges, among them Hans Gerd Techow and Ernst von Salomon, who had spied out Rathenau's habits and kept contact with Organization Consul, as well as the commander of Organization Consul in western Germany, Karl Tillessen, a brother of Erzberger's assassin Heinrich Tillessen, and his adjutant Hartmut Plaas. The prosecution left aside the political implications of the plot but focused upon the issue of anti-Semitism. Before his assassination, Rathenau had been the frequent target of vicious anti-Semitic attacks, and the assassins had also been members of the violently anti-Semitic *Deutschvölkischer Schutz- und Trutzbund.* Kern had, according to Ernst Werner Techow, argued that Rathenau had to be murdered, because he had intimate relations with Bolshevik Russia, so that he had even married off his sister to the Communist Karl Radek—a complete fabrication—and that Rathenau himself had confessed to be one of the three hundred "Elders of Zion" as described in the notorious anti-Semitic Russian forgery *The Protocols of the Elders of Zion.* But the defendants vigorously denied they had killed Rathenau because he was Jewish. Neither was the prosecution able to fully uncover the involvement of the Organization Consul in the plot. Thus, Tillessen and Plaas were only convicted of non-notification of a crime and sentenced to three and two years in prison, respectively. Salomon received five-years imprisonment for accessory to murder. Ernst Werner Techow narrowly escaped the death penalty, because in a last-minute confession he managed to convince the court that he had only acted under the threat of death by Kern. Instead, he was sentenced to fifteen years in prison for accessory to murder.

After the failed Kapp-Lüttwitz *Putsch*, Bavaria and particularly Munich became the primary crucible, in which many of the worst, escalating Romantic Nationalist, xenophobic, *völkisch*, anti-Semitic, and reactionary elements of inter-bellum Germany were catalyzed by mushrooming revolutionary Marxism and the shame of military defeat in the war and combusted over the flames of incompetent political leadership, economic crisis, and a short-sighted, vengeful Versailles Treaty. Although at the turn of the century, Germany had lagged behind the rest of Europe in social upheaval and revolutionary transformation, Germany rocketed to the exosphere and underwent a socio-political paradigm shift during the inter-bellum period that astonished not only the rest of Europe but the entire world. No one knew quite how to view and interact with this sea change in Germany. However, one thing was certain, the world was exhausted and withdrawn from war and had no appetite to seriously confront any burgeoning belligerent power.

CHAPTER 12

National Socialism's Rise to Power 1919–1933

The Führer was a mirror held up to a greater Germany. When we fell in love with him, it was really our greater selves that he was enabling everyone to see.

— ADOLF EICHMANN*

It is offensive both to our reason and to our experience to be asked to believe that the [young] Hitler . . . was the stuff of which . . . Caesars and Bonapartes, are made. Yet the record is there to prove us wrong.

— ALAN BULLOCK

To know Hitler, means to know him before he came to power.

— OTTO STRASSER

To say that Hitler was a mad man is to make a very serious mistake.

— ALBERT SPEER

It being my purpose to write the lives of Alexander the king, and of Cesar, by whom Pompey was destroyed, the multitude of their great actions affords so large a field that I were to blame . . . When once Alexander had given way to fears of supernatural influence, his mind grew so disturbed and so easily alarmed . . . But a diseased habit of body,

---

* While at Camp Iyyar in Yagur, Israel 1960–1961 (Israeli Police Bureau 06 interrogation tapes).

*caused by drugs which Olympias gave him, had ruined not only his health, but his understanding.**

— PLUTARCH, *Parallel Lives*

ADOLF HITLER (20 APRIL 1889–30 APRIL 1945)

ADOLF HITLER WAS BORN ON 20 APRIL 1889 IN BRAUNAU AM INN, A town in Austro-Hungary (present-day Austria), on the river Inn at the border of the German Empire (124 km / 77 mi east of Munich). Adolf's father Alois Hitler, Sr. (1837–1903) was the illegitimate child of unmarried forty-one-year-old Maria Anna Schicklgruber (15 April 1795–7 January 1847). Maria was born in the village of Strones in the *Waldviertel* region of Archduchy of Austria. The Schickgrubers had resided in Strones for generations. She was the daughter of Theresia Pfeisinger (7 September 1769–11 November 1821), and farmer Johannes Schicklgruber (29 May 1764–12 November 1847). Maria was a Catholic; what is known about her is based on church and other public records. Maria was one of eleven children, only six of whom survived infancy. Her early life was that of a poor peasant child in a rural forested area, in the northwest part of Lower Austria, northwest of Vienna. In 1821, Maria's mother died when Maria was 26. She received an inheritance of 74.25 gulden, which she left invested in the Orphans' Fund until 1838. By that time, it had more than doubled to 165 gulden. At that time, a breeding pig cost 4 gulden, a cow 10–12 gulden and an entire inn 500 gulden. Historian Werner Maser wrote she was a "thrifty, reserved, and exceptionally shrewd peasant woman" (Maser 1973).

Other than saving her inheritance, which indicates she was not destitute during that period of her life, little is known about Maria's life until she was over 40. Alois was born on 7 June 1837, in the house of a small farming family named Trommelschläger in Strones, Austrian Empire near the Austrian-Bohemian border. The baptismal register kept in the nearby

* The excerpt is an *exemplum* of the legendary Alexander the Great. The moral point of this narrative is that an individual can change a person's, as well as a whole nation's, destiny for good or bad. *Parallel Lives* is a series of biographies of famous men, arranged in tandem to illuminate their common moral virtues or failings. Plutarch shows how, in history, characters like Alexander the Great have shaped the destinies of states and individuals.

village of Döllersheim did not show the name of his father, and Alois initially bore his mother's surname Schicklgruber. Mr. and Mrs. Trummelschläger were listed as godparents to Alois. Maria soon took up residence with her elderly father Johannes at house number 22 in Strones. After an unknown period, the three Schicklgrubers were joined by Johann Georg Hiedler, an itinerant journeyman miller. On 10 May 1842, five years after Alois was born, Maria Anna Schicklgruber married Johann Georg Hiedler in the nearby village of Döllersheim. Maria was forty-seven, her new husband was fifty.

By the age of ten-years, Alois had been sent to live with Hiedler's brother, Johann Nepomuk Hiedler, who owned a farm in the nearby village of Spital (part of Weitra). Alois attended elementary school and took lessons in shoemaking from a local cobbler. At the age of thirteen-years he left the farm in Spital and went to Vienna as an apprentice cobbler, working there for about five years. In response to a recruitment drive by the Austrian government offering employment in the civil service to people from rural areas, Alois joined the frontier guards (customs service) of the Austrian Finance Ministry in 1855 at the age of eighteen-years.

Historians have proposed various candidates as Alois's biological father:

1. Johann Georg Hiedler, whose name was added to Alois's birth certificate later in his life and who was officially accepted as the father of Alois (i.e., as the paternal grandfather of Adolf Hitler) by the Third *Reich*.
2. Johann Nepomuk Hiedler, Georg's brother and Alois's step-uncle, who raised Alois through adolescence and later willed him a considerable portion of his life savings but who, if he was the real father of Alois, never found it expedient to admit it publicly.
3. And a Jew named Leopold Frankenberger, as reported by ex-Nazi Hans Frank during the Nuremberg Trials.

In some academic quarters, there remains controversy over whether Maria Schicklgruber was raped by the son of her Jewish employer in Graz, Austro-Hungary. Adolf Hitler's one-time personal attorney Hans Frank reportedly discovered evidence suggesting that Alois's mother had been employed as a housekeeper for a Jewish family in Graz, and that the family's nineteen-year-old son Leopold Frankenberger had fathered Alois. In 1930, Hitler received a letter from the son (William Patrick Hitler) of a half-brother

(Alois Hitler, Jr.), possibly an attempt at blackmail, which darkly hinted at "very definite facts concerning our family history." Hans Frank was tasked with investigating the matter confidentially. Frank concluded:

> Hitler's father was the illegitimate child of a cook named Schicklgruber from Leonding, near Linz, employed in a household at Graz. This cook Schicklgruber, the grandmother of Adolf Hitler, was working for a Jewish family named Frankenberger when she gave birth to her child [this should read "when she became pregnant"]. At that time—this happened in the 1830s—Frankenberger paid Schicklgruber on behalf of his son, then about nineteen, a paternity allowance from the time of her child's birth up to his fourteenth year. There was also a correspondence between these Frankenbergers and Hitler's grandmother, the general trend of which was the unexpressed common knowledge of the correspondents that Schicklgruber's child had been conceived in circumstances which rendered the Frankenbergers liable to pay a paternity allowance.[1]

However, all Jews had been reportedly expelled from the province of Styria (which includes Graz) in the fifteenth century; they were not allowed to return until the 1860s, when Alois was around 30-years old. Also, there is no evidence of a Frankenberger family living in Graz at that time, and no record has been produced of Leopold Frankenberger's existence, so historians dismiss the claim that Alois's father was Jewish.

According to Frank, Hitler declared that he knew, from what his father and grandmother had said, that his grandfather was not the Jew from Graz, but because his grandmother and her subsequent husband were so poor they had conned the Jew into believing he was the father and into paying for the boy's support.

Frank's story gained wide circulation in the 1950s. But it simply does not stand up. However, a family named Frankenreiter did live in Graz, but was not Jewish. There is no evidence that Maria Anna was ever in Graz, let alone was employed by the butcher Leopold *Frankenreiter*. No correspondence between Maria Anna and a family called Frankenberg or Frankenreiter has ever turned up. The son of Leopold Frankenreiter and alleged father of the baby (according to Frank's story and accepting that he had merely confused names) for whom Frankenreiter was seemingly prepared to pay child support for thirteen years was only ten-years old at the time of Alois's birth. The Frankenreiter family had moreover hit upon such hard times that payment of any support to Maria Anna Schicklgruber would have been inconceivable. Equally lacking in credibility is Frank's comment that Hitler had learned from his grandmother that there was no truth in the Graz story—his grandmother had been dead for over forty years at the time of Hitler's birth—unless Frank meant to say that Alois was informed by his mother that the Graz story was untrue. And whether in fact Adolf Hitler received a blackmail letter from his nephew in 1930 is also doubtful. If such was the case, then Patrick—who repeatedly made a nuisance of himself by scrounging from his famous uncle—was lucky to survive the next few years which he spent for the most part in Germany, and to be able to leave the country for good in December 1938. His "revelations," when they came in a Paris journal in August 1939, contained nothing about the Graz story. Nor did a number of different *Gestapo* inquiries into Hitler's family background in the 1930s and 1940s contain any reference to the alleged Graz background. Indeed, they discovered no new skeletons in the cupboard. Hans Frank's memoirs, dictated at a time when he was waiting for the hangman and plainly undergoing a psychological crisis, are full of inaccuracies and have to be used with caution.

However, for reasons that remain unclear to date, in May 1938, just two months after the *Anschluß* (the annexation of Austria), Adolf Hitler gave the order to the Land Registries in the region to carry out a survey of Döllersheim (Alois Hitler's birthplace) as to its suitability as a battle training area for the *Wehrmacht*. In the following year, the inhabitants of Döllersheim were forcibly evacuated and the village together with the surrounding countryside was blasted and withered by German artillery and infantry weapons. Interestingly, Adolf Hitler also ordered confiscation and destruction of all original genealogical records of his family before burning the village's storage of genealogical records and archives to the ground and plowing under the cemetery where his mother, father, and many other relatives were buried.

In 1842, Johann Georg Hiedler married Alois's mother Maria Anna Schicklgruber. For reasons that remain unclear, Alois was brought up in the family of Hiedler's brother, Johann Nepomuk Hiedler. Alois Schicklgruber learned the shoemaker's trade and then entered the Austrian revenue office. His intelligence and ambition took him to the highest grade in the Imperial and Royal Customs Authority. In January 1877, at the age of thirty-nine-years, Alois adopted the surname Hiedler, and the baptismal register was changed to register Johann Georg Hiedler as Alois's father (recorded erroneously as "Georg Hitler"). Alois then assumed the surname "Hitler," also spelled Hiedler, Hütter, or Hüttler. The Hitler surname is probably based on "one who lives in a hut" (German Hütte for "hut"). On 7 January 1885, in Braunau am Inn, Alois married his housemaid and third wife, twenty-four-year-old Klara Pölzl (Alois's first cousin once removed—see Fest's footnote to Hans Frank's conclusions, *supra*) who was four months pregnant with their first child Gustav who died in infancy. Adolf was their fourth of six children.

When Adolf was three-years old, the family moved to Passau, Germany. In 1894, the family returned to Austria and settled in Leonding. In June 1895, Alois retired to Hafeld, near Lambach, where he farmed and kept bees. While in Hafeld, Adolf attended *Volksschule* (a state-owned school) in nearby Fischlham. The move to Hafeld coincided with the onset of intense father-son conflicts caused by Hitler's refusal to conform to the strict discipline of his school. In 1897, the family moved to Lambach. The eight-year-old Adolf took singing lessons, sang in the church choir, and even considered becoming a priest. In 1898, the family returned permanently to Leonding, Austro-Hungary. Hitler was deeply affected by the death of his younger brother Edmund, who died in 1900 from measles. Hitler changed from a confident, outgoing, conscientious student to a morose, detached boy who constantly fought with his father and teachers. At eleven-years-old, Alois sent Adolf to the *Realschule gymnasium* in Linz in September 1900. Adolf rebelled against this decision, and in *Mein Kampf* states that he intentionally did poorly in school, hoping that once his father saw "what little progress I was making at the technical school he would let me devote myself to my dream" (art).

After Alois's sudden death on 3 January 1903, Adolf's performance at school deteriorated and his mother allowed him to leave. Soon after her husband's death, Klara Hitler sold the house in Leonding and moved the family into an apartment in Linz. At fifteen-years-old, he enrolled at the *Realschule* in Steyr in September 1904, where his behavior and performance improved. In 1905, after passing a repeat of the final exam, Hitler left the school without any ambitions for further education or clear plans for a career. Teenage Adolf now sat about in Linz, occupied only with amateurish painting exercises; aimless, clumsy designs for sumptuous villas and public buildings. For a time, he took piano lessons, until he grew tired of them and gave them up. He visited cafés, the theatre, and the opera. It was the life half of a man of private means, half of a good-for-nothing, and he was able to lead it thanks to his mother's pension as a widow. He refused to take up any definite work, a "bread-and-butter job," as he contemptuously described it. In 1907, now in his nineteenth year, Adolf traveled to Vienna to enroll in the painting class at the Academy of Fine Arts, but he failed the entrance examination and was rejected; he returned home to Linz. On 21 December 1907, his mother died of breast cancer at the age of 47 and was buried alongside Alois in Döllersheim. In February 1908, Adolf left Linz to live and study fine art in Vienna, financed by orphan's benefits and support from his mother's leftover widow's pension. He applied for admission to the Academy of Fine Arts Vienna but was rejected a second time. A precise calculation of his income at the time has shown that with the inheritance from his father, his mother's estate, an orphan's pension gained by false pretenses (that he was enrolled as an art student), and later with support from an aunt, he had an average monthly income of almost 100 *Kronen*.

In 1909, Hitler ran out of money and was forced to live a bohemian life in homeless shelters and *Meldemannstraße* dormitory (a charity ward). He would hang around night shelters, living on the bread and soup served there, and discussing politics, often getting into heated arguments. In the charity wards he befriended another homeless tramp Reinhold Hanisch. The two eventually moved into the Brigittenau hostel for men. In his landmark work, *The Face of the Third Reich: Portraits of the Nazi Leadership*, historian Joachim Fest performs a sober, masterful job describing the depressing circumstances of Hitler's five years in Vienna. In Part One ("Adolf Hitler's Path from Men's Hostel to Reich Chancellery"), Chapter 1 ("The Incubation Period") of his book, Fest notes the following:

> In the hierarchy of the dregs of society, Hitler's move from the charity ward to the men's hostel was a step up. He probably owed it to the help of his Aunt Johanna, who had once lived with his parents. But here too he was for the most part surrounded by the shiftless and homeless. Among the social flotsam washed up in the city's wards and hostels of the multi-nation state were impoverished Hungarian nobles, bankrupt traders, down-and-outs from the dual monarchy's Italian provinces, petty clerks and moneylenders, gone-to-seed artists and so-called Handelees, Jews from the eastern regions of the Empire trying laboriously to rise in the world as old-clothes men, hosiers or pedlars. This pathological, evil-smelling world of envy, spite and egotism, where

> everyone was on edge for a chance to scramble upwards and only ruthlessness guaranteed escape, became for the next few years Hitler's home and formative background. Here his idea of mankind and his picture of society were moulded; here he received his first political impressions and asked his first political questions, to which he responded with the growing resentment, the hate and impotence of the outcast. He found here the reverse of the world of dreams and fantasies he had erected as a shelter for his frustrated hopes as an artist; he found it equally unreal and removed from the normal life which was becoming more and more closed to him. (Fest 1970, 8.)

The living conditions and experiences of almost six years spent in Vienna left their mark on Hitler's character. He himself declared later in *Mein Kampf* (Hitler 1942, 30):

> During those years a view of life and a definite outlook on the world took shape in my mind. These became the granite basis of my conduct at that time. Since then I have extended that foundation only very little, and I have changed nothing in it.
>
> On the contrary: . . . .

This *post hoc* claim made decades later contradicts the tectonic and unprecedented developments in education, public speaking, self-confidence, leadership skills, and *Weltanschauung* that Hitler underwent in the years immediately following the war and German Revolution of 1919, which were the direct consequence of the intimate influences of central figures in the *völkisch* anti-Semitic Ariosophical Thule Society. Hitler had no familial legacy of anti-Semitism or personal reasons to hate Jews. Historians are generally in agreement that Ariosophy was at the root of Hitler's anti-Semitism. Turn-of-the-century Vienna was the birthplace of Ariosophy and home to its founders, the Nationalist, occultist, journalist, playwright, and novelist Guido von List and *völkisch* political and racial theorist, occultist, anti-Semite, and former Cistercian monk Jörg Lanz von Liebenfels. Hitler's Vienna years provided his first exposure to Ariosophy through Jörg Lanz von Liebenfels's magazine *Ostara, Briefbücherei der Blonden und*

Mannesrechtler,[2] of which Hitler was an avid reader and collector during his years in Vienna. His time in Vienna laid the foundation for a generic anti-Semitism found among many Europeans at the time, albeit with a peculiar occult *völkisch* Viennese twist. However, Hitler's generic anti-Semitism remained dormant and nascent throughout the war years only to reawaken and make significant advancement shifting from romantic neo-pagan occultism to intellectual rationalism and materialism in the years immediately following the war and German Revolution of 1919. This occurred in no small part because of his introduction to and deepening connections with key figures of the Thule Society, particularly Dietrich Eckart.

During these days in Vienna, Hitler supplemented his meager orphan's student stipend by painting and selling watercolors of Vienna's sights. During his time in Vienna, he pursued a growing passion for two interests—architecture and music. Hitler received the final part of his father's estate in May 1913 and moved to Munich, Germany. Hitler's reason for finally leaving Vienna, as expressed in *Mein Kampf*, after years of brooding inactivity, eccentric daydreams, and continual flight into extravagant fantasy: "The gigantic city seemed to me the incarnation of mongrel depravity" (Hitler 1942, 106).

In Munich, Hitler learned he was called up for conscription into the Austro-Hungarian Army, so he journeyed to Salzburg on 5 February 1914 for medical assessment. After he was deemed by the medical examiners as unfit for service, he returned to Munich relieved he did not have to serve in what he viewed as an inferior army relative to Germany's.

News of declaration of war on 1 August 1914 kindled intense emotions in Hitler and his fellow adopted young Bavarians in Munich. A snapshot has been preserved showing Hitler on 1 August 1914 among the enthusiastic crowd in the *Odeonsplatz*, Munich, during the proclamation of a state of war. His face is clearly discernible with the parted lips, and the excited eyes that at last have an aim and see a future. He wrote later in *Mein Kampf* (Hitler 1942, 135):

> For me these hours came as a deliverance from the distress that had weighed upon me during the days of my youth. I am not ashamed to acknowledge to-day that I was carried away by the enthusiasm of the moment and that I sank down upon my knees and thanked Heaven out of the fullness of

> my heart for the favour of having been permitted to live in such a time.

Joachim Fest observed on page 13 of his book *The Face of the Third Reich: Portraits of the Nazi Leadership*:

> For this war promised an end to his loneliness, despondency and mistakes. At last he could flee from the misery of his aimless hate, his misunderstood and dammed-up emotions, his exaltations, into the security of a great community. For the first time in his life he had work to do, could feel solidarity with others, could identify himself with the strength and prestige of a powerful institution. For the first time Adolf Hitler, 25-years-old, without a trade, for years the inmate of a men's hostel and a copier of postcards, knew where he belonged. The war was his second great formative experience, his positive one. He himself asserted with the telltale arrogance of the drop-out: "The war caused me to think deeply on all things human. Four years of war give a man more than thirty years at a university in the way of education in the problems of life."

In Munich, Hitler voluntarily enlisted in the Bavarian Army. According to a 1924 report by the Bavarian authorities, allowing Hitler to serve was almost certainly an administrative error, since as an Austrian citizen, he should have been returned to Austria. On 16 August 1914, he was posted to the Bavarian Reserve Infantry Regiment 16 (First Company of the *List Regiment*) and he served as a dispatch runner on the Western Front in France and Belgium, spending nearly half his time at the regimental headquarters in Fournes-en-Weppes, well behind the front lines. He was an infantryman in the First Company during the First Battle of Ypres (October 1914) where his regiment suffered 83 percent losses, including his regimental commander Julius List (regiment named in his honor). By December 1914, Hitler's First Company of 250 was reduced to 42. After the battle, Hitler was promoted from *Schütze* (private) to *Gefreiter* (lance corporal) and assigned to be a regimental message-runner (courier). The *List Regiment* saw action at the Battle of Fromelles (July 1916), the Battle of the Somme (July–November 1916), the Battle of Arras (April–May 1917), and the Battle of Passchendaele (July–November 1917). During the Battle of

Fromelles on 19–20 July 1916, the Bavarians repulsed the attackers, suffering the second-highest losses they had on any day on the Western Front, about 7,000 men. The history of the *List Regiment* hailed this brilliant defense as the "personification of the German Army on the Western Front." During the Battle of the Somme, Hitler suffered a wound in his left thigh when a shell exploded at the entrance to the dispatch runners' dugout. He was sent for almost two months to the Red Cross hospital at Beelitz in Brandenburg and returned to his regiment on 5 March 1917. He was decorated with the Iron Cross, Second Class, in 1914. On a recommendation by Lieutenant Hugo Gutmann, Hitler's Jewish superior, he received the Iron Cross, First Class on 4 August 1918—a decoration rarely awarded to a *Gefreiter* (lance corporal). However, those like Hitler who served as couriers for more senior officers at regimental headquarters several miles from the front and living in relative comfort (as opposed to battalion or company runners, who had to brave machine-gun fire between trenches) were more readily awarded the Iron Cross, First Class merely for long-term service without the requirement of bravery. Hitler also received the Black (Third Class for those wounded once or twice by hostile action) Wound Badge (*Verwundetenabzeichen*) on 18 May 1918, the Bavarian Military Merit Cross, Third Class with crossed swords (*Militär-Verdienstkreuz*), and the Bavarian Medal of Military Service, 3rd Class. On 15 October 1918, he and several comrades were temporarily blinded, and Hitler also lost his voice, due to a British mustard-gas attack. After initial treatment, Hitler was hospitalized in Pasewalk in Pomerania where on 10 November 1918, Hitler learned of Germany's defeat, and—by his own account—on receiving this news he suffered an exacerbation of his blindness. The Armistice was signed on 11 November 1918 and all army units began demobilization. Hitler was devasted by the outcome of the war. During 10–13 November, Hitler underwent intensive hypnotic therapy by Dr. Forster, who was known to treat hysterics as scoundrels and malingerers, often employing Draconian methods for which he was criticized by his professional colleagues (Binion, *Hitler Among Germans*). On 19 November 1919, Hitler was diagnosed as unfit for military service and was discharged from the Pasewalk Hospital and transferred to the Second Bavarian Infantry Regiment garrisoned in Munich.

Gefreiter Adolf Hitler returned to Munich "[t]owards the end of November" (Hitler 1942, 167). Without formal education or career prospects, he remained in the army, although under the terms of the Armistice, the army was effectively transformed into a limited military force known as the *Vorläufige Reichswehr* (Provisional National Defense). During the intervening six months of December 1918 and May 1919, Hitler found himself surrounded by the anarchy and chaos that filled German society during the collapse of the German Empire and consequent revolution and civil war. Kurt Eisner, a member of the *USPD*, declared the Socialist People's State of Bavaria, seized power, and ushered out the Bavarian monarchy on 8 November 1918. Simultaneously in Berlin, *SPD* leaders Friedrich Ebert and Phillip Scheidemann filled the void left by departing Emperor Wilhelm II and declared the Social Democratic Weimar Republic. Demobilized and demoralized army units returning from the front reported to their respective garrisons only to discover enlisted leadership in the barracks had also transformed into "Soldiers' Councils." In *Mein Kampf* (Hitler 1942, 167), Hitler recalls:

> I went to the depot of my regiment, which was now in the hands of the "Soldiers' Councils." As the whole administration was quite repulsive to me, I decided to leave it as soon as I possibly could. With my faithful war-comrade, Ernst-Schmidt, I came to Traunstein and remained there until the camp was broken up. In March 1919 we were back again in Munich.

By order of the Revolutionary Council, a detachment of soldiers including Hitler and Ernst Schmidt are transferred on 6 December 1918 for guard duty to Traunstein (108 km southeast of Munich) where a prisoner-of-war camp holding Russian soldiers from the Eastern Front was located. The bulk of POWs left Traunstein before the end of January 1919. Between 23 January and 12 February 1919, Hitler returns to the Munich garrison and by mid-February, he successfully candidates for "spokesman" (*Vertrauensmann*) to represent his battalion at the self-governing regimental "Soldier's Council" recognized by the *SPD* branch headquarters in Munich. Hitler's main responsibility was to "enlighten" his unit through pro-Republican propaganda. Between 20 February and 8 March 1919, Hitler begins guard duty at the Munich railway station.

On 21 February 1919, Kurt Eisner was assassinated, and the Socialist People's State of Bavaria quickly collapsed. On 26 February 1919, Hitler and his *Ersatz* Battalion of the Second Infantry Regiment participate in the state funeral of Kurt Eisner walking directly behind the coffin-bearing carriage wearing the black band of mourning on the left arm and the red revolutionary brassard on the right. Recent scholarship has taken the tack that Hitler chose publicly to side with a fallen Jewish Socialist revolutionary leader rather than with his friends in the Thule Society, among whose members were several future Nazi leaders, and continued to serve as deputy battalion representative after the Bavarian Soviet Republic was declared in the wake of the riots following Eisner's death. Thomas Weber, Professor of History and International Affairs at the University of Aberdeen in Scotland, published in 2010 his biography: *Hitler's First War: Adolf Hitler, the Men of the List Regiment, and the First World War* (Oxford University Press). Weber goes to pains to show how all the traditional explanations for Hitler's tergiversations of this period—that he was a Socialist, or an agent *provocateur*, or a secret Nationalist counter-revolutionary, and so on—simply do not stand up to the kind of rigorous analysis steeped in the realities of the contemporary political scene to which historians and biographers ought to have subjected them. "If he really had been a committed dyed-in-the-wool Pan-German anti-Socialist, anti-Semite and hyper-Nationalist and had only overtly cooperated with the new regime to steer the men around him away from Communism and Social Democracy," Weber points out, "he would have done what many right-wing Germans were doing at the time and joined, even in secret while serving in the *Reichswehr*, a *Freikorps*, or one of the many Nationalist anti-Bolshevik political organizations that sprouted in 1919 Bavaria." Although some evidence exists that during the summer of 1919, Hitler was introduced to and granted a "guest" membership in the Thule Society, Hitler was never an official member of any *völkisch* or anti-Bolshevik German organization during the inter-war period. But it appears that during the five months after the war, Hitler remained confused relative to his loyalties, political beliefs, and the proper course of action to pursue his evolving political *Weltanschauung*. Events in Germany, particularly in Bavaria, were changing weekly during those five months of revolution and civil war. No one knew for certain how things would end. Hitler could have laid low and out of site as a corporal in the *Vorläufige Reichswehr*. But, in his deep longing for acceptance and purpose, he chose to be noticed among his veteran peers by speaking openly and pursuing leadership positions. These actions belie the narrative relative to this period promoted by him in *Mein Kampf* and by the Nazi Party. In fact, some of those decidedly Nationalist anti-Socialist and anti-Bolshevik individuals who later became prominent Nazis boldly criticized Hitler in the early 1930s for his failure to be on the right side of history during the turbulent months of the German Revolution and civil war.

In his *Bevor Hitler kam*, an account of the Thule Society published several months after the Nazis took power in Germany, von Sebottendorff claimed the Society was a primary root of the National Socialist movement: "Thule people were to whom Hitler first came, and it was Thule people who joined him in the beginning" (von Sebottendorff 1933, 13). Von Sebottendorff's assertion has considerable merit. Several Thulists became prominent in the emerging Nazi Party, and his claim for Hitler's involvement in the Society does not break the bounds of plausibility (Luhrssen 2012, 149). Von Sebottendorff neither crowned himself Hitler's personal mentor nor claimed to be a Nazi himself; he wrote only that the future *führer* "entered the halls of Thule" a few weeks after von Sebottendorff resigned as the Society's master in the summer of 1919 (Luhrssen 2012, 167).* He described Hitler as a "guest" rather than a full Thule member (Luhrssen 2012, 220). This too speaks for the plausibility of his assertions. Because regulations restricted soldiers from pledging an oath to any organization but the army, many Nationalist groups admitted active military personnel as "guests." This designation, circumventing army rules, applied to any lodge or secret society that Hitler, who was in no hurry to be demobilized, cared to join before his formal discharge from the army on 1 April 1920 (Luhrssen 2012, 149).

Although Hitler's participation in the Thule Society as its guest cannot be verified, and there is no record of him referring directly to Thule, Hitler did try to establish a relationship with one of Thule's front organizations, the *Münchener Beobachter*, by offering to become a correspondent and coeditor in the summer of 1919 (Phelps 1963b, 245, 256).† Certainly, Hitler's closest mentor in his early years in politics was none other than Thule ideologue Dietrich Eckart, to whom Hitler dedicated the closing sentence of his second volume of *Mein Kampf*. There is no dispute about his eventual role in another group that began as a Thule front, the German Workers' Party (*Deutsche Arbeiterpartei, DAP*), which under his leadership became the National Socialist German Workers' Party (*Nationalsozialistische Deutsche Arbeiterpartei, NSDAP*).

---

* Von Sebottendorff gave no precise date for his resignation but his chronology is congruent with the 22 June 1919 departure date given by Goodrick-Clarke 1993, 51.
† His offer was rejected.

TRANSFORMATION FROM *DAP* TO *NSDAP* AND HITLER'S CONSOLIDATION OF POWER

THE INFORMATION IN THIS SECTION WAS MOSTLY EXCERPTED FROM Walter Smoter Frank's 310-page biography of the young Adolf Hitler and the early Nazi era, titled: *Adolf Hitler: The Making of a Fuhrer* (2004), publicly accessible at http://smoter.com. Other publicly accessible sources, as cited, were also used to clarify and enrich the history.

It is not necessary to trace Hitler's remarkable and rapid ascent to leadership of the German Workers' Party (*DAP*), spurred as it was by the increasingly persuasive power of his public speaking, except to note that his rise was accompanied by conflict between him and the party's cofounders, Thulists Karl Harrer and Anton Drexler. Within months after joining the *DAP*, Hitler began to make the party more public and organized its biggest rally to date of 2,000 people on 24 February 1920 in what was to become a frequent gathering place for the party, the *Festsaal* (Festival Hall) of the *Staatliches Hofbräuhaus* in Munich. Such was the significance of this particular planed move in publicity that Karl Harrer resigned from the party in disagreement in January 1920 and was replaced by Drexler as national chairman.

Drexler sought to shore up attendance for the still little-known Hitler by inviting a well-known Munich homeopathic physician and Thule Society member, Johannes Dingfelder, who wrote for Nationalist and *völkisch* publications and often gave anti-Jewish speeches, to deliver the main address. Although Drexler informed Dingfelder that the expected crowd at the meeting might be "partly hostile," the Communist death threat looming over the meeting was never mentioned. Dingfelder agreed to be the first speaker, but he was never informed that Adolf Hitler was to follow him (Phelps 1963, 983). Hitler, meanwhile, set about getting the word out on the upcoming meeting. Bright red posters and leaflets along with newspaper ads addressed to "The Suffering Public," (Flood 1989, 101) with headlines like "The True Causes of the World War," "The Peace Treaty of Versailles," and "War Guilt" announced the coming event (Hitler 1941, 703, 696, 695). Possibly because Hitler still did not consider himself a big enough draw, or because of the Communist death threat, his name did not appear on any of the promotional material; nor was there any mention of the Twenty-Five Points program.

In his keynote address, Doctor Dingfelder complained that "we have lost touch with the powers of nature . . . the God-given Sun-order . . . and have chased after the good life." Hitler then followed. It was in this speech that Hitler enunciated the Twenty-Five Points of the German Workers' Party manifesto that had been drawn up by Drexler, Feder, Eckart, and himself. Hitler's role at the meeting may have been to reiterate ideas circulating in Thule Society circles in more table-pounding language, just as his role in editing earlier drafts of the Twenty-Five Points may have been to add such forceful assertions as "Wir forden" ("We demand").

In Nazi Party legend, Hitler's proclamation of the Twenty-Five Points would be compared to the bold strokes of Martin Luther who, as legend holds, nailed his Ninety-Five Theses to the church door in Wittenberg. Hitler would later recall "violent clashes" with Communist hecklers even as his speech "was accepted with steadily mounting joy" by most spectators, suddenly "united by a new conviction, a new faith, a new will." Through these points he gave the organization a much bolder stratagem with a clear foreign policy (abrogation of the Treaty of Versailles, a greater Germany, eastern expansion, and exclusion of Jews from citizenship) and among his specific points were: confiscation of war profits, abolition of unearned incomes, the State to share profits of land, and land for national needs to be taken away without compensation. In general, the manifesto was anti-Semitic, anti-Capitalist, anti-Democratic, anti-Marxist, and anti-Liberal.

The same day, the party changed its name by adding two words: "National" and "Socialist" either at Hitler's suggestion or over his objection—the history remains unclear on this matter. The new name of the party became *Nationalsozialistische Deutsche Arbeiterpartei* (*NSDAP*, National Socialist German Workers [Nazi] Party). The new name was borrowed from an Austrian party active at the time in Germany (*Deutsche Nationalsozialistische Arbeiterpartei*, German National Socialist Workers' Party). Hitler had always been hostile to Socialist ideas, especially those that involved racial or sexual equality. However, Socialism was a popular political movement, particularly among workers in Germany after the First World War. This was reflected in the growth in the Social Democrat Party of Germany (*SPD*), the largest and oldest political party in Germany. Adding the word "Socialist" would appeal to workers that may otherwise be attracted to Socialist or Communist parties to represent their rights. Earlier, Hitler suggested the party be renamed the "Social Revolutionary Party"; it was Sudeten German Rudolf Jung (1882–1945, a German political theorist born in Bohemia, later working for Hitler's Third *Reich* in Germany) who persuaded Hitler to adopt the *NSDAP* naming. By adding the word

"National," Hitler redefined the traditional understanding of Socialism. And by the word "National," Hitler claimed he was only in favor of equality for those who had "German blood." Jews and other "aliens" would lose their rights of citizenship, and immigration of non-Germans would cease.

At the beginning of 1920, the German Workers' Party had 190 dues-paying (a half Mark monthly) members. Their ranks were made up of fifty-six skilled tradesmen from the railroad shops along with a sampling of minor civil servants, grade schoolteachers, shopkeepers, salesmen and office workers. There were also twelve university students, six engineers, three doctors, and seven members associated with journalism and publishing. There were also nineteen women—occupations unknown. The military was represented by four *Vorläufige Reichswehr* officers along with twenty soldiers (Flood 1989, 86; see also Hanser 1971, 203). Because the military made up only thirteen percent of the membership, and there were only four unskilled members that could truly be called "workers," the party was in reality a lower middle-class party and contrary to popular belief would continue to remain so during its entire existence.

"In 1920," Hitler would later recall, "when I organized my first big assemblies in Munich . . . I was in search of starched collars, in the hope that they'd help me to reach the intellectual class" (Hitler 1961, 359; see also Picker 1976, 159). Hitler now had second doubts. Since his Vienna days he had always had contempt for the intellectual class, and that included Conservatives as well as Liberals and moderates. He saw the intellectuals of the Conservatives as a bunch of "wandering German folkish scholars" who had been doing the same thing for "thirty or even forty years" while the country became more Marxist every year (Hitler 1971, 360). He believed that most of the upper classes were driven by "stupidity and pride" (Picker 1976, 458), and that they really "believed in nothing" (Hitler 1961, 572). Because of his earlier dealings with the legal system, he especially singled out lawyers and judges and felt that "jurists are either born defective or become so through practice" (Picker 1976, 161). Hitler often talked about the "stupidity of lawyers" and pointed out that: "They're the people who used to burn witches!" (Hitler 1961, 262). Hitler, consequently, took one of the most decisive steps in his political career. Instead of attempting to find acceptance among the upper classes at this time, he decided to do what Vienna Mayor Karl Lueger (1844–1910) had done years before and reach out for more of the crowd.

Hitler knew that to succeed in the politics of the time, sooner or later, he would have to take his "struggle" out into the streets. Large outdoor meetings, rallies and marches announced the success of a political group. A hall or meeting room could be defended by a handful of "buddies," however, the streets were controlled by the Socialists and Communists. The Social Democrats had their "defense organizations" (united under the *Reichsbanner* in 1924) while the Communists had their *Rotfrontkampfer* (Red Front Fighters). These gangs not only fought against one another but raided the meetings and street rallies or anyone else who opposed them. The Communists were especially skilled at assembling unemployed workers and these groups seldom dispersed peacefully. Many of the participants were former soldiers and sailors who were now trained organizers and street fighters. They gathered together with short pieces of lead pipe, wood clubs, knives, and guns. They did not hide their intentions of clashing with any opponent and that included the police. Hitler felt that the "cowardly" intellectual and upper classes (who "lived in perpetual fear of irritating the Reds" [Hitler 1961, 572] and fled when "the first communist cudgel appears") (Hitler 1941, 499), would never succeed in attracting a mass following with their "weapons of the mind" (Hitler 1942, 204). He had great admiration for many of the Communist and Socialist party members who were willing to fight, physically, for what they believed in (de Jonge 1986, 40). He was determined to attract those men to him.

With the National Chairman (Harrer) gone, the first thing Hitler did in reshaping the movement was to set about getting rid of any "intellectual" airs. To appeal to the working classes Hitler wore "disheveled clothes" and "made sure that all the members of the movement came to meetings without fancy clothes and ties, but in casual dress so as to win the trust of the working class" (Picker 1976, 205). To appeal to the ex-soldiers, who made up a large part of the Marxist parties, Hitler never attempted to hide the fact that he had served in the army. Like any common soldier he used gutter language and "latrine" phraseology in his speeches that ex-soldiers understood immediately (Remarque 1958, 13, 21, 41, 128). For as much as to attract the workers, as well as to rid the party of "scared rabbits" or "fraidy-cats" (Picker 1976, 205), Hitler also adapted the slogan: "Whoever attacks us with violence, we will defend against with violence" (Hitler 1937, 399). On the other hand, Hitler never attempted to reach down to the lowest strata of society. He was determined to attract the "better elements of the working classes" (Picker 1976, 206). As he would state, "we do not want millions of indifferent rabble, we want a hundred thousand men—headstrong, defiant men. Our success will force the millions to follow us" (Heiden 1944, 112).

Hitler, with his anti-Jewish anti-Marxist outcries, was from the very beginning, as he saw it, an attempt to "educate" (Picker 1976, 378) the workers and change "public opinion." He was determined to drive a wedge between the Marxist parties' leaders (many of whom were Jewish) and the workers. Unlike most "Jew baiters," Hitler had nothing against Jews he met personally and behaved the same toward them as he did anyone (Toland 1976, 108 fn). Most of his attacks against the Jews were, as one observer saw it, "not so much on a racial basis, as on an accusation of black marketeering and waxing fat on the misery round them, a charge which was only too easy to make stick" (Hanfstaengl 1957, 35–6). As Hitler saw it, "constant grumbling against the Jews succeeded in alienating the working class from their Jewish leaders" (Picker 1976, 206).

In Jan 1920, Hitler held his sixth and seventh meetings at the German *Reich* Tavern. Hitler's speeches remained unprepared, and he spoke with primitive force and emotion. Moderation in politics suggests a lack of conviction and in this matter, Hitler was not lacking. He hammered home the incompetence of the new liberal government's policies, he attacked Germany's enemies, he degraded the peace treaty, he defended the army, and his attacks against the Reds were unrelenting. His attacks against the Jews were directed against those of wealth, recent immigrants from Russia, and especially those who played a leadership role in the Marxist parties during and after the war. Over 250 people attended the first meeting and over 400 attended the second. "The hall," Hitler would later state, "could barely hold the crowd." Shortly after, thirty-seven new members joined the party in one day (Phelps 1963b, footnote at 985).

Hans Frank, a twenty-year-old law student was overwhelmed by Hitler's deep sincerity and fearlessness: "The first thing you felt," stated Frank, "was that there was a man who spoke honestly about how he felt and was not trying to put something across of which he himself was not absolutely convinced" (Toland 1976, 101). Frank also felt that Hitler made his beliefs understandable and went to the core of things. He was convinced that "if anyone could master the fate of Germany, Hitler was that man" (Toland 1976, 101).

The Communists' mouthpiece in Munich, *Der Kampf* (*The Struggle*), would call the Twenty-Five Points "a stolen program." Before the next open meeting was held, party membership would rise by an additional hundred. Although Hitler's speech was played down in the major Munich newspapers (Phelps 1963b, 984–5), Hitler had won the hearts of hundreds of converts. Many saw the beginning of a speaker who knew how to "move" the masses. Word of the new party began to spread, but it was not the program that received the most attention—it was Adolf Hitler.

Hitler's disgust at what he had seen in Munich, concerning morals, sex, and tradition, seemed trivial to what he observed in Berlin during the Kapp *Putsch* in March 1920. Since the days of the Roman circuses, inadequate governments have always looked for ways to defuse the public's attention. The Weimar government was "corrupt," "confused," "inept," "shaky," and "self-serving." Its capitol had become a cesspool of super liberal permissiveness. As Marx had wanted, nearly "all morality" was "abolished" (Marx and Engels 1963, 53), and in its place reigned lawlessness and perversion. Berlin had become the center of the Dadaist movement (Toland 1976, 104), and writers and artist wrote "manifestos" against civilization and tradition (Roth 1968, 43). Destructive antisocial and anti-cultural tendencies were viewed as natural. The streets had become unsafe, and criminals went unpunished. Dope pushers openly sold cocaine, called *Schnee* (snow), or any other drug one wanted in the streets. From dusk to dawn, girl prostitutes, ten- and eleven-years-old, heavily rouged and wearing short baby-doll dresses, competed against lush blondes and whip toting Amazon types (Hanser 1971, 224). The Marquis de Sade had been rediscovered and his views that sexual cruelty was "natural" opened the closets of sadist and masochists alike who preached an alternative way of life. Nudity became boring and heterosexuals, homosexuals, and bisexuals did what they could to shock the "philistine" and "good" citizens. Sexual licentiousness became "a triumph of chaos over law and order" (Roth 1968, 43). Hitler believed that the only way to "cleanse" Berlin was to "destroy" the Weimar Republic.

On 29 March 1920, Hitler and Eckart returned to Munich from Berlin. Kapp's failed *putsch* convinced Hitler that a military backed uprising against the government would never succeed without the support of the worker. He was certain from what he witnessed, that Berlin, and then all of northern Germany would, sooner or later, fall to the Communists. Hitler called the *NSDAP* party committee members together at the *Sternecker* Brewery and on three consecutive evenings, 29–31 March (Flood 1989, 125), lectured them on the importance of his views. The only way to save Germany, he believed, was to unite the common workers and those engaged in the higher occupations. With their backing, Hitler believed, a popular Nationalist party could take control of Bavaria's government and then march on Berlin. (This was the reason for Hitler's attempted Beer Hall *Putsch* in 1923.)

Hitler was aware that his present connection with the army, if known, would be a stumbling block in attracting followers. Because of the army's connections with the failed *putsch,* it had become discredited among most northern Germans and even many southerners regarded it with suspicion. Hitler had already taken steps to disguise his position (he registered with the party as an "artist"), but if he continued with his political career, his position was bound to become public knowledge. There can be little doubt that Hitler had considered resigning from the army, but he was reluctant to do so. Outside of the barracks, millions of unemployed were experiencing hunger and uncertainty. The army not only provided Hitler with a comfortable and secure lifestyle, but a prestigious position. Leaving the army was not a decision Hitler could make on his own. "Fate," however, would again come to his aid.

The Versailles Treaty, forced on Germany by the Allies in 1919, demanded that the German Army (after reducing to 200,000) "by a date which must not be later than March 31, 1920 . . . must not exceed 100,000 men, including officers."* Although the army had been stalling on its reduction commitments and would fail to reach its obligations by the prescribed date, it now had to accelerate its demobilization because of rising pressures by the Allies and the Berlin government. Hitler may have been considered too important to the 200,000-man army a year earlier to let go, but an army limited to 100,000 hardly had room for Hitler on its muster roll. Hitler's decision was made for him.

On 31 March 1920, after over four years on the front lines and a year and one-half as a propagandist, he received his "discharge" (Maser 1973, 325). To take him in to civilian life the army officially provided Hitler with fifty Marks along with a suit of clothes: cap; shirt; jacket; coat; underwear; pants; socks; and shoes (Toland 1976, 106). Unofficially however, the army had been providing financial support to Nationalist groups and individuals since the end of the war. They were not about to abandon anyone who served their purposes as well as Adolf Hitler has.

As Hitler became more and more visible, he began attracting more and more risky attention from the Communist opposition. "Indeed," Hitler would later write, "how often in those days were they led in, literally in columns, those supporters of the Red Flag with instructions to smash up everything and put an end to our meetings. And how often was everything touch and go, and only the ruthless determination of our meetings' leaders

---

* Part V, Section I, Chapter I, Article 160.

and the brutal handling by our guards was able again and again to thwart our adversary's intentions" (Hanfstaengl 1957, 186).

Because of the attacks launched against the party by the "Left" (Fest 1974, 150) (usually the Red Front), Hitler was forced to take more elaborate precautions to safeguard himself and his meetings. At this time there were about 150 former soldiers who belonged to the party who could be relied on occasionally to act as bouncers against "Communist and Social Democrat intruders" (Hanser 1971, 266). Because each man had to earn a living, they could not be on call all the time. Hitler, therefore, organized them into squads responsible for certain sections of Munich. When a meeting was held in their part of town, they were required to be ready on short notice to support in defending Hitler and the meeting.

During the years 1920 and 1921, the squads became known as *Saalschutzabteilung* (meeting hall protection detachment) or *Ordnentruppen* (Order Troops) and their first uniform was little more than a swastika arm band. On 3 August of 1921, Hitler would rename the group *Turn- und Sportabteilung* (Gymnastics and Sport-Section or *SA*) so as to disguise their true function. Although many historians contend that the *SA* was created as a paramilitary group to be used against political rivals, the reverse was the purpose at its creation. As Hitler would later state: "The SA was born in 1920 . . . but I had no ideas concerning paramilitary organizations. I began by creating a service to keep order. . . . It was confined to that" (Hitler 1961, 265). Later, as the party became more powerful and the ranks of the *SA* grew, the squads would be used to protect Nazi outdoor activities and also "storm" the meetings of Communists and other rivals who used to threaten Hitler meetings. By 10 September 1921, the *SA* would come to stand for *Sturmabteilung* (Storm-Section). "Terror will be smashed by terror," Hitler would later tell an acquaintance, "I learned that principle in the street battles between the SA and the Red Front" (Speer 1981, 43).

In 1920, most people had no qualms with Hitler's *Ordnentruppen* beating up Communists, Social Democrats, or "Marxist Jews" who had come to disrupt his meetings. But, when it was reported that the Order Troops were also beating up on "harmless" Jews, Hitler used the occasion to bar all Jews from attending any future meetings. "Jews only go to the meetings," Hitler would state, "in order to provoke trouble, and thus try to portray the party as a brutal rapist of 'harmless' participants" (Flood 1989, 162). In one of his speeches shortly after, Hitler voiced the same opinion and a few Nationalists in the audience shouted out that "Negroes" should also be banned. Hitler shouted back: "I would rather have one hundred Negroes in the hall than one Jew" (Flood 1989, 162). The audience erupted into applause. All future advertisements for party meetings would carry the notation: "Jews not admitted" (Hitler 1941, 517–58). Opposition groups and newspapers already incensed over Hitler's swastika flag saw grave undertones in Hitler's proclamation. Rumors began circulating as to the extent of his "anti-Semitism." Hitler was unmoved and considered his proclamation to be a positive act. Opposition only fed his growing anti-Semitism.

The party was now holding a public meeting in Munich nearly every week, and Hitler was the featured or supporting speaker at over sixty percent of the meetings (Flood 1989, 163; Fest 1974, 136). When Hitler was not speaking in Munich, he was normally out of town giving speeches at the four other locals the party had established by this time. His ability as a Nationalist speaker became sought after and he was also paid, in a private capacity, by various veteran or Nationalist groups to deliver his message. Drexler, Eckart, Feder, or invited outsiders were normally the main attraction at party functions when Hitler was not scheduled.

With the exception of Eckart, Hitler felt that most of those who spoke for the party were tiresome "preachers" who failed to arouse the people. He understood that if the party was to continue to grow, he could not do it all on his own. Speakers like himself, capable of "moving the crowd," as he put it, would have to be found.

As the party's propaganda chief, Hitler began coaching a few men who he felt showed promise. One of these was twenty-year-old Hermann Esser who joined the party around the same time as Hitler in late 1919. The son of a railroad official, Esser had been a "press secretary" for the army propaganda group Hitler joined after the war and Esser now wrote for various newspapers and magazines. His writings—normally attacks against Jews and liberals (he harbored ideas of hanging the *bourgeoisie*) (Hanser 1971, 275)—were capable of raising the eyebrows of even the staunchest Nationalists. Esser, as well as the other early followers of Hitler, would later become known as "those Bavarian vulgarians" by newer members of Hitler's circle (Speer 1981, 443). Next to Hitler, however, Esser was the only other effective speaker in the party capable of appealing to the lower classes. Some of his speeches, however, were of such a "primitive" nature that even Hitler found him embarrassing at times (Fest 1974, 144). Esser however, was intelligent, persuasive, and had a gift for reaching the younger lower-class workers that Hitler never truly reached down to. Handsome and sophisticated looking, Esser could have passed himself off as a romantic film star. A great lady's man (Heiden 1944, 292; Hanfstaengl 1957, 191) he often boasted of his ability to live off his mistresses (Shirer 1962, 79). Esser became part of Hitler's inner circle and would shortly become one of the party's main speakers—second only to Hitler.

In October of 1920, Hitler could take satisfaction in his year with the *NSDAP*. He had raised the small group of six part-time debaters to a party with over a thousand dedicated dues-paying members and tens of thousands of sympathizers. Hitler's effect was now becoming felt and when he returned to Austria on a speaking tour (including a stop at Braunau am Inn where he was born), it was he and not Drexler that drew the attention. After a speech in Vienna, a newspaper for the working classes wrote that Hitler spoke for two hours but the audience "could have listened to him for days" (Flood 1989, 160). When he got back to Munich, Hitler held a mass meeting at the *Münchner Kindl-Keller*, a beer garden and eating establishment, which had the largest single feast hall in Munich. He nearly packed the place with 3,500 people.

Röhm, Heß, Eckart, and von Scheubner-Richter made certain that Hitler's achievements did not go unnoticed by military and government leaders who now began to take serious note. Hitler, however, had not as yet linked himself with a prominent personality (or group) that would give him the credibility he sought. (As one of Hitler's friends later remarked: "There was still no room for self-made men in the Germany of those days and Hitler's fight against this attitude was to take him years" [Hanfstaengl 1957, 102].) Such a link would not only open the doors to respectability but large sums of money. In Germany, at the time, the real big money for political purposes did not come so much from individuals, but from large associations of big industrialists, employers, and bankers (Heiden 1944, 113) who considered it beneficial to establish links with any group or individual which might become politically powerful (Nicholls 1970, 158 fn). Hitler did not have long to wait. He was about to receive some unexpected assistance from Moscow—the "worker's paradise."

In the early Fall of 1920, Grigori Zinoviev (born Hirsch Apfelbaum), president of the Communist International, met with the leaders of the Independent Social Democratic Party of Germany (*USPD*) ninety miles outside of Berlin. Zinoviev had been sent by Lenin and Trotsky to get the Independent Socialists to join with Moscow and foment revolution throughout Germany. The ranks of the Independent Socialists were composed primarily of workers which Moscow believed held the key to revolution—the strike.

Lenin and Trotsky regarded strikes as a weapon to be used against all non-Communist governments. A continuous wave of strikes would disrupt Germany's system of industrial production and deepen the nation's economic crisis. The brutal breakup of strikes by the *Freikorps* and other forces did not deter Moscow which viewed any strike, even the most hopeless, as a victory. That men lost their jobs, were put in jail, or ended up dead meant nothing. Continual waves of even minor strikes, which heaped additional hardships upon the lower classes, would lead to upsurges of popular discontent. Every strike, no matter how it ended was seen as a political triumph or training for civil war. With enough strikes the rift between the lower and upper classes would deepen and the influence of the present "false leaders" would be destroyed. Then, Lenin and Trotsky believed, the victory of a Communist takeover would be assured (Valtin 1941, 202).

Zinoviev's appeal to the Independent Socialist fell on receptive ears and he was embraced enthusiastically. Most Communists decided to come out of the closet and over sixty percent of the 393 *USPD* delegates voted to join with Moscow. For various reasons, the remaining delegates walked out, but the Communists picked up over a half a million new converts in one meeting. It appeared to many that it would be only a matter of time before Moscow dominated, to one degree or another, over Germany.

General Ludendorff, a fierce anti-Communist and the symbol to all patriotic and Nationalist groups, was convinced that there was not a single political party in Germany which could turn the tide of Communist growth. He believed that a new Nationalist party had to be found, which could appeal to the millions of Nationalist minded veterans who were now part of the working class.

After the failed Kapp *Putsch,* Ludendorff had fled northern Germany for Munich. He did not fail to notice that throughout Germany all of the conservative politicians were failing to establish any contact with veteran soldiers and ordinary people. Hitler, on the other hand, was not only attracting ordinary people, but was "clearly succeeding in presenting a non-Communist program" (Hanfstaengl 1957, 38).

Ludendorff was closely associated with von Scheubner-Richter (Hanfstaengl 1957, 91) from their Baltic days, and the important contact between Hitler and Ludendorff was established (Bracher 1971, 90). The plan that Ludendorff revealed to Hitler was simple. Five months after the Kapp *Putsch* and the last Communist revolt, the Weimar Republic in Berlin disbanded the *Freikorps* again. Bavaria, consequently, had become home to thousands of former *Freikorps* troops who had poured into the various Bavarian militias and private armies which now numbered 300,000 men. Their ranks were made up for the most part of veterans, but also disgruntled idealists, Nationalist revolutionaries, and disillusioned Socialists. They were united in their hatred of the Communists and in their determination to overthrow the existing government in Berlin which they referred to, like millions of other Germans, as the "Jews' Republic" (Fest 1974, 138). (By 1922, the reference to the Weimar Republic as the "Jews' Republic" or "Jew Republic" became so commonplace that a "Law [for the Defense of the Republic]" was actually passed making it an offense punishable by a stiff prison sentence. There were also "serious prison sentences" for anyone referring to the president as a "brothel-keeper" or the Republic's flag as "a filthy rag" [Heiden 1944, 117].) The inept Weimar government, and the Allies, had demanded that these paramilitary groups be disbanded, but the von Kahr government in Bavaria considered them a "Civil Guard" against the Socialists and refused. Ludendorff's idea, therefore, was to unite all of the Nationalist groups in Bavaria using Hitler's party as a core on which to build an even larger following. Ludendorff would then take over the military leadership with Hitler as political head (Toland 1976, 111; Hanfstaengl 1957, 79).

A few days after Moscow had captured the majority of the Independent Socialists, Ludendorff brought Hitler, dressed in his old blue suit, to meet with Gregor Straßer at Landshut forty miles northeast of Munich. Straßer had a small but vigorous following, including his own *Freikorps*-type army with infantry, artillery, and machine gun companies. A twenty-eight-year-old pharmacist and war veteran, Straßer, like Hitler, had performed heroically during the war and had also won the Iron Cross First Class. Opposed to both Communism and Capitalism, Straßer sought a "German type" of Socialism free of foreign interference. Most of his followers were like himself, Nationalist ex-military men from the trenches who desired a form of government based on the wartime comradeship of brotherhood and patriotism. Although many among the liberal upper classes laughed as such ideas, Straßer spoke for many of the veterans who now made up a substantial part of the civilian population. Ludendorff revealed his plans to Straßer while Hitler promised to make him the first "national" party district leader of the *NSDAP*. Straßer was not particularly impressed with Hitler (nor was his brother Otto who found Hitler too "servile" toward Ludendorff who Hitler repeatedly addressed as "Your Excellency") but he had great "trust" in Ludendorff and made up his mind to join Hitler's party before the day was over.

Hitler had accomplished what only a year before seemed impossible. He had not only linked himself to one of Germany's most revered men among upper military, Nationalist, and conservative circles, but also to a group whose leader, Straßer, was highly respected among lower circles.

By December 1920, the party had established ten locals in different Bavarian towns and could boast of over 2,000 dues-paying members (Flood 1989, 163; Toland 1976, 112). The membership numbers, however, veiled the true strength of Hitler and the *NSDAP*. As an example, Straßer (like other group leaders) may have joined the party, but his followers were under no obligation to do so. This was especially the case with the members of the paramilitary ranks which normally functioned as fairly independent groups. Consequently, the Nazi Party would primarily continue to consist of members of the lower-middle class with paramilitary (*SA*) members normally accounting for only ten to fifteen percent of party strength. But, because of Hitler's links with "Civil Guard" organizations, his influence was far reaching, and he would shortly be in a position to call on thousands of veterans and *Freikorps* troops who were never members of his party.

As Propaganda Chief, the party's newly acquired paper *Völkischer Beobachter* fell completely under Hitler's control and he replaced the old management with members of his inner circle. Hermann Esser was made the First Editor and he and Hitler retained the paper's hate peddling, anti-Marxist, fanatical style as an opposition to Marx's hate peddling *Manifesto* and current hate peddling anti-Nationalist publications. As 1920 drew to an end, Hitler and his friends took up the pen (for which each received a small salary) and spewed out their own version of events.

As with his speeches, Hitler also took his writing seriously. During this period (1919–1921) he borrowed over 100 books and pamphlets from one source alone. As any public speaker or writer quickly learns, when you start speaking or writing to thousands of people, your "facts" better have a sound foundation. Some of the books Hitler read (or skimmed-through) during this period were: *Luther and the Jews*, *Schopenhauer and the Jews*, *Wagner and the Jews*, Henry Ford's *The International Jew*, *Bolshevism and Jewry*, also books on medieval and modern Germany, church history, the Talmud, Montesquieu, and Rousseau (Waite 1977, 69. Kenneth Galbraith as quoted in Toland 1976, 424 fn).

Hitler's articles, like those in the Communist press, appealed to emotion and were merciless against opponents. Socialists and Marxists often called on boycotts of the paper and its street sellers were often beaten up (Hitler 1961, 224). When Hitler was later criticized for his journalistic talents, he asked what someone would say about an advertisement that was intended to promote a new soap but also described competing soaps as good. The crowd, Hitler insisted, could only be won over by a "ruthless and fanatical one-sided orientation" and not by "a so-called objective viewpoint" (Hitler 1941, 467).

The huge debt that came with the paper would burden party finances for years. With the expert guidance of Max Amann, and by exhorting members to subscribe and encouraging them to solicit subscribers, Hitler would finally turn the paper into a profitable venture. The experience filled a void in Hitler's knowledge that would later pay huge dividends. As he would later say: "I would understand nothing about business methods if it had not been, thankfully, for the constant worries about the Party press" (Picker 1976, 270; Hitler 1941, 438). ("Hitler . . . anticipated modern economic policy" (Kenneth Galbraith as quoted in Toland 1976, 424 fn), and when he came to power in 1933, his knowledge of "business methods" turned a bankrupt nation into a respected economic power in three years while most nations languished in the world-wide Great Depression.)

As 1921 began, Hitler felt that it was time for the party to begin to do more than "just talk." He knew that most ordinary Germans were "full of disgust and revulsion" because of the "cowardice" (Hitler 1971, 491) displayed by the middle-class parties who refused to take a stand against unpopular causes and endeavors. Although Hitler had no direct control over Straßer's *Freikorps*, or any of the other paramilitary groups at this time, his association with them was enough to give him the courage to set the party on a revolutionary course. Hitler understood, even in these early days, that one had to have some control of the streets since that is where the "reporters" where. In the first week of January, he gave a speech at the *Münchner Kindl-Keller* to two thousand enthusiastic listeners and promised that in the future the party would "ruthlessly prevent—by force, if necessary—all meetings and lectures intended to have an undermining effect on our already sick fellow Germans" (Flood 1989, 175).

Hitler was in no position at this early stage to carry out his threat against any political party, but he understood that threats in themselves produced effects. The Socialists and Marxists, on more than one occasion, had been responsible for the police informing Hitler, "in writing" (Hitler 1941, 725; Hitler 1971, 487), to cancel his meetings because of "possible violence." Hitler hoped that his threats would have the same effect on his adversaries until his party was strong enough to take the threatened action. The ordinary citizens of Bavaria knew the tactics of the Socialists and Marxists and were pleased to hear of a Nationalist politician who was not only willing to fight back but take the offensive. In the meantime, Hitler satisfied himself with having the *SA* section of his party disrupt or picket controversial plays and performances (Flood 1989, 175) that the majority of Germans found offensive. After a few Nazi demonstrations and "minor" brawls (Toland 1976, 118), Hitler undoubtedly took great satisfaction when later, even the threat of a protest from his group, was enough to cause the Munich police to close down, under the guise of preventing "possible violence," performances that the majority of people found offensive (Flood 1989, 175–6). Hitler's action had a positive effect among the majority of Bavarians who had heard of him and did much to enhance his popularity in Munich. Shortly thereafter, the Allies handed Hitler an issue that would send his popularity soaring.

Because of Allied policy, the winter of 1920–21 was severe with large segments of the German working population going hungry. Food riots erupted and soon spread throughout Germany. Public indignation reached the boiling point at the end of January when the Allies forced on Germany a new "reasonable" formula for paying her war debts—set at 132 billion Gold Marks for all the Central Powers combined. Besides staggering annual fixed payments which threatened to bankrupt the nation, Germany was also expected to hand over to the Allies twenty-six percent of her exports for the next forty-two years. The first bond payment was to be on 1 May 1921. By 5 May, Germany still had not complied with the reparations demands of the treaty and an ultimatum was sent to Germany. If Germany did not comply, the Ruhr Basin would be occupied on 12 May 1921 and the occupation would continue until Germany had made the undertakings required by the ultimatum. Notwithstanding an internal political crisis occasioned by the Allied demands, Germany accepted the conditions just before the expiration of the ultimatum. Such reparations would not only aggravate the already horrid plight of the working classes but would also create hardships for volatile members of the middle class.

In Munich, the "great parties," ignored the Allied ultimatum (Hitler 1941, 739). The Nationalist, center, and Socialist-Marxist parties believed that to refuse payment would give France the excuse it was looking for to invade and occupy the Ruhr, while the Communists, even though their worker members would bear the brunt of the reparations, supported any Allied demand that created discontent. The Nationalist parties, on the other hand, were outraged. A "Workers' Community" of "*völkisch* associations," Hitler wrote, decided to have a combined "demonstration of protest" (Hitler 1941, 739).

The Nationalist coalition first considered holding their demonstration on the *Königsplatz* in front of the *Reichstag*, but the wide, open space was too difficult to defend, and the idea was called off because of fear it would be "broken up by the Reds" (Toland 1976, 114; Hitler 1971, 498–9). The coalition next proposed holding their demonstration in front of the *Feldherrnhalle* (which was protected by buildings on three sides) but this idea was also abandoned. They finally decided to hold their protest indoors at the *Münchner Kindl-Keller* but wavered as to the exact date. Hitler, no doubt sensing that public indignation was high, would later write. "I decided to carry out the demonstration of protest on my own" (Hitler 1941, 739).

At noon, on Wednesday, 2 February 1921, Hitler reserved the largest auditorium in Munich, the *Zirkus Krone*. The building, located northwest of Munich's central railway station, sprawled over an entire block. The central arena was capable of holding 8,000 people. Hitler quickly had posters printed, announcing the meeting for the next day, Thursday, 3 February 1921, at 9 p.m. Never before had the party attempted to attract such a large audience, and never before on such short notice.

Without party sanction, posters appeared throughout Munich announcing a meeting of "NATIONAL SOCIALISTS, MANUAL AND WHITE-COLLAR WORKERS" at the *Zirkus Krone* (Hitler 1941, 534). Though Hitler continued to use the typical stock of anti-Semitic catchphrases, never before had a Hitler poster struck out so hard against the Jews. "Like a giant spider," read the first line of text, "the Jewish international world stock exchange capital creeps over the peoples of this earth, gradually sucking their marrow and blood" (Hitler 1941, 534). The poster then suggests that 300 Jews, "who know one another, dominate the world." Hitler then warns that an "inexorable war of destruction against our people has already set in" (Hitler 1941, 535), and uses the fighting in Upper Silesia between Germans and Poles to prove his point. He then scolds the German people for their lack of concern. He charges that they are being misled by "thousands and thousands" of Jewish agents who "are untiringly active in the press and in political parties" (Hitler 1941, 534). To exemplify his charges, he points to a recent happening in Hungary where the new government under Vice Admiral Miklós Horthy was taking harsh measures ("White Terror") in retaliation to what occurred under Communist revolutionary Béla Kun and his "Jewish Mafia" ("Red Terror"):

> If the Hungarian government hangs ten Jewish stock exchange profiteers, whose money is sticky with the blood and the sweat of hundreds of thousands of honest people, we protest, we cry about pogroms and we demand the boycott of an entire state. In this way one has made fools of our people. (Hitler 1941, 535.)

Hitler proclaims that while the German people's attention is directed toward such events, "Germany's merciless oppressors" were tearing the country apart. He denounces the present republican form of government and the men behind it for the deteriorating state of the nation. He then states that the National Socialist Party is the "only" true anti-republican movement, and the nation needs to follow its "iron-like" principles.

After giving a hint of the infighting within the movement, he calls on those who are opposed to republican principles to attend the meeting as a show of support for his ideas—"To harden the principles of the movement from which alone we hope for the resurrection of the German people" (Hitler 1941, 536). The poster unabashedly announced: "Entry 1 Mark. War invalids free. Jews not admitted" (Jäckel 1981, 309–12).

Hitler knew that if his poster attracted a large enough audience his position would be greatly enhanced. On the other hand, if he failed to attract a large crowd he would look like a fool and his chances of ousting Drexler and his circle from their leading positions would never succeed. Calling such a meeting was a great gamble.

Hitler however, possessed the gambler's instinct to know when to play his hand. He had not given a speech in front of a mass audience in Munich for over two months—last major speech in Munich was before 2,000 attendees at the *Hofbräuhaus* on 24 November 1920, titled: "Versailles – Germany's Destruction"—and undoubtedly knew that thousands of admirers, and opponents, wished to know what he had to say.

Party members were shocked at Hitler's audacity and knew that the action could set the party back by years if the gamble failed. Two thousand people jammed into the *Hofbräuhaus*, or three thousand in the *Münchner Kindl-Keller* gave an image of a huge crowd. But, in the *Zirkus Krone* they would seem insignificant, and the party might lose its credibility. Party members, as well as Hitler, also worried that the Order Troops, which consisted of no more than 250 men at this time, would not be able to protect such a large hall. (Even as late as the summer of 1922, there were only around 400 *SA* men [Jäckel 1981, 168].) By evening, nevertheless, some of the posters were already going up around town and Hitler was confident that his posters would bring success.

The poster headlines proclaimed that "with diabolic cunning" the Allies had perpetrated a "swindle of honesty" on the German people and now, after two years, were going to "rape" them. "We, to, are human beings and not dogs," proclaimed another headline, "there is no place for negotiations." Hitler then invited all Germans—"manual and white-collar workers, laborers and students, officials and employees"—to attend his meeting so as to show German politicians that if they agree to the Allied terms, they would lose their jobs. For "1 Mark," the poster proclaimed, those that attended would hear "*Herr* Adolf Hitler" speak on "FUTURE [PROSPECTS] OR RUIN" (Hitler 1941, 519, 521–3).

By the next morning Hitler's optimism had waned. Bad weather had moved into Munich and Hitler worried "whether under such circumstance many people would not prefer to stay at home instead of going to a meeting in rain and sleet where it was possible that assault and murder would take place" (Hitler 1941, 740). Determined not to be "disgraced in the eyes of the Workers' Community" (Hitler 1941, 740), Hitler decided to adopt a few more tactics used by the Marxists.

Hitler hurriedly dictated some leaflets and had about 20,000 printed. He then rented two trucks and had them draped in as much red material as possible. The party possessed about fifteen large swastika flags at this time and Hitler had them mounted on the two trucks. That afternoon, each truck was loaded with fifteen to twenty men who were given instructions to drive through the streets, shouting slogans and catchwords while throwing the leaflets from the trucks. "It was the first time that flag-adorned trucks on which no Marxists were found, where driven through the streets of town," Hitler would later write. The upper classes "gaped" at the trucks, Hitler stated, while the Marxists raised their fists in anger as though they were "the sole owners of this monopoly" (Hitler 1941, 741).

Hitler knew that his daring tactics would outrage the Communists and become the talk of the town within hours. With enough public attention, a sufficient number of people might be persuaded to attend his meeting. Even with the bad weather, the one thing Hitler had going for him was that all of Munich's trolleys stopped at the *Hauptbahnhof* (central railway station) and the *Zirkus Krone* was only three blocks up *Mars Straße*.

For most of the day Hitler sat nervously at party headquarters. Starting around seven in the evening he was kept informed, by telephone every ten minutes, as to what kind of a crowd was entering the *Zirkus Krone*.

At 7:45 p.m., he left party headquarters and was driven to the *Zirkus Krone*. By the time the meeting started at 9 p.m., over 6,000 people had paid a Mark to hear him speak. He would later write:

> Two minutes past eight, I arrived in front of the circus. . . . Upon entering the enormous hall I was seized with the same joy as a year previously on the occasion of the first meeting in the Munich Hofbrauhaus. But only after I had pushed my way through the walls of people and had reached the high stage, I saw the success in all its greatness. Like a gigantic shell the hall lay before my eyes, filled with thousands and thousands of people. Even the arena was black with crowds. More than five thousand six hundred tickets had been issued, and if one included the entire number of unemployed, of poor students and our supervising troops, about six and a half thousand people may have been present. (Hitler 1941, 741–2.)

The meeting got underway and Drexler introduced Hitler to the audience. Within minutes Hitler began to establish a "connection" between his listeners and himself. Any possibility of Red violence was also quickly put to rest. Hitler observed that in an enormous coliseum it "was actually easier to overpower a group of disturbers than was the case in tightly crowded halls" (Hitler 1941, 740). Within a half-hour of beginning his speech, Hitler had the absolute attention of the audience.

Many of the people who attended Hitler meetings had served in the army or had loved ones who did. They were resentful of the contempt shown the veterans who fought in the war and also the path the Berlin government had embarked on. Under Democracy they had seen the values they believed in as well as their economic condition deteriorate. They had seen their country reduced from one of the greatest powers in the world to one where hunger and chaos reigned. They attended Hitler's meetings because he addressed the issues that they believed in. Other people attended out of curiosity, concern, or because they saw the beginning of a new political force. Whatever their reasons, most people came under the spell of Hitler's oratorical gifts and encouraged others to attend.

By the time Hitler left the platform in the *Zirkus Krone*, he had everyone agreeing with everything he said (Hanfstaengl 1957, 72). Police reports from the time are riddled with "long raging cheers" and "thunderous applause." Onlookers reported "enthusiastic applause," and "frenzied cheering, hand clapping." Educated at Harvard, aristocratic, and from a rich German American family of art dealers, Ernst Hanfstaengl came away "really impressed beyond measure" (Hanfstaengl 1957, 37). Otto Straßer noted that Hitler liberates "the mass unconscious, expressing its innermost aspirations, telling it what it most wants to hear" (Hanser 1971, 236).

Critics also fell under Hitler's spell and described his speeches as "intoxicating" and "overwhelming." Even those who hated him were captivated. American war correspondent William Shirer wrote in his diary: "Hitler's voice 'sounds' tremendously sincere and convincing." Konrad Heiden (whose mother was Jewish) stated: "In this unlikely looking creature . . . there dwelt a miracle: his voice" (Hanser 1971, 236). Heiden heard Hitler speak many times and wrote:

> This miserable human nothing could think only in public terms, feel only the feelings of the mass, and when the nothing spoke with the people, it was as though the voice of the people were speaking. . . . One scarcely need ask with what arts he conquered the masses; he did not conquer them, he portrayed and represented them. His speeches are day-dreams of this mass soul; they are chaotic, full of contradictions, if their words are taken literally, often senseless, as dreams are, and yet charged with deeper meaning.
>
> Vulgar vilification, flat jokes alternate with ringing, sometimes exalted, phrases. The speeches began always with deep pessimism and end in overjoyed redemption, a triumphant happy ending; often they can be refuted by reason, but they follow the far mightier logic of the subconscious, which no refutation can touch. (Heiden 1944, 106.)

Hitler's speeches often still had their lingering affect long after Hitler had left the platform. The audience would file out of the meeting halls and carry the emotion with them into the streets. Columns would form and march through Munich singing patriotic songs.

Before the meeting ended on 3 February 1921 in the *Zirkus Krone*, Hitler viciously attacked the Berlin government. He accused the politicians, "those swindlers and time-servers" (Payne 1973, 169), of allowing Germany to be exploited by "Jewish-Allied interest."

The huge success of the meeting launched Hitler into the limelight. The party had truly broken the bonds of an insignificant group and as Hitler later wrote: "We could no longer be ignored" (Hitler 1942, 278; Hitler 1971, 501).

Hitler now began holding meetings in Munich about every five days. Whether at the *Hofbräuhaus*, the *Münchner Kindl-Keller*, or the *Zirkus Krone*, the place was usually packed. Hitler also began holding meetings at the *Bürgerbräukeller* on *Rosenheimer Straße*, "an eminently respectable beer hall much frequented by a better class of people" (Hanfstaengl 1957, 100).

On Sunday, 6 March 1921 at 10 a.m., Hitler held another meeting at the *Zirkus Krone*. Four thousand people paid a Mark to hear his speech, titled: "London and Us." The speech was a rejection of the Western powers' dictation of terms to Germany. He dismissed contemptuously the accusation of German war guilt by pointing out that "nobody today wants to know that England conducted 43 wars in order to subject three-quarters of the world." He accused England of hypocrisy for proclaiming a people's right of self-determination while, on the other hand, she "is swinging the hunger whip over 250 million Indians." He warned against "the enslaving of the world by international speculative money." The Allied demands and terms should have been "resisted to the last" by Germany, and the government should never have promised to pay reparations; "it should have asked the German people through a referendum" (Jäckel 1981, 329–37).

On 8 March 1921, the French ignited the flames of Nationalism throughout Germany. Still looking for an excuse to fulfill their prewar dreams, the French Army began the occupation of three northern German cities east of the Rhine (Düsseldorf, Duisburg, and Ruhrort). The action was made under the guise that Germany had failed to deliver reparations payments but was in reality a preliminary move to occupy Germany's industrial heartland, the Ruhr—ultimately, executed by French and Belgian forces on 11 January 1923. Even in Bavaria, which by now was at serious odds with northern Germany, Hitler was still able to draw 5,000 paying men and women into Munich's *Hofbräuhaus* to protest France's "breach of the Peace Treaty" and the "NATIONAL CRIMINALS" who were selling out Germany "in doglike submissiveness" (Hitler 1941, 528).

On 13 March 1921, Hitler attacked the Minister for Reconstruction, Walther Rathenau, in an article published by the *Völkischer Beobachter*. He exploited Rathenau's Jewish origin for a full-scale attack against the Jews: "One has to prevent the Jewish subversion of our people, if necessary by putting its instigators in concentration camps." This is the first mention of imprisoning Jews in concentration camps as part of his intended "cleansing" of the German people (Jäckel 1981, 341–8).

On 8 April 1921, Hitler was able to pack the *Hofbräuhaus* for an *NSDAP* meeting (5,000 capacity), and "educate," as he saw it, his "fellow citizens" as to how they were being robbed of their "freedom." In his speech, he accurately predicted that the Allies would ignore the Treaty and the coal producing areas of Upper Silesia would be lost to Germany. "GERMANY AWAKE," proclaimed his poster (Jäckel 1981, 529).

For the next four weeks, Hitler turned his attention to attracting the "thinking" Red worker. His posters, advertising upcoming meetings, proclaimed that the worker's dream of a "dictatorship of the proletariat" had been supplanted by a "Capitalist constitution." He blamed the Jews in power in Berlin for the "fraud" and asked the workers to "recognize the Jewish Democratic swindle." Still determined to drive a wedge between the Marxist leaders and the workers, his poster proclaimed that "a workers movement has to keep itself free from Jews and Capitalists," His posters stated that only the "National Socialist movement of Greater Germany" could give the workers what they wanted.

At the end of the April 1921, the Allies fanned the flames of German Nationalism again. The long-awaited plebiscite in Upper Silesia was held with the majority in favor of remaining with Germany. The British and French governments could not reach a consensus on the interpretation of the plebiscite. The primary problem was the disposition of the "Industrial Triangle" east of the Oder River, whose corners was defined by the cities of Beuthen (Bytom), Gleiwitz (Gliwice) and Kattowitz (Katowice), all three of which were mostly inhabited by ethnic Germans. The French wanted to weaken Germany, and thus supported Polish claims on the territory; the British and the Italians disagreed, in part because the German government declared that a loss of the Silesian industries would render Germany incapable of paying the demanded war reparations. The Allies appointed their own "Commission" which began looking for loopholes to deny Germany as much as possible.

In late April 1921, rumors spread that the British position would prevail. This caused the local Polish activists to organize a third uprising (first: 16–26 August 1919; second: 19–25 August 1920). Having learned from previous failures, the Third Uprising was carefully planned and organized under the leadership of Polish *Reichstag* member Wojciech Korfanty. It started on 2 May 1921 with the destruction of German rail bridges in order to slow the movement of German reinforcements. A particular concern was to prevent a recurrence of violent acts against Polish civilians by members of the *Freikorps* that had refused to disband.

The new Weimar Republic was saddled with a massive war debt that it could not afford. That was worsened by the fact that it was printing money without economic resources to back it. The Treaty of Versailles, with its demand for reparations, further accelerated the decline in the value of the *papiermark*, so that 48 *papiermarks* were required to buy a U.S. dollar by late 1919. By the first half of 1921, German currency had recovered and relatively stabilized at about 90 *papiermarks* per dollar. Because the Western Front was mostly in France and Belgium, Germany came out of the war with most of its industrial infrastructure intact. It was in a better position to become the dominant economic force on the European continent.

In April 1921, the Reparations Commission announced the "London payment plan,"[3] under which Germany would pay reparations in gold or foreign currency in annual installments of 2 billion gold marks, plus twenty-six percent of the value of Germany's exports; this was accepted by Germany after an Allied ultimatum the following month.

On 3 May 1921, in a speech before an *NSDAP* audience delivered in the *Hofbräuhaus*, Hitler demanded that Matthias Erzberger, the former *Reich* Minister in charge of Armistice Negotiations and Finance, should be arrested if he enters Bavaria. "If the Bavarian Government is unable to do it," he exclaims, "we will do it ourselves!" Conservative patriots regarded Erzberger as Germany's chief villain for signing the armistice with the Allies, and for his acceptance of the Treaty of Versailles. He was assassinated later that year, on 26 August, by members of the former *Freikorps Marinebrigade Ehrhardt* under a new name "Organization Consul" (Maser 1965, 288).

Hitler also appealed to the German "youth," especially students, and welcomed them to his meetings. On 6 May 1921, 4,800 people attended one of the meetings at the *Hofbräuhaus* (Hitler 1941, 530–2).

By now the military, paramilitary, and the lower middle classes in Bavaria looked upon Hitler with favor. He was also beginning to make noticeable inroads among the workers. As he proved himself increasingly successful, the government in Munich felt it could no longer ignore him. Rudolf Heß, whose Bavarian family was known to Bavarian Minister-President Gustav Ritter von Kahr, established the important connection. On

14 May 1921, shortly after Hitler's thirty-second birthday, Hitler expresses his fury in *Völkischer Beobachter* at the unconditional acceptance of the Allied ultimatum on reparations (5 May) by the German government. On the same day, Bavarian Minister-President von Kahr received Heß, Drexler, and Hitler. Although von Kahr was not particularly impressed with the "Austrian," he felt Hitler could be used as a propagandist in Bavaria's struggle with the Weimar regime. The reception gave notice that Hitler was becoming a respectable political force.

Hitler began receiving support from the police president and the head of the department's Political Division. They did what they could to suppress complaints against the party and promote its expansion. "We did do that," a spokesperson would later testify, "because we were convinced from the start that this movement was the one most likely to take root among the workers infected with the Marxist plague and win them back into the nationalist camp. That is why we held our protecting hands over the National Socialist Party and *Herr* Hitler" (Toland 1976, 115–16).

With his sudden jump up the social ladder, more important doors began to open to Hitler, and he began to move among circles far more influential than any that the old party committee members provided. There were many among the upper crust however, who were repulsed by Hitler. They sneered at his place of residence, his clothing, his vocabulary, and his background. From the beginning, Hitler was aware what the upper crust thought of him, and he had nothing but "contempt" for them (Hitler 1961, 126). He knew that from their point of view he lacked those "outward qualifications" of formal education and family background which mean so much to them (Hitler 1961, 155). He scorned their pretentious ways and phony airs and stated: "Hasn't everyone in this land sprung from the peasantry" (Picker 1976, 97).

In order to compensate for Hitler's background, Heß wrote a letter to von Kahr shortly after their reception in an attempt to enhance Hitler's position and background. In part he wrote:

> The central point is that [Hitler] is convinced that a recovery is possible only if it proves possible to lead the masses, particularly the workers, back to the nationalist cause. . . . I know Herr Hitler very well personally and am quite close to him. He has a rarely honorable, pure character, full of profound kindness, is religious, a good Catholic. His one

> goal is the welfare of his country. For this he is sacrificing himself in the most selfless fashion. (Fest 1974, 139.)

Heß then gave an account of Hitler's war record and stated: "Your Excellency can unconditionally trust Hitler" (Flood 1989, 190).

Heß was stretching things when he referred to Hitler as a good Catholic. Hitler privately criticized the church (especially the Jesuits) and the Pope more than he praised them. However, he openly scorned the Bavarian separatist movement (with its religious overtones), which undoubtedly appealed to von Kahr. Shortly thereafter, von Kahr mentioned Hitler "in terms of praise" in the Bavarian congress (Fest 1974, 139).

The praise bestowed upon Hitler had the effect of opening a few more heavy doors, but Hitler hated the idea of having to put himself in a subordinate position when dealing with the *bourgeoisie* (Hanfstaengl 1957, 43–4). He knew that their main objective was to use him, and the thought embittered him (Schramm 1971, 41 fn). "The elite," Hitler would later groan, "whatever they do is a result of calculation. Some of them see me as an attraction to their drawing-rooms, others seek various advantages" (Hitler 1961, 224). He nevertheless was learning what any aspiring politician in a Republic must accept—hobnobbing with members of the upper crust, however regretful, is the only way to power—no successful revolution has ever occurred strictly from the bottom up. Hitler would later excuse his association with such people by stating: "The bourgeois with whom we flirted at the time of our struggle were simply aesthetes" (Hitler 1961, 127).

On 29 May 1921, three articles by Hitler appeared in the *Völkischer Beobachter* attacking Weimar President Ebert and the acceptance of the plebiscite in Upper Silesia.

On 31 May, Hitler speaks on "Versailles and the German Worker" in the *Hofbräuhaus*. For the first time he makes public his solution to the dilemma of the German geopolitical position in Central Europe. He rejects the four previous attempts as failures (birth control, overseas colonization, emigration, industrial exports) and argues that the only way to solve the perennial disproportion between the growing population and the diminishing land supply is through acquisition of territories in the East at the expense of Russia. Hitler skillfully contrasts the humiliating terms of the Versailles Treaty with the allegedly fair conditions stipulated by Germany in the Brest–Litovsk Peace Treaty of 1918, which would have secured enough nourishment for Germany's population through the acquisition of land and soil, enough work for the country's industry and trade through the imports of raw materials and provided the foundation for friendly relations with Russia (Hauner 2008, 29).

By the Summer of 1921, Hitler had turned the *NSDAP* into a fairly respectable Nationalist force. Since he was the driving force behind the party, he ran it as he pleased. The six members of the Executive Committee, including Drexler, were resentful. Thrust into the background, they became dissatisfied with the direction the party was going. They knew that Hitler was intent on embarking on a more radical revolutionary course for which they had no taste. Drexler's highest ambition was a seat in congress, and, like the rest of the Committee, he wished to project the image of a mainstream Nationalist party so as to further his own ambitions. Drexler had attempted to get Hitler to listen to the Committee, but Hitler ignored them. Fearful of Hitler's strong personal following, the Committee began plotting to weaken his position.

The more Socialist-wing members of the Executive Committee in the *NSDAP* had since February 1921 commenced a series of moves against Hitler in an attempt to marginalize or completely neutralize him. They began by attacking Hitler's way of life. Moreover, two spokesmen of the German Socialist Party (*DSP*), which was to merge later with the *NSDAP*, Julius Streicher and Hans Vey from Nuremberg, reported after a visit to Munich that Hitler was seen being driven through the city "with smoking ladies" (Tyrell 1975, 40).

Hitler's legitimate position within the party was not one of strength. He had abandoned his place on the Executive Committee and the only position he held was that of Propaganda Chief. It was Hitler however, who found the party funds, who brought in new members, who wrote the party propaganda, who designed the party regalia, who brought the party its publicity, and who had a hand in every other branch of party activity. His name and the party had become inseparable. The Committee had to be careful not to overstep their limits of influence. Hitler could call for a vote of the membership, and since Germans normally voted for "lists" of candidates, Hitler and his inner circle might oust them. If the vote went against Hitler, however unlikely, he might just take his followers with him and start his own party. Whatever the outcome, the Committee knew that without Hitler, they would end up in the back rooms where they started. They consequently did not have the courage to attempt to get rid of Hitler but were intent on using him to further their ambitions.

To assure their positions and recapture the direction of a much-enhanced party, the Committee had offered Hitler the position of "First

Chairman," but with Drexler as "coadjutor in the executive committee" (Fest 1974, 148). Hitler knew that the old Democratic principle of six against one would prevail and ignored the offer. Undaunted, the Committee embarked on another scheme.

Since Hitler's association with Ludendorff, negotiations aimed at consolidation had been going on between the party and other Nationalist organizations. Hitler insisted that the other groups dissolve and/or their members join his party on an individual basis. Outside of Munich a few small groups had been induced to abandon their party platforms and, like Straßer, become locals of Hitler's National Socialists. With its acquisition of individuals and groups, the party had acquired certain "officers and men of academic education," the "so-called fine people" of the movement, who secretly despised Hitler "for his lack of higher education" (Heiden 1944, 253) and background. They began conspiring with the Committee members to attempt a merger with a rival Nationalist group. A merger, they felt, would curb Hitler's freedom of action (Bullock 1961, 49), while still giving them the advantage of using him for their own purposes. The Committee, consequently, began talks with the German Socialist Party (*DSP*).

The *DSP* had been founded in northern Germany shortly after the war and was larger than Hitler's Party which confined its activities primarily to Bavaria. The German Socialists had thirty-five locals throughout Germany, including one in Munich (Flood 1989, 164). Because the ideas and goals of the German Socialist leaders were similar to Hitler's, the Committee, and the "quality people" associated with them, were ecstatic over the possibilities. If a merger was concluded, the main office of the combined group would shortly be shifted to Berlin. All of the locals, along with the Munich group, would be answerable to Berlin. Hitler, the undisputed best speaker, would most likely be kicked upstairs to become a main speaker for the combined party. The Committee members in Munich would then recapture their prominent positions. Certain that Hitler would not pass up the chance to find a nationwide audience, the Committee notified him of their plan.

Hitler was not enthusiastic and saw through their manipulations. A merger called for concessions which would threaten his platform and also jeopardize his fragile leadership role. He knew that with a merger the "western," as he called it, Democratic concept of debate and compromise would prevail. He would also have to fight his way up the ranks of an already established pecking order in an attempt to find a place at the top. He had the perception to know that the academic and "quality people" within the combined movement would never let him enter the higher ranks. Like the great "rabble rousers" of the French and American revolutions (who were used so successfully and then quickly forgotten), Hitler knew that he would only be used to further the ambitions of "people of quality." Hitler demanded that all talks of merger be stopped. When the Committee balked, Hitler threatened to resign. The committee now faced a dilemma. If Hitler resigned and took the party faithful with him, there would be little to negotiate, and they would be right back where they started. All open discussions of mergers ceased.

This was not the first time Hitler threatened to resign from the *NSDAP* over the issue of merging with the *DSP*. On 9 December 1920, internal disputes as to whether the *NSDAP* should work in close alliance with other Nationalist parties and groups inside and outside Germany, specifically with the *Deutschsozialistische Partei* (*DSP*), lead Hitler to threaten resignation. Opposing such an alliance forcefully, he writes to the party chairman, Anton Drexler: "I declare herewith in writing once and for all my withdrawal from the Party Committee . . . and from 15 December my resignation from the Press Committee." However, Hitler offered to remain at the disposal of the party as a speaker, without fees, "as long as I can manage to pay for my expenses incurred on trips outside" (Jäckel 1981, 277).

In early June 1921, Hitler left Munich on an extended fund-raising trip to Berlin. The anti-Hitler faction in the *NSDAP* and *DSP* saw their chance to cut the "would-be big shot," as they saw it, down to size (Fest 1974, 147).

In the previous year, the party had established a local in Augsburg, a town 35 miles northwest of Munich. Some of the "fine" members of the Augsburg local were critical of Hitler and were determined to curb his influence. Working with the Committee in Munich, they resumed negotiations with the *DSP*, but this time in secret. The Committee, headed by Drexler (who was "weak and uncertain" according to Hitler) (Hitler 1941, 493), empowered the Augsburg local to hold the negotiations on behalf of the party (Flood 1989, 199). If the merger could be completed during Hitler's absence, he would almost certainly be forced into the position where his enemies wanted him. By the second week of July 1921, negotiations were well under way.

In Berlin, in the meantime, Hitler was spending his time taking advanced lessons in public speaking, establishing ties with other Nationalist groups, and raising money. While in Berlin, Hitler was also introduced to the anti-Communist Count Peter Yorck von Wartenburg—executed by

Hitler on 8 August 1944 for his role in Operation Valkyrie—who offered Hitler financial support if he would move his party headquarters to Berlin (Whetton 2004, 26). Hitler, well aware that most of his support was in the south and equally aware of the competition in the north from the Straßer brothers (Gregor [1892–1934] and Otto [1897–1974]), declined the offer. Hitler also met Dr. Emil Gansser, a former employee of the industrial giant *Siemens und Halske* (Whetton 2004, 26). Gansser, who moved in wealthy, conservative Protestant circles and would later play an important part in Hitler's finances, took Hitler to speak at Berlin's National Club. Hitler addressed the prestigious National Club of industrial figures and upper-class landowners (*Junkers*) where he insincerely tossed about the possibility of transferring his party headquarters to Berlin. Hitler, however, did all the talking and the *Junkers*, "who had expected to do all the talking," were forced into the demeaning position of having to listen. The meeting led to nothing (Hitler 1941, footnote at 483). It was through Gansser that Hitler met Admiral Schröder, former commander of the German marines, who was one of the first high-ranking officers to join the *NSDAP*. Schröder is known to have channeled funds from the Navy via J. F. Lehmann—a publisher with close links to the Navy and to the *Thule-Gesellschaft*—to Hitler and the *NSDAP* (Whetton 2004, 26).

Someone in Hitler's inner circle found out about the negotiations in Augsburg and tipped Hitler off. Smelling a rat, Hitler hurried back to Bavaria. He went straight to Augsburg on 10 July and descended on the hall where the negotiations were taking place. He found leading representatives of the *DSP* and his party's Augsburg delegation discussing a prearranged plan which had been worked out in detail (Flood 1989, 199). By now the German Socialists were negotiating from strength and their aim was no longer a merger but a complete takeover of Hitler's party (Bracher 1971, 94). Their plan basically called for the same conditions that Hitler expected from groups which joined his party. Hitler's National Socialist program as well as the party name was to be abandoned and all members and locals were to accept the name and program of the German Socialists.

After arguing for hours against the proposed plan, Hitler found that the "official representatives of the Party who were present not only did not support me, but on the contrary continued the negotiations." Unable to accomplish anything in Augsburg, Hitler departed for Munich.

Hitler arrived home the next day on 11 July 1921 and immediately confronted the Committee which, during his absence, had gained some self-assurance. They not only refused to listen to Hitler but called on him to justify his single-minded past actions (Fest 1974, 148). Confronted by six incompetents—who, if not for him, would still be toting their treasury around in a cigar box—Hitler promptly resigned from the party.

Because Hitler was capable of taking most of the party members with him, the Committee lost its negotiating strength and the talks with the German Socialists stalled. Worried that they might lose everything, the Committee quickly lost their new-found self-assurance and sent an emissary to find out what Hitler's conditions were for returning to the party.

Three days later, in a lengthy written statement, Hitler accused the Committee of a lack of leadership and summarized his conditions. He demanded the immediate resignation of the Committee from their positions and the expulsion of all "foreign elements," especially the Augsburg group from the Party (Bracher 1971, 91). He insisted that any talk of altering the party program be stopped, and anyone supporting such a measure in the future be purged from the party. "Concessions on our part," Hitler wrote, "are totally out of the question" (Fest 1974, 148; Flood 1989, 200). He demanded that there be no more talk of mergers in the future but only "annexations" of other groups.

The main point of Hitler's letter, however, was a "demand" for complete power. He insisted on the sole right to make all future decisions and appointments within the party and without mincing words wrote: "I demand the position of First Chairman with dictatorial authority" (Flood 1989, 200).

"I make these demands," Hitler wrote, "not because I am power hungry, but because recent events have more than convinced me that without an iron leadership, the party . . . will within a short time cease to be what it was supposed to be—a National Socialist German Workers Party and not a western association" (Toland 1976, 116). He therefore called for a special meeting of all party members where a majority vote would give him the powers he wanted. Hitler gave the Committee eight days (until 22 July) to respond to his demands (Whetton 2004, 26).

The Committee, fearful of being ousted and replaced by Hitler's inner circle, refused to call a special meeting. Instead, the very next day they wrote Hitler an intentionally submissive letter which was leaked to the general membership. Their hope was to turn the general membership against Hitler by making themselves look rational and giving. In part the letter read: "The committee is prepared—in acknowledgment of your tremendous knowledge, your singular dedication, and selfless service to the Movement, and your rare oratorical gift—to concede to you dictatorial powers, and will be most delighted if after your reentry you will take over the position of First Chairman, which Drexler long ago and repeatedly offered you" (Fest 1974, 148). The letter then goes on to make it appear that Hitler wanted to purge Drexler, the founder of the party, from the movement and continues: "If you should consider it desirable to have him [Drexler] completely excluded from the Movement, the next annual meeting would have to be consulted on that matter" (Flood 1989, 201).

The Committee's answer to Hitler was little more than an attempt to make him appear unreasonable, power hungry, and irrational. About the only thing the Committee was really sincere about was not calling up a special meeting. The "annual meeting" was not to be held for six months. The Committee's only goal was an attempt to silence Hitler so they could conclude the stalled merger.

The Committee persuaded Dietrich Eckart, Hitler's closest friend, to act as moderator (Payne 1973, 158) but Hitler would not compromise. He had made up his mind to take the party in a direction that the Committee and the fine people in the movement would never understand, yet alone approve. Hitler knew that men like Drexler and his circle lacked the temperament and courage to embark on a new course. Hitler accurately saw that millions of Germans, Conservatives and Liberals, were becoming disillusioned with the "bourgeois-romantic sectarian groups" with their Western styled "pseudo-democratic" organizations (Bracher 1971, 91). He was determined to "cash in on the trend of the times toward a 'strong man'" who could reshape the "shattered postwar world by a 'dictatorship of order'" (Bracher 1971, 91).

Hitler's thinking (which would later be more concretely exposed in *Mein Kampf*) was dominated by the class theme again. He believed that most "ordinary people" could be productive and law-abiding citizens. But, the intellectuals and other malcontents, for their own gains, were leading the people into "decadence, idleness, and selfishness." He also knew that the interest of the working class was not that of the upper class and he sought to curb "upper-class government." To achieve that goal, he was determined to unite the working masses and the lower middle class (which together could check the power of "quality people").

The common thread that drew the masses and the lower middle class together was their service in the trenches. Hitler knew these men were looking for a leader to point them in the right direction. He knew that Drexler and his circle were unable to understand the passions of the war veterans and even looked on him as a "stranger" (Hitler 1942, 202). Drexler, Hitler felt, had never been a soldier, "even during the war," and like the other founders of the party, lacked the necessary qualities, as he wrote, "to stir up an ardent and indomitable faith in the ultimate triumph of the movement and to brush aside, with obstinate force and if necessary with brutal ruthlessness, all obstacles that stood in the path of the new idea. Such a task could be carried out only by men who had been trained, body and soul, in those military virtues which make a man, so to speak, agile as a greyhound, tough as leather, and hard as Krupp steel." On the other hand, Hitler wrote of himself: "Physically and mentally I had the polish of six years of service. . . . I had forgotten such phrases as: 'That will not go,' or 'That is not possible,' or 'We ought not to take such a risk; it is too dangerous'" (Hitler 1942, 202).

By 16 July 1921, Hitler was pressing hard for the special meeting of the membership to address his demands, but the Committee kept stalling. It soon became apparent why. Thousands of leaflets were circulated about Munich attacking Hitler (Hanser 1971, 274). The leaflet, titled "Adolf Hitler—Traitor?" was drafted and printed by radical Socialist members of the Executive Committee and later published in a special edition of the Socialist *Münchener Post* on 3 August 1921 (Whetton 2004, 26). The leaflet, a concoction of fact and fancy (Toland 1976, 117), was clearly an attempt to turn rank-and-file party membership against Hitler.

The leaflet defended the Executive Committee and accused Hitler of using the party "as a springboard for his own immoral purposes" (Bullock 1961, 49). It stated that when questioned about his background, Hitler "became agitated and flew into a rage" (Fest 1974, 149). It accused him of being a secret supporter of the monarchy. It claimed that he associated with "criminal elements"—namely Hermann Esser (Payne 1973, 159). It implied that he was embezzling party funds to spend on his "excessive relations with ladies." It claimed that when it came to women, Hitler referred to himself as the "King of Munich" (Hanser 1971, 274).

The leaflet also accused Hitler of "personal ambition and a lust for power" who was "relying only on his gift as a speaker" (Hanser 1971, 274). Hitler, the leaflet charged, "believes the time has come to introduce disunity and dissension into our ranks at the behest of his shady backers . . . and thus to promote the interest of Jewry and its henchmen. . . . And how is he conducting this struggle? Like a real Jew" (Maser 1973, 9–10).

The insinuation that Hitler might be working for the Jews, or even be Jewish, was the standard practice of moderate and conservative elements, including the "fine ones," for casting doubt on their rivals. It would be the first time, of many, that Hitler's political enemies would use the big lie in an attempt to discredit him. That Hitler's enemies could make such statements was because Hitler's attacks against the Jews, at the time, were not extraordinary. He held most of the traditional anti-Semitic ideas and conceptions of the German and Austrian Pan-Germans, and other European Nationalists. Hitler, however, knew that a movement could not be built on racial issues alone and his anti-Jewish rhetoric ebbed and flowed in relation to current events. As an example, when anti-Jewish sentiment reached a peak after the publication of the *Protocols*, Hitler hopped on the bandwagon; but, once the *Protocols* were exposed as a hoax (even though he refused to believe it), he concentrated for the most part, on attacks against "the Jewish millionaire" (Hitler 1941, 530) and "Jewish international stock exchange capital" (Hitler 1941, 527). Such a theme found a ready audience throughout Europe and was used by a wide range of political thinkers—even Jewish Marxists (Socialists and Communists) sought the destruction of "Jewish millionaires" and "capital." Attacks against rich Jews did not automatically eliminate one from being accused of being a tool of the Jews, or a Jew. (So-called "anti-Semitic Jews," labeled even by Jews, had been around for decades.) The fact that Hitler was pursuing a revolutionary course and beginning to go after the masses added validity to the charge. The leaflet was the first in a series of rumors (that persisted throughout the 1920s and into the 1930s) that Hitler was a Jew and/or Communist working for the Jews.

The rumor of "Hitler's Jewish descent" quickly spread though Munich that July (Maser 1973, 10). Hitler was outraged over his betrayal. Over the next few days in the latter half of July 1921, Hitler pressed the Committee hard to call a special meeting where his demands would be met. Because of the rumors started by the pamphlet, he also demanded a public apology from the anti-Hitler faction. When the Committee balked, Hitler himself called for a meeting of the membership.

Drexler, sensing that his days were numbered, went to the Munich police to complain that Hitler had no right to call such a meeting. In attempting to gain sympathy he pointed out that he and his circle were attempting to carry out party aims by "legal, parliamentary procedures," while Hitler and his circle were "aiming at revolution and violence" (Fest 1974, 149). The police refused to get involved since it was an inner party matter. Knowing that Hitler's request for "papal" powers would probably be accepted by the rank and file, Drexler began to weaken. Over the next few days negotiations were carried out and little by little Drexler and the rest of the anti-Hitler faction caved in (Taylor 1983, 65).

During the afternoon of Friday, 29 July 1921, the special meeting finally took place in the hall at the *Sterneckerbräu* above the party office

(Flood 1989, 202). Since Friday was a working day, only 544 party members were present, but Hitler was greeted with applause that would not stop (Fest 1974, 149). Hitler's version of the party infighting was so masterful he swung nearly everyone over to his side. He then stated his goals which included the annexation of other parties and not their destruction. His most poignant statement left little doubt as to what he intended to accomplish: "We will proceed ruthlessly. The salvation of Germany can be brought about only by Germans, not by parliament, but by revolution" (Flood 1989, 203).

When the vote was taken, 543 members voted to give Hitler dictatorial powers. Only one person (a librarian) voted against him. Few parties ever gave its leader the powers that the Nazi Party gave Adolf Hitler in the summer of 1921, and they would continue to elect him every year (as original party statutes specified) until he became absolute ruler of all Germany (Dietrich 1955, 129). Drexler was kicked upstairs to become "honorary chairman for life" and Hitler's inner circle took over all major posts. As in the church Hitler had attended as a boy, a "party papacy" began to take shape (Bracher 1971, 94).

On the evening of 29 July 1921, another mass meeting was held at the *Zirkus Krone*. For the first time ever, Hitler was introduced by Hermann Esser as "*unser Führer*" (Fest 1974, 149). Max Amann, who served with Hitler in the same *List Regiment*, could not recognize him in his new role as a political leader. He testified in 1947 in Nuremberg that Hitler appeared as if "seized by a strange fire . . . he shouted . . . water was dripping down his body, he was completely wet . . . it was unbelievable" (Joachimsthaler 1989, 253). Hitler knew he made himself indispensable to the Nazi Movement by attracting larger crowds than any other speaker (Kershaw 1998, 149). The next day Hitler wrote a letter to one of his acquaintances and for the first time, confidently signing it "*der Führer*."

Despite growing inflation and unemployment in Germany, a reparations payment was made to the Allies in June 1921. It marked the beginning of an increasingly rapid devaluation of the *papiermark*, which fell in value to approximately 330 *papiermarks* per U.S. dollar. Since reparations were required to be repaid in hard currency, not the rapidly depreciating *papiermark*, one strategy that Germany's *Reichsbank* used was the mass printing of bank notes to buy foreign currency, which was then used to pay reparations. That greatly exacerbated the inflation of the *papiermark*.

From August 1921, Germany began to buy foreign currency with *papiermarks* at any price, but that only increased the speed of devaluation of the *papiermark*. As the *papiermark* sank in international markets, more and more *papiermarks* were required to buy the foreign currency that was demanded by the Reparations Commission.

In the first half of 1922, the *papiermark* stabilized at about 320 *papiermarks* per U.S. dollar. International reparations conferences were being held. One, in June 1922, was organized by U.S. investment banker J. P. Morgan, Jr. The meetings produced no workable solution, and inflation in Germany erupted into hyperinflation, the *papiermark* falling to 7,400 *papiermarks* per U.S. dollar by December 1922. The cost-of-living index was 41 in June 1922 and 685 in December, a fifteen-fold increase.

By fall 1922, Germany found itself unable to make reparations payments. The *papiermark* was by now practically worthless, making it impossible for Germany to buy foreign exchange or gold using *papiermarks*. Instead, reparations were to be paid in goods such as coal. On 11 January 1923, French and Belgian troops occupied the industrial region of Germany in the Ruhr valley to ensure reparations payments. Inflation was exacerbated when workers in the Ruhr went on a general strike and the German government printed more money to continue paying for their passive resistance. By November 1923, the U.S. dollar was worth 4.2 billion *papiermarks*. Hyperinflation caused considerable internal political instability in the country, the occupation of the Ruhr by France and Belgium, as well as misery for the general German populace.

Over the ensuing months of the latter half of 1921 and throughout 1922 and most of 1923, Hitler tirelessly delivers speech after speech to a growing audience with a crescendo call to revolt against the Weimar government. During this time, he also manages to marginalize his Nationalist political opponents and competitors while building a small army of militant enforcers called the *Sturmabteilung* (*SA*) and *Kampfbund*.

The following is a chronologic list of important events exhibiting Hitler's incredible indefatigability and how he and the *NSDAP* consolidated power leading up to the Beer Hall *Putsch*. This list of events was taken from German-Czech historian Professor Milan Hauner's book, titled: *Hitler: A Chronology of His Life and Time* (NY: Palgrave Macmillan, 2008, pages 31–45, the footnotes are his with some corrections).

On 4 August 1921, Dietrich Eckart writes a eulogy on Hitler as the nation's selfless *Führer* in the *Völkischer Beobachter*. On the same evening, Hitler speaks in *Zirkus Krone* on the subject "The Dying Soviet Russia."

On 9 August, Hitler and his closest followers interrupt a meeting of the separatist Bavarian League. In the ensuing tumult, its speaker, Otto Ballerstedt, is beaten up and Hitler taken to the police for questioning.

On 12 August, at an *NSDAP* meeting in the *Hofbräuhaus*, Hitler speaks on Germany's dire financial situation.

On 19 August, Hitler speaks at an *NSDAP* meeting in Rosenheim.

On 25 August, about 7,000 people hear Hitler speaking at an *NSDAP* rally on "Jewish Rule and the Starvation of the People."

On 3 September, Hitler speaks at an *NSDAP* meeting in Weilheim.

On 6 September, in a letter to Gustav Seifert, chairman of the local *NSDAP* branch in Hanover, Hitler gives advice on party tactics. He is against setting up new local groups without first strengthening the existing ones. Specifically, he warns against still-simmering tendencies for a merger with the *DSP*, which he calls a "fantasy creation" without much practical value. "What we need," Hitler underlines, "is to attract first strong masses from the most leftist and most rightist wings" (Tyrell 1969, 37–8).

On 8 September, at an *NSDAP* meeting in the *Hofbräuhaus*, Hitler delivers a morbid and tasteless attack on Matthias Erzberger, the former *Reich* Minister of Finance, who was murdered by Nationalist thugs belonging to *Aufbau Vereinigung*'s and *Deutschvölkischer Schutz- und Trutzbund*'s Organization Consul only two weeks earlier (26 August).

On 10 September 1921, Hitler announces the establishment of the *Sturmabteilung* (*SA*) for the protection of political meetings. The *SA* developed from the "Gymnastic and Sports Detachment" (*Turn- und Sportabteilung*), which itself was born of the *Ordnentruppen*, and was designed primarily to attract young men between the ages of 17 and 23 (Tyrell 1969, 29–31).

On 14 September, Otto Ballerstedt, leader of the separatist Bavarian League, held a meeting entitled "We Shall Not Betray Bavaria," which Hitler decides to break up. He provokes Ballerstedt, who is subsequently beaten up and thrown out of the beerhall by *SA* thugs.

On 16 September, Hitler speaks at an *NSDAP* meeting in the *Münchener Kindl-Keller* against Bavarian separatism.

On 17 September, Hitler repeated his strict order that Jews were not to be tolerated at *NSDAP* meetings. All posters must have a printed warning "Jews keep out." "We have nothing to talk about with the Jews," reiterates Hitler, "since these aliens have no right to interfere in our affairs." In the same document, Circular No. 5, Hitler underlines the importance of party insignia and prescribes in detail how the red armband with black swastika should be worn (Deuerlein 1969, 145). On the same day, Hitler also issued the party Communiqué No. 1, on the resignation of the Bavarian Minister-President von Kahr, his Minister of Justice Rohr, and the Munich Chief of

Police Pöhner, all three of them known for their sympathy with the Nazi movement. (Von Kahr resigned in protest against the emergency decree of 29 August, which Weimar President Ebert had proclaimed following the assassination of Erzberger.) In response, Hitler launched a vulgar attack on the Weimar government, accusing them of being part of a Jewish-Bolshevik conspiracy against freedom and the God-loving Bavarians. He called on his supporters to march in the streets and, if necessary, "to show your Bavarian fist to the Berlin Asians" (Franz-Willing 1962, 208–9).

On 21 September, the Munich police arrest Hitler, who is held on suspicion of wanting to turn the demonstration into a *putsch.* He is released the following day for lack of evidence.

On 24 September, Hitler issues Circular No. 6 to *NSDAP* groups reflecting the intensity of the political struggle between the Nazis and other political groups (that is, warning against spying and acts of terrorism). He also issues party Communiqué No. 2, on the political situation in the country at large and in Bavaria in particular. He describes *Reich* Chancellor Dr. Wirth as a friend of Jews and Bolsheviks and takes a stand on "the case Ballerstedt."

On 30 September, at an *NSDAP* meeting held in the *Hofbräuhaus* Hitler speaks on how Germany should oppose Bolshevism.

On 1 October, in the party Communiqué No. 3 Hitler claims that Nazi propaganda has scored a great success and that in the previous 35 days about 30,000 persons attended *NSDAP* meetings.

On 8 October, in the party Circular No. 8 and Communiqué No. 4, Hitler deals with finances, which lag behind the party's activities. He announces that the *Völkischer Beobachter* still carries a debt of 250,000 Marks, which must be balanced by an extra "press tax" of 50 pfennigs. Party members are urged to purchase special debt bonds which will be issued at the same time.

Mid-October: Hitler visits Vienna for five days.

On 21 October, before a half-filled *Zirkus Krone*, Hitler speaks on the defense of Upper Silesia and against the Berlin government.

On 22 October, Hitler announces in party Circular No. 10 that from 1 November the party will open new larger offices at 12 *Cornelius Straße.*

On 25 October, Hitler is again summoned by the Munich police for questioning in connection with the acts of violence committed by his *SA* after the mass meeting at *Zirkus Krone*.

On 26 October, "We must not get into trouble with the police," Hitler tells a group of about sixty *SA* stormtroopers in the Munich restaurant

Adelmann. "Privately, they like us because they, too, hate the Jews. We mustn't, therefore, call them Jewish servants . . . Otherwise, it might come thus far that the SA will be banned by the police. Should this happen, all our work would be in vain . . . I understand you, your blood runs faster . . . but you must restrain yourselves. A half million means nothing to the Jews if they can purchase the dissolution of the SA" (Jäckel 1981, 508).

On 4 November, Hitler's *SA* received the first baptism of fire in a beerhall battle in the *Hofbräuhaus*. "I made it clear to the lads," Hitler said later,

> that today probably for the first time they would have to show themselves loyal to the movement through thick and thin and that not a man of us must leave the hall unless we were carried out dead . . . if I should see anyone playing the coward, I myself would personally tear off his armband and take away his insignia . . . In front of me, especially to the left of me, only enemies were sitting and standing. They were all robust men and young fellows, in large part from the Maffei factory, from Kustermann's, from Isaria Meter Works . . . In a few seconds the whole hall was filled with a roaring, screaming crowd, over which, like Howitzer shells, flew innumerable beer mugs . . . It was an idiotic spectacle . . . I should have liked to see a bourgeois meeting under such circumstances . . . For twenty minutes the hellish tumult lasted, but then our enemies, who must have numbered seven or eight hundred men, had for the most part been beaten out of the hall and chased down the stairs by my men, numbering not even fifty . . . Then suddenly two shots were fired from the hall entrance towards the platform, and wild shooting started. Your heart almost rejoiced at such a revival of old war experience. (Hitler 1969, 458–61.)

On 9 November, Hitler congratulates the *SA* in the Munich restaurant *Adelmann* on their successful "baptism of fire." "Comrades! We have won a battle," he tells them. He conveys an extremely distorted picture of the recent brawl, as if the *SA* were not fighting the Munich workers but the Jews themselves, who had come to the beerhall with the sole intention of killing him (Jäckel 1981, 514).

On 11 November, Hitler speaks at an *NSDAP* meeting in the *Hofbräuhaus* on the theme "Who is Threatening the Republic?"

On 25 and 28 November, Hitler makes two statements at the Munich Police Directorate. The first is in defense against the allegations made in *Münchener Post*, which published the pamphlet entitled *Adolf Hitler—Traitor?*; the second concerns *NSDAP* leaflets that were distributed against police orders.

On 30 November, Hitler tells the *SA* in the Munich restaurant *Liebherr* that he hopes by disrupting political meetings of other parties, the *NSDAP* could expect a massive increase in membership. The party has recently been referred to as "a bunch of brutal rowdies, who do not hesitate to use any means." "This," Hitler admits, "gives me enormous pleasure, because in this manner my own intentions and my party will become at the same time popular and feared." He announces that a well-known boxing champion has just joined the *SA* and will give lessons to stormtroopers each week (Jäckel 1981, 527).

On 2 December, Hitler speaks on the subject "The Jew as People's Friend" at an *NSDAP* meeting in the *Hofbräuhaus*.

On 5 December, Hitler appears as a plaintiff-witness at the court proceedings against the *Münchener Post,* a Socialist newspaper, which he is suing for publishing the libelous pamphlet *Adolf Hitler—Traitor?* When asked about his financial position, he admits that "he receives, on a modest scale, support from party comrades, including an occasional free meal" (*Münchener Post,* no. 284, 7 December 1921).

On 8 December, Hitler is invited to Berlin, where he delivers a speech at the National Club of 1919 on "the Jewish and Marxist Question." This happens without the knowledge of the Berlin police, since the *NSDAP* has been banned in Prussia. Hitler declares that in the event of seizing power he would erect concentration camps in order to shed as little blood as possible (Jäckel 1981, 530).

On 16 December, Hitler speaks at an *NSDAP* meeting in the *Hofbräuhaus* on "the German Woman and the Jew," in which he earnestly insists that a Jew is incapable of affection because he only follows his carnal instincts.

On 19 December, in party Communiqué No. 9, Hitler explains why the *NSDAP* decided not to attend the All-German Congress of National Socialists, held in Magdeburg on 6 December; he did not like the idea of patching together tiny groups and wanted instead a "planned creation of a united, strong, and strictly disciplined movement" (Jäckel 1981, 531–3).

On 20 December, Hitler has to testify again before the Munich police on charges brought against him ten days earlier that some *NSDAP* leaflets and brochures caused unnecessary excitement among the public. He put up an eloquent and skillful defense, arguing that printing and distributing pamphlets and leaflets was not illegal, and was done by all other political parties. He turned the charge into a libel suit against the distributors of the pamphlet *Adolf Hitler—Traitor?*

On 28 December 1921, Hitler is invited to Vienna to speak at a mass protest meeting in front of the Old Town Hall against the signing of the Czech-Austrian Treaty of 16 December, in which Austria endorsed the territorial changes imposed by the Peace Treaties of St Germain and Trianon in favor of Czechoslovakia. Hitler denounces the Treaty as a further step in the post-World-World-War-I encirclement of Germany by the Entente Powers.

1922

IN PARTY COMMUNIQUÉ NO. 10, DATED 7 JANUARY 1922, HITLER SUMMED up the reasons for the failure of the *bourgeois* Nationalist movement in its main task of winning the broad masses for the national cause, how this led to the founding of the *NSDAP*, and what his party can offer the nation and the others cannot: "A Nationalist movement with a firm social base, a hold over the broad masses, welded together in an iron-hard organization, instilled with blind obedience and inspired by brutal will, a party of struggle and action" (Jäckel 1981, 542).

On 12 January 1922, the People's Court of Munich pronounces suspended sentences of three months' imprisonment on Hitler, Hermann Esser, and Oskar Körner for having disrupted the Bavarian League's meeting on 14 September 1921.

The first *Parteitag* (party congress) of the *NSDAP* was held in Munich 29–30 January, representing some 6,000 registered members. About 1,000 delegates are present, including delegations from Austria and Czechoslovakia. In his address, Hitler wants to implement the leadership principle and tight discipline. The party's statutes are formally amended to enable Hitler, as the first chairman, to expel not only individual members but also entire local branches at will.

On 2 February, Rudolf Jung from Czechoslovakia and Hitler jointly address some 4,000 persons in *Zirkus Krone*. Hitler's speech, "Germany in Her Deepest Humiliation," is an anti-Jewish tirade: "Our German girls are being seduced by Jews who contaminated the whole nation. Every Jew caught up with a blond girl should be . . . (interrupted by shouts of 'hanged' from the audience) . . . I would not say hanged but brought to trial that will sentence him to death (applause)" (Jäckel 1981, 565).

During a meeting in Munich on 8 February, Hitler tells the *SA* that the Jewish question (*Judenfrage*) is the only thing that matters.

On 17 February, Hitler speaks before 2,300 people in the *Bürgerbräukeller* on "People's Republic or a Jewish State."

At an *NSDAP* meeting in the *Hofbräuhaus* on 1 March, Hitler speaks before an audience of 2,000 on "The Class Struggle—a Stock-Exchange Fraud." He rejects the Marxist concept of class struggle and offers as an alternative a Nationalist struggle for the liberation of Germany (Hauner 2008, 34).

In the *NSDAP* Circular No. 13, dated 4 March 1922, Hitler instructs his supporters not to take part in the Munich railway worker's strike: "The Party rejects any provoked strike, which serves non-German political aims . . . and sees in any strike an instrument that paralyses economic development of the nation at large" (Hitler 1969, 548–9).

On 8 March 1922, Hitler announces in *Völkischer Beobachter* the foundation of the *Jugendbund* (*NSDAP* Youth Branch).

On 17 March, the Bavarian Minister of the Interior Dr. Franz Xaver Schweyer discussed with the leaders of political parties in the Bavarian *Landtag* the deportation of Hitler, who is stateless, to Austria. Hitler's activities and those of his *NSDAP* party have become very problematic to the maintenance of law and order. The Social Democratic Party leader and editor of the Socialist *Münchener Post* Erhard Auer opposed expulsion on the grounds that Hitler was not to be taken seriously. He succeeded in convincing his Bavarian colleagues in the *Landtag* and Dr. Schweyer.

Hitler's indignant reply to the plans of the Bavarian Government to expel him is published in *Völkischer Beobachter* on 12 April 1922. The same evening, he spoke on a variety of topics in the *Bürgerbräukeller* under the title "The Agitator and the Truth." He denounced the plans to expel him from Bavaria with references to his own sacrifice on the battlefield; explained that he follows the example of Jesus Christ in his struggle against the Jews, whom he calls "the ferment of decomposition"; and is particularly outraged that the

Bavarian Premier, Count Lerchenfeld, called anti-Semitism an anti-Christian attitude incompatible with Christian behavior.

Before an audience of 2,600 on 21 April 1922, Hitler spoke in the *Bürgerbräukeller* against the Russo-German agreement of Rapallo, which he regards as a Jewish conspiracy concocted against the defeated German and Russian peoples. He called upon the Russian people to shake off their tormentors (Hauner 2008, 34–5).

In the *NSDAP* Circular No. 14, dated 26 April 1922, Hitler sets out his aim of creating 250 to 300 local Nazi cells (Hauner 2008, 35).

On 5 May 1922, Hitler spoke in Landshut before an audience of 700–800 on the subject "Is Our Struggle Against the Jewish World Dictatorship in Its Form Capitalist, Reactionary, Trade-Unionist, etc., or One Which Is in the Interest of Workers?"

On 10 May, Hitler spoke on the subject of the 'Unknown Soldier' in the *Bürgerbräukeller*.

On 29 May, Hitler spoke in Berlin to the National Club of 1919 on the necessity to "oppose terror with terror." He claimed that, in contrast to the rightwing Nationalist parties, only the *NSDAP* represented the best guarantee for winning mass support, especially among the working class. As for himself, Hitler said that he wanted nothing, no personal benefits, for he considered himself to be a mere "drummer of the national freedom movement" (Jäckel 1981, 642–3).

On 17 June 1922, Hitler addressed the Inter-State Congress of National Socialist parties in Vienna on the subject: "National Socialism and Germany's Future." Leaders of Nazi organizations in Austria and Czechoslovakia, Walter Riehl and Rudolf Jung, respectively, are also present. The Munich-based *NSDAP* is represented by Drexler, Esser, Hitler, and Rosenberg. Hitler urges the participants to free the world from Jewish tyranny. Hitler is clearly recognized as the dominant figure by Riehl, who calls him at the opening session "our *Reich* German *Führer*" (Hauner 2008, 35).

Walter Rathenau, the German Foreign Minister, is assassinated on 24 June 1922. Hitler was arrested under the hastily passed law for the Protection of the Republic and imprisoned in Munich-*Stadelheim*. He was still under three-months' suspended sentence from 12 January 1922 regarding the 14 September 1921 violent incident involving Otto Bellerstedt and his *Bayernbund*.

On 27 July 1922, Hitler was released from *Stadelheim* Prison.

On 28 July, Hitler spoke in the *Bürgerbräukeller* on "The Free State or Slavery." His main device throughout the speech, which has been hailed as his most successful of the year, was to identify Jews with Capitalist exploiters and Bolshevik agitators alike: "How long can this continue? The Jew knows precisely that his system is no blessing, that he is no master race, that he is an exploiter, that the Jews are a people of robbers. The Jew has never yet founded a civilization, but he has destroyed hundreds. He can show nothing of his own creation. Everything that he has is stolen" (Jäckel 1981, 656–71).

Hitler spoke in Passau, Germany on 7 August 1922 about "National Socialism as Germany's Future."

On 16 August 1922, 70,000 people, belonging to fifty or so extremist Nationalist organizations active in Bavaria, gathered in Munich's *Königsplatz* to protest against the Berlin government and the Law for the Protection of the Republic. Hitler, who was one of the speakers, was conspiring with Dr. Otto Pittinger, the leader of the largest among the patriotic associations, the *Bund Bayern und Reich* (League Bavaria and the *Reich*), to bring about a *putsch* against the *Reich* government in Bavaria (Hitler 1969, 498).

The following day on 17 August, Hitler spoke before an audience of 6,000 in *Zirkus Krone*. Before this meeting, Count Reventlow, the Nationalist anti-Semitic writer from Berlin, introduced Kurt Lüdecke to Hitler. Lüdecke became Hitler's first unofficial ambassador and fund-raiser abroad. Within a few weeks, Lüdecke, acting on Ludendorff's and Hitler's instructions, met Mussolini in Milan, Italy (Lüdecke 1937, 11–73).

On 25 August 1922, Hitler and Pittinger gathered some 5,000 members of patriotic associations for another street demonstration in Munich. Since Munich police banned street processions, the demonstrators marched to the *Münchener Kindl-Keller*, where some 1,000 Communists were waiting for them. They were, however, dispersed by the police, who feared that any disturbance might encourage the *putschists* to go ahead and bring down the existing Bavarian government. At about 11 p.m., Hitler called off the demonstration and urged the participants to go home.

Before an audience of 6,000 in *Zirkus Krone* on 18 September 1922, Hitler spoke on "The Stock Exchange Revolution of 1918 as the Cause of the Rising Cost of Living." Apart from the unconditional expulsion of Jews, he demanded that the "November Criminals be called to account, betrayers of the Fatherland be sent to the gallows, the state administration cleared of rabble, usury stopped, the Peace Treaty abolished, inflation stopped, and the housing crisis solved" (Jäckel 1981, 690–3).

A passionate appeal to *NSDAP* members by Hitler appeared in *Völkischer Beobachter* on 23 September 1922 to support the party paper, which was facing bankruptcy again.

On 28 September, Hitler spoke in the *Bürgerbräukeller* in favor of preserving the middle classes.

On so-called "German Day" (14–15 October), Hitler organized a march on Coburg, a Socialist stronghold in central Germany. His entourage included Max Amann, Dietrich Eckart, Hermann Esser, Ulrich Graf, Kurt Lüdecke, Alfred Rosenberg, Christian Weber, and Julius Streicher (a violent Jew-baiter and leader of the *DSP* splinter group *Völksgemeinschaft* in Nuremberg, who recently joined Hitler's movement). They traveled to Coburg in a special train with 800 *SA* members and a brass band. The Social Democrats failed to stop the train, and on the following day, Sunday, the Coburg residents cheered the marching Nazis, who were led by the triumphant Hitler, clad in his belted trench coat, high boots and slouch hat, and waving his whip (Hitler 1968, 499–502).

On 22 October 1922, Hitler produced a detailed memorandum entitled "Expansion of the *NSDAP*." In it he declared that the aim of his movement should not be "winning a majority or what is called political power," but "a life-and-death struggle between two irreconcilable world views." What the *bourgeoisie* has failed to recognize, Hitler claimed, is that "a victory of the Marxist idea means the total extermination of its opponents." Although Jews are linked with Bolshevism, the main thrust of the memorandum was clearly the struggle against Marxism. In more practical terms, Hitler insisted the main effort must go into propaganda to make *Völkischer Beobachter* into a daily paper with a circulation of at least 25,000 to 30,000, instead of the current 15,000 copies. Under the budget estimate, Hitler proposed to purchase six lorries in order to carry *SA* members to exposed mass meetings. The total cost of Hitler's expansion program was estimated at 53 million Marks, a small price, Hitler maintained, for the *NSDAP* to fulfil its aim: "The destruction and extirpation of the Marxist . . . *Weltanschauung*" (Tyrell 1969, 47–55).

On 28 October 1922, Hitler spoke at an *NSDAP* meeting in Rosenheim on the subject "Can Germany Be Saved Today from the Parliamentarians?" Mussolini marches on Rome.

On 2 November, Hitler spoke before some 2,000 people in the Munich *Gebrüder Thomas Bierbrauerei* on "The Positive Anti-Semitism of the Bavarian People's Party."

A few days after Mussolini's march on Rome, Hermann Esser, at an *NSDAP* meeting in the *Hofbräuhaus* on 3 November 1922, proclaimed Hitler the "German Mussolini" (Maser 1965, 356).

The Munich evening paper, *Acht-Uhr Blatt*, published an interview with Hitler on 11 November 1922, in which he denied resolutely any preparations for a *putsch.* He said that he was fighting against Marxism and the German Republic because both are Jewish-influenced, and explained why he considered Jesus Christ to be German, but Pope Alexander VI, Emperor William II, and King Edward VII to be Jewish. The latter's mother, Queen Victoria, might have had a liaison with her private doctor, a Jew named Wolf (Jäckel 1981, 726–7).

At an *NSDAP* discussion in Munich's *Café Neumayr* on the evening of 13 November, Hitler explained the essence of the party program: "Only a party member can become a German citizen; only a person of German blood can become a member of the party. No Jew, therefore, can become a party member" (Jäckel 1981, 727).

On 14 November, Hitler takes part in another discussion evening sponsored by the *NSDAP*. He not only demanded the formation of a national government based on the Fascist model, but also made several important statements on future foreign policy. Since no great successes can be achieved in the economic sphere, the future national government must gain them in the realm of political expansion by annexing Austria. For this, Hitler believed, British and Italian approval will be necessary. Since Italy was experiencing a national revival, Germany must collaborate with her and renounce her claims on South Tyrol. In politics, Hitler asserted, sentiments must not prevail over astuteness. In exchange for renouncing South Tyrol, Germany will obtain Italy's support for the *Anschluß* of Austria and for reintroducing conscription (Jäckel 1981, 728).

On 19 November 1922, Hitler sought to repeat his success at Coburg by leading a march on Regensburg, but the Munich railway men prevented the departure of his train.

On 20 November 1922, United States Assistant Military Attaché, Captain Truman Smith, met Hitler in Munich. Hitler skillfully underlined his anti-Marxism and played down his anti-Semitism. Hitler told Smith that his movement was "a union of manual and cerebral workers to oppose Marxism." As for reparations, these must be paid, since it was a question of

German honor, but they must first be reduced to "a realistic sum" and "a National Government can alone carry a task like this through." Furthermore, "parliament and parliamentarism must go . . . only a dictatorship can bring Germany to its feet." America and England should realize that it is much better that "the decisive struggle between our civilization and Marxism be fought out on German soil." America must therefore help Nationalist Germany against Bolshevism. Finally, Hitler denounced the institution of monarchy in Germany as an absurdity and declares that he wants understanding with France and not a war of revenge (Toland 1976, 173; Jäckel 1981, 733).

On 21 November, Hitler delivered a speech in Munich's *Salvatorkeller* titled "Why Must the National Socialist Movement Win?" before an audience of some 4,000. Ernst (nicknamed "Putzi") Hanfstaengl, who was to become Hitler's close associate in the following years, recalled the impact of his oratory: For innuendo and irony, I have never heard [him] matched . . . On this evening he was at his best. I looked around at the audience. Where was the nondescript crowd I had seen only an hour before? What was suddenly holding these people who, on the hopeless incline of the falling Mark, were engaged in a daily struggle to keep themselves within the line of decency? The hubbub and the mug-clattering had stopped, and they were drinking in every word. Only a few yards away was a young woman, her eyes fastened on the speaker. Transfixed as though in some devotional ecstasy, she had ceased to be herself, and was completely under the spell of Hitler's despotic faith in Germany's future greatness" (Hanfstaengl 1957, 31–7).

Bavarian Minister of the Interior Dr. Schweyer had a private conversation with Hitler in late November 1922 and extracted from him a promise not to attempt a *putsch* (Maser 1965, 363).

On 30 November, Hitler delivered a series of marathon speeches in quick succession at five simultaneously held *NSDAP* meetings in Munich beerhalls before a combined audience of 50,000 listeners on "The Breakdown of Marxism."

Between 8.30 p.m. and midnight on 13 December 1922, Hitler tirelessly appeared as a speaker in ten Munich beerhalls and inns, delivering the same oration: "Jews and Marxists as the Single Grave-Diggers of the German Nation and the Reich" (Hauner 2008, 37).

In late December 1922, Hitler revealed for the first time in a recorded conversation to Eduard August Scharrer, a confidant of Chancellor

Cuno, his views on future German policy in Russia. He was convinced that his cause will win, first in Bavaria, where the parliamentary government was in shambles and the security and state police support the *NSDAP*. He predicted that civil war between Marxist and Nationalist organizations in Germany will follow and that at this stage only Bavaria could provide a conservative dictatorship—the rest of Germany might succumb to Bolshevism. Hence the importance of gaining the support of those European nations who were interested in the preservation of Germany. France will intervene but only to assist in the disintegration of Germany by occupying the Ruhr. America is not interested, and Italy will help but only after settling the South Tyrol question. England remained the only hope. "In foreign policy," Hitler maintained, "Germany would have to adopt a purely Continental policy and avoid damaging British interests. What should be attempted is the destruction of Russia with British help. Russia could provide enough soil for German settlers and offer a wide field of activity for German industry. In our reckoning with France there will be then no British interference." Finally, Hitler insisted that a solution to the Jewish question in Germany must be found. It is the most important factor in the orientation of the masses in the National Socialist Party. "This slogan cannot be given up," Hitler concludes, "because in this manner the masses will see in every opponent, which will be pointed out to them, their deadly enemy and will act accordingly" (Jäckel 1981, 770–5).

1923

ON 3 JANUARY 1923, HITLER SPOKE AT AN *NSDAP* MEETING IN Nuremberg. As usual, he singled out Jews as the chief enemies of the German nation, both as international bankers and as Bolshevik agitators.

On 11 January 1923, French and Belgian troops occupied the Rhineland. The same evening, Hitler spoke at a mass rally in *Zirkus Krone*. In his view, it was not the French but the Berlin government who signed the peace treaty and therefore must be resisted. "If at the beginning of the War," he would later repeat:

> twelve or fifteen thousand of these Hebrew corrupters of the people had been held under poison gas, as happened to hundreds of thousands of our very best German workers in

> the field, the sacrifice of millions at the front would not have been in vain. . . . And in 1923 [Hitler continued], we faced exactly the same situation . . . the first requirement was always the elimination of the Marxist poison from our national body . . . at that time a true national government should have desired disorder and unrest, provided only that amid the confusion a basic reckoning with Marxism at last became possible. . . . If this were not done, any thought of resistance, regardless of what type, was pure madness (Hitler 1968, 620–1).

Hitler spoke at *Zirkus Krone* again on 18 January before 7,000 people on the struggle of "Two Fronts in Germany."

On 25 January, Hitler met the Munich Chief of Police, Eduard Nortz, who warned him against the idea of instigating a *putsch* and told him that the twelve simultaneous rallies and the march he was planning are to be banned.

The following day on 26 January, the Bavarian government, headed by Minister-President Eugen von Knilling, declared a state of emergency to forestall the likelihood of Hitler's *putsch.* However, advised by General von Epp and Captain Röhm, Hitler pledged not to stage a *putsch.* The *NSDAP* was thus allowed not only to hold the planned rallies but also to continue to function legally in Bavaria, in contrast to its prohibition in virtually all other German states.

On 27 January 1923, the first *NSDAP* national rally (*Reichsparteitag*) opened in Munich, attended by hundreds of Nazi delegates from both inside and outside Germany. For three days and nights, Hitler and the *NSDAP* dominated Munich. Hitler spoke at twelve different party meetings held simultaneously during the evening.

On 28 January, Hitler consecrated swastika banners on Munich's Field of Mars during a procession of some 6,000 *SA* members.

At a general meeting of *NSDAP* delegates on 29 January, Hitler outlined three essential elements of National Socialism: (1) THE SOCIAL PRINCIPLE, based on the idea of duty to serve, as incorporated in the armed forces and the civil service, both being "model examples of socialist organization"; (2) THE NATIONAL PRINCIPLE, which is identical with Socialism for the Germans; and (3) THE PRINCIPLE OF ANTI-SEMITISM. In the evening he delivered a speech in *Zirkus Krone*.

On Röhm's initiative, the leaders of four Nationalist organizations met Hitler on 4 February 1923. They issue a joint proclamation announcing the foundation of the *Arbeitsgemeinschaft der vaterländischen Kamfverbände* (Working Association of Patriotic Combat Formations). Their common goal was the struggle against Marxism. There was no unified political leadership, only a military coordinator, a retired Colonel Hermann Kriebel (Hauner 2008, 39).

Beginning 8 February 1923, *NSDAP*'s *Völkischer Beobachter* appeared daily instead of twice a week thanks to Hanfstaengl's large financial contribution, which enabled Hitler to buy two American rotary presses. During this period, Hanfstaengl became Hitler's steadiest companion and introduced him to wealthy industrialists in Munich. Hitler also felt drawn to Hanfstaengl's beautiful wife, Helene, and their children. His own private life remained spartan; he continued to live in a small, shabby sublet flat at 41 *Thierschstraße*, which he shared with an Alsatian dog named Wolf.

On 20 February, Hitler spoke in Munich to the National Association of German Officers. He rejected the tactics of passive resistance against the French in the Rhineland, as pursued by the Berlin government.

Hitler spoke in Munich's *Löwenbräukeller* on 26 February before an audience of 5,000 on "German Student and German Worker as Carriers of German Future." He sought to bring Marxist students and workers under the banner of his own organization.

In March 1923, Hitler reached an agreement with the German Nationalist leader, Albrecht von Gräfe, by which von Gräfe's *Deutschvölkische Freiheitspartei* incorporated National Socialists in northern Germany (mainly Prussia), where the *NSDAP* remained banned; south Germany was claimed by Hitler's own *Völkischsozialer Block.*

During a visit to Munich on 11 March 1923, General von Seeckt, Chief of the *Reichswehr*, met Hitler. According to Hanfstaengl, who is not always a reliable witness, the two men discussed joint measures in the event of war with France, but no agreement was reached. Hitler demanded that priority should be given to the internal struggle against Marxism. Moreover, he wanted to create a militia force under the *SA*, expand the *Reichswehr*, breach the Versailles Treaty and push the French out of the Ruhr. When von Seeckt asked what Hitler's attitude was to the soldier's oath of allegiance, he allegedly received the answer:

> Herr General, my offer was not intended to conflict with your present oath of loyalty . . . We National Socialists will see to it that the members of the present Marxist regime in Berlin will hang from the lamp-posts. We will send the *Reichstag* up in flames and when all is in flux, we will turn to you, Herr General, to assume leadership of all German workers.

Von Seeckt allegedly responded: "In that case, you and I, *Herr* Hitler, have nothing more to say to each other!" (Hanfstaengl 1957, 85–6).

On 14 March 1923, the Supreme Court in Leipzig rejected Hitler's appeal for the ban on the *NSDAP* to be lifted in Prussia, Saxony, Baden, Mecklenburg-Schwerin, Hamburg, and Bremen.

On 17 March, American diplomat Robert D. Murphy held an interview with Hitler. He asked him whether Henry Ford contributed money to the *NSDAP*. Hitler denied it and maintained that most of the party funds came from Germans overseas.

On 25 March, Hitler spoke at a *SA* meeting in the *Bürgerbräukeller* on the need to replace passive by active resistance against the French occupation of the Rhineland.

On 27 March 1923, *NSDAP*'s *Völkischer Beobachter* published Hitler's answer to a critical article in the *Münchener Post* a few days earlier, titled "Hitler and the November Criminals." Hitler rejected contemptuously the charges of cowardice in the trenches, and of political treachery for joining the Soviets in Munich after November 1918. This latter fact haunted Hitler among his *NSDAP* associates for several years until he was declared absolute ruler of Germany in 1933.

On 6 April, Hitler gave a speech on "The National Socialist Movement and Public Servants and Employees" at an *NSDAP* meeting in the *Löwenbräukeller* before 4,000–5,000 people. The Spanish newspaper *ABC* in Madrid published an article entitled "Hitler, el Jefe del Fascismo Bávaro," written by Antonio Azpeitua: "He seemed to be obsessed by one problem—how to obtain funds for his work: 'I must have money and much money too!' . . . His main program is the renaissance of the 1914 spirit . . . to crush Marxism . . . but also the attack upon capital." There was nothing about Hitler's anti-Semitism.

"Germany at the Crossroads" is the title of Hitler's speech delivered in *Zirkus Krone* before almost 10,000 people on 10 April 1923. Hitler demanded "land and soil for the nation." This was the first of eight speeches Hitler delivered on the subject of the Ruhr occupation during the spring.

On 13 April, Hitler and the leaders of the *Arbeitsgemeinschaft* present an ultimatum to Bavarian Minister-President Eugen von Knilling, demanding the repudiation of the arrest order on four National Socialists and the nullification of the Law for the Defense of the Republic at the next meeting of the *Reichsrat* (the first chamber of the German Parliament representing the state governments). Von Knilling rejected the ultimatum. The same evening, Hitler spoke again in *Zirkus Krone* on "The World Jew and the World Stock-Exchange—the Arch-Culprits of the World War" (Hauner 2008, 40).

On 16 April, Hitler and the leaders of the *Arbeitsgemeinschaft* were again received by von Knilling who affirms that the Law for the Defense of the Republic will be applied against them.

On 17 April, Hitler again returns to *Zirkus Krone* to speak on "The Peace Betrayal of Versailles as the Perpetual Curse of the November Republic." He summed up the purpose of the Nazi movement in three points: abrogation of the Peace Treaty; unification of all Germans; acquisition of land and soil to feed the German nation.

On 19 April, Hitler drafted a memorandum on Nazi tactics in connection with Captain Röhm's efforts to expand the *Arbeitsgemeinschaft.* The ultimate aim should be "the liberation of Germany from internal and external enemies and the unification of all Germans in a great common Fatherland" through the activities of the *Kampfverbände* (Combat Formations); but only the army can be the real unifying factor (Röhm 1928, 175–8).

On 20 April, Hitler spoke on "Politics and Race: Why are We Anti-Semites?" at *Zirkus Krone* before some 9,000 people. It was his birthday. Hitler's little flat was filled from floor to ceiling with flowers and cakes, yet he refused to touch a single one of them from fear that they could have been poisoned (Hanfstaengl 1957, 66).

On 24 April, Hitler speaks on "Race and Economics—the German Workman in the National Socialist State" again at *Zirkus Krone*.

On 27 April 1923, Hitler speaks on "The Jews' Paradise or German People's State" in *Zirkus Krone*.

During a trip to Berlin near the end of April 1923, Hitler's car was stopped at a roadblock near Leipzig by Communist guards. Hanfstaengl rescued Hitler by showing his U.S. passport, declaring that he is an American paper manufacturer and Hitler his valet (Hanfstaengl 1957, 67–8). Hitler reportedly tells Heinrich Claß, the leader of the *Alldeutscher Verband* (Pan-German League), that in three days he will conquer Munich, in three weeks Bavaria, and in three months the *Reich* (Gordon 1972, 207).

On 1 May 1923, the *Arbeitsgemeinschaft*, at Hitler's instigation, organized "The Great German May Celebration," to prevent the Marxists from marching in the streets and to place the Bavarian authorities in a dilemma. In Munich–*Oberwiesenfeld*, hundreds of *Kampfbund* members, some armed as auxiliary police with weapons provided by Captain Ernst Röhm, were waiting ready to strike. Hitler was forced to accept the *Reichswehr* ultimatum to return the requisitioned arms, but a limited confrontation between the *SA* and Marxist workers does take place later and several people are injured. In the evening, Hitler speaks in the maximum capacity *Zirkus Krone*.

On 4 May, Hitler speaks at an *NSDAP* meeting in *Zirkus Krone* on "The Morass of Parliament or the Fight for Freedom," urging that Germany must rearm against France and that the country can be saved only through a national dictatorship (Hauner 2008, 40).

On 6 May, Hitler spoke in Murnau, outside Munich.

On 17 May, Hitler spoke at an *NSDAP* meeting in Erlangen.

On 29 May, Hitler spoke at an *NSDAP* meeting in Augsburg.

In late May, Hitler and his associates spent a few days in the *Moritz* boarding house at Berchtesgaden. According to Eckart, Hitler paced the courtyard one evening, cracking his rhinoceros whip, and repeating aloud: "I must enter Berlin like Christ in the Temple of Jerusalem and scourge out the moneylenders!" (Hanfstaengl 1957, 83).

On 1 June, in a speech entitled "Hammer or Anvil," delivered at *Zirkus Krone*, Hitler declared that the common aim of National Socialists in the *Reich*, Austria and Bohemia, was to create a unified Greater German *Reich* (Hauner 2008, 41).

In early June, Admiral von Tirpitz, the creator of the modern German Navy, met Hitler secretly in Munich.

On 10 June, in memory of Leo Schlageter (executed by the French military in the Rhineland on 26 May for having participated in sabotage activities) the *NSDAP* staged a meeting with other *Kampfbund* groups in Munich in the presence of Hitler, Ludendorff, and others.

On 17 June, Hitler spoke at an *NSDAP* meeting in Passau.

On 20 June, the French announce seizure of the Rhineland for war reparations.

On 23 June, the French impose a blockade on trade between the Ruhr and the rest of Germany. The same evening, Hitler spoke at an *NSDAP* meeting in Regensburg.

On 1 July, Hitler gave two speeches in the *Zur Krone* inn and the *Hotel Watzmann* in Berchtesgaden.

On 6 July, Hitler spoke at an *NSDAP* meeting in Augsburg.

On 8 July, Hitler spoke at an *NSDAP* meeting in Ingolstadt.

On 14 July, at a giant rally in *Zirkus Krone* convened by the *NSDAP* on the occasion of the *Deutsches Turnfest* (German Gymnastic Organizations) in Munich, Hitler spoke on "The Curse of the November Revolution"; clashes with police in the streets follow.

On 17–24 July 1923, *NSDAP*'s *Völkischer Beobachter* is suspended from circulation.

On 1 August, before an audience of 8,500, Hitler delivered a violent speech in *Zirkus Krone* against the Cuno government in favor of a genuine national government which would have the courage to declare to the foreign powers: "The Treaty of Versailles is founded on a monstrous lie. We refuse to carry out its terms any longer. Do what you will! If you wish for war, go and get it! Then we shall see whether you can turn seventy million Germans into serfs and slaves!" (Baynes 1942, 75–9).

On 5 August, Hitler spoke in Neustadt an der Aisch.

On 12–14 August 1923, Hitler and Hermann Göring represent the Munich *NSDAP* at the Inter-State Congress of National Socialists in Salzburg. Hitler made it clear to Sudeten-German Jung and Austrian Riehl that the *NSDAP* now wields more power than the Sudeten and Austrian branches put together, and that from now on they are to be subordinate only to him. After the Salzburg meeting, Hitler visited Linz for two days. There he told Lüdecke about his determination to settle the Jewish question: "I shall settle that problem for good and all. Let them try to make trouble—terrorism and bombs will stop their mouths. No fear, we'll take the power and we'll use it. But if we can't do that, we'll drag all Europe with us into the abyss—at least we have that much force!" (Lüdecke 1937, 133).

On 20 August 1923, the American newspaper *The World* published an interview with Hitler in which he said: "Democracy is a joke. There are only two possibilities—either its reign will be smashed by the Soviet hammer, or it will be swept by an organized minority of Nationalists. With fanatic determination we Fascists must pursue our goal. History has always been made by an organized minority which seized power for the benefit of the majority." On the same day, Hitler received from Richard Frank, a coffee merchant, a loan of 60,000 Swiss francs for his movement, using as security a collection of highly praised jewels received from his female benefactors (Franz-Willing 1962, 192).

On 21 August, Hitler signed a letter of credential for Kurt Lüdecke, who was going to Rome to negotiate with Mussolini on behalf of the *NSDAP* (Lüdecke 1937, 140). In the evening, Hitler spoke to a packed audience of almost 9,000 in *Zirkus Krone* on "The Triumph of the Stock-Exchange Dictatorship." Knowing that the new Berlin government of Gustav Stresemann (Chancellor Cuno resigned on 13 August 1923) was anxious to end the passive resistance in the Rhineland, Hitler now reverses his tactics and accuses the new government of betraying the national resistance and allowing inflation to accelerate.

On 1–2 September 1923, on the anniversary of the German victory over France at Sedan in 1870 (so-called "German Day"), Hitler delivered in Nuremberg, in the presence of General Ludendorff, a firebrand oration at a mass meeting of some 25,000 attendees: "We must have a new dictatorship. We need no parliament, no government like the present." (*The New York Times,* 3 September 1923). A new patriotic association called *Deutscher Kampfbund* (German Fighting Union or Combat League), composed of the *SA* (Hitler), *Reichsflagge* (Adolf Heiß) and *Bund Oberland* (Dr. Friedrich Weber), was set up. In a joint manifesto, it calls for an immediate overthrow of the Berlin government (Hauner 2008, 42).

On 5 September, Hitler spoke in *Zirkus Krone* against the "November Criminals" before some 8,000 people.

On 12 September, Hitler delivered another vitriolic attack on the Berlin government in *Zirkus Krone*.

On 16 September, Hitler speaks in Hof before a procession of 75,000 members of patriotic associations.

On 22 September, General von Lossow, commanding the *Reichswehr* in Bavaria, met Hitler and agrees with nine out of the ten points in the *NSDAP* program (Röhm 1928, 205).

On 25 September, Hitler assumed the political leadership of the *Kampfbund.* He issued a proclamation calling upon all members of the patriotic associations to join the *Kampfbund* through the *SA* (*NSDAP*), *Reichsflagge*, or *Bund Oberland.* Those party comrades who do not join within ten days are to be expelled from the ranks altogether.

On 26 September, the *Kampfbund* under Hitler's leadership was preparing for action as the Stresemann government calls off the campaign of passive resistance in the Ruhr. This is deeply resented by the political

Conservatives in Bavaria, where the government proclaimed a state of emergency and appointed Gustav von Kahr as Bavarian State Commissioner with dictatorial powers. As Socialist governments in Saxony and Thuringia decide to form red paramilitary units, Hitler fears that a Communist takeover will soon occur in Germany (Hauner 2008, 42).

On 27 September, Weimar President Ebert invoked Article 48 of the Weimar Constitution and conferred emergency powers on the *Reichswehr.* Hitler was, nevertheless, determined to carry out preparations for the *putsch* under the slogan "March on Berlin." Despite the ban on political meetings imposed by von Kahr, the *Kampfbund* held one meeting in the evening where Hitler spoke (Hauner 2008, 42).

On 28 September, *Reich* Defense Minister Otto Gessler orders the Bavarian *Reichswehr* to ban by force Hitler's newspaper, the *Völkischer Beobachter.* General von Lossow, supported by von Kahr, refused to comply with the order and was subsequently sacked, but was promptly reinstated by von Kahr in defiance of the Berlin government (Hauner 2008, 42).

On 30 September, 4,000 *SA* men marched in front of Hitler in Bayreuth. Hitler met Siegfried and Winifred Wagner for the first time, as well as Houston Stewart Chamberlain (son-in-law of composer Wilhelm Richard Wagner). Interviewed by a United Press journalist, Hitler declared: "The Bavarian population will stick to me if I should have a conflict with *Herr* von Kahr . . . Our programme is that of a national dictatorship. If Munich does not march now on Berlin, Berlin will march on Munich" (Jäckel 1981, 1022).

In early October 1923, in an interview published in *The American Monthly* (October 1923, pages 235–8; see also Jäckel 1981, 1023–6). Hitler said that Marxism is not Socialism but a Jewish invention. Since the Marxists have stolen the term and confused its meaning, Hitler wants to "take Socialism away from the Socialists." Socialism, Hitler insists, is an ancient Aryan and Germanic institution. Unlike Marxism, it does not repudiate private property, involves no negation of personality and is patriotic.

> We demand the fulfilment of the just demands of the productive classes by the state on the basis of race solidarity. To us, race and state are one. . . . No healthy man is a Marxist, for, being healthy, he recognizes the value of personality. We contend against the forces of disease and degeneration. Bavaria is comparatively healthy, because it is not completely industrialized. . . . If we wish to save

> Germany, we must see to it that our farmers remain faithful to the land. To do so, they must have room to breathe and room to work. We must regain our colonies and we must expand eastward. . . . Parliamentary government is the spawn of hell. It opens the gate to Bolshevism, which is . . . our greatest menace. Kill Bolshevism in Germany and you restore seventy million people to power. . . . The Peace Treaty and Bolshevism are two heads of one monster. We must decapitate both.

When the American journalist, G. S. Viereck, asked Hitler what he would do with the Jews, he received the answer that Jews will be disenfranchised even if born in Germany. "The Jew," Hitler asserts, "is destructive by nature."

> Unable to lead a national existence of his own; his presence in the modern state provides the ferment of decomposition. . . . Birth in itself is no sufficient qualification for citizenship. . . . The Jews are not German. They are an alien people in our midst and manifest themselves as such. . . . I look upon the Jews as you look upon the Japanese. Both are an alien race. Both are an ancient people. Both have an ancient culture. Nevertheless, you do not admit the Japanese to citizenship. . . . Mixed breeds lack vitality. We would forbid mixed marriages hereafter. . . . The issue that confronts us is one between Jew and Aryan. The mixed breed dies; it is a valueless product. Rome fell, when it ceased to keep its race pure.

Hitler admitted that he believed in eugenics and that:

> Syphilitics and alcoholics must be isolated; they must not be permitted to reproduce. The Jews, being weak, have made a virtue of weakness. They have invented a false humanitarianism that teaches us to preserve the unfit. This false humanitarianism is the most diabolically cruel invention of the human brain. . . . I would isolate the criminal as well as the person suffering from some physical taint. One disease breeds many. One pimp makes

> ten. . . . The Bible tells us, "If thy right eye offend thee, pluck it out." I look upon those that teach us otherwise as criminals against the race. The preservation of a nation is more important than the preservation of its unfortunates. That, to me, is the essence of humanity. In my scheme of the German State, there will be no room for the alien, no use for the criminal, no use for the diseased, no use for the wastrel, for the usurer or speculator, or anyone incapable of productive work. (Hauner 2008, 43.)

On 3 October 1923, the *Daily Mail* of London published an interview, "A Visit to Hittler" [*sic*].

On 6 October, Hitler attended a meeting of the *Reichsflagge* in Nuremberg. Disagreements between him and Captain Heiß, the *Reichsflagge* leader, culminated in the dissolution of the *Kampfbund.* But Röhm consolidates it by founding the *Reichskriegsflagge* a few days later (Hauner 2008, 43).

On 7 October, Hitler attacked von Kahr violently in a speech in Bamberg, stating: "We need a revolutionary to lead a march on Berlin! . . . If Kahr is going to march forward, we shall march with him, if he retreats, we shall stay beside" (Jäckel 1981, 1028, 1267).

On 14 October, Hitler spoke at an *NSDAP* meeting in Nuremberg. In the evening he gave an interview in Munich to Leo Negrelli for the *Corriere Italiano* (published on 16 October 1923).

On 16 October, replying to a letter from Fritz Seidl, an old schoolmate from Linz, Hitler writes: "As far as my family is concerned, it consists, for the present, of one wonderful German Alsatian dog. I have not managed to get any further so far. The ringleader of the past is also the ringleader of today" (Jäckel 1981, 1038).

On 19 October, Hitler spoke at an *NSDAP* meeting in the *Löwenbräukeller*, and gave another interview to the *Corriere Italiano* (published on 26 October 1923).

On 20 October, Hitler spoke at an *NSDAP* meeting in Nuremberg.

On 23 October, at a meeting of selected *SA* leaders, Hitler described the three political options left: (1) Bolshevization of Bavaria by the intervention of Berlin; (2) Bavaria will fight against Bolshevization under the present "sulking-corner" party of separatists. Lacking popular support, this alternative will of necessity invite foreign intervention, most probably by the despicable French, who are already waiting in the wings; (3) Bavaria will proclaim an All-German Government and call up an army of liberation under the swastika flag, against Berlin. "The *Kampfbund*," Hitler declares, "with our *SA* men in the forefront, will march . . . only the third path, till the final victory!" (Jäckel 1981, 1043). Hitler also met with the leaders of the *Kampfbund* and revealed his plans for the military uprising to set up a national dictatorship in Bavaria through cooperation between the *Kampfbund,* the Bavarian *Reichswehr*, and the *Landespolizei* (state police). Hitler declared emphatically that without close cooperation between the amateur soldiers and the professionals, the national uprising would fail (Deuerlein 1968, 187–8).

On 24 October, Hitler gave a four-hour lecture on his aims to Colonel von Seißer, chief of the Bavarian State Police and the third member (together with von Kahr and General von Lossow) of the Bavarian political triumvirate.

On 25 October, Hitler tries in vain to persuade von Lossow and von Seißer that von Kahr is unfit for dictatorial powers. He proposes General Ludendorff as the future Commander-in-Chief of the *Reichswehr.* Despite the opposition from senior officers, Hitler believes that the junior officers and the ranks will obey Ludendorff enthusiastically.

On 30 October, at an *NSDAP* rally in *Zirkus Krone*, Hitler told the audience: "The German problem will be solved for me only when the black-white-red swastika flag floats on the Berlin Castle. There can be no retreat, we can only march forward. We all feel that the hour has come" (Röhm 1928, 207).

On 31 October, the *Völkischer Beobachter* published a letter from Hitler to Edmund D. Morel, a British journalist, in which he denounced as an infamous lie the allegation that his movement has received French money. However, there is evidence that, apart from the Swiss money Hitler received in August 1923, he had received financial support from Gertrud von Seidlitz, Edwin and Helene Bechstein, the locomotive manufacturer Borsig, and Hermann Aust, a Munich industrialist. The largest single contribution made in October 1923 to his movement was the sum of 100,000 gold Marks from Fritz Thyssen of the United Steelworks, which Hitler received through Ludendorff.

On 1 November, in a final effort to split the Bavarian triumvirate, Hitler meets von Seißer again and proposes that he and von Lossow abandon von Kahr. Hitler warned that "the time is critical . . . the economic misery is pushing our people so that we must either act now or our followers will run over to the Communists" (Franz-Willing 1962, 136). He gave an interview to Gustavo Traglia for the Italian paper *L'Epoca* (published on 4 November 1923).

On 4 November, on the German Memorial Day to the Dead, Hitler reviewed the *Kampfbund* in Munich. He rejected the plan put forward by his associates Rosenberg and von Scheubner-Richter to use armed stormtroopers to force the members of the triumvirate and the Bavarian ex-Crown Prince Rupprecht to collaborate in the *putsch.*

On 6 November, riots broke out in major cities throughout Germany as hyperinflation reached new heights. A mob of poor and unemployed Berliners stormed the *Schuenenviertel* on *Grenadierstraße* (one of Berlin's oldest and most charismatic neighborhoods) and attacked Jews and their places of business that they blamed for the high prices of food. Members of the Bavarian triumvirate conferred with the leaders of the patriotic associations and declared their readiness to establish a conservative dictatorship in Bavaria, but which will exclude Hitler and Ludendorff. They warned that any separate *putsch*, such as contemplated by the *Kampfbund*, will be suppressed by the force of arms. On learning this, Hitler issued directives to his followers that the *putsch* was to be launched on Sunday, 11 November, the fifth anniversary of Germany's deepest humiliation.

On 7 November 1923, Hitler, Göring, and von Scheubner-Richter met the leaders of the *Kampfbund* to make the final arrangements for the *putsch*—that is, the seizure of key buildings and communication centers, and the arrest of Communists, Socialists, and trade unionists. Hitler calculated that the *Kampfbund* had the numerical edge over security forces in Munich: perhaps some 4,000 armed *putschists* against 2,600 *Landespolizei* and loyal *Reichswehr* troops. Later in the evening, Hitler convened a second meeting. This was attended by the ex-Police Chief of Munich Ernst Pöhner and his assistant Wilhelm Frick, both Nazi supporters who reported that von Kahr had decided unexpectedly to hold a meeting of patriotic associations in the *Bürgerbräukeller* the following evening. Hitler declared that this news is a heaven-sent opportunity and decided to launch the *putsch* the next day (Toland 1976, 207).

BEER HALL *PUTSCH* ("HITLER *PUTSCH*")

ON 26 SEPTEMBER 1923, FOLLOWING A PERIOD OF TURMOIL AND POLITICAL violence, Bavarian Minister-President Eugen von Knilling declared a state of emergency and appointed Gustav Ritter von Kahr *Staatskomissar*, or state commissioner, with dictatorial powers to govern the Bavarian state. Since 1 January 1923, *Reichswehr Generalmajor* Otto Herman von Lossow had been the commander (*Befehlshaber*) in *Wehrkreis VII* (Defense District 7), the *Reichswehr* military district which covered Bavaria. Colonel Hans Ritter von Seißer, head of the Bavarian State Police (*Landespolizei*), together with von Kahr and von Lossow became briefly prominent in German history as being the triumvirate who in 1923–1924 exercised political control in Bavaria.

The Bavarian Government under *Staatskomissar* von Kahr tended to take a line independent of that of the national government of the Weimar Republic in Berlin. When ordered to arrest three of the leaders of the *SA*, Nazis, and their *Kampfbund* operating in Bavaria, the triumvirate refused. General von Lossow was ordered by the commander-in-chief of the republic's *Reichswehr*, General Hans von Seeckt in Berlin, to arrest the three men and to suppress the daily newspaper of the Nazi Party, the *Völkischer Beobachter*. Again, he hesitated to do this and was sacked from his command by General von Seeckt and replaced by General Friedrich Freiherr Kress von Kressenstein. However, Bavarian State Commissioner von Kahr defied von Seeckt and announced that General von Lossow would retain the command in Bavaria.

Shortly after the triumvirate took power in Bavaria, Hitler announced that he would hold fourteen mass meetings beginning on 27 September 1923. Afraid of the potential disruption, one of von Kahr's first actions was to ban the announced meetings. Hitler was under pressure to act. The Nazis, with other leaders in the *Kampfbund*, felt they had to march upon Berlin and seize power or their followers would turn to the Communists. Hitler enlisted the help of General Erich Ludendorff in an attempt to gain the support of von Kahr and his triumvirate. However, von Kahr had his own plan with von Seißer and von Lossow to install a Nationalist dictatorship without Hitler. November 1923 was the height of hyperinflation in the Weimar Republic. In 1923, many Nationalist groups wanted to emulate Mussolini's "March on Rome" (October 1922) by a "March on Berlin." Among these were General Erich Ludendorff and the Nazi (*NSDAP*) Party, led by Adolf Hitler. Hitler decided to try to seize power in what was later known as the "Hitler *Putsch*" or Beer Hall *Putsch.*

On 8 November 1923, at about 8.45 p.m., 606 *SA* storm troopers crashed a public meeting of 3,000 people which had been organized by von Kahr in the *Bürgerbräukeller*, a large beer hall in Munich. They burst into the hall just as von Kahr was speaking. A machine gun was quickly set up in the auditorium. Hitler, surrounded by his associates Hermann Göring, Alfred Rosenberg, Rudolf Heß, Ernst Hanfstaengl, Ulrich Graf, Johann Aigner, Adolf Lenk, Max Amann, Max Erwin von Scheubner-Richter, Wilhelm Adam, and others (some twenty in all), advanced through the crowded auditorium. Unable to be heard above the crowd, with a theatrical gesture Hitler climbs on to a chair, fires a few bullets into the ceiling and screams: "The national revolution has broken out! The hall is filled with six hundred men. Nobody is allowed to leave." By mixture of threat and bluff he proclaims the suspension of the Berlin and Bavarian governments and the establishment of a "provisional German National Government," of which he declares himself to be the leader, von Kahr to be the Regent of Bavaria, Pöhner Bavaria's prime minister, General von Lossow the *Reichswehr* Minister, von Seißer the police minister, and General Ludendorff, who arrives later, the head of the German National Army.

Hitler, accompanied by Heß, Lenk, and Graf, ordered the triumvirate of von Kahr, von Seißer, and von Lossow into an adjoining room at gunpoint and demanded they support the *putsch.* "I know this step is a difficult one for you, gentlemen, but it must be taken," Hitler tells them. "It must be made easier for the gentlemen to take the jump. Everybody must take up the post which he is allotted. If he does not, then he has no right to exist. You must fight with me, achieve victory with me, or die with me. If things go wrong, I have four bullets in my pistol, three for my colleagues if they desert me, the last bullet for myself!" (Deuerlein 1962, 496). Hitler demanded they accept government positions he assigned them. Hitler had promised von Lossow a few days earlier that he would not attempt a *coup*, but now thought that he would get an immediate response of affirmation from them, imploring von Kahr to accept the position of Regent of Bavaria. Von Kahr replied that he could not be expected to collaborate, especially as he had been taken out of the auditorium under heavy guard.

Heinz Pernet, Johann Aigne, and von Scheubner-Richter were dispatched to pick up Ludendorff, whose personal prestige was being harnessed to give the Nazis credibility. A telephone call was made from the kitchen by Hermann Kriebel to Ernst Röhm, who was waiting with his *Bund*

Reichskriegsflagge in the *Löwenbräukeller*, another beer hall nearby, and he was ordered to seize key buildings throughout the city. At the same time, co-conspirators under Gerhard Rossbach mobilized the students of a nearby Officers Infantry school to seize other objectives.

In preparation for the *putsch*, Röhm rented the cavernous main hall of the *Löwenbräukeller* under the guise of a reunion and festive comradeship. It was here that Röhm planned to use the units at his disposal to obtain weapons from secret caches with which to occupy crucial points in the center of the city. Röhm led the *Reichskriegsflagge* militia at the time of the *putsch*. When Hitler's call came from the *Bürgerbräukeller*, Röhm led his force of over 2,000 men to join with Hitler's group at the *Bürgerbräukeller* and led them to the War Ministry, which they occupied for sixteen hours.

While Hitler is negotiating with the triumvirate behind closed doors, Göring sensibly promises the *Bürgerbräukeller* audience that whatever the outcome of the National Revolution, the Bavarians will always get their beer.

Meanwhile, Hitler became irritated by von Kahr and summoned Ernst Pöhner, Friedrich Weber, and Hermann Kriebel to stand guard for him while he returned to the auditorium flanked by Rudolf Heß and Adolf Lenk. Hitler followed up on Göring's speech to the large crowd and stated that the action was not directed at the police and *Reichswehr*, but against ". . . the Berlin Jew government and the November criminals of 1918." Dr. Karl Alexander von Müller, a professor of modern history and political science at the University of Munich and a supporter of von Kahr, was an eyewitness. He reported:

> I cannot remember in my entire life such a change in the attitude of a crowd in a few minutes, almost a few seconds. . . . Hitler had turned them inside out, as one turns a glove inside out, with a few sentences. It had almost something of hocus-pocus, or magic about it.

Hitler ended his speech with: "Outside are Kahr, Lossow and Seißer. They are struggling hard to reach a decision. May I say to them that you will stand behind them?"

The crowd in the hall backed Hitler with a roar of approval. He finished triumphantly:

> You can see that what motivates us is neither self-conceit or self-interest, but only a burning desire to join the battle in this grave eleventh hour for our German Fatherland. . . . One last thing I can tell you. Either the German revolution begins tonight or we will all be dead by dawn!

Hitler returned to the anteroom where the triumvirs remained under guard, to ear-shattering acclaim, which the triumvirs could not have failed to notice. On his way back, Hitler ordered Göring and Heß to take Minister-President Eugen von Knilling and seven other members of the Bavarian government into custody.

During Hitler's speech, Pöhner, Weber, and Kriebel had been trying in a conciliatory fashion to bring the triumvirate round to their point of view. The atmosphere in the room had become lighter but von Kahr continued to dig in his heels. Ludendorff showed up a little before 9:00 p.m. and, being shown into the anteroom, concentrated on von Lossow and von Seißer, appealing to their sense of duty. Eventually the triumvirate reluctantly gave in.

Hitler, Ludendorff, *et al.* returned to the main hall's podium, where they gave speeches and shook hands. The crowd was then allowed to leave the hall. In a tactical mistake, Hitler decided to leave the *Bürgerbräukeller* shortly thereafter to deal with a crisis elsewhere. Around 10:30 p.m., Ludendorff released von Kahr and his two associates.

After Hitler left the beer hall to supervise the activities of the *putschists*, von Kahr, von Seißer, and von Lossow were released, ostensibly to fulfill Hitler's orders in their respective new positions. Instead, the men fled to join the opposition. They went to the barracks of the local infantry regiment, where General Jakob Ritter von Danner, Munich garrison commandant and technically von Lossow's deputy, met them. Von Danner, who had been directed independently by General von Seeckt to put down the *coup*, asked if their statements at the beer hall were merely a ruse to escape Nazi custody. The triumvirate agreed, fearing the consequences of their initial cooperation with the *putschists*, and acted to put down the *putsch* attempt. Von Lossow ultimately escaped any disciplinary action for his behavior during the *putsch* attempt, but never held another command.

The night was marked by confusion and unrest among government officials, armed forces, police units, and individuals deciding where their loyalties lay. Units of the *Kampfbund* were scurrying around to arm themselves from secret caches and seizing buildings. At around 3:00 a.m., the first casualties of the *putsch* occurred when the local garrison of the *Reichswehr* spotted Röhm's men coming out of the *Löwenbräukeller*. They were ambushed while trying to reach the *Reichswehr* barracks by soldiers and state police; shots were fired, but there were no fatalities on either side. Encountering heavy resistance, Röhm and his men were forced to fall back. In the meantime, the *Reichswehr* officers put the whole garrison on alert and called for reinforcements. Foreign attachés were seized in their hotel rooms and put under house arrest.

In the early morning of 9 November, Hitler ordered the seizure of the Munich city council as hostages. He further sent the communications officer of the *Kampfbund*, Max Neunzert, to enlist the aid of Crown Prince Rupprecht of Bavaria to mediate between von Kahr and the *putschists*. Neunzert failed in the mission.

Despite the fact that the *Kampfbund* has occupied some important buildings in the city (Ministry of War and Post and Telegraph offices), the majority of the *Reichswehr* units refuse to join the *putschists*. Von Kahr, General von Lossow, and von Seißer revoke their agreement with Hitler, declaring that they had been forced to agree at gunpoint. Von Kahr bans the *Kampfbund*, the *NSDAP*, and the *Völkischer Beobachter*.

By midmorning on 9 November, Hitler realized that the *putsch* was going nowhere. The *putschists* did not know what to do and were about to give up. At this moment, Ludendorff cried out, "Wir marschieren!" (We will march!). Röhm's force together with Hitler's (a total of over 2,000 men) marched out from the *Bürgerbräukeller* to the center of Munich, overpowering a police cordon guarding the bridge—but with no specific plan of where to go. On the spur of the moment, Ludendorff led them to the Bavarian Defense Ministry. However, at the *Odeonsplatz* in front of the *Feldherrnhalle* they met a force of 130 soldiers blocking the way under the command of State Police Senior Lieutenant Baron Michael von Godin. The two groups exchanged fire, killing four state police officers and sixteen Nazis. According to Ernst Röhm, Martin Faust, and Theodor Casella, both members of the armed militia organization *Reichskriegsflagge*, were shot down accidentally in a burst of machine gun fire during the occupation of the War Ministry as the result of a misunderstanding with Second Infantry Regiment (Hitler's former regiment).

This was the origin of the *Blutfahne* (blood-flag), which became stained with the blood of two *SA* members who were also shot: the flagbearer Heinrich Trambauer, who was badly wounded, and Andreas Bauriedl, who fell dead and bled on the fallen flag. A bullet penetrated the chest and instantly killed Max von Scheubner-Richter who was marching directly on Hitler's right. When von Scheubner-Richter fell he grabbed Hitler's right arm bringing him down and dislocating Hitler's shoulder. Hitler goes into hiding but refuses to flee abroad. Göring was shot in the leg but managed to escape. Ludendorff was arrested, but immediately released after giving his word of honor. The rest of the Nazis scattered or were arrested. Warrants for the arrest of the *Kampfbund* leaders were issued without delay.

In a description of Ludendorff's funeral at the *Feldherrnhalle* in 1937 (which Hitler attended but without speaking), Berlin news correspondent William L. Shirer wrote: "The World War [One] hero [Ludendorff] had refused to have anything to do with him [Hitler] ever since he had fled from in front of the Feldherrnhalle after the volley of bullets during the Beer Hall Putsch." However, when a consignment of papers relating to Landsberg Prison (including the visitor book) were later sold at auction, it was noted that Ludendorff had visited Hitler a number of times. The case of the resurfacing papers was reported in *Der Spiegel* ("The Mirror," a German news magazine) on 23 June 2006; the new information (which came out more than 30 years after Shirer wrote his now-famous book, and which Shirer did not have access to) nullifies Shirer's statement.

State Police and local police units were first notified of trouble by three police detectives stationed at the *Löwenbräukeller*. These reports reached Major Sigmund von Imhoff of the State Police. He immediately called all his green police units and had them seize the central telegraph office and the telephone exchange, although his most important act was to notify Major General Jakob von Danner, the *Reichswehr* city commandant of Munich. As a staunch aristocrat, von Danner loathed the "little corporal" [Hitler] and those "*Freikorps* bands of rowdies." He also did not much like his commanding officer, *Generalleutnant* Otto von Lossow, "a sorry figure of a man." He was determined to put down the *putsch* with or without von Lossow. Von Danner set up a command post at the Nineteenth Infantry Regiment barracks and alerted all military units.

Meanwhile, Captain Karl Wild, learning of the *putsch* from marchers, mobilized his command to guard von Kahr's government building, the Commissariat, with orders to shoot.

Around 11:00 p.m., Major General von Danner, along with fellow generals Adolf Ritter von Ruith and Friedrich Freiherr Kress von Kressenstein, compelled General von Lossow to repudiate the *putsch*.

There was one member of the cabinet who was not at the *Bürgerbräukeller*: Franz Matt, the vice-premier and minister of education and culture. A staunchly conservative Roman Catholic, he was having dinner with the Archbishop of Munich, Cardinal Michael von Faulhaber, and with the Nuncio to Bavaria, Archbishop Eugenio Pacelli (who would later become Pope Pius XII), when he learned of the *putsch*. He immediately telephoned von Kahr. When Matt found the man vacillating and unsure, Matt decisively began plans to set up a rump government-in-exile in Regensburg and composed a proclamation calling upon all police officers, members of the armed forces, and civil servants to remain loyal to the von Kahr government. The action of these few men spelled doom for those attempting the *putsch*.

On 11 November 1923, Hitler is arrested while hiding in Hanfstaengl's house at Uffig near Staffelsee outside Munich. According to one version, he attempts to shoot himself in order to avoid arrest, but *Frau* Hanfstaengl manages to wrest the gun from him (Hanfstaengl 1957, 108). He is taken to the fortress prison of Landsberg, south of Munich, where he remains detained on remand until the trial (February 1924).

On Wednesday, 14 November 1923, 3,000 students from the University of Munich rioted and marched to the *Feldherrnhalle* to lay wreaths. They continued to riot until Friday when they learned of Hitler's arrest. Von Kahr and von Lossow were called Judases and traitors.

Two days after the *putsch*, Hitler was charged with high treason in the special People's Court. Some of his fellow conspirators, including Rudolf Heß, were also arrested, while others, including Hermann Göring and Ernst Hanfstaengl, escaped to Austria. The Nazi Party's headquarters was raided, and its newspaper, the *Völkischer Beobachter*, was closed and banned.

On 23 November 1923, both the *NSDAP* and *KPD* were declared illegal.

THE TRIAL

In January 1924, the Emminger Reform, an emergency decree, abolished the jury as trier of fact and replaced it with a mixed system of judges and lay judges in Germany's judiciary, which still exists today.

This was not the first time Hitler had been in trouble with the law. In an incident on 14 September 1921, he and some men of the *SA* had disrupted a meeting of the *Bayernbund* (Bavaria Union) which Otto Ballerstedt, a Bavarian federalist, was to have addressed, and the Nazis who had gone there to cause trouble were arrested as a result. Hitler ended up serving a little over a month (24 June to 27 July 1922) of a suspended three-month jail sentence in Munich's *Stadelheim* Prison. Judge Georg Neithardt was the presiding judge at Hitler's trial in January 1922 and again in February 1924.

On 8 January 1924, Landsberg Prison physician Dr. Brinsteiner signed an attestation stating that Hitler is physically and mentally able to stand trial, despite the fact that during the *putsch* he had "suffered from a dislocation of the left shoulder with a break in the upper arm's joint and, as a result, from a very painful traumatic neurosis." "Of psychic disorders or psychopathic tendencies," Dr. Brinsteiner states, "the patient has no symptoms" (Lurker 1933, 9–11).

Hitler's trial began on 26 February 1924 and lasted until 1 April 1924. Apart from Hitler and General Ludendorff, the two most prominent defendants, eight other men were accused of high treason against the state: Pöhner; Frick; Weber; Röhm; Kriebel; Brückner; Wagner; and Pernet.

General von Lossow acted as chief witness for the prosecution.

Hitler moderated his tone for the trial, centering his defense on his selfless devotion to the good of the people and the need for bold action to save them, dropping his usual anti-Semitism. He claimed the *putsch* had been his sole responsibility, inspiring the title *Führer* or Leader. Hitler opens his speech by explaining why he joined the Nazi Party in Munich:

> The other political parties abandoned their responsibility of dealing with the whole problem which will cause the death of Germany if not tackled, namely the Marxist movement. In my opinion, this is the vital question for the German nation. By Marxism I understand a teaching which rejects in principle the value of personality . . . and makes it possible that a German considers his own blood brother a mortal enemy and a class enemy, while he looks upon our real enemies, the English, the French, and even the completely racially alien Hottentots, as his own brothers. The second tool of Marxism is indiscriminate terror. No other movement has ever worked with such a thorough

> knowledge of the masses as Marxism . . . it offers the worker the following alternative: either you become my brother or I crush your skull . . . We can never conclude peace with this *Weltanschauung*; as far as we are concerned, Germany will be rescued on the day when the last Marxist has been converted or smashed. There is no middle way. Not the bourgeoisie, but the German working people, the masses, must again become nationalistic! . . . If I stand here as a revolutionary, it is against the Revolution and crime. I am not guilty . . . there is no such thing as high treason against those who betrayed the country in 1918 . . . If I am really accused of high treason, then I must wonder why those who did exactly the same as I did are not sitting here with me . . . I mean the gentlemen Kahr, Lossow, Seisser and all the others . . . I feel myself to be not a traitor but the best of Germans who wanted the best for his people. (Jäckel 1981, 1064–6, 1102.)

One of Hitler's greatest worries at the trial was that he was at risk of being deported back to his native Austria by the Bavarian government. On 26 March 1924, the Munich police sent an enquiry to the provincial authorities of Lower Austria in Linz as to whether Hitler should be expelled to Austria after the trial (Hauner 2008, 62).

On 27 March 1924, Hitler delivers his closing statement at the trial with a sharp condemnation of the Weimar Republic. He sums up the Nazi aims: neither republic nor monarchy; abolition of the Peace Treaty; against international "stock-exchange" enslavement; against the domination of corporations over the national economy; against the transformation of trade unions into political bodies; and for the re-introduction of compulsory military service. Hitler rejects General von Lossow's accusation that he was led by ambition when he staged the *putsch*:

> How petty are the thoughts of small men! My aim, from the very first day, was a thousand times more than becoming a minister. What I wanted to become was the destroyer of Marxism. This is my task, and I know when I settle this question—which I will—then the title of minister will become ridiculous. . . . It was not from modesty that I wanted to become a "drummer" in those days. That was the

> highest aspiration; the rest is a trifle . . . The man who is born to be a dictator is not compelled, he wants it; he does not allow himself to be pushed, he drives himself forward. There is nothing immodest about it! . . . We face punishment today because the attempt failed. The deed of 8 November did not fail! . . . I believe that the time will come when the masses which today stand with our swastika flags on the streets will join forces with those who fired on us on 9 November . . . that the hour will come when the *Reichswehr* soldiers will stand on our side . . . and that the old cockade will be taken from the dirt and the old banners will wave again. . . . For it is not you, esteemed gentlemen, who pass the ultimate verdict on us . . . but the eternal court of history. What verdict you will hand down, I know . . . You may pronounce us "guilty" a thousand times over, but the goddess of the eternal court of history will smile and tear to tatters the brief of the state prosecutor and the verdict of this court, for *she* will acquit us (Jäckel 1981, 1210–16).

The Court's verdict was handed down on 1 April 1924. Although the state prosecutor demanded eight years' imprisonment for Hitler, presiding Judge Georg Neithardt handed him a mild, minimum sentence of five years. The same sentence was passed on Kriebel, Pöhner, and Weber, while Brückner, Frick, Röhm, Pernet, and Wagner received a reduced sentence of fifteen months' imprisonment but were immediately released on probation. Röhm's resignation from the *Reichswehr* was accepted in November 1923 during his time as a prisoner at Stadelheim Prison. Presiding trial judge Georg Neithardt was very sympathetic towards Hitler and held that the relevant laws of the Weimar Republic could not be applied to a man "who thinks and feels like a German, as Hitler does." On the grounds of his wartime service, the court dismissed the claim made by the Prosecution that Hitler should be extradited to Austria as an undesirable alien. The result was that the Nazi leader remained in Germany, despite his Austrian citizenship.

The lay judges were fanatically pro-Nazi and had to be dissuaded by Judge Neithardt from acquitting Hitler. Hitler and Heß were both sentenced to five years in *Festungshaft* (*custodia honesta* or honorary custody) and was fined 500 *Reichsmarks* for treason. *Festungshaft* was the mildest of the three types of confinement sentences available in German law at the time; it excluded forced labor, provided reasonably comfortable cells, and allowed the prisoner to receive visitors almost daily for many hours. This was the customary sentence for those whom the judge believed to have had honorable but misguided motives, and it did not carry the stigma of a sentence of *Gefängnisstrafe* (ordinaly imprisonment) or *Zuchthaus* (hard labor). In the end, Hitler served only a little over eight months of this sentence before his early release for good behavior.

By late afternoon, Hitler was back in his cell in Landsberg Prison. "The trial of common narrowmindedness and personal spite is over," he comments, "and today starts *My Struggle* [*Mein Kampf*]" (Toland 1976, 261).

Due to his story that he was present by accident, an explanation he had also used in the Kapp *Putsch,* along with his war service and connections, General Ludendorff was acquitted. Hermann Göring, meanwhile, had fled to Austria after suffering a bullet wound to his leg, which led him to become increasingly dependent on morphine and other painkilling drugs. This addiction continued throughout his life.

As the *NSDAP* had been banned since the failure of the November *putsch,* substitute organizations emerge during Hitler's imprisonment. The *Völkischsozialer Block* (*VSB*), a national bloc consisting of *Deutsche Arbeiterpartei*, *Nationalsozialistische Arbeiterpartei*, and *Deutschvölkische Freiheitspartei*, was founded in Bavaria, led by Alfred Rosenberg, whom Hitler designated his deputy. Rosenberg's rivals, Hermann Esser and Julius Streicher, founded the *Großdeutsche Volksgemeinschaft* (Greater German People's Community), which agitated against participation in elections. Nazi sympathizers outside Bavaria joined the *Deutschvölkische Freiheitspartei* (German Nationalist Freedom Party), which was later to change its name to the *Nationalsozialistische Freiheitsbewegung*, represented by the triumvirate of Ludendorff, Albrecht von Gräfe, and Gregor Straßer (victim of the Night of the Long Knives and brother of Otto Straßer). The imprisoned Hitler had very little influence on these movements.

While imprisoned, Hitler appointed Alfred Rosenberg to replace him as the underground *NSDAP* leader, with Max Amann, Hermann Esser, and Julius Streicher as his deputies. "It was the greatest good fortune for us National Socialists that this *Putsch* collapsed," Hitler declared in 1933. He gave three reasons: "(1) Cooperation with Ludendorff would have been absolutely impossible; (2) the sudden takeover of power in the whole of Germany would have led to the greatest of difficulties in 1923 because the essential preparations by the *NSDAP* had not even begun; and (3) the events of 9 November 1923 in front of the *Feldherrnhalle,* with their blood sacrifice, have proven to be the most effective propaganda for National Socialism" (Gordon 1972, 408–9). Hitler also nominated Ernst Röhm as the military leader of the *Kampfbund*.

Though Hitler failed to achieve his immediate stated goal, the *putsch* did give the Nazis their first exposure to national attention and a propaganda victory. While serving their honorary "fortress confinement" sentences at Landsberg Prison, Hitler, Emil Maurice, and Rudolf Heß wrote *Mein Kampf.* Also, the *putsch* changed Hitler's outlook on violent revolution to effect change. From then on, he thought that in order to win the German heart, he must do everything by the book, "strictly legal."

The process of *combination*, where the conservative-Nationalist-monarchist faction thought that its members could piggyback onto and control the National Socialist movement to gain the seats of power, was to repeat itself ten years later after the 1933 federal election when Franz von Papen would legally ask Hitler to form a coalition government.

"SABBATICAL" IN LANDSBERG AM LECH 11 NOVEMBER 1923–20 DECEMBER 1924

SINCE HIS ARREST ON 11 NOVEMBER 1923, HITLER HAD BEEN CONFINED AT the fortress prison in Landsberg am Lech. Shortly after his trial and return to Landsberg Prison, Hitler completed an article "Why did the 8th November Have to Come?" which was published in the monthly *Deutschlands Erneuerung*. Apart from his justification of the November *putsch,* Hitler presents his view of Germany's foreign policy which, he believes, has only two options, just as before 1914: "Either one opted for winning farm land, giving up maritime trade and colonies, giving up over-industrialization, etc. . . . in league with England against the Soviet Union. Or one opted for sea power and world trade, in which case the only alternative, was an alliance with the Soviet Union against England." Although some forty other Nazis served time in prison with Hitler, only he and a handful of others (Kriebel, Weber, Hitler's chauffeur Emil Maurice, and later Rudolf Heß, who worked for him as his secretary) enjoy special privileges. He eats well and puts on weight. He is allowed to spend much of his time outdoors in the garden and to receive as many visitors as he wishes for a total length of about six hours weekly. Hardly a day passes without a visitor calling on him. Meals are served three times a day at a common table over which he presides. An unlimited number of food parcels was permitted. Although mail was in theory censored, Hitler and his companions manage to hectograph every week an underground magazine, for which Hitler usually writes the leading article and contributes caricatures. No manual work was required from the prisoners, who are allowed to wear their civilian clothes. Visitors confirmed that when they saw Hitler in Landsberg Prison, they felt that he was in a sanatorium rather than in a prison (Lurker 1933, 18, 31, 51–6; Lüdecke 1937, 232–3).

On 1 March 1924, the government's ban on the Communist Party of Germany (*KPD*) was rescinded the *KPD* was fully reinstated.

On 13 March 1924, owing to the insistence of the minority parties in altering the Weimar government's emergency decrees, President Ebert dissolved the *Reichstage* and called for new federal elections.

On 20 April, the provincial government of Lower Austria replied to Munich police that there was no objection to Hitler's deportation. On his thirty-fifth birthday, Hitler received twenty visitors and so many parcels and flowers that they fill several rooms in Landsberg Prison.

On 4 May, *Reichstag* federal elections produce significant gains for the German National People's Party (*DNVP*, up 24 seats to 95) and the Communist Party (*KPD*, up 58 seats to 62). *NSDAP* members, running as the National Socialist Freedom Movement (*NSFB*), win a total of 32 seats; ten Nazis become deputies. Hitler seems genuinely surprised but not overjoyed. "From now on we must follow a new line of action," he tells Lüdecke, who visited him shortly after the election (Hauner 2008, 48).

> It is best to attempt no large organization until I am freed, which may be a matter of months rather than years. . . . I am not going to stay here much longer. When I resume active work, it will be necessary to pursue a new policy. Instead of working to achieve power by an armed coup, we shall have to hold our noses and enter the *Reichstag* against the Catholic and Marxist deputies. If out-voting them takes longer than out-shooting them, at least the results will be guaranteed by their own Constitution! Already we have 32 deputies under this new programme, and are the second largest party in the Bavarian Diet. Sooner or later we shall have a majority—and after that, Germany. I am convinced

> this is our best line of action, now that conditions in the country have changed so radically (Lüdecke 1937, 234).

By 8 May, it was becoming increasingly evident that Hitler's deportation to Austria, which was requested by the Bavarian State Police, was being obstructed by the Minister of Justice (Hauner 2008, 48).

On 16 August, *Der Nationalsozialist*, a Nazi magazine published in Leipzig, carried an interview between Hitler and Hermann Kügler, a National Socialist from Czechoslovakia, who visited Hitler in Landsberg Prison (on 29 July). To the question of whether he had changed his position on the Jewish question, Hitler answered: "I have been far too soft up to now! While working on my book, I have finally come to realize that the harshest methods of fighting must be employed in the future if we are to win. I am convinced that this is not only a matter of life and death for our people but for all peoples. The Jew is a world plague" (Jäckel 1981, 1242).

On 15 September 1924, the director of Landsberg Prison writes a favorable report on Hitler to the State Prosecutor in Munich, stressing his exemplary behavior and pleading that Hitler should be released on 1 October, when he will be eligible for parole. Hitler is portrayed as a remarkable political figure of the first magnitude, deeply dedicated to the salvation of nationalist Germany and "very much convinced now that a State cannot exist without firm order" (Lurker 1933, 60–2).

In a report to the Ministry of Justice in Munich, dated 18 September 1924, the director of Landsberg Prison sums up his observations of Hitler: "From the very beginning Hitler did not reply, or only very briefly, to written questions. . . . After making some bitter statements about being misquoted in the press, Hitler announced that he wanted to refrain from giving political statements." Over the last couple of weeks, the director emphasized, Hitler had indeed abstained from party politics (Tyrell 1969, 76–7).

On 22 September, the Bavarian State Police submit another request for Hitler's deportation to Austria, which was effectively thwarted by the Ministry of Justice despite the argument that 'the moment he is set free, Hitler will, because of his energy, again become the driving force of new and serious public riots and a menace to the security of the state" (Bullock 1968, 127).

Three days later on 25 September, the Bavarian Supreme Court recommends Hitler for parole, but the Office of the State Prosecutor rules against it.

By 16 October 1924, Hitler completed the first part of his book dedicated to sixteen fallen party comrades who died on 9 November 1923. The original title, "Four and a Half Years of Struggle Against Lies, Stupidity, and Cowardice," sounded so clumsy that Max Amann suggested a brief title, *Mein Kampf* (*My Struggle*), which Hitler grudgingly accepted. In preparing the manuscript, Hitler was assisted greatly by Heß, who not only did most of the typing but also helped Hitler to improve his style. The prison staff allowed the lights in Hitler's cell to burn until midnight so they could work on the book.

On 18 October, *Der Völkische Kurier* publishes Hitler's reaction to the recent decision by the Austrian government to take away his citizenship. The withdrawal of Austrian nationality should not be taken too seriously, replied Hitler, since he "never felt as an Austrian citizen, but always as a German" (Jäckel 1981, 1247).

On 14 December, the director of Landsberg Prison writes another extremely favorable letter on Hitler's behalf, pleading that he should be released on parole, since he was not politically dangerous anymore and set such "a good example to his fellow-prisoners" (Lurker 1933, 63).

On 19 December at about 10 p.m., Hitler is awakened by the prison director who personally brings him the long-awaited news: "Herr Hitler, you are free" (Jäckel 1981, 1249).

The following day on 20 December 1924, Hitler says goodbye to his fellow prisoners. "When I left Landsberg Prison, everybody wept—but not I!" he recalled later and described his imprisonment as: "my university at state expense." A brand-new Mercedes awaited him at the gates—a gift from Albert Pietsch, the president of the Chamber of Commerce of Munich. When he arrived at his apartment at 41 *Thierschstraße*, he found it decorated with flowers and laurel wreaths (Hauner 2008, 50).

1925
REPRISE

ON 12 FEBRUARY 1925, HITLER'S RIVALS, GENERAL LUDENDORFF AND Albrecht von Gräfe, resign from the leadership of the National Socialist Freedom Movement. Four days later on 16 February, emergency legislation against the *NSDAP* is lifted in Bavaria.

The first issue of *NSDAP*'s *Völkischer Beobachter* reappears on 26 February 1925 after the ban, carrying Hitler's "Fundamental Directives for the Reconstitution of the *NSDAP*," in which he rejected past quarrels between individual Nazi leaders, welcomed General Ludendorff, who had agreed to stand as the Nazi candidate in the forthcoming Weimar presidential election, and reiterated his demand for unconditional obedience. In his second article, "A New Beginning for Our Movement," Hitler discussed the relationship with the ruling Bavarian People's Party and made it clear that he did not wish to fight against Christianity, but against "that power which is the deadly enemy of every form of Christianity, no matter what confession," namely Bolshevism (Noakes and Pridham 1974, 68–70).

On 27 February 1925, Hitler delivered the first speech after his release from prison, which was considered masterful, at a mass gathering of *NSDAP* members and sympathizers in Munich's *Bürgerbräukeller*. He declared the *NSDAP* to be reconstituted. As usual, he attacked the Jews: "Their poisoning of pure Aryan blood is the greatest danger. All other dangers can be overcome but once the blood is poisoned it can no longer be changed; it remains and multiplies and presses us lower from year to year." About his own position as the irreplaceable *Führer*, he said: "If anyone comes and wants to impose conditions on me, I shall say to him: "Just wait, my little friend, and see what conditions I impose on you" . . . I am not contending for the favors of the masses . . . I alone lead the Movement, fand no one can impose conditions on me so long as I personally bear the responsibility!" (Heiden 1944, 205–10). The rank-and-file members enthusiastically accepted Hitler's claim that the future of the Movement depended on his personal control. His lieutenants—Buttmann, Esser, Feder, Frick, Streicher—rushed to the stage to pledge loyal support. But there were also noticeable absentees: Drexler, Röhm, Rosenberg, Straßer and, of course, Ludendorff, who thus demonstrated their disagreement. The reconstitution of the *NSDAP* meant a further disintegration of the once-united Nationalist movement; in the *Reichstag*, the four remaining Nazi deputies separated themselves from the Nationalist coalition and the same process took place in the Bavarian *Landtag* (Hauner 2008, 51).

On 25 April, Paul von Hindenburg becomes president of the republic.

On 18 July, the first edition of *Mein Kampf* is published and sold out nearly as fast as it could be printed.

On 25 August 1925, the last Belgian troops leave Germany.

On 9 November, the *Schutzstaffel* (*SS*) is formally established.

1 December, after seven years of occupation, British troops finally depart the city of Cologne (Rhineland).

From 1925 (actually, from 1920) to 1933, Hitler and the *NSDAP* navigate around one obstacle after another and by shear will execute a series of unlikely victories unwitnessed before in world political history to rise from complete obscurity and insignificance against seemingly insurmountable odds and to seize control of an industrialized nation of 67 million people in the heart of Old Europe. Like the Greek *phoenix* or the Egyptian *bennu*, twentieth-century Greater Germany in its smoldering cauldron of tumult, tragedy, and downfall gives birth to an unlikely leader who seizes the reins of his desperate and directionless people to lift them from the ashes of defeat to glory and world dominance and, eventually, deliver them to the gates of hell in only twenty-five years. Theirs is truly a rare story in human history. Unlike the familiar history of the great empires that have also risen from obscurity to glory and then fallen back to obscurity but over many centuries, Germany's twentieth-century story is unprecedented in what it achieved and delivered in such a short term.

THE BLOODLESS *COUP*

We do not know whether Hitler is going to found a new Islam. He is already on the way; he is like Mohammad. The emotion in Germany is Islamic; warlike and Islamic. They are all drunk with wild god. That can be the historic future.

— Swiss psychiatrist CARL JUNG, 1939
The Symbolic Life

Then will come a National Socialist State tribunal; then will November 1918 [Armistice of Compiègne], *be expiated; then the heads will roll.*

— Hitler's testimony at a trial of German Officers, Leipzig, 1930

How fortunate for leaders that men do not think.

— ADOLF HITLER

AFTER THE MURDERS OF 15 JANUARY 1919 (SPARTACIST UPRISING), THE animosity between the Social Democratic Party of Germany (*SPD*) and Communist Party of Germany (*KPD*) grew even deeper. The *USPD* (Independent Social Democratic Party of Germany) dissolved on 24 September 1922 when it merged back into the *SPD* adopting the name United Social Democratic Party of Germany (*Vereinigte Sozialdemokratische Partei Deutschlands*, *VSPD*), which was soon shortened back to *SPD* in 1924. In the following years, the *SPD*, *KPD*, Catholic Center Party, and German National People's Party (*DNVP*) were the only political parties in a position to form a coalition to block the rising Nazi Party from taking power, but out of mutual distrust between *KPD* and *SPD* stemming from the days of the Spartacist Uprising, they were unable to agree on joint action against the Nazi Party, which as of 1930 dramatically grew in strength.

Political Parties in the *Reichstag*	**Jun 1920**	**May 1924**	**Dec 1924**	**May 1928**	**Sep 1930**	**Jul 1932**	**Nov 1932**	**Mar 1933**
KPD	4	62	45	54	77	89	100	81
SPD	102	100	131	153	143	133	121	120
Catholic Center Party	65	81	88	78	87	97	90	93
DNVP	71	95	103	73	41	37	52	52
NSDAP	-	-	-	12	107	230	196	288
Other Parties	98	92	73	121	122	22	35	23

StJbDR (Statistisches Jahrbuch für das Deutsche Reich) Statistical Yearbook for the German *Reich*, 1933, page 539.

As described earlier, the German National People's Party (*DNVP*) was formed in December 1918 from the merger of German Conservative Party, Free Conservative Party, German Fatherland Party, and the radically conservative remnants of the National Liberal Party and Christian Social Party (see Figure 2, *supra*). The *DNVP* was mainly funded by wealthy German industrialist Hugo Stinnes. This Nationalist party opposed the Versailles Treaty, supported the restoration of the monarchy, and was critical of the power of the trade unions. Led in part by the wealthy media magnate

Alfred Hugenberg, the *DNVP* won 71 seats in the *Reichstag* in the 1920 general election, including Hugenberg himself. Ernst Oberfohren was one of those elected to represent the *DNVP* in the *Reichstag*, and in the December 1924 election the *DNVP* won 103 seats. In 1929, Oberfohren was appointed parliamentary leader and Hugenberg was made sole party chairman, but by the 1930 election the Nazi Party became the dominant Nationalist movement in Germany.

The German Youth Movement was an important objective of and contributing element to the Nazi movement. The **Young German Order** (*Jungdeutsche Orden*, often abbreviated as *Jungdo*) was a large paramilitary organization founded in 1920 in Weimar Germany. Its name and symbol were inspired by the Teutonic Knights (*Deutscher Orden*). The pseudo-chivalric group was involved in Nationalistic German politics. Its youth organization was called *Jungdeutsche Jugend* (*Young German Youth*). *Jungdo*'s political arm, the *Volksnationale Reichsvereinigung* (*People's National Reich Association*) merged with the German Democratic Party (*DDP*) and parts of the Christian Social People's Service in July 1930 to become the German State Party (*DStP*). The group was founded by Artur Mahraun in May 1920 in Kassel (Hesse, Weimar Republic). The organization tried to revive ideals of the pre-war *Wandervogel* youth movement.[4] Very soon it reached 70,000 members, was temporarily banned in early 1921 and, being one of the largest paramilitary groups in the 1920s, later expanded to almost 300,000 members. After the Enabling Act on 23 March 1933, *Jungdo* was banned by the Nazis. Most members were absorbed into the Nazi Party.

The **German State Party** (*Deutsche Staatspartei, DStP*) was a short-lived German political party of the Weimar Republic formed by the merger of the German Democratic Party (*DDP*) with the Young German Order in July 1930. The need to reach across generational lines to those who had just begun to exercise their political rights played a far more important role in the strategy for the September 1930 federal election than in any previous election. The Conservative People's Party (*KVP*), for example, was every bit as determined as the *DStP* to achieve a breakthrough into the ranks of the German Youth Movement and set the task of freeing German youth from the hypnotic spell of National Socialism as one of its major campaign goals. By the same token, the leaders of the German People's Party of 1918 (Gustav Stresemann) were desperate to contain the damage that the founding of the *DStP* and the *KVP* had done to their party's own youth organizations and made a more concerted bid for the support of the younger generation than they had done in any previous campaign.

The merger of the Social Liberalism of the *DDP* with the Nationalist corporatism of the Young German Order (*Jungdo*) did not prove a successful one. As the outcome of the 1930 federal election so poignantly revealed, the principal beneficiary of the generational cleavages that had become so deeply embedded in the fabric of Weimar electoral politics was neither the more traditional *bourgeois* parties nor any of the myriad middle-class splinter parties that had appeared on the German political landscape since the middle of the 1920s, but the National Socialist German Workers' Party under Adolf Hitler. At the very least, it was clear that the efforts to build a bridge between the younger generation and the existing party system had ended in failure. The *DStP* went down to a devasting defeat in the 1930 election, in which it lost a fifth of the seats the *DDP* had received just two years earlier, sixteen additional seats in the July 1932 federal election, and two more seats lost in the November 1932 federal election, leaving the *DStP* with only two seats, down from 25 seats the *DStP* inherited at the time of its founding. The German People's Party of 1918, in the meantime, had lost more than a third of its 1928 seats. Nor had it been possible, as the *KVP*'s fate so stunningly demonstrated, to rally the younger generation to the support of the more moderate elements among German Conservatives. The *KVP* had managed to elect only four representatives to the *Reichstag* in 1930.

The outcome of the 1930 federal election dealt a devastating psychological blow to those who had pinned their hopes on overcoming the generational cleavages that had become so deeply embedded in Weimar's political culture. Following its defeat at the polls, the tenuous alliance upon which the *DStP* had been founded began to unravel, and in the first week of October 1930 the *Jungdo* announced its secession from the *DStP*. *Jungdo* had been severely chastened by the way in which their venture into the realm of German party politics had ended, and they moved quickly to put their ill-fated alliance with the *DStP* behind them in the hope of repairing the damage their role in the founding of that party had done to their credibility as a spokesman for the young generation. Meanwhile, the Young Democratic movement had become irreparably divided between those who supported the *DStP* and those who joined the Association of Independent Democrats to establish the Radical Democratic Party (*Radikaldemokratische Partei*, *RDP*) in November 1930. Fate of the *RDP* was the same as for all other political parties in Germany after the passage of the Enabling Act in March 1933.

The German Youth Movement's foray into politics among non-Socialist parties failed at nearly every turn. By the summer of 1932, virtually all of Germany's political youth organizations, except for the Catholic Windthorst Leagues and the rapidly growing Hitler Youth (*Hitler-Jugend*), were on the verge of complete collapse. The net effect of these developments was to leave the younger politically-active generation—many of whom had survived the terror of trench warfare on the fronts only to return home to discover their Socialist political leadership in Berlin had sold them out—with little alternative but to turn to the *NSDAP* and its various associated student and youth organizations that it had created as part of its own crusade for popular support. Among the youth veterans, the invocation of the front experience, with its juxtaposition of the selfless heroism and brotherhood of the trenches to the discord and flabbiness of the home front, represented part of a concerted attempt by the self-appointed leaders of the "front generation" to redefine the polis on essentially male terms and to exclude those whom they held responsible for the collapse of 1918 from any sort of meaningful role in determining Germany's political future. The susceptibility of the younger generation to this sort of rhetoric was greatly enhanced not only by the strong sense of Nationalism to which defeat and the humiliation of Versailles had given rise but, more importantly, by its profound disaffection from the older generation of political leaders who had led the ship of state into the troubled waters of materialist interest politics. In their efforts to free German public life from the tyranny of economic self-interest that the political parties were pursuing in 1918, however, the leaders of the younger generation unwittingly fertilized the soil in which the seeds of Nazism could take root and flourish. For as the fate of the *DStP* and the People's Conservative movement so clearly revealed, the campaign to rebaptize the German party system in the spirit of the "front generation" did little to reconcile the generational cleavages that had become such a prominent feature of Weimar political culture. On the contrary, the net effect of this push was only to accelerate the drift of Germany's younger voters into the ranks of those who sought the nation's salvation not in the reform but in the destruction of the existing political system (Jones 1992, 365–9).

After the 1932 federal election, all requests by the *DStP* to merge with other parties were turned down. It ran on a joint list with the Social Democratic Party of Germany in the March 1933 election. However, this saw little change in the party's fortunes; it only won five seats. The party supported the Enabling Act of 1933, though with significant reservations. Following the Enabling Act's passage, the party was the target of severe harassment, as was the case with the other remaining parties. Pro-*DStP* civil servants defected to the Nazis out of fear for their jobs. Soon after the government banned the *SPD*, it stripped the State Party of its *Reichstag* seats, taking the line that since the *DStP* ran on the *SPD* ballot, they were effectively *SPD* deputies. What remained of the party dissolved on 28 June 1933.

Between 1925 and 1928, the German National People's Party (*DNVP*) slightly moderated its tone and actively cooperated in successive governments. In the presidential election of 1925, the *DNVP* supported Karl Jarres for president, who was defeated in the first round by Center Party's Wilhelm Marx, who however failed to gain a majority. Fearing that Marx would win the second round (something made the more likely by the fact that the *SPD*'s Otto Braun had dropped out to endorse Marx), Admiral Alfred von Tirpitz made a dramatic visit to the home of the retired Field Marshal Paul von Hindenburg to ask him to run for the second round in order to "save" Germany by gaining the presidency for the right. Von Tirpitz persuaded von Hindenburg to run, and though von Hindenburg won the election as a non-party candidate, the *DNVP* strongly supported the Field Marshal. General Otto von Feldmann of the *DNVP* worked very closely with von Hindenburg during the 1925 election as von Hindenburg's "political agent." Despite the move to the Center, the grassroots of the party moved in the opposite direction. Beginning in 1924, the *DNVP*'s newsletter for women (which was written entirely by female volunteers) started to vehemently insist that German women only marry a "Nordic man" and raise their children to be racists. From the mid-1920s onwards, the women party activists started to draft plans calling for the end of all "Jewish cultural influence" in Germany, banning Jews from working as teachers and writers, making eugenics into state policy with a new class of bureaucrats to be called "racial guardians" to be created in order to assess a couple's "racial worth" before allowing them to marry or not, and breaking German citizenship into two grades of those allowed to marry and those who would not.

A further problem for the *DNVP* was the rise of rural rage in the late 1920s. By 1927, though Germany itself was overall very prosperous, a steep economic decline had begun in rural areas, which was only to worsen with the coming of the Great Depression in 1929. By late 1927, it was clear that the increases in agrarian tariffs that the *DNVP* ministers had forced through had made no impact on the continuing economic decline in the countryside, and as result a mood of palpable anger and resentment had set in the countryside of northern Germany with many *DNVP* voters damning their own party. The political repercussion of rural rage was the rise of a number of small parties representing rural voters in northern Germany such as the Agricultural League, German Farmers' Party, and the Christian-National Peasants' and Farmers' Party, which all took away traditional *DNVP* voters, a development that contributed significantly to *DNVP*'s poor showing in the 1928 elections. Finally, Admiral von Tirpitz who had done so much for the *DNVP*'s good showing in the 1924 elections, had often come into conflict with *DNVP* Chairman Count Kuno von Westarp over his policy of half-hearted participation in the government, and chose not to run in 1928, claiming very publicly that the *DNVP* needed more aggressive leaders than von Westarp. The man von Tirpitz chose to continue his work of winning Bavaria for the *DNVP*, General Paul von Lettow-Vorbeck did not have the same mass appeal and in 1928, the *DNVP* won only half the vote in Bavaria that it managed to do in December 1924.

Despite winning a majority in the Bavarian *Landtag* elections on 5 March 1928, the disastrous showing at the polls in the *Reichstag* election of 20 May 1928 (the party's share of votes fell from 21 percent in 1924 to 14 percent in 1928) led to a new outbreak of party infighting. The immediate cause of the infighting was an article published in July 1928 entitled "Monarchism" (*Monarchismus*) by Walther Lambach, an important representative of the liberal social wing in the Nationalist *DNVP* and a board member of the German National Association of Commercial Employees (*DHV*). In his article, Lambach stated that the restoration of the monarchy was no longer possible and that for almost all Germans under the age of thirty the *DNVP*'s incessant talk of bringing back the monarchy was irrelevant at best and downright off-putting at worse. Lambach wrote that for conservative Germans President von Hindenburg had long since replaced the former Kaiser as the object of their affections and that the *DNVP*'s poor showing in the May 1928 elections was a result of the party running on a platform of restoring the monarchy, a goal that most Germans were simply not interested in. Lambach's article with its call for the *DNVP* to transform itself into a party of conservative republicans set off a storm, with the party's core monarchist supporters successfully pressuring its chairman von Westarp to expel Lambach. Led by Alfred Hugenberg, the enraged monarchists then turned their sights on von Westarp himself, claiming he was a weak leader who let republican elements into the party.

In October 1928, Hugenberg, leader of the *DNVP*'s hardliner wing, became chairman. Hugenberg returned the party to a course of fundamental opposition against the Weimar Republic with a greater emphasis on

Nationalism and reluctant cooperation with the Nazi Party. Hugenberg was utterly devoid of personal charisma or charm, but he was a successful industrialist and media magnate, a fabulously wealthy man whose talents at devising business strategies which had made him a millionaire many times over were felt to be equally applicable to the arena of politics.

ALFRED ERNST CHRISTIAN ALEXANDER HUGENBERG (1865–1951)

ALFRED HUGENBERG WAS AN INFLUENTIAL GERMAN BUSINESSMAN AND politician. A leading figure in Nationalist politics in Germany for the first few decades of the twentieth century, he became the country's leading media proprietor during the inter-war period. As leader of the German National People's Party (*DNVP*) he was instrumental in helping Adolf Hitler become Chancellor of Germany and served in his first cabinet in 1933, hoping to control Hitler and use him as his "tool." Those plans backfired, and by the end of 1933, Hugenberg had been marginalized. Although Hugenberg continued to serve as a "guest" member of the *Reichstag* until 1945, he wielded no political influence.

Born in Hanover to Carl Hugenberg, a royal Hanoverian official who in 1867 entered the Prussian *Landtag* as a member of the National Liberal Party, Alfred studied law in Göttingen, Heidelberg, and Berlin, as well as economics in Straßburg. In 1891, Alfred was awarded a doctorate at Straßburg for his dissertation *Internal Colonization in Northwest Germany*, in which he set out three principles that guided his political thought for the rest of his life:

- The necessity for statist economic policies to allow German farmers to be successful.
- Despite the necessity for the state to assist farmers, the German farmer should be encouraged to act as an entrepreneur thereby creating a class of successful farmers/small businessmen who would act as a bulwark against the appeal of the Marxist Social Democrats, whom Hugenberg viewed as a grave threat to the *status quo*.
- Finally, to allow the German farmers to be successful required a policy of imperialism, as Hugenberg argued on Social Darwinist grounds that the "power and significance of the German race" could

> be secured if Germany colonized other nations. Hugenberg maintained that Germany's prosperity depended upon having a great empire, and argued that in the coming twentieth century, Germany would have to battle three great rivals, namely Britain, the United States, and Russia for world supremacy.

From 1894 to 1899, Hugenberg worked as a Prussian civil servant in Posen (modern Poznań, Poland). At the same time, he was also involved in a scheme in the Province of Posen, in which the Prussian Settlement Commission bought up land from Poles in order to settle ethnic Germans there. In 1899, Hugenberg had called for "annihilation of Polish population." Hugenberg was strongly anti-Polish and criticized the Prussian government for its "inadequate" Polish policies, favoring a more vigorous policy of Germanization.

Hugenberg initially took a role organizing agricultural societies before entering the civil service in the Prussian Ministry of Finance in 1903. Again, Hugenberg came into conflict with his superiors, who opposed his plans to confiscate all the non-productive estates of the *Junkers* (landed nobility) to settle hundreds of thousands of ethnic Germans, who would become his idealized farmer-small businessmen and "Germanize" the East. He left the public sector to pursue a career in business, and in 1909 he was appointed chairman of the supervisory board of Krupp Steel, and built up a close personal and political relationship with Baron Gustav Krupp von Bohlen und Halbach—the heir of Friedrich Krupp *AG* (*Aktiengesellschaft*) through marriage and declared by imperial proclamation and *primogeniture*. Krupp *AG* had been "in search of a man of really superior intelligence" to run the finance department and found that man in form of Hugenberg, with his "extraordinary" intelligence and work ethic. In 1902, Friedrich Alfred Krupp—Krupp *AG*'s heir preceding his daughter Berta and her husband Gustav—was ousted, and allegedly committed suicide after the *SPD* newspaper *Vorwärts!* published love letters he had written to his Italian lovers—adolescent boys. After his death, the entire firm of Krupp *AG* was left to his daughter, Bertha Krupp. As Krupp *AG* was one of the world's largest arms manufactures, and the biggest supplier of weapons to the German Empire, the management of Krupp *AG* was of some interest to the state, and Emperor Wilhelm II did not believe that a woman was capable of running a business. To solve this perceived problem, the Kaiser had Bertha marry a career diplomat Gustav von Bohlen und Halbach, who was regarded by the Kaiser as a safe man to run Krupp *AG*. Gustav Krupp, as he was renamed by Wilhelm, did not know much about running a business, and so depended very much on his board to assist him. Hugenberg's role in the management of Krupp *AG* was thus considerably larger than what his title of Director of Finance would indicate, and in many ways, Hugenberg was the man who effectively ran the Krupp corporation during his ten years at the firm between 1908 and 1918.

In 1914, Hugenberg welcomed the war and resumed his work with his close friend Heinrich Claß of the Pan-German League. During the war, Hugenberg was an annexationist who wanted the war to end with Germany annexing much of Europe, Africa, and Asia to make the *Reich* into the world's greatest power. In September 1914, Hugenberg and Claß co-authored a memorandum setting out the annexationist platform, which demanded that, once the war was won, Germany would annex Belgium and northern France, British sea power would end, and Russia would be reduced to the "frontiers existing at the time of Peter the Great" (Leopold 1977, 6). Beyond that, Germany was to annex all of the British, French, and Belgian colonies in sub-Saharan Africa, and create an "economic union" embracing Germany, France, Austro-Hungary, Italy, the Scandinavian nations, and the nations of the Balkans, that would be dominated by the *Deutsches Reich.* Finally, the Hugenberg-Claß memo called for a policy of colonization in Eastern Europe, where the German state would deport indigenous Slavs and settle thousands of German farmers in the land annexed from the Russian Empire.

Hugenberg remained at Krupp *AG* until 1918, when he set out to build his own business, and during the Great Depression he was able to buy up dozens of local newspapers. Hugenberg's increasing involvement in pan-German and annexationist causes together with his interest in building a media empire, caused him to depart from Krupp *AG*, which he found to be a distraction from what really interested him. These newspapers became the basis of his publishing firm, Scherl House and, after he added controlling interests in Universum Film *AG*, advertiser Ala-Anzeiger *AG*, newspaper conglomerate Vera Verlag, and publisher Telegraphen Union, he had a near monopoly on the media, which he used to agitate Germany's middle classes against the Weimar Republic. Given the absence of antitrust laws in Imperial Germany (Schwartz 1957, 635 fn 67; see also Ballersted 1911, 15–17),* this

* The Imperial Administration opposed such legislation for different reasons, one of which was the view that German industry, unless cartelized, would be too weak in the competitive struggle with cartelized foreign industries. For a survey of the

was the greatest concentration of power influencing German public opinion, and it was mobilized to support an ultra-Nationalist program while declaring war on pacifism, internationalism, Socialism, and parliamentary Democracy.

Hugenberg was one of several pan-Germans to become involved in the National Liberal Party in the run up to the First World War. During the war, his views shifted sharply to the right. Accordingly, he switched his allegiance to the Fatherland Party and became one of its leading members, emphasizing territorial expansion and anti-Semitism as his two main political issues. In 1919, Hugenberg followed most of the Fatherland Party into the German National People's Party (*DNVP*), which he represented in the National Assembly (that produced the 1919 Weimar Constitution). He was elected to the *Reichstag* in the 1920 elections. The *DNVP* suffered heavy losses in the 1928 election, leading to the appointment of Hugenberg as sole chairman on 21 October that same year.

Conflict in the streets between Communists and National Socialists continued at a steady pace. On 1 May 1929 (May Day), Berlin police shot thirty-two Communists illegally demonstrating. The massacre became known as *Blutmai* ("Bloody May").

Hugenberg moved the *DNVP* in a far more radical direction than it had taken under its previous leader, Kuno Graf von Westarp. He hoped to use sectarian Nationalism to restore the party's fortunes, and eventually, to overthrow the Weimar Constitution and install an authoritarian form of government. Up to this point, conservative politics outside sectarian Nationalism was going through a process of reconciliation with the Weimar Republic, but this ended under Hugenberg, who renewed earlier *DNVP* calls for its immediate destruction. Under his direction, a new *DNVP* manifesto appeared in 1931, demonstrating the shift to sectarian Nationalism. Among its demands were immediate restoration of the Hohenzollern monarchy, a reversal of the terms of the Treaty of Versailles, compulsory military conscription, repossession of the German colonial empire, a concerted effort to build up closer links with German speaking people outside Germany (especially in Austria), a dilution of the role of the *Reichstag* from that of a supervisory body to a newly-established professional house of appointees reminiscent of Mussolini's corporative state, and reduction in the perceived over-representation of Jews in German public life. Hugenberg also sought to eliminate internal party Democracy and instill a *führerprinzip* within the

---

attempts made by several *Reichstag* parties to introduce anti-cartel legislation, see Michels 1928, 34 and *Denkschrift* 1905–1907.

DNVP, leading some members to break away and establish the Conservative People's Party (*KVP*) in early 1930. More were to follow in June 1930, appalled by Hugenberg's extreme opposition to the cabinet of Heinrich Brüning, a moderate whom some within the *DNVP* wanted to support. Under Hugenberg's leadership, the *DNVP* toned down and later abandoned the monarchism which had characterized the party in its earlier years. Despite Hugenberg's background in industry, that constituency gradually deserted the *DNVP* under his leadership, largely due to a general feeling among industrialists that Hugenberg was too inflexible, and soon the party became the main voice of agrarian interests in the *Reichstag*.

In July 1929, the consummate pan-Germanist Hugenberg decided that the best way of regaining popularity was to use the section of the Weimar Constitution that allowed upon collecting a certain number of signatures a referendum to be held, in this case on the Young Plan.[5] As part of his polarizing strategy, Hugenberg created the *Reichsausschuß* (national committee) for the People's Rebellion Against the Young Plan in the summer of 1929, which was intended to be a sort of counter-parliament to the *Reichstag*. The *Reichsausschuß* comprised Hugenberg, Heinrich Claß of the Pan-German League, Franz Seldte of the *Stahlhelm, Bund der Frontsoldaten* (The Steel Helmet, Association of Frontline Soldiers), and Adolf Hitler of the *NSDAP*. Hugenberg saw himself as the leader of the *Reichsausschuß* and believed through the *Reichsausschuß* he would become the leader of the entire Nationalist bloc and in turn the bloc he intended to create would at last win enough seats in the *Reichstag* to have a majority.

Hugenberg successfully collected enough signatures to initiate a referendum on his "Freedom Law" which called for cancelling the Young Plan together with all reparations. The fact that the Young Plan reduced reparations and committed the Allies to exiting the Rhineland in June 1930 (which was five years earlier than what Versailles had called for) was irrelevant to Hugenberg. He argued that a truly patriotic government would not pay any reparations at all and would force the Allies to leave the Rhineland at once. As such, Hugenberg drafted "A Bill against the Enslavement of the German People" which declared acceptance of the Young Plan to be high treason under the grounds that Germany should not have to pay any reparations, and that those ministers who signed the Young Plan on behalf of the *Reich* government and those who voted for the Young Plan in the *Reichstag* should be prosecuted for high treason.

Hugenberg was vehemently opposed to the Young Plan, and he set up a "*Reich* Committee for the German People's Petition" to oppose it, featuring the likes of Franz Seldte, Heinrich Claß, Theodor Duesterberg, and steel magnate Fritz Thyssen. However, Hugenberg recognized that the *DNVP* and their elite band of allies did not have enough popular support to carry out the scheme to reject the Young Plan. As such, Hugenberg felt that he needed a Nationalist with support among the working classes, whom he could use to whip up popular sentiment against the Plan. Adolf Hitler was the only realistic candidate, and Hugenberg decided that he would use the Nazi Party leader to achieve his goals. As a result, the Nazi Party soon became the recipients of Hugenberg's largesse, both in terms of monetary donations and of favorable coverage from the Hugenberg-owned media, which had previously largely ignored Hitler or denounced him as a Socialist. Joseph Goebbels, who had a deep hatred of Hugenberg, initially spoke privately of breaking away from Hitler over the alliance, but he changed his mind when Hugenberg agreed that Goebbels should handle the propaganda for the campaign, giving the Nazi Party access to Hugenberg's media empire.

Hugenberg's efforts led to the Young Plan referendum on 22 December 1929. The *NSDAP* was one of the groups which joined Hugenberg's campaign against the Young Plan, and the resulting wave of publicity brought Adolf Hitler back into the limelight after five years of obscurity following his trial for high treason in 1924. The 1929 edition of the diaries of Lord D'Abernon, the British ambassador to Germany 1920–26, had a footnote that read: "He [Hitler] was finally released after six months and bound over for the rest of his sentence, thereafter fading into oblivion" (Shirer 1960, 112). At the various campaign rallies against the Young Plan in the autumn of 1929, the charismatic Hitler easily outshone the stuffy Hugenberg, who as one of his aides Reinhold Quaatz wrote in his diary had "no political sex appeal" (Turner 2003, 137). Hugenberg was such an inept speaker that he almost never spoke before the *Reichstag* because his speeches induced laughter among those who listened to them (Beck 2009, 50). The fact that Admiral von Tirpitz of the *DNVP* appeared alongside and spoke with Hitler at the anti-Young Plan rallies was taken by many of the *DNVP* voters as a sign that Hitler was now a respectable figure who was rubbing shoulders with war heroes (Hamilton 1982, 556). The referendum of 1929 brought about a major surge of interest in the National Socialists. Indeed, for many it marked the first time that they ever heard of Hitler, and it led during the winter of 1929–30 to a huge influx of new members into the *NSDAP*. The Canadian historian Richard Hamilton wrote that it was the 1929 referendum, which the National Socialists had treated as a gigantic five-month-long free political ad (Hugenberg had paid for the entire referendum out of his own pocket) running from July to December 1929 that had enabled them to enter the political mainstream just as the Great Depression was beginning (Hamilton 1982, 235–7).

Hitler successfully exploited Hugenberg to push himself into the political mainstream, and once the campaign against the Young Plan failed by referendum, Hitler promptly ended his links with Hugenberg. Hitler publicly blamed Hugenberg for the failure of the campaign, but he retained the links with big business that the *Reichsausschuß* had allowed him to cultivate, and this began a process of business magnates deserting the *DNVP* for the Nazis. Hitler's handling of the affair was marred in one way, however, and that was the premature announcement in the *Völkischer Beobachter* of Hitler's repudiation of the alliance with the Straßer brothers (Gregor and Otto), whose Socialist economics were incompatible with Hugenberg's arch-Capitalism.

Reflecting the changed political dynamics caused by the Young Plan referendum, in the election of 14 September 1930, *DNVP*'s share of the vote dropped dramatically to seven percent while *NSDAP*'s share rose equally dramatically to 107 seats or seventeen percent (compared to *NSDAP*'s 2.6 percent of the vote in 1928). This marked the *NSDAP*'s electoral breakthrough to the mainstream (Broszat 1987, 84). Since the *NSDAP* did very well in areas that had traditionally voted for the *DNVP* like East Prussia and Pomerania, the German historian Martin Broszat wrote that would strongly suggest that most of the *DNVP* voters had deserted their old party for the *NSDAP* (Broszat 1987, 84–5). Broszat argued that what happened between 1929–1932 was that the supporters of the sectarian Nationalist *DNVP* had abandoned it for the radically sectarian Nationalist *NSDAP* (Broszat 1987, 76). The *DNVP* was declining rapidly as many workers and peasants began to support the more populist and less aristocratic *NSDAP* while upper- and middle-class *DNVP* voters supported the *NSDAP* as the "party of order" best able to crush Marxism (Hamilton 1982, 418–19). During the 1930 federal election, the *DNVP* issued a statement proclaiming that there were no important differences between them and the *NSDAP* on the "Jewish Question," arguing that the few differences that did exist concerned a small number of the "radical demands of the *NSDAP*" which were "hardly important since in practice they cannot be implemented" (Childers 1983, 188).

Despite the bitterness caused by the 1930 election, in February 1931, Hugenberg met with Hitler to discuss common cooperation on a referendum for early elections in Prussia that were intended to defeat the government of the Social Democrat Otto Braun, and thereby allow an *NSDAP-DNVP* coalition to win the resulting elections. As part of their efforts to cooperate, the *NSDAP* and the *DNVP* members of parliament walked out of the *Reichstag* on 11 February 1931 to protest the high-handed ways of Chancellor Heinrich Brüning's government (1930–1932). By then, the two parties were in a very loose federation, known as the "National Opposition." This was followed in July of the same year by the release of a joint statement, with Hitler guaranteeing that the pair would cooperate for the overthrow of the Weimar "system." Between June and August 1931, Germany experienced a run on the banking system leading to a crisis.

On 11 October 1931, the *DNVP*, the *NSDAP*, the Pan-German League, the *Reichslandbund*, the German People's Party, and the *Stahlhelm, Bund der Frontsoldaten* briefly formed an uneasy alliance known as the *Harzburg Front*. The *Harzburg Front* was Hugenberg's attempt to create on a more institutional basis the *Reichsausschuß* of 1929, and under his leadership, thereby form the "national bloc" that he confidently believed would sweep him into power in the near future (Beck 2009, 72). The Harzburg rally was "the formal declaration of war by the parties of the Right against the Brüning government—a concentration of all the forces of reaction, both past and present, in one great demonstration of hostility to the Weimar System" (Wheeler-Bennett 1967, 233).

The *Harzburg Front* proved to be a failure, and by the end of 1931 the National Socialists were increasingly lashing out against their nominal allies. Unemployment in Germany had reached six million. In February 1932, over the course of long talks, the *DNVP* and the *NSDAP* failed to agree on a common candidate for the presidential elections, and on 17 February 1932, Hitler unilaterally announced in a press release that he was running for president. This action effectively destroyed the *Harzburg Front* as Hugenberg had not been consulted beforehand.

On 25 February 1932, Hitler successfully obtained German citizenship. Hitler and Hugenberg soon clashed, and Hugenberg's refusal to endorse Hitler in the German presidential election of 13 March1932 deepened their differences. Indeed, the rift between the two opened further when Hugenberg, fearing that Hitler might win the presidency, persuaded Theodor Duesterberg to run as a *Junker* candidate. Although Duesterberg was eliminated on the first vote, due largely to Nazi allegations regarding his Jewish parentage, Hitler nonetheless failed to secure the presidency (Hitler 30.1 percent to von Hindenburg's 49.6 percent). The results required a runoff in April. On 10 April 1932, von Hindenburg wins the runoff with 53 percent of the vote over Hitler's thirty-six percent. Within four days of the election, von Hindenburg and his Chancellor Brüning outlaw the *SA* and *SS*.

In parliamentary elections held on 24 April 1932, the *NSDAP* wins 36.3 percent of the vote prompting President von Hindenburg to dissolve the *Reichstag* on 3 June 1932. On 16 June, the ban on the *SA* and *SS* is lifted by the new von Papen government. In parliamentary elections on 31 July 1932, the *NSDAP* wins 37.3 percent of the vote forcing von Hindenburg to offer Hitler the vice chancellorship under von Papen. Hitler refuses the offer seeking only to be Chancellor of Germany. Given the new seats occupied by the *NSDAP*, Göring is elected *Reichstag* President on 30 August 1932.

Twelve days after assuming the presidency of the parliament, Göring calls for a "no-confidence" vote against von Papen. In response, von Papen dissolves the *Reichstag*.

The 6 November 1932 federal parliamentary election results gave Hugenberg's *DNVP* party a growth in support (15 seats) at the expense of the Nazis (loss of 34 seats), leading to a secret meeting between the two in which a reconciliation of sorts was agreed upon. Hugenberg cautiously opened talks with Hitler in December 1932 with the aim of reviving the *Harzburg Front* of 1931. This reflected the fact that it was now very hard to imagine that the *DNVP* could come to power without the *NSDAP* (Jones 1992, 70). Hugenberg hoped to harness the Nazis for his own ends once again, and as such he dropped his attacks on them during the lead up to the campaign for the March 1933 federal election.

Before the 5 March 1933 federal election, Chancellor von Papen urged President von Hindenburg to continue to govern by emergency decrees (Article 48 of the Weimar Constitution). Von Hindenburg refused to do so, and von Papen resigned as chancellor on 17 November 1932. On 3 December, von Papen was superseded by his defense minister General Kurt von Schleicher who in talks with the left wing of the Nazi Party led by Gregor Straßer tried to build up a Third Position (*Querfront*) strategy. These plans failed when in turn Hitler disempowered Straßer and approached von Papen for coalition talks. On 4 January 1933, von Papen met Hitler at the home of German banker Kurt von Schroeder where a coalition agreement had been brokered. On January 28, von Schleicher resigned as Chancellor when von Hindenburg refused to grant him another dissolution of the *Reichstag*. Von Papen then obtained von Hindenburg's consent to form a new government under Hitler on 30 January 1933.

When Adolf Hitler was sworn in as *Reich* Chancellor on 30 January 1933, the Nazis only had a third of the seats in the *Reichstag* and needed to form a coalition with other political parties such as *DNVP*. On 30 January 1933, *DNVP* Chairman Hugenberg became Minister of Agriculture and Economics under Chancellor Hitler. Hugenberg agreed to participate in the Hitler Cabinet only under the condition that Hitler promise not to dissolve the *Reichstag* and call for early elections—a move that would favor the Nazi Party. Under Hitler's chancellorship in January 1933, the Nazis were limited to three seats in cabinet, and only two with portfolios—the chancellorship for Hitler and the then-powerless Interior Ministry for Wilhelm Frick (Göring was a minister without portfolio). The cabinet's makeup was conceived by former *Reich* Chancellor Franz von Papen and *Reichspräsident* Paul von Hindenburg in hopes of keeping Hitler in check and making him their puppet (Shirer 1960, 181).

On 30 January 1933, Hugenberg was sworn in by von Hindenburg to serve in Hitler's government as Economics and Agriculture minister, as he had requested. During his time in Hitler's cabinet, Hugenberg did not stand in the way of Hitler's efforts and machinations to make himself a dictator. Many prominent *DNVP* members had long favored scrapping Weimar's Democracy in favor of, if not a monarchy, then an authoritarian system under the *Führerprinzip*. Reneging his promise to Hugenberg two days after being named *Reichskanzler*, Hitler announced his "Proclamation to the German People" and promised new elections for 5 March. President von Hindenburg then dissolved the *Reichstag*.

Over the ensuing weeks in February 1933, the new Hitler government with the support of President von Hindenburg ushered in a rapid series of events against established liberal policies and laws: on 4 February, a decree "For the Protection of the German People" gave Hitler the power to ban political meetings and the newspapers of his political rivals; on 17 February, Göring issued a decree in the *Reichstag* that ordered the police to make "good relations" with Nationalist associations (*SA* and *SS*) but to make free use of their weapons against the Socialists and Marxists; on 22 February, Göring united the *SA*, *SS*, and *Stahlhelm, Bund der Frontsoldaten* into a single police force; on 23 February, the first restrictions on homosexual rights groups were introduced into law; and on the night of 27 February, a mysterious fire broke out that gutted the *Reichstag* building; arson was suspected.

After the *Reichstag* fire, Hugenberg gave a speech that spoke of the necessity for "draconic measures" and of "exterminating the hotbeds in which Bolshevism can flourish" (Leopold 1977, 143–4). Hugenberg argued that "in these earnest times there can no longer be any half-measures . . . no compromise, no cowardice." At a cabinet meeting held on 28 February, Hugenberg together with the other *DNVP* cabinet ministers voted for the *Reichstag* Fire Decree ("The Emergency Decree for the Protection of People and State"), which effectively wiped out civil liberties (Leopold 1977, 144). The decree was based largely on a proposal by Ludwig Grauert, a *DNVP* member who had recently been named chief of the Prussian state police, to provide legal cover for the mass arrests of Communists on the night of the fire. On the afternoon of 27 February—hours before the fire—Justice Minister Franz Gürtner (another *DNVP* member) had submitted a draft decree which, like the *Reichstag* Fire Decree, would have imposed draconian restrictions on civil liberties in the name of curbing Communist violence (Evans 2003, 331–2). President von Hindenburg signed the Emergency Decree into law by using emergency Article 48 of the Weimar Constitution. The *Reichstag* Fire Decree banned the *KPD* and suspended most civil liberties in Germany, including *habeas corpus*, freedom of expression, freedom of the press, the right of free association and public assembly, the secrecy of the post and telephone. These rights were not reinstated during Nazi rule.

In the 5 March 1933 federal elections, the Nazi Party won 43.9 percent of the popular vote resulting in 288 seats in the *Reichstag*, while the *DNVP* won 7.97 percent and 52 seats. The Nazis fell just six percentage points of claiming the majority in parliament. To hold the majority, the Nazis had to form a coalition. In March 1933, leading *DNVP* member Ernst Oberfohren resigned from the *Reichstag*. It is claimed that Oberfohren was against doing a deal with Hitler (Hett 2014, 134). Soon after, letters written by Oberfohren and other *DNVP* members that were critical of Alfred Hugenberg were seized by Göring's men and appeared in pro-Nazi newspaper *Braunschweiger Landeszeitung* in April 1933 (Beck 2009, 224–5). Oberfohren disagreed with Hugenberg about the future of the party. He told one journalist, that he pleaded with Hugenberg not to do a deal with Hitler, "but Hugenberg deluded himself that the Nazis could be taught better." He went on to tell the journalist about the "embarrassing police raids on his homes in Kiel and Berlin, the interrogations and the countless threats he had received" and he "prophesied the complete victory of bestiality." (*Neuer Vorwärts*, Prague, 29 October 1933.)

Beginning in 1929, Alfred Hugenberg and his media empire had joined forces with the Nazi movement in a massive campaign against the reparations outlined in the Young Plan and placed his huge propaganda machine for the first time at Hitler's (and Goebbels's) disposal. Thus, at the outset of the world economic crisis, Hitler's name became widely known to the German people, thanks to the short-sightedness of an old-fashioned, self-serving, diehard Conservative leader convinced that he could manipulate the Nazis for his own ends. The *DNVP*, which essentially represented the agrarian lobby in the *Reichstag*—the industrial backers of the *DNVP* were increasingly alienated by Hugenberg's high-handed, inflexible policies—proved, however, to be no match for the Nazis in this tactical alliance between 1929 and 1933. After the 5 March 1933 election, Hitler still needed Hugenberg's *DNVP* to bring the Nazi Party over the 50-percent threshold in the *Reichstag* required to gain majority control. Had the political parties in opposition to the National Socialists and Adolf Hitler overcome their ideological and personal differences in 1933, they could have formed a coalition large enough to claim the majority in the *Reichstag* and locked the National Socialists (Nazis) out of power, thereby avoiding the Enabling Act.

Despite achieving a much better result than in the November 1932 election, the Nazis did not do as well as Hitler had hoped. And despite massive violence and intimidation, the Nazis won only 43.9 percent of the popular vote, rather than the majority that he had expected. Therefore, Hitler was forced to maintain his coalition with the *DNVP* to control a majority of seats. The Communists (*KPD*) lost about 20 percent of their seats, while the Social Democrats only lost one seat. Although the *KPD* had not been formally banned, it was a foregone conclusion that the *KPD* deputies would never be allowed to take their seats. Within a few days, all *KPD*'s members of parliament were either under arrest or in hiding. By 9 March 1933, all states that were previously not loyal to the Nazis now had Nazi-loyal state administrations.

On 13 March 1933, Paul Joseph Goebbels became *Reichsminister für Volksaufklärung und Propaganda* (Minister for Public Enlightenment and Propaganda) in Hitler's Cabinet.

On 21 March 1933, the newly elected *Reichstag* opened a new session. Although the Nazi-*DNVP* coalition had enough seats to claim parliamentary majority and conduct the basic business of government, Hitler needed a two-thirds majority to pass the Enabling Act, a law which allowed the Cabinet—in effect, the Chancellor—to enact laws without the approval of the *Reichstag* for a four-year period. With certain exceptions, such laws were legally permitted to deviate from the Weimar Constitution. Leaving nothing to chance, the Nazis used the provisions of the *Reichstag* Fire Decree to arrest all eighty-one Communist deputies and keep several Social Democrats out of the chamber. Hitler then obtained the necessary supermajority by persuading the Catholic Center Party to vote with him in the spirit of the anticipated *Reichskonkordat*.* The Enabling Act was passed on 23 March 1933 with 444 votes in favor and 94 against. Only the Social Democrats led by Otto Wels opposed the measure, which came into effect on 27 March 1933. As it turned out, the atmosphere of that session was so intimidating that the measure would have still passed even if all Communist and Social Democratic deputies had been present and voting. The provisions of the bill turned the Hitler government into a *de facto* legal dictatorship.

On 28 March 1933, the first open attacks by the *SA* against Jewish businesses occurred. *Gleichschaltung*† was introduced—the forcible removal of all known opponents to the Nazis. On 1 April, an official one-day boycott of Jewish shops took place. Literature produced by the Jehovah's Witnesses was banned. On 7 April, Nazi officials were put in charge of all local government in the provinces and the law for the "Restoration of the Professional Civil Service" was introduced that banned all Jews and non-Germans from public service. On 26 April, the *Gestapo* (*Geheime Staatspolizei*, State Secret Police) was established by Göring. On

---

* *Reichskonkordat* – a highly controversial treaty negotiated between the Vatican and the emergent Nazi Germany. It was signed on 20 July 1933 by Cardinal Secretary of State Eugenio Pacelli, who later became Pope Pius XII, on behalf of Pope Pius XI and Vice Chancellor Franz von Papen on behalf of President Paul von Hindenburg and the German government. It was ratified on 10 September 1933, and it has been in force from that date onward. The treaty guarantees the rights of the Roman Catholic Church in Germany. When bishops take office, Article 16 states they are required to take an oath of loyalty to the Governor or President of the German *Reich* established according to the Constitution. The treaty also requires all clergy to abstain from working in and for political parties. Most of the German church hierarchy regarded the treaty as a symbol of peace between church and state. From a Roman Catholic ghetto Church perspective, it has been argued that the Concordat prevented even greater evils being unleashed against the Church. Though some German bishops were unenthusiastic, and the Allies at the end of World War II felt it inappropriate, Pope Pius XII successfully argued to keep the Concordat in force. It is still in force today. Regardless of the ongoing debate, the Concordat and the Center Party's support for the Enabling Act placed the Vatican among the first legal partners to Hitler's regime.

† *Gleichschaltung* – the coordination, synchronization, and standardization of political, economic, and social institutions under the process of Nazification establishing a system of totalitarian control over all aspects of German society.

2 May, trades unions were abolished, their funds confiscated, and their leaders put in prison. On 6 May, the *Deutsche Arbeitsfront* (German Workers' Front) was introduced to replace trade unions. On 10 May, "Un-German" books were publicly burned in major cities throughout Germany. On 19 May, the *Reich* government took on the task of regulating workers contracts. On 22 June, the Social Democratic Party of Germany (*SPD*) was officially banned. On 5 July, all political parties other than the Nazi Party were banned. Within four months of the Enabling Act, the other parties had been shuttered either by outright banning or Nazi terror, and Germany was firmly a one-party state. Although three more elections were held during the Nazi era, voters were presented with a single list of Nazis and guest candidates, and voting was by open ballot. On 14 July, two laws were passed: the first, making the Nazi Party the only legal political party in Germany; and the second, "Law for the Prevention of Progeny with Hereditary Diseases," forcing the sterilization of all persons who suffered from diseases considered hereditary, such as mental illness (schizophrenia and manic depression), retardation ("congenital feeble-mindedness"), physical deformity, epilepsy, congenital blindness and deafness, and severe alcoholism.

An increasingly isolated figure, Hugenberg was finally forced to resign from the cabinet after a campaign of harassment and arrest was launched by Hitler against his *DNVP* coalition partners (Evans 2005, 13). The *SA* was also turned against the *DNVP*, with youth movements loyal to Hugenberg becoming the focus of attacks (Snyder 1998, 177). He announced his formal resignation on 29 June 1933, and he was replaced by others who were loyal to the Nazi Party, Kurt Schmitt in the Economy Ministry and Richard Walther Darré in the Agriculture Ministry (Evans 2005, 27). A "Friendship Agreement" was signed between the Nazis and the *DNVP* immediately afterwards, the terms of which effectively dissolved the *DNVP* with a few members whose loyalty could be guaranteed absorbed into the Nazi Party (Evans 2003, 373–4). Indeed, the German National Front, as the *DNVP* had officially been called since May 1933, had officially dissolved on 27 June 1933 (Kershaw 1998, 477).

On 20 July 1933, Hitler agreed to the *Reichskonkordat* with the Vatican. Signatories were: Cardinal Secretary of State Eugenio Pacelli on behalf of Pope Pius XI and *Reichs* Vice Chancellor Franz von Papen on behalf of President Paul von Hindenburg. On 14 October 1933, Hitler withdrew Nazi Germany from the League of Nations and the Disarmament

Conference. And in the federal elections on 17 November 1933, the Nazi Party won 92 percent of the votes cast.

In December 1933, the Telegraph Union, the news agency owned by Hugenberg, was taken over by Goebbels' new Propaganda Ministry (established 13 March 1933) and merged into a new German News Office (Evans 2005, 146). Hugenberg was allowed to retain control of the remainder of his newspaper and publishing businesses until 1943. Even then, when the Nazi-controlled Eher Verlag entered negotiations to take over his Scherl Verlag, Hugenberg drove a hard bargain, coming out with a substantial block of shares of Rhenish-Westphalian industry in his briefcase. Hugenberg was able to retain this property after the war and emerge scot-free, since the Detmold de-Nazification court classified him in 1949 as a "fellow-traveler" (*Mitläufer*) rather than a Nazi and chose not to prosecute him for his role as a gravedigger of Weimar Democracy and an accomplice of Hitler (Wistrich 2002, 128). This designation permitted him and his family to keep his property and business interests (Bookbinder 1996, 222–3). He died on 12 March 1951 in Kükenbruch bei Rinteln (present-day Extertal) near Detmold, Germany (Wistrich 2002, 128).

THE DOWNFALL OF ERNST RÖHM

IN APRIL 1924, ERNST RÖHM BECAME A *REICHSTAG* DEPUTY FOR THE *völkisch* National Socialist Freedom Movement. He made only one speech, urging the release from prison of Lieutenant Colonel Kriebel. The seats won by his party were much reduced in the December 1924 election, and his name was too far down the list to return him to the *Reichstag*. While Hitler was in prison, Röhm helped to create the *Frontbann* as a legal alternative to the then-outlawed *Sturmabteilung*. At Landsberg Prison in April 1924, Röhm had been given authority by Hitler to rebuild the *SA* in any way he saw fit. When in April 1925 Hitler and Ludendorff disapproved of the proposals under which Röhm was prepared to integrate the 30,000-strong *Frontbann* into the *SA*, Röhm resigned from all political groups and military brigades on 1 May 1925 and sought seclusion from public life. In 1928, he accepted a post in Bolivia as adviser to the Bolivian Army, where he was given the rank of lieutenant colonel and went to work after six months' acclimatization and language tutoring. After the 1930 revolt in Bolivia, Röhm was forced to seek sanctuary in the German Embassy. After the election results in

Germany that September, Röhm received a telephone call from Hitler in which the latter told him "I need you," paving the way for Röhm's return to Germany.

In September 1930, as a consequence of the Stennes Revolt in Berlin, Hitler assumed supreme command of the *SA* as its new *Oberster SA-Führer*. He sent a personal request to Röhm, asking him to return to serve as the *SA*'s Chief of Staff. Röhm accepted this offer and began his new assignment on 5 January 1931. He brought radical new ideas to the *SA* and appointed several close friends to its senior leadership. Previously, the *SA* formations were subordinate to the Nazi Party leadership of each provincial region. Röhm established new *Gruppe*, which had no regional Nazi Party oversight. Each *Gruppe* extended over several regions and was commanded by a *SA-Gruppenführer* who answered only to Röhm or Hitler.

The *SA* by this time numbered over a million members. Its traditional function of party leader escort had been given to the *Schutzstaffel* (*SS*; established 9 November 1925), but it continued its street battles with "Reds" and its attacks on Jews. The *SA* also attacked or intimidated anyone deemed hostile to the Nazi agenda, including uncooperative editors, professors, politicians, other local officials, and businessmen.

Under Röhm, the *SA* often took the side of workers in strikes and other labor disputes, attacking strikebreakers and supporting picket lines. *SA* intimidation contributed to the rise of the Nazis and the violent suppression of other Nationalist parties during electoral campaigns, but its reputation for street violence and heavy drinking was a hindrance, as was the open homosexuality of Röhm and other *SA* leaders such as his deputy Edmund Heines. In 1931, the *Münchener Post*, a Social Democrat newspaper, obtained and published Röhm's letters to a friend discussing his homosexual affairs. Captain Karl Mayr played a role in the release of this scandalous information to defame the *SA* and the Nazi Party.

Hitler was aware of Röhm's homosexuality. At this point they were so close that they addressed each other as *du* (the German familiar form of "you"). No other top Nazi leader enjoyed that privilege, and their close association led to rumors that Hitler himself was homosexual. Röhm was the only Nazi leader who dared to address Hitler by his first name "Adolf" or his nickname "Adi" rather than "mein *Führer*."

As Hitler rose to national power with his appointment as chancellor in January 1933, *SA* members were appointed auxiliary police and ordered by Göring to sweep aside "all enemies of the state." Thereby, local government offices had to surrender their authority to the Nazis.

Röhm and the *SA* regarded themselves as the vanguard of the National Socialist revolution. After Hitler's national takeover they expected radical changes in Germany, including power and rewards for themselves, unaware that, as chancellor, Hitler no longer needed their street-fighting capabilities. Nevertheless, Hitler did name Röhm to the cabinet on 1 December 1933 as a minister without portfolio.

Along with Gregor and Otto Straßer, Joseph Goebbels, Gottfried Feder, and Walther Darré, Ernst Röhm was a prominent member of the party's radical faction. This group put emphasis on the words "Socialist" and "workers" in the party's name, which put them ideologically closer to the Communists. They largely rejected Capitalism (which they associated with Jews), and pushed for nationalization of major industrial firms, expansion of worker control, confiscation and redistribution of the estates of the old aristocracy, and social equality—effectively a Socialist agenda. Röhm spoke of a "second revolution" against the *Reaktion* (the National Socialist label for Conservatives).

These plans were threatening to the business community in general, and to Hitler's corporate financial backers in particular, including many German industrial leaders who hoped to reap huge profits from the coming Nazi military buildup. So, Hitler swiftly reassured his powerful industrial allies that there would be no "second revolution." Many *SA* storm troopers had working-class origins and expected a radical program. They were disappointed by the new regime's lack of Socialist direction and its failure to provide the lavish patronage they had expected. Furthermore, Röhm and his *SA* colleagues thought of their force as the core of the future German Army, and saw themselves as replacing the *Reichswehr* and its established professional officer corps. By then, the *SA* had swollen to over three million men, dwarfing the *Reichswehr*, which was limited to 100,000 men by the Treaty of Versailles. Although Röhm had been a member of the officer corps, he viewed them as "old fogies" who lacked "revolutionary spirit." He believed that the *Reichswehr* should be merged into the *SA* to form a true "people's army" under his command. At a February 1934 cabinet meeting, Röhm demanded that the merger be made under his leadership as Minister of Defense.

This horrified the army, with its traditions going back to Frederick the Great. The army officer corps viewed the *SA* as an "undisciplined mob" of "brawling" street thugs and was also concerned by the pervasiveness of "corrupt morals" within the ranks of the *SA*. Reports of a huge cache of weapons in the hands of *SA* members caused additional concern to the army leadership. Not surprisingly, the officer corps opposed Röhm's proposal. They insisted that discipline and honor would vanish if the *SA* gained control, but Röhm and the *SA* would settle for nothing less. In addition, the army leadership was eager to co-operate with Hitler given his plan of re-armament and expansion of the established professional military forces.

In February 1934, Hitler told British diplomat Anthony Eden of his plan to reduce the *SA* by two-thirds. That same month, Hitler announced that the *SA* would be left with only a few minor military functions. Röhm responded with complaints and began expanding the armed elements of the *SA*. Speculation that the *SA* was planning or threatening a *coup* against Hitler became widespread in Berlin. In March, Röhm offered a compromise in which only a few thousand *SA* leaders would be taken into the army, but the army promptly rejected that idea.

On 11 April 1934, Hitler exhibited his keen political sense and opportunistic nose and met with German military leaders on the ship *Deutschland*. By that time, he knew President Paul von Hindenburg would likely die before the end of the year. Hitler informed the army hierarchy of von Hindenburg's declining health and proposed that the *Reichswehr* support him as von Hindenburg's successor. In exchange, he offered to reduce the *SA*, check Röhm's ambitions, and guarantee the *Reichswehr* would be Germany's only military force. According to American war correspondent in Berlin William L. Shirer, Hitler also promised to expand the army and navy.

Despite that, both the *Reichswehr* and the conservative business community continued to complain to von Hindenburg about the *SA*. In early June 1934, Defense Minister Werner von Blomberg issued an ultimatum to Hitler from von Hindenburg: unless Hitler took immediate steps to end the growing tension in Germany, von Hindenburg would declare martial law and turn over control of the country to the army. Knowing such a step could forever deprive him of power, Hitler decided to carry out his pact with the *Reichswehr* to suppress the *SA*. This meant a showdown with Röhm. In Hitler's view, because the army was willing to submit, the *SA* constituted the only remaining power center in Germany that was independent of his National Socialist state. Von Blomberg had the swastika added to the *Reichswehr*'s insignia in February 1934 and ended the army's practice of preference for "old army" descent (patrimonial cronyism) in new officers, replacing it with a requirement of "consonance with the new government."

OPPORTUNISM AND INTRIGUE
FINAL CONSOLIDATION OF POWER (*COUP DE GRÂCE*)
THE NIGHT OF THE LONG KNIVES

MURDERERS, PIMPS, HOMOSEXUAL PERVERTS, DRUG ADDICTS OR JUST plain rowdies were all the same to Hitler if they served his purposes (Shirer 1960, 45). No other political party in Germany came near to attracting so many shady characters. When he emerged from Landsberg Prison he found not only that they were at each other's throats but that there was a demand from the more prim and respectable leaders such as Rosenberg and Ludendorff that the criminals and especially the perverts be expelled from the movement. This Hitler frankly refused to do. "I do not consider it to be the task of a political leader," he wrote in his editorial, "A New Beginning," in the *Völkischer Beobachter* of 26 February 1925, "to attempt to improve upon, or even to fuse together, the human material lying ready to his hand" (Shirer 1960, 117). This policy, however, changed after coming to political power when Hitler realized he needed the support of industrial leaders and the traditional military establishment in order to not only hold on to power but to advance towards his greater objectives. The traditional military establishment was disgusted with Hitler's street-thug paramilitary—the *SA*—and was determined to see it destroyed before Hitler permitted it to infect the *Reichswehr*.

Although determined to curb the power of the *SA*, Hitler put off doing away with his close long-time ally. A political struggle intensified within the party's inner circle closest to Hitler, including Prussian Premier Hermann Göring, Propaganda Minister Joseph Goebbels, and *SS-Reichsführer* Heinrich Himmler, positioning themselves against their chief rival Ernst Röhm. To isolate Röhm, on 20 April 1934, Göring transferred control of the Prussian political police (*Gestapo*) to Himmler, who he believed could be counted on to move against Röhm.

In preparation for the purge known as the Night of the Long Knives (*Unternehmen Kolibri*, Operation Hummingbird), both Himmler and his deputy *SS-Obergruppenführer* Reinhard Heydrich, Chief of the *Gestapo* (*Geheime Staatspolizei*, Secret State Police) and the *SD* (*Sicherheitsdienst des Reichsführers-SS*, Security Service of the *SS-Reichsführer*), assembled a dossier of fabricated evidence to suggest that Röhm had been paid 12 million *Reichsmarks* (56 million dollars in 2018) by France to overthrow Hitler. Leading officers in the *SS* were shown falsified evidence on 24 June that Röhm planned to use the *SA* to launch a plot against the government (Röhm-

Putsch). At Hitler's direction, Göring, Himmler, Heydrich, and Victor Lutze drew up lists of people in and outside the *SA* to be arrested and killed. One of the men Göring recruited to assist him was Willi Lehmann, a *Gestapo* official and *NKVD* spy. On 25 June 1934, General Werner von Fritsch placed the *Reichswehr* on the highest level of alert. On 27 June, Hitler moved to secure the army's cooperation. Von Blomberg and General Walther von Reichenau, the army's liaison to the party, gave it to him by expelling Röhm from the German Officers' League. On 28 June, Hitler went to Essen to attend a wedding celebration and reception; from there he called Röhm's adjutant at Bad Wiessee and ordered *SA* leaders to meet with him on 30 June at 11:00 a.m. On 29 June, a signed article in *Völkischer Beobachter* by von Blomberg appeared in which von Blomberg stated with great fervor that the *Reichswehr* stood behind Hitler.

On 30 June 1934, Hitler and a large group of *SS* and regular police flew to Munich and arrived between 06:00 and 07:00 at Hanselbauer Hotel in Bad Wiessee, where Ernst Röhm and his followers were staying. With Hitler's early arrival, the *SA* leadership, still in bed, were taken by surprise. *SS* men stormed the hotel and Hitler personally placed Röhm and other high-ranking *SA* leaders under arrest. According to Erich Kempka, Hitler turned Röhm over to "two detectives holding pistols with the safety catch removed." The *SS* found Breslau *SA* leader Edmund Heines in bed with an unidentified eighteen-year-old male *SA* senior troop leader. Goebbels emphasized this aspect in subsequent propaganda justifying the purge as a crackdown on moral turpitude. Hitler ordered both Heines and his partner taken outside of the hotel and shot. Meanwhile, the *SS* arrested the other *SA* leaders as they left their train for the planned meeting with Röhm and Hitler.

Although Hitler presented no evidence of a plot by Röhm to overthrow the regime, he nevertheless denounced the leadership of the *SA*. Arriving back at party headquarters in Munich, Hitler addressed the assembled crowd. Consumed with rage, Hitler denounced "the worst treachery in world history." Hitler told the crowd that "undisciplined and disobedient characters and asocial or diseased elements" would be annihilated. The crowd, which included party members and many *SA* members fortunate enough to escape arrest, shouted its approval. Joseph Goebbels, who had been with Hitler at Bad Wiessee, set the final phase of the plan in motion. Upon returning to Berlin, Goebbels telephoned Göring at 10:00 a.m. with the codeword *Kolibri* ("hummingbird") to let loose the execution squads on the rest of their unsuspecting victims. Commander of Hitler's personal bodyguard unit, *Leibstandarte-SS Adolf Hitler*, Sepp

Dietrich, received orders from Hitler to form an "execution squad" and go to *Stadelheim* Prison in Munich where Röhm and other *SA* leaders were being held under arrest. There in the prison courtyard, the *Leibstandarte* firing squad shot five *SA* generals and a *SA* colonel. Several of those not immediately executed were taken back to the *Leibstandarte-SS* barracks at Lichterfelde (Berlin), given one-minute kangaroo "trials," and shot by a firing squad. Röhm himself, however, was kept prisoner in Cell 70—the same prison cell occupied by Kurt Eisner's assassin, Count von Arco auf Valley in 1919–1922 and by Adolf Hitler from 24 June to 27 July 1922.

Hitler was hesitant in authorizing Röhm's execution and gave him the option of suicide. On 1 July 1934, *SS-Brigadeführer* Theodor Eicke (later *Kommandant* of the Dachau Concentration Camp) and *SS-Obersturmbannführer* Michael Lippert visited Röhm. Once inside Röhm's cell, they handed him a Browning pistol loaded with a single bullet and told him he had ten minutes to kill himself or they would do it for him. Röhm demurred, telling them, "If I am to be killed, let Adolf do it himself." Having heard nothing in the allotted time, Eicke and Lippert returned to Röhm's cell at 14:50 to find him standing with his bare chest puffed out in a gesture of defiance. Eicke and Lippert then shot Röhm, killing him. He was buried in *Westfriedhof* ("Western Cemetery") in Munich. In 1957, the German authorities tried Lippert in Munich for Röhm's murder. Until then, Lippert had been one of the few executioners of the purge to evade trial. Lippert was convicted and sentenced to 18 months in prison.

The purge of the *SA* was legalized on 3 July 1934 with a one-paragraph decree in the Law Regarding Measures of State Self-Defense, which declared, "The measures taken on 30 June, 1 and 2 July to suppress treasonous assaults are legal as acts of self-defense by the State." At this time, no public reference was made to the alleged *SA* rebellion, but only generalized references to misconduct, perversion, and some sort of plot. In a nationally broadcast speech to the *Reichstag* on 13 July 1934, Hitler justified the purge as a defense against treason.

In an attempt to erase Röhm from German history, all known copies of the 1933 propaganda film *The Victory of Faith* (*Der Sieg des Glaubens*), in which Röhm appeared, were ordered to be destroyed in 1934. *The Victory of Faith* was long thought to have been lost until a single copy was found in storage in Britain in the 1990s. The 1935 film *Triumph of the Will* (*Triumph des Willens*), produced in 1934, showed the new Nazi hierarchy, with the *SS* as the Nazi's premier uniformed paramilitary group and Röhm replaced by Viktor Lutze as the far less powerful new head of the *SA*.

CHAPTER 13

The Storm Begins

By the time Jesse Owens, Helen Stephens, and many other soon-to-be heroes of the 1936 Berlin Olympics arrived in Berlin, the gathering storm that had been approaching over the horizon of the European continent and manifesting with the following foretelling political developments in Germany had finally arrived:

1. 30 January 1933: Adolf Hitler named Chancellor of Germany as his National Socialist German Workers (Nazi) Party forms a coalition and assumes control of the German state.
2. 27 February 1933. Arson of the *Reichstag* building of the German Parliament sets the stage for the *Reichstag* Fire Decree suspending most rights guaranteed under the 1919 Weimar Constitution, allowing the Nazis to arrest Communists and increase police action throughout Germany.
3. 22 March 1933. The *SS* (*Schutzstaffel*) establishes the Dachau Concentration Camp for political prisoners in southern Germany.
4. 23 March 1933. The Enabling Act, formally titled *Gesetz zur Behebung der Not von Volk und Reich* ("Law to Remedy the Distress of People and Reich"), was passed as an amendment to the Weimar Constitution that gave the German Cabinet—in effect, Chancellor Adolf Hitler—the power to enact laws without the involvement of the *Reichstag*. The Enabling Act gave Hitler plenary powers that effectively transform Hitler's government into a legal dictatorship.
5. 1 April 1933. Members of the Nazi Party and its affiliated organizations organize a nationwide boycott of Jewish-owned businesses in Germany.
6. 7 April 1933. The *Reichstag* passes the Law for the Restoration of the Professional Civil Service (*Gesetz zur Wiederherstellung des Berufsbeamtentums*), which excludes Jews and other political opponents of the Nazis from all civil service positions and disbarment of non-"Aryan" lawyers by 30 September 1933.

7. 25 April 1933. The *Reichstag* passes the Law against Overcrowding in Schools and Universities, which dramatically limits the number of Jewish students attending public schools to five percent of total student population.
8. 10 May 1933. German university students burn upwards of 25,000 "un-German" books in Berlin's Opera Square (*Opernplatz*). Some 40,000 people gather to hear *Reich* Propaganda Minister Joseph Goebbels deliver a fiery address: "No to decadence and moral corruption!"
9. 14 July 1933. The *Reichstag* passes the Law for the Prevention of Offspring with Hereditary Diseases (*Gesetz zur Verhütung erbkranken Nachwuchses*), mandating the forced sterilization of certain individuals with physical and mental disabilities, as well as sterilization of Roma (Gypsies), "asocial elements," and Afro-Germans.
10. 20 July 1933. The Vatican signs a Concordat with Germany, whereby all German bishops are obligated to swear an oath of loyalty and respect to either the *Reich* governor of the state concerned or to the President of the *Reich*.
11. 4 October 1933. The *Reichstag* passes The Editors Law (*Schriftleitergesetz*) forbiding non-"Aryans" to work in journalism.
12. 24 November 1933. The *Reichstag* passes the Law against Dangerous Habitual Criminals (*Gewohnheitsverbrechergesetz*). The new law allows courts to order the indefinite imprisonment of "habitual criminals" if they deem the person dangerous to society. It also provides for the castration of sex offenders. The same day, Adolf Hitler signed "the world's most comprehensive animal protection legislation" which outlawed various inhumane practices against animals used in industry and medicine. As war crimes prosecutors would note later at the Nuremberg Trials, the same regime tolerated and promoted cruelty to human beings interned in concentration camps.
13. 2 August 1934. German President Paul von Hindenburg dies.
14. 19 August 1934. With the support of the German armed forces and 84 percent vote in the National Referendum, Hitler assumes the powers of *Reich* President in addition to his position as *Reich* Chancellor, abolishes the office of the President, and declares himself *Führer* of the German *Reich* and people. In this expanded

capacity, Hitler now becomes the absolute dictator of Germany; there are no legal or constitutional limits to his authority.

15. 16 March 1935. Hitler reintroduces military conscription; the peacetime strength of the *Wehrmacht* is fixed at 36 divisions, or 580,000 men. The proclamation denies any aggressive intention and claims that the new German Army will become "exclusively an instrument of defense and therefore an instrument for the maintenance of peace." After the proclamation, Hitler reviews the troops on *Unter den Linden Straße* and departs for Munich. Leaders across the globe condemn this act, but do not confront Germany beyond words. They do, however, begin to repeat the mistakes of the years leading up to the First World War by negotiating mutual defense treaties among themselves, which they have little means and intent to fulfill. Most of the former Entente Powers have neglected their military forces and defenses in the aftermath of the First World War.
16. 2 May 1935. The Franco-Soviet Treaty of Mutual Assistance is drafted in Paris. Each party undertakes to assist the other in case of an unprovoked attack. (The Treaty is not ratified until 27 February 1936, and effective on 27 March 1936.)
17. 16 May 1935. The Czechoslovak–Soviet Treaty is signed, obliging the Soviet Union to aid Czechoslovakia militarily, pending French action to the same effect.
18. 18 June 1935. The Anglo-German Naval Agreement is signed in London, whereby Germany will be permitted to build its navy up to 35 percent of the Royal Navy's strength.
19. 26 June 1935. The *Reichstag* passes the Law for the Alteration of the Law for the Prevention of Hereditarily Diseased Progeny (*Gesetz zur Änderung des Gesetzes zur Verhütung erbkranken Nachwuchses*) sanctioning abortion within the first six months of pregnancy in cases of women categorized as "hereditarily ill" by the Hereditary Health Courts and stipulates sterilization or the termination of pregnancy if the physician has decided that this would forestall a threat to the life or health of the mother.
20. 15 September 1935. Meeting in Nuremberg, the *Reichstag* passes the Nuremberg Race Laws, formally known as Law for the Protection of German Blood and German Honor (*Gesetz zum Schutz des deutschen Blutes und der deutschen Here*), laying the foundation for and legalizing much of what was to engross most of Europe in

the 1940s concluding with the Final Solution to the Jewish Question (*die Endlösung der Judenfrage*). Also passed on this day in Nuremberg was the Citizenship Law (*Reichsbürgergesetz*) limiting citizenship to "Germans or those of related blood."

21. 16 September 1935. Hitler introduces the "*Wehrmacht* Day" for the first time; he appeals to assembled soldiers. All three services of the *Wehrmacht* parade in front of Hitler who is acknowledged as the Supreme Commander (*Oberster Befehslhaber*). They are led by the Minister of War, General von Blomberg, the Army Commander-in-Chief, General von Fritsch; the Commander-in-Chief of the Navy, Admiral Raeder; and the Commander-in-Chief of the new *Luftwaffe*, General Göring. The Army's prerogative to become the "sole bearer of arms" is being seriously challenged by the appearance of two special *SS* regiments (*SS-Verfügungstruppen*), the forerunner of the *Waffen-SS*.
22. 18 October 1935. On Hitler's orders, student fraternities are dissolved. They meet for the last time at the historical castle Wartburg. The Law for the Protection of Hereditary Health of the German People (*Gesetz zum Schutze der Erbgesundheit des deutschen Volkes*), discussed within the Cabinet in Hitler's presence since March, is promulgated with the aim of regulating marriages as well as abortions on medical and racial grounds. The law introduced sterilization (under Nazi terminology, called euphemistically *Entfruchtbarmachung*) of people with mental schizophrenia, epilepsy, congenital blindness and deafness, etc., to be determined by special "health hereditary tribunals" (*Erbgesundheitsgerichte*). Between 250,000 and 300,000 were sterilized in the Third *Reich* without arousing any protest—unlike the euthanasia of mentally handicapped, which led to serious protests and succeeded in bringing "mercy killing" to a halt.
23. 25 January 1936. In a speech to the National Socialist Student Union at Munich, Hitler calls for the perpetual domination of the world by the white race, which "has been ordained to rule, to lead and to dominate the rest of the world."
24. 12 July 1936. The *SS* begins construction of the Sachsenhausen concentration camp in Oranienberg (35 km north of Berlin).

In 1935 and 1936, Hitler makes a series of aggressive overtures to England and France for an alliance. On 21 February 1936, Bertrand de

Jouvenel of *Paris Midi* interviews Hitler, who states: "I wish to succeed in making a *detente* with France." Asked why he does not amend his strong anti-French comments in *Mein Kampf*, Hitler replies: "But I am no writer, I am a politician. How am I going to rectify it? I am doing it every day in my foreign policy directed towards friendship with France!" Hitler warns the French about the consequences of their recent pact with the Soviet Union:

> Do you realize what you are doing?! You let yourselves become involved in a diplomatic game of a power which has only one desire and this is to create disorder among the great European nations. . . . Soviet Russia is a political factor which has at its disposal an explosive revolutionary idea and gigantic armaments. . . . In Germany Bolshevism has no chance of succeeding. But there are other great nations which are less immune to the Bolshevik virus. . . . You'd better think seriously about my offer of an agreement. Never has a German leader made such an overture, neither has he repeated it so many times. And from whom is this offer coming? From a pacifist charlatan who has become specialized in international relations? No, it is coming from the greatest Nationalist who has ever led Germany! I am offering you something which no one could have ever offered you: an agreement which will be approved by 90 percent of the German nation, 90 percent which follow me! . . . Here is your chance. If you don't take it, think of your responsibility towards your children! You're confronting a Germany where nine-tenths show full confidence in their leader, and this leader is telling you: "Let's be friends!" (*Paris Midi* 28 February 1936).

The publication of this interview in French was held back until the day after the ratification of the Franco–Soviet Pact by the Chamber of Deputies in Paris on 27 February 1936.

On 28 February 1936, Hitler has a meeting with the historian Arnold J. Toynbee, director of the Royal Institute of International Affairs, whom he assured that in return for an alliance with London, he would be prepared to assist in the protection of the British empire. Hitler offers specifically to defend India from a possible Japanese attack, with a force of up to twelve infantry divisions and the entire German Navy to be sent to Singapore (Toynbee 1967, 276–95).

On 2 March 1936, The French ambassador François-Poncet has a meeting with Hitler, who subsequently holds a secret conference with his military commanders—von Blomberg, Fritsch, Raeder, and Göring. Von Ribbentrop and Goebbels are also present. They discuss the reoccupation of the demilitarized zone in the Rhineland in response to the Franco-Soviet Treaty. Thereafter, von Blomberg issues the order for starting the operation coded "Winter Exercise."

On 6 March 1936, at a Cabinet meeting on Friday at 9:15 p.m., Hitler orders the *Wehrmacht* to march into the Rhineland the next morning. The actual crossing of the Rhine was carried out by a mere three battalions of infantry under orders to withdraw if the French Army intervened. "I asked myself the same question," Hitler recalled later: "What will France do? Will she oppose the advance of my handful of battalions? I know what I would have done, if I'd been the French: I should have struck and I would not have allowed a single German soldier to cross the Rhine" (Hoffmann 1979, 84).

On 7 March 1936, while German troops are marching into the Rhineland, Hitler orders his Foreign Minister, Konstantin von Neurath, to summon the ambassadors of England, France, and Italy, who are presented with a far-reaching peace proposal that Hitler repeats in his speech delivered at noon before the *Reichstag*. In place of the Locarno Pact, Hitler suggests Germany would sign a series of bilateral non-aggression treaties with all her neighbors, in East and West, valid for twenty-five years; then Germany would re-enter the League of Nations, unconditionally. Not he, but France broke the Locarno Pact by its recent agreement with the Soviet Union: "This new Franco–Soviet Agreement introduces the threatening military power of a mighty empire into the center of Europe by the roundabout way of bolstering Czechoslovakia, the latter country having also signed an agreement with the Soviet Union." This, Hitler says, he would never tolerate. He further claims that the Red Army had a peace strength of 1,350,000 men, which could be brought up to 17,500,000 in times of war. Moreover, it has the largest tank and air forces in the world. "The introduction of this most powerful military machine into Central Europe," Hitler emphasizes, "would destroy the European equilibrium." He concludes his speech by pronouncing a sacred vow: "We will never yield before a foreign power," and quickly adds his standard reassurance, "we have no territorial demands to make in Europe" (Baynes 1942, 1271–1302). After frenetic applause, the *Reichstag* is dissolved because the *Führer* wishes new elections on 29 March. Goebbels comments: "The Führer's joy has no limits . . . we all swim in happiness . . . England remains passive, France does not want to act alone, Italy is disappointed, and America disinterested" (Reuth 1992, 935).

Between 12–29 March 1936, Hitler speaks in eleven cities in preparation for the upcoming *Reichstag* election campaign and national referendum in support of the *Führer*'s domestic and foreign policies. Addressing factory workers in Essen on 27 March 1936, Hitler says:

> I have not upheld the rearming of the German people because I am a shareholder. I am perhaps the only statesman in the world who has no banking account. . . . You yourselves know how often I have held out the hand to the other powers; always I met only with rebuffs. I proposed, in order that no one could feel himself threatened, that all should disarm completely. We are prepared to disarm if the others will do the same. That proposal was rejected. I declared my readiness to accept an army of 200,000 men. That was also rejected. I then declared that I would be content with an army of 300,000 men. That too was rejected. Finally, I declared myself ready for an agreement on an air force under equal conditions. Once again that was rejected. . . . The German people desires peace, desires understanding, desires calm. It wishes to work . . . to earn its bread and live decently. If anyone does not believe this, we cannot help him. . . . I have within my own nation so many tasks . . . I have no time to puzzle out what ought to be done in France. . . . What concern is that of mine? Germany is my concern! I have work to do here in abundance, work for peace of unimaginable extent. Millions are badly housed, millions are badly clothed. . . . To help them, that is my program. . . . I must draw German people nearer to each other; it is in that sphere that there are possibilities of equalizing social conditions. . . . Let the statesmen go into factories, let them ask the workmen "Do you wish to reject this offer?" And I am convinced that everywhere they will find one single answer: "Don't speak of gestures and symbolic acts, but make and keep peace. That is the wish of the people!" (*Völkischer Beobachter*, 29 March 1936).

On 29 March 1936, the national referendum is held on Hitler's policies; he receives almost 44,500,000 votes (98.8 percent) of approval. Goebbels comments: "The first votes are coming in . . . a historic victory . . . the Nation has spoken. The *Führer* has united the Nation. Even in our wildest dreams we couldn't imagine something like that. . . . The *Führer* has won a mandate *vis-à-vis* the outside world" (Fröhlich 1993–1998, 3:52).

Three days later on 1 April, German Ambassador to the United Kingdom Joachim von Ribbentrop presents to Anthony Eden, the British foreign secretary, Hitler's new and very detailed "Peace Plan." On 4 April, Hitler issues a secret order to improve Germany's combat readiness by a series of autarchic measures affecting the national economy. He makes Göring responsible for the control of raw materials and foreign exchange. On 14 May, British Ambassador Sir Eric Phipps discusses with Hitler the latter's "Peace Plan" of 1 April. The British government under Conservative Party Prime Minister Stanley Baldwin refused to take it seriously, wondering whether Hitler was capable of honoring any signed treaty.

On 25 July 1936, after listening to Wagner's *Siegfried*, Hitler received two Germans arriving from Spanish Morocco with a personal letter from General Francisco Franco, who had started an insurgence against Madrid and was asking for military help. Hitler immediately sends for Göring and von Blomberg to discuss Franco's urgent appeal. Initially, von Neurath, von Ribbentrop, and even Göring were against giving assistance. Hitler, however, was able to turn Göring around, and he seized the chance of testing the young *Luftwaffe*. "If Spain really goes Communist," Hitler speculated, "France . . . will also be Bolshevized in due course, and then Germany is finished. Wedged between the powerful Soviet bloc in the East and a strong Communist French–Spanish bloc in the West, we could do hardly anything if Moscow chose to attack us." Under the appropriate Wagnerian codename "Operation *Feuerzauber*" (Magic Fire) Hitler orders the dispatch of twenty Junkers-52 transport aircraft to ferry Franco's troops from Morocco to Spain. In the course of the next three years, Germany was to equip and send the Condor Air Legion, large quantities of material, and up to 6,500 personnel to help Franco (Kershaw 2000, 15–17; Toland 1976, 534).

After the close of the Berlin Olympics at the end of August 1936, Hitler composed a detailed memorandum on long-term rearmament and economic policy, which will form the foundation of the new Four-Year Plan.

The threat against which Hitler wants Germany to be ready is clearly Communism, which:

> through its victory in Russia has established one of the greatest empires as a forward base for its future operations. . . . For a victory of Bolshevism over Germany would lead not to a Versailles Treaty, but to the final destruction, indeed to the annihilation, of the German people. . . . If we do not succeed in bringing the German *Wehrmacht* in the shortest time to the rank of the premier army in the world, so far as its training, raising of units, armaments, and above all its spiritual education also is concerned, Germany will be lost! The German Army and the German economy must be operational within four years (Michaelis and Schraepler 1958, 10:534–42).

On 24 October 1936, Count Galeazzo Ciano, the new Italian foreign minister and Mussolini's son-in-law, meets Hitler in Obersalzberg to discuss the creation of a common front against Bolshevism. Hitler promises that Germany will recognize the Italian conquest of Abyssinia and the Franco regime in Spain. There should be no clash of interest between Germany and Italy. The Mediterranean, Hitler assured Ciano, was an Italian Sea (Ciano 1945).

On 15 November 1936, Hitler tells Goebbels he is happy about the pace of rearmament. On this conversation, Goebbels notes in his diary:

> . . . which is costing us a fabulous amount of money. We should be ready by 1938 when the showdown with Bolshevism comes. . . . The army is now completely won over by us. *Führer* is untouchable. . . . It is as good as certain that we shall dominate Europe. Thus rearm. *Führer* is ready for anything. He must, therefore, win in the end. . . . I am heading home after four hours of discussion. What a wonderful man. I am completely taken in by him."

Hitler also tells Goebbels that, regarding Austria, a new secret propaganda campaign will be launched. On the other hand, Goebbels notes in his diary, he is unwilling to give money to Mosley, the leader of the

Fascists in England, stating: "It is impossible at the moment; he is asking too much" (Fröhlich 1987, 2:727).

Over the ensuing two years (1937–1939), Hitler and sixty-seven million German people worked tirelessly against all odds to fulfill the Four-Year Plan and, once again, prepare for the likelihood of war. In just three years, they achieved an incredible recovery from their devasting losses from the First World War and the Versailles Treaty, the chaos and anarchy of the German Revolution of 1918–1919, the directionless and foundering Weimar Republic, and the Great Depression. For some it is tempting to consider had Hitler been satisfied with these tremendous accomplishments and had England and France allied with Germany in non-aggression pacts permitting Germany to equally rearm with its allies and rest confident in its security, the Second World War would quite probably have been averted and Germany would have become a formidable world economic and military power that may have peacefully achieved many, if not most, of the more rational domestic and geopolitical objectives Hitler envisioned for the German people. However, had this course been taken, Hitler would have inexorably become the Capitalist he so doggedly disdained—this unwitting proselytization remains, to date, the geopolitical principle behind Democratic Capitalism. Moreover, had England and France aligned with Germany in the years 1933–1936, their power to influence Hitler's racial policies may have increased and resulted in their moderation, if not significantly curtailing them. Moderation or reversal of racist policies in 1930s Germany would, more likely than not, have naturally occurred as a consequence of a strong economy integrated into the European economy, national security, and international peace—under such prosperous conditions, the general populace would have lost interest in militant racism forcing the Nazis to alter their domestic political program. And finally, had the West worked with Hitler in lifting the oppressive sanctions of the Versailles Treaty permitting Germany to grow into an economic powerhouse integrating with Western economies, Stalin's National Front Strategy to spread Communism throughout Europe, particularly Eastern Europe given Poland's and Czechoslovakia's strong Democratic leaning, would have been effectively neutered. Unfortunately, and understandably, Western powers were unwilling to take this leap of faith with an autocrat so devoted to sectarian Nationalism and German imperialism. To do so would have first required convincing Hitler that Capitalism and international finance were not Jewish conspiracies to dominate the world. Moreover, to want to work with Hitler would have required a sober understanding of precisely who Stalin (another autocrat) was and the existential threat he and Bolshevism posed to Western Democracies. By the time Hitler came to power, most Western Democracies remained in the dark as to what was really happening in Soviet Russia and Ukraine. Many British and American reporters traveling to the Soviet Union in the 1930s returned with stories of the "great achievements" of Communism. Western Democracies were themselves flirting with Socialism and perceived no real threat from its natural brother Communism. It was not until the passing of President Franklin D. Roosevelt (together with his wife Eleanor, both admirers of Socialism) and the Cold War that Americans began to sense the threat of Communism. This is what led to the unfortunate amnesty of so many Nazi war criminals in the early years of the Cold War—see section "AMNESTY TO OPPOSE COMMUNISM," in the closing chapter of this book, *infra*.

CHAPTER 14

HITLER'S DICHOTOMOUS ANTI-SEMITISM: JUDEO-BOLSHEVISM AND JUDEO-CAPITALISM

The internationalization of our German economic system, that is to say, the transference of our productive forces to the control of Jewish international finance, can be completely carried out only in a State that has been politically Bolshevized. . . . The Jewish way of reasoning thus becomes quite clear. The Bolshevization of Germany, that is to say, the extermination of the patriotic and national German intellectuals, thus making it possible to force German Labor to bear the yoke of international Jewish finance—that is only the overture to the movement for expanding Jewish power on a wider scale and finally subjugating the world to its rule.

— ADOLF HITLER, *Mein Kampf*

The railway is the living proof that one can satisfactorily carry out an undertaking in the interest of the community without any private-Capitalistic tendency. (Baynes 1942, 921)

— ADOLF HITLER, 8 December 1935, speaking at Nuremberg on the centenary of the *Deutsche Reichsbahn*

It was the Jews, of course, who invented the economic system of constant fluctuation and expansion that we call Capitalism. . . . Let us make no mistake about it—it is an invention of genius, the Devil's own ingenuity.

— ADOLF HITLER, 1934

A BRIEF SURVEY OF THE HISTORY AND ETIOLOGY OF MODERN ANTI-SEMITISM

MUCH SCHOLARSHIP, DEBATE, SPECULATION, AND JUDGMENT HAS BEEN made on the topic of anti-Semitism over the past 140 years since the Anti-Semites' Petition (*Antisemitenpetition*) was submitted to Otto von Bismarck, Chancellor of the *Deutsches Reich*, on 13 April 1881. Modern Western literature is replete with viewpoints on this controversial subject and much of it is driven by ideology and shame in response to the twentieth-century European Holocaust and plight of the Palestinians since the 1948 establishment of the State of Israel. Theories that subscribe to theological and/or economic anti-Semitism have dominated academia and the published literature on the topic. Other popular theories such as xenophobia and racism are ubiquitous and common among all peoples and therefore have little to add to the conversation on anti-Semitism. Some theories have included social (Jew as socially inferior, "pushy," vulgar, therefore excluded from personal contact), cultural (Jews regarded as undermining the moral and structural fiber of civilization), and ideological (Jews regarded as subversive or revolutionary) bases for anti-Semitism; however, these forms are more representative of the manifestations rather than root causes of anti-Semitism. An exhaustive examination of this topic, which would require a sociological review of history to the first civilizations and a psychological autopsy of human nature, is far beyond the objective of this segment. The intent of our discussion here is to briefly define anti-Semitism, state some viewpoints on its suspected root causes, debunk mainstream theories, make some reasoned conclusions, and explain the seemingly contradictory and inconsistent dichotomy of Hitler's anti-Semitism.

The term anti-Semitism comes from the Greek Σημ (*Sēm*) which comes from the Hebrew שֵׁם (*Šēm*, "Shem"), the name of the eldest son of Noah. Semites are descendants of Noah's son Shem and the lineage of both Jews (Isaac) and Arabs (Ishmael); Abraham (Abram, Avraham, Ibrahim) being the father of both Isaac and Ishmael. The term "anti-Semitism" is misleading as Semites represent both Jews and Arabs. A more accurate term for hatred of the Jews is "anti-Judaism" or "anti-Jewish," with the understanding that the term "Jew" represents the descendants of the tribes of Judah, Levi, and Benjamin—the three remaining of the original twelve tribes of the Egyptian Exodus that established the first nation of Israel. Being the largest of the remaining three tribes, "Jew" was adopted from the word Judah.

Not long ago, a PBS News Hour book review (Solman 2013) was presented on a 2012 work titled: *The Chosen Few: How Education Shaped Jewish History, 70–1492* (Princeton University Press), written by Maristella Botticini and Zvi Eckstein—two eminent economic historians who teach in Italy and Israel, respectively. Although the book was not written to address the issue of anti-Semitism, it inherently sparks the issue that has vexed many minds for decades since the twentieth-century Holocaust. Given that *Homo economicus judaicus* has been one of the classic myths or canards against Jews (*i.e.*, Shakespeare's *The Merchant of Venice*), it is only natural for many descendants of rescuers of Jews and of survivors of Nazi concentration camps to interpret Botticini's and Eckstein's book in the wider context of the issue of anti-Semitism.

Another book, *The Anguish of the Jews: Twenty-Three Centuries of Anti-Semitism*, written by Roman Catholic priest Edward Flannery and first published in 1965 (Macmillan & Co. Ltd.), claims the root cause of anti-Semitism is what Christians have been told over the centuries was "deicide" by the Jews ("Slayers and rejectors of God in the person of His Son [Jesus]") (Flannery 1985, 284–95). The author argues and a majority of Jews and mainstream academia have bought into the theory that "Christian antisemitism thus has always remained in its core theological" (Flannery 1985, 284–95). Given the widespread embrace of Islam, Buddhism, and many other non-Christian religions by Westerners, this conclusion could not be further from the truth. Throughout his book, Flannery's underlying tone and objective is clearly evident as being a long-overdue apology for organized, sanctioned Christian (especially Roman Catholic) anti-Semitism over the past two millennia. The book's apparent intention is more insightful on a personal subjective psychological rather than general objective academic level. Despite his incorrect conclusion on the root cause of anti-Semitism, Father Flannery appropriately dismisses the longstanding theory or myth that anti-Semitism stems from a medieval view of the Jew as "*homo economicus* ('man of money') . . . a born usurer, a cruel creditor, an addict of sharp practices," while at the same time the author accurately admits: "It cannot be denied, on the other hand, that Jewish involvement in economic affairs has served as a precipitating or aggravating cause of antisemitism," exploiting the Jew as a scapegoat in troubled economic and political times. However, by attributing the real historical and psychological root of anti-Semitism to "deicide," the author has missed the mark.

Scholarly research has produced other conclusions on the root causes of anti-Semitism that are supported by the foundational findings of

Botticini and Eckstein in their book *The Chosen Few* that are right in line with historical facts and the logical argument for the economic success of the Jews over the centuries. The conclusions of these two authors can be appropriately integrated into a theory on the roots of anti-Semitism that are based more in psychology and sociology of personal relationships than theology, race, or macro-/microeconomics. This theory sees anti-Semitism as an irrational psychological response to Jewish efforts to preserve their cultural, religious, and hereditary identity during the second Diaspora (ca. 70 CE–present).

Legalistic Judaism with the codification and standardization of *mitzvot* (613 moral, ceremonial, and civil [juridical] laws), particularly the *kashrut* (dietary laws of Leviticus chapter 11 and Deuteronomy chapter 14), that can be traced back to Rabbi Simlai (ca. third century CE) who was a devoted anti-Christian polemicist, plays a central role in medieval diasporic anti-Semitism. Many scholars over the centuries have opined that the *kashrut* was intended for hygienic and health reasons. However, this theory is without merit given the fact that God instructed Noah after the flood that he and his family may eat "all the birds in the sky . . . every creature that moves along the ground, and . . . all the fish in the sea; they are given into your hands. Everything that lives and moves about [כָּל־רֶמֶשׂ אֲשֶׁר הוּא־חַי (*kol remes asher hu chay*)] will be food for you. Just as I gave you the green plants, I now give you everything."[*] Before the flood, Noah was instructed to bring "clean animals" הַבְּהֵמָה הַטְּהוֹרָה (*habehemah hatehorah*) in sevens and "the animals that are not clean" הַבְּהֵמָה אֲשֶׁר לֹא טְהֹרָה (*habehemah asher lo tehorah*) by pairs into the Ark (Genesis 7:2–3). Curiously, animals were categorized this way even before they were considered a food source. After the flood, Noah and his family were permitted by God to eat those animals that were before the flood considered as "unclean," yet Noah remained righteous[†] in God's eyes. If any of the animals that God permitted Noah and his family to eat after the flood were indeed detrimental to their health, it would be inconsistent with God's love for and view of Noah as a "righteous" man and God's commandment to Noah and his family to "be fruitful and increase in number; multiply on the earth and increase upon it" (Genesis 9:7). Moreover, God permitted Jews to provide "unclean" animals as food to non-Jews visiting or living among them (Deuteronomy 14:21), yet Jewish Law was abundantly clear that Jews were not to mistreat non-Jews in any way. If these

---

[*] Genesis chapter 9 verses 2–3.

[†] Righteous – a legal term meaning free from guilt.

creatures were detrimental to a person's health and unfit for people to eat, God would not have permitted Jews to give or sell them to non-Jews as food.

According to British Old Testament scholar Gordon J. Wenham, the true purpose of *kashrut* was to help Jews maintain a distinct and separate existence from other peoples (Deuteronomy 14:2); he says that the effect of the laws was to prevent socialization and intermarriage with non-Jews, preventing Jewish identity from being diluted. Wenham argued that since the impact of the dietary laws was a public affair, this would have enhanced Jewish attachment to them as a reminder of their distinct status as Jews.

Botticini and Eckstein argue in their book that one to two centuries prior to the Jewish revolts under Roman rule, the Pharisees began requiring Jewish male children attend school to learn to read and study the Torah. This practice dramatically expanded after the destruction of the second temple in Jerusalem in 70 CE. The natural migration over land and sea of the post-Roman Jewish Diaspora followed mostly along lines of economic opportunity in established or growing communities across the globe. Despite primarily relying on agriculture and peddling to earn a living in the first through seventh centuries during the post-Roman Diaspora, Jews carried with them and continued their practice of learning to read and study the Torah. According to Botticini and Eckstein, the opportunity to finally fully exploit their uncommon literacy skills came during the rule of the Umayyad (661–750), and later, the Abbasid (750–1517) Muslim caliphates. "The economic changes prompted by the geographical expansion, the commercial growth and the vast urbanization in the newly established Muslim caliphates had a profound and lasting impact on the occupational structure of the large Jewish community dwelling in this enormous empire" (Solman 2013). This was also true in Christendom beginning in the eleventh century with a return of urbanization and the appearance of the burgher class. Consequently, Jews possessed an uncommon advantage over most other groups in that they had established skills and assets, including general literacy, the ability to understand texts, analytical reasoning, mobility, networking abilities, and contract-enforcement institutions that would become the lever of the transition into high-skill occupations and specializations like crafts, trade, entrepreneurial activities, finance, medicine, and the law. Because of the difficulties faced early in the Diaspora and the heightened awareness of continual persecution and the need to constantly be prepared to pick up and move on, Jews frequently chose professions based on trading that are "portable" or involve duties as middleman that could easily append to existing commerce. In a similar vein, many medieval Jews were especially well suited for commerce because the Jewish Diaspora caused many Jews to have far-flung networks of friends and family, which facilitated trade.

The Jewish Diaspora forced a profound and sudden change on the Jewish character from that of a homeland farmer who bartered for goods to that of a nomadic peddler, hustler, street merchant, and middleman—essentially, a professional beggar who scrapes a living out of whatever opportunity comes his way and makes something out of nothing—much like the gypsy or other nomadic peoples who are constantly searching but never really finding the roots and sense of belonging that they deeply long for. The early centuries of the post-Roman Diaspora were a traumatic adjustment that left lasting effects on the Jewish psyche. People under such tremendous strain naturally gravitate to means of survival and search for anything that will in the smallest way alleviate or ease the burden. Some things the Jews had going for them were religion, literacy, and culture. The religion and culture that they carried with them on their distant travels across the globe were an instrument by which they gravitated to and networked with each other in numbers. This provided a sense of empowerment, safety, familiarity, ingenuity, and comfort. It created a medium by which they could put their minds together to face and solve difficult challenges. Some of these same instruments were to become important means of survival in the *ghettos* and concentration camps of ages to come. Literacy was another gift the Jews took with them when they fled occupied Israel beginning in 70 CE. Literacy was the most important vehicle by which the Jews slowly lifted themselves from nomadic beggar, peddler, and street merchant to coveted manager, bookkeeper, scribe, civic administrator, entrepreneur, inventor, lawyer, physician, professor, banker, financier, and politician.

As Jews slowly climbed the occupational ladders during the Middle Ages in the East (Umayyad and Abbasid caliphates), their economic mobility and influence also slowly rose. Jews were accepted into non-Jewish institutions of higher education as colleges were established (*i.e.*, University of al-Qarawiyyin—ninth century, al-Azhar University—tenth century, *Niẓāmīyah* institutions—eleventh century). During the High Middle Ages, which began after 1000 CE, the population of Europe increased greatly as technological and agricultural innovations allowed trade to flourish and the medieval Warm Period climate change allowed crop yields to increase. Manorialism, the organization of peasants into villages that owed rent and labor services to the nobles, and feudalism, the political structure whereby knights and lower-status nobles owed military service to their overlords in return for the right to rent from lands and manors, were two of the ways society was organized in the European High Middle Ages. This was a period of migratory waves to Europe that drew labor, entrepreneurs, and the intelligentsia away from the Abbasid caliphate in the East. Non-Jewish entrepreneurs, business owners, bankers, tradesmen, professionals, nobility, etc. in both the Muslim and Christian worlds often found themselves interacting with Jews who on the basis of their commercial skills and literacy were more and more in positions of influence and economic power.

Initially, this professional interaction between non-Jews and Jews was collegial as the Middle Ages in Europe and lands controlled by the Muslim caliphates brought together many different cultures from distant lands. The natural evolution of such business interactions prompts cultural, sociological, and familial class integration; business interaction often begets social interaction that eventually leads to integration, *viz.*, breaking bread together, courting, marriage, and family union. This is where on a personal level the friction started between non-Jew and Jew. Upon their immigration into foreign lands, Jews often had the means to find and collaborate with fellow Jewish émigrés (refugees). Over time, these Jews, sensing no need or desire to assimilate, established their own communities separate from non-Jewish communities. They established their own schools, civil laws and law enforcement, system of justice, and community leadership. A Jewish quarter was the area of a city traditionally inhabited by Jews of the Diaspora. Jewish quarters were often the outgrowths of segregated *ghettos* instituted by the Jewish leadership or by non-Jewish civil authorities. A Yiddish term for a Jewish quarter or neighborhood is *Di yiddishe gas* (די ייִדדישע גאַס), or "The Jewish street." Many European and Middle Eastern cities once had a vibrant historical Jewish quarter. Jewish quarters and *ghettos* in Europe existed because Jews placed great importance on maintaining their separate identity (believing it to be a religious commandment) and because they faced a growing view by non-Jews as being alien. In some cases, the *ghetto* was a Jewish quarter with a relatively affluent population (for instance, the Jewish *ghetto* in Venice). In other cases, *ghettos* were places of terrible poverty, particularly during periods of rapid, unabated population growth; such *ghettos* (as that of Rome), had narrow streets and tall, crowded houses. Like in Jewish quarters, residents of these *ghettos* had their own justice system.

Many *ghettos* and *mellahs* (fortified Moroccan *ghettos*) were initially established by government authorities to protect the Jews, but later became tools of segregation, isolation, and punishment. The first *ghetto* was documented in 1084 by Rüdiger Huzmann, Bishop of Speyer (Rhenish Palatinate) from 1073 to 1090. They possibly came at the instigation of

Bishop Rüdiger Huzmann, who invited a larger number of Jews to live in his town with the expressed approval of emperor Henry IV. Jews fleeing from pogroms in Mainz and Worms in the lead up to the First Crusade in 1096 took refuge with their relatives in Speyer under the protection of Rüdiger's successor, Bishop John. Eventually, however, Jews were increasingly placed under strict regulations throughout many European cities.

Deeply rooted in the Jewish culture, faith, and identity was a strict sense of separateness from "unbelievers." Orthodox and other religiously observant Jews believed that non-Jews were in a religious sense "unclean"* and therefore off limits in marriage and more intimate personal and social interactions. Clearly, worship and exercise of faith remained separate for Jews, Christians, and Muslims, despite many shared beliefs. As professional or commercial interactions evolved and deepened, Jewish moral, ceremonial, and civil (juridical) laws (*mitzvot*), particularly dietary law (*kashrut*), prevented the closer and closer personal ties with non-Jews that naturally sprouted from the growing commercial interactions. This unsurprisingly created a sense of inferiority and distrust among non-Jews having regular professional and commercial interaction with Jews. Jews as a minority became the object of scorn and distrust in the majority non-Jewish communities that they worked and interacted. Cultural and social segregation deepened while professional interaction grew creating a dichotomous, paradoxical society among Jews and non-Jews. Non-Jews

* Historically and theologically, the concept of "unclean" referred to the spiritual state of a person, or when referring to an animal or inanimate object or practice, "unclean" related to its hygienic state. Likewise, the Hebrew word "goi" meant "nation" or "people" that was historically used to refer to any nation or people, including the Jews. In the fourth century, St. Jerome translated the Old and New Testaments from their original language into the Latin Vulgate and for the first time used the Latin word "gentilis" for the Hebrew "goi" in the Old Testament and for the Greek "ethne" in the New Testament. When King James I commissioned that the Vulgate be translated into English in 1611, the word "gentilis" became "gentile" and for the first time took on the meaning of "pagan." Between the eighteenth and twentieth centuries, "gentile" reverted to mean "Christian." During this same period, Yiddish-speaking European Jews suffering discrimination and persecution adopted a pejorative meaning of the word "goy" for anyone who was not Jewish and was viewed as being "unclean." So, the Hebrew word for nation or people eventually came to mean "unclean." As non-Jews heard themselves being referred to as *goy* (pleural, *goyim*), and realized it meant "unclean," non-Jews took deep offense to the slur and collectively with other Jewish elitist behaviors of separatism, began to naturally view Jews as racists.

naturally interpreted the growing dichotomy and deliberate separatism of the Jews as elitism, racism, and personally offensive—as an attack on their sense of worth and virtue—particularly when non-Jews learned of and misunderstood their being labeled as "unclean." Needless to say, as a matter of course, these dangerous misunderstandings led to a palpable contempt. Once Jews sensed the growing disdain against them and the eventual resulting injustices that they faced (informal and codified discrimination in social and professional spheres), the more powerful among them revolted in revenge against their anti-Semitic commercial competitors and critics, circled their wagons, insulated themselves and their businesses against foreign invasion and takeover, and pursued a strategy of targeted annihilation in the commercial spirit of Sun Tzu.* This undeclared "cold war" resulted in a general distrust (fear) between the parties and refusal to enter into proprietary partnerships in Jewish and non-Jewish firms, businesses, or financial institutions that would otherwise be natural and economically beneficial to all. Moreover, the rank-and-file Jews and non-Jews that were employed at each other's businesses were often discriminated against and passed over for advancement. Economic or career privileges were often granted based on religious or ethnic grounds. This manner of conducting business from the streets to the boardrooms created a deepening culture and atmosphere of fear and disdain among the disparate parties. Jews began practicing the same contemptuous discrimination that their enemies imposed on them, and their mutual segregation and isolation only deepened. Eventually, this strategy proved in many ways self-defeating to both parties. However, the animus and distrust were too deep for any one side to yield or

* Sun Tzu (544–496 BC) – a Chinese general, military strategist, writer, and philosopher who lived in the Eastern Zhou period (771–476 BC) of ancient China. Sun Tzu is traditionally credited as the author of *The Art of War*, an influential work of military strategy that has affected Western and East Asian philosophy and military thinking. *The Art of War* has been applied to many fields well outside of the military. Much of the text is about how to fight wars without actually having to do battle: It gives tips on how to outsmart one's opponent so that physical battle is not necessary. As such, it has found application as a training guide for many competitive endeavors that do not involve actual combat. Many business books have applied the lessons taken from the book to office politics and corporate business strategy. The book is also popular among Western business circles citing its utilitarian value regarding management practices. Many entrepreneurs and corporate executives have turned to it for inspiration and advice on how to succeed in competitive business situations.

acquiesce and negotiate a lasting truce. Over the course of centuries, the dichotomous and paradoxical nature of Jewish life among non-Jews led to deepening distrust and contempt for each other. The interpersonal gulf between Jews and non-Jews deepened as this anti-Semitism eventually became an inbred subculture among future generations. Yet, commerce between these enemies was so deeply interwoven and mutually beneficial, it proceeded, despite the growing animus. Given their minority status, many Jews responded by adopting the vernacular given and surnames of their ethnic European or Middle Eastern hosts to disguise their Jewish backgrounds. Many also converted from Judaism to Christianity or Islam, either genuinely or insincerely.

Certainly, and inevitably under ordinary circumstances and regardless of differences in personal identity, increasing commercial interaction results in occasional disagreement and may eventually lead to conflict among the parties involved. Given the underlying distrust of Jews due to their perceived separatist elitism, such commercial conflicts easily deteriorated into personal and sectarian conflicts. This growing conflict and the beginning of modern anti-Semitism can be dated to about *AD* eleventh to twelfth centuries.[1] This is not the type of personal interaction and psychopathology that ends up in history books focusing on anti-Semitism. More superficial, palpable, materialistic, and simplistic etiological formulations of anti-Semitism are proffered in conventional history books and their apologetics. But they have missed the mark as their formulations and conclusions are more reflective of the natural manifestations and rationalizations rather than root causes of anti-Semitism.

What was originally intended to be a sign of their "chosen" status as a separate people (nation) and a symbolic means of their sacrificial worship (obedience of faith) of their God (*Yahweh*) as they were emerging from the Sinai and about to enter the Promised Land to live among other nations—analogous or parallel to God's commandment relative to the fruit of the Tree of Knowledge of Good and Evil (see *Epimythium*, *infra*)—the *mitzvot* (particularly, *kashrut* in this case of the history of modern anti-Semitism), the Old Covenant, eventually became a legalism in which the Jews placed their faith and viewed as a means of identity and righteousness. They severed Mosaic law from its foundation of faith in God's promise (Genesis 3:15; Jeremiah 31:31–34), failed to stress dependence on the power of God's Spirit to effectuate righteousness, and thus turned the commandments into a job description or algorithm for how to earn the wages of salvation (individual reconciliation with God and the reversal of the curse brought on all posterity by Adam and Eve). The Law that was to mark them as God's chosen, separate people based on their faith and the promise of the New Covenant* was over time misused and twisted into a false legalistic means of achieving righteousness.† Hence, what was once a *sign* of Abrahamic faith and righteousness (not a means of achieving it) became a proximate cause of punishment in the form of anti-Semitism and all its associated consequences. As Moses misused and twisted God's commandment to speak to the rock at Meribah Kadesh in the Desert of Zin (Numbers 20) resulting in his prohibition to enter the Promised Land (Deuteronomy 32:51–52), so too the misuse of the *mitzvot* led to great suffering and punishment of diasporic Jews. Rejection of the New Covenant and misuse of the Old Covenant (Mosaic law) led, in part, to the unnecessary and avoidable tragedies suffered by the Jews over the nearly two millennia since destruction of the second temple.

No one should misconstrue this misuse of the *mitzvot* (or in the wider sense, *halakha*‡) as laying the blame for historical anti-Semitism solely on the shoulders of the Jews. If it has not already been made absolutely clear here, the remainder of our discussion on this topic should elucidate the fact that non-Jews were equally responsible for anti-Semitism by their irrational response to Jewish separateness. That irrational response was based in

---

* The New Covenant was foretold by the prophet Jeremiah (Jeremiah 31:31); see also: Luke 22:20; 1 Corinthians 11:25; 2 Corinthians 3:6; Hebrews chapters 7–9; and Hebrews 12:24. Jeremiah's prophecy was a clear judgment on the fact that God had expected humanity to uphold their end of the contract, but humanity failed. By the New Covenant, God acknowledged that humanity was incapable of fulfilling their end of the bargain and that in His great love, God had to do it all by Himself on behalf of humanity in order to reconcile with humanity—hence, the writing of God's Law on the hearts of all humanity to convict everyone of their breaching of the contract followed by God's payment of the penalty for humanity's breach. The Law of the New Covenant was no longer a *sign* of Abrahamic faith and righteousness, but an *indictment* of guilt.

† Apostle Paul's letter to the Christians in Rome (Romans) chapter 9, verses 30–32.

‡ *Halakha* (Hebrew: הֲלָכָה) – the collective body of Jewish religious laws derived from the written and Oral Torah. *Halakha* is based on biblical commandments (*mitzvot*), subsequent Talmudic and rabbinic law, and the customs and traditions compiled in the many books such as the *Shulchan Aruch*. *Halakha* is often translated as "Jewish Law," although a more literal translation might be "the way to behave" or "the way of walking." The word derives from the root that means "to behave" (also "to go" or "to walk"). *Halakha* guides not only religious practices and beliefs, but also numerous aspects of day-to-day life.

ignorance and miscomprehension of Jewish history and theology. Non-Jews, meaning Christians, during the Middle Ages suffered from a pervasive ignorance of their own faith and religious doctrine. The blame for this can be squarely placed on the shoulders of the Roman Catholic Church, as Martin Luther so aptly and forcefully argued at the time. Not surprisingly, we would expect non-Jews to know even less about the faith and doctrines of Judaism. Yet, it is, in part, this very ignorance that the growing anti-Semitism of the Middle Ages is based in. Ignorance and misunderstanding are often at the root of most conflicts. They remain so on this issue, to date.

The practical manifestations of this ignorance and misunderstanding of Jewish history and theology came in many forms. Official acts against Jews came from the secular and parochial powerbrokers and authorities wherever Jews lived. During the late Middle Ages as one calamity after another hit Europeans and controversy, heresy, and schism within the Christian Church paralleled the growing warfare between states, civil wars, and peasant revolts in the kingdoms, Jews were increasingly seen as instigators and exploited as scapegoats. Jewish communities were expelled from England in 1290 and from France in 1306. Although some were allowed back into France, most were not, and many Jews emigrated eastwards to more welcoming realms, settling in Poland and Hungary. The Jews were expelled from Spain in 1492, and dispersed to Turkey, France, Italy, and the Netherlands. The rise of banking in Italy during the thirteenth century continued throughout the fourteenth century, fueled partly by the increasing warfare of the period and the needs of the papacy to move money between kingdoms. Unlike Christians and Muslims, Jews were not prohibited by their religious tenets to practice usury in their financial transactions. Therefore, many Jews were employed in the growing financial industry. Kings and prelates, noblemen and farmers, all needed money and could obtain it only from the Jews, to whom they paid from twenty to twenty-five percent interest. This business, which, in a manner, the Jews were forced to pursue in order to pay the many taxes imposed upon them, as well as to raise the compulsory loans demanded of them by the kings, led to their being employed in special positions, as "almonries," bailiffs, tax farmers (tax collectors). Many banking firms loaned money to royalty, at great risk, as some were bankrupted when kings defaulted on their loans. Jews working in finance were the first to be blamed for these financial calamities.

One form of reactionary anti-Semitism in the Middle Ages was a mass of legal restrictions imposed on the occupations and professions of Jews. Local rulers and church officials closed many professions to the Jews, pushing them into marginal occupations considered socially inferior, such as tax- and rent-collecting and moneylending, but tolerated them as a "necessary evil." The reasons behind these discriminatory practices originally stemmed from the aura of elitism and separateness that the Jews projected in their host communities that infuriated and offended non-Jews. More refined excuses such as Jewish economic abuses in commerce were the formal reason often given by the secular authorities for their discriminatory and oppressive laws. The pious layman and cleric typically officially employed religious or theological reasons as a basis of their hatred of the Jews. But these were merely a façade to mask the remote humiliation stemming from suspected Jewish elitism and racism. Eventually, these deceptive superficial reasons for hating the Jews gained a veracity and legitimacy of their own and generations of anti-Semites lost clarity relative to the root causes of their anti-Semitism.

Catholic doctrine held that lending money for interest was a sin and forbade it to Christians. Again, not being subject to that restriction, Jews dominated this business. The Torah and the later sections of the Hebrew Bible criticize usury, but interpretations of the Biblical prohibition vary. Since few other occupations were open to them, Jews were motivated to take up moneylending that proved lucrative. That was said to show Jews were usurers, leading to many negative stereotypes, canards, and propaganda, some of which persist to date. Natural tensions between creditors, typically Jews, and debtors, typically Christians were added to social, political, religious, and economic strains. Peasants who were forced to pay their taxes to Jews could personify them as the people taking their hard-won earnings and loyalists to the lords on whose behalf the Jews worked.

Previously, in the early second millennium, Jews became an asset for rulers who regarded them as a reliable and steady source of taxes and fees, as well as a source of economic stimuli stemming from their exemption from Christian and Islamic prohibitions against usury. Rulers often went to great lengths to have Jews settle in their realm, offering protected settlements and endowing them with special privileges, but short of full citizenship. Throughout much of European history, Jews have been strongly associated with commerce and the money trade, rendered both visible and vulnerable, like Shakespeare's Shylock, by their economic distinctiveness. Jews in modern Europe developed the notion of a distinct "Jewish economic man," an image that grew ever-more complex and nuanced between the eighteenth and twentieth centuries.

Also present in the Middle Ages was the coercion of Jews into being economic objects, possessions, and even slaves by groups of nobles, as is evident in examples from the English code *Leges Edwardi Confessoris* (twelfth century). Jews were re-cast into various economic occupational roles and so became a people that could be coveted, sold, or traded for economic purposes by those in power at the time. That use of Jews also had political causes and ramifications in the time period, but the economic practice of exploiting Jews to fill particular roles in economic sectors was prevalent.

As nation states were established and conflicts increased among nations and with the Ottoman Empire, Jews who conducted transnational business in finance and trade were increasingly seen as instigators or merchants of conflict. Both the Christian Church and the Mosque turned against the Jew leading to state inquisitions and forced conversions. By the end of the Middle Ages, anti-Semitism was in full force. The Renaissance, however, brought a small degree of respite for European Jews as Hebrew grew into an international language among Christian scholars and theologians.

A BRIEF HISTORY OF CAPITALISM

THE ORIGINS OF CAPITALISM HAVE BEEN MUCH DEBATED AND depend partly on how one defines Capitalism. The traditional account, originating in classical eighteenth-century liberal economic thought and still often articulated, is the "commercialization model." This sees Capitalism originating in trade. Since evidence for trade is found even in paleolithic culture, it can be seen as natural to human societies. In this sense, Capitalism emerged from earlier trade once merchants had acquired sufficient wealth to begin investing in increasingly productive technology. This account tends to see Capitalism as a natural continuation of trade, arising when people's natural entrepreneurialism was freed from the constraints of feudalism, partly by urbanization (Wood 2002, 11–21). Thus, Capitalism can be traced to early forms of merchant Capitalism practiced in Western Europe during the Middle Ages (Banaj 2007, 47–74).

The earliest recorded activity of long-distance profit-seeking merchants can be traced back to the Old Assyrian merchants active in the second millennium before the common era (CE). The Roman Empire developed more advanced forms of commerce, and similarly widespread networks existed in Islamic nations, but Capitalism took shape in Europe in the late Middle Ages and Renaissance. However, while trade has existed since early in human history, it was not Capitalism (Wood 2002, 73–94).

Libertarians tend to view Capitalism as an expression of natural human behaviors which have been in evidence for millennia, and the most beneficial way of promoting human wellbeing. They tend to see Capitalism as originating in trade and commerce, and freeing people to exercise their entrepreneurial natures. Marxists tend to view Capitalism as a historically unusual system of exploitive relationships between classes, which could be replaced by other economic systems that would serve human wellbeing better. Both Liberals and Marxists tend to see Capitalism as originating in more powerful people taking control of the means of production, and compelling others to sell their labor as a commodity (Wood 2002). For these reasons, much of the work on the history of Capitalism has been broadly Marxist.

Feudalism (ninth through fifteenth centuries) and the manorial system began to lay some of the foundations necessary for the development of mercantilism, a precursor of Capitalism. Feudal manors were almost entirely self-sufficient, and therefore limited the role of the market. This stifled any incipient tendency towards Capitalism. However, the relatively sudden emergence of new technologies and discoveries, particularly in agriculture and exploration, facilitated the growth of Capitalism. The most important development at the end of feudalism (1500) was the emergence of what Professor of Economics Robert Degan calls "the dichotomy between wage earners and Capitalist merchants" (Degen 2011, 12). Karl Marx labeled this period the "pre-history of Capitalism" (Marx 1976, 875). The competitive nature meant there are always winners and losers, and this became clear as feudalism evolved into mercantilism, an economic system characterized by the private or corporate ownership of capital goods, investments determined by private decisions, and by prices, production, and the distribution of goods determined mainly by competition in a free market.

An early emergence of mercantilism occurred on monastic estates in Italy and France and in the independent city republics of Italy during the late Middle Ages. Innovations in banking, insurance, accountancy, and various production and commercial practices linked closely to a "spirit" of frugality, reinvestment, and city life, promoted attitudes which sociologists have tended to associate only with northern Europe, Protestantism, and a much later age. The city republics maintained their political independence from

Empire and Church, traded with North Africa, the Middle East, and Asia, and introduced Eastern practices. They were also considerably different from the absolutist monarchies of Spain and France and were strongly attached to civic liberty.

In its modern form, Capitalism began to develop during the Early Modern period (1500–1800) in the Protestant countries of northwestern Europe, especially the Netherlands (Dutch Republic) and England with the establishment of mercantilism or merchant Capitalism: traders in Amsterdam and London created the first chartered joint-stock companies driving up commerce and trade, and the first stock exchanges and banking and insurance institutions were established.

England began a large-scale and integrative approach to mercantilism during the Elizabethan Era (1558–1603). An early statement on national balance of trade appeared in *Discourse of the Common Wealth of this Realm of England, 1549*: "We must always take heed that we buy no more from strangers than we sell them, for so should we impoverish ourselves and enrich them."* The period featured various but often disjointed efforts by the court of Queen Elizabeth I to develop a naval and merchant fleet capable of challenging the Spanish stranglehold on trade and of expanding the growth of bullion at home. In 1563, Queen Elizabeth I promoted the Navigation Laws and Statute of Artificers in Parliament and issued orders to her navy for the protection and promotion of English shipping. In 1571, Queen Elizabeth promoted the legalization of usury. These efforts organized national resources sufficiently in the defense of England against the far larger and more powerful Spanish Empire, and in turn paved the foundation for establishing a global empire in the nineteenth century.

Among the major tenets of mercantilist theory was bullionism, a doctrine stressing the importance of accumulating precious metals. Mercantilists argued that a state should export more goods than it imported so that foreigners would have to pay the difference in precious metals. Mercantilists asserted that only raw materials that could not be extracted at home should be imported; and promoted government subsidies, such as the granting of monopolies and protective tariffs, that were deemed necessary to encourage home production of manufactured goods.

Proponents of mercantilism emphasized state power and overseas conquest as the principal aim of economic policy. If a state could not supply

---

* Now attributed to Sir Thomas Smith; quoted in Braudel 1979, 204.

its own raw materials, according to the mercantilists, it should acquire colonies from which they could be extracted. Colonies constituted not only sources of supply for raw materials but also markets for finished products. Because it was not in the interests of the state to allow competition, to help the mercantilists, colonies should be prevented from engaging in manufacturing and trading with foreign powers.

Mercantilism was a system of trade for profit, although commodities were still largely produced by non-Capitalist production methods. Noting the various pre-Capitalist features of mercantilism, Austro-Hungarian economic historian and political economist Karl Polanyi argued that "mercantilism, with all its tendency toward commercialization, never attacked the safeguards which protected [the] two basic elements of production—labor and land—from becoming the elements of commerce"; thus with mercantilism regulation was more akin to feudalism than Capitalism. According to Polanyi, "not until 1834 was a competitive labor market established in England, hence industrial Capitalism as a social system cannot be said to have existed before that date" (Polanyi 1944, 87).

Mercantilism declined in Great Britain in the mid-eighteenth century, when a new group of economic theorists, led by Adam Smith (1723–1790), challenged fundamental mercantilist doctrines. The mid-eighteenth century gave rise to industrial Capitalism, made possible by: (1) the accumulation of vast amounts of capital under the merchant phase of Capitalism and its investment in machinery; and (2) the fact that the Enclosures meant that Britain had a large population of people with no access to subsistence agriculture, who needed to buy basic commodities via the market, thus ensuring a mass consumer market (Wood 2002, 142–6). Industrial Capitalism, which Marx dated from the last third of the eighteenth century, marked the development of the factory system of manufacturing, characterized by a complex division of labor between and within work process and the routinization of work tasks; and finally established the global domination of the Capitalist mode of production (Burnham 2003).

During the resulting Industrial Revolution (1760–1840), the industrialist replaced the merchant as a dominant actor in the Capitalist system and effected the decline of the traditional handicraft skills of artisans, guilds, and journeymen. Also during this period, Capitalism marked the transformation of relations between the British landowning gentry and peasants, giving rise to the production of cash crops for the market rather than for subsistence on a feudal manor. The surplus generated by the rise of commercial agriculture encouraged increased mechanization of agriculture.

The world's earliest recorded speculative bubbles and stock market crashes have their roots in seventeenth-century Holland. The Dutch Republic was also an early industrialized nation-state in its Golden Age (seventeenth century) and, thus, the first Capitalist nation-state. The title of the world's first stock market deservedly goes to that of seventeenth-century Amsterdam, where an active secondary market in company shares emerged. The two major publicly traded companies were the Dutch East India Company and the Dutch West India Company, founded in 1602 and 1621, respectively. The Dutch East India Company's fame as the first public company, which heralded the transition from feudalism to modern Capitalism, and its remarkable financial success for nearly two centuries ensure its importance in the history of Capitalism. If one looks closely at the Dutch in the seventeenth century, we can see virtually every major feature of large-scale industry credited to the English two centuries later. Production was increasingly mechanized, as in sawmilling; standardized parts were deployed in manufacturing, especially in shipbuilding; modern financial markets were developed, underscored by the formation of the Amsterdam Bourse in 1602. And it was all underwritten by an agricultural system that did what all Capitalist agricultures must do: produce more and more food with fewer and fewer manhours.

The Dutch also played a pioneering role in the rise of the Capitalist world-system. The economic and financial supremacy of seventeenth-century Dutch Republic was the first historical model of the Capitalist hegemon. After becoming *de facto* independent from the empire of Philip II of Spain around 1585 the Dutch Republic experienced almost a century of explosive economic growth. A technological revolution in shipbuilding led to a competitive advantage in shipping that helped the young republic become the dominant trade power by the mid-seventeenth century. In 1670, the Dutch merchant marine totaled 568,000 tons of shipping—about half the European total. Pillars of this position were the dominance of the Amsterdam *Entrepôt* (trade system) in European trade, and that of the Dutch East and West India Companies in intercontinental trade. Beside trade, an early industrial revolution (powered by wind, water, and peat), land reclamation from the sea, and agricultural revolution helped the Dutch economy achieve the highest standard of living in Europe (and probably the world) by the middle of the seventeenth century. Affluence facilitated a Golden Age in culture typified by the great artist Rembrandt van Rijn (1606–1669).

THE SEPHARDIM

A DISCUSSION ON THE HISTORY OF CAPITALISM, NO MATTER HOW BRIEF, without a discussion on the history of Jewish migration to the Dutch Republic would be incomplete and inaccurate. These two histories are inextricable. The history of Jewish immigration to the Dutch Republic (founded in 1581 and lasting until 1795) is well documented. Sephardic* Jews have been known to settle in the Iberian Peninsula (Spain and Portugal) well before the Jewish Diaspora.† Their numbers, prosperity, enfranchisement significantly increased under the Umayyad Emirate (756–929) and Caliphate (929–1031) of Córdoba. The Jews of Spain had been utterly embittered and alienated by Catholic Visigoth rule by the time of the Muslim invasion (711–788). To them, the Moors were perceived as, and indeed were, a liberating force. Just prior to and during the invasion, many Jews closely conspired with the Moors against Catholic Visigoths. Wherever they went, the Muslims were greeted by Jews eager to aid them in administering the country. In many conquered towns the garrison was left in the hands of the Jews before the Muslims proceeded further north. Thus was initiated the period that became known as the "Golden Age" for the Sephardim. During this period, Sephardic Jews openly practiced their religion in Spain and Portugal over the centuries until the late Middle Ages.

In the early eleventh century, centralized authority based at Córdoba broke down following the Berber invasion and the ousting of the Umayyads. The Granada massacre of 1066 resulted in the death of nearly 4,000 Jews, including Joseph ibn Nagrela (one of only two Jews in history to command Muslim armies—Joseph's father Sh'muel being the other). Many Muslims, envious of Joseph's position of authority and influence as vizier (high-ranking political advisor or minister) to Abd al-Rahman III, first Caliph of

---

* Sephardi Jews, also known as Sephardic Jews or Sephardim (Hebrew: סְפָרַדִּים) are a Jewish ethnic division that settled in the Iberian Peninsula (Spain and Portugal). The existence of these émigré Jews in Spain was one of the reasons why Apostle Paul wrote that he intended to visit them (see Apostle Paul's letter to the Christians in Rome, chapter 15, verses 23–28).

† Jewish Diaspora – over the course of the history of ancient Israel, several diasporas or exiles took place. In this work, we are only referring to the Diaspora that occurred from Roman Judea (*Iudæa*) after the Jewish Revolt (first Roman-Jewish War), sacking of Jerusalem, and destruction of the Second Temple in 70 CE by Titus, the Roman general of the V, X, XII, and XV Legions, during the reign of Roman Emperor Vespasian (69–79 CE).

Córdoba from 912–929, and unhappy with Joseph's excesses, accused him of using his office to benefit Jewish friends. Joseph was assassinated in a mob uprising against him on 30 December 1066. The mob then proceeded to crucify his body upon the city's main gate. The following morning on 31 December 1066, the massacre of Granada's Jews began as the mob went on a rampage. The Granada massacre was one of the earliest signs of a decline in the status of Sephardim, which resulted largely from the penetration and influence of increasingly zealous, fundamentalist Islamic sects from North Africa.

The Moroccan Berber Almohads, who had taken control of much of Islamic Iberia by 1172, far surpassed the previous Muslim occupiers of Spain, the Almoravides, in fundamentalist practice, and they treated the *dhimmis* (specific individuals living in Muslim lands, who were granted special status and safety in Islamic law in return for paying the capital tax) harshly. Large-scale conversions were forced on Jews and Christians. Those who refused were expelled from Morocco and Islamic Spain (southern Iberian Peninsula).

Meanwhile, the Christian *Reconquista* of the Iberian Peninsula continued in the north. By the early twelfth century, conditions for some Sephardim in the emerging Christian kingdoms became increasingly favorable. As had happened during the reconstruction of towns following the breakdown of authority under the Umayyads, the services of Jews were employed by the Christian leaders who were increasingly emerging victorious during the later *Reconquista*. Their knowledge of the language and culture of the enemy, their skills as diplomats and professionals, as well as their desire for relief from intolerable conditions, rendered their services of great value to the Christians during the *Reconquista*—the very same reasons that they had proved useful to the Arabs in the early stages of the Muslim invasion. The necessity to have conquerors settle in reclaimed territories also outweighed the prejudices of anti-Semitism, at least while the Muslim threat was imminent. Thus, as conditions in Islamic Iberia worsened, immigration to Christian reconquered principalities increased (Assis 1988, 17). As conditions became more oppressive in the areas under Muslim rule during the twelfth and thirteenth centuries, Jews again looked to an outside culture for relief. Christian leaders of reconquered cities granted them extensive autonomy, and Jewish scholarship recovered and developed as communities grew in size and importance (Assis 1988, 18). However, the *Reconquista* Jews never reached the same heights as had those of the Golden Age.

In the beginning of the fourteenth century the position of Jews became precarious throughout Spain as anti-Semitism increased. A series of Jewish massacres beginning in 1328 in Navarre (Northern Spain) where 5,000 Sephardim were killed led to many more massacres. Jews were mandated to wear a yellow badge on their clothing. In 1385, John I, King of Castile and León (1370–1390) issued an order prohibiting the employment of Jews as financial agents or tax-farmers to the king, queen, *enfants*, or *grandees*. To this was added the resolution adopted by the Council of Palencia in 1388 ordering the complete separation of Jews and Saracens (Muslims) from Catholics and the prevention of any association between them, now codified in cannon law.

> The year 1391 forms a turning-point in the history of the Spanish Jews. The persecution was the immediate forerunner of the Inquisition, which, ninety years later, was introduced as a means of watching heresy and converted Jews. The number of those who had embraced Catholicism, in order to escape death, was very large—over half of Spain's Jews according to Joseph Pérez, 200,000 converts with only 100,000 openly practicing Jews remaining by 1410. (Gottheil, Kayserling, and Jacobs 1906.)

As soon as the Catholic monarchs Ferdinand and Isabella ascended their respective thrones for Aragon (1474–1504) and Castile (1479–1516), steps were taken to segregate the Jews both from the *conversos* (Jewish converts to Catholicism) and from their fellow countrymen. At the Cortes (legislative body) of Toledo in 1480, all Jews were ordered to be separated in special *barrios* (impoverished quarter of a town), and at the Cortes of Fraga two years later, the same law was enforced in Navarre, where they were ordered to be confined to the Jewries (*ghettos*) at night. The year 1478 saw the establishment of the Inquisition in Spain, the main object of which was to deal with the *conversos*. One of the reasons for the increased persecution of the Sephardim by the Catholic monarchs was the disappearance of the fear of any united action by Jews and Moors, the kingdom of Granada being at its last gasp. The rulers did, however, promise the Jews of the Moorish kingdom that they could continue to enjoy their existing rights in exchange for aiding the Spaniards in overthrowing the Moors. This promise, dated 11 February 1490, was repudiated, however, by the decree of expulsion of 1492.

As a result of the Alhambra Decree of 1492 expelling all Jews from Spain, the Portuguese Edict of Expulsion in 1497, the Spanish Inquisition (1478), and the Portuguese Inquisition (1536), many Sephardim left the Iberian Peninsula at the end of the fifteenth century and throughout the sixteenth century in search of religious freedom. In 1497, the Portuguese forcibly converted all Jews in Portugal, including many who had returned to Judaism after fleeing Spain and its Inquisition. Following the establishment in 1536 of the Portuguese Inquisition, descendants of Jews who had converted to Catholicism between the forced conversions in Spain in 1391 and the Portuguese forced conversion in 1497, were looked upon with great suspicion. In search of greater religious and economic freedoms, many crypto-Jews left Portugal for places with more lenient religious legislation and opportunities where their unique skillsets could thrive. Many of the Sephardim immigrated to North Africa and France. The newly independent Dutch Republic (established 1581) welcomed these Sephardic Jews. Many of the Sephardim who left for the Dutch provinces were crypto-Jews or *Marranos*, persons who had converted to Catholicism but continued to secretly practice Judaism. After they settled in the safety of the Netherlands, many of them resumed practicing their Jewish religion.

Much of the toleration expressed by the Amsterdam officials was rooted in the economic assets the new Sephardic Jewish community could provide, as well as the officials' lack of prior experience with Jewish residents. These factors made Amsterdam officials and residents less susceptible to labeling the entire Jewish community by their negatively perceived history in Christian tradition (Swetschinski 2000, 14). While the Jews of Amsterdam enjoyed greater freedoms in the religious and economic spheres of everyday life, which helped them assimilate more quickly and efficiently into Amsterdam society, they were denied certain political privileges, like participation in municipal government.

The migration of Sephardim from the Iberian Peninsula to many places other than Amsterdam allowed them to build a strong international trading network that was unique to Diaspora Jews. Because of the business and family relations many Amsterdam Jews had in light of their former community's dispersal, they established trading connections with the Levant and Morocco. The relations between the Dutch and South America were established by Sephardic Jews; they contributed to the establishment of the Dutch West Indies Company in 1621, and some of them were members of its directorate. The ambitious schemes of the Dutch for the conquest of Brazil were carried into effect through Francisco Ribeiro, a Portuguese captain, who is said to have had Jewish relations in Holland. After the Dutch in Brazil appealed to Holland for craftsmen of all kinds, many Jews went to Brazil; about 600 Jews left Amsterdam in 1642. In the struggle between Holland and Portugal for the possession of Brazil, the Dutch were supported by the Jews. After the loss of the Dutch colony of Recife in northeastern Brazil to the Portuguese in 1654, they sought refuge in other Dutch colonies, including the island of Curaçao in the Caribbean and New Amsterdam (Manhattan) in North America. The Jews of Amsterdam also established commercial relations with various countries in Europe. In a letter dated 25 November 1622, King Christian IV of Denmark invited Jews from Amsterdam to settle in Glückstadt, where, among other privileges, the free exercise of their religion would be guaranteed.

Amsterdam became one of the most favored destinations in the Netherlands for Sephardic Jews. Because many of the refugees were traders, Amsterdam benefited greatly from their arrival. Under the influence of Sephardic Jews, Amsterdam grew rapidly. Many Jews supported the House of Orange and were in return protected by the *stadtholder*. Under the influence and economic ingenuity of the Sephardim, Capitalism flourished in the Dutch Republic. England took note and during the Commonwealth of England under Oliver Cromwell in the mid-1650s Jews were permitted to return to England and practice their faith openly. It was not until 1890, however, that Jews achieved full rights and *égalité* as British citizens.

As a group, Jews of the Diaspora learned over the centuries to adapt to the challenges they continually faced since leaving their homeland. Their acquired talents in trade, sales (peddling), finance, negotiation, contracts, networking, opportunism, and risk assessment, combined with the literacy skills they possessed, presented unprecedented economic benefits to any country willing to adopt them. There was no better match made in heaven than Capitalism and the Jews of the Diaspora. Capitalism was a perfect vehicle, by which to maximize the acquired talents that Diaspora Jews possessed at a time in history during the Age of Discovery, Age of Sail, and the Enlightenment when new economic and political models were emerging and creating great opportunities.

Sephardic contributions to modern Capitalism in England and the Netherlands facilitated the spread and success of this economic model throughout the world. Without the tremendous contributions of Diaspora Jews, Capitalism might not have taken hold as solidly as it did during its early decades. Jews became integral constituents to the infrastructure of Capitalism and the communities that practiced it, and thereby also reaped the economic, social, cultural, and political rewards. However, this success also contributed to existential challenges to Jewish communities in the form of economic anti-Semitism.

ECONOMIC ANTI-SEMITISM

THE UNDERLYING PREMISE OF ECONOMIC ANTI-SEMITISM IS THAT JEWS perform harmful economic activities or that economic activities become harmful when they are performed by Jews—a veiled reference to unethical (exploitive) practice. Economic anti-Semitism functions under the assertion that Jews do not produce anything of value but instead tend to serve as middlemen (distributors, shoppers, wholesalers, brokers, financiers, and retailers), acting as "parasites in the production line" seeking to get a piece of the action of the real work being done by non-Jews. Economic anti-Semitism subscribes to the myth that Jews control the world finances, a theory promoted in the fraudulent *The Protocols of the Elders of Zion*, and later repeated by Henry Ford and his *Dearborn Independent*.

Derek Penslar, William Lee Frost Professor of Jewish History at Harvard University, writes that there are two components to the financial canards: a) Jews are savages that "are temperamentally incapable of performing honest labor"; and b) Jews are "leaders of a financial cabal seeking world domination." These premises and canards are all based more in envy, focusing on "excessive" Jewish wealth and power growing out of the Jews' success in commerce, banking, and professional careers, than they are in factual unethical or harmful business practice.

Non-Jews in medieval or Renaissance Europe had feelings of fear, vulnerability, and hostility towards Jews because they resented being beholden to Jewish lenders. Economic anti-Semitism is most often a result of resentment and jealousy of Jews. Their ability to make money where others saw no opportunity stirs jealousy and hate in non-Jews, contributing to a fear that Jews will "ascend too high" in the economic sphere and begin to manipulate and control world finances.

Prevailing economic factors can and often do *exacerbate* anti-Semitism; however, economic factors do not *cause* Jew-hatred; they only provide opportunities for it to be expressed. This is evident by the fact that wealthy non-Jews often do not face the same acerbic hatred from the economically less fortunate as Jews have faced over the centuries.

Furthermore, over the course of history, Jews have often suffered the worst anti-Semitic acts when they were poor, as was true with the overwhelming majority of Jews in Poland and Russia and have encountered the least amount of anti-Semitism when affluent as in the United States and Canada today (Prager and Telushkin 2003, 59–60). In general, however, economic anti-Semitism increases in times of recession or economic hardship, such as during the Depression of 1873. Therefore, economic anti-Semitism must be rooted in something other than wealth and the means employed to obtain it.

The flourishing of commercial and industrial Capitalism in nineteenth-century Europe strengthened the historic association between Jews and trade. For Jews, as for any ethnic minority that falls into a particular economic niche, economic distinctiveness engendered or reinforced group identity. The *Homo economicus judaicus*, who was glorified by middle-class Jews in Western Europe, was one of their own kind or a heroic progenitor of *bourgeois* Jewish society (Penslar 2001, 173).

In the nineteenth century, Jews came to be so closely associated with Capitalism that some even viewed the Jews as the "creators of Capitalism" (Foxman 2010, 98; see also Krefetz 1982, 41–4). According to Professor of History Jerry Muller, those who embraced Capitalism tended to be sympathetic to Jews, and those who rejected Capitalism tended to be hostile to Jews (Muller 2010, 12).

Richard Levy, Professor of Modern German History, writes that although there were local variations, most modern economic anti-Semitism is defined by "the scapegoating of Jews for Capitalism's ills" (Levy 2005, vol. 1, 55). Similarly, historian Steven Beller writes that economic anti-Semitism at the turn of the twentieth century was "based on fear and envy at the supposed stranglehold of 'the Jews' over finance and accused Jews of being behind the depredations of Capitalism on the traditional economy" (Beller 2007).

Laurel Plapp (doctorate in French and German literature) attributes anti-Semitic attitudes that extend back to the Middle Ages for the tendency to blame Jews for the problems of Capitalism and urbanization that arose in the late nineteenth century (Plapp 2008, 20).

Scholars have noted the anti-Semitic attitudes of mid-nineteenth-century French Socialists such as Charles Fourier and Pierre-Joseph Proudhon. Fourier vilified the Jews as the "incarnation of commerce: parasitical, deceitful, traitorous and unproductive." Proudhon used even more vehement invective, attacking Jews as the "incarnation of finance Capitalism" and characterizing them as anti-producers by temperament.

Alphonse Toussenel, a follower of Fourier, argued in *Les Juifs rois de l'époque* that finance, that is to say, Jews, were dominating and ruining France. Similarly, Auguste Blanqui commented in his correspondence on Jews as being usurers and "Shylocks." In the late 1860s, Gustave Tridon, who was a close follower of Blanqui, wrote a book entitled *Du Molochisme juif*, in which he also attacked the Jews on anti-religious as well as racial grounds, in addition to using the usual economic terms of disparagement (Green 1985, 374–99).

Karl Marx argued that earning a living from collecting interest or acting as a middleman was an unjust and exploitive aspect of Capitalism (Perry and Schweitzer 2002, 153–6). Because many Jews were employed in occupations that Marx considered "non-productive," he singled out Jews for particular criticism and blamed Judaism for the exploitation and alienation of workers (Perry & Schweitzer 2002, 153–6). Eighteenth-century German Jewish philosopher and founding leader of the *Haskalah* (the Jewish Enlightenment) Moses Mendelssohn argued to the contrary that commercial activity was just as valid and beneficial as manual labor: "Many a merchant, while quietly engaged at his desk in forming commercial speculations . . . produces . . . more than the most active and noisy mechanic or tradesman" (Muller 2010, 112).

Derek Penslar wrote that Marx argued not that Jews merely embraced Capitalism but that they "embodied" it. Penslar stated that: "Marx [in his *On the Jewish Question*] did not argue that Jews engendered Capitalism but rather that they embodied it. That is, whereas other anti-Semites of his generation saw Jews as particularly shrewd and successful traders, Marx claimed that the essence of commercial Capitalism bore all the characteristics that had long typified Jewish religious culture: egoism, materialism, and a cold, instrumental view of nature" (Penslar 2001, 44).

Marx concluded that Judaism was responsible for the alienation of many workers. That idea became a component of his theory of Communism. According to Perry and Schweitzer:

> Because of Judaism, money has become [quoting Marx] "the essence of man's life and work, which have become alienated from him. This alien monster rules him and he worships it. . . . Only then [under the rule of Judaized Christianity] could Jewry become universally dominant and turn alienated man and alienated nature into alienable, salable objects, subject to the serfdom of egotistical needs

> and to usury. Sale is the practice of alienation." Jews are the embodiment of capitalism (money-system) in action and the creators of all its evil consequences for humanity. Judaism is not a theology but the commercial and industrial practice of a money-system. (Perry & Schweitzer 2002, 153–6.)

Marx's views were shared by fellow Communist Bruno Bauer:

> [Marx believes] that Jews lack a sense of "higher values," are materialistic and thus are devoted only to material survival. . . . [Bruno] Bauer and Marx . . . make egoism the essence of Judaism and who denounced Judaism of imparting a loathsome lust for gain to Christianity. . . . In his essay "On the Jewish Question" published in 1844, Marx saw zeal for money as the essential feature of historic Judaism and the Jew of his day: "What is the Jew's foundation in our world? Material necessity, private advantage. What is the object of the Jew's worship in this world? Usury/huckstering. What is his worldly god? Money?" (Muller 2010, 36; Perry and Schweitzer 2002, 153–5.)

JUDEO-BOLSHEVISM

JEWISH BOLSHEVISM IS ANOTHER OF HITLER'S ANTI-SEMITIC CANARDS that is based on the claim that Jews have been the driving force behind or are disproportionately involved in Communism, sometimes more specifically Russian Bolshevism. This connection has already been thoroughly addressed earlier in this segment on the Origins of the Nazi Movement (see: "Dietrich Eckart's Role in Reshaping Hitler's Anti-Semitism," *supra*).

Judeo-Bolshevism was inferred in the title of Dietrich Eckart's March 1924 posthumously-published pamphlet, "Der Bolschewismus von Moses bis Lenin: Zwiegespräch zwischen Hitler und mir" ("Bolshevism from Moses to Lenin: Dialogue Between Hitler and Me"), and the expression became current after the 1917 October Revolution in Russia, featuring prominently in the propaganda of the anti-Bolshevik "White" forces during the Russian Civil War. That idea spread worldwide in the 1920s with the publication and circulation of *The Protocols of the Elders of Zion*. The expression was legitimized by the Jewish ancestry of many leading Bolsheviks, most notably Vladimír Lenin and Leon Trotsky, during and after the October Revolution. American historian and President of the Middle East Forum Daniel Pipes says that "primarily through *The Protocols of the Elders of Zion*, the Whites spread these charges to an international audience" (Pipes 1997, 93). Scottish historian James Webb wrote that it is rare to find an anti-Semitic source after 1917 that "does not stand in debt to the White Russian analysis of the Revolution" (Webb 1976, 295).

The label "Judeo-Bolshevism" was used in Nazi Germany to equate Jews with Communists, implying that Communism served Jewish interests and/or that all Jews were Communists. Jews and Communists leading the Social Democratic Party were blamed for having allegedly betrayed Germany during the First World War resulting in Germany signing The Treaty of Versailles, in what is known as General Erich Ludendorff's "stab-in-the-back legend." In Poland before the Second World War, *Żydokomuna* was used in the same way to allege that Jews were conspiring with the Soviet Union to invade Poland. According to André Gerrits, associate professor in East European studies and Jean Monnet Chair in European Integration, and Senior Research Fellow at the Netherlands Institute of International Relations, "The myth of Jewish Communism was one of the most popular and widespread political prejudices in the first half of the 20th century, in Eastern Europe in particular" (Gerrits 2009, 195). The allegation still sees use in anti-Semitic publications and websites today.

In summary, unlike popular belief, the theory that "deicide" was the root of early anti-Semitism is a shallow one that ignores the actual operation of human interaction on an individual and local level. Given the chasm in the religious and social spheres that existed between Diaspora Jews and their non-Jewish hosts, the only remaining nexus linking these two groups was commerce. When individual Jews and non-Jews interacted in professional settings during the rise of the Middle Ages and Umayyad and Abbasid caliphates no one had a 1,000-year-old event on their mind, even as the religious orders of Christianity and Islam were growing in power and influence. Human interactions and relationships are established and measured in a much more practical way on an individual level. Geopolitics and history of foreign peoples play little to no role in the establishment of human relationships that have mutual economic interests. Likewise, conflict among individuals engaging in commerce is rarely based in geopolitics and remote historical religious events, particularly when the politics and historical events have no commonality between the two parties. Such conflicts almost always originate in contractual and monetary disputes. In other words, Europeans and Muslims conducting business with individual Jews during the Middle Ages did not give a damn about what transpired between the Jews and Romans in far-away Israel (Roman Judea) during the first century. Moreover, the European Jew was not even on the Christian Church's radar when the first manifestations of anti-Semitism emerged in Europe in the eleventh and twelfth centuries. The Inquisition, as a church-court, had no jurisdiction over Moors and Jews. Generally, the Inquisition was concerned only with the heretical behavior of Catholic adherents or converts. It was not until the fifteenth century that the Catholic Church turned its attention to and targeted the Jews and Muslims with its Spanish and Portuguese inquisitions that focused particularly on the issue of Jewish *anusim* and Muslim converts to Catholicism, partly because these minority groups were more numerous in Spain and Portugal than in many other parts of Europe, and partly because they were often considered suspect due to the assumption that they had secretly reverted to their previous religions.

Homo economicus judaicus, Christ slayers, and many other expressed reasons for anti-Semitism were primarily used as an excuse or false pretense for persecuting Jews once conflict between Jews and non-Jews had started due to other reasons already discussed. Finally, it is separatism that is at the heart of elitism and xenophobia, and the original self-imposed separatism that the Jews practiced in order to preserve their heritage and identity eventually evolved into an externally imposed segregation and genocide. The argument that Jews separated themselves from non-Jews only as a response to anti-Semitism is without historical merit. This superficial, sophomoric analysis of cause and effect is reminiscent of those Western Socialists and Communist apologists who claimed that Stalin's clamp-down on Central and Eastern Europe during the Cold War was primarily a response to America's development of the atomic bomb and that had the bomb not been developed Stalin would not have brought Central and Eastern Europe under Soviet domination (see THE SOVIET UNION'S ROLE IN THE SLOVAK NATIONAL UPRISING, *infra*).

From the very beginning of the post-Roman Jewish Diaspora, Jews naturally flocked to prosperous regions where other Jews had already established themselves, and émigré Jews naturally sought out familiar social, religious, linguistic, and communal settings among their own kind that made their plight easier to bear and success in their new homelands more likely. However, Jews also carried with them a sober memory of their many exiles over the course of their history and how their segregation was commanded by God to preserve their faith and identity but how it also turned out to be a dual-edged sword for good and bad.

This dichotomy also became a source of conflict among the Jewish-Christian Apostles Peter and Paul during the early years of Christianity ("The Way") when they mixed with Greek and other non-Jewish converts to Christianity, particularly over the Jewish religious laws for diet and circumcision (see New Testament book: *Acts of the Apostles*). Before his conversion, Paul (Saul in Hebrew) was a Pharisee scholar in Jewish Law tutored by the great Rabban Gamaliel the Elder, Pharisee doctor of Mosaic Law and leading authority in the Great Sanhedrin of Jerusalem in the first century CE. Paul was thoroughly indoctrinated in *halakha* (הֲלָכָה) including *mitzvot* and *kashrut*. However, after his conversion and subsequent life as a Christian missionary to non-Jews, Paul often spoke, wrote, and practiced in a manner that countered traditional Jewish dietary and circumcision laws. This was the heart of the conflict between Paul and Peter—who believed adherence to Jewish Law was essential to righteousness and holiness—until they resolved it. Christian dogmatic theology holds that throughout his writings, Paul clarifies Jesus's teachings on the true purpose of God's Law as not being a means of attaining righteousness before God but as operating as a *mirror* (revealing to us the sin that we all possess), a *curb* (by means of its fearful denunciations and the consequent dread of punishment, a force keeping sinful nature in check), and a *guide* (helping to remind believers of or lead unbelievers to the Gospel—the realization how we are incapable of perfectly fulfilling the Law and how only God has completely and impeccably fulfilled the Law for believers through His plan of redemption and reconciliation). According to Paul's teachings, no one ever became righteous in God's eyes by adhering to God's Law (see Paul's letter to the Christians in Rome chapter 3 verse 20). Peter and the rest of the Apostles eventually accepted this doctrine of salvation and the proper distinction between Law and Gospel as the five *solae*: *sola fide*; *sola gracia*; *sola scriptura*; *solus Christus*; and *soli Deo gloria*.

Finally, let us examine how all of this applies to Hitler's dichotomous anti-Semitism. Hitler's writings, speeches, and laws regarding the Jews between 1919 and 1945 generally fell into two categories—Judeo-Bolshevism and Judeo-Capitalism—that on the surface appear contradictory, diametrically opposite, and oxymoronic. This dichotomy goes to the heart of Hitler's anti-Semitism. As previously discussed, Hitler had no familial legacy of anti-Semitism or personal reasons to hate Jews. Legitimate controversy still remains over whether Hitler's father Alois was the bastard product of the Jew Leopold Frankenberger raping Adolf Hitler's Aryan housemaid grandmother Maria Anna Schicklgruber. Hitler's first real exposure to anti-Semitism occurred during his Vienna years (1905–1914). However, the anti-Semitism he adopted in Vienna was generic, albeit with a peculiar mythical, occult *völkisch* Viennese twist. It was not until after the First World War and the German Revolution of 1918–1919 that Hitler's anti-Semitism made a paradigm shift from romantic neo-pagan occultism to intellectual rationalism and materialism. This was in no small part due to the influence of his new friends at the Thule Society and the *Aufbau Vereinigung* whose subscription to the Imperial Russian forgery *The Protocols of the Elders of Zion* permitted resurrection of age-old myths and canards about scheming, lying, manipulative Jews influencing geopolitics and dominating the world. Hitler's new, refined dichotomous anti-Semitism saw a close alliance between international finance and Bolshevism viewing the Jew as Shylock or Capitalist exploiter, on one hand, and as Marxist revolutionary or Socialist agitator, on the other, with the two meeting as international Jewish financiers conspiring with international Jewish Bolsheviks to destroy, enslave, and dominate the world by the techniques of *The Protocols of the Elders of Zion*.

In Hitler's mind, Communism was a major enemy of Germany, an enemy he often mentioned in *Mein Kampf*. During the trial for his involvement in the Beer Hall *Putsch*, Hitler claimed that his singular goal was to assist the German government in "fighting Marxism." Marxism, Bolshevism, and Communism were interchangeable terms for Hitler as evidenced by their use throughout *Mein Kampf*:

> In the years 1913 and 1914 I expressed my opinion for the first time in various circles, some of which are now members of the National Socialist Movement, that the problem of how the future of the German nation can be secured is the problem of how Marxism can be exterminated (Hitler 1941, 203).

Later in his seminal tome, Hitler advocated for "the destruction of Marxism in all its shapes and forms" (Hitler 1939, 419). According to Hitler, Marxism was a Jewish strategy to subjugate Germany and the world and saw Marxism as a mental and political form of slavery. From Hitler's vantage point, Bolsheviks existed to serve "Jewish international finance" (Hitler

1939, 475). When the British tried negotiating with Hitler in 1935 by including Germany in the extension of the Locarno Pact, he rejected their offer and instead assured them that German rearmament was important in safeguarding Europe against Communism (Bullock 1962, 334), a move which clearly showed his anti-Communist proclivities.

In 1939, Hitler told the Swiss Commissioner to the League of Nations, Carl Burckhardt, that everything he was undertaking was "directed against Russia" and continued with, "if those in the West are too stupid or too blind to understand this, then I shall be forced to come to an understanding with the Russians to beat the West, and then, after its defeat, turn with all my concerted force against the Soviet Union" (Hildebrand 1973, 88). When Hitler finally ordered the attack against the Soviet Union, it was the fulfillment of his ultimate goal and the most important campaign in his estimation, as it comprised a struggle of "the chosen Aryan people against Jewish Bolsheviks" (Victor 2007, 198).

Alan Bullock avows, Hitler "laid great stress" on the need to concentrate on a single enemy, an enemy he lumps together as "Marxism and the Jew" (Bullock 1962, 130). Shortly in the wake of the Commissar Order, a directive pursuant to the German invasion of the Soviet Union, *SS* Deputy Reinhard Heydrich informed the *SS* of Hitler's geopolitical philosophy, which conflated Bolshevism and Jews, writing "eastern Jewry is the intellectual reservoir of Bolshevism and in the *Führer*'s view must therefore be annihilated" (Binion 1991, 61).

Because Nazism co-opted the popular success of Communism among working people while simultaneously promising to destroy Communism and offer an alternative to it, Hitler's anti-Communist program allowed industrialists with traditional conservative views (tending toward monarchism, aristocracy, and *laissez-faire* Capitalism) to cast their lot with, and help underwrite, the Nazi rise to power. In the 1920s and 1930s, there was a fear among German industrialists, not wholly unfounded, that Germany would likely suffer an October-style Bolshevik revolution at some point and become a Soviet republic of the "World Soviet Federation" envisioned by the Communist International, unless drastic anti-Communist measures were taken. For example, industrialist magnate Fritz Thyssen, who had been arrested by German "Reds" in 1918, did not trust that the Weimar Republic would indefinitely succeed in fending off a Bolshevik-type revolution.

Hitler blamed Germany's parliamentary government for many of the nation's ills. The Nazis and Hitler especially, associated Democracy with the failed Weimar government and the punitive Treaty of Versailles (Stern 1992, 14). Hitler often denounced Democracy, equating it with internationalism. Since Democratic ideals espoused equality for all men, it represented to Hitler and his Nazi ideologues the notion of mob rule and the hatred of excellence (Stern 1992, 88). Not only was Democracy antithetical to their social-Darwinist abstractions, but its international-Capitalist framework was considered an exclusively Jewish-derived conception (Gellately 2007, 13). Hitler also thought Democracy was nothing more than a preliminary stage of Bolshevism (Hilgruber 1981, 51). Both of these concepts were not invented by Hitler; he adopted Karl Marx's views on the natural marriage of Capitalism and Judaism (from Marx's 1844 essay "On the Jewish Question") and the natural political evolution of liberal Capitalistic Democracy to Communism (from Marx's *Das Kapital*). Moreover, popular reactions to the perceived nexus between Jews and finance or Capitalism long predate Eckart and Hitler. The Berlin Movement in the 1880s was a reaction to the six-year financial Panic of 1873 that led to a recession in the United States and parts of the Western European economy. The Berlin Movement assailed Jews and Capitalism; along with this critique it opposed Liberalism and it represented a fear of Social Democracy. The movement came out of a racial conception of national identity on the part of the German middle class. Journalist and author Otto Glagau led a journal, *Der Kulturkämpfer* (*The Culture Warrior*), that propagated these ideas. The pietist Lutheran theologian and politician, Adolf Stöcker, led the Christian Social Party in support of the movement with the Anti-Semites' Petition of 1881. The significance of the movement laid in its being the first anti-Semitic populist movement in modern Germany.

Hitler believed in the leader principle (hence his title, the Leader, *der Führer*), and he considered it ludicrous that an idea of governance or morality could be held by the people above the power of the leader. As Joachim Fest described a 1930 confrontation between Hitler and Otto Straßer, "Now Hitler took Straßer to task for placing 'the idea' above the *Führer* and wanting 'to give every party comrade the right to decide the nature of the idea, even to decide whether or not the *Führer* is true to the so-called idea.' That, he cried angrily, was the worst kind of Democracy, for which there was no place in their movement. 'With us the *Führer* and the idea are one and the same, and every party comrade has to do what the *Führer* commands, for he embodies the idea and he alone knows its ultimate goal'" (Fest 2002, 279; see also Kershaw 2000, 294).

Although Hitler realized that his ascension to power required the use of the Weimar Republic's parliamentary system (founded on Democratic principles), he never intended for the continuation of Democratic governance once in control. To the contrary, Hitler proclaimed that he would "destroy Democracy with the weapons of Democracy" (Grunfeld 1974, 109). The rapid transition from Democracy to dictatorship made by the Nazis once they assumed control clearly reveals that Hitler succeeded in this regard. Likewise, for the most part, Democracy was never embraced by the German masses or by the elite over the short period it existed in interbellum Germany (Kershaw 2008, 258). The ill-fated Weimar Democracy's inability to provide economic relief to the German people during the Great Depression further enhanced its image as an ineffectual system of government amid the masses (Kershaw 2008, 258). Hitler enticed the masses with the promise of a "new and better society" (Kershaw 2008, 258–9). He exploited the conditions in Germany in the ultimate expression of political opportunism when he brought his dictatorial and totalitarian government to power; thereafter, attempting to impose himself and his system upon the world in the process (Kershaw 2008, 258).

Part Two

BASHERT

א"ר שמואל בר רב יצחק: כי הוה פתח ריש לקיש בסוטה, אמר הכי: אין מזווגין לו לאדם אשה אלא לפי מעשיו, שנא': +תהלים קכה+ כי לא ינוח שבט הרשע על גורל הצדיקים. אמר רבה בר בר חנה אמר ר' יוחנן: וקשין לזווגן כקריעת ים סוף, שנאמר: +תהלים סח+ אלהים מושיב יחידים ביתה מוציא אסירים בכושרות. איני? והא אמר רב יהודה אמר רב: ארבעים יום קודם יצירת הולד, בת קול יוצאת ואומרת: בת פלוני לפלוני בית פלוני לפלוני שדה פלוני לפלוני! לא קשיא: הא בזוג ראשון, הא בזוג שני.

(Rabbi Shmuel Bar-Rav Yitzchak said: When Resh Lakish began to expound [the subject of] Sotah, he spoke thus: They only pair a woman with a man according to his deeds; as it is said: For the scepter of wickedness shall not rest upon the lot of the righteous [Psalm 125:3]. Rabbah b. Bar Hanah said in the name of R. Johanan: It is as difficult to pair them as was the division of the Red Sea; as it is said: God setteth the solitary in families: He bringeth out the prisoners into prosperity! [Psalm 68:7] But it is not so; for Rav Judah has said in the name of Rav: Forty days before the creation of a child, a *Bath Kol* [heavenly voice] issues forth and proclaims, The daughter of this person is for that person; the house of this person is for that person; the field of this person is for that person! — There is no contradiction, the latter dictum referring to a first marriage and the former to a second marriage.)

— Babylonian Talmud (Vilna edition): B. Sotah 2a

ACCORDING TO TALMUDIC TRADITION, *BASHERT* MEANS "destiny." It is often used to refer to one's divinely foreordained spouse or soulmate, who is called one's *basherte* (female) or *basherter* (male). It can also be used to express the seeming fate or destiny of an auspicious or important event, friendship, or happening. In modern usage, Jewish singles will say that they are looking for their *bashert*, meaning they are looking for that person who will complement them perfectly, and whom they will complement perfectly. Since it is considered to have been heavenly foreordained whom one will marry, one's spouse is considered to be one's *bashert* by definition, independent of whether the couple's marital life works out well or not.* The unlikely encounter leading to marriage between Roman Catholic Slovak Army officer Peter Vlčko and Hungarian-Slovak Neolog[1] Jew Georgina Reichsfeld in the midst of 1940s Europe can only be considered preordained. This improbable union resulted in the rescue of many lives that produced generations of families across the globe.

* Yevamot, 63b. Yevamot (יבמות, "Brother's Widow") is a tractate of the Talmud that deals with, among other concepts, the laws of Yibbum, loosely translated in English as the levirate marriage, and, briefly, with conversion to Judaism. This tractate is the first in the order of Nashim (נשים, "Women")—Nashim being the third of six orders of the Mishnah containing family law.

CHAPTER 15

PETER EMILIUS VLČKO (1912–2004) THE FIRST THIRTY YEARS

SLOVAKIA UNDER HUNGARIAN RULE

SLOVAKIA IS A LANDLOCKED AGRICULTURAL TERRITORY COMPRISED OF fertile plains and valleys, rolling hills, alpine mountains, great rivers and streams, diverse forests and animals, glacial and mineral rock caves, and fascinating peoples sharing a common Slavic language with many dialects. Slovaks can boast of great kings, princes, and lords beginning with Samo, the first *Rex Sclavorum* (King of the Slavs), in *AD* 623, and ending with the deaths of Mojmír II and Svätopluk II, sons of the infamous Moravian King Svätopluk the Great,* at the Battle of Bratislava† (German: Pressburg;

---

* Svätopluk I (Svätopluk the Great) (c. 840–894) became ruler of the Great Moravian Empire (833–907) in 870 and was Duke Rastislav's nephew and third in the line of the Moravian Mojmirid dynasty after Mojmír I (?–846) and Mojmír I's nephew Rastislav (?–870). After the breakup of the Great Moravian Empire in 907, the Moravian tribe was divided between the new states Duchy of Bohemia and Duchy of Hungary. The western Moravians were assimilated by the Bohemians and presently identify as Czechs. The modern nation of the Slovaks was formed in part out of the eastern portions of the Moravian tribe within the Kingdom of Hungary.

† Battle of Pressburg (*Brezalauspurc*, Bratislava) was a three-day-long battle, fought between 4–6 July 907, during which the East Francian army, consisting mainly of Bavarian troops led by Margrave Luitpold, was annihilated by Hungarian forces under Grand Prince Árpád. An important result of the Battle of Pressburg was the Kingdom of East Francia could not regain control over the Carolingian March of Pannonia, including the territory of the later *marchia orientalis* (March of Austria), lost in 900. The most significant result of the Battle of Pressburg is that the Hungarians secured the lands they gained during the Hungarian conquest of the Carpathian Basin (894–907), prevented a German invasion that would have jeopardized their future, and established the Kingdom of Hungary in AD 1000. This battle is considered one of the most significant in the history of Hungary creating the possibility of an independent Hungarian state with its own church and culture

Hungarian: Pozsony) in *AD* July 907 and the arrival of the Finno-Ugric Magyars (Hungarians) from the Pannonian plains and east of the Carpathian Mountains.

Under Magyar rule (Hungarian Kingdom) since the coronation of Hungary's first king, István (975?–1038) (Stephen I, House of Árpád), on Christmas Day *AD* 1000, Slovakia remained unchanged like a land trapped in time under the heel of one overlord after another. Slovakia's geographic location placed it at the crossroads of major ancient trade routes between eastern, western, northern, and southern European cultures. Strong medieval fortifications and princely estates were built throughout Slovakia at strategic points that controlled the trade routes. Lords and princes of powerful kingdoms and empires competed and fought over its rich and abundant raw materials and minerals. Artisans and skilled labor came from far and wide to serve the lords that over the centuries exploited this strategically important, beautiful, and rich land.

Unlike its Bohemian and Moravian brothers in the west, who were vassals of the Austrian Habsburgs since 1526, Slovakia had been under the rule of the Magyars for nearly a millennium when Peter Vlčko and his father were born. Contrary to how Bohemia and Moravia faired under Habsburg rule, Slovakia was treated more like a colony whose primary value was its rich raw materials and minerals, skilled and unskilled labor force, geographic position as a strategic buffer between the powerful kingdoms of Poland and Germany, and a highland hunting and playground for the aristocracy of Hungary. For much of the millennium under Magyar rule, the Slavic peoples of Slovakia were forbidden to develop their own unique culture, identity, language, system of higher education, self-governance, industry, finance, or any other basis commonly associated with a distinct culture. The Magyars ruled Slovakia with an iron fist while the Habsburgs granted Bohemia and Moravia much latitude, freedom, and self-determination to maintain and grow their own unique identity separate from Austria. The result of this great disparity over the centuries left Slovakia a backward, undeveloped region of uneducated people who were generally illiterate and limited to agriculture and physical labor relative to its neighbors and especially relative to its brothers in Bohemia and Moravia. Things began to change, however, in the mid-nineteenth century when Slovak pride and Nationalism were reborn.

---

and the premise of the survival of the Hungarians until this day. The battle marks the conclusion of the Hungarian conquest for control of the Carpathian Basin.

During the eighteenth century the Slovak National Movement emerged, partially inspired by the broader Pan-Slavic movement (see *infra*) with the aim of fostering a sense of national identity among the Slovak people. Advanced mainly by Slovak religious leaders, the movement grew during the nineteenth century. Hungarian control remained strict after the Austro-Hungarian Compromise of 1867 and the movement was constrained by the official policy of Magyarization (see *infra*).

Austrian-Hungarian Relations

THE ROYAL HUNGARIAN HOUSE OF THE ÁRPÁDS DIED OUT IN 1301 WITH the death of Andrew III. Subsequently, Hungary was ruled by the French Angevins (Anjou Age) until the end of the fourteenth century, and then by several non-dynastic rulers—notably Sigismund of Luxemburg and Matthias Corvinus (Hungarian House of Hunyadi)—until the early sixteenth century. In the Middle Ages, the Duchy of Austria was an autonomous state within the Holy Roman Empire, ruled by the Austrian House of Habsburg (*AD* eleventh century to 1780), and the Kingdom of Hungary was a sovereign state outside the empire.* On 29 August 1526, at the Battle of Mohács, the forces of the Ottoman Empire led by Suleiman I annihilated the Hungarian Army. After the Ottoman siege of Austria failed in 1683, the Habsburgs went on the offensive against the Turks. By the end of the seventeenth century, they managed to invade the remainder of the historical Kingdom of Hungary

* The Habsburg Monarchy is an unofficial umbrella term among historians for the kingdoms and countries in personal union with the Habsburg Archduchy of Austria between 1526 and 1804, when it was succeeded by the Austrian Empire. The Monarchy was a composite state of territories within and outside the Holy Roman Empire, united only in the person of the monarch. The dynastic capital was Vienna, except from 1583 to 1611, when it was moved to Prague. From 1804 to 1867, the Habsburg Monarchy was formally unified as the Austrian Empire, and from 1867 to 1918 as the Austro-Hungarian Empire. The head of the Austrian branch of the House of Habsburg was often elected Holy Roman Emperor: from 1452 until the Empire's dissolution in 1806, Charles VII of Bavaria (1742–1745) was the only Holy Roman Emperor who was not Habsburg ruler of Austria. The two entities were never coterminous, as the Habsburg Monarchy covered many lands beyond the Holy Roman Empire, and most of the Empire was ruled by other dynasties. The Habsburg Monarchy must not be confused with the Habsburg Empire, another unofficial umbrella term for all the territories of the House of Habsburg, divided in 1556 between the Austrian branch and a Spanish branch after the abdication of Charles V, Holy Roman Emperor.

and the principality of Transylvania. By 1686, the capital Buda was again free from the Ottoman Empire, with the aid of other Europeans. The Ottomans were eventually driven out of Hungary by international Western Christian forces led by Prince Eugene of Savoy between 1686 and 1699. From 1526 to 1804, Hungary was ruled by the Habsburg Dynasty as kings of Hungary but remained nominally and legally separate from the other lands of the Habsburg Monarchy.

Francis II (12 February 1768–2 March 1835) was the last Holy Roman Emperor, ruling from 1792 until 6 August 1806, when he dissolved the Holy Roman Empire of the German Nation after the decisive defeat at the hands of the First French Empire led by Napoléon at the Battle of Austerlitz. In 1804, he had founded the Austrian Empire and became Francis I, the first Emperor of Austria, ruling from 1804 to 1835, so later he was named the one and only *Doppelkaiser* (double emperor) in history (1804–1806). Francis II was also ruler of the lands of the Habsburg Monarchy, which included the Kingdom of Hungary. In 1804, Francis II created a formal overarching structure for the Habsburg Monarchy, which had functioned as a composite monarchy for about 300 years.* Thus Hungary formally became part of the Empire of Austria.

Until the 1848 Revolutions, the workings of the overarching structure and the status of Hungary stayed much the same as they had been before 1804. The Kingdom of Hungary had always been considered a separate realm, the country's status was affirmed by Article X, which was added to Hungary's constitution in 1790 during the phase of the composite monarchy; it described the state as a *Regnum Independens*. Hungary's affairs continued to be administered by its own institutions (king and diet) as they had been previously. Thus, under the new arrangements, no imperial Austrian institutions were involved in its internal government. From the

---

* A composite monarchy (or composite state or unions of the crowns) is a historical category, introduced by H. G. Koenigsberger in 1975 and popularized by J. H. Elliott, that describes early modern states consisting of several countries under one ruler, sometimes designated as a personal union, who governs his territories as if they were separate kingdoms, in accordance with local traditions and legal structures. The composite state was the most common and dominant type of states in the early modern era Europe. Koenigsberger divides composite states into two classes: those, like the Spanish Empire, that consisted of countries separated by either other states or by the sea, and those, like Poland–Lithuania, that were contiguous. A famous medieval example for composite monarchy was the Angevin Empire. A modern example is the United Kingdom.

perspective of the Austrian Court since 1723, *regnum Hungariae* had been a hereditary province of the Habsburg Dynasty's three main branches on both lines. From the perspective of the *ország* (the country), Hungary was *regnum independens*, a separate land as Article X of 1790 stipulated.

The Holy Roman Empire was abolished after the Battle of Jena and Auerstedt when Napoléon Bonaparte defeated the Prussians on 14 October 1806. The Austrian Court reassured the Hungarian Diet, however, that the assumption of the monarch's new title (Francis I Emperor of Austria) did not in any sense affect the laws and the constitution of Hungary. Although the Kingdom of Hungary had its own diet (parliament) and constitution, the members of the Governor's Council (*Helytartótanács*, the office of the palatine) were appointed by the Habsburg monarch, and the superior economic institution, the Hungarian Chamber, was directly subordinated to the Austrian Court Chamber in Vienna. The Hungarian legal system and judicial system remained separated and independent from the unified legal and judicial systems of the other Habsburg ruled areas. Moreover, from 1526 to 1851, the Kingdom of Hungary maintained its own customs borders, which separated Hungary from the united customs system of other Habsburg ruled territories. Despite these reassurances, ninety percent of ethnic Magyars, as well as all Slovaks, constituted the lower stratum of society in the Kingdom of Hungary: they were serfs and consequently did not participate in the mainstream of the political life. Throughout the period of the composite monarchy, any ethnic Magyars that achieved nobility status and served in imperial leadership positions in the Kingdom of Hungary were Magyars who were Germanized.

The humiliation felt by ethnic Hungarians over their lower status in the Kingdom and greater Austrian Empire festered for centuries. Similar sentiment existed among the many disenfranchised ethnic groups throughout Europe that were delegated to common status and barred from ruling their own realms. This was all challenged by the 1848 Spring of Nations Revolutions that confronted monarchies and aristocratic classes across Continental Europe.

Nationalist Hungarian revolutionary forces under General Artúr Görgey (1818–1916) won victory after victory against the Austrians. Fearing defeat, the Austrians pleaded for Russian help. The combined forces of the two empires quelled the revolution. The desired political changes of 1848 were again suppressed until the Austro-Hungarian Compromise of 1867. The Magyars came close to regaining independence and were defeated by the Austrian Empire only by the military intervention of the Russian Empire.

After the restoration of Habsburg rule, Hungary was placed under martial law. Prime Minister Prince Felix of Schwarzenberg and his government, operating from November 1848, pursued a radically new imperial policy. It wanted to develop a uniform empire in the spirit of the imperial constitution issued by Franz Joseph I (reign: 2 December 1848–21 November 1916)* in Olmütz (Czech: Olomouc) on 4 March 1849, and as a result, Hungary's constitution and territorial integrity were abolished. The centralist March Constitution of Austria introduced the neo-absolutism in Habsburg ruled territories, and it concentrated absolute power for the Austrian monarch. The Austrian constitution was accepted by the Imperial Diet of Austria, in which Hungary had no representation and traditionally had no legislative power in the territory of Kingdom of Hungary; still, it also tried to abolish the Diet of Hungary, which existed as the legislative power in Hungary since the late twelfth century. The new Austrian constitution also went against the historical constitution of Hungary and tried to nullify it. A military dictatorship was created in Hungary. Every aspect of Hungarian life was put under close scrutiny and Austrian governmental control.

German became the official language of public administration and Germanization the official policy of the Empire. An edict issued on 9 October 1849 placed education under state control, the curriculum was prescribed and controlled by the state, the teaching of national history was restricted, and history was taught from a Habsburg viewpoint. Even the bastion of Hungarian culture, the Academy, was kept under control: the institution was staffed with foreigners, mostly Germans, and the institution was practically defunct until the end of 1858. Hungarians responded with passive resistance. Anti-Habsburg and anti-German sentiments were strong. In the following years, the empire instituted several reforms but failed to resolve problems. After the Hungarian revolution of 1848–49, the independent customs system of Hungary was abolished, and Hungary became part of the unified imperial customs system on 1 October 1851.

---

* Franz Joseph I (18 August 1830–21 November 1916) was Emperor of Austria along with his wife Empress Elizabeth of Austria, Queen of Hungary. He was also King of Hungary, King of Bohemia, and monarch of many other states of the Austro-Hungarian Empire, from 2 December 1848 to his death. From 1 May 1850 to 24 August 1866, he was also President of the German Confederation. He was the longest-reigning Emperor of Austria and King of Hungary, as well as the third-longest-reigning monarch of any country in European history, after Louis XIV of France and Johann II of Liechtenstein.

In 1866, Hungary's fate began to change. Austria was completely defeated in the Austro-Prussian War. Its position as the leading state of a Greater Germany (*Großdeutschland*) ended, and the remaining German minor states were soon absorbed into the Northern German Confederation created by Prussia. Austria also lost much of its remaining claims and influence in Italy, which had been its chief foreign policy interest.

After a period of Greater Germany ambitions, when Austria tried to establish itself as the leading German power, Austria again needed to redefine itself to maintain unity in the face of Nationalism. As a consequence of the Second Italian War of Independence and the Austro-Prussian War, the Habsburg Empire was on the verge of collapse in 1866, as these wars caused monumental state debt and a financial crisis. The Habsburgs were forced to reconcile with Hungary, to save their empire and dynasty. The Habsburgs and part of the Hungarian political elite arranged the Austro-Hungarian Compromise of 1867.

The Austro-Hungarian Compromise of 1867 established the dual monarchy of Austria-Hungary. The Compromise partially re-established the sovereignty of the Kingdom of Hungary, separate from, and no longer subject to the Austrian Empire. The agreement also restored the old historic constitution of the Kingdom of Hungary. Under the Compromise, the lands of the House of Habsburg were reorganized as a real union between the Austrian Empire and the Kingdom of Hungary, headed by a single monarch who reigned as Emperor of Austria in the Austrian half of the empire, and as King of Hungary in Kingdom of Hungary. The Cisleithanian (Austrian) and Transleithanian (Hungarian) states were governed by separate parliaments and prime ministers. The two countries conducted unified foreign diplomatic and defense policies. For these purposes, "common" ministries of foreign affairs and defense were maintained under the monarch's direct authority, as was a third ministry responsible only for financing the two "common" portfolios.

Pan-Slavism

PAN-SLAVISM, A MOVEMENT WHICH CRYSTALLIZED IN THE MID-nineteenth century, is the political ideology dedicated to the advancement of integrity and unity for the Slavic-speaking peoples. Pan-Slavism began much like Pan-Germanism, both of which grew from the sense of unity and Nationalism experienced within ethnic groups after the 1789 French Revolution and the consequent Napoleonic Wars against European monarchies. Like other Romantic Nationalist movements, Slavic intellectuals and scholars in the developing fields of history, philology, and folklore actively encouraged the passion of their shared identity and ancestry.

The first Pan-Slavic Congress was held in Prague on 2–16 June 1848. The delegates at the Congress were specifically both anti-Austrian and anti-Russian. Nonetheless, "the Right"—the moderately liberal wing of the Congress—under the leadership of František Palacký (1798–1876), a Czech historian and politician, and Pavol Jozef Šafárik (1795–1861), a Slovak philologist, historian, and archaeologist, favored autonomy of the Slav lands within the framework of the Austrian (Habsburg) monarchy. In contrast, "the Left"—the radical wing of the Congress—under the leadership of Karel Sabina (1813–1877), a Czech writer and journalist, Josef Václav Frič, a Czech nationalist, Karol Libelt (1817–1861), a Polish writer and politician, and others, pressed for a close alliance with the revolutionary Democratic movement going on in Germany and Hungary in 1848.

A national rebirth in the Hungarian "Highlands" (now Slovakia) awoke in a completely new light, both before and after the 1848 Slovak Uprising (September 1848 to November 1849). The driving force of this rebirth movement were Slovak writers and politicians who called themselves Štúrovci, the followers of Ľudovít Štúr (1815–1856). As the Slovak nobility was Magyarized (see *infra*) and most Slovaks were merely farmers or priests, this movement failed to attract much attention. Nonetheless, the campaign was successful as a brotherly cooperation between Croats and Slovaks that bore its fruit throughout the 1848–49 war. Most of the battles between Slovaks and Hungarians, however, did not turn out well for the Slovaks who were logistically supported by the Austrians but far short of what was needed.

During the 1848 Revolutions, the Slovak National Council brought its demands to the young Austrian Emperor, Franz Joseph I, who seemed to take note of it and promised support for the Slovaks against the revolutionary radical Hungarians. However, the moment the revolution was over, Slovak demands and aspirations were forgotten. These demands included an autonomous land within the Austrian Empire called *Slovenský kraj*. This act of ignorance from the emperor convinced Slovak and Czech elite to declare Austroslavism dead.

Disgusted by the emperor's policy, Ľudovít Štúr, who codified the first official Slovak language, wrote a book in 1849 titled *Slavism and the World of the Future*. This book served as a manifesto, by which he declared that Austroslavism was not the way to go anymore. He also wrote a sentence that often serves as a quote until this day: "Every nation has its time under God's sun, and the linden [a symbol of the Slavs] is blossoming, while the oak [a symbol of the Teutons] bloomed long ago" (*Každý národ má svoj čas pod Božím slnkom, a lipa kvitne až dub už dávno odkvitol*) (Štúr 1993, 59).

Štúr expressed confidence in the Russian Empire, however, as it was the only country of Slavs that was not dominated by anybody else, yet it was one of the most powerful nations in the world. He often symbolized Slavs as being a tree, with "minor" Slavic nations being branches while the trunk of the tree was Russian. His Pan-Slavic views were unleashed in his book, where he stated that the land of Slovaks should be annexed by the Tsar's empire and that eventually the population could be not only Russified but also converted into the rite of Orthodoxy, the religion originally spread by Cyril and Methodius during the times of the Great Moravian Empire, which served as an opposition to the Catholic missionaries from the Franks. After the Hungarian invasion of Pannonia, the Magyars converted to Catholicism, which effectively influenced the Slavs living in Pannonia and in the land south of the Lechs.

However, the Russian Empire often claimed Pan-Slavism as a justification for its imperialistic actions in the Balkans against the Ottoman Empire, which conquered and held the Slavic lands for centuries. This eventually led to the Russian Balkan campaign resulting in Balkan independence from the Ottoman Empire.

During World War I, captured Slavic soldiers were asked to fight against "oppression in the Austrian Empire." Consequently, some did (see Czechoslovak Legion, *infra*). Finally, the long-anticipated creation of an independent Czechoslovakia in 1918 made the old ideals of Pan-Slavism anachronistic. After collapse of the Russian Empire and rise of Bolshevism, Pan-Slavism was revived and exploited before and after the Second World War as a pretext for Stalin's National Front Strategy to dominate Europe. Pan-Slavism remained a potent ideology among dedicated Marxists throughout the Cold War and like Pan-Germanism remains a latent force to this day.

Hungarian Reaction to Pan-Slavism – Magyarization

DURING THE PERIODS 1000–1784 AND 1790–1844, LATIN WAS THE official language of administration, legislation, jurisprudence, and schooling in the Kingdom of Hungary. Habsburg Holy Roman Emperor Joseph II (1780–90), a monarch influenced by the Enlightenment, sought to centralize control of the empire and to rule it as an enlightened despot. More than two and one-half centuries after the publication of Martin Luther's Ninety-Five Theses (1517), Joseph II decreed that German replace Latin as the empire's official language. Hungarians perceived Joseph's language reform as German cultural hegemony, and they reacted by insisting on the right to use their own tongue. As a result, Hungarian lesser nobles sparked a renaissance of the Hungarian language and culture. The lesser nobles questioned the loyalty of the magnates, of whom less than half were ethnic Magyars, and even those had become French- and German-speaking courtiers.

The Magyarization policy actually took shape as early as the 1830s, when Hungarian started replacing Latin and German in education. Magyarization lacked any religious or racial motivation. Language and national identity were the only issues. The enthusiasm of the Hungarian government in its Magyarization efforts was comparable to that of tsarist Russification of the late nineteenth century.

In the early 1840s, Lajos Kossuth pleaded in the newspaper *Pesti Hirlap* for rapid Magyarization: "Let us hurry, let us hurry to Magyarize the Croats, the Romanians, and the Saxons, for otherwise we shall perish." In 1842, he argued that Hungarian had to be the exclusive language in public life. He also stated that in one country it is impossible to speak a hundred different languages. There must be one language and in Hungary this must be Hungarian. Zsigmond Kemény supported a multinational state led by Magyars, but he disapproved Kossuth's assimilatory ambitions. István Széchenyi, who was more conciliatory toward other ethnic groups, criticized Kossuth for "pitting one nationality against another." He promoted the Magyarization of non-Hungarians on the basis of the alleged "moral and intellectual supremacy" inherent in the Hungarian population. But he felt that first Hungary itself must be made worthy of emulation if Magyarization was to succeed. However, the radical version of Magyarization proposed by Kossuth gained more popular support than the moderate version of Széchenyi. The slogan of the Magyarization campaign was *One country – one language – one nation.*

The Austro-Hungarian Compromise of 1867 emboldened Hungarian elite. However, the first Hungarian government after the Compromise of 1867, the 1867–1871 liberal government led by Count Gyula Andrássy and sustained by Ferenc Deák and his followers, passed the 1868 Nationality Act, that declared "all citizens of Hungary form, politically, one nation, the indivisible unitary Hungarian nation (*nemzet*), of which every citizen of the country, whatever his personal nationality (*nemzetiség*), is a member equal in rights." The Education Act, passed the same year, shared this view as the Magyars simply being *primus inter pares* ("first among equals"). At this time ethnic minorities *de jure* had a great deal of cultural and linguistic autonomy, including in education, religion, and local government.

As the Andrássy-Deák administration ended, Menyhért Lónyay was appointed prime minister of Hungary. He became steadily more allied with the Magyar gentry, and the notion of a Hungarian political nation increasingly became one of a Magyar nation. "[A]ny political or social movement which challenged the hegemonic position of the Magyar ruling classes was liable to be repressed or charged with 'treason . . . , 'libel' or 'incitement of national hatred.' This was to be the fate of various Slovak, South Slav [e.g., Serb], Romanian and Ruthene cultural societies and nationalist parties from 1876 onward . . ." (Bideleux and Jeffries 1998, 363–4). All of this only intensified after 1875, with the rise of Kálmán Tisza, who as minister of the Interior had ordered the closing of *Matica slovenská* on 6 April 1875. Until 1890, Kálmán Tisza imposed upon the Slovaks many other oppressive measures which prevented them from keeping pace with the progress of other European nations. It is ironic that just after receiving political autonomy from the Hapsburg Empire under the "Compromise," or *Ausgleich*, the Hungarians quickly turned on their still disenfranchised neighbors in the region. Countless Croats, Rumanians, Serbs, Slovaks, Slovenes, and Ukrainians were subjected to Magyarization, or forced assimilation. The Hungarians proved crueler than their previous Teutonic adversaries who employed a similar practice of Germanization decades and centuries before.

Throughout most of its history, the number of non-Hungarians that lived in the Kingdom of Hungary was much larger than the number of ethnic Hungarians. According to statistics recorded in 1787, the population of the Kingdom of Hungary numbered 2.3 million Hungarians (29 percent) and 5.7 million non-Hungarians (71 percent). In 1809, the population numbered 3.0 million Hungarians (30 percent) and 7.0 non-Hungarians (70 percent). An increasingly intense Magyarization policy was implemented after 1867.

It was in 1878 that active Magyarization of Greater Hungary reached its zenith. Magyarization was not just about the forced use of the Hungarian language. The program's supposed justifications have root in the Hungarian notion that a native of the Kingdom of Hungary could not be a patriot unless he spoke, thought, felt, and totally identified as a Magyar. Slovaks who remained true to their ancestry—Slovaks were in the region long before Hungarian tribes arrived—were considered deficient in patriotism. The official political view was that a compromise with the Slovaks was impossible; that there was but one expedient, to "ethnically cleanse" them, to wipe them out as far as possible by assimilation with the Magyars. Slovak schools and institutions were ordered to be closed, the charter of the *Matica slovenská* was annulled, and its library and rich historical and artistic collections, as well as its funds, were confiscated. Inequalities of every kind under the law were devised for the undoing of Slovak heritage, language, and culture and turning them into "proper" Hungarians.

Over two million Slovaks clung to their language and Slavic customs. The clergy, however, were educated in their seminaries through the Magyar tongue and required in their parishes to conform to state-imposed restrictions. Among the 750,000 Protestant Slovaks, the government went even further by taking control of their synods and bishops. Slovak family names were Magyarized, and any vocational advancement was only given through Hungarian channels.

Slovak Patriots Remain Steadfast

THE FIRST CODIFICATION OF A SLOVAK LITERARY LANGUAGE BY ANTON Bernolák (1762–1813) in the 1780s was based on the dialect from western Slovakia. It was supported by mainly Roman Catholic intellectuals, with its center in Trnava. Lutheran intellectuals continued to use a Slovakized form of the Czech language. Especially Ján Kollár (1793–1852) and Pavel Jozef Šafárik (1795–1861) were adherents of Pan-Slavic concepts that stressed the unity of all Slavic peoples. They considered Czechs and Slovaks members of a single nation and they attempted to draw the languages closer together.

In the 1840s, the Protestants split as Ľudovít Štúr developed a literal language based on the dialect from central Slovakia (centered in Banská Bystrica). His followers stressed the separate identity of the Slovak nation and uniqueness of its language. Štúr's version was finally approved by both the Catholics and the Lutherans in 1847 and, after several reforms, it remains the official Slovak language.

In the Hungarian Revolution of 1848 (part of the greater 1848 Spring of Nations), Slovak Nationalist leaders sided with the Austrians in order to promote their separation from the Kingdom of Hungary within the Austrian monarchy. On 28 July 1849, the Hungarian Revolutionary Parliament acknowledged and enacted the strongest ethnic and minority rights in the world, but it was too late: to counter the successes of the Hungarian revolutionary army, Austrian Emperor Franz Joseph asked for help from the "Gendarme of Europe," Tsar Nicholas I, whose Russian armies invaded Hungary. The Russian and Austrian forces proved too powerful for the Hungarians, and General Artúr Görgey surrendered in August 1849. The Slovak National Council—a political body created in Vienna on 15–16 September 1848—even took part in the Austrian military campaign by setting up auxiliary troops against the rebel government of the Hungarian Revolution of 1848. In September 1848, it managed to organize a short-lived administration of the captured territories. However, Slovak troops were later disbanded by the Vienna Imperial Court. Simultaneously, tens of thousands of volunteers from the territory of Slovakia, among them a great number of Slovaks, fought in the Hungarian revolutionary army.

After the defeat of the Hungarian Revolution, the Hungarian political elite was oppressed by Austrian authorities and many participants of the Revolution were executed, imprisoned, or forced to emigrate. In 1850, the Kingdom of Hungary was divided into five military districts or provinces, two of which had administrative centers in the territory of present-day Slovakia—Military District of Pressburg (Bratislava) and Military District of Košice.

Austrian authorities abolished both provinces in 1860. The Slovak political elite made use of the period of neo-absolutism of the Vienna court and the weakness of the traditional Hungarian elite to promote their national goals. Turz-Sankt Martin (present-day Martin, Slovakia) became the foremost center of the Slovak National Movement with founding of the national cultural association *Matica slovenská* (1863) and the Slovak National Party (1871).

The heyday of the Slovak National Movement came to an abrupt halt after 1867, when the Habsburg domains in central Europe underwent a constitutional transformation into the dual monarchy of Austria-Hungary as a result of the Austro-Hungarian Compromise of 1867. The territory of Slovakia was included into the Hungarian part of the dual Monarchy dominated by the Hungarian political elite which distrusted the Slovak elite due to its Pan-Slavism, separatism, and its recent stand against the Hungarian Revolution of 1848. *Matica slovenská* was accused of Pan-Slavic separatism and was dissolved by the authorities in 1875 along with other Slovak institutions (including primary and secondary schools).

New signs of national and political life appeared only at the very end of the nineteenth century. Slovaks became aware that they needed to ally themselves with others in their struggle. One result of this awareness, the Congress of Oppressed Peoples of the Kingdom of Hungary, held in Budapest in 1895, alarmed the government. In their struggle, Slovaks received a great deal of help from the Czechs. In 1896, the concept of Czecho-Slovak Mutuality was established in Prague to strengthen Czecho-Slovak cooperation and support the secession of Slovaks from the Kingdom of Hungary.

At the beginning of the twentieth century, growing democratization of political and social life threatened to overwhelm the monarchy. The call for universal suffrage became the main rallying cry. In the Kingdom of Hungary, only five percent of inhabitants could vote. Slovaks saw in the trend towards representative Democracy a possibility of easing ethnic oppression and a break-through into renewed political activity.

The Slovak political camp, at the beginning of the twentieth century, split into different factions. The leaders of the Slovak National Party based in Martin expected the international situation to change in the Slovaks' favor, and they put great hopes in Russia. The Roman Catholic faction of Slovak politicians led by Father Andrej Hlinka focused on small undertakings among the Slovak public and on 29 July 1913 established a political party named the Hlinka's Slovak People's Party (*Hlinkova slovenská ľudová strana, HSĽS*). The liberal intelligentsia rallying around the journal *Hlas* (*Voice*), followed a similar political path, but attached more importance to Czecho-Slovak cooperation. An independent Social Democratic Party emerged in 1905.

The Slovaks achieved some results. One of the greatest of these occurred with the election success in 1906, when, despite continued oppression, seven Slovaks managed to get seats in the Diet of Hungary (*Országgyűlés*). This success alarmed the Hungarian government and increased what was regarded by Slovaks as its oppressive measures. Magyarization achieved its climax with a new Education Act of 1868 known as the Apponyi Act, named after education minister Count Albert Apponyi (1846–1933). The new act stipulated that the teaching of the Hungarian language must be included in the curriculum of non-state-owned elementary schools as a condition to receive state-financing. As a part of Magyarization, from 1883 to 1919, Nitra was the seat of the Upper Hungarian Teaching Association (*FEMKE*), a government-sponsored association whose main goal was to apply Magyarization policies on Slovaks.

Before the outbreak of World War I, the idea of Slovak autonomy became part of Austrian Archduke Franz Ferdinand's plan of federalization of the monarchy, developed with help of Slovak journalist and politician Milan Hodža. This last attempt to maintain Slovakia's ties to Austro-Hungary was abandoned because of the Archduke's assassination, which in turn triggered the First World War.

The Magyar national reawakening that manifested in the 1848 revolution triggered national revivals among the Slovak, Romanian, Serbian, and Croatian minorities within Hungary and Transylvania, who felt threatened by both German and Magyar cultural hegemony. These national revivals later blossomed into the Nationalist movements of the nineteenth and twentieth centuries that contributed to the Austro-Hungarian Empire's ultimate collapse.

PETER EMILIUS VLČKO (1912–2004)

TWELVE YEARS HAD PASSED SINCE THE TURN OF THE CENTURY WHEN Peter Emilius Vlčko was born on 28 May 1912 in the mountainous central Slovak village of Brehy, district of Nová Baňa—at the time, the highlands of Austro-Hungary. His father, also Peter Vlčko, was born on 12 November 1889 in the village of Tekovská Breznica (four kilometers southwest of Brehy) in the mountain range known as Štiavnické Vrchy.* Likely seeking employment in the coal mines or lumber industry of the region, he moved from Tekovská Breznica to Brehy where he met his future wife Adela Jakubíková (born 8 December 1895). Adela was the daughter of Joseph and Anna (née Medveďová). Adela had four siblings: Gregor, Peter, Pavlina, and Julia.

---

* Štiavnické Vrchy are a volcanic mountain range southern central Slovakia. They are part of Inner Western Carpathians and the Slovenské stredohorie Mountains. The area is protected by Štiavnické Vrchy Protected Landscape Area. They are bordered by the Kremnické vrchy in the north, Pliešovce and Krupina basins (Krupinská kotlina) in the east, Danubian Hills (Podunajská pahorkatina) in the south and Pohronský Inovec, Vtáčnik and Žiar Basin (Žiarska kotlina) in the west. The highest point is Sitno (1,009 meters). Štiavnické Vrchy are an immense caldera created by the collapse of an ancient volcano. Due to their volcanic origin, they are mineral-rich, with around 140 kinds of minerals. In the past, silver mining flourished in the area around the town of Banská Štiavnica. From originally over 60 lakes called tajchy in Štiavnické Vrchy, there are over 30 still existing today. Although they are now integrated in their natural environment, they were originally built as water reservoirs serving the mining industry, most of them in the 18th century.

Twenty-four-year-old Peter Vlčko and eighteen-year-old Adela bore their first child Peter Emilius. When Peter Emilius was only two-years old, the Great War broke out and his twenty-six-year-old father was conscripted by the Austro-Hungarian Army as part of the Central Powers. He fought in Russia during the First World War but was captured in Ivangorod (160 kilometers west of St. Petersburg) by the Russian Imperial Army and became a prisoner of war from 26 October 1914 until 27 June 1918. Conditions as a prisoner of war in Russia were primitive, overcrowded, and harsh. Despite the fact that the death rate of prisoners of war in Russia was among the highest of all countries, he managed to remain strong and healthy over the four years of his captivity.

JAKUBÍK LINEAGE

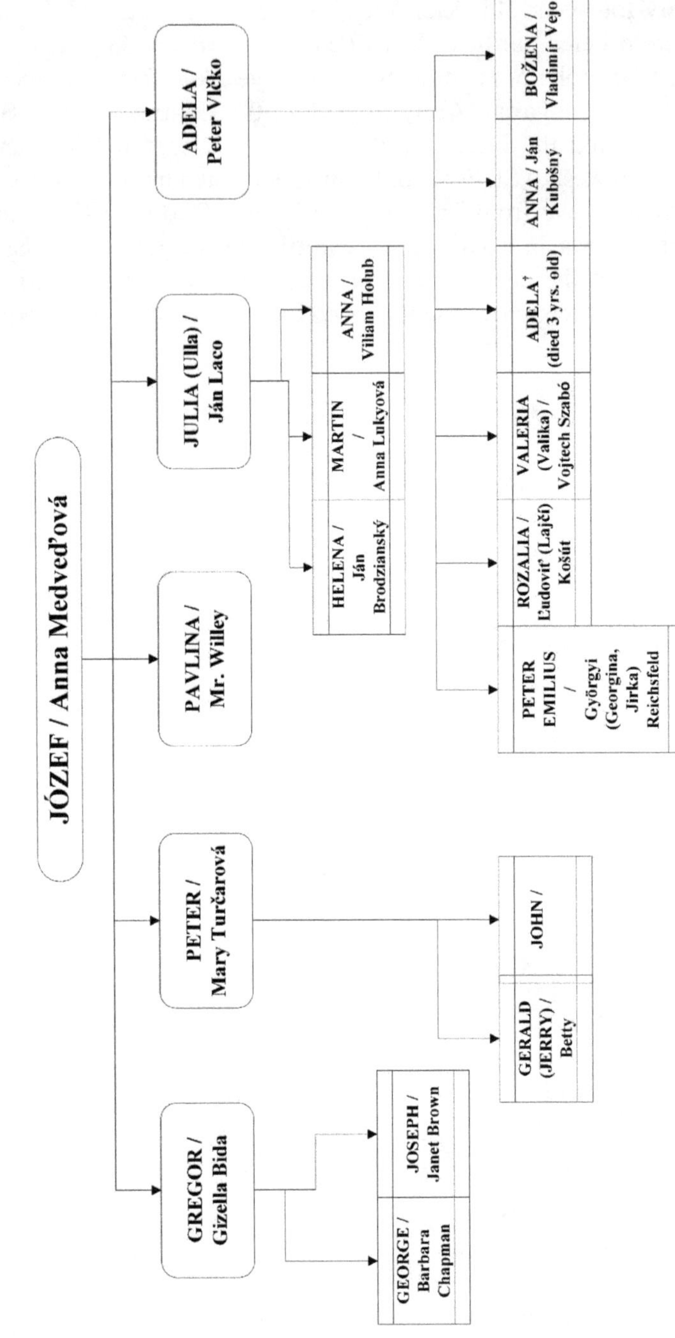

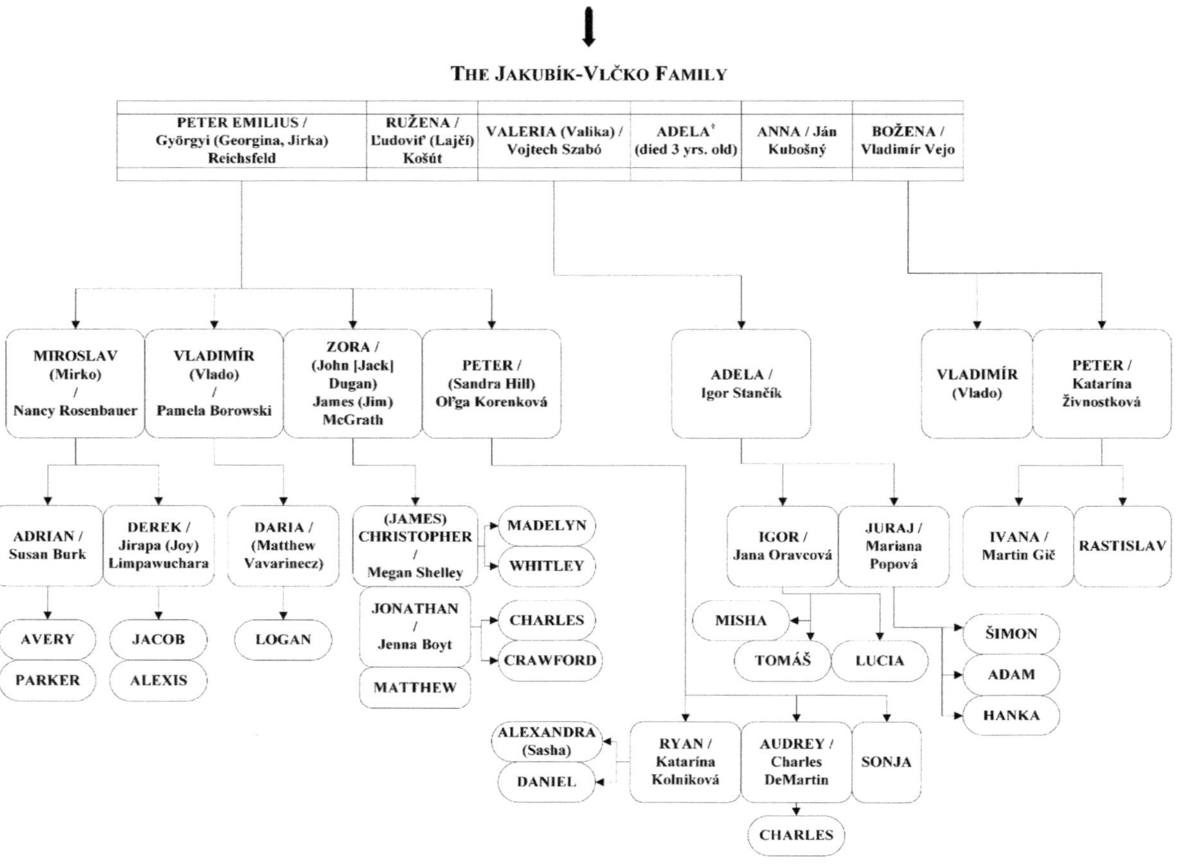
THE JAKUBÍK-VLČKO FAMILY
PETER EMILIUS / Györgyi (Georgina, Jirka) Reichsfeld
RUŽENA / Ľudovíť (Lajčí) Košút
VALERIA (Valika) / Vojtech Szabó
ADELA† (died 3 yrs. old)
ANNA / Ján Kubošný
BOŽENA / Vladimír Vejo
MIROSLAV (Mirko) / Nancy Rosenbauer
VLADIMÍR (Vlado) / Pamela Borowski
ZORA / (John [Jack] Dugan) James (Jim) McGrath
PETER / (Sandra Hill) Oľga Korenková
ADELA / Igor Stančík
VLADIMÍR (Vlado)
PETER / Katarína Živnostková
ADRIAN / Susan Burk
DEREK / Jirapa (Joy) Limpawuchara
DARIA / (Matthew Vavarinecz)
(JAMES) CHRISTOPHER / Megan Shelley
MADELYN
WHITLEY
JONATHAN / Jenna Boyt
CHARLES
CRAWFORD
MATTHEW
IGOR / Jana Oravcová
JURAJ / Mariana Popová
IVANA / Martin Gič
RASTISLAV
AVERY
PARKER
JACOB
ALEXIS
LOGAN
MISHA
TOMÁŠ
LUCIA
ŠIMON
ADAM
HANKA
ALEXANDRA (Sasha)
DANIEL
RYAN / Katarína Kolníková
AUDREY / Charles DeMartin
SONJA
CHARLES

The Russian Civil War and the Fate of Peter E. Vlčko's Father

EIGHT DAYS AFTER COMMENCEMENT OF THE WORKERS' STRIKES AND THE launch of the Russian Revolution in Petrograd (the seat of the Russian throne), Tsar Nicholas II (House of Romanov) was forced to abdicate his throne on 15 March 1917. The following day, a Provisional Government was announced under Georgy Yevgenyevich, Prince Lvov (1861–1925) and later Aleksandr Kerensky (1881–1970). Four days earlier, the Petrograd Soviet of Workers' and Soldiers' Deputies revived its 1905 organization and formed a parallel government under Menshevik Nikolay Chkheidze, Bolshevik Leon Trotsky, and Bolshevik Grigory Zinoviev. Leading Imperial Duma member Aleksandr Kerensky of the Social Revolutionary Party held leadership roles in both the Provisional Government (Minister-President, Minister of War and Navy) and the Petrograd Soviet (Vice-Chairman). Initially, these two bodies, the Provisional Government (comprised of Democrats, Socialists, and Monarchists) and the Petrograd Soviet (Marxists), or—rather—their respective executive committees (Provisional Committee of the State Duma and *Ispolkom*), worked together but soon became each other's antagonists. Between March and November 1917, the two powers ruled Russia under a "Dual Power" (*dvoevlastie*) arrangement. While the Democratic Socialist leaning Provisional Government attempted to bring law and order to Russia, the Marxist Petrograd Soviet progressively worked to undermine the Provisional Government.

During the initial months after its reestablishment, the struggle for leadership of the Petrograd Soviet played out between the Mensheviks and the Bolsheviks. Eventually, the Bolsheviks under Leon Trotsky were victorious in this internal struggle. With the assistance of the German Empire, Lenin managed to return to Russia from exile in Zurich on 16 April 1917. Lenin immediately joined Trotsky to lead the Petrograd Soviet and eventually took over the leadership after the November Revolution.

On 7–8 November 1917, the Bolsheviks managed to finally seize power from Kerensky's Provisional Government. Kerensky escaped the Winter Palace raid and fled to Pskov, where he rallied some loyal troops for an attempt to retake the capital. His troops managed to capture Tsarskoe Selo but were beaten the next day at Pulkovo. Kerensky spent the next few weeks in hiding before fleeing the country. He went into exile in France and eventually emigrated to the U.S.

Kerensky faced a major challenge: three years of participation in World War had exhausted Russia, while the Provisional Government offered little motivation for a victory outside of continuing Russia's obligations towards its allies. Russia's continued involvement in the war was not popular among the lower and middle classes, and especially not popular among the soldiers. They had all believed that Russia would stop fighting when the Provisional Government took power, and subsequently felt deceived. Furthermore, Vladimír Lenin and his Bolshevik party were promising "peace, land, and bread" under a Communist regime. The Russian Army, war-weary, ill-equipped, dispirited, and ill-disciplined, was disintegrating, with soldiers deserting in large numbers. By autumn 1917, an estimated two million men had unofficially left the army.

After the fall of the Tsar, Kerensky and the other non-Marxist leaders of the Provisional Government continued Russia's involvement in World War I, thinking that nothing but a glorious Entente victory was imperative to legitimize the new Democratic Socialist government, and fearing that the economy, already under huge stress from the war effort, might become increasingly unstable if vital supplies from France, the United Kingdom, and the United States ceased flowing. The dilemma of whether to withdraw was a great one, and Kerensky's inconsistent and impractical policies further destabilized the army and the country at large.

Furthermore, Kerensky adopted a policy that isolated the Conservatives, both Democratic and monarchist oriented. His philosophy of "no enemies to the left" greatly empowered the Bolsheviks and gave them a free hand, allowing them to take over the military arm or *voyenka* (Военка) of the Petrograd and Moscow Soviets. In the mass discontent following the July Days (3–7 July 1917), the Russian populace grew highly skeptical about the Provisional Government's abilities to alleviate the economic distress and social resentment among the lower classes. Pavel Milyukov, the Kadet leader, described the situation in Russia in late July as, "Chaos in the army, chaos in foreign policy, chaos in industry and chaos in the nationalist questions" (Siegelbaum 2015). Cossack General Lavr Georgiyevich Kornilov, appointed Commander-in-Chief of the Russian Army in July 1917, considered the Petrograd Soviet responsible for the breakdown in the military in recent times and believed that the Provisional Government lacked the power and confidence to dissolve the Petrograd Soviet. Following several ambiguous correspondences between Kornilov and Aleksandr Kerensky, Kornilov commanded an assault on the Petrograd Soviet (Siegelbaum 2014).

Because the Petrograd Soviet was able to quickly gather a powerful army of workers and soldiers in defense of the Revolution, Kornilov's *coup d'état* was an abysmal failure, and he was placed under arrest by the Kerensky government. The Kornilov Affair resulted in significantly increased distrust among Russians towards the Provisional Government. Kerensky's arrest of Kornilov and other officers left him without strong allies against the Bolsheviks, who ended up being Kerensky's most formidable and determined adversaries, as opposed to the monarchists and republicans, who evolved into the White movement. Kornilov managed to escape captivity but eventually died on 13 April 1918 in the Kuban (southern Russia on the east coast of the Black Sea) under Bolshevik shelling. His and the death of several of his like-minded peers such as General Aleksandr Krymov left the anti-Bolshevik cause to Admiral Aleksandr Kolchak (1874–1920).

In light of the incredible drain on the national treasury, the casualties and crushed *esprit de corps* of the Imperial Russian Army, and the need to reorganize and redeploy the army for the widening civil war, the Bolsheviks, having ousted the Provisional Government, proceeded to negotiate with Germany Russia's exit from the First World War and its alliance in the Triple Entente Powers. Lenin's Bolshevik government finally withdrew from the Entente Powers on 3 March 1918 with the signing of the Peace Treaty of Brest-Litovsk. An estimated 2.4 million prisoners of war remained confined in Russia, of which two million belonged to Austro-Hungary. Among these, Slavs (Poles, Ruthenians, Czechs, Slovaks, Serbs, Croats, Slovenes) made up about one half; ethnic Germans and Hungarians each around one quarter; and Italians and Rumanians constituted the rest. Five months after the collapse of the Kerensky Provisional Government, revolution and civil war broke out in Russia between the Whites (monarchists and Democrats) and Reds (Bolsheviks).

The October (November by modern calendar) Revolution drastically altered the conditions for the prisoners of war. After initial chaos, the Bolsheviks declared POWs free citizens and officers were theoretically declared class enemies. However, "freedom" also meant that POWs no longer received a government stipend and were obliged to fend for themselves. The Bolsheviks turned camp economies into cooperatives with stocks and commodity-based currencies. Former POWs were now on par with Russian workers and received representation on all political levels. A large number of POWs welcomed the Bolsheviks, albeit less for political reasons than from a longing for peace and rapid repatriation. Only a minority of POWs joined the Russian Communist Party or fought in Internationalist divisions of the Red Army during the Civil War.

When the Bolsheviks took power in November 1917, they controlled only a fraction of Russia, mostly in the west. The White forces under the command of Admiral Aleksandr Kolchak, controlling most of the east and north, viewed the POWs as potential Bolshevik recruits and proxies. The Whites initially sent POWs back to prison camps and halted the repatriation process that was expected with the signing of the Brest-Litovsk Peace Treaty. Soon, however, the Whites gained the support of Western Powers and exploited the POWs for their own cause.

The chairman of the Czecho-Slovak National Council, Tomáš G. Masaryk, along with his Foreign Minister Eduard Beneš and Minister of War General Milan Rastislav Štefánik, arrived in Russia in May 1917 to help organize Slavic resistance to the Austrians and begin planning for the unification and transformation of the Czecho-Slavic Army serving in the Russian Imperial Army and the Czech and Slovak prisoners of war from the Austro-Hungarian Army into the Czechoslovak Legion. Three years earlier, on 5 August 1914, the Imperial Russian High Command authorized the formation of a battalion, recruited from expatriate Czechs and Slovaks living in Russia. The unit went to the front in October 1914 and was attached to the Russian Third Army. This unit was called the "Czech Companions" (*Česká družina* or *Družina*) (Kalvoda 1986, 62–3). From its start, Masaryk desired to expand the *Družina* from a battalion into a formidable military formation—Masaryk was convinced such a force joining the Entente struggle would convince Western Powers to grant independence to Czechoslovakia from its Austro-Hungarian overlord. To achieve this goal, however, they recognized that they would need to recruit from Czech and Slovak POWs in Russian camps.

In early 1916, the *Družina* was reorganized as the First Czecho-Slovak Rifle Regiment. During that year, two more infantry regiments were added, creating the Czechoslovak Rifle Brigade (*Československá střelecká brigáda*). This unit distinguished itself during the Kerensky Offensive in July 1917, when the Czecho-Slovak troops overran Austrian trenches during the Battle of Zborov. Thereafter, Kerensky and the Russian Provisional Government finally granted to Masaryk and the Czecho-Slovak National Council permission to recruit and mobilize Czech and Slovak volunteers from the POW camps. Later that summer, a fourth regiment was added to the brigade, which was renamed the First Division of the Czechoslovak Corps in Russia (*Československý sbor na Rusi*), also known as the Czechoslovak Legion (*Československá legie*) in Russia. A second division consisting of four regiments was added to the Legion in October 1917, raising its strength to about 60,000 troops by 1918.

Clearly, these war-hardened soldiers had the potential of being a formidable foundation for the future army of an independent Czechoslovakia. The Czecho-Slovak National Council, however, first needed to consolidate and transfer the Legion away from the Russian Civil War, in which the Czecho-Slovak National Council mandated them to remain neutral, to the Western Front in France so they could join the fight against the Central Powers and earn their right to independence.

The Allied decree signed by French President Raymond Poincaré in Paris on 16 December 1917, formally recognized the autonomous Czecho-Slovak Army under French military command but under the political direction of the Czecho-Slovak National Council. This decree served as acknowledgment by the European Allies that the Czechs and Slovaks represented a national political entity. On 7 February 1918, the Czechoslovak Legion was proclaimed as an autonomous part of the Czecho-Slovak Army, and negotiations with the Bolsheviks to allow movement of the Legion to France intensified. However, on 18 February 1918, before the Czechoslovaks left Ukraine, the German Army launched Operation *Faustschlag* (fist punch) on the Eastern Front to force the Soviet government to accept its harsh terms for peace—this was in preparation for the Brest-Litovsk Treaty. Under threat of further aggression by the Central Powers (Germany, Austro-Hungary, Bulgaria, and the Ottoman Empire), Bolshevik-controlled Russia under Lenin and Trotsky signed the Treaty of Brest-Litovsk on 3 March 1918, that ended Russia's participation in World War I. In compliance with the treaty, the Bolshevik government caved to German pressure to obstruct any further transfer of the Czechoslovak Legion to France where it was joining the Entente Powers against Germany and the Central Powers. This developing obstacle forced Masaryk, Beneš, and General Štefánik to turn the Legion against the Central Powers in the infamous Battle of Bakhmach.

On 8 March 1918, Germans reached Bakhmach, an important railroad hub 220 kilometers northeast of Kiev. The Legion was in danger of being encircled. The threat was grave because captured Legionnaires were summarily being executed as traitors of Austro-Hungary. After nearly one week of bloody battles, the Legion was victorious forcing the Germans to negotiate a truce on 13 March 1918. Since most of Russia's western routes were blockaded, Masaryk decided that the Legion should travel 9,600 kilometers from central Ukraine via rail to the Pacific port of Vladivostok in

Soviet-controlled Russia, where the men would embark on transport vessels that would carry them to the United States and then on to France.

After leaving Ukraine and entering Soviet Russia, representatives of the Czecho-Slovak National Council continued to negotiate with Bolshevik authorities in Moscow and Penza to iron out the details of the Legion's evacuation. Masaryk had departed Russia on 7 March for his long-anticipated trip to the U.S. On 25 March 1918, the two sides signed the Penza Agreement, in which the Legionaries were to surrender most of their weapons in exchange for unmolested passage to Vladivostok. On 26 March, People's Commissar for Nationalities' Affairs Joseph Stalin signed the order to permit the evacuation of the Czechoslovak Legion. During the truce, the Legion with their weapons and their armored trains freely passed through Bakhmach railway junction to Chelyabinsk, where they prepared for their eastern escape from Russia via the Trans-Siberian railroad.

By May 1918, the Czechoslovak Legion was strung out along the Trans-Siberian Railway from Penza to Vladivostok. Their evacuation was proving much slower than expected due to dilapidated railway conditions, a shortage of locomotives, and the recurring need to negotiate with local soviets along the route, while at the same time the Bolsheviks were repatriating German, Austrian, and Hungarian prisoners of war from Siberia. The early stages of the Legion's movement eastward were marked by an atmosphere of tension and mistrust. The Germans were charging the Bolsheviks with violating the treaty arrangement for allowing the Legion to leave. The Czechoslovaks were afraid the Bolsheviks would cave to German pressure and intern them again. The Bolsheviks doubted the good faith of the Legionnaires because they were associated with the French and were capable of becoming a very effective counter-revolutionary force in Russia. As the Legionnaires gained control over the Trans-Siberian Railway, the Bolsheviks became increasingly alarmed.

Throughout May 1918, growing tensions with the Bolsheviks provoked the infamous Revolt of the Legions. Conflict already existed between trains of Legionaries going east to fight for the Entente Powers and German and Austro-Hungarian prisoners going west to fight for the Central Powers. On 14 May 1918, the eastbound train carrying members of the Sixth Regiment of the First Czechoslovak Army Corp was coming to a stop in Chelyabinsk. A second, westbound train just slowly leaving the station carried Central Powers prisoners of war. One of the Hungarian soldiers on the train threw a broken cast-iron portion of a stove out the window and killed a Czechoslovak soldier in the other train. Members of the Legionnaires quickly exited their train and overpowered the westbound train. The responsible Hungarian was identified and was summarily hung by the Legionnaires. Local Bolsheviks arrested the responsible Legionnaire soldiers and placed them in the local jail waiting for instructions from Moscow.

Finally, on 25 May 1918, Leon Trotsky, then People's Commissar of War, under intense pressure from the Germans, ordered the execution of the jailed Legionnaires and disarming and arrest of the entire Legion, thus betraying his promise of safe passage. Trotsky's message, however, was intercepted by the Legionnaires. Based on this intelligence, the Legionnaires overpowered the Bolsheviks and seized weapons, ammunition, sixteen locomotives, and released all arrested Czech and Slovak soldiers. At the time, the Soviet Red Army totaling less than 50,000 was no match against the well organized and disciplined Czechoslovak Legion. This incident triggered further hostilities between the Legion and the Bolsheviks. Czechoslovaks began to occupy the cities on their route: Chelyabinsk, Petropavlovsk, Kurgan, Novonikolaevsk (Novosibirsk), Mariinsk, Nizhneudinsk, and Kansk. At the same time as the Legionnaires moved in, White Russian officers overthrew the Bolsheviks in Petropavlovsk and Omsk. The White Russians under Admiral Aleksandr Kolchak joined up with the Legionnaires to fight the Bolsheviks. Within a month, the Legionnaires controlled most of the Trans-Siberian Railway from Lake Baikal to the Ural Mountains. By June 1918, the two sides were fighting along the railway from Penza to Krasnoyarsk. On 7 June 1918, the Legion's Second and Sixth Rifle Regiments capture and occupy Omsk making it the seat of the new Provisional Siberian Government (PSG) and eventual headquarters of the White Army under Admiral Kolchak. By the end of the month, Legionaries under White Russian General Mikhail Diterikhs had taken control of Vladivostok, overthrowing the local Bolshevik administration. On 6 July, the Legion declared the city to be an Allied protectorate, and Legionnaires began returning across the Trans-Siberian Railway to support their comrades fighting to their west. Generally, the Czechoslovaks were the victors in their early engagements against the fledgling Red Army. The same day, the Legion had seized control of the 2,600-mile section of the Trans-Siberian Railway from Samara on the Volga River to Irkutsk, joining all Czechoslovak Legion units located to the west of lake Baikal. One day earlier, the Legion's Fifth and Eighth Regiments captured and occupied Nikolsk-Ussuriysky.

Upon his conditional release as a prisoner of war in Ivangorod on 27 June 1918, Peter Vlčko volunteered to join the Czechoslovak Legion. Political and military allegiances in Russia during the Civil War were fluid, rapidly evolving, chaotic, and extremely confusing to the world powers, both those at war and those non-combatant powers looking to exploit their opportunities (i.e., Japan and China).

Between 14 July and 16 August 1918, the Legion gained control of the railway tunnels near Lake Baikal by means of an end run over mountains and the lake. By the beginning of September 1918, the Legion had cleared Bolshevik forces from the entire length of the Trans-Siberian Railway—St. Petersburg to Vladivostok (6,000 miles). Legionnaires conquered all the large cities of Siberia, including Yekaterinburg, but Tsar Nicholas II and his family were executed on 17 July 1918 on the direct orders of Vladimír Lenin and Jakov Sverdlov less than a week before the arrival of the Legion. During the summer of 1918, Bolshevik power in Siberia was totally neutralized. From this point on, the fate of the Czechoslovak Legion became inextricably tied to the final Allied decision to intervene in Russia—"North Russia Intervention."

News of the Czechoslovak Legion's campaign in Siberia during the summer of 1918 was welcomed by Allied statesmen in Great Britain and France, who saw the operation as a means to reconstitute an eastern front against Germany. President Woodrow Wilson, who had resisted earlier Allied proposals to intervene in Russia, gave in to domestic and foreign pressure to support the Legionaries' evacuation from Siberia. In early July 1918, he published an *aide-mémoire* calling for a limited intervention in Siberia by the U.S. and Japan to rescue the Czechoslovak troops, who were then blocked by Bolshevik forces in Transbaikal (Kennan 1958, 395–408). But by the time most American and Japanese units landed in Vladivostok, the Czechoslovaks were already there to welcome them. The Allied intervention in Siberia continued so that by autumn 1918, there were 70,000 Japanese, 829 British, 1,400 Italian, 5,300 American, and 107 French colonial (Vietnamese) troops in the region. Many of these contingents supported anti-Bolshevik White Russians and Cossack warlords who had established regional governments in the wake of the Czechoslovak seizure of the Trans-Siberian Railway.

From May to November 1918, Masaryk visited the United States (starting from Moscow 7 March to Vladivostok, Fusan, Tokyo, and then to Vancouver by steam liner, and from Canada to Chicago), where he convinced President Woodrow Wilson of the righteousness of his cause. On

5 May 1918, more than 150,000 Chicagoans filled the streets to give a triumphant welcome to the future President of Czechoslovakia. Chicago was then the center of Czechoslovak immigration to the United States and the city gave Masaryk an enthusiastic reception, which echoed Masaryk's earlier visits to the city and his visiting professorship at the University of Chicago where he lectured in 1902 and 1907. He also had strong personal links with the U.S. since 1878 by his marriage with an American citizen, the Unitarian Brooklynite Charlotte Garrigue (1850–1923), and his friendship with Charles R. Crane, a Chicago industrialist. Crane arranged for Masaryk to be invited to the University of Chicago and introduced him to the highest political circles, including Woodrow Wilson.

The Czechoslovak Legion's campaign in Siberia impressed Allied statesmen and attracted them to the idea of an independent Czechoslovak state. As the Legionnaires cruised from one victory to another the summer of 1918, the Czecho-Slovak National Council began receiving official statements of recognition from various Allied governments. On 29 May 1918, U.S. Secretary of State Robert Lansing declared that the "nationalistic aspirations of Czechoslovaks and Yugo-Slavs for freedom" had the "earnest sympathy" of the U.S. government. On 31 May 1918, in Pittsburgh, Pennsylvania, Czech and Slovak organizations in America signed, under the provisional presidency of Masaryk, an agreement regarding the creation of a Czecho-Slovak state on an equal basis for both nations. Three days later on 3 June, the French, British, and Italian prime ministers noted the American declaration "with pleasure" and hastened to "associate themselves" with it. By Masaryk's request for assistance, on 6 July 1918, Wilson approved sending American troops "to help the Czecho-Slovaks consolidate their forces and get into successful cooperation with their Slavic kinsmen and to steady any efforts at self-government or self-defense in which the Russians themselves may be willing to accept assistance" (Murphy 1999, 44; see also Mamatey 1989, 70).

American Military Intervention in the Russian Civil War

PARIS WAS UNDER THREAT OF FALLING TO THE GERMANS IN MAY 1918 as the first major deployments of the American Expeditionary Forces were landing in France. The Allied armies in Western Europe were in great need of reinforcements and the American Expeditionary Forces served a tremendous relief. The Allied intervention in Russia, however, was a multinational military expedition launched during the Russian Civil War in

August 1918. Countries contributing to the Allied Expeditionary Forces in Russia included: France; United Kingdom; United States; Canada; Romania; Greece; Estonia; Italy; Australia; Japan; China; Serbia; and Poland. The approximate total Allied force strength in Russia, excluding the Czechoslovak Legion, approached 120,000. The initial goals of the intervention in Russia before the armistice ended World War I were to secure the Czechoslovak Legion, protect large caches of Allied munitions and armaments in Russian ports before the Germans or Bolsheviks captured them, re-establish the Eastern Front to force the Central Powers to divert soldiers and war matériel from the Western Front, and to bolster anti-Bolshevik forces (White Russians and Cossacks) in their fight against Communism. By December 1918, all naval and ground forces of the Allied Expeditionary Forces, including the Czechoslovak Legion, were placed under the supreme command of French General Pierre-Thiébaut-Charles-Maurice Janin (1862–1946). The Allied Expeditionary Forces finally departed Russian soil in late 1920, though Japanese forces occupied parts of Siberia until 1922 and the northern half of Sakhalin until 1925. Over time, the Allied intervention in Russia was used effectively by the Bolsheviks for propaganda purposes to argue that their enemies were backed by western *bourgeois* Capitalism.

The North Russia Intervention (Archangel Campaign, Murman Deployment) was America's part of the multi-national Allied intervention in the Russian Civil War. The North Russia Intervention was comprised of two components: American Expeditionary Force (AEF, North Russia), North Russia (also known as the Polar Bear Expedition); and the American Expeditionary Force, Siberia (AEF, Siberia). Several motivating factors drove the Allies to intervene in the Russian Civil War. Under Lenin's directive, the Bolsheviks signed the Brest-Litovsk Peace Treaty with the Central Powers on 3 March 1918, thereby withdrawing from the Great War and coalition with the Entente Powers. This provided the failing German Army the opportunity to redeploy its eastern armies to the Western Front to concentrate on the Entente Powers main forces. This opportunity manifested as the 1918 Spring Offensive, or *Kaiserschlacht* ("Kaiser's Battle"), also known as the Ludendorff Offensive under the codenames *Michael* (21 March), *Georgette* (9 April), *Blücher-Yorck* (27 May), and *Gneisenau* (9 June). The Entente Powers were shocked by the possibility the Germans could turn the tide in the war and win, despite the recent involvement of American forces on the Western Front.

Before the collapse of Kerensky's Provisional Government, which was allied to the Entente Powers, Russia was receiving large quantities of war matériel, railroad rolling stock, and other support in the war effort from the United Kingdom, France, and the United States. After the fall of the Provisional Government and rise of the Bolshevik Soviets, the Entente Powers were deeply concerned the war matériel would be forever lost, or worse, captured by enemy forces. Moreover, the Entente Powers were increasingly recognizing the formidable strength and capabilities of the Czechoslovak Legion in Russia. Receiving tenable intelligence and pressure from the Czecho-Slovak political and military leadership that the Czechoslovak Legion wants to join the Entente cause in the war, the Entente Powers began making plans to rescue the Legion trapped in Russia along with the large quantities of stockpiled war matériel the Western Powers sent to Russia. Equally stressed by President Wilson was the need to "steady any efforts at self-government or self-defense in which the Russians themselves may be willing to accept assistance." At the time, Bolshevik forces controlled only small pockets in Siberia and President Wilson wanted to make sure that neither Cossack marauders nor the Japanese military would take advantage of the unstable political environment along the strategic railroad lines and in the resource-rich Siberian regions that straddled it. Also worrisome to the Entente Powers was the fact that in April 1918, a division of German troops had landed in Finland, creating fears they might try to capture the Murmansk-Petrograd railroad, the strategic port of Murmansk, and possibly even the city of Arkhangelsk (Archangel) where a large stockpile of Allied military equipment was kept. The leaders of the British and French governments had three objectives: they hoped to prevent the Allied war matériel stockpiles in Arkhangelsk from falling into German or Bolshevik hands; to mount an offensive to rescue the Czechoslovak Legion, which was stranded along the Trans-Siberian Railroad and resurrect the Eastern Front; and by defeating the Bolshevik army with the assistance of the Czechoslovak Legion, to expand anti-Communist forces drawn from the local citizenry. Severely short of troops to spare, the British and French requested that U.S. President Woodrow Wilson provide troops for the campaign.

The Polar Bear Expedition's objectives were to: 1) secure the strategic port of Archangel and the stockpile of military equipment held there; 2) prevent a German advance from Finland and loss of the important Murmansk-Petrograd railroad; 3) secure the strategic port of Murmansk; 4) help reopen the Eastern Front by linking up with the Czechoslovak Legion;

and 5) in cooperation with AEF, Siberia help rescue the Czechoslovak Legion in their withdrawal from Russia to redeploy on the Western Front, particularly if the aforementioned objectives fail.

On 14 July 1918, the U.S. Army's Eighty-Fifth Division, made up primarily of men from Michigan and Wisconsin, completed its training at Fort Custer, outside of Battle Creek, Michigan, and proceeded to England. Three days later, President Wilson signed the orders for a limited participation by American troops in the Allied North Russia Intervention with the stipulation that they would only be used for guarding the stockpiled war matériel. When U.S. Army General John J. Pershing received the directive from President Wilson, he changed the orders for the 339th Infantry Regiment, along with the First Battalion of the 310th Engineers plus a few other ancillary units from the Eighty-Fifth Division. The 339th Infantry Regiment was known as Detroit's Own. Most of the 3,800 car-factory workers, tax attorneys, farm laborers, shopkeepers and other conscripts who filled its ranks hailed from Michigan. These men also underwent a month or so of infantry training at Camp Custer in Battle Creek, Michigan before traveling to New York and embarking on ships to England in July 1918. The ships put in at Liverpool on 4 August 1918 and then boarded a train to a tent camp set up on the estate of the widow of Henry Stanley, the Africa explorer. A week later, the 339th, along with engineering, ambulance, and medical companies, loaded aboard three camouflage-painted steamers at Newcastle upon Tyne and set out on the eight-day journey to the port of Archangel, a Russian port on the White Sea, 600 miles north of Moscow. Instead of heading for France, these units were trained and re-outfitted in England with Russian guns and then sent to North Russia.

The Polar Bear Expedition under U.S. Brigadier General Wilds P. Richardson comprised some 5,300 troops, including: the 339th Infantry Regiment and support units (one battalion of the 310th Engineers, the 337th Field Hospital, and the 337th Ambulance Company); the 167th and 168th Railroad Companies, which were sent to Murmansk to operate the Murmansk-Petrograd line; and navy cruiser USS *Olympia* attached to British naval units. On the gray afternoon of 4 September 1918, the men disembarked at Archangel, a crescent-shaped port with neglected, shabby docks, muddy streets, and a cathedral dome painted blue with gold stars. The city had been wrested from Bolshevik hands just a month earlier on 2 August 1918 in an operation led by French, British, and White Russian forces. As the American soldiers walked down the gangplank, they were greeted by the

University of Michigan fight song, “The Victors,” played by the band from the warship USS *Olympia.*[*]

Hail to the victors valiant
Hail to the conquering heroes
Hail! Hail! To Michigan
The champions of the West!

When the British arrived at Archangel in August, they discovered that the Allied war matériel had already been moved up the Dvina River by the retreating Bolshevik forces. Therefore, when the American troops arrived one month later, they were immediately used in offensive operations to aid in the rescue of the Czechoslovak Legion. President Wilson made plain that Americans would not intervene in the civil war, saying that would only “add to the sad confusion in Russia rather than cure it.” However, AEF, North Russia was under British command and the British commanders had other ideas. They envisioned British, American, French, and other Allied forces pushing south from Archangel to link up with the Czechoslovak Legion and reverse the Russian Revolution. Almost as soon as the 339th set foot on the dock in Archangel, the British ground commander, Lieutenant General Frederick Poole, ordered two U.S. battalions to reinforce his men against the Bolsheviks. The 339th Infantry Regiment under U.S. Colonel George Stewart (a Congressional Medal of Honor recipient for braving enemy fire to save a drowning man during the Philippine insurrection in

---

[*] “The Victors” is the fight song of the University of Michigan written and composed by UM music student Louis Elbel in celebration of a last minute 12–11 Michigan victory over rival Chicago, giving UM its first Western Conference football championship in 1898. “The Victors” was first played in public by John Philip Sousa’s band in May of 1899 in Ann Arbor. Sousa later called it the “best college march ever written.” An abbreviated version of the fight song, based on the final refrain, is played after the football team either scores or makes a decisive defense play, such as an interception. Its full lyrics span several verses that run of more than two-minute duration. The melody of the fight song is very similar to the trio section from “The Spirit of Liberty March,” published seven months earlier by *Tin Pan Alley* composer George “Rosey” Rosenberg. The phrase “champions of the West” is often misunderstood; it is a reference to Michigan’s membership in the Western Conference, later renamed the Big Ten. “The Victors” is considered one of the top fight songs ever written and considered the first significant fight song to be written. The fight song is written as a military march format.

1899) was then sent up the Dvina River and the Third Battalion of the 339th boarded the railway to Vologda, a transportation hub about 460 miles south of Archangel, where they engaged and pushed back the Bolshevik forces for the next six weeks.

However, the two fronts between Archangel and the closest Czechoslovak Legion units were stretched over hundreds of miles and were extremely narrow and difficult to supply, maintain, and protect. By the end of October 1918, they were no longer able to maintain the offensive and acknowledging their precarious situation and the rapid onset of winter, the Allies began to adopt a defensive posture. The Allied commanders also soon realized they would be unable to raise an effective local force of anti-Bolshevik soldiers. Thus, they gave up the goal of linking up with the Czechoslovak Legion and settled in to hold their gains over the coming winter. During that winter, the Bolshevik army went on the offensive, especially along the Vaga River portion of the Dvina River Front, where they inflicted numerous casualties and caused the Allies to retreat a considerable distance. During the battle, twenty-nine Americans were killed and fifty-eight wounded; nineteen went missing. "Most of those missing are believed to have been wounded and probably frozen," the regimental commander reported to headquarters. Colonel James Ruggles, the U.S. military attaché in Archangel, declared the situation around Archangel critical: Too few American troops were spread over too wide a front, facing an enemy superior in numbers, arms, and moral.

The Armistice ended the war on 11 November 1918, but the port of Arkhangelsk was now frozen and closed to shipping leaving the Americans bereft of hope. Colonel Ruggles told headquarters that neither enlisted men nor their officers could understand why they were still fighting. With so many U.S. field units under the command of British officers, American soldiers on the front lines believed they were "being used to further selfish designs of England upon Russian territory," Colonel Ruggles reported. Several soldiers mutinied; others threatened to mutiny. It was not until early June that the bulk of the AEF in North Russia sailed for Brest, France, and then for New York City and home—which for two-thirds of them was in the state of Michigan. During the withdrawal, the men of AEF, North Russia decided to call themselves "Polar Bears" and were authorized to wear the Polar Bear insignia on their left sleeve. AEF, North Russia officially disbanded on 5 August 1919. In the end, 6,083 Americans served in northern Russia, suffering more than 210 casualties, including at least 110 deaths from combat, thirty missing in action, and seventy deaths from disease, 90 percent of which were caused by the Spanish flu. An October 1919 report lists the casualties as 553: 109 killed in action; thirty-five died of wounds; eighty-one from disease; nineteen from accidents and other causes; 305 wounded and four POWS (released).

British forces withdrew from Archangel by the end of September 1919, and the Bolsheviks took the city from the remaining White Russian defenders in February 1920. The humbling U.S. withdrawal led to finger-pointing. A military memo buried in the National Archives summed up the undeclared war-within-a-war. In it, Captain Hugh S. Martin wrote to the U.S. military attaché in Archangel:

> The real truth was, we were waging war against Bolshevism. Everybody knew that. Yet no Allied government ever stated that that was its policy in intervening. . . . The result was that in the course of a day the ordinary soldier would hear any number of varying—and sometimes contradictory—replies to the questions which were constantly being asked; for example, why were they being called upon to fight here after the fighting on the Western Front had ceased . . . what were our reasons for making war on the Bolsheviks; why not let Russia take care of her own internal affairs, etc.

Three thousand five hundred miles east of Archangel, the objectives of the American Expeditionary Force, Siberia (AEF, Siberia) were to: 1) capture and secure the Russian eastern port city of Vladivostok, from which the Czechoslovak Legion could safely withdraw and redeploy to the Western Front; 2) to repatriate the large quantities of military supplies and railroad rolling stock that the United States had sent to the Russian Far East in support of the Russian Empire's war efforts on the Eastern Front; and finally 3) to "steady any efforts at self-government or self-defense in which the [anti-Bolshevik] Russians themselves may be willing to accept assistance."

AEF, Siberia was commanded by Major General William S. Graves and eventually totaled 7,950 officers and enlisted men. The force included the U.S. Army's Twenty-Seventh and Thirty-First Infantry Regiments, plus large numbers of volunteers from the Twelfth, Thirteenth, and Sixty-Second Infantry Regiments of the Eighth Division, Graves's former division command. The first 3,000 American troops disembarked in Vladivostok between 15 and 21 August 1918 only to discover units of Czechoslovak

Legionnaires had already captured and secured the port city. The Americans were quickly assigned guard duty along segments of the railway between Vladivostok and Nikolsk-Ussuriysky in the north. The last American soldiers left Siberia on 1 April 1920. During their nineteen months in Siberia, 189 soldiers of the force died from all causes.

On 18 October 1918, Masaryk published in Washington, D.C. the Declaration of Czechoslovak Independence, and personally handed it to President Wilson. On 28 October, the Czecho-Slovak National Council in Prague proclaimed the independence of Czechoslovakia and established its power in Bohemia and Moravia. Masaryk was elected in absentia as the first president of the state. In November 1918, Masaryk left the U.S. for Europe. The main goals of his visit had been achieved. The third one—the return of the Czechoslovak Legion from Russia was partially completed. The U.S. promised to promote its transportation across the Pacific Ocean, through continental America, and across the Atlantic to France.

The Struggle of the Czechoslovak Legion in Russia

IN JUNE 1918, AND AFTER INTENSE NEGOTIATIONS WITH THE Czecho-Slovak National Council and Masaryk, most of the remaining Legionnaire prisoners of war, including Peter Vlčko's father, were finally paroled by the Bolshevik government with the understanding they would leave Russia. However, this understanding would soon be mired by the rapidly changing political winds. Still owing a debt of gratitude to the Germans for aiding and abetting Lenin's leadership of the Russian Revolution, and under treaty obligation to prevent any prisoners of war in Russia from joining the Entente armies on the Western Front, the Bolsheviks breached their promise of safe passage to the Czechoslovak Legion while simultaneously aiding in the rapid redeployment to the West of prisoners of war belonging to the Central Powers. Upon his release, he volunteered for the Legion and joined in their struggle against the Bolsheviks while attempting to leave Russia.

Nearly 70,000 former POWs joined the Czechoslovak Legion, which now constituted a major military and political force against the Bolsheviks. The seizure of the Trans-Siberian railroad by the Czechoslovak Legion in May 1918 blocked off Siberia from Europe and halted the official repatriation of POWs until 1920.

Shortly after they entered into hostilities against the Bolsheviks, the Legionnaires began making common cause with anti-Bolshevik, or White Russians who began forming their own governments behind the

Legionnaires' lines. The most important of these governments were the Komuch in Samara and the Provisional Siberian Government in Omsk. With substantial Czechoslovak help, the People's Army of Komuch won several important victories, including the capture of Kazan and an Imperial state gold reserve on 5 August 1918. Czechoslovak pressure was also crucial in convincing the White Russians in Siberia to nominally unify behind the Socialist Revolutionary Party's All-Russian Provisional Government, formed at a conference in Ufa during September 1918.

In November 1918, the unpopular Socialist Revolutionary government in Omsk was overthrown in a British sponsored *coup d'etat.* Kolchak had returned to Omsk on 16 November from an inspection tour. He was approached and refused to take power. The Socialist-Revolutionary (SR) directory leader and members were arrested on 18 November by a troop of Cossacks under Ataman Krasilnikov. The remaining cabinet members met and voted for Kolchak to become the head of government with emergency powers. He was named Supreme Ruler (*Verkhovnyi Pravitel*) on 18 November, and he promoted himself to full admiral. The arrested SR politicians were expelled from Siberia and ended up in Europe. The Left SR leaders in Russia denounced Kolchak and called for his assassination. Their activities resulted in a small revolt in Omsk on 22 December 1918, which was quickly put down by Cossacks and the Czechoslovak Legion, who summarily executed almost 500 rebels. Subsequently, the SRs opened negotiations with the Bolsheviks and in January 1919 the SR People's Army joined the Red Army.

The Brest-Litovsk Treaty was effectively terminated on 11 November 1918, when Germany surrendered to the Allies. However, over the eight and one-half months it was in effect, the treaty did provide some relief to the Bolsheviks, already fighting the Russian Civil War, by the renouncement of Russia's claims on Poland, Finland, Estonia, Latvia, Belarus, Ukraine, and Lithuania. The fragmented Bolshevik army could regroup and concentrate its efforts against the opposing factions in the civil war, such as the White Russians.

In the autumn of 1918, the Bolshevik Red Army began its counter offensive and defeated the Whites on the Eastern Front in Siberia. However, between autumn 1918 and spring 1919, the Whites under Aleksandr Kolchak enjoyed significant success in European Russia. The northern White Army under the Russian Anatoly Pepelyayev (younger brother of Kolchak's Prime Minister Viktor Pepelyayev) and the Czech Rudolf Gajda seized Perm (near the Ural Mountains) in late December 1918. The plan was for three main advances—Gajda to take Archangel, Khanzhin to capture Ufa (southeastern European Russia) and the Cossacks under Alexander Dutov to capture Samara and Saratov (southeastern European Russia).

The White forces took Ufa in March 1919 and pushed on from there to take Kazan (on the Volga River in southwest Russia) and approach Samara on the Volga River. Anti-Communist risings in Simbirsk, Kazan, Viatka, and Samara assisted their advancement. The newly formed Red Army proved unwilling to fight and instead retreated, allowing the Whites to advance to a line stretching from Glazov (just west of Perm near the Ural Mountains) through Orenburg to Uralsk (deep southern Russia). Kolchak's territories covered over 300,000 square kilometers where nearly seven million people lived. In April 1919, the alarmed Bolshevik Central Executive Committee made defeating Kolchak its top priority. As the spring thaw arrived Kolchak's position degenerated—his armies had outrun their supply lines, they were exhausted, and the Red Army poured newly raised troops into the area.

Kolchak had also aroused the dislike of potential allies, including the Czechoslovak Legion and the Polish Fifth Rifle Division. The Czechoslovak Legion withdrew from the conflict in October 1918 but remained a presence; their supreme commander as of December 1918, French General Maurice Janin, regarded Kolchak as an instrument of the British—Janin, himself, was pro-SR. Kolchak could not count on Japanese aid either; the Japanese feared he would interfere with their occupation of Far Eastern Russia and refused him assistance, creating a buffer state to the east of Lake Baikal under Cossack Ataman General Grigory Mikhaylovich Semyonov. The 7,000 or so American troops comprising AEF, Siberia were officially strictly neutral regarding "internal Russian affairs" and officially served only to maintain the operation of the Trans-Siberian railroad in the Far East. The American commander of AEF, Siberia, General William S. Graves, personally disliked the Kolchak government, which he saw as monarchist and autocratic, a view that was shared by President Woodrow Wilson. British War Secretary Winston Churchill pressed very strongly in the cabinet for British recognition of Kolchak's government, but Prime Minister David Lloyd George would only do so if the United States likewise recognized Kolchak. President Woodrow Wilson was strongly hostile towards Kolchak, openly doubted his word, and was against diplomatic recognition. Wilson's main adviser on Russia was the former head of the Provisional Government, Alexander Kerensky, who told Wilson that

Kolchak was a "reactionary" who would "inaugurate a regime hardly less sanguinary and repressive than that of the Bolsheviks."

Czechoslovak Legionaries' enthusiasm for fighting in Russia in late 1918, mostly confined along the Volga and Urals, dropped precipitously. The rapidly growing Red Army was getting stronger by the day, retaking Kazan on 10 September, followed by Samara a month later. The Legionaries were lacking reliable reinforcements from POW camps and were disappointed by the failure of Allied soldiers from other countries to join them on the front lines. Having learned about the creation of an independent Czechoslovakia on 28 October 1918, Legionaries began to ask why they had to fight in the Russian Civil War; they now only wanted to return to their new and independent homeland. The final blow to Czechoslovak morale arrived on 18 November 1918, when a military *coup d'état* in Omsk overthrew the All-Russian Provisional Government and proclaimed Admiral Aleksandr Kolchak Supreme Ruler of Russia.

At the beginning of 1919, all Czechoslovak troops dispersed throughout Ukraine and Soviet Russia began to retreat via the Trans-Siberian Railway. On 27 January 1919, Jan Bohumír Syrový (1888–1970)—at that time commander of all Czechoslovak troops in Russia—claimed the Trans-Siberian Railway between Novonikolaevsk (Novosibirsk) and Irkutsk as a "Czechoslovak zone of operation." This made it nearly impossible for Admiral Kolchak and his White Army to use the railway for retreating in mid to late 1919.

During the winter of 1918–1919, Czechoslovak troops were redeployed from the front to guard the route of the Trans-Siberian Railway between Novonikolaevsk and Irkutsk from partisan attacks. Alongside other legions formed from Polish, Romanian, and Yugoslav POWs in Siberia, the Czechoslovaks defended the Kolchak government's only supply route for the duration of 1919.

During the summer and autumn of 1919, Kolchak's armies were in a steady retreat from the Red Eastern Army Group. One of Kolchak's commanders, Radola (Rudolf) Gajda, had fallen out of Kolchak's favor and was dismissed on 5 July 1919. Kolchak had left Omsk on the 13 November 1919 for Irkutsk along the Trans-Siberian Railroad. Travelling a section of track controlled by the Czechoslovak Legion, he was sidetracked and stopped; by December his train had only reached Nizhneudinsk. On 14 November, the Reds took Omsk, Kolchak's capital, initiating a desperate eastward flight by the White Army, the wounded, and refugees along the Trans-Siberian Railway. In the following weeks, the Whites' rear was further disorganized by widespread outbreaks of uprisings and partisan activity. The White Army eventually collapsed. With the anti-Bolshevik movement in chaos and no clear remaining objectives, the Legionnaires finally declared neutrality in the Russian Civil War. The homesick Legionnaires simply wanted to leave Siberia without incurring any more casualties than necessary.

In late December, Irkutsk fell under the control of the Political Centre and Socialist Revolutionary Party (Left SRs).[1] One of their first actions was to dismiss Kolchak. When he heard of this on 4 January 1920, he announced his resignation, giving his office to General Anton Ivanovich Denikin and passing control of his remaining forces around Irkutsk to the Baikal Cossack Ataman, General Grigory Mikhaylovich Semyonov. Meanwhile, Admiral Kolchak's trains, which included an enormous cache (350 tonnes) of Imperial gold bullion captured from Kazan, were stranded along the railway near Nizhneudinsk. After his bodyguard deserted him there, the Legionaries were ordered by Allied representatives in Siberia to safely escort the admiral to Irkutsk where the British military mission under General Sir Alfred Knox, K.C.B., Military Attaché in Russia, was waiting to assist him out of the country. This plan was resisted by Bolshevik units along the route, and as a result the Legionaries, after consulting their commanders, Generals Janin and Jan Syrový, made the controversial decision to turn Kolchak over to the Political Centre, a government formed by Socialists in Irkutsk whose primary mission was to eliminate Aleksandr Kolchak.

On 14 January 1920, after giving his word to guarantee the safety of Admiral Kolchak to the British military mission in Irkutsk, General Janin ordered the Czechoslovak Legion to hand him over to the Left SRs in Irkutsk.

On 20 January 1920, the Provisional All-Russian Government in Irkutsk—a short-lived regional White government centered in Omsk—surrendered power to the Left SRs and a Bolshevik military committee. Upon hearing of Admiral Kolchak's capture, the White's Second Army[2] under the command of General Vladimír Kappel marched days and nights toward Irkutsk in subzero temperatures while Kolchak was being interrogated by a commission of five men representing the Revolutionary Committee (*REVKOM*) during nine days between 21 January and 6 February. Despite the arrival of a contrary order from Moscow, Admiral Kolchak was condemned to death along with his Prime Minister Viktor Pepelyayev.

Both prisoners were brought before a Cheka firing squad in the early morning hours of 7 February 1920 to prevent his rescue by a unit of White Army soldiers on the outskirts of the city preparing an attack. According to eyewitnesses, Kolchak was entirely calm and unafraid, “like an Englishman.” The Admiral asked the commander of the firing squad, “Would you be so good as to get a message sent to my wife in Paris to say that I bless my son?” The commander responded, “I’ll see what can be done, if I don’t forget about it.” Because of this, and also an earlier attempted rebellion against the Whites organized by Legionnaire and veteran of the Battle of Zborov Captain Radola (Rudolf) Gajda in coordination with members of the Socialist Revolutionary Party in Vladivostok on 17 November 1919, the Whites accused the Czechoslovaks of being traitors. (Radola Gajda [1892–1948] would go on the become a controversial military and political leader and personality in Czechoslovakia.)

On General Janin’s return to France, he was brought before a court-martial with delegates from all Allies present. The allied majority wanted him to be hanged, had it not been for his efforts during the Great War, it would have been the case. But despite his previous heroics, he was now a disgrace to the entire French Army and the French Ministry of War. It was decided that he would be stripped of all rank and titles and be sentenced to life in military prison. He was later released when he was diagnosed with a fatal tuberculosis.

Many saw him and see him today as the reason why the counter-revolution failed. If Admiral Kolchak and his staff and government in exile had been successfully evacuated, they could have regrouped and launched a new invasion with help of the Allies—perhaps this time better equipped and better coordinated.

On 7 February 1920, the Legionaries had signed an armistice with the Fifth Red Army at Kutin, whereby the latter allowed the Czechoslovaks unmolested passage to Vladivostok. In exchange, the Legionaries confirmed their agreement to not try to rescue Kolchak (although at this point it was a moot issue) and to leave 285 tonnes of Imperial Russian gold bullion captured from Kazan with the authorities in Irkutsk. (Unbeknownst to the authorities in Irkutsk, the rest of the gold was used to charter ships and set up the Legion Bank in 1920. The bank’s headquarters on *Na poříčí* Street, in the center of Prague, is a masterpiece of Czech cubist architecture with its façade featuring scenes of the Legion’s arduous retreat through Siberia. When the Soviets liberated Prague in May 1945, Red Army troops raided the bank’s vaults, sending much of the gold reserves there to Moscow.)

By March 1920, all Legionnaires and their trains in Irkutsk had been transferred to Vladivostok. From December 1919, the Czechoslovak Legion started to leave Russia through Vladivostok, and the evacuation was completed in September 1920. The total number of people evacuated with the Czechoslovak Legion in Russia was 67,739, including 56,455 soldiers, 3,004 officers, 6,714 civilians, 1,716 wives, 717 children, 1,935 foreigners, and 198 others. After their return to Czechoslovakia, many formed the core of the new Czechoslovak Army. The number of Legionaries killed in Russia during World War I and the Russian Civil War amounted to 4,112. An unknown number went missing or deserted the Legion, either to make an arduous journey to return home or to join the Czechoslovak Communists fighting in support of the Bolsheviks. Among the latter was Jaroslav Hašek, later the author of the popular satirical novel *The Good Soldier Švejk*.

The Legionnaires' 6,000-mile land journey across a hostile continent from Kiev in the Ukraine to Vladivostok on the Pacific coast of Soviet Russia, then by ship crossing the Pacific Ocean to San Francisco (8,335 km/5,179 mi), then by rail through continental United States to the eastern seaboard (5,467 km/3,400 mi), on to France (6,782 km/4,214 mi), and finally to Prague, Czechoslovakia (1,238 km/770 mi), for a total of 31,484 kilometers or 19,563 miles, has no parallel in history. The infamous retreat of the *Ten Thousand* Greeks under soldier-historian Xenophon (431 BC to 354 BC) was conducted over only a comparatively small portion of Asia Minor (approximately 1,600 miles). Relatively speaking, the retreat of the *Ten Thousand* was but a cub scout undertaking when measured against the tremendous feat triumphantly accomplished by the Czechoslovak Legionnaires (Horne 1923).

Peter's father's journey home in late 1920 had to proceed from Vladivostok to San Francisco through the American continent via railway to the eastern seaboard where he again boarded a ship to Western Europe and back to his home in the newly established and independent Czechoslovakia. He did not reach home until 1921.

Youth and Early Military Career

DURING PETER SENIOR'S SEVEN-YEAR ABSENCE, PETER'S MOTHER, ADELA, moved in with her mother, Anna Jakubíková (née Medveďová), in the village of Brehy and, as the oldest child among five (Gregor, Peter, Pavlina, and Julia or Ulla as she was affectionately known), she had to travel to work in the fields of wealthy Hungarian landlords to help the family survive the war and the uncertain fate of her husband. During his parents' absence, Peter was in the care of his maternal grandmother Anna and aunt Julia (Ulla). He initially attended primary school connected with the village Catholic Parish of St. Joseph Church. Later, he continued his primary education in the public school associated with the mining town of Nová Baňa just across the river Hron that separated the two mountain communities.

When Peter was nine years old, he first came to know his father who recently returned from Siberia. Peter Emilius Vlčko was the first-born and only male child of five living children (Rozalia, Valeria, Anna, and Božena)—a sister Adela had died at the age of three-years. At the age of twelve-years, Peter was sent to live with an unrelated family in Levice, a city thirty kilometers south of his native village, in order to attend *gymnázium* (college preparatory high school). Later, when his father was hired to work there for the state-owned railroad, his parents and younger sisters also moved to Levice in a home of their own where young Peter rejoined them.

In his adolescent years, Peter loved soccer and gymnastics. He became a member of Sokol, a Czechoslovak national gymnastics organization, at the age of fourteen. Though he was always a very good student, his plans for studying medicine were thwarted when he failed the *maturita*, a state examination, administered upon graduation from *gymnázium* in 1931. Some faculty members viewed Peter dimly. They considered him to be a rebel, entirely too free and independent in thought. When the examination in natural sciences was given to him, he answered all the questions correctly, except one in paleontology. It was this question which Jozef Zeman, a teacher of natural science, had deliberately chosen so that he might justifiably fail Vlčko. Peter's case came before a review board, and when a vote to pass or fail him was taken, it was Father Štefan Bolcek who cast the deciding vote. Vlčko's future was sealed. As a consequence of this failure, he lost the opportunity to acquire the state scholarship for university studies in Bratislava.

Embittered by such undeserved treatment, even after passing the reparative examination in October of the same year, Peter chose to volunteer for the army. What else could he do? He lost scholarship eligibility and could not possibly finance his university education without state aid.

Shortly thereafter, Peter Vlčko volunteered for the Czechoslovak Army and entered the Reserve Cavalry Officer's School in Pardubice, present-day Czech Republic. Vlčko's first military assignment was with the Third Cavalry Regiment at Nové Zámky in southern Slovakia. After basic training, he advanced to reserve cavalry officers school located at Pardubice in Bohemia. In October 1932, he enrolled in the Military Academy in Hranice, Moravia. After two years of rigorous training and studies, he was commissioned second lieutenant of the cavalry and assigned to the Fifth Dragoon Regiment at Košice in eastern Slovakia. There, at the age of twenty-two-years he commanded a cavalry squad of thirty men, thirty-two horses, two light machine guns, twenty-eight rifles, thirty sabers, and six pistols.

Two years later in 1934, Vlčko was sent to National Military Equestrian School in Pardubice (modern day Czech Republic). After graduation, he joined his regiment, which during his schooling had moved to Stará Boleslav, about thirty kilometers north of Prague. Soon Vlčko was promoted to first lieutenant and made commander of an anti-tank cannon squad. In January 1935, he again was sent to Pardubice, this time as an anti-tank cannon instructor at the Reserve Cavalry Officer's School. Within one year, he was given the position of platoon commander of the cavalry. It was at Pardubice that Vlčko experienced the tragic moment in history when the German Army crossed the Czechoslovak border on 15 March 1939 and occupied the western half of the Republic, declaring Bohemia and Moravia a German Protectorate. One day earlier, Slovakia declared itself independent and allied to Nazi Germany. On command of Interim Prime Minister and Minister of National Defense, General Jan Syrový, all officers had to immediately surrender their arms and remain quarantined in their barracks until further orders. In a speech to the nation, he stated Czechoslovakia had no choice but to accept the terms because without British or French support, the country was outnumbered, and any conflict would result in severe casualties. "We were abandoned," he said. "We stand alone." Syrový felt that had the allies of Czechoslovakia upheld their treaty obligations with Czechoslovakia, he would never have agreed to the Munich Dictate and order the army to stand down, but that, under the circumstances, the Czechoslovak Army on its own had no chance of success. Vlčko and his fellow soldiers were disarmed and demobilized. Several days later, Vlčko was sent to Bratislava, the capital of the newly independent Slovakia.

During the second half of 1939, Vlčko served as adjutant to the commander of a cavalry regiment stationed in Nitra in central Slovakia. There, he was promoted to captain of the cavalry. His assignment, however, did not last very long. Within six months Captain Vlčko entered the Slovak National War College (*Vysoká vojenná škola*) for general staff and quartermaster officers in 1940 in Bratislava, the capital of the newly independent Slovak Republic.

Peter Vlčko might give the impression of being a small man, for he was not particularly tall. But he was a strong, healthy specimen of the army officer corps. Physical fitness was part of his character. He had developed a solid, trim body, lean and sinewy, which enabled him to withstand the toughest and most rigorous military training and discipline. His compact size was ideal for a cavalry officer. On foot, he was light and fast having played goalie for the army's national soccer team. His normal walk was rapid, even a little staccato. There was a kind of electricity to his movements. Peter was energy, himself. His head and face were testimony of strength and vitality. If slightly gaunt, his face was virile and masculine. Though his dark, straight hair was gradually receding, he retained a youthful appearance. Heavy brows accentuated his deep-set hazel eyes, which could only be called luminous. They seemed always to emit a gleam, a brightness, incandescent when he was angry, or sparkling when he was happy and pleased. His straight nose, firm chin, and ample mouth gave him a resolute quality, absent only when he smiled. And Peter's smile was irresistible, the perfect complement to his flashing eyes. If he was a fraction less than handsome, his military uniform made up for this deficiency. In his officer's dress uniform, he could even be called dashing.

CHAPTER 16

GEORGINA REICHSFELD (1920–2020) THE FIRST TWENTY YEARS

THE FISCHERS

GEORGINA'S MATERNAL GRANDPARENTS WERE JÁKÓB AND JOZEFINA (née Österreicher) Fischer. A branch of the Österreichers in Austria settled in Transylvania (modern-day Romania) while the Fischers lived in Budapest. Jozefina was born in the Austro-Hungarian (Kingdom of Hungary) city of Nagy-Várad (modern day Oradea, Transylvania). The history of how the two met, courted, and married has been lost, but they settled in Budapest where Jákób and Jozefina inherited the Fischer family's bakery whose biggest customer was the Austro-Hungarian Army.

The Fischers had two children: Árpád was firstborn followed three years later by Helena on 17 April 1900. The Fischer children were raised in secular Hungarian schools. Helena attended a trade school until the age of fourteen-years and then began working in the retail arm of the family's bakery.

Soon after commencing work at the bakery, Jákób Fischer died of complications of diabetes mellitus. Unable to manage the large bakery, Jozefina sold the business and raised the two teenagers alone in Budapest.

Upon the outbreak of the First World War, Árpád was conscripted by the Austro-Hungarian Army. His years as a soldier and young adult are unknown to this writer, other than the fact that he met a young non-Jewish woman, with whom he married and fathered a son, Robert, who immigrated to Israel before the Second World War as part of *Aliya Bilty Legalit* (*Aliyah Bet*; Hebrew: *Ha'apalah* הַעְפָּלָה). Soon thereafter, as the Second World War approached, Árpád also emigrated to Israel sparing himself the tragedy of the Holocaust.

At the age of sixteen-years, Helena met Berthold Reichsfeld, a young Austro-Hungarian officer serving in the medical corps during the Great War. He was on leave at the time to attend his sister Julia's wedding in Slovakia. Why he exploited this time to also visit Budapest remains unclear. However, while in Budapest, Berthold met his future bride. The two courted until the war ended, and then twenty-three-year-old Berthold and eighteen-year-old Helena were married.

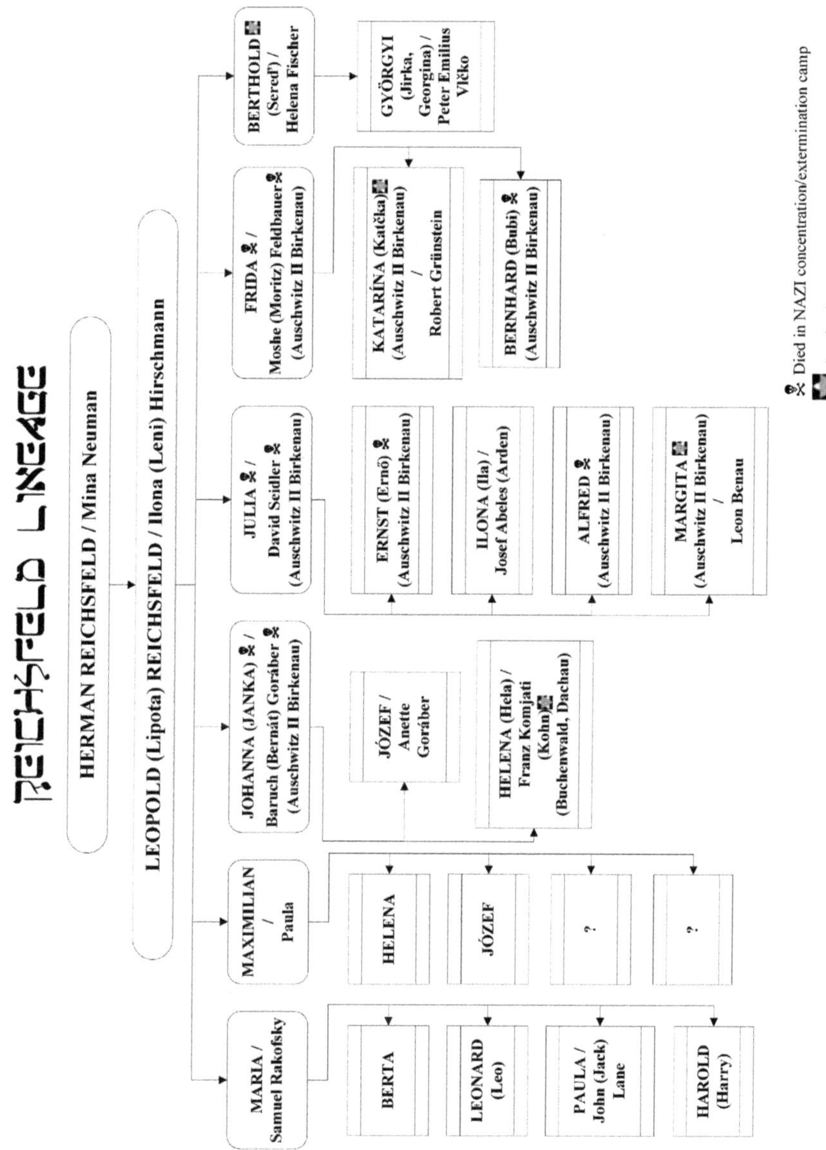
REICHSFELD LINEAGE
HERMAN REICHSFELD / Mina Neuman
LEOPOLD (Lipota) REICHSFELD / Ilona (Leni) Hirschmann
MARIA / Samuel Rakofsky
BERTA
LEONARD (Leo)
PAULA / John (Jack) Lane
HAROLD (Harry)
MAXIMILIAN / Paula
HELENA
JÓZEF
?
?
JOHANNA (JANKA) / Baruch (Bernát) Goráber (Auschwitz II Birkenau)
JÓZEF / Anette Goráber
HELENA (Hela) / Franz Komjati (Kohn) (Buchenwald, Dachau)
JULIA / David Seidler (Auschwitz II Birkenau)
ERNST (Ernő) (Auschwitz II Birkenau)
ILONA (Ila) / Josef Abeles (Arden)
ALFRED (Auschwitz II Birkenau)
MARGITA (Auschwitz II Birkenau) / Leon Benau
FRIDA / Moshe (Moritz) Feldbauer (Auschwitz II Birkenau)
KATARÍNA (Katčka) (Auschwitz II Birkenau) / Robert Grünstein
BERNHARD (Bubi) (Auschwitz II Birkenau)
BERTHOLD (Sereď) / Helena Fischer
GYÖRGYI (Jirka, Georgina) / Peter Emilius Vlčko
Died in NAZI concentration/extermination camp
Survived NAZI concentration/labor camp

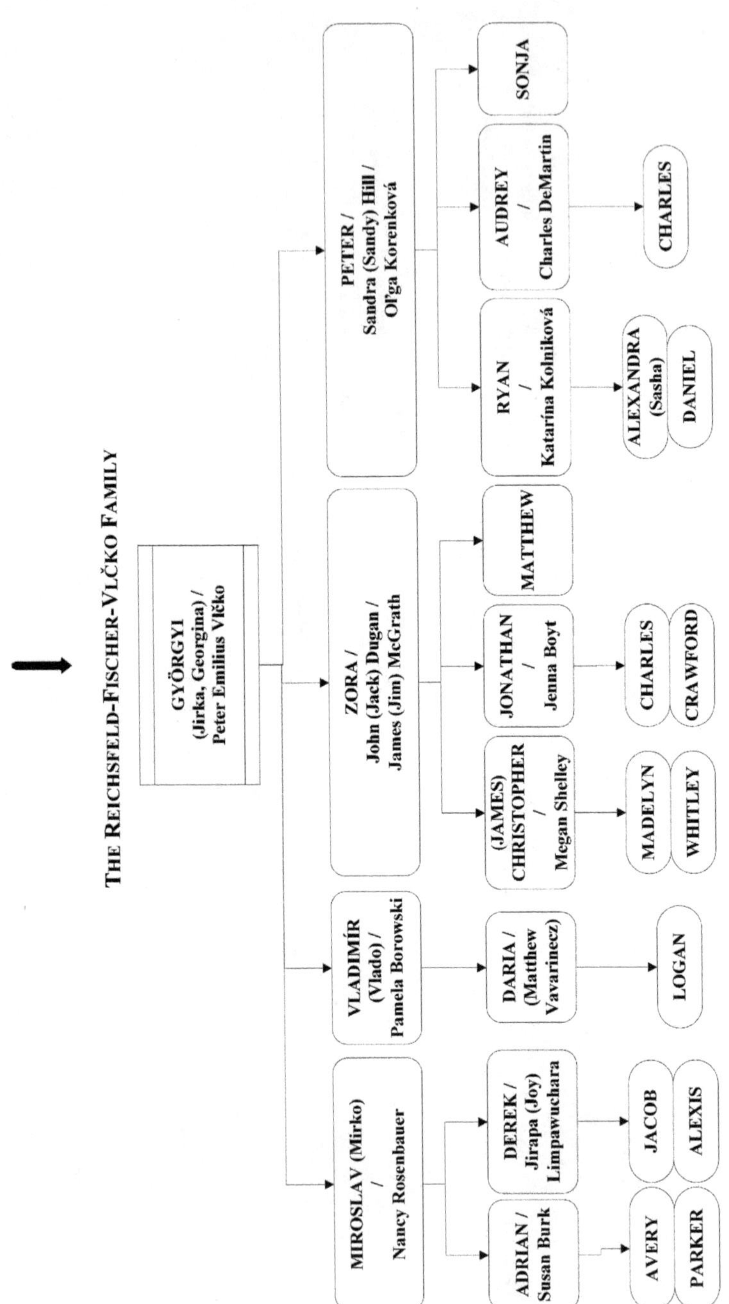
THE REICHSFELD-FISCHER-VLČKO FAMILY
GYÖRGYI
(Jirka, Georgina) /
Peter Emilius Vlčko
MIROSLAV (Mirko)
/
Nancy Rosenbauer
VLADIMÍR
(Vlado) /
Pamela Borowski
ZORA /
John (Jack) Dugan /
James (Jim) McGrath
PETER /
Sandra (Sandy) Hill /
Oľga Korenková
ADRIAN /
Susan Burk
DEREK /
Jirapa (Joy)
Limpawuchara
DARIA /
(Matthew
Vavarinecz)
(JAMES)
CHRISTOPHER
/
Megan Shelley
JONATHAN
/
Jenna Boyt
MATTHEW
RYAN
/
Katarína Kolníková
AUDREY
/
Charles DeMartin
SONJA
AVERY
PARKER
JACOB
ALEXIS
LOGAN
MADELYN
WHITLEY
CHARLES
CRAWFORD
ALEXANDRA
(Sasha)
DANIEL
CHARLES

THE REICHSFELD-GORÁBER FAMILY

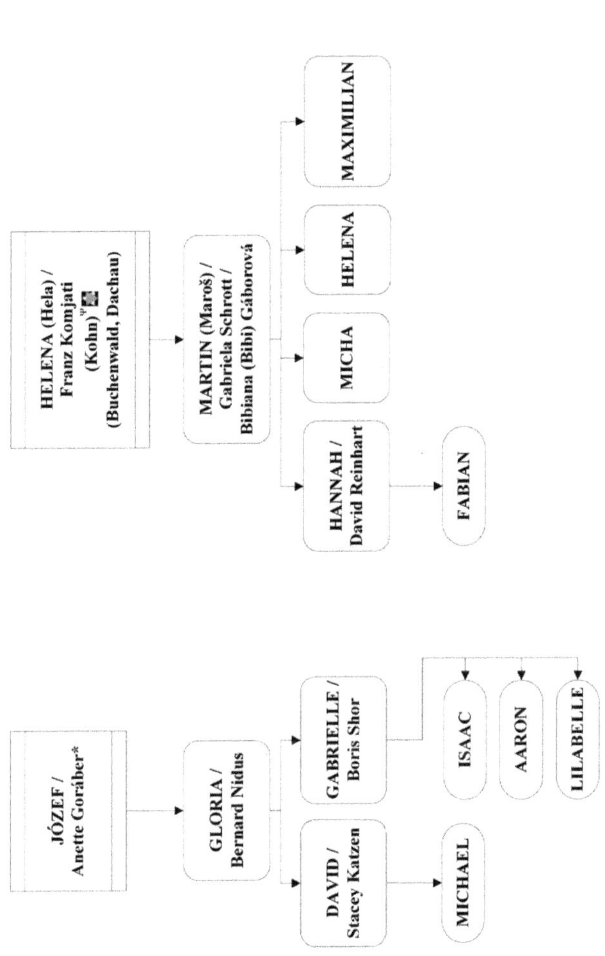

* Annette (daughter of David Goráber) and Józef (son of Bernát Goráber) were 1st degree cousins

Ψ Franz's father changed his surname from Kohn to Komjati

THE REICHSFELD-SEIDLER FAMILY

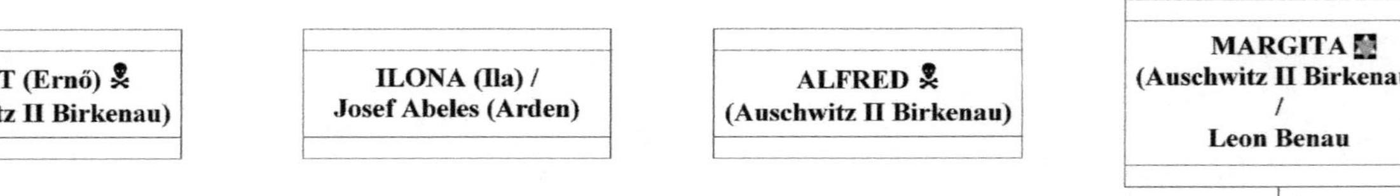

THE REICHSFELD-FELDBAUER FAMILY

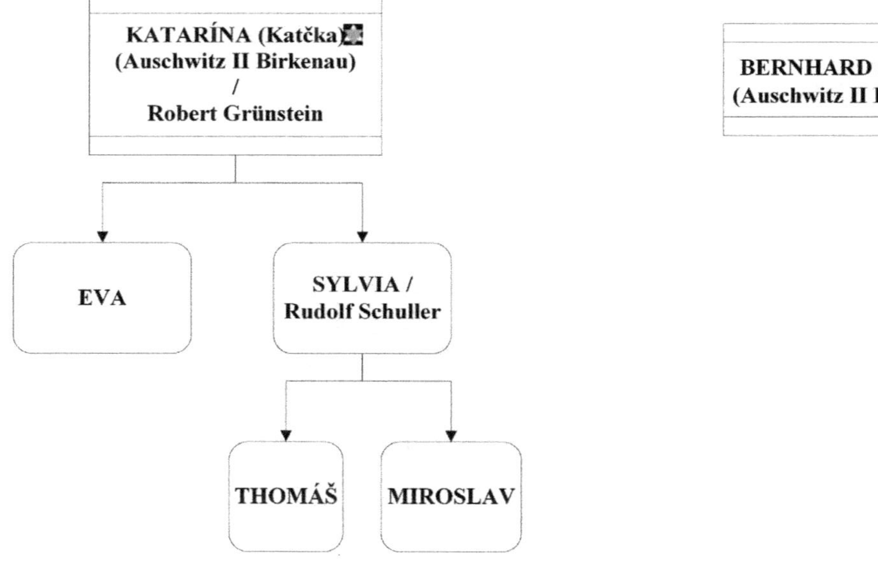

THE REICHSFELDS

THE REICHSFELD ANCESTORS SETTLED IN THE AUSTRO-HUNGARIAN (Slovak) village of Dehtice, district Trnava, where Herman Reichsfeld was born in 1822. Herman and Mina (née Neuman) bore a son Leopold (Lipota) in Dehtice on 14 November 1850. In adulthood, Leopold moved two and one-half kilometers south to Kátlovce, a neighboring village where he took a wife Helene (Leni) Hirschmann and together they established and ran a local tavern (*hostinec*) that became a popular gathering place. On 10 April 1895, Berthold, the couple's sixth and last child and second boy, was born. His siblings were: Maria; Maximillian; Johanna (Janka); Julia; and Frida. While still a young boy, Berthold's mother Leni died. Janka, being considerably older than Berthold, managed to raise Berthold in the absence of their mother. At age seven-years, Berthold was enrolled in a Slovak school administered by Jesuits in Trnava (22 km south of Dehtice). This was the only school available in the area, even to Jewish families. He later entered *gymnázium* in Skalica (56 km northwest of Dehtice). Subjects in this school, as in all Slovak schools at this time, particularly after the Austro-Hungarian Compromise of 1867, were taught in compulsory Hungarian. During this time, Berthold's older brother Maximillian while still only a teenager left the family and his homeland to immigrate to Argentina to work in the lucrative energy and mineral industry. In Argentina, Max eventually met his bride with whom they had three children. Likewise, Berthold's eldest sister Mary left the family and homeland with her Slovak fiancé, Mr. Rakovsky, and immigrated to New York where they married and had four children.

Shortly after graduating from *gymnázium* in 1913 and with the financial support of his father, Berthold also left his family and Slovak homeland and began his medical studies (five-year program) at the Royal Hungarian University of Science in Budapest (Budapesti Királyi Magyar Tudományegyetem—known since 1969 as Semmelweis University in honor of the brilliant obstetrician and early pioneer of antiseptic procedures Professor Ignác Fülöp Semmelweis). The Royal Hungarian University of Science in Budapest originated in 1769, when Holy Roman Empress Maria Theresa added a medical faculty to the University of Nagyszombat (now Trnva, Slovakia). In 1777, the university moved first to Buda (Royal University of Buda) then in 1784 to Pest (Royal University of Hungary) and once the university settled in its permanent location a period of great development commenced.

Berthold chose Budapest over Vienna or Charles University in Prague for a number of reasons. At the turn of the century, Budapest was a thriving metropolis on the scale of Vienna and Berlin. However, Budapest was not always the vibrant Central European city that it is sometimes shown to have been, at least not under that name. It was essentially three separate municipalities within the Austro-Hungarian Empire until the districts of Buda, Pest, and Obuda were combined in 1873. This, together with the earlier Compromise Agreement of 1867, which set up the dual monarchy, and the Emancipation Decree of the same year, which "granted Jews full political and civic equality in the Hapsburg lands," led to the rapid development of Budapest as a rival to Vienna and much more hospitable to Jews. Showcasing the city was meant to send a signal to the world that Hungary was a major power in the region. And the high percentage of Jews in Budapest (professor of history and Judaic studies Mary Gluck gives a figure of twenty-three percent by 1900) indicated that they played a prominent part in the life of the city. In the decades between 1880 and 1914, Budapest became famous for its edgy music halls, opulent Orpheums, and titillating all-night coffee houses, which were widely admired and emulated throughout Central Europe.

The Budapest Royal Orpheum—a decadent cabaret that hosted the best acts of its time, including the American dancer and French vedette singer Josephine Baker, one of the most celebrated performers at the Folies Bergère in Paris and an icon of the jazz age—was infamous among European variété theaters. The Royal Orpheum, built by Hermann Keleti and Oszkár Fodor, opened its doors on 3 October 1908. The European Orpheum circuit enjoyed its golden age between 1880 and 1914 and pioneered one of the most important and innovative entertainment industries of its age. Widely emulated in Vienna and Berlin, the Budapest Orpheum helped transform the Hungarian capital into the popular entertainment center of German-speaking Central Europe. Less widely known is the close identification between the Orpheum and the city's lower middle-class Jewish population, which supplied the owners, directors, writers, actors, and most of the audiences of these popular musical reviews.

While Jews in Vienna and less so in Prague were often on the defensive, the vibrant Jewish community and open, liberal acceptance of assimilated Jews in cosmopolitan Budapest provided a welcoming attraction to young Jewish university students from the hinterlands of the Kingdom of Hungary. The university in Budapest including the faculty of medicine also grew in international stature in parallel with the city's cultural development.

For these reasons, many Slovak Jews chose to study in Budapest rather than Prague or Vienna. For Berthold, Budapest being only a mere 200 kilometers (130 mi) from home was the right choice.

During the First World War, a majority of university professors and students voluntarily enlisted in the Austro-Hungarian Army. As a first-year medical student, Berthold Reichsfeld was among those who enlisted.

During his early years in the Army Medical Corps, Berthold was stationed in Italy. Towards the end of the war, he was stationed in Molnos (modern day Mlynárce-Nitra, Slovakia) 145 kilometers (90 mi) northwest of Budapest. He managed to complete limited medical studies through the military while serving in the medical corps during the war and successfully passed his military medical certification examination in April 1917. This certification, however, was not equivalent to a full medical diploma awarded by the university, and he could not practice as a physician in civilian life.

After their wedding in 1918, the two took up residence in Budapest during the interwar period and tumultuous events in Hungary.

The Hungarian Revolution

EVENTS IN HUNGARY TOOK A RAPID TURN FOR THE WORSE AFTER THE devastating loss of the First World War and Treaty of Trianon that cost Hungary two-thirds of its territory and one-third of its native Hungarian speakers. While a prisoner of war in an Imperial Russian prison cell in the Urals, Austro-Hungarian soldier Béla Kun (born Kohn; 1886–1938) became interested in Communism and envisioned a Bolshevik Revolution in Hungary. With the collapse of Imperial Russia and withdrawal of Russia from the Entente Powers' involvement in the First World War, Kun was released from prison by his sworn oath not to rejoin the Central Powers. In March 1918, in Moscow, Kun co-founded the Hungarian Group of the Russian Communist Party (the predecessor to the Hungarian Communist Party). He travelled widely, including to Petrograd and Moscow where he befriended Vladimír Lenin. In the Russian Civil War in 1918, Kun fought for the Bolsheviks. During this time, he initiated concrete plans for a communist revolution in Hungary. In November 1918, with at least several hundred other Hungarian Communists and with a large sum of money provided by the Soviets, he returned to Hungary and managed to establish the Hungarian Soviet Republic (the first Communist government in Europe outside of Russia) ousting Hungary's first Democratic government on 21 March 1919.

The first action of the new Hungarian Soviet Republic was the nationalization of most of the private property in Hungary. Despite advice from Lenin and the Bolsheviks, Béla Kun's government chose not to redistribute land to the peasantry, which fragmented their support in Hungary. Instead, all land was to be converted into collective farms and former estate owners, managers, and bailiffs were to be retained as the new collective farm managers. This resulted in the dissolution of the balance of power between the old elite and the peasantry which made up the majority of Kun's support. In an effort to win peasant support, Kun cancelled all taxes in rural areas. To provide food for the cities, the Soviet Republic requisitioned food in the countryside through a red militia known as the Lenin Boys. This caused additional conflict between Kun and his supporters in the countryside. On 24 June, an attempt to overthrow the communist regime failed. A brutal retaliation for the *coup* attempt was exacted by the secret police, revolutionary tribunals, and semiregular detachments—such as Commissar for Military Affairs Tibor Szamuely's bodyguards, known as the Lenin Boys and commanded by József Cserny—and became known as the *Red Terror*. Of those arrested, an estimated 600 were killed, mostly anti-Communist intellectuals. Former Social Democrats such as József Pogány, relatively moderate supporters of Kun, played a major limiting factor on the reprisals, which would have otherwise been far more extensive.

In late May 1919, Kun attempted to fulfill his promise to restore Hungary's borders. The Hungarian Red Army marched northward and reoccupied part of Slovakia. Despite initial military success, however, Kun withdrew his troops about three weeks later when the French threatened to intervene. This concession shook his popular support. Kun then unsuccessfully turned the Hungarian Red Army on the Romanians, who with the help of the French broke through Hungarian lines on 30 July, occupied Budapest, and ousted Kun's Soviet Republic on 1 August 1919. On 6 August, Kun fled to Vienna and then made his way to the Russian Soviet Federative Socialist Republic (precursor to the Union of Soviet Socialist Republics), where he was welcomed back. He settled and worked in the Soviet Union as a functionary in the Communist International bureaucracy as the head of the Crimean Revolutionary Committee from 1920. He was an organizer and an active participant of the Red Terror in Crimea (1920–1921) but was later executed during Stalin's Great Purge of foreign Communists in the late 1930s.

The short-lived Hungarian Soviet Republic precipitated the formation of the intensely anti-communist movement under Vice Admiral

Miklós Horthy de Nagybanya (1868–1957) and his National Army (*Nemzeti Hadsereg*). Admiral Horthy led the counterrevolutionaries and their government from the southern city of Szeged and entered Budapest with the help of Romanian soldiers in November 1919. In January 1920, Hungarian men and women cast the first secret ballots in the country's political history and elected a large counterrevolutionary and agrarian majority to a unicameral parliament. Two main political parties emerged: Social Conservative Christian National Union and the Independent Smallholders' Party, which advocated land reform. On 1 March 1920, the parliament annulled both the Pragmatic Sanction of 1723 and the Compromise of 1867, and it restored the Hungarian monarchy but postponed choosing a king until civil disorder had subsided. Meanwhile the same day, the Hungarian Parliament elected Miklós Horthy regent and empowered him, among other things, to appoint Hungary's prime minister, veto legislation, convene or dissolve the parliament, and command the armed forces.

Hungary's forced signing of the Treaty of Trianon on 4 June 1920, ratified the country's dismemberment, limited the size of its armed forces, and required reparations payments. The territorial provisions of the treaty, which ensured continued discord between Hungary and its neighbors, required the Hungarians to surrender more than two-thirds of their prewar lands. Romania acquired Transylvania; Yugoslavia gained Croatia, Slavonia, and Vojvodina; Slovakia (known for nearly a millennium as the Hungarian highlands) became a part of Czechoslovakia; and Austria also acquired a small piece of pre-war Hungarian territory. Hungary also lost about sixty percent of its pre-war population, and about one-third of the ten million ethnic Hungarians found themselves outside the diminished homeland.

The new international borders separated Hungary's industrial base from its sources of raw materials and its former markets for agricultural and industrial products. These new circumstances forced Hungary to become a trading nation. Hungary lost eighty-four percent of its timber resources, forty-three percent of its arable land, and eighty-three percent of its iron ore. Because most of the country's prewar industry was concentrated near Budapest, Hungary retained about fifty-one percent of its industrial population, fifty-six percent of its industry, eighty-two percent of its heavy industry, and seventy percent of its banks.

At the end of the First Word War, anti-Semitism became an element of the competition between the various Hungarian elites. Prior to the First World War, social roles in Hungary had been very distinct: the Christian middle classes had sent their sons to work for the state or for local government offices, while the Jewish middle classes had sent their sons to work in non-state-controlled sectors. Among market-controlled professions, the ratio of middle-class Jews was very high. Nationally, Jews comprised forty-two percent of all journalists, and in Budapest the ratio was forty-eight percent. Jews also accounted for fifty-three percent of Hungary's commercial executives, and sixty-four percent in Budapest. Moreover, forty-five percent of lawyers and forty-three percent of legal staff were Jewish. On the other hand, the Christian middle classes were over-represented amongst public officials. After the 1920 Treaty of Trianon, which greatly reduced Hungary's territory, the country needed far fewer public officials. This meant that the Christian middle classes were obliged to secure positions outside state-controlled sectors. When they could not obtain work in the commercial market, either because they lacked useful skills or because the commercial market was saturated with Jews, the Christian middle classes would invariably blame their bad luck on Jews.

The Treaty of Trianon was followed by the mass migration into Hungary of middle-class Hungarian speakers from the successor states, resulting in stiff competition for positions and jobs. Against this backdrop of increased competition, the Christian middle classes turned to the executive power for assistance in their struggle against the Jews. Nevertheless, the increased level of competition was not enough to persuade the Hungarian middle classes—so proud of their *Corpus Iuris*, the symbol of their adherence to Europe—to transform the Hungarian legislative into a means of violently suppressing the Jews. Nationalist public opinion began to argue that Liberalism, radicalism, and Social Democracy—all of which it perceived as manifestations of "Jewish cosmopolitism"—were responsible for the collapse of the historical kingdom of Hungary. "National sentiment," which had been a natural associate of the neo-Liberalism of the nineteenth century, became locked in a conflict with "liberal sentiment," a natural associate of classical Liberalism. In the end, the middle classes chose sectarian Nationalism rather than classical Liberalism, discarding the old principles of equality and human rights and giving the green light to discrimination and restrictions against Jews. Although it was evidently the extreme wing rather than the political center that gave the concrete impetus to the adoption of the *Numerus Clausus* Act of 1920 (Law No. XXV), nevertheless without this "state of competition" and the "contradiction between Nationalism and Liberalism," the country's elite might never have been willing to tolerate anti-Semitism in the form of a parliamentary act.

These developments would contribute to a growing anti-Semitism in Hungary that would ultimately produce tragic consequences in the 1940s.

On 19 July 1920, Regent Horthy appointed reactionary Transylvanian nobleman and former Minister of Foreign Affairs Count Pál János Ede Teleki de Szék (1879–1941, from a noble family from Alsótelek in Transylvania) as Prime Minister of the newly re-established Kingdom of Hungary. Teleki's sectarian Nationalist government nearly immediately passed the *Numerus Clausus* Act on 22 September 1920. The law formally placed limits on the number of minority students at universities, legalized corporal punishment, and, to quiet rural discontent, took initial steps toward fulfilling a promise of major land reform by dividing about 385,000 hectares from the largest estates into small holdings. Though the text of the law did not use the term Jew, it was nearly the only group overrepresented in higher education. The policy is often seen as the first anti-Jewish Public Act of twentieth century Europe. Its aim was to restrict the number of Jews in higher education to six percent, which was their proportion in Hungary at that time. Before the First World War, the percentage of Jews among university students was around twenty-five percent, and by 1918 reached thirty-six percent.

In retaliation for Kun's *Red Terror*, responsible for up to 600 deaths, reactionary military units of the counterrevolutionary government exacted revenge in a two-year wave of violent repression later known as the *White Terror*. These reprisals were organized and carried out by sectarian Nationalist officer detachments of Horthy's National Army, particularly Baron Maj. Pál Prónay de Tótpróna et Blatnicza (1874–1946), Count Capt. Gyula Ostenburg-Moravek (1884–1944), and Lt. Iván Héjjas (1890–1950). Horthy's foreknowledge and involvement in the *White Terror* remains controversial. The degree of Horthy's responsibility for the excesses of one of the most zealous of the reactionary leaders, Maj. Prónay, is disputed. On several occasions, Horthy reached out to stop Prónay from a particularly intense burst of anti-Jewish cruelty, and the Jews of Pest went on record absolving Horthy of the *White Terror* as early as autumn 1919, when they released a statement disavowing the Kun revolution and blaming the terror on a few rogue units within the National Army. Horthy has never been found to have personally engaged in *White Terror* atrocities. But biographer Thomas L. Sakmyster concluded that he "tacitly supported the right-wing officer detachments" who carried out the terror; Horthy called them "my best men" who helped restore stability to Hungary.

The aims of the reactionary officers' junta were revealed by reports published in Vienna newspapers concerning a meeting held in the War Office in Budapest that was attended by the Minister of War, General Vitéz Károly Soós de Bádok (1869–1953), General Béla Berzeviczy von Berzevicze und Kakas-Lomnitz (1870–1922), and Lt. General in reserve Adalbert Dani von Gyarmata und Magyar-Cséke (1868–April 1920), Regent Horthy's *aide-de-camp* László Magasházy (1879–1959), several General Staff officers, the commanders of the various White Guard terror detachments previously mentioned, and by the zealously racist, Nationalistic President of the Hungarian National Defense Association (*Magyar Országos Véderő Egylet*) and President of the Association of Awakening Hungarians (*Ébredő Magyarok Egyesűlete*), the future prime minister Capt. Gyula Gömbös de Jákfa (1886–1936). Captain Gömbös was a protégé of Lajos Méhely (1862–1953), the notorious Darwinian eugenicist and Hungarian racial hygienist (*fajvédők*) recognized as a visionary guru by the various associations and societies of the Hungarian Race Protection movement (*Magyar Tudományos Fajvédő Egyesület*, *Magyar Fajmentő Misszió*). During this meeting, a resolution was presented by Count Capt. Ostenburg-Moravek that called for the establishment of a military dictatorship, and recommended, as preliminary measures, the seizure of the railroad terminals, post and telegraph offices and telephone exchanges, disarmament of the police, confiscation of all property owned by Jews, destruction of the plants of liberal and Jew-owned newspapers, and the general massacre of all radicals, Socialists, and Jews ("Hungary and Her Neighbors" 1920, 1067–8).

The victims of the *White Terror* were primarily Communists, Social Democrats, and Jews. Most Hungarian Jews were not supporters of the Bolsheviks, but a majority of the leadership of the Hungarian Soviet Republic was comprised of young Jewish intellectuals, and anger over the Communist revolution easily translated into anti-Semitic hostility. In 1920 and 1921, internal chaos afflicted Hungary. Under Prime Minister Teleki, the *White Terror* continued unabatedly to plague Jews, Socialists, and Liberals. Unemployment and inflation soared, and penniless Hungarian refugees poured across the border from neighboring countries burdening the floundering Hungarian economy. The government offered the population little succor. Ultimately, tens of thousands were imprisoned, up to 5,000 were murdered, and nearly 100,000 people were forced to leave the country, most of them Socialists, intellectuals, and middle-class Jews.

In March and October 1921, Horthy thwarted two attempts by Austrian Emperor Charles I (1887–1922) to regain the Hungarian throne. After the first failed attempt, Teleki's government resigned on 14 April 1921. King Charles' attempted return split parties between monarchists who favored a Habsburg restoration and sectarian Nationalist radicals who supported coronation of a Hungarian king. Count István Bethlen de Bethlen (1874–1946), a nonaffiliated Nationalist member of the parliament, took advantage of this rift by convincing members of the Christian National Union who opposed Charles' re-enthronement to merge with the Smallholders' Party and form a new Party of Unity with Bethlen as its leader. Horthy then appointed Bethlen Prime Minister.

After Maj. Prónay's men were implicated in the murder of a Budapest policeman in November 1920, his superiors' permissiveness declined sharply. The following summer, Prónay was put on trial for extorting a wealthy Jewish politician, and for "insulting the President of the Parliament" by trying to cover up the extortion. Found guilty on both charges, Prónay was now a liability and an embarrassment. His command was revoked, and he was denounced as a common criminal on the floor of the Hungarian parliament.

After serving short sentences, Prónay tried to convince Horthy to restore his battalion command. The regent turned him down. Furious with his former patron, whom he now condemned as a useless windbag, Prónay moved to the Austrian border, where he continued his atrocities, and proclaimed himself Supreme Leader of a buffer state (the Banat of Leitha). Finally, in the fall of 1921, Prónay joined in the second failed attempt to oust Horthy and restore the Habsburg Charles I to the throne. Horthy at last permanently severed his ties with Prónay.

The Prónay Battalion lingered for a few months longer under the command of a junior officer, but the government officially dissolved the unit in January 1922 and expelled its members from the army. Prónay entered politics as a member of the government's radical Nationalist opposition. In the 1930s, he sought and failed to emulate the Nazis by generating a Hungarian Fascist mass movement. In 1932, he was charged with incitement, sentenced to six months in prison and stripped of his rank of lieutenant colonel.

In October 1944, as Budapest fell under siege by the Soviet Red Army and descended into chaos at the end of the Second World War, sixty-nine-year-old Prónay assembled a death squad and resumed his hunt for the old objects of his hatred, Hungarian Jews. He vanished in the war's final weeks and was formerly believed to have fallen during the siege of Budapest. Declassification of the Soviet archives revealed that Prónay was captured on 20 March 1945, held as a prisoner of war, sentenced by the Soviet authorities to twenty-years forced labor on charges of sabotage and espionage, and died in the *gulag* in 1947–48.

As Prime Minister, Bethlen dominated Hungarian politics between 1921 and 1931. He fashioned a political machine by amending the electoral law, eliminating peasants from the Party of Unity, providing jobs in the bureaucracy to his supporters, and manipulating elections in rural areas. Bethlen restored order to the country by giving the radical counterrevolutionaries payoffs and government jobs in exchange for ceasing their campaign of terror against Jews and Liberals. In 1921, Bethlen made a deal with the Social Democrats and trade unions, agreeing, among other things, to legalize their activities and free political prisoners in return for their pledge to refrain from spreading anti-Hungarian propaganda, calling political strikes, and organizing the peasantry. In May 1922, the Party of Unity captured a large parliamentary majority. Emperor Charles's death in October 1921 promoted to the top of Hungary's political agenda the revision of the Treaty of Trianon. Bethlen's strategy to win approval for the treaty's revision was first to strengthen his country's economy and then to build relations with stronger nations that could facilitate Hungary's goals. Revision of the treaty had such a broad backing in Hungary that Bethlen used it, at least in part, to deflect criticism of his failing economic, social, and political policies. However, in the end Bethlen's only foreign policy successes were entry into the League of Nations in 1922 and a treaty of friendship with Italy in 1927, which had little immediate impact.

When Bethlen took office, the government was all but bankrupt. Tax revenues were so paltry that he turned to domestic gold and foreign-currency reserves to meet about half of the 1921–1922 budget and almost eighty percent of the 1922–1923 budget. To improve his country's economic circumstances, Bethlen undertook development of industry. He imposed tariffs on finished goods and earmarked the revenues to subsidize new industries. Bethlen squeezed the agricultural sector to increase cereal exports, which generated foreign currency to pay for imports critical to the industrial sector. Further compounding Hungary's problems was the fact that of its four neighbors, three (Czechoslovakia, Romania, and Yugoslavia) were enemies and kept troops stationed on their borders at all times, even though Hungary had an army of only 20,000 men. The fourth, Austria, was a struggling nation and little more than an economic competitor.

In 1924, after the *White Terror* had waned and Hungary had gained admission to the League of Nations, the Bethlen government was able to borrow fifty million U.S. dollars from the League, which in order to protect its investment placed the country in effective receivership, even placing an American banker, Jeremiah Smith, in charge of the country's finances. Hungary's outcast status had prevented it from obtaining any foreign aid in the immediate postwar period, but by the middle of the 1920s, the British decided to extend the hand of friendship to the losers of World War I. Hungary also obtained sympathy from the United States and Mussolini's Italy. Meanwhile, France's and Hungary's neighbors vigorously objected.

By the late 1920s, Bethlen's policies had brought some order to the economy. The number of factories increased by about sixty-six percent, inflation subsided, and the national income climbed twenty percent. However, the apparent stability was supported by a rickety framework of constantly revolving foreign credits and high world grain prices; therefore, Hungary remained undeveloped in comparison with the wealthier Western European countries, as most of the foreign loans went for non-productive purposes such as graft, expanding bureaucracy, and monumental public works projects. Agricultural products were subject to unstable prices and the vagaries of the weather. Furthermore, tariffs were commonplace in America and Europe during the 1920s, which frequently made it difficult to export. Hungary was no exception and liberally employed trade barriers to protect its manufacturing base. Exports also had to pass through Hungary's neighbors to reach the West, and as already noted, all but one was hostile.

Despite economic progress, workers' standard of living remained poor. Consequently, the working class never gave Bethlen its political support. The labor movement had never developed in pre-World War I Hungary the way it did in Austria, and the Horthy government remained resolutely opposed to organized labor or social reforms. There was no minimum wage or any sort of labor laws in Hungary until shortly before the start of the Second World War, and wages were further undercut by peasants flocking into Budapest who were willing to work for a pittance. On the whole, workers fared more poorly in interbellum Hungary then they had before the First World War. The peasants were even worse off than the working class. In the 1920s, about sixty percent of the peasants were either landless or were cultivating plots too small to provide a decent living. Real wages for agricultural workers remained below prewar levels, and the peasants had practically no political voice. Moreover, once Bethlen had consolidated his power, he ignored calls for land reform. The industrial sector failed to expand fast enough to provide jobs for all the peasants and university graduates seeking work. Most peasants lingered in the villages, and in the 1930s Hungarians in rural areas were extremely dissatisfied. Hungary's foreign debt ballooned as Bethlen expanded the bureaucracy to absorb the university graduates who, if left idle, might have threatened civil order. This was because Hungary, like the rest of Eastern Europe, had an educational system primarily focused on the liberal arts and law rather than science, engineering, or other practical disciplines that might have helped the country's development.

Following the armistice, disarmed former students returned to the university from the trenches *en masse*, creating an impossible situation for the institutions that had effectively shuttered. Consequently, Berthold decided to remain in the army for as long as he could. The so-called Aster (or Chrysanthemum) Revolution of 1919 under Count Mihály Károlyi, which led to the foundation of the short-lived Social Democratic First Hungarian People's Republic, also caused severe problems, as did the brief proletarian Communist dictatorship which followed soon thereafter, and which almost immediately withdrew the university's autonomy and intruded deeply into its internal affairs. This provided a small taste of the methods the Communist dictatorship would employ some thirty years later.

The war, the Communist experiment, the Romanian occupation of Budapest, the truncation of the country through the Treaty of Trianon, the Horthy-Teleki reign of terror, and the general political uncertainty gave rise to extremely serious economic and social tensions, which had an impact on the university as well. Fraternal societies began to form with the participation of the veteran students, anti-Semitic riots broke out, and the university, for the first time in its history, had to limit the number of students that could be admitted.

Georgina is Born

THE WORSENING CONDITIONS IN HUNGARY CLEARLY INFLUENCED THE stability of the Reichsfeld household in Budapest and was the final chapter in Berthold's hopes of returning to the university and finishing his medical degree. Instead of a doctorate in medicine, Berthold Reichsfeld was blessed and burdened with a child on 16 December 1920—Györgyi (pronounced "Dyurdy"; known as Jirka—pronounced "Yirka"—in Slavic languages and Georgina in English).

Despite the unstable and threatening times, Georgina's eight years in Budapest were relatively typical for a young girl living in blissful ignorance and protected from the turmoil that surrounded her. The Reichsfelds were as assimilated as a Jew could be and the gold Star of David was not yet in vogue, so, Georgina freely enjoyed all that Budapest and her secular primary school had to offer girls of her age.

Georgina was enrolled in ballet and theater at the Budapest Royal Orpheum Theater (on Elizabeth Boulevard just down the street from the infamous Grand Hotel Royal) where she pantomimed Harlequin at the age of seven-years. A beautiful lakeside resort was not far from Budapest at Lake Balaton. Her parents often took Georgina to Lake Balaton for holiday. Her cousin Helena Gorábor (two years her senior) lived a three-hour drive north in the village of Hradište pod Vrátnom (100 km northeast of Bratislava). When Berthold's older sister Janka with husband Bernát Gorábor and daughter Hela would visit her brother and his family in Budapest, they would often go to Lake Balaton for holiday. Likewise, when Berthold took his family to visit his sister Janka in Slovakia, Georgina would enjoy the blissful and intriguing life in the country village of Hradište pod Vrátnom with Hela. The two young cousins were like sisters.

Only his former officer's position and service in the Austro-Hungarian Army during the First World War provided a modicum of protection during the *Red* and *White Terror*. However, during the rule of the Teleki government he faced increasing pressure to denounce his Czechoslovak citizenship and adopt Hungarian citizenship. He refused and rebuffed this pressure. Consequently, he was unemployed for the most part.

In 1928, one year before the Great Depression, the Reichsfelds concluded they needed to leave Hungary and move to the more stable and Democratic Czechoslovakia—the homeland of Berthold's modern ancestors—where they could settle in Bratislava. However, before moving to Bratislava permanently, they temporarily lived with Berthold's older sister Johanna and her family, the Gorábers, in the village of Hradište pod Vrátnom (100 km northeast of Bratislava and 16 km southeast of Senica where Berthold's sister Frida lived with her husband Moritz Feldbauer). Berthold's widowed father Leopold was also living with the Gorábers at the time. In Hradište pod Vrátnom, Georgina enrolled in the village primary school exchanging her native Hungarian for Slovak. The Reichsfelds remained in Hradište pod Vrátnom until the end of the academic year in 1929 when they moved to Bratislava. The ambitions of her parents demanded that their daughter receive a better education than they felt the Slovak schools could offer. And so, before Georgina could learn to speak fluently the language of her adopted country, she was sent to a summer language camp near Vienna to acquire a working knowledge of German.

New Life in Bratislava

ONCE SETTLED IN BRATISLAVA, BERTHOLD'S EMPLOYMENT opportunities improved. He trained for and took a position as an insurance agent with the Bratislava branch of the Italian insurance company Riunione Adriatica di Sicurtà. Living in Bratislava also presented Berthold the opportunity to explore resuming his medical studies. He enrolled in gross anatomy courses with the Faculty of Medicine at Comenius University (Lekárska fakulta Univerzity Komenského) located at Sasinkova Street No. 2—established only ten years earlier on 21 September 1919, and named in November 1919 after the Moravian world-renowned "father of modern education" Jan Amos Komenský (1592–1670, Latin: *Iohannes Amos Comenius*). As a preteen, Georgina would sometimes accompany her father to his cadaver dissection sessions. Unfortunately for the Reichsfelds, economic and political constraints forced Berthold to permanently relinquish his dream of becoming a physician.

Berthold Reichsfeld could not be considered anything but a man with an imposing physique—not corpulent or massive, yet large-boned and sturdy. His stature impressed those who met him, except when he walked. He walked with shoulders dropped and head bent forward. Blue, inquisitive eyes revealed a determined man, a man who distrusted others, a man who could be merciless if circumstances forced him to revenge his injured pride. Though his nose dominated his face, it was Berthold's squared chin which betrayed his stubborn nature. Black hair, now streaked with gray, grew thick and straight from his rather highbrow. He always kept his hair combed back smoothly, with frequent applications of tap water in an attempt to cool his head, which produced sufficient perspiration from constantly moving about like a man who was late for an important engagement.

Reichsfeld was an excellent mathematician, and generally intelligent. He spoke Slovak, German, and Hungarian fluently. His consistency and rational thinking characterized all his actions. Given to over-deliberation, certainly, due in no small part to his life's experiences, Berthold thoroughly analyzed each situation that confronted him. Friends respected him because he was very reliable and always kept his word. At the same time, he could not tolerate insincerity or broken promises. This intolerance caused many arguments and brought lawsuits. Berthold would sue people for any slight deviation from a mutually consented agreement, even though it was evident he had no chance of winning. Since he hated to be a loser, he never gave up easily, but fought as long as he could. Since he rarely trusted anyone, he never failed to keep an ace up his sleeve.

Paradoxically, Reichsfeld proudly displayed a sign in his bedroom reading, "Jesus, not Caesar." Yet, he found it hard to forgive and easy to punish his enemy. Not even his daughter escaped his tyranny. If she violated his edicts, he could be unsympathetically cruel. But as a man of extremes, he could shower her with love and attention, particularly when she followed his dictates.

Despite all his imperfections, Berthold Reichsfeld was very concerned about the welfare of his family. Each time his luck increased as an insurance agent, he would not hesitate to spend the extra money on his wife and daughter. If this luck diminished, he would only work that much harder to find another way of getting enough money to make his family happy. In his wife's eyes, Berthold was too generous. She exerted her influence to curb this passion.

Helena Reichsfeld was a small, rather plump woman, with a pleasant face. Deep brown eyes and chestnut hair complemented her olive skin. In manner of dress, she always showed good taste and conservative style. This neat appearance carried over into her home, which was never disorderly. She could be considered a hard-working and spotless housekeeper. The presence of a live-in maid was more a status symbol of the European middle-class woman than a necessity in their moderate-sized apartment.

From the time she was a young girl, she had only one ambition—to run her own business. Before the war her parents owned and managed a bakery in Budapest with some large accounts like the Hungarian Army, and she had not forgotten it or the security that a successful merchant's life provided. Helena was by nature more interested in materialism than she was in education and culture. It was partly her fault that her husband did not promptly return to medical school and finish his studies after returning home from serving in World War I. Although the chances of realizing this in Budapest after the Great War were slim, given the prevailing revolutionary chaos and anti-Semitism, Berthold had the choice of continuing his medical studies at Charles University in Prague or the University of Vienna. However, the funding his father was able to provide for his education before the Great War was no longer the same after the war. By her own lack of academic talent, Helena Reichsfeld never really learned either the Czech or

Slovak language with any degree of fluency, preferring to speak only Hungarian, even after thirty years in her adopted country. Her German was as poor as her Slovak.

The relationship between mother and daughter was never very close. Despite the fact that Helena was only twenty-years old when Georgina was born, the generational differences between them resulted in their failure to understand one another. In fact, Helena Reichsfeld seemed unsuited for her role as a mother and often exhibited a jealous reaction to her husband's attention to his own child. More self-centered than she had a right to be as a mother, she did little or nothing to prepare Georgina for marriage, and not much more for adult life in general. She viewed men with a jaundiced eye and constantly warned her daughter not to let any man take advantage of her. Helena was a contradiction, since she did not want to lose her child and at the same time, she seemed only interested that Georgina make an economically secure marriage. Had Peter Vlčko not come along, she might have sacrificed her daughter to someone financially much better situated than they, even if he were twenty years Georgina's senior.

Helena Reichsfeld's social etiquette was always polite and gracious, if sometimes exaggerated. Moreover, she was addicted to bestowing flattery on everyone she met, so that one could never be certain when she was sincere and when she was merely observing the rules of courtesy. She definitely loved her husband. But she prodded him every time she felt he was not aggressive enough to take advantage of opportunities which came their way. She was more pushy than nagging and had an inordinate need to see him produce. His strong will and stubbornness conflicted often with her dominating personality, and many serious arguments disturbed their marriage. It was her fear of his temper that restrained her from going too far. If she had any legitimate fears, they were the same ones all Jews felt during those terrible years of the Thirties and Forties in Europe's crucible.

As a pre-adolescent, Georgina participated in Sokol. Sokol was and continues to be a Czechoslovak cultural and gymnastics organization founded in Prague in 1862 by Miroslav Tyrš and Jindřich Fügner. It is based upon the principle of "a strong mind in a sound body." Through lectures, discussions, and group outings, Sokol provides what Tyrš viewed as physical, moral, and intellectual training for the nation. This training extended to men of all ages and classes, and eventually to women and children.

Georgina loved dogs and adopted a fox terrier puppy that she raised and enjoyed for years. She also loved the water. With her schoolmates and occasionally her cousin Hela, Georgina would spend time across the Danube River in the Bratislava suburb of Petržalka where the newly opened (1928) Lido gravel and river beach was located just east (downstream) of the *Štefánikov most* (Štefánik's Bridge).*

In Bratislava, Georgina continued her elementary education in a German school. Two years at the German elementary school enabled her at the age of ten-years (autumn 1931) to test for and be accepted to the 1931–1932 academic year at *Deutsches Staatsrealgymnasium* (now known as *Deutsche Schule Bratislava*) at the intersection of Palasády and Kuzmányho streets—a fifteen-minute walk from her parents' apartment on Hviezdoslavovo námestie[1] near the Danube River. Georgina, however, most often took the electric tram from Carlton Hotel to and from school each day. Because of Bratislava's close geographical and historical proximity to Austria and Hungary, the citizenry spoke three languages, Slovak (Bratislavans spoke a mix of Czech and Slovak at the time), Hungarian, and German. The Jewish population,† which controlled most of the city's business, favored a knowledge of all three languages. By 1939, the year Georgina graduated from *gymnázium*, she had mastered German, French, and Latin, and had working knowledge of Czechoslovak and Hungarian.

Her summer vacations were usually spent at Hradište pod Vrátnom with her Aunt Janka (Berthold's older sister), Uncle Bernát Goráber, and her two cousins Hela and Józef. She dearly loved the little village, located in a deep valley in the western Carpathian Mountains, just west of Trnava. Tall granite peaks enclosed the rich, moist, green valley. The meadows and pastures surrounding the village reached out in all directions to meet forests of beech, oak, and pine that climbed the mountain slopes. Down the side of one mountain crawled a clear, cold, rock-strewn brook, which crossed the meadows and passed through the village on its way southward. In the fresh,

---

* *Štefánikov most* (*Franz-Joseph Brücke* / *Ferencz József-híd* / *Most Františka Jozefa* [Franz-Joseph Bridge; 1891–1918], *Štefánikov most* [Štefánik's Bridge; 1918–1945], *Most Červenej armády* [Red Army Bridge; 1945–1990], *Starý most* [Old Bridge; 1990–2013]). The 460-meter-long (1,510 ft) bridge included a wooden pathway for pedestrians and a two-lane road and railway track, connecting the historic old city of Bratislava with the newer region Petržalka south of the old city. In 2013, the bridge was permanently closed for demolition in 2014. A new bridge was built to replace the Old Bridge and opened to traffic in 2016.

† In the early 1920s there were approximately 11,000 Jews in Bratislava: 3,000 Neolog and 8,000 Orthodox. In the 1930s there were 14,882 Jews in the city (12% of the total population).

vibrant air, half-naked boys gathered beside the stream to fish for trout or hunt for crabs that lay hidden among the willow tree roots in the shadowy waters. Patches of mountain flowers colored the fields and mingled with the verdant grass. Young girls often wandered happily in the warm summer sun across these fields, collecting fragrant bouquets of daisies, bluebells, and Forget-Me-Nots (*Vergissmeinnicht*). Sometimes, they would stop to rest on the grass and weave lovely garlands of flowers for their heads. Or, they would stretch out on the cool, damp ground and lazily watch the clouds drift by. In this carefree setting Georgina passed her summer holidays, content with her surroundings. Her cousin, Hela, and her aunt and uncle were Georgina's friends, and she was happy here. Hradište pod Vrátnom was her second home.

The Gorábers owned and managed the only general store in the village. It provided the village farmers with whatever necessities, and a few luxuries as well, they could not themselves provide on their small farms. It was also a collection agency for local handicraft work that her aunt bought from the village women and sold throughout Europe and even in America. Georgina loved to sell candy and pretty ribbons from behind the counter during those hours when she wasn't off in the meadows or down at the stables with the farmers at milking time. Best of all for Georgina, the village store was a social center, where the farmers would gather after the day's work had ended. The men and women would drop by to visit with friends and exchange the news of the day. Girls and boys would sit out on the stairs at the entrance to the store and talk and giggle and sing. Boys strutted in manly fashion before innocent girls who blushed and whispered secretly, for they knew the boys sought to impress them. Sometimes the village youth teased Georgina because she was a city girl who never tired of catching frogs and mice for pets. She would bathe her captives, feed them generously, give them abundant love, and then set them free again. These were gentle days which she would remember always.

A Summer to Remember

IN THE SUMMER OF 1936, GEORGINA AND HER PARENTS TRAVELED TO Berlin, Germany along with Georgina's eighteen-year-old cousin Helena Goráber, to attend the XI Olympiad summer games and travel through Europe. They boarded a train in Bratislava and rode through Prague on to Berlin. In Berlin, they had prearranged accommodations with a private family to stay in their home. Months earlier, Berthold discovered at a local railroad station in Bratislava a posted announcement of the availability of some rooms in a private Berlin home. Upon their arrival in Berlin, they took a taxi to the private home where the owners welcomed and hosted them.

During the Berlin Olympics, Georgina and her family witnessed many historic events and visited many historic sites. On several occasions, they saw *Reich* Chancellor Adolf Hitler and his closest associates in the Nazi regime. They witnessed the historic achievements of American Olympic Champion Jesse Owens and other Olympic athletes.

The Reichsfelds remained in Berlin and attended the Olympic events for several days, toured Berlin, and then proceeded on their European vacation, first to Potsdam, Germany, then Warnemünde seaside resort in Rostock, Germany on the Baltic Sea, and finally Copenhagen, Denmark. From Denmark they returned home to Bratislava, Czechoslovakia.

At the time of the Berlin Olympics, few living outside Germany recognized and really understood the gathering storm that was approaching over the horizon of the European continent. However, the signs were clearly evident to the Germans who already by 1936 witnessed the following foretelling political developments in Germany:

1. 30 January 1933: Adolf Hitler named Chancellor of Germany as his National Socialist German Workers' Party (Nazi) assumes control of the German state.
2. 27 February 1933: Arson of the *Reichstag* building (German Parliament) setting the stage for the *Reichstag* Fire Decree suspending of most rights guaranteed under the 1919 Weimar Constitution, allowing the Nazis to arrest Communists and increase police action throughout Germany.
3. 22 March 1933: The *SS* (*Schutzstaffel*) establishes the Dachau Concentration Camp for political prisoners in southern Germany.
4. 1 April 1933: Members of the Nazi Party and its affiliated organizations organize a nationwide boycott of Jewish-owned businesses in Germany.
5. 7 April 1933: The German government issues the Law for the Restoration of the Professional Civil Service (*Gesetz zur Wiederherstellung des Berufsbeamtentums*), which excludes Jews and other political opponents of the Nazis from all civil service positions and disbarment of non-"Aryan" lawyers by 30 September 1933.

6. 25 April 1933: The German government issues the Law against Overcrowding in Schools and Universities, which dramatically limits the number of Jewish students attending public schools to five percent of total student population.
7. 10 May 1933: German university students burn upwards of 25,000 “un-German” books in Berlin’s Opera Square (*Opernplatz*). Some 40,000 people gather to hear *Reich* Propaganda Minister Joseph Goebbels deliver a fiery address: “No to decadence and moral corruption!”
8. 14 July 1933: The German government passes the Law for the Prevention of Offspring with Hereditary Diseases (*Gesetz zur Verhütung erbkranken Nachwuchses*), mandating the forced sterilization of certain individuals with physical and mental disabilities, as well as sterilization of Roma (Gypsies), “asocial elements,” and Afro-Germans.
9. 4 October 1933: The German government passes The Editors Law (*Schriftleitergesetz*) forbidding non-“Aryans” to work in journalism.
10. 24 November 1933: The German government passes the Law against Dangerous Habitual Criminals. The new law allows courts to order the indefinite imprisonment of “habitual criminals” if they deem the person dangerous to society. It also provides for the castration of sex offenders.
11. 2 August 1934: German President Paul von Hindenburg dies. With the support of the German armed forces, Hitler becomes President of Germany. On 19 August 1934, Hitler abolishes the office of President and declares himself *Führer* of the *Deutsches Reich und Volk*, in addition to his position as Chancellor. In this expanded capacity, Hitler now becomes the absolute dictator of Germany; there are no legal or constitutional limits to his authority.
12. 15 September 1935: The *Reichstag* passes the Nuremberg Race Laws laying the foundation for and legalizing much of what was to engross most of Europe in the 1940s and concluding with the Final Solution to the Jewish Question (*die Endlösung der Judenfrage*).
13. June 1936: The *SS* establishes the Sachsenhausen concentration camp in Oranienberg (35 km north of Berlin).

The 1936 Olympic Games (both the IV Olympic Winter Games in Garmisch-Partenkirchen, Germany and the XI Olympic Summer Games in Berlin) were a propaganda success for the Nazi government, as German officials made every effort to portray Germany as a respectable member of the international community. They removed anti-Jewish signs from public display and restrained anti-Jewish activities. In response to pressure from foreign Olympic delegations, Germany also included one part-Jew, the fencer Helene Mayer, on its Olympic team. Germany also lifted anti-homosexuality laws for foreign visitors for the duration of both games. Although, in hindsight it was bold of the Reichsfelds to visit Germany in August 1936, like many Jews of the time, they failed to grasp the growing danger in their midst.

Georgina and her family witnessed many historical events and places in Berlin during the summer Games. An innovation in 1936 was the Olympic torch relay, lit by the rays of the sun at Olympia in Greece and carried by over 3,000 relay runners to the *Olympiastadion* in Berlin. In all, the torch was transported over 3,187 kilometers by 3,331 runners in twelve days and eleven nights from Greece to Berlin. It is a tradition that has continued at every subsequent Olympic Games. The last of the relay runners lit the Olympic cauldrons in central Berlin and the Olympic Stadium, both of which Georgina and her family visited and photographed. The lighting of the two cauldrons on *Unter den Linden* Boulevard at twelve noon on the opening day of the games by twenty-six-year-old 400-meter runner Siegfried Eifrig remains an iconic event of the Games. Eifrig sprinted 1,500 meters east on *Unter den Linden* from in front of the Soviet Embassy (Nos. 63–65 at the southeast corner of *Wilhelmstraße* and *Unter den Linden*), past the equestrian statue of Frederick the Great, crossing the Spree River over the *Schlossbrücke* bridge, turning north into *Lustgarten* where he lit the cauldron in front of the *Altes Musuem* and a packed crowd of tens of thousands. He then proceeded to light the cauldron on *Unter den Linden* Boulevard directly opposite *Lustgarten* and in front of the *Stadtschloss*.

The flame at *Lustgarten* served as the starting point for the final twelve and one-half kilometer relay to *Olympiastadion* for the opening ceremonies four hours later at 1600 hours. The final relay team lit a torch in the cauldron in *Lustgarten* and began their trek westward down *Unter den Linden* Boulevard (north traffic lane), past the statue of Frederick the Great, under the Brandenburg Gate, through *Hindenburg Platz*, *Charlottenburger Chaussee*, *Bismarckstraße*, *Kaiserdamm*, *Adolf Hitler Platz* (now *Theodor Heuss Platz*), *Reichsstraße*, *Olympische Straße*, *Olympischer Platz* (north traffic lane), to the eastern Olympic Gate. Fritz Schilgen, a three-time 1500-meter champion, awaited at the eastern Olympic Gate to carry the Olympic Torch the final 500 meters. As the last strains of Strauss's composition faded in the stadium, cheers were heard from outside when the torch bearer passed the burning torch to Schilgen. He then proceeded between the two stone pillars at the eastern gate on to the entrance to *Olympiastadion* where he paused for a moment at the gap at the top of the stairs as the crowd gasped and then fell silent. The athletes of all participating nations filled the field below with the German delegation in all white dress next to the U.S. delegation in blue blazers and white trousers directly in front of Schilgen. To the Nazi salute by the majority of the audience, Schilgen descended the eastern steps into the arena, ran 200 meters counterclockwise along the southern running track to the western gate where he climbed the Marathon Steps to light the Olympic Cauldron to signify the formal commencement of the XI Olympiad. The Reichsfelds' seats on this occasion were on the north edge of the west gate below the Olympic Cauldron down close to the field. This was the very same gate the Reichsfelds witnessed only a few feet away the entrance and descent down the Marathon Steps of Count Henri de Baillet-Latour (President of the International Olympic Committee), walking next to *Reich* Chancellor Adolf Hitler along with Dr. Theodor Lewald (Ceremonial President of German Olympic Organizing Committee and Secretary of IOC), walking to the right of and slightly behind Hitler.

Over the course of the Games, Georgina and her family witnessed the historic achievements of Jesse Owens on the field. She remembers it to the day of this writing, as it was the first time that she had ever laid eyes on a Negro.

Jesse Owens won the gold in the long jump with a new Olympic record of 26 feet 5 ¼ inches. In addition to the gold medals won for the infamous 100-meter dash (tying the world record with 10.3 seconds) and the long jump, Jesse Owens won two more gold medals at the Berlin games for the 200-meter dash with a new Olympic record of 20.7 seconds and the 400-meter relay (first leg) with a new Olympic and world record of 39.8 seconds.

The long jump on 4 August was Germany's Lutz Long's first event against Owens, and Long met his expectations by setting an Olympic record during the preliminary round. In contrast, Owens fouled on his first two jumps. While speaking with Long's son Kai decades later during a return visit to Berlin in 1964, Owens admitted that during qualifying rounds of the long jump, Lutz approached him and told him to try to jump from a spot several inches behind the take-off board to safely qualify for the finals. Owens went on to win the gold medal in the long jump with 8.06 meters while besting Long's own record of 7.87 meters. Long won the silver medal for second place and was the first to congratulate Owens: they posed together for photos and walked arm-in-arm to the dressing room. Owens said in 1964, "It took a lot of courage for him to befriend me in front of Hitler . . . You can melt down all the medals and cups I have, and they wouldn't be a plating on the twenty-four-karat friendship that I felt for Luz Long at that moment." Long's competition with Owens is recorded in Leni Riefenstahl's infamous documentary *Olympia – Fest der Völker*.

Long served in the Wehrmacht during World War II. During the Allied invasion of Sicily, Long was killed in action on 14 July 1943. He was survived by two sons, Kai-Heinrich and Wolfgang. Wolfgang died at 9-months old. Long and Owens corresponded after 1936. In his last letter, Long wrote to Owens and asked him to contact his son after the war and tell him about his father and "what times were like when we were not separated by war. I am saying—tell him how things can be between men on this earth." After the war, Owens travelled to Germany to meet Kai Long, who is seen with Owens in the 1966 documentary *Jesse Owens Returns to Berlin*, where he is in conversation with Owens in the Berlin Olympic Stadium. Owens later served as Kai Long's best man at his wedding.

Between attending Olympic events, Georgina and her family toured throughout central Berlin on foot to photograph the historic architecture and statuary, much of which was destroyed during the Allied bombardment beginning in 1943 and the Russian siege of Berlin in May 1945. *Unter den Linden Straße* was and remains one of Europe's most famous boulevards in historic *Mitte* Berlin. Composer Johann Strauss III wrote the waltz "*Unter den Linden*" in 1900 commemorating the cultural importance of this boulevard. Running from the City Palace (*Stadtschloss*) to Brandenburg Gate, it is named after the linden trees that have lined the pedestrian mall on the median and the two broad carriageways since 1647. The avenue links numerous historic Berlin sights, landmarks, and river tours. Since 1937, the numbering of the properties on the boulevard has started on the east end with the *Zeuhaus* just west of the *Schlossbrücke* (Palace Bridge), which connects *Unter den Linden* with the *Lustgarten* and Museum Island. In the course of the building of the north-south tunnel for the rapid-transit train in 1934–35, most of the linden trees were cut down and during the last days of World War II the remaining trees were destroyed or cut down for firewood. The present-day linden trees were replanted in the 1950s.

Just to the south of the statue of Frederick the Great lied the historic *Altes Palais* (Old Palace), No. 9 on the boulevard, the favorite residence of Emperor Wilhelm I (rebuilt after the war and now the *Alte Bibliothek* of the Humboldt University law faculty). Adjacent to and directly east of the palace lied the *Opernplatz* (now known as *Bebelplatz* after the Socialist politician August Bebel). *Opernplatz*, a public square bordered by the *Staatsoper* (Berlin State Opera House) on the east, *Altes Palais* on the west and by St. Hedwig's Cathedral (the first Catholic church built in Prussia after the Reformation), was where on 10 March 1933, the Nationalist German Student Association hosted the infamous *bücherverbrennung* (book burning) of 25,000 books considered subversive or representing ideologies opposed to Nazism. There, some 40,000 people heard *Reich* Propaganda Minister Joseph Goebbels deliver a fiery address: "No to decadence and moral corruption!" Goebbels enjoined the crowd. "Yes to decency and morality in family and state!"

Further east from the *Altes Palais* on *Unter den Linden* Boulevard is the *Schlossbrücke* (Palace Bridge), which connects *Unter den Linden* with Museum Island (named for the complex of internationally significant museums on the northern half of an island in the Spree River in the central district of Berlin on the UNESCO list of World Heritage Sites). On the north side of *Unter den Linden* just east of the Palace Bridge lied the *Lustgarten* (Palace Garden). The *Lustgarten* is bordered on the east by The Berlin Cathedral (*Berliner Dom*, officially known as the Evangelical Supreme Parish and Collegiate Church) and on the north by the *Altes Museum* (Old Museum). The *Altes Museum* was and remains world-renowned for its extraordinary collection of classical antiquities (Egyptian, Etruscan, Roman, and Greek), many of which the Russians pilfered and transported to Russia via Soviet Trophy Brigades where they are currently on display in museums throughout the country. Among the looted artifacts was the legendary Priam's Treasure from the lost city of Troy discovered by German archeologist Heinrich Schliemann in 1837. During the war, the treasure was removed to a bunker under the Berlin Zoo where it remained until 1945. The treasure was secretly removed to the Soviet Union by the Red Army. During the Cold War, the government of the Soviet Union denied any knowledge of the fate of Priam's Treasure. However, in September 1993, the treasure turned up at the Pushkin Museum in Moscow. The return of items taken from German museums has been arranged in a treaty with Germany but, as of January 2010, is being blocked by museum directors in Russia. They are keeping the looted art, they say, as compensation for the destruction of Russian cities and looting of Russian museums by Nazi Germany in World War II. A 1998 Russian law, the "Federal Law on Cultural Valuables Displaced to the USSR as a Result of the Second World War and Located on the Territory of the Russian Federation," legalizes the looting in Germany as compensation and prevents Russian authorities from proceeding with restitutions.

During World War II, the *Altes Museum* suffered significant damage and burned out almost completely when a fuel truck exploded in front of the museum, and the frescoes designed by Schinkel and Peter Cornelius, which adorned the vestibule and the back wall of the portico, were largely lost. After the war, only a portion of the damage was restored.

During the years of the Weimar Republic, the *Lustgarten* was frequently used for political demonstrations. The Socialists and Communists held frequent rallies there. In August 1921, 500,000 people demonstrated against right-wing extremist violence. After the murder of Foreign Minister Walther Rathenau, on 25 June 1922, 250,000 protested in the *Lustgarten*. On 7 February 1933, 200,000 people demonstrated against the new Nazi Party regime of Adolf Hitler; shortly afterwards public opposition to the regime was banned. Under the Nazis, the *Lustgarten* was converted into a site for mass rallies. In 1934, it was paved over and the equestrian statue of Friedrich Wilhelm III was removed by the Nazis (in 1944 melted down for war materiél). Hitler addressed mass rallies of up to a million people there. By the end of World War II, the *Lustgarten* was a bomb-pitted wasteland. Located in the new East Germany, the German Democratic Republic (*DDR*) left Hitler's paving in place but planted linden trees around the parade ground to reduce its militaristic appearance. The whole area was renamed *Marx-Engels-Platz*. Since the reunification of Germany in 1990, the *Lustgarten* was in 1998 finally restored to a park and once again features fountains in the heart of Berlin.

On the south side opposite *Lustgarten* lied the *Stadtschloss* (City Palace). The *Stadtschloss*, originally built in the fifteenth century, was a royal and imperial palace, and served as the winter residence of the Electors of Brandenburg, the Kings of Prussia, and the German Emperors. During World War II, the *Stadtschloss* was twice struck by Allied bombs: on 3 February and 24 February 1945. On the latter occasion, when the air defense and fire-fighting systems of Berlin had been destroyed, the building was struck by incendiaries, lost its roof, and was largely burnt out; the external structure remained intact. The building was used for a 1950 Soviet war film ("The Fall of Berlin") in which the *Stadtschloss* served as a backdrop, with live artillery shells fired at it for the realistic cinematic impact. The East German communist regime then leveled the ruins in late 1950. The palace is currently being rebuilt with completion expected in 2020.

The Reichsfelds were privileged to view and photograph the National Kaiser Wilhelm Monument on the northwest corner of the *Stadtschloss* off the *Kupfergraben* canal. The National Kaiser Wilhelm Monument was dedicated to Wilhelm I, first Emperor of a unified Germany. It rested on the *Kupfergraben* canal opposite the west main entrance to the *Stadtschloss* from 1897 through 1950. East German Communists destroyed the monument along with the remains of the *Stadtschloss* in 1950.

The Reichsfelds were also privileged to see and photograph the historic *Reichstag* building, albeit after the fire that gutted the building three years earlier. The *Reichstag* building (short for *Reichstagsgebäude*), intended to house the Imperial Diet (*Reichstag*) of the newly formed German Empire, is located on the east end of *Königsplatz* (King's Square) where the Palace of Prussian Count Atanazy Raczyński had stood since 1842. Construction of the *Reichstag* building began in 1884 and completed in 1894. In 1916, the iconic words *Dem Deutschen Volke* ("[To] the German people") were placed above the main façade of the building.

The building caught fire on 27 February 1933, under circumstances still not entirely known. This gave a pretext for the Nazis to suspend most rights provided for by the 1919 Weimar Constitution in the *Reichstag* Fire Decree, allowing them to arrest Communists and increase police action throughout Germany. The burning of *Reichstag* had also created fear in the U.S. and Western Europe of the rise of Communism in Germany. This furthered the West's Policy of Appeasement towards Hitler (who had portrayed himself as anti-Communist).

During the twelve years of Nazi rule, the *Reichstag* building was not used for parliamentary sessions. Instead, the few times that the *Reichstag* convened at all, it did so in the Kroll Opera House, west of the *Reichstag* building. This applied particularly to the session of 23 March 1933, in which the *Reichstag* surrendered its powers to Adolf Hitler in the Enabling Act, another step in the so-called *Gleichschaltung* ("coordination"). The main meeting hall of the building (which was unusable after the fire) was instead used for propaganda presentations and, during World War II, for military purposes.

The building, never fully repaired after the fire, was further damaged by air raids. During the Battle of Berlin in 1945, it became one of the central targets for the Red Army to capture, due to its perceived symbolic significance. Today, visitors to the building can still see Soviet graffiti on smoky walls inside as well as on part of the roof, which was preserved during the reconstructions after reunification.

On 2 May 1945, Red Army photographer Yevgeny Khaldei (born to a Jewish family in Yuzovka, now Donetsk, Ukraine) took the iconic photograph *Raising a flag over the Reichstag* showing 18-year-old Private Alexei Kovalyov from Kiev holding the Soviet flag, which symbolized the victory of the USSR over Nazi Germany. The photograph was taken over the southeast cornice of the *Reichstag* before Soviet tanks completed shelling the long-abandoned building. Visible on the now infamous photograph below on the corner of *Hermann Göring Straße* and *Dorotheenstraße* are the remains of the historic *Französisches Gymnasium*—a French school established in 1689 by Elector Frederick III of Brandenburg for the children of the Huguenot families who had settled in Brandenburg-Prussia by his invitation, being persecuted for their Protestant beliefs in the Catholic Kingdom of France after the Revocation of the Edict of Nantes by King Louis XIV in October 1685. The school was attended by an above-average number of Jewish pupils until 1938 when the Nazis expelled all Jews from academia in Germany.

The official German reunification ceremony on 3 October 1990, was held at the *Reichstag* building. One day later, the parliament of the united Germany would assemble in an act of symbolism in the *Reichstag* building. Only after a fierce debate did the German parliament (*Bundestag*) conclude, on 20 June 1991, with quite a slim majority in favor of moving the capital of the newly reunited Germany back to Berlin from Bonn. Reconstruction of the building was completed in 1999, with the *Bundestag* convening there officially for the first time on 19 April of that year.

The Reichsfelds photographed the famous Victory Column. The Victory Column, originally located in the center of *Königsplatz* opposite Raczyński's palace, was built to commemorate the Prussian victory in the Danish-Prussian War, known as the Second Schleswig War (February–October 1864). But by the time it was inaugurated on 2 September 1873, Prussia had also defeated Austria and its German allies in the Austro-Prussian War (1866) and France in the Franco-Prussian War (1870–71), giving the statue a new purpose. Different from the original plans, these later victories in the so-called unification wars inspired the addition of the twenty-seven-foot, 38.5-ton bronze sculpture of Victoria.

Built on a base of polished red granite, the column sits on a hall of pillars with a glass mosaic designed by Anton von Werner. The column itself consists of four solid blocks of sandstone, three of which are decorated by cannon barrels captured from the enemies of the three aforementioned wars. The fourth and highest block is decorated with golden garlands and was added in 1938–39 when the whole monument was relocated as part of the preparation of the monumental plans to redesign Berlin into *Welthauptstadt Germania*. Hitler's chief architect Albert Speer relocated the column two kilometers west of the *Reichstag* to its present site at the *Großer Stern* (Great Star), a large intersection in Tiergarten Park (equivalent to New York's Central Park) on the city axis that leads from the former *Stadtschloss* (Berlin City Palace) through the Brandenburg Gate to the western parts of the city.

During their travels in the summer of 1936, the Reichsfelds managed to visit several other European destinations, including Potsdam, Germany (35 km southwest of Berlin), and Warnemünde seaside resort in Rostock, Germany on the Baltic Sea (3 ½ to 4 hours by train from Potsdam), and Copenhagen, Denmark (220 km by Gedser-Rostock Ferry and train from Rostock, Germany). In Potsdam, they visited the Sans Souci Palace—the former summer palace of Frederick the Great, King of Prussia, built between 1745 and 1747 to rival the French Versailles. Sans Souci and its extensive gardens became a World Heritage Site in 1990 under the protection of UNESCO. On the Gedser-Rostock ferry departing Rostock, Germany to Gedser, Denmark Georgina and Hela befriended two young male Japanese tourists. Little did they know what the future held for these two young men in the upcoming war.

Georgina's Pre-War Years in Bratislava, Czechoslovakia

IN THE AUTUMN OF 1938, GEORGINA AND HER PARENTS ATTENDED A formal Hungarian ball in Bratislava. On the same evening, a young Czechoslovak Army Lieutenant Viliam Procházka (born in Bohemia) was walking near the *Reprezentak* building on the Danube River and noticed an attractive young woman in her evening gown enter the building with her parents to attend the ball. With peaked interest in the beautiful young woman who captured his eye, Lieutenant Procházka decided to investigate further. Although only dressed in his working officer's uniform, he purchased entry to the ball and proceeded to search for the young woman and her family in the ballroom. Some time passed before he could locate them among the large crowd. In the meantime, Berthold Reichsfeld attempted to engage several young men inviting them to ask his daughter to dance. Lieutenant Procházka finally spotted them sitting at their table and approached the young woman and introduced himself to her and her parents. After introduction, he invited her to dance. The young couple danced the evening away. Thereafter, Villi and

Jirka (Slovak version of her name) often met and courted. Eventually, Lieutenant Procházka proposed to Jirka with the permission of her father.

At eighteen, Georgina was a young and lovely woman. Though small, nearly petite, her slender body reflected womanly grace. Long chestnut hair with highlights of gold framed her delicate, oval face. A classic brow and large, wide-set eyes—sometimes misty gray and other times intense blue—softened her aquiline nose. High cheekbones, a gently turned chin, and a nearly sensuous mouth completed the harmony of her face. She was reserved with strangers, but she had only to smile to reveal an inner warmth that easily encouraged friendship. There was little deception in her face. It was innocent and candid, a face people naturally trusted. Yet, it was not without a certain mystery which attracted young men and made some women envious. Expressive and animated, her face seldom concealed those deeper feelings which gave her personality its individual, vibrant quality.

At nineteen, on the threshold of adult life, Georgina should have been able to look forward to a future of expectant happiness, hope, and fulfillment. But events beyond her control would interfere, altering any plans she may have made.

DISMEMBERMENT OF CZECHOSLOVAKIA AND THE RISE OF THE SLOVAK FASCIST STATE

AS 1939 APPROACHED, POLITICAL EVENTS IN EUROPE BEGAN TO RAPIDLY unravel, particularly in Czechoslovakia. On 13 March 1938, while the Slovak state was still incubating, Adolf Hitler, *Reichsmarshall* Hermann Göring, and Reich Minister for Foreign Affairs Joachim von Ribbentrop met with Slovak *JUDr.* (*Juris doktor*) Ferdinand Ďurčanský and Hlinka's Slovak People's Party (*HSĽS*) Deputy Chairman Monsignor Jozef Tiso in Berlin (Tiso went instead of *HSĽS* founder and Chairman Andrej Hlinka because of Hlinka's opinion of Hitler being a "cultural beast"). During this meeting, Ďurčanský promised Hitler that Slovak Jews would be treated in the same manner as in Germany. Upon the urging of Ďurčanský, they arranged for Slovakia's eventual secession from the Republic and independence—a century-old dream—hence laying the foundation for Hitler's pretense to invade Bohemia and Moravia one year later on 15 March 1939. A steady progression of anti-Semitic developments in Slovakia occurred leading up to Slovakia's independence on 14 March 1939. After declaration of Slovak independence, Ďurčanský became Minister of Interior and Foreign Affairs. Gaining their long-sought independence with the help of the Nazis, the Slovaks were now called upon to pay their debts to the Germans, and one of these debts was "the solution of the Jewish question" in Slovakia. A wave of anti-Semitic terror swept Slovakia. Slovak leadership began speeding up the drafting of a long series of legislation that would introduce strict limitations of Jews in public service, the professions, and trade, and eventually legalize the deportation of Jews from Slovakia. The laws would be based on the 1935 Nuremberg Law and a compromise between Slovak religious and racial anti-Jewish theories.

Nearly twenty German "advisers" were placed in the highest political, economic, and administrative institutions in Slovakia as a result of the Salzburg Conference on 28 July 1940, attended by Hitler, Jozef Tiso, Vojtech Tuka, Alexander (Šaňo) Mach, and Franz Karmasin (the leader of the German minority in Slovakia). At the Salzburg Conference, it was decided to incorporate Slovakia into the *Reich* as a satellite state by setting up a National Socialist regime in Slovakia that partnered with the Nazi regime in Germany. The most anti-Semitic Slovak radicals were emboldened and empowered by the Salzburg Conference. The genocidal program of Aryanization began in Slovakia culminating with the *Judenkodex* (*Codex Judaicus* or Jewish Code) promulgated 9 September 1941, which comprised 270 articles comprehensively denying civil and human rights to Slovak Jews. The Code was longer than the Slovak Constitution and Nuremberg Laws, combined, and as legislation, far exceeded the Nuremberg Laws in its racist and genocidal objectives.

About two months before the end of the 1938–1939 school year at the *Deutsches Staatsrealgymnasium*, Georgina Reichsfeld learned the true character of Slovak Germans. Her graduating class numbered over sixty students with twenty of them being Jewish. With the exception of the Czech principal, the faculty was German and all male. In fact, this was the only German administered *gymnázium* in the newly independent Slovakia. One day, when Georgina arrived at school, she saw that the entrance doors were blocked by a line of students. None among them was Jewish. The leader of this student group informed all Jews who tried to enter the building that it had been decided by students and faculty that no Jews would be permitted to attend classes. Several Jewish students requested to talk with the principal. When they met with him, they realized nothing could be resolved without their parents. Expulsion of Jewish students from the *Deutsches Staatsrealgymnasium* long preceded the official law passed by the Slovak parliament on 4 September 1940 that banned Jews from education in public and private high schools because Georgina's private school was owned and administered by Germans. Hela Goráber, Georgina's cousin, attended the pedagogical public school for training teachers across the street from Georgina's school. Although Hela graduated two years before Georgina, the Jews in her school completed their studies and graduated in 1939.

In a few days, an agreement was finally reached between the administrators of Georgina's school and the approximately twenty families of Jewish students. The parents would rent an apartment where classes could be held for Jewish students until graduation. The teachers would conduct these special classes in the afternoons, after their morning classes in the *gymnázium*, and would be paid for their services by the parents, themselves. The Reichsfelds managed to convince Georgina's teachers to come to their home on Hviezdoslavovo námestie to tutor Georgina over the two months before her *maturita* examination. A different professor for each subject would visit her on separate evenings. The segregated students would take their final examinations at the *gymnázium* and would receive their diplomas separately and privately. German racist policy had arrived in Bratislava.

With arrangements for the separate classes completed, Georgina Reichsfeld was ready to make the best of an otherwise unbearable situation. She set out for the school to collect her books, papers, and other belongings. She didn't know what she would find there, but since the incident that day when the other students prevented Jews from attending classes, conditions in general had deteriorated. Anti-Jewish propaganda appeared everywhere, and fairly frequently—in print, on the radio, and in conversations overheard at shops and cafés, and even in the streets of Bratislava. Yet, somehow, she could not believe that lies about the Jews would affect her. Most of her friends had been non-Jews. She lived in a non-segregated neighborhood. She could not, therefore, bring herself to accept the terrible changes which were taking place. Surely, none of her friends believed the vicious accusations leveled against her people. Georgina tried to tell herself that her friends at the *gymnázium* had not really changed. Thirty minutes later, Georgina entered the school and headed directly for her classroom. In the dim hallway, several groups of students stood idly talking. She knew most of them.

"I've come for my things," Georgina remarked, speaking to no one in particular in the group just outside her classroom door. "Hello, Dietrich," she said. "How are you, Maria?" They all had been good friends in history class this past year. No reply came. Georgina then walked around them, attempting an inconspicuous entrance into the room. At that moment,

Dietrich called out. "What are you doing here? Don't you know Jews aren't allowed in this building?" His voice was harsh and unfriendly. Georgina could not believe that she had heard him correctly. She went to her desk, hesitated, and then commenced to gather her belongings. A hostile murmur of student voices rose up. The next words she could distinguish split the air around her.

"Look, Jewish pig! Get the hell out of here!" Dietrich shouted, his eyes focused on Georgina, who stood with her back to them, frozen in disbelief. It was not possible. This could not be happening to her. These were her friends. She had known one or two of them, Hans and Ilsa, since first coming to this school eight years earlier. What was the matter with them? Had they suddenly lost their senses and forgotten who she was and who they were? She still said nothing. The books and papers rested on her desk. Georgina picked them up, cradled them in her arms, and turned to leave. Just then Maria broke out from the crowd and rushed toward her, grabbing Georgina's arms forcefully in an attempt to knock the books to the floor.

"Don't touch those books, Jew!" Maria almost screamed, "They're not yours!"

"Maria, let go of me. You don't know what you're saying." Georgina held her ground firmly and at the same time managed to hold onto the books. "You know perfectly well these are mine. I paid for them and I mean to take them." She wrenched herself free from Maria's grasp, struggling to maintain her present, relatively calm exterior. But she knew full well the situation had become threatening. Not one person in the group had come to her defense. Not one friend was there to help her. She knew she had to get out as quickly as possible. "Now, please, let me go," Georgina said without losing control, "before I regret ever having known you, Maria." With these words she headed for the door. Momentarily, an unhealthy silence fell upon the room. The students stood transfixed as Georgina passed in front of them. She reached the door and was now out in the hallway leading to the street exit. Without warning she was kicked from behind and pushed up against the wall. Her books fell to the floor, scattering papers in every direction. Shouts of derision crashed in upon her.

"Jewish pig! Dirty swine!" pierced her brain. Georgina breathed heavily; afraid she might not escape unharmed. When she saw the hate filled eyes which held her at bay, she forced herself to stoop down and retrieve her things. She scooped them up and sped for the door, dropping books and papers as she ran. The angry students were not far behind, shouting abuse and throwing the books she had lost. By this time several teachers appeared in the doorways, but not one did anything to stop the attack. There could be no mistaking whose side they were on.

In the street, Georgina continued to run, heedless of the stares from passersby. She choked for air, clutching her books close to her body. She could not stop now for there was no telling what the half-crazed students might do next. Reason and civility had vanished, and they had become a pack of hungry wolves in pursuit of their prey. Georgina could still hear their strident cries as she disappeared among the crowd in the shopping concourse several blocks away. In a few minutes, she found refuge in a lady's washroom at the back of a small cafe. She explained to the manager as she emerged from the lavatory that she had suddenly become sick to her stomach. Thanking him, she excused herself and hurried out of the café. Her only thought was to get home safely.

For a long time, Georgina Reichsfeld had dreamed of studying medicine at the university. Her father had not finished medical school when he returned from the front and often had talked of his regret. He related his experiences to Georgina, who listened with interest. And like so many idealistic young people, she considered medicine the highest vocation a devoted person could pursue. Georgina even thought that by becoming a doctor she would in some way fulfill her father's desire for a medical career. Besides, she was an only child and there would be no one else who could. But now it was not possible for Jewish girls and boys to pursue their dreams. The Slovak government had forbidden the continuation of any form of higher education for Jews. Only elementary and a few rabbinical schools remained accessible to Jews. By denying them the opportunity to enter the university, the Nazi controlled Slovak government would reduce the Jewry to semi-literacy and common labor. This method of cultural apartheid was deliberately designed to bring about the extinction of Jewish intelligentsia.

After the German Army occupied Bohemia and Moravia on 15 March 1939, Czech Lieutenant Procházka was disarmed and deported home to Prague, as many other Czechs were. Later, with the assistance of the Czech underground, he managed to escape north to Poland and eventually join the French Army to fight the Nazi occupiers of his homeland. Before his escape, Georgina and Berthold traveled to Prague to deliver an emotional farewell to her fiancé.

With the aid of her parents, Georgina managed to timely graduate from *gymnázium* in 1939. In the years following her graduation, Georgina had no chance of employment or further education. The growing violence against Jews in public prevented Georgina from venturing out very often.

Over the course of the ensuing nearly two years after her graduation, Georgina limited her activities away from her home by joining the famous Jewish swim club *Bar Kochba** at the Grössling pool in Bratislava and getting together with her Jewish friends on occasion at each other's homes where they would gather, gossip, and party. On occasion, during the day, she and a couple of her friends would go to the local *cukrárna* (pastry shop) for some gossip over a piece of pastry and mineral water. On a rare occasion, she and her friends would venture out for an evening to the café Luxor at Grösslingová 5 street to listen to live music, sip on some mineral water, enjoy some *koláčiky*, and await an invitation to dance. During the summers of 1939 and 1940, the Reichsfelds would make short visits to the Gorábors in Hradište pod Vrátnom. And on a rare occasion, Berthold would take the family to Vienna by train to attend a theater performance. However, by September 1940, Slovak Jews had to surrender their passports to government officials (Law number 215/1940) and were prohibited from driving motor vehicles (Law number 216/1940). These were very scary and uncertain times for the Reichsfelds. Any punctuated moment of enjoyment helped ease the stress of the growing threat engulfing them.

* Jewish Swim and Sport Club Bar Kochba Bratislava (*Židovský plavecký a športový klub, ŽPŠK*) was founded on 12 September 1929 by swimmers affiliated with the Maccabi Sport Club of Czechoslovakia—an international Jewish amateur sport organization. The club was the home of several world class swimmers and water polo players who were slated as Olympic favorites in their respective specialties for the upcoming 1936 Berlin Olympic Games. However, as the Berlin Olympics approached, the Maccabi World Union (MWU) elected to boycott the games. Soon, many Jewish sport clubs across Central and Eastern Europe supported the MWU decision by joining the boycott. Bar Kochba Bratislava was one of those supporting the boycott. As a consequence, the Czechoslovak Amateur Swimming Union, the national oversight body for all amateur swimmers and water polo teams and their respective clubs, sanctioned and fined those clubs boycotting the Berlin Olympics. After the 1936 Olympics, Bar Kochba Bratislava continued to compete in regional and national competitions and was most often crowned champions in water polo and various swimming events. However, as the Second World War approached and anti-Jewish laws were enacted, competitive members of Bar Kochba Bratislava made plans to leave the club. By January 1939, the majority of world-class competitors in Bar Kochba Bratislava had left for London. The club slowly disintegrated and by 26 September 1940, the club officially closed by law. (Bučka 2018, 86–99.)

CHAPTER 17

FATEFUL MEETING

IT WAS MONDAY, 6 JANUARY 1941, THE FEAST OF THE THREE WISE MEN. Most of the officers attending the War College (*Vysoká vojenná škola*) in Bratislava took advantage of the day off to recover from their Sunday night carousing at the local cafes. Only a few of the more industrious were studying for the next day's class in military strategy. Captain Vlčko was not one of them. "Peter, where would you like to go tonight?" asked infantry Captain Štefan Murgaš. They had been friends at the Military Academy in Hranice, and by their chance meeting at the War College they again struck up their old friendship. Both had been promoted to the rank of captain the previous year. Now they were here to advance their military careers.

"I don't know. The Luxor might be the best amusement," answered Peter who was well aware that this cafe was the favorite meeting place for the young crowd, particularly girls. It was a respectable establishment just the same. The girls always came in groups, never alone, and expected only to enjoy a casual sociable evening. Young officers were often a part of the lively gathering and fraternized easily with the girls, who were eager to dance with them, or to quietly sip a coffee and talk of things which made the war in Europe lose its importance. Some had boyfriends in the Slovak Army stationed elsewhere in the country, and these exchanges with the officers at the Luxor seemed to make the separations more bearable.

"Then let's go!" With this Štefan and Peter walked out of the day room and left the barracks.

The early evening air was cold and invigorating. Streetlights stood like patient sentinels along the road leading into the business district, nearly deserted because of the holiday closing. In the usually busy square only a few shops were open, indicating that their owners either did not honor the religious observance, or were perhaps more enterprising than their competitors who remained at home for the day. A small tobacconist's light welcomed Peter as he stepped in to buy cigarettes while Štefan waited outside.

"Here, you owe me twenty-five *haliers*," said Peter, slipping the Egyptian cigarettes into Štefan's hand. The name referred to one of the better brands of imported tobacco.

Five minutes later they found themselves inside the entrance to the Luxor. As Peter had suspected, the place was packed. There was nothing to do but wait for one of the tables to be vacated. Meanwhile, they removed their overcoats and sidearms, deposited them in the checkroom, and took a position just inside the large, modern dining room on the second floor, which gave them a good view of all the tables. Family groups and couples occupied most of the tables. Here and there were soldiers sitting and drinking beer from large glass steins. Only two or three tables held lone occupants, and these were older men who sat quietly reading the day's newspaper, absentmindedly lifting a drink to withered lips or drawing smoke through mellowed pipes. Peter found no tables of unescorted girls.

"Peter, over there. That group's leaving," Štefan indicated. They immediately made their way through the crowd to a table which commanded an excellent view of the café and the street. No sooner had they sat down than a waiter appeared.

"Roast pork, dumplings, and sauerkraut for me," Peter ordered without hesitating.

"We're out of the dumplings. Perhaps you'd like potatoes?"

"Fine," agreed Peter, never one to fuss about food as long as it was well-prepared.

"I'll have the veal cutlets," Štefan decided, taking out a cigarette and lighting it.

"Would you gentlemen like something to drink?"

"Do you have *Plzenské*?" asked Peter, who favored a light beer. A sour stomach and the doctor's prescription had led him to enjoy this acid-neutralizing drink.

"Make it two," Štefan added, drawing on his cigarette.

They were hungry from just thinking about food. The meal they were given back at the mess hall that day was quite inadequate—Swiss cheese, bread, butter, and black coffee—hardly enough for two officers out on the town to raise a little innocent hell.

After the waiter served them, they ate heartily and in silence. Dinner finished, they paid their bill and took the stairs to the souterrain level of the café. There the gypsy orchestra played for dancing in an atmosphere more subdued than in the dining room. Smaller tables, softer lights, whispered conversations and the strains of violins gave the room an intimate and romantic air. Peter and Štefan found a table close to the dance floor. From there they could easily survey the entire dancing square and catch the glance of any young lady in distress, eager for someone to rescue her from an uncoordinated dancer.

Looking around the room, Peter noticed three girls sitting at a table on the opposite side of the dance floor. He brought Murgaš's attention to them.

"Štefan, what do you think of the one sitting in the middle."

"The one in the black and white striped sweater?"

"Exactly."

"I think they're all Jewish."

"Who, cares, as long as they're good looking," countered Peter. Štefan was not yet openly anti-Semitic. However, since the anti-Jewish campaign had begun, Peter observed his friend's increasing resentment toward the Jews and his more than passive acceptance of current propaganda.

"Order a bottle of *Pezinok*, Štefan," Peter asked as he rose from the table. "And wish me luck."

Impressively, Captain Vlčko presented himself before the young ladies, bowed to the one in the striped sweater, and with the words: "May I," he asked her to dance. Without hesitation she rose from her seat as if drawn by the magnetism which an officer's uniform produces, no matter what the country or the time. On the dance floor Peter tuned himself in to the tempo of a tango, drew her close to him, and with a slow but deliberate step began to dance. For a short while he purposely said nothing. He could feel the slightly unsure movements of her slender body and the rapid beating of her heart. When he noticed that she didn't resist his firm grasp, he drew her even closer and brought his cheek against hers. With this she missed a step. Taking advantage of the pause, Peter broke the silence.

"We tango well together."

"Do you think so, *Kapitán*?" Her voice revealed nothing of her momentary embarrassment.

"Yes, I do. Where did you learn to dance?" he asked, hoping now to keep the conversation going.

"In dancing class," she replied simply.

"Do you come here regularly?"

"No. As a matter of fact this is the first time I've ever been here," she answered. Peter had not expected this reply.

"Who are the other two girls with you?"

"My cousins, Kačka and Hela. Kačka is from Senica and Hela's home is in Hradište pod Vrátnom. They're visiting during the holidays."

"And where do you live?" Peter inquired.

"On Hviezdoslav Square opposite the National Theater."

"Do you like the theater?" Peter anticipated her answer.

"Yes, very much. I like the operetta best, though." She had lost her initial uneasiness and discovered that they did in fact dance well together.

"Recently, I heard *The Gypsy Baron*, by the Vienna City Opera Company."

"Dušik's *Under a Foreign Flag* opens next month. Would you like to see it with me?" There was no hesitation in his enticement.

"Maybe. But isn't that a little too far in advance?" With that the dance ended and Peter escorted her back to the table with the waiting cousins. He didn't know her name and he hadn't received a definite answer to his invitation, but he had asked for the next dance, and she accepted. After thanking her politely, he returned to his own table.

"Well, Štefan, what do you think? How do you like my new girl?" Peter had formulated his own opinion, but he still wanted to hear what his friend had to say.

"Not bad, Peter. She's got a good figure. Nice legs, too, like a young doe's."

"Who did you dance with?"

"That redhead over there." Štefan inclined his head in the direction of the girl in question.

"She seems cute enough. Did you ask her for a date?"

"Not yet. But I can tell she's eager," Štefan was always the less inhibited one in dealing with girls. "Give me one more dance. You'll see."

This time it was a waltz. Peter hurried over to the waiting girl. At the same time, another man also approached her. Simultaneously, they both bowed, but since she had already promised Peter this dance, she excused herself and accepted the arm which he extended to her.

"Thanks. You won't regret your choice." Then they began to dance to the lilting strains of *The Blue Danube*.

"I told my friend you have dark eyes," Peter started the conversation.

"Maybe you are mistaken, *Kapitán*." She hadn't expected this comment.

"Show them to me, up close," Peter urged lightly. He was confident in the power of his own eyes.

"Don't look at me so strangely or you'll have me under your spell." He was not entirely convinced that he wasn't capable of taking advantage of her susceptibility to his obvious charms. After all, he was good-looking, he was young, and he was an officer.

"That's exactly what I'd like," Peter thought.

"I was right. Your eyes *are* dark, and mysterious."

She laughed at this. "Your imagination is playing tricks."

"I feel they're hiding something." He seemed determined.

"Really, *Kapitán*, there's nothing for them to hide." She was equally determined. "You know, I don't even know your name." Better to change the subject than encourage him, she thought.

"Peter Vlčko. What's yours?"

"Georgina Reichsfeld. But everyone calls me Jirka. My parents and Hungarian friends prefer to call me Györgyi."*

"Then I'll call you Jirka." Introductions were complete. "Will you still be here for the next few dances?" Gradually, he became more assured they were compatible, and that he should pursue her further.

"No, I'm sorry, my cousins and I have to leave."

"Then may I walk you home?" Peter persisted.

"Thank you, *Kapitán*, but not tonight. Perhaps some other time."

Still not discouraged by her refusal, Peter asked if he might see her tomorrow evening.

"I'm not sure I can."

"Well, try. I'll wait for you in the Central Passage at seven."

"We'll see." The hesitation in her voice was still evident. With this they exchanged goodnights. Jirka thanked him for a pleasant evening, and he replied with a bow before joining Štefan.

"So, are you satisfied?" Štefan immediately inquired.

"'Definitely. I hope to see her tomorrow," Peter's answer carried a confident ring. "How did you fare?"

"Pretty well. In fact, I think I've got this pigeon in my grasp," Štefan added with no immodesty. Though Murgaš was anything but handsome. He was short and balding but had a way with the opposite sex. His appeal was psychological rather than physical.

Jirka rose from her chair, followed by her two cousins, and headed for the exit. Before she disappeared up the stairs, she turned toward Peter,

---

* Hungarian: Györgyi – pronounced "Dyurdy"; Slavic: Jirka (Jiržina) – pronounced "Yirka (Yirzhina)"; English: Georgina.

who had not taken his eyes off of her. Then she winked at him impishly. He grinned broadly and nodded his head. His gaze held her retreating form until she was out of sight. Tonight, he felt as never before. Something had happened to him without his knowing quite yet what it was. But he sensed that Jirka Reichsfeld and Peter Vlčko would meet again.

"Peter, who's next?" suddenly Murgaš interrupted his thoughts.

"Štefan, I don't care to dance with anyone else tonight."

"Well, well, well," Murgaš teased, a little disbelieving.

"In that case, let's go. My chick's flown away, too."

After paying their bill, they collected their belongings at the checkroom and stepped out into the cold night. The clock struck ten as they headed back to the *kaserne* (barracks).

NEARING THE APARTMENT BUILDING ON HVIEZDOSLAV SQUARE, Georgina grew apprehensive. She and two cousins had walked from the Luxor without incident, it was true, but the confrontation with her parents was still before them.

In the afternoon, Györgyi's parents had gone to visit friends in the outskirts of Bratislava and would surely be back before the nine o'clock curfew for Jews. It was now after ten; and if she and her cousins had eluded the police, they would not be so lucky with her parents. Besides, there was also the matter of why they had left the apartment in the first place. Györgyi's mother had even locked all the closets so that the girls would be forced to remain at home, lacking any appropriate dress. But a determined daughter will always find a way to circumvent parents' wishes—and Györgyi did. She found a heavy skirt and sweater of her mother's which somehow had escaped being locked up in the wardrobe, and these Györgyi wore to the Luxor. Her cousins were similarly attired but did not look as dowdy as Györgyi in her mother's things.

To explain her escape costume was one thing, but to say why she had gone out at all was another. Could she say simply that she wanted a little innocent fun? Or would she dare reveal the deeper feelings she harbored against her parents? She had become depressed of late because her mother and father seemed not to want her to grow up and away from them. They seemed oppressively near and watchful of her every move. She could not be a separate person free to explore even the immediate world around her without her parents' interference. They did not want to let her go, and she ached to fly from the nest. Györgyi was twenty, and at this age a girl has to believe she will someday soon become a woman. Moreover, Georgina Reichsfeld was bored; and boredom alone was enough to inspire her to challenge her parents' authority, particularly since Hela and Kačka offered moral support and were just as eager as their cousin to find adventure, maybe even romance, in Bratislava after dark. There was no particular reason for choosing the Luxor Cafe for this adventure, except that it was a new place to go dancing not far from the Reichsfeld apartment. The chance Georgina had taken tonight was worthwhile, she thought. She was thrilled when Peter asked her to dance. His manners and uniform impressed her, too. In her eyes he was handsome. But she could not figure out why she appealed to him in her mother's apparel. She wondered why an officer would dance with a Jewish girl. Maybe she was only feeling guilty because she might cause trouble for him, since Jews were prohibited from patronizing public places.

Once inside the foyer, they took the elevator to the sixth floor, got off and stood before the door to their apartment. Suppressing their new fears, they rang the bell. Immediately, Bobby, Georgina's miniature fox terrier, started yapping. As soon as the door opened, he jumped excitedly around the three girls while Mrs. Reichsfeld snapped, "where have you been?" Her anger erupted like a volcano. "And what are you doing in my clothes?"

"Aunt Icza (diminutive form of Illona, the Slovak version of Helena), we were bored staying at home," Hela offered lamely in defense.

"Bored! We thought we would never see any of you again." Mrs. Reichsfeld's anger could not suppress the fears she felt when she discovered the girls were gone.

"I tried to tell Györgyi it was too late to go to the Luxor Cafe, but she wouldn't listen." Kačka interfered, trying to save herself from her aunt's wrath. She insisted, "so what could we do?"

Nervously, Mr. Reichsfeld motioned the girls into the living room while his wife closed and secured the door.

"That's no excuse. Uncle and I have been frantic, imagining the things that could have happened to you."

"But Auntie," Hela interrupted, "you should have seen who danced with Györgyi tonight."

"Don't change the subject, Hela," She would not be sidetracked, yet she was curious to hear her niece's report.

"A young cavalry officer . . . ," Helena ignored her protest, as if certain a romance was destined to begin, ". . . who had eyes only for Györgyi."

"How could you, Györgyi? Have you lost your mind? Play with fire and you'll get burned."

"Mama, I didn't ask him to dance with me. He invited me, and I couldn't refuse."

"Icza, be reasonable," interrupted her father. "Györgyi had no choice but to accept him. But she should never have gone out in the first place."

Decidedly, the Reichsfelds were strict parents, and Georgina was their only child, so they quite naturally exercised their parental prerogatives, with little concern for her need to be independent. This strictness was not without its physical manifestation, for Father Reichsfeld firmly believed that to spare the rod was to spoil the child. His temper burst meteorically, and at such times he would shake his daughter or strike her across the face. Once, when he discovered that she had failed to attend synagogue services, he searched the neighborhood until he trapped her in the park. Mindless of the crowd, he grabbed her by the ear and pulled her down the street, depositing her with the rabbi. Georgina was only thirteen at the time, but her humiliation, to say nothing of the fear she experienced, was complete. Her only defense was submission. But her father's discipline had made her determined to survive. Lately, Georgina had observed, though, that her father was less threatening; and she perceived in him a rather more solicitous concern for her welfare. No doubt the times were dangerous for all of them, and their fate marked with uncertainty. This drew them closer together in spite of the emotional damage she had sustained during childhood and adolescence.

"I hope you didn't bite his nose off," Mr. Reichsfeld commented. Such levity would have been absent under like circumstances a few years earlier. But it did ease the tension for everyone, particularly Györgyi, who smiled at her father's remark.

"No, Apuka [Hungarian for 'daddy']."

"Then we've got nothing to worry about," concluded Mr. Reichsfeld, apparently more relieved than angry. "Now, is anyone hungry?"

"I'm starved," Hela was quick to offer.

"Icza, get that supper. We can be thankful they're safe."

The meal had been kept warm until the girls arrived.

"Helka, your father called this evening to say he'll pick you up tomorrow. Kačka can ride with you if she wants. She can't go home by herself with things as bad as they are nowadays," Reichsfeld informed his niece.

"Would someone help me set the table?" Mrs. Reichsfeld's tone had changed, revealing little of the agitation she had displayed earlier.

"Right away, Auntie," Kačka called from the lavatory, where she had gone to freshen up a bit. Georgina had slipped out of the living room to return her mother's clothes and change into her own.

The Reichsfeld apartment building stood in a pleasant neighborhood. By modern standards, their unit was fairly small, but when compared to others in Bratislava it was quite comfortable. The five rooms, immaculately clean, included a sitting room, kitchen, dining room, bedroom, bath, and an unusually small room where Georgina slept. The sitting room was only used on special occasions or for important guests. It was the dining room where the family ate their meals, read the paper, entertained informally, and held their discussions. It was a simple yet tastefully decorated room, distinguished only by a small brass chandelier, several modern paintings, and a fine Persian rug. Two very comfortable looking chairs, an indestructible looking sofa, a buffet, and an oval dining table flanked by six padded chairs, completed the furnishings. A series of curtained French doors concealed the Reichsfelds' bedroom, which opened into the dining room.

A short prayer of thanksgiving opened the meal. In relative silence they ate cold cuts, and white bread. Meals were necessarily Spartan in times like these, but soon would be regarded as feasts.

After supper the girls washed and dried the dishes while Mr. and Mrs. Reichsfeld prepared for bed. By midnight, the apartment was still. Georgina laid wide awake. Sleep would not come. She could not forget the events of the evening. Nor could she forget Peter. She wondered if he really wanted to see her the following evening. Why had she danced with him at all? The more she thought about Peter, the more she came to reject her mother's feelings of alarm. Nothing in his manner warranted distrust. Still, she was uncertain about accepting his invitation. These thoughts disturbed her, and yet she was unable to sort them out satisfactorily. Then she thought of Willy, her Czech fiancé, now serving somewhere in North Africa with the French Foreign Legion. She wondered what he would say. She hadn't heard from him in over a year. Did he still think of her? Was he injured, or worse, had he been killed?

Georgina had met Czech artillery Lieutenant Viliam Procházka while he was stationed in Bratislava before the formation of the Slovak state. After the Germans occupied Bohemia and Moravia, he was disarmed and deported home to Prague, as many other Czechs were. Later, with the assistance of the Czech underground, he managed to escape north to Poland and join the French Army to fight the Nazi occupiers of his homeland. Because the memory of Villi had not dimmed, Georgina could harbor no thoughts that might endanger their love. She would remain faithful to him. She told herself she would, and yet. . . .

WHEN VLČKO AND MURGAŠ ARRIVED BACK AT THE WAR COLLEGE, THEY saw that a number of their colleagues were still working on Colonel Lavota's assignment. Others were just lounging on their bunks, talking the small talk heard in military barracks everywhere. They were quartered in a starkly simple room, about fifty feet long and twenty-five feet wide. From opposite white-washed walls, steel bunks extended into the middle of the room, forming a corridor which ran the length of the sleeping quarters. A tall, narrow window with a view of the Danube Bridge was set in the wall at one end of the room. The opposite wall contained a door which opened into a hallway. The large light bulbs hung from the ceiling. The building was a solid structure of mortar, brick, and stone, erected during the days of Austro-Hungarian rule.

Cavalry Lieutenant Ján Straka looked up from his book and remarked, "Have a good time?" Straka, the nephew of Defense Minister *Generál* Čatloš, seldom did.

"We had." Murgaš remembered the good dinner, but even more he remembered his redheaded Anna. "We discovered some new girls tonight."

"I suppose they're going to do your lessons, too." Straka couldn't hide the subtle envy.

"Janko, don't worry about us," Vlčko smiled, detecting his feelings. "Have you forgotten the cavalry maxim?"

"Which one?"

"A cavalry officer squeezes a girl in a bar all night, and when he returns to his barracks in the morning, he squeezes his mare."

"Do you agree, Julo?" Straka directed his question to Captain Julius Nosko. He was an older, more experienced cavalry officer, known for his seriousness and respected among the students.

"Well, I decided that while I'm here, I'm going to squeeze the books first, then my mare and the girls last. That's if I have any strength left. Too much girl-squeezing's bad for a soldier. Besides, Colonel Lavota will be the one to squeeze our brains tomorrow."

"Gentlemen, please. It's late. We'd like to sleep. Argue in the hallway if you must," artillery Major Ondrej Hreblaj chastised. He was also an older officer, even more serious than Nosko.

"Ondrej's right. You've had enough fun for one night," Captain Anton Cyprich added, not without some irritation, always the exemplary infantry officer.

"All right, all right. Don't get your dander up. You know, Anton, you're a bit sensitive these days since the Germans forced your fiancée to remain in Silesia. If she were here, you'd speak differently," said Murgaš, attempting to even the score. Even though Cyprich's girl was of German descent, he was having trouble arranging her passport to Slovakia. "It's irrelevant where she is," cut in Lieutenant Jozef Dvornak. "If I know Anton, he'll convince the Germans, regardless." Dvornak's own love affair was complicated by the present military situation in a like measure. His fiancée was Czech, and she was having more than her share of difficulties in convincing the Protectorate Government to allow her to travel to Slovakia.

"Well, I gave up on Christine," Vlčko announced, "after her request was denied. Besides, she found herself a German officer, and that was the end of our little romance."

Before the occupation of the Czech lands, Bohemia, Moravia, and Silesia, and the declaration of independent Slovakia, most of the officers of Slovak origin had served in those provinces of the Czechoslovak Republic. Now they were cut off from personal contact with their most intimate friends. Time, place, and circumstances had seriously altered their lives. And perhaps they knew that life would never be the way it was. The Germans would see to that.

Peter tried to forget Christine Svobodová. They had met in Prague. He was stationed in Stará Boleslav and she was studying social science in the Vinohrady district. Headquarters of Slovak Army ground forces in Banská Bystrica refused Vlčko permission to marry her several months earlier because he was not yet twenty-eight, the minimum age for entering into marriage as stipulated by army regulations. When Christine learned this, she stopped writing. It was that simple.

Tonight, Peter met Jirka. It was a fortuitous meeting. And tonight, she helped him forget Christina, at least for a while. For this, he was grateful. Besides, there was the prospect of tomorrow night. She made no promises, but neither did she refuse to see him again. Thoughts of Jirka occupied his mind and he was unable to concentrate on the next day's lessons. He tossed his books aside, laid down on his bed, and tried to sleep. The church clock struck two when sleep finally came.

The War College in Bratislava consisted of two departments—one for preparation of officers for the General Staff, and the other for officers of the Quartermaster Corps. Due to limited space in the Danube *Kaserne* (barracks), men from both departments lived together, most in one large room, the rest in two small adjoining rooms. Colonel Augustín Malár, Commandant and Inspector General of the War College, was assisted by Colonel Ladislav Lavota and Lieutenant Colonel Rudolf Kanák. They functioned as administrators and professors. Along with these officers, there were other notables such as Colonel Rudolf Pilfousek and Colonel Pavel Bauman who served as instructors. Officers of the German General Staff assigned the faculty at the War College.

Because the Slovak Army suffered a shortage of commanding officers with higher military education, students at the War College were fast-tracked and subjected to intensive schooling lasting two years. The German command exerted great pressure on everyone at the school to condense and accelerate its training program.

On the day after Vlčko met Georgina, life went on as usual in the school. Reveille was at six in the morning and the first class started at eight. During these two hours, the officers washed, dressed, and put their quarters in impeccable order. Then, they assembled for breakfast in the mess hall. From eight o'clock until nine-thirty, they attended horseback riding class. This course was set up mainly for infantry officers who seldom rode horses. It was not unusual to see them sweat it out every morning while cavalry and artillery officers blithely took each exercise in stride.

The next class was a course in macroeconomics that was taught only twice a week by Dr. Peter Karváš, president of the Slovak National Bank. During the last three hours of morning classes, the students were schooled in sociology and geography, taught by Dr. Vladimír Hromádka, professor at Comenius University in Bratislava. Following the noon break for lunch were two hours of military tactics and strategy. On days when weather permitted, this class was held outdoors, and then it usually lasted until five o'clock. Today, however, Peter was lucky. The lecture was given indoors and ended at four. There was enough time left for him to study his political science text and still clean up for his date with Georgina.

THE JANUARY 1941 SKY OF LUSTROUS STARS STOOD SILENT. ONLY THE rhythmic sound of Peter's steps upon the snow-packed pavement disturbed the night. Without warning, the wind rose up, sending swirling shafts of white powder into the air. Peter closed his eyes and bent his head against the chilling wind. Once he crossed the square, he would find relative shelter from the buildings that lined the narrow street leading to the central passage. As he approached the Umlauf hardware store, he turned into the shopping concourse, grateful for the protection it offered from the cold. He passed the brightly lighted shop windows along the passageway but did not give them a glance. When he came to the end of the concourse, he stopped to check his watch. It was nearly seven. Anxiously, he looked around for Georgina, but he could see no one that resembled her. He reasoned she had probably been detained in the sewing class (the word in the Jewish community was that young women sent to concentration camps could avoid harsh treatment or worse if they possessed a skill needed by the Nazis—Georgina chose sewing); so, he decided to walk the length of the concourse once more. Turning, he noticed a girl in the distance. She was wearing a burgundy wool suit, which clung close to her body, revealing her slim, lithe figure. A large-brimmed hat of the same color was pulled down slightly over her forehead and eyes. The brim tilted to one side gave her a coquettish appearance. Gracefully draped about her neck and shoulders was a matching wool stole which cascaded down her back. Before completing his inspection of the young lady, Peter recognized that she was Georgina. Immediately, he hurried to meet her.

"Good evening, Jirka," he addressed her, smiling victoriously.

"Good evening, *Kapitán*." Her voice was pleasant and rather soft.

"So, you did come after all." Peter sounded not a little triumphant.

"I really didn't want to, except my curiosity brought me." Jirka paused. "I wanted to find out if you were serious, or if you were merely joking with me."

Georgina still remembered Kurt Fochem, who had been her best boyfriend in the last year at the *gymnázium*. He was charming and attentive, and they both thought they were in love. Then the anti-Jewish campaign broke. She never saw him again except for that afternoon in Blumenthal Street when he crossed to the other side in an obvious effort to avoid her. She had called to him, but he never turned around.

"Jirka, I'm not in the habit of lying to anyone, especially girls. Nor do I try to make fools of them either." Momentarily, Peter was a little hurt by her remark. "I was quite serious when I asked you to meet me here tonight."

"I'm sorry, *Kapitán*." Jirka was both apologetic and upset. She had not wanted to judge Peter unfairly and yet she had. Perhaps, girls of twenty are normally cautious about the young men they meet for the first time. Then, again, it could be that since she had been hurt before, she still carried the pain unconsciously and was somewhat defensive. Besides, Peter was not Jewish, and she was. These days it was easy for a Jewish girl to be sensitive. And her feelings for Willy made her feel guilty. To relieve the tension, she added, "Believe me, *Kapitán*, I'm sorry if I offended you." Her eyes told him she was sincere. They both smiled, relieved to know that neither had been deceived.

"Have you been home yet, Jirka?"

"No. I was just on my way back from sewing class. If you hadn't come on time, I would have gone straight home." Aside from her desire to let him know she was usually punctual, she wanted to conceal her interest in him—at least on their first date.

"Then you must be starved. I haven't eaten yet either. How about dinner?"

"Well, if you are really hungry, I can't refuse." Jirka had eaten very little that day, but the prospect of dinner with Peter increased her appetite. "There's a little restaurant around the corner where they serve excellent food."

From the concourse they turned left, and after few steps entered the restaurant. A circular stairway took them down into a cozy room. reminiscent of a Slovak peasant's hut. Folklore painting decorated the walls. Coarse wooden benches and tables were informally arranged about the low-ceilinged room. The place was crowded with young couples sitting close to each other, who spoke in whispered tones. No one seemed to notice the newcomers. Peter led Jirka to a vacant table near the back of the room. Colorful, hand-embroidered linen cloths covered the tables. On each stood a tiny vase which held a pine sprig.

Scanning the menu, Peter asked what Jirka would like. The veal cutlet appealed to her, but secretly she confided she could make a meal of *Wiener Schnitzel*.

Peter gave the waiter their order and asked that he bring a bottle of *Modranské vino*. Turning to Jirka, "Did you get home all right yesterday?"

"Yes, and it wasn't as bad as I'd expected. Mother reprimanded us, but we still ate dinner."

"Your cousins . . . are they in town for long?"

"No. In fact, they left this morning. Hela's father picked them up. She was the taller one," Jirka explained.

"Do you have brothers and sisters?"

"No, unfortunately. I'm an only child. I've always wanted a sister or brother, but mother couldn't have any more children."

"I see."

"She had an operation. It seems now it's really better that way. My parents have enough trouble just taking care of themselves these days. They worry about me and what will happen to us."

"What do you mean?"

"The war has touched all of us. Perhaps in the end, at least, things will be better for those who survive. I just don't know." Then Jirka fell silent. When the waiter brought their food and filled their glasses with the white wine, Peter immediately offered a toast.

"To you, Jirka. And to our close friendship."

Na zdravie! Jirka raised her glass. She was glad Peter had not taken offense because of her unwillingness to discuss conditions in her life which were painful. Yet, why should she resist his questions? He did seem genuinely interested.

"Jirka, if you don't mind my asking, why are you taking sewing lessons?" He imagined she might be a university student instead.

"Because I'm not allowed to study at the university. I had planned to enter medical school, but Jews are prohibited."

"Couldn't you study abroad?"

"I wanted to leave in '39 and go to study in London where my older cousin Ila Seidler lived, but Father wouldn't let me. He himself didn't want to leave Slovakia because he hoped things would improve. But they didn't. Now the borders are closed, and we're trapped." Jirka sounded fatalistic.

"But laws against Jews aren't as bad here as they are in Germany," Peter injected.

"True. But where will Hitler's insanity end? He's brought so much unhappiness to so many people that I'm afraid it won't be long before. . . ." Jirka could not finish saying what was on her mind.

"President Tiso would never permit Nazi atrocities in Slovakia." Peter was reasonably convinced for the time being of the veracity of his words. "I know the German Nazis have been cruel," he continued, "but Slovakia is not Germany. We will not persecute the Jews." He had to believe this, for he could not conceive of a world built upon hate and discrimination.

"Yes, but can we forget what's happened in Poland, as well as in Germany? Thousands of Jews, even Aryans, have been sent to resettlement camps. From all that I hear, they're beaten brutally, and even murdered!" Her voice rose angrily. "The Nazis have confiscated private property and simply given it away to whomever they pleased. Is this justice, *Kapitán*?"

"No, but I still say conditions aren't as bad here. I find it hard to think of Slovaks going that far to solve the 'Jewish Problem'." Yet, as he spoke these words, Peter wondered himself when and where it all would lead to. Politely, their waiter removed the plates and inquired if they wished coffee. Peter replied in the affirmative. When the coffee arrived, he poured some for Jirka and himself. For a moment neither said anything. Peter took out his cigarettes, offered Jirka one, lit them, and let the smoke trail off. He extinguished the match and dropped it into the ashtray. Jirka sat opposite, her eyes lowered, conscious that Peter was staring at her. His gaze was intense.

"Jirka."

"Peter." They spoke in unison. This was the first time she had used his given name.

"We're being pretty serious, don't you think?" Peter interrupted their amorous silence.

"I suppose we are."

"Something inside makes me want to protect you," Peter found himself saying without hesitation.

"And something in my heart tells me to turn to you." Jirka was not surprised by her words. "When I look at our meeting realistically, I can't see why we met or why we should ever meet again. This is what my head says. But not my heart. Oh, Peter, I don't know which one to listen to." She could not suppress her feelings, for she knew she had to be honest with him. Strangely enough, too, she no longer felt guilty about Willy. A year had passed since she heard from him, and a year was surely sufficient time to make up one's mind about another person. Yet, she was confused and needed time to think.

"Jirka, sometimes a person has to listen to his heart. Logic doesn't solve everything, you know." Peter, too, was being honest with her.

"What time is it?" Jirka changed the subject. Something was telling her that it was getting late.

"A quarter to nine." Peter was not happy that the time was running fast.

"I must go now. You know I must be home by nine." Peter motioned for his check, disappointed the evening was ending so soon. After paying the bill, they quickly left the restaurant and set out for Jirka's place. In front of the apartment building, outside the gate, Peter stopped Jirka. Standing beside her in the shadows, he turned Jirka around to face him and looked into her eyes for what seemed like a long time. Then he spoke.

"When can I see you again?"

"I don't know, but not tomorrow, Peter. I promised a girlfriend I'd go to the movies with her."

"What about Thursday?"

"Peter, I really have to think whether we should see each other at all. Let's wait until Saturday. By then one of us will surely have changed his mind about everything. Let's give our heads time to weigh what our hearts keep saying we should do. Agreed?" Jirka smiled, but seriousness was there.

"If that's really the way you want it, I guess I'll have to agree." Peter was resigned. "Where shall we meet on Saturday?"

"I'll call you and tell you what I've decided. Thank you for dinner." She opened the door and turned toward Peter. "I'll phone you later this week."

"Until then I'll be thinking about you, Jirka." Peter stood by the gate for a few minutes and waited for her to disappear inside the elevator. Then he returned directly to his quarters.

FOLLOWING THE FALL AND DISINTEGRATION OF CZECHOSLOVAKIA, THE next sacrifice to German aggression was Poland. On 1 September 1939, the Polish army valiantly attempted to halt Hitler's mechanized divisions, but an attack from the east by the Soviets shattered any hopes of a successful Polish resistance. Within three weeks, Poland surrendered. Fulfilling the terms of their mutual alliance only in word, France and England declared war on Germany on 3 September 1939, which did not help the Polish people. This was the beginning of the Second World War.

After signing a non-aggression pact (Molotov-Ribbentrop Pact) on 23 August 1939, with Nazi Germany that included a secret protocol to divide territories of Romania, Poland, Lithuania, Latvia, Estonia, and Finland into German and Soviet "spheres of influence," the Soviet Union proceeded to invade and annex much of eastern Poland, parts of Finland, Estonia, Latvia,

Lithuania, and parts of Romania (Bessarabia, Northern Bukovina, and the Hertza region).

Shortly after the fall of France in June 1940, the long arm of the *Luftwaffe* reached out for England. It was that same England which had appeased Hitler in 1938 by sacrificing Czechoslovakia in order to insure British and European peace and security. In mid-August 1940, a thousand German warplanes bombed England in Operation Eagle Attack (*Unternehmen Adlerangriff*). They continued their assault on the British Isles day and night, in preparation for an ultimate land invasion by ground forces in Operation Sealion (*Unternehmen Seelöwe*). The losses in property and lives incurred by both sides during these aerial battles were tremendous. The British bravely bore these attacks, aided by Polish and Czechoslovakian pilots who managed to escape from their occupied countries to join the Royal Air Force.

Near the end of September 1940, due to great losses inflicted on them by the British RAF, the Germans halted their massive air raids. Instead, they deployed dive bombers, torpedo boats, and submarines in a series of *Blitzkrieg* attacks on British shipping and land objectives. Nevertheless, not even these frenzied tactics broke the spirit of the English. It was during these critical months that Sir Winston Churchill began to prepare his people for an offensive war.

Simultaneously with German aggression, Italy invaded Albania. A year later her hostility extended to British Somalia. In September 1940, Italy attacked Libya and Egypt.

Since 1937, Japan had been at war with China. Of great advantage was her Tripartite Pact with Germany and Italy (signed in Berlin on 27 September 1940). This agreement called for total German conquest of Europe, Italian control of the Mediterranean countries, and Japanese domination of the Far East. In November 1940, Hungary willingly joined this alliance. Rumania was forced to do the same.

IN THE MIDDLE OF FEBRUARY 1941, GEORGINA REICHSFELD INVITED Captain Vlčko to meet her family and several of her closest friends. Her parents especially wanted to know Peter. Over the previous month, his name had become a household word, and they wanted to see who it was that deserved their daughter's attention.

It was four o'clock in the afternoon when Vlčko knocked on the door of the apartment in Hviezdoslav Square. Georgina herself appeared in the vestibule.

"Hello, Jirka."

"Peter, how are you?" She welcomed him in, took his long coat and cap, and hung them up on the rack in the outer hallway. "Mama come here. I want you to meet *Kapitán* Peter Vlčko."

"I'm happy to meet you, *Pán Kapitán*." Mrs. Reichsfeld extended her ample hand to him.

"Here's Father, Peter." Mr. Reichsfeld walked briskly into the hallway when he heard Vlčko had arrived. He shook his hand warmly.

"How do you do, *Pán Kapitán*? I am glad I finally have the chance to meet you. I've tried to picture you from Jirka's descriptions. Now at last, I can complete my image of you. Please feel welcome in our home." His raw-boned figure towered over the young officer.

"Thank you. I'm happy to be here, *Pán* Reichsfeld." Peter's manner was friendly and respectful.

"'Father, will you please excuse us? I want Peter to meet my friends." She led him by the hand into the adjoining sitting room.

"May I present *Kapitán* Peter Vlčko?" Going around the room, she introduced him to each of her friends. The girls, Duci Hecht and Eva Yust, were about her age. The men, Beno Gubi, Gyuri Bondi, and Alexander Braun, were somewhat older. In fact, Gubi was nearing forty, but this had not prevented him from making advances toward Georgina. He often sent her flowers and candy that she graciously accepted, but never did she encourage him.

After an exchange of greetings, Beno Gubi studied Vlčko. "*Pán Kapitán*, I suspect you're in a position to know—and I hope you don't mind my asking—what is the latest news?"

"I'm sure I don't know any more than you, Mr. Gubi. What precisely do you want to know?"

"Well, everything. Since our radios have been confiscated, we've been cut off from the outside world. We only have one another and a few gentile friends, of course. God knows when we will lose them, too."

Georgina had already told her friends that Peter could be trusted. They could speak freely with him. Moreover, he was understanding and sympathetic with their problems. "If you've had no news of any kind, the international situation would certainly interest you." Vlčko told of British victories over the Italians at Tobruk and Benghazi in Libya, of landings in

Somalia and Eritrea in northeastern Africa, and of Hitler's plans for some kind of surprise maneuver in the Balkans. Since Hungary and Rumania had joined forces with Germany, army convoys were moving in that direction, day and night.

"As for your situation, I came to a conclusion," Vlčko continued. "The longer you remain here, the worse it will get. If you escaped now to Yugoslavia, you could travel to Greece or Turkey, and from there to Palestine."

The fears Peter had tried to allay the first night Jirka and he discussed them, the speculation over the spread of Nazi racism, came back to haunt him as he advised her friends.

"*Pán Kapitán*, you sound sincere enough, but are you being practical?" Bondi objected.

"What choice is left? You can't depend much longer on the little freedom you still enjoy. What's occurred to the Jews throughout German-occupied Europe is an ugly reality you can't afford to ignore and feel immune to. The concentration camps are a fact of life, *Pán* Bondi. How far our government will go is anybody's guess. There are radicals seeking a rapid and effective solution to the Jewish question. Vlčko was referring to the well-known radical members of the Slovak Fascist government, namely, Prime Minister and Minister of Foreign Affairs *JUDr.* (*Juris doktor*—Doctor of Law) Vojtech Tuka and Interior Minister Alexander Mach who were in lockstep with Hitler on the "Jewish question." So, everyone has to secure his own safety. The sooner, the better. To do otherwise is inexcusable and dangerous."

"*Kapitán* Vlčko, believe me, I would be happiest if I could grab a rifle and openly fight our enemies." Alexander Braun, an athletic-looking enthusiast, showed unusual courage.

"Organized, armed resistance would be futile and suicidal. This is not the time for heroism." Peter wished he could offer them more hope.

"What else can we do, then?" Duci Hecht, a dark-complexioned, charming girl, did not relish escaping to Yugoslavia, for this, too, presented certain unknown dangers.

"Prepare for the unexpected. Make arrangements with gentile friends to help you when the critical moment arrives. Alone, the Jews are powerless. You'll need your Christian friends." Peter knew he would be there when Jirka and her parents needed him. What this would entail he could not possibly foresee.

"Györgyi, I think we all need a drink," Beno Gubi interrupted. "I'm sure *Kapitán* Vlčko does."

"What would you like, *Tokaji* or *Modranské*?" Georgina liked the idea.

"*Tokaji*, in deference to our Hungarian friends." Eva displayed the right amount of sarcasm. Everyone appreciated her remark and accepted the wine of their Hungarian neighbor who had joined forces with the Germans. When the wine was served, they toasted to their mutual friendship and to the victory of England and France. Georgina wound up the gramophone, selected a record, and for a while they danced and forgot how dangerous the times were in which they lived.

Exactly at six, the party broke up. Georgina's friends said their goodbyes. Each shook Peter's hand warmly in appreciation of his frankness and understanding. Beno Gubi, the last to leave, turned to Vlčko. "*Pán Kapitán*, are you leaving now?" It was apparent he did not wish to see him remain.

"I suppose I really should be going," Vlčko answered, not too convincingly.

"You have time yet, Peter. Besides, you were the last to arrive, so you should be the last to depart." Jirka hoped to detain him.

"I accept your logic, Jirka." He picked up her cue. "Good night, Mr. Gubi. I trust we will meet again?" Peter amicably extended his hand.

"Perhaps. Goodbye, Györgyi. Thanks for everything." Gubi left both standing in the entrance hall. When the door closed, they joined Jirka's parents in the dining room.

"Why don't you have dinner with us, *Kapitán* Vlčko? I think we all are a little hungry," remarked Mr. Reichsfeld at their return. His clear blue eyes revealed the sincerity of his invitation.

"Why, thank you, *Pán* Reichsfeld. I'm not really very hungry but I would like to stay a bit longer," Peter gladly accepted the opportunity and smiled at Jirka.

The dinner was simple—chicken *paprikas* and *halušky*—but delicious. As they sat around the table drinking the strong, aromatic after dinner coffee, the father offered everyone a cigarette. He then turned the conversation in a different direction than it had taken during the meal.

"*Pán Kapitán*, aren't you afraid to be seen associating with Jewish people?"

"Why? I'm not breaking any laws, *Pán* Reichsfeld. Besides, no one knows yet that I've been seeing Jirka. And she knows how I feel." Peter, from early youth, had rejected any form of prejudice which violated human rights and his Christian ethics. Moreover, he was convinced that Christian love was not a mere abstraction. It was a reality by which a person should live his life.

"Didn't you swear to obey the president and the government?" Mr. Reichsfeld inquired, "and to fight the enemies of Slovakia?"

"Yes. I did take that oath. But I was not told that unjust laws would threaten innocent citizen's lives."

"Let's pray the government will resist Nazi mandates." Reichsfeld's optimism had diminished in recent months. Vlčko's words offered only slight encouragement.

"I think you two have had enough of politics," interrupted Georgina, who had been listening attentively. "How about a game of rummy? The youth against the elders." Jirka longed to have Peter on her side.

"If you'd like. But not for long. I still have to study when I get back to the barracks."

"Györgyi, don't detain the *Kapitán* any longer. If he has studying to do, you shouldn't prevent him." Mrs. Reichsfeld was always more practical than her daughter. Of course, her heart was not involved.

"What time *is* it?" Peter asked, looking at his watch. "Oh, it's eight-thirty. I really should go, Jirka. Forgive me. We can play cards another time."

Peter rose from the table, thanked, the Reichsfelds, and said good night. Jirka escorted him to the door, where she helped him with his coat. Instead of handing Peter his cap, she set it on his head for him, adjusting the visor at a rakish angle.

"I can't say for sure when I'll see you, but certainly the first opportunity after I return from the Tatras," Peter answered Jirka's inquiring expression.

"Oh, I completely forgot. The skiing course. It's a shame we have to be separated for that long."

"It's only for three weeks, Jirka."

"That's like three months to me, Peter."

"I know. It will be hard on me, too. Meanwhile, take care until I get back."

"You too, Peter, and be careful. Drop me a card if you have time."

"I will." He pulled her closer to him. For a moment they stood with the door opened and said nothing. His intention to kiss her was foiled when two women emerged from the opposite apartment and took them by surprise. Everyone smiled and nodded a greeting. He instead extended his hand to

Jirka, who accepted it responsively. Then he said good night and took the stairs to the ground floor.

CHAPTER 18

SLOVAK MOUNTAINS GIVE INSPIRATION

IN THE SECOND HALF OF FEBRUARY 1941, ALL THE STUDENTS AND THEIR instructors left for the Low Tatra Mountains. The army bus delivered the group to the main railway station in Bratislava, where they boarded the Košice-bound express, scheduled to leave at eight that morning. Everyone looked forward to this trip, especially those who had never been on skis before. For them this was a vacation rather than a continuation of their schooling.

"All aboard!" called the conductors, going from door to door and locking the safety latches. Just as the train began to move, they quickly jumped on board.

The train appeared brand new. It was exceptionally clean and comfortable. Finding seats in the compartments, which had been reserved for them, the students and their instructors settled down for the five-hour journey which lay ahead.

Sixty kilometers northeast of Bratislava, on the eastern slopes of the Carpathian (Tatra) Mountains, the train made its first stop in Trnava. After the usual exchange of passengers and the mail, the train continued on its way to Leopoldov. Hardly anyone was unfamiliar with this city, for it was famous for its fortress built in the last half of the seventeenth century as protection against Turkish invasion. In 1865, it was converted into a state political prison. There were now many prisoners here who were Czechoslovak patriots and who had fought for the liberation of Czechs and Slovaks from Austro-Hungarian domination prior to and during the First World War. They had recently fallen into disfavor with the new Slovak state because of their determined opposition to the dissolution of Czechoslovakia after the Nazi invasion.

From Leopoldov the train headed north to Trenčín. This city was proud of its ancient castle ruins, impressive for its size and historic importance. On the cliff wall far beneath the castle is engraved one of the most important Roman epigraphic monuments in Central Europe north of the Danube River. In the last third of *AD* second century, the invasion of

Germanic tribes of Marcomanni and Quadi started one of the most notable conflicts between the Roman Empire and tribes of the Danube River. In *AD* 179, the last year of the war, a detachment of troops of the Second Auxiliary Legion (*II legio Adiutrix*) penetrated from a garrison in *Aquincum* (modern day Budapest) through the Vah River valley as far as *Laugaricio* (modern day Trenčín), the northernmost Roman border outpost in Central Europe–*limes Romanus*. The final battle of the Second Marcomannic War was fought between the Second Auxiliary Legion and the Germanic tribes in *Laugaricio* and is commemorated by a Latin inscription on the castle rock:

> "To the victory of emperors [Marcus Aurelius and his son Commodus], dedicated by 855 soldiers of II. Legion of an army stationed in Laugaricio. Made to order of Marcus Valerius Maximianus, a legate [General] of the Second Auxiliary Legion."

British film director and producer Sir Ridley Scott attempted to recreate a portion of this battle in the opening scene of his 2000 film *Gladiator*.

Leaving Trenčín, the train picked up speed. The railroad track closely followed the route of the Vah River, which flowed through a delightful valley of small farms and gentle hills. Occasionally, somber forests of spruce, pine, and oak were visible in the distance. As the valley widened, the train began to slow as it entered the city of Žilina, situated at the center of the main railroad lines connecting Bratislava with Ostrava and Těšín at the Polish border, as well as Košice and Prešov to the east.

Once out of Žilina, the train turned eastward in the direction of the Tatra Mountains. As the valley narrowed, the surrounding hills rose more abruptly toward the sky and the trees pressed in beside the margin of the river. The frozen earth lay silent beneath the windless patches of snow, disturbed only by the turbulent, icy waters of the river Vah which raced southwestward through Trenčín to join the Danube River at Komárno. If the landscape appeared deserted now, within a month it would come alive. Peasant farmers and sheepherders would emerge from their quiet villages to answer the call of spring. Loggers would take to their rafts and guide their floating cargo downriver, singing old folk songs about lovely forest nymphs who roamed the eternal woods. Fresh, green grass would soon carpet the meadows and red poppies would invade the land, recalling for some the stories of Turkish invaders whose blood stained the earth as they fell in mortal combat.

The first leg of the journey ended at Ružomberok, where the men transferred to a local train which served the villages along the route to Korytnica, a popular spa and health resort in the Low Tatras. In less than an hour they disembarked at Liptovská Osada and were ready to hike six kilometers north on foot to Smrekovica (1,428 meters above sea level), the army mountain retreat and recreation center that would be their home for the next three weeks.

The party, depositing their gear on a large, wooden, horse drawn sled, struck out along a narrow trail that wound back and forth across stubborn inclines. It was difficult going, the bitter air stinging their faces. Heavy-crusted snow underfoot made walking arduous. For the horses it was even more difficult. They sank to their bellies and remained immobile until the students formed a human chain and freed them.

After nearly three hours, the weary caravan sighted a large stone structure, isolated at the top of Velká Fatra, a lonely mountain ridge. One hundred meters away stood a smaller wooden building. The military occupied the stone structure; the other was privately owned and used by tourists who came to Smrekovica to ski. It was an ideal location. Even in their now weakened condition, the students were eager for the mountain course to begin.

THE WAR COLLEGE HAD PROGRAMMED THREE WEEKS OF INTENSIVE training and study. During this time everyone would learn to ski and would attend daily lectures in military science. Captain Jozef Artim was assigned to teach physical fitness and skiing. Lavota and Kanák would handle the lectures.

After a short briefing, the students either retired to their quarters or braved the cold to inspect the mountain slopes they would soon challenge. Those who already knew how to ski were permitted to take to the runs before dinner at six.

Unable to ski, Vlčko decided he would write Jirka. He found pen and paper, went outdoors, and sat down on a log which lay along the path that bordered the mountain ridge. Glistening in the late afternoon sun, the mountains burned gold and ember. He put on his sunglasses to reduce the glare. The sun slanted across his face as he raised his head to look into the distance. He wanted to tell Jirka how much he thought about her. The separation would not be easy, he knew this, and it had only just begun.

Exactly at six o'clock the first evening all the members of the school gathered in the mess hall where they heard the first Order of the Day, officially opening the three-week course.

The orders given, the students and staff took their places for the evening meal. Everyone ate with gusto and filled his plate more than once. Appetites had increased considerably in the bracing mountain air. Besides, the effects of the workout from climbing the path that afternoon were beginning to show. No one complained about army cooking when the meal was finished.

OUTSIDE IN THE BLACKNESS, RIBBONS OF YELLOWED LIGHT CASCADED over the drifting snow that collected beneath the windows of the military lodge. Beyond, the trees echoed the bitter, wanton wind. A door opened suddenly, and a shaft of splintered light slanted across the path leading to the tourist lodge. Two figures stepped into the light, closed the door behind them, and stood for a moment in the dark. Then, only the squeak and crack of their heavy boots as they tramped upon the snow stirred the cadent wind. Minutes later, men's voices mingled with the night as the door to the lodge opened and the figures stamped the snow from their boots before closing the door against the night.

Once inside, Peter Vlčko and Jozef Dvornak took a table a little removed from the pot-bellied stove that heated the snug public lounge. There were hardly any customers, which was not unusual during the middle of the week. The proprietor, standing behind a simple counter cluttered with inexpensive souvenirs and picture postcards, advanced to greet the new arrivals.

"Good evening, gentlemen. What can I do for you?" "A liter of *Prevareného*, please!" Dvornak ordered his cold-weather drink.

"Fine. Hot wine tonight sounds like a good idea." Peter liked to drink wine boiled with sugar and cinnamon bark.

He was all smiles as he scanned the lounge, which served as dining room, bar, and warming station for those who came to ski in this part of the Low Tatras. His eyes came to rest on his friend, Jozef, and he thought how good it was to be in his company. This husky young officer, three years Peter's junior, was always cheerful. Though his thin blond hair and nearly square face with the wide jaw gave him a serious, and typically Slavic, appearance, his lively blue eyes made his face anything but ordinary. Dvornak's eyes smiled even when the rest of his face remained immobile. They were smiling now as he started to speak. "There don't seem to be any girls here tonight. Fact is, I don't even see too many men around," Jozef quipped, having himself made a careful inspection of the room. He seldom demonstrated a keen interest in girls. However, he sought their company when he wanted to forget what troubled him.

"I hadn't noticed," Peter agreed somewhat vacantly.

"You mean you failed to notice a thing like that? Peter, since when has the female of the species failed to interest you? I seem to remember you and Murgaš having frequent nocturnal excursions into Bratislava." Jozef enjoyed this harmless teasing. They had become friends at the War College and often discussed their mutual problems, particularly those where young ladies were involved.

Before Peter could comment, the proprietor appeared, carrying a jug full of wine and two empty glasses. He poured the hot, red liquid into transparent tumblers and set the pitcher down on the table.

"Will there be anything else?"

"No, thank you," Peter replied. His tone was serious and thoughtful, as if Dvornak's gentle bantering about girls had not been heard and the waiter had not come at all.

"Jozef, you remember me telling you Christina and I were no longer communicating. That she'd also returned my engagement ring when permission to marry was refused?"

"Yes, but that was some time ago," Jozef recalled. "Don't tell me you haven't gotten over Christina? Didn't she find a German officer and. . . ."

"The answer is yes," Peter picked up before the subject of Christina proceeded further.

"Wait a minute! I'm beginning to understand. The night you and Murgaš went to the Luxor—after the holidays, wasn't it?—Štefan said something about meeting some really nice girls." His eyes met Peter's and flashed an *I-know-something-you're-not-telling* signal.

"The truth is, I have met someone."

"Well?"

"Well, what?"

"Peter, you always are the lucky one."

"Lucky? Maybe. She's beautiful, intelligent, charming, but she's Jewish."

"What's wrong with that? I wouldn't care if she were a gypsy. Does she love you?"

"That's not the point. I'm afraid I'm going to have problems keeping company with her in public. Then, there is her family."

"What's her name?"

"Georgina Reichsfeld. Her Slovak friends call her Jirka."

"It's really conspicuous. How does she feel about you and the problem you are concerned about?"

"She's interested in me. I don't know about the other."

"That's the main thing, Peter. If she's interested, any barriers will seem small. My fiancée is still trying to get a transfer from Prague, but the German authorities have yet to give their approval. It's getting on my nerves."

"Jozef, as long as she's faithful, you have nothing to worry about."

"Oh, I'm pretty certain she's faithful. But two years! We want to get married." Dvornak had never liked the idea of separation in the first place. "And it's pointless looking around for other girls. I'm just lonely, I guess." His eyes darkened, and the perpetual smile faded as he and Peter lapsed into silence.

Jozef Dvornak was the sort of person everyone thought of as sincere. He had integrity, people said. Never one to be anything but fair with others, he thought it was grossly unfair that he shouldn't be permitted to see the person he loved most. For two years his personal life had been interfered with by the authoritarian Nazi occupation forces which brought suffering and grief to so many Czechs. There were times when the kind, gentle, loving Jozef hated—no, despised—the Germans. He wondered how long a person could be patient before his optimism would succumb to pessimism, how long before his life would take on the meaning he looked for. He wanted very little. A wife, children, a home of their own. He loved flowers and wanted someday to open a little shop. He hated war and killing and oppression. He wasn't really cut out to be in the military. He was just doing his duty; and though he would fight for his country, if necessary, Dvornak wasn't interested in military science. Even in the army he was not part of the General Staff but in the Quartermaster Corps dealing with supplies and procurement. This was not very aggressive work and did not require a combative spirit as a frontline soldier needed; he liked it that way. He knew that once he left the army he would go into business and try to forget the military and politics.

Well, not altogether—he was a Democrat by inclination and would resist, if he had to, any Fascist tyranny. Right now, Jozef wanted his fiancée with him in Bratislava. Better yet, right here beside him at Smrekovica.

Peter saw Jozef's spirits slipping during the past few minutes and knew he had to rescue his friend from a state of depression.

"Come, Jozef, let's drink to reunion in Bratislava!"

"I'll drink to that anytime," Dvornak snapped back almost instantly. He lifted his glass. "To reunion with our sweethearts."

"Are you in love, Peter?"

"I don't know. But I do know that if Jirka needs me, I'll be there to protect her."

"Peter, if it matters, I'm on your side. If you should ever need any help from me, you know you can count on it." There was no doubt about Jozef's sincerity.

"Thanks, Jozef. For the time being, I'd rather no one knew what I told you tonight." In those days, it was unhealthy to be seen with or have Jewish friends. Therefore, the fewer people who knew about Peter and Jirka the better it was for everyone concerned.

"Of course, you can trust me, Peter."

They finished their wine, paid the check, and bundled up before returning to their lodge. Peter felt he had a good friend he could trust and depend on in any circumstances. For this, he was grateful.

AT SEVEN THE NEXT MORNING, THE BUGLER SOUNDED REVEILLE. "Well, how did you sleep on that straw mattress?" Murgaš asked Vlčko. They were roommates.

"Fine. Better than at the Danube barracks."

"Why is that, Peter?" Štefan began to dress as they talked.

"No bedbugs here." He couldn't resist smiling. "Besides, the mountain air and the wine last night worked like a sleeping pill."

"I exercised all night. I dreamed I was learning to ski. I learned to jump, stop, to do the telemark and the stem christie. It was quite a night."

"That's what I need."

"What?"

"To be able to dream and learn to ski at the same time."

Peter slipped on his shirt, buttoned it and reached for his trousers. The room was far from warm, so both men worked fast to get into their uniforms.

"Štefan, how long does it take a beginner to learn?"

"Oh, skiing every day as we will be, I'd say you should be pretty good within a week—that's if nothing happens to you." There was a chance Peter might get a broken leg.

"How long have you been skiing?"

"As a student I skied often. Actually, I was pretty good. But from the time I joined the army I've done very little skiing. I miss it, too."

"This will be my first time today. I'm looking forward to the experience. When I was young, I never had enough money to buy the equipment, and then later I never had the opportunity to learn. There was always something, the army, the Academy. But I think I'm going to love it. Skiing seems like such a beautiful sport, maybe the most exciting of all sports." Peter admired grace and skill in anyone, an athlete, a horseman, a dancer. He himself was more than competent in athletics, as a cavalry officer, and on the dance floor. He felt skiing would be something quite natural to him, and he had no apprehensions about falling and getting injured. At least, he thought he didn't.

"Peter, I couldn't agree with you more. Yesterday, I skied for the first time in several years. I was a little rusty, but I still had the same excitement and exhilaration coming down the slopes as I used to have. In a few days I'll be back in shape, you'll see." Murgaš was proudly confident he could fulfill his expectations.

"Štefan, let's go. I'm starved and don't want to miss breakfast."

After the morning lectures and the lunch break, everyone gathered on the slope nearest their lodge. There under the guidance of Captain Artim students and professors took their first skiing lesson.

At three, after an exhausting afternoon of elementary skiing, everyone assembled for the trip back to the lodge. The column of men moved slowly along the trail through the woods adjacent to the recreation center. It had been a good first day and the officers agreed that skiing was indeed a great sport. Anyone listening to their conversation would have gotten the impression that these were all expert skiers. But the most satisfied of all was Artim. Lesson one had been successful. Only Stanek had been injured, and not too badly either.

During the first week of intensive training the class learned the fundamentals of skiing. They learned how to turn, left or right, on a downhill run and how to use the snowplow method for stopping. They practiced turning completely around from a standing position. Getting uphill sometimes proved difficult for the novices, but after a short time they were able to make an ascent by using either the herringbone method for short slopes or the zigzag one for longer slopes. The sidestep method, where the weight is placed on the uphill edge of the skis, was the best for steep, long climbs or for especially slippery ones. By the end of the week confidence and skill had developed to such a degree that most of the men were really enjoying their training program.

The second week they began to tackle bigger hills. This meant their speed increased. They then had to learn how to make sudden stops which would not send them sprawling to the ground. Since these stops could be dangerous, only the better skiers were permitted to use the long and steeper slopes. The best skiers, however, improved until they were ready to practice jumps.

By the third week everyone had become reasonably competent. Now the students were allowed to set out in groups of three or four, in any direction. These exploratory trips in the mountains were excursions in cross-country skiing which acquainted the men with the local terrain and also provided them with many scenic delights.

The landscape was ruggedly beautiful. Noble evergreens, frosted and glazed from the winter snows, interrupted the undulating lines of interlocking hills which converged and then fell away to reveal the awesome sweep of a silent valley far below. In the distance a strangely muted stream gleamed in the midday sun, iridescent and blinding. Sequestered villages, like delicate cameos, embellished the bosom of the whitened earth.

"Let's head for that village," Peter said, pointing to a cluster of small huts nestled below in the valley. Štefan, Jozef, and Peter had embarked that morning in a different direction from that of their fellow students and had chosen to explore on their own. In a moment the threesome disappeared beneath the crown of the hill where they had paused to rest and enjoy the view. They raced against the wind, sending a fine spray of dry snow into the air. Their bodies were alive with excitement in an atmosphere of sensuous, cosmic involvement. Freely, without inhibition, they coursed downward, dominating each curve and contour of the snow-blanched earth. With their ski poles barely skimming the surface of the snow, they angled in toward the collection of timbered cottages which huddled together near a stand of birch trees that leaned in the wind. A short distance away, a narrow wooden bridge crossed a tiny stream. There was no sign of life in the village, except for sinewy curls of smoke which unfurled above the snow swept rooftops and faded against the pale sky. The trio banked, like splendid eagles coming to rest, and came to an abrupt halt only meters from the nearest cottage.

Peter and the other two were silent. He knew something had happened to him as he sped down that mountainside. It was more than an exercise in skiing, more than simple physical sensation. He had somehow become spiritually united to the land, to his beloved Slovakia, in a way as yet unknown to him. Mastering a mountainside had transformed him. He was infused with a new love of country which would sustain him throughout the uncertain and terrible days that lay ahead. He knew now he had the strength, the courage, the determination to resist any and all enemies who sought to subjugate or to destroy the land and the people he loved. Today, Peter had been free as never before, and he vowed he would do all in his power to preserve this freedom.

"Let's stop here and rest awhile," Murgaš addressed his comrades, removing his skis, which he set against the wall of the cottage. "Maybe the farmer who owns this place will offer us some hot tea."

"I could use some, with good strong slivovica," Peter almost drooled.

"Me, too," Dvornak was eager to take advantage of the warmth which the peasant's house promised.

AT THE END OF THE THIRD WEEK, THE ENTIRE SCHOOL PACKED UP AND embarked on their return journey to Bratislava. They took the same trail they had traveled on arrival, except that this time it proved easier going downhill. Some of the men sat on the wooden sleigh, singing as they descended to the valley station at Liptovská Osada. Others, along with Captain Artim, skied down the mountain trails leading to Ružomberok, where they would join the main party and board the train together. They had learned their lessons well and were a satisfied, happy lot. Smrekovica had been, for most, the experience of a lifetime. For Peter Vlčko, it was a prelude—deeply significant, even prophetic.

CHAPTER 19

UNDERCOVER MISSION TO BUDAPEST

DAVID MANDLER, A PRACTICING PHYSICIAN, AND HIS BROTHER OTTO, A chemical engineer, had for quite some time thought about leaving their native Prague. Nazi racist policies had become far too threatening for them to remain any longer. If they hoped to escape with their lives, they had to do it now.

In the third week of January 1941, the Mandler brothers and two of their friends, Jozef Stein and Ludvik Grossman, boarded a train for Bratislava. Immediately upon their arrival, they contacted the local Jewish authorities, who gave them the names of Dr. Julius Werner and Berthold Reichsfeld. Either, they were told, would be able to offer assistance.

The plan they worked out was quite simple. They would go to Budapest and contact the American or British embassies, obtain visas, and then travel either to the United States or to England. But there were certain obstacles to overcome first before their plan could be accomplished.

The greatest difficulty in getting to Hungary was acquiring valid passes which would allow them to cross the border and travel at least up to ten kilometers within the country. To obtain such passes was hard even for non-Jews. For Jews, it was practically impossible. Fortunately, *JUDr.* (*Juris doktor*—Doctor of Law) Pavel Macháček was Chief of State Security Police in Bratislava and a friend and former gymnázium classmate of Berthold Reichsfeld—as close a friend as was possible under existing circumstances. He was contacted, and within a week four sets of identity papers and the necessary border passes arrived.

Another difficulty was the language barrier. Neither the Mandlers nor their friends spoke Hungarian. Someone would have to accompany them on their journey if they hoped to clear the Hungarian border control successfully. To find such a person was a real problem, since no one knew who could be trusted these days. Failing to come up with even one likely candidate and ready to abandon their scheme, it was suggested to Reichsfeld that his daughter accompany them. At first, he rejected the idea, for there was too much at stake. But the more he thought about it the more he was convinced it was their only hope. Georgina could be trusted, and she spoke fluent Hungarian. Besides, this might be just the opportunity she was waiting for—to escape to England where she could join her cousin Ila Seidler, who left Slovakia a few years back when travel restrictions did not exist.

Reichsfeld explained the nature and purpose of the trip to his daughter, its potential dangers, and its prospects of success. He reasoned that it was more for her safety than for the Mandlers' convenience that she take the assignment. Reichsfeld thought this also would prevent his daughter from getting further involved in the affair with Peter, a gentile and officer of the Fascist Slovak state.

Georgina in recent months had grown more distrustful of Slovak government officialdom. She wondered how long it would be before Nazi racism would infect the power structure of her own country. Perhaps this was her last opportunity to escape, one she could not afford to ignore. However, it was not so simple. She had met Peter less than six weeks ago and had become very fond of him. Though their relationship was one of friendship and faced many obstacles, Georgina could not bring herself to say that love was an impossibility. She could not make up her mind; Peter Vlčko, of course, knew nothing of this plan. The secrecy with which Reichsfeld prepared the journey demanded that no one, not directly involved, have any knowledge of the arrangements. The most opportune time for carrying out this plan was during Vlčko's absence, while he was at Smrekovica.

IT WAS THE THIRD WEEK IN FEBRUARY WHEN GEORGINA AND THE FOUR men boarded the local train. This would take them to Galánta, the nearest station to board the express train going to Budapest.

The weather on the morning of their departure was far from ideal. It had snowed the night before and the temperature had dropped to below freezing. They were prepared for these conditions with heavy fur coats, woolen ear mufflers, gloves, and caps. On their feet they wore ski socks and sturdy boots. Each man carried a small briefcase, while Georgina took a leather satchel and her handbag. Any additional baggage would have aroused suspicion, particularly since their passes were only valid for twenty-four hours.

The Slovak border control and customs officials passed through the train checking documents and asking questions of the passengers who were traveling to Hungary. During this time the train rattled along the narrow-gauge track which led to the border.

Quietly, Georgina and her companions had taken seats near the exit door. They did not talk to one another, purposely. The Mandler brothers sat with their eyes closed, pretending to doze. Jozef Stein, normally reticent anyway, stared out the window, seemingly hypnotized by the frozen landscape. Ludvik Grossman held a wrinkled newspaper in front of him but found it difficult to read. Georgina, occupying a seat on the opposite side of the coupe, rummaged through her handbag and rearranged the contents in an effort to appear nonchalant.

"Good morning, Miss." A young, uniformed Slovak addressed her in a pleasant and friendly voice. His partner, a lightly older man, stood a short distance away, impassive, and silent. "May I see your pass?" Discreetly, Georgina smiled and handed him the paper.

"You're going only as far as Galánta?"

"Yes."

"And what is the purpose of your trip?"

"I'm going to visit a girl friend of mine. She's invited me for an overnight stay," Georgina was sure this officer could not verify her statement.

"I see. Then you'll be returning this way tomorrow?" He in no way indicated he doubted her answer. On the contrary, he seemed to imply that he looked forward to seeing her again. A bit of innocent conversation followed, which led nowhere but must have helped to break the monotony of his job. Actually, she found him quite charming and said she would see him on her return trip.

"Enjoy your visit, Miss. Don't forget, I'll see you tomorrow." Georgina half expected that tomorrow, should tomorrow ever come, he would ask her for a date. He politely tipped his hat and turned to her friends across the compartment. The first hurdle had been a success and she, almost inadvertently, had primed the Slovak official for his next interrogation.

"May I please see your passes, gentlemen?" The four men acknowledged the request, handing the fake documents to the train customs official. He kept two himself and gave the other two to his co-worker assisting him. They examined the papers carefully before returning them.

"All of you are going to Galánta?" His question sounded commonplace. They each replied with either a vocal 'Yes' or a nod of the head.

"What is the nature of your trip? You're all traveling together, I take it?"

David Mandler took the initiative and spoke. "We want to buy some goose feathers in Hungary. People say there are plenty and of good quality in Galánta." His manner revealed none of the nervousness which he felt at this moment.

"I see. Well, we have no objections."

"Yes, thank you." Mandler was glad the questioning was so short.

"Oh, by the way. You'll be returning this way tonight?"

"Yes, on the last train." Grossman assured them.

The interrogation ended. They moved to the exit door, opened it, and proceeded to the next car. Hurdle number two had been easier than anyone expected. When the train reached the border, a pair of Hungarian customs officers entered and commenced the questioning all over again as they passed from one car to the next. Until the formalities were completed the train was required to remain at the border station. This time, Georgina Reichsfeld would act as spokesman for the group. When the Hungarian officials stopped beside them in the aisle way, she calmly handed over all five passes, remembering to flash her most ravishing smile. But neither officer reacted. Both were rather dour and hardly gave her a second glance as they checked the papers one by one.

Turning to Otto Mandler, one of the officers asked, "Why are you entering Hungary?" The question was direct and apparently without emotion.

"We like your country," Georgina interrupted, replying to the question. Her compliment was well chosen. Hungarians were always pleased with such remarks.

"That's nice, young lady, but is there any reason why this gentleman cannot speak for himself?" The words rang metallically, disturbing Georgina unpleasantly. However, she could not afford to lose her composure now.

"No, except that he and his friends don't speak Hungarian—only Slovak and Czech." This was the truth; to lie and say they were deaf-mutes, which she considered saying, would be foolish and easily disproven.

"Are all these gentlemen friends of yours?" There was a note of suspicion in his question.

"Yes and no. Actually, they are friends of my cousins in Bratislava. Since I speak Hungarian, they thought it would be easier if I helped them in their business deal in Galánta. They are going to buy some down feathering. They manufacture pillows and feather quilts. Our stay is short, and they don't have time to spend learning the language." Her story did sound convincing, or so she thought, for it certainly was not unusual. Yet, she felt she was a little too sarcastic. Fortunately, neither one of them noticed it.

"Are you all returning to Bratislava together?"

"Of course. If they finish early enough, we'll be returning on the last train tonight." Georgina actually began to believe her own words. She had to, if ever she were to convince these two inquisitive Hungarians.

"Are you bringing anything into the country?" The other fellow picked up the questioning, apparently not interested in the reason for their journey.

"No, just enough for the short visit." Georgina prayed now as never before that they would not ask to see anybody's wallet. She was delegated to carry all their funds in a billfold in her handbag. It contained sufficient Slovak and Hungarian currency to last them for several weeks—far in excess of the import allotment.

The officials surveyed the group once more and then started to leave. Nearing the exit door at the opposite end of the car they stopped and exchanged words which could not be heard by Georgina. Their gaze came to rest on her once again. Apparently satisfied, they stepped down onto the platform. As the train slowly pulled out of the bleak border station, Georgina noticed they had disappeared inside the station to wait for the next train which would pass into Hungary. Little did they suspect that a young Jewish girl had deceived them.

"Galánta!" shouted the conductor as he moved up the aisle hurrying to the next car.

"Let's get off as quickly as possible," Georgina said. She was in charge, of this there was no doubt.

After disembarking, they followed the arrows which pointed to the railroad station waiting room. Georgina asked her companions to take a seat while she went over to buy tickets for Budapest. This time they would ride in relative comfort, even in third class, aboard an international express which was scheduled to arrive from Vienna within the hour. She returned shortly and distributed the tickets. Eyeing the wall clock which hung above the exit doors, she suggested they get a bite to eat in the station restaurant.

One entrance to the restaurant opened off the waiting room and another from the street in front. When Georgina and her friends entered the crowded, smoke-filled restaurant, they took only a minute to spot an empty table near the door leading to the kitchen. The floor was wet from the snow that clung to the many boots which tramped in and out. The dirty windows, steamed in a cheerless gray from too many bodies breathing the foul air, obscured their view of the street outside. A blur of voices resounded within the rather small enclosure as Georgina motioned to her friends to follow. They filed past four or five tables of animated conversation before reaching the other side of the room. When they had seated themselves, David Mandler broke the silence which Georgina had imposed from necessity for fear someone would hear them speaking Slovak to one another.

"I've a great idea! Jirka can treat us all." It was their first bit of levity since Bratislava. Everyone managed a smile. It was essential they maintain a normal exterior.

"That'll be easy. You've already made me treasurer of this expedition." Her eyes glistened, reflecting the white light which fell from naked bulbs illuminating the hazy interior. "Perhaps you'd like to order, Dr. Mandler?"

"Impossible. You know I don't speak Hungarian."

"Let me teach you then." Georgina almost seemed to forget where they were. "Repeat after me, *Pán* Doctor. '*Öt rumos teját kérem.*'"

"*Öt urmos teját kérek,*" the doctor stuttered.

"Oh, how funny it sounds when you say it! You certainly wouldn't get very far with that vocabulary."

"I think you'd better stick to your job as spokesman, Jirka."

"I believe you're right. If I hadn't come along, you'd probably end up in prison rather than the American Embassy. However, when we speak Slovak, we must be careful not to be overheard. These Hungarians are fanatically Nationalistic and would quickly turn us over to the authorities if they for a moment thought we were foreigners."

They cut their conversation off when they saw the waiter approaching. Georgina gave the order of tea and breakfast rolls and also asked if the kitchen might prepare five ham sandwiches for them to take on the train. She knew they would be hungry before arriving in Budapest and thought it wise if they avoided the dining car during the two-hour journey—anything not to draw undue attention to themselves. The waiter, eager to please, took the order and hurried out to the kitchen. It is a well-known fact that in Hungary everyone demands good service and good food. All waiters and chefs are aware of this and do everything they can to satisfy their guests. In what seemed like a very short time, the waiter returned, served them their tea and rolls, and set a small package containing the sandwiches on the table.

"Would you please pay now, *Kisaszony*?"

Georgina pulled out a black wallet from her purse and paid the check. She had previously separated her Slovak and Hungarian money into different compartments so that she would not make the fatal mistake of drawing out the wrong currency.

Suddenly, two *Csendörök* (gendarmes) appeared in the doorway. They began to sternly scrutinize the noisy crowd, as if looking for someone in particular. Dressed in khaki uniforms, with dark blue rooster-tail feathers jutting from their caps, they carried rifles slung over their broad shoulders. Their knee-high black boots shone immaculately. Pompous, arrogant, and sinister were entirely suitable adjectives to describe these representatives of the redoubtable Hungarian state police. Their physical presence alone produced a noticeably disquieting effect on everyone in the restaurant. Conversations subsided until only a low murmur of voices pervaded the room.

"Do you suppose they're looking for us?" Ludvik Grossman managed to ask his companions, unable to remove their eyes from the two figures who had entered the restaurant. Without shifting her position or changing the expression on her face, Georgina whispered a cautious reprimand to Grossman, seated beside her. "Quiet. Act normal. Do you want to draw their attention to our table?" They could only wait, like spectators at a fireworks display, holding their breath until the rockets exploded. But nothing happened. The *Csendörök*, satisfied with their inspection, left by the lobby door without speaking to anyone. And almost instantly the general atmosphere changed. People relaxed, and conversations resumed. The rising din of human voices reassured Georgina and her companions that for the time being they were safe.

"Phew! That was close," Grossman sighed, wiping the perspiration from his brow with a large white handkerchief. Georgina was relieved, too, now that the police had gone.

"We have to remain calm, or we'll ruin everything," Otto Mandler cautioned them inconspicuously.

Just as they prepared to leave, the loudspeaker carried an announcement that the Budapest Express would arrive on track number 3 in five minutes.

"Let's hurry. Our train is due any minute. And don't forget your briefcases."

"Don't you forget the treasury," Stein reminded Georgina. The express line was half empty. This meant they could choose seats they wanted. Wooden partitions divided the car into separate sections, affording some degree of privacy. They selected seats as far removed from the other passengers as possible. After they sat down, the train started to move. Once out of the station, Georgina and her friends relaxed. Outside, the flat country was blanketed with clean, white snow. Occasionally, a deer scampered across an open field, or a jackrabbit ran and hid among the dead grass which poked through the frozen snowdrifts. Small stands of scrub oak zipped by their window. Now and then a lonely village appeared in the distance, an oasis of humanity in an otherwise lifeless countryside. A strange melancholy paralyzed the lowering clouds. Georgina and her four comrades sat in self-imposed silence while the train sped on toward its destination.

Two hours later the express approached Párkán-Nána, a famous rail station on the main line connecting Vienna-Bratislava-Budapest with tracks connecting in all directions. (After World War I, the town where the station was located was called Párkán or Párkány in Hungarian, a border town of Czechoslovakia. In 1938, as a result of the First Vienna Award, Párkány and parts of southern Slovakia were returned to Hungary. After World War II, by the annulment of the Vienna Awards, the town became a part of Czechoslovakia again. It was renamed to Štúrovo in 1948. The formerly independent villages of Nána and Obid were merged with the town in 1960 and 1972 respectively.)

The city of Esztergom was visible through the coach window on the opposite shore of the Danube. Georgina could see on Esztergom's Castle Hill the beautiful Roman Catholic basilica *Cathedral of Our Lady of the Assumption and Saint Adalbert*, the Episcopal seat of Bishop (and future Cardinal) József Mindszenty, Prince Primate (*hercegprímás*) of Hungary.*

From Párkán the tracks paralleled the north bank of the Danube eastward as it wound its way through the Novohrad (Hungarian: *Nógrád*) County and entered Hungary. At Vác, Hungary, the Danube River turned

---

* Cardinal Mindszenty personified uncompromising opposition to Fascism and Communism in Hungary in support of religious freedom. During World War II, he was imprisoned by the pro-Nazi Arrow Cross Party. After the war, he opposed Communism and the Communist persecution in his country. As a result, he was tortured and given a life sentence in a 1949 show trial that generated worldwide condemnation, including a United Nations resolution and papal excommunication of all authorities involved. After eight years in prison, he was freed in the Hungarian Revolution of 1956, but after Soviet forces crushed the Revolution, he sought and was granted political asylum by the United States Embassy in Budapest, where Mindszenty lived for the ensuing fifteen years. He was finally allowed to leave the country in 1971. He died in exile in 1975 in Vienna, Austria.

directly south, cutting Hungary in half along the 19th meridian. In another hour the express arrived in Budapest, city of a million people, the Paris on the Danube.

At Budapest's west end railway terminal, Nyugati pályaudvar, the train discharged its passengers on track number 1, adjacent to the terminal building.

"Let's hurry now and leave with the crowd," Grossman advised, trying to correct his reputation of having been panicky before.

"But let me do the talking, and have your tickets ready," Georgina added.

Squeezing through the busy terminal lobby, they reached the street. Georgina flagged a cab and directed the driver to take them to *Szabadság tér* (Liberty Square), where they would find the American Embassy. The four men sat in the back, and she sat up front beside the driver, so she could quickly answer any questions he might ask. Her companions were to remain silent.

"This your first trip to Budapest?" The driver questioned Georgina as soon as they drove off from the station.

"No, I used to live here," she replied self-consciously. "Then you know the city?"

"A little. I haven't been back in a dozen years. But one never forgets Budapest." She tried to please him. Why did he want to carry on a conversation? There was something unsettling about his manner. She sensed he was questioning her, though no further words came. When they stopped at the first busy intersection, Georgina observed that he was staring intently at the reflection in the rearview mirror, studying the occupants in the back seat. He shifted gears.

"Is there any particular place you'd like me to leave you off in *Szabadság tér, Kisaszony*?" The question was more speculative than casual. "The American Embassy, perhaps?" Georgina's body stiffened. His words had stunned her.

"My God," she thought, "he suspects something! I've got to think fast."

"We're getting off in the block beyond, if I remember correctly." She didn't know whether this would check his curiosity or not. She only knew that she had to appear calm.

"Yes, *Kisaszony*. The block beyond the Embassy." His response was insinuating, or so she thought. Georgina's mind began to imagine all sorts of things. He suspected them and would turn them in to the Security Police. But why when nothing had been said to arouse his suspicions? Had her mute companions given them away? Cab drivers, after all, were accustomed to passengers who talked freely with one another. They must have looked rather odd—a lone girl and four men traveling together. What did he have to gain by delivering them to the police? Was he a misguided patriot, or could he be an agent of the state security apparatus? She had no answers to these questions. They had to get to the Embassy. Looking up she saw the *Szabadság tér* sign, which meant they couldn't be far now. The driver began to slow down as they passed a building flying the United States flag. In the next block he pulled up to the curb and brought the taxi to a complete stop.

"Here we are, *Kisaszony.*" Georgina paid the fare without comment and then opened the door and got out. The Mandlers and their friends emerged at the same time. They waited on the sidewalk until the cab skidded around the corner out of sight.

"Let's hurry. I think that driver suspected something."

"What do you mean, Jirka?" Grossman trembled more from fear than from the cold wind which stung their faces.

"We haven't time to talk now. I only know he disturbed me."

They crossed the street and were inside the Embassy at the stroke of one. All the seats in the reception room were filled. People even stood wherever they could find space. It seemed everyone who wanted to escape the Nazi or Fascist danger now sought help from the Americans. Apparently, the Yugoslav and British Embassies had failed—how else would one explain the crowd?

Georgina was not encouraged. With so many people ahead of them there was but a slim chance they would receive any assistance today.

"There's nothing we can do but wait," David Mandler said. "At least we'll have plenty of time to formulate our request before presenting it to the Ambassador."

"Then we'd better announce ourselves to the secretary and make an appointment or we'll never get an audience with Mr. Ambassador," Grossman reminded his companions. His anxiety was obviously coupled with fears that by taking such chances he might miss the last boat.

Then the agony began. Locating a small reading room, they sat down to wait until their names were called. Those ahead were ushered into the Ambassador's office in small groups of three or four. Each entered with hopeful trust.

However, only a few came out smiling. Georgina, the Mandlers, Grossman, and Stein became increasingly alarmed. Their optimism slowly disappeared as they questioned those who had already talked with the Ambassador. It was not that the Americans refused to help these refugees. They could not. The State Department had not issued instructions to the Embassy for assisting refugees seeking asylum in the United States.

Finally, Georgina's group was called. Their interview lasted ten minutes: the course of their entire futures had been determined. In ten minutes, their plans for freedom disappeared like a wisp of smoke on a windy day.

Completely disillusioned, they saw no purpose in remaining one minute longer. To return to Bratislava on the early evening express was their only course.

"Will you excuse me?" Georgina said. "I'd like to go to the restroom before we leave."

"Of course. We'll wait for you outside." Otto Mandler spoke impassively. No one seemed to feel anything at all. They had been thoroughly numbed by today's experience with the Americans. Now, with no other place they could turn to, they knew total helplessness.

WHEN GEORGINA LEFT THE EMBASSY, SHE WAS SURPRISED TO FIND THE street empty of even one familiar face. She looked in both directions but was unable to pick out any of her friends in the crowd. In five minutes, they had vanished. "But where have they gone?" Georgina asked herself.

"I'm positive they said they'd wait outside."

She rushed back into the Embassy, inspected the reading and reception room, and then hurried back out onto the street. Just at that moment she noticed a dark green police van at the end of the block. Two uniformed men were forcing a third man into the van. In the struggle to free himself, he wheeled around so that Georgina could see his face. It was Ludvik Grossman. His cries for help went unheeded, and the struggle ended with a blow across his head. After he was hauled inside the rear doors of the vehicle were secured. Then the guards went around front, jumped in, slammed the doors and sped away.

Confused, frightened thoughts swarmed about in Georgina's brain. Had she actually seen Ludvik Grossman being dragged off in a police van or had her eyes deceived her? The fur coat the man was wearing and the leather briefcase in his hand, wasn't this evidence enough that it was him? And the Mandlers—and Stein! Had they been arrested, too? Or had they managed to escape? She could not stop to answer these questions now. She had to get away from here before the police returned to look for her. She couldn't take a taxi, not now. It must have been that taxi driver who reported them. If she could only disappear. She would take a streetcar. It was her only chance. She had to leave distance between her and the Embassy and the sooner the better.

When she finally boarded a streetcar, Georgina realized she had no idea in which direction she was headed. She bought a ticket to the end of the line and walked to the rear of the car, where she sat down.

The ride lasted over an hour. For panic-stricken Georgina it had been an eternity. She checked her watch, but it showed the same time it had shown back at the Embassy. "My watch must have frozen from fright, the same as I did," Georgina thought.

"Last stop. Everybody out!" the conductor called out from a position beside the exit door. As they prepared to face the bitter night, the passengers bundled up before stepping down from the car.

Crossing in front of the streetcar, Georgina noticed a sign over the driver's window: "Rákospalota." "Thank God! At least I'm in the northern part of the city and on the east side of the Danube." She would head for the Slovak border and pray that no one had followed her this far.

"My satchel! Where is my satchel?" Georgina heard herself saying. She remembered she had left it on the streetcar. But she could not return now to reclaim it. It was already dark, and she had to locate a village soon. Besides, the authorities would ask to see her identification—and there would be questions which she did not want to answer. She would get by without it. Checking her purse, she heaved a sigh, grateful for the money safely tucked away in her wallet.

ON THE ROAD LEADING NORTH, GEORGINA WAS A LONELY PEDESTRIAN. At this hour she passed no one traveling in either direction. Mechanically, she paced her steps through the loosely packed snow and breathed deeply the clear night air. The wind had eased since afternoon, though the temperature remained unchanged. It was forty-five minutes before Georgina glimpsed a tiny light shining through a grove of trees, naked and dormant in the winter night.

"A light! I wonder what time it is?" Georgina knew she had to reach the burning light before the owner extinguished it and made off for bed. Imperceptibly, the bitter cold had exhausted her strength. Just a few minutes longer. She quickened her step and headed for the small farmhouse. Her breath came in short gasps. Sharp pains gripped her sides and a mounting fear choked in her throat. The day's events were beginning to close in on her as she approached the farmer's yard.

"Hello! Hello!" Her trembling voice called out. A distant sound of a dog barking answered her cries. "Please, let me in."

Shortly the door to the house opened.

"Hello! Who is it?" The man's voice was gruff but not unfriendly.

"It's me."

"Who are you? What do you want at this hour?"

"Please let me in and I'll explain everything."

"All right, come in." A man of about fifty invited Georgina in through the doorway, shining a lamp in her face. "Quickly. It's cold out there."

"I don't have any idea how late it is," Georgina managed to ask once the porch door was closed.

"It's nine o'clock." The man motioned her to enter the kitchen where she could warm herself at the wood-burning stove while they talked.

"Eržika, here's a young *Kisaszony* who just wandered in from out of nowhere," the farmer said to his wife who was sitting at the kitchen table.

"*Isten hozott!*" she welcomed Georgina warmly.

"Thank you. I'm surprised you're still up at this hour." She could think of nothing else to say. Her brain was stiff as her whole body.

"My wife is writing a letter to our son. I was finishing the newspaper."

"Then I'm fortunate."

"Sit down. Tell us what brings you way out here at this time of night," said the farmer with as much friendliness as curiosity.

Georgina decided she would tell no one any more than was necessary of the truth. She began without hesitation. "I'm looking for someone who will take me to the Slovak border."

"Why do you want to go there?" asked the farmer.

"I want to get back to Slovakia."

"Why don't you take the train?"

"Because." Georgina hesitated for a moment. "I'm afraid, I'm afraid the police will catch me and put me in jail. You see. I secretly visited my aunt in Rákospalota."

"How did you ever get there, young lady?" The farmer looked with slight distrust at Georgina's conduct.

"With a one-day pass to Galánta, and from there to Budapest by car."

"Couldn't you return by car, the way you came?" He was not content with her illegal border crossing.

"No, the car broke down this afternoon, and my friends are staying on in Budapest until it is repaired. But I must get back home. Please, help me. I was hoping you might take me back by horse cart. It would not be for nothing. I will pay you well. Besides, during the winter, you must be a little bored with nothing to do and the horses could probably do with some exercise." Her voice revealed a quiet determination which demanded the farmer's trust. Georgina's eyes held a resolute gaze which would not release him.

"Well, maybe I can help you. What do you say, Eržika?" His hesitation diminished as his doubts disappeared. What he needed was a slight encouragement.

"Do what you think is best, but I have no objections." She didn't want to take the blame if something went wrong.

"All right. But we won't be able to leave tonight. We'll go tomorrow, the first thing in the morning," he finally agreed.

"How long do you think the trip will take?"

"Where exactly do you want me to take you, *Kisaszony*?"

"Anywhere, as long as it's near the border. I can manage alone from there."

"In that case, I'll take you to Surány. It's closer than Galánta. Still, it will take about two or three days."

"How much do you want?" Georgina was very business minded now that she had secured his cooperation.

"Oh, three hundred *Pengö* should be more than satisfactory."

"I'll give you half now and the other half when we get to Surány. All right?" Even though she was happy with this progress, the deal still required some cautiousness.

"Agreed. Now, why don't you eat something? You must be starved. Then we will get some sleep." The man was glad the opportunity was so favorable. "Eržika, warm up your *Székely goulas* for our visitor."

"*Kisaszony*, do you like this kind of goulash?" asked his wife.

"Oh, yes. Very much. My mother makes it often at home." Georgina pulled out her wallet and gave the farmer one hundred-fifty *Pengö* which he happily accepted and immediately deposited in his bedroom for safekeeping.

"What is your name?" The farmer's wife was the first to ask. "Györgyi."

"Then you must be Hungarian."

"Only partly. My mother is. She was born and raised in Budapest. My father is Slovak." She could see no sense in withholding this bit of innocent information.

"Here," she said, putting the delicious smelling meal in front of Györgyi. "I hope you enjoy it. And take some bread."

"Thank you. I'm really starved."

"I'll go make your bed. You'll have to sleep in the back room. It's not heated, but you can cover up with the goose down quilt. It'll keep you plenty warm."

"Fine. I like to sleep in a cold room anyway." With this she began to eat in silence.

When the meal was over, her hostess took Györgyi to the little room which would be hers for the first night following a day of disappointment and fear. She thanked the woman, complimented her good cooking, and retired for the night.

Georgina Reichsfeld was grateful for having found such good people. Or perhaps they were just being kind because they expected the money. It didn't really matter. It was more important that they were going to help her. Certainly, things could have turned out much worse. At least for the time she was safe and warm. But she was not completely sure of anything. In the morning either she would find a horse cart out front or a police wagon waiting to take her back to Budapest to join the Mandlers and their friends. Nevertheless, she would try to sleep. These thoughts crossed her mind as she settled beneath the cold quilt. Her body shook more from cold than from fear, a healthy sign. In a little while her eyes closed, and she was asleep.

"*KISASZONY*, IT'S TIME TO GET UP. MY HUSBAND IS READY AND WAITING outside," the farmer's wife called from behind the bedroom door.

"I'll be right out," Georgina replied as she opened her eyes. Jumping out of bed, she washed her face in a small basin filled with clear, cold water. She had lost her toilet articles, so she rubbed some soap on her finger and scrubbed her teeth with it, mindless of the strange tasting dentifrice. "How did you sleep?" The woman smiled as she greeted Györgyi, who had entered the kitchen.

"Like a baby. I didn't wake until you called me this morning."

"Here. Some hot coffee and bread and butter. This should give you strength and warm you up, too. I've fixed a little food for you to take on your journey. Three days is a long time in this weather."

"What is your name?" asked Georgina as she began her simple breakfast.

"Mészáros, Eržebet."

"Mészárosné, I can't thank you and your husband enough for your hospitality. It was very nice of you to take me in last night. And now, your husband taking me to the border. You have no idea how grateful I am. I wish you the best of everything."

"There's nothing to thank me for, *Kisaszony*. I wish you luck. I hope you get home soon—and safely."

With breakfast over, Georgina bid goodbye to Mészáros' wife and hurried out into the yard where her husband was impatiently waiting. The sight of his ancient cart was a relief to Györgyi, who still could not erase the picture of the Budapest police van from her mind.

The farmer extended his hand and helped her up onto the seat beside him and gave her two blankets to protect her from the cold. She put one beneath her and wrapped the other around her legs. Mészáros himself was dressed in a long sheepskin coat, a fur hat, and long, heavy felt boots. His thick, bushy mustache was further protection against the freezing air. Cracking the long whip he held in his hand, he shook the rains with his left and let out a loud "Hi-yo!" The horses began moving out of the farmyard into the road. He pulled on the right rein, and they turned in the direction of Vác.

In the early morning air, crisp and biting, the horses snorted often to clear the ice which collected on their nostrils and mouths. They were reluctant to travel in the penetrating cold but had only to hear the crack of Mészáros' whip to pick up speed. The wooden wagon wheels crunched through the dry snow, slicing the silence of a slumbering world.

Györgyi realized that to travel in this kind of bitter cold, in an open wagon was foolhardy. But she also knew she had no choice. She would certainly face several serious charges if she was apprehended by the Hungarian police: helping others to illegally cross the border; carrying a large sum of foreign currency without an official permit; traveling on an expired border pass; and most serious of all, being Jewish. She was on her way home, and for that she was grateful.

THE JOURNEY WAS PROVING TO BE LONGER AND MORE DIFFICULT THAN Georgina had expected. It was made even more arduous by the fact that her companion was so much older and was an uneducated man with whom conversation was nearly impossible. Yet, it was probably better this way than if she had to resist the advances of an overly eager Hungarian lad.

During the trip no one stopped them, and they encountered few people using the back roads. Georgina imagined the police were searching for her, but she reasoned they would never expect her to travel in this manner when she could have returned to Slovakia on a comfortable train within two hours.

At the end of the first day, they reached a little village north of Párkán near the big bend in the Danube. Here they spent the night. By nightfall of the second day, they made Surany but continued to the outskirts of town until they located another small village where they learned the border was twenty kilometers away.

After traveling for seven hours on the third day, Georgina and the farmer came within sight of the border and could make out the villages which lay outside Nitra in Slovakia. It would be, but a short time and Georgina would be safely across. She could hardly restrain herself from running through the field, deep with snow, soon to be home. "Thank you for bringing me here," she said to the farmer, who had fulfilled his agreement, and she paid him the rest of the money she had promised.

"Don't go near the guard hut. It's off this road parallel to the railroad tracks. Keep to the left and try to stay hidden. Good luck!" With these words he turned the wagon around and headed for home. Now Georgina was alone, and the most critical leg of her journey lay before her.

GEORGINA STOOD IN SILENCE ON THE SNOW PACKED ROAD. She looked in every direction to see if anyone had observed her getting off the wagon. No one appeared. Without delay she left the road and set out through the open field on her left. She made her way from one group of small trees and bushes to the next. This concealment offered her the opportunity to rest a little and to enjoy at least momentary protection. In the flat and open countryside, the winds piled the snow in long dune-like drifts, sometimes a full meter high. Unfortunately, they collected across Georgina's direction of travel. Slowly, she waded through the snow barriers. When she sank into the deeper ones, she struggled free and crawled on her knees, fighting shortness of breath which froze in the frigid air. Her appearance would have been almost laughable if the circumstances were different. She was covered with snow from head to toe. Her face wore a mottled mask which she brushed away with her gloved hands. Loose snow slipped down into her boots, freezing her feet and legs. The numbness increased until she feared she might collapse, only to die before reaching the border. But she continued to move, almost crazed with the idea that safety was minutes away. A frozen brook appeared. Swirling snow funnels rose from the ice which imprisoned the waters. These would help to hide her as she made her last steps into Slovakia.

"The brook must be the boundary line," Georgina thought, crossing to the other side. But she couldn't be certain. Exhausted, she stopped to rest within the shelter of a clump of trees. Fatigue threatened to take her mind from her objective when in the distance she heard the whistle of a train that seemed to be going in the direction from which she came. Then she heard the metallic sound of brakes, screeching across the field. The train stopped, and she recovered enough strength to continue. She could only think of being dry and warm and of finding someplace to sleep. The railroad tracks lay only a few meters ahead. She quickened her step and literally dragged herself into the heated waiting room of the Slovak border station. Half dazed, she pulled a chair up to the coal-burning stove, removed her frozen boots, and fell asleep as her clothes dried on her body.

"HEY, MISS, WHERE ARE YOU HEADED?" ASKED THE STATION-MASTER, shaking her shoulder.

"Home!" Georgina answered, still half-asleep and not yet conscious of her surroundings.

"Where's home?"

"'Bratislava."

"Do you have your ticket yet?"

"No."

"Then you better hurry up. The last train will be returning soon." Georgina pulled on her dry boots and went to the ticket counter. She purchased a second class one-way to Bratislava. When the train pulled into the station, she boarded and took a seat beside the window. "Thank God, I'm free again!" She was grateful she had managed to return safely.

When the train arrived in Nitra, where it made a short stop, the stationmaster came aboard and walked directly to where Georgina was sitting.

"Excuse me, Miss. Are you Georgina Reichsfeld?"

"Yes, I am," she replied, a little wary about answering. She was surprised he knew her name. What did he want, she wondered?

"Step this way, please," he asked, indicating that they were to leave the train.

"My God, what now?" She was afraid to ask any questions.

A few minutes later they entered the station-master's small office. No police were waiting. That was some consolation, but still she was disturbed.

"We have been looking for you for several days now," the stationmaster spoke first.

"It is true," she thought. "The police have been looking for me." Perhaps if she made a break. . . . But the stationmaster continued.

"Your parents have been frantic. They called several border stations trying to locate you." Now Georgina recalled that she failed to send a message to her parents from Budapest about how they made it there.

"You had better phone them now to let them know you're all right."

He handed her the telephone, which she accepted with relief. Her spirits were lifted for the first time in four days. Finally, she could breathe freely. Maybe she would even enjoy the ride back to Bratislava.

CHAPTER 20

THEIR RELIGIOUS CONTEMPLATION

WESTERN POWERS ANSWERED GERMAN ACTS OF AGGRESSION WITH THEIR own counter measures. The Allies' weakness in Europe for the time being was at least partially counter balanced by their strength on other battlefields elsewhere in the world. The English began a counteroffensive in Egypt in December 1940 against the advancing Italians reaching El Agheila. By January 1941, the British captured the port of Tobruk in Libya, inflicting such heavy losses on the enemy that the Italian army was almost completely destroyed. This prompted the arrival of Rommel and his *Afrika Korps* in Tripoli in February 1941.

The United States, although not yet in the war, was not asleep. In September 1940, the first military conscription law was passed, and in October 1941, extraordinary tonnage of food, oil, war matériel, military transports, raw industrial materials, and medical supplies began to leave American ports under the first protocol of the Lend-Lease Act. With these steps, the United States clearly decided to emerge from isolationism and help the allied nations, including the Soviet Union, opposing the Axis powers, while at the same time begin to build itself into a powerful "Arsenal of Democracy."

In January 1941, the British also landed forces in East Africa. During the ensuing four months, they occupied Eritrea, Somalia, and Abyssinia.

Failing to attack the English directly, Germany turned to aggressive action against the weaker European continental countries. In March 1941, they forced Bulgaria to join the Axis, enabling the *Wehrmacht* to occupy the Balkans. Then in the beginning of April, Yugoslavia and Greece fell into German hands. The desperate resistance of these two countries was broken in two weeks. The defeat of Yugoslavia and Greece climaxed the fall of western and central European countries. Hitler had far greater plans, however, and did not rest on the laurels of his victories for even a moment. Beginning in February 1941, Hitler decided to commence execution of the ultimate goal of *Generalplan Ost* against his August 1939 agreement of friendship and non-aggression with the Soviet Union, when he began massing troops near the Soviet border even before the campaign in the Balkans had finished.

NEWS OF GREAT GERMAN VICTORIES WAS BROADCAST WITH MUCH fanfare all over Europe, and the effect on the people of the occupied countries was depressing. The Jewish population especially began to lose hope for the future. When increased persecution and oppression reached the stage of despair and helplessness, they simply laid their fate in the hands of the Almighty. The military news was alarming enough, but announcements that the Jews, even in Slovakia, were to be further restricted and controlled shattered all faith.

Vlčko visited the Reichsfeld family more often these days. He sought every opportunity to see Jirka, and their relationship grew deeper and stronger. Only his studies kept him from seeing her every day.

Jirka's parents, however, failed to see anything sensible in Vlčko's courtship of their daughter. In fact, they were afraid the relationship would be exposed, and serious consequences would ensue for all involved because of Peter's close association. Moreover, they repeatedly brought up the religious differences that inherently existed between the two families, differences they considered irreconcilable. Györgyi was their only child. Although they were not pious Jews, they tried to raise her in the Jewish faith and traditions. But as she grew into an adult woman, they could not control her thoughts and feelings. She was a determined person with a mind of her own. Now, when she had found a man in whom she could confide, she saw her opportunity to unshackle herself from the smothering protection of her parents and their "antiquated" ways, and to gain at least some of the independence she longed for.

Georgina described her relationship with Peter to her Jewish friends by pointing out his sympathy for and understanding of their common plight, particularly the misfortune of being Jewish in a racist society. When they asked if she would go so far as to marry him, she replied that she could solve whatever religious problems might arise. Her conscience permitted her this much. To their next question whether she would change her religion for Peter, she answered with a firm and decisive "Yes!" suspecting she may one day face this dilemma in order to save her life.

Beno Gubi then asked if she was certain she could trust a gentile like Peter, and whether she views the present racist policies as the fault of the Jews. He probed her for possible indoctrination by anti-Semitic Aryanites.

"Of course I don't think we Jews are to blame for our present troubles. There's absolutely no rational excuse for Hitler's actions. No one in the world has the right to punish anyone, let alone a whole nation or race, for their faith or traditions. Nor is it right to blame the Jews for Europe's problems. Hitler is just using the Jews as scapegoats for European problems that have been building for a long time."

Although somewhat simplistic, Georgina was not too far off in her assessment of Hitler's motives.

Georgina continued, "I think at this moment in history everyone needs to carefully and critically examine themselves, but particularly us Jews. Personal experience tells me I'm right."

"Perhaps, but there's one thing you must not forget. Regardless of everything being said about the Jews, we are the chosen people. God will not let anything happen to us." Georgina often heard this response from Jews who felt they were special in the eyes of God.

IT WAS THE MIDDLE OF MARCH 1941 WHEN GEORGINA FAILED TO KEEP AN appointment with Peter.

"I wonder what could have happened?" he asked himself. "Maybe she'll phone me tomorrow." He tried to remember if he'd said or done anything to make her angry the last time they were together. He couldn't think of anything. It was late, and he still had some studying to finish, so he headed back to the barracks. When no news came from her the next day, or the day after that, he decided to call her from the payphone outside his quarters. Jirka's mother answered.

"Oh, I'm sorry, *Kapitán* Vlčko, but Györgyi has been in bed with the flu the past three days."

"That's too bad, Mrs. Reichsfeld. Would you tell her how unhappy I am to hear she's not well? I hope she'll be better soon." Intentionally, Peter did not mention that he would like to see Jirka.

"Would you like to drop by tomorrow, *Pán Kapitán*?" Her invitation sounded genuinely understanding of his feelings.

"If you think it'll be all right. I'll be there around two."

"Jirka will be pleased to see you, I'm sure."

"Fine. Well, goodbye," Vlčko said, unable to think of anything else to add.

"Goodbye," Mrs. Reichsfeld said, and hung up the receiver.

Peter wondered why he hadn't thought of the possibility that Jirka might be sick. He could have kicked himself for not calling sooner. She was probably waiting for him to phone or to visit her. He had to check the impulse to run over this very moment. He wished he had said he would be there this evening, but he would simply have to wait until tomorrow. "At least she knows I called, and I'll be there Sunday." Reasonably satisfied, Peter slipped back into the *kaserne* to finish his studies to have more time the next day with his sweetheart.

SUNDAY WAS USUALLY A DAY OF REST AND RELAXATION FOR THOSE WHO had completed their duties on Saturday. For those who spent Saturday evening on the town, Sunday morning was for sleeping. Some went to church every Sunday. Afterwards they normally took a stroll down the city *korzo* (promenade), which started at St. Michael's Gate and ended at the Danube River. Here young people walked leisurely, discussing controversial topics, and exchanging opinions frankly, often loudly. The more romantic couples walked hand in hand. Groups of young men scanned the narrow walkways for single, unattached girls. Most had learned through experience that if a girl returned their attentive gaze, nothing prevented a closer relationship from developing. Those who were afraid or clumsy had to content themselves with a brief flirtation and nothing more. If one were really serious, a little bouquet of snowdrops or violets purchased at a flower stand helped.

Captain Vlčko was one of the most enthusiastic Sunday habitués. On these occasions, he dressed in his formal uniform with high black, polished riding boots, red riding breeches, a neatly sheathed dagger hanging from his left waist, white wool suit jacket with polished, gold buttons, and a stiff, high brim white officer's cap. If the weather was cool, he wore a long army wool overcoat, snugly tailored. He presented a figure straight from the pages of *The Student Prince*. So taken was he by her charms that from the time he met Jirka, his interest in the *korzo* had declined rapidly. And so, today after Sunday Mass in the chapel opposite the Sturzer sweet shop, he went to the Blaha Café near the Danube Bridge for a generous lunch. Lunch over, he read the latest papers and looked through some picture magazines in order to kill time before calling on Jirka. He checked his watch continually so as to not be late. At fifteen minutes before two, he got up from his table, paid the check and left the café, hurrying to where his heart drew him.

"Good afternoon, *Pani* Reichsfeld," Peter greeted Jirka's mother as she opened the door of their apartment.

"*Pán Kapitán*. How have you been?" She was all smiles.

"'Quite well, thank you. How is the patient?"

"She's still in bed but feeling much better today. Let me take your things, and you can go to her room and see for yourself. She's been waiting for you. Not too patiently, I'm afraid." Peter could not tell whether this was a good sign, for Mrs. Reichsfeld's voice revealed little more than the words themselves.

He stopped in front of Jirka's door, peeked inside, and whispered the warmest "Hello" he could manage. Jirka smiled in return and answered back.

"Hello, Peter."

"Have you moved in here permanently?"

"I didn't move; I was sentenced!" Her irritation was only superficial now that Peter had arrived.

"What heartless judge sentenced you to so cruel a fate?" Why not continue their little game, he thought? It was enough to be with Jirka that it didn't really matter what words were exchanged.

"The flu bug. That's who. I've been imprisoned for four days."

"That's not awfully long. When I get the flu, I wind up in bed for at least a week, sometimes longer."

"Were you lonely without me, Peter?" Jirka abruptly changed the subject.

"What do you think?"

"Tell me. I want to know." Her face was serious now except for an unmistakable sparkle in her lustrous eyes. They still appeared brown to Peter in the dim light of her bedroom.

"When you didn't show up the other evening, I couldn't imagine what had happened. I hoped you'd call but you didn't. At first, I was hurt, but then I began to worry about everything and nothing. I was afraid you had changed your mind about us."

"Peter, I'd never do anything that silly. What reason would I have?" she said, giving particular stress to her reply. Then her eyes held him fast.

"Come here, Peter. Let me give you a kiss." She took his face in her hands and brushed his lips gently with hers. "I'm glad you came. You'll help me more than the medicine I'm taking." Her innocent smile reflected in his eyes, and for a brief moment they said nothing.

"I think you need a different prescription."

"What would you recommend, Doctor Vlčko?"

"Well, first let me explain. Your loneliness became my ally."

"I don't understand."

"It's simple. Your mother invited me over and unwittingly revealed you'd be very glad to see me."

"*Pán Kapitán*, you sound overconfident. Maybe I just wanted you to come because I was bored with so much time on my hands and nothing to do, chained to this miserable bed."

"I don't believe that. You could have just as easily invited some of your girlfriends over. Instead, you picked me. Now that, my dear young lady, is significant." He then took Jirka in his arms and kissed her passionately, holding her firmly against his body. His pounding heart echoed hers. Suddenly, a spark had burst into flame. The fire of suppressed desires illuminated the room with an incandescence that only lovers can produce. Just as quickly as he had taken Jirka in his arms, he released her.

"Peter!"

"Jirka!"

"I'm breathless, I . . . I don't know what to say."

"Then don't say anything, my darling." This time he drew her delicate body toward him and waited before he brought his lips against her warm cheek. He kissed her eyes, which were closed now, and sought her expectant mouth, as eager as his own.

"Györgyi! Do you two want a snack?" Mrs. Reichsfeld's voice intruded.

"Yes, I am a little hungry," Jirka recovered enough to reply.

"You see. My treatment is beginning to take effect. Your hunger is proof of that," gloated Peter, who had risen to a standing position beside Jirka's bed.

"'You think so?" Jirka smiled, for she could not conceal her true feelings. His presence had been therapeutic.

Mrs. Reichsfeld entered carrying a tray with coffee and apple strudel which she set on a little table next to the bed.

"The strudel is excellent," Peter remarked after the first bite.

"Don't be bashful. Take as much as you want. Mother will bring us more."

"This beats army fare." Peter really enjoyed home cooking, which he seldom received.

"Mama! More strudel!"

The conversation then shifted to the mundane, and both Peter and Jirka seemed not to notice.

"Mother makes the world's best strudel. And the walnuts add just the right touch."

"I wish I would. . . ." Peter wanted to say how happy he would be to become a steady customer in their kitchen, when the door opened.

"What's going on?" Mrs. Reichsfeld asked, surprised Jirka was eating at all. "At noon you weren't a bit hungry."

"I wasn't, but Peter has improved my appetite."

"In that case, maybe the *Kapitán* should move in with us. You might get better faster." Was it possible mother was wise to Peter's curative powers, Jirka wondered?

"You really think it would help?" Peter asked in complete innocence.

"Certainly. I haven't seen her like this in a long time."

"Mama, which room are we going to give to Peter?"

"I hadn't thought of that. We really don't have any spare room. The two of you certainly couldn't stay here together."

"That wouldn't be a bad idea, *Pani* Reichsfeld," Peter teased, sneaking a wink at Jirka.

"I know what you men are always thinking about."

"Mama, could we be alone for a while? Peter is especially entertaining today."

"Well, all right. If you need anything, just call."

"Certainly, *Pani* Reichsfeld," Peter assured her. One thing neither he nor Jirka wanted was a chaperone.

"Peter, you've no idea how much trouble I have with my parents. I can't make a move without them. They're like my shadow. There's hardly anywhere they'll let me go alone. Sometimes, I feel like a puppet on a string. It's beginning to get on my nerves and, frankly, I don't know what to do any more."

"I understand, Jirka. It looks as if your independence won't come easily."

"Well, I'm running out of excuses. I even have to lie. But there just doesn't seem to be any other way. I want more freedom, which they refuse to give me. When I'm truthful, I get even less." Peter listened sympathetically. He held Jirka's hands in his own and tried to comfort her as she spoke. She was unusually candid.

"I feel like a fox terrier we used to have. Everywhere my parents went, they took him along inside a large handbag, with only his little head sticking out of the top so as not to suffocate. When they went to a movie, or travelled on a train, even his head didn't show."

"What happened to him?"

"She died of a heart attack. Old age. That's how I lost one of my closest friends."

"You don't need a pet, Jirka. You have me instead."

"But I can't always have you by my side to entertain me." Jirka and Peter were enjoying this simple interchange.

"Then you still want another dog?"

"Yes, I guess I do."

"Maybe I can get one for you. Right now, I have to go. I don't want to overstay my welcome."

"What do you mean, Peter? You only just arrived."

"Not quite. It's almost four-thirty."

"So!"

"I've been here over two hours."

"Do you have any regrets?" She sounded disappointed.

"No regrets. It's been wonderful being here with you. But I've some tests tomorrow, and I have to prepare a little for them, or I'll surely fail. If that weren't the case, I'd have been over yesterday. It wasn't easy waiting an extra day."

"When will I see you again?"

"'It depends on the assignment I pull tomorrow. In any case, I'll call you." With that he kissed her again and went out into the hallway to get his coat.

"*Kapitán* Vlčko. Leaving so soon? Wouldn't you like to stay for dinner? My husband will be home shortly."

"Thank you, *Pani* Reichsfeld. I'd like to, but my books are waiting for me."

"Yes, I know your studies should come before anything else. They, more than socializing, will determine your future. Then I won't detain you." She helped him with his coat and hat, and he thanked her once again for her kind hospitality and said goodbye.

ONE SUNDAY IN MAY, PETER INVITED JIRKA TO CHURCH WITH HIM.

"Why, sure, Peter. I'd like to. But I'll need a rehearsal. I don't want to panic because I can't follow what everyone else is doing during the service."

"Don't worry. I'll be at your side every minute."

At eleven o'clock they entered the historic St. Martin's Cathedral for mass. It was filled to capacity. People lined the walls along the side aisles and overflowed to the back of the church. There was nothing for Peter and Jirka to do but find a place to stand. St. Martin's Cathedral is situated on Staromestská street at the western border of the historical city center below Bratislava Castle (*podhradie*) near the old Jewish quarter and Neolog Jewish Synagogue where the Reichsfelds attended. It is the largest and one of the oldest churches in Bratislava, dating to 1311, known especially for being the coronation church of the Kingdom of Hungary between 1563 and 1830 during a period when the Ottomans captured Budapest and threatened Vienna. In total, the coronations of eleven kings and queens plus eight of their consorts took place there.

"At least you don't have to worry about when to stand and when to kneel or sit. The rest is easy," Peter whispered to Jirka. She smiled, a little relieved. Leaning her head forward she surveyed the impressive Gothic interior. The slender pillars rose majestically like trees reaching up to heaven.

"'This is a lovely church, Peter. As beautiful as the pictures I've seen."

"Have you ever been inside a Christian church before?"

"No, never. This is my first time."

"Now we're supposed to make the sign of the cross. The priest will read today's Gospel."

"The Gospel according to St. Matthew, chapter 22, verses 34–40:

> *34Hearing that Jesus had silenced the Sadducees, the*
> *Pharisees got together. 35One of them, an expert in the law,*
> *tested him with this question: 36"Teacher, which is the*
> *greatest commandment in the Law?" 37Jesus replied:*
> *"'Love the Lord your God with all your heart and with all*
> *your soul and with all your mind.' 38This is the first and*
> *greatest commandment. 39And the second is like it: 'Love*
> *your neighbor as yourself.' 40All the Law and the Prophets*
> *hang on these two commandments.*

"Peter, how sad, really! Mankind seems to have forgotten these words."

"Unfortunately, yes. Let's hear the sermon. I think this is no ordinary priest. He's wearing a monk's habit under his vestments."

> My dear friends in Christ . . . Jesus Christ clearly explained to the Pharisees which is the greatest and most fundamental of His laws, and which should be followed before all others. He not only stated the first law about loving God, but also the second law, which He said was like the first and about loving your neighbor. And He made them into one by calling them the "greatest commandment." The entire world is dependent on these two laws. Fulfilling one and ignoring the other is as serious a sin as ignoring both, because loving God is nothing less than loving your fellow man. "Truly I tell you, whatever you did for one of the least of these brothers and sisters of mine, you did for me," Christ said in Matthew, chapter 25. Plainly, love for our fellow man is synonymous with love for God.

He ended his sermon with these words:

> I say to you once again; your neighbor is anyone who needs your help. It doesn't matter whether he's Christian, Jew, Muslim, or a Samaritan. We were all created by the same God in His image. Therefore, we are all equally His children. In the name of the Father, the Son, and the Holy Ghost. Amen.

"Well," Peter spoke in a low voice, "what did you think?"

"I've waited to hear someone speak like this for a long time. I only wonder how many here took his words to heart."

"Pray that they do. What the world needs now is love, not hate."

At the consecration Jirka interrupted Peter. "What's the priest raising up now?"

"The host, made from unleavened bread, is Christ's body. The wine in the chalice is Christ's blood, shed for the sins of mankind. At the consecration the mystery of the Eucharist says the bread and wine are the body and blood of Jesus Christ."

When the congregation began to file up to the altar for Holy Communion, Jirka asked Peter if they were supposed to follow, too.

"Not everyone receives communion. Only those who have a guilty conscience and are sorry for their sins."

"What do you mean?"

"In their last confession these people admitted their sins and repented. They were forgiven by the priest, who is God's representative on Earth. By receiving communion, they replenish themselves spiritually in order to be able to resist further temptation to sin."

The Mass ended, and people began to pour out of the cathedral into the street. Peter took Jirka's hand and led her away from the crowd, so they could walk quietly together in the May sunlight.

"Peter," Jirka began, "how can one person forgive the sins of another?"

"Christian doctrine teaches that Jesus Christ conferred to His disciples the power to exonerate the sins of the penitent and to sustain the sins of the impenitent as taken from Christ's own recorded words in Matthew chapter 16, verse 19 regarding the 'Keys of the Kingdom of Heaven' and the instructions Jesus gave His disciples in John chapter 20, verses 21 and 23 ('As the Father has sent me, I am sending you. . . . If you forgive anyone's sins, their sins are forgiven; if you do not forgive them, they are not forgiven')."

"Do you believe that?"

"Absolutely."

"What do you mean by that?"

"'Don't be impatient. There are better places to discuss religion than out on the street. You know what? It's noon and we should be thinking about getting something to eat. Let's continue our discussion over lunch. I'm hungry."

"But I'm not hungry."

"Wait a minute. Do you remember what you told your mother when we ate all that strudel at your place?"

"No . . . but then I was sick."

"Now that you're well, you'll enjoy food twice as much. And I'm willing to wager that, as soon as I start eating, you'll develop a ravenous appetite. No excuses now. Call your mother and tell her you won't be home for lunch. You can phone her from the restaurant."

"Mother isn't preparing lunch today, anyhow. If you really want me to have lunch with you, I will."

"Good! We'll go to the Carlton Hotel."

"The Carlton! Why so exclusive? Isn't the Blaha Café good enough? The Carlton will cost too much and it's really not necessary."

"Nonsense. I think we need an elegant environment today."

THE HOTEL CARLTON WAS THE LARGEST ESTABLISHMENT OF ITS KIND IN Bratislava. Guest lodgings had existed on this location since the thirteenth century. Known originally as *At the Swan*, and later as *At the Green Tree*, the complex was rebuilt and expanded in 1908, and became known as the *Savoy-Carlton* in 1913. The Carlton was located on Hviezdoslav Square—named after Pavol Országh de Felsőkubin Hviezdoslav (1849–1921) a Slovak poet, dramatist, translator, and for a short time, member of the Czechoslovak parliament—within view of the Slovak National Theatre. The building was three stories high and served the most demanding customers who could afford the astronomical fares. Because of its reputation for excellent accommodations, food, and service, many famous dignitaries have been guests at the Carlton, including Holy Roman Empress Maria Theresa, Jules Verne, Albert Einstein, Franklin Roosevelt, Ludovit Štúr, Alfred Nobel, Thomas Edison, and Tomáš G. Masaryk. The main dining room was illuminated by large crystal chandeliers which bathed the room in a glamorous light. Handsome Old-World furniture, exquisite china, delicately engraved silverware, and formally attired waiters gave the room a striking yet restrained appearance. To dine in this atmosphere always made one feel important.

Captain Vlčko and his lady were greeted with a deep bow by the *maître d'hôtel*, who stood at the entrance to the dining room. He personally escorted them to a small table set for two. After they were seated a waiter appeared and took their coats to a nearby cloak room. While Peter ordered lunch, Jirka slipped out to phone her mother and then returned. "Well, is everything all right?" Peter asked.

"I think so. I told Mother since she hadn't prepared lunch, I was quite hungry and decided to accept your invitation. She could only object weakly. So, I guess everything is fine."

"Good."

When Jirka settled herself and they waited for the meal to be served, she and Peter talked the small talk of two people who obviously enjoyed one another's company. Then he stopped somewhat abruptly and said, "What do you think of the dress that lady is wearing? At the third table by the window."

"Very beautiful. It's the kind I'd like to have someday."

"After you're my wife, you'll have one like that."

"*Kapitán* Vlčko! Is that a promise or a proposal?"

"Both, my dear."

"I think it's a bit early for either."

"Maybe you're right. But I can dream, can't I?"

"Yes, I suppose so. Much depends on how things work out for us." She did not want to discourage him, and yet it would be unfair to encourage him unless she were sure of herself, of him, and of the world in which they found themselves.

"Peter, look at those two German officers who just came in." They stood at the entrance to the room and saluted with Nazi greeting.

"Yes, I see them. I know the blond one. He's the personal adjutant of General Otto, the chief of the German Mission."

"He's certainly handsome."

"You can be sure he thinks he's God's gift to a race of supermen."

Then they ate their meal in silence, except for an occasional comment about the excellence of the food. When the waiter cleared the table, Peter ordered a bottle of wine. *Na zdravie!* Peter toasted, clinking his glass against Jirka's.

"To friendship, Peter," she added, taking a long drink from her glass. "This wine is excellent. Neither too dry nor too sweet. It's just right."

"I agree. It's light and crystal-clear. As good to the eye as to the palate."

"So, tell me about those sins, Peter." The theological dialogue was about to begin, since it was a conversation that they both knew must come sooner or later.

"According to the Church, Christ gave His Apostles the power to forgive sins and the keys to the Kingdom of Heaven." Peter spoke simply. "However, as the Church grew and expanded, her powers also increased, I believe beyond what was intended by Christ. Even kings were sworn to obey Rome, so you can only imagine how the common man was held in spiritual serfdom. That's what the Reformation was all about. The Reformation was never intended to establish a separate Christian religion. It was always intended to remain the universal "catholic" faith with Christ at the center."

Peter sipped his wine slowly. He reached inside his pocket for a cigarette, offered one to Jirka and lit both of them before continuing.

Peter continued, "I don't always agree with the Church. I believe people can confess their sins directly to God and ask Him for forgiveness without a priest acting as intermediary. But it seems, in order to ensure control over the masses, the Church corrupted itself with powers beyond those originally intended by God. I believe Christ and the Apostles, although not unexpectedly, would not recognize Christianity today. As much of history is subject to agenda-driven revisionism, so too, is religion. Over the centuries Church leaders continually directed theologians to reinterpret the message of Christ in order to achieve a set of agendas, thereby changing what was initially intended to be a message of the free gift of undeserved forgiveness by Christ's self-sacrifice to a recipe of laws to which the faithful found themselves shackled in a spiritual enslavement. If you say the Jews need to reevaluate their religion, the Catholic Church needs major surgery."

"'How can the Prime Minister (Vojtech Tuka) go to communion when he issues inhumane mandates against the Jews?" Georgina asked.

"Not surprisingly, this contradiction exists among the highly placed as well as ordinary people. Hypocrites are found everywhere, even among the so-called faithful. What some profess in church doesn't always correspond with what they do outside of church. But I'm sure God sees lip service for what it really is. He wants true contrition from us, not empty words. Only true contrition and God's forgiveness bear forth good deeds. A person should worship God freely and spontaneously under God's influence, without temporal forces dictating the rules of our relationship with God. We should see God as the source of love and ethical and moral truth giving us the courage to say no to what is wrong and to lead just and loving lives." Peter paused and drew deeply on his cigarette, allowing the smoke to trail from his mouth.

"Well, I will say I felt comfortable in church. In the synagogue, I never experienced this sense. Instead, I was always apprehensive and rather depressed. The closeness of God, His compassion and love, were somehow missing. He was forever the angry judge, the God of vengeance. Christ's love for humanity appeals to me. His understanding of human frailty and suffering, His mercy and forgiveness—these I like. To love and help one's neighbor is particularly beautiful."

"Jirka, I know the Jews don't acknowledge Christ's divinity—that He was both God and man. They are still awaiting the coming of the Messiah. Nevertheless, as I see it, the crucifixion was not the responsibility of all Jews, but only of the priests and a segment of the people at that time. Our own priests have made gross errors in judgment in the past. Just look at

Jan Hus, the great fifteenth-century Czech evangelist and reformer, and others like him. We can't whitewash their tragedies. All religions have at least one thing in common—they all involve human beings. And human beings are fallible. The essential thing is that religions teach love for one another. This can only be accomplished after we grasp the depth and breadth of God's love for us and our condition without it. Then all humanity can prosper in an atmosphere of love, peace, and mutual understanding."

"Peter, I fully agree. Complex theories and dogmas are a distraction as is any myth that conceals the essential truth and only creates mysteries."

"Precisely. And Sunday sermons should show us how we need God's love, the wondrous gift of forgiveness given freely, though undeservedly, to us, and how that love teaches us to love one another. Without recognizing our need for God's forgiving love, we can never truly love our fellow man. A person should receive spiritual refreshment and strength in this regard instead of sleepy, dry-bones dissertations on lofty mysteries or dogmas. Law and Gospel, distinct, yet inseparable, these are the essential nutrition required for love and Truth to be victorious."

"Speaking of sleepy, this wine has gone to my head. I think I need a little fresh air. Do you mind if we leave?" Jirka stifled a yawn as she reached for her purse and gloves.

"Not at all. We can't be accused of putting one another to sleep with too much intellectualizing about religion on a day as beautiful as this." Peter rose to help Jirka with her chair. In a moment, they were walking in the warm spring air.

Outside, their thoughts and conversation changed completely. The gentle warmth which greeted them brought a closeness both satisfying and reassuring. Nature was restorative.

The streets were crowded with people enjoying the reawakening of nature. Happy faces were everywhere. Jirka and Peter relaxed in the warm sunshine as they walked aimlessly down the narrow lanes. Feeling a little tired, they debated whether or not they should take in a movie. Peter suggested he check the advertisement outside the theater across the street.

"Go ahead, I'll wait here. I want to see this little dog coming along the road." Jirka usually wanted to stop and pet every animal she saw. A short distance away a young boy led a small, spotted dog. It tugged at the leash as the boy neared Jirka. When they came alongside, the dog stopped abruptly and jumped up to greet Jirka, affectionately licking her outstretched hand. It was love at first sight. She smiled and talked kindly to the little bundle of animated joy whose tail began wagging swiftly as he barked in a friendly tone with each word that she spoke to him.

"What's his name?" Jirka was all smiles.

"Peggy. He's a fox terrier," the boy replied proudly. "How old is Peggy?"

"Four months."

"Why, he's just a puppy. May I pick him up?"

"Be careful. He'll mess."

"Oh, that's no problem. I can always clean it off." She picked up the puppy and began to pet and hug it lovingly. Overcome with childlike excitement, she called to Peter, who was approaching. "Peter! Look what I've got."

"Yes, I see. Where did he come from?"

"Peggy belongs to this boy."

"I see you and Peggy are pals already."

"Isn't he beautiful, Peter? Look at the roof of his mouth. It's black. Does that mean he's a pedigree?" Jirka did not stop to take a breath.

"Young man. Would you consider selling your dog? Peter was direct in his question.

"Hmm, maybe. How much will you give me for him?"

"How much do you want?"

"One hundred twenty-five *korun*."

"One hundred."

"Agreed. He's yours."

"Ya-a-a-y!" Jirka squealed in uncontrolled rapture. She kissed Peter and then Peggy. "Oh, thank you, Peter. I'm so happy. I've wanted a dog just like this for so long. How kind you are!"

"I'm glad you're pleased." Then, turning to the young man waiting for his money, Peter counted off the bills.

"Thank you, sir," said the boy. So happy was he at his quick profit, he ran down the street, disappearing beyond the next corner.

Jirka received no papers with Peggy, but she was content to know the dog was hers. A close friendship had already begun between them, one which time would only strengthen.

"Well, we can't take Peggy to the movie," Peter remarked.

"Let's head for home. My puppy is probably hungry anyway.

"I won't be able to stay. I've got to get back to the barracks."

"That's too bad." Jirka would gladly see Peter going with her, but since she had a new friend, she did not force him.

"Duty calls. I'd much rather be with you—you hold a spell no book could ever hold, Jirka."

She accepted the compliment with genuine pleasure as she took Peter's arm for the journey home. They talked mostly about little Peggy, forgetting all else for the time being. When Peter left her at her apartment, he kissed her tenderly, reluctant to leave but fully aware that to delay would not erase the picture of his colleagues busily poring over military assignments in ponderous texts.

ON 22 JUNE 1941, ABOUT EIGHT IN THE MORNING, PETER AND JIRKA SET out for an excursion to Grinava, a little town on the eastern slopes of the Carpathian Mountains, north of Bratislava. There, an outdoor swimming pool was popular with young couples from the surrounding area.

It was Sunday, and from all indications it promised to be a beautiful day. The sky, a Wedgewood blue overhead, faded to a powdery gray in the distance. Sunshine even this early in the day penetrated the brick and stone of the city.

"What a lovely morning. I hope the weather lasts," Peter said as they were leaving the Reichsfelds' apartment building.

"I do, too."

"Do we have everything?"

"Yes, I think so. Fried chicken and my bathing suit and towel. You didn't forget your suit, did you?"

"No, I have it on," Peter replied. "Let's hurry. I see a streetcar coming. If we miss this one, we'll have to wait fifteen minutes for the next one." They ran hand-in-hand to the nearest stop, arriving just in time.

The ride from the apartment to the end of the line lasted about an hour. From there they had to go on foot another hour, reaching the outskirts of Grinava around ten in the morning. As they walked through the town, they laughed the carefree laughter of those who understood the simple joy of being alive. But then it ceased. They heard the German National Anthem over a radio playing in one of the flats which looked out onto the narrow street. The anthem finished. An announcer began in German, his voice heavy with emotion.

"Today begins the most important chapter in the history of the German *Reich*. On command of our *Führer*, Adolph Hitler, early this morning the *Wehrmacht* attacked our greatest enemy, the Soviet Union, in order to destroy the menace of world Communism and the dangerous Jewish-Bolshevik conspiracy. *Sieg Heil! Sieg Heil! Sieg Heil!*" the voice had reached a frenzied pitch.

"I'm frightened. Will the Slovak Army be affected? What will happen to you, Peter?"

"My God! We'll find out soon enough."

"This means things will get even worse for us. If you have to go away, I'll be alone. With you here, I feel safe."

"Let's not think about my leaving you yet, Jirka. Perhaps it won't be necessary." Peter tried to change the subject to lessen Jirka's fears.

"You know, I never even asked if you liked to swim. Do you?"

"Yes, very much. It's my favorite sport."

"You swim well, then?"

"Pretty good. I took lessons at the Grössling pool in Bratislava." Jirka obliged by keeping the conversation going—anything to forget the unsettling news they both just heard.

"'How about you, Peter?"

"I've been swimming ever since I was a little boy. When I was eight, I fell into the Hron River from a pontoon rig. The water was over my head, and I couldn't swim a stroke. Luckily, a man jumped in and pulled me to safety. I was unconscious. After I came to, I remember a couple of men holding me upside down by my feet to let the water out of my lungs. I vowed then I would learn to swim."

By this time, they had reached the pool entrance gate. Peter purchased two admission tickets and gave one to Jirka, who entered the women's locker area to change while he searched out a pleasant spot on the grass. He laid out the blanket in a corner which was protected from the wind by a wooden fence. He quickly slipped out of his clothes, folded them neatly and rolled them up to use as a pillow under their heads. His body accepted the sun's rays greedily as he stretched out full length across the coarse woolen army blanket. He was not tanned, but it wouldn't be long before the winter pale skin would mellow tawny in the summer sun.

Soon, Jirka appeared. He had never seen her this undressed before. Her red flowered bathing suit was perfect, he thought. Cut deep in front, it revealed a sufficient amount of cleavage to be tempting and yet not overly seductive. The snug fit emphasized her narrow waist and graceful hips. Her legs looked much longer, too. All in all, she was not in the least bit disappointing to the eye.

"Hmmm! You look great, Jirka."

"Thank you. I bought this suit yesterday. I'm glad you like it." She was rather pleased with her choice, too, and was complimented, as any woman is, by male approval.

"Here," Peter said, patting the blanket, "sit down next to me and rest awhile. We can get a little sun first and then take a dip to cool off."

No sooner had Jirka positioned herself comfortably on her back, then Peter moved right beside her so that their outstretched bodies came into contact.

"Peter, I thought you wanted to rest." Playfully, she pushed him away.

"Being near you doesn't tire me in the least. It excites me!"

"Well, stay over on your side of the blanket or people will begin to stare." She seemed only a little embarrassed.

Instead of doing as she asked, Peter pulled her over to him and they lay on their sides so that he could look closely into her eyes. He pressed his body against hers and could feel the rapid beating of her heart. She, too, seemed to yield under the pressure of his embrace. Neither wanted to interrupt this ecstatic interlude. Neither seemed to care that someone might be watching.

"Jirka," Peter began, his voice tender yet passionate, "when I'm close to you, your warmth gives me the courage to say what I've felt for a long time. I'm very much in love with you." Gently he brushed aside a strand of her hair which the wind had disturbed. "At first, I thought what I felt was only sympathy—I mean, the fact that you're Jewish, and the way things are lately. But the longer we see each other the more I'm convinced I really love you. There's no use hiding it. I can't hold back, Jirka. I was afraid to tell you before. I thought I might frighten you off."

"Peter, is this love, or merely the passion of the moment which we both feel?"

"I'm absolutely sure. More than I've been about anything in my life before."

"What about Christina?" Jirka could not forget that Peter once loved her. "Have you completely forgotten her?" She searched his face for the answer she wanted so desperately to hear.

"Christina, have I forgotten her? No. But she's a memory now. You have all my love. My thoughts and feelings revolve around you and no one else. You must believe this."

She began to speak, but Peter placed his fingers against her lips.

"No, don't speak. Don't say anything now. I want your answer to be entirely unbiased. This moment shouldn't influence a reply. Think over what I've said and let your heart answer honestly. But know that you now have a man that belongs to you completely, that is, if you'll have him." Overcome with Peter's words, she could find none herself to answer him, not yet at any rate. Her eyes mirrored her joy, but still she was uncertain. She had to have time to think. Somehow, though, she knew how she would answer him once she found the words.

"Let's cool off, Peter. You're much too heated up right now." She rose quickly and darted toward the inviting pool.

"All right. But no water can put out the fire you started in me." Peter laughed, picked himself up, and took a running dive into the water.

Alternating for the remainder of the day between sunning themselves and swimming, they soon were exhausted. By late afternoon, with no further reference to Peter's admission of his love for Jirka, they collected their belongings and headed for home.

THE STREETCAR PETER AND JIRKA BOARDED OVERFLOWED WITH returning Sunday excursionists. No seats remained, but they found a place to stand. Heads bobbed up and down as weary passengers fought to stay awake. In one part of the car, fatigue was absent. A lively debate was in progress. There, a middle-aged couple, obviously man and wife, sat was dressed in leather shorts held up by suspenders. He wore a white shirt and thick white knee socks. On his head a peaked green hat, complete with jaunty feather, perched comically. His wife wore a bold flowered skirt protected by a neat white apron. Her plain white blouse showed from underneath a colorfully embroidered vest. Their costumes testified they were local Germans—Karmasins, after their leader Franz Karmasin.

Germans in Bohemia and Moravia were, for the most part, organized into the Henlein political party. Those along the border fondly called themselves Sudeten Germans, after the name of the geographic area. Whether Czechs or Slovaks, these Germans considered themselves part of the Third *Reich*, which, in turn, recognized them as allies and full-fledged citizens. If they yearned to return to their original homeland or their forefathers, they also wanted to take with them the land on which they now lived. German superiority had caught on with these people, and they felt themselves better than Czechs and Slovaks, in whose country they made their homes.

Certain politicians and opportunists looked for friends and support among this group of displaced Germans. But the majority of Slovak intelligentsia rejected this attitude and hated its concept of racial superiority, fearing increasing German control. This fear caused many fights to break out and ultimately ended with the German representatives in Slovakia interceding by extracting promises that no further incidents of this kind occur against the Germans.

The Slovak students were in their early twenties, and they were strongly patriotic. Peter could not help but overhear them.

"Do you know the German Army broke through Soviet defenses in Poland and is right now marching victoriously eastward? If this keeps up, we'll be in Moscow within a month or two," boasted the German.

"That's what Napoléon thought when he invaded Russia, and you know what happened to him. His glorious army froze to death," retorted one student.

"Napoléon didn't have Stukas or Panzer divisions to clear the way for him, not to mention the triumphant German spirit," countered the Nazi supporter.

"True," said the other student, "but Napoléon was no less aggressive than Hitler. He tried to unify and rule all of Europe. Fortunately, he underestimated the reactions of other nations, which finally brought about his downfall. He was defeated by his own megalomania."

"So, that was Napoléon. You'll see what the mighty German Command and the *Führer* will accomplish. History will not repeat itself," snapped the German, fully convinced of his kinsmen's superiority.

"Yes, everyone knows that wherever a German boot falls, no grass will grow again. Your adversaries will sweat blood, fearing the invincible Nazis," the other student jibed.

"Slander! You speak nothing but lies. We Germans only want to institute a new order. We want to reorganize the labor force, for example," he said, fairly bursting with Teutonic pride. "After all, didn't we rid the Fatherland of all Jews and other parasites? We will do the same for all countries. We are not working fast enough here in Slovakia. The government should begin shipping the Jews to labor camps in Poland to teach them how to do an honest day's work."

"Not before you strip every Jew naked and extract the gold from his teeth."

"Are you accusing Germans of barbarism? We are not robbers," interrupted the German woman, who had remained silent as long as she could. "Jews are crooks. Look at how much gold jewelry their women wear. And where does it come from? From the poor. They are the thieves, and we have a right to take from them."

"'Perhaps you're only jealous," one of the students suggested.

"Jealous! We don't need to drape ourselves in gold to impress others. What the Jews accomplish with gold, we accomplish with good, honest labor. Why, look what Hitler has done in Germany. The finest roads in the world. And did he use gold to build them? No, he didn't," argued the woman, who had become obsessed with her line of reasoning.

"Oh, he built excellent roads all right, but with money and property he stole from the Jews!" one of the students shot back, livid with anger.

"Young man, you'd better watch that sharp tongue of yours," interrupted the husband. "Let's see if you speak so boldly to the *Hlinka* Guard." With that the couple rose quickly to search for a *Guardist*, half expecting to find one in the car with them. The students pushed through the crowd and made their escape out the doors at the opposite end of the car, only moments after it had come to a stop.

Peter and Jirka enjoyed the debate thoroughly, especially the needling which the German couple bore so badly. Out the window they could see the young men lose themselves in the crowd. Spontaneously, the remaining occupants of the streetcar broke into loud cheers and applause. Slovak patriotism and pride had won out over Nazi arrogance, at least in this instance.

CHAPTER 21

FROM FRIENDSHIP TO LOVE

THE POLITICAL EVENTS OF THAT SUNDAY HAD CREATED QUITE A STIR among the students at the War College. Those who sympathized with the Germans and the puppet Slovak government were joyfully optimistic about the future. They had high hopes the war would soon take a more positive and aggressive direction, which they regarded as absolutely necessary for a complete German victory.

Others were not so optimistic. They foresaw a long and cruel war, one with an uncertain outcome.

"A war on two fronts, in the east against the Soviet Union and in the west against the British, will be difficult for the Germans to win. The vast Russian plains and her giant armies will swallow every single German. She cannot be easily overrun and occupied. The farther east the Germans go, the harder it will be for them to maintain supply and communication lines," they argued. Simple military strategy proved the scheme just wouldn't work.

These students predicted that if the Germans didn't defeat Russia by November, it would mean the end of any chance for victory in the eastern campaign. The severe Russian winters would see to that.

"Peter, did you hear the news today?" Second Lieutenant Jan Stanek asked. His fiancée was in occupied Bohemia, and he had reason to be more than casually interested in what the Germans were doing next. He also took Peter's side in any discussion of world affairs.

"Yes, this morning in Grinava. I also heard that the Germans broke through the Russian defenses and are marching eastward to glory." Peter's sarcasm was obvious.

"That's not all," interrupted Hreblaj enthusiastically. He was always an admirer of the Germans and their successes. "Most of the Russian tanks and artillery were destroyed by Stukas while retreating."

"Andrej. I'd be willing to bet if the Germans announced tomorrow that they had defeated the English, you'd believe it," interjected Dvornak, who was allied with the second group at the college.

"Dvornak, I don't think you quite expressed yourself fully." Air Force Captain Ladislav Ďurčanský corrected. He loathed Hreblaj for his Germanophilia. "I would be willing to wager if the Germans asked Andrej to lick their asses, he would, and eagerly."

"Cut out these smart remarks, Ďurčanský. Things are far too serious to be arguing as we are," said Captain Nosko.

"Julo, no one's arguing. We're just expressing our views of the situation," explained Peter, defending the group who shared his sympathies.

"Well, what do you have to say, Peter?" Second Lieutenant Jan Kužel was on the neutral side in the dispute. "Well, in the first place, I never believe German Nazi propaganda. It's based on lies and deceit. This war, like all German wars, is a war of aggression. And you can rest assured that those nations which have been occupied by the Nazis don't believe Hitler is their savior. They may be winning now, but I doubt they will be victorious in the end."

"Peter, tell me, who can beat the Germans?" Hreblaj questioned smugly.

"Russia is huge. Her population alone is enormous. If one of her armies falls, another will arise to take its place. The size of the Soviet territory will allow the Russians to reorganize their defenses and build new fronts. Time is on their side. And so are the terrible winters. Moreover, it's only a matter of time before the United States backs Russia like they're helping the British. Besides, Germany has already been stopped in the west. Its strength was not sufficient to defeat England. Fortunately, I think Hitler blundered when he attacked Russia before first eliminating the British threat."

Peter was on to something. Had Hitler more carefully assessed all the political and military options before him in 1939 and resisted his deep desire for revenge over Compiègne and Versailles, he would have recognized that attacking Poland would more likely than not push France, England, and possibly the Soviet Union into the war. Given that Hitler's objectives of German hegemony over Europe lied on his eastern as well as his western flank, each for different reasons, a closer examination of likely scenarios and his options should have yielded some obvious conclusions different to those ultimately made by Hitler at the outset of the war. Considering the political will, foreign relations and treaties, and state of military preparedness of Germany's Eurasian neighbors in 1939, Hitler should have more accurately envisioned the risks of opening up a two-front war by invading Poland first. The August surprise of the Molotov-

Ribbentrop Pact (officially: *Treaty of Non-aggression between Germany and the Union of Soviet Socialist Republics*) bought Hitler (and Stalin) some time. However, soon enough (prematurely and anachronistically, in reality) Hitler faced a two-front war that ultimately decided the outcome of the Second World War. Had Hitler more carefully planned the order of invasion, the outcome may have been entirely different. Well before the outset of the war, Hitler's objectives included conquering the Soviet Union, Northern Africa, and mainland Europe to create a Greater Germany. He could have accomplished these objectives had Hitler first attacked the Soviet Union via Czechoslovakia, Hungary, and Romania rather than Poland while Stalin was totally unprepared before tackling Western Europe. Having already succeeded in dividing and conquering Czechoslovakia in 1938, in mid-1939 Hitler should have accelerated the expansion of the Tripartite Pack (Berlin Pact) to include Hungary and Romania (signatories to the Pack on 20 and 23 November 1940, respectively). Granted, Romania only acceded to Germany's will after the *Blitzkrieg* Poland Campaign and the signing of the Molotov-Ribbentrop Pact. However, Hitler could have conscripted Romania much earlier simply with the Molotov-Ribbentrop Pact and ceding Bessarabia, and Northern Bukovina to the Soviet Union and Northern Transylvania to Hungary. Had he taken these moves, by September 1939, Hitler would have controlled a continuous friendly land bridge from Germany to Southern Ukraine along with the rich oil fields in Romania. Given the extant treaty obligations at the time, England and France would have remained neutral relative to Germany. And while Stalin invaded Poland, Hitler's invasion of the Soviet Union from Romania would have pleased Western elites and caught Stalin completely off guard and unprepared militarily. Hitler's *Blitzkrieg* war would have rapidly overtaken the Ukraine, Crimea with its rich oil fields, and Stalingrad by December 1939, and Moscow by summer 1940, thereby occupying European Russia and controlling most of Russian heavy industry. This would have avoided drawing England, France, and the United States into the war. Under these circumstances, Hitler may have even succeeded in convincing Chamberlain (an anti-Bolshevik) to sign a non-aggression pact, as Hitler romanticized that he would. Moreover, before turning his sites on Western Europe, Hitler could have pushed Japan to attack the United States earlier in 1941 to occupy them in the Pacific and not draw them to the defense of England, permitting Hitler to open the inevitable two-front war under more promising circumstances shifting many of his divisions in the Soviet Union to Western

Europe. By invading Poland first, Hitler incensed Chamberlain thereby shattering any hope of an Anglo-German non-aggression pact.

Peter thought seriously about his views and could not be accused of taking the situation lightly. He was convinced he was right. Before he could be interrupted, he continued.

"Though the Americans have managed to stay out of the war, their help to England testifies that sooner or later they will enter. They may have no choice. Besides, these initial German victories have to be considered in context of the extensive war preparations that Germany has made. These latest Nazi victories are to be expected. When the rest of the world finally mobilizes, when its industrial potential converts from peacetime to war production, then we will see who is really superior."

"Peter, your opinions are pretty bold and speculative. Germany's our ally. And you are a Slovak officer." Hreblaj's tone was intimidating.

"We're not speaking politically. We're merely assessing the situation from an academic viewpoint," retorted Nosko, trying to mitigate the anti-German impression created by Vlčko's statements. "The future will decide whose military judgment was correct. To question Peter's national loyalty is a bit rash, don't you think?"

"'I think all of you should begin packing your bags tonight. You will be needing them soon. Now, turn off the lights, it's ten o'clock," snapped Captain Juraj Greguška, another neutral among the students.

"All right. Discussion's ended. Besides, my biggest worry is the bedbugs in this room," Peter conceded for the moment. "They never give me any peace."

"Peter, spray some insecticide on your bed. And on the walls, too. Then, rub this ointment on your body. They'll stop bothering you," Ďurčanský offered as he handed him his own pest-control remedies.

"Fortunately, I won't be suffering much longer. I've found a private home and I'm moving soon," Peter said as he sprayed everything around him within sight.

"No excuses, Peter. We all know why you're leaving us," Murgaš remarked knowingly. "I wouldn't stay here either if I had a good-looking girlfriend like yours."

"Hey, watch it, Stefan. You sound jealous. Are you?" Peter resented any innuendo where Jirka was concerned.

"No, I'm not jealous. In fact, I wish you the best, Peter. Take advantage of a good opportunity as long as you can. We'll all probably be at the front soon anyway."

"Kill the lights. We've had enough talk for one night." Nosko was irritated from being disturbed in his sleep. His colleagues finally gave in.

After exchange of "goodnights" they either dozed off or pondered the day's momentous events, which would affect them all in the not distant future.

THE GOVERNMENT OF DR. JÓZEF TISO DIDN'T WASTE ANY TIME IN demonstrating its loyalty to the Third *Reich*. With the news of the attack on the Soviets came the following announcement:

> All Christian Europe recognizes the historical significance of the present struggle between the two giants. There does not exist a country in Europe unwilling to join in this fight. The Slovak nation again, with weapon in hand, seals its fateful friendship with Germany. We are the first to join the war to save the Christian world and to liberate the many subjugated nations. We want to prove ourselves before ourselves, our consciences and history. We want to avenge the millions of martyrs murdered by the communists and to liberate the enslaved countries of the U.S.S.R. After we free them from these tyrants, they will join the ranks of National Socialistic oriented nations and will become the pillars in our fight for a new world order.
>
> God is on our side and those who are against us will be damned!

Hungary, Rumania, and Finland followed the example set by this tiny German satellite. Bulgaria was the only country, though controlled by Germany, not to declare war against Russia. Nazi pressure could not force this Balkan nation to reject its Slavic brother who once had saved it from Turkish rule.

In line with the government's position, the Minister of Defense *Generál* Čatloš, decided that the college should participate in the military campaign against the Soviet Union—codenamed by Germany as Operation Barbarossa after the charismatic medieval German Holy Roman Emperor

Frederick Barbarossa (Frederick I). This news was received by the members of the school with mixed emotion.

Even though the government in Russia had been in Communist hands since 1917, and the country was isolated from other Slavic nations, it was still a land inhabited by Slavs, toward whom the majority of Czechs and Slovaks felt kinship. For the Slovak Army to fight against its fellow Slavs alongside Germany was unthinkable to many in Slovakia. Some officers strongly criticized Čatloš for this move, while others condemned it. However, any overt resistance was impossible. Another way had to be found. Forthcoming events provided many examples of contradictory feelings shared by the soldier and officer alike.

After the declaration of war, Captain Vlčko also made an important decision. He moved from the War College dormitory to a private apartment located off the central concourse. Increasingly, aware of the worsening situation for Jirka and her family because of stepped up anti-Semitism, he felt the apartment would come in handy should he ever have to hide them on short notice if their safety was in jeopardy.

WHEN VLČKO FINALLY LEARNED OF HIS ASSIGNMENT AND DEPARTURE date, he telephoned Jirka at the sewing school and asked her to meet him after class.

"Peter, I've missed you. It's been three days since I saw you last," Georgina exclaimed as they met.

"I've been very busy, as you probably can imagine. I moved to the apartment finally. And there's something that's been bothering me."

"Is it something serious?" She searched for bad news in his eyes.

"Yesterday, we were informed that all of us would be going to the Russian front. We're supposed to depart the twenty sixth of June. Tomorrow, I'm going to Zlaté Moravce to see my parents, but I'll return late Wednesday. Tonight, and Wednesday night are all we have left together until I get back from Russia."

"Oh, Peter, I'm so worried!"

"It won't be bad. We'll be at Command Headquarters, away from the shooting. I'm sure nothing will happen to me. I won't stick my neck out unless I have to. Come up to my apartment for a little while where we can talk in privacy."

"Do you think I should?"

"Why not? It'll be much more comfortable there. I've prepared supper. There won't be anyone in my room except the two of us."

"That's where the greatest danger lies. And what I'm most afraid of."

"Jirka, don't fret. Let's go."

"Promise me you'll behave."

"Word of honor."

When they arrived at his new quarters, he led her up a winding staircase to the second floor. From there they had to walk along an outdoor balcony in front of several other apartments. This made Jirka very uncomfortable. Public opinion condemned any actions by a single girl which appeared compromising. Sadly enough, moral misjudgments can be heartless and often unfair. Their usual targets are those in love, whose desire makes postponement difficult. Quick to see and judge, a cynical world watches slyly and lies in wait to condemn sincere acts of love. It is ironic that in a world dominated by hate, fear, and danger, so many found time to be suspicious of love.

Drawn tightly against Peter so no one would see her, Jirka glanced around as they made their way to his place. When they stopped in front of his door, he quickly opened it. Once inside he locked the door securely behind them. Jirka heaved a sigh of relief. Peter took her in his arms and began to kiss her passionately, his imagination seeking out the mysteries of her face.

"Peter, you said we were going to come up here to talk and not to make love. You promised you'd behave."

"I'm sorry. It's just that I haven't seen you for so long and so much has happened since then. I had to show you I still love you. Doesn't that matter to you?"

"You said you had dinner ready. I think we should eat now." The meal was prepared by his military orderly and spread out on the table.

PETER'S APARTMENT CONSISTED OF ONE LARGE ROOM, WHICH WAS entered by way of the balcony outside. It was furnished simply, with a wooden bed on one side of the room, and a small nightstand next to it. On the opposite wall were a desk and chair. Against the third wall was a small table with two chairs, used for eating. Next to that was an old armchair. In the corner between the table and the desk was a small sink with hot and cold running water, and above it a mirror and medicine cabinet. At the foot of the bed stood a portable wooden closet. Beside the door a tall potted plant gave the room a breath of freshness. The long window adjacent to the door was covered with a curtain from the ceiling to the floor. The smooth mortared walls were decorated with multicolored designs. A two-bulb lamp hung from the center of the ceiling.

When Peter had at least partially satisfied his hunger, he began to talk seriously to Jirka about the day's events. "Soviet involvement in this war will definitely improve our future outlook."

"Peter, I'm afraid things won't happen as you'd like them to," objected Jirka pessimistically.

"Russia is enormous," continued Peter, ignoring her interruption. "Even if the Soviets have to retreat all the way back to the Urals, they'll still have Siberia behind them. And where will the Germans be? Thousands of kilometers from their homeland with their divisions dispersed throughout Russia. Some just defending their lines of supply and communication. You can't win a war this way, particularly on two fronts."

"In the meantime, what will happen to us?" For Jirka, the war was more a personal matter affecting her and her family, and less a global predicament.

"As long as the Germans are experiencing success at the front, they won't bother anybody back here. As soon as they meet any strong resistance, they'll take their frustrations out on the people they've conquered. Then, the Jews will be the first to suffer. If this happens and I'm not here to protect you, you'll have to go into hiding."

"But I'm thinking of you, not myself."

"I'll be careful because I know you need and are waiting for me." With that he opened a bottle of wine and filled their glasses. "Let's drink a toast to our eternal love."

"I thought we were going to drink coffee. Wine will weaken my defenses."

"One glass won't disarm you."

"Well then, *Na zdravie!*" She took a long sip of the dry wine. After the first glass she felt the wine going to her head and stifled a yawn.

"Peter, this wine is making me sleepy."

"I don't feel a thing. Why not stretch out on the bed for a while and rest? Maybe you're tired from sewing today."

"For a little while. Until this drowsiness passes."

"Just make yourself comfortable. I'll take your shoes off for you and lie down for a moment myself." He manufactured a yawn as he carefully placed her shoes at the foot of the bed.

"Not too close, Peter," she said as she held him away from her with both hands.

"I want to look into your eyes, Jirka. They are lovely, even dazed with sleep. I've waited for this moment more than you know. I planned what I would say, and how you would look, but now all I manage is, I love you." He paused a moment before continuing. "We probably won't have another chance to be alone like this for a long time." She listened to his voice and found it was what she most wanted to hear. "Jirka, I'm very happy right now. I feel we are free to decide our future for ourselves. That day at the pool I told you about my love, and today I hope you can answer me. As for me, I'm sure I love you very, very much. In three days, I'll be leaving for the front. I don't know what's waiting for me there. I'd like to take your love with me to give me the strength I'll need in the difficult days ahead." She realized for the first time that their love was an island of peace in a hostile world.

"Peter, where will all this lead?"

"Love is a powerful force. It can overcome the impossible. I just have to know if you love me as much as I love you."

"I don't think you have to worry about that anymore, Peter. I do love you, very much." Her eyes met his. "At first, when we met, I was looking for a companion. I was lonely and needed someone to talk with. Then you appeared. After I got to know you, my feelings changed, and I experienced something quite different from friendship. The more we saw each other, the more I needed and wanted you. Would I have dared come up to your apartment if I didn't love you?"

Peter stopped her speech by pressing his thighs firmly against her. He took her in his arms and began to cover her mouth with his kisses. His breathing echoed their mounting passion. Jirka responded eagerly, reaching out for the happiness which she knew he would bring. Her hands gripped his shoulders as they lay locked in the wonder of their embrace.

"Oh, Peter," Jirka managed to whisper, drawing herself only slightly away from him. "You promised." Her words were a half-hearted final token of resistance. "You said you would behave."

"I know, I promised. But how can I prove how much I love you? When we're this close, my body becomes its own master. It's as if we were in another world where nothing else mattered except our love for each other. God gave us minds and bodies to express love. Please, don't shut me out. I love you and I want you. It's that simple. I'll be leaving soon, and this moment may never come again. Now, while it is here, don't waste it. Trust me. I'll never do anything to hurt you." While he spoke softly, he caressed her breasts gently. She stiffened slightly, but then relaxed and responded to his desire. The combination of the wine and his words of love worked to lessen her restraint. With an ardor rising to match his own, she surrendered.

THE FOLLOWING EVENING PETER WAS ON HIS WAY TO SEE HIS PARENTS IN Zlaté Moravce, a pleasant town in the Žitava River valley where vineyards and peach orchards were tended by the local farmers. Nearby, the town of Topolčianky with its beautiful castle, the President's summer residence, attracted many visitors. After the loss of southern Slovakia to Hungary in 1938, Zlaté Moravce became an important rail center and the main hub for east-west passenger trains.

Three of Vlčko's sisters lived there, fourteen-year-old Božena with her parents, twenty-three-year-old Valeria, and twenty-one-year-old Anna with their respective husbands. Twenty-Seven-year-old Ružena, the eldest of the sisters, was also married but lived with her husband Lajči in Krivaň near Detva.

Peter walked from the station to his parents' home as crimson streaks stretched across the evening sky. Peach orchards perfumed the dry air. Only the intermittent barking of a dog and the tolling of a distant church bell broke the silence.

When Peter appeared in the doorway, the first to notice him was Božena. She let out a squeal of delight and ran up and threw her arms around her brother. After kissing his youngest sister, he greeted his parents, who were overjoyed to see their only son.

"Mama, do you have something for me to eat? I'm starved." Peter could think of nothing else but the gnawing in his stomach.

"Certainly, my boy. I made noodles with *lekvár* this afternoon, almost as if I knew you were coming."

"Good. I haven't had them in a long time. It's wonderful to be home."

"Tell us what's new, my son." His father joined him at the table.

"I'm leaving for the Russian front Sunday. You know we've declared war on Russia, and since I'm an officer in the army I have to go where my country sends me."

"Isn't there any way you can avoid going?" Senior Vlčko was not happy to see his son fighting the Slav brothers on the German side.

"Unfortunately, no. The whole school is leaving."

"Peter, you know I fought in Russia with the Austro-Hungarian Army and was a prisoner of war for four years there during the First World War. After my release in 1918, I joined the Czechoslovak Legion and fought alongside the Entente Powers against the Bolsheviks until 1920. We weren't permitted to return home through the Ukraine, so, we had to travel east on the Trans-Siberian Railway to Vladivostok where we boarded a ship to America on our journey back home. I know the Russians pretty well. They're fierce but good people and understand our language. The Germans are strangers to us. I don't understand them or their language."

"Apik, I know, I didn't really know you until you returned home when I was nine years old. But there's nothing I can do now. I've been ordered to go. Remember, the shirt is closer than the coat. The Russians are my shirt, and the Germans are only my coat. I won't be carrying a rifle, so I certainly can't shoot any Russians."

"That's good but take care of yourself so no one shoots you. Try to avoid the front line. Bullets don't pick their targets. They don't know you're a friend of the Russians."

"What will Jirka do while you're gone?" Božena interrupted. "You wrote us you had a new girl, and you sounded serious." She deliberately changed their topic, for she was more interested in love than in politics.

"I *am* serious, and worried. She'll have to be careful until I return. You know, the Jews are in great danger now. Any day they might all be deported, or worse."

"Yes, it's terrible. But why couldn't you find a Christian girl? Then you wouldn't have so many worries," objected his mother. She was concerned for her son's happiness and safety. How would this girl affect his future?

"Maminka, every girl not only brings a man happiness, but also worries. Some bring one kind of trouble, while others bring another. Some are attractive, others are not. Mine happens to be beautiful. Her religion doesn't matter," Peter maintained stubbornly.

"Peter, when can we meet her?" Božena already thought of Peter's girl as her future sister-in-law.

"'As soon as I get back."

"But a Jewish girl? Their religion is different from ours, his mother complained.

"Mother be reasonable. Religion influences character, but there's no guarantee the person will be moral. Look at some of our national leaders. Prime Minister Tuka goes to church and communion every Sunday, yet he approves unjust laws, and jails innocent people. Then there's Tiso, a Catholic priest. What does he preach every Sunday? Hatred for Czechs and Jews. He's sold his soul to Hitler for a political career. Throughout history there are those who have fought for right and justice, and they weren't all Catholics. We don't have a monopoly where honor and morality are concerned."

"Aren't you afraid someone will make trouble because you're going with a Jewish girl?" His mother didn't give up her effort to convince him.

"That's not the point. I hate the government because it's persecuting innocent, helpless people who are citizens of Slovakia. Maminka, you know how I am. I've always sided with the weak, the oppressed, regardless of the consequences. Right now, Jirka needs me and I intend to help her in whatever way I can." Peter made it clear that his mind was made up. "How are my other sisters?"

"'Valika is doing very well. She works with her husband in the Baťa shoe store.* They have plenty of money, and where there is an abundance everything else works."

"Is she really happy?" Peter inquired.

"I think she is. She hasn't complained to me about anything yet."

"What about the difference in ages?" Peter knew her husband was more than twice as old as Valeria.

"That doesn't matter to her. He loves Valika and would do anything for her."

"Is that all you wanted when you advised marriage to such an old man? Didn't you care about her love and happiness?" It bothered Peter to see his mother so disturbed about his relationship with Jirka, and yet so oblivious to Valeria's frustrations.

---

* The Baťa Shoe Company was founded on 24 August 1894 in the Moravian town of Zlín, Austria-Hungary (today the Czech Republic) by Tomáš Baťa, his brother Antonín, and his sister Anna, whose family had been cobblers for generations. The company became one of the world's biggest multinational retailers, manufacturers and distributors of footwear and accessories. As of 1934, the firm owned 300 stores in North America, a thousand in Asia, and more than 4,000 in Europe. In 1938, the Group employed just over 65,000 people worldwide, including 36% outside Czechoslovakia, and had stakes in the tanning, agriculture, newspaper publishing, railway and air transport, textile production, coal mining, and aviation industries.

"Valika was never one to worry about such things or to make extravagant demands." Peter's mother preferred a financial security in marriage before anything else. She had worked hard in her youth and earned so little. Now at least her daughter was spared such a bitter deal.

"Well, I don't want to seem pessimistic, but I doubt their marriage will last. And how about Anička? Is she still in Nitra? She hasn't written to me in months."

"She's fine. She's working for the District Army Induction Center, and Štefan is an administrative clerk at the District Court, in Nitra."

"And Ruženka?"

"Lajci has a job with the railroad, and she helps out by raising some pigs and growing vegetables. They had a small house built which they're trying to pay off." Mother realized this was a love marriage—as opposed to an arranged marriage—and was only too glad to help her daughter and son-in-law establish themselves financially.

"And you, Apik, how is your job?"

"Very good, son. Ever since I was transferred from Levice, my tours have been much shorter, and I've been working day shift mostly. I'm getting ready to take a test for Train Crew Foreman. I have been substituting in that position for a while now, and they want to promote me permanently."

"I hope you get it. Then, you'll soon be foreman on a passenger train."

"I could if I wanted to, but I'd rather just stay on freight trains. There is not as much trouble with people and the freights run slower."

After testing his mother's cooking again and catching up on family news, Peter realized how exhausted he was. "Mama, where do you want me to sleep?"

"In the front room, Peterko. Your bed is ready."

"It's eleven-thirty, I'm pretty tired. Apik, are you working tomorrow?"

"No, I've got the day off, but I'm sleepy myself."

"Well then, goodnight, everyone. See you in the morning."

The Vlčkos were only renting their present house. The family home in Levice still belonged to them. Peter Senior considered the Hungarian occupation only temporary and felt there was no sense in buying a new place somewhere else. After the war ended with the defeat of Nazi Germany, as the family believed it would, they planned to move back to their own home in Levice.

THE SEPTEMBER 1938 MUNICH CONFERENCE DICTATED THAT Czechoslovakia give to Germany its border territories in the western half of the Republic, while the First Vienna Award in November 1938, transferred the southern border region of Slovakia to Hungary. The far eastern province of Carpathian Ruthenia was occupied and annexed by Hungary when Hitler invaded Bohemia and Moravia. The Second Vienna Award in August 1940 forced Romania to surrender northern Transylvania to Hungary, thereby assuring Hitler of another subservient country (Hungary) in central Europe and free access to the Balkans.

By these and other geographical manipulations, Hungary grew to its pre-World War I size. For this friendly gesture by Hitler and Mussolini, Hungary felt not only grateful but also obligated to close cooperation with Axis powers, economically and militarily.

Hungary was much stronger than her northern neighbor Slovakia. So, disputes quickly erupted along the Slovak-Hungarian border. Hitler stopped these quarrels with little effort, exerting a yet much tighter control over Slovakia.

With partial mobilization of Slovak defensive forces in June 1941, the military was in a position to deploy two infantry divisions (about twenty thousand men), one motorized brigade (about six thousand men), and the field army command (about three thousand men).

Four days after the German invasion of the Soviet Union, Slovakia sent its own independent units forward against the Russian lines in the form of the Slovakian Expeditionary Army Group. Students and professors at the War College headed divisional departments or were assigned directly to the army command staff departments. Minister of National Defense *Generál* Ferdinand Čatloš took command of the Slovak Expeditionary Army Group.

Early in the operation, Slovak forces began to fall behind the massive German blitz. This was mainly because of a general lack of mobile forces able to transport the 45,000 strong Slovak Army Group alongside the German advance. As a result, it was decided to create a mobile unit that would be capable of doing so. This was done by forming all the motorized units of the former Slovak Army Group into a single formation termed the Slovak Mobile Command, otherwise known as Brigade Pilfousek, commanded by the former commander of the Second Slovak Division and former instructor at the War College, Colonel Rudolf Pilfousek. His brigade was equipped with the most modern weapons and consisted exclusively of active service army contingents: the I/6 Motorized Infantry Battalion; I/11 Motorized Artillery Battalion; the First Tank Battalion with the First and Second Tank Company and the First and Second Anti-Tank Company; Second Reconnaissance Battalion; First Weapons Company; Second Motorcycle Company; and the I/3/I Motorized Engineer Platoon. As soon as Pilfousek's Brigade achieved battle readiness, they received orders to move out.

The preparation of the two infantry divisions required a little more time as they consisted mainly of reservists called to active duty by partial mobilization.

The scene of Peter's farewell visit to his parents was common among almost all of the officers being sent to the front. Those who didn't see their families spent their last leave with girlfriends or fiancées. A general state of restive uncertainty prevailed. Whispered propaganda circulated by loyal Czechoslovaks disrupted the fluent military mobilization and weakened the government position. The Free Czechoslovak Government in exile in London under former President Edvard Beneš broadcasted radio messages sharply criticizing and condemning the actions of the Slovak Fascists in power. It called on Slovak soldiers and officers to resist, passively or actively, the alliance with Germany, and to either slow down or stop the army buildup for the invasion of Russia. These broadcasts were not in vain, as later actions of many Slovak soldiers and officers proved.

"WHERE HAVE YOU BEEN? WE'VE BEEN COMBING BRATISLAVA, LOOKING for you," Štefan Murgaš said when Vlčko returned from Zlaté Moravce.

"Why, what happened? I told Lavota I was going to see my parents. Must I hang signs all over the barracks announcing my whereabouts?" Peter was irritated the message was not conveyed.

"No, but don't you think you should have at least told me?"

"Then *you* conducted the search and not the entire school? What in the hell for?"

"I want you to double with me tonight. I have a date, and she has a friend. She's supposed to be very good looking. You'll probably have a pretty good time."

"Before I answer you, Štefan, when do we leave for Poland?"

"At ten tomorrow morning. In full battle dress with all bags packed. But if I know the Army we won't pull out until after lunch. I thought you knew this information already."

"I did, but I just wanted to confirm there weren't any changes while I was gone."

"Well, what about tonight?"

"Štefan, I'd like to help you out. You know I like beautiful women, but this time I have to refuse. Why not ask Šimko or Cyprich?" Peter suggested, trying to get off the hook.

"I did. Šimko won't go because his girl's in from Prague. Cyprich's still morning over his beloved, so there's no talking to him. And you know the others, they're just not the type. Why can't you go? Don't tell me you're going to sleep."

"Don't be naïve."

"Oh, I completely forgot. Are you really serious about her?"

"Štefan, wait a minute. I'll call Jirka. Be right back." He hurried to the pay phone outside the barracks.

"Jirka. Peter."

"Peter, how are you? When did you get back?" The ardor in her voice made his heart beat faster.

"About six o'clock. Murgaš told me we're leaving tomorrow around lunch time. Can I see you tonight?"

"'What time is it now?"

"Six forty-five."

"Have you eaten supper yet?"

"No."

"Then have dinner with us. Come over right away.

"Okay. See you in thirty minutes."

"Bye." Jirka hung up the phone.

"Was she at home?" Štefan asked impatiently when Peter returned.

"Where else would she be? She doesn't go anywhere without me, especially at night. She just invited me over for dinner."

"I should be so lucky. For supper tonight a hunk of smoked salami, some cheese, dry bread, and bitter coffee. The salami reeked. I was afraid even to smell it because of my date tonight."

Peter laughed. "Well, Jirka's menus are more imaginative and less corrosive, you can be sure of that."

"Peter, are you two engaged yet?"

"You know it's not that simple. In the first place, I don't think her parents are ready yet, and neither is the army." Unofficially, government agencies discouraged Aryans from even associating with Jews. They certainly would not sanction Vlčko's engagement to Georgina.

"You'll have to face it someday, one way or the other. I feel sorry for you, though. You got yourself into a situation that really has no future."

"Štefan, don't tell me you think the Germans are going to win fighting on two fronts simultaneously against western powers and Russia?"

"No. I don't think that; I'm just not sure they'll lose."

"I'm certainly not going to wait that long to marry her. If I see the Nazis are winning, I'll take Jirka with me and disappear, even if I have to steal her away."

"Peter, you must be crazy. Why tie yourself down? Pretty soon you won't even be able to walk down the street with her. Rumor has it all Jews will have to wear the Star of David insignia. How can you go anywhere with her then?"

"If you have to ask, you certainly don't know me. Once my mind's made up, I'll manage, no matter what it takes."

"Just keep playing with fire. Do you really want to risk your career or your life for her? Why don't you find some nice gentile girl? Have your fun now, if you must, but for heaven's sake don't get serious."

"Štefan, I never realized before, You're anti-Semitic. Lord knows, I've seen you dance with Jewish girls often enough."

"Yes, and I still do, but if it's strictly forbidden, I won't even glance at one. It's time someone put the squeeze on the Jews. They've begun to overstep their bounds anyway."

"I'm shocked. You can't be serious."

"Listen, do the Jews amass their fortunes by honest work? No, they don't, Peter, have you ever seen a Jew work hard in a field, or in a factory? Or serve in the army as an enlisted soldier? Hell, no! A Jew is either a storekeeper, doctor, or lawyer. In the army they're always in an office somewhere, even if they're only bookkeepers or just common clerks. 'Leave the hard work to the stupid.' That's the Jewish view on life."

"Štefan, all this proves that Jews are much smarter and cleverer than we are. How can you blame them for that? The only people who work the fields are those who like to or those who have to. Anyway, it's not easy to become a doctor or lawyer. Both professions involve a great deal of intense study, sacrifice, and patience. Even a storekeeper works hard, takes risks, and uses his business skills to maximize profits. Why must people forever envy others' success?" Peter's voice became more emotional as he spoke. It was as though he answered not only Štefan, but all those who shared Murgaš' prejudices.

"Peter, you're mistaken. Christians don't know how to lie or steal like the Jews. That's why they aren't in the lucrative professions. A Christian hasn't the heart to rob a fellow Christian. Only a Jew can do that."

"Well, we could argue until morning. Just go into any Christian store. For the same item you buy at a Jewish store for five *koruny*, you'll pay the Christian eight. Who's robbing whom and getting richer for it? Štefan, don't be blinded and let other people put these kinds of crazy ideas in your head. You are simply parroting vicious lies the Nazis want you to believe."

"Then why does everyone hate the Jews so much?" countered Murgaš.

"For several reasons. First, people are jealous of them. Some resent all foreigners who were never really assimilated by the local culture. Should we condemn them because their ancestors were forced by circumstances to leave their homeland? If they choose to not forget their heritage and faith, and long to return someday to their rightful place, Palestine, we should recognize their aspirations, and admire their persistence. It doesn't mean they are a threat to Christians. We have to understand them before we can judge or criticize them. Their traditions unite them and fulfills their family and cultural life."

"Peter, I think we understand each other completely. The only difference is that above all I'm a soldier. I obey the government and my commanders. You're an individual who acts according to his heart. The question is, which one of us is right?"

"I may be emotionally involved with Georgina, but I am not a person strictly driven by emotion. I am a man of conscience. When my conscience tells me something is wrong, I am not the type of person who can blindly execute injustice even if I am an instrument of the government to which I swore loyalty. I have to oppose injustice, otherwise I am nothing more than an accomplice. Who was it that once said: 'The penalty good men pay for indifference to public affairs is to be ruled by evil men'; or 'Bad men need nothing more to compass their ends, than that good men should look on and do nothing.' Even soldiers must be guided by conscience. The future will prove one of us right and the other wrong. Now, I have to leave. It's five to seven, and I'm going to be late as it is. Štefan, we're still friends, aren't we?" Although Peter was quite disappointed in his friend, Peter was silently concerned Murgaš may one day betray him and Georgina.

Murgaš nodded affirmatively. "I trust I won't have to comb the town for you tomorrow because you stayed out all night. Remember, tomorrow we march into the field against our Jewish-Bolshevik enemies," he needled Peter good-naturedly.

"Yours, not mine, Štefan. Someday, you may regret those words." Then, Peter set out for the Reichsfelds.

WHEN PETER GOT TO THE REICHSFELDS' APARTMENT, HE FOUND THE elevator out of service, so he took the stairs, two or three at a time, to the sixth floor. Out of breath, he knocked on the door. Jirka opened it immediately and hurried him inside. "Where have you been? We thought you'd been shipped to the front early."

"I was held up by one of my friends. Everyone is excited because we're leaving. There's lots of talk at the barracks. When I checked my watch, it was already seven. By the way, your elevator's out of order. I'm sorry I'm late."

"Let me take your things. Dinner's waiting."

"Good evening, *Pán* and *Pani* Reichsfeld. Please accept my apologies, but I was unavoidably detained."

"Never mind. Come sit down so that the food doesn't get cold," Mr. Reichsfeld motioned Peter to a chair next to him. They all sat down to eat. After dinner, Mr. Reichsfeld filled everyone's wineglass and lifting his own offered a toast.

"*Pán Kapitán*, to your safe return."

"Thank you. To the health and happiness of us all," Peter added.

"Jirka told us you're leaving for the Russian front tomorrow." Mr. Reichsfeld did not approve of the Slovak decision to fight the Russians. He knew his and his family's future depended on a German defeat.

"Yes, sad, but true."

"Couldn't you have done something to avoid going?"

"My parents posed the same question. Not really. Part of our job there is continuing our military studies. Those who stay behind will not graduate." Vlčko's military career depended on his graduating from War College as soon as possible.

"Doesn't it bother you that you'll be fighting fellow Slavs?"

"Very much, but I have no choice at this time."

"*Pán Kapitán*, do you think there's any hope we'll survive this war?"

"Before the Germans attacked the Soviet Union the situation was bleak for all Jews. All Germany had to do was reach another accord with England, and Europe would probably have been hers. The invasion of Russia changes the entire calculus. Now, hope for the total defeat of the Nazis is realistic."

"Pray God you're right. England in the past few years has disillusioned me. She's always generous giving away what belongs to others, and France has been worse. France deserted us in '38 and '39 when we needed her most, despite a mutual defense treaty [*Treaty of Mutual Assistance Between the Czechoslovak Republic and the Union of Soviet Socialist Republics*, signed 16 May 1935, that made France the determining factor in the defense of Czechoslovakia]. Now the French Communists will have to defend their country against the Germans, instead of undermining the French war effort and sabotaging the Republic."

"Meanwhile, what'll happen to us?" Mrs. Reichsfeld spoke up.

"That all depends on how far the government will go in complying with Nazi pressures in solving the so-called 'Jewish question.' But if they start acting, conditions will worsen," Peter conjectured.

"And what then?" asked Jirka, frightened by Peter's sober assessment.

"Prepare for the worst. As I said once before, make connections with people you know you can depend on in an emergency."

"*Pán Kapitán*, it's not easy to find someone who will help. You know yourself there's hardly anyone left nowadays who can be trusted."

"I realize this, and it worries me that I must go when I'd rather stay. I can do this much, however. I'll give you the key to my apartment. Use it if you ever need to. The safety of this family rests completely on your shoulders, *Pán* Reichsfeld."

"Yes, I know, and it's too heavy a burden." Though he was aware of the difficulty, he was not afraid to carry it.

"Well, it's getting late. I'd better leave."

"You forgot to eat your strudel and drink your coffee." Jirka did not want to see him leave.

"I can't leave without having some of your mother's delicious strudel. Memory of this strudel alone will keep me alive, so I can return from the front and enjoy it again."

"*Pán Kapitán*, I'd like to ask you one other thing," said Mr. Reichsfeld.

"Yes?"

"Why are you helping us? Isn't it your duty to fight the enemies of the State? We Jews have been declared enemies of the Third *Reich*; and since Germany is an ally of Slovakia, we are also the enemies of this country."

"*Pán* Reichsfeld, I don't obey orders blindly. I'm a rational human being first and a soldier second. To help you and anyone else who is in need, in times like these, is my real duty. Well, I've got to go now. I'd just like to say; I expect to see you all when I return."

"God be with you, *Pán Kapitán*," Jirka's father added with obvious emotion. Jirka walked to the door and handed him his holster and cap. They went out into the hall, happy to be alone if only for a few more minutes. Peter encircled Jirka's waist with his arms, pulled her tight against him, and kissed her mouth hungrily.

"Think of me and write as soon as possible, Peter." She spoke breathlessly, locked in his ardent embrace. Pushing him away gently from her, she looked into his eyes. "You must come back to me, darling."

"God knows I will, for I love you more than life itself." Tears welled up in her eyes, which she fought to hold back. One escaped and traced its course down her face. Suddenly, Peter realized her vulnerability and his own responsibility for her future. "*Au revoir!*" she said, releasing herself from the comfort of his protecting arms.

"*Au revoir*." He spoke these words and knew they would see each other again. Then he took the stairs which led him away from his beloved Jirka.

Part Three

SLOVAKIA NO LONGER ABOVE THE FRAY

POLITICAL EVENTS IN EUROPE TOOK A RAPID TURN FOR THE worse when Adolf Hitler assumed power in Germany in 1933. His philosophy of the supremacy of the German race was directed not only against Communists, pacifists, and Jews, all of whom he designated as enemies of the Third *Reich*, but also against anyone who dared to stand in the way of Nazi expansion and conquest. With this ideology he succeeded in transforming Germany into a completely totalitarian state, and with his allies, Italy and Japan, he set out on the road of gregarious imperialism. With the aid of his army, which he built into the most terrible and powerful military force in the world, he gained control of almost all of Europe.

On 12 March 1938, Hitler annexed Austria to the *Reich* (*Anschluß Österreichs*), thereby extending the southern portion of his iron pincers aimed at the future bisection of neighboring Czechoslovakia. This young republic, conceived from the debris of the disintegrated Austro-Hungarian Empire after the First World War, was the most Democratic state in Central Europe. Her founder and first president, Tomáš Garrigue Masaryk, was not only a philosopher of Democracy but also a great humanitarian of his time. His teachings regarding the equality of nations permeated the very marrow of the bones of each and every citizen of the Republic. All rules and laws of the state were also strongly dedicated to this proposition of justice and equality.

The Czechoslovak Republic was an example of cooperation between citizens of different ethnicities, and a beacon of Democratic principles guaranteeing individual human rights, as well as personal safety and security. Economic stability was secured through her prosperity as the Czechoslovak *Koruna* was considered a valuable and desirable currency in Europe. While in neighboring Germany the Jewish population was facing persecution, there existed in Czechoslovakia religious and ethnic freedom and tolerance. The effect of these national policies on citizens manifested in their great love for President Masaryk and their loyalty to the state.

A republic which advocated such principles and was also allied with the other Democratic powers of the West necessarily stood in the way of the German *Drang nach Osten* and had to be eradicated from the map of Europe. With Hitler's rise to power, Czechoslovak citizens of German extraction who enjoyed the full benefits of humanitarian laws became the instrument of Hitler's aggressive diplomacy.

The decision at the Munich Conference, which Hitler extorted from Czechoslovakia's allies France and England on 29 September 1938, finally broke the back of the young republic. The guarantee of the new boundaries that Hitler gave after annexing the Sudeten Land was not worth the paper on which it was written. On 15 March 1939, the German army invaded Czechoslovakia and occupied Bohemia and Moravia, the western provinces of the country. Under pressure from the German *Führer*, the eastern part of the republic, Slovakia, declared its independence from the Czechoslovak state only the day before. Meanwhile, with Hitler's assent, Carpathian Ruthenia (Ukraine)—part of Czechoslovakia since 1918—was annexed by Hungary. Thus, declaration of Slovak independence would support Hitler's contention that Czechoslovakia had fallen apart from within and not because of his intervention. By this act, he was able to confiscate all state property and wealth including the stockpile of industrial resources, money, and gold that had been saved since the end of the First World War.

For years this small nation of approximately fifteen and one-third million people had been patiently building their prosperity. The Czechoslovak people asked only that their God-given right to life, liberty, and the pursuit of happiness be guaranteed within their own national boundaries. Against them, Hitler committed one of the more brutal acts of his political career.

Five months before the Munich Agreement, a proposal had been offered to Czechoslovakia to relinquish a large portion of her territory in the interest of world peace. Actually, she was being coerced by several great powers into not fighting for her freedom, integrity, and sovereignty in order to "save" the rest of the world from another terrible war. If she refused to submit, these powers threatened to leave her to the mercy of the Hitler's Germany. However, no sacrifice at that time was enough to satiate Nazi Germany. What various statesmen called peace was only wishful thinking. At the time, few in Europe and the United States recognized Hitler's true *modus cogitandi et operandi*. The European officials that pushed to delegate

Democratic Czechoslovakia the "sacrificial lamb" to appease Hitler were self-serving elitists, political opportunists, and Brutuses in the worst sense, but not true national leaders of high principles.

After the occupation of the western half of Czechoslovakia, it was literally impossible to speak of Slovak sovereignty because of the emerging intentions of the German *Reich*. Every act of the Slovak government was coordinated with Nazi political and economic planning, and as a result was ultimately controlled by German officials in Slovakia.

With Hitler's insistence, the Hlinka's Slovak People's Party (*Hlinkova slovenská ľudová strana, HSĽS*), which had continuously opposed Czechoslovak unity since 1925 and claimed the right to speak on behalf of all Slovaks, finally accomplished its prime objective on 14 March 1939—the creation of an independent Slovak state. The *Hlinka* Guard, the extreme paramilitary faction of the party, became the political elite in the new state and the guardian of the Fascist state order. Its black uniforms were supposed to spread not only fear but terror to all who would not cooperate with the new political system.

The current upheavals had a chilling effect on the majority of the population, especially officers of the Slovak Army who had grown up in and served with the Czechoslovak Army. The dilemma which the Slovak Army officer faced was one of divided loyalty. Should he remain faithful to the ideals of the former Democratic republic, or should he support the new Slovak Fascist state, which at least offered him some palpable sense of security and a promise for the future? Among these officers was a young cavalry captain, Peter Vlčko.

CHAPTER 22

SETTING THE SCENE

FROM THE MOMENT OF ITS DECLARED INDEPENDENCE ON 14 MARCH 1939, Slovakia was spared the tumultuous fate that Austria, Bohemia, and Moravia were subjected to under the Nazi boot. Soon, however, Slovakia could not escape Hitler's demands calling in debts owed. In his cathartic *Mein Kampf*, Hitler set before the world his central arguments and primary objectives to correct the West's alleged injustices against Germany for its role in the Great War. Secondarily, he laid down a marker on behalf of the German *Volk* and their destiny for a Greater Germany that included *lebensraum* to the East. Misjudging the resolve of the West's commitment to Poland (much of which historically belonged to Prussia and Austria), Hitler counterproductively chose to undertake only the first phase of the *lebensraum* objective before his much greater objective of reversing the humiliation of Compiègne and Versailles. In fecklessly doing so, Hitler managed to simultaneously alarm both the Soviets and the Western powers, prematurely placing them on a war footing.

To predicate his moves in the East, Hitler had to first set the scene for his *Drang nach Osten*. Throughout 1938, a series of international disputes provoked and cleverly orchestrated by Hitler took place between Czechoslovakia, Germany, Poland, and Hungary over the borders created by the Versailles (21 January 1920) and Trianon (31 July 1921) treaties. The nations that lost significant territories to create Czechoslovakia in the aftermath of the First World War now demanded return of much of the lost territory. Germany demanded the Sudetenland nearly encircling Bohemia and Moravia (although this territory was not part of Wilhelmine Germany), Poland demanded scattered northern border regions from Czechoslovakia, and Hungary the southeastern regions of Slovakia and Carpathian Ruthenia, thereby restoring, at least in part, the Hungarian-Polish border. To accomplish the breakup of Czechoslovakia, Hitler exploited long-standing ethnic conflict between the Czechs and Slovaks, and the Slovaks and the Hungarians.

Hitler first set his sights on the Sudetenland where an ethnic German majority had existed since the Middle Ages. The increasing aggressiveness of Hitler prompted the Czechoslovak military to build extensive concrete border fortifications starting in 1936 to defend the troubled border region. Immediately after the *Anschluß* of Austria in March 1938, Hitler made himself the advocate of ethnic Germans living in Czechoslovakia, triggering the "Sudeten Crisis." The following month, Sudeten Nazis, led by Konrad Henlein, agitated for autonomy. The "Sudeten Crisis" ultimately culminated in appeasement of Hitler by the French and British governments and the Munich Agreement. As a consequence of the Munich Agreement of 29 September 1938, Germany occupied the Sudetenland on 1 October 1938. One day after the Munich Agreement, however, Hitler sought to further destabilize Czechoslovakia by adding new demands, insisting that the territorial claims of Poland and Hungary also be satisfied. The Polish side argued that Poles in the Zaolzie region bordering northern Bohemia, Moravia, and Poland deserved the same ethnic rights and freedom as the Sudeten Germans under the Munich Agreement. Hungarians sought to restore large portions of their prewar northern territories in Slovakia. Intuitively, Hitler was playing on the political instability within Czechoslovakia among its various ethnic groups and respective neighboring states.

While Germany was swallowing up the Sudetenland on 1 October 1938, Polish armed forces invaded and occupied the northern town of Český Těšín and the Zaolzie region and annexed the entire region totaling some 801.5 square kilometers (309.5 mi^2) with 227,399 inhabitants, of which Poles made up about thirty-six percent.*

---

* Zaolzie ("lands beyond the Olza River" or "trans-Olza Silesia") is a historical region that has been in dispute since AD ninth century. It is in southeastern Silesia, centered on the towns of Cieszyn and Český Těšín and bisected by the Olza River. It comprises a total of 2,280 km^2 (880 mi^2) and has about 810,000 inhabitants, of which 1,002 km^2 (387 mi^2) or 44% is in Poland, while 1,280 km^2 (494 mi^2) or 56% is in the Czech Republic. Zaolzie forms the eastern part of the Czech portion of Cieszyn Silesia. It was formally created in 1920, when Cieszyn Silesia (Těšínské Slezsko) was divided between Czechoslovakia and Poland. The 1920 division of Zaolzie did not satisfy any side, and conflict over the region persisted through the interwar period. The area was important for the Czechs as the crucial railway line connecting Czech Silesia with Slovakia crossed the area (the Košíce-Bohumín Railway, which was one of only two railroads that linked the Czech provinces to Slovakia at that time). The area is also very rich in black coal. Many important coal

In southeastern Czechoslovakia, another drama was unfolding. The Hungarian Minister of the Interior, Miklós Kozma, had been born in Carpathian Ruthenia (part of Czechoslovakia since 1918), and in mid-1938 his ministry armed the *Rongyos Gárda* ("Ragged Guard"), which began to infiltrate southern Slovakia and Carpathian Ruthenia. The situation was approaching open war. From the German and Italian perspectives, this would be premature, so they pressured the Czechoslovak government to accept the joint Arbitration of Vienna. Since the "Sudeten Crisis," Hungarian forces remained poised threateningly on the Slovak border. They reportedly had artillery ammunition for only thirty-six hours of operations and were clearly engaged in a bluff, but it was one that Hitler had encouraged and one that the Hungarians would have been obliged to support militarily if the much larger and better equipped Czechoslovak Army chose to reject the Munich Pact. Responding to the growing calls by Slovakia's neighbors for reclamation of borders, the Czechoslovak Army began in 1936 building 2,000 small, well-positioned concrete emplacements along the border in places where rivers did not serve as natural obstacles to help repel an enemy invasion.

On 2 November 1938, after it had failed to reach a diplomatic compromise with Hungary and Poland, Czechoslovakia under its new president Emil Hácha (and later Slovakia under Jozef Tiso) was forced by Germany and Italy under the First Vienna Award—the illegitimate child of the Munich Agreement—to cede southern Slovakia (one third of Slovak territory) to Hungary. The partition also cost Slovakia Užhorod (Ungvár) and southern portions of Carpathian Ruthenia, as well as Košice, Slovakia's second largest city, and left the capital, Bratislava, vulnerable to further Hungarian pressure. The Hungarian Army immediately acted on this reward. Under the Vienna Award, the remainder of Carpathian Ruthenia received autonomy, and in December 1938, was renamed Carpathian Ukraine. The First Vienna Award did not fully satisfy Hungary, so twenty-two minor border clashes occurred with Czechoslovakia between 2 November 1938 and 12 January 1939, during which five Czechoslovaks were killed and six were wounded. The Slovak national militia *Hlinka* Guard participated in these clashes.

On 1 December 1938, Poland annexed an additional three areas on their border with Slovakia in the northern sectors of Kysuce (just east of

---

mines, facilities, and metallurgy factories are located there. At one point, many Germans resided in the Zaolzie region making it one more target for Hitler's Greater Germany. He advocated it belonged to Poland just before invading Poland.

Zaolzie), Orava (just east of Kysuce), and Spiš regions totaling 226 square kilometers (87 mi^2) and comprising 4,280 inhabitants with only 0.3 percent Poles.

As a result of these border disputes, Bohemia and Moravia lost about thirty-eight percent of their combined area to Germany totaling 28,500 square kilometers (11,004 mi^2), with some 3.2 million German and 750,000 Czech inhabitants. Hungary, in turn, received 11,927 square kilometers (4,605 mi^2) comprising 869,299 inhabitants in southern Slovakia and southern Ruthenia; according to a 1941 census, about 86.5 percent of the population in this territory was Hungarian. And Poland gained over 1,000 square kilometers (386 mi^2) with 231,679 inhabitants, including some important sources of raw materials and infrastructure.

The Germans were delighted with this outcome for its strategic and propaganda benefits. It laid the foundation for Hitler's argument in March 1939 that the Republic of Czechoslovakia had fallen apart and spread the blame for the partition of Czechoslovakia by making the Western Ally Poland a participant in the process. Poland was accused of being an accomplice of Nazi Germany—a charge that Warsaw was hard put to deny.

After achieving victory with the Munich Agreement in September 1938, Hitler continued to masterfully orchestrate the unlikely series of events leading to the bloodless collapse of the young Czechoslovak Republic. In order for Germany to adhere to the Munich Agreement, Czechoslovakia had to fall apart on its own and not by foreign invasion. In March 1939, a new crisis hit the political scene in Czechoslovakia. President of Czechoslovakia Emil Hácha (replaced Edvard Beneš on 30 November 1938) dismissed the Slovak government of Jozef Tiso and appointed a new Slovak prime minister, Karol Sidor. Hitler decided to take advantage of the situation and inflict a final blow to the weakened Czechoslovak state. His emissary approached Sidor with the goal of dividing Czechs and Slovaks to make the final blow easier. Hitler made it absolutely clear that either Slovakia would declare independence immediately and place itself under Nazi Germany's "protection" or he would let Hungary, whose forces were positioned on the border, to repossess Slovakia as Hungary had before the First World War. However, Sidor refused the coercion and what would be considered treason. Hitler then summoned the dismissed prime minister Monsignor Jozef Tiso. On the evening of 13 March 1939, Tiso and Ferdinand Ďurčanský secretly met with Hitler, von Ribbentrop, and Generals Walther von Brauchitsch and Wilhelm Keitel in Berlin. During this time, being aware of the German position, Hungary was preparing for action on the adjacent Ruthenian border. The meeting resulted in not only in Tiso's and Ďurčanský's enthusiastic endorsement of declaring Slovak independence and alliance with Germany but also agreeing, albeit reluctantly, to Germany's and Hungary's demands for a territorial revision along ethnic majority lines that included a large swath of southern Slovakia and Carpathian Ruthenia.

During the afternoon and night of 14 March, the parliament of Slovakia proclaimed Slovakia's independence from Czechoslovakia. Czechoslovak president Hácha, in an attempt to save the country, travelled to Berlin to persuade Hitler not to intervene in Czechoslovak affairs. Instead, Hitler forced him to surrender the army and accept the occupation. At 5:00 a.m. on 15 March, declaring that Czechoslovakia's collapse from internal strife was a threat to German security, Hitler ordered his troops into Bohemia and Moravia encountering little to no resistance because the Czechoslovak armed forces were ordered to stand down by Defense Minister General Ján Sirový. Simultaneously, in an effort to restore the old Polish-Hungarian border, Hungary invaded and occupied the remainder of autonomous Carpathian Ukraine—total Ruthenian soil incorporated into Hungary was 12,097 square kilometers (4,671 mi^2). Bohemia and Moravia were declared a German protectorate and Carpathian Ukraine ceased to exist. Young Czechoslovakia, the "dagger in the side of Germany," had collapsed and was now entirely in Hitler's palm.

Slovakia was surprised when Hungary formally recognized its new statehood as early as 15 March 1939. However, only two days after recognizing independent Slovakia and still unsatisfied with their frontier borders, Hungarian forces attempted to seize Hill 212.9 deeper in Slovak territory just west of Užhorod (Ungvár). Hungarian authorities ordered their armed forces to push westward into Slovak territory as far as they could go. Weak elements of the Slovak Twentieth Infantry Regiment and frontier Guards had to repulse the Hungarians. In this and the subsequent shelling and bombing of the border villages of Nižné Nemecké and Vyšné Nemecké, Slovakia claimed to have suffered thirteen dead, and it promptly petitioned Germany, invoking Hitler's promise of protection made a few days earlier in Berlin.

On 17 March, the Hungarian Foreign Ministry told Germany that Hungary wanted to negotiate with the Slovaks over the eastern Slovak boundary on the pretext that the existing line was only an internal Czechoslovak administrative division, not a recognized international boundary, and therefore needed defining now that Carpathian Ukraine had passed to Hungary. The Hungarians enclosed a map of their proposal that shifted the frontier about ten kilometers (6 mi) west of Užhorod (Ungvár), beyond Sobrance, and then ran almost due north to the Polish border.

Germany let Hungary know that it would agree to such a border revision and informed Bratislava of their decision. On 18 March 1939, while in Vienna for the signing of the Treaty of Protection with Germany,* Slovak leaders were forced to accept this additional loss of territory to Hungary, though grudgingly, and Bratislava ordered Slovak civil and military authorities to pull back. All other potential Hungarian territorial requests were supposed to be illegal.

Hungary was aware that Slovakia had signed a treaty guaranteeing Slovakia's borders on 18 March and that it would only come into force when Germany countersigned it. Hungary, therefore, decided to act immediately and take advantage of the disorganized Slovak Army, which had not yet fully consolidated its redeploying assets from Bohemia and Moravia (including Lieutenant Peter Vlčko). At dawn on 23 March 1939, Hungarian forces in western Carpathian Ukraine began to advance from the Uzh River into eastern Slovakia starting the Slovak-Hungarian War, also known as the "Little War," some six hours before German Foreign Minister Joachim von Ribbentrop countersigned the Treaty of Protection (*Schutzvertrag*) in Berlin. A truce was agreed on 24 March but fighting continued until 31 March (stopping just east of Snina) resulting in 807 total casualties: eighty-one killed (Hungary: 8 military, 15 civilians; Slovakia: 22 military, 36 civilians), more than fifty-five Hungarians wounded (Slovak wounded unknown), and 671 captured (360 Slovaks, 311 Czechs).

On 23 March 1939, Hungary annexed these newly occupied parts of eastern Slovakia bordering with former Carpathian Ukraine. On 4 April, Slovakia acquiesced to the new reality of losing even more territory to Hungary when a peace treaty was signed in Budapest, which forced Slovakia to cede 1,697 square kilometers of territory to Hungary, despite the Treaty of Protection with Germany. The Hungarian invasion of Carpathian Ukraine was followed by weeks of terror in which more than 27,000 people were shot dead without trial and investigation. Over 75,000 Ukrainians decided to seek

---

* Treaty of Protection (*Schutzvertrag*) included a secret protocol that granted Germany the right to build military bases in the so-called "Zone of Protection" (*Schutzzone*) located in western Slovakia between the White Carpathian Mountains and the border of the Protectorate of Bohemia and Moravia. The secret protocol also required Slovakia to conduct its foreign and defense policies according to the interests of Germany, as well as subordinate the Slovak economy to Germany's needs in anticipation of the war. (Nižňanský et al. 2009, 305–8 doc. 96.)

asylum in the Soviet Union; of those, almost 60,000 died in *gulag* prison camps. Others joined the Czechoslovak Army.

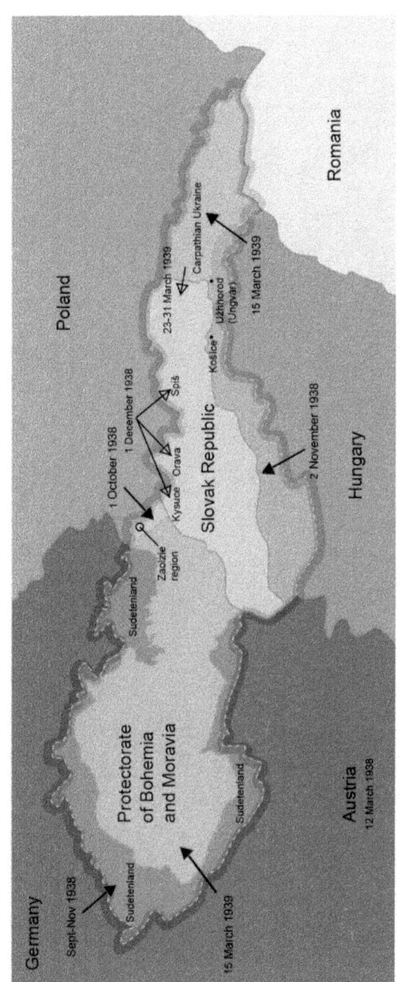
Germany
Sept-Nov 1938
Sudetenland
Protectorate of Bohemia and Moravia
15 March 1939
Sudetenland
Austria
12 March 1938
Sudetenland
Zaolzie region
1 October 1938
1 December 1938
Kysuce
Orava
Spiš
Slovak Republic
Poland
23-31 March 1939
Košice
Užhorod (Ungvár)
Carpathian Ukraine
15 March 1939
2 November 1938
Hungary
Romania

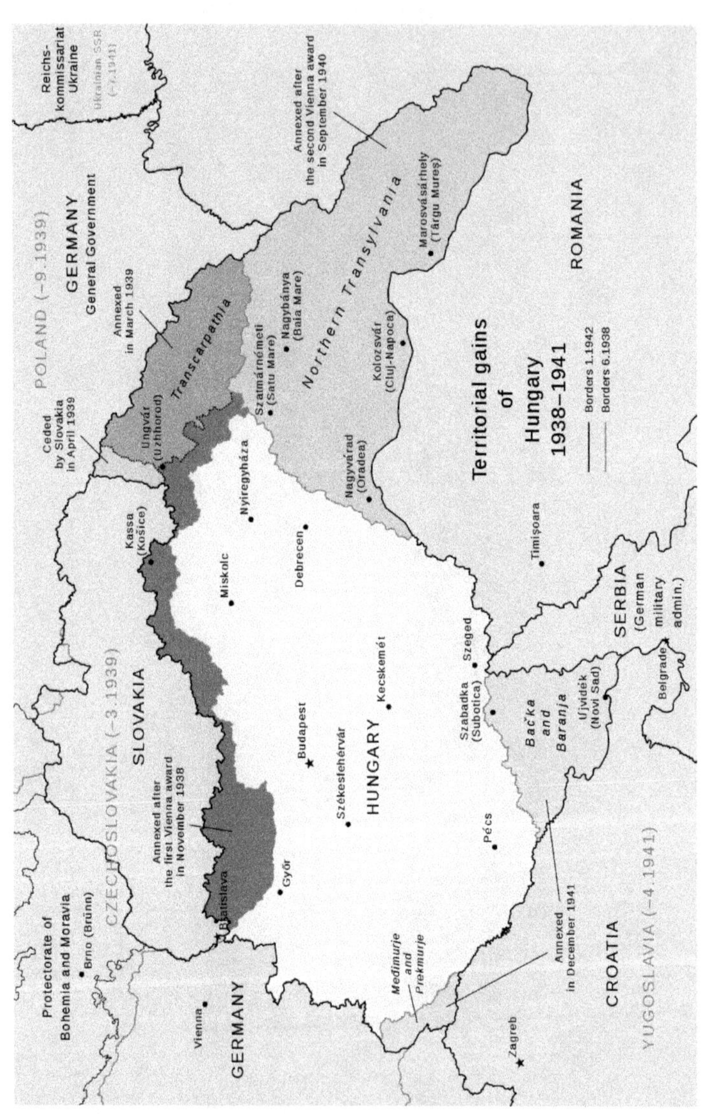
Territorial gains of Hungary 1938–1941
Borders 1.1942
Borders 6.1938
Protectorate of Bohemia and Moravia
Brno (Brünn)
CZECHOSLOVAKIA (–3.1939)
SLOVAKIA
Vienna
GERMANY
Bratislava
Annexed after the first Vienna award in November 1938
Győr
Budapest
Székesfehérvár
HUNGARY
Miskolc
Kassa (Košice)
Ceded by Slovakia in April 1939
POLAND (–9.1939)
GERMANY
General Government
Annexed in March 1939
Ungvár (Uzhhorod)
Transcarpathia
Reichs-kommissariat Ukraine
Nyíregyháza
Debrecen
Szatmárnémeti (Satu Mare)
Nagybánya (Baia Mare)
Northern Transylvania
Annexed after the second Vienna award in September 1940
Kolozsvár (Cluj-Napoca)
Nagyvárad (Oradea)
Marosvásárhely (Târgu Mureș)
ROMANIA
Timișoara
Kecskemét
Szeged
Szabadka (Subotica)
Bačka and Baranja
Újvidék (Novi Sad)
Belgrade
SERBIA (German military admin.)
Pécs
Annexed in December 1941
Međimurje and Prekmurje
CROATIA
YUGOSLAVIA (–4.1941)
Zagreb

THE SLOVAK ARMY

ATTEMPTS TO BUILD SEPARATE SLOVAK MILITARY UNITS UNDER THE command of Slovak officers within the framework of the Czechoslovak armed forces already existed in the period of autonomy between 6 October 1938 and 14 March 1939. The government in Prague refused such demands; however, since many conscripts and officers of Slovak nationality were allowed to serve in Slovakia this later enabled the relatively fast formation of Slovak army units. During this same period, the Hlinka Slovak People's Party or *HSĽS* (*Hlinkova slovenská ľudová strana*) had a party militia called the *Hlinka* Guard *(Hlinkova garda, HG*). The *HG*-men *(gardisti)* belonged to the radical separatists among *HSĽS*, and later became known for their terrorist acts against Czechs, Jews, and opponents of the Slovak regime. The units of the newly established Slovak army and the volunteers of the *HG* took part in the "Little War" against Hungary in March 1939 (see *supra*). However, Slovak Army officers considered the *HG* as dangerous fanatics with little training and ardently opposed their inclusion in the armed forces. Only in autumn of 1944, after the suppression of the Slovak National Uprising, did the *HG* (which took part in the suppression), become part of the Slovak armed forces.

At its beginning, the newly established Slovak Army was only a smaller copy of the Czechoslovak Army, which the Germans had just dissolved. The transition from the Czechoslovak organizational model (new ranks, emblems, and symbols, etc.) was a relatively long process. The army initially used Czechoslovak uniforms and was equipped mainly with the same weapons and machinery, which were later partly replaced by German models. Like the Czechoslovak Army, it was based on a conscription system and compulsory military service for all able-bodied men, usually for two years. Reservists, men who had already completed their regular service, could be summoned for military training and, in the case of a national emergency, for additional service (Eséfalvay et al. 2008, 16–24). The main problem of the Slovak Army was a lack of officers. In August 1938, there were only 435 officers of Slovak nationality in the Czechoslovak Army, which constituted just 3.4 percent of the officer corps (Cséfalvay et al. 2008, 14). Some officers of Czech nationality, mainly those who had Slovak wives, were allowed to continue their service in the Slovak Army and some ethnic Germans, also former Czechoslovak officers, were likewise accepted. New officers were recruited from the pool of reservists, some against their will. A Slovak military academy was opened in Banská Bystrica, and command schools in Bratislava and Nitra. In July 1939, the Slovak Army had 29,683 men; in February 1940, 33,741 (including 1,010 officers), and in June 1941, 33,676 men, including 1,347 officers, forty-two of them Czechs (Cséfalvay et al. 2008, 22–3). Jews, according to governmental decree of 21 June 1939, served only in military labor units and the same applied to Roma (gypsies). Ethnic Germans living in Slovakia, who were Slovak citizens, served first in the Slovak Army in special units, but were later allowed to fulfil their military service in the German Army or *SS*. In 1944, their service in the *SS* became mandatory (Rychlík 2018, 119).

As one would expect, the Slovak officer corps reflected different political opinions. Certainly, there were officers devoted to the cause of Slovak independence and even to the close cooperation of Slovakia with Nazi Germany (Cséfalvay et al. 2013, 153–4, 197–8, 250–1). Generally speaking, however, Slovak officers were not supporters of the *ľudák* (people's) regime—as they were known after their political party—and were indifferent to the idea of an independent Slovakia or even openly hostile to it. Some Slovak officers joined the underground resistance movement. The Czech underground organization National Defense *(Obrana naroda, ON*), which was based in the Protectorate but operated in Slovakia with the support of Slovak officers, specialized in sabotage and military intelligence. The basis for such actions was rather simple; former Czechoslovak officers, who had graduated from Czechoslovak military schools (most notably the Military Academy in Hranice, Moravia), were educated with pro-Democratic values (Rychlík 2018, 120). Professional Slovak officers before 1938 were often stationed in Czech lands and took Czech wives (Mičianik 2007–2012). They were therefore integrated into the Czech secular milieu. Some former Czechoslovak officers of Slovak nationality belonged to the Czechoslovak Legionnaires. The former Legionnaires formed the elite of the interwar Czechoslovak Army. Some among them were supporters of the *ľudák* regime (e.g., Slovak Defense Minister General Ferdinand Čatloš), but, in principle, former Legionnaires were rather hostile to it going so far as to sign a memorandum to the Slovak parliament on 14 March 1939 protesting the decision to break away from Czechoslovakia—see THE SOVIET UNION'S ROLE IN THE SLOVAK NATIONAL UPRISING, *infra*. Some even deserted from the Slovak Army and joined the Czechoslovak Army abroad. This was the case with General Rudolf Viest, the only general of Slovak nationality who escaped to Paris and subsequently became the commander of the Czechoslovak Army in France (Rychlík 2018, 120). This army fought the

Germans on the Western Front in May and June 1940, and after the Allied defeat, the remnants fled to Great Britain.

OPERATION *FALL WEIß*

AS CZECHOSLOVAKIA GAINED INDEPENDENCE IN THE AFTERMATH OF THE First World War, Poland also regained independence as the Second Polish Republic after 123 years of partitions imposed by foreign powers and internal divisions. Both emerging countries shared a long border, and soon became embroiled in a border conflict. Although it never developed into an open war, this conflict led to foul relations between both nations in the interwar period.

The Treaty of Protection in fact meant that Slovakia could be forced to participate in a war alongside Germany if the German government so decided. On 20–21 July 1939, secret discussions between the German and Slovak governments took place, during which Slovakia informally agreed to participate in Germany's planned invasion of Poland—Operation *Fall Weiß* (Case White). The Slovaks also agreed to allow Germany to use its territory as the staging area for its troops. On 21 August, the German Foreign Ministry Office prepared a *Note verbale* informing the Slovak government that German armed forces would enter Slovakia to protect Slovakia from the danger of Polish attack (Nižňanský et al. 2009, 576–7). The content of the note (approved by Adolf Hitler) was presented to the Slovak government first unofficially by the German ambassador to Slovakia Hans Bernard on 24 August 1939 (Nižňanský et al. 2009, doc. 209, pages 589–90). The Slovak government was also asked to take part in the military operations against Poland (with assurances that the Slovak Army would not be used outside Slovak territory (Nižňanský et al. 2009, doc. 205, page 583), but this promise was not fulfilled). In exchange, Germany promised to guarantee the integrity of the Slovak-Hungarian border. Once Poland was defeated, Slovakia would regain the territories lost in the fall of 1938, and eventually also those which were lost to Poland in 1920 (Nižňanský et al. 2009, doc. 210, pages 590–1). After a short hesitation, the Slovak government accepted the German requirements. The German request was officially presented on 27 August 1939 and the Slovak government officially consented the next day (Nižňanský et al. 2009, doc. 216, pages 604–5, 610).

The Slovak Army had two infantry divisions and another division with partially motorized reconnaissance and artillery and support units. The Slovak Air Force had 139 combat and sixty auxiliary aircraft.

On 26 August 1939, the Slovak Republic mobilized its armed forces and established a new field army, codenamed *Bernolák* after the famous Slovak linguist, comprising 51,306 soldiers divided into three infantry divisions and a motorized group, which participated in the invasion. Additionally, 160,000 reservists were called up with 115,000 entering service on 20 September 1939.

The *Bernolák* Field Army was led by Slovak Minister of Defense Ferdinand Čatloš and had its initial headquarters in Spišská Nová Ves, though after 8 September this was moved to Solivar near Prešov. The Army Group consisted of:

- First Infantry Division *Jánošík* led by General Anton Pulanich in sector Spišská Nová Ves-Prešov. In October 1939, it returned to Slovakia and was upgraded to a fully motorized division.
- Second Infantry Division *Škultéty* led by Lieutenant Colonel Ján Imro, later General Alexander Čunderlík in sector Brezno-Poprad.
- Third Infantry Division *Rázus* led by General Augustín Malár in the sector east of the High Tatras.
- A motorized unit *Kalinčiak* under Lieutenant Colonel Ján Imro was created on 5 September in Humenné but its participation in the campaign was limited to mopping up operations.

Bernolák was part of the German Fourteenth Army led by *Generaloberst* Wilhelm List under Army Group South commanded by Field Marshal Karl Rudolf Gerd von Rundstedt. The Fourteenth Army consisted of four corps with infantry, mountain, and panzer divisions, as well as Slovakia's Field Army *Bernolák*. The Fourteenth Army was based in Moravia and Slovakia. *Bernolák*'s task was to support German troops and prevent a Polish incursion into Slovakia.

The official political pretext for Slovak participation in the Polish Campaign was a disagreement over the disputed areas in Kysuce, Orava, and Spiš on the Polish-Slovak border. Poland had annexed these areas on 1 December 1938, in the aftermath of the Munich Agreement. Moreover, some Polish politicians openly supported Hungary in their effort to retake parts of southern and eastern Slovakia inhabited mostly by Hungarians.

Bernolák's primary opponent was the Polish Karpaty Army (Carpathian Army), which mainly consisted of infantry units with some light artillery support. The attack started at 0500 hours on 1 September 1939—historians view this as the official date for the opening of the Second World War. First Infantry Division *Janošík* occupied the village of Javorina and the town of Zakopane, then continued toward Nowy Targ protecting the left flank of the German Second Mountain Division. During 4–5 September, *Janošík* engaged regular Polish Army units. On 7 September, *Janošík* stopped its advance thirty kilometers inside Polish territory. Later, *Janošík* was pulled back with one of its battalions remaining until 29 September to occupy Zakopane, Jurgów, and Javorina.

Second Infantry Division *Škultéty* was kept in reserve and participated only in mopping-up operations. In this, it was supported by the *Kalinčiak* motorized group. The Third Infantry Division *Rázus* had to protect 170 kilometers of the Slovak border between Stará Ľubovňa in the north and the southeastern border with Hungary. *Rázus* fought minor skirmishes, and after several days moved into Polish territory ending its advance on 11 September 1939.

Two or three Slovak air squadrons, codenamed *Ľalia* (Lily), were used for reconnaissance, bombing, and close support for German fighters. Two planes were lost (one to anti-aircraft fire, one to an accidental crash), and one Polish plane was shot down. Total Slovak losses during the campaign were eighteen dead, forty-six wounded, and eleven missing.

Field Army *Bernolák* was demobilized and disbanded on 7 October 1939. The Slovak Army took around 1,350 civilian prisoners in Poland. In February 1940, around 1,200 of these were handed to Germans and some of the remainder to the Soviets. The rest were kept in a Slovak prison camp in Lešť.

All the disputed northern territories bordering Poland, both from 1920 and 1938, were given by Germany to Slovakia (formalized by a Slovak parliamentary resolution on 22 December 1939). This lasted until 20 May 1945, when the border was returned to its 1920 position.

With the only exception of one week of armed conflict by Slovak First Infantry Division *Janošík* resulting in 162 Slovak casualties, Slovakia and its professional armed forces evaded combat and generally enjoyed peacetime at home during the Second World War. This all changed on 22 June 1941 when Germany attacked the Soviet Union in Operation Barbarossa.

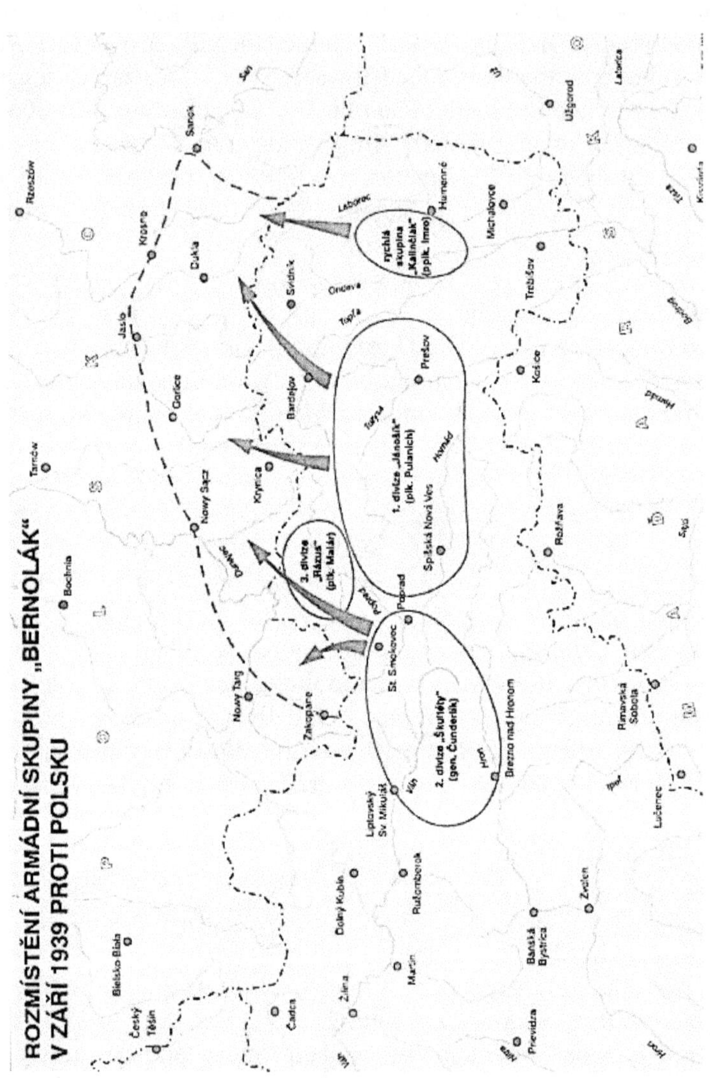
ROZMÍSTĚNÍ ARMÁDNÍ SKUPINY „BERNOLÁK“
V ZÁŘÍ 1939 PROTI POLSKU

OPERATION BARBAROSSA

Preparations for War Against the Soviet Union

AFTER THE DEFEAT OF POLAND, GERMANY DID NOT REQUIRE FURTHER Slovak participation in German military operations and Slovakia entered a phase of quiet and peace on the home front. After France was defeated in June of 1940, Berlin had a free hand to purge the Slovak government of "unreliable elements." It was in this phase that Minister of Foreign Affairs and Minister of the Interior Ferdinand Ďurčanský, who in the spring of 1940 had tried to secretly contact the British government and negotiate the recognition of the neutral status of Slovakia, was replaced (Rychlík 2018, 115, 121). The new government, with Vojtech Tuka and Alexander Mach in leading roles, oriented definitively and exclusively towards Germany. On 24 November 1940, Slovakia, together with Hungary and Romania, joined the Tripartite Pact (Berlin Pact) (Nižňanský et al. 2009, 270–2). In April 1941, Slovakia did not participate in the military campaign against Yugoslavia and Greece. On the other hand, when the campaign stared on 6 April, Bratislava severed diplomatic relations with Belgrade and on 10 April, expressed a willingness to recognize the new independent Croatian state (Rychlík 2018, 122).

On 21 June 1941, Chief of the German General Staff General Franz Halder secretly visited Bratislava to inform the head of the German military mission in Slovakia, General Paul von Otto, that Hitler expected the participation of the Slovak army in the war against the Soviet Union (Nižňanský et al. 2009, 1092). On the following day, 22 June 1941, Operation Barbarossa commenced. German Minister to Slovakia Hans Elard Ludin (1905–1947) visited President Tiso and Prime Minister Tuka to present them with the German request for Slovakian participation. Tuka agreed and offered military aid (Nižňanský et al. 2011, 95). On the same day, diplomatic relations between the USSR and Slovakia were broken off (Nižňanský et al. 2011, 98) and Defense Minister General Ferdinand Čatloš ordered reservists to report for "extraordinary military training." Not until 24 June 1941 did the government approve participation in the war, which was then officially announced by radio broadcast. The Slovak Parliament, which according to the Constitution was the only body competent to declare war, was not informed (Rychlík 2018, 122). Therefore, Slovakia's participation in Operation Barbarossa was unconstitutional. On 26 June 1941, Slovakia declared war on the USSR.

Slovak Armed Forces Order of Battle

SLOVAK ARMED FORCES WERE NOT INCLUDED IN THE EARLY PLANS FOR the German invasion of the Soviet Union, Operation Barbarossa. But Slovakia threw itself into the campaign to a greater extent than any other member of the Axis. Some preparations began in May 1941, when a German corps moved into Poprad and Prešov, Slovakia for the upcoming campaign, but mobilization was not formally declared until 22 June. Early preparations before formal mobilization created the Slovak Expeditionary Army Group that was organized, much like Field Army *Bernolák*, into a field corps of First and Second Infantry Divisions under Colonels Jozef Turanec (1892–1957) and Augustín Malár (1894–1945), respectively, plus a smaller supporting division comprised of two brigades: motorized artillery brigade (regiment); and another brigade consisting of three battalions (Eleventh Engineer Battalion, Eleventh Motorized Signals Battalion, Eleventh Armored Company, Eleventh Armored Car Reconnaissance Company, Twelfth Motorized Antitank Company, Eighth Motorized Heavy Antiaircraft Company, Eleventh Quartermaster, Eleventh Army Hospital, and Eleventh Ambulance)—see Figure 1.

Jozef Turanec was born in north central Slovakia (then Kingdom of Hungary) in 1892, attended *gymnázium* in Ružomberok and Comenius University for undergraduate and law school in Bratislava. Some years after completing law school, he enlisted in the Czechoslovak Army in 1919 and graduated from War College in 1920. On 1 November 1921, he was promoted to captain. In 1928, he served as intelligence officer in the Tenth Infantry Division in Banská Bystrica. He was rapidly promoted in rank: captain of the general staff on 1 August 1930; major on 1 July 1937; lieutenant colonel on 17 May 1939; and colonel on 1 January 1940. From 1939 until 1941, he served in various military functions in Ružomberok, Bratislava, and Trenčín. From 19 November 1940 until 22 June 1941, he served as commander of the First Divisional District Command in Bratislava. From 22 June until 3 August 1941, he commanded the First Infantry Division of the Slovak Expeditionary Army Group (SEAG). From 3 August until 27 November 1941, he commanded the Slovak Rapid Division in SEAG and earned the German Iron Cross, Second Class on 5 November 1941. In gratitude for his successes on the front and military qualities, he was honored and promoted to general II. class on 1 January 1942. From 25 April until 23 September 1942, he resumed command of the Rapid Division and earned the Knight's Cross of the Iron Cross on 7 August

1942. During the year 1943, he served in an administrative capacity in the Slovak Ministry of Defense in Bratislava. From 1 January until 27 August 1944, he commanded all ground forces in the Slovak Ministry of Defense. Two days before the outbreak of the military uprising in Slovakia, he was entrusted as a devoted supporter of the Tiso government and Nazi Germany with the command of all Slovak forces and anti-partisan activities. On 29 August 1944, he arrived from Trenčianske Biskupice at Tri Duby Airport (now Sliač Airport), where he was arrested on the order of his former Chief of Staff Colonel Ján Golian (commander of the insurrectional army in Slovakia during the Slovak National Uprising) and handed over to the partisans who arranged for his and recently captured Slovak Minister of Defense Ferdinand Čatloš's transport to the U.S.S.R. In 1947, he was returned to Czechoslovakia and sentenced to death by the National Court. However, the court's verdict was soon changed to thirty-years in prison. Jozef Turanec died in Leopoldov Prison on 9 March 1957 at the age of sixty-five-years.

Augustín Malár was born in Reitern, Austro-Hungary (107 km / 66 mi west of Vienna) on 18 July 1894. After graduating from gymnasium in 1914, he enlisted in the Austro-Hungarian Army as a one-year volunteer and on 8 May 1915 he joined the Seventy-Second Regiment in Bratislava. Malár then transferred to the Sixty-Fourth Regiment, with which on 1 December 1915 he arrived on the Russian front in command of the Third Platoon of the Fifteenth Field Company, Fourth Battalion. At the time of the Brusilov offensive, he participated in the fighting at Gorodišči. At the beginning of April 1916, he was transferred to the Italian front where on 10 October 1916 he fell into captivity. After two months captivity, Malár was paroled to join the Czechoslovak Legion in Italy. On 13 February 1918, he was promoted to second lieutenant and served as commander of platoons in the Thirty-Third and Thirty-Fourth Infantry Regiments. Soon he was promoted to first lieutenant in 1918. After returning to newly independent Czechoslovakia, Malár participated in border combat with Hungary from 27 December 1918 to 15 October 1919, during which he was promoted to captain on 1 May 1919. From 1927–1930, he attended military academy in Prague. On 1 January 1931, he was promoted to major of the general staff and assigned Chief of the 1st and 4th Departments (personnel and matériel) of the Ninth Infantry Division in Bratislava. Thereafter, until 15 February 1935, he served in various other functions at Provincial Army Headquarters in Bratislava, followed by placement at the Military Geographical Institute, where he worked until 13 March 1939 as a member of the Commission for the adjustment of the Slovak-Hungarian border. Before declaration of Slovak independence, Malár became commander of the Sixth Corps and remained in this position throughout the fighting over borders with Hungary in eastern Slovakia. After declaration of Slovak independence on 14 March 1939, and despite his formal condemnation of the breakup of Czechoslovakia, he served as a government representative to the Slovak Army's Sixth Corps in Spišská Nová Ves (northeastern Slovakia). On 17 May 1939, Malár was promoted to full colonel. When fighting broke out against Poland on 1 September 1939 in Operation *Fall Weiß*, Colonel Malár commanded the Third Infantry Division *Rázus*, which from 6 to 11 September 1939 advanced to the Bukowsko-Kulzne-Baligród-Jabłonki-Ciszna line. This command ended on 1 October 1939. His next engagement was the establishment and management of the War College in Bratislava. At the same time from 20 October 1939 to 9 January 1940, he held the position of Commander of Third Divisional Headquarters in Prešov. While still serving at the War College from 1 August to 1 October 1940, he also commanded First Divisional Headquarters in Trenčín. From 22 June 1941 to 12 August 1941, he commanded the Second Division of the Slovak Expeditionary Forces in Ukraine. From 17 September to 19 November 1941, he commanded the Slovak Security Division in Ukraine. From 27 November 1941 to 25 April 1942, Malár commanded the army's Rapid Division on the Eastern Front, where on 2 January 1942 he was promoted to General II. class and on 6 February 1942, he was awarded the Knight's Cross of the Iron Cross. During June 1942–1944, he served as Slovak military attaché in Rome, Budapest, and Berlin where in November 1943 Captain Peter Vlčko met with and confided in him. In June 1944, General Malár took command of the Eastern Slovak Army Corps headquartered in Prešov. On the day before the outbreak of the Slovak National Uprising, Malár suddenly left his post in Prešov and flew to Bratislava. On 30 August 1944, the day after the outbreak of the uprising, in a radio speech Malár ordered rebelling Slovak soldiers to return to their barracks and not support the uprising. Paradoxically, he employed the word "premature" suggesting the possibility of fighting the Germans in the future. Aware of this gaffe, the Germans arrested Malár at Išla airport near Prešov on 31 August as he returned from Bratislava. He was taken to Germany for interrogation and executed in 1945 in Sachsenhausen Concentration Camp; the precise date of his death remains unknown.

The Slovak Expeditionary Army Group (SEAG) was not part of the initial Axis invasion of the Soviet Union, which began on 22 June 1941. However, the Slovaks immediately reorganized their expeditionary force (originally created in early June 1941) and mobilized 68,000 personnel (18,000 active duty, 50,000 reserves) at staging areas in Prešov and Medzilaborce east of the Tatra Mountains near the Polish border. SEAG (actually, a corps) was commanded by Slovak Defense Minister General Ferdinand Čatloš and was attached to the German Seventeenth Army under *Generaloberst* Carl-Heinrich von Stülpnagel, which itself was part of Army Group South commanded by Field Marshal Karl Rudolf Gerd von Rundstedt. Although Čatloš served as commander of SEAG, he made only two brief visits to his troops in the theater during this period, choosing instead to execute command from his offices at the Ministry of National Defense (*MNO*) in Bratislava.

The Seventeenth Army consisted of five corps: Forth Corps with five infantry divisions; Forty-Ninth Corps with three mountain divisions; Fifty-Second Corps with three light infantry divisions; the Hungarian Fast Corps (*Gyorshadtest*; actually, a division with 25,000 personnel) with two motorized and one cavalry brigades; and the Slovak Expeditionary Group (actually, a corps with over 68,000 personnel) comprising operational units depicted in Figure 2.

Before entering the theater of operations, General Čatloš ordered the formation of a "Mobile Group" for use on the Eastern Front. Colonel Rudolf Pilfousek was named as its commander.

Rudolf Pilfousek was born on 2 January 1899 in Habartice, Austro-Hungary to a Sudeten German family, attended War College in Prague, and served in the Austro-Hungarian Army during the First World War. He rose to the rank of lieutenant colonel in the Czechoslovak Army during the interwar period. Due to his Sudeten German descent, he was released from the Czechoslovak Army on 8 October 1938, after which in 1939 he joined the newly formed army of the Slovak Republic and led the Slovak Second Infantry Divisional Command in Prešov as lieutenant colonel. In September 1939, this division took part in the invasion of Poland. While serving in Operation Barbarossa in Ukraine in 1940, he was promoted to colonel of the general staff. After reorganization of the Slovak Expeditionary Army Group, Pilfousek took command of the Slovak Rapid Brigade on 7 July 1941 and the divisional strength Mobile Command on 25 July 1941. On 3 August 1941, Pilfousek was reassigned commander of antiaircraft artillery. On 5 August 1942, he was again reassigned as commander of the Security Division in southern Russia. On 1 August 1943, he was made commander of the Second Infantry Divisional Headquarters back in Slovakia. Shortly thereafter from August 1944 until May 1945, he fought against the insurgent

Slovak Army during the Slovak National Uprising and the advancing Soviet Red Army. During this time in October 1944, Pilfousek joined the Germans as *Standartenführer* in the Sixteenth *SS-Panzergrenadier* Division *Reichsführer SS*. At the beginning of 1945, he took command of a unit of Slovak and German troops to fight against the Soviet Red Army in Slovakia. He retreated with the Germans to Germany and survived the war. He died in Germany in 1980.

The Mobile Group consisted of the Headquarters, the Second Cavalry Reconnaissance Squadron JPO-2 (Michalovce), a tank battalion with two tank companies and two companies of antitank guns (Turčianský Svätý Martin), a motorized artillery battalion from the Eleventh Artillery Regiment (Žilina), First Battalion of the Sixth Infantry Regiment mounted on trucks (Trebišov), and auxiliary units supplied by the Second Infantry Division (staff platoon, telegraph company, engineer platoon and staff automobile unit). A total compliment for the Mobile Group was: fifty-nine officers; twenty-seven NCOs; 1824 men; 813 rifles; 661 pistols; eighty-five light machine-guns; ninety-eight heavy machine-guns; sixteen 3.7-cm vz. 37 antitank guns; four 7.5-cm vz. 15 mountain guns; nine vz. 30 10-cm howitzers; three OA vz. 30 armored cars; thirty LT vz. 35 tanks; ten LT vz. 38 tanks; seven LT vz. 40 tanks; 183 trucks; forty-nine passenger cars; three fuel trucks; three ambulances; thirty-three motorcycles; and 112 bicycles (Kliment and Nakládal 1997, 66–7). All the units were ready by midnight of 22 June, and on 23 June started assembling in the vicinity of Medzilaborce. The unit was tactically subordinated to the German Seventh Army and was assigned to German liaison officers.

Only the Mobile Group of SEAG crossed the Slovak-Polish border on 24 June making its way to Sanok that same afternoon where they joined the German Seventeenth Army, the day after Slovakia declared war on the U.S.S.R. SEAG's structure was as depicted in Figure 2.

In the meantime, the bulk of SEAG was still forming in northeastern Slovakia. It consisted of two infantry divisions, two artillery regiments, an engineer battalion, communications battalion and companies of tanks, armored cars, and antitank guns. The field corps was 50,698 strong. Its weakness was a lack of transport, which forced most of its infantry units to proceed to the front on foot. The corps started to Dukla Pass on 30 June and reached the Soviet border three days later. Its progress was so slow that by the time it reached Sanok the front was already at Lviv. From Sanok, the corps moved slowly to Sambor, where in the meantime on 4 July, General

Čatloš visited with Colonel Pilfousek's Mobile Group. (Kliment and Nakládal 1997, 68.)

Figure 1 (7 June 1941)

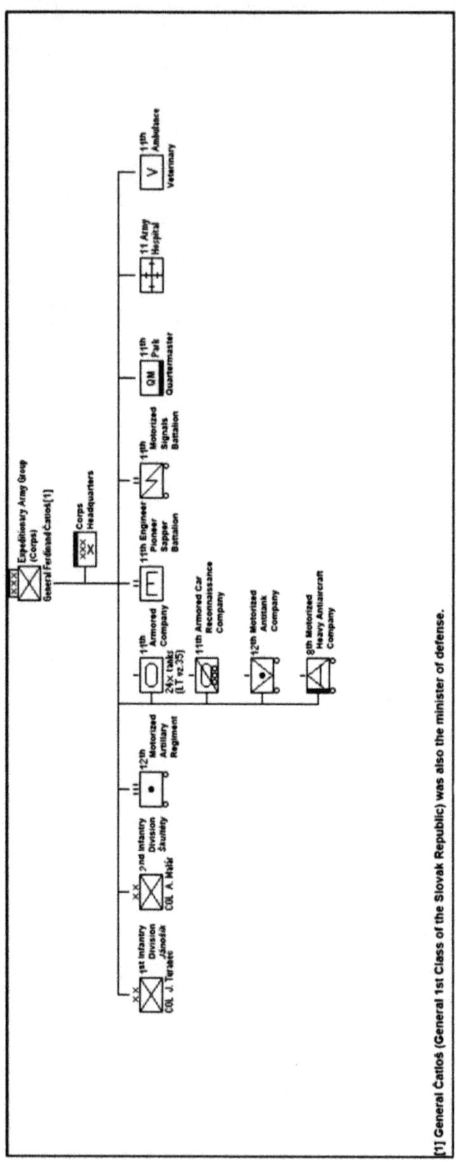

Figure 2

Slovak Expeditionary Army Group 6/26/41

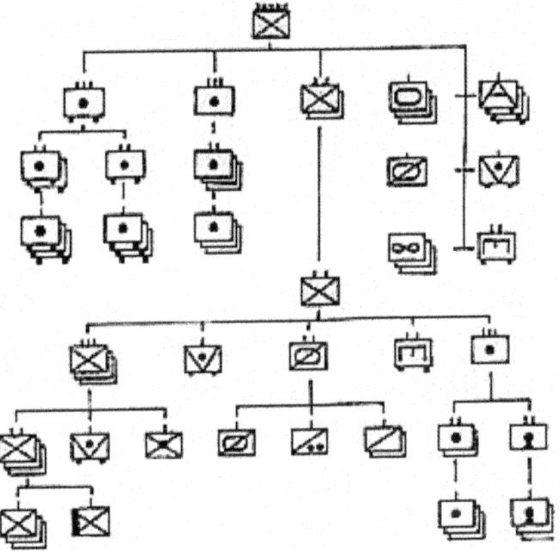

Initial Phase

THE SEVENTEENTH ARMY ENGAGED THE SOVIET TWENTY-SIXTH ARMY OF the Southwest Front. From nearly the beginning of the operation, Slovak infantry divisions had difficulty keeping up with the rapidly advancing German units. A general lack of mobile forces, logistical capabilities, and transport equipment caused the Slovak units to fall behind. The corps was 50,698 strong. Its lack of transport forced most of its infantry units to proceed to the front on foot. The corps left Prešov, Slovakia for the Polish border via Dukla Pass on 30 June and reached the Soviet border three days later. By the time it reached Sanok, the front was already at Lviv. The corps moved slowly east towards Sambor (97 km / 60 mi), where in the meantime on 4 July, General Čatloš visited the Mobile Group—the only Slovak unit managing to keep pace with the Germans. General Čatloš decided to elevate the Mobile Group to a Mobile Brigade by transferring to it all available motorized units of the Field Corps (Kliment and Nakládal 1997, 68).

Before reaching the Soviet border, the Mobile Group met their first armed resistance at Wojtkowa, Poland, where there were units of the Red Army in prepared positions. The tanks and antitank guns managed to partially paralyze the defense, but the group was heavily engaged by Russian artillery and had to retreat to Trzcianiec. This brief action cost the group one dead and six wounded.

On the 27 June, the Mobile Group was ordered back to the San River, where it was supposed to neutralize the remaining Soviet bunkers in the vicinity of Sanok. Before moving to Sanok, a company of tanks drove again to Wojtkowa, but found that the Soviet units have retreated during the night. The bulk of the Slovak Mobile Group moved to Załuż near the San River, where it met with the command group of the German Rapid Group Coretti under the command of Colonel Julius Coretti, with which it was supposed to attack the bunkers. While moving from Załuż to Sanok, the Slovak reconnaissance platoon and their German cars drew heavy fire from the fortifications. Most of the German soft-skin vehicles were hit and burned up. The Slovak Mobile Group sent two tank companies against the bunkers. Five LT vz. 38 tanks from the First Armored Company and five LT vz. 35 tanks from the Second Armored Company moved up the hill. One LT vz. 38 fell into a ditch and had to be abandoned, while another was repeatedly hit by a 4.5-cm antitank gun from one of the bunkers. This tank (V-3006) burned and was a total loss; its crew perished as well.

As the Field Corps could not keep pace with the motorized units, it fell behind. At the beginning of July 1941, its headquarters was in Chyrow. The infantry was used for consolidating the conquered area and for some limited anti-partisan duties. As the corps was clearly not utilized, General Čatloš eventually ordered that it be reorganized to form a Rapid Division and a Security Division, and to send the rest of the reservist home in time for the autumn harvest. In all, 35,523 men were demobilized and sent back to Slovakia (Kliment and Nakládal 1997, 68).

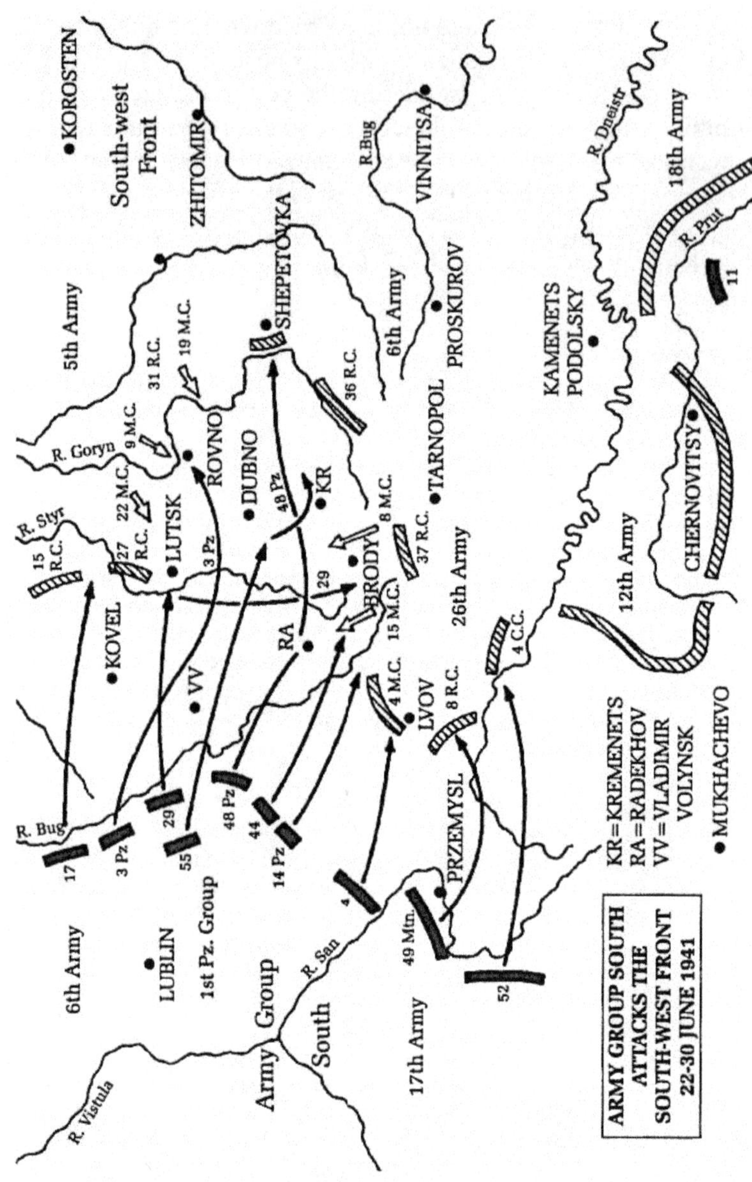
KOROSTEN
South-west Front
ZHITOMIR
VINNITSA
R. Bug
R. Dneistr
18th Army
R. Prut
11
5th Army
SHEPETOVKA
6th Army
PROSKUROV
KAMENETS PODOLSKY
31 R.C.
19 M.C.
36 R.C.
R. Goryn
9 M.C.
ROVNO
DUBNO
TARNOPOL
CHERNOVITSY
12th Army
R. Styr
15 R.C.
27 R.C.
22 M.C.
LUTSK
3 Pz
48 Pz
KR
8 M.C.
37 R.C.
26th Army
29
BRODY
KOVEL
RA
15 M.C.
4 C.C.
VV
4 M.C.
LVOV
8 R.C.
R. Bug
17
3 Pz
29
55
48 Pz
44
14 Pz
PRZEMYSL
4
49 Mtn.
52
6th Army
LUBLIN
1st Pz. Group
Army Group South
R. San
17th Army
R. Vistula
KR=KREMENETS
RA=RADEKHOV
VV=VLADIMIR VOLYNSK
MUKHACHEVO
ARMY GROUP SOUTH ATTACKS THE SOUTH-WEST FRONT 22-30 JUNE 1941

"Rolling in The Deep"*

ON 7 JULY 1941, THE SLOVAK EXPEDITIONARY ARMY GROUP WAS reorganized with the best motorized units of both infantry divisions, including Pilfousek's Mobile Group, forming a brigade size rapid Mobile Command that came to be known as Pilfousek Brigade after its commander. The brigade received additional artillery units—the rest of the I/11 on 8 July, the entire Eleventh Armored Regiment on 12 July, with twenty-four 10-cm howitzers and twelve 10.5-cm cannons—additional armor (10 OA vz. 30 armored cars, 22 LT vz. 35 tanks and 12 3.7-cm antitank guns), and over 200 additional trucks. Its manpower was increased to 3,546 officers and men (Kliment and Nakládal 1997, 68).

Around 8 July 1941, the brigade had advanced beyond the tactical control of the Slovak command, so control of the unit was handed over to the German Seventeenth Army. The remaining forces of SEAG, no longer an independent formation, were eventually used behind German lines in conjunction with the 103rd Rear Area Command of Army Group South in security duties and helping to eliminate pockets of Soviet resistance.

On 9 July, the brigade moved forward from Sambor to the Rudky-Lviv-Vynnyky line and then to the area between Shopky-Kurovychi (Kliment and Nakládal 1997, 70). On 10 July, the brigade was reinforced by the Fifteenth Light Antiaircraft Battery with 2-cm vz. 36 antiaircraft guns (Kliment and Nakládal 1997, 70). On 11 July, the brigade moved to the area east of Ternopil. On 12 July, it incorporated the rest of the Eleventh Armored Regiment and II/6 Infantry Battalion was augmented to a motorized infantry group (Kliment and Nakládal 1997, 70).

---

* During the Battle of the Hornburg (a fictional battle in J. R. R. Tolkien's epic *The Lord of the Rings*), Saruman's army of Uruk-hai was able to penetrate the outer wall of Helm's Deep using a "blasting-fire." As they began to break down the door to King Theoden's inner chamber, the King gives a rousing speech indicating that, as per Aragorn's suggestion, the forces of good should ride out and face their enemies head on. He finishes the speech by shouting, "the Horn of Helm Hammerhand shall sound in The Deep one last time!" It is the sound waves from this horn which were "rolling in The Deep" that this phrase refers to. It was the sound of the Horn of Helm Hammerhand that rolled over the forces of good and strengthened their resolve, ultimately leading to their victory over Saruman's seemingly unconquerable mass of Uruk-hai. The phrase "rolling in The Deep" is thus an expression of resolve or determination in one's course.

Under German orders, Pilfousek Brigade rapidly advanced eastward through Lviv, Ternopil, and towards Vinnytsia to challenge a mounting Soviet counteroffensive east of there. On 15 July, the brigade moved to Buchach (formerly, Buczacz, Poland)* and on 16 July to Grodky, thus reaching the prewar territory of the Soviet Union (Kliment and Nakládal 1997, 70). During 17–18 July, all vehicles were repaired, and fuel and munitions were replenished (Kliment and Nakládal 1997, 70). On 19 July, General Čatloš and Šaňo Mach visited the brigade for a last review, and on 20 July the brigade set off again (Kliment and Nakládal 1997, 70).

By 22 July, the brigade had passed Vinnytsia and its staff set up command headquarters about eight kilometers (5 mi) west of Lypovets while combat units pushed on towards Lypovets, a small town 212 kilometers (131 mi) southwest of the metropolis of Kyiv and 151 kilometers (94 mi) due south of Zhytomyr. Near Lypovets, Pilfousek's Brigade experienced heavy fighting with the Soviets, who were mounting a counteroffensive to stop the *Blitzkrieg* the Germans were executing—see BATTLE OF LYPOVETS in Chapter 24, *infra*.

After the bloody Battle of Lypovets, the Pilfousek Brigade was expanded to a division on 25 July 1941 and later merged with the Slovak First Infantry Division and changed its name to the Rapid Division. Before merging, it consisted of the following: 156 light machine guns; twenty-seven heavy machine guns; thirty-nine 37-mm antitank guns; two mortars; four 75-

---

* The Germans occupied Buczacz on 7 July 1941. Before the Germans entered the city, Ukrainian Nationalists began to assault Jews, killing several. In mid-July, Ukrainian nationalist militia murdered 40 people, both Jews and non-Jews. In August 1941, between 350 and 450 Jewish men were murdered outside the city. Between May and August 1942, the Germans concentrated the Jews of the nearby towns and villages into Buczacz, raising the number of Jewish inhabitants to at least 11,000-12,000. At the end of 1942, a *ghetto* was established in the city. Most Buczacz Jews were murdered in major operations between the fall of 1942 and the summer of 1943: on 17 October and 27 November 1942, a total of 3,800 Buczacz Jews were deported to the Bełżec extermination camp in Poland; during preparations for the deportations several hundred Jews were shot. In operations on 1–2 February and 13–15 April 1943, between 6,400 and 7,200 Jews were murdered outside the city. At the end of June 1943, those remaining in the *ghetto* were murdered in the vicinity of Buczacz. The Red Army entered the city on 23 March 1944, but shortly afterwards the Germans temporarily reoccupied Buczacz. They then murdered between 600 and 800 Jews who had come out of hiding in the area and returned to the city. Buczacz was finally liberated by the Red Army on 21 July 1944. (Yad Vashem 2019.)

mm infantry guns; twenty-four 10-cm vz. 30 Howitzer canons; twelve 10.5-cm vz. 35 cannons; five armored cars; eight 20-mm antiaircraft guns; forty-three tanks; 459 trucks; five artillery tractors; 137 light transports; and just under 5,000 personnel. The Mobile Command remained under Colonel Pilfousek's leadership. In early August 1941, the divisional strength Mobile Command fought at Uman with the German Seventeenth Army helping to annihilate the encircled Soviet Sixth and Twelfth Armies.

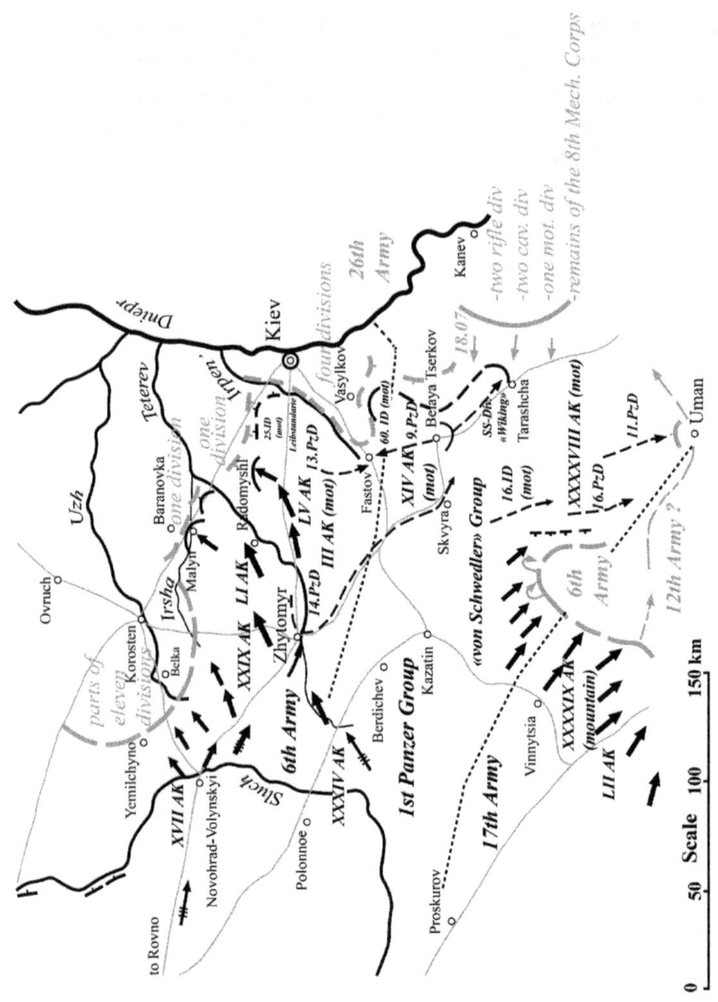

Wikipedia contributors, " Battle of Uman," Wikipedia, The Free Encyclopedia, https://en.wikipedia.org/w/index.php?title=Battle_of_Uman&oldid=916563613

During the Battle of Uman (15 July to 8 August 1941), a mechanized body of Army Group South formed double wings encircling the Sixth (Lieutenant General Ivan Nikolayevich Muzychenko) and Twelfth (Major General Pavel Grigorevich Ponedelin) Soviet Armies at the city of Uman. During this struggle, twenty Soviet divisions were destroyed or surrendered. The battle occurred during the Kyiv defensive operation between the elements of Red Army's Southwestern Front, retreating from the Lviv salient, and German Army Group South.

The command of the encircled Soviet armies realized the gravity of the situation and asked for help but did not receive it. The troops of the Southern Front retreated; their battle line was broken several times. By the evening of 4 August, the Soviet High Command (*Stavka*) had virtually lost interest in the fate of the remnants of encircled armies. In his communications with the commander of the Southwestern Front, Colonel General Mikhail Kirponos, Stalin demanded the creation of a powerful defensive line along the Dnieper and mentioned the fate of the Sixth and Twelfth Armies only in response to the question by Kirponos. Kirponos later died in the First Battle of Kyiv, which immediately followed the Battle of Uman and was a scaled-up version of the disaster at Uman. Formally, on 6 August, another Soviet offensive towards Uman from the northeast was planned, but in reality, the armies were left to their own fate. The two armies were systematically annulated. The commanders of both the Sixth and Twelfth Armies along with the commanders of four corps and eleven divisions were taken prisoner. The Soviets suffered 203,000 casualties (100,000 dead or wounded, 103,000 captured) with the loss of 317 tanks. The Germans suffered 20,853 casualties (4,610 dead, 15,458 wounded, 785 captured or missing).

During or shortly after the Battle of Uman, the Slovak Expeditionary Army Group was again reorganized by Defense Minister Čatloš. The Mobile Command (divisional strength) merged with the remnants of the Slovak First Infantry Division on 3 August 1941 to form the Slovak Rapid Division (*RD*) under the command of Colonel Jozef Turanec (former commander of First Infantry Division). Simultaneously, remnants of the First and Second Infantry Divisions were reorganized into a Security Division (*ZD*) for mopping-up operations in the rear areas of northern Ukraine and Belarus. The new Rapid Division had two small, motorized infantry regiments and an artillery regiment; all the Slovak tanks had already been sent back to the home country for repairs.

These units were concentrated near Lviv and for the next three weeks trained the infantry for coordination with artillery. After the final exercise, the Rapid Division was transferred on 18 August to Proskurivka (150 km / 92.6 mi southwest of Vinnytsia) and on to Bila Tserkva (85.5 km / 53 mi south of Kyiv).[1] (Kliment and Nakládal 1997, 73.)

The Rapid Division was organized into its final form by 22 August and moved to Skvyra (124 km / 77 mi northeast of Vinnytsia), where it trained for several more weeks. It did not witness or take part in the massacre at Bila Tserkva. At this time, it was subordinated to the German Thirty-Fourth Corps (General Friedrich Koch), which was part of the Sixth Army (Colonel General Walther von Reichenau) of the Southern Army Group. (Kliment and Nakládal 1997, 73.)

The composition of the Rapid Division was (Kliment and Nakládal 1997, 73–5):

- **Headquarters**: 43 officers; 16 NCOs; 200 men; 120 rifles; 93 pistols; 4 light machine-guns (MG); 22 trucks; 20 passenger cars; 2 motorcycles with sidecars; 6 motorcycles; and 1 bicycle.
- **Twentieth Infantry Regiment**: 57 officers; 12 NCOs; 1954 men; 1552 rifles; 623 pistols; 101 light MG; 24 heavy MG; 12 mortars; 12 3.7-cm antitank guns; 4 7.5-cm guns; 169 trucks; 51 passenger cars; 2 motorcycle combinations; 30 motorcycles; and 50 bicycles.
- **Twenty-First Infantry Regiment**: 63 officers; 13 NCOs; 1752 men; 1183 rifles; 493 pistols; 63 light MG; 25 heavy MG; 10 mortars; 12 3.7-cm antitank guns; 4 7.5-cm guns; 171 trucks; 35 passenger cars; 2 motorcycle combinations; 26 motorcycles; and 62 bicycles.
- **Eleventh Artillery Regiment**: 36 officers; 12 NCOs; 1051 men; 714 rifles; 294 pistols; 28 light MG; 28 heavy MG; 16 10-cm vz. 30 howitzers; 4 10.5-cm vz. 35 cannons; 116 trucks; 32 passenger cars; 24 motorcycles; and 27 bicycles.
- **Eleventh Reconnaissance Group**: 13 officers; 9 NCOs; 425 men; 253 rifles; 155 pistols; 19 light MG; 6 heavy MG; 4 3.7-cm antitank guns; 54 trucks; 9 passenger cars; 14 motorcycles; and 140 bicycles.
- **Second Communications Battalion**: 20 officers; 6 NCOs; 395 men; 334 rifles; 113 pistols; 12 light MG; 47 trucks; 22 passenger cars; and 8 motorcycles.

- **Eleventh Engineer Battalion**: 14 officers; 8 NCOs; 525 men; 291 rifles; 41 pistols; 19 light MG; 65 trucks; 7 passenger cars; and 5 motorcycles.
- **Eleventh Mountain Battery**: 2 officers; 3 NCOs; 96 men; 40 rifles; 23 pistols; 2 heavy MG 4 7.5-cm vz. 15 mountain guns; and 9 trucks.
- **Eleventh Antitank Company**: 4 officers; 164 men; 55 rifles; 114 pistols; 6 light MG; 12 3.7-cm antitank guns; 19 trucks; 4 passenger cars; and 4 motorcycles.
- **Antiaircraft Group**: 10 officers; 3 NCOs; 362 men; 4 light MG; 12 2-cm antiaircraft guns; 4 8.8-cm antiaircraft guns; 46 trucks; 11 passenger cars; and 6 motorcycles.
- **Automotive Workshop**: 1 officer; 1 NCO; 37 men; 9 rifles; 7 pistols; 7 trucks; 1 passenger car; and 1 motorcycle.
- **Quartermaster**: 38 officers; 7 NCOs; 1099 men; 347 rifles; 155 pistols; 9 light MG; 168 trucks; 13 passenger cars; 9 motorcycles; and 2 bicycles.
- **The total complement of the Rapid Division on 22 August 1941 was**: 301 officers; 90 NCOs; 8,060 men 4,898 rifles; 2,111 pistols; 265 light MG; 57 heavy MG; 22 mortars; 12 2-cm Oerlikon antiaircraft guns; 40 3.7-cm antitank guns; 12 7.5-cm vz. 15 mountain guns; 4 8.8-cm antiaircraft guns; 16 10-cm vz. 30 howitzers; 4 10.5-cm vz. 35 cannons; 893 trucks; 201 passenger cars; 6 motorcycle combinations; 133 motorcycles; and 282 bicycles. (Note: no armored vehicles, no submachine guns.)

The Rapid Division obtained its first assignment on 14 September 1941, when it was ordered to relieve the 514th Regiment of the 294th Division, which was holding the west (right) bank of the Dnieper River between Ukrainka (49.6 km / 31 mi south of Kyiv) and Khodosivka (25 km / 15.5 mi south of Kyiv) (Kliment and Nakládal 1997, 75). The Rapid Division built its positions above the river, and lent one engineer platoon with a bridge unit, one battery of the Eleventh Artillery Regiment and one platoon of the Thirteenth Antiaircraft battery to the Thirty-Fourth Corps for a forced crossing of the river in the First Battle of Kyiv (23 August to 26 September 1941) resulting in the largest military encirclement in the history of warfare (Kliment and Nakládal 1997, 75).* The Rapid Division was spared a role in the battle and remained in the rear as reserve.

The Soviets tried to cross the river on 16 September but were repulsed. In the next four days, the Rapid Division broadened its sector, as its neighboring German units were pulled into the attack. The division secured the banks of the Dnieper and captured 1,650 Soviet soldiers without suffering any casualties (Kliment and Nakládal 1997, 75).

After concluding the Battle of Kyiv, German Army Group South advanced south along the right bank of the Dnieper River through Horodyshche, crossing the Dnieper River at Checheleve, entering Kremenchuk, and on to Magdalynivka, where heavy fighting took place, then and on to the Sea of Azov coast where at the beginning of October took part of the envelopment of Soviet units. The Rapid Division began moving east across the miserable, muddy Russian roads, following the leading German units.

As of 2 October 1941, the Rapid Division was a part of the First Panzer Army under *Generaloberst* Paul Ludwig Ewald von Kleist fighting on the eastern side of Dnieper River near the region of Pereshchepyne (just northeast of Magdalynivka). The First Panzer Army advanced further south along the eastern banks of the Dnieper River and encircled Soviet troops at Melitopol in October. Melitopol became strategically important due to its location near the Sea of Azov. The Red Army was routed and had to retreat. The German Army occupied Melitopol on 6 October 1941. Within one week the entire remaining Jewish population of Melitopol (2,000 men, women, and children) were murdered by *Einsatzgruppe D*—see *EINSATZGRUPPEN*, *infra*.

* First Battle of Kyiv – The battle was an unprecedented defeat for the Red Army, exceeding even the Battle of Białystok–Minsk of June–July 1941. The encirclement trapped 452,700 soldiers, 2,642 guns and mortars and 64 tanks, of which scarcely 15,000 escaped from the encirclement by 2 October. The Southwestern Front suffered 700,544 casualties, including 616,304 killed, captured, or missing during the battle including the death of its lauded commander Mikhail Kirponos. The 5th, 37th, 26th, 21st, and 38th Armies, consisting of 43 divisions, were almost annihilated and the 40th Army suffered many losses. Like the Western Front before it, the Southwestern Front had to be recreated almost from scratch.

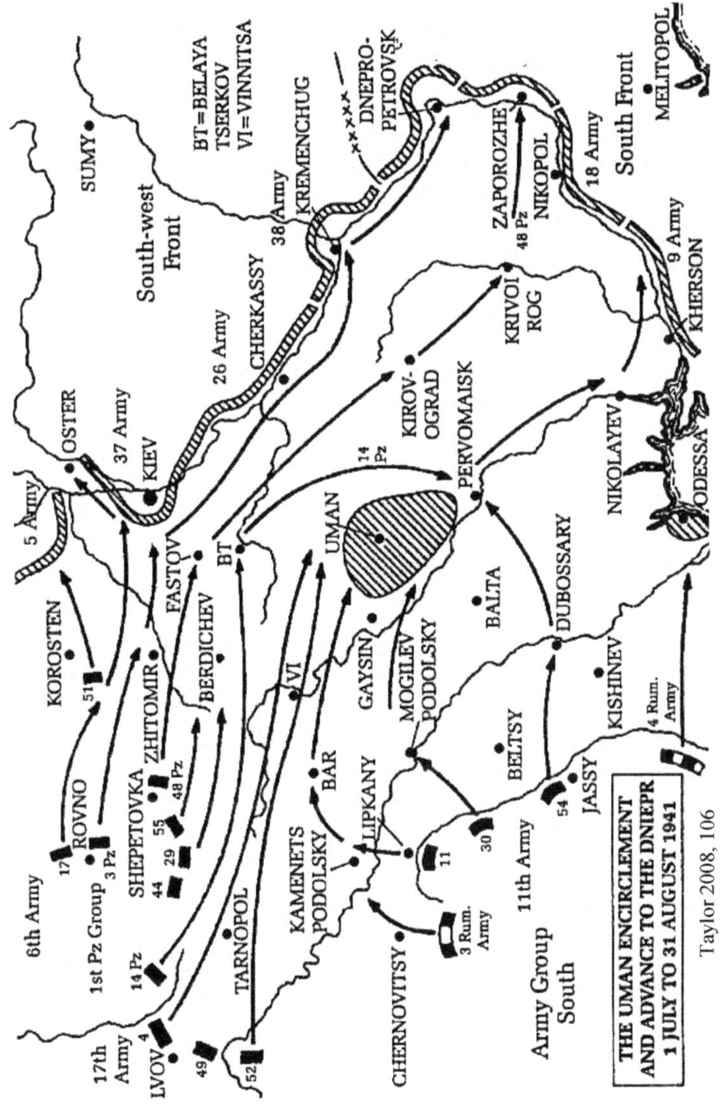

THE UMAN ENCIRCLEMENT AND ADVANCE TO THE DNIEPR 1 JULY TO 31 AUGUST 1941

Taylor 2008, 106

The Rapid Division fought its way along the northern banks of the Sea of Azov to Mariupol and Taganrog. By 17 October 1941, the Mius River was crossed, and Taganrog was captured by German troops. The First Panzer Army continued further east along the northern shore of the Sea of Azov toward Rostov at the mouth of the Don River, known as the gateway to the Caucasus. However, the autumn rains had begun, and the *Rasputitsa* (literally, "slush"; "time without roads") had set in slowing the First Panzer Army's advance to a crawl. This meant that the leading German units did not reach the outskirts of Rostov until mid-November, having lost contact with the Red Army in the meantime.

The assault on Rostov began on 17 November 1941, and on 21 November the Germans took the strategic city. However, the German lines were over-extended, and warnings by First Panzer Army's commander von Kleist that his left flank was vulnerable and that his tanks were ineffective in the freezing weather were ignored by the German High Command. On 27 November, the Soviet Thirty-Seventh Army, commanded by Lieutenant General Anton Ivanovich Lopatin, as part of the Rostov Strategic Offensive Operation (17 November 1941 to 2 December 1941), counter-attacked the First Panzer Army's spearhead from the north, forcing them to pull out of Rostov-on-Don. Adolf Hitler countermanded the retreat. When Army Group South's commander von Rundstedt refused to obey, Hitler sacked him, and replaced him with Field Marshal Walther von Reichenau. However, von Reichenau saw at once that von Rundstedt was right and succeeded in persuading Hitler to authorize the withdrawal. The First Panzer Army was forced back to the Mius River at Taganrog where it took up defensive positions throughout the winter of 1941–1942. It was the first significant German withdrawal of the war.

At the end of November 1941, one infantry battalion and its support units were left at the Azov shore, while the three infantry and one artillery battalions were ordered by the Fourteenth Corps to form a defense line on the Mius River close to the village of Zolotarevo. Shortly after manning their new positions, these units found themselves in the middle of heavy Soviet attacks, when the frontal German divisions retreated around their positions. The division held its line and even managed several counterattacks in the face of heavy Soviet pressure. By the beginning of December 1941, the situation stabilized, and the division constructed new defensive positions on the hills at the western bank of Mius River. At the same time, Colonel Turanec was replaced by Colonel Augustín Malár, an experienced and popular officer.

The Rapid Division fought bravely as part of the First Panzer Group in Ukraine for the rest of the 1941 campaign, ending it in defensive positions along the Mius River. During this time Colonel Turanec was honored with the German Iron Cross, II. class for his leadership of the Rapid Division. By this point, most of RD's vehicles had broken down and it was no longer a true motorized unit. But it compiled a good combat record during that span. On 1 January 1942, Colonel Turanec was promoted to General, II. class.

From 27 November 1941 to 25 April 1942, Colonel Augustín Malár commanded the Rapid Division and was promoted to General, II. class on 2 January 1942 and awarded the Knight's Cross of the Iron Cross on 6 February 1942. The Rapid Division remained in its defensive positions on the western bank of the Mius River for seven and a half months (November 1941–May 1942). It defended twelve kilometers of the line, while the Soviets tried repeatedly to puncture its line with groups of various sizes. During Christmas 1941, the Soviet army staged a massive attack with tank support, but the Rapid Division held. The Soviet attacks lasted into the spring of 1942, and only the German second offensive against Kharkov (May 1942) brought some respite. The Rapid Division was taken out of the line in June 1942, and some of its soldiers were able to return home when replacements became available. During more than seven months of this static defense, the Rapid Division's casualties were 119 dead, 576 wounded, and 89 missing.

The front line started moving east again on 19 July 1942 as part of Operation *Edelweiß* to capture the major oil fields in the Caucasus (Maykop, Grozny, and Baku), and so did the Rapid Division. Its new automotive repair team was so efficient that its truck columns moved sometimes even faster than the German armored formations. The Rapid Division reached the suburbs of Rostov-on-Don on 22 July recapturing the city on 25 July. In the next few days, the Rapid Division was the first to form a bridgehead on the south bank of the Don River. The advance of Army Group South was fast, and the Rapid Division, still part of the Fourteenth Corps, was very successful. By September 1942, it had advanced over 800 kilometers from its winter positions at the Mius River.

These were challenging times for the Rapid Division as the Germans faced a strong Soviet counteroffensive at Rostov-on-Don (Rostov Strategic Offensive Operation). The Rapid Division was well thought of by the Germans and was used as a front-line unit fighting in the campaigns of 1941 and 1942, reaching the Caucasus with Army Group B. Army Group B was established when Army Group South was divided for the summer offensive of 1942 on the Eastern Front. Army Group B was given the task of protecting the northern flank of Army Group A and included the Sixth Army during the Battle of Stalingrad (August 1942 to January 1943).*

From 25 April to 23 September 1942, General Turanec resumed command of the Rapid Division and earned the Knight's Cross of the Iron Cross on 7 August 1942. During the summer of 1942, General Turanec led the Rapid Division across the Kuban River and into the Taupse district on the eastern shore of the Black Sea just north of the seaside resort of Sochi. In late 1942, the Thirty-First Artillery Regiment from the Security Division (formerly, Second Infantry Division) was transferred to the Rapid Division. Command of the Rapid Division changed again on 23 September 1942, when Lieutenant General Štefan Jurech took over. Jurech, who was promoted to General in December 1941, was a strong adversary of the Slovak Fascist government, and he planned the defection of the entire Rapid Division to the Soviets (Kliment and Nakládal 1997, 77). The Division took up a defensive position sixty-eight kilometers south of Krasnodar, in the area of Kutaisskaya, and remained there for several months. Jurech soon began to seek out individuals among his division with anti-Fascist orientation. Officers holding the same views as General Jurech contacted the Red Army and planned for the defection, which was to occur on 28 January 1943. The plan included deliberately being outflanked by the Red Army near Taupse leading to a staged surrender and capture.

In the meantime, the Rapid Division finally received its long-promised armor. On 17 October 1942, a company of tanks left the railway station in Martin, Slovakia. It had two platoons of tanks (seven LT vz. 38s and six LT vz. 40s), four trucks and one workshop truck. The transport reached Kerch on 27 October. The next day, the tanks were ferried to Taman and on 29 October, they set off for Krasnodar. The company reached Kutaisskaya on 2 November. In the following weeks, the tanks were used piecemeal for patrol, for recovering stalled trucks, and even as munitions carriers for artillery when trucks could not get through. (Kliment and Nakládal 1997, 79.)

---

* Operation Case Blue (*Unternehmen Fall Blau*), launched 28 June 1942, saw Army Group South divided into two Army Groups, Army Group A and Army Group B, the former participating in the Battle of the Caucasus. Throughout the operation the German situation, especially that of Army Group B centered on Stalingrad, began to deteriorate. As Army Group B began collapsing in the North, Army Group A quickly found itself at risk of being flanked. It was forced to abandon its task of securing the oilfields of the Caspian and began withdrawing down the Terek River toward the Taman Peninsula.

The Soviet North Caucasian Strategic Offensive Operation started on 1 January 1943 and lasted until 4 February 1943. The Strategic Offensive involved the following operations:

- Salsk-Rostov Offensive Operation (1 January 1943–4 February 1943)
- Mozdok-Stavropol Offensive Operation (1 January 1943–24 January 1943)
- Novorossiysk-Maykop Offensive Operation (11 January 1943–4 February 1943)
- Tikhoretsk-Eisk Offensive Operation (24 January 1943–4 February 1943)

By these operations, the Soviets succeeded in the following:

- Mozdok: 3 January 1943
- Stavropol: 21 January 1943
- Armavir: 23 January 1943
- Maykop: 29 January 1943
- Soviet marines beat off a German attempt to land at Malaya Zemlya on 4 February 1943
- Soviet forces landed in the port of Novorossiysk on 5 February 1943
- Krasnodar: 12 February 1943
- Germans begin to retreat from the *Blue Line* defensive positions on 9 September 1943
- Novorossiysk: 16 September 1943
- Red Army controls the whole of the Taman Peninsula by 9 October 1943

The Taman Peninsula was not completely cleared of German forces until early October 1943. The First Taman Offensive Operation (4 April 1943 to 10 May 1943) failed to push German forces out of the Taman Peninsula. A German counterattack forced the Red Army in the northern Caucasus on the defensive again during 26 May 1943 to 22 August 1944. This was, however, followed up with a new Novorossiysk-Taman Strategic Offensive Operation (10 September 1943 to 9 October 1943) which, following the Novorossiysk Amphibious Operation (10 September 1943 to 16 September 1943) resulted in the successful Second Taman Offensive

Operation (10 September 1943 to 9 October 1943), whereby the Red Army breached the Blue Line.*

Breaching the Blue Line (depicted below by thick fenestrated line)
Where Iron Crosses grow

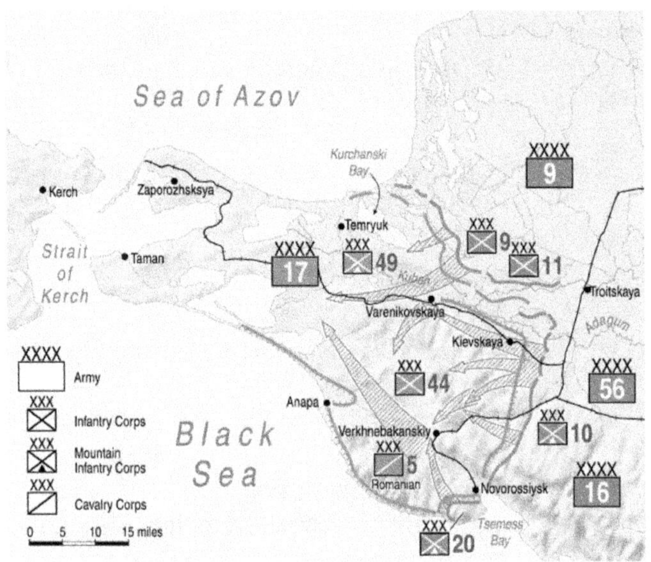

* "Blue Line" – a heavily fortified frontier, which German forces had created on the outskirts of the Taman peninsula in January 1943 to aid in retreat from the Caucasus and to keep the possibility of launching a new offensive to achieve Hitler's objective of taking the oil fields in the Caucasus. Much of the defensive works of the *Blue Line* were actually the former defensive engineering work of the Soviets as they retreated from rapidly advancing German forces entering the Kuban and Caucasus regions.

General Jurech's plan to defect to the Soviets ultimately did not materialize because the Germans responded extremely quickly and effectively to the movements of the Red Army. At the same time, the unexpected order to retreat forced the Rapid Division to leave its vulnerable position between Kutaisskaya and Taupse. Jurech tried again to defect shortly thereafter, at least with part of the division, but by that time he no longer had the support and approval of those Slovak commanders who had a decisive role in the defection. General Jurech was later captured in Bratislava during the Slovak National Uprising (29 August to 28 October 1944) and taken to Germany where he was brutally interrogated and eventually met the same fate as General Augustín Malár in the closing weeks of the war in 1945.

In February 1943, Army Group B and Army Group Don were combined to create a new Army Group South. After the disaster at Stalingrad in the winter of 1942–1943, the entire position of the Germans in the Caucasus was altered, making any further advance south a certain complete loss of all forces south of the Mius River if the Soviets reached Rostov, thus trapping them. As a direct result of the losses in the north, the forces in the Caucasus, including the Rapid Division, were quickly pulled back north to escape this possible entrapment.

The Rapid Division retreated to a new line on 27 January 1943. It was again ordered out of the defensive line on 31 January, and on 2 February obtained its transfer order to Crimea. The Rapid Division was nearly encircled and trapped near Saratowskaya (inland north of Taupse) but managed to escape. It was supposed to take all its heavy weapons with it. Damaged vehicles were destroyed, and superfluous crews were flown to Crimea from the Slavyanskiy airfield. (Kliment and Nakládal 1997, 79.)

About half of the Rapid Division's manpower was airlifted to Crimea with just small weapons, the remaining 2,500 men were rushed with their remaining heavy weapons to Taman. In Taman Harbor the Rapid Division withstood several Soviet air attacks, but finally managed to board the ships and was ferried to Crimea. The division's material losses were substantial. After the evacuation, the division was left with one tank, 237 trucks, twenty-nine passenger cars, and ten motorcycles. It transferred part of its heavy guns to German units and lost quite a few. In Crimea, it was left with two 10.5-cm vz. 35 cannons and five 10-cm vz. 30 howitzers. The Germans gave the division 1,000 Soviet rifles, ten 82-mm mortars and fourteen 4.5-cm Soviet antitank guns.

The Rapid Division shared the fate of the reunited Army Group South with the Seventeenth Army, losing their heavy equipment in the Kuban bridgehead* as they withdrew across the Kerch Straight into the Crimean Peninsula (January to October 1943). The Rapid Division was then used to help cover the retreat of over the Isthmus of Perekop connecting the Crimean Peninsula to mainland Ukraine. During this retreat, its last tank was used for a while as a mobile reserve, but on 23 June it was returned to Slovakia, together with ten tank guns and twenty heavy machine-guns that were removed from the abandoned tanks and the Armored Company's damaged trucks. Most of the Armored Company's personnel went back with the vehicles, but some of the officers remained in Crimea (Kliment and Nakládal 1997, 80–1). The remainder of the Rapid Division—officially converted into an infantry division on 1 August 1943—was then badly hammered in the second battle of Melitopol (September to November 1943).

The Slovak division retreated together with German units from Crimea back to Romania. As its personnel and equipment were no longer adequate, it was converted into the First Technical Division, utilized mostly for fortification work behind the front lines. In February 1944, it was stationed in Hungary between Balaton and Nezired lakes. At the beginning of September 1944, it was completely disarmed (the officers were left only with pistols and soldiers with their bayonets) and was used as a labor unit. At the end of the war, the division was taken prisoner by the Soviet Army and its men were interned in POW camps in the Soviet Union. (Kliment and Nakládal 1997, 84.)

After some initial setbacks, both the Slovak officer and men proved their fighting qualities. The Rapid Division performed well both in attack and in defense, often against superior enemy forces, and was respected by both the Germans and the Soviets. In the second year of the invasion of the Soviet Union, a large number of its men began to realize that they were fighting on the wrong side, and defections to the Soviets began to mount. In

---

* Kuban bridgehead (*Gotenkopf Stellung* or Goth's Head Position) was a German position on the Taman Peninsula, in southern Russia, between the Sea of Azov and the Black Sea. The bridgehead's defensive line was demarcated by what the Soviets called the "Blue Line." Existing from January to October 1943, the bridgehead formed after the Germans were pushed out of the Caucasus. The heavily fortified position was intended as a staging area for the *Wehrmacht* which was to be used to renew attacks towards the oil fields of the Caucasus. The bridgehead was abandoned when the Red Army breached the Panther-Wotan line, forcing an evacuation of the German forces across the Kerch Strait to Crimea.

some instances, whole small units crossed over. Two hundred Slovak defectors were in Crimea and another 300 in the catacombs in Odessa. This may have contributed to the downgrading of the division, as the Germans realized that the Slovaks could not be trusted any more. (Kliment and Nakládal 1997, 84–5.)

After breaking through at the Mius River and defeating Axis troops in the Donbas and Taganrog, armies of the Soviet Southern Front pursuing the retreating enemy came to the Molochna River on 22 September 1943. There, in the basin of the Milk River, German troops had built a strong long-term defense which they called the *Panther-Wotan* line. It was on this line that the fate of the Crimean Peninsula and the whole course of offensive operations in the southern Soviet Union were decided.

The German defense consisted of four lines, covered with solid antitank ditches and land mines. The first attempt of the Soviets to break through was unsuccessful. Soviet commanders decided to prepare completely new attack plan: the so-called "Melitopol Operation," which was carried out successfully from 26 September to 5 November 1943.

Despite the courage and heroism of Soviet soldiers, fighting lasted long, as the Germans introduced fresh reserves in order to hold on to Melitopol. Finally, after many days of heavy street fighting against vastly superior numbers of men and equipment, German resistance was broken and on 23 October the Red Army took complete control of the city. By decrees of the Presidium of the U.S.S.R. Supreme Soviet, eighty-seven Red Army soldiers and airmen were awarded the title of "Hero of the Soviet Union" for their actions in the reconquest of Melitopol.

In September 1944, the remnant of the Rapid Division, no longer considered fit for combat due to low morale, was disarmed and the personnel reassigned to construction and logistical work, a fate which had already earlier befallen the Slovak Security Division for the same reason.

The Slovak Security Division (formerly, Second Infantry Division) was stationed in northern Ukraine and south Belarus where it was charged with protecting roads and railways, especially the line between Pinsk and Gomel, against attacks from partisans. At the end of 1941, the majority of guerrilla fighters belonged to Ukrainian Nationalists, later known as the Ukrainian Insurgent Army (*UPA*) and former soldiers of the Red Army who had been caught behind German lines. The Ukrainian Nationalists also fought against the Red Army for an independent Ukraine, but when the German authorities rejected this idea the *UPA* started to target German troops, as well. Generally speaking, however, Slovak units did not have much contact with the *UPA* (Stahel 2018, 271–5).

Only at the end of 1942 and mainly in 1943 did the Slovak Security Division's area of operations see large numbers of Soviet partisans. The attitude toward partisans of the officers and soldiers of the Slovak Security Division was rather complicated. Regiments, battalions, and even companies were scattered across an area almost as large as Slovakia. Units of a single battalion were often situated along the railway lines many kilometers apart. Therefore, it is difficult to generalize about relationships between Slovak soldiers, the local civilian population, and various partisan groups. For example, units of the 102nd Regiment of the Security Division took part in brutal "pacification" actions against Soviet partisans with special battalions destroying several villages suspected of supporting partisans. In so-called "punishable expeditions," the commander of the regiment, Lieutenant Colonel Michael Lokšík, was especially active and the excesses of his men extended to summarily executing captured and disarmed partisans and their abetting civilian suspects. In contrast, the situation in the 101st Regiment of the Security Division was very different. Here, most of the officers turned a blind eye when their soldiers established friendly relations with the local population. Yet, some commanders in far-flung locations, even up to battalion-sized formations, concluded unofficial armistices with Soviet partisans. There were also some instances of Slovak soldiers defecting to the partisans. One of the more notorious cases involved Captain Ján Nálepka, Chief of Staff of the 101st Regiment, established contact with the partisan leader General Saburov. When this activity as discovered, he defected on 15 May 1943 with two other officers and organized the First Czechoslovak Partisan Unit. When Nálepka died in a raid on 16 November 1943, he was posthumously awarded the "Hero of the Soviet Union" by Stalin. Generally speaking, however, desertions to the partisans were not very numerous, altogether about 400 Slovak soldiers changed sides during the war before the Slovak National Uprising in August–October 1944. (Rychlík 2018; Šimko 2017.)

Given the deteriorating success in security operations, the Security Division reverted to its former name the Second Infantry Division on 1 August 1943 under the command of Colonel Karol Peknik. Slovak desertions and low moral eventually had consequences; the German command considered the Security Division unreliable and unable (or unwilling) to fight against the partisans and decided to remove it from the Ukrainian-Belorussian theater. Lieutenant General Fritz Schlieper, a representative of the *Wehrmacht* at the Slovak Ministry of National Defense, negatively assessed the suitability of the division to fight the partisans and urged the Slovak Defense Minister assign the Second Division to rear duties. On 5 October 1943, at the council of General Čatloš, it was decided that the Second Infantry Division should be withdrawn from Belarus. Earlier, a similar view was expressed by the head of the German Supreme Command, Field Marshal Wilhelm Keitel, who suggested using it to build fortifications in Italy. On 10 October 1943, the decision of the German Supreme Command was made.

As with the Rapid Division, the Security Division was eventually transformed into a labor unit under the name Second Technical Brigade (later, Second Technical Division). The majority of Slovak soldiers were returned to Slovakia in late 1943 and early 1944. The number of remaining Slovak soldiers in these labor brigades was ultimately reduced to 3,413 by October 1943 and sent to work in Italy under the command of Slovak Lieutenant Colonel Ján Krnáč. (Rychlík 2018; Šimko 2017.)

CHAPTER 23

THROUGH THE CARPATHIANS TO POLAND

ON WEDNESDAY, 26 JUNE 1941, THE ENTIRE WAR COLLEGE BOARDED A military transport train at Malá Station in Bratislava. It was a long train—thirty railroad cars—which carried not only the school but also troops and supplies from the Bratislava Garrison. The only two passenger cars of the train were assigned for the officers; another ten enclosed freight cars were loaded with enlisted men, horses, and ammunition; the rest were flat cars carrying artillery, tanks, and other military vehicles.

After Vlčko put his gear on the overhead rack, he stretched out on one side of the compartment. His companion for the trip was Ján Straka. He was standing in the hallway of the car talking with his girlfriend through an open window. She came to see him off. Peter would have liked Jirka to do the same, but it was much better this way.

A little weary from the emotional strain he had been under, Peter decided to rest. Instead of falling asleep, however, he found a myriad of thoughts running through his head. He thought of Jirka and her family, their safety and their future. That Jirka might be lost to him when he returned was frightening and depressing. He pushed this thought to the back of his mind, but it haunted him like a specter. Then he thought about the approaching action at the front. Could he resolve both his military obligations and still not violate his conscience? He recalled the promise to his father during his visit yesterday. The Russians were still his Slavic brothers, regardless of the politics and what the government said. He assured Jirka's father, too, about not helping the Germans, and had consoled Jirka by telling her he would return safely. With devilish speed, doubts and questions chased one another within Peter's brain. The future seemed bleak and forbidding. Then into his awareness returned the picture of Jirka as she had been that night at his apartment. With the memory of her calming love and serene beauty, he relaxed until, lips in a half-smile, he fell peacefully asleep.

THE TRAIN FINALLY BEGAN TO MOVE AFTER NEARLY SIX HOURS IN THE station. Lieutenant Straka waved to his girlfriend, his head sticking out the window, until she was lost from view. Returning to his compartment, Straka found Vlčko stretched out on the opposite seat of the car, sleeping soundly. Careful not to wake him, he arranged his own seat, so he could lie down when he got tired. The compartment felt stuffy. Straka pushed open the window and drew in huge gasps of fresh night air. The welcome drafts helped clear his mind. But he knew they could not drive Eva from his heart. Squinting against the onrushing air, he barely made out the terrain in the settling darkness. Because of blackout regulations, there were no lights to reveal passing farms and towns. A thick blanket lay across the countryside. His eyes caught sight of thousands of tiny sparks emitting from the train's smokestack. They streaked above the cars like the tail of some huge meteor. Even the engine lights were extinguished. The only warning of the speeding train was the intermittent sound of the steam whistle, which, like the cry of a sick child, disturbed the night.

Straka stepped away from the window and made himself comfortable on his seat. Like Peter, he too fell asleep. The movement of the train was not interrupted by any delays. Top priority over all other trains insured prompt transport of the troops. Short stops for water or coal were made in Zlaté Moravce and Banská Bystrica in central Slovakia. At six the next morning the train arrived in Prešov in northeastern Slovakia where a longer stop for breakfast was scheduled.

Straka arose first. "Morning, Peter. How did you sleep?"

"Great."

"You know a train will put anyone to sleep. Let's hurry. The others are already eating breakfast."

"I'm starved. Mountain air sure gives me an appetite."

"Hey, are you up?" Stanek called, sticking his head in through the doorway. "If you guys don't hurry, you'll miss breakfast."

"Not on your life," replied Straka, grinning.

"Jano, I'm afraid to ask. What's for breakfast?" Vlčko knew he could not expect much.

"Fried chicken and frog legs. You have your choice," Stanek mimicked.

"Why are you always dreaming of legs? Can't you think of anything except women?"

"I said frog legs, not women's legs."

"Yes, and you used to call your girl, 'My little frog!'" said Peter, still jesting.

"All right, all right. Black coffee and dark bread will be served buffet style." With that he bowed and backed away from his colleagues.

"If that clown thinks I'll hurry to eat a breakfast like that," said Vlčko, turning to Straka, "he can have my portion."

"Never mind. A little hot coffee won't hurt our empty stomachs," Straka advised.

The field kitchen reminded Peter of the Fifth Dragoon Regiment in Košice. On maneuvers with the Cavalry Brigade and the Infantry Division he had often napped on his horse during night-long rides while the animal continued to walk along without any direction from him. Then, in the morning, all chilled, he would devour the hot, black coffee and dry bread, letting them warm him from the inside out. At other times, commanding his unit at the outpost, he would pace back and forth in the open, waiting for the field kitchen to arrive. Often, it would not serve supper until three in the morning. This was real military life. Vlčko always felt content with his troop. Since he entered War College, he lost contact with that kind of Spartan military life. With the General Staff he missed those moments of camaraderie with his men. Only memories remained.

The departure whistle of the train interrupted Vlčko's thoughts. Gulping his coffee to wash down the bread, he hurried to his car. The train signaled one more whistle and, on our way, we went.

"Colonel, how much longer do we have?" Vlčko asked Lavota, whom he met on the way back to his seat.

"About five hours. Then we'll disembark," he answered, suppressing a yawn. "Say, Vlčko, where have you been hiding yourself? I haven't seen you the last couple of days."

"I was in Moravce to say goodbye to my family."

"I see." Lavota hesitated. "Something else I want to ask you, Vlčko, I hear you're in love."

"Who told you that?" Peter was taken aback by the directness of Lavota's question.

"Military intelligence. Is it true?" Lavota smiled knowingly.

Trying to evade a direct reply, Peter countered, "Well, your intelligence certainly hasn't been napping."

"That's right. They don't miss much. Anyway, I hope you know what you're doing." Then he entered his compartment and slid the door closed.

Who in the world would have told him? Who was so indiscreet with a superior? After another moment, it suddenly struck Peter that it must have been Murgaš, for only he and Dvornak knew Jirka personally. And Dvornak was never one to reveal a secret. "From now on I'll have to be on guard. At least I know how things stand between us." Uneasy, he went back to his car and sat next to the window, trying not to think of Lavota's question. He turned to face the landscape, which would distract him temporarily. Mounds of freshly dug earth gave evidence that the track was just recently completed. The decision for its construction was made by the Czechoslovak government when it realized the strategic importance of a railroad leading to the east. The only other east-west track ran along the southern border, and it was now in Hungarian hands as a result of the Vienna Awards. All other rail lines in the eastern Slovakia ran north and south and offered only short distance transportation.

Winding lazily across the foothills and tunneling through the Carpathian Bezkid Mountains in northeastern Slovakia, the train reached the Topľa River at Bystré, Pavlovce District, and then headed south toward Vranov. From there it turned eastward, crossed two mountain ridges, and followed the valley of the Ondava and Laborec Rivers. Passing through Humenné, the train made its way north along the Laborec River, to Medzilaborce. The track continued past this point across the Carpathians by way of Lupkovský (Łupków) Pass into Poland. However, the tunnel pass had been destroyed by the retreating Soviets and all traffic ended at Medzilaborce, three miles from the nearest Polish border.

Unloading began at one in the afternoon. When assignments were announced, Vlčko learned he was to work with the third department of the army. His commanding officer was General Staff Colonel Viliam Talský, professor at the War College. The command consisted of four departments* in the following order: 1) personnel; 2) intelligence; 3) operations†; and 4)

---

* Military Staff Department – (often referred to as general staff) is a group of officers, enlisted, and civilian personnel that are responsible for the administrative, operational, and logistical needs of its unit. It provides bi-directional flow of information between a commanding officer and subordinate military units. A staff also provides an executive function where it filters information needed by the commander or shunts unnecessary information.

† Operations – involves planning the operations for the forces' provisions, services, training, and administrative functions enabling them to commence, insert, then egress from combat. The general staff of military operations deals with the planning,

matériel. Additionally, representatives from the German Military Mission acted as coordinators between the Slovak Army and the German Command.

Military trucks arrived hourly at the Medzilaborce station to take the men into town for billeting. Officers were quartered in private homes while troops were quartered in schools and other public buildings. Horses were sheltered in farmers' barns along with their grooms. Henceforth, the War College ceased to function as an independent military institution. All further duties it had previously performed would take place within their respective detachments.

AFTER SETTING UP CAMP OUTSIDE MEDZILABORCE, THE ARMY BEGAN TO transfer men and supplies to Sanok on the San River in Poland, about twenty-five kilometers north of the Slovak border. Their arrival evoked mixed emotions from the local population. Though the natives were happy to be rid of the Communists, they nevertheless viewed with contempt the Slovak alliance with Nazi Germany. Later, many changed their views, for the Slovaks were Slavs, and the similarity of their languages eased communication and softened initial suspicions and mistrust. The German Command was prepared for these sympathies.

Aware of the Slovak soldier's dislike of fighting other Slavs and understanding his deep religious beliefs, the Nazis knew exactly how to manipulate his sentiments.

In Sanok, on the northern Carpathian slopes loomed a large historic Franciscan cathedral and monastery. An imperious Communist star hung from the cathedral tower facing the market square. Portraits of Marx, Engels, Lenin, Stalin, and Trotsky decorated the interior. In place of the main altar stood a curtained stage. Outside the church entrance on the grass were the bloated bodies of about twenty people, mutilated beyond recognition, some with severed arms and legs, others brutally decapitated. One can only imagine the brutal insanity with which these people were massacred. According to the German explanation, the bodies were found in a nearby well and pulled out as evidence of Communist atrocities. Slovak soldiers were encouraged to examine the church and monastery that had been desecrated and transformed into a propaganda theater and torture chamber.

---

process, collection, and analyzing of information. Its major function is responsible in the allocating of resources and determining time requirements.

The Nazi propagandists made one classic, hypocritical mistake. Although they denounced Communist atrocities, they failed to conceal their own bestiality.

A group of German soldiers were gathered beside a nearby pond. In the middle of it, up to his waist in water, stood a trembling Jewish boy wearing a large, brimmed hat, eyes gaping in terror, not knowing what was going to happen next. As if playing a schoolyard game, the soldiers threw rocks and stones at him, laughing at his futile attempts to evade the flying objects. In this manner they chased him from one side of the pond to the other, forcing him to duck under the water for protection. When he submerged, they stopped pelting him, but as soon as he raised his head for air, a shower of rocks struck again. Once more he disappeared beneath the surface of the water. When a stone hit its target, the men shouted and clapped, pleased to have scored. The purpose of this sadistic game was either to drown the boy or to kill him with the stones, whichever came first.

Vlčko heard rumors of this kind of treatment of the Jews but considered them exaggerations. No longer could he disregard the cold facts. Shocked by what he saw, he suppressed a wave of anger which caused his temples to swell with blood.

"Should I stop them or keep on walking?" he asked himself. "If I interfere, the army may label me undependable because I stood up for a Jew. But if I fail to help this boy, I'll be an accomplice to the murder."

Approaching the nearest soldier, he inquired what was going on.

"The boy is a Jewish spy. This is his punishment."

"How do you know he's a spy?" Vlčko was coldly authoritative.

"'Sergeant Heinz told us before he pushed him into the pool."

That was enough for Vlčko. He knew Heinz had taken it upon himself to stage this performance. Peter angrily called the Sergeant forward.

"Sergeant, let me see your orders for this public execution." Heinz remained motionless. "Can you show me your papers?" Vlčko's voice in German was threatening.

"This is not your business, *Herr Kapitän*," the Sergeant managed weakly.

"Pull this boy out of the water. If he's guilty of something, take him to your nearest command post. If not, set him free. I'll make certain the German Commander with the Slovak Army finds out about your impromptu court. There are many of our own soldiers here who will testify to what they have just seen."

Vlčko spun around and left with a quick, determined step so that he looked as if he were going straight to the German Commander. When he rounded the corner by the nearest building, he stopped and glanced back to see what was happening. Sergeant Heinz had called one of his soldiers over and said something to him, motioning in the direction Peter had taken. He must have given an order, for the soldier walked to the edge of the pool and gestured to the boy. Together with another soldier, they pulled him out. One ripped the hat off the dripping boy's head and slapped him hard across the back. The other smashed him across the rear with a stick and shouted, "Get the hell out of here, Jewish pig!"

Vlčko was satisfied. The youth was alive and free. He never did find out whether the boy reached home safely. Nor did he tangle with the German Command over the incident, for he could easily have gotten both of them, himself, and the boy, into deeper trouble. The boy was safely out of the pond, and that was all Peter had tried to do.

THE SAME DAY, HAVING COMPLETED HIS DUTIES AT THE ARMY Headquarters, Vlčko had his orderly drive him to his new lodging. "*Pán Kapitán*, it's a nice home. I've already taken your gear over," the orderly answered when Peter asked if he had found him a place to stay.

"Where is it?"

"Not far. We'll be there shortly."

"Ďurko, what kind of people are they?"

"I only saw a young lady. She's very pretty."

"Well, that's not important, as long as I have a decent bed."

"The lady was pleased that an officer would be staying at her home. Said she'd feel a lot safer. When I told her you were thirty, she seemed satisfied. She only speaks Polish, though. But I understood her pretty well."

"Ďurko, are you plotting something?"

"No, sir. But all the officers are looking for a place exactly like this one. You were lucky. Besides, she may be single."

"Well, if I have any trouble with her, you'll take care of it, understand?"

"Don't tell me you're afraid of women, *Pán Kapitán*," the orderly teased his boss.

"No," retorted Peter, "but anything can happen. Perhaps you've had no experience along those lines." Peter grinned as his orderly blushed. "Besides, this is no time for love games. Have you ever had a girl?"

"Yes, in my hometown, about two years ago."

"How far did it go?"

"Not very far. I went with her for two months. Then it ended."

"How?" Peter asked curiously, pursuing the matter.

"Badly. She suddenly left me."

"Why did she do that?"

"Because I used to see her almost every night and never kissed her. Every time I tried, she'd push me away and threaten to stop seeing me if I didn't quit. So, all I could do was hold her hand and maybe sometimes sneak my arm around her waist. She wouldn't let me go any further. Then one night she didn't show up for a date, and I never saw her after that. I later discovered she found herself a new boyfriend."

"The same thing happened to me, in Levice when I was eighteen. Our *gymnázium* was at the end of the street where this girl lived. Every morning on my way to school I'd meet her at her house. I don't know if she planned it that way or if it was pure coincidence. Once in class, my friend Štefan Knapp asked if I'd like to meet his cousin Suzy Steiner. That's how we got acquainted. She was a pretty Jewish girl with a small, thin body and large, dark eyes and long black hair. Even though she wasn't Christian, she attended the Hungarian Catholic school. I suppose because it was across the street from her house. Our relationship lasted about six months. We saw each other at least three times a week. We'd meet at the edge of town. I used to take her to all the intimate places with beautiful views overlooking the city and the surrounding countryside. I was very romantic and worshipful with her. Often in the evening we'd sit and listen to the thrushes and nightingales singing. On our way home, we'd part outside the town, so no one would see us together. We wanted to keep our love a secret from everyone. When we walked, I'd put my arm around her waist. Often, I wanted to kiss her, but she reacted the way your girl did. She'd push me away and threaten to stop seeing me. So, I didn't try any more. But she stopped going with me after all. The fact that I was miserable without her didn't faze her in the least. Within a month, she started going with a friend of mine, Jaroslav Bruckner. I don't know how he met her. She probably saw him with me and asked her cousin, Štefan, to introduce them. Zuzka went everywhere with him, and I was left alone."

"Women sure are strange!"

"Not really. You and I were fools. I'll tell you where I think we made our mistakes. In the first place, we should have ignored our girls' objections when we tried to kiss them. They wanted to be kissed almost as much as we wanted to kiss them, only for appearance's sake they had to pretend resistance. That's how they are raised. Besides, what if they didn't protest? How would a nice young man feel if a girl let him do whatever he wanted the first time he tried? He'd lose all respect for her. A hard-fought victory is sweeter. It's the same with love. The fact that a girl goes with a young man for a longer period of time should be enough proof she's interested. If she goes for walks with him and allows his arm around her waist and looks lovingly into his eyes, this is a positive sign. Our girls dropped us because they got tired of us. We were clumsy and afraid, and the girls could see we weren't capable of even one good kiss. If we ask for a kiss, they feel compelled to say no. If we just take the kiss, then they can feel guiltless. When a naïve young man falls into the clutches of an experienced woman, it's all over for him. She usually ends up twisting him around her finger, laughing at his amateur behavior. Now do you see why I'm a little apprehensive about this young woman in the house you've found for me?"

"Perhaps you'll have luck now, *Kapitán*. If not, then I'll take care of her. I've learned to handle myself around girls since I've been in the army." Peter laughed aloud, and the two basked in the light of their smug masculine egos. By this time, they had reached the house and Ďurko let Peter out of the car, saluted and drove away.

A TALL, BLOND, ATTRACTIVE WOMAN OF ABOUT THIRTY ANSWERED THE door in response to Peter's knock.

"What can I do for you, sir?"

"My orderly tells me I'm quartered here and that my things have arrived. I'm *Kapitán* Peter Vlčko."

"Oh, *Pán Kapitán*. Please come in. Let me show you to your room." She led him through the kitchen and living room. "The bath is here. If you would like something to eat, we have supper ready."

"Thank you, I've already eaten. If you have some tea, though, I'd be grateful."

"Of course. Perhaps you would like to wash up and make yourself more comfortable. When you're through come back into the dining room and I'll have your tea waiting. By the way, what would you like in it, lemon or liquor?"

Her look was disarming, Peter thought. Really, she was more than attractive, she was seductive. Her well-formed breasts amply filled the tight blouse which she had neglected to button to the neck. There was just enough cleavage to start a man wondering what she would look like had she failed to button it at all. Momentarily, Peter forgot his conversation with Ďurko, and his susceptibility to earthy women took hold of him.

"Do you have rum?" Some magic power invited him to take advantage of the occasion. A lemon tea was no drink to encourage a romantic interlude.

"I think there's still some. We'll see you shortly." She smiled, turned away and left Peter alone.

"Did she say, 'We'll see you'? Then she is not alone," he thought, disappointed to know there was a husband around. The plan Peter was concocting collapsed. Removing his tunic, he washed himself down to the waist in the small enamel basin and dried himself with a clean towel left there for him. He decided to put on his pajamas and robe, since he had had a long day and planned to retire early. After combing his hair, he went to join his hosts.

"'Good evening!" said Vlčko, entering the dining room where a man was seated with the woman.

"This is my husband, Władysław Kozlowski," she said. He was tall and quite slender. A thatch of black hair fell across his forehead.

"I'm *Kapitán* Peter Vlčko with the Slovak Army Command."

"How do you do, *Kapitán*? Welcome to our home. Please sit down. Wanda, you may serve the tea. Do you have any news, *Kapitán*?"

"What are you interested in hearing?"

"Nothing in particular. You know civilians aren't supposed to concern themselves with military matters. The authorities become suspicious."

"We just arrived here yesterday. We hope you think of us as friends, not invaders. Despite certain misunderstandings between our governments over border changes, I see nothing that should separate our two countries."

"A close friendship between the Polish people and the Slovaks should not be difficult. We understand your troubled and unfortunate political position. In politics, for the lips to speak what the heart feels is sometimes inexpedient."

Peter respected the man but was in no hurry to commit himself. "*Pán* Kozlowski, what do you do for a living?"

"I'm an engineer. I was with the state-owned radio in Warsaw. However, since the Germans arrived, I've been working here in a small electrical store."

"Were you at the station in '39 when the Germans attacked?"

"Yes. That was a terrible day. The worst I've ever lived through. As soon as we announced the raid to warn the people, the bombs started falling. We were soon knocked off the air. Many people were killed, and thousands were injured. I was lucky to get away without a scratch."

"Yes, I remember your distress call. It's strange, but at that moment I understood your plight completely, and my heart went out to you. Your people fought so gallantly to stop the Nazis. How I admired your resistance."

"That wasn't all, *Kapitán*," interrupted his wife. "As soon as the army was reorganized across the Vistula River to defend Warsaw, the Russians attacked us from behind and killed or captured every man. Since then, nearly two years ago, not one of our officers has returned home from prison in Ukraine. In fact, we haven't had any news from them at all."

"I can't comprehend why they haven't given you any news of your officers. I think when the Russians saw the Nazis were hurrying to take as much of Poland as they could, they decided to grab some for themselves. Using Poland as a buffer, they probably hoped to protect their own country on your territory. I'm not suggesting they were justified; they should have made reparations. It looks as if they've treated you even worse than the Nazis."

"I feel the same way." Kozlowski was pleased that Vlčko understood and sympathized.

"How were things under the Soviets?"

"Well, we certainly weren't happy. It might have been better had the Germans occupied us. In order to make you understand this, I should tell you exactly what happened. The first thing the Soviets did after they arrived was eliminate all local and public governments and replace them with National Committees, staffed exclusively with Communists. They then investigated all citizens. Under this administration, many people disappeared, without explanation. One day you saw them, the next day they were gone. The churches were either closed or turned into 'cultural centers.' Every student was forced to learn all about Lenin and Stalin. The clergy was shipped to labor camps or worse, to Siberia, depending on how vehemently they resisted the new order. We learned to live in fear, and terror became almost routine. Only since the Germans came, have we been able to breathe a little easier and feel a little safer."

"Then what the Nazis have been saying about Communism is true. It is a real danger to western culture."

"Nazi propaganda this time is all too true," Kozlowski admitted.

"'Today, they showed us the monastery church and how the Communists had desecrated it." Then, Vlčko told the couple about what he witnessed earlier that day.

"Yes, we often heard of such horrible things. How incredible, those poor souls lying there, innocent victims, unable to protest!" Kozlowski did not like to think about Communist atrocities.

"It's barbaric! The Soviets knew why they had to cut off the heads of these victims. They were afraid of what the eyes and faces would disclose. But their agonized cries were heard in heaven and will one day be avenged." Wanda Kozlowski said, fighting back the tears.

"I'm glad we've had the chance to get better acquainted and that you've spoken so frankly. Now I'm more secure, knowing we feel similarly about many things. I hope we can talk again soon. I'm due at headquarters by seven, so I'd better say good night. Thanks for everything."

"Good night," the Kozlowskis replied.

"Would you like breakfast in the morning?" Mrs. Kozlowski asked.

"If you would be so kind, I'd appreciate it very much."

"What would you like?"

"I know food is pretty hard to come by. Coffee and bread will be just fine." With that Vlčko left them alone.

CHAPTER 24

IN UKRAINE

WITHIN A FEW DAYS, THE SLOVAK ARMY WAS AGAIN TRANSFERRED, THIS time near Sambor, Drohobycz, and Komarno, the region southwest of Lviv (Polish: Lwów; Russian: Lvov). The transfer took place during the day, made possible by the *Luftwaffe*, which had complete control of the air. Along their march were towns scarred by German and Russian clashes. Dead bodies, destroyed cannons and abandoned tanks lined both sides of the main road, testifying to the great losses of the Soviet Army and to the overwhelming strength of the Germans. Slovak soldiers, most of whom had never before seen this much carnage, were now exposed to the brutality and horror of war. The mangled bunkers with their silent occupants told the sad story better than words.

The short stops which Slovak soldiers made at these bloodied memorials to heroism produced just the opposite effect the Germans hoped for. Instead of admiration for the mighty Nazi war machine, they felt pity and horror for their dead Slavic brothers. Even though there were many officers who strongly supported a total German victory, the ordinary Slovak soldier had no interest in it whatsoever.

The subsequent friendly contact between Slovak soldiers and the local Polish and Ukrainian inhabitants was not only a psychological challenge to the Nazis, but also a subject of repeated complaints from the German Command. The Slovak commanders brought up these grievances daily to the troops and gave strict orders that no signs of disloyalty to the Germans would be tolerated, but to no avail. Their sympathies went deeper than even the Germans had guessed.

Many Slovak soldiers shared their rations with the local population and even supplied partisan units with guns and ammunition. Later, some Slovak soldiers began to desert and join these units.

The Nazis *SS* excelled in cruelty and bestiality. A mother, infant in her arms, who did not disclose the whereabouts of her husband suspected of being a partisan was forced to witness her child being shot to death by the *SS*, the elite *Waffen Schutzstaffel Verfügungstruppen* (Armed *SS* Disposal

Troops) racially indoctrinated and fanatical fighters hardened to human suffering. The executioner puffed on a cigarette as he pulled the trigger. When her child's death failed to break her, he coldly emptied his pistol into her body.

These cruel and inhumane tactics did not succeed in breaking the will of the people. Instead, a deep hatred for the Germans developed. Rather than respect and cooperation, the occupied people offered resistance. At first, resistance was only passive in the form of dissatisfaction and grumbling, but later it intensified. Whole partisan units were organized to fight the Germans openly.

In the beginning, only a random lone German soldier was attacked here or there. Later, small transport units were ambushed, and finally command posts and isolated fighting units were targeted and destroyed by the partisans. Their activity reached such proportions that no German felt safe. As a result, German military police and security forces had to be reinforced, leaving the front lines short of reserves. Furthermore, two Slovak divisions remained to help secure the occupied territory.

The unwritten understanding between Russian patriots and Slovak soldiers was strange indeed, and fully incomprehensible to the Germans. Nevertheless, the Germans had to tolerate it, for it was far better than the harassment they received from Russian partisans in areas exclusively controlled by their own divisions.

A REPORT CAME IN ONE DAY AT SLOVAK ARMY HEADQUARTERS THAT Russian paratroopers had been sighted in the vicinity of Sambor. Slovak Intelligence was to investigate such reports in this region. Captain Ján Cisarik, one of Vlčko's colleagues from the War College, was assigned by Colonel Lavota to carry out the action. He set up a small patrol with Vlčko and Stanek as his assistants. They left for the designated area in a transport truck. North of Sambor, they stopped at a German occupation post, where they learned that the local Ukrainian Militia, previously organized by the Germans, had already caught one paratrooper, and shot another. A third paratrooper who refused to surrender shot himself. Before he died, he raised his clenched fist and shouted, "For Lenin and Stalin." The Militia buried him under a large bush on the spot. The captured paratrooper had been turned over to the nearest German Command.

When the Nazis entered the Ukrainian Soviet Socialist Republic at the outset of Operation Barbarossa, many Ukrainians welcomed them as liberators and volunteered for various paramilitary units under the supervision of the Germans, as well as the Ukrainian Army. In total, the Germans enlisted 250,000 native Ukrainians for duty in five separate formations including the Nationalist Military Detachments (*VVN*), the Brotherhoods of Ukrainian Nationalists (*DUN*), the Galician Division of the *Waffen-SS*, the Ukrainian Liberation Army (*UVV*), and the Ukrainian National Army (*Ukrainische Nationalarmee*, *UNA*). Several of these formations performed the Nazis' dirty work on the battlefield and in concentration camps and were involved in some of the worst crimes against humanity of the war. Historically, the reasons behind enthusiastic collaboration with the Nazis were based in a deep rooted hatred for Russian oppression and included Ukrainian political aspirations for regaining independence from the Russian Empire and Soviet Union, resurgent Nationalism strangulated since Russian annexation in 1775 and 1793 under Empress Catherine II, and widespread anger and resentment against the Russians over the genocide-by-famine (Holodomor) engineered by Stalin in 1932–1933 to eliminate the Ukrainian independence movement. The Holodomor was a man-made famine (genocide) that killed an estimated 3.5 to 7.5 million Ukrainians in Ukraine alone, with millions more counted in birth loss estimates and Ukrainians living in other Soviet Republics—Kuban, the North Caucasus, Lower Volga, and Kazakhstan. Conditions during the Holodomor were indescribable with more than 2,500 people convicted of cannibalism.

When Captain Cisarik protested Ukrainian militia interference with Slovak military security, he was arrogantly rebuffed and reminded that the entire Slovak Army was subordinate to the Germans. That was all Cisarik needed to hear. This incident, one in a long line of many to follow, revealed how unimportant the Slovak Army was to the Nazis.

Several days later, the Ukrainian Militia captured a Polish student, a professor's son traveling without the necessary papers. According to regulations, they turned him over to the military authorities. However, a mistake was made in maintaining proper channels. Instead of the German Command it was Slovak Intelligence that accepted the captive. In the report sent to the Germans, the Ukrainians were not aware of this error. In the meantime, Slovaks questioned the student. Finding nothing to arouse suspicion, they were prepared to release him but first had to apprise the Germans of their decision. When they received the report, German

Intelligence insisted they be present for another interrogation. To convince the Germans that the interrogation had been handled properly, the Slovaks made a few quick changes to deceive them. The prisoner was tied to a chair with his head upside down. When the Intelligence officer arrived, he was informed they were unable to get a confession despite the torture the prisoner received. Fortunately for the student, the officer had no time to witness the interrogation or to examine the youth himself, since almost immediately he was summoned to investigate a more urgent case at Sambor. He left instructions for the Slovaks to carry on, and after they finished to transfer the prisoner to German custody.

Captain Cisarik could not have asked for more. As soon as the German departed, he untied the boy and told him the questioning was over. He then ordered his aide to take him to the enlisted men's quarters where he would be housed and fed. Cisarik hoped to stall the Germans as long as possible, or better, to let the matter ride until his case got lost in bureaucratic red tape. But things did not work out as Cisarik had hoped. In a few days the Germans returned and removed the prisoner. Later, Cisarik learned that after intensive questioning they also were unable to wring any confession from the youth. In characteristic fashion he was shot in the head as the simplest way of closing the investigation.

10 July 1941
My beloved Jirka,

You can't imagine how difficult it's been for me to steal a few moments to write you.

The trip to Poland seemed to go by quickly because everything we saw was new to us. The life we had been leading at the College was so routine most of the men had become bored.

As soon as we arrived, we saw a church the Communists had converted to a theater. It showed us the godlessness of Communist philosophy, and the total subordination of the human soul to materialism. A number of mutilated bodies were displayed publicly by the Germans, who said they found them in a nearby well. According to the local people, everything the Germans say about the Communists is true.

Right now, we are stationed in the vicinity of a small town southwest of Lviv. Most of the people here are Ukrainians, and we seem to get along with them quite well. Because we can understand their language, it almost seems as if we were back home in Carpathian Ruthenia.

After seeing that church, I had a terrible nightmare. I dreamt that the Germans in Bratislava, along with the *Hlinka* Guard, rounded up all Jewish girls and herded them onto a train destined to deliver them to German officers for their pleasure. I saved you from the train, only to end up surrounded by the guards and police. Then, I awoke from the hellish dream. I never did find out what happened to you. Ever since, I have been thinking about how things are going back home for you and your family.

When I hear of human suffering, I think of you and the danger you're in. It's hard for me to imagine how it is to be happy and secure in a normal world. I know you can't write to me, but I'm frustrated not knowing how you are. You are my greatest concern.

Know that I love you, I miss you, I want you.

Eternally,
Peter.

"*KAPITÁN* VLČKO, COME IN," COLONEL TALSKÝ SAID, WITHOUT LOOKING up from his desk.

"Yes, sir," as Peter closed the door behind him.

"Sit down. I'll be right with you." Talský continued to read a file which he held in his hands.

"Vlčko, as you know, our Rapid Brigade has been fighting for several days now and the casualties have been high." He stood up and moved to an armchair next to Peter. "According to information we received yesterday, we're running low on medical supplies. We must relieve this shortage immediately. The Command is sending another doctor, too. You're to deliver the supplies. The doctor will go with you. Headquarters is waiting for certain orders which you will convey personally. The trip should take a couple of days by truck. You'll travel to Tarnopol, then eastward to Vinnytsia [212 km southwest of Kyiv], where you'll pick up further instructions from the German dispatch officer there. I'm assigning two drivers and three soldiers for security. They'll be out front within the hour, so you don't have much time to prepare. As soon as you're ready, report to *Generál* Čatloš. He has some instructions for you. This sealed envelope is for Colonel Pilfousek. Guard it with your life, and be sure to give it to him personally, and to no one else. Any questions?"

"No, sir, everything is quite clear."

"Then, you're dismissed."

Vlčko went straight to his room and packed his gear. He checked and loaded his 9-mm sidearm and put it back in its leather holster. Then, he slipped his field glasses, a cowhide map case, and a camera over his shoulder. His long overcoat, a small suitcase, and extra ammunition he gave to his assistant Ďurko and told him to deposit them in the truck while he stopped to see *Generál* Čatloš.

"*Pán Generál*, you wished to see me." Vlčko saluted his commander.

"*Kapitán*, I'll not detain you very long. I do want to say that you should be extremely careful on this mission. Stop only at German units and command posts. They will supply you with gasoline. Avoid civilians at all costs. Partisans are everywhere. This goes for your men, as well. You are to tell no one you have orders for the division commander. The Germans only have to know about the medical supplies. Since all our vehicles carry German insignia, you should have no difficulties getting through. My orders for Colonel Pilfousek emphasize that he is to spare our men and not send them out to be slaughtered. I also want you to impress upon him that he should take better care of himself. I can't replace field commanders at will. I understand he's been acting as a forward artillery observer, even commanding the men at the frontline instead of directing from his command post to the rear. As soon as you return, you are to provide a full report to me. The best of luck, Vlčko."

"Thank you, *Pán Generál*."

Vlčko spotted the loaded truck waiting in front of headquarters. He hopped in alongside the doctor. The driver had the motor running. The relief driver, Ďurko, and the three infantry men sat in the open in back. At exactly ten in the morning, they began the 360 km journey south and east deep into Ukrainian territory down the dusty road toward Tarnopol.

Brigade Pilfousek advanced through Lviv, Ternopil, and towards Vinnytsia. Around 8 July 1941, the brigade had advanced beyond the tactical control of the Slovak command, so control of the unit was handed over to the German Seventeenth Army with Army Group South under the command of General Carl-Heinrich von Stülpnagel. The remaining forces of the former Slovak Expeditionary Army Group (no longer an independent formation) were used behind the German lines in conjunction with the 103rd Rear Area Command of Army Group South in security duties and helping to eliminate pockets of Soviet resistance. By 22 July 1941, the brigade had passed Vinnytsia and its staff set up command headquarters about eight kilometers (5 mi) west of Lypovets while combat units pushed on towards Lypovets, a small town 212 kilometers (131 mi) southwest of the metropolis of Kyiv and 151 kilometers (94 mi) due south of Žytomyr. Near Lypovets, the Brigade experienced heavy fighting with the Soviets, who mounted a counteroffensive to stop the *Blitzkrieg* the Germans were executing.

THE TRUCK BOUNCED ALONG THE HARD-PACKED GRAVEL ROAD, DODGING potholes which heavy military vehicles had made. At the Dniester River the road improved. The country they drove through was flat, yet resplendent with fields of ripening grain, tall corn, and hardy potato plants. Peter wondered who would harvest the fields.

There was no sign of life anywhere. The sun, high in the cloudless sky, beat down mercilessly. And there was an uneasy silence about, the silence of death. Somewhere ahead, a battle raged, and thousands of men lay dying, torn apart by impersonal apparatus of war. Disabled Soviet tanks along the roadside and crippled trucks abandoned in haste spoke mutely of the relentless *Luftwaffe*. The Russians were in retreat.

Around five o'clock, Vlčko's group reached Tarnopol. This city of about eighty thousand was known for its historic fortifications and remembered as the site of bloody battles during the First World War when the Russian and Austro-Hungarian armies clashed. Since they had traveled three hundred kilometers, Vlčko decided to stop here for a short break.

"Don't venture off. Two men must stay to guard the truck. If you need me, I'll be in that barber shop getting a haircut." And he pointed to the familiar red and white barber pole (dating to medieval times) that hung outside the doorway.

"*Zdravstvuyte*," the barber greeted Vlčko.

"*Zdravstvuyte*." Peter responded.

"Please sit down," said the barber, indicating the chair nearest the window. "How would you like your hair cut?"

"Cut it close, please. And a shave, as well."

"Same as the Germans like?"

"Not that short. I'm Slovak, not German."

"What's your rank?"

"I'm a cavalry captain."

"How did you get way out here, so far from your own country?"

"We're helping the Germans defeat the Red Army," Vlčko assured him. He assumed Ukrainians would welcome such optimistic boasting.

"We are indebted to you. Without your intervention the Soviets would still have their boots on our necks."

Now Peter knew he could relax. What if this man had been a Soviet partisan? His razor could easily have slipped and cut Peter's throat. Čatloš was right about not talking with civilians, though. One never knew who the enemy might be.

"Are you serious or are you just making conversation?"

"I'm very serious, *Pán Kapitán*. From the time the Germans arrived in Tarnopol, I've felt much safer. I can again be a proud Ukrainian. At night I can sleep peacefully, knowing I'll still be alive the next morning."

"I hope you'll always be able to enjoy this freedom."

"And why not? The Germans promised they would give us independence. They even organized our militia," the barber said. His self-respect was apparent.

The Ukrainians have always despised the Russians. Their country of 586,000 square kilometers and thirty-seven million inhabitants is the richest republic in the Soviet Union. Until the twelfth century, Ukraine was an empire with its center in Kyiv. From there the rulers dominated Russia for 800 years. Under Empress Catherine II, the Russians seized the country and divested it of sovereignty. Now, when the Germans came, it seemed to many that their long-lost independence had finally been restored. They welcomed the German "liberators" with open arms and kisses, offering gifts of bread and wine. Their cities were festooned with garlands of wildflowers. Bands played, and people danced joyously. These dreams of a free Ukraine slowly faded. Instead of gaining independence, they became a colony under a German governor who received his orders from Berlin.

Vlčko got up when the barber had finished with him. He paid the man and wondered at the same time what his fate would be. How long would the Ukrainians remain jubilant?

"*Do svidaniya.*" And with this farewell, Vlčko left the barber shop.

Back at the truck the men were ready to leave. On the way out of the city they stopped and refueled at the first German petrol station. It was only a matter of minutes, and they were again on their way toward the front.

WHEN THE TRAFFIC GREW HEAVIER AND THE ROAD NARROWED, THEY slowed down. Then as the sun neared the western horizon driving was easier. Twilight came gradually, and evening was night. The sky ahead looked as if heaven were drawing a shroud over the earth. As darkness settled in, they could see light flashes against the sky. It was either an approaching storm, or artillery fire. They heard nothing yet, so they did not know which it was. Each man's thoughts and fears were his own.

"We'll drive another hour, and then stop for the night," said Vlčko, breaking the long silence.

"Do you think we'll find a suitable place in exactly an hour?" Dr. Darvaš asked.

"No, I don't. That's why we'll have to start looking right now." In Ukraine, one can travel thirty or forty kilometers before seeing any signs of life.

"Then let's keep our eyes open," the doctor remarked.

"How do you feel about your new assignment? Vlčko kept the conversation going.

"I'm really not too happy about it. There will probably be more work than I can handle. The experience may be valuable, but I'd rather not see a really serious casualty. Anyway, I'll do the job, regardless of whether I get one of our men, a German, or a Russian. I'm a doctor, not a soldier or a politician. There's nothing I can do to stop these lunatics from killing one another, but maybe I can save their lives. What are you going to do once you reach the front?"

"I'm supposed to deliver you and the supplies. Then, I have to see Colonel Pilfousek. Čatloš is mad because Pilfousek is trying to play the hero by wasting Slovak blood. After that, I'll return to Army Command."

"You seem much happier than me. I envy you a little." Then, he paused. "Look, there's a light over there. Up ahead."

"Hey, guys, are you asleep yet?" Vlčko called out.

"Yes, sir. We were dozing off," came a tired answer.

"'Then, wake up and get ready. We'll be stopping soon. We're not going any further, even if we have to sleep in the barn." Vlčko made up his mind.

"Ondrej, turn here. I see some trucks already parked."

Two armed German guards stopped them at the entrance gate. After inspecting everyone's papers, they waved them on. The driver was barely able to squeeze their truck in between the parked German vehicles. Then, he stopped the motor. Vlčko exited the truck and proceeded to look for the German officer in charge who would give his group permission to spend the night.

The place was not an ordinary farm, but an estate. The buildings were not visible from the road because they were hidden behind tall, majestic pines. If that were not enough to ensure privacy, there was a small, thick stand of birches between the pines and the road. The little house they had spotted first was merely the guard house. The main structure was a stately, if ancient, manor house. Grey stone walls, weather worn from countless seasons of wind, rain, and snow, rose gracefully upward. The classic façade suggested a long, dignified history of Ukrainian nobility that lived here before the Revolution. Light came from only a few windows inside on the first floor. The remainder was in total darkness. At the top of the stairs in front of the main entrance, additional guards kept watch. Vlčko approached and asked to be taken to their commanding officer. Again, his papers were inspected.

"Excellent security," Peter thought.

"*HERR MAJOR*, I'M *KAPITÄN* VLČKO, OF THE SLOVAK ARMY."

"Good evening. Major Henkel. My colleagues, *Kapitän* Hochnagel and *Oberleutnant* Würtz," he said, introducing his companions.

"My pleasure, *Herr Kapitän*," said Hochnagel. The other clicked his heels and bowed stiffly.

"How can I be of service?" asked the Major after completing the formalities.

"*Herr Major*, I'd be grateful if you would permit us to spend the night here. We're on our way to join the Rapid Brigade at Vinnytsia."

"How many of you are there?"

"Me, a military doctor, and five enlisted men."

"We have an extra room for you two. The soldiers can sleep in the kitchen with our men. Have you eaten anything yet, *Herr Kapitän*?"

"Not yet. This is our first stop since Tarnopol. We have some rations, so we won't trouble you.

"It's no trouble, *Herr Kapitän*. As soon as you're situated in your room," pointing to a door to Vlčko's right, "our cook will fix something to eat. We have plenty of food. The provisions officer will take care of your men. *Leutnant* Würtz, would you handle this matter?"

"*Jawohl*, *Herr Major*." And he left.

"When you're ready, we'll meet in the dining room. It's just off the reception hall."

"Thank you, *Herr Major*." Immediately, he went out to the truck. After giving instructions to his men, Vlčko set the time of departure for seven the next morning. Then, he returned with the doctor, and they put their gear into their assigned room. When they went into the dining room their dinner was already on the table.

"*Meine Herren*, may I present Dr. Štefan Darvaš," said Vlčko. Each in turn introduced himself.

"Please, be seated and eat while the food is still warm. What would you like to drink, beer or wine?" the Major asked.

"I think I'll have wine," Vlčko replied.

"The same for me, please," added Dr. Darvaš.

"*Herr Oberleutnant*, two bottles of Rhine wine for our guests."

The dinner consisted of vegetable soup, roast beef, and potatoes. Although prepared simply, it was very tasty. The pity was, there wasn't more of it.

"It seems Hitler's austerity measures and the war taught these Germans to eat small portions. We Slovaks require more food and like to leave a little something on our plates when we've finished," thought Peter as he ate.

"Well, did you have enough?" asked the major.

"Yes. It was excellent," answered Darvaš for both. "All day we thought about opening our cans of meat and eating them cold. We never expected to be offered such a treat."

"You are our allies. We take care of our friends," said the Major, smiling. "We fight together; we eat together. I've heard your soldiers fight bravely."

"True. We also have an excellent commander, who at this moment is at the frontline alongside his men," said Vlčko in agreement. He knew the men had to fight well because the German commanders were always standing behind them, pushing them forward.

"That's as it should be. A commander should set an example for his troops with his own bravery."

"*Herr Major*, don't you think a division commander should lead the entire division, and not just one small unit right at the battle line?" Vlčko objected.

"What you say is true, but sometimes it's important that he show himself to his troops to encourage them."

"It's a pretty desperate situation when a commander has to grab a rifle to get his men to fight," Vlčko thought to himself. He nearly voiced his disagreement but decided instead to take another tack. "However, if this commander were killed, it would be hard to find a replacement. Colonel Pilfousek is someone we simply cannot afford to lose."

"Well, I don't think it's all that dangerous there. In any case, the war will not be won or lost just because of a single commander. Besides, it won't last long anyway. By the end of October, we'll be in Moscow, and we'll all be home by Christmas." Major Henkel expressed the prevailing opinion of among the Germans.

"I'm afraid my profession sees the individual in a less expendable light. But as to the war's conclusion, I can only hope you're right." Darvaš lit a fuse without foreseeing the effect on his host.

"Do you doubt me, *Herr Doktor*?" asked the Major stiffly.

"I have no doubts about the might of the German Army. I'm afraid of the giant vacuum in front of us, and that our goal is not really Moscow, but Vladivostok." The doctor smiled. His sarcasm was obvious, but the major still ignored it.

"That won't be hard either. Remember how quickly we defeated France and occupied all of Europe," he boasted instead.

"That was possible only because those countries weren't resolved to fight as the Russians are. You know what the situation was in Europe. One country was forever arguing with another, and the stronger would sacrifice the weaker in order to save itself."

"That's exactly what we Germans want to put an end to. France is not going to hold itself above Germany anymore, the Polish aren't going to curse the Czechs for Cieszyn, the Rumanians aren't going to hassle with the Hungarians because of Transylvania, and the Czechs aren't going to dominate the Slovaks. There will be one united Europe, and she will have only one *Führer*." He was convinced it would be Adolf Hitler.

"Do you really think that is so desirable? What will happen to Nationalism and the thousand-year-old culture of the individual countries?" The doctor pursued the discussion with yet greater animation.

"That all can be stored in their museums. People will learn to get along better without these disparate identities. We have plenty of able German professors and scientists, politicians, and statesmen, who will assist. Only strong German national directives can offer a healthy basis for the existence of a United Europe. This can be accomplished only with blood and iron and sweat, not with futile arguments in some parliament. Everywhere, as far as our boundaries will extend, there will be one union." This was a dream of all German Nazis.

"What do tyrants know about uniting Europe? Under their dictatorship all existence would be meaningless," he thought. He rephrased his comment before adding, "*Herr Major*, do you think a dictatorship is better for Europe than Democracy?"

"Of course! Europe needs a strong leader. Democracy has proven incapable of doing the job properly. The Third *Reich* can accomplish with the European countries what has always seemed impossible."

"You are right, *Herr Major*. Yours are an intelligent and industrious people, and you can achieve many things which other nations cannot. But you're forgetting one thing. Real friendship is nurtured by friendship and not by weapons or the use of force," continued the doctor, losing control of his feelings.

"*Herr Doktor*, the force we use is only temporary and will last so long as we have to fight this war. When the war is over, conditions will moderate, and our methods will be more humane. Providing no one gives us any opposition," the major answered as if by rote.

"Let's hope our mutual sacrifices will not be in vain, and that we all live to see victory," interrupted Vlčko, trying to mitigate the growing adversarial atmosphere created by Darvaš. "Allow me to make a toast to this victory. *Prost!*" he wished, lifting the glass.

"*Prost!*" All three German officers joined in.

Na zdravie! added the doctor, and their discussion ended on that note.

"I think we've had enough debating. Besides, it's time to retire," Vlčko suggested. "We have a long day ahead of us tomorrow."

"It's a good idea, *Herr Kapitän. Gute nacht.*" The Major extended his hand, and everyone rose from the table to say good night.

In their bedroom, Peter mentally reviewed the day's journey, and recalled the smug confidence of the German officers. Then, he turned his thoughts to Jirka. With her image before him, he lapsed into sleep.

THE NEXT MORNING ON 22 JULY 1941 AT EXACTLY SEVEN O'CLOCK, Vlčko's group continued on their way eastward. The sun was already quite high and shone brightly into their faces. Its rays sparkled on the dew-covered grass, revealing tiny cobwebs woven overnight between the blades. Butterflies fluttered above the grain fields, while birds rested after their early morning songs. Now they were about the important business of gathering food for their young. Farmers had not yet begun their day in the fields. Aside from the birds and butterflies, life appeared to be either purposely hidden, or it had been destroyed by the recent battles that had raged across the land.

"Why haven't we seen any animals grazing?" the doctor asked Peter.

"The Red Army probably took everything with them during their retreat."

"Look over there behind that clump of bushes. No, on your right near that little hill. Are those cows?" asked the doctor.

"I'll have a look with my field glasses." He focused on the objects in question. "Good God! Doctor, those aren't cows. They're prisoners!"

When Vlčko and his party reached the top of the next rise in the road, they saw in front of them a long dark line that moved very slowly, like a wounded snake. It stretched out along the side of the road they were traveling and moved toward them. After driving on they could finally see that the men were captured Russians. Their shirts were open; some were bareheaded and shoeless, and exhausted to the point of dropping. German guards, armed with sub-machine guns, prodded them onward. At the head of the column was a Russian officer who looked up at the approaching truck, then turned away as if to conceal his present shame. But there were those who raised their hands, expecting whatever help might be offered them.

Captain Vlčko ordered his driver to slow down. In an instant they were mobbed by the prisoners, begging for food and water. When the German guards saw the clamoring men, they began shouting and ordering them back into line, firing shots above their heads. Submissively, they continued their march, glancing back at the truck every now and then.

Noticing that the guards were also tired and emaciated, Peter pulled out a can of meat and handed it to the first one they passed. He wanted to eliminate any resistance the guards might show if he distributed some food among the prisoners. When Peter questioned the German if it would be all right to give food to the prisoners, the German acquiesced. And, as the truck slowly moved along, Peter's men handed out all their rations. Two of his men even gave two bareheaded prisoners their caps. They didn't have enough to feed nearly ten thousand prisoners, but they did all they could. The only thing they had to offer the rest was a wave of their caps as a symbol of friendship and hope. It was a tragic sight even more tragic because nothing good awaited these unfortunate men at their destination.

Feeding prisoners of war on the Eastern Front was the last thing the German Army troubled itself over. In the fury of war, who is there with sufficient power to enforce justice, let alone charity? Until final victory, what kind of principles motivate the belligerents? Even when both sides are fully aware of the total disregard for the Geneva Convention rules, neither wants to acknowledge or accept the consequences, for each expects to win, and each hopes to sit in judgment over the other.

When the truck passed the end of the column, it picked up speed, as if to flee this depressing scene as quickly as possible. Peter and his men knew they would never be able to forget this tragic incident. It would remain in their memories the rest of their lives. In his nightmares, Peter envisioned Jirka imprisoned, in a railroad car, like a farm animal being shipped to slaughter. That was only a bad dream, and it was over. But today was no dream. This was cruel reality from which there was no escape.

THE BATTLE OF LYPOVETS
22–23 JULY 1941

Preliminaries

ON 10 JULY 1941, THE SLOVAK RAPID BRIGADE WAS INCORPORATED INTO the German Seventeenth Army's Forty-Ninth Mountain Corps of General Ludwig Kübler. On 21 July, Kübler ordered the brigade to move to the Lypovets-Ilintsi area, both on the west bank of the Sob River, with the goal of preventing the escape of Red Army units to the south or southeast (Kliment and Nakládal 1997, 70). Their advantage was that the Forty-Ninth Corps consisted mostly of soldiers from the Caucasus and Central Asia, so it could be said that they were acclimatized to life in the mountains as

Lypovets, albeit not mountainous, was higher elevation terrain (Maslov 2001).

On the eve of the battle, the brigade's order of battle was (Kliment and Nakládal 1997, 71):

- **Headquarters** with staff company in Shchaslyva (eight kilometers west of Lypovets): 30 officers; 10 NCOs; 149 men; 109 rifles; 73 pistols; 2 light machine-guns (MG); 26 trucks; 12 passenger cars; 4 ambulances; and 11 motorcycles.
- **Motorized Reconnaissance Group**: 2 bicyclist and 2 heavy squadrons and supporting units; a total of 25 officers; 11 NCOs; 734 men; 452 rifles; 302 pistols; 53 light MG; 9 heavy MG; 6 3.7-cm antitank guns; 5 OA vz. 30 armored cars; 53 trucks; 13 passenger cars; 1 ambulance; 13 motorcycles; and 241 bicycles.
- **Motorized Infantry Group**: 3 infantry and 1 machine-gun companies; 1 antitank and 1 mortar platoons; 1 battery of 7.5-cm mountain guns; radio squad and supporting units; a total of 22 officers; 1 NCO; 821 men; 488 rifles; 189 pistols; 38 light MG; 12 heavy MG; 2 mortars; 4 3.7-cm antitank guns; 4 7.5-cm mountain guns; 40 trucks; 7 passenger cars; 1 ambulance; 1 motorcycle; and 8 bicycles.
- **Artillery Regiment**: 110 officers; 13 NCOs; 1476 men; 1078 rifles; 354 pistols; 23 light MG; 24 10-cm vz. 30 howitzers; 12 10.5-cm vz. 35 cannons; 149 trucks; 39 passenger cars; 1 fuel truck; 5 artillery tractors; 30 motorcycles; and 42 bicycles.
- **Armored Battalion**: staff company; 3 tank and 3 antitank guns companies; for a total of 33 officers; 15 NCOs; 876 men; 333 rifles; 617 pistols; 41 light MG; 92 heavy MG (86 in the tanks); 65 3.7-cm antitank guns (36 in tanks); 43 tanks (27 LT vz. 35s, 9 LT vz. 38s, 7 LT vz. 40s); 89 trucks; 56 passenger cars; 4 ambulances; 3 fuel trucks; and 29 motorcycles.
- **Engineer Company**: 5 officers; 1 NCO; 248 men; 186 rifles; 24 pistols; 4 light MG; 26 trucks; 1 passenger car; 2 motorcycles; and 1 bicycle.
- **Antiaircraft Battery**: 154 officers; 139 men; 65 rifles; 63 pistols; 4 light MG; 8 2-cm vz. 36 antiaircraft guns; 17 trucks; 3 passenger cars; 3 motorcycles; and 1 bicycle.
- **Communications Company**: 4 officers; 118 men; 71 rifles; 30 pistols; 1 light MG; 14 trucks; 3 passenger cars; and 3 bicycles.

- **Automobile Repair Shop**: 1 infantry platoon consisting of 1 officer; 1 NCO; 43 men; 10 rifles; 7 pistols; 6 trucks; and 1 passenger car.
- **315th Truck Column**: 1 officer; 51 men; 23 rifles; 7 pistols; 23 trucks; 1 passenger car; and 1 motorcycle.
- **The full complement of the Mobile Brigade on 21 July 1941 was**: 195 officers (including Colonel Pilfousek and Major Julius Nosko); 52 NCOs; 4,655 men; 2,815 rifles; 1,666 pistols; 166 light MG (ten in armored cars); 113 heavy MG (86 in tanks); 4 7.5-cm vz. 15 mountain guns; 24 10-cm vz. 30 howitzers; 12 10.5-cm vz. 35 cannons; 8 2-cm antiaircraft guns; 2 mortars; 75 3.7-cm antitank guns (36 in tanks); 5 armored cars OA vz. 30; 43 tanks; 445 trucks; 10 ambulances; 4 fuel trucks; 5 artillery tractors; 137 passenger cars; 90 motorcycles; and 296 bicycles.

Lypovets was defended by the Red Army's Forty-Fourth Mountain Rifle Division, which was assigned to the Southwestern Front's Twelfth Army's Thirteenth Rifle Corps (Kiev Special Military District). The Soviet commander of the rifle division was Major General Semyon Akimovich Tkachenko, a Ukrainian. With a total of 7,500 battle-hardened men, Tkachenko's Rifle Division was superior to the young and inexperienced Rapid Brigade, but had few heavy machine guns, artillery, and no armored vehicles. General Tkachenko's Rifle Division had been engulfed in heavy combat along the borders of Ukraine from nearly the beginning of Operation Barbarossa and immediately suffered heavy losses. The division also experienced widespread desertion during the initial days of the war. Between 22–30 June, nineteen men willfully deserted from its artillery units. Subsequently, the combat morale of most of the division's soldiers and officers deteriorated sharply, largely due to the seemingly endless series of military misfortunes it experienced.

In mid-July the commander of the Forty-Fourth Mountain Rifle Division's 179th Howitzer Regiment sent a report to the division's chief of artillery that vividly documented the declining state of morale. In his report, the artillery commander wrote, "The conditions are terrible. People have lost heart, especially the command cadre. I am putting things in order, [but] it requires considerable effort just to tighten up this lack of discipline a little." (Mazlov 2001.)

By 21 July 1941, the division was already short of its establishment (*shtat* or Table of Organization and Equipment) strength by 4,013 rank-and-file soldiers, 1,025 junior command cadre, 199 cargo trucks, 3,000 rifles and carbines, and sixty-six heavy machine guns (Mazlov 2001).

Despite suffering defeat after defeat during the opening month of the war with Germany, the Forty-Fourth Mountain Rifle Division did achieve some small combat successes. The division recorded one of these successes in late July when it was engaged in heavy fighting for possession of the town of Lypovets. In this instance, the division's combat reports record a successful counterattack on 22 July, when the division's soldiers reportedly captured two 3.7-cm antitank guns and 116 shells from the enemy. The following day, the journal records that the division seized another nine guns, three tanks, two heavy machine guns, and several prisoners from the enemy. (Mazlov 2001.)

Ultimately, however, General Tkachenko's Forty-Fourth Mountain Rifle Division was encircled and destroyed during fierce combat for the village of Podvyskoe in the Kirovograd and Uman region. General Tkachenko was wounded in the head and arms and taken prisoner by the Germans while attempting to escape from the encirclement. Tkachenko died in German captivity in February 1945. (Mazlov 2001.)

The Battle

IN PREPARATION FOR THE BATTLE OF LYPOVETS, RATHER THAN constructing a maze of trenchworks, the Slovak Rapid Brigade built a series of U-shaped foxholes just west of Lypovets intended for two to six standing soldiers facing the enemy. The foxholes were camouflaged, especially at the edges of the flax fields, causing difficulties for enemy artillery spotters.

According to German reconnaissance, there were approximately two Soviet infantry regiments in Lypovets. Colonel Pilfousek met with the Commander of the German Ninety-Seventh Infantry Division, which was to the south of the brigade, and found that a reconnaissance unit of the division had reached the village of Shchaslyva (8 km / 5 mi west of Lypovets) without encountering the enemy (Kliment and Nakládal 1997, 70). He decided to move the brigade to Shchaslyva and leave it there overnight for rest and preparations.

During the early morning hours of 22 July 1941 before the battle, General Tkachenko sent scouts to gather intelligence on the adversary. Alert Slovak soldiers, however, captured the Soviet patrol.

The Rapid Brigade's motorized reconnaissance units commenced attack on Lypovets at 0430 hours. The leading unit was one company of three armored cars and one platoon of bicyclists. They encountered the first Soviet unit about three kilometers in front of Lypovets. It was approximately a company of infantry in foxholes (Kliment and Nakládal 1997, 72). The initial attack was a disaster as dug-in camouflaged Soviet troops were waiting and caught the inexperienced, young Slovaks off guard with small arms fire and grenades. The Slovaks panicked and ran away. The chaos was so great, according to Slovak historian Pavel Mičianik, that some officers had to stop the soldiers by firing in the air. Among them was Major Julius Nosko, later a commander during the Slovak National Uprising (Mičianik 2007).

The main force of the advanced units started at 0500 hours. By 0600 hours, the motorized reconnaissance group was fully engaged in the fighting. It was now augmented by two platoons of tanks from the Third Armored Company, one company of infantry, two platoons of bicyclists, and one battery of I/11 (Kliment and Nakládal 1997, 72). This skirmish concentrated on a low hill governing the western approach to Lypovets. The two tank platoons approached the hill across the open country, as the Soviet artillery was well zeroed in on the road. The tanks in hull-down positions started firing both on Lypovets and Kamyunka (a small village on the southern outskirts of Lypovets). Two of them separated out and went to the aid of the reconnaissance group. As the Soviet infantry did not have any antitank guns, the Slovak tanks easily overcame the Soviet resistance and helped the Slovak infantry to penetrate part of the main Soviet line (Kliment and Nakládal 1997, 72).

In the meantime, eight LT vz. 35 tanks from the main body came to help the reconnaissance group bicyclists (part of the first wave in the battle), who were pinned down by the Soviet infantry in the foxholes. The tanks had originally run over the foxholes without firing but returned at the infantry's order and helped to neutralize this area (Kliment and Nakládal 1997, 72).

Soviet mortars and artillery were firing from the area of Kamyunka and from a hill east of Feliksovka (a village 5 km west of Lypovets) behind the advanced units. Their fire notwithstanding, the advance units of the brigade took the hill between Lypovets and Feliksovka around 1000 hours. The rest of the Rapid Brigade formed a column and was ready to follow its advance units to Lypovets (Kliment and Nakládal 1997, 72). Colonel Pilfousek ordered a general assault on Lypovets at 1015 hours but Pilfousek then hesitated for two hours to regroup and reassess the enemy, and then at 1230 hours ordered a new attack on Lypovets with all forces.

The attack began with a powerful artillery bombardment followed by infantry attack. The tanks and their supporting infantry captured the hills on both sides of the road to Lypovets. The motorized infantry and antitank guns followed the tanks on the main road, but the Soviet artillery started firing at them and started destroying the trucks, one after another. The brigade's artillery commenced a counter-battery fire, which the Soviets returned, and the ensuing artillery duel lasted for about an hour. (Kliment and Nakládal 1997, 72.)

Soviet resistance was getting stronger. The hill on the right side of the road was strongly contested, and it had proven impossible to dislodge the Russians. Finally, Slovak soldiers managed to completely scatter the units of the Forty-Fourth Mountain Rifle Division on the hills. Around 1600 hours, the advance units of the Rapid Brigade reached the outskirts of Lypovets and pushed on to the railway station, which they managed to occupy shortly thereafter (Kliment and Nakládal 1997, 72).

The armored battalion lost two tanks during this fight. LT vz. 35 (13846) was hit by a mortar mine on its open turret hatch, its commander was killed, and the crew had to abandon the tank. The front part of one LT vz. 40 (V-3037) was hit by an antitank round in Lypovets. The round broke the driveshaft and destroyed the clutches. (Kliment and Nakládal 1997, 72.)

Around this time, the tanks were pulled back to an area one kilometer south of Feliksovka to replenish their fuel and munitions. The tanks of the Third Armored Company fought at Kamyunka. During their pull-back two LT vz. 35 bogged down in the wet terrain and had to be abandoned. One of them was destroyed during the night and could not be salvaged. (Kliment and Nakládal 1997, 72.)

Under the impression that Lypovets had been already taken, Colonel Pilfousek ordered the whole brigade to move to the town at 1700 hours. While the brigade was advancing across the only road, the Red Army counterattacked with two infantry battalions and strong artillery support from the Kamyunka area (Kliment and Nakládal 1997, 72). Soviet artillery hit the Shchaslyva-Lypovets road and the brigade's right flank. They succeeded in cutting the brigade in half. The units fighting in or nearing Lypovets were cut off from the main body, which started withdrawing in panic (Kliment and Nakládal 1997, 72). Colonel Pilfousek realized there were no reserves available to stop such an extensive attack. Therefore, by 1800 hours he ordered the advance units to retreat to a defensive position eight kilometers (5 mi) west to the village of Shchaslyva. At the same time, Soviet infantry attacked separated units caught in Lypovets from the left bank of the river Sob (just east of Lypovets). However, when the bulk of the attacking Soviet forces approached the Slovaks at 500 meters, Slovak howitzers and cannons started firing with brush shots. The approaching wall of human bodies suddenly spilled. The survivors began to run in retreat (Mičianik 2007). The Soviet counterattack was finally stopped about two kilometers east of Shchaslyva (Kliment and Nakládal 1997, 72).

Notwithstanding the foolhardy Soviet infantry charge into enemy artillery, the Soviet counteroffensive threatened to encircle and destroy forward assault units of the Rapid Brigade within Lypovets. Over 250 Slovak soldiers and officers with armored vehicles remained cut off in Lypovets. To help the units fighting in Lypovets, five tanks of the Second Armored Company and one tank from the First Armored Company were sent around 1800 hours (Kliment and Nakládal 1997, 72). They reached Lypovets safely and were joined there by one tank from the Third Armored Company. The fighting in Lypovets was very tough, house-to-house. The tanks reached the trapped antitank guns company and, further on, the Slovak armored cars. One of them was already burned out, one was captured by the Soviets and was recovered only the next day (with red stars already painted on), and the third was damaged (Kliment and Nakládal 1997, 72). The tanks and the armored cars fought in the village until 2200 hours, when they executed a fighting withdrawal. Soviet antitank guns were quite active during the withdrawal and managed to hit one LT vz. 35, which had to be left behind, and one LT vz. 38 (V-3000), which exploded and was totally destroyed (Kliment and Nakládal 1997, 72).

By 2300 hours, Lypovets was again in Soviet hands but Tkachenko failed to meet the main objective—a strong attack to completely destroy the Rapid Brigade. The Rapid Brigade did not conquer Lypovets that day and, moreover, suffered significant losses.

At 0400 hours on 23 July 1941, Slovak artillery began a forty-five-minute bombardment in preparation for another attack on Lypovets. When the artillery barrage ended, Slovak tanks and infantry staged in Shchaslyva advanced to Lypovets while vanguard units of the German 295th Infantry Division approached from the village of Vakhnivka (20 km / 12 mi northwest of Lypovets). Running low on ammunition and with waning morale of his troops, General Tkachenko realized that after a two-day exhaustive fight his division could not withstand a concentrated attack from two sides. Therefore, he ordered his troops to subtly withdraw twenty kilometers (13 mi) southward from Lypovets to Ilintsi. By 1200 hours, German and Slovak artillery launched another strong barrage at the retreating Soviets in

Lypovets. At the same time, the German infantry on the northern edge of Lypovets attacked and by 1600 hours Lypovets was completely under German control.

The Rapid Brigade helped take Lypovets with less than 5,000 soldiers, 43 tanks, and 123 artillery pieces. Total losses of the Rapid Brigade were seventy-five dead (including seven officers), 167 wounded (including nine officers) and nineteen captured (including one officer). Of the original fifty captured men, twenty-seven succeeded in escaping from Soviet captivity and four fell in an attempt to escape. Material losses included five light tanks (three LT vz. 35, one LT vz. 38, and one LT vz. 40), one OA vz. 30 armored car, and twenty-five trucks. (Kliment and Nakládal 1997, 72.)

The automotive workshop of the brigade had enough spare parts for repairing most of the damaged vehicles, but their personnel faked a lack of spare parts and finally caused the withdrawal of the whole armored battalion back to Slovakia under the pretext that the tanks could not be repaired in the field. In this they were supported by most of the officers with anti-Fascist leanings. The battalion formed a column, the running tanks towed the damaged ones all the way to Ternopil, where all the vehicles were loaded on flat cars and sent to Sambor. There, the battalion was organized for transport home and eleven days later was shipped on two trains back to Turčianský Svätý Martin. The battalion also brought home nine armored Komsomolec artillery tractors, two Soviet trucks and two TB tanks. The rest of the brigade was assigned to help the German 295th Infantry Division (Fourth Corps of the Seventeenth Army). The Rapid Brigade's artillery supported its advance, while the infantry formed advance guard all the way to Kalnik (16.6 km southeast of Ilintsi). (Kliment and Nakládal 1997, 72–3.)

It can be said that Slovak losses in the Battle of Lypovets were the result of an underestimation of the enemy, of whom the command of the Rapid Brigade practically knew nothing during the entire fight. The brigade was sent to fight without adequate reconnaissance intelligence and air support. Estimated losses by the Soviet Forty-Fourth Mountain Rifle Division were over 700 dead, nearly 1,000 wounded, and 150 captured.

For Slovak soldiers, the Battle of Lypovets was not only baptism by fire but also the bloodiest battle in the campaign against the U.S.S.R. The Germans discovered that following the battle for Lypovets, the Slovak infantry had become very sensitive to artillery and especially mortar fire, which caused them to panic and leave their positions. Colonel Turanec, himself, wrote in his diary: "The men are generally cowardly, once the Russian artillery starts firing, they run back. The officers are in the rear during an attack, but in the front during the retreat!" (Kliment and Nakládal 1997, 73.)

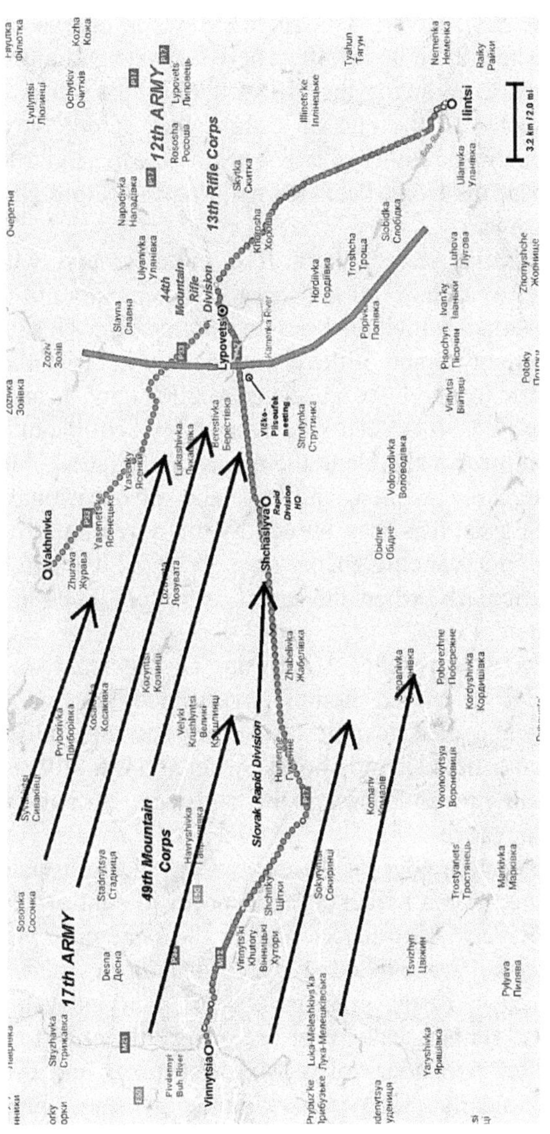
17th ARMY
49th Mountain Corps
Slovak Rapid Division
12th ARMY
13th Rifle Corps
44th Mountain Rifle Division
Vinnytsia
Vakhnivka
Shchaslyva
Rapid Division HQ
Lypovets
Ilintsi
3.2 km / 2.0 mi

ABOUT MID-MORNING THEY REACHED THE WESTERN BANK OF THE Southern Bug (*Pivdennyi Buh*) River. A German officer in charge of traffic on the pontoon bridge held them up briefly. There were several units waiting ahead of Vlčko's truck. Convincing the officer about the urgency of his mission, Vlčko was directed to the end of a short line of other trucks ready for crossing. The bustling activity of tanks, armored cars, and trucks meant they were not far from the front. Peter learned that the Rapid Division was less than four hours away.

The crossing lasted about five minutes, and without incident. Several batteries of antiaircraft guns on the eastern shore of the river would take care of any attack which the Russians might stage. This left the Germans free to carry on their pursuit of the enemy openly in broad daylight.

The tactic in which the Russians excelled now, as well as in the past, was retreat. The Red Army destroyed everything it could not take with them. Whatever might prove valuable to them was taken in tow. All that remained undestroyed were the women, children, and an occasional field crop. In places, even the grain had been burned by the retreating Soviets. This kind of retreat from an advancing enemy does the most damage to the enemy's war effort, particularly when the enemy's supply lines extend over two thousand kilometers.

At noon, they reached Vinnytsia. The signs of war were evident everywhere. Half-destroyed homes, overturned streetcars, knocked-out telephone lines and electric poles, smoking rooftops, all testified to the raging battle that concluded only hours earlier and was still near at hand. The thunder of distant guns rolled across the landscape, earmarking the direction of the German advance.

On the eastern edge of the city was the last obstacle Vlčko's men had to overcome, a small river running north to south (*Pivdennyi Buh* or Southern Bug River). All traffic forded at the same crossing point. On the other side, Peter's driver picked up speed, leaving a cloud of dust behind. Once again, because of the great number of men and vehicles using this narrow field road running east toward Lypovets, they had to slow down and yield often. After two hours of passing transports and evading disabled vehicles over nearly forty-five kilometers, they reached division headquarters.

"This is a surprise. What are you doing here, Peter?" Julius Nosko asked.

"I came to check up on you to see if you're behaving. Čatloš had reports you weren't the best," Peter joked with his friend.

"You won't talk like that when you've been here for a couple of hours."

"Julko, I know any division where you are chief of staff has to be first-rate. I brought medical supplies and another doctor."

"That sounds better. What else did you bring?" Nosko interrupted.

"The *Generál* has orders I'm to hand deliver to Pilfousek."

"Do you want to see Pilfousek immediately, or would you rather rest awhile?"

"I'd better go to him right now, but do you have something to drink? My throat feels like parchment." On this, Nosko immediately called on his orderly to bring two bottles of beer. "Julko, fill me in quickly on the situation here and how do I find Pilfousek."

"Well," Nosko said as he spread a map out on his desk, "we're eight kilometers southwest of Lypovets. The front line is about five kilometers from here. If you follow this road," pointing to a red line on the map, "it will take you to him. Between his post and Lypovets is a small (*Kamenka*) river that runs through a gully. Our vanguard encountered the Russian defenses there. Since this morning, we've suffered eighty-two men killed in action and over two hundred wounded. Lieutenant Lehotsky was killed today. He stuck his head out of the turret hatch of his tank [LT vz. 35-13846] to have a look around and was hit by a Ruský mortar round. The upper part of his body was torn away. It was terrible. Anyway, use this trench along the road for cover and stay down. The Russians have a good view of our positions. The staff car will take you as far as it can go, but then you'll have to move the rest of the way on foot."

"Julko, can you get us some provisions for the return trip? There are seven of us. I'd like rations for ten days." Peter was thinking of Russian prisoners. "As soon as I deliver these orders to Pilfousek, I have to start back."

"Sure, I'll take care of it. Now drink up." With that he handed Peter a beer. "I'll get the mail ready also, along with my report, so you can deliver it to Army Staff Headquarters."

"Are you getting along with Pilfousek?" Peter inquired.

"Not too well. He seems completely mad. He'd like to defeat the whole Red Army himself, even though he has only a handful of soldiers. He'll sacrifice anyone for the sake of the Germans. Maybe he thinks the greater the losses, the more medals he'll receive."

"How's your field hospital?"

"That's becoming a real problem, too. We're certainly grateful you came when you did. We're completely out of bandages and some very essential drugs. We don't have enough stretchers, either. The wounded have to lie on the ground until they're transferred to a German Army hospital. There aren't even enough ambulances to transport all the wounded."

"'Do you have any prisoners?"

"No. We have to turn them over to the Germans immediately."

"On our way here, we saw thousands of Russian prisoners being marched back by the Germans. They were a pitiful sight."

Nosko's face reflected his own concern. "Peter, you know there isn't anything I'd like more than to be able to go back to Bratislava right now and get back to my studies at the college. I don't have the heart for all this killing of our Slavic brothers, especially when I see how our men are dying for a victory that is completely foreign to us. It seems so pointless. Pilfousek no longer thinks rationally about the welfare of his men. Because he's so willing to die, he thinks all of us share his feeling."

"Julko, if you don't have to stick your neck out, stay here in relative safety. I want to see you after the war in good health and in one piece. Well, I must be going. See you later."

Nosko's situation disturbed him. It was bad enough for men to have to die when the cause was right and just. But the sacrifice of young men in a struggle alien to ours was bitter medicine to swallow.

THEY FOLLOWED A WIDE GRAVEL ROAD WITH DEEP DITCHES ON BOTH SIDES and devoid of either trees or bushes, an indication it had been built recently. In five minutes, they came across Slovak troops, no doubt waiting to be sent into battle. Behind a grove of trees, a short distance from the road men were loading a cannon, firing at irregular intervals. To the west, another battery was just now camouflaging its position. Ahead, the road grew steeper. Near a small rise, Peter observed the movement of individual men and small groups as they ran back and forth, keeping their heads down in a half crouch, to the accompaniment of explosions from enemy artillery shells. About three hundred meters before they reached the highest point of the rise, they were stopped by an officer who came out of the ditch.

"Where can I find the brigade commander?" asked Vlčko, getting out of his car.

"You see those two mounds of earth over there?" he asked, pointing toward the crest of the hill.

"Yes, I see them."

"Colonel Pilfousek is in one of those two large foxholes next to the mounds. Be careful, the Russians have our range. As soon as anyone appears on the hill, the shells begin falling. Take the ditch on the other side of the road, and for God's sake, keep your head down."

"Thanks, Major." Vlčko returned to the car.

"Move the car about a hundred meters back and wait for me there." Then, Peter made his way toward the crest of the hill as he had been advised. The whirr of a flying artillery shell forced him to hit the ground. He waited for a lull in the enemy fire before getting up and racing for the mounds.

"Colonel Pilfousek!" he called out.

"Over here!" And he popped his head up. Peter took a few quick steps, and, in a sprint, he reached their dugout. "Vlčko, what are you doing here?" the commander greeted him cheerfully as he extended his hand. His adjutant was with him. An artillery lieutenant was in the next hole looking through his field glasses. After greeting the men, Peter explained why he had come.

"*Pán plukovník*, I've brought orders from *Generál* Čatloš, along with his most hearty greetings to all the troops."

He drew the envelope from his pocket and handed it to Pilfousek. While Pilfousek was busy reading, Peter took his binoculars and scanned the field in front of them.

"Vlčko, let me tell you what the situation is here."

"Yes, sir."

"Straight ahead of us behind that hill is Lypovets. The Russians are hidden along the river which runs between us and the city. This morning our units were pinned down by enemy machine-gun fire. We can't go forward until we find those nests and destroy them. We've been at this since four-thirty this morning, and it's now three in the afternoon. We lost eighty-two of our men. About two hundred more were wounded. One of my best tank officers [Lieutenant Lehotsky] was killed today. He died in front of that bean field over there."

Suddenly, two enemy shells exploded about twenty meters off to the left. Peter immediately grabbed his camera and began taking pictures.

"If you want some really good pictures, keep your camera focused and ready to click the shutter when a shell explodes. In the meantime, I'll write Čatloš a report."

"Colonel, before you do, I'd like to mention one thing. The *Generál* asked me to tell you not to take so many chances with your life. He doesn't want to lose you. He said he has a special assignment for you far more important than your present command. He was quite alarmed when he learned you were right on the battle line." Peter tried to be as tactful as possible.

"Vlčko, tell Čatloš that as long as I'm in charge of this brigade, I'll command it as I see fit. If he doesn't like what I'm doing, he can damn well come here and take it over. I'm not doing more or less than the Germans have ordered. Certain sacrifices just have to be made. What the hell does he want me to do, disobey the German Command or surrender?"

"I understand, Colonel. I'm quite sure the *Generál* is aware of this. But he knows these sacrifices must be justified to the government back home."

"Sometimes I feel I'm fighting two different wars. Look out, Vlčko! Hit the dirt." No sooner had he said this than a deafening "kaboom" resonated as a shell hit ten meters from their position.

"Damn, I should've had a picture of that one" Peter exclaimed, raising his head above the edge of the dugout.

"You would've had a piece of shrapnel in your skull to send home along with the picture," the adjutant remarked. "*Kapitán*, that wasn't the last one. There will be many more like it."

Peter didn't have to wait long. In the next few moments three more shells exploded within several meters of the dugout. No one saw them because each man lay on the ground with his face buried in the dirt.

It was about one and one-half kilometers from their position to the Russian-held hill. On the north side of the river, variegated strips of green climbed up and down the incline. As Peter looked toward Lypovets, he thought how wrong it was for Slovaks to be helping the Germans take Russian soil. How much better he would feel alongside the Russians. Through his field glasses, Peter noticed more men moving around. Then a disturbing thought entered his mind—what if there weren't any Russians over there, only Mongolians? What if they shot him on sight before he had a chance to explain? If he really wanted to join the Russians, this wasn't the way to go about it. He would have to wait for a better occasion. Suddenly, he was drawn from his thoughts by Pilfousek's voice.

"I'm through with my report to *Generál* Čatloš. Lieutenant, write a statement to the effect that I received the *Generál*'s orders from *Kapitán* Vlčko at 1500 hours about three kilometers southwest of Lypovets. Then give it to Vlčko." A few minutes later, Peter put the receipt and Pilfousek's report in his pocket and started to leave.

"I wish all of you the best of luck," he said.

"Thanks, *Kapitán*. You have a safe return," the lieutenant replied.

Peter then crawled out of the hole and headed back, stooping down as low as he could. At the road, he rolled over into the ditch that ran alongside. Here, it offered little protection, so he scampered to get away from the enemy's line of fire. Suddenly, a powerful blow hurled Peter through the air to the ground knocking him unconscious. Then, there was silence. When he recovered from the shock, he raised himself to one knee, flexing the muscles in his back to see if he was still in one piece. "Thank God! I'm all right." He flattened himself back against the ground and breathed deeply to clear the cobwebs in his head and steady his nerves. Sweat poured down his face as he began to slowly relieve the strain and slow his pulse.

"Vlčko, are you hurt?" A voice called to Peter from the ditch on the opposite side of the road.

"I'm okay." He was still shaking from the experience, his face a pale white.

"That was close. We thought it was all over for you when we heard the explosion and saw you thrown to the ground," another voice joined the first. As if on cue they all stuck their heads up cautiously.

"What the hell happened?" asked Vlčko.

"While you were running, a shell exploded behind you on the side of the road. You're lucky no shrapnel happened to be flying in your direction, or you wouldn't be alive right now. When you left Pilfousek, the Russians must have spotted you and fired."

"God protected me at that moment. I'd better get out of here before He changes His mind," said Peter, regaining his composure.

"Yes, I think you'd better," said one of the officers, still amazed at what he had just seen.

"So long. The best of luck until we meet again in Slovakia."

It was now about four in the afternoon. The sky was clear, except for a few cirrus clouds that floated gently overhead. A fresh breeze blew from the north and cooled Peter's body, which was bathed in sweat. Increasingly for him, war became less an academic subject and more a flesh and blood reality. In some dim way he had always assumed his own invulnerability. Now he grasped the reality of his vulnerability; he, too, could at any unexpected moment be torn apart and shattered by a whining bullet or screaming piece of shrapnel.

On the way back to his car, Vlčko noticed a Slovak soldier leading two Russian prisoners.

"Hey, private, where are you going?" he asked.

"I'm taking them to headquarters, sir. We captured them by the river this morning."

"Why, they're both wounded!" exclaimed Peter, as he walked over for a closer look.

"Yes, *Pán Kapitán*. One has a serious stomach wound. The other nearly got his hand shot off." The soldier was helping the Russian with the stomach wound with one hand, holding his gun in the other. The other prisoner was walking alongside supporting his bleeding hand.

"You don't think they can make it in that condition, do you? They'll bleed to death before you reach headquarters. My car is right over here. I'll take them there. Let's have a look at their wounds first."

The soldier with the injured hand looked as if he would lose at least two fingers. The other man showed an opening in his stomach just above the navel. Blood was seeping from the hole in a thick red flow. Both looked at Peter with pleading eyes. The pain showed in their faces and the prisoner with the abdominal wound trembled, indicating impending shock. Overcome with concern, Peter wanted to do all he could to help. He took one arm of the man with the stomach wound, while the private took the other. Slowly, they made their way to the car. Then, he and the private eased the Russians into the back seat. When they were ready, he got in himself and ordered the driver to take off.

"Be careful. This is a bumpy road." Vlčko cautioned his driver when he stepped on the gas.

In ten minutes, they reached headquarters. Peter found Dr. Darvaš and asked him to look after the men. Then, he went to say goodbye to Nosko. He also picked up the mail before making his departure.

"Let's go," he said to his soldiers, who by now were waiting beside the truck. "Sambor will seem like a resort after today." He smiled, and they all piled into the truck and were on their way.

Unbeknownst to Captain Vlčko during this mission deep into Ukraine, he visited areas that would soon become infamous in history.

EINSATZGRUPPEN

THE *EINSATZGRUPPEN DER SICHERHEITSPOLIZEI UND DES SD* WERE FORMED under the direction of *SS-Obergruppenführer* Reinhard Heydrich and operated by the *SS* before and during World War II (Edeiken 2000). The *Einsatzgruppen* had their origins in the *ad hoc Einsatzkommando* formed by Heydrich to secure government buildings and documents following the *Anschluß* in Austria in March 1938 (Streim 1999, 436–54). Originally part of the *Sicherheitspolizei* (Security Police; *SiPo*), two units of *Einsatzgruppen* were stationed in the Sudetenland in October 1938. When military action turned out not to be necessary due to the Munich Agreement, the *Einsatzgruppen* were assigned to confiscate government papers and police documents. They also secured government buildings, questioned senior civil servants, and arrested as many as 10,000 Czech Communists and German citizens (Longerich 2012, 405, 412; see also Streim 1999, 436–54). From September 1939, the *Reichssicherheitshauptamt* (*Reich* Main Security Office; *RSHA*) had overall command of the *Einsatzgruppen* ("Nuremberg Trial Proceedings").

As part of the drive to remove so-called "undesirable" elements from the German population, from September to December 1939 the *Einsatzgruppen* and others took part in *Action T4*, a program of systematic murder undertaken by the Nazi regime of persons with physical and mental disabilities and patients of psychiatric hospitals. *Action T4* mainly took place from 1939 to 1941, but the killings continued until the end of the war. Initially the victims were shot by the *Einsatzgruppen* and others, but gas chambers were put into use by spring 1940 (Longerich 2010, 138–41).

In response to Adolf Hitler's plan to invade Poland on 1 September 1939, Heydrich reformed the *Einsatzgruppen* to travel in the wake of the German Army Groups (Longerich 2012, 425). Membership at this point was drawn from the *SS*, the *Sicherheitsdienst* (Security Service; *SD*), the *Sicherheitspolizei*, and the *Gestapo* (Rossino 2003, 11; see also Longerich 2010, 144). Heydrich placed *SS-Obergruppenführer* Werner Best in command, who assigned Hans-Joachim Tesmer to choose personnel for the task forces and their subgroups, called *Einsatzkommandos*, from among educated people with military experience and a strong ideological commitment to Nazism (Rossino 2003, 11, 20). Some had previously been members of paramilitary groups such as the *Freikorps* (Evans 2008, 17). Heydrich instructed First Quartermaster of the *Wehrmacht Heer*, General

Eduard Wagner* in meetings in late July that the *Einsatzgruppen* should undertake their operations in cooperation with the *Ordnungspolizei* (Order Police; *Orpo*) and military commanders in the area (Rossino 2003, 14). Army intelligence was in constant contact with *Einsatzgruppen* to coordinate their activities with other units (Rossino 2003, 17).

Initially numbering 2,700 men (and ultimately 4,250 in Poland) (Evans 2008, 17; Rossino 2003, 12), the *Einsatzgruppen*'s mission was to kill members of the Polish leadership most clearly identified with Polish national identity: the intelligentsia, members of the clergy, teachers, and members of the nobility (Browning and Matthäus 2004, 16–18; see also Longerich 2010, 144). As stated by Hitler: "there must be no Polish leaders; where Polish leaders exist they must be killed, however harsh that sounds" (Longerich 2010, 143). *SS-Brigadeführer* Lothar Beutel, commander of *Einsatzgruppe IV*, later testified that Heydrich gave the order for these killings at a series of meetings in mid-August 1939 (Rossino 2003, 15). The *Sonderfahndungsbuch Polen*—lists of people to be killed—had been drawn up by the *SS* as early as May 1939, using dossiers collected by the *SD* from 1936 forward (Longerich 2010, 144; Rossino 2003, 16). The *Einsatzgruppen* performed these murders with the support of the *Volksdeutscher Selbstschutz*, a paramilitary group consisting of ethnic Germans living in Poland (Longerich 2010, 144–5). Members of the *SS*, the *Wehrmacht*, and the *Ordnungspolizei* also shot civilians during the Polish campaign (Longerich 2012, 429). Approximately 65,000 civilians were killed by the end of 1939. In addition to leaders of Polish society, they killed Jews, prostitutes, Romani people, and the mentally ill. Psychiatric patients in Poland were initially killed by shooting, but by spring 1941 gas vans were widely used (Evans 2008, 15; Longerich 2012, 430–2).

Seven *Einsatzgruppen* of battalion strength (around 500 men) operated in Poland. Each was subdivided into five *Einsatzkommandos* of company strength (around 100 men).

- *Einsatzgruppe I*, commanded by *SS-Standartenführer* Bruno Streckenbach, under the Fourteenth Army

* Eduard Wagner (1 April 1894–23 July 1944) was a General-of-the-Artillery in the *Wehrmacht* who served as Quartermaster-General in World War II. He had the overall responsibility for security in the Army Group Rear Areas, and thus bore responsibility for the war crimes committed by the rear-security units in the occupied areas under the army's jurisdiction.

- *Einsatzgruppe II, SS-Obersturmbannführer* Emanuel Schäfer, under the Tenth Army
- *Einsatzgruppe III, SS-Obersturmbannführer und Regierungsrat* Herbert Fischer, under the Eighth Army
- *Einsatzgruppe IV, SS-Brigadeführer* Lothar Beutel, under the Fourth Army
- *Einsatzgruppe V, SS-Standartenfürer* Ernst Damzog, under the Third Army
- *Einsatzgruppe VI, SS-Oberführer* Erich Naumann, acted in *Wielkopolska*
- *Einsatzgruppe VII, SS-Obergruppenführer* Udo von Woyrsch and *SS-Gruppenführer* Emil Otto Rasch, acted in Upper Silesia and Cieszyn Silesia (Weale 2012, 225).

Though they were formally under the command of the army, the *Einsatzgruppen* received their orders from Heydrich and for the most part acted independently of the army (Gerwarth 2011, 147; see also Evans 2008, 18). Many senior *Wehrmacht* officers were only too glad to leave these genocidal actions to the task forces, as the killings violated the rules of warfare as set down in the Geneva Conventions. However, Hitler had decreed that the army would have to tolerate and even offer logistical support to the *Einsatzgruppen* when it was tactically possible to do so. Some army commanders complained about unauthorized shootings, looting, and rapes committed by members of the *Einsatzgruppen* and the *Volksdeutscher Selbstschutz*, to little effect (Longerich 2010, 146). For example, when *Generaloberst* Johannes Blaskowitz sent a memorandum of complaint to Hitler about the atrocities, Hitler dismissed his concerns as "childish," and Blaskowitz was relieved of his post in May 1940. He continued to serve in the army but never received promotion to field marshal (Evans 2008, 25–6).

The final task of the *Einsatzgruppen* in Poland was to round up the remaining Jews and concentrate them in ghettos within major cities with good railway connections. The intention was to eventually remove all the Jews from Poland, but at this point their final destination had not yet been determined (Weale 2012, 227–8, 242–5). Together, the *Wehrmacht* and the *Einsatzgruppen* also drove tens of thousands of Jews eastward into Soviet-controlled territory (Longerich 2012, 429).

On 13 March 1941, in the lead-up to Operation Barbarossa, Hitler dictated his "Guidelines in Special Spheres re: Directive No. 21 (Operation Barbarossa)." Sub-paragraph B specified that *Reichsführer-SS* Heinrich

Himmler would be given "special tasks" on direct orders from the *Führer*, which he would carry out independently (Hillgruber 1989, 95; see also Wette 2007, 93). This directive was intended to prevent friction between the *Wehrmacht* and the *SS* in the upcoming offensive (Hillgruber 1989, 95). Hitler also specified that criminal acts against civilians perpetrated by members of the *Wehrmacht* during the upcoming campaign would not be prosecuted in the military courts, and thus would go unpunished (Longerich 2012, 521–2).

In a speech to his leading generals on 30 March 1941, Hitler described his envisioned war against the Soviet Union. General Franz Halder, the Army's Chief of Staff, described the speech:

> Struggle between two ideologies. Scathing evaluation of Bolshevism, equals antisocial criminality. Communism immense future danger . . . This a fight to the finish. If we do not accept this, we shall beat the enemy, but in thirty years we shall again confront the Communist foe. We don't make war to preserve the enemy . . . Struggle against Russia: Extermination of Bolshevik Commissars and of the Communist intelligentsia . . . Commissars and GPU personnel are criminals and must be treated as such. The struggle will differ from that in the west. In the east harshness now means mildness for the future. (Hillgruber 1989, 95–6.)

Though General Halder did not record any mention of Jews, German historian Andreas Hillgruber argued that because of Hitler's frequent contemporary statements about the coming war of annihilation against "Judeo-Bolshevism," his generals would have understood Hitler's call for the destruction of the Soviet Union as also comprising a call for the destruction of its Jewish population (Hillgruber 1989, 95–6). The genocide was often described using euphemisms such as "special tasks" and "executive measures"; *Einsatzgruppe* victims were often described as having been shot while trying to escape (Rhodes 2002, 14, 48). In May 1941, Heydrich verbally passed on the order to kill the Soviet Jews to the *SiPo* NCO School in Pretzsch, where the commanders of the reorganized *Einsatzgruppen* were being trained for Operation Barbarossa (Hillgruber 1989, 94–5). In spring 1941, Heydrich and General Eduard Wagner, successfully completed negotiations for cooperation between the

Einsatzgruppen and the *Wehrmacht* to allow the implementation of the "special tasks" (Hillgruber 1989, 94–6). Following the Heydrich-Wagner agreement on 28 April 1941, Field Marshal Walther von Brauchitsch ordered that when Operation Barbarossa began, all *Wehrmacht* commanders were to immediately identify and register all Jews in occupied areas in the Soviet Union, and fully cooperate with the *Einsatzgruppen* (Hillgruber 1989, 96).

In further meetings held in June 1941, Himmler outlined to top *SS* leaders the regime's intention to reduce the population of the Soviet Union by thirty million people, not only through direct killing of those considered racially inferior, but by depriving the remainder of food and other necessities of life (Longerich 2010, 181).

For Operation Barbarossa, initially four *Einsatzgruppen* were created, each numbering 500–990 men to comprise a total force of 3,000 (Longerich 2010, 185). *Einsatzgruppen A*, *B*, and *C* were to be attached to Army Groups North, Center, and South, respectively; *Einsatzgruppe D* was assigned to the Eleventh Army. The *Einsatzgruppe* for Special Purposes operated in eastern Poland starting in July 1941 (Longerich 2010, 185). The *Einsatzgruppen* were under the control of the *RSHA*, headed by Heydrich and later by his successor, *SS-Obergruppenführer* Ernst Kaltenbrunner. Heydrich gave them a mandate to secure the offices and papers of the Soviet state and Communist Party (Thomas 1987, 261–301); to liquidate all the higher cadres of the Soviet state; and to instigate and encourage pogroms against Jewish populations (Rees 1997, 177).

These special units were established in the spring of 1941 and were each given a geographic area of operation:

- *Einsatzgruppe A*: lead by *SS-Brigadeführer und Generalmajor der Polizei* Franz Walter Stahlecker; The Baltic countries of Estonia, Latvia, and Lithuania; subgroups—*Sonderkommandos 1a* and *1b*, *Einsatzkommandos 2* and *3*. Attached to Army Group North during Operation Barbarossa.
- *Einsatzgruppe B*: lead by *SS-Gruppenführer und Generalleutnant der Polizei* Arthur Nebe; Byelorussia; subgroups—*Sonderkommandos 7a* and *7b*, *Einsatzkommandos 8* and *9*. Attached to Army Group Center.
- *Einsatzgruppe C*: lead by *SS-Gruppenführer* Juris Dr. Emil Otto Rasch; northern and central Ukraine; subgroups—*Sonderkommandos 4a* and *4b* (*Sonderkommando 4a* was commanded by *SS-Standartenführer* Paul Blobel reported to be

responsible for 59,000 murders), *Einsatzkommandos 5* and *6*. Attached to Army Group South.

- *Einsatzgruppe D*: lead by *SS-Gruppenführer* Professor Otto Ohlendorf; southern Ukraine, Crimea, and eventually Caucasia; subgroups—*Sonderkommandos 10a* and *10b*, *Einsatzkommandos 11a*, *11b*, and *12*. Attached to Eleventh Army.

Additional *Einsatzgruppen* were created as additional territories were occupied (see *infra*).

The men of the *Einsatzgruppen* were recruited from the *SD*, *Gestapo*, *Kriminalpolizei* (*Kripo*), *Orpo*, and *Waffen-SS* (Longerich 2010, 185). Each *Einsatzgruppe* was under the operational control of the Higher *SS* Police Chiefs in its area of operations (Hillgruber 1989, 96). In May 1941, General Wagner and *SS-Brigadeführer* Walter Schellenberg agreed that the *Einsatzgruppen* in front-line areas were to operate under army command, while the army provided the *Einsatzgruppen* with all necessary logistical support (Rhodes 2002, 15). Given their main task was defeating the enemy, the army left the pacification of the civilian population to the *Einsatzgruppen*, who offered support as well as prevented subversion (Langerbein 2004, 30–1). This did not preclude their participation in acts of violence against civilians, as many members of the *Wehrmacht* assisted the *Einsatzgruppen* in rounding up and killing Jews of their own accord (Langerbein 2004, 31–2).

Heydrich acted under orders from *Reichsführer-SS* Himmler, who supplied security forces on an "as needed" basis to the local *SS* and Police Leaders (Edeiken 2000). Led by *SD*, *Gestapo*, and *Kripo* officers, *Einsatzgruppen* included recruits from the *Orpo*, Security Service, and *Waffen-SS*, augmented by uniformed volunteers from the local auxiliary police force (Browning 1998, 10–12). Each *Einsatzgruppe* was supplemented with a reserve battalion of *Orpos* and *Waffen-SS* as well as support personnel such as drivers and radio operators (Longerich 2010, 185). On average, the *Orpo* formations were larger and better armed, with heavy machine-gun detachments, which enabled them to carry out operations beyond the capability of the *SS* (Browning 1998, 10–12). Each death squad followed an assigned army group as they advanced into the Soviet Union ("Einsatzgruppen Case" 414–16). As later revealed during the Nuremberg trials, during the course of their operations, the *Einsatzgruppen* commanders received assistance from the *Wehrmacht* ("Einsatzgruppen Case" 414–16)—see GERMAN OCCUPATION, NUREMBERG TRIALS, THE COLD WAR, AND

AMNESTY in the final chapter of this book. Activities ranged from the murder of targeted groups of individuals named on carefully prepared lists, to joint citywide operations with *SS Einsatzgruppen* which lasted for two or more days, such as the massacres at Babi Yar, perpetrated by the *Orpo* Reserve Battalion 45, and at Rumbula, by Battalion 22, reinforced by local *Schutzmannschaften* (auxiliary police) (Robertson 2008; see also Browning 1998, 135–6, 141–2). The *SS* brigades, wrote historian Christopher Browning, were "only the thin cutting edge of German units that became involved in political and racial mass murder" (Browning 1998, 10).

Many *Einsatzgruppe* leaders were highly educated; for example, nine of seventeen leaders of *Einsatzgruppe A* held doctorate degrees (Longerich 2010, 186), one of whom (*SS-Gruppenführer Juris Dr.* Emil Otto Rasch) held a double doctorate in law and political economy (Browning & Matthäus 2004, 225–6).

Additional *Einsatzgruppen* were created as additional territories were occupied. *Einsatzgruppe E* operated in Independent State of Croatia under three commanders, *SS-Obersturmbannführer* Ludwig Teichmann, *SS-Standartenführer* Günther Herrmann, and lastly *SS-Standartenführer* Wilhelm Fuchs. The unit was subdivided into five *Einsatzkommandos* located in Vinkovci, Sarajevo, Banja Luka, Knin, and Zagreb (MacLean 1999, 23; see also Simon Wiesenthal Center staff 1987). *Einsatzgruppe F* worked with Army Group South (Museum of Tolerance). *Einsatzgruppe G* operated in Romania, Hungary, and Ukraine, commanded by *SS-Standartenführer* Josef Kreuzer (MacLean 1999, 23). *Einsatzgruppe H* was assigned to Slovakia (Longerich 2010, 419). *Einsatzgruppen K* and *L*, under *SS-Oberführer* Emanuel Schäfer and *SS-Standartenführer* Ludwig Hahn, worked alongside Fifth and Sixth Panzer Armies during the Ardennes Counteroffensive (Dams and Stolle 2012, 168). Hahn had previously been in command of *Einsatzgruppe Griechenland* in Greece (Conze et al. 2010).

Other *Einsatzgruppen* and *Einsatzkommandos* included *Einsatzgruppe Iltis* (operated in Carinthia on the border between Slovenia and Austria) under *SS-Standartenführer* Paul Blobel (Crowe 2007, 267), *Einsatzgruppe Jugoslawien* (Yugoslavia) (Mallmann and Cüppers 2006, 97), *Einsatzkommando Luxemburg* (Luxembourg) (Museum of Tolerance), *Einsatzgruppe Norwegen* (Norway) commanded by *SS-Oberführer* Franz Walter Stahlecker (Larsen 2008, xi), *Einsatzgruppe Serbien* (Yugoslavia) under *SS-Standartenführer* Wilhelm Fuchs and *SS-Gruppenführer* August Meysner (Shelach 1989, 1169), *Einsatzkommando Tilsit* (Lithuania, Poland) (Longerich 2010, 197), and *Einsatzgruppe Tunis* (Tunis), commanded by

SS-Obersturmbannführer Walter Rauff (Mallmann, Cüppers, and Smith 2010, 130).

After the invasion of the Soviet Union on 22 June 1941, the *Einsatzgruppen*'s main assignment was to kill civilians, as in Poland, but this time its targets specifically included Soviet Communist Party commissars and Jews (Rees 1997, 177). In a letter dated 2 July 1941, Heydrich communicated to his *SS* and police leaders that the *Einsatzgruppen* were to execute all senior and middle ranking Comintern officials; all senior and middle ranking members of the central, provincial, and district committees of the Communist Party; extremist and radical Communist Party members; people's commissars; and Jews in party and government posts. Open-ended instructions were given to execute "other radical elements (saboteurs, propagandists, snipers, assassins, agitators, etc.)." He instructed that any pogroms spontaneously initiated by the population of the occupied territories were to be quietly encouraged (Longerich 2012, 523).

On 8 July 1941, Heydrich announced that all Jews were to be regarded as partisans and gave the order for all male Jews between the ages of 15 and 45 to be shot (Longerich 2010, 198). On 17 July Heydrich ordered that the *Einsatzgruppen* were to kill all Jewish Red Army prisoners of war, plus all Red Army prisoners of war from Georgia and Central Asia, as they too might be Jews (Hillgruber 1989, 97). Unlike in Germany, where the Nuremberg Laws of 1935 defined as Jewish anyone with at least three Jewish grandparents, the *Einsatzgruppen* defined as Jewish anyone with at least one Jewish grandparent; in either case, whether or not the person practiced the religion was irrelevant (Hilberg 1985, 368). The unit was also assigned to exterminate Romani people and the mentally ill. It was common practice for the *Einsatzgruppen* to shoot hostages (Headland 1992, 62–70).

As the invasion began, the Germans pursued the fleeing Red Army, leaving a security vacuum. Reports surfaced of Soviet guerrilla activity in the area, with local Jews immediately suspected of collaboration. Heydrich ordered his officers to incite anti-Jewish pogroms in the newly occupied territories (Urban 2001). Pogroms, some of which were orchestrated by the *Einsatzgruppen*, broke out in Latvia, Lithuania, and Ukraine (Longerich 2012, 526). Within the first few weeks of Operation Barbarossa, forty pogroms led to the deaths of 10,000 Jews, and by the end of 1941 some sixty pogroms had taken place, claiming as many as 24,000 victims (Haberer 2001, 68; see also Longerich 2012, 526). However, *SS-Brigadeführer* Franz Walter Stahlecker, commander of *Einsatzgruppe A*, reported to his superiors in mid-October 1941 that the residents of Kaunas were not spontaneously starting pogroms, and secret assistance by the Germans was required (Longerich 2010, 193–5). A similar reticence was noted by *Einsatzgruppe B* in Russia and Belarus and *Einsatzgruppe C* in Ukraine; the further east the *Einsatzgruppen* travelled, the less likely the residents were to be prompted into killing their Jewish neighbors (Longerich 2010, 208).

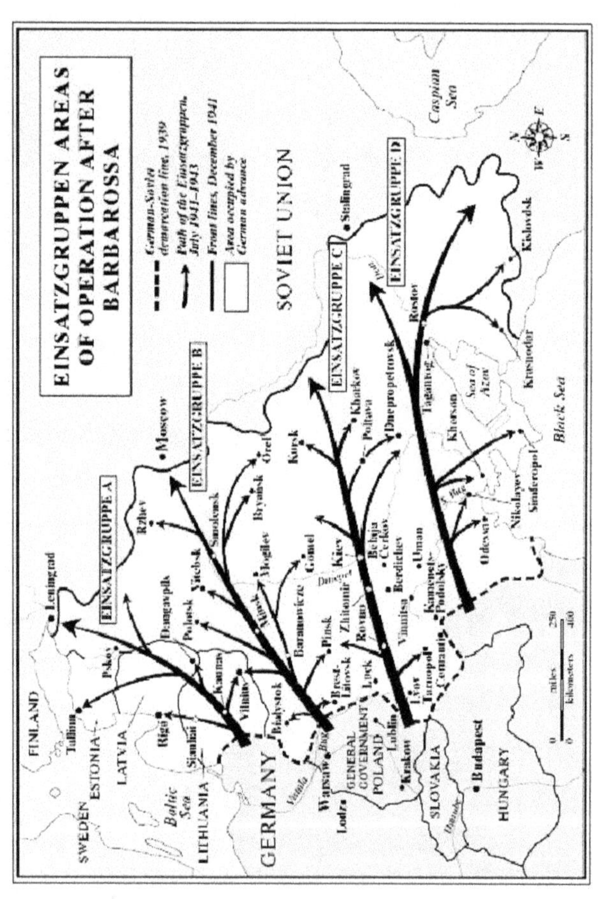
EINSATZGRUPPEN AREAS OF OPERATION AFTER BARBAROSSA
German-Soviet demarcation line, 1939
Path of the Einsatzgruppen, July 1941–1943
Front lines, December 1941
Area occupied by German advance
SOVIET UNION
EINSATZGRUPPE A
EINSATZGRUPPE B
EINSATZGRUPPE C
EINSATZGRUPPE D
FINLAND
SWEDEN
ESTONIA
LATVIA
LITHUANIA
Baltic Sea
GERMANY
GENERAL GOVERNMENT
POLAND
SLOVAKIA
HUNGARY
Black Sea
Sea of Azov
Caspian Sea
Leningrad
Tallinn
Pskov
Riga
Kaunas
Vilnius
Minsk
Smolensk
Moscow
Rzhev
Orel
Kursk
Bryansk
Mogilev
Gomel
Vitebsk
Polotsk
Pinsk
Bialystok
Warsaw
Lodz
Lublin
Krakow
Lvov
Tarnopol
Rovno
Zhitomir
Kiev
Berdichev
Vinnitsa
Uman
Kharkov
Poltava
Dnepropetrovsk
Stalingrad
Rostov
Taganrog
Kherson
Nikolayev
Odessa
Simferopol
Krasnodar
Kislovodsk
Budapest
Vistula
Bug
Dnieper
Danube
miles
kilometers

All four main *Einsatzgruppen* took part in mass shootings from the early days of the war (Longerich 2010, 196–202). Initially the targets were adult Jewish men, but by August the net had been widened to include women, children, and the elderly—the entire Jewish population. Initially there was a semblance of legality given to the shootings, with trumped-up charges being read out (arson, sabotage, black marketeering, or refusal to work, for example) and victims being killed by a firing squad. As this method proved too slow, the *Einsatzkommandos* began to take their victims out in larger groups and shot them next to, or even inside, mass graves that had been prepared. Some *Einsatzkommandos* started to use automatic weapons, with survivors being killed with a pistol shot (Longerich 2010, 207).

As word of the massacres got out, many Jews fled; in Ukraine, seventy to ninety percent of the Jews ran away. This was seen by the leader of *Einsatzkommando VI* as beneficial, as it would save the regime the costs of deporting the victims further east over the Urals (Longerich 2010, 208, 211). A situation report from *Einsatzgruppe C* in September 1941 noted that not all Jews were members of the Bolshevist apparatus and suggested that the total elimination of Jewry would have a negative impact on the economy and the food supply. The Nazis began to round their victims up into concentration camps and *ghettos* and rural districts were for the most part rendered *Judenfrei* (free of Jews) (Longerich 2010, 211–12). Jewish councils were set up in major cities and forced labor gangs were established to make use of the Jews as slave labor until they were totally liquidated, a goal that was postponed until 1942 (Longerich 2010, 212–13).

The *Einsatzgruppen* used public hangings as a terror tactic against the local population. An *Einsatzgruppe B* report, dated 9 October 1941, described one such hanging. Due to suspected partisan activity near Demidov, all male residents aged fifteen to fifty-five were put in a camp to be screened. The screening produced seventeen people who were identified as "partisans" and "Communists." Five members of the group were hanged while 400 local residents were assembled to watch; the rest were shot (Headland 1992, 57–8).

The largest mass shooting perpetrated by the *Einsatzgruppen* took place on 29 and 30 September 1941 at Babi Yar, a ravine northwest of Kyiv, a city in Ukraine that had fallen to the Germans on 19 September (Rhodes 2002, 179; Evans 2008, 227). The perpetrators included a company of *Waffen-SS* attached to *Einsatzgruppe C* under *SS-Gruppenführer* Juris Dr. Emil Otto Rasch, members of *Sonderkommando 4a* under *SS-*

Obergruppenführer Friedrich Jeckeln, and some Ukrainian auxiliary police (Weale 2012, 315). The Jews of Kyiv were told to report to a certain street corner on 29 September; anyone who disobeyed would be shot. Since word of massacres in other areas had not yet reached Kyiv and the assembly point was near the train station, they assumed they were being deported. People showed up at the rendezvous point in large numbers, laden with possessions and food for the journey (Rhodes 2002, 172–3).

After being marched two miles northwest of the city center, the victims encountered a barbed wire barrier and numerous Ukrainian police and German troops. Thirty or forty people at a time were told to leave their possessions and were escorted through a narrow passageway lined with soldiers brandishing clubs. Anyone who tried to escape was beaten. Soon the victims reached an open area, where they were forced to strip, and then were herded down into the ravine. People were forced to lie down in rows on top of the bodies of other victims, and they were shot in the back of the head or the neck by members of the execution squads (Rhodes 2002, 173–6).

The murders continued for two days, claiming a total of 33,771 victims (Evans 2008, 227). Sand was shoveled and bulldozed over the bodies and the sides of the ravine were dynamited to bring down more material (Rhodes 2002, 178). Anton Heidborn, a member of *Sonderkommando 4a*, later testified that three days later there were still people alive among the corpses. Heidborn spent the next few days helping smooth out the "millions" of banknotes taken from the victims' possessions (Weale 2012, 317). The clothing was taken away, destined to be reused by German citizens (Rhodes 2002, 178). Jeckeln's troops shot more than 100,000 Jews by the end of October 1941 (Evans 2008, 227).

Einsatzgruppe A operated in the formerly Soviet-occupied Baltic states of Estonia, Latvia, and Lithuania. According to its own reports to Himmler, *Einsatzgruppe A* killed almost 140,000 people in the five months following the invasion: 136,421 Jews, 1,064 Communists, 653 people with mental illnesses, fifty-six partisans, forty-four Poles, five Romani, and one Armenian were reported killed between 22 June and 25 November 1941 (Hillgruber 1989, 98).

Upon entering Kaunas, Lithuania on 25 June 1941, the *Einsatzgruppe* released the criminals from the local jail and encouraged them to join the pogrom which was underway (Rhodes 2002, 41). Between 23–27 June 1941, 4,000 Jews were killed on the streets of Kaunas and in nearby open pits and ditches (Haberer 2001, 67–8). Particularly active in the Kaunas pogrom was the so-called "Death Dealer of Kaunas," a young man who murdered Jews with a crowbar at the Lietukis Garage before a large crowd that cheered each killing with much applause; he occasionally paused to play the Lithuanian national anthem *Tautiška giesmė* on his accordion before resuming the killings (Haberer 2001, 67–8; Rees 1997, 179).

As *Einsatzgruppe A* advanced into Lithuania, it actively recruited local Nationalists and anti-Semitic groups. In July 1941, members of the *Baltaraisciai* movement joined the massacres (Haberer 2001, 68). A pogrom in Riga in early July killed 400 Jews. Latvian Nationalist Viktors Arājs and his supporters undertook a campaign of arson against synagogues (Haberer 2001, 68–9). On 2 July, *Einsatzgruppe A* commander Stahlecker appointed Arājs to head the *Arājs Kommando* (Haberer 2001, 68), a *Sonderkommando* of about 300 men, mostly university students. Together, *Einsatzgruppe A* and the *Arājs Kommando* killed 2,300 Jews in Riga on 6–7 July (Haberer 2001, 68–9). Within six months, Arājs and his men would kill about half of Latvia's Jewish population (Haberer 2001, 69).

Local officials, the *Selbstschutz*, and the *Hilfspolizei* (Auxiliary Police) played a key role in rounding up and massacring Jewish Lithuanians, Latvians, and Estonians (Haberer 2001, 71). These groups helped the *Einsatzgruppen* and other killing units to quickly identify Jews (Haberer 2001, 71). The *Hilfspolizei*, consisting of auxiliary police organized by the Germans and recruited from former Latvian Army and police officers, ex-*Aizsargi*, members of the *Pērkonkrusts*, and university students, assisted in the murder of Latvia's Jewish citizens (Haberer 2001, 69). Similar units were created elsewhere and provided much of the manpower for the Holocaust in Eastern Europe (Haberer 2001, 69–70).

With the creation of units such as the *Arājs Kommando* and the *Rollkommando Hamann* in Lithuania (Haberer 2001, 70), the attacks changed from the spontaneous mob violence of the pogroms to more systematic massacres (Haberer 2001, 69). With extensive local help, *Einsatzgruppe A* was the first *Einsatzgruppe* to attempt to systematically exterminate all the Jews in its area (Rees 1997, 182; Haberer 2001, 71). Latvian historian Modris Eksteins wrote:

> Of the roughly 83,000 Jews who fell into German hands in Latvia, not more than 900 survived; and of the more than 20,000 Western Jews sent into Latvia, only some 800 lived through the deportation until liberation. This was the highest percentage of eradication in all of Europe. (Haberer 2001, 66.)

In late 1941, the *Einsatzkommandos* settled into headquarters in Kovno, Riga, and Tallinn. *Einsatzgruppe A* grew less mobile and faced problems because of its small size. The Germans relied increasingly on the *Arājs Kommando* and similar groups to perform massacres of Jews (Haberer 2001, 70).

Such extensive and enthusiastic collaboration with the *Einsatzgruppen* has been attributed to several factors. Since the Russian Revolution of 1905, the *Kresy Wschodnie*—the eastern part of the Second Polish Republic during the interwar period constituting nearly half of the territory of the state—and other borderlands had experienced a political culture of violence (Haberer 2001, 73). The period of Soviet rule had been profoundly traumatic for residents of the Baltic states and areas that had been part of Poland until 1939; the population was brutalized and terrorized by the imposed Soviet rule, and the existing familiar structures of society were destroyed (Haberer 2001, 74–5).

Russian and European historian Dr. Erich Haberer notes that many survived and made sense of the "totalitarian atomization" of society by seeking conformity with Communism (Haberer 2001, 76). As a result, by the time of the German invasion in 1941, many had come to see conformity with a totalitarian regime as socially acceptable behavior; thus, people simply transferred their allegiance to the German regime when it arrived (Haberer 2001, 76). Some who had collaborated with the Soviet regime sought to divert attention from themselves by naming Jews as collaborators and killing them (Haberer 2001, 77).

Most Nazi collaborators in the East, however, suffered tremendously under Soviet collectivization and Stalin's first Five-Year Plan (1928–1932). Millions starved to death or lost nearly every means they had to sustain themselves. This was particularly true in Ukraine and in regions populated with Ukrainians—Kuban, the North Caucasus, Lower Volga, and Kazakhstan—where an estimated ten million Ukrainians (seven million in Ukraine alone) starved to death between 1932 and 1933. This period has come to be known as the Holodomor. When the Nazis arrived in 1941, they were welcomed by many as liberators. What they did not realize was the fact that Nazis viewed all Slavs as *Untermensch* (subhuman) and planned to subjugate them even worse than the Soviets did.

In November 1941, Himmler was dissatisfied with the pace of the exterminations in Latvia, as he intended to move Jews from Germany into the area. He assigned *SS-Obergruppenführer* Jeckeln, one of the perpetrators of the Babi Yar massacre, to liquidate the Riga *ghetto*. Jeckeln selected a site about ten kilometers (6.2 mi) southeast of Riga near the Rumbula railway station and had 300 Russian prisoners of war prepare the site by digging pits in which to bury the victims. Jeckeln organized around 1,700 men, including 300 members of the *Arājs Kommando*, fifty German *SD* men, and fifty Latvian guards, most of whom had already participated in mass killings of civilians. These troops were supplemented by Latvians, including members of the Riga city police, battalion police, and *ghetto* guards. Around 1,500 able-bodied Jews would be spared execution so their slave labor could be exploited; 1,000 men were relocated to a fenced-off area within the *ghetto* and 500 women were temporarily housed in a prison and later moved to a separate nearby *ghetto*, where they were put to work mending uniforms (Rhodes 2002, 206–9).

Although Rumbula was on the rail line, Jeckeln decided that the victims should travel on foot from Riga to the execution ground. Trucks and buses were arranged to carry children and the elderly. The victims were told that they were being relocated and were advised to bring up to twenty kilograms (44 lb) of possessions. The first day of executions, 30 November 1941, began with the perpetrators rousing and assembling the victims at 4:00 a.m. The victims were moved in columns of a thousand people toward the execution ground. As they walked, some *SS* men went up and down the line, shooting people who could not keep up the pace or who tried to run away or rest (Rhodes 2002, 208–10).

When the columns neared the prepared execution site (around 9:00 a.m.), the victims were driven some 270 meters (300 yards) from the road into the forest, where any possessions that had not yet been abandoned were seized. Here, the victims were split into groups of fifty and taken deeper into the forest, near the pits, where they were ordered to strip. The victims were driven into the prepared trenches, made to lie down, and shot in the head or the back of the neck by members of Jeckeln's bodyguard. Around 13,000 Jews from Riga were killed at the pits that day, along with 1,000 Jews from Berlin who had just arrived by train. On the second day of executions, 8 December 1941, the remaining 10,000 Jews of Riga were killed in the same way. About 1,000 were killed on the streets of the city or on the way to the site, bringing the total deaths for the two-day extermination to 25,000 people. For his part in organizing the massacre, Jeckeln was promoted to Leader of the *SS* Upper Section, *Ostland* (Rhodes 2002, 210–14).

Einsatzgruppe B, C, and *D* did not immediately follow *Einsatzgruppe A*'s example in systematically killing all Jews in their areas. The *Einsatzgruppe* commanders, with the exception of *Einsatzgruppe A*'s

Stahlecker, were of the opinion by the fall of 1941 that it was impossible to kill the entire Jewish population of the Soviet Union in one sweep, and thought the killings should stop (Hilberg 1985, 342). An *Einsatzgruppe* report, dated 17 September 1941, advised that the Germans would be better off using any skilled Jews as laborers rather than shooting them (Hilberg 1985, 342). Also, in some areas poor weather and a lack of transportation led to a slowdown in deportations of Jews from points further west (Longerich 2012, 549). Thus, an interval passed between the first round of *Einsatzgruppen* massacres in summer and fall 1941, and what American historian Raul Hilberg called the second sweep, which started in December 1941 and lasted into the summer of 1942 (Hilberg 1985, 342–3). During the interval, the surviving Jews were forced into *ghettos* (Marrus 2000, 64).

Einsatzgruppe A had already murdered almost all Jews in its area, so it shifted its operations into Belarus to assist *Einsatzgruppe B*. In Dnepropetrovsk in February 1942, *Einsatzgruppe D* reduced the city's Jewish population from 30,000 to 702 over the course of four days (Hilberg 1985, 372). The German Order Police (*Ordnungspolizei* or *Orpo*) and local collaborators provided the extra manpower needed to perform all the shootings. Haberer wrote that, as in the Baltic states, the Germans could not have killed so many Jews so quickly without local help. He points out that the ratio of *Orpo* to auxiliaries was one to ten in both Ukraine and Belarus. In rural areas, the proportion was one to twenty. This meant that most Ukrainian and Belarusian Jews were killed by fellow Ukrainians and Belarusians commanded by German officers rather than by Germans (Haberer 2001, 78).

The second wave of exterminations in the Soviet Union met with armed resistance in some areas, though the chance of success was poor. Weapons were typically primitive or homemade. Communications were impossible between *ghettos* in various cities, so there was no way to create a unified strategy. Few in the *ghetto* leadership supported resistance for fear of reprisals on the *ghetto* residents. Mass breakouts were sometimes attempted, though survival in the forest was nearly impossible due to the lack of food and the fact that escapees were often tracked down and killed (Longerich 2010, 353–4).

After a time, Himmler found that the killing methods used by the *Einsatzgruppen* were inefficient: they were costly, demoralizing for the troops, and sometimes did not kill the victims quickly enough (Rees 1997, 197). Many of the troops found the massacres to be difficult if not impossible to perform. Some of the perpetrators suffered physical and mental health problems, and many turned to drink (Rhodes 2002, 52, 124, 168). As much as possible, the *Einsatzgruppen* leaders militarized the genocide. The historian Christian Ingrao notes an attempt was made to make the shootings a collective act without individual responsibility. Framing the shootings in this way was not psychologically sufficient for every perpetrator to feel absolved of guilt (Ingrao 2013, 199–200). Browning notes three categories of potential perpetrators: those who were eager to participate right from the start, those who participated in spite of moral qualms because they were ordered to do so, and a significant minority who refused to take part (Rhodes 2002, 163). A few men spontaneously became excessively brutal in their killing methods and their zeal for the task. Commander of *Einsatzgruppe D*, *SS-Gruppenführer* Otto Ohlendorf, particularly noted this propensity towards excess, and ordered that any man who was too eager to participate or too brutal should not perform any further executions (Rhodes 2002, 165–6).

During a visit to Minsk in August 1941, Himmler witnessed an *Einsatzgruppen* mass execution first-hand and concluded that shooting Jews was too stressful for his men (Longerich 2012, 547–8). By November, he arranged for any *SS* men suffering ill health from having participated in executions to be provided with rest and mental health care (Rhodes 2002, 167). He also decided a transition should be made to gassing the victims, especially the women and children, and ordered the recruitment of expendable native auxiliaries who could assist with the murders (Rhodes 2002, 167; Longerich 2012, 551). Gas vans, which had been used previously to kill mental patients, began to see service by all four main *Einsatzgruppen* from 1942 (Longerich 2012, 548). However, the gas vans were not popular with the *Einsatzkommandos*, because removing the dead bodies from the van and burying them was a horrible ordeal. Prisoners or auxiliaries were often assigned to do this task so as to spare the *SS* men the trauma (Rhodes 2002, 243). Some of the early mass killings at extermination camps used carbon monoxide fumes produced by diesel engines, similar to the method used in gas vans, but by as early as September 1941 experiments were begun at Auschwitz using *Zyklon B*, a cyanide-based pesticide gas (Longerich 2010, 280–1).[1]

Plans for the total eradication of the Jewish population of Europe—eleven million people—were formalized at the Wannsee Conference, held on 20 January 1942. Some would be worked to death, and the rest would be killed in the implementation of the Final Solution of the Jewish question (*Die Endlösung der Judenfrage*) (Longerich 2012, 555–6). Permanent killing centers at Auschwitz, Bełżec, Sobibór, Treblinka, and other Nazi extermination camps replaced mobile death squads as the primary method of mass killing (Longerich 2010, 279–80). The *Einsatzgruppen* remained active, however, and were put to work fighting partisans, particularly in Belarus (Rhodes 2002, 248).

After the fall of Stalingrad in February 1943, Himmler realized that Germany would likely lose the war, and through Reinhard Heydrich ordered the formation of a special task force, *Sonderkommando 1005*, under *SS-Standartenführer* Paul Blobel. The unit's assignment was to visit mass graves all along the Eastern Front to exhume bodies and burn them in an attempt to cover up the genocide—*Sonderaktion 1005* (Special Action 1005), also called *Enterdungsaktion* (Exhumation Action). The task remained unfinished at the end of the war, and many mass graves remain unmarked and unexcavated (Rhodes 2002, 258–60, 262).

By 1944, the Red Army had begun to push the German forces out of Eastern Europe, and the *Einsatzgruppen* retreated alongside the *Wehrmacht*. By late 1944, most *Einsatzgruppen* personnel had been folded into *Waffen-SS* combat units or transferred to permanent death camps. American historian Raul Hilberg estimates that between 1941 and 1945 the *Einsatzgruppen* and related agencies killed more than two million people, including 1.3 million Jews (Rhodes 2002, 257). The total number of Jews murdered during the war is estimated at 5.5 to six million people (Evans 2008, 318).

According to research by German historians Klaus-Michael Mallmann and Martin Cüppers, an *Einsatzgruppe* was created in 1942 to kill the half-million Jews living in the British Mandate of Palestine and the 50,000 Jews of Egypt. *Einsatzgruppe Egypt*, standing by in Athens, was prepared to go to Palestine once German forces arrived there (Mallmann, Cüppers & Smith 2010, 130). *SS-Obersturmbannführer* Walter Rauff was to lead the unit (Mallmann, Cüppers & Smith 2010, 118). Given its small staff of only twenty-four men, *Einsatzgruppe Egypt* would have needed help from local residents and from the *Afrika Korps* to complete their assignment. Its members planned to enlist collaborators from the local Arab population to perform the killings under German leadership (Mallmann, Cüppers & Smith 2010, 124–5). Former Iraqi prime minister Rashid Ali al-Gaylani and the Grand Mufti of Jerusalem Haj Amin al-Husseini played roles, engaging in anti-Semitic radio propaganda, preparing to recruit volunteers, and in raising an Arab-German Battalion that would also follow *Einsatzgruppe Egypt* to the Middle East (Mallmann, Cüppers & Smith 2010, 127–30). On 20 July

1942, Walther Rauff, who was responsible for the unit, was sent to Tobruk to report to Field Marshal Erwin Rommel, Commander of the *Afrika Korps*. However, since Rommel was 500 kilometers away at the First Battle of El Alamein, it is unlikely that the two were able to meet (Mallmann, Cüppers & Smith 2010, 103, 117–8). The plans for *Einsatzgruppe Egypt* were set aside after the Allied victory at the Second Battle of El Alamein (23 October–11 November 1942) (Krumenacker 2006). Historian Jean-Christophe Caron opines that there is no evidence that Rommel knew of or would have supported Rauff's mission (Caron 2007).

Had Operation Sealion, the German plan for an invasion of the United Kingdom been launched, six *Einsatzgruppen* were scheduled to follow the invasion force into Britain. They were provided with a list called *die Sonderfahndungsliste, G.B.* ("Special Search List, G.B."), known as *The Black Book* after the war, of 2,300 people to be immediately imprisoned by the *Gestapo*. The list included Churchill, members of the cabinet, prominent journalists and authors, and members of the Polish and Czechoslovak governments-in-exile (Shirer 1960, 783–4).

The *Einsatzgruppen* kept official records of many of their massacres and provided detailed reports to their superiors. The Jäger Report, filed by Commander *SS-Standartenführer* Karl Jäger on 1 December 1941 to his superior, Stahlecker (head of *Einsatzgruppe A*), covers the activities of *Einsatzkommando III* in Lithuania over the five-month period from 2 July 1941 to 25 November 1941 (Rhodes 2002, 215).

Jäger's report provides an almost daily running total of the liquidations of 137,346 people, the vast majority of them Jews (Rhodes 2002, 215). The report documents the exact date and place of massacres, the number of victims, and their breakdown into categories (Jews, Communists, criminals, and so on) (Rhodes 2002, 126). Women were shot from the very beginning, but initially in fewer numbers than men (Longerich 2010, 230). Children were first included in the tally starting in mid-August, when 3,207 people were murdered in Rokiškis on 15–16 August 1941 (Rhodes 2002, 126). For the most part, the report does not give any military justification for the killings; people were killed solely because they were Jews (Rhodes 2002, 126). In total, the report lists over 100 executions in 71 different locations. Jäger wrote: "I can state today that the goal of solving the Jewish problem in Lithuania has been reached by *Einsatzkommando 3*. There are no more Jews in Lithuania, apart from working Jews and their families" (Rhodes 2002, 215). In a February 1942 addendum to the report, Jäger increased the total number of victims to 138,272, giving a breakdown of 48,252 men, 55,556 women, and 34,464 children. Only 1,851 of the victims were non-Jewish (Rhodes 2002, 216).

Jäger escaped capture by the Allies when the war ended. He lived in Heidelberg under his own name until his report was discovered in March 1959 (Rabitz 2011). Arrested and charged, Jäger committed suicide on 22 June 1959 in a Hohenasperg prison while awaiting trial for his crimes (Rhodes 2002, 276).

Another infamous *Einsatzgruppe* leader was Heinz Jost. Heinz Jost (1904–1964) was born in the northern Hessian village of Homberg (Efze), District Holzhausen—32 km (20 mi) northwest of Hersfeld—in 1904 to a middle-class Catholic and Nationalist family. Heinrich Jost, Heinz's father, was a pharmacist and later became a fellow *NSDAP* member. Heinz attended grammar school in Bensheim, graduating in 1923. As a student he became a member, and eventually a leader, of the *Jungdeutsche Orden* (Young German Order), a Nationalist paramilitary movement. Heinz studied law and economics at the Universities of Giessen and Munich. He completed his civil service examination in May 1927. Heinz's legal career began as a legal civil servant employed in Hesse. He later worked in the district court at Darmstadt.

Jost joined the Nazi Party on 2 February 1928 (Earl 2009, 512–14) with an *NSDAP* membership number of 75,946. He performed various functions for the party's operations in southern Hesse. From 1930, he worked as an independent lawyer in Lorsch, Hesse. After the Nazi seizure of power in March 1933, Jost was appointed Director of Police in the city of Worms (Rhine-Hesse) and then to police director of Giessen, Hesse. During this time, Jost became associated with Werner Best, who eventually brought Jost into the main Nazi intelligence and security agency, the *Sicherheitsdienst* (*SD*). On 25 July 1934, Jost began his full-time career with the *SD*. His *SS* membership number was 36,243. In May 1936, Jost was promoted in the *SD* Main Office to head Department III 2 (Foreign Intelligence Services) ("CV of Jost" in *SS Record Jost*, no. 2896, in Trial, roll 11, frame 0525; see also Browder 1996, 201). In 1938, Jost was head of the *Einsatzgruppe Dresden* which operated in Czechoslovakia (Reitlinger 1957, 117, 138, 145). In August 1939, Jost was tasked by Reinhard Heydrich with obtaining the Polish uniforms needed for the false flag attack on the station in Gleiwitz (*Unternehmen Großmutter gestorben*, Operation Grandmother Died) (Williams 2003, 9).

When the *Reich* Main Security Office (*RSHA*) was organized in September 1939, Jost was appointed Chief of *Amt VI* (Office VI) *Ausland-*

SD (foreign intelligence) (Weale 2012, 140–4; see also Reitlinger 1957, 117, 138, 145). One of the chief purposes of *Amt VI* was to counteract foreign intelligence services that might try to operate in Germany (Kahn 2000, 59). He also served as *SS-Brigadeführer* in the German invasion of Poland in 1939 (Earl 2009, 512–14).

Jost's career suffered by being linked with Werner Best, who was a rival of Reinhard Heydrich. Best lost the power struggle with Heydrich, who went on to become one of the most powerful men in the Nazi state. In March 1942, Jost was fired from his position as Chief of *Ausland-SD* (Doerries 2007, 21, 80; see also Reitlinger 1957, 117, 138, 145). Jost's place was taken by *SS-Brigadeführer* Walter Schellenberg, a deputy of Heydrich. Heydrich had given Schellenberg the task of building up a case for Jost's removal (Doerries 2007, 21, 80). According to Schellenberg, Jost was lacking in bureaucratic skill and drive.

> The general inefficiency of this Amt and the failure of Brigadeführer Heinz Jost in his capacity as chief, to both control his subordinates and manage the department's affairs was common knowledge. In an illuminating pen-picture Jost has been described by Schellenberg as a worn-out, tired, lazy individual lacking initiative or the will to work, who was active at the most for three or four hours a day. During these hours he read a few reports, which he mostly passed on without appreciation or criticism and permitted a small number of individual [advisors] who had often been waiting weeks for an interview, to bring various matters before him. Because of his inability to say "no," Schellenberg says, his subordinates worked without direction needlessly duplicating their work. (Doerries 2007, 21, 80.)

In March 1942, Jost was sent to command *Einsatzgruppe A*, whose previous commander Franz Walter Stahlecker, had recently been killed in a battle with partisans on 23 March 1942. *Einsatzgruppe A* was then operating in the Baltic States and in Belarus. Jost became *Befehlshaber der Sicherheitspolizei und des SD* (Commander of the Security Police and the *SD*) or *BdS in Reichskommissariat Ostland*, with his headquarters at Riga. Jost retained this position until September 1942. According to Jost, this position carried substantial responsibility:

> During my activity as Chief of the Einsatzgruppe A, I was also Commander in Chief of the Security Police and SD in East land (BdS Ostland). Headquarters for the Einsatzgruppe A was located in Krasnogvardeisk, while headquarters for the Commander in Chief for the Security Police and SD Eastland was located in Riga. On the whole, the duties of a Commander in Chief of the Security Police and SD were the same as those of a Chief of an Einsatzgruppe, and the duties of a Commander of the Security Police and SD (KdS) the same as those of a Chief of a Sonderkommando or Einsatzkommando, respectively. (Earl 2009, 512–14.)

While the territory under his jurisdiction was subject to army control, Jost as Chief of *Einsatzgruppe A* cooperated with the army command. When the territory came under civilian administration, he, as Commander in Chief of Security Police and *SD* received his orders from the Higher *SS* and Police Leader Friedrich Jeckeln. In both cases, Jost was responsible for all operations conducted in his territory (Earl 2009, 512–14).

After his *Einsatzgruppe* command, Jost was able to secure a position with the occupation administration for the eastern territories that was run by Alfred Rosenberg, where he acted as a liaison officer between Rosenberg and the *Wehrmacht*'s commander-in-chief of *Heeresgruppe* (Army Group) *A* in southern Russia, *Generalfeldmarschall* Paul Ludwig Ewald von Kleist. At his later trial, Jost claimed that he held this position until May 1944, when as a result of enmity from Heinrich Himmler, he was forced to enlist with the *Waffen-SS* as a second lieutenant (Earl 2009, 512–14; Reitlinger 1957, 117, 138, 145). Himmler decided in January 1945 that Jost should be retired from the *SS* with a pension.

In April 1945, *SS-Brigadeführer* Jost was arrested in Gardelegen, in Saxony-Anhalt. He was eventually charged with murders committed by *Einsatzgruppe A* and was together with his fellow 23 officers of the *Einsatzgruppe* brought before the U.S. Nuremberg Military Tribunal for trial number nine, *Einsatzgruppen* Trial (officially, *The United States of America vs. Otto Ohlendorf, et al.*) held from 29 September 1947 to 10 April 1948 before justices John J. Speight, Michael A. Musmanno (presiding judge), and Richard D. Dixon. Jost tried to avoid responsibility for these crimes by claiming that the murders, or at least some of them, occurred before he came into the command of the unit:

> The prosecution charges the defendant with responsibility for these murders. The item itself does not carry the exact date of its happening, but the latest date revealed in the entire document is 26 March. Thus the execution of the 1,272 persons mentioned therein could not have occurred on a date subsequent to 26 March. The defendant testified that he was in Smolensk when, on 24 or 25 March he received his orders to take over the command of *Einsatzgruppe A* and that he did not arrive in Riga, headquarters of the *Einsatzgruppe*, until 28 and 29 March. (Earl 2009, 512–14.)

This defense was rejected by the tribunal:

> The record shows that *Einsatzgruppe A* had accomplished some hundred thousand murders prior to 29 March and, as late as 26 March as indicated by the report above-mentioned, was still killing Jews. It would be extraordinary that it should suddenly cease this slaughter for no given reason and with the Fuehrer Order still in effect, three days before Jost arrived. . . . The record clearly demonstrates, however, that as Chief of *Einsatzgruppe A*, the defendant was aware of the criminal purpose to which that organization was put, and, as its commander, cannot escape responsibility for its acts. (Earl 2009, 512–14.)

Jost also claimed, through his attorney, that whatever he had done was justified by "self-defense, necessity, and national emergency." He claimed further that he had had nothing to do with carrying out the *Führer* Order (*Führerbefehl*) for the extermination of entire populations. These claims were rejected by the tribunal as being inconsistent with each other: "If, as a matter of fact, the defendant committed or approved of no act which could be interpreted either as a war crime or crime against humanity, the argument of self-defense and necessity is entirely superfluous" (Earl 2009, 512–14).

Jost did testify that when in May 1942 he received an order from Heydrich to surrender Jews under sixteen-years and over thirty-two-years for liquidation, he placed the order in his safe and declined to transmit it. The tribunal found that the evidence contradicted him. According to *Einsatzgruppen* status report number 193, dated 17 April 1942, there was an execution in Kovno (Kaunas, Lithuania) on 7 April 1942 of twenty-two persons "among them 14 Jews who had spread Communist propaganda."

> The defendant was asked on the witness stand—"Do you regard it proper, militarily proper, to shoot fourteen people, or only one person for that matter, because he spreads Communist propaganda?" and he replied—"According to my orders these measures had to be carried out. In that far it was correct and justified." Defense counsel in arguing this phase of the case said that the victims had indulged in Communist propaganda "up to the last moment." But there is nothing in international law which justifies or legalizes the sentence of death for political opinion or propaganda. (Earl 2009, 512–14.)

In addition, the U.S. Nuremberg Military Tribunal found that on 15 June 1942 one of Jost's subordinates wrote to the *RSHA* requesting shipment of a gas van (used by *Einsatzgruppen* for executions by means of carbon monoxide asphyxiation) and gas hoses for three gas vans on hand. Jost denied any knowledge of this letter but admitted that the subordinate in question had the authority to order equipment. (Earl 2009, 512–14.)

In the end, the three-judge panel sentenced Jost to life imprisonment. His sentence was later reviewed by the controversial "Peck Panel."* Based on the recommendations of the Peck Panel, Jost's sentence was commuted to ten years. In 1951, after only six-year's imprisonment, Jost was released from Landsberg Prison due to an amnesty law passed by the new West German *Bundestag*. He then worked in Düsseldorf as a real estate agent and died in 1964 at Bensheim.

The killings by *Einsatzgruppen* took place with the knowledge and support of the German Army in the East (Hillgruber 1989, 102). On 10 October 1941, Field Marshal Walther von Reichenau drafted an order to be read to the German Sixth Army on the Eastern Front. Now known as the Severity Order, it read in part:

> The most important objective of this campaign against the Jewish-Bolshevik system is the complete destruction of its

---

* See section "AMNESTY TO OPPOSE COMMUNISM," in the last chapter of this book, *infra*.

> sources of power and the extermination of the Asiatic influence in European civilization . . . In this eastern theater, the soldier is not only a man fighting in accordance with the rules of the art of war, but also the ruthless standard bearer of a national conception . . . For this reason, the soldier must learn fully to appreciate the necessity for the severe but just retribution that must be meted out to the subhuman species of Jewry (Craig 1973, 10).

Field Marshal Gerd von Rundstedt of Army Group South expressed his "complete agreement" with the order. He sent out a circular to the generals under his command urging them to release their own versions and to impress upon their troops the need to exterminate the Jews (Mayer 1988, 250). General Erich von Manstein, in an order to his troops on 20 November 1941, stated that "the Jewish-Bolshevist system must be exterminated once and for all" (Hillgruber 1989, 102). Von Manstein sent a letter to *Einsatzgruppe D* commanding officer Ohlendorf complaining that it was unfair that the *SS* was keeping all of the murdered Jews' wristwatches for themselves instead of sharing with the army (Smelser and Davies 2008, 43).

Beyond this trivial complaint, the *Wehrmacht* and the *Einsatzgruppen* worked closely and effectively. On 6 July 1941, *Einsatzkommando 4b* of *Einsatzgruppe C* reported that "Armed forces surprisingly welcome hostility against the Jews" (Hilberg 1985, 301). Few complaints about the killings were ever raised by *Wehrmacht* officers (Wette 2007, 131). On 8 September 1941, *Einsatzgruppe D* reported that relations with the German Army were "excellent" (Hilberg 1985, 301). In the same month, Stahlecker of *Einsatzgruppe A* wrote that Army Group North had been exemplary in cooperating with the exterminations and that relations with the Fourth Panzer Army, commanded by General Erich Hoepner, were "very close, almost cordial" (Hilberg 1985, 130). In the south, the Romanian Army worked closely with *Einsatzgruppe D* to massacre Ukrainian Jews (Marrus 2000, 64), killing around 26,000 Jews in the Odessa massacre (Marrus 2000, 79). German historian Peter Longerich thinks it is probable that the *Wehrmacht*, along with the Organization of Ukrainian Nationalists (*OUN*), incited the Lviv pogroms, during which 8,500 to 9,000 Jews were killed by the native population and *Einsatzgruppe C* in July 1941 (Longerich 2010, 194). Moreover, most people on the home front in Germany had some idea of the massacres being committed by the *Einsatzgruppen* (Marrus 2000, 88). British historian Hugh Trevor-Roper noted that although Himmler had forbidden photographs of the killings, it was common for both the men of the *Einsatzgruppen* and for bystanders to take pictures to send to their loved ones, which he felt suggested widespread approval of the massacres (Klee, Dressen, and Riess 1991, xi).

Officers in the field were well aware of the killing operations being conducted by the *Einsatzgruppen* (Wette 2007, 200–1). The *Wehrmacht* tried to justify their considerable involvement in the *Einsatzgruppen* massacres as being anti-partisan operations rather than racist attacks, but Hillgruber wrote that this was just an excuse. He states that those German generals who claimed that the *Einsatzgruppen* were a necessary anti-partisan response were lying and maintained that the slaughter of about 2.2 million defenseless civilians for reasons of racist ideology cannot be justified (Hillgruber 1989, 102–3).

During the Second World War, the Nazis conducted the majority of the genocide against the Jews by deporting them to death camps, located mostly in Poland and operated by a separate division of the *SS* known as *SS-Totenkopfverbände* (*SS-TV*, "death's head formations"). To differentiate themselves from ordinary *SS* units wearing the *Totenkopf* (skull) insignia on their caps, the *SS-TV* wore an additional death's head insignia on their right collar. Poland was chosen by Himmler and his deputy Reinhard Heydrich for a number of reasons. Upon the outbreak of the war in September 1939, the Nazis established camps in Poland for prisoners of war and political prisoners captured in Operation *Fall Weiß*. Due to its central location in the East and strong rail infrastructure connecting many international rail lines, Poland was deemed ideal initially for POW camps and later for labor and extermination camps. Moreover, Poland had the largest Jewish population of any nation in Europe making their transport logistically more convenient. Finally, the complete isolation and encirclement of Poland by occupying forces and the fact that Polish control over organs such as the press, governmental and non-governmental institutions, radio and telegraphic communications, rail, and roads, etc. was so effectively and systematically dismantled and taken over by the Nazis and Soviets that any news of prisoner executions in Poland would face great obstacles in reaching the West. During the invasion of the Soviet Union in June 1941 (Operation Barbarossa), however, the murder was local. Because of the region's inadequate railway systems and the limited capacities of the extermination camps in Poland, the Nazis were unable to easily transport the Jews westward to the camps. Instead, mobile execution units, *Einsatzgruppen I-VII*, that followed *Wehrmacht* army units performed "clean-up" operations by gathering and executing the Jews *en masse* on their home soil. Villages became execution sites and villagers became witnesses. After the executions, the *Einsatzgruppen* buried their victims in mass ditches and continued on to the next village. With bodies and bullets beneath the ground, the perpetrators left behind little indication of the crimes that had occurred.

After the Wannsee Conference on 20 January 1941, Reinhard Heydrich envisioned the need to destroy the evidence of the mass murders. He designed *Sonderaktion 1005* (Special Action 1005), also called *Enterdungsaktion* (Exhumation Action), to redress the buried evidence left by the *SS-Einsatzgruppen* and death camp *Sonderkommandos*. The action plan was to begin in May 1942 in occupied Poland but was delayed until June 1942 due to Heydrich's assassination. The special action, which was conducted in strict secrecy from 1942–1944, was overseen by selected squads from the *Sicherheitspolizei* (*SiPo*) and *Ordnungspolizei* (*Orpo*) and used prisoners to exhume mass graves and burn the bodies. These work groups were officially called *Leichenkommandos* ("corpse units"); inmates were often put in chains in order to prevent escape and then executed upon completion of their work. In May 1943, the operation moved into occupied territories deep in Eastern Europe to destroy the evidence of massacres, as well as to erase the most incriminating evidence of extermination operations in the death camps as Soviet forces approached in 1944.

Knowledge of the murders was limited mostly to the Nazis and the local neighbors that watched or participated. Traumatized and fearful, few of these witnesses spoke about what they had seen. Because of their silence and the lack of visible evidence, there existed over the decades after the war little record of the mass murder that occurred.

Father Patrick Desbois is a Catholic priest and President of *Yahad–In Unum*, a global humanitarian organization he founded in 2004 dedicated to identifying and commemorating the sites of Jewish and Roma mass executions in Eastern Europe during the Second World War. *Yahad–In Unum* identifies mass Jewish killing sites and collects forensic evidence of the executions. Their team videotapes eyewitness testimonies to these killings. To date, *Yahad* has effectuated research concerning 1,902 execution sites and has gathered 4,748 testimonies during the course of its 111 investigative research trips in seven countries (Ukraine, Belarus, Russia, Poland, Romania, Moldova, and Lithuania).

Ternopil, Ukraine was the site of several infamous massacres of the local Jewish population, some of which the local non-Jews participated in. In 1939, there were approximately 18,000 Jews in Ternopil. A few days after

Ternopil was occupied by the German army in July 1941, 5,000 Jews were massacred over eight days. Moreover, the Germans fined the Jewish community 1,500,000 rubles. Sixty-three Jews belonging to the intelligentsia in Ternopil were invited to the local *Gestapo* on the pretext of receiving public appointments but were all murdered in the *Gestapo* office. The *ghetto* established in Ternopil in September 1941 was the first to be set up in Galicia. Over 12,500 people were crowded into a small area. The *ghetto* inmates were gradually murdered; on 25 March 1942, 1,000 Jews were shot in the nearby forest. Thousands of Jews were seized in the streets or taken from their homes for forced labor at camps in the Ternopil district. On 29–31 August 1942, over 4,000 Jews from Ternopil were sent to the Bełżec death camp just north of Lviv. On 30 September 1942, a further 1,000 Jews were sent there. During the following winter, the remaining able-bodied Jews were separated and put into a labor camp near the *ghetto*. The final liquidation of the *ghetto* took place on 20 June 1943, followed by that of the nearby work camp on 6 August 1943. Small numbers of Jews fought from bunkers or joined the partisan fighters in the district. By the end of the war, only 350 Jews remained in Ternopil.

In 1939, the 1,353 Jews of Lypovets comprised nearly fifty-three percent of the town's inhabitants. The town was occupied by German troops on 23 July 1941. Soon after the start of the occupation, the German authorities imposed various restrictions on the Jewish population: e.g., they were forbidden to leave their homes during certain hours and forced to wear white armbands with blue Stars of David. By September 1941, about 200 Jewish men and young boys were shot, while the majority of the town's remaining Jews were murdered in 1942.

On 16 and 22 September 1941, two mass shootings of Jews occurred in Vinnytsia by the Eleventh *SS* Panzer Army's *Einsatzgruppe D* (responsible for 91,728 murders between 1941 and 1943 and comprised in part of Ukrainian militia). A third mass shooting of Jews brought to the town from outside Vinnytsia district followed shortly thereafter. In total, 34,000 Jews from Vinnytsia and its surrounding area were executed. The now infamous photograph known as *Last Jew of Vinnitsa* was taken during these executions.

Preceding these massacres was another infamous mass execution in Vinnytsia during Joseph Stalin's Great Purge in 1937–1938. This time, mostly ethnic Ukrainians were shot by the Soviet secret police (*NKVD*). In July 1943—ironically, near the conclusion of Nazi genocide in the same region—91 mass graves were discovered at three different locations in

Vinnytsia, and 9,432 bodies were exhumed: 149 of them women. Investigation of the three sites first conducted by the international Katyn Commission (comprised of experts in anatomy and forensic pathology from eleven European countries and formed in April 1943 under request by Germany to investigate the Katyn massacre) coincided with the discovery of a similar mass murder site of Polish prisoners of war in Katyn Forest. Because the Germans utilized this evidence, albeit hypocritically, of Communist terror to discredit the Soviet Union internationally, it became one of the better researched sites of the politically motivated *NKVD* massacres among many in Ukraine.

(For postwar prosecution of members of the *Einsatzgruppen*, see Chapter 65, section "MILITARY TRIALS, THE BERLIN BLOCKADE, & REPERCUSSIONS," *infra*.)

ANYONE FAMILIAR WITH CZECHOSLOVAK HISTORY KNOWS THAT THE independence and establishment of this country in 1918 was neither a miracle, a gift, nor a result of chance, but rather the fruit of hard work, perseverance, healthy optimism, and an indestructible hope. No one freed the Czechs and the Slovaks. These people freed themselves. Many generations of national leaders kept alive the Czechoslovak culture, identity, and spirit. For a thousand years, the Slovak people had been dominated and oppressed by autocratic Hungary. From 1620, Austria had dominion over all Czech lands (Bohemia and Moravia). But this would not always be so. During the First World War, many intellectuals, professors, literati, and military leaders escaped abroad or deserted the Austro-Hungarian Army and either organized their own movement or joined the Entente Powers. Later, they formed separate legions and fought under the Czechoslovak flag. Regardless of the consequences, they raised their weapons against Austro-Hungarian tyranny and the Central Powers in the name of freedom. Many gave their lives at Terron in France, on the Piave River and the heights of Doss Alto in Italy, and at Zborov and Bakhmach in the Ukraine. The climax of their long and difficult struggle was reached when they framed their declaration of independence on 28 October 1918, in Prague, and on 30 October 1918, in Turčanský Svätý Martin in Slovakia, less than a month before the end of that horrible war.

On their way back to Sambor, Vlčko had the driver stop at a large sign which read "ZBOROV."

"Why are we stopping?" one of the soldiers asked.

"We're going to see the place where our fathers gave their lives for our liberty twenty-four years ago, at Zborov."

The road led southward to a small Ukrainian village named Cecová (now known as Kalynivka in Zboriv district, Ternopil region). Here, an event took place that was talked about throughout Europe and from the Ukraine to beyond the Urals, all the way to the Pacific. In these gold wheat fields the Czechoslovak Legion fought their way to glory.

The Battle of Zborov was a part of the Kerensky Offensive, (the last Imperial Russian Army offensive in World War I) beginning on 1 July 1917. The battle was the first significant action of the Czechoslovak Legion, originally in 1914 known as the *Družina* and then in 1916 the Czechoslovak Rifle Brigade (*Československá střelecká brigáda*), on the Eastern Front and the only successful action of the failed Kerensky Offensive in Ukraine. The volunteer Czechoslovak Rifle Brigade, formed from three regiments (about 3,500 men) of Czechs and Slovaks recently paroled from Russian prisoner of war camps, fought against four well-entrenched and well-equipped infantry regiments (totaling 12,000 men) of the Austro-Hungarian Army. The brigade was commanded by Russian Colonel Vjačeslav Platonovič Trojanov, but the tactical assault plan was prepared by Czech and Slovak officers serving in the First Czechoslovak Legion. The brigade was low on equipment and training. Moreover, this was the first use of the brigade as a single formation. At 0515 hours on 2 July 1917, after an initial artillery bombardment, small groups of Legionnaires equipped with grenades attacked the enemy. At 0800 hours, the main wave of the attack began. After they breached the barbed wire defenses, follow-up units continued with the attack. By 1500 hours, the Legion had advanced deep into enemy territory, breaking through the enemy's entire trench line. The Czechoslovak Legionnaires proved their bravery to the whole world. Determined to win or fall, they launched an attack almost without ammunition, with bayonets and hand grenades—and they gained a victory over an enemy vastly superior in numbers. Russian General Brusiloff declared: "The Czecho-Slavs, perfidiously abandoned at Tarnopol by our infantry, fought in such a way that the world ought to fall on its knees before them."

The official communiqué from Russian Army Headquarters the following day on 3 July 1917 read:

> On 2 July, at about three o'clock in the afternoon, after a severe and stubborn battle, the gallant troops of the Czecho-

Slavic Brigade occupied the strongly fortified enemy position on the heights to the west and southwest of the village of Zborov and the fortified village of Koroszylow. Three lines of enemy trenches were penetrated. The enemy has retired across the Little Strypa. The Czecho-Slavic Brigade captured 62 officers and 3,150 soldiers, 15 guns and many machine guns. Many of the captured guns were turned against the enemy.

The Zborov monument, built on the spot where 195 Czechoslovak heroes are buried, is constructed in the form of a Russian *Zemlyanka* (earth-house), or hut. On one side is a tablet with the Czech inscription:

> *Zde, na staré slovanské půdě vedle Zborova, spí synové Československa, kteří padli za svobodu, mír, za lepší budoucnost všech slovanských národů. Věčná jim sláva 2. VII. 1917* [Here on ancient Slavic ground near Zborov, rest the sons of Czechoslovakia, who died for freedom, peace, for a better future for all Slavic nations. Eternal glory to them. 2 July 1917]

Peter and his group paid their respect with a salute and a moment of silence. After gazing across the wide, rolling fields of Cecová, fields which had witnessed the decimation of the Austro-Hungarian defensive lines by the Czechoslovaks, he gave the word for them to get back in the truck. Slowly, they returned to the main road. Peter thought how ironic it was that they were now fighting the Russians, who had helped his nation to gain its freedom in the First World War. He wondered who would stop and salute his grave if he were to die in this war fighting with the Germans against his Slavic brothers.

Part Four

PERIL AND FEAR HIT HOME

THE YEAR 1942 WAS A TURNING POINT IN THE WAR BOTH militarily and politically. The seemingly invincible German military machine marching east had finally hit a wall with the defeat at Stalingrad by the end of the year. The Germans had successfully fought nearly a thousand miles across the Soviet Union to get to Stalingrad. But having conquered most of European Russia, this was as far as they would reach into the territory of their enemy. They would spend the next twenty-seven months making a fighting retreat all the way back to the center of Berlin. The first signs of cracks in the German armor surfaced in late 1941 when for the first time in the war the German Army had to retreat when facing determined enemy forces at Rostov-on-Don during the Rostov Strategic Offensive Operation (17 November 1941 to 2 December 1941). This was the telltale sign of things to come.

On the political front, Germany and its Axis partners accelerated what had up until then been only token cooperation on the "Jewish Question." Legalized discrimination against Jews in Germany began immediately after the Nazi seizure of power in January 1933. Violence and economic pressure were used by the Nazi regime to encourage Jews to voluntarily leave the country. The ideology of Nazism brought together elements of anti-Semitism, racial hygiene, and eugenics and combined them with pan-Germanism and territorial expansionism with the goal of obtaining more *Lebensraum* (living space) for the Germanic people. Nazi Germany attempted to obtain this new territory by attacking Poland and the Soviet Union, intending to deport or exterminate the Jews and Slavs living there, who were viewed as being inferior to the Aryan master race.

Discrimination against Jews, long-standing, but extra-legal, throughout much of Europe at the time, was codified in Germany immediately after the Nazi seizure of power on 30 January 1933. The Law for the Restoration of the Professional Civil Service, passed on 7 April of that year, excluded most Jews from the legal profession and the civil service.

Similar legislation soon deprived Jewish members of other professions of the right to practice. Violence and economic pressure were used by the regime to force Jews to leave the country. Jewish businesses were denied access to markets, forbidden to advertise in newspapers, and deprived of access to government contracts. Citizens were harassed and subjected to violent attacks and boycotts of their businesses.

In September 1935, the Nuremberg Laws were enacted, prohibiting marriages between Jews and people of Germanic extraction, extramarital sexual relations between Jews and Germans, and the employment of German women under the age of forty-five years as domestic servants in Jewish households. The *Reich* Citizenship Law stated that only those of German or related blood were defined as citizens; thus, Jews and other minority groups were stripped of their German citizenship. A supplementary decree issued in November 1935 defined as Jewish anyone with three Jewish grandparents, or two grandparents if the Jewish faith was followed. By the start of the Second World War in 1939, around 250,000 of Germany's 437,000 Jews emigrated to the United States, Palestine, Great Britain, and other countries (Longerich 2010, 127).

After the invasion of Poland in September 1939, Hitler ordered that the Polish leadership and intelligentsia be destroyed. The *Sonderfahndungsbuch Polen* (Special Prosecution Book Poland)—lists of people to be killed—had been drawn up by the *SS* as early as May 1939. The *Einsatzgruppen* performed these murders with the support of the *Volksdeutscher Selbstschutz* (Germanic Self-Protection Group), a paramilitary group consisting of ethnic Germans living in Poland (Longerich 2010, 144–5). Members of the *SS*, the *Wehrmacht*, and the *Ordnungspolizei* (Order Police; *Orpo*) also shot civilians during the Polish campaign (Longerich 2012, 429). Approximately 65,000 civilians were killed by the end of 1939. In addition to leaders of Polish society, they killed Jews, prostitutes, Romani people, and the mentally ill (Evans 2008, 15; Longerich 2012, 430–2).

On 31 July 1941, Hermann Göring gave written authorization to *SS-Obergruppenführer* Reinhard Heydrich, Chief of the *Reich* Main Security Office (*RSHA*), to prepare and submit a plan for a "total solution of the Jewish question" in territories under German control and to coordinate the participation of all involved government organizations (Browning and Matthäus 2004, 315). The resulting *Generalplan Ost* (General Plan for the East) called for deporting the population of occupied Eastern Europe and the Soviet Union to Siberia, for use as slave labor or to be murdered (Snyder

2010, 416). The minutes of the Wannsee Conference estimated the Jewish population of the Soviet Union to be five million, including nearly three million in Ukraine (Roseman 2002, 112).

In addition to eliminating Jews, the Nazis also planned to reduce the population of the conquered territories by thirty million people through starvation in an action called the Hunger Plan devised by Herbert Backe (Tooze 2006, 476–86, 538–49). Food supplies would be diverted to the German Army and German civilians. Cities would be razed, and the land allowed to return to forest or resettled by German colonists (Snyder 2010, 162–3, 416). The objective of the Hunger Plan was to inflict deliberate mass starvation on the Slavic civilian populations under German occupation (Tooze 2006, 669). According to historian Timothy Snyder, "4.2 million Soviet citizens (largely Russians, Belarusians, and Ukrainians) were starved" by the Nazis in 1941–1944 as a result of Backe's plan (Gerhard 2009, 57–62; see also Snyder 2010, 411).

Harvests were poor in Germany in 1940 and 1941 and food supplies were short, as large numbers of forced laborers had been brought into the country to work in the armaments industry (Tooze 2006, 539). If these workers—as well as the German people—were to be adequately fed, there had to be a sharp reduction in the number of "useless mouths," of whom the millions of Jews under German rule were, in the light of Nazi ideology, the most obvious example (Tooze 2006, 538–49).

Among Axis partners to Germany, Slovakia was the first and most eager participant seeking a solution to the "Jewish Question." Slovakia was the only country that paid Germany, and by their own proposal as early as 1939 before Germany had any logistical plan or means, to remove its Jewish population. In September 1941, Slovakia codified the most comprehensive anti-Jewish laws (Jewish Codex, *Židovský kódex*) in the world—exceeding those in Germany and Italy.

At the time of the Wannsee Conference (20 January 1942), the killing of Jews in the Soviet Union had already been underway for some months. Right from the start of Operation Barbarossa, *Einsatzgruppen* were assigned to follow the army into the conquered areas and round up and kill Jews. In a letter dated 2 July 1941, Heydrich communicated to his *SS* and Police Leaders that the *Einsatzgruppen* were to execute Comintern officials, ranking members of the Communist Party, extremist and radical Communist Party members, people's commissars, and Jews in party and government posts (Longerich 2012, 523). Open-ended instructions were given to execute "other radical elements (saboteurs, propagandists, snipers, assassins, agitators, etc.)" (Longerich 2012, 523). He instructed that any pogroms spontaneously initiated by the occupants of the conquered territories were to be quietly encouraged (Longerich 2012, 523). On 8 July, he announced that all Jews were to be regarded as partisans and gave the order for all male Jews between the ages of fifteen and forty-five years to be shot (Longerich 2010, 198). By August 1941, the net had been widened to include women, children, and the elderly—the entire Jewish population (Longerich 2010, 207). By the time planning was underway for the Wannsee Conference, hundreds of thousands of Polish, Serbian, and Russian Jews had already been killed (Longerich 2010, 309). The initial plan was to implement *Generalplan Ost* after the conquest of the Soviet Union (Snyder 2010, 416; Kershaw 2008, 683). European Jews would be deported to occupied parts of Russia, where they would be worked to death in road-building projects (Longerich 2010, 309).

On 29 November 1941, Heydrich sent invitations for a ministerial conference to be held on 9 December at the offices of Interpol at 16 Am Kleinen, Wannsee, Germany (Roseman 2002, 57). He changed the venue on 4 December to the eventual location of the meeting (Roseman 2002, 57). He enclosed a copy of a letter from Göring, dated 31 July, that authorized him to plan a so-called "Final Solution to the Jewish Question." The ministries to be represented were Interior, Justice, the Four-Year Plan, Propaganda, and the *Reich* Ministry for the Occupied Eastern Territories (Browning and Matthäus 2004, 406).

Between the date the invitations to the conference went out (29 November) and the date of the cancelled first meeting (9 December), the situation changed. On 5 December 1941, the Soviet Army began a counteroffensive near Moscow ending the prospect of a rapid conquest of the Soviet Union. On 7 December 1941, the Japanese attacked the United States at Pearl Harbor causing the U.S. to declare war on Japan the next day. The *Reich* government declared war on the U.S. on 11 December. Some invitees were involved in these preparations, so Heydrich postponed his meeting (Browning and Matthäus 2004, 407). Somewhere around this time, Hitler resolved that the Jews of Europe were to be exterminated immediately, rather than after the war, which now had no end in sight (Longerich 2000). At the *Reich* Chancellery meeting of 12 December 1941, he met with top party officials and made his intentions plain (Browning and Matthäus 2004, 407–8). On 18 December, Hitler discussed the fate of the Jews with Himmler in the *Wolfsschanze* (Dederichs 2009, 119). Following the meeting, Himmler made a note on his service calendar, which simply stated: "Jewish question/to be destroyed as partisans" (Dederichs 2009, 119).

Transporting masses of people into a combat zone during large-scale military operations was impossible. Thus, Heydrich decided that the Jews currently living in the General Government (the German-occupied area of Poland) would be killed in extermination camps set up back in occupied areas of Poland, as would Jews from the rest of Europe (Longerich 2010, 309–10).

On 8 January 1942, Heydrich sent new invitations to a meeting to be held on 20 January (Browning and Matthäus 2004, 410). The venue for the rescheduled conference was a villa at 56–58 Am Großen, Wannsee, overlooking the *Großer Wannsee* just northeast of Potsdam, Germany.

The Wannsee Conference lasted only about ninety minutes. Heydrich did not call the meeting to make fundamental new decisions on the Jewish question. Massive killings of Jews in the conquered territories in the Soviet Union and Poland were ongoing, and a new extermination camp was already under construction at Bełżec (southeastern Poland) at the time of the conference; other extermination camps were in the planning stages (Breitman 1991, 229–33; see also Longerich 2010, 309). The decision to exterminate the Jews had already been made, and Heydrich, as Himmler's emissary, held the meeting to ensure the cooperation of the various departments in conducting the deportations (Longerich 2010, 310). Observations from historian Laurence Rees support Longerich's position that the decision over the fate of the Jews was determined before the conference; Rees notes that the Wannsee Conference was really a meeting of "second-level functionaries," and stresses that neither Himmler, Goebbels, nor Hitler were present (Rees 2017, 251–2). According to Longerich, a primary goal of the meeting was to emphasize that once the deportations had been completed, the implementation of the "Final Solution" became an internal matter of the *SS*, totally outside the purview of any other agency (Longerich 2000, 14). A secondary goal was to determine the scope of the deportations and arrive at definitions of who was Jewish, who was *Mischling*, and who (if anybody) should be spared (Longerich 2000, 14). "The representatives of the ministerial bureaucracy had made it plain that they had no concerns about the principle of deportation per se. This was indeed the crucial result of the meeting and the main reason why Heydrich had detailed minutes prepared and widely circulated," said Longerich (Longerich 2000, 306, 310). Their presence at the meeting also ensured that all those present were accomplices and accessories to the murders that were about to be undertaken (Longerich 2000, 7).

Eichmann's biographer David Cesarani agrees with Longerich's interpretation; he notes that Heydrich's main purpose was to impose his own authority on the various ministries and agencies involved in Jewish policy matters, and to avoid any repetition of the disputes that had arisen earlier in the annihilation campaign. "The simplest, most decisive way that Heydrich could ensure the smooth flow of deportations," he writes, "was by asserting his total control over the fate of the Jews in the Reich and the east, and [by] cow[ing] other interested parties into toeing the line of the RSHA" (Cesarani 2005, 110–11).

The Jewish Telegraphic Agency (New York) reported on anti-Semitic activities in Slovakia throughout the war. Headlines of just some communiqués describing the events that directly confronted Peter Vlčko and Georgina Reichsfeld were as follows:

- 23 June 1939: Jews to Be Purged from Slovak Army
- 10 July 1939: Slovakia Orders Jews, Aliens to Register Realty by 29 August
- 8 September 1939: Jews and Hungarians Barred from Slovak Military Draft Order
- 7 July 1940: Slovakia Takes Licenses from 1,600 Jewish Firms
- 30 August 1940: Slovakia Mandates Inventory of Jewish Property by 16 September (Law number 203/1940)
- 4 September 1940: Slovakia Bans Jews From Education in Public and Private High Schools
- 14 September 1940: Slovak Jews Have Eight Days to Surrender Their Passports to Government Officials (Law number 215/1940), and Are Prohibited from Driving Motor Vehicles (Law number 216/1940)
- 25 September 1940: 850 Slovak Jews from Prešov Sent to Labor Camp Near Liptov
- 20 November 1940: Slovakia Reported Planning Ban on Inter-Racial Marriage
- 26 March 1941: Slovakia Liquidates 4,100 Jewish Firms Between February 1 and March 15
- 22 May 1941: Jews Ousted from Trade in Slovakia Called Back As 'advisers' to Prevent Complete Breakdown of the Slovak Economy

- 18 August 1941: Total of 7,400 Jewish Enterprises Liquidated to date in Slovakia
- 25 August 1941: Slovakia Releases Jewish Doctors from Camps to Attend Wounded German Soldiers Returning from Russian Front
- 26 August 1941: Jews in Slovakia Evicted from Their Homes
- 2 September 1941: Jewish Property in Slovakia to Be Taxed 25% for Establishment of "Emigration Fund"
- 9 September 1941: Slovak Parliament ratifies the Jewish Codex (*Židovský kódex*) containing 270 articles over 60 pages affecting nearly 90,000 Jews in Slovakia.
- 10 September 1941: Jews Barred from All Theatres, Restaurants, Exhibitions, and Places of Entertainment in Slovakia
- 28 October 1941: Slovakia Will Deport 11,500 Jews from Bratislava to Ghettos in Sereď, Nováky, and Orgulas
- 4 November 1941: 15-hour Curfew Imposed on Jews in Slovakia in Preparation for Wholesale Expulsions
- 7 December 1941: Slovakia Promulgates More Anti-Jewish Laws: Jews Forbidden to Use Telephone
- 17 December 1941: 9,851 Jewish Businesses Confiscated to Date by Slovak Government
- **15 March 1942: Slovakia Deports Jews from "Ghetto Towns" into Nazi-held Galicia**
- 10 April 1942: Arrest of All Outstanding Jewish Central Office Leaders in Slovakia Announced in Nazi Press
- 17 April 1942: German Priests in Slovakia Threatened with Punishment for Baptizing Jews to Save Them from Deportation
- 21 April 1942: Government and Church Battle in Slovakia over Baptizing Jews
- 14 May 1942: Vatican Reported to Have Intervened for Jews in Slovakia
- 18 May 1942: Slovakia Deports 5,000 Jews to Hungary, Hundreds Die in Woods Escaping Raids
- 19 May 1942: Slovak Parliament Approves [retroactive] Bill to Expel All Jews from Country (Law no. 68/1942)

CHAPTER 25

THE ENGAGEMENT

AFTER PETER'S DEPARTURE FOR THE FRONT, LIFE AT THE REICHSFELDS continued without incident. Georgina continued her studies at Madame Green's Sewing School. Her father still had his job at Riunione Adriatica di Sicurtà Insurance Company, which, although Italian owned, was already controlled by the Slovak State. Reichsfeld felt fairly safe with his firm since Jews had not yet been excluded from this enterprise. However, this apparent security did not last long.

On 15 July 1941, Minister of the Interior Alexander Mach issued an edict that no Jews would be allowed in any public place of gathering, including, baths, swimming pools, restaurants, bars, sports events, or parks; they would have to do all their shopping before ten in the morning; they would not be permitted on the streets after nine o'clock at night. They would also be forbidden to have any contacts with non-Jews. The purpose of these restrictions was to further isolate and demoralize them. Most of those affected by this edict observed it closely, but there were, or course, some who completely ignored it, including a segment of the non-Jewish community accompanying Jews. New, more severe restrictions followed soon. All Jews had to move to designated areas of Bratislava within a matter of weeks. Hviezdoslav Square was one of the off-limit areas. Thus, the Reichsfelds moved to their new address, 22 Röhmish Street in Ružinov, a Bratislava suburb.

The house, on the northeast edge of the city, belonged to an elderly Czech pensioner named Nedavaška. It was a grim building consisting of a small apartment on the main floor where the owner lived, and another slightly larger apartment on the lower level that the Reichsfelds occupied. Though their new place had only two tiny rooms and a kitchen, the rent was as high as their more modern apartment in the center of Bratislava. Opportunists exploited desperate Jews whenever they could.

This change did not affect Georgina greatly, for she was young, strong willed, and overcame hardships rather easily. Peter's constant letters from Ukraine helped tremendously. She also had a good friend and close companion in her dog, Peggy.

Georgina, however, remained unaware of the real problem her family faced. Her parents would not tell her their troubles; there was nothing she could do about them anyway other than needlessly worry. They did not want to destroy the little happiness she still enjoyed or to crush the hopes she nurtured. She did not know her father had been dismissed from the insurance company and was now supporting his family as best he could, hustling odd jobs here and there along with the help of his wife who bore these vicissitudes bravely.

The first step he took to ease their financial crisis was to rent their back room to a trio of Bulgarian students. Instead of three people living in two rooms, there were now six. Despite the overcrowded and hectic atmosphere, the students brought a measure of good cheer and youthful zest for life. These feelings at times cheered the Reichsfelds. Instead of being depressed, they were able to smile and even laugh at times. Heart to heart talks and innocent socializing that the family and the students periodically shared led to a mutually warm and close friendship. It eventually reached the point where the Reichsfelds' suffering was also the students' suffering, and the students' hope and optimism became the Reichsfelds' own expectations.

THE CLOSE RELATIONSHIP BETWEEN JIRKA AND PETER WAS THEIR treasured secret. It was the fountain from which they drew their strength. Without each other, life would have little meaning. His letters from Ukraine were to Jirka the cool rain that falls on the hot, parched land after a summer drought. To Peter, they were an opportunity to use the conduit of love to escape the stress and tragedies of his surroundings.

One morning, Georgina's father came across one of Peter's letters that had carelessly been left on the nightstand next to her bed. From the contents of the letter, he learned of their past intimacy. This discovery enraged him. In order to save Georgina from her father's wrath, Mrs. Reichsfeld called her at school to tell her what had happened. She told her to be prepared for her father's anger when she comes home. Coincidentally, Peter returned to Bratislava the same day. Georgina tried contacting him by telephone.

"Peter, I'm in trouble. You have to help me," she said to him on the telephone, breaking into tears.

"What's happened, my love? Don't cry. Tell me about it." Peter tried to calm her.

"Father knows everything about us and now he wants to beat me up."

"How did he find out?"

"Mother told me he found and read all your letters."

"I was afraid something like that would happen. Where are you calling from now?"

"From home, but I'm very afraid of father's anger."

"All right. Just stay there for now. I'm going to explain everything to your father."

"He told mother he doesn't ever want to see you again or hear your name mentioned around the house."

"I'll write and tell him again exactly how I feel about you and what our plans are. Maybe if he sees it in writing he will believe me. I'll convince him he's wrong."

"All right, Peter, I trust you." Her sobs had subsided now. "But I haven't asked how you are. I wasn't even sure you'd be back from Russia when I called."

"I'm fine and glad to be home. I have a lot to tell you. I'm in one piece and I can't wait to see you, dearest. Don't worry about your father. He'll simmer down. Everything will be all right."

"When can I see you?"

"Tomorrow for sure. I have to write the letter first. I heard you're not allowed on the street after nine, and I doubt if I can be finished by then." It was ten minutes to six in the evening. Moreover, Peter still had something to do at the College. "I promise I'll see you tomorrow. My orderly will bring you a message to your school."

"All right, darling, until tomorrow." Relieved now, Jirka echoed his promise and hung up the phone.

16 August 1941

Dear *Pán* Reichsfeld,

Today, when I returned from Ukraine Jirka telephoned me. She was most upset. After I managed to calm her down, she told me you were going to punish her because you discovered in our letters what was sacred to us alone.

As you know, we met in January. Since then, in spite of some difficulties, a very strong love developed between us. Though there remain hurdles ahead, we made plans for our future and will not let anything separate us, for we expect to be married as soon as possible. If unreasonable laws had not stood in our way, we would have already been married.

The night before my departure for the Eastern Front I came over and explained my feelings to you. I wanted to wait until I returned to make a formal request for our engagement.

Now, man to man, tell me, what would you have done in the same situation, if you were in love with a woman, and she were very much in love with you, and you had to leave and might never return? Imagine that both of you wanted to keep in your heart a most beautiful remembrance of your mutual love. Would you have acted differently than me?

We are both adults and completely responsible for our actions.

Now that you know what we didn't just yet want to tell you, if you still consider our intimacy wrong, the only thing I can do is reaffirm my intentions. I love your daughter very much and hope she can become my wife soon with your blessings.

When and how we can marry remains a big question right now, but we're not going to wait forever. My word is as good as my name.

Pán Reichsfeld, please understand and help us to realize the happiness we both seek. At the same time, I beg you to forgive Jirka. She suffers enough without the added agony of a father's anger. Your blessing will set things right.

Awaiting your positive reply, I remain.

Yours, Peter.

He put the letter into an envelope, sealed it, and hurried to the main post office. To ensure there would be no delays, he sent it Express.

"If this doesn't work, nothing will. If Jirka's father continues to be angry over this, I'll have her move in with me and take care of her myself. I will not let anyone hurt her as long as I'm alive," Peter thought, as he returned to his apartment off the Central Passage.

After reading the letter, there were no actual words of forgiveness or apology on Mr. Reichsfeld's part, but his decision to say nothing was tantamount to accepting the facts as they now stood. Peter's departure for two weeks to Trenčín, where he was taking an air reconnaissance course, enabled Reichsfeld to cool down and view his prospective son-in-law in a different light. In time, he recognized his paternal authority had not been seriously damaged, and that Peter was after all an honest man, even if he did not like Peter.

BY THE END OF NOVEMBER 1941, WITH LIGHTNING SWIFTNESS THE German Army reached Moscow. As a dwindling food supply threatened Leningrad, besieged since September 1941, the city bravely held out for 832 days with nearly three and one-half million casualties. It ended up being one of the longest and most destructive sieges in history and possibly the costliest in terms of casualties. In Ukraine, Kharkov and Rostov-on-Don were occupied while Sevastopol, a strategically important port and naval base in Crimea, was surrounded. After taking Kerch Peninsula on the eastern edge of the Crimean Peninsula in May 1942 with Operation *Trappenjagd* ("Bastard Hunt"), the Germans prepared to strike all the way through the Caucasus in July 1942 with Operation *Edelweiß*. However, the onset of a Russian winter halted German advances in late 1942 and had, in fact, forced the Germans to retreat in some places by early 1943. Realizing German unpreparedness for the winter campaign, the Soviets began a series of strong counter-offensives in the Caucasus in January 1943.

On 14 August 1941, President Roosevelt met with Winston Churchill aboard the USS *Augusta* at Placentia Bay off the coast of Newfoundland. There, they agreed to a joint policy statement known as the Atlantic Charter defining the Allied goals for the postwar world, which contained the following eight points:

1. No territorial gains were to be sought by the United States or the United Kingdom.
2. Territorial adjustments must be in accord with the wishes of the peoples concerned.
3. All peoples had a right to self-determination.
4. International trade barriers were to be lowered.
5. There was to be global economic cooperation and advancement of social welfare.
6. Freedom from want and fear;
7. Freedom of the seas;
8. Disarmament of aggressor nations, postwar common disarmament.

On 19 September 1941, the Congress of the United States of America gave permission for all American merchant marine and transport ships to arm themselves for their own protection.

On 7 December 1941, Japan attacked the American Navy at Pearl Harbor, forcing the United States into the war.

On 11 December 1941, Germany and Italy declared war on the United States. They were later joined by Slovakia, Rumania, Bulgaria, and Hungary.

On 1 January 1942, the United States, along with twenty-six other countries, formed the Allied Nations. At the end of January 1942, the first American troops disembarked in Northern Ireland.

In the Far East, a well-armed and trained Japanese military was having great success. Aside from the victories in the Pacific, the Japanese were also making progress in China with whom they had been fighting since 1937.

Under the command of Field Marshal Erwin Rommel, the newly-formed German *Afrika Korps* began Operation *Sonnenblume* (Sunflower) in February 1941 as part of the greater North Africa Campaign to aid the remaining Italian forces in Libya after the Italian Tenth Army was destroyed by British attacks during Operation Compass (9 December 1940–9 February 1941). Rommel quickly began his eastward push across North Africa leading to the Siege of Tobruk, Libya (lasting 241 days) in mid-April 1941. While the Siege of Tobruk played out, Rommel reached the Egyptian-Libyan border at Sollum (El Salloum) on 14 April 1941, pressing Allied forces further into Egypt. Allied forces in Tobruk, however, remained recalcitrant. Without capturing the port at Tobruk, supply lines for the Axis forces ran thin and unsustainable. This prevented Axis forces from seriously penetrating into Egypt. The British attempted a series of minor counter-offenses in May 1941 (Operations Brevity and Battleaxe) that fell short in their goal of repelling Rommel's offensive. On 18 September 1941, a German air raid on Cairo killed thirty-nine Egyptian civilians with nearly an additional 100 injured. This brought immediate condemnation against the Axis from the Arab and Muslim press. Radio Berlin later apologized to its Arab listeners.

By mid-November 1941, the British Eighth Army began a counteroffensive known as Operation Crusader that rescued Tobruk and ultimately drove the Germans back to El Agheila in Libya and within forty-eight kilometers of Tobruk by the second week of January 1942. It was the first victory by British-led forces over German ground forces in the Second World War. The victory was short-lived, however. The ability of the Germans to shift resources to North Africa after stabilizing the Eastern Front in January 1942 and the diversion of British resources to meet the Japanese threat in the Pacific after 7 December 1941, enabled Rommel to launch a second offensive on 21 January 1942. Axis troops reached Al-Gazala, just west of Tobruk, within two weeks and pushed the British back into Egypt all the way to El Alamein by July 1942.

ON 9 SEPTEMBER 1941, SIX YEARS AFTER THE ENACTMENT OF THE Nuremberg Laws, the Slovak government promulgated Law Number 198/1941, titled "Regarding the Legal Standing of Jews" and commonly known as the "Jewish Codex" (*Židovský kódex*). This 270-article, 60-page law was the first major law of its kind in Slovakia and one of the most extensive and calculated set of anti-Jewish state codes in the world—even more so than in Germany or Italy. It included: The definition of a Jew or Jewish organization; the system of monitoring Jews (gold star); marriage and sexual intercourse between Jews and non-Jews; loss of voting rights; working in certain state jobs or professions such as medicine and law was prohibited; there were restrictions on education; Jews had to work only in jobs selected by the government; limitations were imposed on several other freedoms like freedom of privacy (house searches anytime without a warrant), freedom of press (only one Jewish organization was allowed to publish under tight regulation and oversight by the government); Jewish work products could not be sold or exhibited, including Jewish art (even

under a different name); Jewish intellectual property could not be incorporated into the economy (besides scientific achievements); even minor things were forbidden such as fishing, driving a car, riding a bicycle, or owning binoculars.

The majority of the 270 articles addressed the Aryanization process—nationalization and redistribution of Jewish property to non-Jews (which benefited many members and friends of the ruling party in Slovakia). There was also an article which enabled the President of the Slovak Republic to grant exemptions from the Codex law. The majority of those who applied and wrote a letter to the president was not granted an exception. Each of the restrictions of the Nuremberg Laws (especially the first law regarding the mixing of Jewish and German blood) was also included in the Slovak Jewish Codex. Naturally, as they emerged hundreds of other Nazi regulations served as inspiration for possibly the most horrifying law passed in Slovak history with the only exception being *ex post facto* Law Number 68/1942 (that will be addressed later).

"Berci, what are we going to do now?" Mrs. Reichsfeld asked her husband.

"There's nothing we *can* do. We'll just have to wear a gold star like everyone else."

"I won't wear one," said Georgina defiantly. "If the Nazis want to brand their cattle, that's their business, but they're not going to brand me! If I choose to wear the Star of David, I'll hang a gold one around my neck. Anyway, I don't think Peter would let me."

"Just be careful, Györgyi. Don't let your stubbornness get you into trouble even Peter won't be able to save you from," her father warned.

"No one will even know I'm supposed to wear a star if I don't allow them to intimidate me. But Apa, you can't afford to disobey this law. You're too well known. And Mama, whenever you're seen with Apa, you'll have to wear one, too. I think it would be safest if you only pinned the stars on, instead of sewing them. Then, if an occasion ever arose when you'd be better off without them, you could remove them quickly," Georgina advised.

"We'll know what we should do after we see how this new law is accepted by the public. But no good can come from it. There are going to be bad times ahead, you can be sure."

"Berci, you should've seen this coming a long time ago. Now it's too late. A couple of years ago we could've easily left the country like a lot of other people did, but then you were optimistic, or you just didn't want to leave your job."

"I didn't want to drag us somewhere into the unknown. I'm no adventurer. I was used to normal times and to reasonable laws. Who knew things would turn out so badly?"

"I would rather be dead than marked by shame." Georgina was adamant. She would stand up to the devil himself if necessary.

STIRRED BY THE DESIRE TO BE ENGAGED, PETER STOPPED AT A JEWELER'S and ordered a diamond ring for Jirka, to be ready no later than her birthday, 16 December 1941. Apprehensive that the order would not be filled in time, he returned two days prior to the celebration. The ring was ready. After inspecting it under a magnifying glass, Peter was thrilled by the stone's refracting glitter. The clerk set the ring in a velvet box and wrapped it in white paper with a turquoise ribbon. After paying him, Peter slipped the surprise package in his pocket while humming a few bars of Wagner's Bridal March.

On the following day, the eve of Jirka's birthday, he skipped supper and went directly from the college to a little flower shop where he bought a dozen red roses. The narcissi, the December flower, was not available. He hid the engagement ring box in the flower arrangement that he carried in his hand. Then, he headed for their rendezvous. As usual, Jirka was prompt.

"Hello, my love!" Peter exclaimed with great joy as if he had not seen her in years. They embraced, looked into each other's eyes and kissed.

"Peter, I have some good news."

"You do?"

"Mother told me today Father isn't opposed anymore to your coming by. She baked a cake. I want you to have some with us tonight to celebrate my birthday," Jirka said, flashing her most dazzling smile.

"That's great. Your father is finally softening a little. Let's hurry and catch this streetcar. I also have something I want to tell you." This time Peter was serious. He was prepared to make the most delicate decision of his life.

"What? Good or bad?" Jirka asked, overcome by curiosity as they mounted the tramway.

"I wanted to tell you a long time ago but be patient a little while longer. We can't talk here in public. Let's get off at the next stop. We can talk in the park."

In the little park behind Blumenthal Church, he looked for the most intimate spot he could find and then sat Jirka down on a bench and handed her the bouquet of roses.

"Oh, what beautiful flowers. Are they for me?"

"Of course. And look inside the flowers. You'll find something there."

Jirka found the small package, untied the ribbon, and carefully unwrapped the box.

"O-o-o-oh! How beautiful. What does this mean?"

Peter sat down beside her. After what seemed like minutes of looking into her eyes, he asked, "Do you want to be my wife?"

In complete surprise and shock by his proposal, she responded nearly in tears, "Yes! But it's impossible," as she remembered the Jewish Codex recently decreed.

"No worries! Everything will be okay." He pulled her yet closer to him and covered her lips with his. He embraced her until she gently had to hold him back to keep from being swept away by his passionate ardor.

"Careful, someone's coming," she said, and moved discreetly to her side on the bench.

"It's only another young couple, and they're not interested in us," he said reassuringly, and pulled her close again. "Today, I'm the happiest man alive because I know you're mine for always. Let's tell your parents. I don't want our love to be a secret from them anymore. I'll protect and love you the rest of my life."

"I feel dizzy hearing you talk so sweetly. My parents will be just as shocked as I am," Georgina maintained her apprehension over the worsening political atmosphere. Yet, her joy drowned any worries she harbored as she took a deep breath and passionately embraced Peter feeling all so distant from the uncertainties that surrounded them.

"We have to hurry. It's nearly seven, and supper will be ready." She put her arms through his and pulled him toward her once more as they stood from the park bench. Large snowflakes began to fall, as if heaven's inhabitants were showering confetti on their engagement. In truth, they would need all the support heaven would offer. Eyes laughing, they squeezed closer together, and quickened their pace. The snow fell faster now, covering the pavement and decorating the rooftops and cornices. It was a beautiful world at this moment for two people deeply in love. All the daunting obstacles and dangers laying before them seemed distant and irrelevant.

IN THE REICHSFELDS' HOME AT RUŽINOV EVERYTHING WAS READY. There was a large walnut torte sitting on the table, and *gulyás* warming in the oven. It hadn't taken Helena Reichsfeld as long to fix supper as it once did, because now there was less of everything to prepare since Berthold was out of work. They didn't have a maid anymore either, so her husband helped with the housework. Life was more Spartan, but as long as no one threatened them physically, they would get by. Anything that brought a little happiness into their lives was cherished and gave them new strength to go on. Now, Georgina's birthday gave them an occasion to forget everything else, even if for only a few hours.

"Berci, I'm curious to see if Peter will come today," Helena remarked to her husband.

"Well, if he does, we'll find out just how strong the love between them is. We'll see if he really meant what he wrote in that letter."

"If he didn't love her, he could have left her when she had that trouble here at home, don't you think?"

"You don't understand these kinds of things, Ica. Men his age are all the same. They want only one thing—sexual satisfaction. And an officer can get more than his share of girls." He was convinced he was right.

"I think during the time he's been coming over here you have had plenty of opportunity to get to know him. Haven't you noticed he seems to be much more serious than all of Györgyi's other friends?"

"You have a point there. He is definitely more serious, but does that mean he also keeps his word?"

"Györgyi says a man like Peter is very hard to find. She says she believes in him because, whenever he gives his word, he always keeps it." Helena Reichsfeld was seldom on Peter's side, but this time she was.

"If he is as you say, then he is a rare individual. I will believe him when he proves himself," objected Berthold with his usual skepticism.

"Well, I'm sure Györgyi wouldn't have fallen so much in love with Peter if he wasn't worthy."

"I just hope both of you are right. I'd hate to see my daughter deceived. I can't imagine how she would endure that."

"I'm not afraid that will ever happen. What bothers me is how they propose to resolve their religious differences."

"The situation hasn't come to that yet. Don't you know every officer needs permission from the military to get married? As long as this government is in power, he'll never get it. Besides, this war may go on for years, and even the strongest love can falter under such a burden."

"And what if Peter comes up with the suggestion that Györgyi convert and be baptized? Helena surprised her husband with this question.

After a moment he answered her. "If they both really want that, there's very little we can do to stop it. So, we're better off not objecting. They'll need all the help and support they can get, if they decide to marry. Then, who knows? Maybe we will have to face that same decision soon ourselves."

"What do you mean? We'll have to face it, too?" She was the surprised one, now. "You don't mean we should change our religion?"

"I've been thinking about this possibility more than ever before. Everyone's looking for a way to save himself. As long as there's some other way out, I don't even consider it. As a last resort, we would really have no choice."

"I hear someone coming. I think it's Györgyi and Peter. I'll let them in." Helena beamed as she went to the door. Peter came, as she believed he would.

"PETER, GIVE ME YOUR COAT," GEORGINA DIRECTED HIM. This was his first visit to their Ružinov home.

"I'm glad to see you, *Pán Kapitán*," Mr. Reichsfeld greeted him. "Come in and sit down. The ladies are getting impatient."

Peter extended his hand, relieved to see Mr. Reichsfeld in such a good mood.

"How were things at the front?" Mr. Reichsfeld continued.

"Not as bad as I thought they'd be. Jirka must have told you. My stay was really quite short."

"And how was your flying course?" Reichsfeld had no difficulty in talking to Peter now that the ice was broken.

"It was very interesting. I made ten observation flights. I thought at first my stomach would crawl out of my mouth, but I got used to it. The pilots tried to scare us with some acrobatic maneuvers in the old open cockpit airplanes."

"At least now you have an idea of what it's like to fly."

"Yes, I do. It's much more complicated than I thought it would be. To be an observer, that is. The pilot has to fly high enough to be out of range of ground fire, but not too high so as to make it impossible for the observer to gather the necessary intelligence."

"Did you wear a parachute?"

"Yes, both the pilot and I always wore them."

"How high do you have to be before you could use it?"

"At least three hundred meters."

"Okay, let's forget military matters for now and eat," said Mrs. Reichsfeld, bringing the food to the table.

After dinner, Reichsfeld brought out a bottle of domestic wine and poured four glasses.

"To my beloved Jirka on her twenty-first birthday." Peter was the first to offer a toast.

"To my daughter's health," added her father. They all clinked glasses and drank.

"I'd like to add something," said Peter, smiling. "Jirka and I became engaged today. Now, we would like your blessing." Berthold and Helena were astonished.

After a moment of complete silence as the Reichsfelds stared at each other, Mr. Reichsfeld broke the silence in a rather formal, dispassionate tone, "Mama, should we give our daughter to *Kapitán* Vlčko in marriage?"

"I certainly have no objections. I just wish them all the happiness in the world," she replied, her eyes beginning to fill with tears of joy.

"In that case, I wish you both a long and happy life together. May God bless and guard you and your every step," said Reichsfeld, who remained realistically anxious over their uncertain future.

"Thank you very much," said Peter, more than a little relieved. "I hope you will call me Peter from now on instead of *Pán Kapitán*." He then stood from the table and embraced them both warmly.

"This calls for another drink," said Reichsfeld, filling everyone's glass to the brim. "Since we have the engagement behind us, what can we do to help with the wedding? Do you have any suggestions, Peter?"

"Before we can set a wedding date, I'll need special permission from the President. To get it, Jirka will have to formally convert to Catholicism. I hope this will not be an obstacle for you."

"Under the circumstances, do you believe you have a chance of gaining the President's consent?" Reichsfeld was not optimistic at all about the prospects.

"Nothing's impossible if we are determined enough."

"Peter, your faith and optimism are encouraging, but not very realistic in these times. I can only hope you're right."

"*Pán* Reichsfeld, I want you to trust me. Everything will work out for the best. You'll see."

The Reichsfelds' support reinforced Peter's determination to overcome any obstacles that crossed their path. He felt strengthened in heart and sensed a serenity and happiness he had not known for a long time.

SIX JANUARY 1942 HELD SPECIAL SIGNIFICANCE FOR PETER AND JIRKA. This was the anniversary of their first meeting at the Luxor Cafe. "I wonder how we should celebrate it?" thought Peter before he made any suggestions to his fiancée.

"Let's have dinner at the Luxor. Or would you rather go somewhere else a little more private?" he said to her.

"Since we both ski and have never been skiing together, why not go to the mountains?"

"That sounds like a great idea. Let's go to Smrekovica. It's beautiful there and I know the area well. Besides, it will cost us hardly anything since we can stay in the military lodge."

"When can we leave?"

"This week. We can spend New Year's there." Peter didn't need a special leave because his two-week vacation did not end until just after the day of the Three Kings (Epiphany, 6 January). Jirka's parents had no objections either, for they were engaged.

The trip to Smrekovica involved the same hardships Peter and his War College mates encountered when they traveled there for mountain ski training. They had to transfer trains a couple of times, and then make the long hike on foot from the last station to the recreation center. This time, however, the center was filled with young people who had come here for pleasure rather than study. The accommodations also were more comfortable, as each person had a private room.

The first day they rested. A few played cards or chess or lounged around the fireplace in a totally relaxed and lazy setting. The next day was New Year's Eve. A typical celebration was planned to usher in the new year. Wherever there is youth, there is gayety, and so it was at Smrekovica. It was decided that everyone should come in costume. The suggestion was received with great enthusiasm, and instead of just a normal dance they had a masquerade party. Jirka dressed as an Indian prince with turban, and Peter wore a big fur coat and disguised himself as a bear. The merrymaking lasted until morning. Some of the more uninhibited put on their skis at the first sign of dawn and took to the slopes, still a little intoxicated. The saner ones went to bed and slept until midafternoon.

The week that followed was filled with sport and sunbathing. The surrounding hills had never heard such weird cries and yowls as came from these young people. The sounds varied from high-pitched screams of girls on runaway skis to clumsy attempts of young men yodeling. Then, pleasantly exhausted, they would sit around the fireplace and drink hot tea with rum or *slivovica* (plum brandy), or hot wine flavored with cinnamon bark. Later, couples would dance or play cards or just sit and talk, knowing they did not have to go to work the next day.

As the days slipped by Peter and Jirka made their own holiday plans. They wanted to spend the eve of their anniversary completely alone. After wandering about the beautiful hills, among the small stands of evergreens, heavy with pillows of clean snow, they returned to their cottage. With supper finished, they stole away and headed for a distant and secluded spot. There, they settled down on the powdery snow beneath a towering spruce. Whispered words of love passed gently between the lovers. Only the moon above witnessed their sublime contentment. They had each other and they were safe. Even their future seemed, for now, happy and secure.

"Peter, I want us to be happy like this the rest of our lives. Do you think it is possible?"

"As long as we have each other, no hardship can destroy our happiness. And even hardship can strengthen our love if we face it together with faith and hope." His arms enfolded her to emphasize the meaning of his words.

When they were a little chilled, they got up and brushed the snow off and returned to the lodge. Rather than join the others in the lounge, they went to Jirka's room. There, they reminisced about the past year's experiences they had shared together and made tentative plans for the future. It was not long before they crawled in under the huge goose down feather quilt and reached that moment of ecstasy which binds two lovers as one.

THE FIRST SLOVAK WAR COLLEGE, ORGANIZED IN FEBRUARY 1940, prepared officers for higher army command and General Staff duty. There, students gained considerable military and political knowledge for their new assignments. Since the need for these officers had arisen, their graduation was advanced by the Minister of National Defense Ferdinand Čatloš. The first group graduated on 12 February 1942. The ceremony was attended by important government figures and many foreign dignitaries.

Upon graduation, Cavalry Captain Vlčko became Captain of the General Staff, and was assigned to the matériel department of the Ministry of National Defense (*MNO*) in Bratislava for further practical experience.

Captain Vlčko did not intend to take an active part in the war, since he opposed the Slovak collaboration with the Nazis. He would remain passive wherever and whenever possible. His assignment at the *MNO* was ideal because he was near Jirka and her family and could see to it that no harm came to them.

CHAPTER 26

HIDING, THE ONLY RECOURSE

THE HOPE FOR THE 1942 RUSSIAN WINTER OFFENSIVE MELTED AS QUICKLY as the snow. After replacing losses inflicted by the Russians, the Germans drove on eastward. After the Russian defeat, disillusioned Western Allies experienced an even more painful shock.

Like the German *Blitzkrieg*, the Slovak government struck like lightning against Slovak Jewish citizenry. At the end of March 1942, extreme extralegal anti-Jewish measures were implemented. The *Hlinka* Guard, along with German *Ordner*—an ethnic German Slovak paramilitary formation known as *Freiwillige Schutzstaffel* (Volunteer *SS*)—began to round up all Jewish women. Those in the countryside and in smaller villages suffered most since no escape existed for them. Women in larger towns and cities found it easier to hide. In Bratislava, one advantage existed like nowhere else. Bratislava Headquarters State Security Police Chief *JUDr.* Pavel Macháček opposed this new extralegal directive. Through him many families learned of these planned deportations in advance and could prepare for them.

Berthold Reichsfeld wasted no time. He immediately took Georgina to Filip Polivka, a photographer friend who lived on *Hlinka* Square and owned a studio there. The following day, the most dreaded fantasies became realities. In the streets, unsuspecting young women wearing the gold Star of David were the first to be picked up by the *Hlinka* Guard and German *Ordner*. These women would never again see their families. Those found at home were only a little better off. They were allowed to take a few basic necessities with them before saying goodbye to their parents and relatives. Very few were fortunate enough not to be recognized immediately. Forewarned by friends, some were offered a place of safety with them. Eternal gratitude belongs to those who provided at least a temporary refuge, in spite of the danger involved.

Peter learned of this Herod-like enterprise before Reichsfeld called him, for the news had spread amazingly fast through the city. Peter left his office the first chance he had. Outside the apartment his heart pounded, and his moist hands shook. He could hardly get the key into the lock. As he opened the door, he spied an envelope lying on the floor. He ripped it open and read: "Peter! Jirka's in hiding at Polivkas'. Please, go to her today. Be very careful. No one must suspect anything. Berthold."

Peter's heartbeat slowed back to normal. Jirka was safe. Then, he set out for Polivkas' studio. The moment he arrived, Jirka collapsed in his arms and sobbed uncontrollably.

"Don't cry, my love. I won't let them take you. I have my military pistol. I'll kill anyone who tries to harm you."

"Peter, how many bullets do you have?" her father asked. Reichsfeld had stopped by to check if Georgina was still safe.

"Enough to prevent anyone from getting in here."

"Yes, but how long can bullets insure Jirka's safety?"

"Long enough for us to escape to some other hiding place."

"So far, thanks to the Polivkas, that hasn't been necessary. Maybe this awful purge will subside, but when? In any case, Györgyi can't stay here forever. There are too many customers entering and leaving the studio." The worry showed in his face.

"I have a better idea," Peter said with self-reliance.

"Yes?"

"One of my colleagues is leaving for the Eastern Front this week. I'll ask him if I can rent his apartment while he's gone."

"When do you think he'll let you have it?"

"Probably the day after tomorrow."

"Well, Györgyi will have to stay here until then. Right now, I can't think of a better place," her father decided, grateful for any suggestions or help Peter might offer.

"In case Jirka has to run from here, she can stay with me, Peter assured.

"I'd rather she didn't. Everyone can see everyone else coming and going there," her father objected.

"How do you know that?" Peter showed surprise, since Reichsfeld had never been to his apartment.

"I have a friend who lives in the same building. I guess he knows you, too." Reichsfeld did not wish to give Peter the idea he had been spying on him.

"I suppose you're right. There are no secrets with nosy neighbors all around. I'm going to have to find another place soon."

"Be here the same time tomorrow. Maybe you'll have some concrete news about your friend's apartment." With that, their meeting ended.

THE FOLLOWING DAY, THE SLOVAK GOVERNMENT EXPLAINED THEIR latest anti-Jewish campaign as necessary assistance to the German war effort. According to reliable sources, the more beautiful girls were being sent to the Eastern Front for German soldiers' entertainment. Apparently, Hitler's racial policies, strictly forbidding contact between Jews and non-Jews, had been modified to allow such arrangements deemed as necessary morale-builders. Under the Nuremberg Laws, mixing Jewish with German blood was still *verboten*. Plain but healthy Jewish women were shipped to concentration camps to work. Those totally unsuited for either of these programs were administered a lethal injection and then buried. News from the concentration camps testified to this barbaric truth.

Chairman of the *Reich Committee for the Protection of German Blood* and Nazi legal theorist Wilhelm Stuckart along with his Interior Ministry deputies Hans Globke, Franz Albrecht Medicus, and Bernhard Lösener drafted the essential core of the *Law for the Protection of German Blood and German Honor* and the *Reich Citizenship Law* (together known as the Nuremberg Laws or *Nürnberger Gesetze*) that were formally passed by the *Reichstag* in Nuremberg on 15 September 1935.[1] The laws were based on the concept of *Volksgemeinschaft* ("people's community") to which every German was bound by common blood. The individual was not a member of society, a concept viewed by Nazi legal theorists as a Marxist one, but a born member of the German *Volk*, through which he or she acquires rights. Interests of the *Volk* were to always override those of the individual. People born outside of the *Volk* were seen to possess no rights, and in fact to represent a danger to the purity of the people's community. As such, anti-miscegenation legislation was justified, even necessary. Stuckart stated that these laws represented "a preliminary solution of the Jewish question."

"PETER, WHAT'S THE MATTER? YOU LOOK WORRIED," CAPTAIN ŠTEFAN Šimko said when he dropped by his office the following day.

"Štefan, do you really see something in my face, or do you just think you do because of recent events?" asked Peter.

"Well, I was thinking about your fiancée. Has anything happened to her?"

"Nothing so far, thank God. But it was certainly a close call."

"Where is she now?"

"With family friends. But she can't stay there indefinitely. These friends have a business which they operate in their home."

"Do you know that I'm leaving for the front tomorrow?"

"Yes, I've heard you are, but didn't know when."

"My wife is in Prague now with her parents and won't return until I get back. Would you like to use my apartment in Nová Doba? It's completely furnished."

"Would I? It's really nice of you to offer to help us. We'll take good care of everything, and you don't have to worry about the rental or the other bills. I'm really grateful."

"You know, when I learned about the deportations, I immediately thought of the both of you. I only hoped my offer wouldn't be too late."

"Thank God and Dr. Macháček."

"You mean, the Chief of Police?"

"Yes. He's one of the few good people left in the government."

"It's strange how all of us who served in Bohemia together share common problems. I guess we have to help one another as much as we can. It brings us closer together, too." Štefan sympathized with Peter at this moment. "You can move in tomorrow evening. I'll give you the keys before you leave in the afternoon."

"Thank you, again, Štefan. I won't forget this. See you then."

AFTER WORK THE NEXT DAY, VLČKO STAYED CLEAR OF ANY POLITICAL debates and hurried off to the Polivkas'. When Anna Polivka's smile greeted him, he knew everything was all right. She took him to a back room where Georgina was hiding. He knocked twice and then once, as he was instructed by Anna, to signify he was a friend.

"You've come finally." Reichsfeld greeted him. He was like a guardian angel at his daughter's side. He had been at Polivkas' since before noon.

"Yes. I'll take over your sentry duty now, *Pán* Reichsfeld."

"I hope you'll give me a few more privileges than he did. He wouldn't even let me go to the bathroom," Jirka complained.

Georgina's refuge was a small, cold, and colorless room in Polivkas' home, normally used for storing the odds and ends that people usually put away in attics. This little cubbyhole had been cleaned out recently and improvised for human habitation in case of emergency. The only furnishings were a simple folding iron cot, a table, and two chairs. No carpet covered the wooden floor. A narrow window facing an alley offered little light and ventilation. In effect, the room was a prison cell without bars to hold the inmate in. This room was entered from another larger room where Polivka's customers came to have their portraits taken. In a moment of necessity, it was the only place for Georgina to hide.

Every time a customer entered the house, she received a signal from either of the Polivkas. She then crawled under her bed and stayed there until an all-clear signal was given.

"You're safe, which justifies your father's restrictions. Outside, there is still a great uproar. The government pawns are running around like bloodhounds searching for girls to fill their quotas. How did you spend the day?"

"Peter, you know I can't stand confinement. I may be safe here, but it's like a prison. Most of the day I read and thought about you. I wondered if you needed all these troubles." She paused and looked in his eyes. She did not wait for the answer. "Did you find another place for me to stay?"

"I know, my dear. My day dragged for me too. I was thinking more about you than of supplies for our units in Russia. But everything turned out better than I had expected."

"Well, tell us!" Her father was anxious to hear the details.

"Tomorrow night we can take Jirka to her new home."

"Fantastic!" Jirka exclaimed. Her face brightened with the news. "You'll never believe how it happened, though. Šimko came up to me and offered his apartment before I even had a chance to ask him for it. He said he'd been thinking about it for the past two days. He was worried and hoped he wasn't too late. According to him, you'll find everything there you need. It won't cost us much, either."

"It's certainly generous of him," said Jirka, grateful for Šimko's kindness.

"Mother will pack a bag with what she thinks you'll need, and Peter can bring it over tomorrow," said her father. "I'm going to hurry home with the good news. Mother will feel better when she hears it. See you tomorrow evening, Peter. Goodbye."

"How can we get away with this, Peter?" Jirka already suspected Peter had not told her everything. "You're planning for us to live there together, aren't you?"

"Do we have any choice? I can't let you live there alone. Who knows what trouble the other tenants may cause? By yourself, you would arouse the curiosity of the neighbors. If I'm living there with you, no one will think it unusual, for they'll assume we're married. In fact, starting tomorrow we'll have to go around openly as if we were."

"What will my parents say?"

"I'll have to convince them this is the only way. You can't sit on two horses at the same time. If they want you to escape deportation, they'll have to agree. They must realize my main concern is your safety, and to ensure that safety, we have to ignore conventions."

"You must know, darling, how happy this makes me. But I still doubt that my parents will be overjoyed with the arrangement."

"Well, there's not much they can do at this point. They may object on moral grounds, but how do they expect me to protect you by living on the other side of town?"

"Peter, you must be very diplomatic with them. I feel that what we are about to do is not wrong. But they have to feel the same way."

"As soon as it's possible for us to get married officially, we will. I think your parents know this. In the meantime, there are still twenty-four hours before we can move into Nová Doba. Be very careful and don't even stick your nose out of this hole, no matter what. I'll be back tomorrow at about the same time. Until then, goodnight, my little prisoner." He kissed her and left. Jirka locked the door and laid down. She thought of tomorrow and the life it would bring. She knew she loved Peter deeply and felt entirely content with the plans. She was his wife now, regardless of what the world would say if they knew.

"DID EVERYTHING GO SMOOTHLY?" REICHSFELD ASKED AS VLČKO entered their apartment.

"Jirka and I had no difficulties. Is everything ready?"

"Yes, the suitcases are in the hallway."

"*Pán* Reichsfeld, I can't stay long because my driver has to get back to the barracks. Before I go, there is something I have to tell you," said Peter, a little reluctant to begin.

"I have a feeling I know what it is," cut in Reichsfeld. "Even though at first I didn't want to admit it, I know there's nothing else that can be done."

"Thank you. *Pán* Reichsfeld, you make it easier for me to ask for your consent, and I hope that you come to consider us husband and wife."

"Mother and I want you two to be happy and safe. We're sure someday soon you will be able to marry." He put his arms around Peter, tears clouding his eyes. He managed a smile for their future son-in-law.

"Peter, take care and watch over Györgyi so that nothing bad happens to her." Helena Reichsfeld grasped his hands in hers and kissed him on the cheek. Peter picked up two large suitcases and walked to the waiting car.

ŠIMKO'S APARTMENT BUILDING WAS LOCATED IN A LARGE COMPLEX IN THE northeast part of Bratislava, between the Cavalry Barracks and Ružinov. The apartment itself was not spacious, as the Šimkos only needed a place big enough for two with a large sitting room that served also as a bedroom, with separate kitchen and bath. The total furnishings included a studio couch bed, one lounge chair and two end tables, a small dining table and four chairs, plus a generous-sized china cabinet that held several porcelain figures and some cut glass. A traverse drape that provided privacy covered the only window in the room.

Jirka was happy now. The stress which she had recently experienced at the Polivkas dissipated. Though her freedom remained partially limited because of danger in the streets, Peter's everyday presence brought her peace of mind and something to look forward to. The love he lavished on her made her deeply content.

In her new role as housekeeper, she found satisfaction. Living on her own with Peter she felt secure and finally independent from her parents. The most memorable time of their secret life was in the evening, after together they had put the apartment in order, taken their showers and changed into comfortable evening clothes. They often listened to music on the radio from Vienna or Berlin, or to the Czech newscasts from London. Hot tea with lemon or *slivovic* was their favorite nighttime drink. Life was simple and uncomplicated by the world outside. Each night at broadcast sign-off at 9:55 p.m., the voice of Liselotte Wilke, alias Lale Andersen, singing *Lili Marleen* from German forces radio station in Belgrade lulled them to sleep as they lay locked in each other's arms.[2]

CHAPTER 27

ESPIONAGE, THE SECOND DEPARTMENT, CZECHOSLOVAK RESISTANCE, AND THE ASSASSINATION OF REINHARD HEYDRICH

THE NEWLY INDEPENDENT CZECHOSLOVAKIA FORMED ON 28 OCTOBER 1918 was surrounded by countries unhappy with its existence. Germany, Hungary, and Poland laid claim to territories in Czechoslovakia and pursued policy measures supporting these claims. Their national minorities in Czechoslovakia represented a fertile base for espionage and sabotage activities both in peacetime and time of heightened tension. Austria represented a smaller threat; however, it was monitored by the intelligence service since the 1920s with regard to its sentimental longing to restore the Hapsburg monarchy.

Immediately upon declaration of the establishment of the new Czechoslovak Republic on 28 October 1918, German separatists in Bohemia and Moravia were organizing secessionist movements to join Germany and Austria. These movements ultimately culminated in the declaration of four separatist provinces—*Deutschböhmen* in northern Bohemia, *Sudetenland* in Moravia and Silesia, *Deutschsüdmähren* in southern Moravia, and *Böhmenwaldgau* in the Bohemian Forest—and ultimately, the attempt to annex them to Austria when events in 1920s Germany demanded focus on the internal chaos of the Weimar Republic. This separatist movement had to be put down with the deployment of newly organized Czechoslovak military units in the separatist provinces. A similar situation occurred in Slovakia, when the government of the postwar vestiges of Hungary did not want to accept loss of its "highlands" in Slovakia and Carpathian Ruthenia to Czechoslovakia.

In response to the prompt military reaction of the new Czechoslovak government, German Nationalists went underground. An illegal resistance group, the *Deutscher Mitterstandverband*, was established by Dr. Alois Baeran. In 1919, a center for German illegal resistance movement in

Czechoslovakia, the *Hilfsverein für Deutschböhmen*, was established in Vienna.

Furthermore, German Consul General Baron Fritz Freiherr von Gebsattel in Prague was expelled from Czechoslovakia in January 1919 because of espionage. This espionage was a grave signal to the Czechoslovak Administration that real threats to the new republic existed from neighboring countries in the period shortly after the First World War and establishment of diplomatic relations with Germany. Consequently in 1919, the High Command of the Czechoslovak Army moved to establish a military intelligence branch known as the Second Department of the General Staff of the Ministry of National Defense (*MNO*).

Initially, the Second Department suffered a shortage of knowledgeable and experienced intelligence officers since under Austro-Hungarian rule Czechs and Slovaks were unofficially barred from service in the monarchy's military intelligence. Major Čeněk Haužvic was one of the rare exceptions to the practice. Major Haužvic was appointed the first Chief of the Second Department in 1919 with his deputy as Major of the Czechoslovak Legion in Italy, Mojmír Soukup.

With time, a younger generation of officers filled posts in the Second Department. They were educated in the Czechoslovak Military Academy and War College in Prague. By 1930, as a result of its organizational structure of offensive, defensive, and study sections, the Second Department of the General Staff had grown in power and effectiveness surpassing that of long-established intelligence services of many European countries. The Second Department represented the most efficient component of the Czechoslovak security system. The department had cooperated with the British Secret Intelligence Service (SIS, later known as MI6) since the mid-1930s when SIS was under the leadership of Rear Admiral Hugh Sinclair (successor to SIS founder, Royal Navy Captain Sir Mansfield George Smith-Cumming) followed in 1939 by Colonel Stewart Menzies.

František Moravec was chief of the Second Department since 7 January 1937, when he was promoted to Colonel. Organizationally, the Second Department was comprised of two groups—the Search Group, which was subdivided into Offensive and Defensive Intelligence Sections, and the Plan and Study Group. The Offensive Intelligence Section of the Search Group, under the command of Major Emil Strankmüller who was also Moravec's overall deputy, was the most important Section in terms of the preparation and training of Czechoslovak parachutists for operations in the homeland. Between 1941 and 1945, the Offensive Intelligence Section was subdivided into: Intelligence Group (A), Study Group (B), Cipher Group (C), and Special Group (D). Intelligence Group A directed spying activities against Germany, relying upon the spy network of Czechoslovak Military Intelligence. It maintained contacts with the Allies and passed intelligence to them. Study Group B gathered intelligence from Group A, assessed it and formulated it into comprehensive intelligence reports, analyses, and studies of the enemy. Cipher Group C decoded messages from military radio transmissions and, conversely, encoded messages to be sent by military radio.

Special Group D was modeled after SOE Section D (formally part of SIS until 1940) and was responsible for the training of men for special operations. This Group was further subdivided into three Sections: Command, Training, and Support. The Command Section was responsible for the selection of suitable candidates for training, the organizational provision of training in cooperation with British authorities, administration, the targeted training of individuals according to their potential missions, the assessment of preparation and the processing of data for organizational use. Two men heading the Command Section of Special Group D during World War II were General Staff Captain First Class Jaroslav Šustr and General Staff Major Karel Paleček. The second section of Special Group D was the Training Section, responsible for the fulfillment of the requirements of training for Czechoslovak parachutists. The Czechoslovak officers and select personnel of this Training Section participated with British SOE personnel in organizing day-to-day and enhanced training of Czechoslovak parachutists at the sites allocated to SOE called Special Training Schools (STS).

The main role of the Offensive Intelligence Section of the Search Group was to gain extensive information on threats and capabilities of foreign militaries and their political leadership. The Offensive Section primarily functioned outside the borders of the homeland. The Defensive Intelligence Section of the Search Group was tasked with preventing infiltration of foreign espionage groups in the Czechoslovak military and areas important for defense support of the Republic (arms industry, defense facilities development, etc.). The Defensive Section primarily functioned within the homeland and closely cooperated with gendarmerie, all parts of state police, and civil intelligence services of the Interior Ministry.

The Plan and Study Group was primarily tasked with analysis of information obtained by the Search Group. Between the two world wars, approximately 2,000 cases of treason and espionage were discovered, investigated, and prosecuted; and this was just a fraction of the actual total number of hostile actions conducted against First Republic of Czechoslovakia during this time.

ENTER AGENT A-54

ONE OF THE MOST FAMOUS ACCOMPLISHMENTS OF THE SEARCH GROUP in the Second Department was the development and management of assets like German double agent Paul Thümmel. Paul Thümmel was born on 15 January 1902, in Neuhausen (Saxony). He was a baker's apprentice who eventually became a recipient of the coveted Nazi Gold Party Badge and member of the *SA* (*Sturmabteilung*)—original paramilitary wing of the Nazi party and precursor to the *SS*—as well as a Dresden-based high-ranking member of the *Abwehr* (German military intelligence for espionage, counterintelligence, and sabotage). In 1927, He organized the Neuhausen *NSDAP* (Nazi Party) group. Heinrich Himmler came to speak at the formation of the Neuhausen *NSDAP* and reportedly stayed the night at Thümmel's house. Years later, in gratitude, Himmler arranged work for his friend Paul in the Dresden branch of the *Reich*'s military intelligence establishment (*Abwehr*) under Admiral Wilhelm Franz Canaris.

Shortly after joining the *Abwehr* station in Dresden, Thümmel crossed the Czechoslovak-German border to mail a letter in Chomutov (65 km from Chemnitz, 120 km from Dresden) offering his services to the Czechoslovak intelligence service. The letter was postmarked 8 March 1937. In his memoirs, *Master of Spies: The Memoirs of General Frantisek Moravec*, published in the United States and London in 1975, František Moravec recalls his introduction to Paul Thümmel. The following is an extended excerpt from Colonel Moravec's fascinating memoir relative to this fateful and historic event.

> I found in my mail a fat blue envelope which my staff captain had not opened because it was addressed to "The Chief of the Czechoslovak Intelligence Service, General Staff, Prague. Personal." The postmark was that of the frontier town of Chomutov. The handwriting was educated, but unknown to me. There was no return address.
>
> I opened it—three closely typed pages in German,

addressed as on the envelope but with the German words for "Very Secret" added.

The letter began: "I offer you my services. First of all, I shall state what my possibilities are: 1. The build-up of the German Army. (a) The infantry. . . ."

Surprised, I glanced through the other pages. There were nine such numbered paragraphs, each with its own precise heading. The subjects covered were such things as "German mobilization plans" ("partly documentary," the writer had noted); "Detailed battle order and deployment"; "German defense plan for the Saxonian border"; "Information on German armament, tanks, planes and airfields"; "Information on Sudeten German activities and their support from official German sources"; "Information on German espionage in Czechoslovakia."

I rang for my staff captain. "For an hour," I said, "I must not be disturbed. No telephone calls, no reports, no visitors." Then I turned to the last page of the letter: "I request at the first meeting 100,000 Reichsmarks." (That was the equivalent of about $40,000.) "I suggest the meeting be held in Chemnitz. If you are interested reply to Post Office Box g, Cheb. Then I will give you details." The signature was "Karl."

I read the letter again. I received many offers of various kinds but this one was unique. The first two pages looked like a catalogue of a commercial firm offering its product. The phraseology indicated a professional in military and Intelligence matters.

The risk involved in carrying such a letter across the frontier would be too great. It therefore must have been not only mailed but written on Czechoslovak territory. The typing was even, obviously unhurried, and the tone was almost official. Chemnitz, the suggested meeting place, was a frontier town in Saxony, within the territory of the *Reich*. Clearly this was a proposition to be handled with the utmost care.

Once again, I read the letter. On the face of it, here was an offer to deliver a number of vital secrets of the *Reich* which our organization was trying strenuously to ferret out, in many cases with meager results. The scale of the offer was unprecedented. If the information was in fact delivered as listed, it would be a fantastic Intelligence coup.

On the other hand, it looked too good to be true. There were ample grounds for suspicion. Was it a trap? At first glance, that interpretation seemed the most likely. We had in recent months carried out several successful "provocations" against the *Abwehr*—the German Intelligence organization. Were they furiously looking for an opportunity for revenge on us?

Having considered the whole matter carefully I rang for my assistants—my deputy, Lieutenant-Colonel Tichý, Major Strankmüller and Captain Fryč. They arrived in a few minutes. "I have here an interesting letter," I told them. "I want each of you to read it and give me his evaluation. Each separately, individually, without consultation. As soon as one is finished he will come and tell me his opinion. Include the test for secret writing."

When they had left I walked around the room, thinking. The promise of disclosures about the relationship of the Sudeten Germans to "official sources" in the *Reich* had especially intrigued me. What sources? Political, military, Intelligence? We knew that contacts existed, but we had not been able to document exactly their nature, scope and purpose. I considered the Sudeten German danger immense, but most Czechoslovak politicians still refused to accuse Germany of the flagrant interference in our affairs which such contacts implied. They wanted more proof.

Captain Fryč came in. He was an Intelligence officer of long experience, used to dealing with the inflow of information from various agents' networks. He delivered his report: the tests for secret writing had proved negative. His evaluation was: "Utterly suspect. I deduce provocation. The reasons for my evaluation: the offer is too magnificent and too precise. A bona fide volunteer hints but does not specify. A man of the intelligence of the writer would not risk so much concrete detail. Even the fact that the letter was posted on our own territory makes it suspect. It is not probable that a would-be spy would use a go-between for an offer of this type, and who has the facilities to cross the frontier at will? The answer is, the *Abwehr*. The proposal of Chemnitz as a meeting place clinches the matter. My conclusion therefore is that it is a provocation. I would disregard it."

"You see nothing positive?" I asked him. "Nothing that would make you feel we should explore the offer?"

"In my opinion," said Fryč, "it is a provocation with a probability ratio of ninety-nine to one, and I cannot even evaluate that one. I do not trust it."

Major Strankmüller followed—an able officer who directed our espionage service against Germany. His opinion was basically the same as Fryč's. He added that, while I might disagree, he personally was convinced we would be losing any officer sent to Chemnitz. In his opinion, the man would be going straight to a German prison.

Tichý, my deputy, a nervous, talkative but persuasive man, came in next with a similar judgment. "I don't believe that anything of this scope is possible. It is transparent—the *Abwehr* is behind it. They want to get one of our men. My opinion is, let us not react."

I said I would make my decision by the afternoon.

As my officers had pointed out, the offer contained in the letter was concrete and well-informed. This was no letter from a crank. It was written by a military, probably Intelligence, professional. The question was why was it written? In the opinion of three experts in Intelligence it was a German trick.

But I continued to think about the possibility of the offer being genuine. I was well aware of all the suspicious circumstances. I was thinking, however, of two further factors. If it was a trap, surely it was a very inept attempt. It is a very poor trap that looks so much like one. Surely the Abwehr could have prepared a trick of greater subtlety.

Now suppose it was not a trick? The indisputable fact was that the Karl who wrote our letter had access to unique material. If he *could* deliver what he was promising. . . . The odds against it were heavy but I felt we simply could not afford to pass up the chance.

I decided to react to the offer—with reservations. I called in Captain Fryč and instructed him to reply that we were willing to meet, but somewhere other than on German territory.

The gamble—and gambles at times are necessary—was on. The next letter from Karl did little to satisfy our basic doubts. He proposed a meeting in Austria—at Linz. Austria, nearing its *Anschluss* with Germany, was now the scene of intensive Nazi agitation, and one of the centers of this was Linz, the hometown of Adolf Hitler, an industrial city lying but a few miles from the southern Bavarian frontier of Germany.

We replied to Karl's second letter that Linz was also not a suitable rendezvous. We insisted that the personal contact be made within Czechoslovakia. Although our letters were being sent to a Sudetenland post office box, easy for us to watch, I had decided deliberately against any move which might scare off our man Karl. If the matter was worth pursuing, it also was only sensible to nurse Karl along.

The third letter from Karl proposed as a meeting place the Czechoslovak town of Kraslice [on the German-Czechoslovak border directly opposite from the German border town of Klingenthal/Sa. and about 90 km from Chemnitz, 175–212 km from Dresden]. The correspondence up to this time had been fairly rapid: less than a month had passed in this initial fencing. But Karl's latest proposition did not really solve our problem. The town he proposed presented almost as much danger for us as Linz or Chemnitz. Kraslice, a town with a population of 8,000, lay in the heart of Sudetenland, whose inhabitants had been whipped up by Hitler's henchman Henlein into an efficient tool of *Reich* foreign policy. The Henlein stronghold was virtually enemy territory. It also lay as close to German soil as physically possible, in fact one end of its central square was within a stone's throw of the frontier [border].

Only three years before one of my men had been the victim of a frontier kidnapping and this was very fresh in my memory. However, I felt we had raised enough objections with Karl already. If we were going to find out the truth about him, certain irreducible risks would have to be faced. We replied, accepting Kraslice.

So, at last the place and the time for the meeting were set. In his final reply, which came back promptly, Karl stipulated that the rendezvous should be at 11:00 P.M., that he would enter the square of Kraslice from the sloping upper end of the German frontier and that he would identify himself to us by stopping in front of the church in the square and setting his watch by the clock on the steeple. We accepted at the same time I had also arrived at a further decision about this meeting. I would go myself.

I did not like the melodrama of the arrangements, but all I could do was to order every possible precaution to be taken. The day before the meeting I sent two officers to reconnoiter. I asked the state police for a dozen men who knew the locality to be assigned to me and posted in adjacent streets around the square. I selected twelve officers from my department, all of them experts on Germany, with various specializations in technical fields, such as photography and mimeographing, secret writing and document testing, to be included in the party.

The Czechoslovak military Intelligence had a house in Chomutov—the Sudetenland border town, about thirty miles north of Kraslice, from which Karl's original letter had been posted. In this house we put the men and the equipment we would need. For myself, I decided to go not only to Chomutov but to Kraslice as well. I felt it was only right that I should share with my men whatever dangers arose as a result of my decision to contact Karl.

By April 1937 the Czechoslovak Intelligence service had obtained from a variety of sources a fairly good picture of the makeup and disposition of the German Army and the *Luftwaffe*. We deduced that these forces would soon be employed against Czechoslovakia. To know in complete detail the deployment of the forces, of Hitler's plans in general and his timetable—all of which Karl was promising—was now of paramount importance. The urgent need in Prague in 1937 was documentary proof that Hitler was using the Sudeten Germans for his own ends as an international issue. We had to prove to our own people, to France, Britain and other allies, that Hitler intended to cripple Czechoslovakia, that the Sudeten German agitation was a means to that end, that all his propaganda was based on military ambitions and that no concessions on our part would alter his purpose.

On the day of the proposed meeting I went to the house in Chomutov and waited there until evening. At 9:30 P.M. I left in a black civilian car with Captain Fryč and arrived in Kraslice at ten o'clock. My first move there was to make a tour of inspection. The police had been assigned to their places by one of my staff who had gone on ahead. We now manned three sides of a quadrangle, the square being the center of it. The slope at the far end of the square led to the German frontier. Our men had been placed far enough apart in dark places so that they were in general contact but not obtrusive. I took up a position at the edge of the square with Strankmüller, Tichý and Fryč near me. It was now 10:45 P.M., fifteen minutes before the hour set by Karl for the meeting.

It was a gloomy scene. The houses and small shops around the tree-lined square were dark. The few gas streetlamps flickered and gave little light. If any citizens of Kraslice were still awake they gave no evidence of it. The silence was so intense that the only sound was the wind stirring the trees. I noticed that the clock on the church steeple had stopped.

Impatient, consulting my watch constantly, I now began pacing under the trees. I had decided to wait an hour, but every minute that passed increased my uncertainty, especially when eleven o'clock had come and gone. I had to fight back the inclination to call my men off and abandon the entire project.

I was not armed but all the other officers had revolvers. As I walked back and forth under the trees, Lieutenant-Colonel Tichý, my second-in-command, walked with me, his hands in his pockets. We were talking quietly when suddenly a shot rang out. Tichý, in the steadily mounting tension, had pressed the trigger of his revolver. A bullet, I discovered later, had passed through the cloth of my trouser leg. I whirled on Tichý, who was more shocked than I was, and told him—among other things—to put the safety catch on his revolver.

Now it was not only twenty minutes past the hour but the quiet had been shattered by a gunshot. It seemed almost impossible that any man, bringing with him such material as Karl had indicated, would dare now to come into the square.

But the square remained as undisturbed as it had been. No lights came on, no windows opened. If any of the citizens of Kraslice had heard the shot, they chose to ignore it and remain discreetly indoors.

By 11:30 P.M. I was convinced the meeting had been a trick and that it had been called off because of our security measures. I was just about to say this to Strankmüller when I saw a man suddenly emerge from the darkness at the lower—or wrong—end of the square. When he reached the church, he put down the large suitcases and long rolls of paper he was carrying and, looking up at the stopped clock, seemed to set his watch by it. I realized this figure in plus fours, who had arrived half an hour overdue, was the man we had come to meet. I told Strankmüller, "Go to him."

Events now moved rapidly. Strankmüller, a small, slightly built man, walked across the square to the man, said something to him and then motioned with his hand. I immediately started walking to our cars, which were waiting nearby. Strankmüller and Karl followed. As we reached the vehicles the German, who had been told by Strankmüller that I was the senior officer, said to me in German, "Good evening, I am Karl. I am in a hurry."

The man was deliberate in his movements absolutely calm and he spoke as though he had known me for years. "All right, Karl," I said. "We will now take you to a place where we can talk."

When we reached the Chomutov villa I was able to get a close look at the German. He was about five feet eight inches in height. He was slightly bowlegged, but militarily erect. He had light brown hair, cut short, almost in the Prussian way. He was clean-shaven. I saw that his blue eyes were rather prominent his chin slightly cleft. I could see again that he appeared to be as completely at ease as if we were in a club room.

That he was an officer was very probable from the way he held himself, from the way he walked and later from the way he talked. That he was an expert in Intelligence matters and had access to highly important German secret documents also became obvious almost at once. The two suitcases he carried contained a bulging mass of papers. The paper-wrapped rolls he had held under his arms were also documents. Incredibly, this man had dared to cross the German frontier openly loaded with documents stamped "secret" virtually on every page. If he was a bona fide volunteer this could only mean, that he had the status to pass the German border guards without challenge. Not only had he apparently crossed once but he intended to go through yet again. "I must get back with my samples by six-thirty this morning," he told me.

Upon arrival at the villa, Karl handed his suitcases and rolls to my officers. While the experts sorted, photographed and assessed his samples in other rooms, Major Strankmüller and I sat down in the living room to, talk with Karl. The room was wired so that everything that was said could be recorded and later played back for the assessment of experts.

We had coffee and brandy and our conversation lasted for nearly four hours. From time to time officers came in with documents they thought to be of particular importance. As one such report followed another the atmosphere of suppressed excitement—and astonishment—grew.

I began by asking Karl formally if he was the author of the letters. He answered that he was. I asked him, "How do you explain the possibilities you outline in the letters?"

He answered, "I am doing this after thorough consideration. I have a definite plan." He added that he wanted to earn money but that he also wanted to live as long as possible. He would refuse to take assignments from us. "I have my limits," he said. "When these limits are exceeded in cases like mine it usually ends very quickly and very badly."

His manner was calm and matter-of-fact. With the same unruffled calm, he then refused to give any information about his identity or his official position, refusing even to give his name. All he would say was, "The material I brought tonight and the material I shall be bringing in the future will speak for itself."

I asked about his motive. He repeated that he needed money, adding that he had a fiancée whom he intended to marry soon and that he wanted to buy furniture and "such things." He added that his fiancée was a Luzitian Serb and as a member of that oppressed Slavonic minority in East Prussia hated the Nazis. "I don't like the regime myself," he said. "You see, Colonel, my motives are not entirely pecuniary."

I was not impressed. Spies, being human, often invent a better-sounding motive if their sole reason for betraying their country is money. I said that 100,000 Reichsmarks was a lot of money and that to pay it to an anonymous person was a great responsibility. His reply was that I should make that decision after I had examined what he had brought. In his businesslike way Karl added that he did not expect to be paid the entire sum for what he had brought with him at the moment, although he wanted the money at once. The total would stand, he explained, as a credit—and he and I would decide when he had brought me 100,000 Reichsmarks' worth of military secrets.

As the conversation went on I received more and more indications from my experts of the bona fide nature of his documents, so I moved on to the question of future co-operation and what it would produce. Obviously, his reports would be of two kinds: oral and written. I pointed out that oral reports were important but only with agents of whom something was known or who had been tested and proved. Karl retorted that his "samples" would take care of that problem. He said that he would deliver in person at future meetings further documentary material which he judged would be of interest to us.

I asked where he would send his letters from. "Not from Germany," he replied. "They will be sent from Czechoslovak territory."

However, he agreed to my proposal that in a case of extreme urgency he would write from Germany in secret ink. At this moment he unwittingly gave me proof of his professional knowledge. He said he would write in water, then the latest method in secret writing. He suggested a code and I called in our code expert, Captain Fryč. It was to be simple—one sentence would stand for another. For example, if he wrote "I am ill" it would mean "I cannot come to the meeting." This was still further proof that he knew what he was talking about—such coding was usual procedure in Intelligence operations at that time.

Then we settled some other points—and Karl certainly knew his own mind. Because he would be working from across the frontier he refused to use microphotography. He also rejected the idea of using his own radio transmitter. He declined to be assigned a contact man. As for further meetings, he proposed that they should take place at roughly bimonthly intervals, that he would notify us in good time by letter and that if anything urgent arose in the meantime he would ask for a special meeting.

It was not possible for us to photograph the great mass of "sample" material in time for Karl's departure. When one of my officers came in to confirm this, Karl said that he would sort through some of it himself and select certain documents which would not be missed and which he could leave with us until the next meeting. When he returned from doing this he resumed the making of arrangements. Item: as an address for our letters we could use three post office boxes—he gave us the numbers, in Cheb, Falknov and Chomutov. Item: our letters should be sent "care of Karl Schneider." Item: future meetings would be in both Chomutov and Prague and the date and place of the next meeting should be the beginning of July, in

Chomutov.

Throughout these nearly four hours Karl had been constantly asked for explanations of certain parts of the documents—for example, with regard to abbreviations—to test his knowledge. I was passing judgment, on my part, on the value of the material. It was obvious, in the first place, that the documents he had selected were those directly bearing on matters concerning Czechoslovakia.

In the papers there was one of particularly great importance. This was the German *Grenzschutz*, or Frontier Defense Plan, for the border of Saxony. The rolls he had been carrying under his arm were a part of it. As we bent over the drawings he told me it had taken him two months to assemble them. This one document alone was priceless, not only for Czechoslovakia but also for other European countries, especially France. Leafing through the papers I noticed that missing from the documentation was the section dealing with Intelligence. This would contain details of the *Abwehr*'s *Grenzschutz* arrangements, including the names and addresses of spies and the location in Czechoslovakia of German clandestine radio transmitters. I asked Karl where the Plan's Intelligence section was.

"That is not so simple," he replied. "But in time I may deliver that also." This evasive answer immediately confirmed for me that Karl was an experienced officer in German Intelligence. As such he would avoid putting Intelligence documentation into our hands because any resulting investigation of it, first on our part and then on the part of the Germans, would come dangerously close to him.

I said that the *Grenzschutz* would have to be studied to determine its authenticity and instructed two of my experts to examine it in detail. Karl agreed at once, smiling for the first time. He reached into his breast pocket, pulled out several sheets of paper and, handing them to me, said, "Now that you know our *Grenzschutz* I want you to see that we also know yours."

What he gave me was a digest, in about twelve pages, of the Czechoslovak Frontier Defense Plan for our northeastern region. I studied these papers with a sinking feeling. Even at a cursory glance the information looked authentic, which meant that vital data about our plan were in the hands of the Germans. Here was a situation of the utmost gravity for us, because the betrayal of such a plan is naturally much more dangerous for a country planning to defend itself, like Czechoslovakia, than to an aggressor, such as Germany. (When I put this information before our Chief of Staff he was ill for two days.)

In reply to my questions Karl said that what I held in my hand was a copy of the original pages sent the previous summer to the *Abwehr* office in Berlin in an unsigned letter from the Czechoslovak frontier town of Cheb. The *Abwehr*, according to Karl, had been trying ever since to trace the anonymous sender. "So far they have not been able to find him," said Karl. "Perhaps you can."

Another sensational item in Karl's "samples" concerned the Sudeten Germans. It consisted of two original documents, directives from the *Abwehr*'s HQ in Berlin to its branch office in Chemnitz, which proved the *Abwehr*'s role in directing and organizing "incidents" in the Sudetenland—the same incidents on which the violent Nazi propaganda against Czechoslovakia was based.

In the days to come every one of Karl's documents would naturally be subjected to the most careful scrutiny and tests. But the experts with me were already expressing confidence in their authenticity. Unorthodox as he was, Karl had spoken the truth. His "samples" were more than enough to establish his bona fides. I paid him his money without further ado. He signed the receipt simply "Karl"—thus producing a document our department's auditor wouldn't like at all—but his formal registration in our files would henceforth be A-54.

I did not go with Karl when he left. It was now nearly dawn. A staff officer drove him back to Kraslice. There he stepped out into the square where we had met-and disappeared, 100,000 Reichsmarks in his pocket, his bags of documents in his hands. (Moravec 1975, 58–69.)

As it turned out, Moravec enlisted that night one of the most valuable secret agents in the history of espionage. The spy provided much of the material he promised in his letter, and the Czechoslovak intelligence officers were sure he was a professional and genuine. Through agent A-54, Moravec learned and passed on to the British, French, and Soviets an extraordinary mass of vital information about Hitler's aggressive plans. Thümmel's motives for betraying his friend Himmler and his country remain, to date, unclear whether based merely on financial grounds, ideology, or worsening relations with his peers in the Nazi party. Former Inspector General of the Central Intelligence Agency John H. Waller opined in his 1996 book, *The Unseen War in Europe: Espionage and Conspiracy in the Second World War* that:

> While Thümmel always claimed to have been willing to spy against the Nazi regime on his own volition, there remains the possibility that Canaris had put him up to it. [With the execution of Admiral Canaris on 9 April 1945] [t]his point was never resolved, but he was a good friend of the admiral's, and for all his dislike of the Nazis, he would have been unlikely to deceive him. . . . Moreover, his services for the Czechs fitted the pattern of other Abwehr agents secretly dispatched by Canaris to provide Hitler's victims or potential victims with valuable fore-warning as to Nazi intentions. . . . (Waller 1996, 67.)

However, the money he received, albeit considerable (amounting to about $400,000 in total, according to Moravec), clearly did not amount to enough to compensate for the dangers to which he exposed himself, and much of the information he passed was too valuable to be considered disinformation. For example, he told Czechoslovak intelligence the exact date and time of invasion of Czechoslovakia on 15 March 1939, information on the core of the first German offensive in France and Holland, information on German observers on the Finnish-German war, preparations and main points of operation against Yugoslavia, German intelligence on the Soviet Air Force, crucial information on the German invasion of Great Britain (Operation Sealion), development and deployment of V-1 rockets, Soviet generals working for the Nazis, etc. For the Second Department, Thümmel provided, among other things, detailed information on mobilization against Czechoslovakia, list of receivers of German radio stations in Czechoslovak territory, organization of the *Abwehr*, conclusive espionage material coming from Nazi agents in Czechoslovakia to *abwehrstelle* Dresden and later Prague, and a map revealing locations of German agents operating in Czechoslovak territory that in several cases the Second Department was able to successfully act on.

The most effective contribution for Czechoslovak Intelligence was what he did from spring 1937 to the occupation of Czechoslovakia in 1939. Thümmel was part of a conspiracy along with his friend Heinrich Himmler to falsely discredit high-ranking Soviet officers that led to the notorious purge of many Soviet Red Army officers in 1937 and 1938. In his 1968 book, *The Great Terror*, British historian Robert Conquest accuses Nazi Party leaders Heinrich Himmler and Reinhard Heydrich of forging documents, which implicated Marshal Mikhail Tukhachevsky in an anti-Stalinist conspiracy with the *Wehrmacht* General Staff, to weaken the Soviet Union's defense capacity. These documents, Conquest said, were leaked to Czechoslovakian military intelligence, who passed them to Soviet Russia through diplomatic channels. Marshal Tukhachevsky was a leading Soviet military leader and theoretician who helped direct the modernization of Soviet armament and army force structure in the 1920s and 1930s and became instrumental in the development of aviation, mechanized, and airborne forces. Conquest's thesis of an *SS* conspiracy to frame Tukhachevsky was based upon the memoirs of Himmler's personal adjutant Walter Schellenberg and Czechoslovak President Edvard Beneš. In 1989, the Politburo of the Communist Party of the Soviet Union announced that new evidence had been found in Stalin's archives indicating German intelligence intentions to fabricate disinformation about Tukhachevsky with the goal of eliminating him. The purge of the Red Army and Military Maritime Fleet removed three of five marshals (then equivalent to six-star generals), thirteen of fifteen army commanders (then equivalent to three- and four-star generals), eight of nine admirals, fifty of fifty-seven army corps commanders, 154 out of 186 division commanders, sixteen of sixteen army commissars, and twenty five of twenty-eight army corps commissars. Between 3.7 and 7.7 percent of Soviet military officers had been purged.

In June 1937, Moravec and Thümmel met again, this time at Hotel Pošt in Karlsbad (Karlovy Vary). The relationship only deepened from there. Another meeting with Thümmel in Chomutov on 14 July 1937, revealed that the German General Staff held war games in preparation for invasion of Czechoslovakia codenamed "Case Green" (Operation *Fall Grün*). The exercise was based on reliable intelligence that France will not provide any effective military assistance if Germany invades Czechoslovakia. During this meeting, Thümmel also agreed to sign a commitment to collaboration, stating: "I hereby declare that I voluntarily entered the service of the Czechoslovak intelligence service. I will faithfully perform all assigned tasks and give possession of all things and documentary material, to which I have access. Prague, 14 July 1937. Joachim Wedel, lieutenant, Dresden N., Carola-Allee 14."

Again, a new alias. However, it was not important—clandestine intelligence services expected as much. Throughout 1938, Thümmel also met frequently with Lieutenant Colonel František Fryč of the Second Department at the Manes restaurant in Prague. He told Fryč he hated the *SS* but did not explain why. He also told Fryč that his mother was descended from the Wenden of Lausitz (referring to the Serbian Slavs [Sorbs] who settled in southern Brandenburg and northern Saxony regions in *AD* fifth century), and he felt close to the Czechs, because he had Slav blood. Czechoslovak intelligence did not discover agent A-54's true name until after the war when it also was discovered that neither Thümmel's fiancée nor his mother came from Lausitz. As a matter of fact, he had no fiancée; he was married.

On 12 May 1938, agent A-54 called an emergency meeting with the Second Department in the Sudetenland. During this meeting, agent A-54 revealed the Germans were preparing a campaign of sabotage and agitation against Czechoslovakia designed to precipitate a *coup* in the Sudetenland on 22 May. He also reported that weapons, ammunition, and explosives were being secretly transported into the Sudetenland for Sudeten Germans that were trained in the *Reich* by senior officers of the *SS* and *SD*. On 20 May 1938, German radio broadcast the code word *Altvater* to commence Case Green to take the Sudetenland. Colonel Moravec and the Czechoslovak Army was already aware of the details of Case Green and had made their own plans to counter it. President Beneš ordered a partial mobilization, in which 176,000 soldiers were sent into the threatened regions of the Sudetenland to preserve order and prepare for armed conflict. Demonstrations in the Sudetenland ceased with the arrival of the military units. The crisis was averted, for now. However, to the rest of the world, it appeared as an "overreaction" on the part of the Czechoslovak government to some local demonstrations against discrimination of the Sudeten Germans. Over the ensuing months of 1938, the British put tremendous pressure on the Beneš government to grant ever greater concessions to Henlein and the Sudeten Germans.

On 30 May 1938, Hitler signed a new Case Green directive to

"smash Czechoslovakia by military action" by no later than 1 October 1938. Five army groups with thirty-six divisions were placed on the northern and southern borders of Moravia. Czechoslovakia ordered general mobilization on 22 September. France ordered partial mobilization on 24 September while Britain ordered mobilization of their navy on 27 September. Stalin ordered a partial mobilization in eastern Belarus and the Ukrainian SSR on 22 September and threatened Poland with the dissolution of the Soviet-Polish non-aggression pact, because at this time, Poland was supporting the Nazis in their territorial claims against Czechoslovakia. By 29 September, 330,000 reservists were mobilized throughout the western Soviet Union.

Opposing the Germans were thirty-two Czechoslovak divisions in Bohemia and Moravia, and seven divisions in Slovakia to counter Hungarian divisions mobilized on the southern border preparing to reclaim territory in Slovakia. Poland mobilized forces north of Ostrava in preparation to claim the Zaolzie (southeastern Selesia or *Moravsko-sliezsky kraj*) region of northern Moravia, over which the two countries briefly skirmished in 1920. All Czechoslovak divisions were first-class, well-equipped with the most modern weapons, including four armored divisions. They only lacked a meaningful air force. However, Stalin offered 700 planes. By 28 September, Czechoslovakia had more than one million men in arms. The French had sixty-five of its potential 100 division ready. This tally, of course, did not include the 120 divisions promised by Stalin.

Out of fear of a repeat of the Great War, France and Britain ultimately caved to Hitler's demands. These events gave birth to the Munich Agreement on 29 September 1938, followed by German military units entering the Sudetenland on 1 October 1938, with Poland marching into and annexing the Zaolzie region the same day. As a result of the illegitimate child of the Munich Agreement, the First Vienna Award gave Hungary the green light to march into southern Slovakia on 2 November 1938, followed by Hitler's gifting the Carpathian Ruthenia region of eastern Slovakia to Hungary on 15 March 1939, thus re-establishing the Hungarian-Polish border, as it had existed since *AD* tenth century.

As a result of these border disputes, Bohemia and Moravia lost about thirty-eight percent of their combined area to Germany totaling 28,500 square kilometers (11,004 mi^2), with some 3.2 million German and 750,000 Czech inhabitants. Hungary, in turn, received 11,927 square kilometers (4,605 mi^2) comprising 869,299 inhabitants in southern Slovakia and 12,097 square kilometers (4,671 mi^2) of Carpathian Ruthenia. And Poland gained over 1,000 square kilometers (386 mi^2) with 231,679 inhabitants, including some important sources of raw materials and infrastructure.

Colonel Moravec expressed the following in his book, *Master of Spies: The Memoirs of General Frantisek Moravec*:

> In the opinion of the Czechoslovak General Staff, the situation was such that had France and Britain stood firm, and France kept her word [treaty obligations], Hitler would have been compelled to back down, with probably fatal results for his regime, or, had he gone to war, he would have suffered a military defeat. This opinion has since been supported by analyses of German military strengths and weaknesses as revealed by captured documents. The information from Intelligence sources on which the Czechoslovak opinion was based was, in virtually every detail, in the possession of the British and the French, but their interpretation of it apparently differed from ours.
>
> The same was not true of the evaluation by Hitler's own top commanders. General Alfred Jodl, chief of operations on the German General Staff, has since said [in his testimony during the Nuremberg trials], "It was out of the question. With five fighting divisions and seven reserve divisions in the western fortifications—which were nothing but a large construction site—to hold against a hundred French divisions . . . It was militarily impossible."*
>
> Nor was Jodl by any means alone. General Fritz Mannstein [*sic*, Erich von Manstein], one of the greatest of Germany's field commanders, said [in his testimony during the Nuremberg trials], "If a war had broken out, neither our western frontier nor our Polish frontier could really have been effectively defended by us, and there is no doubt whatsoever that had Czechoslovakia defended herself we would have been held up by her fortifications, for we did not have the means to break through."† And General Wilhelm Keitel himself later asserted [in his testimony

* [Footnote in original] Jodl's testimony at Nuremberg, June 4, 1946, *Trial of Major War Criminals*, Vol. XV, 361.

† [Footnote in original] Mannstein's testimony at Nuremberg, August 9, 1946, *Trial of Major War Criminals*, Vol. XX, 606.

> during the Nuremberg trials], "We were extraordinarily happy that it had not come to a military operation because . . . we had always been of the opinion that our means of attack against the frontier fortifications of Czechoslovakia were insufficient. From a purely military point of view we lacked the means for an attack involving the piercing of the frontier fortifications."*
>
> Hitler himself, looking at the details of the Czechoslovak military fortifications which were handed to him gratuitously [by the British and French] at Munich, said, "What we saw greatly disturbed us; we had run a serious risk. The plan prepared by the Czech generals was formidable. I now understand why my generals urged restraint."† (Moravec 1975, 121–2.)

BETRAYAL AND DIPLOMATIC CHAOS IN EUROPE

FROM THE RISE TO POWER OF HITLER AND THE NAZI PARTY BEGINNING IN 1933, the growing fear of many European countries over growing racism, Nationalism, and imperialism in Germany, as well as Germany's expanding military strength contrary to the Treaty of Versailles, led to a frenzy of diplomatic efforts to establish treaties of mutual assistance and cooperation among European anti-Fascist governments. Professor of History and International Relations Igor Lukes summarizes the following in his writings about Stalin and Beneš relative to the *Zeitgeist* leading up to the Munich crisis (Lukes 1990; see also Lukes 1996).

> This general mood was summarized by the Swiss national daily *Journal de Genève*: "The fear which the Hitlerian regime inspires everywhere in Europe, its racist doctrine and its Nationalistic claims have recently made many a Government turn to the Soviets for support and even

* [Footnote in original] Keitel's testimony at Nuremberg, April 4, 1946, *Trial of Major War Criminals*, Vol. XX, 606.

† [Footnote in original] André Géraud Pertinax, *The Gravediggers of France* (New York, NY: Doubleday, Doran & Company, Inc. 1944), 5.

alliance. Democracies and autocracies alike vie with one another in paying court to the Kremlin." This fully applied to Beneš. In June 1934, disregarding all domestic and international tensions, the Czechoslovak Government recognized the Soviet Government *de jure,* exactly twelve years after its *de facto* recognition. In September 1934, Beneš achieved his next objective: successfully co-sponsoring with France the Soviet Union's membership in the League of Nations. Simultaneously, Beneš started working toward achieving a mutual assistance pact with Moscow. Only a political *connoisseur* can appreciate fully the clever steps that Beneš took. Instead of approaching the Soviet Union directly, Beneš had first sought to bring Paris and Moscow together. This was meant to have two advantages. First, French involvement with the Soviet Union would stretch the field of *Quai d'Orsay*'s operations so as to cover Czechoslovakia, left in a limbo by the Locarno Pact of 1925; second, the French action would legitimatize Beneš' own Soviet initiative, especially in the eyes of his opposition at home.

Overall, Beneš's political legacy is one of crucial strategic defeats (1938, 1948) resulting, paradoxically, from scores of tactical successes. The Franco-Soviet Treaty of Mutual Assistance, signed in Paris on 2 May 1935, was one of his many tactical victories. Only now, when the scene had been prepared and the principal actor insured, was Beneš ready to solidify his nation's position with the *Treaty of Mutual Assistance Between the Czechoslovak Republic and the Union of Soviet Socialist Republics*, signed in Prague on 16 May 1935. The following day, Stalin extended a hearty invitation for Beneš to visit Moscow. On 8 June 1935, Beneš was given a red-carpet welcome in Moscow by Stalin with People's Commissar for Foreign Affairs of the Soviet Union Maxim Litvinov announcing Beneš was welcome "as an outstanding champion of international collaboration and of reinforcing universal peace."

By intention, the Franco-Soviet and Czechoslovak-Soviet treaties were intimately intertwined: Article II of the Czechoslovak-Soviet Treaty's Protocol of Signature

> stipulates that Czechoslovak and Soviet armies would be required to come to each other's defense "only insofar as . . . assistance will be accorded by France to the Party victim of the aggression." It remains unclear who insisted on the stipulation. It may have been added by the careful Beneš who feared that, in an emergency, Moscow could seize the initiative, force a corridor through Romania (Poland had already made quite clear its position against permitting any Soviet army through its territory to assist Czechoslovakia), and occupy Czechoslovakia on the invitation of a "provisional government," consisting of a few Moscow-trained "revolutionary workers." This explanation is less likely than Beneš's concerns at the time that the internationally respected Czechoslovak Army would be obligated to come to Stalin's assistance in his growing tensions with Japan and China in the Far East.

Between the years 1938 and 1940, the repeated betrayal by the French and unreliable commitment from the British forced President Beneš again to play a dangerous and unpredictable diplomatic game with Stalin and the Soviets in order to push the British to firm up their commitment to ensure the Pittsburgh Agreement of 31 May 1918; the territorial and political integrity of a united and sovereign Czechoslovakia.

Declassified Soviet archives covering the period of early 1938 to the outbreak of war in September 1939 reveal that the Kremlin was aware of the unprecedented pressure Britain and France placed on Czechoslovakia in 1938 to appease Hitler with the Munich Agreement. Russian foreign intelligence service Major General Lev Sotskov, who sorted the 700 pages of declassified documents, stated:

> At every stage of the appeasement process, from the earliest top-secret meetings between the British and French, we understood exactly and in detail what was going on. It was clear that appeasement would not stop with Czechoslovakia's surrender of the Sudetenland and that neither the British nor the French would lift a finger when Hitler dismembered the rest of the country. (Holdsworth 2008; see also Sotskov 2018.)

The declassified Soviet archives reveal that on 15 August 1939, the Soviet Union proposed sending a powerful military force in an effort to entice Britain and France into an anti-Nazi alliance. The offer of a military force to help contain Hitler was made by a senior Soviet military delegation at a Kremlin meeting with senior British and French officers two weeks before war broke out. But the British and French side—briefed by their governments to talk, but not authorized to commit to binding deals—did not respond to the Soviet offer. Instead, Stalin turned to Germany, signing the notorious and seismic Molotov-Ribbentrop *Treaty of Non-aggression Between Germany and the Union of Soviet Socialist Republics* with Hitler barely a week after proposing to help fight Hitler. The Molotov-Ribbentrop pact would never have happened if Stalin's offer of a western alliance had been accepted, according to retired General Sotskov. The declassified documents also reveal the Soviet offer, made by People's Commissar (Minister) for Defense Marshall Klement Voroshilov and Chief of the General Staff of the Red Army Boris Shaposhnikov, would have put up to 120 infantry divisions (each with some 19,000 troops), sixteen cavalry divisions, 5,000 heavy artillery pieces, 9,500 tanks, and up to 5,500 fighter aircraft and bombers on Germany's borders in the event of war in the west. Shaposhnikov at the time was in charge of modernizing and rebuilding the Red Army and its leadership after Stalin's purges of 1937–1938. Deemed necessary for this operation, he obtained the release of 4,000 Soviet officers imprisoned in Gulags. In 1939, Stalin accepted Shaposhnikov's plan for a rapid buildup of the Red Army's strength. Although the plan was not completed before the German invasion of June 1941, it was sufficiently advanced to save the Soviet Union from complete disaster. Shaposhnikov elaborated: "Had the British, French, and their European ally Poland taken this offer seriously then together we [combined with the Allied powers] could have put some 300 or more divisions into the field on two fronts against Germany—double the number Hitler had at the time. This was a chance to save the world or at least stop the wolf in its tracks" (Holdsworth 2008). A desperate attempt by the French on 21 August 1939 to revive the talks was rebuffed, as secret Soviet-Nazi talks were about to conclude with signing of the Molotov-Ribbentrop Pact on 23 August 1939.

Professor of Law and Political Science *JUDr.* Jan F. Tříska and Professor of Russian and Soviet history Dr. Robert M. Slusser published their book, *Theory, Law and Policy of Soviet Treaties* in 1962 in which they proffer the following:

Both these pacts [Franco-Soviet Treaty and Czechoslovak-USSR Treaty], the first Soviet mutual assistance treaties, suffered a lamentable fate. According to [Sergeĭ Borisovich] Krylov [Professor of Law and first Soviet judge on the International Court of Justice], "The capitulation of the French at Munich actually robbed [both of] them of their force."

In the view of Soviet scholars, at the time of the "Munich conspiracy which surrendered the Czechoslovak people to Nazi torture, only the Soviet Union remained loyal to its treaty obligations to Czechoslovakia." At the beginning of September 1938, the Soviet government proposed to the governments of Britain, France, and Czechoslovakia the immediate convocation of representatives of the USSR, France, and Britain and the publication of a declaration in the name of those powers warning that Czechoslovakia would receive assistance if she were the victim of German attack; the Soviet government proposed that the problem be submitted to the League of Nations for discussion of ways of defending Czechoslovakia and arranging for technical consultation among the Soviet, French, and Czechoslovak General Staffs to work out a plan of joint military operations. "At the time it was emphasized that the USSR would extend aid to Czechoslovakia by every means and through all available channels in accordance with the Soviet-Czechoslovak Mutual Assistance Treaty." However, "the refusal of the Anglo-French imperialists to join the USSR in measures of collective defense against the Fascist aggressors, the Munich deal and subsequent concessions made by the imperialists of Britain, France, and the U.S.A. to Nazi Germany and Fascist Italy *in an effort to draw Germany into a war against the USSR* [*sic*], which was anathema to them, plunged the peoples into the maelstrom of World War II."

Declared Stalin: "How could it happen that the nonaggressive countries, which have enormous potential, so easily and without offering any resistance yielded their positions and repudiated their obligations in favor of the aggressors? . . . The main reason was that the majority of nonaggressive countries, Britain and France in the first instance, refused to enter into a policy of collective security, a policy of collective rebuff to the aggressors, and took up an attitude of nonintervention and 'neutrality.'"

At the twentieth anniversary of Munich in 1958, Nikita Khrushchev spoke again, according to Walter Lippmann, "with passionate conviction," of the Soviet readiness in 1938 to help Czechoslovakia under the Mutual Assistance Treaty. However, according to a Czechoslovak journalist, Ivo D. Duchaček, the Chairman of the Foreign Affairs Committee in the Czechoslovak Parliament and a personal friend of President Beneš, in September 1938, "President Beneš and his Foreign Minister, Kamil Krofta, pressed the Soviet Ambassador in Prague, Alexandrovskii, for concrete information as to the scope, rapidity, and technique of assistance if Czechoslovakia were to decide to go on its own and fight Hitler without French assistance. The Soviet government and its Ambassador took refuge in very general assurances as to the traditional Soviet faithfulness to all their international obligations. The Czechoslovak government was thus convinced that the Soviet government was to honor its signature provided France first honored hers; the Soviet government, however, appeared reluctant to be fully involved if Czechoslovakia was not to be assisted by France."

In the summer of 1945, Mr. Duchaček reported, he discussed the matter with Beneš. What kind of help might have been expected from the USSR if, despite France's default, Czechoslovakia had decided to fight? "Beneš suggested that the Soviet Union, to save face, would have helped Czechoslovakia, in the same insignificant way she had assisted the Republicans during the Spanish civil war. Some plans, some weapons, and plenty of commissars, said President Beneš. This would not have altered the outcome: Czechoslovakia would have become a Nazi protectorate as she did—with one difference; her economic wealth would have been devastated by war and her population decimated."

Clinging to the letter rather than the spirit of the

> Soviet-Czechoslovak Mutual Assistance Treaty, however, the Soviet government was in the clear. The Soviet answer to the question, "why was not the mechanism of the 1935 pacts ever brought into play in the 1938–39 period," has always been unanimous: simply "through the fault of the French government of that day, which refused to come to the aid of the victim of aggression, in spite of its accepted obligation to do so."
>
> Said [Feodor Ivanovich] Kozhevnikov [Moscow University Professor of Law and judge on International Court of Justice]: "In this connection one must especially underscore the commonly known fact that, despite the elimination of the obligations of the mentioned treaty, owing to the refusal of France to come to the aid of Czechoslovakia, the Soviet government, nevertheless, invariably expressed its readiness to defend the people of Czechoslovakia; this, however, could not be realized through the fault of the ruling circles of Poland of that time and, partly, of Czechoslovakia itself."
>
> This contention includes an element of truth; however, the Soviet Union thereafter adjusted itself rapidly to the new situation and (1) asked that the Czechoslovak embassy in Moscow be closed and its members leave the country, (2) recognized *de jure* the new German-sponsored state of Slovakia, (3) did not come to the aid of Czechoslovakia when part of its territory—Ruthenia—was invaded by Hungary, and (4) in the secret Soviet-German Additional Protocol (to the Nonaggression Treaty of August 23, 1939) ceded Czechoslovakia to the German "sphere of influence." (Tříska and Slusser 1962.)

The Soviet high command's own Marshal Mikhail Tukhachevsky secretly admitted in 1936 to William Bullitt, first U.S. Ambassador to the Soviet Union, that "at the present moment the Soviet Union would be unable to bring any military aid to Czechoslovakia in case of German attack." One year later Tukhachevsky was executed in the notorious 1937–1938 purge of Red Army officers and Military Maritime Fleet admirals.

When the Soviets offered to help create a two-front threat with the British and French against Hitler, no one in either the British or French governments, backed by extant intelligence, believed Stalin and the Soviet Red Army was capable of and serious about actually executing such a feat. Their suspicions were soon to be proven correct in June 1941.

Finally, Stalin himself believed wars among Capitalists are likely to weaken them and therefore speed "Socialist encirclement." Soviet poet and biographer Felix Chuev recalls in his diaries many conversations he had with Stalin's close confident and foreign minister, Viacheslav Molotov: "'Stalin looked at it this way,' his foreign minister, Viacheslav Molotov recalled: 'World War I has wrested one country from Capitalist slavery; World War II has created a Socialist system; and the third will finish off imperialism forever'" (Resis 1993, 63). For Stalin, encouraging "bourgeois" Capitalist powers to battle it out with Hitler would help pave the way for his domination of Europe. "The idea of propagating world Communist revolution was an ideological screen to hide our desire for world domination," one of his secret agents Sudoplatov recalled decades later (Sudoplatov et al. 1994, 102). "This war is not as in the past," Stalin himself explained to the Yugoslav Communist Milovan Djilas in 1945: "Whoever occupies a territory also imposes his own social system. . . . It cannot be otherwise" (Djilas 1962, 114).

Like his many ruses to foreign political leaders in Poland, Czechoslovakia, Britain, France, and Germany, Stalin's offer to the British and French in August 1939 was just another ruse. He had no real intentions of sacrificing his own armies before the armies of Capitalism were seriously weakened and brought to their knees. Stalin would have much rather had it that Capitalist armies beat each other into the ground paving the easy path for the armies of Bolshevism to victoriously reshape the political landscape and liberate the proletariat of the world. Any argument that it was the failure of Capitalist "imperialistic" governments to join with Stalin before the war to defeat the Fascists are purely a diversion to deflect the harsh criticism and shame the Molotov-Ribbentrop Pact continues to generate in Russia today. This is no more evident than in the decision to selectively declassify former Soviet documents relative to the events surrounding Czechoslovakia in 1939 and the revisionist propaganda the Russian government has been pushing during the recent seventieth anniversary remembrance of the signing of the Molotov-Ribbentrop Pact.

RETREAT TO ENGLAND

IN 1938, THE 1,500,000 STRONG CZECHOSLOVAK ARMY WAS AMONG THE largest in Europe, and fairly well-equipped with modern weapons, including locally produced tanks and aircraft. One day after the conclusion of the Munich Conference, German troops entered the Sudetenland area of Czechoslovakia on 1 October 1938, occupying the entire region with almost no resistance from the Czechoslovak forces—only the Third Battalion of the Eighth Border Regiment briefly resisted advancing German troops before being ordered to stand down by Czechoslovak High Command. The Czechoslovak Armed Forces had been fully mobilized since late September 1938 and counted a total of twenty infantry divisions (each with three infantry brigades and one or two artillery regiments), two motorized divisions, and four armored cavalry divisions, each with one tank and one cavalry brigade (modeled on the "fast divisions" used in the French army at the time). In addition, there were a total of 138 battalions manning border fortresses along the borders, split into twelve border sections and seven "defensive regional groups" responsible for securing lines of communication behind the border fortresses. A formidable force, on paper.

Adolf Hitler made a triumphant visit to the border areas (Cheb) on 3 October 1938, to an enthusiastic Sudeten welcome. On 5 October 1938, President Dr. Edvard Beneš handed in his resignation. On 22 October 1938, accompanied by his wife Hana (née Vlčková), President Beneš secretly flew from Prague to England. Before leaving Czechoslovakia, Beneš had a short meeting with what became the first cell of the Czechoslovak resistance to Nazi aggression. The group meeting with him consisted of some of his immediate collaborators and trusted political friends. Convinced as he was (in part, based on information provided by agent A-54), that war would start in May or June 1939 with an attack on Poland, Beneš told his friends: "As soon as the second European war starts, we must again begin an all-out struggle as in 1914." He urged the creation of an organization for overall resistance at home and abroad to Nazi Germany as well as large-scale political and military emigration to countries in Europe "which will be forced to go to war in spite of the Munich treason or rather because of it."

On 3 March 1939, at an urgent meeting in Prague requested by agent A-54, Moravec and several of his close subordinate officers in the Second Department learned from A-54 of German plans to occupy the rest of Bohemia and Moravia in twelve days. Furthermore, simultaneously with the occupation of Bohemia and Moravia, an "independent" Slovakia would be created under the protection of the German *Reich*. The *Gestapo* accompanying the invading armies were ordered to arrest all Czechoslovak intelligence officers and subject them to interrogation "with great severity" to learn the identity of their source agents in Germany. A-54 asked what Colonel Moravec and the Second Department intended to do to escape the *Gestapo*. This inquiry was probably out of concern that his identity as a source agent for the Czechoslovak intelligence would be discovered by the *Gestapo* if members of the Second Department and their files were captured. Moravec told him that they had made plans for such a scenario to prevent any documents or intelligence from falling into the hands of the *Gestapo*. Agent A-54 then warned the group meeting with him in Prague not to go to France if they planned on leaving Czechoslovakia. He did not explain why at this time. However, after the invasion, rapid capitulation of France in June 1940 made this warning entirely clear to Moravec and his compatriots in the Second Department. At the end of the meeting, Colonel Moravec again assured him nothing would be left behind about A-54 for the *Gestapo* to find. Agent A-54 then wished them "good luck . . . this is not goodbye but *auf Wiedersehen*" (Moravec 1975, 138–9).

On 10 March 1939, Thümmel met personally with Chief of the Offensive Section of the Second Department General Staff Major Emil Strankmüller and further solidified the precise date and time of German invasion of Bohemia and Moravia. At the time of occupation, he moved into Czechoslovakia and took an apartment in Břevnov, a northern district of Prague. There, he was assigned, most likely by Admiral Canaris, himself, as *Leiter* (Chief) of the Counterintelligence Bureau III.F, of the Prague *abwehrstelle* station responsible for Czechoslovakia, the Balkans, and the Near East. Division III was responsible for counterintelligence operations in industry, planting false information, penetration of foreign intelligence services, and investigating acts of sabotage and treason. Bureau III.F (*Feind*) was the counter espionage agent's bureau responsible for penetration of enemy intelligence services.

Having gleaned much information about the impending occupation of Czechoslovakia after taking the Sudetenland, the growing unrest in Slovakia, and intelligence from agent A-54 about the planned German invasion, the Second Department informed Major Harold Charles Lehr Gibson, the SIS representative in Prague. He passed this information to his superiors at SIS headquarters in London and was instructed to offer the Czechoslovak Military Intelligence the transfer of a certain number of their staff to the United Kingdom. On 11 March 1939, it was agreed with Major

Gibson that the British would enable some chosen Czechoslovak operatives to leave for London, where they would continue their activities against Germany. It was also agreed that Colonel Moravec would take eleven members of his group based on his own selection. Information provided by agent A-54 was allegedly a decisive factor in Moravec's choice of the officers to accompany him to London. On the evening of 14 March 1939, Colonel Moravec secretly left Prague for London accompanied by eleven of his subordinate officers and staff aboard a diverted chartered KLM plane, which landed at London's civil airport Croydon at 2240 hours the same day. This daring escape occurred just seven hours before the full invasion of Bohemia and Moravia by German forces. They took with them large portions of the archives of the Second Department, including operatives' registers and the most important intelligence files. Further materials were transmitted to Major Gibson who was also departing Prague so that he could arrange their transport to England via diplomatic mail. The departure of the Moravec group can be considered the beginning of the Czechoslovak organized military resistance abroad during the Second World War. The group of eleven Czechoslovak intelligence officers headed by Colonel František Moravec has been referred to as "Moravec's XI." Admittedly, one of the most difficult decisions in his life, Colonel Moravec had to leave his wife and two young daughters behind in Prague since there were only twelve seats aboard the Dutch KLM plane that took them to England and of the hundreds of people working in the Second Department, he had to make the agonizing decision as which eleven were the most crucial to the future of Czechoslovakia.

THE DIPLOMATIC GAME

ON 15 MARCH 1939, GERMANY OCCUPIED THE REST OF Czechoslovakia—essentially the regions of Bohemia and Moravia. Although the Czechoslovak Army was formally disbanded as part of this process, many army personnel still wanted to fight the Germans. Despite feeling betrayed by the Allies, the only option was to volunteer to fight in one of the Allied armies at the time. Thus, many Czechs and Slovaks made their way to Romania and Poland before borders were closed completely. However, many of the Czech and Slovak soldiers (and civilians) that had managed to escape from Czechoslovakia when Germany invaded, decided not to stay in Poland and made their way to France instead to join the new First Czechoslovak Infantry Division in Agde.

In an effort to organize and garner support of the Americans and Czechoslovak-Americans (as he and Dr. Tomáš G. Masaryk so successfully did in 1918) against the tragedy of Munich, President Edvard Beneš left London and traveled to the United States between February and July 1939. On 28 May 1939, Beneš secretly held a lengthy meeting with President Franklin D. Roosevelt at his Hyde Park residence. In reply to Roosevelt's questions, Beneš predicted a German *Blitzkrieg* against Poland any time after the middle of the summer and Poland's collapse within two weeks because of "the total unpreparedness, lack of seriousness and empty megalomania" of the Polish leadership. He expressed his confidence that Britain would oppose German aggression against Poland and his hope that France would do so, too. To the President's question, on whose side the Soviet Union would enter the war, Dr. Beneš answered: "Of course on our side." For his part, Roosevelt told him: "We have helped you once. We will help you again."

When Beneš returned to Britain six weeks before the outbreak of war, the British Foreign Office intimated to him that it would not be advisable to air his views in public. Yet, a growing number of British politicians flocked to his modest residence in Putney. On 27 July 1939, a private luncheon was held in his honor on the initiative of Winston Churchill and Anthony Eden (both former members of the British government were, like Beneš, in a period of political exile at the time), at which leading members of Britain's three political parties came out wholeheartedly in support of the cause of Czechoslovakia. Churchill stated that there would be no peace in Europe as long as Czechoslovakia remained enslaved. And Britain's future war leader concluded: "I do not know how events will develop. And I cannot say that Great Britain will now go to war for Czechoslovakia. I only know for certain that the peace which still has to be established will not be made without Czechoslovakia." Sir Archibald Sinclair, for the Liberals, promised Britain's continued loyalty to the ideals of Democracy, while Laborite Arthur Henderson stressed that there were no differences between the various political parties in Britain with respect to removing the "injustice" done to Czechoslovakia. Most outspoken was the ageing Lord Robert Cecil, who considered Munich the "shameful betrayal" by Britain of her great past. Beneš in his reply asked those present not to forget "the unmerited sufferings of his people." Describing his impressions of the United States' attitude, he said that both the President and the

Secretary of State had assured him that "America would never recognize the violence done to Czechoslovakia."

Meanwhile in Paris, the Munich-ites Daladier and Georges Bonnet continued to hold office. As British Foreign Office liaison to the exiled Czechoslovak government Robert Bruce Lockhart later put it, the position of the Czechoslovaks in France at the outbreak of the war was "the tragic illustration of the dislike that men feel for those whom they have wronged." There was in fact what amounted to a Daladier veto on Beneš's policies. The French Premier apparently considered that Beneš had not been pliable enough during the 1938 crisis and had forced him to Munich. He refused to receive him when he visited Paris in October 1939 to discuss details of the Czechoslovak-French Treaty on the Reconstitution of the Czechoslovak Army in France. Before departing London, Beneš's foreign minister Štefan Osusky warned Beneš he would not be welcome by the French in Paris. Georges Mandel, then Minister of Colonies, told Beneš at the time in Paris that after what Daladier had done to Czechoslovakia, he did not dare to look Beneš in the face. There were also diplomatic considerations behind this attitude. Polish Foreign Minister Colonel Józef Beck was still bent on splitting the Czechs and Slovaks by creating a common Polish-Hungarian border and with war on the horizon, there was no desire in Paris (or London, for that matter) to alienate Poland. Moreover, Beck sent the British Foreign Secretary a letter opposing any recognition of the Czechoslovak government in exile. Beneš and his government in exile in London faced formidable opposition to formal recognition not only from Britain and France over the legacy of the Munich disaster, but also from Poland and Hungary for their respective self-serving political motivations. For centuries, Hungary and Poland have had a uniquely congenial relationship in spite of their disparate ethnic and linguistic backgrounds. The Magyars and Poles shared much common ground in their ties through marriages among the noble class, and both were under Habsburg rule sharing a mutual border until the Treaty of Versailles. This historical association persevered during World War II, even though the two nations were on opposite sides. They both believed they could restore their pre-World War I borders and only needed the pretext or opportunity to do so. Both the Polish government in exile in London and existing Hungarian government held positions of influence over British foreign policy. This was made clear by the British Foreign Office under Viscount Halifax in their internal communiqués and legal analyses of the Munich Agreement. At this time, the status of the Czechoslovak Provisional Government, in comparison with the other Governments in exile in Britain clearly was not the same, and this was primarily due to the Munich Agreement which the British under Chamberlain and French under Daladier were not ready to capitulate and disavow. This opposition to recognizing Czechoslovakia, the defeat of France, and the impending German attack on Britain would eventually precipitate the fall of the Chamberlain-Halifax government, rise of Churchill, the infamous War Cabinet crisis of May 1940, and the appointment of Anthony Eden as Secretary of State for War and again as Foreign Secretary. However, full British diplomatic recognition of the Czechoslovak government in exile under President Beneš did not materialize until 18 July 1940.

THE PRICE OF RECOGNITION

ONCE GERMANY ATTACKED POLAND IN SEPTEMBER 1939, ACTION TO restore Czechoslovak government legitimacy centered primarily in France. There were several politically expedient reasons for this. Continental France bordered on Germany, the Czechoslovak embassy was still recognized by the French government, and the thousands of Czechoslovak refugees reaching the country of their former ally were allowed to join the French Foreign Legion. Later, when an agreement on the recognition of a Czechoslovak National Committee was reached, these Czech and Slovak *légionnaires* were to form the nucleus of the Czechoslovak Army abroad. As early as September 1939, the French government set up the First Infantry Battalion of the Czechoslovak Armed Forces abroad in Agde, France.

In Paris on 2 October 1939, French Prime Minister Édouard Daladier and Czechoslovak Foreign Minister Štefan Osusky signed the Czechoslovak-French Treaty on the Reconstitution of the Czechoslovak Army in France (*Accord relatif à la reconstitution en France de l'armée tchéchoslovaque*) permitting a general mobilization of Czech and Slovak soldiers in the territory of France. On 16 October 1939, the First Czechoslovak Infantry Battalion expanded into a regiment and, a month later, the Second Infantry Regiment was formed from new arrivals. Soon, these units at the Foreign Legion base at Agde in southern France formed the First Czechoslovak Infantry Division. This new infantry division was included in the French Order of Battle on 15 January 1940. The treaty, reluctantly signed by Daladier (with refusal to acknowledge Edvard Beneš as President of the Czechoslovak government in exile), was born in the setting of imminent invasion and in the wake of his country's betrayal of Czechoslovakia a few months earlier when France failed to fulfill its obligations to the *Treaty of Alliance and Friendship Between France and Czechoslovakia* signed in Paris on 25 January 1924, wherein France promised to come to the aid of Czechoslovakia if threatened by Germany or Hungary, and the *de facto* tripartite *Treaty of Mutual Assistance Between the Czechoslovak Republic and the Union of Soviet Socialist Republics* signed in Prague on 16 May 1935, making France the determining factor in the defense of Czechoslovakia.

The First Czechoslovak Infantry Division in France initially had two infantry regiments, with a combined strength of 5,000 men, but had no artillery, only a handful of 81-mm mortars, and only two 25-mm antiaircraft guns, rendering its combat usefulness limited. However, by the end of May 1940, the division comprised a mixed reconnaissance unit, a field artillery regiment, an antitank troop, an antitank company, a headquarters squadron, two signal companies, a company of field engineers, and divisional rear. The organization, equipment, and armaments were French, and mostly leftovers from the First World War. This amounted to 120 pieces of artillery, including mortars, 1,800 horses, 900 motorized vehicles, and 11,495 men. Of these, 3,326 volunteers were from the homeland and 8,169 were mobilized expatriates living abroad that made their way to France via the Balkans and Middle East, since the way through Poland had been cut off by that country's surrender.

During the Battle of France in 1940, the First Czechoslovak Regiment (at Coulommiers) and the Second Regiment (on the Marne) tried to halt the Sixteenth Panzer Division, but had their flanks turned and had to fight a rearguard action back across France. Being left seriously underequipped by the French, the division was steadily driven back by the Germans until only a brigade remained and had to be emergently evacuated to Britain when the French government and army collapsed in June 1940. They were eventually re-grouped at Narbonne before being evacuated from Selte.

It had been a long and difficult journey from Czechoslovakia to England. No one among them from general to private knew if he would ever see his homeland again. The remaining brigade landed in Britain bitter and demoralized. Rushed into battle in France inadequately equipped against the modern, rapidly advancing German forces in May 1940, the First Czechoslovak Infantry Division was mired in the French military defeat. When France surrendered on 17 June 1940, its former allies were left to fend for themselves. Many soldiers with wives and families in France returned to Agde where they were demobilized. The remainder, exiles who could not risk falling into the hands of the *Gestapo*, determined to escape to Britain and continue the fight. Under the command of *Generál* Sergej Ingr, these elements retreated towards the Mediterranean coast along roads strewn with refugees and broken remnants of the French Army while President Beneš in London desperately lobbied the British authorities to secure evacuation ships. Despite his best efforts, the troops were nearly abandoned in the general confusion of defeat and retreat. The situation was only salvaged by Robert Bruce Lockhart, British Foreign Office liaison with the Czechoslovak provisional government-in-exile, who pulled strings at the British Admiralty to rescue the remnants of the First Czechoslovak Infantry Division. The men sailed without their heavy equipment but with a deep and abiding contempt for France which was seen as guilty of a triple betrayal—first at Munich, then when Hitler invaded Czechoslovakia and occupied all of Bohemia and Moravia, and again in the recent fighting when it had once more abandoned its Czechoslovak allies.

CZECH HOME RESISTANCE

DURING THREE HUNDRED YEARS OF AUSTRIAN RULE BEGINNING WITH Habsburg Holy Roman Emperor Ferdinand II's victory over Bohemian forces at the Battle of White Mountain on 8 November 1620, the Czechs had not lost their identity or given up attempts to regain their sovereignty; they would continue to resist this new German enslavement with courage and determination. The promise, "We shall remain faithful," given to President Tomáš Masaryk when his remains were interred in Prague on 21 September 1937, throbbed deeply within the hearts of all Czechs and Slovaks who were united under one nation by Dr. Masaryk. Before his death, he had directed the nation to resist any spiritual or material oppressor.

Czechoslovak resistance organizations abroad, particularly in the United Kingdom, were now prepared for this new phase in the war and could at last join their fellow countrymen in the struggle to defeat the enemy.

The Czech resistance network that existed during the early years of the Second World War operated under the leadership of Czechoslovak President Edvard Beneš, who together with the head of Czechoslovak military intelligence, Colonel František Moravec, coordinated resistance activity while in exile in London. In the context of German persecution, the major resistance groups consolidated under the Central Leadership of Home Resistance (*Ústřední vedení odboje domácího, ÚVOD*). It served as the principal clandestine intermediary between Beneš and the Protectorate and operated through 1941. Its long-term purpose was to serve as a shadow government until Czechoslovakia's liberation from Nazi occupation.

The three major resistance groups that consolidated under *ÚVOD* were the Political Center (*Politické ústředí, PÚ*), the Committee of the Petition "We Remain Faithful" (*Petiční výbor Věrni zůstaneme, PVVZ*), and the Defense of the Nation (*Obrana národa, ON*—consisting mostly of former professional soldiers and reserve officers). These groups were all Democratic in political ideology, as opposed to the fourth official resistance group, the Communist Party of Czechoslovakia (*KSČ*). In 1941, *ÚVOD* endorsed the political platform designed by the Leftist group *PVVZ*, titled "For Freedom: Into a New Czechoslovak Republic." In it, *ÚVOD* professed allegiance to the Democratic ideals of Czechoslovakia's first president Tomáš G. Masaryk, called for the establishment of a republic with a Socialist platform, and urged all those in exile to stay in step with the Socialist advances at home.

In addition to serving as the means of communication between London and Prague, *ÚVOD* was also responsible for the transmission of intelligence and military reports. It did so primarily through the use of several secret radio transmitters known as the Sparta network. The Sparta network consisted of eleven wireless radio transmitters, three of which were codenamed "Sparta I" in Jinonice district of Prague, "Sparta II" also in Prague, and "Libuše" near Pardubice, all of which could reach London and the Czech population. Between 1939 and 1941, the network provided some twenty thousand intelligence messages. Sparta I and Sparta II were responsible for 6,000 of those messages.

ARRIVAL OF THE "BUTCHER OF PRAGUE"

IMMEDIATELY AFTER THE NAZI OCCUPATION OF BOHEMIA AND MORAVIA on 15 March 1939, these territories were annexed to the Third *Reich* as *Reichsprotectorat Böhmen und Mähren* under the supervision of *Reichsprotektor* Baronet Konstantin von Neurath as the first territorial administrator serving the *Reich* in Prague. Hitler ignored all Czech

Nationalistic feelings when he made this appointment. To Neurath's appeals for cooperation, the Czechs responded with either passive resistance or outright sabotage. Neurath had failed to win the support of the Czech population. As a consequence, Hitler lost confidence in Neurath. In September 1941, Neurath requested an extended leave of absence because of poor health. He was quickly replaced by intensely dedicated and deeply ideological *SS-Obergruppenführer und General der Polizei* Reinhard Heydrich, second in command only to *Reichsführer* of the *Schutzstaffel* (*SS*) Heinrich Himmler.

On 27 September 1941, Heydrich arrived in Prague, immediately declared a state of emergency, and issued a number of directives. The surprise elements in this intervention were speed and cruelty, calculated to have a strong psychological effect on the population. The rule of terror and fear cast a shadow over the country. On 28 September 1941, Heydrich was formally inaugurated into office and he immediately announced martial law for the *Oberlandrats* (regional governors) in Prague, Brno, Moravská Ostrava, Olomouc, Kladno, and Hradec Králové. Martial law courts had only three options—carry out the death sentence, hand the accused over to the *Gestapo*, and/or vindicate the person. The sentences of the martial law courts were irrevocable and were executed immediately. The first to fall victim to his new measures were Czech General and Prime Minister of the Protectorate of Bohemia and Moravia Alois Eliáš and a number of other former Czech generals who were known anti-Nazis. On 29 September 1941, two acting leaders of the Czech military resistance organization, the Defense of the Nation (*Obrana národa, ON*), *Generál* Josef Bílý and *Major Generál* Hugo Vojta, Commander of the Bohemian Provincial Headquarters, were sentenced under martial law and executed by a firing squad at Ruzyně Barracks. These brutal measures were meant to break anti-German resistance in the Czech Lands. The last words of *Generál* Bílý were: "Long live the Czechoslovak Republic! Fire, you dogs!" Their deaths only provoked the Czech populace, who from then on sought revenge. As persons convicted by martial law courts burgeoned, local capacity to carry out executions was overwhelmed. On 30 September 1941, Heydrich advised the Commander of the Berlin headquarters of the *Gestapo*, *SS-Brigadeführer* Henrich Müller that all persons sentenced by martial law courts should be placed exclusively in the Mauthausen Concentration Camp. In Mauthausen, a total of 4,473 of Czechoslovak citizens were tortured to death or executed during the war. Arrests and executions increased daily, but the Czechs refused to be terrorized into submission. Resistance groups sprang up like mushrooms after a heavy rain.

When terror did not bring the Czechs to their knees, Heydrich offered bribes. The *Reich* needed labor to mass produce materials for the war effort. Improved living quarters and provisions were promised to those who would cooperate. In this effort to break the passive resistance, the Germans failed to foresee the lengths to which a conquered people will go to resist tyranny.

TRAINING OF CZECHOSLOVAK PARACHUTISTS IN THE UNITED KINGDOM

AFTER ARRIVING AT LIVERPOOL DOCKS IN BRITAIN IN JUNE 1940, THE remnants of the former members of the First Czechoslovak Infantry Division in France gathered in a camp in Cholmondeley Park near Chester. In August 1940, the Czechoslovak provisional government concluded a military agreement with the British and a liaison military mission under British Colonel Pollock was assigned to the Czechoslovak Army. Out of the remnants of the First Czechoslovak Infantry Division, the First Czechoslovak Mixed Brigade was formed on 12 August 1940, with Brigadier General Bedřich Neumann-Miroslav as Commanding Officer. Soon afterwards, morale and *esprit de corps* greatly improved among the Czechoslovak soldiers. This brigade was composed largely of volunteers, well-educated men who had sacrificed everything for their country. The men were motivated by two deep seated sentiments. The first was to reestablish in postwar Czechoslovakia the Democratic society founded by President Tomáš G. Masaryk in the First Republic. However, beyond this, they wanted a better society free of racism and discrimination among ethnic groups, particularly between Czechs and Slovaks. The second sentiment driving the men was a bitter hatred of the Germans who the Czechoslovaks considered as obstinate racists, elitists, and imperialists. The men wanted to fight and win to invalidate the verdict of Munich and Prague. These sentiments were partly fueled by a haunting sense of guilt at being in a safe place while the home population suffered at the mercy of Sudeten German Karl Hermann Frank and Reinhard Heydrich. Together, they executed a reign of terror in the Bohemian and Moravian Protectorate, arresting and killing dozens of opponents and ramping up the deportation of Jews to concentration camps. The men of the First Czechoslovak Mixed Brigade believed the only way they could ever hope to return to their homeland with pride was to fight their way back, sharing with the resistance movement a common victory against the Nazis. As one British observer remarked, the soldiers could "never hold up their heads in Prague unless they have been in actual combat with the Germans. . . . [T]he men themselves realize full well that they will receive no welcome in their own country unless they have fought the Germans in the later stages of the war; and of course, it is the urgent wish of every man in that Brigade to have a go. . . ."

The First Czechoslovak Mixed Brigade numbered 3,276 men and comprised: the headquarters; two infantry battalions; a machine gun company; an artillery division; an antiaircraft battery; an antitank battery; engineer and telegraph platoons; a motorized company; a motorcycle platoon; a heavy equipment repair shop; and a replacement unit. In the autumn of 1940, this brigade relocated to Leamington Spa, where it was stationed until the spring of 1942. As in France a few months before their arrival in Britain, the burden of combat for the First Czechoslovak Mixed Brigade rested on the Czechoslovak pilots, who immediately joined the ongoing battle that raged over the British Isles. The first Czechoslovak fighter squadron (No. 310) was formed on 10 July 1940, and its sister squadron (No. 312) on 29 August 1940. Also, in July a Czechoslovak bomber squadron became part of No. 3 Group. No. 310 Squadron was soon involved in the Battle of Britain while No. 312 Squadron fought over Liverpool. Josef František, a Czechoslovak pilot flying in a Polish squadron, was the top Allied ace. In all, eighty-seven Czechoslovak pilots participated in the Battle of Britain and eight were killed. By the end of 1940, Czechoslovak fighter pilots had shot down 129 enemy aircraft, plus twenty-five probable hits, and seriously damaged fourteen German aircraft. By this date, a Czechoslovak Inspectorate General was established to coordinate the activities of the Czechoslovak Air Force, which now formed a semi-independent section of the Royal Air Force Volunteer Reserve.

British Special Operations Executive

ALL OF OCCUPIED MAINLAND EUROPE, FROM THE ENGLISH CHANNEL TO beyond the plains of Ukraine, became the field for intelligence activity. To supplement this effort, allied military units were organized in England. Only those physically capable men who were the bravest and most dedicated patriots were selected for this task. They all were thoroughly instructed in various sabotage skills and were put into top physical condition by the

British SOE (Special Operations Executive) at various Special Training Schools (STS) and Experimental Stations.

The Czechoslovak groups were organized by the Czechoslovak Ministry of National Defense in Exile in London under the leadership of Minister of Defense General Sergej Ingr, General Rudolf Viest, and Colonel František Moravec, master spy and chief of the Czechoslovak Military Intelligence Service—Second Department of the General Staff of the Ministry of National Defense (*MNO*)—in exile. The official headquarters of the Second Department was at the Czechoslovak Ministry of National Defense, 131 Piccadilly, but Colonel Moravec eventually formed the real center in Porchester Gate on Bayswater Road in London.

On 16 July 1940, Prime Minister Winston Churchill appointed a civilian, Sir Dr. Edward Hugh John Neale Dalton (simply known as Hugh Dalton), as Minister of Economic Warfare, as well as SOE's political master, and then promptly ordered him to "set Europe ablaze!" Special Operations Executive was founded on 22 July 1940 at a time when Great Britain was the only enemy of Hitler on the European continent actively deploying military units abroad while defending the homeland against the Germans. Few people were aware of SOE's existence. Among those who were part of it or liaised with it, it was sometimes referred to as "the Baker Street Irregulars," after the location of its London headquarters, "Churchill's Secret Army," or the "Ministry of Ungentlemanly Warfare." Its main task was irregular warfare. The main idea of irregular warfare was to use any method available to undermine the enemy's strength. Among the types of irregular fighting was a whole spectrum of activities—partisan warfare, sabotage, espionage, the formation of indigenous resistance movements, assassinations, and all these were to take place directly in the enemy's backyard. The SOE was initially also involved in the formation of the Auxiliary Units, a top secret "stay-behind" resistance organization, which would have been activated in the event of a German invasion of Britain. At its height of activity, the organization directly employed or controlled just over 13,000 people, of whom about 3,200 were women. Of SOE's fifty-five female operatives, thirteen were killed in action or died in Nazi concentration camps. Unlike British SIS (Secret Intelligence Services, also known as MI6, was founded in July 1909), which preferred placid conditions in which it could gather intelligence and work through influential persons or authorities, the SOE was intended to create unrest and turbulence. At times, these disparate missions resulted in tension between SIS and SOE.

The Czechoslovaks were highly recommended to Sir Hugh Dalton by Robert Bruce Lockhart, who was then co-director of SO.1 (Section 1 of SOE) for propaganda, as well as the British Foreign Office liaison with the Czechoslovak provisional government-in-exile. After a meeting with President Beneš in October 1940, Lockhart sent Dalton an enthusiastic report on the Czech resistance movement, which Lockhart described as the most "formidable subversive movement now available to us in Europe." By their sheer skill and determination in sabotage, passive resistance, and an eventual uprising, the Czechoslovak underground was seen as capable of doing incalculable harm to the German war machine. Lockhart argued that SOE must assist the Czechoslovak resistance movement with money and arms, combining maximum support with minimum interference. Dalton was an opponent of the Munich Agreement and sympathized with the Czechoslovak cause. In the Autumn of 1940, Colonel Moravec and the Second Department began working with the newly created British SOE developed by Dalton and this close and productive relationship lasted until the end of the war. No other European country provided more helpful intelligence to the Allies on the Germans than the Czechoslovak Second Department. This was in no small part due to the Second Department's ability to develop and manage assets like A-54 and execute operations behind enemy lines like Anthropoid.

On 17 March 1941, the Chief of the British Ministry for Economic Warfare, Sir Hugh Dalton, who was also still in charge of SOE, inspected Czechoslovak army units in Britain accompanied by the Czechoslovak Minister of National Defense, Major General Sergej Ingr. A decision had been made by British Joint Intelligence Committee to select and train Czechoslovak operatives for missions behind enemy lines in Czechoslovakia and elsewhere in Europe. In April 1941, Major Emil Strankmüller, deputy to Colonel Moravec and head of the Offensive Intelligence Section of the Search Group in the Second Department, Major Karel Paleček (a Legionnaire veteran of the Battle of Zborov) and Captain Jaroslav Šustr, co-commanders of Special Group D in the Offensive Intelligence Section, arrived at headquarters of the First Czechoslovak Mixed Brigade at Leamington Spa charged with a special mission. They were to screen, select, and recruit suitable men for secret operations in the occupied homeland. The requirements were strict. The men to be selected were to be patriotic, fearless, intelligent, capable of controlling their emotions under extreme stress, and keeping secrets under torture. No one with a history of drunkenness or womanizing was eligible. By early May 1941, thirty-six candidates were identified—fourteen commissioned officers and twenty-two non-commissioned officers. Plans worked out with SOE leadership in early spring 1941 were to send three-man teams of Czechoslovak operatives to the Protectorate of Bohemia and Moravia with the primary objective of reestablishing radio communications with the resistance movement under *ÚVOD* and the flow of information from Agent A-54. As these operations progressed, the missions evolved from support to sabotage to assassination.

As the dawn of Operation Barbarossa approached in 1941, the Germans heightened security as a precaution. Secretary of State and Chief of Police Karl Frank, the radical Sudeten German National Socialist in the Protectorate of Bohemia and Moravia, anticipated the Czechs would react violently to an assault on their fellow Slavs to the east (the Russians). He was determined to preempt any such possible reaction by stamping out all resistance in advance. In February 1941, the occupation German security apparatus arrested almost the entire central committee of the Czech Communist party and destroyed its radio links to Moscow. The Czech home army under *ÚVOD* and *ON* also suffered serious losses, including the members of the "Three Kings" with their Sparta I wireless transmitter that functioned as agent A-54's primary communication conduit with the Beneš government in London. On 22 April 1941, Lieutenant Colonel Josef Balabán was arrested by the *Gestapo*. Three weeks later, on 13 May, his comrades Lieutenant Colonel Josef Mašín, Captain Václav Morávek, and radio operator František Peltán were discovered in Jinonice District of Prague in the middle of a transmission of critical information on the impending invasion of the Soviet Union. They were discovered by the transmission signal detector station (*Funkmesstellen*) in southeast Prague and search vehicles equipped with mobile goniometers and detailed street maps that pinpointed them to their apartment.[1,2] These setbacks forced a period of silence between A-54, the Czech resistance, and the Second Department in London. Reestablishment of these lines of communication was crucial to many of the Allies desperate for intelligence information on the Germans. To facilitate reestablishment of communications with the home army and resistance, the Second Department had to select the best volunteer candidates from the First Czechoslovak Mixed Brigade, train them for covert operations, and drop them behind enemy lines in the homeland with new radio transmitters provided by the British SOE.

The men selected from the First Czechoslovak Mixed Brigade in Leamington Spa received the following special operations training: 1) assault course in the Scottish Highlands in the county of Inverness-shire at Garramor House (STS 25a) in the village of South Morar, Camusdarach House (STS 25b) in South Morar, Traigh House (STS 25c) in South Morar, and Arisaig House (STS 21) in the village of Arisaig; 2) parachute training at Royal Air Force station in Ringway, Cheshire, near Manchester, at Dunham House (STS 51a) in the city of Altrincham, and at Fulshaw Hall (STS 51b) in the town of Wilmslow; 3) explosives and special diversion training in the county of Hertfordshire at Brickendonbury Manor (Experimental Station XVII) in the village of Brickendon just north of London; and finally 4) an advanced finishing graduate course in the town of Dorking, Surrey County, covering sabotage, extreme use of motorized vehicles, Morse code, orientation in unfamiliar territory, marksmanship, and use of modified grenades at Villa Bellasis (STS 2) just southwest of London. It was at the training Centre STS 2 where final selection of the team for Operation Anthropoid was made, as well as other operations, after a biography of each man was compiled. It was necessary to determine the individual's absolute fitness and preparedness for the hazardous missions ahead. Just prior to each team's departure, individual last will and testaments were drafted. From 1942 to 1943, the Czechoslovaks had their own Special Training School (STS) at Chicheley Hall in Buckinghamshire. In 1944, SOE sent men to support the Slovak National Uprising.

By the summer of 1943, the 200th Czechoslovak Light Antiaircraft Regiment arrived in England. Czechoslovak forces in the Near East were organized into the Eleventh Czechoslovak Infantry Battalion East on 1 November 1940, at Gedera camp, near Tel Aviv in Palestine where it trained and served various duties throughout Palestine and Egypt until May 1941. From 30 May 1941 to 6 October 1941, the Eleventh Battalion moved to the Western Desert with British Twenty-Third Infantry Brigade and participated in Operations Battleaxe and Exporter. On 20 October 1942, the battalion was shipped to Tobruk where it served for the remainder of the siege under the Polish Carpathian Brigade, until 13 December 1941. During the siege of Tobruk, the battalion suffered fourteen killed and eighty-one wounded. Following the siege, the battalion stayed in the Tobruk area, first under British XIII Corps, then Thirty-Eighth Indian Infantry Brigade until that brigade departed for Egypt on 27 March 1942. On 7 April 1942, the battalion returned to Palestine for conversion to 200th Light Antiaircraft Regiment East in May 1942. When arriving in England in mid-1943, the 200th Czechoslovak Light Antiaircraft Regiment had some 1,500 men. Many of these units in England eventually joined the First Czechoslovak Independent Armored Brigade that landed in Normandy in August 1944.[3]

Between 1940 and 1945, the British SOE-Czechoslovak Second Department relationship in England produced thirty-one airborne operations tasked with "special" missions into the Protectorate of Bohemia and Moravia, Slovakia, France, and northern Italy. It comprised intelligence, demolition, courier, organizational, and assassination missions, the most famous among them being Operation Anthropoid, the successful assassination of *Reich*'s Protector Reinhard Heydrich in Prague on 27 May 1942. In total, ninety-one volunteer Czechoslovak operative paratroopers trained in England were dropped in the homeland and elsewhere throughout Europe. Only forty-five survived the war. Of those that died, they died in action in direct contact with the enemy. Some fell being hit by enemy fire or grenade, some took their own life in order to prevent capture, interrogation, and certain death. Only seven operatives betrayed their mission. Warrant Officers Karel Čurda, Bohuslav Grabovský, and Vilém Gerik, First Lieutenants Václav Kindl and Adolf Horák, and Corporals Libor Zapletal and Vítězslav Lepařík informed on their comrades to the Nazis. All these traitors were executed either during or after the war. Below is a list of the Czechoslovak-SOE operations originating from England, in chronologic order:

1941–1942:
BENJAMIN – 16 April 1941: Sergeant Otmar Riedl

PERCENTAGE – 3 October 1941: Lance Corporal Cadet František Pavelka

ANTHROPOID – 28 December 1941: Warrant Officers Josef Gabčík and Jan Kubiš

> *SILVER A* - First Lieutenant Alfréd Bartoš, Warrant Officer Josef Valčík, and Lance Corporal Jiří Potůček
>
> *SILVER B* – Staff Sergeant Jan Zemek and Sergeant Vladimír Škácha

ZINC – 27 March 1942: First Lieutenant Oldřich Pechal, Warrant Officer Arnošt Mikš, radio operator Sergeant Vilém Gerik

OUT DISTANCE – 27 March 1942: First Lieutenant Adolf Opálka, Warrant Officer Karel Čurda, Corporal Cadet Ivan Kolařík

BIOSCOP – 27 April 1942: Warrant Officer Bohuslav Kouba, Sergeant Jan Hrubý, Sergeant Aspirant Josef Bublík

BIVOUAC – 27 April 1942: Warrant Officer František Pospíšil, Staff Sergeant Jindřich Čoupek, Corporal Cadet Libor Zapletal, Corporal Cadet

Václav Málek

STEEL – 27 April 1942: Lance Corporal Oldřich Dvořák

INTRANSITIVE – 29 April 1942: First Lieutenant Václav Kindl, Sergeant Bohuslav Grabovský, and Corporal Vojtěch Lukaštík

TIN – 29 April 1942: Staff Sergeant Ludvík Cupal, Staff Sergeant Jaroslav Švarc

1942–1943:
ANTIMONY – 23 October 1942: Second Lieutenant František Závorka, Sergeant Stanislav Srazil, Corporal Lubomír Jasínek

IRIDIUM – 14 March 1943: First Lieutenant Miroslav Špot, First Lieutenant Miroslav Křičenský, Sergeant Vladislav Soukup, radio operator Corporal Bohumír Kobylka

BRONSE – 14 March 1943: First Lieutenant Bohumír Martínek, Sergeant Aspirant František Vrbka, radio operator Corporal Antonín Kubec

1943–1945:
CALCIUM – 3 April 1944: Second Lieutenant JUDr. Jaroslav Odstrčil, Staff Sergeant Josef Gemrot, Staff Sergeant František Široký, Staff Sergeant Karel Niemczyk

BARIUM – 3 April 1944: First Lieutenant Josef Šandera, radio operator Sergeant Aspirant Josef Žižka, cryptographer Sergeant Tomáš Býček

SULPHUR – 8 April 1944: First Lieutenant Adolf Horák, radio operator Staff Sergeant Oldřich Janko

CHALK – 8 April 1944: First Lieutenant Bohumil Bednařík, Staff Sergeant Vladimír Hauptvogel, radio operator Staff Sergeant František Nedělka, Sergeant Josef Künzl

CLAY – 13 April 1944: Staff Sergeant Antonín Bartoš, Staff Sergeant Jiří Štokman, radio operator Sergeant Aspirant Čestmír Šikola

CARBON – 13 April 1944: Captain František Bogataj, radio operator Sergeant Aspirant Jaroslav Šperl, parachutists František Kobzík and Josef Vanc

POTASH – 4 May 1944: First Lieutenant Jan Bartejs, radio operator Sergeant Aspirant Josef Machovský, Staff Sergeant Oldřich Pelc, Staff Sergeant

Stanislav Zuvač

SPELTER – 4 May 1944: Staff Captain Břetislav Chrastina, Staff Sergeant Jaroslav Kotásek, radio operator Staff Sergeant Rudolf Novotný, Sergeant Jan Vavrda

MANGANESE – 9 June 1944: radio operator Staff Sergeant František Bíroš, Staff Sergeant Štefan Košina, radio operator Sergeant Aspirant Drahomír Vaňura

GLUCINIUM – 2 July 1944: First Lieutenant Vítězslav Lepařík, Staff Sergeant Ludvík Hanina, radio operator Staff Sergeant František Trpík, Sergeant Josef Cikán

DESTROYER (Paris) – 2 July 1944: Staff Sergeant Karel Tichý

SILICA NORTH (Italy) – 8 September 1944: Major Wittakera (Great Britain), Captain Rudolf Hrubec, radio operator Sergeant Bohuslav Nocar

SILICA SOUTH (Italy) – 9 September 1944: Lieutenant Colonel C. B. Cope (Great Britain), Corporal W. Williamson (Great Britain), Captain Rudolf Krzák

WOLFRAM – 14 September 1944: Captain Josef Otisk, Staff Sergeant Josef Bierský, Staff Sergeant Josef Černota, Staff Sergeant Vladimír Řezníček, radio operator Staff Sergeant Karel Svoboda, Sergeant Robert Matula

TUNGSTEN – 21 December 1944: First Lieutenant Rudolf Pernický and Warrant Officer Leopold Musil

EMBASSY – 21 December 1944: radio operator Staff Sergeant Karol Mladý, Sergeant Jozef Haríň, radio operator Sergeant Ján Grajzel

PLATINUM–PEWTER – 16 February 1945: Captain Jaromír Nechanský, Staff Sergeant Jaroslav Pešán, radio operator Staff Sergeant Alois Vyhňák, radio operator Sergeant Jaroslav Klemeš

BAUXITE – 22 March 1945: Captain Pavel Hromko

Other operations, some unnamed:
COTTAGE – 19 February 1944: American OSS operation from Italy to Prague with Vlastislav Žuk.

NICKEL – Cancelled operation to Bohemia, Vojmír Matuš dropped April 1944 ended up joining groups *CALCIUM* and *BARIUM*.

OCHRE – Cancelled operation to Bohemia, Václav Michal dropped April 1944 ended up joining groups *CALCIUM* and *BARIUM*.

ROTHMAN – Cancelled operation to Moravia in May 1944, Corporal Cadet Klement Hlásenský, Corporal Cadet Osvald Peroutka, radio operator Sergeant Antonín Stolařík, Corporal Vladimír Ruml.

FOUR SQUARE – Cancelled operation to Plzen, attempted between March and May 1945 with Second Lieutenant Jaroslav Bublík, Corporal Josef Špinka, Corporal Karel Hubl, Lance Corporal Josef Krist.

CHROMIUM – Cancelled operation to Prague, attempted between April and May 1945 with Captain Václav Knotek, Lieutenant Karel Tichý, radio operator Second Lieutenant Jan Štursa.

MORTAR – Cancelled operation to eastern Bohemia, attempted between April and May 1945 with Second Lieutenant Václav Modrák, Corporal Alois Horáček, Lance Corporal Jan Sekerka.

CHURCHMAN – Cancelled operation to Prague, attempted between April and May 1945 with Captain Vladimír Hanuš, Sergeant Ladislav Vyskočil, radio operators Lance Corporal Jaroslav Krsek and Lance Corporal Alois Hladík.

IRON – Cancelled operation to Prague between April 1943 and December 1944, team moved to Italy where they waited for deployment that never came, returned to London. Team with Sergeant Rudolf Turšner and Sergeant Josef Modřanský, who was later replaced by Sergeant John Švachulou in Italy.

JAN KOZINA – Soviet partisan operation directed by Marshal Koňev and First Ukrainian Front. First plan was to drop seventeen parachutists in Beskydy, Slovakia to organize local partisan groups for sabotage missions and Communist political committees; plan changed to drop in Bohemia on 16 October 1944.

UNNAMED – 19 July 1944: four Czech parachutists dropped in Chrudim, Eastern Bohemia.

UNNAMED – 20 July 1944: eleven Slovak parachutists dropped near Ružomberok, Slovakia for impending Slovak National Uprising.

UNNAMED – 17 September 1944: twelve parachutists dropped at Tri Duby airfield during Slovak National Uprising.

UNNAMED – September 1944: forty-eight parachutists dropped in Medzilaborce, Slovakia near Dukla Pass on the Slovak-Polish border during the Carpatho-Dukla Operation and Slovak National Uprising.

THE DOWNFALL OF AGENT A-54

AFTER A PERIOD OF SILENCE DURING THE EARLY MONTHS OF THE GERMAN occupation of Bohemia and Moravia, Paul Thümmel reestablished contact through the Czech underground with the Second Department now in exile in London. Agent A-54—as he is codenamed by the Second Department (cover names: Karl Schneider; Jochen Breitner; Voral; Franta; René; Dr. Holm; Dr. Steinberg; Eva; Bear; Raab; Joachim Wedel; František) and ULTRA, his British SOE codename—informed Czechoslovak intelligence of German plans to invade Poland (Operation *Fall Weiß*), and sent them the complete German plan of attack on Holland, Belgium, and France (Operations *Fall Gelb* and *Fall Rot*, respectively). Thümmel's intelligence was passed by the Second Department to both MI6 and the USSR—during 1936–1939: via Soviet Embassy in Prague, during 1941–1945: via *NKVD* liaison in London Colonel Ivan Andreyevich Chichayev (codename JOHN), as well as via the Soviet Consulate in Istanbul (primarily, by Slovak Ministry of National Defense agents)—which helped maintain the credibility of Edvard Beneš with the British and Soviet governments. In June 1940, the Second Department in Britain put Thümmel in contact with certain leaders of the home army resistance who stayed behind in Prague after the German occupation, respectfully codenamed by the *Gestapo* as "Three Czech Kings of the resistance," referring to Captain First Class Václav Morávek (codenames Ota, León, Mladý, and Vojta), Lieutenant Colonel Josef Balabán, and Lieutenant Colonel Josef Mašín. Thümmel had close contact with Staff Captain Václav Morávek, one of Czechoslovak intelligence's best men in Prague. Asset A-54 made almost daily reports to his handler Morávek, providing details on the postponement of Operation *Seelöwe* (Sealion), and the timing of the German invasion of the Soviet Union (Operation Barbarossa).

The *Gestapo* had been trying to shut down Morávek's network since 1940, and they finally captured his radio transmitter, and decoded information about agent A-54. Once the *Gestapo* broke the code, they discovered they had a high-ranking German intelligence member providing secrets to the Czechoslovaks. Heydrich took over the case personally and learned from two captured Czechoslovak agents of the "Three Kings" with their Sparta I transmitter that the high-ranking German intelligence official codenamed *René* lived in a northern district of Prague. This led the *Gestapo* to Thümmel, who was living in northern Prague, Břevnov district. He was arrested on 19 October 1941. However, due to insufficient evidence to prosecute him and under an avalanche of protest from his immediate superior Admiral Canaris, who traveled to Prague explicitly to defend Thümmel, as well as pressure from *SS* Chief Heinrich Himmler a long-time friend of Thümmel, Chief of the Nazi Party Chancellery Martin Bormann, and other prominent representatives of the Nazi Party, Heydrich reluctantly had to release him on 25 November 1941.

Wilhelm Franz Canaris (1887–1945) was head of the *Abwehr* from 1935 to 1944. Until 1938, Canaris was a supporter of Hitler's Nazi regime as the only available political entity capable of stopping the spread of Communism from the Soviet Union. However, Canaris was never a member of the Nazi Party. In the latter half of the 1930s, it became clearly evident to several high-ranking officers of the German high command (*OKW*) that Hitler's policies were leading Germany in a dangerous direction and opposite to what these officers believed necessary to reestablish Germany's domestic and international respect that was destroyed by the First World War and the Versailles Treaty. During the 1938 crisis over Czechoslovakia that culminated in the Munich Agreement, Admiral Canaris was a leading figure in the anti-Hitler group in Germany together with the army chief of staff, General Ludwig Beck, Foreign Office State Secretary Ernst von Weizsäcker, and *Abwehr* Central Division Chief Colonel Hans Oster. These individuals were determined to avoid another war in 1938 that they felt Germany would lose. In 1938, Colonel Oster became head of *Abwehr*'s central division (*Z*) in Berlin, who turned it into a center of activity for opponents of the regime. The following year, Osler became Chief of Staff to Admiral Canaris. Canaris made sure that *Abwehr* was stocked with anti-Nazis. However, Canaris and his associates were loosely allied to another, more radical group, the "anti-Nazi" faction led by Colonel Hans Oster and Hans Bernd Gisevius that wanted to use the crisis as an excuse for executing a *coup* to overthrow the Nazi regime. The most audacious plan contemplated by Canaris, in collaboration with Ewald von Kleist-Schmenzin (1890–1945),* was to

* Ewald Albert Friedrich Karl Lepold Arnold von Kleist-Schmenzin was a German lawyer, a conservative politician, opponent of Nazism, and a member of the 20 July

capture and eliminate Hitler and the entire Nazi party leadership before the invasion of Czechoslovakia. At this particular moment, von Kleist-Schmenzin visited Britain secretly and discussed the situation with MI6 and some high-ranking politicians. There, the name of Canaris became widely known as von Kleist-Schmenzin's executive officer in the event of an anti-Nazi plot. Several high-ranking German military leaders believed that if Hitler invaded Czechoslovakia, or any other country, Britain would declare war on Germany. MI6 was of the same opinion. The British declaration of war would have given the German General Staff, in their belief, both the pretext and support for an overthrow of Hitler. Canaris tried to hinder Hitler's attempts to absorb Czechoslovakia, and he also advised Spain's Franco not to permit German passage through Spain for the purpose of capturing Gibraltar, a vital strategic location in Hitler's view. After hearing reports of massacres in Poland and even witnessing war crimes himself, Canaris visited Hitler's headquarters train on 12 September 1939, at the time in Upper Silesia, to register his objection to the atrocities. Before getting to see Hitler, he met General Wilhelm Keitel, whom he informed, "I have information that mass executions are being planned in Poland, and that members of the Polish nobility and the Roman Catholic bishops and priests have been singled out for extermination." Keitel warned Canaris to go no further with his protest, as the detailed plan of atrocities came directly from Hitler himself. Shocked by these incidents and at increasing risk to himself, Canaris began working more actively to overthrow Hitler's regime, although he also cooperated with the *SD* to create a decoy. This made it possible for

---

Plot to assassinate Hitler, for which he was executed. As a conservative, he supported the idea of monarchy and Christian ideals, shown in part through his membership of the Order of Saint John (Bailiwick of Brandenburg), to which he was admitted as a Knight of Honor in 1922 and in which he was promoted to Knight of Justice in 1935. He was a staunch, active opponent of Nazism even before Hitler came to power in 1933. He was arrested as a result in May and June of that year, although he was never held very long. He refused to fly the Nazi flag over his castle. He went to the UK in 1938 as Admiral Wilhelm Canaris's and Colonel-General Ludwig Beck's secret emissary. He was to make the British government aware of the resistance to Hitler's rule inside Germany. He used his contacts with Winston Churchill and Robert Vansittart to try to shift British policy away from one of appeasement to one based more on the use of force. He believed that only if the British were seen to be willing to use force to support Czechoslovakia would the opposition in Germany have the support that it needed among Germany's High Command to move against Hitler.

him to pose as a trusted man for some time. He was promoted to the rank of full Admiral in January 1940. With his subordinate Erwin Lahousen, he formed a circle of like-minded *Wehrmacht* officers, many of whom were executed or forced to commit suicide after the failure of the 20 July 1944 plot in Operation Valkyrie (*Unternehmen Walküre*). At a conference of senior officers in Berlin in December 1941, Canaris is quoted as saying "the *Abwehr* has nothing to do with the persecution of Jews . . . no concern of ours, we hold ourselves aloof from it." Canaris was in contact with British intelligence during this time, despite the war between the two countries. It is thought that during the invasion of the Soviet Union, he received a detailed report of all the enemy positions that was known only to the British. The head of MI6, Stewart Menzies, who shared Canaris's strong anti-Communist beliefs, praised Canaris's courage and bravery at the end of the war. After 1942, Canaris visited Spain frequently and was frequently in contact with British agents from Gibraltar. In 1943, while in occupied France, Canaris is said to have contacted British agents. He was taken blindfolded to the Convent of the Nuns of the Passion of our Blessed Lord on 127 Rue de la Santé where he met the local head of the British Secret Intelligence Services, Colonel Claude Olivier, codename "Jade Amicol." Canaris wanted to know the terms for peace if Germany removed Hitler. Churchill's reply at this point in the war, sent to him two weeks later, was simple: "Unconditional surrender." Canaris also intervened to save a number of victims of Nazi persecution, including Jews, some by getting them to Spain. Many such people were given token training as *Abwehr* "agents" and then issued papers allowing them to leave Germany. One notable person he is said to have assisted was the then Lubavitcher Rebbe in Warsaw, Rabbi Yosef Yitzchok Schneersohn.[4] This has led Chabad-Lubavitch to campaign for his recognition as a Righteous Gentile by the Yad Vashem Martyrs' and Heroes' Remembrance Authority in Jerusalem. Throughout the war, Canaris managed to send the Allies crucial intelligence to help either foil or greatly reduce the likelihood of success of several of Hitler's objectives. Canaris was arrested on 23 July 1944, on the basis of the interrogation of his successor at Military Intelligence, Georg Hansen. Hansen had admitted his own role in the 20 July Valkyrie Plot and accused Canaris of being its "spiritual instigator." He was charged with and found guilty of a variety of acts of treason or knowledge of treason going back to 1938. Together with his deputy General Hans Oster, military jurist General Karl Sack, Lutheran theologian Reverend Dietrich Bonhoeffer, and *Abwehr* Captain Ludwig Gehre, Canaris was humiliated before witnesses by being led to the gallows naked and then executed on 9 April 1945, in Flossenbürg Concentration Camp, just weeks before the end of the war.

Back in Prague during a meeting between Canaris and Heydrich, the two agreed that Thümmel would be released from custody but kept under close surveillance. After more evidence was gathered and Heydrich's patience wore thin seeing they were no closer to capturing the third and final member of the "Three Kings," Thümmel was arrested again on 22 February 1942. He confessed and managed to convince Heydrich he was playing a double game with Morávek and needed more time to lure him into his trap and roll up his entire operation. On 2 March 1942, he was released on condition that he would bring Captain Morávek to a meeting where he could be captured. Thümmel tried to warn Moravec in London but without success. He did, however, reach Morávek without meeting him personally, and when Morávek did not arrive at a scheduled meeting at Thümmel's apartment, the *Gestapo* rearrested Thümmel on 20 March 1942. Thümmel informed Heydrich of an upcoming Saturday evening meeting on 21 March 1942, between Morávek and *ÚVOD* agent Sergeant Václav Řehák (known as "The Dandy") in a small park next to the Convent of Loretta in Prague. The *Gestapo* clandestinely staked out the park and captured Řehák as he approached. The waiting Morávek jumped into a bush and began firing both pistols. Morávek was shot in the leg and tried to run, but the arterial hemorrhaging was too much for him and he collapsed. The *Gestapo* approached, and he fired into his own temple. The *Gestapo* officially reported it a suicide. Morávek had fired over seventy shots at his assailants before committing suicide. He was found with two semi-automatic pistols (probably version 27 of the 7.65 x 17 mm Browning SR Česká zbrojovka) and nine empty clips of ammunition. Thümmel was rearrested and jailed in Prague, then moved to Theresienstadt Concentration Camp (midway between Prague and Dresden), where he was held under the false name of Peter Toman so that other members of the *Abwehr* could not locate him. There is some speculation that early in this final imprisonment in exchange for his life he was offered, or forced to take, a chance to help Heydrich in his campaign against Admiral Canaris and the *Abwehr*. In any event, Heydrich had only about ten more weeks to live before he was assassinated by Czechoslovak paratroopers in Prague.

On 20 April 1945, as Soviet forces were on the outskirts of Berlin and American forces (Lieutenant General S. LeRoy Irwin's XII Corps of Patton's Third Army) crossed the western Czech border at Aš (rushing towards Prague until, at the insistence of Marshal Koňev, General

Eisenhower halted them), reportedly several drunk *SS* guards at Theresienstadt were instructed to start randomly selecting 40 prisoners at a time for execution by firing squad. To his misfortune, Paul Thümmel was one of those selected. When he was led out of his cell to the courtyard, he stopped and asked one of their more fortunate fellow prisoners to give Colonel Moravec his cordial greetings and the following message: "It was a real pleasure to work with the Czechoslovak intelligence service. I'm sorry it had to end like this. Comforted by the knowledge that our work might not be in vain" (Moravec 1975, 215). The message was ultimately delivered.

OPERATION ANTHROPOID AND ITS COST

FROM THE MOMENT OF HIS ARRIVAL IN PRAGUE ON 28 SEPTEMBER 1941, the speed and brutality of Heydrich's reign of terror, especially in instituting martial law, the mass arrests of thousands of Czech citizens, the setup of martial law courts, and the immediate implementation of executions created an atmosphere of fear and terror among the populace of the "Protectorate." In this atmosphere, Prime Minister of the Protectorate *Generál* Alois Eliáš was summarily sentenced to death on 1 October 1941. He was the first and only Premier of a Nazi occupied state that was executed during the Second World War. Thus, began an era of the bloodiest terror in the Czech nation's recent history.

Immediately after his arrival in Prague, Heydrich also began to execute his idea of "the final solution to the Jewish problem." As Hitler's primary author of this "final solution," Hitler was intending to put Heydrich in charge of dealing with Europe's Jews. Only four months after exhibiting his plan in Bohemia and Moravia, Heydrich was tasked by Hitler to upscale the plan for all of Europe and the Soviet Union at the Wannsee Conference on 20 January 1942.

One of his first decrees in the Protectorate, dated 29 September 1941, concerned measures against Czech Jews in mixed marriages, Czechs who were friends of Jews, and the closing of synagogues. It stated, among other things:

> Jewish synagogues and places of prayer have not been used for religious purposes for some time. Instead, they have become centers for all kinds of Jewish subversive elements

> and focal points of illegal whispered propaganda. For this reason, I have ordered the closing of all Jewish synagogues and places of prayer. This is to take effect immediately. . . . Certain Czech circles are behaving in a very friendly manner toward the Jews, especially in recent times. They are mainly the Czech elements that are trying to demonstrate their anti-*Reich* thinking. I am ordering the State Police to intervene against the Czechs who openly demonstrate their friendship with the Jews in the streets and public places (protective custody!).

This measure was brought about because of gestures of support from some Czechs towards Jews after all Jewish citizens were forced to wear the gold Star of David from September 1941. Some Czechs had started to demonstratively wear the Star of David, thus openly showing friendship to the Jews. At the same time, Heydrich started preparing to establish a Jewish *ghetto* in Terezín, north of Prague. The German army left the town as early as October 1941. The first prisoners arrived in Terezín on 24 November 1941. From 9 January 1942, a total of 86,934 prisoners were shipped out from Terezín (German: Theresienstadt) to extermination camps set up in the former Polish territory. Only 3,097 lived to see the end of the war.

From his quarters in Černín Palace in Prague on 2 October 1941, Reinhard Heydrich presented a convincing answer to anyone with any doubts about his mission in a speech delivered to leading representatives of the occupying forces.

> I must unambiguously and with unflinching hardness bring the citizens of this country, Czech or otherwise, to the understanding that there is no avoiding the fact they are members of the *Reich* and as such they owe allegiance to the *Reich*. . . . This is a task of priority required by the war. I must have peace of mind that every Czech worker works at his maximum for the German war effort. . . . This includes feeding the Czech worker—to put it frankly—so that he can do his work.

In the part of his speech relative to the "final solution," he said that the Protectorate must once and for all be settled by the German element:

> To be able to make a decision as to who is suited to be Germanized, I need their racial inventory . . . We have all kinds of people here, some of them are showing racial quality and good judgment. It's going to be simple to work on them—we can Germanize them. On the other hand, we have racially inferior elements and, what's worse, they demonstrate wrong judgment. These we must get out. There is a lot of space eastwards. Between these two extremes, there are those in the middle that we have to examine thoroughly. We have racially inferior people but with good judgment, then we have racially unacceptable people with bad judgment. As to the first kind, we must resettle them in the *Reich* or somewhere else, but we have to make sure they no longer breed, because we don't care to develop them in this area. . . . One group remains, though, these people are racially acceptable but hostile in their thinking—that is the most dangerous group, because it is a racially pure class of leaders. We have to think through carefully what to do with them. We can relocate some of them into the *Reich*, put them in a purely German environment, and then Germanize and reeducate them. If this cannot be done, we must put them against the wall.

The "Butcher of Prague," as Heydrich quickly became to be affectionately known, managed to arouse resistance in all quarters of the Protectorate and among Czechoslovaks abroad. On 3 October 1941, the Czechoslovak press in Britain published the first news about the bloody terror unleashed by Reinhard Heydrich in the occupied homeland. Around the same time, between September and October 1941, the idea of eliminating one of the leading figures of the German occupying power and Nazi Party was born within the circle of President Edvard Beneš's colleagues. Given the struggle for recognition and legitimacy the Czechoslovak government in exile faced in London under Chamberlain and Halifax, it was necessary to prepare an enterprise that would clearly show the home resistance movement's anti-German stance while simultaneously demonstrating President Beneš's control over the home country. The terror unleashed by Heydrich in the Protectorate was another reason for planning his assassination. The assassination was considered an act of just retribution. At the same time, it was meant to prove to the Nazis that none of them was untouchable, and any one of them might at any time be called to account for their actions. Initially, the plan considered either Reinhard Heydrich or Karl Hermann Frank as the target.

The operation designed to carry out the assassination was given the codename Anthropoid. Actual preparations began on 2 October 1941, in coordination with British SOE. The selection process was conducted by General Staff Captain First Class Jaroslav Šustr and General Staff Major Karel Paleček of the Command Section of Special Group D in the Second Department. The selection process finally resulted in the choice of Slovak Warrant Officer Josef Gabčík (8 April 1912–18 June 1942) and Czech Staff Sergeant Karel Svoboda (18 October 1912–3 April 1982) to carry out the assassination. Target date for the operation was 28 October 1941; appropriately, Czechoslovakia's founding and Independence Day (1918).

In preparation for Operation Barbarossa, the Germans successfully swept up and cut critical radio communications between the homeland and London. This communication link was maintained from the autumn of 1939 through a series of radio transmitters operated by members of the home front resistance movement. Contact between London and the home front resistance was crucial for the success of all planned operations in the Protectorate, including Operation Anthropoid. This need to bolster communications led to Operation Percentage.

During the night of 3 October 1941, Lance Corporal František Pavelka parachuted over Koudelov near Čáslav, Bohemia. His goal was to establish contact with the leading representatives of the home front, deliver a message from General Ingr, and crystals for new radio transmitters, telegraph keys, and new enciphering key. Pavelka was also equipped with a transmitter, model MARK III, supplied by the British SOE, with which he was to help maintain communication between the home front and London. Although Pavelka landed thirty-five kilometers away from the intended drop zone near Nasavrky, he was able to establish contact with the underground at the alternative address of Václav Doležal in Chrudim on 4 October 1941. He managed to get to Prague and hand over all his materials to the resistance. However, over the ensuing three weeks in Prague, the *Gestapo* caught up with him and the resistance group he collaborated with and arrested them on 25 October 1941. It was later discovered, the *Gestapo* obtained their identities and location from a captured Soviet intelligence officer, Major Jedlička. Corporal Pavelka was the first Czechoslovak parachutist the Germans were able to capture in the Protectorate. He was subjected to intense physical and psychological torture at the hands of the *Gestapo* and along with other members of his resistance group was executed in Berlin on 11 January 1943. During his interrogation, the name "Lidice" was first mentioned together with the families of Stříbrný and Horák and their alternative addresses, which Pavelka had received in London before his departure.

Anthropoid was originally targeted for 7–10 October 1941, however, during parachute training Staff Sergeant Svoboda suffered a serious head injury during a jump. He was transferred to a hospital in London and the next day on 6 October 1941, a doctor examined him for persistent headaches. On 7 October 1941, Warrant Officer Gabčík completed the advanced finishing graduate course alone. General Staff Captain First Class Šustr immediately informed the Chief of Intelligence, Colonel Moravec, suggesting that Staff Sergeant Svoboda be replaced by Czech Warrant Officer Jan Kubiš at Gabčík's request with the consent of Major Karel Paleček, who was in charge of the selection of the paratroopers. This switch was agreed to, but the planned timing of the operation could not be met because Warrant Officer Kubiš's false Protectorate identity documents were not yet complete. Moreover, he had not yet completed the upgraded parachuting and shooting courses. Operation Anthropoid had to be postponed. The failure of Operation Percentage further postponed the departure of the Anthropoid Group. The failure to reestablish communication with the home resistance movement led the Second Department in London to prioritize the SILVER program. This operation comprised two groups (A and B), equipped with communications equipment and radio operators.

With the postponement of the operation, both members of the Anthropoid group gained enough time to improve their training and to plan the entire mission more thoroughly. Warrant Officers Jan Kubiš and Josef Gabčík spent the days between 14 and 18 October 1941, in Scotland, where they graduated from the Special SOE Course. The aim of this Special Course was accurate shooting and grenade and bomb throwing. Part of the course's objective was aiming and instinctive shooting in action with a Sten (acronym after designers Shepherd and Turpin at Enfield Royal Small Arms Factory) gun, a Colt (after Samuel Colt of Connecticut) pistol, and a Bren light machine gun. This demanding training took place in a variety of situations that the two men might encounter in the occupied homeland. They practiced on fixed and moving targets in open terrain as well as in enclosed buildings and rooms.

On 20 October 1941, both paratroopers were moved to Experimental

Station XVII in Brickendonbury Manor, near London, which specialized in diversionist training. There, they continued their practical exercises in handling explosives. The paratroopers learned to create all sorts of explosive booby traps on roads, railroads, and in buildings. They learned to use pressure, mechanical, chemical, and electrical fuses. Under the watchful eyes of British SOE Captain Pritchard, they also learned to handle special bombs with very sensitive contact fuses made from modified antitank grenades, model 73. One such grenade was used six months later in the assassination of Reinhard Heydrich.

From 8 November 1941, both paratroopers forming the Anthropoid group stayed in STS 2 in Villa Bellasis near Dorking. Czechoslovak First Lieutenant Rudolf Hrubec organized a graduate course there for sabotage groups. Warrant Officers Jan Kubiš and Josef Gabčík were in Villa Bellasis to improve their skills in the use of motorized vehicles, the Morse code, and orientation in unknown territory. They drilled the necessary procedures after landing, demarcating drop zones for supply airdrops, practiced shooting with pistols and machine guns, and throwing hand grenades.

On 28 December 1941, shortly before departure for the occupied homeland, Josef Gabčík and Jan Kubiš made out their last will. On the same day at 2200 hours, a heavily laden airplane carrying fifteen men took off from Tangmere Airport in Sussex in southern England. The historic airdrop was carried out during the night of 28–29 December 1941, by the crew of a four-engine Handley-Page Halifax from the No. 138 Special Duties Squadron under the command of Flight Lieutenant Ronald C. Hockey. In addition to the seven-member crew on board were a dispatcher, General Staff Captain First Class Jaroslav Šustr, and seven Czechoslovak paratroopers. In order to maximize the full capacity of this powerful plane, Anthropoid was joined by groups Silver A and Silver B. The Halifax flew over the French coast to the Le Crotoy area of northern France, and from there headed for Darmstadt, where they arrived at 0042 hours on 29 December. During their flight, they twice met enemy night interceptor planes, which the Halifax was able to shake off. Orientation for the crew was made very difficult because most of the reference points, such as railroad tracks, rivers, and even small towns, had disappeared under heavy snow cover. This fact contributed to a navigation mistake as the crew mistook Prague for Plzeň (from which they were shot at by an antiaircraft battery at 0212 hours). As a result, the Anthropoid group was airdropped at 0224 hours close to Nehvizdy, a village near Čelákovice, east of Prague, instead of east of Plzeň. At 0237 hours, Silver A group was airdropped (First Lieutenant Alfréd Bartoš, Warrant

Officer Josef Valčík, and Lance Corporal Jiří Potůček). According to the navigator, this happened east of Čáslav but, in reality, it was between Poděbrady and Městec Králové. The Silver B crew (Staff Sergeant Jan Zemek and Sergeant Vladimír Škácha) was airdropped at 0256 hours but, instead of landing northwest of Ždírec, they landed near Kasaličky, not far from Přelouč. The mission of the Silver groups was to search out members of the home resistance and to renew radio communication with London. After finishing this dangerous and demanding mission, the Halifax headed for Darmstadt and was shot at twice by antiaircraft batteries. The Halifax flew over the French coast at 0720 hours and the English coast at 0807 hours, and finally touched down at Tangmere Airport at 0819 hours on 29 December 1941.

Silver A operated primarily in the area of Pardubice. Here, they could rely on a wide illegal network of colleagues, who not only helped them to hide but also supplied them with the information that was awaited by London headquarters. One the most important mission objectives of the Silver A group was to establish contact with Captain First Class Václav Morávek. Through this last member of the most famous section of the Defense of the Nation (*ON*) still on the run, who the *Gestapo* respectfully called "the three Czech kings of the resistance," the Czechoslovak Second Department in London was trying to reestablish the flow of information from agent A-54. Sparta A commander Alfréd Bartoš, recently promoted to Captain, had been trying to contact Morávek for a long time without any success. No one could have suspected that the effort to gain more information from A-54 was pointless given the fact that the *Gestapo* had since 19 October 1941 A-54's identity and had subjected him to a series of arrests and constant surveillance.

All the news sent out from the occupied homeland was received by military radio headquarters, set up on Duke's Hill in Woldingham, approximately fifty kilometers from London. An experienced radio telegrapher, Jiří Potůček, with the help of the radio transmitter model MARK III, codenamed Libuše—named either in honor of Bedřich Smetana's famous mythical opera about the founding of Prague or after Colonel Moravec's wife's aunt Libuše Formánková from Nová Huť near Plzeň—was able to establish contact with the military radio headquarters at Woldingham as early as the night of 14 January 1942. Agent A-54 was released from custody on 2 March 1942 on condition he would help capture Morávek. The same month, the Silver A group was finally able to establish contact with Captain Václav Morávek. On 14 March, the Libuše radio station was able to inform London that contact was established and added eagerly awaited dispatches from Morávek with news from agent A-54. During this time, Morávek met with Captain Alfréd Bartoš in Prague for the last time to give him more messages for the Libuše radio transmitter. In turn, Bartoš gave him photographs of the paratroopers in Silver A group for their new false documents to be prepared by the resistance. With the establishment of contact with Morávek (and agent A-54) and the representatives of *ÚVOD*, about which London had heard no news since 4 October 1941, Silver A fulfilled its mission and became one of the most successful paratroop groups ever sent to the Protectorate. However, it was no longer possible to send new information from agent A-54. Paul Thümmel was already under constant surveillance by the *Gestapo.*

Silver A's activities were ultimately disrupted by Karel Čurda's betrayal. Warrant Officer Karel Čurda, member of Operation Out Distance (27 March 1942), informed the *Gestapo* about the hiding places of other paratroopers. Silver A's commander Captain Alfréd Bartoš, on the run from the *Gestapo*, shot himself in Pardubice on 21 June 1942, but did not succumb to his self-inflicted wound until the following night on 22 June. The final message from the Libuše transmitter sent by Jiří Potůček to London on the night of 25 June 1942, stated: "Instead of my radio station, they have leveled Ležáky [5 km southwest of Vrbatův Kostelec] to the ground. People helping us arrested. Fred's location unknown. People suspicious. Impossible to establish contacts. I am alone. . . ." Less than one week of life was left for Jiří Potůček at that point. On 2 July 1942, Lance Corporal Jiří Potůček died on the run after being shot to death by a Protectorate gendarme, Sergeant Karel Pulpán, while sleeping in a hideout near Rosice. A photograph of Josef Valčík was found on Morávek's dead body by the *Gestapo* and led to an extensive search action. The announcement was posted in all cities and villages of the Protectorate. Valčík was forced to leave Silver A and began hiding in Prague where he started to collaborate with the Anthropoid group.

On the early morning of 29 December 1941, Silver B also landed near Přelouč. The mission of the two-member team, Staff Sergeant Jan Zemek and Sergeant Vladimír Škácha, was to deliver a radio transmitter to the home front resistance movement and help them maintain contact with London. The radio station was damaged during the jump and the group was unable to establish contact with London or with the local resistance. Silver B was unsuccessful in its mission. Both paratroopers lived to see the end of the war: Zemek in the underground, Škácha (arrested by the *Gestapo* in January 1945) in Flossenbürg Concentration Camp.

On 28 March 1942, the Out Distance group was airdropped near Ořechov. This sabotage group was made up of First Lieutenant Adolf Opálka, Warrant Officer Karel Čurda, and Corporal Cadet Ivan Kolařík, who were to join up with the Silver A group. Most importantly, they brought into the Protectorate a Beacon radio to guide incoming flights (forerunner of the better-known Rebecca/Eureka transponding radar) and a Mark III radio transponder. Ivan Kolařík lost his false documents upon landing, which later put the *Gestapo* on his trail. In an attempt to save his relatives from retribution, he poisoned himself near Zlín on 1 April 1942. The *Gestapo* managed to find all of the group's operational material, hidden in a dugout pit. Adolf Opálka contacted Captain Alfréd Bartoš of Sparta A in Pardubice, who was in charge of the paratroopers hiding in Prague. Karel Čurda found his way to Prague in the same manner.

On 29 December 1941, at approximately 0230 hours, Jan Kubiš and Josef Gabčík landed on a snow-covered field near Nehvizdy not far from Prague. Their contacts, however, were in Plzeň, 120 kilometers southwest of Nehvizdy. They hid their materials in a local garden shed and headed to Plzen where the first people to help the paratroopers were State Secret Police Inspector Václav Král (password: "Adina greets Plzeň – March 8th is good") and the retired railway man Václav Stehlík at Rokycany (password: "Greetings from Hradecký"). They then made their way back to Nehvizdy by way of Prague and gathered their hidden operational materials, gradually relocated it into hiding places in Prague and the surrounding area. With the help of the local resistance, they were provided with safe houses in Prague. Over the ensuing months, Kubiš and Gabčík spent their time investigating various aspects of their mission and collaborating with the resistance. The paratroopers devised various plans for the assassination of Reinhard Heydrich. Finally, at the beginning of April 1942, Heydrich himself contributed to the options for his own assassination when he moved from his temporary quarters in Prague Castle to a Château in Panenské Břežany. In the end, a sharp right-hand curve straddling the streets Kirchmayerova and V Holešovičkách below a school in Kobylisy was chosen for the attack. It was known that his car was driven through this curve daily on the way to Prague Castle and that his chauffeur, *SS-Oberscharführer* Johannes Klein, had to slow down significantly around the curve.

Up to this point Czech home resistance was in the dark as to the precise objective of Operation Anthropoid. When home resistance discovered from the detailed preparations by the paratroopers that they were trying to assassinate Reinhard Heydrich, they feared a major reprisal from the Germans and decided to contact London through the Libuše transmitter with a dispatch warning not to continue with the assassination plan. In an operation directed against the Silver A group, the *Gestapo* intercepted one of these warnings on 12 May 1942:

> From the preparations that Ota and Zdeněk are working on and the place where it is happening, we guess, despite their silence, that they're preparing to assassinate H. This assassination would not help the Allies and would bring immense consequences upon our nation . . . we ask you to give an order through SILVER not to carry out the assassination. There is a danger of delay, issue the order immediately. If necessary, for international reasons, assassinate a local Quisling . . . the first choice would be E[manuel] M[oravec].

The reply from Colonel František Moravec (unrelated to Emanuel Moravec, collaborationist Minister of Education) was sent two days later using the radio transmitter of Professor Vladimír Krajina: "Don't worry when it comes to terrorist actions. We believe we see the situation clearly, therefore, given the situation, any actions against officials of the German *Reich* do not come into consideration. Let *ÚVOD* know. . . ." To date, it remains an unexplained mystery why Colonel Moravec did not order, through Silver A, the cancellation of Operation Anthropoid right then.

In his book, *The Assassination of Reinhard Heydrich*, originally published in Britain in 1989 under the title, *The Killing of SS Obergruppenführer Reinhard Heydrich 27 May 1942*, Callum MacDonald provides a well-researched and excellent description of the scene of the assassination. The following is a paraphrased excerpt from Macdonald's book (MacDonald 2011).

On the morning of 27 May 1942, a black Mercedes 320 C with the convertible bonnet retracted, chauffeured by *SS-Oberscharführer* Johannes Klein, approached Kirchmayer Street from Kobylisy. The red standard of the *Reich* Protector on the right fender and the license plates *SS*-3 indicated who was sitting in the front seat next to the driver. *SS-Obergruppenführer* Reinhard Heydrich was arriving from his summer residence in Panenské Břežany about twenty kilometers northeast of Prague and on his way to his office in Prague Castle. It was 10:35 a.m. and the vehicle was braking in the sharp curve leading into V Holešovičkách Street. Josef Gabčík, waiting for several hours at the curve, dropped his overcoat and raised his assembled Sten machine gun with which he was to spray Heydrich with bullets. At the critical moment, however, the machine gun jammed. Gabčík was left helplessly standing at the curb as the Mercedes swept by. Heydrich then made a fatal error of hubris. Instead of ordering Klein to accelerate away from the ambush, he ordered him to stop, and he stood up in the open convertible. Neither he nor Klein had spotted the concealed Jan Kubiš across the street and believed that they were dealing with a lone assassin. As the car came to a stop, Kubiš stepped out of the shadows and tossed a modified antitank grenade at the two men in the front seat. It was fitted with a highly sensitive impact fuse which, after a safety device is pulled out, triggers an explosion upon the slightest of impacts. It was a British number 73 antitank grenade, the lower two-thirds of which had been removed to make it lighter and easier to handle. The bottom of the remaining upper one-third had been sealed with adhesive tape and the whole body was wrapped in more tape. German explosives experts, who later examined Kubiš's spare grenade left at the scene, judged its powerful explosive Polar Ammon Gelatin Dynamite, a nitroglycerine-based explosive, to be extremely dangerous to handle.

Kubiš unscrewed the bake-like cap, set the fuse, and threw the grenade with a pre-rehearsed underhand toss in the direction of the *Reich* Protector's vehicle. Unfortunately, the grenade missed the target and fell short just outside the vehicle near the right rear fender. If the powerful bomb had exploded in the vehicle, Heydrich and Klein would have died instantly. The bomb exploded above the running board just in front of the right rear fender throwing shrapnel into Kubiš's face and shattering the windows of the electric street tram that had stopped at the curve near the car. There were screams as tram passengers were hit by shards of flying glass and metal. Marie Sochmanová, a young woman who was standing nearby at the moment of the explosion sustained a large calf wound from a grenade fragment. Heydrich's Mercedes lurched violently and came to rest near the curb. The two *SS* overcoats, which had been folded and placed on the back seat of the car were thrown into the air by the blast and landed draped across the electric trolley wire, above the street. The explosion punctured the right rear tire, ripped the vehicle's body, and dislodged the right door from its hinges.

As the noise of the explosion abated, Heydrich and Klein leaped from the wrecked car with drawn pistols. While Klein ran towards Kubiš, who had staggered against the street railings half-blinded by blood, Heydrich turned uphill where Gabčík stood paralyzed, holding his Sten gun. As Klein came towards him, Kubiš recovered and, grabbing his bicycle, forced his way through the crowd of shocked passengers spilling from the tram. While Gabčík scattered the crowd by firing in the air with his Colt pistol, Klein tried to bring him down with his semi-automatic but, dazed by the explosion, he pressed the magazine release catch and the gun jammed. Kubiš pedaled furiously downhill, outpacing his pursuer. Within minutes of the bomb explosion, he had reached a safe house in the suburbs of Žižkov. There, his bloodstained bicycle was hidden, and he was given the uniform of a railway worker. Then, mingling with the lunchtime crowds, he made his way to another safe house where his shrapnel wounds were treated by Dr. Břetislav Lyčka. This important member of the Sokol resistance organization Jindra had supplied the paratroopers in previous months with many important contacts. He treated Kubiš's head wound created by a fragment of the vehicle's shell. He escaped, believing that the assassination had failed. His last sight of Heydrich was of the German jumping from the shattered car to pursue his companion. On 21 July 1942, the *Gestapo* in Ouběnice discovered Dr. Břetislav Lyčka. In a hopeless situation, Lyčka chose suicide.

Gabčík found escape less easy. As Heydrich came toward him through the dust from the explosion, lurching and weaving like a drunken man, Gabčík dropped his Sten and tried to reach his bicycle. He was forced to abandon this attempt, however, and took cover behind a telegraph pole, exchanging shots with Heydrich who ducked behind the stalled tram. The situation grew more dangerous with every passing second. The longer Heydrich kept Gabčík pinned down, the greater the chance the agent would be killed or captured when the police arrived at the scene. Suddenly, Heydrich doubled over and staggered to the side of the road, obviously wounded and in pain. Unknown to Kubiš, the bomb had severely injured the German breaking a rib and driving fragments of horsehair and wire from the upholstery of the car upwards into his spleen. As Heydrich collapsed against the railings, holding himself up with one hand, Gabčík seized his opportunity and began to run uphill to his right. But he was not yet out of danger. As he sprinted away from the scene of the ambush, Klein returned from his unsuccessful pursuit of Kubiš to help his wounded superior. Heydrich, his face white with pain, gestured with his free hand and gasped: "Get that bastard." As Klein ran after the fleeing assassin, Heydrich staggered along the pavement and fell against the bonnet of the wrecked car. His painful progress was watched by the crowd of tram passengers. Nobody stepped forward to help the crippled figure in the torn *SS* uniform.

At the top of the hill, Gabčík turned down a side street and hid in a butcher's shop. He could not have made a worse choice. The owner, a man named Brauer, was a Nazi sympathizer and had a brother who worked for the *Gestapo*. Ignoring Gabčík's request for help, he ran out into the road attracting Klein's attention by shouting and pointing. His Sten still jammed and useless, the *SS* man rushed into the shop, perhaps believing that his opponent was escaping by a rear entrance. In fact, Gabčík had discovered there was only one way out and doubled back, colliding with his pursuer in the doorway. In the confusion, he shot Klein through the legs with his Colt pistol and the *SS* man fell forward, dropping his gun. Gabčík leaped over the sprawling figure, firing as he went, and reached the safety of the street. In a desperate attempt to prevent his escape, Klein ordered the butcher to take his gun and pursue his fleeing assailant. Hardly surprisingly, the shopkeeper showed no enthusiasm for this task, taking a few hesitant steps down the road before abandoning the enterprise. Gabčík disappeared into the side streets. Shortly afterwards he arrived at a safe house where he rinsed his hair with boiled chamomile tea to lighten its color. He was limping as a result of a fall during his escape from Klein and was bitterly disappointed about the failure of his Sten gun.

At the scene of the attack, the crowd began to recover from the shock of the explosion. A young blonde woman recognized Heydrich and took charge, shouting for a car to take him to the hospital. One of the tram passengers, an off-duty Czech policeman, halted a passing baker's van. The driver was reluctant to become involved in the affair and an argument ensued while Heydrich remained slumped against his car, an ominous dark stain spreading across his uniform. A second vehicle was stopped and commandeered, a small truck carrying a load of floor polish. With the help of the policeman, Heydrich was squeezed into the tiny cab and the truck set off down the hill, jolting heavily on the tram tracks. The vibration was too much for Heydrich and he asked the driver to stop. He was transferred into the back where he sprawled on his stomach among the crates of wax and floor polish, one hand across his face, the other pressed against his wound. In this way, the most powerful man in Czechoslovakia arrived at the Bulovka hospital. It was just after eleven o'clock.

Heydrich was immediately taken to the emergency room where his wounds were cleaned by a young Czech doctor, Vladimír Šnajdr. He was conscious and had regained his icy self-control. As Šnajdr later recalled: "I took forceps and a few swabs and tried to see whether the wound was deep . . . he did not flinch although it must have hurt him." Dr. Šnadjr had the nurse call Dr. Walter Dick, the Sudeten German Chief of Surgery at

Bulovka Hospital since 1940 and an experienced thoracic surgeon. Dr. Slalina, Dr. Dick's assistant, was the first to arrive. He found a 10-cm by 5-cm wound in the left T_8–T_{10} paravertebral area, upon which he applied a pressure dressing. Dr. Dick then walked in with an entourage of German physicians. After clicking his heels and giving the Hitler salute, he examined the wound, filled with blood, pieces of metal and car upholstery. At first, he thought that the wound was limited to the chest wall and could be debrided and sutured under local anesthesia in the minor surgery room, but nonetheless, he ordered a radiograph. Heydrich was taken to the radiology suite in a wheelchair but walked unassisted to the X-ray machine. The film showed a left pneumothorax, a fractured left eleventh rib, a diaphragmatic tear, and a metal fragment in the spleen. They were injuries which could have been avoided by the recommended installation of armor plating in the seatbacks of the Mercedes. Told that he needed immediate surgery, Heydrich refused and insisted on a Berlin surgeon. Dr. Dick repeated that the operation was urgent and offered to call Professor Josef Hohlbaum, the Chairman of the Surgery Department at the nearby Charles University, a Silesian German. Heydrich accepted after a few minutes of hesitation and Professor Hohlbaum was summoned. Drs. Slalina and Mach brought the patient to an operating room which had just been vacated by Dr. Alois V. Honek, who had hurriedly finished a gastrectomy when told that his room was needed for an important patient. Thirty minutes later, Dr. Honek was called back to administer Heydrich's anesthetic. Apparently, he was the only surgeon familiar with the new British anesthesia machine equipped with a closed-circuit system for positive pressure ventilation.

Entering the operating room, Dr. Honek found Heydrich silent and aloof, lying undressed on the operating table. He ignored Dr. Honek's questions about loose teeth and dental prostheses but let him examine his mouth. He was then anesthetized with ether by mask and the left lung was reinflated by positive pressure. An endotracheal tube was not inserted. The anesthetic was administered by Mr. Müller, an operating room orderly, helped by nurse Zavadilová and supervised by Dr. Honek.

The operation started around noon and ended shortly after 1:00 p.m. Drs. Dick and Slalina had started scrubbing when Professor Hohlbaum walked in with two assistants. As he was ready to scrub, Dr. Hohlbaum noticed that in his haste he had forgotten his glasses and an aid was sent to fetch them. He told Dr. Dick to start the procedure and that he would assist him until he had his glasses. Dr. Mach gave the patient a transfusion of type A blood at the beginning of the operation and another at the end, along with tetanus and gas gangrene antitoxins.

Once asleep, Heydrich was turned on his right side and Dr. Dick debrided the back wound, resected the tip of the fractured eleventh rib, inserted a pleural Petzer catheter and closed the wound over the expanded left lung. The pleural catheter was later attached to a *Bülau* bottle to keep the lung expanded postoperatively. Whether the 10-cm diaphragmatic tear was sutured through the back wound or during the laparotomy is unclear in the operative report.

The patient was then turned on his back and the abdomen was prepared for a laparotomy. Dr. Hohlbaum, now wearing his glasses, made an incision from sternum to mid-abdomen. As he was reaching the umbilicus, Dr. Honek noticed that he was perspiring profusely. Dr. Dick reacted at once, and in his usual quiet and courteous manner whispered, "Professor Hohlbaum, you are not well, allow me to take over." He then extended the incision under the left costal margin and finished the procedure with Drs. Hohlbaum's and Slalina's assistance. The peritoneal cavity was filled with blood coming from the spleen. The other abdominal organs and the left kidney were intact. The damaged spleen was removed; it contained an 8-cm by 8-cm grenade splinter and a lot of car upholstery material. Dr. Dick sutured the pancreatic tail, inserted a peritoneal drain, and closed the abdomen. Heydrich tolerated the surgery well, with normal vital signs.

At 12:30 p.m. on 27 May, Hitler, at his headquarters in Rastenburg (East Prussia), was informed of the attack and immediately telephoned the hospital and spoke with Karl Frank who was on the scene. Hitler expressed anger that Heydrich dared to travel without armed escort. Hitler ordered that one million *Reichsmarks* was to be offered for the arrest of the assassins, anyone associated with the plot was to be shot along with their entire family, ten thousand Czechs were to be arrested, and all prisoners already in custody for political offenses were to be executed immediately.

The same afternoon, Hitler held a meeting with Himmler in Berlin during which they decided that General Kurt Daluege already in Prague was to be interim *Reichsprotektor* instead of Frank who they viewed as too soft for the task of reprisal.

SS-Standartenführer Horst Böhme, chief of *SiPo* (Security Police) for the Protectorate of Bohemia and Moravia, reported to Berlin, at 3:26 p.m. on 27 May 1942, the results of Heydrich's first operation via teleprint:

> [A] lacerated wound to the left of the back vertebrae without damage to the spinal cord. The projectile, a piece of sheet

> metal, shattered the 11th rib, punctured the stomach lining, and finally lodged in the spleen. The wound contains a number of horsehair and hair, probably material originating from the upholstery. The dangers: festering of the pleura due to pleurisy. During the operation the spleen was removed.

On the afternoon of 27 May, Czechoslovak exiles in England learned of the attack from Prague radio. President Beneš immediately congratulated Colonel Moravec. As a result of the crackdown in the Protectorate, Beneš and all exiles in England lost radio contact with the parachutists and resistance in and around Prague, but Silver A with their transmitter Libuše in Pardubice remained functional. On 3 June, Beneš sent Captain Bartoš of Silver A the following congratulatory message:

> From the President. I am delighted that you are maintaining contact and I thank you sincerely. I can see that you and your friends are absolutely determined. It is proof to me that the whole nation is solidly together. I can assure you that it will bring success. The events over there have a great effect here and attract recognition for the resistance of the Czech people.

The same day at 9:05 p.m., Himmler sent Frank a teleprinter message reiterating Hitler's orders for reprisal, adding: "Among the . . . ten thousand hostages arrest . . . all Czech intelligentsia, shoot this very night one hundred of the most important." At the same time, Himmler sent to Prague his personal physician, Professor and Chief of Orthopedic Surgery at Berlin University, Chief Surgeon in the Staff of the *Reich* Physician *SS* and Police, and Consulting Surgeon to the *Waffen-SS*, Dr. med. Karl Franz Gebhardt.

Dr. med. Gebhardt landed in Prague the evening of 27 May, accompanied by his *SS* deputy, Dr. med. Ludwig Stumpfegger, the renowned Berlin surgeon Dr. med. Ernst Ferdinand Sauerbruch, Chairman of the Department of Surgery at Charité Hospital in Berlin, and Professor of Surgery in Breslau and Munich. Professor Dr. med. Sauerbruch had been Gebhardt's teacher and was a close friend of the Heydrich family. Dr. med. Morell, Hitler's physician, never came to Prague. Gebhardt followed Heydrich closely and phoned Himmler twice a day to report on his patient's progress. Heydrich probably never received sulfonamides. The Bulovka nurses and pharmacists later commented on the enormous amounts of morphine ordered for Heydrich and even suspected that one of his physicians was an addict. It is plausible, however, that large amounts of narcotics were needed for a 38-year-old, six-foot-three-inch, 205-pound male patient with painful back and abdominal injuries. Gebhardt may have also tried to keep his patient comfortable during the numerous visits of his wife and his *SS* colleagues, including Himmler.

On the evening of 27 May, Frank declared martial law throughout the Protectorate. Curfew was 9:00 p.m. and all road and rail traffic in and out of Prague was halted. A massive house-to-house search operation began in Prague, using Czech and German police assisted by *Waffen-SS* troops and three battalions of regular soldiers. Approximately 21,000 men were involved in checking over 36,000 houses.

By 30 May, the reward for the assassins was doubled. A wave of executions in Prague and concentration camps in Germany and Poland spread like a wildfire. A week after the ambush, however, all the searches and terror failed to produce a single worthwhile lead on the whereabouts of Heydrich's assailants. All safe houses throughout the city were no longer safe. Through their contacts in the resistance, Gabčík and Kubiš along with five other parachutists who ended up joining the Anthropoid group (Josef Valčík of Silver A, Adolf Opálka of Out Distance, Jaroslav Švarc of Tin, and Josef Bublík and Jan Hrubý of Bioscop) eventually found refuge in the crypt under the Karel Boromejsky Greek Orthodox Church, also known as the Saints Cyril and Methodius Church. Gabčík was the last to join the group in the crypt on 1 June.

Over the ensuing days, chaos beset governmental and security offices throughout the Protectorate.

In his book *The Assassination of Reinhard Heydrich*, Callum MacDonald poignantly summarized the final thoughts of the man known as "The Butcher of Prague," as follows:

> On 2 June, a worried Himmler flew to Prague to speak to his protégé for the last time. During the conversation, which centered on the themes of fate and death, Heydrich quoted some lines from his father's opera, *Amen*: "The world is just a barrel-organ which the Lord God turns Himself. We all have to dance to the tune which is already on the drum." In one sense, this piece of sentimental doggerel, which reflected all his father's faults as a composer, was a fitting

> epitaph for a life that was ultimately devoid of either morality or meaning. In death, Heydrich was unable to invoke any great cause or idea. The man who held power over millions was forced to descend at last to the level of the trivial and the second-rate. He was as devoid of a coherent intellectual or moral centre as the movement which had shaped him. In another sense, the words reflected a staggering evasion of personal responsibility. For Heydrich, who had murdered thousands in the pursuit of total power, to appeal to fate or predestination was hypocrisy on the grand scale (MacDonald 2011, 218–9).

Within days of the operation, Heydrich's condition deteriorated. He developed peritonitis followed by septicemia. With spiking fevers and use of morphine to control his pain, his blood pressure dropped. Blood transfusions only temporarily helped stabilize him. Gebhardt refused to consider a second operation. In the early hours of 3 June 1942, Gebhardt reported to Himmler that the fever and the drainage had subsided, and that the patient was improving. However, around noon, while Heydrich was sitting in bed eating a late breakfast, he suddenly went into shock and soon lapsed into a deep coma.

At 4:30 a.m. on 4 June 1942, Reinhard Heydrich died. Heydrich's death was recorded in the Bulovka death register as "Nr 348/1942, Reinhard Tristan Heydrich. Cause of death: gunshot wound/murder attempt/wound infection."

A postmortem examination, ordered by Heydrich's office, was performed at noon on 4 June 1942, at the Bulovka Hospital morgue. Professors Dr. med. Herwig Hamperl, Director of the Department of Pathology and Dr. med. Günther Weyrich, Director of the Department of Forensic Medicine, both at Charles University, conducted the autopsy. Present were the surgeons Drs. med. Dick, Hohlbaum, Gebhardt, and Sauerbruch, as well as several *SS* physicians. The essential findings included:

1. The surgical sutures were intact and there had been no postoperative bleeding, a reassuring finding for the surgeons.
2. There were small abscesses in the splenic bed, in the thoracic wall and diaphragmatic wounds, and around the pleural drain, but there were no large collections of pus in the abdominal or thoracic

cavities.

3. The pericardial sac contained 100 mL of sero-fibrinous fluid.
4. The coronary arteries and aorta were normal, except for a few small atheromatous plaques.
5. The right ventricle, the pulmonary artery, and its main branches were filled with fat particles and blood clots. The cardiac valves were intact.
6. The esophagus contained foul-smelling, regurgitated gastric content.
7. The lungs showed the most significant changes:
   a. The bronchi were filled with foamy mucus.
   b. The upper lobes of both lungs revealed severe pulmonary edema whereas the lower lobes and the left lingula were markedly atelectatic.
   c. There was a right hydrothorax (170 mL sero-fibrinous fluid).
   d. The anterior and lateral surfaces of the left lung were fused to the parietal pleura by thick, fibrinous adhesions. A pocket of 50 mL of cloudy, brownish fluid separated the left lung from the mediastinum. Another larger pocket (650 mL) lay under the left lung, covering the costo-diaphragmatic recess.

The main microscopic and bacteriological findings in the autopsy report included:

1. Cloudy swelling of the hepatic, renal, and myocardial cells.
2. The diaphragmatic wound, the left pleural cavity and the pericardial sac showed an abundance of gram-positive bacilli and cocci (mainly *streptococci*) and, especially, of *proteus* bacteria.

Based on this limited autopsy, the final cause of death remains a point of debate. The late Professor Emeritus Ray J. Defalque, M.D. and Associate Professor Amos J. Wright, III, M.L.S. in the Department of Anesthesiology at the University of Alabama, Birmingham published an article in the *Bulletin of Anesthesia History* in 2009 titled, *The Puzzling Death of Reinhard Heydrich*. In their article, the following is described:

> The autopsy findings belie Dr. Hamperl's diagnoses of "septic organ failure" (1942) and, [later in his revised conclusions,] of "anemic shock" (1970 and 1972).

> Mediastinitis was never substantiated. Fatal cardiac tamponade generally occurs with larger pericardial effusions than the 100 mL found by the pathologists. Sudden postoperative cardiovascular collapse and coma suggest either a cerebral embolism or severe brain ischemia following a massive pulmonary embolism with acute cor pulmonale and impaired cardiac output. The embolus may have been a large fat particle or a blood clot, since both materials were found in the right ventricle and in the pulmonary artery. In the absence of examination of the brain and of a search for evidence of pulmonary embolus, deep vein thromboses, and foramen ovale in the heart, an accurate diagnosis is impossible. However, sudden cardiovascular collapse and coma occurring several days after surgery in a young, previously healthy patient without long bone fractures suggests a pulmonary embolism with acute cor pulmonale and brain anoxia. In the absence of important data, however, this diagnosis must remain a speculation. (Defalque and Wright 2009, 1, 4–7.)

At midnight on 5 June 1942, Heydrich's coffin was transported by torchlight procession to Prague Castle where it lay in state for two days surrounded by blazing funeral urns and guarded by senior officers of the police, *SS*, and *Wehrmacht*. On the morning of 7 June 1942, Heydrich's coffin was exhibited in the courtyard in front of Matthias Gate, where crowds of German and Czech citizens streamed past until late afternoon. Then, the coffin was loaded on a gun carriage (caisson) and conveyed solemnly via the Charles Bridge to the Central Railway Station, from where the coffin was placed on a train and transported to Berlin. The grandiose funeral in Berlin on 9 June 1942 included a eulogy by Himmler in which he sought to immortalize Heydrich for all of posterity. However, Heydrich managed to do that best, himself. Hitler was too overcome to say more than a few words, but he recognized Heydrich's contribution to the Nazi cause by awarding him the "greatest honor which I can bestow," the highest class of the German Order (*Deutscher Orden* or "Hitler Order"). It was the second of eleven such decorations to be bestowed during the entire war.

CHAPTER 28

NAZI REVENGE

LIDICE

FOLLOWING A TENUOUS SERIES OF INDIRECT AND AMBIGUOUS LEADS FROM various sources starting with the addresses of two families living in the village of Lidice found on captured parachutist Corporal Pavelka of Operation Percentage in October 1941, the *Gestapo*, under great pressure to come up with something, focused on the village of Lidice as a possible hideout for Heydrich's assassins. Chief of Security Police (*SiPo*) for Bohemia and Moravia *SS-Standartenführer* Horst Böhme informed Himmler in Berlin on 9 June of the evidence they had on Lidice and recommended harsh retaliation. Himmler discussed the matter with Hitler that evening after a reception. Then, Himmler informed Frank of Hitler's decision. At 7:45 p.m. on 9 June, Frank telephoned Böhme from Berlin to pass on the *Führer*'s instructions. Lidice was to be razed. The men were to be shot on the spot and the women sent to Ravensbrück Concentration Camp (94 km north of Berlin and 440 km north of Prague). Children worthy of Germanization were to be handed over to *SS* families as part of the *SS-Lebensborn* program; the fate of the rest was the be determined.

The population of the village of Lidice (9 km northwest from Prague city limits) in 1942 was 503 (195 adult males, 203 adult females, and 105 children). On the morning of 10 June, all the men fifteen-years old and older were taken to a farm in the village belonging to Stanislav Horák and Anastázie Horáková, where they were systematically executed by a *Schupo* (*Schutzpolizei*) unit of twenty soldiers and three officers brought from Heydrich's birthplace, Halle an der Saale in southern Saxony. The *Schupo* unit was provided hard liquor to enable the task at hand. A total of 203 women and 105 children (all females and only those males less than fourteen-years old) were first taken to the Lidice village school, then transported aboard trucks five kilometers west to the town of Kladno and detained there in the grammar school gymnasium for three days. One by one the village houses in Lidice were set on fire with the help of incendiary liquids. Initially, the executions of the males were conducted by firing squad in groups of five, but then Böhme felt that their "work of art" was progressing too slowly. Böhme ordered them to double the firing squad, executing ten males at a time. The murdering continued, with short breaks for meals and more alcohol, until the next afternoon on 11 June. A total of 173 males were killed in the village on 10–11 June. Eleven village men who happened to be outside the village on the fatal night—mainly because of night shift work in the local mine—and two boys who were discovered to have recently turned fifteen were also executed later in Prague on 16 June. The remaining eight men were captured and executed elsewhere (three Lidice men were never apprehended). In total, 192 males were killed.

In Kladno, the children were separated from their mothers. Of the 203 Lidice women, nineteen did not make the trip to Ravensbrück Concentration Camp. Four in late stages of their pregnancy were immediately sent to the same hospital where Heydrich died, forced to undergo abortions, and then sent to different concentration camps. The four fetuses were murdered. Other pregnant women in various stages of pregnancy were identified in Kladno and reportedly sent to an asylum in Prague where they were permitted to proceed to term and give natural birth. Their children were then reportedly sent to orphanages in Prague and Svatobořice (300 km southeast of Prague) but their fates remain mostly a mystery, to date. The fate of other Lidice women taken to Kladno but not to Ravensbrück Concentration Camp remains also a mystery. Other Lidice women whose pregnancy was either unknown or not evident at the time, ended up delivering in Ravensbrück Concentration Camp. All of their newborns were murdered on site. Of the total 203 Lidice women, 184 were transported from Kladno to Lovosice and then north via rail 380 kilometers to Ravensbrück Concentration Camp on 13–14 June 1942.

Of the 105 Lidice children, eighty-eight boarded buses in Kladno on 13 June and were transported sixty kilometers north to Lovosice where they boarded a train and were transported 560 kilometers northeast to the transit camp in Łódź, Poland (*Generalgouvernement*). The fate of seventeen Lidice children that failed to make this trip remains unclear, but some reports place them in orphanages in Prague and Svatobořice. Shortly after their arrival in Łódź, officials from the Central Race and Settlement branch of the *SS* chose seven of the eighty-eight children for Germanization and eventually turned them over to *SS* families as part of the *Lebensborn* program. Of those seven children, six died in German orphanages. The international outcry over

Lidice caused some hesitation over the fate of the remaining children but in late June 1942, Adolf Eichmann ordered the massacre of the remainder of the children in custody in Łódź. On 4 July 1942, eighty-one to eighty-two of the remaining Lidice children in the transit camp in Łódź were boarded into specialized box trucks equipped with redirected motor exhaust (Magirus gas vans) and commenced their final journey fifty kilometers northwest to the extermination camp in the Polish village of Chełmno nad Nerem. All eighty-one to eighty-two died of carbon monoxide poisoning. Their bodies were never discovered.

Fifty-three of the 184 Lidice women sent to Ravensbrück Concentration Camp did not survive. Out of the 105 original living Lidice children, eighty-two died in Chełmno, six died in the German *Lebensborn* orphanages, and seventeen eventually returned home to Lidice after the war.

On 10 June 1942, the Protectorate government issued the following proclamation:

> Be it officially announced:
> During the search for the murderers of *SS-Obergruppenfuehrer* Heydrich, incontestable evidence was found that the inhabitants of the village of Lidice, near Kladno, were aiding and abetting the perpetrators of the crime. The relevant evidence was proven despite questioning and without the help of local residents. The attitude of the population in regard to the assassination is also evidenced by other anti-*Reich* measures, such as discoveries of subversive literature, stores of weapons and ammunition, an illegal [radio] transmitter and a large quantity of rationed goods held in unlawful possession indicting the local residents in the active service of the enemy abroad. After the inhabitants of this village violated the laws passed by their activity and support of the killers of *SS-Obergruppenführer* Heydrich, the male adults were shot, the women were sent to a concentration camp, and the children were given a proper education. The buildings of the village have been razed to the ground and the name of the village has been obliterated.*

* Official transcript of the Nuremberg Trial Proceedings, Volume 7, Fifty-Fourth Day, Friday, 8 February 1946.

HUNTING DOWN THE PERPETRATORS

IN EARLY JUNE 1942, THE GERMAN POLICE RECEIVED INFORMATION FROM a local informer that certain parachutists had spent a night in a local mill and stored some weapons there. Normally, this incident would have ended with the imprisonment of the mill owners. However, the Nazis were abnormal and did not respect the rules of armed conflict or the Geneva Convention.

Shortly after the death of Reinhard Heydrich, a "Special Committee" was created by the commander of the *Gestapo* in Prague, *SS-Standartenführer* Jurist Hans Ulrich Geschke on Karel Frank's orders. The Committee worked under direct supervision of a commissar, who from June 1942 held a rank of senior criminal investigator in the state police, *SS-Hauptsturmführer* Heinz Pannwitz (who also commanded the II.g department of *Gestapo* Prague). On 21 July 1942, this Special Committee prepared the closing report of *SD* Department IV about the current status of the Heydrich assassination investigation, titled, *Atentat auf Heydrich,* otherwise known as the "Pannwitz Report," intended for Chief of *Gestapo SS-Gruppenführer* and Lieutenant General Heinrich Müller in Berlin. The report found the contraband in Lidice merely consisted of two hunting rifles, several tins of bullets, and a photograph of a soldier in a foreign uniform. On this basis, the security apparatus in occupied Bohemia and Moravia embarked on a killing spree of innocent Czech civilians.

While the others were gathering in the crypt under Saints Cyril and Methodius Church, Warrant Officer Karel Čurda of Out Distance could not be found. Čurda managed to flee Prague and get to his family's home in Nová Hlína near Třeboň in southern Bohemia, where he hid in his mother's barn. After nearly two weeks, he finally gave in to his own fear, the weight of his conscience over all the innocent deaths the Nazis were causing in their search for Heydrich's assassins, and the reproaches of those closest to him, and ended up betraying his comrades in arms and all those associated with them. First, on 13 June 1942, he wrote an anonymous letter to the Czech police in Benešov—a town forty-five kilometers south of Prague and about 100 kilometers north of where he was hiding—stating: "cease searching for the assassins of Heydrich; cease arresting and executing innocent people. I can't stand it anymore. The perpetrators of the assassination are a certain Gabčík from Slovakia, and Jan Kubiš, whose brother is an innkeeper from Moravia." When the expected reaction did not materialize, he took a train to Prague on 16 June 1942, and, shortly before noon, reported to the *Gestapo* administrative headquarters in Peček Palace. There he caused a sensation with his all-encompassing testimony, because up to that point, all of the Nazis' efforts to find the assassins had proved fruitless. Čurda betrayed to the *Gestapo* everyone he knew personally who had assisted the paratroopers, not only in Prague but in Pardubice, Lázně Bělohrad, and Plzeň. Through his betrayal he caused the deaths of dozens of patriots and their families.

However, Čurda was unable to lead the *Gestapo* directly to the parachutists because he did not know where they were hiding, but he betrayed several of the safe houses provided by the Jindra (Sokol) group, most importantly the flat in Žižkov occupied by the Moravec family (unrelated to Colonel Moravec in England or Emanuel Moravec working with the Nazis in Prague) which lay at the center of the network. The very next morning, the *Gestapo* began extended raids on the apartments of the people who had assisted the paratroopers. The first in line was the Moravec family on Biskupcova Street in Prague. At 5:00 a.m. on 17 June, the Moravec family was awakened by the thunder of gun butts on their apartment door. In their night clothes, they were marched out into the hallway while the *Gestapo* searched their flat. In the confusion, Mrs. Moravec asked to go to the toilet, a request that was surprisingly granted. There she locked herself in and swallowed a cyanide capsule. The door was broken down and a doctor summoned, but by the time he arrived she was dead. Mr. Moravec and their son Vlastimil "Ata" (born 17 March 1921) were taken to *Gestapo* headquarters for interrogation. They were tortured and when Ata's resistance appeared to be at its lowest, he was presented the severed head of his mother. Broken, he gave his torturers the first real clue of the whereabouts of the assassins, revealing that his mother told him to go the catacombs of the Karel Boromejsky church if he was ever in trouble. By using the most brutal interrogation techniques, the *Gestapo* succeeded near midnight of 17 June 1942, in finding out where the paratroopers were hiding.

At 3:45 a.m. on 18 June 1942, the Commander of the *SS* forces in Bohemia and Moravia, *SS-Brigadeführer* Karl von Treuenfeld, issued an order to the Reserve Battalion *Deutschland* and the Guard Battalion *Prag* to surround the area around the Church of St. Cyril and Methodius. The inner and outer perimeters were closed at 4:15 a.m. with 700 *Waffen-SS* troops. Chief of State Security Police *Gestapo* Unit II.g *SS-Hauptsturmführer* Heinz Pannwitz was responsible for investigating assassinations, illegal weapons possession, and sabotage. Pannwitz and his *Gestapo* police were the first to enter the church's main entrance. Inside the church, as they broke open the locked gate to the stairway leading to the choir loft, a grenade came rolling down followed by a burst of fire from atop the stairs. The explosion injured one German and extinguished the lights. *Waffen-SS* shooters on the neighboring rooftops began firing indiscriminately into the church shattering the stained-glass windows and ricocheting bullets on the pillars. Pannwitz and his detachment retreated, and the *Waffen-SS* commander von Treuenfeld restored discipline and the random firing ceased.

The *Waffen-SS* was sent in to storm the choir loft. Orders were to take the parachutists alive. However, only after two hours of shooting and the use of grenades, were they able to fight their way up and finally reach the choir loft where they found two dead parachutists who had taken poison and a third severely wounded and unconscious. This man was Kubiš who also apparently tried to take poison but lost consciousness before he could do so. Although he was immediately transferred to the hospital, none of the doctors' attempts to save him succeeded. He died within twenty minutes of his arrival. The other two agents were identified by Čurda, who, along with Ata Moravec, was on the scene, as being Bublík of Bioscop and Opálka of Out Distance. None of the corpses fitted the description of Gabčík, so, the search continued. Parish priest Vladimír Petřek was interrogated and revealed there were four more men in the catacombs. An argument broke out between Pannwitz and *Waffen-SS* commander von Treuenfeld about the need to capture the assassins alive. The *Waffen-SS* commander wanted to storm the crypt regardless of the consequences. By now, the crypt was filled with tear gas and partially flooded with water by the Prague Fire Department. The first attempt under these conditions resulted in two severely wounded *SS* soldiers. They were planning to blow open the narrow entrance to the crypt when suddenly four shots rang out from the crypt followed by silence. A soldier was sent down to investigate and emerged a few moments later shouting *Fertig* ("Finished!"). According to Pannwitz's report on the operation: "Four dead criminals were found in the crypt. Apart from serious injuries, they had wounds in the temple demonstrating they had killed themselves with their own pistols." The parachutists had resisted their assailants for over six hours and committed suicide with their last bullets rather than surrender. The bodies were brought out to the street where Čurda identified them and Gabčík as the second assassin. Three days later, Captain Alfréd Bartoš of Silver A was apprehended by the *Gestapo* in Pardubice. He attempted to kill himself but only succumbed to his self-inflicted wound the following night on 22 June 1942.

MORE NAZI REPRISALS

THE VILLAGE OF LEŽÁKY WHICH CONCEALED SILVER A'S RADIO transmitter "Libuše" suffered even a grimmer fate than Lidice. On 24 June 1942, an assault was carried out against the entire village of Ležáky, in which members of the *Gestapo*, *Schupo*, and *SS* from Pardubice and Hradec Králové took part. The entire village was cordoned off, and its inhabitants were crowded into an abandoned quarry from where they were later transported to Pardubice. All nine dwellings in the village were raided and subsequently set on fire. At the Pardubice Château the children were separated from the women, and they were later sent to Prague and from there to Łódź and then to Chełmno extermination camp in Poland, where all traces of them disappear—after the war only sisters Jarmila and Marie Šulíková were found. On the evening of 24 June, thirty-three adult inhabitants of Ležáky were shot on the execution grounds of the Pardubice Château. The remaining adults were murdered in the same place later, or they died in a concentration camp. The Ležáky tragedy hence cost the lives of a total of fifty-seven people.

In the village of Bernartice near Tábor (91 km / 56.5 mi south of Prague), which collaborated with the Intransitive group, twenty-four people were executed under martial law (twenty-two in Luby near Klatovy and two in Tábor). Another twenty-two citizens of Bernartice did not return from concentration camps. The Nazis carried out a number of punitive measures against the villages of Bohdašín and Končiny in the Náchod district, which were connected with Silver A paratroop's Libuše transmitter, where radio telegrapher Jiří Potůček had hidden. They arrested eighteen people during the operation. Fifteen of them were executed on 9 July 1942, at the execution grounds of the Pardubice Château. A total of 194 citizens and patriots were murdered on the execution grounds of Pardubice Château, including *Major Generál* Alois Eliáš, General Staff Colonel Josef Churavý, *Brigádny Generál* Otakar Zahálka, and General Staff *Major* František Kopuletý.

After the capture of the Libuše and Baroš's message files in Pardubice which gave details of codes and cover names of operatives, the Germans initiated an operation intended to deceive British and Czechoslovak intelligence in England. The Czechoslovak transmitters in Woldingham responded to Silver A's call sign, but the *Gestapo* lacked a captured parachutist radio operator who knew proper radio procedures, so, the operation was eventually shut down in September 1942 (MacDonald 2011, 237).

Nazi reprisals continued throughout the summer of 1942. Between 28 May and 1 September, 3,188 Czechs were arrested and 1,357 condemned to death by the emergency martial law courts (MacDonald 2011, 237). Over twenty percent of those executed were former military officers or members of the intelligentsia, groups defined by the Nazis as recalcitrant representatives of the "national idea," an independent Czechoslovak state. This total did not include the victims of Lidice or Ležáky or the 3,000 Jews deported to the East. Nor did it include the 252 relatives and helpers of the parachutists condemned in Prague on 29 September. During their interrogation, they were beaten and confronted with the heads of seven operatives, impaled on spikes (MacDonald 2011, 237). Their conduct in the face of such brutal treatment impressed even their jailers. As the chief of the Prague *Gestapo* reported on 25 June: "Most of the people who helped the assassins took a pronounced Czech, chauvinist, anti-German stance, especially the women. . . . They were often heard saying: 'We are proud to die for our country'" (MacDonald 2011, 237). Sentence was carried out on 24 October 1942 at Mauthausen Concentration Camp. The men were shot, and the women and children sent to the gas chambers. Among the victims were twelve relatives of Kubiš and thirteen of Valčik. Gabčík's family escaped reprisal because he was Slovak, and the Nazis found it convenient to maintain the fiction that their satellite state of Slovakia was independent and loyal to Germany. After arriving in Mauthausen, none of the large group of people who had helped the paratroopers and their relatives suspected that they only had a few hours of life left. The largest execution in the history of the camp began on 24 October 1942, at 8:30 a.m. Shortly before 5:45 p.m., it was over. On that day, 257 collaborators and family of the parachutists were murdered by a shot to the back of the head. A second group of thirty-one members had its turn in Mauthausen on 26 January 1943. Among the victims of this time, 3,000 citizens of Jewish origin must not be forgotten, who on the days between 10 and 13 June 1942, were shipped from the Protectorate in three transports (AAh, AAi, AAk) to extermination camps in Poland, where they were eventually murdered.

During Nazi occupation of Bohemia and Moravia, Pankrác Prison just south of Prague became the largest prison in the Protectorate housing up to 2,200 prisoners. Between 5 April 1943 and 26 April 1945, a total of 1,079 people (including 175 women) were beheaded by guillotine in Pankrác by Nazi executioners; the number of people executed by hanging during this period is unknown. The chief Nazi executioner was Alois Weiss. The three rooms used for this purpose (colloquially referred to as the *sekyrárna*, or axe room) have been preserved (including the guillotine execution device that was recovered from Vltava River, where it was disposed of by the German Nazis fleeing Prague in May 1945) and serve as a memorial that is occasionally accessible to schools and the public. Kurt Daluege, the interim *Reichsprotektor* responsible for the Lidice and Ležáky massacres, was hanged at Pankrác Prison on 24 October 1946.

THE LEGACY OF ANTHROPOID

KAREL ČURDA WAS PAID A REWARD OF HALF A MILLION *REICHSMARKS* (five million Czech crowns)—a quarter of the total Nazi bounty of two million *Reichsmarks* (the same amount was paid to another traitor, Viliam Gerik—the rest was divided among seven citizens of the *Reich*, and fifty-three lesser informers from the Protectorate). His mother and sister were released from custody and avoided the grim fate awaiting the families of the other parachutists. Čurda continued to live in Prague under the German name Karl Jerhot, adopted German citizenship, married the sister of a German *SS* officer, and pursued a career as a *Gestapo* spy. He toured the Protectorate posing as a parachutist, a role he knew well, reporting those who offered to assist him. He helped the *Gestapo* track down the radio group of Operation Antimony, dropped in October 1942. Convinced the Nazis would win the war, he hoped to settle in the East as one of the warrior peasants of Hitler's imperial dreams. Upon liberation of southwestern Bohemia by Patton's Third Army, Čurda had the audacity on 15 May 1945, to show up at the police station in Manětín (Plzeň region) seeking a job. His true identity was verified, and he was arrested and later sentenced to death. On 29 April 1947, he was hanged in Pankrác Prison. Čurda, in his closing statement refused to ask for mercy. His German wife and son emigrated to Austria.

The widespread public sympathy for Czechoslovakia created by the killing was reinforced by the crime of Lidice, which condemned as an act of barbarism throughout the civilized world. In a speech typical of allied comment, the U.S. Secretary of the Navy, Frank Knox, proclaimed: "If future generations ask us what we were fighting for in this war, we shall tell them the story of Lidice." According to Jan Masaryk, Nazi reprisals played straight into the hands of the exiles: "I was in the U.S. at the time of Lidice and making no progress in our propaganda, having exhausted all the possibilities of the situation. Then came Lidice, and I had a new lease on life.

Czechoslovakia was put on the map again and we had an easy time." In Britain, Beneš was able to use the favorable atmosphere to political advantage, securing the concessions for which he had fought tenaciously since 1939. On Wednesday, 5 August 1942, the British Foreign Secretary Anthony Eden sent Czechoslovak Foreign Minister Jan Masaryk a letter containing an extraordinarily important statement regarding the standpoint of Her Majesty's Government on the Munich Agreement. The statement, as recorded in the House of Commons, was as follows:

> HC Deb 05 August 1942 vol 382 cc1004–5
>
> 3. **Major Sir Derrick Gunston** asked the Secretary of State for Foreign Affairs whether, having regard to the recognition of the Czechoslovak Government in July, 1941, and to the resistance being offered to German oppression by the Czechoslovak people, His Majesty's Government still consider themselves bound in any way by the terms of the Munich Agreement?
>
> **Mr. Eden**: I am glad to have this opportunity to inform the House that I have today exchanged notes with the Czechoslovak Minister for Foreign Affairs in which I stated that the policy of His Majesty's Government in the United Kingdom in regard to Czechoslovakia was guided by the formal act of recognition of the Czechoslovak Government by His Majesty's Government in July, 1941, and by the Prime Minister's statement on 30th September, 1940, that the Munich Agreement had been destroyed by the Germans. I added that, as Germany had deliberately destroyed the arrangements concerning Czechoslovakia reached in 1938, His Majesty's Government regarded themselves as free from any engagements in this respect, and that at the final settlement of the Czechoslovak frontiers to be reached at the end of the war, His Majesty's Government would not be influenced by any changes effected in and since 1938.
>
> In his reply Monsieur Masaryk informed me that the Czechoslovak Government accepted my note as a practical solution of the questions and difficulties of vital importance for Czechoslovakia which emerged between our

> two countries as the consequence of the Munich Agreement, while maintaining their political and juridical position with regard to that Agreement and to the events which followed it.
>
> The text of this exchange of notes is being laid as a White Paper.
>
> I should not like to let this occasion pass without paying tribute on behalf of His Majesty's Government to the tenacious and courageous stand which the Czechoslovak people are making against their ruthless German oppressors. Acts such as the destruction of Lidice have stirred the conscience of the civilised world and will not be forgotten when the time comes to settle accounts with their perpetrators.

It was through this act, following Heydrich's assassination and bloody repressions of the Nazis on the Czech citizenry, that Britain finally unequivocally revoked the Munich Agreement, and made it clear that the legal status of the Czech government was in no way inferior to that of the other exile regimes by raising the British legation to the rank of an embassy. Less than two months later, on 29 September 1942, in the presence of General Charles de Gaulle and the Prime Minister of the Czechoslovak Government in exile, Monsignor Jan Šrámek and Foreign Minister Jan Masaryk (son of former President Tomáš G. Masaryk) signed the proclamation of the French National Assembly that it considered the Munich Agreement null and void from the very beginning. The mission assigned to the Anthropoid paratroopers and their supporting groups was accomplished.

Operation Anthropoid was the only successful government-directed targeted killing of a top-ranking Nazi during the Second World War. Reinhard Heydrich was first deputy to *Reichsführer* of the *SS* Heinrich Himmler, who himself was commonly considered third in line to Hitler after Heß and Göring. The closest any operation came to the Heydrich assassination were Operations Kutschera and Bürkl when Polish underground killed two senior *SS* officers in the General Government. Also, *SS-Generalkommissar* of Belarus Wilhelm Kube was assassinated in Operation Blowup by Soviet partisan Yelena Mazanik, a Belarusian woman employed in his household. However, these individuals were not even close to the same class of Nazi hierarchy as Reinhard Heydrich.

(*Story continues in Volume Two*) . . .

www.ingramcontent.com/pod-product-compliance
Lightning Source LLC
Chambersburg PA
CBHW070837020826
48982CB00020B/1393/J

* 9 7 8 1 7 3 4 3 7 7 7 6 7 *